A SHORT HISTORY OF
WESTERN CIVILIZATION

A SHORT HISTORY OF
WESTERN

John B. Harrison
Richard E. Sullivan
MICHIGAN STATE UNIVERSITY

CIVILIZATION

FOURTH EDITION

Alfred A. Knopf   New York

FOURTH EDITION

9 8 7 6 5 4 3 2 1

Copyright © 1960, 1966, 1971, 1975 by John B. Harrison and Richard E. Sullivan

Copyright © 1971, 1975 by Alfred A. Knopf, Inc.

First Edition published 1960
Second Edition published 1966
Third Edition published 1971

Library of Congress Cataloging in Publication Data

Harrison, John Baugham.
    A short history of Western civilization.

    Includes bibliographies.
    1. Civilization—History. 2. Civilization, Occidental—History. I. Sullivan, Richard Eugene, 1921- joint author. II. Title.
CB59.H37   1975   910'.03'1821   74-28206
ISBN 0-394-31901-X

Manufactured in the United States.

Design: James M. Wall
Cover photograph: Steven Phillips

to Mary and Vivian

BIBLIOGRAPHICAL NOTE

In compiling the bibliographies the authors have made no attempt to supply an exhaustive list of the latest titles. Books have been selected chiefly for their readability. Brief descriptions have been supplied for each title to guide the reader. Note that many older classic works, although cited here with the original publishing data, have been reprinted in recent years. A special effort was made to utilize to the fullest the numerous inexpensive books now available. All books published in paperback or inexpensive hardback editions have been designated by an asterisk (*). The series in which each volume has been published (Meridian, Penguin, and so on) has also been noted.

A LETTER TO THE STUDENT READER

DEAR STUDENT READER,

We have written this book primarily for your use in a course in the history of Western civilization, or a survey of world civilization, or humanities. Ever since we were college freshmen we, the authors, have spent much if not most of our time studying, teaching, thinking, and writing about the material in such courses. We have done this because as freshmen we discovered that these courses, more than any others, satisfied our hunger for knowledge in breadth. Since then nothing has changed our minds. Furthermore, as we proceeded with our studying and teaching, we became convinced that nothing is more relevant to the thinking person than knowledge in some depth of the origins and development of our present ideas and institutions. How did the world get to be the way it is? How has man reacted in the past to problems somewhat similar to those we face today?

But why study *Western* civilization in this now interrelated world? This is a good question. It is simply a matter of practicality. We have discovered from bitter experience that it is impossible to study with a reasonable degree of success all the major civilizations—giving them equal and parallel treatment—in a one-year survey. The course becomes either blurred and too watered down or overwhelmingly complex. We hope you will find the time to study some or all of the major non-Western civilizations, but not at the expense of an adequate grasp of our own Western civilization. Meanwhile, we have attempted to give you a brief but meaningful glimpse of these non-Western civilizations at the time of their first major contact with the West. Only since World War I has the world been regarded as one—and we have treated it as such here.

We believe you will soon discover the necessity of one quality we have incorporated into this book—specificity. We and our serious students have found that it is futile to try to generalize and philosophize about the past (or almost anything else for that matter) without a command of the basic facts involved. We have not introduced a single fact into this book that we did not consider to be significant and essential. Without the basic facts there can be no history.

But let's face it—history is a difficult subject, and the survey course is the most difficult of all. Therefore, in planning and writing this book we have brought to bear everything we have learned to make it as clear and meaningful as possible. Clarity has been our sole aim in style. We have organized the material into sixty chapters approximately equal in length, each one designed as an assignment with two chapters per week scheduled throughout the school year. We have attempted to be as brief as practically possible in order to avoid burdening you with more details than you can

CREDITS FOR PART OPENING PHOTOS

absorb and also to give you the time to read some of the suggested collateral books. Furthermore, the brevity of the text should give the instructor time to teach. Even so, man and his history are complex and we would be falsifying history and deceiving you if we tried to make them appear simple. Frankly, we offer you many questions but propose few answers.

This is not a picture book. Much time and money have been spent on the maps and illustrations, by both the authors and the publisher. But we believe you have reached that stage in your education when you need to rely on the written word more than on visual aids for the complex subject matter you will be dealing with as responsible adults.

Now an important word about the suggested readings: Did you know that the majority of the books in any sizable library or bookstore are not worth reading? This is particularly true of history books. Anyone may write a book on any subject. Learning which books and authors to trust and to what extent is one of the most important ingredients of every student's education. We have selected the books in the bibliographies at the end of each chapter with great care and with regard to their reliability and readability. Wherever possible we have suggested inexpensive paperback editions. But do not trust our judgment completely. Rather, we hope you will read this text and the books on the suggested lists with a critical eye. What are the author's prejudices? Be assured that being human like you he has some.

Finally, we would like to point out that a book of this nature is not the product of only one or two persons. No two individuals can possibly be authorities on all the areas of knowledge found between these covers. In preparing this fourth edition we have benefited from the criticism and advice of many distinguished historians and scholars in other fields of knowledge. But of all the critic readers the ones we have appreciated the most are student readers — some of whom have written to us about their reactions and suggestions. We cordially invite you to do the same.

Sincerely,

JOHN B. HARRISON
RICHARD E. SULLIVAN

East Lansing, Michigan
OCTOBER 1974

I The Ancient Near East 4000-300 B.C.

II Greco-Roman Civilization 1200 B.C.-A.D. 200

CONTENTS

VI   The Late Middle Ages 1300-1500

VII   The Beginning of Modern Times   Fifteenth and Sixteenth Centuries

VIII   The Age of Royal Absolutism   Seventeenth and Eighteenth Centuries

IX   The Era of the French Revolution 1776-1830

X   The Industrial Revolution
First Phase: The Dominance of the Middle Class 1830-1871

XI   The Industrial Revolution
Second Phase: The Emergence of the Masses 1871-1914

XII The Era of the Two World Wars 1914-1974

Where Historians Disagree

Maps

A SHORT HISTORY OF
WESTERN CIVILIZATION

I

The Ancient Near East
4000-300 B.C.

The purpose of this work is to describe the evolution of Western civilization and to make its major characteristics intelligible by describing the numerous ingredients which combine chronologically into its basic features. Our story will take us back to a remote age and to earlier civilizations that contributed vital elements to ours. By "civilization" we mean that total pattern of institutions and ideas by which a large group of people conducts a collective life over a long period. Civilizations are characterized primarily by large political organization, complex social groupings, economic systems featuring highly specialized divisions of labor, cultures marked by the expression of conscious thought in writing and a variety of art forms, and the existence of urban life.

Our account of the history of Western civilization will therefore begin with a study of the civilizations that emerged in the great river valleys of the Near East about 6,000 years ago. But first a few introductory remarks must be made about the long era of human history that preceded their birth.

The origin of man is still shrouded in mystery. The story must be deduced from a pathetically meager collection of skeletons found quite by accident at various places on earth. Some of these remains, bearing a remarkable resemblance to modern man, date back over a million years. Enough such remains have been found in Africa to suggest that that continent was the cradle of the human species. Skeletons from more recent dates show that man was the product of a long process of biological evolution, and that it was probably not until about 30,000 years ago that the human species assumed its present physical form. However, even the earliest manlike creatures possessed a superior combination of physical qualities that distinguished them from the other animals: an upright posture, better eyesight, a digestive system capable of utilizing nearly any kind of food, a voice mechanism capable of producing a wide variety of sounds, and a complex brain allowing them to remember and to coordinate their bodies better than other creatures, among other assets.

Even the most primitive manlike creatures of 500,000 or 600,000 years ago were beginning to develop patterns of living. These early societies, traces of which are scattered all over the earth, were all essentially the same and have been given the common name paleolithic which means Old Stone Age. Paleolithic men lived in small groups as hunters and food gatherers; the greatest accomplishment of the era was man's acquisition of the skills to create weapons from stone and wood that made him an effective killer. Scanty bits of evidence suggest he had developed the belief that spirits exist in all things and that survival depended on getting along with these spirits. In all probability these concepts represent the first attempt at organizing knowledge. Evidence in the form of paintings, as in the Altamira caves in Spain, indicates that primitive man had an urge to express his inner feelings—to interpret the world visually as he saw it.

If we date the dawn of human history from the time when tools began to be made by hunting societies, then the paleolithic era stretches over nine-tenths of all human history. Not until about 10,000 B.C. did the hunting life begin to disappear in a few parts of the world; and some remnants of it persist even today in Australia, the Pacific islands, and Alaska. The revolutionary changes that brought hunting societies to an end were the development of agriculture and the domestication of animals. These two developments ushered in the neolithic, or New Stone Age, life. How,

when, and where this first occurred is hotly disputed. The best evidence suggests that agricultural activity first appeared in Southwest Asia about 10,000 years ago. This area was especially favored by climatic changes occurring at this time: The retreat of the ice caps at the end of the last ice age had given much of Europe and parts of Asia heavy forests and created conditions that produced the deserts

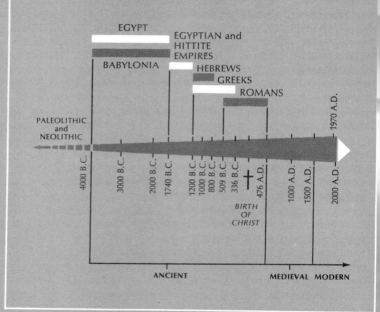

TIME CHART OF WESTERN CIVILIZATION

of North Africa and Arabia. Both areas, formerly the strongholds of hunting societies, grew inhospitable. In the zone between, storms sweeping around the world from west to east brought regular rainfall and a mild climate, both conducive to grass and grain growing. It was here that man the hunter adapted himself to changing conditions and became man the farmer. During the next few thousand years, this mode of life appeared over most of the earth, probably "invented" several times by groups faced with difficulties sustaining a food-gathering economy.

The domestication of plants and animals revolutionized man's living habits. He ceased wandering and settled permanently in villages. He produced new tools and techniques such as houses, hoes, sickles, pottery, and weaving. He could accumulate enough wealth for better dwellings, clothing, and luxuries. Systematic farming yielded sufficient surplus to permit the specialization of labor, with a resultant increase in skill and efficiency and the broadening of the economic base of society. Neolithic man met the new social problems of the village community by creating tribal governments with authority vested in the hands of one or a few men. The family developed into an institution capable of directing the activities of all its members. Neolithic man also had to expand his mind to cope with the demands of his new situation. His religion, which increasingly centered around worship of the forces of nature, challenged him with ideas that were not so tangible as the animal spirits with which he had grappled daily. His answer was to place more trust in religious experts — priests — and to dedicate more energy and wealth to the worship of the spirits that nourished his crops and protected his village.

Neolithic society marked a great advance in human life, but the small isolated village, the limited technology, the routine imposed by nature, the narrowly conceived social system, and the restricted intellectual horizons characteristic of it combined to inhibit further advances. A leap forward occurred during the fourth and third millennia before Christ at a very few spots on the globe. In the great river valley systems of the Near East, China, and India, there existed a physical environment offering opportunity for a more bounteous return from human effort — if men could organize their activities to capitalize on this potential. The response was the development of urban societies embracing much larger groupings of people. Urbanization in the Near and Far East constitutes the crucial event inaugurating the history of civilization in the proper sense of the term.

Before becoming engaged in the tumultuous, complicated, fascinating story of the emergence and maturing of civilized human existence, it would be well to pause for a moment to recognize the debt the human species owes to those primitive hunters and simple farmers of old. Because of them it was already decided that city life would be supported by an agricultural economy. They had realized that man was a social being who must concern himself with the bonds attaching him to other men. They had perfected numerous techniques for controlling the natural world. They had sensed the existence of supernatural powers that affected human affairs and had evolved methods of placating these forces. All this accumulation of economic, social, and political techniques, technical skills, and religious practices served as the basis upon which life in the emergent cities was constructed. Without them, civilization would have been impossible.

In this section attention will be devoted mainly to the civilizations that developed in the Tigris-Euphrates Valley of Mesopotamia and in the Nile Valley of Egypt. By this selection there is no intention of slighting comparable and equally significant advances in China and India. The regions we have chosen require our full attention because their achievements are vital to the central theme of this book: the history of Western civilization. The first task is to characterize the nature of their civilizations. Beyond this, the extension of these civilizations into a large area of Northeast Africa and Southwest Asia must be considered, for numerous other peoples absorbed ideas and institutions from them. Equally significant, many made unique contributions of their own to the expanding stream of civilized life. Until at least 500 B.C., the Near East led the civilized world. Its teeming population created a priceless heritage that was later exploited by other peoples participating in the shaping of Western civilization.

It is now generally agreed that the transition from neolithic village society to urban civilization occurred first in the Tigris-Euphrates Valley. The causes of the transition are still an issue of considerable debate among historians, anthropologists, and archeologists. Some stress the natural evolution of complex city life out of village existence. Others speak of a dramatic leap forward and often cite the development of the use of metals as the decisive factor. Still others argue that an environmental change gripping the entire Near East forced radical changes of life style. And not a few authorities emphasize the intrusion of new peoples into the area as a vital stimulant. There is evidence to give credence to all these views. Whichever prevails, the rather sudden transformation of life in the Tigris-Euphrates Valley about 4000 B.C. set a basic pattern of culture that developed in an unbroken sequence down to about 1750 B.C.

1. THE ENVIRONMENT

The great transformation that occurred about 4000 B.C. is associated with a new relationship between men and their environment: Mesopotamian[1] civilization came into being as a result

'The term "Mesopotamian" will be used to refer to the whole cultural tradition that extends from about 4000 to 1750 B.C. As a label, it is not entirely accurate from any point of view: It does not adequately em-

1

MESOPOTAMIAN CIVILIZATION, 4000–1750 B.C.

of the ability of organized communities to construct an irrigation system.

The Tigris and Euphrates rivers have their sources in the Armenian highlands, from which they flow southward in roughly parallel paths to the Persian Gulf. The land between them is called Mesopotamia, a word of Greek origin meaning "the land between the rivers." In their upper reaches, the rivers traverse a semiarid plateau that was and remains a severe challenge to herders and farmers. Roughly 300 miles north of their mouths, the rivers enter a flat alluvial plain 20 to 50 miles wide. This area, although relatively small, is immensely rich as a result of the silt constantly deposited by the flood waters of the rivers. However, the richness of the soil meant little without an irrigation system, for the hot climate and lack of rainfall made dry-land agriculture nearly impossible.

Tapping the rivers for irrigation confronted primitive farmers with major problems. The Tigris was of little use, for it ran in a deeply cut bed from which it was nearly impossible to draw water. The Euphrates was different. As it flowed slowly across Mesopotamia, it deposited heavy layers of silt in its bed and along its banks. This process lifted the river above the plain, making it necessary only to cut canals in the banks to get water to the adjacent fields and across the flat plain to a large area. But it entailed immense planning and labor to retain the river within its banks, keep the canals free from silt, and control the amount of water flowing through them. Any disruption of the dikes would flood the low-lying fields and destroy the crops. The danger of uncontrolled waters was especially great at flood season, usually April to June, for the rise of the river, dependent upon the thaw of snow in the Caucasus Mountains, was unpredictable. Since this period coincided with the chief growing season, flooding spelled disaster to crops and settlements alike, and archeological finds confirm that it often occurred. Hardly less destructive was the lack of water; the supply in the rivers apparently varied greatly from season to season. If it was short, then the burning sun ruined the crops and brought great suffering. But if it was adequate and if an orderly system of dikes and canals could be maintained, then water could be drawn off throughout the long growing season to nourish a wide variety of crops and to assure a yield far in excess of the yields of dry-land farming. At the same time, the muddy Euphrates eternally re-

brace the total geographical area that will be dealt with; it has no relevance to some of the many peoples involved in the long period being considered; it provides no meaningful clue to the pattern of culture that will be examined. Yet it has become a traditional term, and for this reason it serves better than any other single descriptive term that might be employed.

newed the fertility of the soil by depositing silt on the fields it watered.

No natural barriers protected Mesopotamia; the peoples who first exploited the waters of the rivers and the rich soil of the valley were exposed to constant attacks. To the east the Zagros Mountains sustained tough herdsmen; on the west the Arabian Desert supported equally formidable nomads; hardy farmers inhabited the plateaus along the upper reaches of the rivers. All could and did move into the valley with ease. Their constant assaults had a significant effect on Mesopotamian society, but they also made possible the spread of Mesopotamian influence outward into these more primitive areas.

There is danger in ascribing too much influence to environment in determining the character of a people's history and culture; yet physical conditions in the Tigris-Euphrates Valley did generate a deep sense of insecurity among its inhabitants. The everlasting threats of flood, drought, famine, and invasion bred an attitude of uncertainty and fatalism that is reflected in Mesopotamian literature and art. But the same conditions can and do conversely breed effort and creative thought in an attempt to overcome adversity. Perhaps this is the reason for the intensity with which life was lived in Mesopotamia and the richly varied response to human existence these people managed to develop.

2. MESOPOTAMIAN POLITICAL HISTORY

The development of higher civilization in the Tigris-Euphrates Valley began about 4000 B.C. with the conquest of the ancient inhabitants of the southern part of the area by a new people, the agricultural Sumerians. Their origins have not been established, but they appear to have come from the east, perhaps forced to move by the progressive drying up of the entire Near East. The first settlers almost immediately began to irrigate the lands adjacent to the river. This initial effort required relatively simple techniques, but success apparently attracted more settlers, so that the network of canals had to be extended away from the river. The growing complexities of the irrigation system and the increasing population placed a premium on management and organization skills and led to the formation of the more structured and sophisticated city, in which authority to govern both inhabitants and the agricultural operation was vested in a single person or group. Thus, the first political manifestation of advancing civilization in the land of Sumer (as southern Mesopotamia was called) was the appearance of several city-states consisting of an urban center and the surrounding farmlands. By 3000 B.C. many such communities existed, each with a large population and each jealous of its independence. During this same period Semitic peoples moved from the Arabian Desert into an area of southern Mesopotamia called Akkad, lying immediately north of Sumer. Imitating their more advanced neighbors, the Semites too developed thriving city-states, some of which matched those of the Sumerians in splendor and wealth.

The governance of the typical Sumerian city-state was grounded in religious faith. The Sumerians believed that each city-state was originally created by a god who had rolled back the primeval flood, made the earth appear, and fashioned the city and its inhabitants out of the mud. The city therefore belonged to the god, and its citizens were his slaves, charged with serving him in every way. As the city-states first took form, each was apparently governed by a group of elders who consulted with an assembly of freemen in making the decisions by which the will of the gods was carried out. This "primitive democracy," as it has been characterized, did not last long. Probably for the sake of efficiency, power was more and more concentrated in the hands of a single leader. The system grew into a theocratic kingship in which the ruler's power was based on his role as the agent of the patron god, the true ruler of the community. The priest-king, called *ensi* or *lugal*, centered his activities in the temple and surrounded himself with priest-assistants. From the temple flowed orders directing the numerous communal activities required to farm the lands of the gods. Back to the temple came a huge income gathered from the lands reserved for the support of the god, his house (the temple), and his agents (the priest-king and his aides). Added to this income were the sacrificial offerings made to please the god and to win his favor.

The temple complex became the nerve center of the entire community. Specialists whose skills were needed to conduct the numerous rituals in honor of the god congregated there. So did the ever-increasing hordes of overseers, tax collectors, surveyors, engineers, recordkeepers (scribes), and planners who enacted the directives of the priest-king. Its many activities nourished the arts, architecture, writing, learning, skilled crafts, and trade—all of which combined to elevate life in the city far above the level in neolithic villages. The civilizing aspects of city life were made possible primarily through the ability and willingness of the priestly community to divert surplus wealth from the city-state economy into such undertakings.

There is evidence in the histories of several Sumerian city-states that somewhere in the evolution of their government, the *ensi* or *lugal* began to divorce his activities from the temple community to assume a more secular status. The king did not surrender his role as representative of the patron god; his power was still theocratically based. But he exercised that power more independently by creating a nonpriestly circle of agents to assist him and drawing many civic functions away from the temple to the palace, which became the center of civic life. The priests were increasingly reduced to strictly cult functions. In this transformation, badly understood because of the lack of evidence, lies the roots of a type of government which has been called Oriental despotism. It was destined to play a major role in the history of the Near East and was to exercise a great fascination over men who lusted after power and glory in many other parts of the world.

The changing character of Sumerian city-state government was probably related to new political problems in Mesopotamia after 3000 B.C. By then the city-states were solidly established. Still, Mesopotamia was plagued by a lack of political stability. In part, this resulted from the incessant attacks of outsiders attracted by the riches of the valley communities. Even more disruptive was the violent rivalry among the city-states for land and power. The more successful a certain region

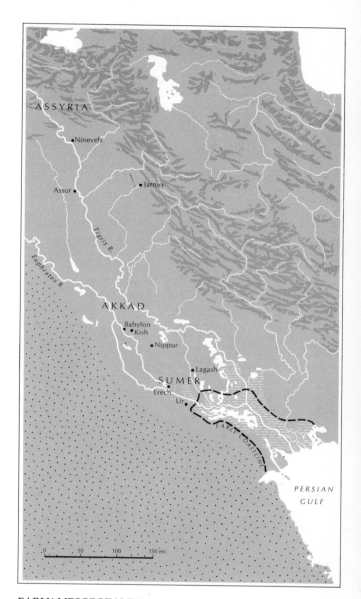

EARLY MESOPOTAMIA

was in ordering its internal structure, the more capable it was of harassing its neighbors. The political history of Mesopotamia during much of the third millennium B.C. centered around coping with the problems of barbarian attacks and incessant intercity warfare. The solution was eventually found in the formation of empires ruled by kings who developed new political techniques for keeping peace and order among smaller political entities. In the course of this search, Oriental despotism, grounded in earlier Sumerian political experience, took mature form.

The first attempts at shaping a new political order were made by Sumerian cities. At various times between 3000 and 2400 B.C., strong military leaders from Ur, Erech, Lagash, and Umma succeeded in establishing temporary mastery over other cities, but these "empires" were short-lived. Ultimately the Semites proved more talented in uniting Mesopotamia.

The first great Semitic empire builder, Sargon I, emerged about 2400 B.C. from the city of Akkad. Ancient legend cast him in the role of a man of humble origin, set adrift in a basket in the bulrushes by an errant mother when he was an infant and rescued and raised as a gardener until the gods called him to greatness. More reliable records indicate that Sargon was a servant in the royal household of a minor Semitic king whose office he usurped. Whatever the case, he proved to be an effective war leader, utilizing his Semitic troops with great skill to subdue the powerful and more advanced city-states of Sumer south of Akkad. He also led his armies into the Zagros Mountains to the east and to the shores of the Mediterranean in the west, thereby curbing the barbarian assaults on the rich valley region and spreading its culture among more backward peoples. Sargon's empire was sustained until about 2200 B.C. by his descendants. Its excessive size made it vulnerable to outside attacks and internal resistance from the Sumerian city-states. The main beneficiaries of its collapse were these cities, which once more entered an era of independence and glory.

By 2000 B.C. the renaissance of the old Sumerian city-stages was apparently ending. Ascendant now was a new group of Semitic people, the Amorites, who had only recently installed themselves in the river valley after migrating from the Arabian Desert. Early in the second millennium B.C., several Amorite chieftains created petty kingdoms at the expense of the Sumerian city-states. Out of this setting emerged the greatest of the Amorite leaders, Hammurabi, ruler of the city-state of Babylon. His reign,

extending from about 1792 to 1750 B.C., was distinguished by military exploits. He repeated the conquests of Sargon I, creating an empire that extended from the Mediterranean to the Zagros. By his own description, he was "King of the Four Quarters of the World." Babylon became a great city, the seat of a government that maintained peace and unity over a broad territory. The Amorite rulers absorbed and spread the high culture of conquered Sumer and under them Mesopotamian civilization reached its apogee.

But the brilliance of Hammurabi and his successors provided the Amorite Empire no safety from outside assaults. Shortly after 1750 B.C. foreign peoples like the Hittites and the Kassites began to push in from the north. They moved as part of an extensive disturbance that upset the political order throughout the Near East. Eventually the Kassites seized control of the Tigris-Euphrates Valley. The Sumerian cities did not have the strength to rise against them; Amorite rule had apparently crushed local patriotism. Never again would the people of the valley itself create a strong political power, although they and the area would serve as a base for large empires built by future conquerors.

The empire builders who dominated the Tigris-Euphrates Valley after 2400 B.C. instituted several new ideas and practices in government that proved to be among the greatest of all Babylonian contributions to civilization. The principal political challenge facing a "king of kings," as Hammurabi called himself, was to overcome the differences that divided the peoples he ruled. He was especially successful in resolving this problem.

One of Hammurabi's achievements was to complete the destruction of the monopoly of power previously held by the priests. He created a new concept in which the king himself was judge, lawgiver, and general in his own right. This powerful figure served as a symbolic center around which his subjects could rally, thus undercutting the dependence upon priests who ruled over small areas that a god was believed to have made sacred.

Hammurabi also developed institutions that enabled him to exercise the powers he claimed.

Backed by a well-organized army ready to curb threats to peace in his empire, he established at Babylon a centralized bureaucracy with specialized departments of finance, public works, justice, and defense. He subdivided his empire into local units and sent out royal servants to collect taxes, raise troops, suppress uprisings, and judge disputes. He emerges as a tireless administrator who paid careful attention to every detail in his extensive realm. Hammurabi used religion as a unifying force, promoting the worship of Marduk, once a deity in Babylon alone, throughout his empire. Marduk was presented as having conquered the other gods and therefore gained the right to rule their lands on earth. Never, however, did Hammurabi's power depend solely on religion.

Probably the most significant of all Hammurabi's measures was his famous code of law. It is no longer possible to hail him as history's first lawgiver, for it is now evident that earlier Sumerian rulers had drawn up codes and that Hammurabi's was a synthesis of these. But by the very act of synthesis, he took an important step toward effacing the diversities in the everyday affairs of his subjects by providing them with a common set of rules for property, wages, marriage and family affairs, crime, commercial exchange, and inheritance. Here was a practical device for unifying his subjects. The great king reveals in the code a passion for peace and justice, a desire "to destroy the wicked and the evil, so that the strong may not oppress the weak." In reading the laws, one senses Hammurabi's appreciation of the fact that a sound legal system based on widely accepted rules was a prime tool for instituting and maintaining a civilized society. A modern reader is sometimes taken aback by the brutal punishments prescribed: death to a builder whose construction falls and kills its owner; loss of a hand for the surgeon whose patient dies; loss of an eye for anyone who puts out the eye of another. But the code is better characterized by its common-sense, humane approach to basic problems: protection for women, children, and slaves; fairness in commercial exchange; protection for the property of soldiers on duty; standard procedures for adjudicating disputes; debt relief for victims of flood and drought. On the whole, the code probably represented an enlightened concept of justice that drew people to accept Hammurabi's rule and to join the larger community of his empire.

3. THE MESOPOTAMIAN SOCIAL AND ECONOMIC SYSTEM

The material base for Mesopotamian society was agriculture. That base was sound, for the fertile soil of the valley and the irrigation system combined to permit a rich return in agricultural produce. A wide variety of crops was cultivated, with barley, sesame (for oil), and date palms being the staples. Aside from the irrigation system, agricultural techniques advanced little beyond neolithic levels. The spade, the crude wooden plow, the clay sickle, and the flail were the prime tools. Much of the labor was provided by human beings, although oxen and asses were used; the horse, while known, seems not to have played any significant role in economic life. Despite this primitive technology, yields seem to have been high—some authorities argue that grain harvests were as great as those in modern North America. Pigs and sheep were also raised in large numbers.

The prime agricultural unit was the large farm. It was tilled by gangs of laborers, some semifree peasants and others slaves, under the careful supervision of the landlord or his agents. This labor force also spent much time repairing the dikes and canals, clearing away the troublesome rushes, and dredging out the silt that constantly threatened the irrigation system. Agricultural laborers were given their pay in produce. There were also some small independent farmers who cultivated their acreage with the aid of a slave or two. On the whole, however, landownership tended to be confined to a small group of nobles. In the early Sumerian period the temple priests nearly monopolized control of the land. By Hammurabi's time, although the myth that all land belonged to the patron god was sustained, a nonpriestly aristocracy—chiefly soldiers and royal agents—had gained possession of a considerable part of the land, usually by grant from the king.

Hammurabi's code. The relief, which shows
Hammurabi receiving his code of laws from a god,
is carved at the top of a cylinder carrying the laws in
cuneiform symbols. *Photo: Giraudon*

Mesopotamian economy was enriched and
variegated by a flourishing trade and industry.
Many cities maintained high production of textiles, pottery, jewelry, metal goods, and especially clay bricks for building. The priests played
an important role in promoting industry, using
the vast religious offerings as capital. Great
rulers also sponsored manufacturing, and by
Hammurabi's time there even existed craftsmen who were able to engage in industrial
enterprises on their own.

Lack of many raw materials, especially stone
and metals, made trade a necessity in Mesopotamia. Every city had a class of people who spent
their lives trading with neighboring cities or in
the uncivilized areas surrounding the river valley. The code of Hammurabi makes it clear that
highly developed business methods had
evolved to aid commerce among them: compli-

cated contracts, standard weights and measures,
credit buying, lending for interest, deeds, and
promissory notes.

Mesopotamian society was dominated by a
small aristocracy of priests and nobles. As we
have seen, the priests were especially powerful
in early Sumerian cities, but laymen had become
more prominent by the time of Hammurabi.
Regardless of who constituted the aristocracy,
this class benefited most from Mesopotamia's
riches and created a glittering life for itself. By
twentieth-century standards much of this wealth
was ill-gotten. Nonetheless, the aristocracy performed an important function in society by directing the efforts of hundreds of thousands of
individuals toward a common end. Without
such a guiding force, the cooperation needed to
control the rivers would have been impossible.
In a very real sense, the aristocrats earned their
rewards. Perhaps their wealth was not too deeply resented by the rest of society; at least we hear
nothing of attempts to overthrow them.

Even though Mesopotamian society was
dominated by a small aristocracy, care was taken
to define and protect the status of other classes.
Hammurabi's code embodied the principle that
nobles should be punished more severely for
certain crimes than other members of society. It
was also careful to state the rights and duties of
slaves, peasants, merchants, and artisans. The
Mesopotamians were class conscious indeed,
but it was understood that each social class had a
role in society, a role that all other classes must
respect.

4. MESOPOTAMIAN RELIGION

Mesopotamian civilization is comprehensible
only in terms of Mesopotamian religion, for religious beliefs and practices permeated every facet of life. But our knowledge is scanty, and there
is no evidence like that available from the writings of theologians of the great modern faiths.
The origins of Mesopotamian religion lie in the
remote and inaccessible past. When records
began to be kept, most religious ideas were already formed and stable, and the scribes were
little concerned with describing their evolution

or content logically. From the evidence we have, however, we can draw some conclusions.

We know, for example, that Mesopotamian religion was polytheistic. Perhaps the most basic conviction of all Mesopotamians was the belief that every phenomenon was caused by spirits living in all things. Then men realized that some of these gods were more powerful than others and thus worthy of greater attention. This heightened awe was felt especially toward the spirits who controlled the forces of nature. Among Sumerians and Semites alike the worship of the forces of nature fixed on Anu, the sky god; Enlil, god of the air; and Enki (called Ea by Semitic peoples), god of the earth and waters. Hardly less important were the astral deities: Nanna (Sin in Semitic), the moon god, and Utu (Shamash to the Semites), the sun god. One of these five was often accepted as the founder and present owner of a city and its inhabitants. Another deity almost universally worshiped in the valley was the goddess of fertility, whose munificent power renewed all nature every spring. This great "mother," called Inanna by Sumerians and Ishtar by Semites, had a special appeal to the ordinary person living close to the soil, to whom the annual miracle of renewal was most obvious.

These gods were all represented as human beings possessing terrible powers and capable of doing great damage to anyone who displeased them. But they were not alone in the universe. Each family and individual worshiped lesser gods who controlled the multitude of activities that surrounded human existence. Each also believed that the world was filled with demons capable of causing no end of discomfort and small misfortune.

During the long period of Mesopotamian history, there was a tendency to clarify the nature and power of these deities and to spell out their relationship to one another and the human community. One suspects that more energy was expended on this quest than on any other intellectual activity. The Mesopotamians' success in this venture may have constituted one of their main accomplishments, for it was probably crucial that man formulate his religion with some precision before turning his creative mind to

other ends. The fruit of this immense effort to know the divine better was a rich and intriguing body of mythology.

Mesopotamians ascribed to their gods a style of life similar to their own: Divine society reflected human society (Mesopotamian "theologians" would have put it the other way around). They also tried to spell out the hierarchy of the gods, a problem made more pressing by the incessant political fluctuations in Mesopotamia. Since the people believed that each city-state was the property of a god, some explanation had to be given when one polity conquered another. Usually this resulted in a myth about a similar war between the gods, with one conquering the other, and the defeated people usually accepted the conquering god as their chief deity, their old god being reduced to subordinate rank. At one time or another most of the great gods mentioned previously were accepted by large numbers of people as a result of conquest. This development culminated in the time of Hammurabi, when the god of the victorious city of Babylon, Marduk, was universally worshiped.

Mythology also grew from an urge to understand how there came to be order in the universe and what that order consisted of. The result was a series of elaborate creation myths explaining how a particular god, such as Marduk, subdued the primeval chaos, fashioned the families of gods, created and positioned the heavens, the stars, the seas, and the land, and filled the universe with living things. The mythologists also dealt with change; for example, by the age of Hammurabi there existed a rich mythology explaining how the goddess Ishtar and her lover, Tammuz, managed to assure the renewal of life each spring. As a body, this primitive "theology" is an impressive venture into answering the questions that face man. It became a rich storehouse from which later peoples drew their religious ideas.

Where did men fit into this religious scene? A man was viewed as a slave of the gods, created by them to carry out their will without question. They were vengeful, angry gods, apt at any moment and for any reason to heap disaster on their slaves. Men therefore bore a terrible burden in trying to keep their unpredictable masters happy. The care and feeding of the gods was crucial in this respect. Magnificent temples were built as dwellings, and every care was lavished on decoration and furnishings. Sumptuous banquets were prepared daily and served with great pomp. Troops of priests and priestesses, organized by specialties, stood constantly ready to feed, bathe, perfume, fan, sing for, and make love to the gods — or those whom the gods designated as their surrogates. Whole city-states labored to provide the building materials, the metals, the bread, the beer, the fruit, and all other things needed to make life comfortable for the gods. Great festivals, like the spring New Year celebration, were organized in their honor. A major part of the wealth and creative talent of the whole community was poured into this effort to make them pleased with their earthly slaves. Aside from the great temples, people gave offerings to placate the spirits at countless smaller temples and shrines in houses, on the farms, and in the streets. No project, great or small, was ever undertaken without a ritual performance, first to ask the gods to look with favor on the venture and later to thank them for its success. For all this elaborate effort, the Mesopotamians were never sure of reward. Thus their view of life was pessimistic; with no certainty of success or even safety, they lived life as a ritual aimed at pleasing the gods, for this was how things had to be.

As one might expect, the Mesopotamians were especially anxious to find out in advance what the gods might be planning. They developed a whole battery of prediction techniques. Dreams were interpreted and the entrails of animals were studied to find signs of the future. The movement of the stars was carefully observed, and the astrologer was a powerful figure in society. By adding these many facts together, it is perhaps safe to say that the Mesopotamians explored nearly every mode of external worship conceivable, creating a set of ritual practices that long remained a model for imitation by later peoples.

Yet the Mesopotamians had no god who placed heavy ethical demands on his believers. Seldom did they give much thought, therefore, to the problem of moral standards as a facet of religious life. Perhaps this lack of concern with morality and ethics was connected with the absence of any deep feeling about immortality. Mesopotamians believed that the dead passed on to a "land of no return" somewhere underground, "where dust is their feed, clay their sustenance; where they see no light and dwell in darkness." Very little attention was paid to expensive burial or to the care for the dead. Religion was concerned chiefly with sustaining earthly life.

5. MESOPOTAMIAN LITERATURE, ART, AND SCIENCE

The achievements of the Mesopotamians in the arts, literature, and science have always seemed less significant than those of the Egyptians, probably because Egyptian cultural monuments have survived so much better. But what has remained of their culture suggests a great deal of creative power and notable advance over peoples who lived in the area prior to them. By and large, the Sumerians were the original artistic creators in Mesopotamia. The Semites sometimes modified and developed Sumerian cultural accomplishments, but more often they merely imitated them. Culturally, the two peoples merged, so that a common pattern of culture rooted in ancient Sumer embraced the entire area of Mesopotamia.

The Sumerians developed a writing system during the fourth millennium B.C. Their original method of writing employed pictographs, but gradually a system of symbols representing sounds was developed. After Sargon I, the Sumerian written language began to be replaced by the Semitic, called Akkadian. However, learned men continued to study Sumerian, so that a considerable body of Sumerian literature has survived. Both peoples wrote on clay tablets, pressing the symbols into soft clay with a wedge-shaped reed stylus and then baking the tablets. This writing has been called *cuneiform*, a term from the Latin word meaning "wedge."

Writing in the early Sumerian cities probably developed for recordkeeping purposes. Once a usable system was perfected, it was employed to preserve an extensive body of literature which can be classified into a few major genres. The most impressive writings were the magnificent religious epics, of which the *Creation Epic* and the *Epic of Gilgamesh* are the best examples. The *Creation Epic* consists of a series of stirring episodes describing how Marduk won supremacy over the spirit world and created the earth and man. The *Epic of Gilgamesh* recounts the doings of a legendary hero named Gilgamesh, ruler of the city of Erech. The story, which centers on the theme of a fruitless search for immortality, leads him through numerous encounters with angry gods and with the forces they create to destroy him. The Mesopotamians also wrote impressive hymns to the gods containing countless references to worldly affairs. Several pieces of "wisdom" literature, embodying advice on how to get along in this world, have survived. There were attempts at historical writing in the form of chronicles recounting the deeds of famous rulers. The Mesopotamians were prolific letter writers, especially toward the end of the period. Unquestionably these works were read by a small circle, since literacy was not general. Nonetheless, Mesopotamian writings clearly indicate a lively cultural atmosphere. In reading this literature one is often struck by the similarities it bears in theme, style, and form to segments of the Old Testament, written down more than a thousand years later. This likeness suggests that the Mesopotamian literary tradition helped shape the minds and esthetics of many later generations.

From the beginning of their civilization, the Mesopotamians were skilled and creative artists. Their art did not survive well because of the lack of stone and the consequent use of more perishable materials. Their major architectural works were temples. From earliest times, every Sumerian city had a large and elaborate temple to the patron deity at its center. Near it was often a temple tower, called a *ziggurat*, designed as a series of terraces one on top of another, each succeeding layer smaller than the one below it. A sanctuary remote from the world was placed atop the final terrace. The purpose of these towers is not clear. Perhaps they served as tombs of some kind, or man-made replicas of the mountains where the valley dwellers used to worship before they came to the lowlands, or bridges to heaven. Around the main temple there usually developed an extensive complex of offices, dwellings, lesser shrines, storehouses, workshops, and market stalls, all comprising a sacred precinct for conducting the activities associated with serving the gods and often of immense size.

Magnificent brick palaces were also built for the kings, especially after the royal establishment began to separate from the temple. The palace at Mari, an important city at the height of the Amorite Empire, covered 6 acres and contained more than two hundred and fifty rooms. Mesopotamian architects knew how to use the column, the dome, the arch, and the vault, but given the limitations of the building materials at their disposal, they were unable to apply these techniques very extensively, especially in the monumental temples and the palaces. On the whole, Mesopotamian architecture was conservative, following set styles over long centuries.

Considerable sculpture has survived, although this art too was restricted by the shortage of good stone in Mesopotamia. Most of the three-dimensional statues are portrayals of gods and kings. Sculptors took some pains to give a distinctive character to a face but concerned themselves little with a realistic rendering of the body; they were governed by ideal geometrical forms—cylinders and cones—in conceiving their work. The statues are solid, stiff, motionless. More realistic and animated scenes were created by sculptors working in low relief. These *steles*, which often depicted historic events or divine exploits, accentuated action. The most exquisite carving was done by the seal makers, who wrought miniaturized scenes on stone that could be used to press an identifying mark into clay. The same skill is also illustrated in the abundant jewelry, metalwork, and decorated pottery. All this work reflects not only a great deal of technical skill but also a strong sense of beauty.

The Mesopotamians produced a body of knowledge that can be called science. They devised a system of time reckoning, with the year based on the sun's movement and the months on the moon's cycles. They also used a seven-day week. Since the solar and lunar phases do not coincide, extra days were added periodically to keep the two systems together. They also developed a standard of weights and measures, used almost universally by the end of Hammurabi's dynasty. Their numbering relied on both a decimal system and units of sixty; we still use the latter, for instance, in our divisions of the hour. They were able to add, subtract, multiply, and divide and to work simple geometry, such as finding the area of a plane surface or the volume of a cylinder. Mesopotamian medicine mixed intelligent observations about diseases and injuries with a quantity of superstition. A rather extensive knowledge of geography resulted from their wide travels. Since the stars played such a large part in religious beliefs, they accumulated considerable accurate information about astral movements, thus laying the basis for astronomy. Their attitude toward this information was typical: Astronomy did not lead them to consider the nature of the heavenly bodies; it merely served as a means of foretelling the future. So it was with all Mesopotamian scientific knowledge. They had no interest in discovering the natural world for its own sake. Theoretical science and the inquiring spirit made little progress of any kind.

Taken together, the achievements of the Mesopotamians in literature, the arts, and science suggest a few general characteristics of the outlook that predominated in this ancient culture. Certainly religion was the integrating force in intellectual life. It supplied the basic assumptions that governed all thought and expression and provided the great overarching truths about existence that gave meaning to every intellectu-al activity. Because the prime aim of religion was to sustain earthly life in good order in the face of powerful, capricious divine forces, Mesopotamian thinkers and artists were basically practical men. They expended their talents on keeping the gods happy and protecting the status quo. There was little room for free expression, experimentation, individual fancy, and speculation. The creative person was conservative, given to saying and doing over and over what had already been proved effective. There is a notable absence of evolution in artistic styles and themes across the two thousand years we have reviewed. Mesopotamians were also basically pessimistic, seldom hopeful that the burdens imposed on the slaves of the gods would lighten in an unstable and uncertain cosmic system. Finally, they were anxious, their minds alert for signs that man's efforts were attuned to the forces that governed existence. Perhaps this anxiety supplied the adaptability that made Mesopotamian civilization durable.

When the semibarbarous Kassites began to occupy the lower Tigris-Euphrates Valley about 1700 B.C., the first phase of Mesopotamian civilization had ended. For two thousand years the Sumerians and their Semitic imitators had struggled successfully to create an orderly society and a highly developed culture. After 1700 B.C., Mesopotamian civilization began to exert a powerful influence over a much wider area. Hardly a single people was to emerge in the later history of the Near East who did not borrow heavily from it. The Mesopotamian impact was felt long after the men from the "land between the rivers" ceased to be politically strong in the Near East.

Suggested Reading*

Overview of Part I
*V. Gordon Childe, *Man Makes Himself* (4th ed., Mentor). A stimulating interpretative work emphasizing economic and technological developments as prime factors in the evolution of Near Eastern civilizations.

Will Durant, *Our Oriental Heritage* (The Story of Civilization, Vol. I, 1935). A well-written survey strongly focused on cultural history.
*Sabatino Moscati, *The Face of the Ancient Orient* (Anchor). An excellent survey which gives particular

*Works available in paperback or inexpensive hardback editions are marked with an asterisk.

attention to the intellectual achievements of ancient Near Eastern civilizations.

C. W. Ceram, *Gods, Graves, and Scholars: The Story of Archaeology* (2nd ed., 1967). A splendid introduction to a science that has contributed greatly to our understanding of ancient Near Eastern history.

*Ignace J. Gelb, *A Study of Writing* (rev. ed., Phoenix). An invaluable guide to the development of writing.

Paleolithic and Neolithic Cultures

*William White Howells, *Back of History: The Story of Our Own Origins* (rev. ed., Anchor).

*Robert J. Braidwood, *Prehistoric Man* (7th ed., Scott Foresman).

*Ralph Linton, *The Tree of Culture* (Vintage). This and the preceding two titles will provide a good introduction to the diverse and always changing interpretations of human prehistory.

*Robert M. Lowie, *Primitive Religion* (Grosset and Dunlap Universal Library). A good description of primitive religion and its role in shaping early cultures.

Mesopotamia

*Henri Frankfort, *The Birth of Civilization in the Near East* (Anchor). A stimulating introduction to the complicated problems associated with the transition from neolithic culture to higher civilization in the Near East.

*H. W. F. Saggs, *The Greatness That Was Babylon: A Sketch of the Ancient Civilization of the Tigris-Euphrates Valley* (Mentor). The best general survey of Mesopotamian civilization, providing a good summary of political history and topical discussions of social, economic, and cultural matters.

H. Frankfort, *Kingship and the Gods: A Study of Ancient Near Eastern Religion as the Integration of Society and Nature* (1948). A brilliant study on the nature of Mesopotamian political institutions and the forces that shaped them.

*Cyrus N. Gordon, *Hammurabi's Code: Quaint or Forward Looking?* (Holt, Rinehart, and Winston). A stimulating introduction to Hammurabi's chief handiwork, useful in interpreting its significance.

*Georges Contenau, *Everyday Life in Babylon and Assyria* (Norton). A storehouse of information on how people in Mesopotamia lived and worked.

S. H. Hooke, *Babylonian and Assyrian Religion* (1963). A full description of the crucial element of Mesopotamian civilization.

*Henri Frankfort et al., *Before Philosophy: The Intellectual Adventure of Ancient Man* (Penguin). Contains a brilliant essay on the mentality dominating Mesopotamian society by T. Jacobsen.

*Otto Neugebauer, *The Exact Sciences in Antiquity* (2nd ed., Dover).

Henry Hodges, *Technology in the Ancient World* (1970). This and the preceding work will provide information on the accomplishments of the Mesopotamians in science and technology.

Sources

The Epic of Gilgamesh: Prose Version, trans. Nancy Sandars (Penguin).

James B. Pritchard, ed., *Ancient Near Eastern Texts Relating to the Old Testament* (1955). A splendid collection of literature representing the accomplishments of the Mesopotamians as well as other peoples of the ancient Near East.

2

ANCIENT EGYPT, 4000–1750 B.C., AND MINOAN CIVILIZATION

Not long after higher civilization had begun to take shape in Mesopotamia, a similar leap forward occurred in Egypt. Somewhat later still, a comparable advance occurred on the island of Crete. There is some evidence that influences from Mesopotamia played a role in shaping these new civilizations, but in the main, developments in each area, especially Egypt, were indigenous and thus assumed unique forms.

1. THE NILE VALLEY

The Greek historian Herodotus uttered a fundamental truth that still must be the starting point for the history of ancient Egypt: Egypt is the gift of the Nile. Rising in the mountains of equatorial Africa, the river ultimately traces a narrow, cliff-lined trough, seldom more than 10 miles wide, cutting through several hundred miles of bleak desert almost devoid of rainfall. As it nears the Mediterranean, the Nile fans out into a series of channels to form the Delta, a triangle about 120 miles on each side. Although the river links the land along its course to create a geographical entity, the Delta differs from the narrow valley to the south. It is less dominated by the desert, more open to the outside world, more comfortable. Geography created "two lands" in Egypt that always remained visible in Egypt's historic development.

The Egyptians themselves described the valley as the "black land," which they contrasted with the terrible "red land" of the desert. The "black land" was deposited by the benevolent river over the ages. With amazing regularity from ancient times until our own, each summer the Nile overflowed its low banks and covered the flat land on each side with floodwaters, soaking the parched soil and spreading a new layer of silt. When the river returned to its normal channel, crops could be planted in the rich, muddy soil. They matured quickly in the hot climate, usually returning high yields because of the fertility of the soil. If the crops needed additional moisture or if a second crop was planted in the same season, it was possible to draw water from the main channel of the river or from reservoirs.

The Nile's gifts were not free. Men had to struggle to keep down the vegetation in the swamps produced by the floods and to push water from the mainstream to drive back the ever-intrusive "red earth." And the river could be capricious, rising too much so that men's handiwork was swept away or too little so that the crops died. But on the whole, exploiting the Nile was less burdensome than controlling the Tigris-Euphrates rivers, which were less predictable in their flooding and which formed a much wider valley to irrigate. The Nile inspired confidence and optimism in those who lived along it. Well might the Egyptians sing: "Hail to Thee, O Nile, that gushest forth from the earth and comest to nourish Egypt!"

The Nile Valley differed from the Tigris-Euphrates Valley in another significant way: It was shielded from invaders by forbidding natural barriers. The deserts flanking it, the rapids (cataracts) that block river traffic about 700 miles south of its mouth, and the Mediterranean isolate the valley. The only readily accessible entry into Egypt is a narrow, easily defensible passage connecting the Delta to Asia. This isolation gave Egypt stability but deprived her of contact with foreigners and limited her ability to influence outsiders.

2. EGYPTIAN POLITICAL HISTORY

From the available evidence, it appears that the Nile Valley began to be occupied as early as 5000 B.C. by peoples who had already mastered agricultural life. Perhaps they were North Africans forced to seek new homes by the emerging desert in that area. Some may also have been from the south or from western Asia, for the Egyptians were surely a mixed people. The earliest settlers built small agricultural villages typical of neolithic peoples a distance from the river — away from the floods, away from the swamps and from the beasts and insects that infested them. Then began a long struggle to tame the land, a struggle that we must presume caused men to develop their skills. By about 4000 B.C., village settlements had spread throughout the valley, and there was an irrigation system that permitted the inhabitants to begin to gather the gifts of the Nile. There seems to have been no great economic pressure to unite the villages in larger communities, for nothing comparable with the Mesopotamian city-states evolved in early Egypt. However, over the centuries several contiguous villages tended to coalesce into petty kingdoms. The survival into later history of many totem symbols and totemic religious ideas from this age suggests that blood ties and shared religious beliefs were factors in this. Also, it is not impossible that aggressive, capable landlords forced their authority on weaker neighboring villages. As larger units formed, it very likely became obvious that greater cooperation brought greater benefits from the land and the river. However, the primitive villages never disappeared in Egypt; for long ages and under many kinds of government, they endured as the basic units of society.

The era of the formation of small kingdoms, called the Predynastic Age, ended suddenly about 3100 B.C., when all Egypt was unified under the *pharaoh*. Egyptian tradition ascribed this amazing feat to Menes, who launched the first dynasty of pharaohs and an era called the Old Kingdom. Certainly the process of unification had begun before Menes' time, for he already ruled a large kingdom in Upper (southern) Egypt when he subdued another in Lower Egypt. It required some time before the unification process was complete. Still, Menes preceded Sargon I by nearly seven centuries, and when Hammurabi built his rather temporary Amorite Empire, Egypt had enjoyed about thirteen centuries of almost uninterrupted unity.

In part, Egypt's unification was helped by the Nile, an easily traveled road from one end of Egypt to the other that draws all life to itself. More important was the absence of strong centers of local patriotism such as the religiously oriented city-states in Mesopotamia. The simple agricultural villages lining the Nile offered no real opposition to a resourceful unifier.

During the Old Kingdom (3100–2200 B.C.), Egypt was ruled by a succession of pharaohs, six dynasties in all. The rulers of the first two seem to have been absorbed chiefly in completing her unification: coercing or persuading the northern people to accept a "foreign" ruler from Upper Egypt, working out the details of an effective administration. Success in this venture set the stage for the glorious third and fourth dynasties, the golden age of the Old Kingdom. The pharaohs' rule, exercised from their capital at Memphis, situated near where the Nile fans out to form the Delta, brought the people peace, good order, and great prosperity. And their influence was felt outside the valley: in the Sinai peninsula; in Syria, where they maintained a trading outpost at Byblos; and in the south toward Nubia. The splendid pyramids built at Gizeh by the powerful pharaohs of the Fourth Dynasty, Menkaure, Kephren, and Khufu (Cheops), reflect not only the immense wealth and power of their builders but also the complex and unique cultur-

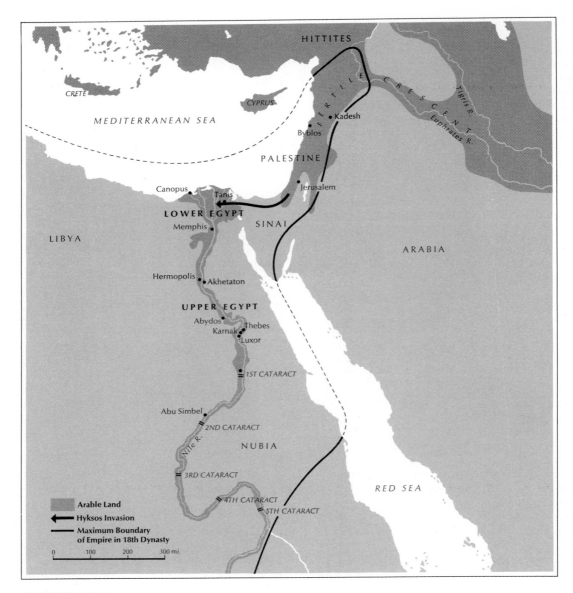

HITTITES

CRETE

MEDITERRANEAN SEA

CYPRUS

FERTILE
CRESCENT

Tigris R.
Euphrates R.

Kadesh

Byblos

PALESTINE

Canopus
Tanis
Jerusalem

LOWER EGYPT

SINAI

LIBYA

Memphis

ARABIA

Hermopolis
Akhetaton

UPPER EGYPT

Abydos
Karnak Thebes
Luxor

1ST CATARACT

Abu Simbel

2ND CATARACT

Nile R.

NUBIA

3RD CATARACT

RED SEA

4TH CATARACT
5TH CATARACT

Arable Land
Hyksos Invasion
Maximum Boundary
of Empire in 18th Dynasty

0   100   200   300 mi.

ANCIENT EGYPT

al pattern that had emerged in Egypt following unification.

By the time of the Third Dynasty, the Egyptian government had assumed the form it was to have for many centuries. Its central feature was the absolute power of the pharaoh. Indeed, he was universally accepted as a god, supposedly sired by the sun god Ra, born in a way different from humans, and destined to eternal life with other gods. The pharaoh owned Egypt and her populace. Every person was his servant, and his word was unchallengeable law. He could not even marry an ordinary mortal, but only his divine sister.

Despite their lofty and remote status, most of the pharaohs of the first four dynasties were active statesmen. They were carefully educated for their office, took an active part in administering the state, and emerge as nearly human. They traveled extensively, were informed about the condition of the irrigation system, directed building programs, took special care to render justice to all their subjects, and sponsored trading projects to acquire needed materials from abroad.

The records of the third and fourth dynasties reveal that a complex and efficient set of institutions had evolved through which the pharaoh exercised his vast powers. At his royal palace in Memphis, he gathered a group of trusted friends and delegated jobs for them to carry out. Among the high officials prominent in the records of the Old Kingdom were a vizier, a treasurer, a chief of irrigation, a chief justice, recordkeepers, and high priests. Most important was the vizier, who served as chief assistant to the pharaoh. Each of these major officials was assisted by numerous lesser state servants. But the government was not confined to the capital; Egypt was divided into forty-two government units, called *nomes*, each controlled by royal officials. Every nome was divided into villages, where the mass of the people lived and where officials appeared from time to time to enforce the pharaoh's orders and to collect taxes.

During the fifth and sixth dynasties, this splendid system began to falter, and Egypt drifted imperceptibly toward disorder. The pyramids built during this time were smaller, suggesting a decline in royal wealth and power. There is evidence of great independence of royal administrators and provincial governors. Complaints about disorder, injustice, and oppression appear in the records. The priests began to challenge the pharaoh's monopoly of the power to intercede with the gods on behalf of the people. The pharaoh's influence outside Egypt disappeared. The causes of the decline are hard to discern. There is no record of any sudden, overpowering internal or external development. Perhaps the pharaohs grew lax in ruling

Egypt and tended to place too much trust in their officials. The administrative machine appears to have become so large and complex as to be beyond the control of a single ruler. The opportunity for bureaucratic empire builders to shape their own little circles of power appears not to have been missed. There is some indication that the pharaohs impoverished themselves by overgenerous grants to the nobles and especially to the priests. And the rulers may have discredited themselves by imposing too great a burden on their subjects for such costly, nonproductive projects as the great pyramids.

By the end of the Sixth Dynasty, Egypt had entered a period of anarchy sometimes called the Feudal Age but more accurately named the First Intermediate Period (2200–2050 B.C.). Power rested in the hands of innumerable local princes who made their old offices and land grants hereditary and did as they pleased. The pharaohs of the seventh through tenth dynasties were shadowy, ineffective figures. Political disunity brought with it internal wars, lawlessness, injustice, and economic depression. Sensitive men reacted to these developments with shock and moral outrage. One writer complained of nobles slaving in the workhouses while "he who never slept on a plank now owned a bed," the robber possessing riches, the land deprived of kingship by irresponsible men, the desert spreading through the land. The end of political unity brought bitter fruit to most Egyptians while the strong and the grasping flourished.

Then, about 2050 B.C., the princes of Thebes, previously an insignificant city far to the south in the valley, undertook the task of reunification, perhaps in the name of the god Amon, heretofore only a minor deity. After a fierce struggle, these princes (designated as the Eleventh Dynasty) established what is known as the Middle Kingdom (2050–1750 B.C.). It reached its peak during the Twelfth Dynasty. Some of these rulers, especially Amenemhet I and Senusret III, remind one of the great pharaohs of the Fourth Dynasty. They restored many of the political institutions characteristic of the Old Kingdom — the divine power of the pharaoh, the centralized bureaucracy, the provincial administration — and labored to revive the economy, reclaim land from the desert, and maintain order. Once again Egypt's influence was felt in Syria, the Sinai region, and Nubia.

However, the divine character of the pharaoh was no longer so predominant. One authority has suggested that the pharaohs of the Middle Kingdom might better be called "good shepherds" than gods. The word ma'at *(justice)* provides a key to the spirit animating their government. They were especially concerned with providing *ma'at* for the lower classes, defining their place in society, ensuring their rights and welfare, and protecting them from greedy and oppressive officials. It appears that the grim experience of the First Intermediate Period had heightened the moral sensitivity of the Egyptians and generated a sense of individual rights. The strongest pharaohs of the Twelfth Dynasty did modify the government to some extent by decreasing the power of the old nobility and giving greater authority to a class of professional civil servants, called *scribes*, to carry out the multitude of functions associated with directing a centralized state.

After nearly three hundred years of orderly government and prosperity, the Middle Kingdom also began to decline. Its end was hastened by the emergence of a threat for which the Egyptians were not prepared. About 1750 B.C. a barbarian horde called the Hyksos swept out of Asia and seized control of the Nile Valley. Lawlessness and violence replaced orderly government. This interlude is usually called the Second Intermediate Period (1750–1580 B.C.). Eventually Egypt recovered from this catastrophe, but that story is a new chapter in the history of the Near East and must be reserved for later.

3. EGYPT'S ECONOMIC AND SOCIAL LIFE

Organized under a strong government, Egyptian society produced tremendous wealth, its chief source agriculture. Two or even three huge harvests of wheat, barley, flax, vegetables, and fruit were gathered each year. Herds of cattle, sheep, pigs, and goats pastured in the valley. The bulk of the Egyptian population devoted itself to farming. The peasants, crowded together in small villages, supplied the farm labor. Their mud huts, their scanty clothing, their monotonous diet of bread, beer, fish, and dried fruit, and their simple furniture certainly do not suggest a high standard of living. Life from one generation to the next consisted of constant labor to keep the irrigation system under control and to cultivate the crops.

Most of the labor was performed by hand and was extremely routinized as a result of the demands imposed by the river. Added to the regular work in the fields was the incessant demand for extra labor on the immense building programs undertaken by the pharaohs and the priests. The peasant was never permitted to keep much of the product of his work. After the owners of the land, the state, and the priests claimed their shares, he had only a bare subsistence. Despite his hard lot and his lack of freedom, he appears in literature and art as a happy, contented, healthy man, pleased to live in the favored land of the Nile under the good rule of the god-kings. Famine and disorder brought him misery, but these were temporary conditions, made up for by the numerous gifts of the Nile.

Although Egyptian civilization rested chiefly on agriculture, a considerable number of artisans and merchants also added to the wealth. They produced primarily luxury goods, working directly for the pharaoh, the rich nobles of his court, or the powerful provincial nobility. Every great household and temple had its own shops where artisans made a variety of items and from which merchants went forth to exchange goods and procure raw materials. In some cases, such as stone quarrying, copper mining, and brick making, production was organized on a large scale. The social status of the craftsman and merchant was usually much like that of the peasant. They were bound to an overlord, granted little freedom of action, and rewarded for their efforts with little more than subsistence. Egypt never developed urban communities comparable to those of Mesopotamia, where merchants and artisans constituted a class with considerable economic freedom to venture into enterprises of their own.

Egypt's economy and society were dominated by a relatively small aristocracy. At the peak stood the pharaoh, whose power gave him command over all elements of society and the total wealth of the state. The rest of the aristocracy consisted of those to whom the pharaoh chose to give high status and to reward with wealth. The priestly class enjoyed an especially high rank. The nonpriestly aristocrats, who served as government officials, played a leading role in organizing the labor of peasants and artisans and enjoyed large incomes derived from land.

In both Egypt and Mesopotamia, economic and social order was marked by certain significant departures from that of neolithic societies. Wealth was produced by extensive division of labor and specialization. Different groups plowed and reaped, built with their hands, traded, ruled, and prayed, to mention only the broadest divisions. The combination of all these specialties, each as necessary as any other, permitted millions of people to exploit successfully a small but rich geographical area. The efforts of these many "specialists" were rigidly directed from the top down, creating a regimented society. Aristocratic leadership was to remain a keynote of civilized people for long ages after Egypt and Mesopotamia had declined.

4. RELIGION IN EGYPT

As in ancient Mesopotamia, every aspect of Egyptian society was given its essential meaning by religious belief and practice. In fact, the modern student of history is forced to agree with Herodotus' conclusion that the Egyptians were the most religious of all peoples. Never has a society sustained more gods, more priests, more temples, or more modes of worship. The problem of the modern historian is to make sense out of Egyptian religious belief and practice. Unfortunately, gathering more information about Egyptian religion has not simplified things, for our increasing knowledge has revealed baffling complexity, persistent confusion, and glaring contradictions.

One basic characteristic does emerge clearly: The Egyptians believed that everything that happened was caused by divine forces. Their religion was thus highly polytheistic, the gods worshiped at various times numbering in the thousands. The origins of most of the gods go far back into history. When reliable historical records finally appear, a great host of deities was already familiar to the Egyptians. They were conceived in a variety of forms—as animals, humans, birds, plants, inanimate objects, abstractions, and mixtures of any two or three of these forms. Most of the gods had a particular sacred place in Egypt or in the skies above it, but all of them roamed about freely and were likely to be present wherever and whenever humans were at work or play. There is some evidence to suggest that Egyptian concepts of the divine forces tended to evolve from a more primitive animal worship toward gods with human forms and cosmic powers and even toward abstract, disembodied gods (such as *ma'at*). But this trend should not be overemphasized, for seldom were even the most primitive deities abandoned. Moreover, any effort to set forth a clear definition of the powers and duties of each (such as is possible, for instance, in Greek religion) is completely frustrating. For example, the Egyptians had several versions of creation, all accepted as equally valid. On the whole it does seem that the Egyptians conceived of their gods as basically benevolent and kindly. In contrast to the Mesopotamians, they did not live in constant fear, but rather viewed the gods and their activities with optimism and hope.

There was, however, an effort to create order among this horde of gods, and especially to decide which were most important. An elaborate body of mythology developed in the centuries preceding the end of the Middle Kingdom. During the Predynastic and Old Kingdom periods, there was a tendency for the gods of victors in war to become supreme. For instance, when Menes unified all Egypt, the falcon god Horus, formerly the god of Upper Egypt, became the supreme god of all Egypt. Even as late as the Middle Kingdom, a relatively unknown deity like Amon could become a powerful force as a result of the political success of the princes of Thebes. By the end of the Old Kingdom, Ra was accepted as a god demanding reverence from all

Egyptians and as the supreme figure in the heavens. His growing popularity was undoubtedly due to the importance of the sun in the life of every Egyptian. The effort to understand how things came to be could exalt a particular god as the prime creator; such was the case with Ptah, brought to prominence by the priests at Memphis as the creator of an ordered universe and all things in it (including other gods). Especially significant was the emergence of Osiris, who was believed to possess the power of granting men a happy life after death. By the end of the Middle Kingdom, this theologizing process had brought some order to religious thought and practice. A few gods, especially Ra and Osiris, were recognized as most powerful, and their widespread acceptance provided a powerful unifying force. Egypt never achieved complete religious unity, however, for local cults persisted.

Since everything from the Nile floods to the smallest household incident was a consequence of the will of some god, Egyptian religion placed heavy emphasis on man's need to do things that would please the gods. Religious obligations became fixed early in Egyptian history and changed little over the centuries. The burden of pleasing the gods fell on all men alike. To the pharaoh belonged the prime responsibility of the care of the great deities, and no little part of the activities of the god-king was devoted to ministering to the needs of other gods. All of society joined the pharaoh in this holy work.

For example, the gods required living quarters. Therefore, the Egyptians built temples and shrines, ranging all the way from the great temples built by the pharaohs in honor of the chief gods to tiny chapels in villages and homes. The gods enjoyed finery, and the Egyptians lovingly decorated the sacred dwellings with their best artistic efforts. The gods required food and physical care; the priests enacted an elaborate ritual to ensure that these needs were met. The daily routine of caring for the gods was carried out privately in the inner sanctuaries of the temples; but on occasion great festivals were organized. The statue of the god being honored was brought forth from the temple with great pomp, and crowds came from all over Egypt to pay their respects and make their sacrifices.

Prayers and songs were a regular part of religious worship and were composed in great numbers to fit any request men had to make of the gods. A rich array of magical practices existed to win the favor of the gods and avoid the consequences of divine annoyance. In contrast with the Mesopotamians, the Egyptians did not devote much effort to ascertaining the future. They seemed confident that the gods would smile on them and therefore felt no pressing need to know divine intentions. The necessity of addressing, caring for, and pleasing the gods was so great that Egypt maintained a vast number of priests who specialized in this job. Probably most Egyptians felt that their efforts to please the gods were fully repaid. The abundant harvests, the peace in the kingdom, and the security with which a man could live his life made it seem that the gods were satisfied with the attentions they received.

Besides earthly benefits, the gods held another precious gift for deserving Egyptians — a happy life after death. Concern with immortality was a unique aspect of Egyptian religion and was the source of some of its most dynamic features. From early times, Egyptians believed that every man had a *ka*, a double for his body that lived on after death in some kind of close association with the divine spirits. The *ka* had to have all it needed to keep it happy after death. In early Egyptian history, that end was met in a rather crude and materialistic fashion. The body was preserved by mummification so that the spirit could return to it. A tomb that would last forever was built to shelter the spirit. Elaborate arrangements were made to ensure that the spirit would have food, drink, luxuries, companions — everything it had enjoyed in life — to make immortal life tolerable. Perhaps only the pharaoh could afford proper provisions; but at least he was willing to help some others live eternally so that they could continue to be his companions and servants. He therefore built tombs for his wives, his children, his officials, and his friends close to his own great tomb. By the end of the Old Kingdom, many nobles were constructing their own tombs. The fate of the common man in this early period is not clear, but one must presume that some kind of afterlife was his lot too, even if he could not make the proper preparations.

This Egyptian funerary papryus from the tomb of a princess shows some of the steps in the transition to afterlife. In the center, the gods weigh her heart in a balance against the figure of the Goddess of Truth. *Ca. 1000 B.C.* *Photo: The Metropolitan Museum of Art*

Gradually, the expectation of gaining immortality was democratized and universalized until the gates of heaven were open to all Egyptians. The crux of this radical transformation came in the troubled First Intermediate Period and was probably part of the moral outrage generated against the materialism and greed of the Old Kingdom's ruling class. The new concept of immortality found its focus in the worship of Osiris, which by the period of the Middle Kingdom had advanced to a central place in religious life and was embodied in a touching myth. Osiris, a good god associated with life forces and the Nile, was murdered by his wicked brother, Seth, who dismembered his body and scattered the parts over the face of the earth. Osiris' wife, Isis, patiently gathered them up, and when her task was finished, Osiris returned to life. Thereafter, he had the power to raise everyone from death to life. When any Egyptian died, he appeared before Osiris and a panel of judges in the other world. Osiris placed the dead man's heart on one pan of a balance and a feather on the other. If the heart was weighted with evil, the dead man was not fit for eternal happiness and was tossed to a ferocious beast. If it was buoyant with goodness, he was allowed to live forever in a heavenly place very much like the earthly Nile Valley.

The radically new element in this concept of immortal life is the idea of the moral worth attached to each man. Osiris was concerned with goodness in evaluating a man's eligibility for eternal life and not with his wealth and social position. In articulating a moral basis for human life, the Egyptians were far in advance of other ancient peoples. This is not to imply that all of Egyptian life was transformed by this birth of conscience and moral sense. Egyptians continued to provide for the material welfare of the dead, although from the Middle Kingdom onward the emphasis was less on the grandeur of the tomb and more on its decoration—a record in pictures and writing to convince Osiris that the occupant had indeed lived a "good" life; and in time, men came to busy themselves devising clever formulas to conceal their moral faults. Still, Osiris worship heightened moral awareness in a way that was unknown in Mesopotamia, and it provided a meaningful place in the cosmic order for all men.

5. EGYPTIAN CULTURAL LIFE

Perhaps the chief glory of Egypt's history down to 1750 B.C. was her intellectual and artistic

cal tool, useful in government. Once it was perfected, however, it allowed the Egyptians to set down their ideas in a clear and artistic fashion.

Because much of Egyptian literature has survived from religious records, we get the impression that religion supplied the chief inspiration for writing. The pyramids were prime repositories for much of Egyptian religious literature. On their walls were carved hymns, prayers, magical incantations, moral exhortations, and bits of mythology, all intended to influence the gods in some way. Although this kind of literature often reflects deep feelings and sophisticated intellectual concepts, on the whole it is traditionalist, bound in form and content by ancient and sacred conventions. Somewhat fresher and more revealing of the character of society were the pyramid texts recounting the splendid deeds of the pharaohs who built the tombs. In a sense, this kind of writing represents an early attempt at history, except that its purpose was religious rather than worldly.

Not all Egyptian literature was intended to serve religious ends. Several kinds of secular writings have survived either in stone carvings or on papyrus. Religious themes are never absent from these works, but their focus is quite different. There are some letters, legal accounts, and business records. The Egyptians appear to have liked collections of moral maxims and wise sayings, often set down in the form of instruction from father to son or teacher to pupil. Lyric poetry was written, and laments expressing disgust with the world circulated in difficult times. Perhaps most appealing today are the marvelous tales of fancy and romance recounting the adventures of travelers, shipwrecked sailors, and soldiers.

What has survived of Egyptian literature—and it certainly comprises only a small fraction of a larger production—shows considerable technical skill and a feel for humanity. The mood

achievement. Her culture is striking for its unity and coherence, an effect that stems from the fact that it was basically a product of a single center—the pharaoh's court. Court ideals dictated a single style and a single set of motifs, and once these had been established, there was little questioning or experimenting over many centuries.

One of Egypt's achievements was her system of hieroglyphic writing, which began to develop about the time of the Old Kingdom (about 3200 B.C.). Gradually, various pictures began to be accepted as representations of sound values, and several of these symbols put together formed words. Writing probably developed as a practi-

is often gay, confident, and carefree, although occasionally a writer could work himself into a state of black despair, especially over the talent of men for sin and greed. On the whole, Egyptian literature is less profound but more versatile than Mesopotamian, which never devised lyric poetry, romances, and tales of fancy. But Egypt produced nothing like the Gilgamesh epic, perhaps because the very concept of a heroic figure seeking to master mysterious cosmic forces and assure immortality for himself was foreign.

It is through the visual arts that the character and quality of Egyptian life are most clearly preserved. Who can view the Egyptian collections in the Louvre or the British Museum without a sense of the marvelous creative power, feeling, and technical skill of the anonymous Egyptian artist? Egyptian art reveals what may have been the keystone of Egyptian civilization: the ability to work for long ages with set forms and subjects and maintain freshness and vitality.

Architecture was the queen of all the arts in Egypt, most of the other forms serving to adorn it. Architects worked in many materials, including mud, reeds, brick, and wood; but the most monumental work was in stone. The first flowering of stonework occurred in the early years of the Old Kingdom and was devoted chiefly to tomb building, which reached its apogee in the construction of the pyramids. The pyramid of Khufu (about 2600 B.C.) stands as one of the great construction feats of all time. It measured 755 feet on each side at the base, falling short of a geometrically perfect square by about 8 inches of difference between the north and south sides and by less than 1/2 inch of difference between the east and west sides. The pyramid once was 480 feet high and contains over two million blocks of stone averaging 2½ tons each but weighing as much as 30 tons. The outside of the structure was covered with polished stone. Most of the stone was precut, probably with copper saws and wedges, in quarries many miles away and floated down the Nile to the pyramid site, a procedure that entailed tremendous planning. The huge blocks were probably elevated into position up dirt ramps built alongside the pyramid. The labor was performed by hand with almost no mechanical aid. The passages and

rooms that honeycomb the interior were skillfully vaulted. Pyramid building continued for many centuries, but later architects never equaled those of the Old Kingdom. Shifting concepts of immortality militated against such massive, complex undertakings as the pyramids at Gizeh.

Although the surviving evidence is not so impressive as the pyramids, it seems quite certain that architects had arrived at the basic forms for temples and palaces by the end of the Old Kingdom; by the Middle Kingdom they were building impressive structures. The basic temple style was the hypostyle hall, consisting of a roof on columns. Typically a high-ceilinged central hall was flanked by side halls, each covered with a roof on columns shorter than the central hall's. The builders achieved splendid artistic effects by modeling their columns after plants—the palm tree, the lotus plant, the papyrus plant, the reed. Within the temple, numerous chambers were grouped to serve the sanctuary, which was the living place of the god. Before the temple was an open court surrounded by a columned portico and entered by a massive gateway. In the center of the court often stood an obelisk in honor of the sun god. (Many of these obelisks have found their way to the cities of Western Europe, the spoils of the nineteenth-century expansion into Africa.) The palaces of the pharaohs were undoubtedly as splendid as the temples and probably utilized the same basic architectural forms.

Egypt's sculptors matched her architects in skill. At a very early date sculptural styles became fixed, and they changed little over most of her history. Sculpture was the handmaiden of religion. The chief subjects of three-dimensional works were the gods, the pharaohs, their families, and their companions, the statues being intended for tombs and temples. Human forms were usually massive, stiff, unemotional portrayals following fixed proportions, but the face was another matter. Here the sculptor tried to show feeling and purpose: the power of a god, the majesty of a pharaoh, the devotion of a royal servant. He was concerned not with realistic portrayal of a particular individual, but with a semblance of the perfection that individual embodied. Thus the face of the typical statue gazes straight out at the viewer as an embodiment of an ideal. Although the sculptor worked within highly conventionalized canons, each face is different—a reflection of the dynamic quality of the Egyptian achievement in art.

Egyptian sculptors were also skilled at relief work. Inside the tombs and on the pillars and walls of temples, endless series of scenes tell us more about daily life in Egypt than does all Egyptian writing. Again, the sculptor seldom tried to be realistic. He let the space he had determine the size and shape of his figures, and he often used conventional designs to represent objects. The human shapes are distorted, the feet and faces usually being shown in profile while the main trunk of the body faces the viewer. Many of the reliefs were painted to heighten the effect. Painting, most of which survives in tombs, bears a striking similarity to relief work in terms of subject matter and form. The artist sketched an outline of the scene to be pictured, often in red, and then filled it in with strong colors of one tone.

Viewed as a whole, Egyptian art suggests certain generalizations about Egyptian thought. It shows how completely thought was dominated by religion. The artist almost always created for eternity—his emphasis on massiveness and solid construction displayed his great confidence in the civilization he was representing. The unchanging artistic canons of Egypt might be interpreted as evidence of the artist's sense of the permanence of his society as well as his satisfaction with the existing order. The accent on size in building and sculpture was in part motivated by the desire to show what tremendous things men could do. The art as a whole portrays a stable, unemotional, proud people, impressed by what they had achieved and eager to maintain it.

The Egyptians made remarkable advances in technology and practical science. They compiled a substantial body of knowledge about the movement of the stars and at an early date devised accurate time reckoning based on the annual appearance of the star Sirius. Their calendar consisted of twelve thirty-day months plus five days added at the end of the year. They perfected a system of numbers by which they could perform the mathematical operations based on addition and subtraction, and while they did not use zero and had great difficulty working with fractions, they did develop a simple form of geometry for computing the areas of triangles, rectangles, and hexagons and the volumes of pyramids and cylinders. Egyptian scientists accumulated considerable information about metals and their properties and a tremendous knowledge of plant and animal life. In medicine they developed surgical techniques and learned to use a wide range of drugs. Their grasp of anatomy was extensive, undoubtedly because of observations from mummification, which required opening the body and removing the internal organs. Egyptian medicine was far in advance of that of other Near Eastern peoples of the age.

However, pure science held little interest for the Egyptians, who seldom sought new scientific knowledge after the modern fashion. Like the Mesopotamians, once they had found a workable solution for a problem of engineering or medicine or metallurgy, they sought no farther. Their thinking was mythological, and they found no reason for questioning what religion revealed. Despite this lack of interest in pure science, credit must be given the Egyptians for gathering considerable information that not only solved some of their own problems but also served later civilizations as a solid base from which to proceed toward more fully developed scientific knowledge.

Egypt's history was not ended when the Hyksos invaded the Nile Valley about 1750 B.C., but her long isolation was: her future role would be played in a much larger frame of reference than the Nile Valley. (We shall return to this subject in a later chapter.) However, the achievements we have just described were to remain the fundamental bases of Egyptian society. The Egyptians had made their creative contributions to the world by the end of the Middle Kingdom; thereafter, their role would be as a model for other peoples.

6. MINOAN CIVILIZATION

While complex and sophisticated cultures were being shaped in the great river valleys of the

Near East, another center of civilization developed on the island of Crete. Although Greek mythology transmits a vague memory of this civilization, its fundamental character was unknown until archeological discoveries fifty years ago. Its emergence came considerably later than did the development of Mesopotamia and Egypt, and in fact, it owed much to the Near Eastern centers and did not represent an independent creation. Yet it is distinctive enough to warrant treatment in conjunction with the older and more powerful societies of the river valleys. Even more important is the fact that the early civilization of Crete provided a link between the cultures of the Near East and the world toward the west, where new peoples were soon to add fresh elements to civilized life.

The island of Crete offered an entirely new setting for the emergence of higher civilization. Here was no flooding river to regenerate the soil. Instead, the inhabitants had to rely on rainfall to nourish crops in the moderately rich earth of small plains interspersed among the mountains that dominate the island. The insular setting, however, gave the Cretans a basic security — and they had the sea. Its mastery provided access to a wider world from which they could buy or borrow without danger of being engulfed by greater political powers. The people of Crete advanced to higher civilization as a consequence of their ability to turn the sea to their advantage.

The roots of that civilization lie in the third millennium B.C., when a flourishing neolithic culture developed on the island as well as in Greece, the Aegean islands, and Asia Minor. Probably it had been imported to Crete about 3000 B.C. by invaders from Asia Minor, and it prevailed for most of the next millennium. Life centered in agricultural villages, and society had a clan structure. There was change, however, generated in part by the creative talents of the Cretans themselves and in part by newcomers from the north who invaded the island from time to time. Technical skills advanced steadily, but the introduction of bronze was of special importance. More complex social organisms developed, the landowners apparently taking the lead in forming larger groupings of people. Cretans learned to sail the seas and came in con-

tact with the new sources of wealth and with the more advanced civilizations in Asia and Egypt. It was their expanding contact with the external world and the resulting influx of techniques, wealth, and ideas that permitted the Cretans to outstrip the peoples with whom they had once shared a relatively simple neolithic culture.

About 2000 B.C. a sudden advance occurred on Crete which marked the beginnings of a mature civilization, named the *Minoan* by modern historians after a legendary Cretan king whom the Greeks called Minos. The new age was heralded by the appearance of great palaces in several cities, especially Knossos, Phaistos, and Mallia. Not only do these palaces bespeak great wealth and technical ability, but they also give evidence of consolidation of society under the direction of kings who had perfected techniques for administering larger areas and numbers of people. The kingdoms coexisted apparently without any serious conflicts; and their energies were devoted largely to overseas trading — in Egypt, Syria, Asia Minor, the Aegean islands, the Greek mainland, and even the western Mediterranean — and to the manufacturing pursuits that supplied this trade. The Minoan thrust into the Greek peninsula was particularly strong and marked a significant period in Greek history to which we will return in a later chapter.

With time, Knossos seems to have outstripped the other cities of Crete and established dominance over them peacefully. Knossos reached the peak of her power between 1600 and 1400 B.C., when she dominated Crete and held sway over a wide circle of the eastern Mediterranean. Then suddenly, the great city was destroyed, and Minoan influence rapidly waned. What brought on this disaster is disputed, but the best explanation seems to be that Crete was invaded by a Greek people called the Mycenaeans, who had learned most of what they knew about civilized life from the Minoans. The Minoans apparently were not prepared to cope with warrior peoples; their talents for centuries had been devoted to peace, trade, and the quest for a comfortable, carefree life.

The nature of Minoan civilization must be derived chiefly from archeological remains. The Minoans developed a system of writing called

A view of the ruins of the palace of Knossos on Crete that gives an indication of the splendor of this island civilization during its golden age. *Photo: Hirmer Verlag*

Linear A, whose origins are uncertain, but evidence suggests a kinship with Akkadian. Some records exist in a language called Linear B, from the last years of Minoan history, but this seems to have been an ancestor of Greek brought to Crete by the Mycenaean intruders. Neither tongue reveals much about Minoan civilization.

From the evidence we have, we know that a well-developed system of monarchy had developed based upon orderly recordkeeping and bureaucratic adminstration. Royal power appears to have depended on religious sanction and on the wealth the kings derived from overseas trade, rather than on military strength. A powerful nobility grouped itself around the kings and helped uphold royal authority. A productive agriculture sustained society, but trade and industry contributed considerable wealth. Innumerable artisans plied their talents in the workshops of the palaces and the cities. Especially skilled were the potters and the metalworkers. Merchants carried these goods abroad in fleets owned by the kings and brought back a variety of raw materials and manufactured goods. Little is known about the condition of the lower classes, but the nobility enjoyed a luxurious life in fine city houses. The Minoans worshiped a variety of gods representing the forces of nature, chiefly the goddess of fertility, whose life-giving powers were evoked by prayer, ceremony, and sacrifice. Religion played an important but not dominant part in Minoan civilization. No great temples were built, nor was a numerous priesthood maintained; worship was carried out on hillsides and in groves with considerable popular participation. There was a belief in an afterlife and some attention was given to the care of the dead, but never on the scale that occurred in Egypt.

The genius of the Minoans was in the arts, which also convey best the character of their civilization. Their considerable architectural skills were lavished on palaces and private dwellings rather than temples and tombs. The immense palace at Knossos was a marvel of technical ability and mixed architectural forms. Palaces and

houses were decorated with paintings and carvings that emphasized nature and humanity. Often the artist sought to capture the action of living things in his work, so that Minoan art is mobile, free of stylization, intense, energy-filled. Minoan decorated pottery reflects their fine sense of form, great ingenuity in decoration, and love of color. In its general character, Minoan art reflects a civilization that was gay, worldly, lacking in fear, eager for change, pleasure loving, and amazingly free. Its spirit contrasts sharply with that underlying Mesopotamian and Egyptian civilization, although the Minoans borrowed considerably from both. It points not east but west toward a world yet to come—to Greece and Europe.

Suggested Reading

Egypt

*Alan H. Gardiner, *Egypt of the Pharaohs* (Galaxy). A well-organized survey of Egyptian political history.

William A. Ward, *The Spirit of Ancient Egypt* (1965). Another excellent survey of ancient Egyptian history, especially valuable for its integrated treatment of all aspects of Egyptian civilization.

*John A. Wilson, *The Culture of Ancient Egypt* (Phoenix). A brilliant analysis of the interactions between political and religious life in ancient Egypt.

*Pierre Montet, *Eternal Egypt* (Mentor). An excellent synthesis treating various aspects of Egyptian civilization topically.

*Jon Manchip White, *Everyday Life in Ancient Egypt* (Capricorn). Provides a wealth of detail about how people of all classes lived in ancient Egypt.

*Henri Frankfort et al., *Before Philosophy: The Intellectual Adventure of Ancient Man* (Penguin). Has an excellent essay by John A. Wilson summarizing the basic Egyptian attitude toward life.

*Henri Frankfort, *Ancient Egyptian Religion: An Interpretation* (Harper Torchbook).

Jaroslav Černy, *Ancient Egyptian Religion* (1952). This and the preceding title will provide a thorough introduction to Egyptian religious ideas and practices. The latter provides more factual material, the former more interpretation.

K. Lange and M. Hirmer, *Egypt: Architecture, Sculpture, Painting in Three Thousand Years* (4th ed., 1968). A

splendid introduction to all phases of Egyptian art with remarkable illustrative material.

*I. E. S. Edwards, *The Pyramids of Egypt* (2nd ed., Penguin). A fascinating description of these marvelous structures, characterized by its clarity and grasp of technical details.

*Otto Neugebauer, *The Exact Sciences in Antiquity* (2nd ed., Dover).

Henry Hodges, *Technology in the Ancient World* (1970). This and the preceding volume provide full details on the Egyptian accomplishment in science and technology.

Minoan Civilization

Sinclair Hood, *The Minoans: The Story of Bronze Age Crete* (1971). A brief, readable treatment solidly based on archeological evidence.

M. P. Nilsson, *Minoan-Mycenaean Religion and Its Survival in Greek Religion* (2nd ed., 1950). A clear description of the main features of Minoan religion.

Sources

*Adolph Erman, *The Ancient Egyptians: A Sourcebook of Their Writings* (Harper Torchbook).

Miriam Lichtheim, *Ancient Egyptian Literature: A Book of Readings*, Vol. I: *The Old and Middle Kingdoms* (1973).

Joseph Kaster, *Wings of the Falcon: Life and Thought in Ancient Egypt* (1968). These three works offer a rich sampling of Egyptian literature which will illuminate some of the ideas and values that animated Egyptian society.

3

THE DIFFUSION OF NEAR EASTERN CIVILIZATION

By the beginning of the second millennium B.C., the institutions, techniques, and ideas that had been born in the great river valleys during the preceding two thousand years had begun to spread outward. Traders, soldiers, travelers, and diplomats were the prime carriers. This process of diffusion was the characteristic feature of the entire second and the early first millennium B.C. It was hastened by invasions of the Near East by new peoples, who upset the existing political system, elevated new leaders, and brought significant changes to basic patterns of life. They were, in the words of one authority, catalysts.

The invaders came in two great waves. The first were Indo-Europeans, who appeared about 1800 B.C. and caused an adjustment of the power structure in the Near East that lasted until about 1200. Then new invasions, involving both Indo-Europeans and Semites, brought about a realignment of power that persisted until about 800 B.C. Underlying the many changes in the political order was a unifying factor of prime historical importance: the civilizing influences spreading outward from the great river valleys to engulf the invaders.

1. THE INDO-EUROPEAN INVASIONS OF THE NEAR EAST

The Indo-Europeans whose invasions opened the era were a people heretofore unknown in the Near East. Although some have argued that they were large, fair-skinned, blond men who contrasted sharply with the smaller, darker peoples of ancient Mesopotamia and Egypt, it is by no means certain that they represented a new physical type. The only sure significance of the term "Indo-European" is linguistic: The newcomers brought with them a new language from which later evolved Sanskrit, Greek, Latin, and most of the modern European languages, including English.

The Indo-European invasions of the Near East originated from the Eurasian steppes north of the great mountain chain that stretches across Europe and Asia to divide each into two parts. Here they had practiced a primitive herding economy and lived under a strong clan system as early as 3000 B.C. During the next thousand years, they slowly adopted a settled agricultural life, but they were still barbarians by Near Eastern standards when they began to move southward about 2000 B.C. They crossed the mountain barrier between Europe and the Near East by several routes—across the straits connecting the Black and Aegean seas into Asia Minor; across the Caucasian Mountains into the area capping the upper reaches of the Tigris and Euphrates; across the mountains east of the Caspian Sea into the vast Iranian plateau. Greece, Italy, Central Europe, and India felt the impact of this vast movement. Probably because of their superior military strength, based on horse-drawn chariots and a skilled warrior class, the Indo-

Europeans were able to establish political dominance over extensive areas of the Near East.

As the invaders moved south, they subdued the natives and formed new political groupings. At first, these groupings consisted of numerous small principalities led by successful Indo-European warlords. Gradually, these principalities coalesced into large kingdoms whose rulers were strongly influenced by the model of river valley monarchies, especially the Amorite Empire of Hammurabi. One powerful group, the Hittites, occupied eastern Asia Minor and began to thrust east and south. The Mitanni emerged as the dominant force in the upper Tigris-Euphrates area. The Kassites, first established in the mountainous area east of the Tigris River, attacked and destroyed the floundering Amorite Empire, once made great by Hammurabi; for over four centuries they dominated Mesopotamia. Still other Indo-Europeans sifted into the Syria-Palestine area, uniting with Semitic marauders from the Arabian Desert to form the Hyksos, who invaded Egypt and destroyed the Middle Kingdom. All these newcomers quickly adopted the techniques, culture, and religious concepts of their conquered subjects, thus divesting themselves of their barbarism. They retained their older militancy, however, and their presence led to strife and incessant flux throughout the Near East.

2. THE EGYPTIAN EMPIRE, 1600–1200 B.C.

Proud Egypt's ordeal lasted about two centuries, an interlude called the Second Intermediate Period (ca. 1750–1580 B.C.). It is difficult to ascertain exactly what happened during this period: Probably the Middle Kingdom was already in decline when the Hyksos invaders began to attack from their base in Palestine; local Egyptian princes may again have begun to assert their independence, making effective defense difficult. The Hyksos never succeeded in taking control of all Egypt; much of Upper Egypt escaped them. The "shepherd kings," as the Egyptians contemptuously called the Hyksos rulers, were pharaohs from the fourteenth through the sixteenth dynasties. Although they assimilated much Egyptian culture, they were pillagers, en-

joying temporary military superiority because they possessed the horse and chariot and because they had attacked Egypt at a moment of weakness.

The chief result of Hyksos rule was revulsion against foreigners, which eventually generated an open revolt, led by the Theban princes, who established the Seventeenth Dynasty. Revolt turned quickly into a war of liberation and then a crusade to smash the oppressors at their source of power in Palestine. Ahmose I (ca. 1580–1546), founder of the Eighteenth Dynasty, crowned this patriotic resurgence with a crushing defeat of the Hyksos in Palestine. His reign opened a third period of glory in Egypt's history—the Egyptian Empire, or New Kingdom, extending from 1580 to 1200 B.C.

During the first century of the Eighteenth Dynasty, a succession of able pharaohs devoted their energies to restoring internal order, "cleansing" the land of the taint of foreign domination, and reestablishing the ancient system, and they succeeded remarkably well. The administrative machine, agricultural regime, tax system, foreign trade connections, religious order, and artistic and intellectual life all revived in patterns closely parallel to those of the Old and Middle Kingdoms. Especially notable was the religious fervor of the age, which manifested itself in the worship of the god Amon, whose priests became ever more powerful.

Amid the restoration, there was a new factor at work, challenging the Egyptians' long-standing sense of superiority: a haunting fear of new invasions. The first pharaohs of the Eighteenth Dynasty responded to this sense of insecurity by conducting raids to the south and into Syria-Palestine. These raids not only restored confidence but also demonstrated that the exploitation of foreigners could be profitable. Fear, pride, greed, and internal strength slowly combined to breed imperialism.

Thutmose III (1484–1447 B.C.), called "the Napoleon of Egypt," launched the policy of conquest and occupation of foreign lands. He led a series of brilliantly executed campaigns into Syria-Palestine, Nubia, and Libya that crushed all resistance to Egyptian domination. The Egyptians had learned the use of the horse and chariot from the Hyksos, so that their armies proved more than equal to the foreign forces they met. Thutmose's diplomats made Egypt's might felt beyond the area of actual conquest, forcing powers such as the Hittites, Mitanni, Kassites, and Assyrians to seek to remain on friendly terms with her. He marshaled Egypt's internal resources, both material and human, to support the enlarged army, and he established an administration to ensure Egyptian domination over conquered lands. For a century Thutmose's successors pursued his policy and kept Egypt the dominant power in the Near East.

Successful imperialism brought Egypt a new period of magnificence. Her government reached peak efficiency in exercising absolute control over the population. Agriculture and trade, coupled with heavy tribute extracted from foreign subjects, produced unprecedented prosperity. Artistic and intellectual life blossomed again, inspired by pride in Egypt's power and supported by her great wealth. The greatest landmarks of Egyptian artistic vigor were magnificent temples built at Luxor and Karnak in honor of Amon-Ra, the chief god at this time. Like the pyramids built a thousand years earlier, these giant pillared structures, brilliantly decorated with carvings and paint, illustrate the Egyptian genius for building. However, artists looked back to earlier times for models, thereby maintaining the static quality in Egyptian art.

Nevertheless, the cultural activity of the New Kingdom kept alive and vital an ancient and rich cultural tradition. And the influences of that culture were felt in a positive way throughout the eastern Mediterranean world. In Nubia huge temples were built in the Egyptian architectural style in honor of Egyptian gods; on their walls were written prayers and hymns in the Egyptian language. In Syria and Palestine artisans began to imitate Egyptian styles and techniques in the manufacturing of pottery, metalwork, and jewelry. The petty princes of this area, many of whom were educated at the Egyptian court, aped the royal style of the pharaohs, as is evident in the considerable body of diplomatic correspondence that has survived from the period (the Amarna letters, discovered in 1887 in the ruins of that city). Egyptian manufactured products were exported in quantity to Mesopotamia, the Hittite kingdom, and Crete. Here was cultural diffusion at work.

The Egypt of the New Kingdom, though, was not quite the Egypt of old. Successful imperialism presented serious problems. One was that of dealing with conquered peoples. Egypt adopted a system of permitting conquered subjects to keep their own rulers, sign treaties with Egypt pledging friendship and loyalty, pay tribute, and furnish hostages as security. She sought to hold this intricate alliance system together by establishing garrisons abroad, organizing periodic displays of military might, and sending diplomats to monitor semi-independent powers. As long as the armies and diplomats were vigilant, the system worked, but each prince always remained a potential source of rebellion.

A second problem facing Egypt was the fear and hostility her expansion aroused among peoples beyond her borders. The Egyptians discovered that expansion did not necessarily safeguard a nation from external attack but instead increased the possibility. Holding her empire thus imposed on her the burden of waging foreign wars against a formidable array of enemies.

Ultimately, the Hittites proved to be Egypt's most dangerous foe. Of all the "new" peoples that had emerged from the Indo-European invasions, the Hittites achieved the greatest power and prominence. Their history had begun in eastern Asia Minor about 1800 B.C., when Indo-European warlords imposed their rule on the natives of the area and formed a series of small kingdoms. By about 1600 B.C., several of these had been drawn together into a consolidated state with its capital at Hattusas (modern Boghazköy in Turkey). Its rulers played an aggressive role in the Near East, as indicated by their attacks on the declining Amorite Empire. The unified Hittite kingdom developed an advanced culture, brought to light by modern excavations at Boghazköy and by the decipherment of Hittite writing. Its political institutions, religion, literature, architecture, and art were strongly influenced by Mesopotamian models, so that in one sense the Hittite kingdom was a cultural outpost of the Tigris-Euphrates Valley. But Hittite cul-

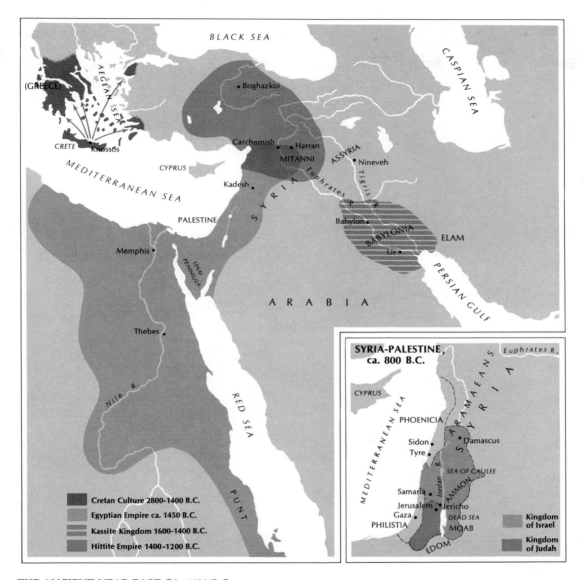

THE ANCIENT NEAR EAST CA. 1450 B.C.

ture also reflects an amalgam of native elements to which the borrowings were added.

Hittite power, spread over a large area in Asia Minor and reaching out east and south, reached its peak about 1400 B.C. The Hittites drew the Mitanni into their orbit and began to attack the northern fringes of the Egyptian Empire. They successfully encouraged rebellion among the princes ruling the numerous petty states within Egypt's sphere of influence in Syria-Palestine. Such interference of course added greatly to Egypt's difficulties in maintaining her empire.

A third problem facing imperial Egypt was the erosion of the social and spiritual bases of society within Egypt. The demands of war resulted in an increasing regimentation of the lower classes by the government. Occupied with military and diplomatic issues and with pleasures, the pharaohs themselves lost contact with their subjects. Their officials, often newcomers into the world of power and greatly enriched by the spoils of imperialism, constituted a heartless, oppressive ruling class. Especially powerful were the priests of Amon-Ra; they amassed immense wealth and even challenged the divine authority of the pharaoh for the right to approach the gods. New ideas and new styles of life, often brought in by foreigners, entered the land to compete with the old and to cause doubts about the validity of ancient ways. Excessive wealth tended to vulgarize life and erode long-established social values. All these trends bred tensions and doubts in a society long accustomed to the confident acceptance of an established set of values.

The troubled society of the New Kingdom was finally brought face to face with its problems by an intriguing individual elevated to the throne in about 1375 as Amenhotep IV. This occupant of the office that was the most sacred symbol of the old order turned out to be a revolutionary. His answer to Egypt's problems lay in a new religion: the worship of Aton as the sun god. According to the new theology, Aton was the sole god, master of the whole universe and the cause of all things. Symbolizing his break with the old order, Amenhotep IV changed his name to Akhenaton. He abandoned the old capital at Thebes, which was also the center of the powerful Amon-Ra cult, and built a new city called Akhetaton. He ordered his subjects to stop worshiping the old gods, destroyed their temples, and demoted their priests. Symbolized by the sun disc, Aton was conceived in more abstract and spiritual terms than the old gods. New rituals, revealing fresh, poetic inspiration, were devised in his honor, and a naturalistic art style, breaking sharply with tradition, was developed to portray his divine powers. Akhenaton personally involved himself in the new cult and the new art; he, his beautiful queen Nefertiti, and his five daughters were the very center of a pul-

sating movement that turned away from imperialism, bureaucracy, and staid modes of thought and art.

Akhenaton's reforms provoked a storm of protest in Egypt and gripped the population in a struggle that consumed everyone's energies. The opposition to Akhenaton, led by the priests of Amon-Ra, found adequate support elsewhere in society. Although no one can now be sure of Akhenaton's motives, his program seemed to offer Egyptian civilization a supreme challenge. Would it continue to progress or would it remain conservative and backward-looking? Akhenaton was trying to hasten his people along a path leading to the worship of one almighty god who demanded moral goodness rather than a welter of gods who asked material offerings. He was seeking to reduce the power of the priests, who had been gaining power and prestige at the pharaoh's expense. He was trying to guide Egypt's intellectuals and artists into new channels, to divert them from worship of the past. In short, he was trying to find in a new religion a means of rousing Egyptians to take the lead in exploiting the new currents that were running strong in Near Eastern society in this era of mixing and mingling of cultures. His efforts were fruitless. By the time of his death, his foes had already forced him to abandon his reforms. His successor, Tutankhamon, sealed the victory of reaction by a vigorous restoration of the pre-Akhenaton order in religion, art, and politics.

These internal disturbances proved fatal to the Egyptian Empire. Even before Akhenaton's reforms, Egypt's grip on Syria-Palestine was loosening. His neglect of military affairs encouraged rebellion. Unfortunately for the Egyptians, Hittite power was at its peak at this critical moment. Under the able king Suppilulimas (1375–1355 B.C.), they applied great pressure on the Egyptian Empire by attacking her Syrian holdings and by encouraging rebellion among Egypt's restless subjects. By the end of the Eighteenth Dynasty, Egypt's power in Asia had been greatly reduced.

The early rulers of the Nineteenth Dynasty (ca. 1320–1200 B.C.), especially Seti I and Rameses II, acted with some success to halt the disintegra-

Akhenaton the Enigma

   Every student of history must learn to recognize generalizations about the past and to view them with a healthy skepticism. One such generalization appears in the section of this text on Akhenaton, where it is argued that he was an innovator seeking to move a tradition-bound, proud, self-centered society wallowing in wealth and power into a new world, larger and more complex than the accustomed one. But was this enigmatic figure a leader of this order? A quick glance at the surviving portraits of him may even raise some doubts: His long-faced, pot-bellied, thick-legged figure does not bespeak vigorous, forward-looking leadership. Indeed, not all who have studied his career accept him as he is presented in this book.

   Akhenaton's contemporaries were extremely harsh on him. To most of them, he was a heretic who denied the ancient gods in his pursuit of a false deity. His defection bred internal strife and external disaster, as one would expect. The other gods, especially the almighty Amon-Ra whose worship had become dominant in Egypt in the two centuries prior to Akhenaton's reign, would surely display their anger. Even before the end of his reign, Akhenaton's mother, Tiy, took the lead in halting his religious reforms and restoring the old order. The pharaoh spent his last years in isolation at his holy city of Akhetaton, while a co-ruler was installed at Thebes to represent the real authority in Egypt. After his death the very name of the "criminal Akhenaton" was dropped from the list of pharaohs, and all traces of his religious ideas were erased from the books and chiseled from the stones (with the exception of some tombs at Akhetaton). Not until these tombs were unearthed in the nineteenth century was the existence of Amenhotep IV, renamed Akhenaton, even known to historians.

   The initial reaction to the discovery of Akhenaton's existence and his religious ideas was to exalt his role in history. The American Egyptologist James Henry Breasted gave wide popularity to this view. He saw the pharaoh as a sensitive, intelligent man of great individual talent with a new religious vision for which he became a prophet. Steeped in the trends of religious development working in imperial Egypt and offended by the pedestrian, routine religious concepts and practices represented by the traditional priesthood, his seminal thought drew him to monotheism. The unlimited power that was his as pharaoh prompted him to impose this exalted religion on his subjects. The formulation of the new faith was his personal achievement, a witness to his intelligence and depth of feeling. Here then was the first monotheist. Breasted's Akhenaton soon prompted others to see the first monotheist as the teacher of Moses, whose career in Egypt came about a century after his reign. In *Moses and Monotheism,* Sigmund Freud argued that Akhenaton was really the progenitor of Hebrew monotheism.

Not all scholars are persuaded that the evidence points where Breasted and Freud thought. Some have found evidence that Akhenaton was an irresponsible, bigoted religious zealot who insisted on imposing his religious "fads" on a populace that had no desire for innovation and when this did not work withdrew to his own little paradise where he could work his will on his docile retainers, leaving the empire to drift toward ruin. Others see him as demented; perhaps he was a victim of disease, since recent studies of his mummified body suggest he suffered a pituitary disorder that led to physical and mental deterioration. The most careful studies of Akhenaton's religious ideas strongly suggest that he was not a monotheist, but rather the propounder of a faith that proclaimed a new god for the pharaoh to worship while insisting that everyone else worship the pharaoh. This may have been a political ploy: the restoration of the pharaoh's absolute power, the focusing of attention on royal splendor as a key to control over the empire, the curbing of the power of the rich priests. These basically conservative goals would make the pharaoh not even a heretic, much less a religious revolutionary.

Like all significant men in history, Akhenaton will undoubtedly continue to provoke differing viewpoints. Each one must draw his own conclusions on the basis of all information he can gather about one of the first "individuals" to emerge in human history.

tion of the empire, but at a heavy price. Incessant warfare between Egypt and the Hittites sapped both powers. Although they made peace about 1271 B.C., their days of greatness had ended. The Hittite kingdom was completely destroyed about 1200 by a new wave of invaders surging through the Near East. Egypt's fate was not quite so drastic. She too came under attacks —from Nubians, Libyans, and the "People of the Sea," seafaring marauders from the Aegean area—that forced her back into her old boundaries and from time to time put foreigners on her throne. After 1200 B.C. she never again stood out as a leader, although her achievements left a permanent mark on history.

3. THE ERA OF SMALL NATIONS, 1200–800 B.C.: PHOENICIANS AND ARAMEANS

The collapse of the Hittite and Egyptian empires around 1200 B.C., coupled with the destruction of Minoan power slightly earlier, resulted in a new alignment of political forces in the Near East. The confusion was compounded by waves of new Indo-European invaders, especially formidable because they possessed iron weapons, who spilled over Asia Minor, the Aegean area, and the waterways of the eastern Mediterranean. Semitic nomads poured out of the Arabian Desert to fill the vacuum created by the collapse of the empires. Several small groups previously under Egyptian or Hittite rule seized the opportunity to establish political independence. For the next four centuries, the Near East was a patchwork of small nations.

The changed political order emerging between 1200 and 800 B.C. did not, however, constitute a break in the broad pattern of historical development. The diffusion of culture remained the basic characteristic of the era. As the small nations struggled to establish and maintain themselves, they borrowed heavily from the Mesopotamian and Egyptian cultures. Their efforts resulted in a continued spread over most of the Near East of ideas and institutions that had originated in the great river valleys.

Two small nations stand out especially as borrowers and disseminators of the older civilizations—the Phoenician and the Aramean. Both

This statue of the pharaoh Akhenaton illustrates the realism and freedom introduced into art by its subject's efforts to revolutionize religious life; the new style contrasts sharply with traditional forms. *Photo: Hirmer Verlag*

these groups were Semitic in origin, migrating from the Arabian Desert into modern Syria prior to 2000 B.C. The Phoenicians settled in the narrow band of territory lying between the Mediterranean Sea and the mountains of Lebanon. The Arameans were located east of these mountains between the northern end of the Arabian Desert and the Euphrates River. Both groups were repeatedly conquered and strongly influenced by the Mesopotamians, Egyptians, and Hittites. Consequently, by 1200 B.C., they were already highly civilized peoples, and when Egyptian and Hittite power declined, both groups were able to establish their political independence. Ultimately, a number of independent city-states emerged in Phoenicia, the chief of which were Tyre and Sidon. The Arameans organized themselves into a number of small kingdoms, centering around cities like Damascus, Kadesh, and Palmyra. For about four centuries these principalities were among the chief states in the Near East. Their independence was finally crushed, however, by the rising power of the Assyrians in the eighth century B.C.

The Phoenicians and the Arameans derived most of their wealth from trading ventures. The Phoenicians took to the seas and established a virtual monopoly on trade in the Mediterranean. Their merchants carried manufactured goods from the whole Near East to the backward peoples of Greece, Italy, North Africa, Spain, and southern France, and brought the raw materials of these areas back. From these merchants many barbarian peoples got their first taste of higher civilization. The Phoenicians, not content to trade, also established colonies abroad, notably the North African city of Carthage, which became one of the leading centers of civilization in the western Mediterranean after 800 B.C. The Arameans were land traders; they exploited the trade routes that linked Egypt, Mesopotamia, Asia Minor, and points beyond. Both Phoenicians and Arameans reaped a rich reward from their trading ventures which was, in part, devoted to patronizing the arts and learning. Neither people was particularly creative, but the Phoenicians did perfect an alphabet that later served as a model for the written languages of the Mediterranean world.

4. THE ERA OF SMALL NATIONS, 1200–800 B.C.: THE HEBREWS

The most significant of the small nations for the history of Western civilization was that of the Hebrews. To do them justice in a brief account is virtually impossible, for few people in history have evoked greater interest or more intensive study. They left one literary record that has been invaluable to the historians of later ages: the Old Testament. This account raises innumerable problems, but it does provide a record far superior to the literature of any other people in the ancient Near East. On the whole, the story it tells has been corroborated by other literary sources and by archeology, and it can be read as a serious introduction to Hebrew history.

The Hebrews originated as Semitic nomads living in the Arabian Desert. About 1800 B.C., roughly at the time of Hammurabi, some tribes led by the patriarch Abraham began a search for a new home. In no sense did they constitute a single people; rather, each tribe retained a spirit of independence. Failing to establish themselves in the Euphrates Valley, the wanderers moved toward Syria-Palestine.

In Palestine the newcomers encountered the well-established and highly civilized Canaanites, whose culture showed heavy Egyptian and Mesopotamian influences. While some Hebrews quickly adopted Canaanite civilization, others, forced to settle in semiarid parts of Palestine, retained their ancient desert way of life. Grouped into small tribes under patriarchal leaders such as Isaac and Jacob and often seminomadic, they sustained a fierce sense of independence and an egalitarian social order.

Some Hebrews made their way into Egypt to escape famines in Palestine, as part of the Hyksos invasions, or as Egyptian prisoners. There they were assigned lands in the Delta region (the Biblical land of Goshen), and some, like Joseph, even enjoyed great favor in the pharaoh's court. Eventually, however, life in Egypt became intolerable, probably because the Hebrews became victims of the increasing oppression of the late eighteenth and nineteenth dynasties. This set the stage for a major turning point in Hebrew history—the Exodus from Egypt, which occurred shortly before 1200 B.C.

The familiar story of the Exodus and of Moses' effective leadership of those Hebrews who fled Egypt does not need detailing here. During forty trying years spent wandering about the Sinai peninsula, Moses' followers underwent a religious experience that laid the basis for a Hebrew nation. The origins and development of Hebrew religious concepts up to the Exodus are extremely obscure and open to debate. The Old Testament probably distorts this development by projecting backward into this early period ideas that developed much later. It cannot be said for sure that the Hebrew tribes had a common religion during the age of the patriarchs; but at least some gave particular allegiance to Yahweh. Yahweh was a powerful and somewhat terrible nature god, capable of caring for the material needs of followers who courted his favor with sacrificial offerings and prayers. The tribes that worshiped him did admit that other gods existed. Therefore, prior to 1200 B.C. some Hebrews appear to have developed *monolatry*, that is, belief in one god for a given community while recognizing other gods proper to other groups. No other Near Eastern people—with the exception of the ill-fated circle around Akhenaton—had ever propounded such a belief.

During their stay in the desert, however, the followers of Moses pledged themselves to the worship of Yahweh and accepted certain ideas about that god and their relationship to him. Prompted by the inspired leadership of Moses, the Hebrews of the Exodus entered into a covenant, or contract, with Yahweh: They pledged themselves to worship only him, and in return, he promised that he would care for them under any circumstances, just as he had done during the escape from Egypt. The Hebrews also accepted from Yahweh a set of laws that were to govern the way each follower conducted himself toward Yahweh and toward his fellowmen. By the acceptance of these ideas, Moses' "mixed multitude" became a "nation," the Israelites, bound together by the exclusive worship of one god. The gradual refinement of these concepts and their adjustment to new historical situations led ultimately to the great contribution of the Hebrews to the history of the world—Judaism.

The first task to which the newly formed Hebrew nation turned was to renew the search for the Promised Land. Armed with the Ark of the Covenant, a wooden chest containing Yahweh's commands, this impoverished band set themselves against the Canaanites and the other Hebrew tribes in Palestine. Shortly after 1200 B.C., they crossed the Jordan to capture the Canaanite city of Jericho. For the next hundred and fifty years, the Hebrews devoted their energies to establishing their dominion over Palestine.

Usually they were successful, although their own disunity made the task difficult. Only in periods of great crisis were they able to overcome tribal jealousies for a united effort. As their control over Palestine widened, the Hebrews enjoyed increasing prosperity. The primitive culture of desert dwellers was greatly modified by the higher culture of settled farmers, which the Hebrews borrowed from the conquered Canaanites.

The worship of Yahweh gained new adherents during the period of conquest, probably because Yahweh seemed to be fulfilling his promise to watch over the interests of those who worshiped him. The Hebrew system of law, still closely allied to the worship of Yahweh, continued to expand and to serve as a common bond among many Hebrew tribes. Another common tie developing in this era was a shared set of religious practices directed by an emerging priesthood and centering around the Ark of the Covenant, which appears to have been located at the town of Shiloh. However, Yahweh worship was still not accepted by all the Hebrews. During the period of conquest, there was a series of leaders who tried to rally backsliding Hebrews to return to the worship of Yahweh. These leaders, called "judges" in the Old Testament and represented by figures like Gideon, Samson, and Samuel, sought to convince the Hebrews that their many military setbacks were punishment for their failure to serve Yahweh and for their tendency to fall under the spell of the Canaanite gods, the Baals.

Although they succeeded in overpowering the Canaanites, the Hebrews eventually met a foe they could not handle so easily. Shortly after 1100 B.C., they began to clash with the Philistines, a people probably from Asia Minor who had recently settled along the Mediterranean shore of southern Palestine after having been rebuffed in an attempt to seize Egypt. By 1050 B.C., most of the Hebrews had been conquered by the Philistines. This disaster eventually proved a blessing for the Hebrews because it forced them into a political union. As a step toward ending Philistine overlordship, several Hebrew tribes agreed to accept a single king. The person they selected for that honor was called Saul.

The reigns of Saul and his successors, David and Solomon (about 1020 to 930 B.C.), mark the high point of Hebrew political history. These kings smashed Philistine power and subdued many other enemies around Syria-Palestine, making the Hebrew nation the leading power in that area. A centralized government developed at Jerusalem, and diplomatic relations were established with most other nations of the Near East. Hebrew traders brought prosperity to the new kingdom. The royal court at Jerusalem patronized the arts and letters. There was occasional dissidence, often in protest against the personal conduct of the kings. Saul's jealousy of the youthful David, David's passion for other men's wives, and Solomon's heavy expenditures outraged the feelings of some Hebrews. For a time, however, the kings were able to curb the dissatisfied elements and to maintain a unified kingdom enjoying power and prestige.

The reigns of Saul, David, and Solomon represented a significant chapter in the history of Judaism. These kings were all active champions of Yahweh, claiming they had been anointed to lead the Hebrews to the victory promised in the Covenant. Nearly all Hebrews now accepted Yahweh worship. David moved the Ark of the Covenant to Jerusalem after he captured that city and made it the seat of his power. Solomon completed the process of making it the religious center of the nation by building a splendid temple. The ritual practices devoted to Yahweh took on elaborate form under the guidance of an expanded priesthood richly supported by the kings. A body of religious writings, much of it later to be incorporated in the final form of the Old Testament, was set down at this time. Yahweh worship was becoming a full-fledged religious system.

Even while Solomon reigned in all his glory, however, deep-seated economic, political, and religious dissension threatened the Hebrew nation. Many Hebrews, remembering their tribal freedom, hated the autocratic methods used by the kings to hold the kingdom together. The old social equality characteristic of tribal life began to be undermined as the Hebrews became more civilized, and a definite aristocracy emerged and sought to subdue the masses. This social and economic inequality was anathema to many

Hebrews. As for their religion, many Hebrews resented the non-Hebraic ideas and practices that had slipped into the rituals at the great temple in Jerusalem. Furthermore, they deplored Solomon's tolerance of the religions of his many non-Jewish wives, for such forbearance of the alien appeared to compromise Yahweh worship. Immediately after Solomon's death, this discontent ended the short-lived unity of the nation. The northern part of the kingdom refused to recognize his son as king and formed a new kingdom called Israel, with its center at Samaria. The southern Hebrews formed a kingdom called Judah, under kings descended from David.

Israel and Judah proceeded steadily toward destruction, both victims of internal disturbances and misrule that sapped their will to resist foreign attack. In 722 B.C. Israel was destroyed by the Assyrians. Her people were carried off into captivity to become the Ten Lost Tribes. Judah survived until 586 B.C., when the Chaldeans captured Jerusalem and carried off large numbers of Jews into captivity in Babylonia. Thus ended the independent political history of the ancient Hebrews. The Persians did free some of the captives in 538 B.C., allowing them to return to Jerusalem and to reestablish the Hebrew religion, but this meant only that Hebrew priests were given permission to exercise a great deal of influence in Palestine, always under Persian supervision.

As Hebrew political glory faded in the centuries after 900 B.C., Hebrew religious life took on new depth. During the period of the divided kingdoms and foreign conquests, religion became the sole force that sustained a sense of nationhood and uniqueness among the harassed Hebrews. The priests fashioned a sober, austere cult that cut away much of the magic and superstition surrounding other Near Eastern religions. Much more significant was the fresh reformulation of the basic concepts of Hebrew religion by a series of powerful religious leaders known as the prophets. Several of these rank among the world's greatest spiritual spokesmen: Elijah (ninth century), Amos and Isaiah (eighth century), Jeremiah (seventh–sixth centuries), Ezekiel and the anonymous second Isaiah (sixth century), and Haggai (late sixth century). As a group, they represent a unique type of religious leader in the ancient Near East. They spoke forth as individuals, often of humble origins, who raised their voices out of personal conviction and spiritual insight. They all proclaimed a common message that the Hebrews were abandoning their covenant with Yahweh and would be punished for their sins. Their prophecies were firmly rooted in Hebrew tradition, but they spoke with such passion and such depth of spiritual understanding that collectively they formulated in nearly final form a set of religious ideas that became the essence of Judaism. Their reformulation of Judaism, put into writing in the prophetic books of the Old Testament, established a base for much of the religious development of the future.

First of all, the prophets proclaimed a true monotheism. They made Yahweh the only god and denied that any other gods existed. Second, they proclaimed a whole new concept of Yahweh. He was a god outside nature, not existing in any natural object; he was a god of justice, acting according to a definite law instead of his own fancy; he was omnipotent, controlling the whole universe and causing everything in the past, present, and future to happen; he was a god with a plan for the world; his will would be worked out in the history of the world. He was a god of righteousness, pleased by those who did good, vengeful toward those who did evil. This was truly the most exalted concept of deity yet expressed in the Near East.

Third, the prophets defined a new basis for human conduct. Just as Yahweh treated men with righteousness and justice, so also must each individual treat his fellowmen according to these same principles. God had handed down to men a code of law (called the Torah) that must serve as the basis for earthly society. Transgression of the law would bring down his punishment on the offender. Decent treatment of other men became a major obligation of each Hebrew. The religion of the prophets thus emphasized ethical concepts far above ritual practices.

Finally, the prophets proclaimed that the Hebrews were the people chosen to carry out Yahweh's will on earth. No matter what disasters might befall them at a given moment, they would ultimately emerge victorious over the other peoples of the earth, and through them the one god would eventually be worshiped by all. Yahweh would aid in this venture, since it was his plan for the world, and eventually he would send a Messiah to lead the Hebrews to victory. While awaiting that final victory, the Hebrews must retain their ties with one another. If they could not all live in an independent kingdom, they could retain their common religious beliefs as a binding tie. The Hebrew "nation" would live on as a religious community, awaiting its victory over the non-Hebrews.

By the fourth century B.C., when the ancient Near East was conquered by Alexander the Great and its civilization submitted to heavy Greek influences, the Hebrews had made no progress toward winning the world to worship of their god. Near Eastern peoples were too accustomed to a multitude of nature gods, their elaborate mythology, and splendid rituals for winning divine favor to listen to Hebrew concepts of a single almighty god living outside nature and expecting men to live by a law requiring high moral standards. But although few men then paid attention to these ideas, they had tremendous impact on later civilizations, serving as the base upon which Christianity and Islam would be built. Despite modest success in the total setting of ancient Near Eastern history, the Hebrews had written one of the great chapters in man's spiritual and moral history.

Suggested Reading

Indo-European and Semitic Invaders
V. Gordon Childe, *The Aryans: A Study of Indo-European Origins* (1926). An objective treatment of a much discussed subject.

*Sabatino Moscati, *Ancient Semitic Civilizations* (Capricorn). An excellent survey providing a balanced discussion of the role of Semitic peoples in establishing Near Eastern civilization.

The Egyptian Empire

*George Steindorff and Karl E. Seele, *When Egypt Ruled the East* (2nd ed., Phoenix). This detailed history of the period of the New Kingdom will add to the material provided by the general histories of ancient Egypt cited in Chapter 2.

Hittites, Phoenicians, and Arameans

*O. R. Guerney, *The Hittites* (2nd ed., Penguin). The best general survey of Hittite history and culture.

C. W. Ceram, *The Secret of the Hittites: The Discovery of the Ancient Empire* (1956). Provides a well-balanced picture of the nature of Hittite civilization and tells a fascinating story of how it was found by archeologists.

Sabatino Moscati, *The World of the Phoenicians*, trans. Alistair Hamilton (1968). The best survey of the history of this fascinating people.

A. T. Olmstead, *History of Palestine and Syria to the Macedonian Conquest* (1939). Although somewhat out of date, this work will be helpful in describing the role of the Arameans.

Hebrews

*Stanley Cook, *Introduction to the Bible* (Penguin). This excellent study is useful in interpreting the Old Testament as a historical source.

*Harry Orlinsky, *Ancient Israel* (2nd ed., Cornell). A concise but well-done survey of the early history of the Hebrews.

*William F. Albright, *The Biblical Period from Abraham to Ezra* (Harper Torchbook). A provocative treatment by a famous archeologist that does an excellent job of reconciling archeology and the Old Testament version of Hebrew history.

Salo Wittmayer Baron, *A Social and Religious History of the Jews* (2nd ed. rev., 12 vols., 1952–67), Vol. I: *Ancient Times: To the Beginning of the Christian Era*. A masterful longer history of the ancient Hebrews.

*Roland de Vaux, *Ancient Israel: Its Life and Institutions* (2 vols., McGraw-Hill). Rich in details about Hebrew society in Old Testament times.

Th. C. Vriezen, *The Religion of Ancient Israel* (1967).

Helmer Ringgren, *Israelite Religion*, trans. D. E. Green (1966). This and the preceding title are excellent in tracing the development of ancient Judaism and highlighting its unique features.

4

THE GREAT EMPIRES:
ASSYRIA AND PERSIA, 800-300 B.C.

During the ninth century B.C., the rising might of Assyria heralded a new era in Near Eastern history. The ground had been prepared in the previous millennium for a cosmopolitan civilization and a universal political order. The diffusion of the river valley cultures had provided large numbers of men with common techniques and ideas. The formation of new political entities, even though many of them were small, had established local stability and order and had created political building blocks out of which great empires could be shaped. Expanding trade had knit distant communities together with common economic interests. These developments invited attempts at political consolidation, and adventuresome men were at hand to respond to the opportunity.

1. THE ASSYRIAN EMPIRE

The Assyrians were a people of Semitic origin who migrated out of the Arabian Desert as early as 3000 B.C. and settled on either side of the upper Tigris Valley. They eventually spread out toward the Zagros Mountains and into the plateau highlands between the Tigris and Euphrates rivers. For centuries after 3000 B.C., the main lines of their history are extremely vague. Perhaps the chief development during this period was the powerful influence exercised by Mesopotamian civilization over the Assyrians, who never demonstrated any ability to create art

styles, writing techniques, religious ideas, or political and economic institutions of their own. In fact, so intimate were the cultural ties that many historians treat the two areas as having one history. At times, such as under Sargon I and Hammurabi, the Assyrians were politically incorporated into empires based in the lower Tigris-Euphrates Valley. However, Assyria never lost her identity completely, and when the Amorite Empire declined after 1750 B.C., Assyria continued as an independent nation.

The era from 1750 to 1000 B.C. was the testing period for Assyria. In an age of general confusion, she was subjected to great pressure from beyond her borders, her location making her a constant target for the invading Kassites, Hittites, and Mitanni, all of whom assaulted Assyria at one time or another, as did new hordes of Semites from the Arabian Desert. The hardy farmers of Assyria met this challenge by subordinating all other interests to a defense of their homeland, and they developed one of the best military forces in the Near East, especially after they adopted the new iron weapons introduced in the late second millennium. The incessant struggle for survival produced a prime motive for later expansion: fear for the safety of the ancestral homeland which encouraged preventive wars against potential enemies.

In the ninth century B.C., a series of capable leaders emerged who harnessed the warlike sentiments of the tough Assyrian farmer-soldiers to

This stele, representing one of Assyria's great conquerors, Esarhaddon (680–669 B.C.), reflects the overpowering might of the Assyrian warrior-king.
Photo: Staatliche Museen, Berlin

alry units. They increased the effectiveness of their military machine by pursuing a deliberate policy of terrorism. The annals recording their exploits are filled with some of the most incredible examples of brutality and inhumanity ever perpetrated by man in his long career of mistreating his fellowmen. Victorious Assyrian kings proclaimed their feats as a matter of course in terms such as these: flaying conquered chiefs to death, covering the walls of conquered cities with the skins of the captured populace, impaling victims on sharp poles, cutting off the ears, noses, fingers, and legs of prisoners, spanning a river with corpses so as to make a bridge, turning cities into pastures. So awesome did the Assyrian reputation become that many peoples refused to resist, preferring to "embrace the feet" of the conquerors.

These ninth-century forays were primarily tribute-collecting raids, not empire-building expeditions. They demonstrated a second powerful motive generating Assyrian expansion: the desire for a larger sweep of territory from which to exact tribute as a way of enriching life in a hard, poor land. The Assyrians were still predators, little concerned with the fate of their victims as long as they turned over their wealth. There thus began a vast flow of wealth from all over the Near East to the modest kingdom astride the Tigris, and the fortunate recipients began to adopt a grandiose style of life. Perhaps the Assyrians would have remained mere predators if the methods employed by their ninth-century rulers had been permanently successful. This was not the case. Rebellion and refusal to pay tribute occurred as soon as the Assyrian armies departed from any pillaged territory, requiring repeated expeditions that strained the never abundant Assyrian manpower resources. The system seems to have set off internal struggles for the division of the booty and bred resentment against the ruler for his distribution of the wealth produced by the new national industry. This internal disarray was so serious that during the early eighth century the raiding nearly stopped.

Shortly after 750 B.C., a ruler who was the real founder of the Assyrian Empire appeared. He was Tiglath-Pileser III (745–727 B.C.), and his

launch a wide-sweeping series of raids on surrounding nations. The Hebrews, the Phoenicians, the Arameans, the Mesopotamians, the mountaineers to the north and east of Assyria, and the nomads of the northern part of the Arabian Desert all felt the lash of Assyrian might. No one was capable of standing up against the Assyrian armies, siege engines, and strong cav-

policy was twofold: Internally, he imposed a new order by strengthening the hand of the king against the great nobles who had been troublesome earlier. Externally, he initiated a policy of establishing permanent, organized, systematic control over conquered subjects. A succession of able kings continued his policy from 722 to 631 B.C.: Sargon II, Sennacherib, Esarhaddon, and Ashurbanipal III. These five rulers, several of whose arrogant visages still stare out from the remarkable stone reliefs wrought by Assyrian artists and all of whom left boastful accounts of their exploits, built the first genuinely ecumenical empire in the Near East.

Tiglath-Pileser III and Sargon II shaped the heartland of the empire. They led the Assyrian armies on a series of expeditions that destroyed the bulk of the political powers from southern Mesopotamia around the great sweep of the Tigris-Euphrates Valley into Syria and Palestine. Only the tiny kingdom of Judah escaped, but at a terrible price in tribute. Assyrian governors were sent to rule the conquered lands and ensure the delivery of tribute. The central administration in Assyria was enlarged to supervise the conduct of imperial affairs, and effective means of communication were devised to keep the royal court informed of affairs in the empire. The army stood ready to crush all signs of resistance, continuing its brutal habits.

Once this base of power was established in the Fertile Crescent, Sennacherib, Esarhaddon, and Ashurbanipal devoted their energies to dealing with outsiders who insisted on interfering with Assyrian rule. Egypt was attacked and forced to accept overlordship. The last remnants of local independence in southern Mesopotamia were crushed. Assyrian influences were extended into Asia Minor. Semibarbaric peoples in northern Arabia, the Zagros Mountains, and the highlands to the north of Assyria were beaten into submission. By 650 B.C. the whole civilized Near East accepted for the first time a single master, the great king of Assyria, "ruler of the four rims of the world."

The Assyrian state, however, was not so strong as its size indicated. The terrorism had aroused an irreconcilable hatred among subject peoples, nowhere better reflected than in the writings of the later prophets in the Old Testament. Constant warfare depleted Assyria's manpower and eventually forced her armies to rely on levies from conquered subjects, who made much less efficient soldiers. Some of the later Assyrian rulers were more inclined to enjoy the fruits of victory than to exercise the active leadership needed to hold their empire together. Worst of all, Assyria encountered the plague of all empire builders—enemies beyond the frontier, aroused by the threat of absorption. Assyria's enemies included the Medes, living east of the Zagros Mountains; Semitic tribes pushing into the lower Tigris-Euphrates Valley; and barbarians pouring into territory north of her.

Assyria herself began to suffer setbacks during the time of Ashurbanipal; they mounted in fury after his death in 631 B.C. The Egyptians successfully revolted and caused discontent among the Assyrian subjects in Syria and Palestine. A Semitic group, the Chaldeans, raised the standard of revolt in southern Mesopotamia. Assyria committed most of her strength to checking this particular liberation movement, weakening herself beyond repair. Then the Medes, who had learned a great deal by imitating Assyrian military techniques, struck out of the east. In 612 B.C. they and the Chaldeans destroyed the Assyrian capital at Nineveh. Assyria's power vanished immediately, leaving her empire at the mercy of her many foes.

No one in the Near East lamented her passing. The Hebrew prophet Nahum spoke for all the world: "All who hear the news of you clap their hands at your downfall." However, Assyria's bad reputation should not conceal her contributions to history. She broke new ground in trying to create a single state out of many different peoples. Her attempt to erect a centralized monarchy was destined to be imitated by others. She wiped out many artificial political boundaries that kept small groups at sword's point. She at least briefly imposed a beneficial peace on the Near East, protecting it for nearly three centuries against barbarians who might have destroyed its civilization had they succeeded in seizing control.

Economically, the Assyrian regime had significant results. The Assyrians themselves added

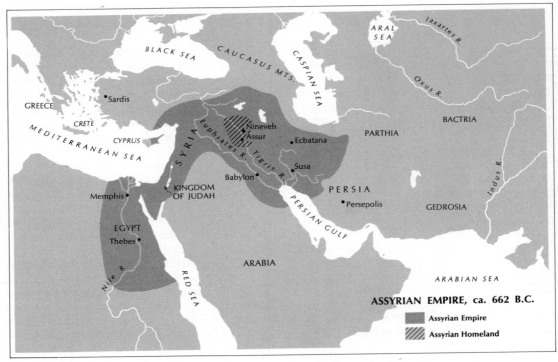

ASSYRIAN EMPIRE, ca. 662 B.C.

Assyrian Empire

Assyrian Homeland

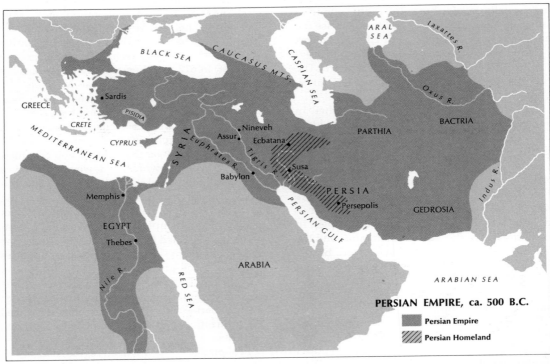

PERSIAN EMPIRE, ca. 500 B.C.

Persian Empire

Persian Homeland

The Assyrian and Persian Empires

very little to Near Eastern economy, but they encouraged trade and assisted it by breaking down barriers against the movement of goods. People like the Arameans, the Phoenicians, and the city dwellers of lower Mesopotamia seized this opportunity: Through their efforts goods flowed freely across the Near East, and technical skills associated with production spread widely among peoples still technologically backward.

In cultural activities, the Assyrians also made a notable contribution. Their efforts were not creative, but their imitations resulted in the continuation of cultural activity. This can be seen best in architecture and sculpture. Assyrian kings were avid builders, constructing the great cities of Nineveh, Sargonsburg, and Ashur as monuments of their power and glory. In these cities earlier Mesopotamian architectural styles were followed closely and thus kept alive. Temples and palaces were decorated with massive sculptured pieces and with excellent stone reliefs. The vigorous application of traditions from the past gave the Near East a new period of artistic glory. In literature, the Assyrians devoted a great deal of effort to collecting and copying older works in Sumerian and Akkadian. One of Assyria's kings, Ashurbanipal, built a huge library at Nineveh as a repository for thousands of copies of cuneiform tablets. Aside from administrative and economic records, most of the writing in Assyrian was merely a re-rendering of earlier literary works, especially the religious epics and creation stories so dear to the Sumerians. The Assyrians did show some originality in compiling accounts of their innumerable military campaigns, thereby making a contribution to the art of historical writing.

Assyrian religion was likewise strongly colored by borrowings from earlier Mesopotamia. The great state god of Assyria, Assur, was very similar to the Amorite Marduk. Assyrian rituals, prayers, and priesthoods are almost indistinguishable from those of the earlier Mesopotamians. Despite the derived character of their religion, there is considerable evidence that the Assyrians were deeply religious. Perhaps even their imperialism was motivated by a genuine desire to assert Assur's dominion over other gods. In all these ways the Assyrians kept alive some of the most precious cultural traditions in the Near East, and their conquests helped to spread those traditions throughout a vast region.

2. SUCCESSORS OF ASSYRIA, 612-550 B.C.

Assyria's sudden collapse opened a brief but spirited era of competition for the spoils of her empire, a struggle that ended when another empire builder, Persia, crushed the other contenders for power.

Egypt was one nation that seemed destined to benefit by the fall of Assyria. Foreign rule had again had the effect of uniting her under a single pharaoh, Psammetichus (also known as Psamtik; 663-609 B.C.), who founded the Twenty-sixth Dynasty. Egypt again briefly enjoyed internal order, prosperity, and international prestige, but she was incapable of meeting the needs of the new era. Her pharaohs had to rely on foreign mercenaries (chiefly Greeks) to man the armies. These troops, thoroughly hated by the antiforeign Egyptians, caused internal trouble. Egyptian artists and writers failed to produce anything new that would establish the Egyptian reputation abroad. The priests were even more reactionary, using religion as a means of resisting necessary changes. Old age had gripped Egypt, making her unable to check Persia. She fell to Persian armies with almost no struggle in 525 B.C.

In Asia Minor, the small kingdom of Lydia, which first emerged after the fall of the Hittites, was the chief beneficiary of Assyria's fall, and she quickly established control over nearly all of Asia Minor. Her rapid rise was especially significant in Greek history, since Lydia lay as a link between the Near East and Greece. During the reign of Croesus (560-546 B.C.), this greatest Lydian king ruled many Greeks living in Asia Minor. However, Lydian power was shaky, succumbing in 546 B.C. to one blow by Persia.

Still another contender for the Assyrian power was Media. The Medes had long been restless dependents of Assyria, and they furnished most of the armed might to destroy her. Once she was defeated, the Medes seized control of a large part of the northern empire and built up a vast state in the Iranian plateau. However, the state was poorly organized. One of the Median vassal princes, Cyrus of Persia, succeeded in deposing the Median king and laying successful claim to old Median territory.

The most spectacular of all Assyria's successors was the empire of the Chaldeans, a Semitic people who had entered lower Mesopotamia while it was under Assyria's rule. On her decline, the Chaldean princes seized some of the most valuable parts of the conquered territory. Under the one great Chaldean ruler, Nebuchadnezzar II (605–562 B.C.), all of Syria-Palestine was joined with the Tigris-Euphrates Valley in a single empire. Among the victims of his conquests was the kingdom of Judah. Jerusalem was destroyed in 586 B.C., and many of its citizens were carried off to Babylon as captives.

Nebuchadnezzar not only prided himself on being a conqueror, but also a champion of culture. In fact, the Chaldean interlude in Mesopotamian history was marked by a cultural renaissance strongly oriented toward the ancient past. The jewel of this revival was Nebuchadnezzar's rebuilding of Babylon as his capital. Its massive walls, its beautiful temples and palaces, its fabulous hanging gardens, and its impressive sculpture and painting made it one of the most splendid of ancient cities. Even the redoubtable Hebrew prophet Jeremiah, amid his lamentations over the calamities that had befallen his people at the hands of Nebuchadnezzar, had to admit that "Babylon was a golden cup in the hands of Yahweh" (Jer. 51:7). A religious revival in this period brought all the ancient Mesopotamian gods, above all Marduk, again to the center of the stage.

Nonetheless, Nebuchadnezzar's empire was not strong. It was guilty of worshiping the past, and its military resources were limited. Nebuchadnezzar's heirs were weak and little interested in political problems, and when the Persians captured Babylon in 539 B.C., the Chaldean state collapsed immediately.

3. THE PERSIAN EMPIRE, 500–328 B.C.

The final victory in the competition to succeed Assyria fell to a people who hardly seemed in the running—the Persians. They were of Indo-European origin, their ancestors having migrated to the Near East about 2000 B.C. from north of the Black Sea. The original Persians settled in the barren plateau of Iran, becoming simple farmers and herders. For many centuries they maintained their own political independence. During these long years, civilizing influences penetrated Persian society, especially from Assyria, so that the Persians began to be drawn into the orbit of the cosmopolitan civilization emerging in the Near East. However, they did retain significant aspects of their old Indo-European pattern of life, especially in religion and language. In the seventh century they were forced to accept the overlordship of the Medes, who were closely akin to them in language and culture. But in 550 the Persian king, Cyrus, overthrew the Median ruler and began to call himself "king of the Medes and the Persians." This event launched the Persians on their spectacular career as masters of the Near East.

Cyrus' accession to power resulted immediately in a rapid extension of Persia's boundaries. Cyrus and his successors Cambyses and Darius (collectively 550–486 B.C.) destroyed all other powers in the Near East. Cyrus was the most successful conqueror, taking first Lydia, the key to control of all Asia Minor, and then the Chaldean Empire, which made him master of the Tigris-Euphrates Valley and of Syria and Palestine. During his last years he subdued various nations in eastern Iran, pushing Persian power to the borders of India. Cambyses conquered Egypt. Darius extended Persian power into Europe by conquering a territory west of the Black Sea. However, this expansion was checked by the Greeks in 490 B.C. in a war we shall describe later. When Darius died in 486 B.C., the Persian Empire stretched from the Aegean and Mediterranean seas to India and from the mountains bounding the Near East on the north to far south in the Nile Valley. It was one of the largest empires ever created.

The first rulers were intelligent statesmen as well as conquerors and laid the basis for sound government of their huge holdings. Cyrus established a good reputation for Persian rule by practicing a policy of tolerance toward defeated people. He avoided slaughtering captured kings, preferring to proclaim himself the legitimate successor of the conquered local dynasty. Especially meaningful was the respect he showed for the religious systems of his conquered subjects, making their gods his own and contributing to their worship with his resources. He earned himself a hero's role by allowing the Hebrew exiles to return to Jerusalem to rebuild the temple of Yahweh. These actions convinced most peoples in the Near East that the Persians did not intend to continue the terrorism and brutality of the Assyrians.

Darius was the most constructive of the Achaemenid dynasty, as this line of rulers was called. Borrowing and adapting old ideas and practices in government, he laid the basis for one of the great political systems of all history. He established himself as absolute ruler, claiming full authority to make laws, to judge, and to command the services of his subjects. At his court in the capital cities of Ecbatana, Susa, and Persepolis, he created a magnificent court etiquette intended to impress upon everyone that he was, as he proclaimed himself, "king of kings." He surrounded his position with powerful religious sanctions, claiming that he was the divinely selected representative of the great Persian god, Ahura-Mazda. Darius gathered around him numerous officials and servants, assigning to each a specific task. These servants, usually of Median or Persian origin, became a kind of aristocracy fanatically devoted to maintaining Persian power.

Darius' greatest political innovation lay in the techniques he devised for ruling widely scattered possessions inhabited by many different peoples. He divided his empire into twenty large districts, called *satrapies*. Over each he appointed a governor, usually a Persian and often a member of the royal family, who was given power sufficient to make him a king in his own right. These satraps were removable at the will of the great king and were held strictly accountable for the administration of their districts. An excellent road system was developed binding the satrapies to the capital, and a constant stream of correspondence flowed to and from the royal court. Periodically, Darius sent out

inspectors to investigate the adminstration and report back. Spies in his pay swarmed through the empire to keep him informed. Contingents of the royal army under trusted commanders were garrisoned in strategic spots. Careful tax records were kept at the capital as a means of accounting for each governor's administration. By these methods Darius managed to create twenty semi-independent governments and still keep an eye on each in a fashion that coordinated policy over the whole empire.

In the final analysis, the armed forces were the key to Darius' power. The Persian army was built around a corps of professional soldiers recruited from the Persians and the Medes and was rounded out with contingents supplied by the conquered peoples in vast numbers that made the Persian armies awe inspiring. The Persians also commanded excellent naval forces, composed largely of hired Phoenician, Egyptian, and Greek ships and crews. In view of this military might, very few peoples were willing to challenge the Persian king.

Darius' imperial system endured about 150 years. The history of Persia after his death contains few events worthy of our attention. There were wars with outsiders that the Persians seldom won; on the other hand, they did not lose much territory. Rebellions occurred within the empire, only to be smashed eventually by the superior power of the king. Perhaps the most significant aspect of this period was the slow erosion of royal power. The Persian royal family declined in vigor and political intelligence, and the court became corrupt, torn by intrigue among the friends and officials of the king. Several later Persian rulers spent more time trying to survive the plots of their many wives and children and ambitious servants than administering their empire. The satraps could not resist the temptation to try to overthrow the king. Often they raised a rebellion by putting themselves forward as champions of subject peoples or by promising great rewards to anyone who would follow them against the king. The only protection against these rebellions was rigid control over the satraps, which the Persian kings were unable to maintain. With the passage of time the Persian army also declined in strength. By the middle of the fourth century B.C., all that was needed to destroy Persian power was a strong attack from the outside. It was soon forthcoming, led by a Macedonian king, Alexander the Great, who was driven in part by an urge to destroy the Persian menace that had haunted the Greeks since the reign of Darius the Great. Alexander was able to take possession of the whole Persian Empire before his untimely death in 323 B.C.

The Persians, emerging suddenly to master the Near East and confronted constantly with the problem of holding their empire together, devoted most of their talents to administrative and military affairs. As a consequence, their contributions to cultural development in the Near East were not spectacular. In general, they played a role similar to that of the Assyrians, borrowing from the cultural treasure that already existed. They utilized already developed written languages, especially Aramean, for administrative purposes. Their kings were lavish in their patronage of the arts, the results showing chiefly in the royal palaces built at Susa, Persepolis, and Ecbatana. They continued the Assyrian practice of commissioning artists to render in stone pictorial records of their military exploits. The Persians welcomed in their cities men who were schooled in the literary and scientific traditions of the past and thereby helped to keep alive ancient traditions. Their tolerant attitude toward the many different cultural elements in their empire is of inestimable importance in the history of Western civilization, because it was from the Persians that the Greeks derived and transmitted westward a knowledge of many ancient Near Eastern ideas and institutions.

The Persians did make one outstanding contribution to Near Eastern history. They created a new religion, Zoroastrianism, and aided in the spread of some of its ideas. Its beginnings seem certainly to have rested on beliefs held by the Persians before they became the rulers of the Near East. Early Persian religion centered around the worship of several gods who represented forces of nature, including especially a god of the sky and a god of fire. Along with the

chief gods, the ancient Persians believed in innumerable lesser spirits who were capable of doing both good and evil. A complicated ritual, including sacrifices, magic, and prayer, had developed as a means of winning the favor of the gods and the spirits. A group of priests called the Magi played a prominent role in the early religious life of the Persians.

Out of this setting came one of history's great religious reformers, Zoroaster (Zarathustra in the Persian language), a worthy member of that potent breed of men who by the vigor and freshness of their insights into man's spiritual nature have left an indelible imprint on other men's minds. Legend has clouded Zoroaster's career, but it seems likely that he lived in the seventh or sixth century before Christ, prior to the emergence of the Persians as masters of the Near East. According to tradition, he spent the early part of his life in contemplation in the desert, finally receiving a revelation of the true way from Ahura, the god of the sky. Fortified by his vision, Zoroaster returned to the world as a preacher urging all to become converts to his beliefs. At first he enjoyed little success and even suffered persecution, but eventually he began to win adherents, and his religion was implanted in Persian society just prior to the emergence of Persia as a world power.

Zoroaster's exact teachings have become as blurred by the passing centuries as are the details of his life. The essence of his religion is contained in a sacred book called the Avesta, compiled over many centuries and consisting largely of interpretations and refinements of his original doctrines. It seems certain that Zoroaster cast his new message in terms of a protest against existing Persian religious beliefs. His central tenet, repudiating the old polytheistic system and the superstitions surrounding it, was monotheism. In this conviction, Zoroaster resembles some of the Hebrew prophets, whose concepts of the divine nature were taking final shape at about the same time. The only god was characterized as the all-powerful, all-pervading lord of creation, Ahura-Mazda (Lord of Wisdom). This good and benevolent spirit presides over human destiny, emanating and personifying such qualities as justice, pure thought, integrity, devotion, good intentions, and immortality. But the good Ahura-Mazda is opposed by the diabolical Ahriman, who struggles to blot out justice, light, wisdom, and good. The warfare between good and evil, going on since the beginning of the world, constitutes the essence of existence. Eventually, in a final day of judgment, Ahura-Mazda will prevail, but in the meantime, the conflict will continue, extending into every soul and demanding that it choose whether to join the good or the evil. On the final day of reckoning, those who have chosen good will be rewarded with perfection and eternal happiness, while those who have elected the way of Ahriman will be damned to eternal misery. This concept of dualism became one of the most fertile grounds for discussion in Zoroastrianism and produced a rich vein of spiritual speculation in later centuries.

By postulating the goodness of Ahura-Mazda and the evil of Ahriman as fundamental to the cosmos, Zoroaster made man's basic obligation clear. Only good conduct could win favor in the eyes of Ahura-Mazda. The worship of the old gods, magic, sacrifices, and priestly intervention were irrelevant and constituted surrender to evil because they diverted attention from doing good. Zoroaster spelled out a vigorous moral code for his followers, derived in its particulars from the qualities of goodness surrounding Ahura-Mazda and including a clear concept of sin. Certainly none of the religions in the world that the Persians were soon to rule, except Judaism, gave such emphasis to ethical issues—and not even Judaism placed the burden so squarely on each individual. Zoroaster did not associate goodness and righteousness with a particular chosen people; his message was aimed at all mankind.

Although the record is again vague, it appears that Zoroaster's religion took hold among the Persians and the Medes after the prophet's death and that it became in some fashion the official religion of the rulers of the Achaemenid dynasty at least from the time of Darius the Great onward. But the Avesta shows that the Zoroastrianism of the Persian Empire was not the religion proclaimed by Zoroaster. Ritual practices aimed at pleasing Ahura-Mazda and warding off Ahriman's evil influences grew increasingly prominent. Polytheism crept back into religious life. Ahriman was elevated to the status of a god, standing equal to Ahura-Mazda in the cosmic order. Many of the old gods reappeared and hosts of angels and devils joined the eternal war between good and evil. The whole concept of the struggle between good and evil tended to associate good with purely spiritual things and evil with material things. This version of dualism had the effect of belittling the practice of virtue in everyday life and of exalting flight from the world to a secluded life. These new currents dulled the sharp edge of monotheism and ethical purity and drew Zoroastrianism back toward the accustomed patterns of ancient Near Eastern religions.

The conquest of the Persian Empire by Alexander the Great represented a setback for Zoroastrianism. Although the Achaemenid dynasty had never supported it fanatically, still Zoroastrianism was the official religion and it suffered from that association when the dynasty collapsed. The general policy of tolerance in the empire had meant that other faiths had maintained their hold, and thus Zoroastrianism did not have a very large base. Despite this defeat—and others in the future—Zoroastrianism survives today; its modern adherents, called Parsees, are located chiefly in Iran and India. During the twenty-five centuries of its existence it has not only satisfied its adherents but has powerfully affected other religions, including Judaism, Christianity, and Islam.

The ignominious end of the Persian Empire must not detract from an appreciation of its importance. The enlightened and tolerant rule of the Achaemenids built a universal empire in the ancient Near East, one that brought all kinds of people at many levels of civilization into a viable community. The benevolent, cosmopolitan Persian spirit permitted local elements to persist while providing instruments through which all could mix and fertilize each other. The resulting amalgam was a fitting climax to a long chapter in history.

Suggested Reading

Assyrians

*Georges Roux, *Ancient Iraq* (Penguin). Provides a clear chronological survey of Assyrian history, treating it as an extension of earlier Mesopotamian civilization.

*A. Leo Oppenheimer, *Ancient Mesopotamia: Portrait of a Dead Civilization* (Phoenix). Covers much of the same ground as the previous work with a stronger emphasis on cultural history.

André Parrot, *Arts of Assyria* (1961). An excellent guide to the Assyrian accomplishment in all of the arts.

Persians

*A. T. Olmstead, *History of the Persian Empire* (Phoenix). A detailed survey that presents a rich picture of the Persian accomplishment.

*R. N. Frye, *Heritage of Persia* (Mentor). A recent study emphasizing the intellectual developments in ancient Persia.

R. C. Zaehner, *Dawn and Twilight of Zoroastrianism* (1961).

R. C. Zaehner, *The Teachings of the Magi* (1956). These two works present a full description of the nature of Zoroastrianism and of its historical evolution.

Retrospect

When in 330 B.C. Alexander the Great stood in triumph over the body of Darius III, a great chapter in the history of the world had ended. The Persians ruled a world that was old and tired, while their youthful conquerer was a fitting symbol of a new world, a world filled with vitality, emerging on the western periphery of the Near East. Before shifting our focus to that new setting, at least an epitaph on the civilizations of the ancient Near East is in order.

For the purposes of this epitaph, let us view the Persians as the last scions of a great family whose origins are rooted in simple neolithic villages and whose members include all the peoples whose history has been reviewed in the preceding pages. The first thing that strikes one is that this family had in the course of five or six millennia put together a great and varied patrimony for the future. The family fortunes had grown especially rich after about 4000 B.C., when men had learned to exploit the river valleys and had adjusted their whole life style to that environment. Their treasure included impressive techniques for controlling large groups of people: absolute monarchy, complex tax systems, effective military establishments, organized bureaucracies, recordkeeping systems, legal codes — all representing great advances in government. These same peoples had devised effective systems for wresting sustenance from nature: organized agriculture, skilled technology, trade, transportation. They had developed complex social systems by which large numbers of individuals could relate to other individuals in an orderly and productive fashion. They had learned to enrich their lives through a magnificent art. They had devised writing systems and put into a permanent record descriptions of their daily activities, their thoughts, and their knowledge about themselves, animals, plants, the stars, and all other matter of things. It is indeed an insensitive man who can view this patrimony in all its shapes and forms without being convinced that the peoples of the ancient Near East were amazing creators, a testimony to the ability of the human species to turn the world to its own support and pleasure. Out of this ancient world had come achievements in government, economics, social organization, art, literature, and science from which all men of future ages could draw. And men of succeeding ages did draw on this treasury and thus did not have to do over again what men in the Near East did so well the first time. In one sense, world history is a story of the diffusion of ancient Near Eastern achievements across much of the face of the earth.

But the Near Eastern patrimony was more than a jumble of things to be borrowed from piecemeal and looked back upon in wonder. The peoples of that area had interrelated the elements of their lives in a pattern that gave meaning to their actions. In a higher sense, the most impressive part of the Near Eastern patrimony was its intellectual component. Men in the ancient Near East had learned how to reflect on the human endeavor and the setting in which it took place. Their reflections resulted in an understanding of the human condition and a sense of its destiny. In the ancient Near East the integrative, unifying, sense-giving aspect of civilized life was supplied by religion. Religion penetrated every facet of life, providing reasons that things happened and justifications for all that was done. All the Near Eastern religions (except Judaism and Zoroastrianism) posited a universe totally occupied and completely directed by powerful cosmic spirits to whose demands men had to adjust in every facet of their existence. Men—even the most powerful—were slaves in this cosmic system, bound forever to repeat in their government, labor, prayer, sacrifice, art, writing, and thinking those kinds of actions and thoughts demanded to sustain harmony in the cosmos. If they acted the part of good slaves, then life went on; the proof that obedience to the established order paid off was the wealth and splendor achieved by the Mesopotamians, the Egyptians, the Persians, and all the rest. The confidence and sense of sureness this approach to existence generated was the vital spark pushing the people of the ancient Near East on to their accomplishments.

Viewed from such a perspective, the achievements of that world were magnificent. Why then did the society grow old and lifeless? Men have for centuries wrestled with the causes of the decline and fall of civilizations. Most great theories on the theme have been discarded soon after their initial expression in favor of newer theories. Here we cannot expect to do more than point to certain limitations on the pattern of civilized life that developed in the ancient Near East by way of suggesting some factors in its decline. The environment imposed a set of limitations, for aside from the river valleys the Near East had limited potential in terms of material resources. Technology imposed another limitation. We must not let the spectacular advances of the last century or two blur a basic fact: Technological advance through most of history has been slow and painful, hindering man's ability to expand his control over nature. The ancient Near East suffered too from the overpowering influence of the river valley peoples. What succeeded so remarkably in early Mesopotamia and early Egypt became the model of civilized life for every people in the Near East. Although they benefited from imitation, those living beyond the valley floodplains became prisoners of modes of life that were creative only in a small geographical setting. This problem became especially serious when the direction of Near Eastern civilization passed from the people of the valleys to the people from the outside—the Hittites, the small Semitic kingdoms, the Assyrians, the Persians. Slavish imitation of the river valley pattern of civilization brought people to a certain point—and then stopped them from further advance. Still another limitation on the ancient Near Eastern world was its waste of human resources. It was a world directed by small elites who achieved wonders but who ultimately failed to call forth fresh creative talent. The social structure was too inflexible, too closed, to permit genius to break through from unexpected sources.

However, the greatest constriction on ancient Near Eastern civilization and the ultimate cause of its stagnation lay in the minds of men. The world view encased in the great religious systems made it extremely difficult for them to use to full capacity their greatest asset: the power to reason. Instead of freeing them to reflect on the nature and potential of themselves and the things around them, the ancient Near Eastern world view required that men pour their intellectual energies into acts of conformity with the directive forces of the cosmos. Because rationality was smothered, men failed to discover themselves. They were reaching in this direction, as the Hebrew prophets and Zoroaster testify, but they never broke through the formidable barriers imposed by the assumptions upon which their civilization was based. Only someone outside their world still had the freedom to discover what man really was. When that discovery was made, the Near Eastern peoples had to surrender the leadership of civilization to others.

Here then is the epitaph of the ancient Near East: It was a world that knew men not well enough.

II

Greco-Roman Civilization
1200 B.C.-A.D. 200

While the civilizations of the Near East were reaching maturity under the political sway of the Assyrians and the Persians, a new civilization was appearing in the lands around the Aegean Sea. It began to emerge about 1200 B.C. and reached its most creative phase in the fifth century B.C., when the city-states of Greece produced literary, artistic, philosophical, and scientific works that departed radically from those of the Near East. The great intellectual and artistic outburst of fifth-century Greece was nourished in a political and social order that was likewise revolutionary.

From its Aegean center the new civilization exerted a powerful influence over other peoples. The Greeks themselves propagated their style of life through trading and colonizing ventures that ringed the Mediterranean with their city-states. More significant was the role played by non-Greeks as missionaries of Greek civilization. In the latter part of the fourth century, the Macedonians under the meteoric Alexander the Great joined with the Greeks to burst out of the Aegean basin and overrun the old centers of civilization in the Near East. All across this vast area Greek ideas and institutions made a profound impression, and in the territory bordering on the eastern rim of the Mediterranean, the Greek way of life became supreme. In the third century B.C. the Romans, just emerging as a world power, became enamored of Hellenic civilization and turned their energies to absorbing and spreading it. The Romans eventually conquered Greece and the Near East but were themselves mastered by the ideas and culture of their victims. The empire that they forged became the setting for a further extension of the Greek pattern of life so that much of Western Europe and North Africa fell under Greek influence. Roman political genius combined with Hellenic cultural patterns to forge a vast community of men living around the

Mediterranean and a civilization that ranks as a great achievement in human history.

In tracing the complex evolution of Greco-Roman civilization through fourteen or fifteen centuries, one should try to identify in an orderly way the main stages of development and the actors responsible for each new stage. One should comprehend the essential ingredients of Greco-Roman civilization, many of which became a permanent part of the total human accomplishment. But perhaps most important, one should grasp the extent to which the Greco-Roman world discovered and unleashed a new range of human talents and turned them to creative ends. To many historians, the key to this chapter of human history was the discovery and development of the idea expressed by the Athenian dramatist Sophocles in his *Antigone:* "Many are the wonders of the world, and none so wonderful as Man."

Greco-Roman civilization was born in a group of small, independent communities around the Aegean Sea. No one can understand that civilization until he grasps the unique nature of these communities, which spurred their inhabitants to creative activities radically different from any that had preceded them. However, no city-state sprang full-grown from a void; each was a product of long experimentation and sometimes painful growth. This chapter will trace that evolution and seek to reveal the nature of these communities by showing how they came into being. After a look at the general pattern of development, a closer study will take Athens and Sparta as examples of city-state society.

Greco-Roman civilization had its origins in the setting provided by the Aegean Sea—the lands to its west, north, and east and the innumerable islands on its surface. The sea and the land merge intimately, so that no inhabitant is far from the sea, and none using the sea is far from land. The whole area is blessed with a beneficent climate, marked by mild winters and long, dry summers, which permits men to sail the Aegean in relative safety and to live on the land without expending great amounts of energy to clothe and house themselves. But its resources are not overabundant. The topography, especially of Greece proper, is dominated by mountains, valleys, bays, and peninsulas that cut the land into many small pockets of tillable soil and create barriers against political unifica-

5

THE ORIGINS AND DEVELOPMENT
OF THE GREEK CITY–STATE POLITY

tion. The limited amount of tillable soil was poor in quality, subject to erosion, and ill-suited to cereal production. As the Greek historian Herodotus said, "Greece has always poverty as her companion."

This restrictive environment might have doomed its inhabitants to a modest historical role had there not been an avenue of escape: the sea. The Aegean provides excellent harbors, and it is tideless, is relatively calm, and has good sailing winds. It thus became a roadway especially to the east and the north. This was an important factor because it drew the Greeks toward the higher civilizations of the Near East and subjected them to the influences of the Indo-European barbarians moving from the north toward the Mediterranean world during the second millennium B.C.

1. PRE-GREEK ORIGINS: THE MYCENAEAN AGE, 2000–1200 B.C.

Greek history in a strict sense did not begin until about 1200 B.C., roughly the time of the era of small nations in the Near East. However, certain events before that time set the stage for the emergence of the Greeks. The first significant advance toward civilization occurred during the fourth millennium B.C., when neolithic culture spread over the Aegean area from the east. During the ensuing centuries, agricultural villages developed everywhere and a typical neolithic

pattern emerged. The archeological record suggests no great innovations in this age; it is important chiefly because the basic population and the fundamental techniques of agricultural life were established as a foundation for later development.

About 2000 B.C. this primitive order was profoundly disturbed by the intrusion of Indo-Europeans from the north. They imposed their political system on the native population, and their language ultimately became predominant. However, the newcomers adopted from the natives the basic features of agricultural life, so that for the next four or five centuries Aegean history centered on the activities of numerous agricultural principalities dominated by aggressive warlords and their retainers who showed little talent for raising their level of civilization.

But about 1500 B.C., there was a change. A series of great fortress-palaces was built in many places in southern and central Greece, the chief one at Mycenae. The kings of the small principalities had increased their power and wealth to the point where they could afford great building projects. The key to their success appears to have been what they learned from their growing contacts as booty-seeking pirates and traders with the civilized societies of the Near East and Crete. From Crete, where Minoan civilization was reaching its apogee, a great influx of Minoan technical skills, art forms, religious ideas, and political techniques swept across Greece, all reflected primarily in the elegant palaces and great tombs built by the kings. The rulers now commanded a centralized bureaucracy capable of imposing strong control over the populations of the principalities. A written language, which modern scholars call Linear B, had been perfected, chiefly to record the kings' dealings with their subjects. The decipherment of that language a few years ago furnishes proof that the Mycenaean world spoke Greek and that its people must therefore be counted as Greeks. Mycenaean culture, which reached its peak about 1300 B.C., was basically derivative. Under its influence the Aegean world appeared to be moving toward a pattern of civilization similar to that characteristic of the ancient Near East. The process of diffusion in the second millennium B.C. seemed about to link the Aegean world to the Near East. Had this happened, the later history of Greece and the West would have been drastically altered.

Mycenaean culture, however, lacked the vigor to advance on its own. The collapse of Minoan civilization about 1400 B.C., perhaps caused by Mycenaean raids, cut off a vital source of inspiration. The movements of peoples that disrupted the Hittite and Egyptian empires about 1200 B.C. blocked access to the Near East. The Mycenaean kings reacted to their shrinking world by turning their aggressiveness on closer neighbors, such as Troy, and on each other. Their culture collapsed shortly after 1200, when a new horde of Indo-Europeans called the Dorians swept through the Aegean world and laid waste their rich fortress-cities.

2. THE FOUNDATIONS OF GREEK SOCIETY: THE DARK AGE, 1200–800 B.C.

From one perspective, the Dorian invasions were catastrophic, sweeping away most of the Mycenaean establishment—the kingdoms, their cities, trade, technical skills, art, and writing. The "Dark Age" that gripped the Aegean world lasted for four centuries. However, for all its retrogressive character, this age had another side. Cut off from external cultural influences, the invaders and their conquered subjects forged a new pattern of life. To some extent, this new culture was derived from the wreckage of Mycenae, but it was basically a Greek creation, and it was the foundation for later Greece in all her glory. Our information about the Dark Age comes chiefly from archeology, but at the very end of the period two literary masterpieces, the *Iliad* and the *Odyssey* of Homer, were set down as witnesses to the age and its vitality.

The Dorian invasions caused an extensive movement of peoples early in the period, and Greeks spread to the Aegean islands and the coast of Asia Minor. Mycenaean culture had never embraced so extensive an area. A common language (with several dialects) spread over this territory, and from it emerged the highly developed written language of the Homeric epics. A common pattern of religion, clearly delineated in the *Iliad* and the *Odyssey*, was a major accomplishment. A set of political, economic, and social institutions took shape. The basic political unit was the small kingdom based on agricultural pursuits and ruled by a chieftain who led his people in war, judged their disputes, and represented them before the gods. In marked contrast with the Mycenaean and with other ancient monarchies, a potent nobility limited royal power. The authority of the nobles was rooted in a powerful clan structure under which extended families shared property and religion. The noble heads of these clans in each kingdom met regularly as a council to advise the king on matters of common interest. Peasants and artisans possessed honorable status by virtue of their membership in a clan and even participated to a degree in political life through an assembly where they could shout their approval or disapproval of the decisions of kings and elders.

By 800 B.C. kinship ties still provided the chief cohesive force in society, but already people were being drawn into another entity that transcended the clan. The communal bonds found their focus in the physical center of each kingdom, and all were so small that every citizen had access to that center. There the king's residence was a fortress where all could gather in times of danger. There temples were built in honor of the gods shared by the members of the kingdom. The same center served as a meeting place for the clan leaders when they gathered from their rural estates to advise the king. A market developed around the fortress. Little by little this "city," called the *polis* by the Greeks, became the center of communal life. Those who became increasingly identified with the *polis* became its "citizens"; *citizenship* constituted the total set of conditions that gave a man membership in a *polis*. Participation in military, religious, political, and economic activities at a single center slowly ingrained in men's minds a sense of belonging to a larger group than their kin group. This combination of physical and psychological involvement in the city-state provided the dynamic element in the Greek world.

Perhaps the Dark Age produced another development as unique and important as these institutional patterns, a development that ultimately allowed the citizens of the *polis* to do something creative for it. On the basis of Homer's epics and the artistry of the pottery fashioned during the later stages of the age, one might venture that the Greeks had assumed a new mental posture. In simplest terms, these sources portray a view of the world that placed a high value on human capability and that took joy in human activity. Moreover, each work shows a sense of harmony, proportion, balance, and order, the product of one of man's special powers, his reason. Dare we suggest that, amid the darkness at the beginnings of Greek history, humanism and rationalism were somehow born, opening wide vistas to men increasingly inclined to serve the *polis*?

3. GROWTH AND DEVELOPMENT: THE ARCHAIC AGE, 800–500 B.C.

By 800 B.C. the foundation was laid for a new civilization; in the succeeding three centuries, the edifice was completed. These were centuries of rapid change, for institutions and ideas became ever more complex and sophisticated. The cultural, intellectual, and religious aspects of change will be treated later. Here the focus of attention will be on the development of the *polis*.

The first manifestation of change affecting the *polis* came during the eighth century, with the replacement of kingship in all but a few communities by a government in which decisive au-

thority rested in a council of nobles and execution of council decisions was entrusted to elective officials. The causes of this change, running quite contrary to historical development elsewhere in the ancient world, are obscure. Perhaps royal authority as reflected in the Homeric epics had become too tradition-bound to respond to new problems. Some historians argue that a military revolution replacing chariot warfare with the *phalanx*, a massed formation of heavily armored infantrymen, was responsible, as the new system called less for individual prowess than for purposeful action by considerable numbers. One suspects that the growing political consciousness of the aristocrats, based on their long experience in advising the kings, was the prime factor. Whatever the causes, the consequences were great in broadening the political base of the *polis*.

Aristocratic domination of most *poleis* persisted at least into the sixth century B.C. During the Archaic Age, few radical changes occurred in the structure of government. However, the hold of the *polis* on its inhabitants continued to expand. Although they were often greedy and jealous of their power, the aristocrats themselves formulated during these centuries an ethos that emphasized justice, courage, loyalty, respect for the gods, and responsibility toward others. These were all basically civic concepts. The aristocrats began to lend their wealth and talents to the propagation of these ideas in art, literature, and education, so that other elements of society caught a sense of the larger community. Most important of all, the aristocratic masters of most city-states were ultimately willing to take political action to resolve basic problems affecting the whole population.

There were indeed serious problems in most *poleis*, arising chiefly from an economic crisis. As reflected so clearly in the lamentations of an eighth-century poet, Hesiod, much of the Greek world began to feel the pinch of severe poverty early in the Archaic Age. The causes were deep-seated and many: the basic poverty of the Greek soil, increasing population, aristocratic exploitation, and a newborn urge for economic gain driving men to compete for limited resources. In many city-states previously free small farmers

EARLY AND CLASSICAL GREECE

were being reduced to dependency and slavery. Because this threatened the bonds attaching the common people to the community, the trend could have spelled disaster for the still immature *poleis*.

The danger was averted in part by overseas settlement. Bold leaders, often of aristocratic origin, and willing followers took to the seas in search of new land where they could assure their livelihood. Often these ventures were civic undertakings, sponsored and organized by the aristocratic governors of the mother city. Between 800 and 500 B.C. this burst of activity dotted the northern Aegean, Black, and Mediterranean shores with a large number of new Greek cities. These communities were not colonies but independent *poleis* with their own governments, citizens, laws, religion, and patriotism.

More significant in reducing the economic pressures was a great expansion of trade and industry. The colonizing undertakings played a part in this by opening opportunities for trade between overseas Greek cities and the homeland. From this kind of trading activity it was but a short step to involvement in the larger trading world already mapped out in the Near East, especially by the Phoenicians. The Greeks proved energetic and enterprising, and by 500 B.C. they had become the leading traders in the Mediterranean world. Trade nourished manufacturing, particularly of excellent pottery. Even the old agricultural system was altered by expanding trade opportunities. Enterprising farmers abandoned the raising of grain in favor of raising grapes, olives, and livestock, all of which found profitable markets overseas and in the Greek cities. Thus for merchants, artisans, and commercial farmers alike, the center of economic life shifted to the marketplace in the city, creating new ties between citizen and *polis*.

The social structure changed under the impact of economic change. Some aristocrats became involved in trade and industry, either as entrepreneurs or as supporters of growth through political action. This development weakened their solidarity as a class and bred disagreement among them. Men from the lower ranks of society succeeded in amassing wealth through trade and industry and became rivals of the landowning aristocracy for power and prestige. Small farmers, unable to engage in capitalistic farming and unwilling to become dependents of great landowners, moved to the cities. This change dissolved ancient family ties, weakened the control of the clan leaders over the populace, and thrust upon public authorities the burden of controlling socially displaced groups.

These mounting tensions evoked from the aristocratic governments of most *poleis* deliberate political actions that had the overall effect of expanding the importance of public life and strengthening the ties binding men to the *polis*. Each city-state ended up with a set of unique political and social institutions, but a broad pattern was discernible throughout the Greek world.

In general, aristocratic regimes tried to relieve mounting tensions by "reforms" that did not require surrender of their monopoly on political power. They enacted legal codes that defined rights and obligations more clearly and devised techniques to limit the arbitrary exercise of power. They encouraged overseas colonization and the expansion of trade. They granted relief to debtors and protection to small landowners. Aristocratic concern for the lower classes was a unique feature of Greek political life, contrasting sharply with the viewpoint of the Egyptian and Mesopotamian ruling classes. The Greek aristocrats were undoubtedly motivated in part by self-interest, but their efforts were perhaps inspired by another force: patriotism, born of a realization in the minds of aristocrats that steps must be taken to retain the allegiance and services of valuable artisans, sailors, shopkeepers, and farmers who each in his own way made a contribution to the welfare of the *polis*.

As important as they were in strengthening the *polis*, aristocratic "reforms" were not usually sufficient to maintain stability. The growing attachment of men of all levels to the city generated demands for greater political participation that the aristocrats were unwilling to grant. Usually, force was required to unseat the nobles. The revolt against them was spearheaded in many city-states by individual leaders called *tyrants* by the Greeks. Tyrants were often men of noble origin and great wealth, acquired in many cases by trading ventures, who were zealous for personal power and pursued policies that would ensure they held it. Once established in control of a *polis,* the typical tyrant struck at the wealthy nobles who were the greatest threat to his power. Nobles were taxed severely, sometimes deprived of their lands, and often driven into exile; most important of all, they were deprived of control of political life. Tyrants usually sought to please the poorer elements in society by creating economic opportunities for them, spending huge sums on beautifying the cities, and increasing trade and industry. Although their political methods were brutal and oppressive, they did increase the economic stake of the common citizen in the *polis*.

The period of tyranny was brief in most cities, chiefly because tyrants had seized power illegally and were incapable of carrying out the changes in political institutions that would prolong and legitimize their rule. The aristocrats who had been their chief victims took the lead in unseating them but were seldom able to restore their old monopoly. In progressive city-states the end of tyranny was accompanied by radical changes in the political system that allowed the total citizen body to take control of civic affairs and to decide for themselves what was in their best interest. With all citizens entitled to participate in government, the last knot binding them to the *polis* was tied.

The perfection of a democratic polity provided the setting for the Golden Age of the Greeks— that glorious era centering in the fifth century B.C. that witnessed the flowering of literature, art, philosophy, and science. Beyond doubt the full participation of citizens in political life provided a major stimulant to the burst of artistic and intellectual energy that made the fifth century a golden age; indeed, the democratic *polis* was one of the prime features of the Golden Age.

4. ATHENS

The history of Athens provides a case study illustrating the process by which a collection of people grew into a democratic *polis*. At an early date, the region called Attica was inhabited by Indo-Europeans living in small agricultural villages led by clan elders. Eventually these Attic villages coalesced into a single unit centering around Athens with a king as the head of this enlarged community. In the process Athens became the focus for governmental, economic, religious, and military affairs for all Attica and thus the embryo of a *polis* that henceforth bore the name of the city at its center. The kings of ancient Athens were assisted by an aristocratic council of clan heads called the Areopagus. Some form of popular assembly also existed, but its role was limited. For political and military purposes, the clans were grouped into four tribes, each divided into three brotherhoods (*phratries*). Citizenship was established by admission to a brotherhood; and since kinship ties were the basis for society, citizenship was hereditary, dependent on clan membership.

About 750 B.C. monarchy began to be replaced by an aristocratic government. Elective officials, the *archon* (for civil affairs) and the *polemarch* (for military leadership), took over the functions of the king. These officials were elected annually by an assembly of all citizens. Only the wealthy of noble birth were eligible for elective office. The directive power in the *polis* rested in the Areopagus, composed of ex-archons who passed from elective office to a life term on the council. The Areopagus supervised the conduct of the archons, deliberated on policy decisions, formulated proposals to be submitted to the assembly, and served as the final court of appeal.

The aristocratic political system formed in the eighth century persisted with minor changes for more than two centuries. However, across these centuries there was mounting internal tension. In large part it arose from economic pressures, especially the tendency of the noble landowners to exploit and enslave the less fortunate farmers. And the increasing involvement of Athens in trade and industry caused shifts in the distribution of wealth and the development of new social groups not easily incorporated into a clan structure rooted in landowning. Within the governing aristocratic circle there developed factions whose rivalries sharpened tensions in the city. Ultimately, the aristocracy responded to these pressures by seeking to adjust the political system.

The first notable reformer was Draco, archon in 621 B.C., somewhat mistakenly enshrined in history as the giver of a harsh code of laws. In fact his enactments sought to limit the power of aristocratic judges to oppress the citizenry and to increase the authority of public courts at the expense of the clan-dominated courts.

A more significant reformer was Solon, archon in 594 B.C. Although an aristocrat by birth, Solon was a man of broad vision, the result perhaps of his experience as a trader and perhaps also of his intellectual interests, reflected in the surviving fragments of his poetry. His reforms seem to have emerged from a conviction that Athens was endangered by aristocratic exploitation of the poor and by the lack of opportunity for many citizens to improve their economic and social lot.

In his effort to aid the lower classes, Solon reformed the debt laws to end the vicious practice of enslavement for debt. Many who had been enslaved were freed, and some who had fled Athens because of debt were repatriated. He carried through legislation to reduce the power of the clan over the individual and substituted the public authority as the vessel of power to which the individual could turn. He initiated measures to promote trade and industry, including the adoption of a new coinage system and the recruitment of artisans from abroad.

To check aristocratic abuses of power, Solon made changes in the structure of government. Previously, citizens had been classified on the basis of land ownership, which meant that one had to be wealthy and of good birth to hold office and enter the Areopagus. Solon changed the basis for classification to income from land or other sources, a significant reform because it opened up offices to men who had achieved wealth but were not of high birth. To stand alongside the powerful Areopagus, he established a new body, called the Council of Four Hundred, made up of a hundred members selected from each of the four tribes. Its main function was to prepare matters for the assembly and provide recommendations on what action that body should take. Probably Solon intended this body as a curb on the assembly, which had great potential power; in any case, the Council did bring new people into public service. To curb judicial abuse, Solon created a new court, called the *Heliaea,* composed theoretically of all citizens sitting in the assembly but constituted in practice by a large panel selected from the total citizen body by lot. It was a court of appeal in which citizens had the power to correct inequities perpetrated in the regular courts.

Solon's whole system of government was designed to prevent abuse of power while still leaving the operation of the *polis* in aristocratic hands. His reforms broadened the political base of the state somewhat, but were not democratic. His main importance for history lay in giving the public a vastly wider role in safeguarding its interests; the government was every citizen's government to a much greater degree.

Solon's reforms were not sufficient to satisfy the Athenians. Strong factionalism, with noble families in the forefront, marked political life during the first half of the sixth century. In broad terms, the basic issue at stake was whether Athens would revert to an oligarchy—rule by a few—or move toward more popular government. The struggle opened the way for tyranny. Athens' first tyrant was a nobleman, Pisistratus, who finally established control in 546 B.C. after some earlier abortive attempts. He held power until his death in 527, and his sons continued the regime until 510. Pisistratus came to power by force, using foreign mercenaries paid out of his own wealth and the contributions of foreigners hostile toward Athens. He and his sons made no changes in the constitutional structure of Athens, but they did direct the overall policy of the government toward safeguarding the interests of the poor. They promoted a foreign policy that greatly expanded Athenian commercial and industrial interests to the advantage of the merchants and artisans. They patronized public works and the arts with vigor, thereby providing jobs for many and making Athens prominent as a cultural center.

Tyranny was overthrown in Athens chiefly through the efforts of the artistocrats whose power had been curbed for thirty-five years; their cause was abetted by foreign help. But they had no chance to restore their old monopoly. Another reformer, Cleisthenes (archon in 508 B.C.), took the initiative in establishing a democratic regime in which power rested with the total citizen body. He carried out this important reform by abolishing the political functions of the twelve brotherhoods and the four tribes they constituted, although leaving them their ancient religious and social functions. To replace the old clan-dominated system, he divided the whole city-state into territorial units called *demes*. All freemen living in a *deme* were registered as citizens, family connections making no difference. The *demes* were combined into ten new tribes. In forming the tribes, Cleisthenes divided the city-state into three regions—the hill country, where poor farmers predominated; the plain, which was the stronghold of the great noble families; and the coast, where the artisans and merchants of the city proper prevailed. Each tribe was composed of *demes* drawn from each of these districts; as a result, each of the basic units of political life contained a cross section of the population. Each *deme* and tribe was a political unit in its own right with officials, courts, taxes, military forces, and so forth, allowing a wide range of opportunity for direct political participation by local citizens.

Cleisthenes then rearranged the main organs of government to fit the new tribal organization. The Council of Four Hundred was replaced by a Council of Five Hundred, fifty citizens of each tribe selected by lot from an elected panel for annual terms. No one could serve on this council more than twice in a lifetime. This body, however, did not have the final authority, which rested with an assembly called the *ecclesia* made up of all male citizens over eighteen years of age voting by tribe. It met at least once a month and decided upon matters prepared for its deliberation by the Council of Five Hundred. Thus the citizen body, consisting of perhaps 30,000 or 40,000 males, had the final power in the state. The citizens were further involved in governing the city through the Heliaea, which remained as Solon had constituted it. Finally, Cleisthenes ensured popular control over the *polis* by introducing the practice of *ostracism*, through which a majority of citizens in the ecclesia could vote an individual dangerous to the state and exile him for ten years. Cleisthenes did not disturb the Areopagus, although it now lacked the authority to guide crucial decisions, and the elected archons remained the executive officers of the city-state. They were elected by the ecclesia and were still usually from aristocratic backgrounds, but now they had to win the support of the total body of citizens. Cleisthenes thus provided political equality for the citizens and devised a way whereby a majority of them could decide all matters. This was democracy.

Cleisthenes' system of government was not much changed in later years. It did require some time for the citizenry to become accustomed to the full exercise of its power. Not until the time of Pericles, the chief political figure in Athens from 461 to 429 B.C., did Athenian democracy reach its full bloom. Pericles was not primarily a lawmaker, although he did enact measures stripping the Areopagus of its last remnants of

power. More important, he introduced payment for service in the Council of Five Hundred, the Heliaea, and the elective magistracies. This enabled the poor to engage in political life without sacrificing their livelihood. Pericles' real importance lay in the encouragement he gave to citizens to participate in political life. Although aristocratic by birth and the companion of the leading intellectuals and artists of his day, he felt no fear in entrusting the political destiny of Athens to the common citizens. His own exemplary conduct as a leader convinced nearly all citizens that public life was a dignified, responsible, and rewarding activity.

In discussing the nature of fifth-century Athenian democracy, we must make one important reservation. Participation in political life was confined to citizens, a severely limited group in Periclean Athens. Only those whose ancestors had been citizens could qualify for that precious right. Large numbers of foreigners (called *metics*) and slaves did not and thus took no part in political life. Since metics and slaves outnumbered citizens, a minority of the population actually governed the city.

5. SPARTA

Other cities followed a pattern of development similar to that of Athens, ending with a system that encouraged participation in civic affairs by all citizens. Still other cities evolved toward different forms, as Sparta's history illustrates.

Sparta was founded by Indo-European invaders who overran Peloponnesus shortly before 1000 B.C. The invaders first settled in many small villages, which then moved toward union in a single city-state. By the seventh century B.C., Sparta was well along in this process, following a development similar to that of Athens and most other Greek *poleis*. But when they began to feel the sharp edge of poverty, Spartans made a decision that determined their future as a city-state: They turned to the conquest of neighboring cities, forcing them to labor for Sparta's benefit. This policy posed the necessity of making Sparta's citizens into a permanent army to stand guard over her subjects.

The reorganization of Spartan society on a

military basis was attributed to a great lawgiver, Lycurgus. The new order probably evolved over several decades in the late seventh and early sixth centuries B.C. Its most fundamental feature was the division of the population into three classes, each with rigidly defined responsibilities. First were the *Spartans,* consisting of about 5 percent of the population. This class served as professional soldiers, each member dedicating his life to ruling the rest of the population. No Spartan was allowed any other occupation. Next were the *perioeci,* a class charged with conducting whatever trading and manufacturing were necessary. Finally there were the *helots,* state slaves who served as laborers on the land or as personal servants. Membership in each class was hereditary, and there was little movement from one class to another.

The Lycurgan reforms prescribed a regimen to be followed by each Spartan to prepare him for his life's service as a soldier. At birth each child of a Spartan citizen was inspected by state officials for physical fitness. If the child was defective, the state ordered death by exposure. If allowed to live, the child lived with his mother until the age of seven. Then the males were sent to barracks, where severe military training was given them until the age of twenty. Girls were likewise rigorously trained to become the mothers and wives of future soldiers.

At twenty, the Spartan youth became a regular soldier, deriving his income from a piece of land that the state assigned to him along with enough helots to farm it. A man could marry after he was twenty, although he was not permitted to live with his wife until he was thirty, when he was also allowed to take part in political life. At sixty he could retire from military service.

The helots and perioeci escaped this regime, but they too were carefully disciplined. Every year the state formally declared war on the helots so that any troublemaker could be killed on the spot. The perioeci had greater freedom, even being allowed to govern themselves in some cases, but they were excluded from decisions affecting the policy of Sparta and therefore never had a chance to command a leading position in Spartan society.

Sparta always remained a monarchy, with two

This bronze statue of a Spartan warrior, about 6 inches high, dates from the late sixth century B.C.
Photo: Courtesy Wadsworth Atheneum, Hartford

kings as the formal heads of the state. Actually their power was very slight; the real power was held by the *gerousia,* a council of elders, consisting of the two kings and twenty-eight other men over sixty years old elected to serve for life. This body formulated all legislation, judged the most important cases, and acted as an advisory body to the administration of the state. Its decisions had to be presented to an assembly made up of all male Spartans over thirty. Theoretically the assembly had the power to repudiate any policy, but one can well imagine that this assembly of citizen soldiers, peopled by men taught from childhood to obey orders and to let their superiors do the thinking, was seldom able to render an independent decision. The execution of laws was entrusted to a board of five *ephors,* elected annually by the assembly, which conducted foreign affairs, supervised military training, policed the helots, and handled all matters of military preparation. Throughout most of Spartan history the ephors exercised virtually dictatorial powers, especially if, as was usually the case, they agreed with the thirty-member council of elders. Sparta was thus ruled by an oligarchy of military commanders.

Once the Lycurgan constitution was finished, it proved effective. The iron discipline of the citizen body resulted in Sparta's possessing the best army in Greece, and by 500 B.C. she had forced most of the city-states in the Peloponnesus to join the Peloponnesian League. The member cities were allowed independence but were forced to follow Spartan leadership in foreign affairs, thereby ensuring Spartan predominance in the Peloponnesus and enhancing her power in all of Greece.

6. THE CHARACTER OF THE POLIS

The two or three hundred other city-states that had been shaped by the fifth century each considered its institutions as excellent and as typically "Greek" as those of Athens and Sparta. In fact, there was infinite variety in the structure of the Greek *poleis;* the Greeks spent much intellectual energy — and sometimes blood — debating the merits of various political systems. But more significant in the grand historical picture are the features common to all *poleis.*

The city-states were all small, intimate organisms, embracing a territory seldom as large as an American county and a populace often less than that of a modern university. In each *polis* life focused on a spot — a town — familiar to all, where were concentrated political, religious, economic, and cultural activities bearing directly on all. Each made citizenship a distinctive and precious condition of life that involved direct and active participation in civic affairs. What the Greek historian Thucydides credited Pericles with saying of Athens can serve as a fundamental characterization of all *poleis:* "We alone regard a man who takes no interest in public affairs, not as harmless, but as a useless character." Whatever its constitutional form might be, the *polis* drew the individual out of himself, his clan, his calling, his class to make him a participant in a community enterprise. It made him, as Aristotle put it, a political animal. Active involvement nourished a psychological state in the political animal, breeding patriotism — fierce pride in and love for his *polis.* Every *polis* was then a pressure chamber compelling men to discover and exercise their talents in the interests of something larger, more enduring, and more splendid than themselves. As such, the *polis* nourished an intensity of life seldom witnessed in history and brought forth achievements which sometimes seem almost superhuman.

Suggested Reading

General Surveys of Greek History
*C. E. Robinson, *Hellas: A Short History of Ancient Greece* (Beacon).
*H. D. F. Kitto, *The Greeks* (Pelican).
*M. I. Finley, *The Ancient Greeks* (Compass). Any of these three titles will provide a stimulating short introduction to the history of the Greeks.
N. G. L. Hammond, *A History of Greece to 322 B.C.* (1959). An excellent longer account treating all aspects of Greek development.

The Mycenaean, Dark, and Archaic Ages

C. G. Starr, *The Origins of Greek Civilization* (1961). A splendid synthesis of the early period in Greek history.

*A. E. Samuel, *The Mycenaeans in History* (Spectrum). A clear presentation of the Mycenaean period and its civilization.

*T. B. L. Webster, *From Mycenae to Homer* (Norton). Especially good on Mycenaean and Dark Age culture.

T. D. Seymour, *Life in the Homeric Age* (1963). Utilizes Homer's poems expertly to create a lively picture of the Dark Age.

The Polis and Its Evolution

*Alfred E. Zimmern, *The Greek Commonwealth: Politics and Economics in Fifth-Century Athens* (Galaxy). A classic treatment of the fundamental nature of the city-state.

*Kathleen Freeman, *Greek City-States* (Norton). A more recent work than Zimmern's, especially good for the information it provides on city-states other than Athens and Sparta.

*W. G. Forrest, *The Emergence of Greek Democracy, 800–400 B.C.* (McGraw-Hill). A brilliant work on the evolution of the Athenian political system.

A. H. M. Jones, *Athenian Democracy* (1957). Excellent for its description of Athenian political institutions and their operation.

*W. G. Forrest, *History of Sparta, 950–192 B.C.* (Norton). A good study of Spartan development.

*A. Andrewes, *Greek Tyrants* (Harper Torchbook). Provides a clear picture of the role of the tyrants in shaping Greek city-states.

Economic and Social History

Hendrik Bolkestein, *Economic Life in Greece's Golden Age* (rev. ed., 1958). An excellent description of the main features of Greek economic life.

J. P. Mahaffy, *Social Life in Greece from Homer to Menander* (7th ed., 1925). Old but still excellent.

Sources

*Homer, *Iliad* and *Odyssey* (many editions; an excellent one is the translation by E. V. Rieu, Penguin). Essential for understanding the origins of a unique Greek society.

Hesiod, *Works and Days,* trans. H. G. Evelyn-White, Loeb Classical Library. A picture by a contemporary of the economic and social stresses of eighth-century Greece.

*Aristotle, *On the Constitution of Athens,* trans. K. von Fritz and E. Kapp (Hafner).

Xenophon, "Constitution of the Lacedomonians," in *Scripta Minora*, trans. E. E. Merchant (1925). This and the preceding work provide descriptions by two Greeks of the constitutions of Athens and Sparta.

Plutarch, *Lives* (many editions). Presents short biographies of Lycurgus, Solon, Themistocles, and Pericles that offer insight into the careers of key political figures associated with the evolution of Greek city-states.

6

THE FAILURE OF THE GREEK CITY-STATE POLITY

In its full bloom in the fifth century B.C., the *polis* was a marvelous institution for spurring its citizens to expend their talents for the good of the commonwealth. But by 500 B.C., another facet of Greek society took the center of the stage. Even while the city-states and especially Athens were pouring forth the many-sided creative effort that marked the Golden Age of Greek culture, the problem of the relationships among them became more critical and difficult. Small, numerous, crowded together on a poor land, the city-states inevitably became rivals of one another. These rivalries were intensified by the fervent patriotism bred in each *polis*. Eventually the city-states surrendered to their parochialism and destroyed themselves in what seem in retrospect to have been senseless internecine struggles. Here was one of those countless ironies that confront the student of history: The very institution that made the Greeks magnificently great turned out to be their nemesis.

1. THE PERSIAN WARS, 490–479 B.C.

Throughout early Greek history, there had been wars among the city-states, but prior to 500 B.C., these had been minor. The Greeks poured their energies into the internal development of each *polis*, colonization, and commerce. In fact, strong pan-Hellenic forces were operating to unite them. Most Greeks worshiped the same gods and gathered together regularly to pay honor to these deities. They held such all-Greek festivities as the Olympic Games. Moreover, most Greeks had a common language which became the vehicle for a literary tradition shared by all the city-states. Common styles and techniques in art were widely shared. Some progress had even been made toward political unions, such as the already noted Peloponnesian League.

The practical need for strong pan-Hellenism was dramatically posed at the beginning of the fifth century by the emergence of the Persian Empire, which threatened to engulf all the Greek city-states. For nearly two centuries prior to 500, the Greeks had been increasing their commercial and cultural contacts with the Near East and had benefited greatly from this highly civilized world. Some of the Greek cities on the Ionian coast had even been drawn politically into the Lydian Empire while it was the dominant force in Asia Minor. But the sudden emergence of Persia after 550 B.C. created entirely new relationships between the Greek world and the Near East. Westward expansion carried Persian rule to the Aegean shores of Asia Minor and into several Greek city-states. It was not unduly harsh, especially under Darius I, but it seemed burdensome to the Greek city-states, long accustomed to independence or the easy overlordship of Lydia. The city-states in Europe sympathized with their captive fellow Greeks and viewed the Persians as a threat to the independence of all Greek cities. They became particularly alarmed when Darius invaded Europe in 512 and established his rule in an area lying north of the Aegean called Thrace.

Hostility between Greeks and Persians grew rapidly after 499, when the Greek cities in Asia Minor revolted against the Persians. The rebels called on the European Greeks for aid and received it from Athens and Eretria. Darius crushed the rebellion, however, and determined to punish those who came from Greece to make trouble in his empire. He was encouraged to believe that this might be an easy task by political factions — usually antidemocratic — in many city-states who saw the Persians as potential allies in their struggle for power and by the neutrality proclaimed by several key city-states. He did not realize, however, that there were equally potent forces emerging in the same cities who saw in the Persians a threat to the new Greek way of life just coming into bloom.

In 490 B.C. Darius sent a fleet bearing a moderate-sized army across the Aegean, ostensibly to punish Athens and Eretria but perhaps to begin the conquest of the Greeks. After destroying Eretria, the Persian army landed in eastern Attica near Marathon, probably expecting that pro-Persian elements in Athens would launch an internal revolt to open the way to the city. But the Athenians, although outnumbered, decided on an attack. Under the brilliant leadership of Miltiades, they mauled the Persian army at Marathon and forced it back to its ships. The Persians then sailed around to Athens, but by the time they arrived Miltiades had marched his army from Marathon and was ready to defend the city. The Persians returned to Asia Minor. Greece had been saved, and Athens was the savior.

The Persians, preoccupied by revolts within the empire and by political disturbances accompanying the accession of a new ruler, Xerxes I, were unable to resume the war for ten years. The Greek city-states meanwhile made better preparations than they had before Marathon. An Athenian leader emerged whose talent suited the approaching ordeal. He was Themistocles, a staunch supporter of democracy and an astute politician. Meanwhile, several city-states responded to Sparta's suggestion to form a league, and in 481 B.C. they agreed to pool their armies and navies in a joint force commanded by Spartan leaders. Ultimately, thirty-one city-states joined this "Greek League"; it was one of the most impressive common undertakings ever agreed to by the individualistic cities. Despite this show of unity, many cities, especially in northern Greece, preferred to remain neutral or to surrender to the Persians.

Early in 480, Xerxes began to move his huge army. It passed across the Hellespont, the strait between the Sea of Marmara and the Aegean, and moved slowly overland around the northern Aegean and into Greece. The Greek League decided to make its stand at Thermopylae, where a narrow pass would allow the smaller Greek army to check the massive Persian forces and where the narrow sea lanes between the mainland and the island of Euboea could be advantageously blocked by the Greek fleet. It seemed that the plan might succeed. The Greek fleet fought the Persians, weakened by severe losses suffered in storms, to a standstill, and the Greek army threw back attack after attack in the pass. But a local traitor showed the Persians a trail around the pass. When the Greek commander, King Leonidas of Sparta, discovered what had happened, he sent the bulk of the Greek army south while he and three hundred Spartans fought to the death to delay the Persians. Once past Thermopylae, the Persians flooded into central Greece. Athens was captured and burned, although her citizens fled to safety.

At this point, Themistocles exercised a deciding influence. There was strong pressure in the council of the Greek League to withdraw the armies to the Peloponnesus and the fleet to the Gulf of Corinth. Seeing clearly that the issue would be decided by sea power, Themistocles combined persuasion and threats of Athenian withdrawal to convince the league to face the Persians in the waters off Attica. In late September 480 B.C., he maneuvered the Persians into an engagement in the narrow strait between Attica and the island of Salamis. Caught where they could not use their full strength effectively, the Persians suffered a shattering defeat. Since the winter season was close at hand, Xerxes ordered

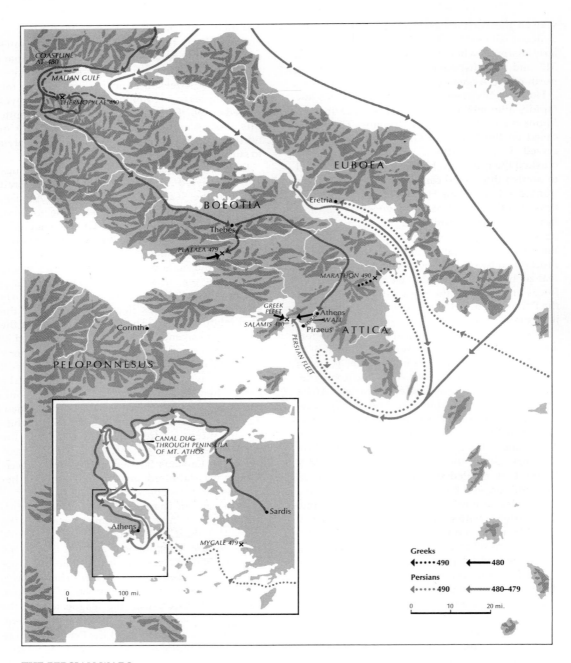

THE PERSIAN WARS

his fleet back to Asia Minor and the withdrawal of his armies to northern Greece, for they could not survive without sea support.

Xerxes undertook a new campaign in the spring of 479. This time a sizable Greek army moved out to meet the Persians and defeated them at Plataea. In the meantime the Greeks sailed boldly across the Aegean and destroyed what was left of the Persian fleet at Mycale. This was a signal for the Greek cities in Asia Minor to revolt once again. Xerxes could do nothing but recall his armies from Europe; the Greek fleet could now cut the path of escape in the straits. The jubilant Greeks had demonstrated their vitality against even so great a foe as Persia.

2. CONFEDERACY OF DELOS

The Greek victories in 480–479 had been magnificent, but the Persians were still a threat. This realization kept alive the spirit of unity among the Greeks, although leadership passed into new hands. The Spartans, who had directed the league in the critical days of 480 and 479, grew increasingly unwilling to commit their limited strength to projects remote from the Peloponnesus. Athens took the lead in summoning a meeting of Greek cities on the island of Delos in 478. It was quickly agreed to form the Confederacy of Delos to continue the war against Persia. Policy decisions were to be made by all the cities meeting annually in an assembly, with Athens executing the decisions. The members pledged to contribute ships and money according to their abilities. And the cherished independence of each *polis* was protected; no city-state was required to surrender its sovereignty.

The confederacy immediately swung into action. An Athenian, Cimon, was placed in command of its forces and enjoyed immediate success against the Persians. Within about ten years, all the Greek city-states in Asia Minor had been freed from Persian rule, while the Aegean and the straits area were cleared of Persian naval power. Athens was obviously the most powerful city in the league, but she conducted herself with marked restraint in her relations with her fellow city-states. Cimon's policy was conciliatory even toward nonmembers such as Sparta. Seldom before or after did the Greek world present a more united front than during the first years following the victory over the Persians.

3. THE ATHENIAN EMPIRE

This happy condition did not last long—and Athens was responsible for altering the situation. As the danger from Persia receded, some members of the confederacy desired to withdraw. Athens was unwilling to allow this to happen. Her leaders and many of her citizens saw that Athenian sea power, developed to check the Persians, could be turned to commercial advantage. Athens slowly began to convert the league into an empire under her control. She refused to allow members to withdraw, used territories won by league forces to establish her own colonies, and forced cities not in the league to join.

Athenian imperialism reached its full tide with the emergence of Pericles as the leader of the city in 461 B.C. He came to power in the wake of the downfall of Cimon, who had tried to restrain Athenian imperialism to a degree. Pericles launched a two-pronged drive to spread Athenian influence. In Greece he used every method available to force more cities into the confederacy under Athenian control. He supported revolts against nondemocratic governments, tried to entice the members of the Peloponnesian League to abandon Sparta, and used Athenian sea power to bottle up such trading powers as Corinth. Meanwhile, he renewed the assault on Persia, carrying the struggle into the eastern Mediterranean. In both offensives, he enjoyed some success. But about 450 B.C. it became obvious that Athens was overextending her power, and in spite of popular opposition, Pericles arranged peace treaties with both Persia and Sparta. In a treaty of 448 B.C. Persia and Athens agreed to respect each other's spheres of influence; and in the Thirty Years' Truce of 445 B.C., Sparta promised to refrain from interfering in the affairs of the Confederacy of Delos while Athens agreed to halt her aggressive policy among free Greek cities and especially those in the Peloponnesian League.

These treaties left Athens with a considerable empire, consisting of about three hundred city-states in the Confederacy of Delos. She continued to collect tribute annually, although the Persian danger had vanished. The money was now used in Athens for whatever the Athenians chose. Athens forced many of the league members to institute democratic governments in the hope that such governments would be more manageable. She forced subject cities to use her money and her weights and measures. By any standard of judgment, she treated these formerly independent cities as her subjects. And she did this for her own profit.

The profit was indeed great and very beneficial to Athens. At the height of the Periclean Age, she had grown to a population of perhaps 400,000, about 160,000 of them citizens and the rest alien artisans (metics) and slaves. The tribute money and the wealth from commerce made her richer than all others. A considerable part went to the citizenry as payment for the service in the many political agencies of the Periclean system of democracy. And it was liberally used to beautify the city and support the writers and artists who made Athens the "school of Hellas." The master hand of Pericles guided this great *polis* with sureness, purpose, and total trust in the citizens, and to his guidance they responded with good judgment and restraint. But fifth-century Athens would not have been the jewel of Hellas had it not been for the price she exacted from her "allies."

The subject city-states, of course, shared the fruits of increased commerce and the security that came from the imposed peace. Still, their hatred for Athens grew steadily. Its source was political. Athens had usurped their one valuable privilege, political independence. She had become a tyrant, endangering liberty everywhere. Even some of the Athenians felt moral aversion at destroying the liberty of any *polis* and raised their voices in protest. But the mass of the people, aware that the economic welfare of Athens was related to imperial power, overrode these voices.

Athens made no attempt to compensate her subjects for limitations on their freedom. They were not permitted to become citizens of Ath-ens, and they were allowed no representation in the Athenian government. Gradually, anti-Athenian feeling spread throughout the Greek world. These city-states now began to look toward Sparta as a champion of freedom. This was a rather strange development, considering Sparta's own record of domination over the cities of Peloponnesus. The anti-Athenian sentiment heralded a serious war in which Greek assaulted Greek, unmindful of the many things the city-states had in common.

4. THE PELOPONNESIAN WAR, 431–404 B.C.

The uneasy peace in the Greek world was finally shattered in 431 B.C. by the outbreak of the Peloponnesian War. Its immediate cause was the success of a few cities, especially Corinth, in convincing Sparta that Athens was violating the Thirty Years' Truce, thereby threatening the independence of all Greek cities. Athens was not unwilling to join the issue, probably feeling that a showdown was inevitable. She had a large fleet and huge financial resources to pit against the superior land forces of Sparta and her allies. Pericles was confident that the Spartans were incapable of a campaign that would strike at the real sources of Athenian power—her maritime empire.

The first ten years of the war were indecisive. Athens refused to commit herself to a land war with Sparta; Pericles persuaded the populace to withdraw within the city's impregnable walls and let the Athenian fleet hold together the empire which the Spartans were ill-equipped to attack. This disciplined strategy proved too much for the Athenians, especially after a plague decimated the cooped-up population in 429 B.C., claiming Pericles as a victim. The restless populace demanded bolder military action; a new leader, Cleon, answered by leading Athenian armies outside Attica. The Spartans produced a leader named Brasidas, who persuaded them to use their military forces to encourage revolt among the subject cities of the Athenian empire rather than waste energy attacking the walls of Athens itself. However, before the new struggle

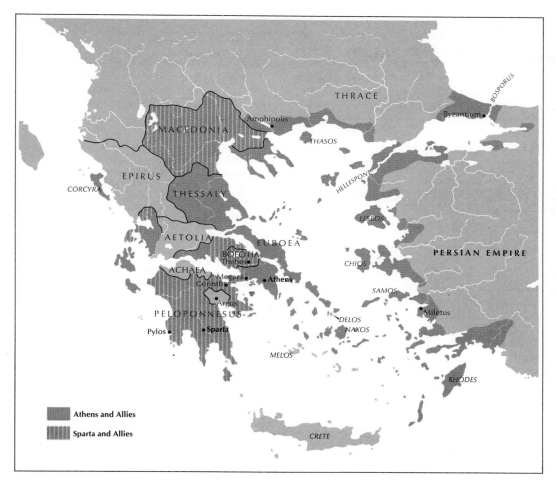

GREECE 431 B.C.

reached a decisive point, Cleon and Brasidas were both killed in 422. This gave powerful peace elements in both cities a chance to end the war. In 421 B.C. they agreed to a Fifty-Year Truce which returned their relations to what they had been before the war.

The truce lasted only until 415. Again, Athens was responsible for ending it. Led by the brilliant and popular but overly ambitious Alcibiades, she launched an ill-conceived expedition against the great Greek city of Syracuse in Sicily, where the Athenians suffered a disastrous defeat after a two-year campaign. Worse, her attack

on Syracuse provoked Sparta and her allies to renew the war against an Athens seriously weakened by the Sicilian venture.

After 413 the fortunes of Athens declined steadily. The main theater of war shifted to the Aegean Sea, where the Spartans, brilliantly led by Lysander, proceeded to destroy Athenian sea power while encouraging the cities of the Confederacy of Delos to revolt. At the same time, Sparta allied herself with the Persian king, who supplied money and ships in return for Spartan permission to reestablish Persian control over the Greek cities in Asia Minor. Athens occasionally won an isolated victory, but the net of Spartan-Persian power continued to close around her. Finally in 404 B.C. she surrendered. The victors forced her to tear down her walls, to destroy all but twelve of her ships, and to submit to a government of oligarchs who were guarded by a Spartan army stationed in the city. Although these Thirty Tyrants, as the Athenians called them, were ousted in 403 and democratic government was restored, Athens never recovered her former power.

5. THE DECLINE OF THE CITY-STATES, 404–336 B.C.

The defeat of Athens in no way solved the problem of intercity rivalry. The Peloponnesian War, which left a legacy of deep hatred, had caused other problems as well. Trade had been badly disturbed, and numerous areas of Greece had been laid waste. In many cities the declining economy bred serious class struggles. Often the lower classes were prevented from stating their case because democracy had suffered a heavy blow with the defeat of its champion, Athens. Many Greeks, especially intellectual leaders, grew pessimistic and sought escape from their civic responsibilities in individual pursuits.

The majority of Greeks failed to realize what was happening. They persisted in engaging one another in fruitless struggles that merely compounded the problems. Sparta, now the greatest power in Greece, behaved even more dishonorably than had Athens. She pursued a reactionary policy of imposing oligarchic government on any city-state she could bully into submission. When the Greek world protested her narrow and often brutal policy, she turned to Persia for help, which only increased Greek hatred of Spartans.

The resentment against Sparta led to a new series of wars. Thebes now became the champion of city-state independence. Under her only great statesman, Epaminondas, Thebes smashed the declining power of Sparta in a single battle in 371 B.C. She established a new league under her control, but was never able to extend it to all Greece. She too succumbed to the lure of Persian money in the attempt to ensure her own supremacy, but even Persian assistance was insuf-

ficient. A new coalition of cities, led once again by Athens, inflicted a fatal defeat on Thebes in 362 B.C.

The incessant warfare went on, but none of the city-states was able to establish the predominant position that might have meant peace. Instead, struggles prompted by the smallest issues continued to waste human and material resources and put the citizens of all the city-states under constant strain. Civic life was being sapped. The engulfing weakness and discouragement were especially dangerous at this moment. For on the northern fringe of the Greek world a powerful giant, the semibarbarous Macedonian kingdom, was casting greedy eyes on the seething turmoil to the south; and in the west, in Italy and Sicily, Carthage and Rome were stirring.

Some Greeks became aware of the dangers of intercity warfare and raised eloquent appeals for some kind of union that would stop it and protect Greece from foreigners. Some of them, like the Athenian orator and statesman Demosthenes, argued that Athens should take the lead in forming a confederation, but his appeal was not effective in view of Athens' past conduct. Others urged that the Macedonian king serve as the head of a Greek league, but this idea was widely looked upon as treason. In general, pan-Hellenism was a lost cause. The Greek city-states were too accustomed to total independence to surrender their sovereignty to a super-organization. Such great philosophers as Plato and Aristotle, who lived during the fourth century, vigorously maintained that only the traditional small city-state was fit for the Greeks. With this attitude, the Greeks did nothing to put a stop to their quarrels.

6. MACEDONIAN CONQUEST OF GREECE

The Greek city-states, unable to check their feuding, grew increasingly ripe for conquest. The conqueror rather unexpectedly turned out to be Macedon. She had not had a particularly brilliant history before the fourth century. The land was poor and inhabited by unruly peoples, far inferior to the Greeks culturally, who resisted organization.

The situation in Macedon changed rapidly as a result of the leadership of Philip II, king from 359 to 336 B.C., a masterful political leader, skilled both as a diplomat and as a general, who genuinely admired Greek culture and wished to preserve it. Once he became king, he welded his wild subjects into a disciplined and loyal army, and he spared no effort to secure an income sufficient to maintain it.

Philip's own love of all things Greek, along with his personal ambition, soon drew him into Greek affairs. His money and his army made him a valuable ally for any Greek city engaged in a war with its neighbors. He was not above intriguing to incite wars in Greece so that his services would be called upon. Wherever he became involved, Philip ended with the upper hand. Gradually the confusion in the Greek world began to clear as the Greeks realized the strength of Macedon and as Philip's growing mastery made itself felt. Athens emerged as the champion against Macedon and tried desperately to rally the rest of the Greeks to that cause, but the struggle was one-sided from the beginning. Demosthenes, whose eloquent pleas to the Athenian population to wake up to the threat from the north can still be read in his *Philippics*, did succeed on occasion in persuading the Athenians to send aid to Greek cities besieged by Philip, but usually too late and always too little. Demosthenes' efforts to form a Greek union fared little better. Slowly Philip advanced, finally forcing the Athenian alliance to commit itself to battle at Chaeronea in 338 B.C. In a single engagement the last strength of the Greeks was destroyed by Philip's well-trained army. Greece lay at his feet to be dealt with as he chose.

Philip II treated his victims with extreme mildness. He did, however, end the old order in Greece. One of his first moves was to call a meeting of all Greek city-states in 338 B.C. and form them into a Hellenic league, formally called the League of Corinth. Members of this league were theoretically entitled to complete independence, but in fact crucial restrictions were placed upon that freedom. No city was allowed to change its existing form of government, and without freedom to change its government a city-state certainly was no longer the city-state of old. The

league held regular meetings at which each city had representatives to debate and decide league policy. Finally, a common army and navy were created, with each state contributing according to its ability. Although Macedon was not a member, Philip required that the league sign a treaty of alliance with her, thereby giving the Macedonian king an important voice in its decisions.

Philip dictated the first undertaking of the League of Corinth: a war on the Persian Empire, a goal most Greeks could approve. But he did not live to lead the union of Greeks and Macedonians in an Asian campaign. One of his own nobles assassinated him in 336 B.C., perhaps at the behest of his wife, who did not fully approve of Philip's lack of respect for the institution of marriage.

Philip II was certainly one of the most farseeing statesmen of the fourth century. He was aware of the folly of the rivalry that had kept the Greek cities in a state of warfare for nearly a century. To end this, he used the superior strength of Macedon to force them into a union sufficiently strong to check the strife, and he sought to divert the martial characteristics of the Greeks into a war against Persia. These policies mark a turning point in Greek history. Philip II has seldom been given full credit, for his son, Alexander, put into practice the policies Philip had conceived.

7. THE SIGNIFICANCE OF THE CITY-STATE

The fateful course toward self-destruction followed by the Greek city-states during the fifth and fourth centuries B.C. is hardly inspiring. It may seem that the history of this period involves a contradiction. Much has been made of the unique vitality and strength of the *polis* — but in view of its precipitous decline, could it have been so great an institution? There can be no doubt that the city-state generated self-destructive warfare. It obviously limited the political capabilities of the Greeks to regulate relations among independent, proud, self-contained political units. But we should recall that man has always had grave difficulty restraining himself

An example of one of the finest of Greek art forms, the painted vase. Here Odysseus is presenting Achilles' armor to his son. *Photo: Kunsthistorischen Museum, Vienna*

from warfare and from the destruction of his best handiwork. The generalization that inter-

city warfare was the nemesis of the Greek *polis* may be too obvious and too easy.

The study of Greek history in this period leads one to suspect that the fatal flaw in the *polis* lay in the superhuman demands it made upon the frail creature that man is. It demanded of its citizens a willingness to recognize the problems of others, to judge these problems rationally, and to sacrifice self-interest in the name of a higher good. Perhaps for brief periods men are capable of such conduct, but in the long run they cannot sustain it. Individuals and classes could not sustain the rational, detached posture—what the Greeks themselves defined as the aristocratic view—demanded to keep the *polis* alive. They descended in human fashion to self-seeking and self-interest and to irrational warfare. It was a failure of men, not institutions, that doomed the *polis*. The city-state suffered from what was perhaps the nemesis of the whole of Greek civilization—too high an estimate of the capabilities of men.

Whatever its flaws, the Greek city-state was amazing, at least for a brief period. For the first time in history, large numbers of people were virtually compelled to rise above themselves to search out and put to work whatever talents they might have. The age-old system of masses of men bent before the will of a few masters was challenged and found wanting. The typical Greek *polis* demonstrated that even the most ordinary man could do remarkable things if he had the freedom.

Suggested Reading

Fifth- and Fourth-Century Greece

M. L. W. Laistner, *A History of the Greek World from 479 to 323 B.C.*, 3rd ed. (1957). An excellent detailed work on this era.

*A. R. Burn, *Persia and the Greeks* (Minerva). An interesting study of the Persian Wars.

*A. R. Burn, *Pericles and Athens* (Collier). Will help to evaluate the policy of Athens in the heyday of its empire.

Sources

*Herodotus, *The Persian Wars*, trans. Aubrey de Selincourt (Penguin). A stirring account of the encounter between Greeks and Persians; one of the great classics of historical writing.

*Thucydides, *The Peloponnesian War*, trans. Rex Warner (Penguin). Another classic describing the bitter struggle between Athens and Sparta.

*Plutarch, *Lives* (many editions). The short biographies of Themistocles, Aristides, Cimon, Pericles, Alcibiades, Lysander, and Demosthenes will add color to the history of this era.

7

GREEK CULTURE

Our examination of the Greek *polis* as a political, social, and economic institution revealed it as an instrument capable of evoking from its citizen members intense activity, activity generally creative and beneficial but sometimes destructive. We must now approach the *polis* from another, more difficult perspective. It provided the setting for one of the most creative cultural outbursts in all history. Living within its confines and interacting with others according to its rules, men were stimulated to modes of thought and expression that still seem amazing for their variety, their quality, and their durability. We must try in this chapter to grasp a sense of the "miracle" of Greek thought and expression as revealed in literature, art, philosophy, and science. It was in this realm that the *polis* produced something shared by all Greeks, something "Hellenic," as they would have said, to balance the divisiveness bred in political life.

1. AN OVERVIEW

The roots of Greek culture lie far back in the history of the Aegean world, the seeds having been planted by neolithic men, early Indo-European invaders, Minoan influences, and Mycenaean achievements. During the long Dark Age, that inheritance was shaped within the isolated Aegean world to produce a uniquely Hellenic culture. The first fruits of this new culture emerged

in the eighth century in highly original pottery decoration and in the Homeric epics. From the eighth through the sixth centuries B.C., the Archaic Age, the new culture developed rapidly, its unique characteristics being nourished by the changes in society which marked the development of the *polis,* overseas colonization, and commercial expansion. New poetic forms, large-scale architecture, and three-dimensional sculpture evolved. By the end of the period, the first signs of rational philosophical inquiry and mature prose literature had appeared.

During a relatively short period in the fifth century B.C. extending from the Persian Wars to the Peloponnesian War, Greek culture reached its Golden Age, with Athens as the chief center. The esthetics and ideas shaped in the Archaic Age were honed to perfection by a remarkable group of artists and thinkers who reflected a strong civic and religious sense but who were powerfully animated by a rational impulse. This was the age of tragic and comic drama, the poetry of Pindar, the history of Herodotus, the architectural and sculptural masterpieces of the Acropolis in Athens, the science of Hippocrates, and the philosophical inquiry of a succession of brilliant thinkers. However, by the end of the fifth century, signs of transformation and decline had appeared. The Sophists and their relativistic concepts, Socrates and his questioning, the dramatist Euripides and his critical attitudes, the historian Thucydides and his disillusionment set the tone of this age. By the fourth century B.C., classical Greek culture had clearly passed its peak. The literature and art between the end of the Peloponnesian War and Alexander the Great were undistinguished. Only in philosophy, dominated by Plato and Aristotle, was there still vitality. The ground was being prepared for a new phase of culture, which is called Hellenistic, one derived from the Hellenic experience but more cosmopolitan, individualistic, and personal.

2. GREEK RELIGION

A description of the cultural achievement of the Greeks must begin with their religion, for their lives were permeated with religious forces, and their main cultural achievements were rooted in religious belief. The origins of Greek religion are buried in the earliest stages of Greek history. By the time the historian can begin to find clear evidence for belief — toward the end of the Dark Age — these concepts were well developed in an elaborate mythology, and religious practices were set in a complex ritual pattern. A study of these myths and rituals makes it clear that in its origins Greek religion was an amalgam of concepts and practices derived from neolithic, Indo-European, Minoan, and Near Eastern sources. But some features do stand out as essential and remain central throughout the classical period.

The Greeks, first of all, were polytheistic. At an early date, at least before the Homeric age, they conceived of most of their gods as having human forms and as conducting themselves much the same as earthly men, except that the gods were immortal and infinitely more powerful. This anthropomorphism was highly significant in shaping Greek thought, for it made human access to the gods easier.

The major deities constituted a tumultuous family living on Mount Olympus under the authority of Zeus, whose position resembled that of an earthly father of a noble household. The activities of this pantheon — their feats, their intrigues against each other, their love lives, their quarrels, their good and evil deeds toward

men, their special likes and dislikes — were perfectly familiar to most Greeks. Most of the Olympian gods were worshiped by all Greeks, so that religion constituted a common element in Greek life. Many of the great gods had assumed a specific role: Zeus was the father and ruler of the gods and the world; Hera, his wife, was the protector of marriage and the family; Athena was the goddess of wisdom; Apollo was the bringer of light and the patron of the arts; and so forth. Several gods had among their functions the protection of particular city-states, so that the worship of the Olympian pantheon provided the basis for civic religion and constituted a powerful force linking men to the *polis*. The great deities honored in mythology were not the only divine forces in the Greek religious system. At a lower, more popular level were innumerable lesser spirits — nymphs, satyrs, muses, demons, spirits of heroes and departed ancestors.

The Greeks generally accepted the basic proposition that the gods controlled all human affairs and therefore that men must attune their activities to divine will. All good things as well as life's misfortunes came from the gods. Basically, the Greeks viewed their gods as capricious and amoral with respect to men, as exemplified in Zeus' insatiable lust for earthly maidens. In the later stages of Greek history considerable intellectual energy was spent trying to discover some higher principle of cosmic order. About all this struggle to "tame" the gods achieved was to posit the rather unappealing idea that over gods and men ruled some inexplicable force of fate that guided all things. In general, the Greeks persisted in their mythology. Yet they saw the gods as basically benevolent, approachable, concerned with human well-being — in short, good. They were too much endowed with life, too human to inflict a burden of terror and helplessness on men. If a man adjusted to their demands, if he did not usurp their powers, he could expect their support in endowing his life with what was good.

Sacrifice and prayer played a part in Greek life at every level: Each home and each clan had its shrines and its rituals. More impressive were the splendid civic cults, for which great temples were built. On occasion, the entire Greek world joined in honoring the Olympian pantheon; the Olympic Games in honor of Zeus, inaugurated in 776 B.C. and held every four years thereafter, represent such a pan-Hellenic ceremony. Greek ritual life was remarkably open. Large numbers of people from all walks of life participated, as is so dramatically evident in the Parthenon sculpture frieze illustrating the annual procession connected with the civic feast in honor of Athena. Almost every kind of human activity was accepted as worthy of offering to the gods—athletic contests, poetry reading, song, dance, drama, prayer. There were no elaborate priesthoods in Greece; fathers conducted rituals in the household and elected officials served as priests in the civic ceremonies. After the Greeks offered their gifts of meat and wine, they immediately ate and drank the offerings, leaving only scraps for the gods. In their prayers, they addressed the gods boldly and confidently and were often answered directly. The search for foreknowledge was institutionalized in the *oracles,* special people through whom the gods spoke. The most famous of these was at Delphi, where all Greeks went to discover everything from personal destinies to great political issues.

From a rather early date in Greek religious history there also developed more emotional, personal movements that are called *mystery* religions. They derived primarily from the ancient worship of the regenerative forces in nature. The mystery cults centered on belief in a god or goddess who died and then arose to become a savior for those initiated into the cult. The god Dionysus was the center of such a cult throughout much of Greece. His worship involved his devotees in a highly emotional initiation ritual and in ecstatic rites such as wild dancing and eating raw flesh. Another mystery cult, centering at Eleusis near Athens, grew up in connection with the fertility goddess Demeter and her daughter Persephone. Over time, the mystery cults tended to grow more subdued, as is illustrated by a poorly understood movement called Orphism, which modified Dionysus worship by emphasizing the need for ethical conduct as a way of pleasing the god. The mystery cults made an important mark on Christianity at a later date.

In the context of this chapter, Greek religion has another dimension: It provided the framework and the stimulus for cultural growth. It postulated a kindly, humane direction of the cosmic order which inspired the Greeks to approach the unknown without fear, for the gods were always fundamentally pleased with what man did. Thus out of religion grew the arts, philosophy, and science, each in its own way a form of religious expression, even when the writer or artist transcended the specific religious belief or ritual that inspired his work. It is symbolic that the Greeks conceived the forces that produced the arts and thought as goddesses, the Muses.

3. LITERATURE

Greek literature is a magnificent artistic creation emerging from a substratum of religious themes. Most of it demands a familiarity with Greek mythology, for literary artists played upon this material to give it new vitality and meaning in terms of the human situation.

Greek literature was born in glory with the two epic poems of Homer, the *Iliad* and the *Odyssey*, probably set down in the eighth century B.C. Behind them lay a long tradition of oral poetry sung by professional bards in aristocratic courts to tell the deeds of heroic figures who lived in the early Dark Age and the legends pertaining to the gods. Homer, who according to tradition lived in Ionia, drew these oral threads together into unified compositions characterized by great artistry and dramatic force. His language is masterful and his verse form reveals a mature esthetic sense. The *Iliad* recounts the deeds of great warriors who went to Troy to avenge the theft of a Greek woman, Helen, by Paris, the prince of Troy. The *Odyssey* is an adventure story recounting the experiences of one of the heroes of the Trojan War, Ulysses, who takes ten years to return to his home and family. Not a little of the appeal of these epics lies in their gripping plots, but they have other dimensions. They create a heroic picture of men endowed with courage, nobility, and a deep love for life; in portraying men in such heroic proportions, Homer wrestles with the thought-provoking problem of the relationship of these demi-gods to the real gods. His epics enshrined a view of gods and men that provided Greeks of all ages with an ideal of heroic greatness.

The epic style of Homer was imitated long after his death, but for all its richness, this one literary form could not contain the Greek literary genius. In about 700 B.C., the poet Hesiod wrote his *Works and Days,* a bitter reflection on the poverty of small landowners and the injustice of the rich and powerful. It is filled with a search for some deeper understanding of divine justice as an antidote to human misery. Hesiod's work pointed the way to an outburst of lyric poetry in which several poets developed new verse forms to express their personal reactions to man, nature, political developments, the gods, love, and a wide variety of other subjects. Among the best were Archilochus of Paros, Alcaeus of Mytilene, and above all the poetess Sappho of Lesbos. Aside from the new literary forms they developed, including the elegy and the choral ode, these lyricists made literature a vehicle for the forceful expression of deep thought and a personal reaction to life. The nobility and force of Greek lyric poetry were perhaps best exemplified by Pindar of Thebes (ca. 518–441 B.C.), most of whose works took the form of choral songs to honor victorious athletes at great religious festivals. His poems set forth the classic view of aristocratic (in the Greek sense of "the best") man in terms seldom equaled in poetry. He convinces one of what many Greeks believed—that great poetry can inspire ordinary men to rise above their own limits to the greatness of the athletes who struggled for personal and civic glory and for the honor of the gods.

The burgeoning poetic talent reflected in epic and lyric poetry reached full fruition in the fifth century with the development of tragic drama, perhaps the greatest literary achievement of the Greeks. The drama was written and produced for large audiences and paid for by the state from public funds. In this respect, it is a product of the democracy of the fifth century. Its profundity and artistry suggest an articulate, sensitive, thoughtful populace that speaks well for the power of democracy.

Tragedy originated in religious ceremony and never lost touch with its seedbed. It began in the dramatic choruses and hymns developed to honor the gods. By the sixth century B.C., the dramatic element in these rituals had grown increasingly important, providing opportunities for poets to portray the deeds of the gods and heroes enshrined in Greek mythology and to comment on the meaning of these deeds through choral interludes interspersed with the dramatic action.

This developing dramatic art suddenly burst forth in full maturity during the fifth century in the work of three of the world's greatest masters. The first was Aeschylus (525–456 B.C.), a writer of deep religious convictions and strong aristocratic sentiments. He wrote about ninety plays, only seven of which survive. His tragedies spell out with great power the consequences that follow human transgressions of the dictates of the divine powers. His most impressive surviving work is a cycle of three plays called the *Oresteia,* which traces the tragic fate of the family of Agamemnon resulting from its crime of spilling the blood of its own kinsmen. Aeschylus had a genius for making his suffering characters noble and admirable, capable of bearing their burden of punishment with dignity and even with understanding.

Sophocles (495–406 B.C.) was less aristocratic. During his long life, centered chiefly in the period of Athens' greatest power, he produced a large number of plays, all but seven now lost. His dramas remained closely bound to the traditional themes provided by myth and religion, but his interest is more human, more intent on searching out the psychological effects of suffering on men who ran afoul of the gods. He portrayed suffering as an experience that uplifted and purified man. Many would argue that Sophocles' *King Oedipus* is the greatest tragedy ever written. Essentially it is a drama that reveals the measure of man by showing his response when he is trapped by fate into committing an act for which the gods must destroy him. Much more than Aeschylus, Sophocles celebrates the greatness of man.

Euripides (480–406 B.C.) was a dramatist profoundly touched by the growing disillusionment, skepticism, and pessimism of the later fifth century—the generation of the Peloponnesian War. He utilized tragedy as a vehicle for posing profound questions, arousing the suspicion that human powers are limited. His plays, especially *Medea,* represent a search for some understanding of the full nature of man, especially his dark and frightening emotional qualities. Again and again he casts doubt on conventional moral values and accepted religious beliefs. But from this incessant probing emerges a picture of man that is fuller and subtler—if not nobler—than the portraits by Aeschylus and Sophocles.

While the tragic drama was developing, the Greeks also perfected comic drama to a highly effective level. Comedy, like tragedy, began as a part of public religious ceremonies, especially the worship of Dionysus. Its origins were rooted in ribald songs evoked by the joy and good humor that apparently surrounded religious feasts. By the fifth century, comedy became independent of religious ceremony and was performed as a distinct art that educated audiences about current affairs by making them laugh. The greatest user of this form was Aristophanes (ca. 445–385 B.C.), a conservative Athenian who despised nearly all the developments of his society. His comedies held up for scorn politicians, artists, democratic institutions, and Athenian social mores. Typical is his play *Lysistrata*, based on the efforts of Athenian women to deny their husbands any pleasures with them until the men gave up warfare.

Prose literature in Greece was long overshadowed by the immense influence of poetry. Its first use came in the sixth century in the works of early philosophical and scientific writers, and it was thus closely associated with emerging rationalism in Greek life. The best Greek prose in the fifth century was historical literature. Two outstanding men, Herodotus and Thucydides, not only produced great literature, but also introduced scientific history to the world.

Herodotus (ca. 484–425 B.C.) wrote a history of the war between the Greeks and Persians. To make his account as accurate as possible, he traveled extensively and searched through written records for evidence concerning the causes and the events of the wars. Herodotus usually tried to sift his material to arrive at the truth; however, he was too good a storyteller to leave out colorful material whether true or not. His finished work was therefore spiced with hundreds of anecdotes and stories, many quite fantastic, intended to illustrate the qualities of the two peoples involved in the war.

Thucydides' masterpiece was a *History of the Peloponnesian War.* With great industry and complete objectivity, he searched out the details of the military campaigns and the political maneuvers associated with the war, which he was convinced was the greatest in Greek history. He tries to let the events illustrate the folly, the nobility, the chicanery, and the bravery of which men under stress are capable. His presentation leads one to the inevitable conclusion that the Athenians lost because of their own mistakes, their pride, their bad judgment. By successfully illustrating what war in any age can do to men and to political institutions, Thucydides did what every modern historian yearns to do: to make the truth about the past enrich our understanding of men in the present.

4. ART

"Painting is silent poetry; poetry is painting that speaks." Greek art drew its basic themes from the same sources as literature—religion and mythology. Artists labored toward the same ends—to discover man and place him meaningfully in the larger cosmos. Artists found their audiences where writers did; and they poured into their work the same talents. Certainly nature provided them with some of the finest materials in the world, especially marble, and with dramatic sites upon which to place their buildings, such as the Athenian Acropolis, but it was their genius that produced the magnificent works that reveal the Greek spirit.

The art of the Golden Age was the product of a long evolution. During the Mycenaean era, a flourishing art, strongly influenced by Minoan models, had developed on mainland Greece. With the onset of the Dark Age, Mycenaean art styles and technical skills were largely lost, although remnants survived to provide a starting point for a uniquely Greek art. The first signs of this new art appeared near the end of the Dark Age: finely executed pottery decorated first with geometric patterns and, by the eighth century B.C., with human forms. These works estab-

Athens' Theseum, one of the best-preserved temples in the Greek world, exemplifies the Doric style of architecture. *Photo: Hirmer Verlag*

lished the basic themes for painters and set conventions for representing human beings and animals in action. During the Archaic period, architects developed a basic style for temples and other public buildings: a rectangular form with surrounding columns and low-pitched roofs; toward the end of the period, most of these structures were being built of stone. At the same time, sculptors were perfecting a unique style of portraying the nude male and the draped female figure. Architects, sculptors, and painters received increasing support from the city-states, whose leaders and citizens were deeply interested in beautifying the cities and in elaborating civic religious ceremonies.

By the beginning of the fifth century, the long apprenticeship was over, and Athens had become the focal point for artistic excellence. Her monuments offer the best examples of Greek art. Unquestionably, the city's crowning glory was the Acropolis, a hill upon which were built three major temples, the Parthenon, the Erectheum, and the temple to Victorious Athena. A splendid gate and stairway, called the Propylaea, gave access to the Acropolis.

The Parthenon, portions of which still stand, was the noblest of the temples. Built in honor of Athena, this structure is of moderate size, measuring 228 by 101 feet. The inner chamber is surrounded by simple, unadorned columns (called Doric columns), seventeen on each side and eight on each end, which support the roof. A series of dignified statues and stone reliefs added a harmonious decorative touch. Many devices were employed by the architects to achieve harmony, balance, and unity. The columns all lean inward slightly and are thickened in the middle to offset the optical illusion that makes a straight column viewed from below seem to tip outward. The middle of every long horizontal line is slightly higher than the ends to avoid the impression of sagging.

The other Acropolis temples and the Propylaea, all built after the Parthenon, incorporate the same features. The only basic departure is the slightly more slender and ornate columns (in the Ionic style), which add a grace lacking in the rather severe Parthenon. Similar temples were built in other cities, although none quite equals the Acropolis group for total effect. The many public buildings constructed in the *poleis* incorporated the principles employed in temple construction, adding to the beauty of the cities.

Greek sculpture was primarily dedicated to the adornment of temples. The most representative sculptors are Phidias (ca. 500–432 B.C.), Polyclitus (ca. 452–412 B.C.), and Praxiteles (ca. 400–320 B.C.). Phidias designed the sculpture adorning the Parthenon and executed some of the individual pieces. His statues in the round have been lost; all the surviving Parthenon sculpture is relief work, and it is difficult to tell whether any particular piece is the work of Phidias or of someone working under his direction. Polyclitus devoted his talents chiefly to shaping bronze statues of young men. Praxiteles created splendid versions of the gods in human form. The work of all these sculptors concentrated on the idealized human body; their figures are dignified, quiet, and beautifully proportioned. However, some artists did portray violent action. For instance, the fifth-century sculptor Myron, in his statue of the discus thrower, manages to catch the body at a moment of tension just before the cast. When looking at any of the statues of Greek sculptors, the viewer feels that he finally sees man as he should be, although he is aware that he has never seen such perfect men.

Little has survived of Greek painting, except for pottery decoration, which had perhaps passed its peak by the fifth century. However, it remained a significant art during the Golden Age. There is evidence from literary sources that artists rendered large-scale paintings to decorate temples and public buildings. For example, the painter Polygnotus decorated a colonnade in the Athenian *agora*, which was the section of the city where major political meetings and market activities took place, with scenes from the Trojan Wars. We may suspect that Greek painting reflected the same idealizing traits seen in sculpture and drew heavily on mythology for its themes.

5. PHILOSOPHY

The Greeks leaped furthest beyond the achievements of earlier cultures in the realm of philosophical and scientific speculation. They left a heritage that has shaped thinking in the West up to the present. Until the sixth century B.C., most Greeks were content to accept the explanations of mythology for the nature of the universe and man's place in it; Homer and Hesiod provided the basic ingredients of their world view. Then during that century, just when the *polis* was reaching maturity, thinkers began to move beyond these limits, initiating one of the great intellectual revolutions in the history of the world. Fundamentally, the new modes of thought were by-products of a growing faith in man's capabilities and of the freedom nourished in the atmosphere of the *polis*. So bold and so cogent was this activity of the mind that the fifth and fourth centuries B.C. are still regarded as the most productive in the entire history of philosophy.

The prime concern of speculative thinkers during the sixth and fifth centuries centered around the discovery of the fundamental force lying behind and giving unity to the universe. Rejecting traditional religious explanations, a series of philosophers tried to give rational answers. One school of thinkers developed a materialistic approach and concluded that such obvious elements as fire, water, and air were the basic substances out of which all other things came. This materialistic tradition continued to be refined until in the early fourth century Democritus expounded an atomic theory, according to which the universe is composed of tiny atoms floating at random in space. By mere chance these atoms compose themselves into beings and objects and by the same chance decompose into floating particles again. Another school of philosophers rejected materialism and sought the key to the universe in some nonmaterial force. Perhaps the source of this approach was the sixth-century thinker Pythagoras, whose career combined deep scientific interest with a strong religious bent. He argued that the key to the universe lay in a numerical relationship among its many parts. Equally influential in shaping this school (flourished ca. 500 B.C.)

was Heraclitus, who insisted that change was the essence of the physical, material world and therefore that no physical explanation of the universe could have meaning. This whole school of thinkers ultimately concluded that a nonmaterial, changeless being, endowed with perfect intelligence, supplied the creative force of order in the universe.

About the middle of the fifth century philosophical inquiry shifted from speculation about the fundamental nature of the universe to an examination of man's nature and his place in that universe. The Sophists, although they were primarily teachers whose interest in philosophy was a by-product of their ideas on education, led the way into this fresh realm of thought. Protagoras (485–410 B.C.), a famous teacher in Periclean Athens, was chiefly responsible for articulating their precepts. He rejected speculative philosophy on the grounds that the many contradictory schemes put forth by the speculative thinkers proved objective truth to be nonexistent. Man was the measure of all things. Human reason, he said, should be dedicated to a search for the kind of knowledge that would be useful to man in his quest for a comfortable, safe, happy life. He therefore spent his time instructing Athenians in those things that would fit them for citizenship in a democratic society—public speaking, politics, grammar, and the art of being respectable. Greece soon swarmed with his disciples. They delivered withering attacks on all things that were accepted as the truth, preaching that truth was relative and encouraging their audiences to live by any rules of conduct that proved beneficial and workable. The Sophists as a group were condemned, with partial justice, as skeptics, troublemakers, and destroyers of morality. But they made the Greeks more aware of human problems than had earlier thinkers, and they prepared the way for the greatest Greek philosophers, Socrates, Plato, and Aristotle.

Probably no one was better known in Athens just before 400 B.C. than a homely, dumpy little stonecutter named Socrates (ca. 469–399 B.C.). Socrates left no writings. He set forth his ideas orally; the Athenian *agora* provided him an ideal setting. Here he locked horns intellectually with anyone interested. But Socrates was more than a street-corner debater. His pupils, especially Plato, recorded enough of his ideas to permit us to grasp the basic thrust of his thought. He believed that objective truth did exist and that man was prevented from discovering it by his own ignorance, which Socrates made it his business to enlighten. The Socratic method consisted of asking questions until the error of those who claimed to know something was exposed and then leading the mind through further questioning to the truth by way of precise definition and exact logic.

Socrates attracted an eager following of youths, including the scions of several of Athens' noblest families—and he earned the anger of many of the elders of his society. His annoying questions finally got him into trouble with the state. In 399 B.C., amid the bitterness surrounding Athens' defeat in the Peloponnesian War, he was accused of corrupting youth and sentenced to die. Although given a chance to escape, he chose to abide by the state's decision of death by drinking hemlock, still convinced that the highest virtue consisted of pursuing knowledge, no matter what the consequences.

Plato (427–347 B.C.) carried on the work of Socrates, his master. He was an Athenian whose career spanned an era filled with defeats for Athens and constant civil strife, all of which discouraged him. Most of his life was spent as a teacher in a school called the Academy, which he founded. His voluminous works, elegantly written in dialogue form, offer a complete although sometimes confusing record of his thought. Plato was a philosophical idealist, his work bringing to a conclusion the nonmaterialistic philosophical movement that had begun with Pythagoras. He argued that the fundamental realities in the universe are *ideas,* or abstract forms, the chief of which is the good. The so-called realities that man perceives with his senses are but imperfect reflections of the perfect universal forms. The justice practiced in Athens was only a shadowy reflection of perfect transcendental justice; a man is but a pale image of higher reality, humanity. The intellect, by reflecting on the imperfect earthly embodiments of ideas, opened the path to contemplation of the ultimate, unchanging realities of the universe.

Much of Plato's writing centers on a search for perfect understanding of universal ideas and an effort to make that wisdom and insight applicable to the problems of human existence. His best-known dialogue, *The Republic,* illustrates his idealism, his method, and his earnest concern for the human condition. This work is devoted to governance. Plato assumes that the purpose of the state is to achieve justice, the ideal state being an earthly embodiment of the perfect idea of justice. He concludes that justice consists in each man's doing that for which he is best fitted. The ideal state is one in which every man holds that station and does that job for which he is qualified. Such a state, Plato argues, must be ruled by a philosopher-king who will be wise enough to know and recognize the talents of his subjects and put these talents to work. A completely socialistic economy controlled by the wise king must be instituted so that each will be rewarded according to his merits and so that competition and greed can be eliminated from society. In short, the perfect society is a dictatorial state. In his other dialogues Plato conducts a comparable search for an understanding of the nature of love, friendship, courage, the soul—in fact, virtually the whole range of those elements that constitute the ultimate reality, perfect good.

Aristotle (384–322 B.C.) was Plato's most brilliant and productive pupil. A Macedonian by birth, he came to Athens as a youth to study at the Academy. After Plato's death, he spent some time as tutor to young Alexander the Great. He then returned to Athens and founded his own school, the Lyceum. His followers were called the Peripatetics because Aristotle often walked about while lecturing.

During his career, Aristotle produced a massive body of philosophical work ranging across the whole spectrum of human knowledge. Perhaps typical of teachers in all ages, he had a passion for systematizing and organizing knowledge, so that his works constitute a kind of encyclopedia of the total learning of the ancient world. Imbedded in his massive scholarship, however, is a basic philosophical position. Aristotle was certainly influenced by Platonic idealism, but his approach is basically different. In

Hermes with the infant Dionysus. Most likely the work of the famed sculptor Praxiteles, this statue is an excellent example of Greek artistic canons; the gods are taken as subject matter and portrayed in an idealized human form that emphasizes physical perfection rather than spiritual qualities. *Photo: Hirmer Verlag*

his seminal *Metaphysics,* he argues that reality consists of a combination of matter and form (or idea). The form makes the object what it is but has no reality except when it exists in matter. Every object has some purpose in a larger universal order, and its perfection consists in serving that purpose. Behind the wilderness of individual objects lies an ultimate "cause," a higher force that animates everything. The philosopher's path is from the study of nature toward the formulation of concepts about the entire universe.

In most of his works, many of which deal with scientific subjects, Aristotle pursued the course laid down in the *Metaphysics*. His *Politics* supplies an illustration of his method. On the basis of a study of the history and organization of more than 150 Greek city-states, he concluded that the state is a natural grouping of men for the purpose of promoting virtue. Man is a political animal and cannot fulfill his true nature unless he is a member of a state. In his *Ethics*, Aristotle asked how man should conduct his individual life and argued that happiness is the proper goal of every human action. Man is happy and therefore good if he controls his passions by use of his reason and if he seeks a mean between extremes. Although Aristotle's principal method is inductive and although he was the most influential exponent of that method among the Greeks, he is also the founder of formal logic, a deductive discipline. The last great thinker of Greece, Aristotle was the most comprehensive.

6. SCIENCE

Aristotle's scientific works were the culmination of a sustained and highly significant interest in science reaching back at least two centuries before him. Because the Greeks made no clear distinction between science and philosophy, it is difficult to treat science as a thing apart. Nearly all thinkers derived their conclusions from observations of nature, but they also borrowed extensively from ancient Mesopotamia and Egypt.

Hippocrates (460–377 B.C.), a leading physician to whom is attributed the famous oath defining the responsibilities of a physician which we still know today, typifies Greek interest in observation. He insisted that nothing could be known about sickness except through observation of sick people and through a search for the natural causes of illness. He repudiated the traditional belief that sickness was due to evil spirits and taught that it was a result of natural causes. Hippocrates had numerous followers who took the same approach and accumulated

an extensive body of knowledge about the human body and its workings.

The collective efforts of Greek astronomers, physicists, geographers, botanists, and zoologists allow us to credit the Greeks with the invention of the scientific method, which relies on observation as the source of knowledge about nature. But of course they lacked precision instruments; and they often made glaring errors in interpreting their discoveries. Moreover, few were interested in using their knowledge for practical purposes. Scientific knowledge was employed chiefly by philosophers who sought to illustrate the operation of the universe by observing how it worked.

7. THE GREEK MIND

Any review of the brilliant work of the Greeks in literature, art, philosophy, and science raises one final question: Did all the leaders of Greek cultural life, whatever their specific interests, share any common ideas that characterize the Greek approach to life? The following basic concepts are offered in answer.

Greek thought was intensely *humanistic*; it placed man on a pedestal for admiration and idealization. Most Greeks believed that the world had been created for man's happiness. They therefore were certain that man was *in harmony with nature* and had no need to struggle against it, try to escape it, or shrink from it in fear. The Greeks were *rationalistic*; they placed a powerful trust in man's ability to understand nature's mysteries through his own intelligence and to act on the basis of his sound judgment to solve any problems that might beset him. The Greeks insisted upon *restraint* and *balance*; nothing was worse than excess in any shape or form. Their *spirit of inquiry* constantly pushed them into new fields in every aspect of life and added an element of *boldness* to their endeavors. Most Greek intellectual leaders were *politically oriented*, ready to offer their talents to the community instead of pursuing individual and introspective ends. Finally, the Greek mind sought *order* and *symmetry* in all things.

No one would insist that the ideals expressed by a few intellectual and artistic giants were attained by all Greeks. Probably most Greeks, engaged in the routine of daily life, seldom

The Irrational
in Greek
Culture

Every historian who tries to reconstruct the grand sweep of history in an account of reasonably modest proportions quickly becomes aware of a disturbing consequence of his effort. He finds himself distorting the past by concentrating on what is dominant in any era at the expense of many facets of a society that in his judgment are less momentous.

Our treatment of Greek culture provides an example of the distortion of selection: We have repeatedly and emphatically stressed that the central and crucial mode of Greek thought and expression was rationalism. Ours is, of course, no new insight. Across long ages, Near Eastern potentates, Roman aristocrats, medieval churchmen, Renaissance artists, early modern scientists, American revolutionaries, and modern intellectuals have all paid obeisance to the Greek confidence that man is preeminently a thinking creature capable of utilizing his rational faculties to make the world into what he "thinks" it should be.

But was what later admirers and interpreters—all in one way or another historians—focused on the whole story? Did all Greeks perceive all things from a rational perspective? Was even the most sophisticated and intellectually enlightened Greek convinced that man was primarily a rational being? Is it possible that the legions of students of the Greek "mind" have been blinded to significant dimensions of the Greek cultural experience as a consequence of their eagerness to make the Greeks models of that desirable human trait, reasonableness?

Investigations of Greek culture have been broadened and deepened over the past century by valuable insights and techniques supplied by social scientists. Especially illuminating has been the work of anthropologists investigating religious life among existing primitive societies and of psychologists seeking to comprehend the nonrational aspects of human behavior. The whole thrust of this approach to the nature of Greek culture has been to cast doubt on the conventional generalization that rationalism is the key to that culture.

One of the most perceptive and learned of contemporary classical scholars, E. R. Dodds of Oxford, has brilliantly posed the issue of the irrationality of Greek civilization and has suggested a viable response in his book *The Greeks and the Irrational* (1951). Dodds begins by asserting a fundamental postulate established by modern anthropologists and psychologists: In the intellectual behavior of all people in all ages there is a powerful element of the primitive mentality, a mentality that often manifests itself in religion. He argues that, in the main, interpreters of the Greek experience have failed (or refused?) to take this fact into account. Quite rightly he asks: "Why should we attribute to the ancient Greeks an immunity from 'primitive' modes of thought which we do not find in any society open to our direct observation?" He thinks the attribution is erroneous, and sets out to demonstrate that the Greeks were not "quite so blind to the importance of nonrational factors in man's experience and behavior as is commonly assumed."

Dodds succeeds in demonstrating persuasively that Greek literary and philosophical spokesmen were always aware of irrational factors governing human conduct and that they expressed their awareness in religious terms. For example, he finds in the Homeric epics, usually interpreted as reflecting no deep religious concepts, significant evidence that Homer saw irrational conduct among his heroes as a case of "psychic intervention" by an outside divine agency. He discerns the sense of despair and insecurity in the Archaic Age as stemming from a conviction that the divine forces were hostile toward man. This religious strain bred a sense of guilt, often associated with the idea of pollution. He examines Greek concepts of madness, positing that to many it represented a state of blessedness because it indicated the infusion of the divine into man. Dodds finds evidence to suggest that the "enlightened" views of the great cultural heroes of the fifth century B.C. were looked upon with suspicion by many intellectuals, who felt that the rationalist concepts being promulgated did not encompass man's whole existence, and by the great mass of the Greeks, who reacted violently by persecuting the intellectuals. Extending his view beyond the Golden Age through Plato to the Hellenistic era, Dodds concludes that the irrational grew increasingly important in accounting for man's actions.

Dodds' powerful synthesis forces us to realize that only a few Greek thinkers affirmed that man was a rational creature, and in the long run their belief was buried under a belief in man as irrational. When one adds to this the obvious fact that the great mass of Greeks always accepted a religious interpretation of man, believing his existence dependent on divine forces, the generalization about rationalism as a key to Greek culture becomes exceedingly suspect.

Thus it turns out that the historian who stresses rationalism as a major feature of Greek culture is overlooking a dimension that had immense importance to the Greeks. This sounds dishonest. Yet in fitting the Greeks into the grand sweep of history, their rationalism is of greater significance than their irrationalism. Their consciousness of man's rational powers marked a fresh insight into human nature, while their awareness of the irrational aspects of human behavior simply provided the common bond with most other societies in history that have tried to cope with the monumental problems of living.

paused to think about what their civilization really meant to them, just as most modern men seldom dwell on this question. But even so, at least Greek ideals were presented to them in poetry, drama, history, sculpture, architecture, and philosophy. Thus values ingrained in the great artistic and philosophical works of Greece became a model of civilized life for numerous peoples who rose to prominence in the Mediterranean area after she was no longer a power.

Suggested Reading

General Cultural Histories

*Edith Hamilton, *The Greek Way* (Norton).

*C. M. Bowra, *The Greek Experience* (Mentor). This and the preceding title represent two splendid introductions to the general features of Greek culture and its underlying spirit.

François Chamoux, *The Civilization of Greece,* trans. W. S. Maguinness (1965). A general survey that is enriched by splendid illustrations.

Werner Jaeger, *Paideia: Ideals of Greek Culture*, 2nd ed. 3 vols. (1943–45). A penetrating analysis of the uniqueness of Greek thought and expression, stressing especially the aristocratic temper of Greek culture.

Religion

*Robert Graves, *The Greek Myths* (2 vols., Penguin). The best starting place in understanding Greek religion is to discover what the Greeks believed about their gods as these beliefs were set forth in mythology; this work provides a full treatment.

H. J. Rose, *Ancient Greek Religion* (1946).

*W. K. C. Guthrie, *Greeks and Their Gods* (Beacon). Either this or the preceding title will provide a description of the content of Greek religious belief and the nature of religious practice.

A. J. Festugière, *Personal Religion Among the Greeks* (1960). Touches on aspects of Greek belief that are sometimes overlooked.

Literature

*M. Hadas, *A History of Greek Literature* (Columbia). A clearly organized survey, especially useful in assessing the contributions of individual authors.

*C. M. Bowra, *Ancient Greek Literature* (Galaxy). Another survey that provides more interpretation than the preceding title.

Art

*J. Boardman, *Greek Art* (Praeger). An outstanding general description.

*J. Barron, *Greek Sculpture* (Dutton).

*A. W. Lawrence, *Greek Architecture* (Penguin).

*P. Devambez, *Greek Painting* (Compass). This and the two preceding titles will provide excellent introductions to specialized aspects of Greek art; all are well illustrated.

John Travlos, *Pictorial Dictionary of Ancient Athens* (1971). A masterful guide to the art of Athens, highlighted by impressive illustrations.

Philosophy and Science

*Rex Warner, *Greek Philosophers* (Mentor).

*W. K. C. Guthrie, *Greek Philosophers: From Thales to Aristotle* (Harper Torchbook).

*F. Copleston, *History of Philosophy*, Vol. 1: *Greece and Rome* (Image). Any of these three works will provide a clear account of the development of Greek philosophy and an assessment of its accomplishments.

*Marshall Claggett, *Greek Science in Antiquity* (Collier). An up-to-date summary of Greek scientific accomplishments.

Sources

*W. H. Auden, ed., *The Portable Greek Reader* (Viking).

*G. Howe and G. A. Harrer, eds., *Greek Literature in Translation* (1948). The most fruitful way to get at the spirit of Greek culture is to read Greek literature. These two anthologies will provide a rich sampling. From this sampling many may wish to read individual authors in their entirety; especially suggested are Homer, Herodotus, and Thucydides, whose works were cited in earlier chapters.

*L. R. Lind, ed., *Ten Greek Plays in Contemporary Translations* (Riverside Editions). Contains representative works of Aeschylus, Sophocles, Euripides, and Aristophanes.

*Scott Buchanan, ed., *The Portable Plato* (Viking). Provides a good selection illustrative of Plato's philosophical position and method; especially worth studying are his dialogues *Protagoras, Phaedo, Symposium,* and *The Republic.*

Richard McKeon, ed., *The Basic Works of Aristotle* (1941). Offers *Politics, Nicomachean Ethics, Metaphysics,* and *Poetics* as representative of Aristotle's philosophical works.

8

GREEK IMPERIALISM: THE HELLENISTIC WORLD, 336–31 B.C.

To many Greeks, the coming of the barbarian Macedonians spelled doom. But, as is so often the case when men judge their own age, they were wrong. The Macedonian conquest set the stage for a new chapter in Greece's history; it liberated her from what was becoming a restrictive milieu. The Greeks were about to discover what one of their own philosophers, Democritus, had argued: that the native land of great souls is the whole earth. Under Macedonian leadership, they exploded out of the Aegean to establish their mastery over a wide circle in Asia and Africa. Their genius and their traditions began to mix with Near Eastern civilizations to produce a new culture that historians have called "Hellenistic."

1. ALEXANDER THE GREAT

The military and political genius of Alexander the Great was chiefly responsible for launching the Greeks on this new phase of their history. Endowed with numerous powers—intelligence, ambition, industry, imagination, physical attractiveness, boldness, an iron will—Alexander has never ceased to fascinate students of history. Although Macedonian by birth, he was a Greek in spirit. His education under Aristotle had instilled in him a thorough knowledge and a fanatical admiration of Greek civilization.

Alexander was twenty when his father was murdered in 336 B.C. Philip had charted the immediate future for his son. Besides being king of Macedon, Alexander was master of the Greek city-states by virtue of his control of the League of Corinth. Philip had prepared for a war against Greece's ancient foe, Persia, perhaps hoping to win the approval of all Greeks by rallying them in a crusade. It was this war that absorbed Alexander's interests.

In 334 B.C. he led his Macedonian-Greek army into Asia Minor in order to attack Persia. Although Persia possessed a huge empire, a rich treasury, and a large army and navy, Alexander was victorious from the beginning. Perhaps mindful of the role naval power had played in the long struggle between Greeks and Persians, his first campaigns were aimed at winning control of Persia's Mediterranean territories. He defeated her army at Granicus in 334 B.C. and occupied the key coastal cities. In 333, following victory at the battle of Issus in Syria, he proceeded to take over Syria, Palestine, and Egypt, thereby wiping out Persian naval power. Then he marched on the center of Persian power in Mesopotamia and in the spring of 331 destroyed the last major military strength of the Persians at the battle of Arbela. Following this victory, he occupied the chief Persian cities and hunted down the fugitive King Darius III, who was finally murdered in 330 by his own officials as Alexander closed in on him.

The end of Persian might did not satisfy Alexander's ambition. Again he drove eastward. Battling vast distances, native resistance, and defection in his own ranks, he pushed across Persia and the Hindu Kush Mountains into Bactria and eventually India, claiming all this territory as his and leaving behind newly founded cities as centers of Greek power. Beyond the Indus Valley his troops refused to go. Alexander therefore turned back westward through southern Persia and into Mesopotamia, where he fell ill and died in June 323 at the age of thirty-three. Tradition has it that he was planning new conquests, including Arabia, Carthage, and Central Asia.

A career so short and so completely occupied with military campaigns left Alexander little time to face the problems of ruling his vast conquests. Probably he had no definite plans when he launched his campaign and formed his policies as circumstances arose. But before he died, he had established certain broad policies that guided his successors. He moved toward creating a style of rulership that cast him in the role of divine autocrat. Seeing that Greeks alone could not rule his vast empire, Alexander began to employ the talents of the conquered peoples. Persians were placed in some army and administrative posts. But from the beginning of his career, he had insisted that the Greeks would remain politically, economically, and culturally supreme within his empire. High positions in the army and the civil administration were reserved for them.

Alexander's death left most of his policies far from fulfilled, and it has often been said that his death was timely for the benefit of his fame, since his reputation might have suffered had he lived to face the task of holding his empire together. The Greek masters sat uneasily atop their vast domain. Greek culture was not firmly planted in the conquered territory, although many Greeks had migrated to the new cities built by Alexander. Furthermore, Alexander left no heir capable of capitalizing on the magic of his name. Aside from his conquests his positive achieve-

ments were few; his influence lay chiefly in what later generations thought he was trying to do. He established for Greek society the ideal that a statesman of ability could create a government capable of bringing peace, harmony, and prosperity to all men living within a vast empire. He also convinced his successors that a great ruler could uplift his subjects by Hellenizing them. The struggle to attain these goals motivated much of the activity of Mediterranean men for centuries after Alexander's death.

2. HELLENISTIC POLITICAL LIFE, 323–31 B.C.

A difficulty surrounds the presentation of Hellenistic political history. It is that more than one approach is possible and instructive, but no one approach succeeds in portraying the whole story.

We can recount Hellenistic political history from the point of view of Alexander's dream of political unity, peace, and harmony. Alexander's successors tried to follow this program, especially in the early years after his death; throughout the Hellenistic period men dreamed of reconstructing the ecumenical empire. From this perspective, the Hellenistic Age tells a story of failure. Hardly was the great conqueror dead

The use of portraits of rulers on coins began with the successors of Alexander the Great, whose idealized image appears on this silver coin issued by a Thracian king around 300 B.C. *Photo: Museum of Fine Arts, Boston*

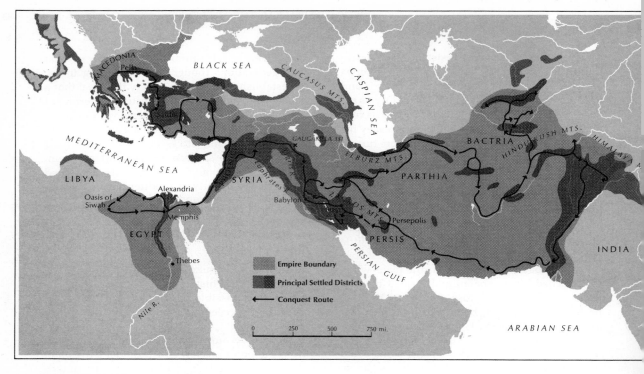

ALEXANDER'S EMPIRE 336–323 B.C.

when the struggle began to divide his empire. Out of the struggle emerged a hodgepodge of political entities of various sizes, strengths, and forms of government. These "successor states" were almost constantly at war; peace and harmony seldom prevailed. Ultimately, Rome was the chief beneficiary of the strife, incorporating into her empire the best parts of Alexander's domains—Macedonia, the Aegean area, Asia Minor, Syria, Palestine, and Egypt.

Or we might approach Hellenistic history by viewing the fate of Alexander's program of establishing a small minority of Greeks and Macedonians as political masters of his vast territory. Again there was partial failure. Large segments escaped Greek control. During the third century B.C. the region lying east of the Tigris-Euphrates Valley was taken over by non-Greeks, who established kingdoms of considerable importance to the future, including Bactria and Parthia. Along the southern Black Sea coast small but virile kingdoms—Pontus, Bithynia, Cappadocia—

were formed by local rulers. Despite these losses, the conquering masters did retain power in a large part of the Near East, especially in Egypt, Syria, Palestine, and the southern shore of Asia Minor. And their power was solidly established; they met little resistance from the native populations. It is true that the ruling elite did to some degree adapt their ways to the political traditions of their subjects, particularly in Egypt. Still, the ability of a relatively few outsiders to hold political power over highly civilized peoples with ancient political traditions of their own is a great achievement.

Still another approach to Hellenistic history—and the one usually taken—is to concentrate on the most prominent states that developed in the period. Immediately after Alexander's sudden death, a council of his generals decided to maintain a united empire under a single monarch. They elected Alexander's incompetent half-brother as king, with the understanding that should the child which Alexander's widow,

Roxanne, was carrying be male, he would share the throne—which is what happened. But this pair could provide no direction for the shaky empire, and the generals were soon engaged in a struggle for control, and each took what he could get. The process of partition was not very rational and the exact boundaries of the emerging states were confused, but by about 275 B.C. there were three major kingdoms. In Egypt Ptolemy had established himself as successor to the ancient pharaohs and had laid claim to territories in Palestine and Syria. Another general, Antigonus, claimed the old kingdom of Macedon plus control over the Greek city-states still theoretically bound to Macedon in the league established by Philip in 338 B.C. Seleucus staked out a third kingdom embracing all the lands from Asia Minor to India; this conglomeration was most nearly similar to Alexander's empire.

Only the briefest summary of the complex histories of these kingdoms can be undertaken here. Macedonian political history centered around the efforts of a succession of kings to maintain control over the Greek city-states and to hold back barbarians constantly pressing on the northern frontiers of the kingdom. These burdens were great for the monarchs, since Macedon was a poor land whose manpower had been badly depleted by the eastern conquests. Shortly before 200 B.C. some of the Greek city-states appealed to Rome for help against Macedon. In the ensuing wars, Roman armies overran and annexed both Macedon and Greece.

The Ptolemaic kingdom was the most stable of the Hellenistic states. The ruling dynasty inherited a homogeneous population and a rich land, established an autocratic regime such as the Egyptians had long known, and exploited the agricultural and commercial potential of Egypt with intelligence and skill. Internal stability and wealth permitted the Ptolemies to play an active role in foreign affairs; they concentrated chiefly on extending their sway in Syria, which involved them in almost constant struggle with the Seleucid kingdom. Not until the second century B.C. did Ptolemaic power begin to decline. In the face of growing internal unrest, the rulers turned to Rome for support. Eventually (in 31 B.C.), Rome annexed Ptolemaic Egypt to her empire.

The history of the Seleucid kingdom is most difficult to tell. Its huge size and mixed populace provided little basis for unity or stability. The burden of its rulers was to supply a common bond, and the task was too great. Rather quickly they lost the territories they claimed east of Mesopotamia. Their hold on Asia Minor was always tenuous and ultimately was compromised by the emergence of petty kingdoms in the northern and western portions, of which Pergamum was the most significant. Most of the royal energy was devoted to creating a viable state embracing Syria and Mesopotamia. The Ptolemies constantly challenged the Seleucids for control of Syria. The kings also had to contend with native uprisings, for example, the Maccabean revolt among the Jews. Ultimately, the Seleucid kingdom was squeezed to death by Parthian pressure from the east and Roman pressure from the west. The last Seleucid king was overthrown in 64 B.C. by the Romans, called into Asia Minor by the petty kingdoms bent on protecting their independence against Seleucid claims.

Numerous smaller realms shared the political scene with these three large kingdoms during the Hellenistic period. Chief among them were several Greek city-states which continued their independent existences and had their own histories. Their internal affairs remained a vital concern, as did their efforts to hold off Macedonian power and their rivalries with other city-states. A noteworthy development in Greek history in this period was the establishment of effective leagues as a means of holding off Macedonian might. The two chief ones were the Aetolian League in central Greece and the Achaean League in the Peloponnesus, both of which demonstrated willingness on the part of some city-states to compromise total autonomy in the interests of common effort. Among the small states of the era, the most successful were the kingdom of Pergamum in western Asia Minor and the Republic of Rhodes, both of which fared well by capitalizing on the commercial activity of the Hellenistic Age.

The mere listing of the chief states suggests another approach to Hellenistic political history: the conduct of interstate relations, an activity that took on an intensity and sophistication new to men. Great and small states developed a battery of techniques designed to gain advantage over others: military force, diplomacy, psychological warfare, internal subversion, economic penetration. In a general way, the Hellenistic world moved toward a balance of power that safeguarded the status quo rather effectively until a major outside power such as Rome moved onto the scene.

Finally, the political history of the Hellenistic Age can be approached from an institutional point of view. The Hellenistic world developed certain common patterns of political thought. The very idea of empire itself was important, especially as so dramatically fleshed out by Alexander. The Near Eastern world was, of course, familiar with this political concept as a result of the efforts of the Amorites, the Egyptians, the Hittites, the Assyrians, and the Persians. But it was new to the Greeks, given their enchantment with the microcosmic world of the *polis*. The experiences of the Hellenistic Age put into the Greek vocabulary and mentality the vision of a great world state where men of many kinds shared a common citizenship and a common destiny. Nowhere was this ideal given more eloquent expression than in the political ideology of the Stoics, who were among the chief philosophical products of the age. And the concept of empire shaped by Greeks in the Hellenistic Age had a powerful impact on Rome.

The chief development in political institutions during the Hellenistic period, however, was the Greek acceptance of the concept of monarchical government. The Greeks had been schooled to think that a *polis* governed by the collective will of equal citizens (or at least the best of them) was the only civilized form of government. In the fourth century, as is obvious in Plato's *Republic*, that idea began to be questioned in favor of a form of government in which only a hero, a philosopher-king, a superman could provide good government. The success of monarchs like Philip and Alexander served as practical demonstrations of the validity of this idea. During the Hellenistic period, monarchy became the standard form of government among the Greek rulers of the Near East. In most Hellenistic kingdoms the king's power was personal: It derived from his feats at arms, his intelligence, his will, and his favor with the gods. By virtue of his abilities, he

could bestow blessings on his subjects. No constitution limited his power. No entrenched nobility acted to check him. No law other than what he decreed set limits to his authority. Only his ability defined the range of his power. Obviously, this kind of monarchy was shaped by the traditions of the ancient Near East, but it reflected a quality of its own, especially to the extent that it was personal and derived from human ability. In this sense, it bore the stamp of ancient Greece.

To exercise his vast powers efficiently, each Hellenistic king developed a well-organized central government featuring a strong army, an elaborate bureaucracy, and a careful tax structure, the chief offices manned by Greeks. Elitism supplied a bond of loyalty to the monarch. The old structures of local government were left largely intact, except that again Greeks manned the key posts. One major effect of this was the spread of Greek institutions into the cities of the Near East. Assemblies, councils, popular courts, and elected officials were instituted in such a way as to give the Greek communities considerable local autonomy.

While centralized, absolutist monarchy gained the upper hand in the Hellenistic world , the older city-state polity persisted with considerable vitality in Greece and western Asia Minor. Many *poleis* remained completely autonomous during much of the Hellenistic Age. The accustomed forms of city-state government continued—democracies, oligarchies, tyrannies. The city-state world even demonstrated the power to innovate, as illustrated by the Aetolian and Achaean leagues, both of which were better organized and more effective than earlier Greek confederations. But if the *polis* lived on, it was overshadowed in every way by monarchy. In war, in beautification of cities, in patronage of the arts, in wealth, in security, Athens and Sparta could not match the Seleucid or the Ptolemaic kingdoms.

For all its confusion, the Hellenistic period was of great importance politically. The Greeks demonstrated an ability to turn their considerable talents to the creation of units larger than the city-state. They put their own stamp on monarchy, yet were willing to utilize the political experience of conquered peoples to refine the art of government. They experimented with establishing local autonomy in a larger framework and with international relations. The whole complex of Hellenistic government prepared the ground for the Romans, who did so much to perpetuate the Greek political experience and to make many of its features applicable to a world far larger than the Aegean basin.

3. HELLENISTIC PROSPERITY

Greek rule in the Hellenistic world resulted in vigorous economic growth, so that one of the highlights of the period was great prosperity. Alexander's conquest might well be compared to Columbus' discovery in the sense that it opened up for Greek exploitation a vast territory endowed with vast riches. The Greeks migrated from their native cities in large numbers and applied themselves with vigor to the exploitation of these new lands. As they broke away from their native *poleis*, many discarded the old attitudes that had placed a higher value on political and cultural life than on economic enterprise and became skilled entrepreneurs. All over the Near East they found a native population accustomed to economic domination by a narrow ruling group and were therefore able to seize economic control without much resistance. In many areas of the Hellenistic world well-organized agriculture, skilled industry, and well-developed trading systems already existed, again supplying openings for Greek enterprise. The energetic Greeks missed few of these opportunities.

Agriculture continued to be the basic source of wealth. The new Greek masters did not fundamentally change the established systems, but they did promote greater efficiency and productivity. Greek entrepreneurs, including the kings, sponsored land clearance, directed new irrigation projects, encouraged crop rotation and fertilization, introduced new crops and better breeds of livestock, and organized production more effectively. One senses here an application of the rational spirit of the Greeks at a very mundane level.

The chief advance was in trade and industry. Extensive capital came into Greek hands as a result of their seizure of the treasury of the Persian king and of the wealth controlled by the rich all over the Near East. The Greeks put this capital to work in large-scale trading and industrial ventures, centered chiefly in the great seaboard cities of the eastern Mediterranean but extending outward to the entire Mediterranean world. The Hellenistic kings led in this activity by creating state monopolies for the exchange and production of many items. They also helped trade by clearing the seas of pirates, keeping roads safe, building canals and harbors, improving marketing facilities in their cities, establishing sound money systems, and abolishing artificial political barriers to trade. The horizons of commerce were considerably extended by geographical exploration which expanded Greek contacts eastward to India and out of the western Mediterranean to the coasts of Africa, Western Europe, and Britain.

Hellenistic prosperity, however, benefited only a few—princes, civil servants, landowners, great merchants, and priests. The mass of the population on the farms and in the cities still labored for small gain. The Greeks who spread over the Near East were usually predominant in the favored upper classes, the natives generally economically oppressed. As the Hellenistic era progressed, this gap between rich and poor caused increasing social conflict. Moreover, the prosperity was not evenly distributed geographically. The great centers of wealth were in a belt stretching from Asia Minor to Egypt. Here were the great cities, like Alexandria and Antioch, the best farms, the chief trade routes, the most skilled workers, and the most capital. Greece herself suffered a constant impoverishment during the Hellenistic Age as economic leadership moved eastward and southward. This situation bred deep hostility and boded ill for the long-run stability of Hellenistic society.

The increasing maldistribution of wealth constituted a serious failure on the part of the Greek masters. In many of the ancient Greek city-states, intelligent leadership had directed economic and social development toward the improvement of the lot of the deprived, a policy that had strengthened the whole fabric of society. But the Greek rulers and entrepreneurs of the Hellenistic Age chose to be exploiters. Perhaps this new posture was a natural product of

This statue of an old market woman, a second-century Hellenistic marble found in Rome, reflects an emotionalism and realism far removed from the serene, idealized figures of classical Greece. *Photo: The Metropolitan Museum of Art*

their position as overlords rather than sharers of power with fellow citizens. Perhaps too it was the inevitable consequence of their migration from the ancient *poleis*, a process that trans-

formed them from aristocratic political animals into entrepreneurial economic animals.

4. LITERATURE AND ART

The three centuries following Alexander's conquests mark an important era in cultural history. The Greeks were convinced they had conquered "barbarians," and they retained their feeling of superiority over, and sought to impress their ideas on, their subjects. Nevertheless, expansion brought the Greeks face to face with new ideas and made them aware of their own limitations. The result was a new outburst of activity in art, literature, and philosophy which broadened the older Greek culture.

The literary output of the Hellenistic Age was massive. The outpouring was due in part to the patronage of wealthy monarchs, officials, and private individuals and in part to the increased demand for literature by a growing reading public. Greek became the common tongue of the Hellenistic world of government, commerce, and learning; the Old Testament was translated into Greek (the Septuagint) in Alexandria in the third and second centuries B.C. for the use of Jews living there. While the writers of the Hellenistic Age were prolific, they were not especially inventive. They imitated the epic and lyric poems, the tragedies and comedies, and the histories of classical Greece. Most, especially the poets, were chiefly concerned with style. They often reworked old subject matter in an attempt to achieve stylistic perfection. As a consequence, later ages found Hellenistic literature of little interest, and almost none of it has survived. It did, however, serve as a model for the Romans in developing their literary styles in Latin.

The Hellenistic Age also produced a multitude of scholars who spent their lives reconstructing earlier Greek literary masterpieces, writing extensive commentaries on their meaning, analyzing their grammar, and defining their stylistic features. This patient labor played an important role in establishing and preserving the texts of the Greek classics. Scholarly activity tended to concentrate in a few great cities, of which Alexandria and Pergamum were the most important and Athens the most prestigious. Supported by royal patronage, scholars at Alexandria and Pergamum collected great libraries. The scholarly establishment provided endless grist for an education system that was expanding in the Hellenistic Age and becoming increasingly literary and formal. Education played a major role in preparing the Greek ruling elite to discharge its duties and to sustain the cultural brand that was its mark of superiority.

The artists of the Hellenistic period were no less active than the literary men. Again classical Greek models exerted a powerful influence, completely overshadowing the artistic traditions of the Near East. Architecture enjoyed a great boom because of the numerous new cities built by the Greeks and filled with the traditional buildings—temples, gymnasiums, theaters, and centers for public business. There was a tendency to stress size and ornateness in these buildings. Most Hellenistic cities were much better planned than the older Greek cities, with emphasis on wide streets, adequate water supplies, commercial conveniences, and parks. As a result, Alexandria and the like were more impressive than Athens.

Most Hellenistic sculptures were mere copies of the masters of fifth-century Greece. Occasionally one caught the full spirit of the classical style, such as the famous *Winged Victory of Samothrace* or the *Aphrodite of Melos* (more commonly known as the *Venus de Milo*). But some works took on important new features. In place of the classic quest to create idealized perfection, Hellenistic sculptors tended toward realism. They came down into the streets for their subjects instead of ascending to the abode of the gods. Children, old people, common laborers, and barbarians occupied their attention, and they gave vent to emotions, seeking to portray action and violence, passion, sorrow, and suffering.

5. PHILOSOPHY AND SCIENCE

The major contributions of the Hellenistic Age were in the fields of science and philosophy. Often these thinkers moved beyond their predecessors, a development that seldom occurred in the fields of literature and art.

The moment was especially ripe for scientific advance. The Greek philosophers of the sixth, fifth, and fourth centuries had made brilliant hypotheses about the natural world. Some of them, especially Hippocrates and Aristotle, had introduced the idea that the world could best be understood by observing it and classifying the results rationally. Many educated men shared a sense of the importance of this approach; Alexander, for example, had strange natural specimens collected during his military ventures into the distant east. His conquest put the Greeks in touch with a huge body of data compiled over many centuries by learned men in the ancient Near East. The general use of Greek as the language of learning permitted scientific advances to spread widely. Royal patronage, especially by the Ptolemies, who built a great library and museum at Alexandria, helped to create an interest in science and to provide the necessary facilities. In this favorable climate the quest for knowledge about the natural world was actively pursued.

The new geography, of great interest in the Hellenistic period, was summed up by Eratosthenes (ca. 275–200 B.C.), who worked at Alexandria. He calculated the circumference of the earth as 24,662 miles, about 200 less than the actual figure. On the basis of his study of tides, he insisted that the Atlantic and Indian oceans were joined and that India could be reached by boat around Africa. He made maps using lines of longitude and latitude and divided the earth into zones still used by geographers. Seleucus (second century B.C.), along with others, studied the tides and came close to relating them to the gravitational force of the moon.

Astronomy likewise attracted attention. The two greatest names were Aristarchus (ca. 310–230 B.C.) and Hipparchus (ca. 185–120 B.C.). Aristarchus insisted that the earth revolved around the sun. Hipparchus denied this, and his opinion carried the day. He compiled an extensive atlas of the stars and from observation of their movement arrived at an extremely accurate calculation of the solar year. Both these great astronomers tried to calculate the size of the sun and its distance from the earth, but with little success.

Much was also done to advance mathematics. Euclid (323–285 B.C.) compiled a textbook of geometry that remained standard until the twentieth century. Archimedes (287–212 B.C.) calculated the value of pi (the ratio between the circumference and the diameter of a circle). He also devised a system for expressing large numbers, solved the problem of the relative volumes of a cylinder and sphere, and laid the foundations for calculus. Trigonometry was perfected by Hipparchus, and a fundamental work on conic sections was done by Apollonius of Perga (third century).

Scientific medicine was of great interest to the scholars of this period. Following the lead of Hippocrates, Hellenistic physicians made important progress in anatomy and physiology. Among the chief accomplishments of these men were the discovery of the nerves and the exploration of the function of arteries and the brain. Surgery advanced considerably; so did the use of medicines.

Comparatively little work was done in physics, chemistry, zoology, and botany. Archimedes, however, discovered the laws governing floating bodies and developed the theory of the lever; and Theophrastus (ca. 372–287 B.C.) wrote an important descriptive work on botany that summarized most of the knowledge of plants in his day.

Most of the important work of Hellenistic scientists had been completed by the end of the second century B.C. Thereafter, interest shifted to magic, astrology, and empty repetition of past accomplishments. The Hellenistic Greeks, like their predecessors in classical Greece, were limited in their scientific progress by lack of proper instruments. And there was still no widespread interest in the practical application of scientific ideas, although a few scientists did distinguish themselves as inventors. Archimedes, for instance, invented the windlass, the double pulley, the endless screw, and several devices for defending his native city, Syracuse, against Roman attack.

The last significant development in ancient science was the compilation of great scientific encyclopedias. Among these works were those of Ptolemy (ca. A.D. 85–160) in astronomy and geography, Strabo (ca. 63 B.C.–A.D. 21) in geography, and Galen (A.D. 130–201) in medicine. The bulk of the material in these manuals was derived from the labors of Hellenistic scientists, so that each is a monument to their accomplishments. These encyclopedias served as guides until the beginning of the great scientific revolution in early modern times; little was added in the nearly two millennia separating the Hellenistic scientists from Galileo and Copernicus.

For vigor and creativity, Hellenistic science was rivaled by Hellenistic philosophy. The old philosophical interests lived on, as evidenced by the continued activity of Plato's Academy and Aristotle's Lyceum in Athens. However, the older Hellenic quest for absolute truth about the cosmic order gave way to concern with problems of human conduct, ethical principles, and above all the human soul—the individual and his personal destiny. This trend was already evident among the Sophists of the fifth century B.C. In the Hellenistic Age it was given new impetus by the Greeks projected into a cosmopolitan world where men were on their own among strangers of many kinds. Left with only his own resources, man needed self-knowledge and reassurance.

The search for individual identity and guidance produced several schools of thought. Some caught popular fancy or aroused popular ire for their eccentricity and excess. One such group was the Skeptics, who made a principle of doubting everything and argued that men should live with no concern for truth or values. The Cynics were more spectacular; they advocated that society should abandon all its civilized conventions and wealth to return to nature. In search of converts, they took to the streets in filthy rags to deliver diatribes against the "establishment."

More profound and influential was the teaching of Epicurus (ca. 341–270 B.C.), who taught at Athens. He built his ethical concepts on a strictly materialistic basis. He argued that the universe consisted of atoms, which by chance formed themselves into beings and things. The gods, if they existed, had nothing to do with this process and therefore need be of no concern to men. Given such a cosmos, men should occupy themselves only with happiness and pleasure. Epicurus argued that mere physical pleasure is not the path to happiness but rather those things that bring a peaceful, undisturbed mind. He pleaded with his disciples to withdraw into themselves and avoid excessive wealth, politics, superstition, and too great contact with the world. This philosophy was welcome to many educated men who saw little use struggling in a world where great kings and great wealth determined most things. Although some turned Epicurus' teachings into an excuse for seeking purely physical pleasure, most Epicureans were admirable men, learned and refined, obedient to public authority, calm, and long-suffering.

Even more influential in shaping the moral atmosphere of the Hellenistic Age were the Stoics, whose founder, Zeno (336-264 B.C.), taught in Athens while Epicurus was there. Zeno was of Semitic origin and thus an interesting product of the Greek impact on the Near East. Stoicism was based on Zeno's conviction that the universe is ruled by a Divine Reason, which for many Stoics was a great god who had ordained a perfect world; harmony and order would result if the laws of nature were adhered to by all creatures. Man's moral duty was thus clear. He must use his reason to attune himself and his actions to the unchanging laws of nature. He must bear all misfortune with patience, since everything that happens has been ordained by an all-knowing Providence. And he must bear his good fortune without pride, since he is not responsible for it. The Stoic was schooled to adjust himself to circumstances; his life was a pilgrimage in which he disciplined himself to accept whatever came.

6. HELLENISTIC RELIGION

In at least one realm of life, the Greek way suffered an eclipse: religion. The old civic religion of the Greeks had already been weakened by the blows suffered by the city-states in the fifth and fourth centuries and by the assaults of the philosophers. The old gods and the communal rites in their honor ceased to have meaning to the Greeks who migrated into the Near East. From Alexander's time on, there was an attempt to encourage the worship of kings, but it took no root.

Permeating the Near East were powerful religious forces rooted deep in the past. These forces had evolved into definable cults that we shall call collectively *mystery religions.* With the passing of time, they simply overpowered Greek civic religion and drew increasing numbers of Greeks into their orbits. Many mystery cults flourished in the Near East in the Hellenistic Age: Isis worship, Mithraism, the Earth Mother cult; and the Greeks still had their own Dionysus worship. Whatever their origin, all shared certain fundamental ideas that clashed sharply with the communally oriented, humanistic cults of the *polis.* They centered around the worship of a savior whose death and resurrection provided salvation for each individual. Thus they appealed to men of all classes and nations. The mystery religions involved elaborate, emotional ritual practices and stressed the moral conduct of each believer. In the cosmopolitan atmosphere of the Hellenistic world, ideas from various mystery religions constantly mingled; this syncretism pointed toward the growth of a common faith shared especially by common men throughout the Hellenistic world. Here was the seedbed for two new religions soon to arise in the Near East — Christianity and Islam.

The mystery cults powerfully influenced several aspects of thought and expression. Science and philosophy were put to the service of these religions. Astronomy was transformed into astrology, the "scientists" studying the stars to know the future rather than to find new information, while the philosophers' efforts to understand the universe became an attempt to achieve contact with the powerful deities of the mystery cults. In this sense the peoples of the Near East conquered the Greeks during the Hellenistic Age.

This "religionizing" of thought had brought Greek culture and its Hellenistic continuation full circle: A culture born out of religion was now being absorbed back into religion. A real possibility existed that some of the finest achievements of the Greeks would be swallowed up and twisted out of shape in their losing encounter with Near Eastern religious ideas. This trend was checked at least temporarily by the emergence of Rome as a new champion of Greek civilization. Under Roman auspices Greek culture enjoyed a renaissance and increased its geographical sway considerably.

Suggested Reading

Political History

Max Cary, *A History of the Greek World from 323 to 146 B.C.*, 2nd ed. rev. (1963). A standard survey; excellent for political history.

F. E. Peters, *The Harvest of Hellenism: A History of the Near East from Alexander the Great to the Triumph of Christianity* (1970). A balanced, judicious treatment of all aspects of Hellenistic history.

*C. Bradford Welles, *Alexander and the Hellenistic World* (University of Toronto Press). Especially good in this up-to-date survey are the chapters on social and economic conditions.

*W. W. Tarn, *Alexander the Great* (2 vols., 1948; vol. I has been published as a paperback by Beacon).

*A. R. Burn, *Alexander the Great and the Hellenistic World* (Collier).

Peter Green, *Alexander the Great* (1970). These three biographies, all outstanding, present Alexander in quite different ways. The last, by a novelist, may be of greatest interest.

Hellenistic Cultural Life

Moses Hadas, *Hellenistic Culture: Fusion and Diffusion* (1959). The best general survey touching the major aspects of Hellenistic culture.

*W. W. Tarn and G. T. Griffith, *Hellenistic Civilization* (3rd ed., Meridian). A generally successful survey; some of its chapters on special topics are particularly stimulating and informative.

*George Sarton, *A History of Science: Hellenistic Science and Culture in the Last Three Centuries B.C.* (Wiley). A monumental treatment filled with detailed discussions of Hellenistic science.

*O. Neugebauer, *The Exact Sciences in Antiquity* (2nd ed., Dover). Provides a brief treatment of Hellenistic science.

*N. W. DeWitt, *Epicurus and His Philosophy* (Meridian).

Edwyn Bevan, *Stoics and Sceptics* (1913). These two volumes, neither of which is easy to read, will summarize Hellenistic achievements in philosophy.

Sources

*Arrian, *The Life of Alexander the Great,* trans. A. de Selincourt (Penguin). A colorful biography by a second-century A.D. author who used materials written in the time of Alexander, but since lost.

W. J. Oates, ed., *The Stoic and Epicurean Philosophers* (1940). A collection of nearly all the writings of the Stoic and Epicurean writers of the Hellenistic period.

*F. C. Grant, *Hellenistic Religion: The Age of Syncreticism* (Liberal Arts). A collection of ancient writings that will help to understand the nature of the major religious movements of the Hellenistic Age.

9

THE RISE OF ROME TO DOMINATION OF THE MEDITERRANEAN WORLD

The failure of the Greek city-states and the Hellenistic kingdoms to establish permanent order in the eastern Mediterranean opened the way by the end of the third century B.C. for the intrusion of a new power from the West: Rome. Down to about 4000 B.C., there had been few differences between eastern and western Mediterranean peoples, but after that date the West had fallen far behind. The rise of Rome to a position where she could challenge eastern powers marks the first time western Mediterranean peoples were able to play a decisive role in history.

1. THE EARLY ITALIANS

The city of Rome was the catalytic force that organized the peoples of the western Mediterranean and especially Italy for their new role, but Rome relied primarily on the Italians for the human resources to achieve her greatness. The formation of the Italian people was a long, complex process. At a very ancient date Italy was inhabited by paleolithic hunters. During the third millennium B.C., farming culture, strongly affected by influences from the east, spread over Italy, probably brought by peoples migrating to Italy, perhaps from North Africa. These stocky, swarthy newcomers were to be the basic population of the future. Between about 2000 and 1000 B.C., successive waves of Indo-Europeans moved into Italy from north of the Alps and fused with the neolithic stock. They brought with them

superior technical skills, especially the use of copper, bronze, and iron, and the military and political ability to impose their authority on the natives. Various Indo-European dialects emerged, of which Latin was one. In the second millennium B.C., the level of life in Italy steadily advanced, although it still lagged far behind that of the eastern Mediterranean.

Beginning approximately 800 B.C., the backward western Mediterranean world was powerfully stimulated by the appearance of highly civilized easterners in the West—the Phoenicians, the Greeks, and the Etruscans. The Phoenician impact was slight in Italy but decisive in North Africa, where it gave rise to the powerful city of Carthage. As we have seen, Greeks settled in Sicily and southern Italy, from whence powerful cultural forces flowed through the entire peninsula. It was the Etruscans, however, who had the most immediate and direct influence on Italy and especially on Rome. This people is still an enigma to historians, in large part because their language has not yet been deciphered. They probably came from Asia Minor during the eighth century B.C. and established a series of cities along the western coast of Italy north of the Tiber. These cities remained politically independent, but were bound together by strong economic, religious, and cultural ties. Within a short time Etruscan influence began to expand so that between about 650 and 500 B.C., they ruled supreme over western Italy from the Po

Valley to Naples. After 500 B.C. their power declined as a result of native resistance and Greek and Carthaginian opposition. However, they transmitted a wide range of knowledge that prepared the peoples of Italy for a major historical role. Their most precocious pupils were some villagers living along the Tiber.

2. THE HISTORY OF ROME TO 509 B.C.

The colorful legends enshrined in the works of the Roman historian Livy—including the story of the founding of Rome by Romulus and Remus in 753 B.C.—are undoubtedly beguiling, but they have little relationship to fact. The future "head of the world" was initially the creation of backward herder-farmers living in a poor area known as Latium who established villages about 750 B.C. on a cluster of seven hills lying south of the Tiber some 15 miles upstream. Perhaps these Latins were attracted by the convenient ford at this point, but more likely they sought the protection and pastures offered by the hills. The villages ultimately formed a loose league; and tradition spoke of a common king, but nothing substantiates this legend.

Shortly after 600 B.C., the several villages were rather suddenly transformed into a single city-state. What brought about this decisive event is not clear, but it was probably the consequence of Etruscan domination imposed in the course of the sixth century. During this period a single government under a king was established. The king was advised by a council of elders, called the Senate, composed of men of wealth who drew their authority from their headship of families. There was also an assembly of freemen who were grouped into thirty units called *curiae*, but it was severely limited in its power and did little more than approve the decisions of the king and the Senate. The city-state populace was divided into two distinct classes, *patricians* and *plebeians*, with the former exercising a predominant influence over society. Many plebeians were closely tied to patrician families as *clients*, an institution under which a noble *patron* protected a plebeian and assisted him materially, and the client in return performed various services, including following political directions.

Etruscan techniques, especially in trade and industry, were adopted by the fledgling Roman city-state, greatly strengthening its primitive economy. An alphabet was derived from Etruscan models, resulting in the rapid development of written Latin. Etruscan architecture and decoration served as models for the temples and public buildings in the burgeoning city. Primitive Latin religious practices took on more sophisticated patterns reflecting Etruscan usages. Rome was rapidly becoming the center of an advanced culture.

Despite their debt to the Etruscans, the Romans chafed under their domination. Shortly before 500 B.C. Etruscan power began to be contested by her dependent subjects everywhere in western Italy, while Greeks and Carthaginians vied with Etruscan forces in the larger setting of the western Mediterranean. The challenge was too much for the Etruscans. In Rome the patricians took the lead in a revolution that dethroned the Etruscan king and established in his place two *consuls* elected annually from patrician ranks to wield the *imperium*, that is, the highest authority of the state. This revolution marked the beginning of the Roman Republic, an episode long celebrated by the Romans as the greatest event in their history.

3. THE EARLY REPUBLIC, 509—265 B.C.

The two and a half centuries following the founding of the republic put the Romans to a severe test. From 509 to about 340 B.C. the Romans were chiefly occupied defending themselves in Latium, especially against neighboring peoples. Immediately after the revolt against the Etruscans, the other cities of Latium forced Rome to accept a position as their equal in the Latin League. This league fought to hold back the Etruscans and the tough mountain peoples of central Italy. About 400 B.C. a new menace emerged—Celtic invaders from Gaul, who captured and sacked Rome in 390. Out of this long struggle for survival, Rome slowly emerged as the dominant force in Latium; her success bred fear in the Latin League and caused several of its members to rise against Rome in 340. The rebels were subdued within two years, and the league was dissolved, leaving Rome in control of Latium.

From this base, she turned her attention to the troublesome mountaineers. In a series of campaigns known as the Samnite Wars, stretching from 326 to 290 B.C., she systematically crushed these tribes and incorporated their territory into her expanding state. In the meantime, Roman influence was expanding northward at the expense of the Etruscans and the Gauls. In fighting these various peoples simultaneously, the Romans showed considerable diplomatic skill and succeeded in keeping their foes isolated from one another. Hardly had the Samnite Wars ended when Rome was drawn into the strife-torn world of the Greek city-states in southern Italy. A series of victories in that area ended in 265 B.C. with the Romans in complete control. All Italy south of the Po Valley was hers, constituting the base for a new—although still unproved—world power.

Many factors combined to bring the tiny city on the Tiber these victories. But two were crucial: Rome's enlightened treatment of her victims and her ability to adjust her internal political system to retain and deepen the loyalty of her citizens.

The victorious Romans spurned the usual methods of brutal subjugation and exploitation of conquered peoples. Rather, they applied a variety of solutions, usually dictated by the practical demands of the situation, to bring their victims under their direction. To some peoples, especially those in Latium, Rome extended outright citizenship. Others, especially those already organized as city-states, were made partial citizens without rights to participate in Roman public life but with rights to trade and intermarry. These cities continued to govern themselves in most matters, but their half-Roman citizens owed financial and military obligations to Rome. Still other communities were made allies of Rome, each group signing a formal treaty which left it considerable local independence but which deprived it of control over foreign affairs and imposed on it the obligation to provide men and money for Rome's wars. These arrangements for partial citizenship and alliances were based on the assumption that the subject peoples would eventually earn full citizenship when they demonstrated their loyalty and their capability to participate fully in Roman political and social life. Rome moved to hasten the process by planting numerous colonies of her citizens at various places in Italy. This complex set of arrangements meant that by 265 B.C. Rome ruled over a loose confederation of Italians, most of whom enjoyed a considerable degree of independence, but all of whom were tied to Rome by virtue of an obligation to serve in her armies and of a promise to achieve full citizenship. A system that made Rome's yoke relatively light soon paid off richly in her favor.

The intelligent program for conquered people was matched by a constant modification of the Roman constitution which promoted allegiance and loyalty among the citizens. When the Romans threw off Etruscan rule in 509 B.C., power fell to a narrow patrician aristocracy which controlled the elective offices, the Senate, and the assembly of the *curiae*. During the following two and a half centuries there ensued what is referred to as the "struggle of the orders." The patrician oligarchy came under constant pressure from the plebeians and grudgingly surrendered its monopoly over political life by conceding a larger share of power to the plebeians. Plebeian gains were won gradually, but they came in vital areas. Their role in the army was expanded. New assemblies emerged permitting a plebeian voice in passing laws, electing magistrates, and vetoing arbitrary decisions. One by one elective offices were opened to plebeians. Ancient legal customs were codified to guard citizens from unfair decisions by patrician judges. New legislation was enacted to protect debtors, permit intermarriage between patricians and plebeians, curb patrician monopoly on the control of public land, and encourage colonizing ventures, all promoting the economic interests of the plebeians. The cumulative results of the "struggle of the orders" can best be seen by examining the constitution of the republic in 265 B.C.

Theoretically, Rome was governed in 265 by the decisions of the total citizen body acting through the assemblies, of which two were especially important. The Assembly of Centuries was based on a grouping of the citizenry into

ITALY 265 B.C.

193 military units called *centuries;* each citizen was assigned to one according to his wealth. The majority of the centuries were composed of the wealthier citizens. Since each century cast a single vote in the Assembly of Centuries, that body was dominated by a numerical minority of the total citizen body. However, all citizens did participate through it in such vital functions as approving all laws and electing all officials. The other important assembly was the Assembly of Tribes. It originated as a plebeian body constituted to advise special plebeian officials, called *tribunes,* who were granted the power to veto the acts of regularly elected magistrates dangerous

to plebeian interests. It was based on territorial units called *tribes*, of which there were eventually thirty-five. Male citizens were enrolled in the tribes on a basis of equality, greatly reducing the importance of wealth and social status in the assembly's deliberations. Eventually, the Assembly of Tribes gained the power to enact laws, called *plebiscites*, binding on the entire state; thus it became the chief instrument for the expression of the popular will.

The decisions of the citizenry enacted in the assemblies were executed by an elected magistracy, collegiate in form: With minor exceptions, every office was occupied by a board of at least two members of equal rank, each of whom had the power to veto the acts of his colleagues. The highest executive authority in the state—the *imperium*—was exercised by two consuls who were charged with the management of all civil and military affairs. Below them were the *praetors*, elected primarily to administer justice, but under special circumstances capable of exercising the *imperium*. The *quaestors* handled the financial matters of the state. The *aediles* managed the policing of the city, the repair of streets and public buildings, the city's food supply, and the conduct of religious ceremonies. Priestly colleges were elected to carry out worship of the civic gods. All these officials were elected for one-year terms. *Censors* were elected every five years to classify the citizens for military service and to judge the moral fitness of citizens for public functions. In times of grave crisis, a *dictator* could be elected for a term of six months with unlimited powers to rule the state. According to law, any citizen was eligible for election to these offices, but since there was no pay for service and electioneering was expensive, few men of humble means aspired to high office and even fewer gained it.

Especially potent in the republican system of government was the Senate, a body of about three hundred men who served for life. New members were recruited almost exclusively from the ranks of ex-magistrates. Election to the consulship and praetorship automatically qualified a man for the Senate. Theoretically, the Senate was an advisory body, counseling the magistrates and the assemblies in all public matters. But its decisions were almost invariably accept-

ed by the magistrates and the assemblies because of the prestige of the senators.

Although ostensibly a democracy by 265 B.C., the Roman Republic was dominated by a small, wealthy, landed aristocracy, still largely hereditary. This tightly knit group acted consciously to control the machinery of government. From its ranks came most of the elected magistrates, who passed from these offices into the Senate. That body, with its extensive role in decision making, was the bastion of aristocratic control. The patricians carefully managed the election process and skillfully manipulated the assemblies, relying heavily on the institution of clientage as a means of controlling the votes of the plebeians. The chief threat to the political power of the patrician families came from able, enterprising plebeians who managed to gain wealth by exploiting the opportunities arising from Roman expansion. These "new men" had their appetite for power whetted by the opportunity for broader political participation created during the "struggle of the orders." The patricians met their challenge chiefly by absorbing the new men into their ranks, usually through carefully managed marriage alliances. This process tended to shift the basis for aristocratic status from birth to wealth, but it in no way weakened aristocratic control over political life.

Most Romans were content to entrust the fate of the city to the aristocrats, satisfied that means were at hand to curb them if they abused their power. The history of Rome from 509 to 265 B.C. justified that confidence. The aristocrats led her to mastery over Italy. They were not guilty of prolonged periods of abuse of power, and they were usually responsive to popular demands for change. They also proved capable of pursuing a consistent policy to a successful conclusion, especially in the vital areas of war and diplomacy. Seldom did Rome suffer from the indecision that hampered so many of the more democratic Greek city-states.

4. OVERSEAS EXPANSION: THE PUNIC WARS, 264–201 B.C.

For many decades after 265 B.C., Rome's energy was directed toward establishing her place

This relief, now in the Musée Calvet in Avignon, shows a towboat carrying casks of wine drawn by slaves. *Photo: Alinari/Art Reference Bureau*

among the other Mediterranean powers. She ended by conquering them and welding them into a vast empire.

The first important Roman encounter with a major overseas power was with the African city of Carthage. Originally a Phoenician colony, Carthage had gone her own way after Phoenicia's defeat by Assyria. She created a thriving commercial empire in the western Mediterranean, where by the third century she was the greatest power. On several occasions Rome and Carthage had signed friendly treaties that recognized Carthaginian dominance in the western Mediterranean while conceding Rome's control over Italy.

The two powers stumbled almost accidentally into their first clash. In 265, the Sicilian city of Messana, seeking to escape domination by Syracuse, appealed to both for help. Carthage, eager to contain the Greeks so she could maintain her position in Sicily, moved quickly to help Messana. The Roman Senate was indecisive, apparently reluctant to become involved in a war outside Italy with a major sea power. When the issue was referred to the people in assembly, they voted for intervention. One ancient historian says they were beguiled by promises of rich spoils, but some Romans apparently felt that a Carthaginian stronghold so close to Italy would give the Carthaginians an opportunity to inter-

vene in the affairs of Rome's recently conquered Greek allies in southern Italy.

The First Punic War (264–241 B.C.) centered around a struggle for Sicily. To offset Carthage's control over sea routes and key seaports, Rome was driven to build a navy—and in this venture she succeeded almost miraculously. So confident did the Romans become that they invaded Africa in 255, but this move ended in a disaster that prolonged the war many years. The Romans continued their efforts to dislodge the Carthaginians from the fortress cities in Sicily, suffering a series of naval disasters in the course of the struggle. But they persisted, building fleet after fleet to threaten Carthaginian sea power. Eventually, in 241 Carthage sued for peace. In the treaty ending the war, Rome gained Sicily and received sizable monetary reparations for her losses.

But the issue was far from settled. In the years that followed the peace of 241, the Carthaginians turned their energies to rebuilding their forces for a new showdown. Under the leadership of Hamilcar Barca, Spain was made the base for the next war. Hamilcar successfully subdued the native Spanish population, collected a huge war chest, and recruited and trained an excellent army of Spaniards. After his death in 229, his policy was carried on first by his son-in-law and later by his son, Hannibal. In the meantime, Rome was too involved with other issues to pay much attention to the revival of Carthage. She organized a provincial government for Sicily and then for Corsica and Sardinia, which she seized from Carthage in the aftermath of the first war. Her forces were deeply involved in extending Roman authority into the Po Valley against the bitter resistance of the natives and in curbing the activities of pirates operating along the Dalmatian coast. And so a determined Carthage and a busy Rome headed for a new war, which finally began in 218 B.C., when Hannibal attacked a Roman ally in Spain.

The Second Punic War (218–201 B.C.) was certainly Rome's sternest military test, due in large part to the genius of Hannibal. He boldly led an army from Spain across southern Gaul into northern Italy. On three different occasions between 218 and 216 the Romans challenged him with large armies, only to be crushed each time. The last of these battles, Cannae, convinced the Romans that Hannibal was superior in open battle. They therefore adopted a policy of harassing his army, otherwise leaving him free to do as he pleased in Italy. For fifteen years Hannibal maintained an army on Italian soil, spreading destruction up and down the peninsula—a remarkable feat, especially in view of the fact that he received almost no replacements or supplies from Carthage or Spain. But he could not win: He could not persuade a decisive number of Rome's Italian allies to desert so that he could isolate Rome.

While holding Hannibal at bay in Italy, Rome resolutely undertook the long struggle to crush Carthage. She fought on many fronts, and actually won the war outside Italy. Large armies sent to Spain slowly crushed Carthaginian power and cut off Hannibal's reinforcements. Another Roman force was dispatched to Sicily to choke off a rebellion in support of Carthage. Roman naval forces patrolled the western Mediterranean and the Adriatic, preventing Hannibal from getting help from Carthage or from her ally, Macedon. She encouraged African peoples to attack Carthaginian territories. Her counteroffensive culminated in 205 B.C., when a large army under Scipio Africanus was sent to Africa. In him, Rome had found a military talent equal to that of Hannibal. He attacked Carthage, and Hannibal was recalled from Italy in 203 to save the city. But even he could no longer stem the tide: He met Scipio in a battle in 202 at Zama and suffered a complete defeat.

After Zama, Carthage sued for peace. She was forced to surrender Spain to Rome, to destroy her navy, to accept a heavy fine to be paid over the next fifty years, and to agree never again to wage war outside Africa and within Africa only with Rome's permission. Part of her African territory was turned over to Numidia, a state Rome hoped would balance Carthaginian power in Africa. Carthage was reduced to a minor power; victorious Rome was mistress of the western Mediterranean.

5. OVERSEAS EXPANSION: DOMINATION OVER THE EAST, 200–133 B.C.

The peace of 201 left Rome with many problems: new provinces to organize, a ravaged Italy to repair, war weariness, rebellious subjects to subdue. But these matters had to go unattended, for her new role as a world power drew her toward the turbulent eastern Mediterranean. By 200, the uneasy balance of power in the Hellenistic world was breaking down, chiefly as a result of two factors. First, Egypt grew weak under the rule of the Ptolemies. Second, a pair of ambitious kings, Philip V in Macedon and Antiochus III of the Seleucid Empire, sought to capitalize on Egypt's weakness by seizing her territory and subduing the other independent states in the Near East. Each dreamed of reconstituting Alexander's empire. Their aggressive policies frightened their intended victims into a frantic search for help. They turned to the "rising cloud in the West."

In 200 Pergamum and Rhodes appealed to Rome for help against Philip V. The war-weary Roman populace, speaking in the assembly of *curiae*, refused to become involved, but the Senate was more bellicose. Many Roman leaders feared Philip of Macedon, who had been an ally of Hannibal in the Second Punic War. Perhaps more significantly, many aristocrats, including no less a person than Scipio Africanus, had become ardent admirers of the Greeks. They felt a need to do something to save them and their civilization from Macedonian aggression. Senatorial power asserted itself, and Rome declared war on Philip V in 200 B.C. Although her military performance was not brilliant, Rome managed to defeat him in three years. He was required to evacuate all Greece and confine his activities to

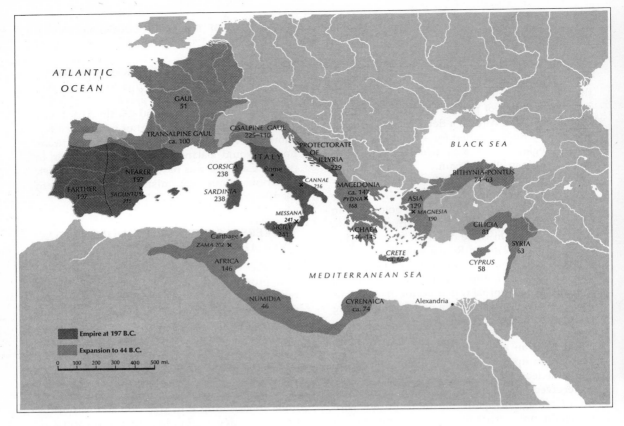

THE ROMAN EMPIRE 197–44 B.C.

his own kingdom. Rome then proceeded to restore peace in Greece, chiefly by bending every
effort to reaffirm the autonomy of each city-
state. She finally withdrew without having imposed any overlordship on the Greeks.

But Roman involvement in the East was hardly over. In 192 B.C. Antiochus III, who had sat by
innocently while his fellow aggressor, Philip V,
was beaten, invaded the Greek peninsula at the
urging of some of the city-states displeased with
Rome's settlement. Rome again sent her troops
east, and Antiochus fared no better than had
Philip V. Roman legions drove him into Asia
Minor, where a crushing defeat was inflicted on
his army in 190. Once again, Rome tried to establish order. Antiochus was required to keep
out of Asia Minor. His navy was destroyed, and
a staggering fine was imposed. Rome turned
over large territories in Asia Minor to Pergamum
and Rhodes, sanctioning them as Roman-backed
peacekeepers. Most of the Greek cities were

again restored to independence, although those
who had aided Antiochus were fined and deprived of some territory. Again, the victors took
nothing except the fines.

With both Macedon and the Seleucid state
reduced to secondary importance, peace in the
East seemed guaranteed. However, the trouble
had only started. With the destruction of the old
balance of power, warfare among the petty states
became chronic, as did calls for Rome's attention. Even the Greeks, whom she had "saved,"
proved treacherous, quarrelsome, and unreliable. Plainly, a new order was needed in the
Near East. With a mixture of idealism, fear, and
increasing greed, the Romans accepted the only
possible solution—Roman rule in the East.

The first evidence of the new policy came in
171–167 B.C., when Macedon provoked another
war with the collaboration of a number of Greek
city-states. Rome easily crushed this alliance.
She now virtually took over Macedon, leaving

her only nominal independence. A few years later a minor disturbance in Macedon resulted in the annexation of the whole kingdom as a Roman province under a Roman governor. Persistent trouble in Greece resulted in stern reprisals, culminating in 146 with the complete destruction of Corinth as an example to the Greeks. By that date Rome had managed to force pro-Roman governments on most Greek cities.

Rome's allies in Asia Minor had proved equally unreliable and troublesome. Such harsh measures had to be taken against them that the most important states, Rhodes and Pergamum, were virtually ruined. Finally, in 133 Rome took over Pergamum as a province. Once established in Asia Minor, a rich world beckoned Rome. And there was no one to stay her hand: The Seleucid kingdom and Egypt were in precipitate decline.

While concentrating her attention chiefly on the East between 200 and 133 B.C., Rome continued to solidify her power in the West. The occupation of Spain was begun; and northern Italy between the Alps and the Apennines, called Cisalpine Gaul, was reconquered and reorganized in the wake of the rebellions there during the Second Punic War. Although no longer a serious threat, Carthage continued to haunt Rome as a potential enemy. With politicians shouting "Carthage must be destroyed" as a solution to every problem, it was only a matter of time until Rome vented her fear and vengeance on her old foe. The final blow came in 149, when Rome again declared war on Carthage for no apparent reason. In 146 Carthage was captured after a heroic defense, destroyed completely, and the site sown with salt. Her territory was annexed as a Roman province.

The passing of her most formidable foe was a fitting symbol of Rome's position in the Mediterranean world as the second century B.C. neared its close. But her success posed questions: What would it profit Rome to conquer so large a world? How would she use her new power and authority?

Selected Reading

Overview

A. E. R. Boak and W. G. Sinnigen, *A History of Rome to A.D. 565*, 5th ed. (1965). The best general survey of Roman history.

Donald R. Dudley, *The Romans: 850 B.C.–A.D. 337* (1970). An attempt to provide a picture of the basic conditions of daily life conditioning Roman development.

Early Italy and Rome

*Massimo Pallottino, *The Etruscans* (Penguin). An excellent treatment of the history of this mysterious people.

E. H. Richardson, *The Etruscans: Their Art and Civilization* (1964). Covers much of the ground as the preceding volume with a greater emphasis on the cultural achievement of the Etruscans.

Raymond Bloch, *Origins of Rome* (1960). Presents a clear picture of the confused history of the early Romans.

The Republic to 265 B.C.

*H. H. Scullard, *History of the Roman World from 753 B.C. to 146 B.C.*, 3rd ed. (University Paperbacks). The best detailed history of the development of the republic.

Leon Homo, *Roman Political Institutions from City to State* (1929). Provides a clear description of the political institutions of the republic and their evolution.

Tenney Frank, *Roman Imperialism* (1921). Supplies a good treatment of Roman expansion and clarifies the forces motivating it.

*B. H. Warmington, *Carthage* (Penguin). A superb treatment of the history of Rome's greatest enemy.

G. P. Baker, *Hannibal* (1929).

H. H. Scullard, *Scipio Africanus: Soldier and Politician* (1970). This and the preceding biography provide interesting insights into the Punic Wars and the men who fought them.

Sources

*Livy, *Early History of Rome*, trans. A. de Selincourt (Penguin).

*Livy, *War with Hannibal*, trans. A. de Selincourt (Penguin). These two works, representing selections from Livy's *History of Rome*, will provide an excellent introduction to how the Romans interpreted their own past.

*Polybius, *The Histories*, ed. E. Bedian and trans. M. Chambers (Washington Square Press). An abridged version of a longer work which describes Rome's rise to world power.

10

THE FAILURE OF THE ROMAN REPUBLIC 133-31 B.C.

Rome's long succession of wars leading to domination of the Mediterranean area had generated profound problems that inevitably had to be faced. Prior to 133, the problems had been neglected by a populace increasingly intoxicated with military success and power; the century following was dominated by a succession of crises emerging from them. Before that century had passed, the republic was in ruins.

1. THE BURDENS OF A WORLD POWER

Certain of the problems emerging prior to the period 133–31 B.C. were especially dangerous to the Roman Republic.

First, Rome's military success left her with a long frontier exposed to hostile foreigners and with a variety of conquered subjects to govern. Her citizen army was ill-suited and badly organized for the tedious burden of defending the distant frontiers. Moreover, the system developed to govern the conquered peoples was largely improvised. The Romans were inclined to view conquered non-Italians simply as subjects to be exploited. Provincial administration gave absolute military and civil power to governors who were seldom held accountable for their conduct. The residents of each province were subject to heavy tribute, the collection of which was entrusted to tax farmers who paid the Roman government what it expected from the provinces and then proceeded to extort all they could from the provincials. No serious effort was made to establish a provincial civil service responsible to the Roman government to impose order and justice. Almost from the beginning, the provincials were exploited and abused with impunity.

Second, Rome's allies in Italy, who had fought loyally and suffered much in the wars of conquest, were ill-rewarded for their efforts. The prospect of citizenship implicit in Rome's earlier arrangements with them grew increasingly remote, and the allies became proportionately restless and rebellious.

Third, Rome's economy was subjected to major strains and transformations. The traditional backbone of the republican economy was the small, independent farm which raised grain primarily for the owner-family and the city market. This style of farming became increasingly unprofitable, chiefly as a result of the competition of cheaper grain imported from more productive lands in the provinces. Moreover, many small farms were devastated by the wars in Italy and depopulated to fill the incessant demand for soldiers. Also, enterprising Romans with capital began creating large estates (*latifundia*) devoted to raising grapes, olives, and livestock to be sold as cash crops, with slaves, a prime prize of successful conquest, providing the labor force. Rome's involvement in the larger economy of the entire Mediterranean world provided new opportunities for trade and industry, further upsetting the simple economic order of the early republican era.

These fundamental economic changes created a fourth set of problems of a social nature. Impoverished small farmers flocked to Rome, where they became a rootless and restless proletariat, endowed with the rights of citizenship but deprived of an opportunity for gainful employment in a city that increasingly lived from tribute and slave labor. This city "mob" was forced to depend on the state or on rich patrons for its livelihood; its members "earned" their living by selling their votes and political support. The "new" Rome also produced a new breed who grew rich as contractors for army supplies, provincial tax collectors, bankers, and organizers of trading enterprises. The members of this class, called *equites*, began to agitate for a share of political power.

Finally, Rome's citizens were profoundly unsettled by new ideological factors impinging on their lives. Society was deeply affected by the sophisticated concepts and styles of Hellenistic culture, which became irresistible from the third century onward. The wealth that flowed into Rome from conquest bred a taste for comfort and luxury and a lust for more of both. Incessant military involvement engendered a disturbing tolerance for violence and corruption. These currents made men less willing to abide by the moral standards and rustic simplicity characteristic of the early republic.

In many ways, these vast forces of change spelled progress for Rome and Italy—greater wealth, greater sophistication, greater opportunities. But their impact called for adjustments that could only be effected by innovative political action. Here the Romans failed. During the long and difficult era of conquest, the Roman government remained essentially what it had been in 265 B.C. The narrow aristocracy dominating the government steadily increased its power. Most citizens, little understanding the complicated issues of war and diplomacy, willingly allowed the patricians to decide Rome's fate. By 133 B.C., the aristocrats had become so accustomed to unquestioned authority that they thought only in terms of their own interests. The conservative, narrowly based government, designed to rule a small city-state, was faced with the problems of a world empire. The fuse was set for an upheaval. When it came, it was so violent that the republican form of government was destroyed.

2. THE PARTIES AT WAR, 133–79 B.C.

The first phase in the ordeal of the republic was a violent party struggle for control of the government. On one side was the old ruling oligarchy, calling themselves the *optimates*—the best—and standing for the established order. Opposed was a shifting alliance of the poor and middle classes, the *populares*, usually led by strong leaders from the patrician ranks. These leaders were often men moved by a genuine urge to reform in order to safeguard the state, but they were also driven by an urge for personal power denied them by the "establishment."

The initial engagement in the power struggle occurred between 133 and 121 B.C. The champions of the *populares* were the brothers Tiberius and Gaius Gracchus. Aristocratic (Scipio Africanus was their grandfather), well educated, and politically conscious, the Gracchi were deeply troubled by the decline of Rome's free farmers and the plight of the proletariat. Elected tribune in 133, Tiberius proposed that public land be redistributed in small parcels for the use of the landless populace of Rome. Plutarch's remark that "no milder or gentler program was ever devised in the face of such injustice and greed" found no backers among the ruling clique, which used its powers to induce another tribune to veto the proposal. Tiberius then persuaded the Assembly of Tribes to oust the offensive tribune and pass his law. Rather than accept the will of the people, the senatorial party, resorting to violence, murdered Tiberius on the pretext that he was trying to be a dictator.

Ten years later, Gaius Gracchus took up the same cause, adding more radical proposals. Elected tribune in 124 B.C., he persuaded the Assembly of Tribes to pass new land laws, to provide cheap grain for the masses, to establish colonies for the resettlement of impoverished Romans, and to extend political privileges to the Italian allies. His legislation also granted extensive privileges in tax collection to the nonnoble capitalist *(equites)*, whose support he sought.

But ultimately he failed to hold together the alliance of poor farmers, *equites*, and city proletariat, and lost his bid for election as tribune in 122. Shortly after, in order to escape senatorial retribution, he commanded a slave to kill him; three thousand of his followers were murdered by the senatorial forces.

Although the careers of the Gracchi ended tragically, their leadership had reminded the populace of its potential power, raised the issue of reform, and bequeathed a series of "causes" to the future. The Senate was impervious to the demands of the people and proved willing to resort to violence to remove those who threatened it. Its posture promised bitter days ahead.

The death of Gaius Gracchus left the *populares* leaderless for a decade. Then a new popular hero arose to turn popular fury against the Senate. The man of the hour was a peasant's son, Marius (ca. 155–86 B.C.), who had held minor offices and who had served in the army in an unsuccessful war in Africa against Jugurtha, a contender for the Numidian throne. In 108 Marius ran for consul, building his campaign around an attack on the Senate; although bitterly opposed by the patricians on the grounds that he was a man of no position or family connection, he was elected to serve for the year 107 B.C. He persuaded the Assembly of Tribes to vote him command of the army in Africa, and once in office, he took a bold and fateful step: He recruited an army of volunteers to fight under his command. His control of this personal army virtually put him beyond the reach of the Senate, which could no longer safely rely on assassination as a convenient way of disposing of threats to its power.

Marius quickly justified the trust placed in him by crushing Jugurtha in 105 B.C. He was ably assisted by a young nobleman named Sulla, soon to play a major role in Rome. So great was Marius' reputation that he was reelected consul during the years 104–101 to fight Germanic tribes threatening the Roman position in northern Italy. Again he was successful, and so he was in the running for consul for the sixth time for the year 100 as the leader of a powerful faction proposing broad reforms that contained most of the elements of the Gracchan program. But Marius proved inept as a political leader. Before his term ended, his party collapsed and he lost most of his great prestige. The *optimates* returned to power, having learned what even an unskilled politician could do to control Rome when backed by an army.

The next decade was relatively quiet, perhaps because moderate elements in the Senate made some effort to resolve critical problems. Two issues defied their efforts, however, and provided the fuel for the next crises. One was the situation of the Roman allies in Italy, who had long been pressing for citizenship but were repeatedly frustrated by opposition from most elements in Rome. In 90 B.C. their disillusionment finally generated a great rebellion that threatened Rome's survival. She responded by granting citizenship to the Italians, a momentous act that ended the days of the simple city-state. In order to meet the military threat posed by the rebels, the Senate then entrusted Sulla (138–78 B.C.) with an army; by 87, he had dispersed the rebels, demonstrated his considerable abilities, and greatly enhanced his influence.

The Italian revolt triggered another crisis which was a by-product of a second problem, that of a provincial administration which had aroused deepening discontent in nearly every part of the Mediterranean world. In 88 B.C. Mithradates, king of the small state of Pontus in Asia Minor and widely accepted in Asia Minor and Greece as a liberator, took up arms against Rome. Despite the critical situation, there was virtual civil war in Rome over the question of who would command the desperately needed army. The Senate favored Sulla; the *populares* clamored for Marius. Sulla finally resolved the issue by marching the army he had commanded in the campaign against the Italians into Rome and securing the command in Asia by force, a procedure that was neither constitutional nor customary, but effective.

Sulla defeated Mithradates and his allies, forced the king to return to his old kingdom, and reestablished Roman dominance in the eastern provinces. But he made no final settlement of affairs in the East; his eyes were on Rome. Immediately after his departure, the *populares* under Marius had forced their way back into power and imposed a reign of terror on the Senate.

They ruled supreme until 83, when Sulla and his army finally reappeared in Italy, well fortified with booty seized in the East. His battle-tested soldiers easily routed the Marians, whose leader had died in 86, and assured Sulla complete mastery over the city.

Once in control, Sulla set about a program aimed at avoiding the violence and illegality that had surrounded Roman political life so often since the Gracchi and at restoring direction of the state to the Senate. He sought to eliminate *populares* leadership by launching a brutal proscription that led to the execution of thousands of Romans who had been associated with the Marian faction. The powers of the tribunes and the Assembly of Tribes were severely limited, and the Senate was enlarged and the new seats given over to *equites.* Sulla took steps to regularize the election procedures for the magistracies, improve the working of justice, and reorganize provincial administration. Having restored the ancient constitution with the Senate in charge, Sulla retired from public life in 79 to pursue his intellectual interests and enjoy the great wealth he had accumulated. He obviously hoped that the Senate could find means of resolving Rome's problems now that it was free of rabble-rousers.

Although it might seem that Sulla's restoration of the Senate left the situation just where it had been in 133 B.C., his retirement actually ended an era. The Senate was in power in 79 not because of its own virtues, prestige, or accomplishments but because a successful military leader decreed so. It was clear that bold individuals, properly armed, might topple it as easily as Sulla had restored it. The long, bitter, indecisive clash between the *optimates* and the *populares* favored the emergence of such individuals by encouraging disregard for the law and reliance on force. The republican form of government had suffered a mortal blow.

3. THE ERA OF STRONG MEN, 79–44 B.C.

New opportunities for "strong men" were quick in coming, for the Senate proved itself completely unworthy of Sulla's confidence. Between 79 and 70 B.C. it was faced in rapid succession by a revolt in Italy led by a disaffected Roman consul,

a revolt in Spain directed by a Roman governor, a slave revolt in Italy led by Spartacus, and a new war with Mithradates of Pontus. A protégé of Sulla's, Pompey (106–48 B.C.), was given command of forces to deal with the Italian revolt and then the Spanish insurrection; he did his job well and thus emerged as a key figure. The slave revolt was handled by Marcus Licinius Crassus (ca. 115–53 B.C.), a rich and unscrupulous capitalist who aspired to political greatness. These two ascending political stars were elected consuls for the year 70 largely because both were supported by loyal armies.

During their co-consulship, Pompey and Crassus negated most of Sulla's legislation by enactments that won the applause of the remnants of the *populares* and raised suspicions among the senators. But neither was satisfied. Pompey was the first to move toward more decisive power. By manipulation he persuaded the people and the Senate to vote him two important military commands: In 67 he was granted powers to clear the Mediterranean of pirates, which he did in a matter of months. And in 66 he was given even greater power to deal with Mithradates, who since 74 had again been defying Rome in the East. Pompey very shortly eliminated him, and then, while in the East, did some things for which he had no authority: He conquered new territories around the Eastern end of the Mediterranean, organized new provinces, cleaned up the administration of the old provinces, and put friends in key spots. By 63 B.C. he was virtually the ruler of the East.

Pompey's success, reminiscent of Sulla's rise to power, caused constant concern in Rome and drove other aspiring politicians to a series of maneuvers to check him. Crassus emerged as a major figure. He found a skilled ally in young Julius Caesar (100–44 B.C.), who demonstrated remarkable talents as a political manipulator. Crassus and Caesar promoted various laws to attract popular support and spent huge sums in an attempt to get the people of Rome to vote them armies and authority such as Pompey possessed. The Senate resisted their maneuvers. A major obstacle was Cicero (106–43 B.C.), a talented, ambitious lawyer who skillfully worked his way to the consulship in 63 and who advocated an alliance between Pompey and the Senate as the solution to Rome's problems. His finest hour came when he foiled a conspiracy by Catiline, a frustrated power seeker and sometime agent of Crassus. Cicero proclaimed that he had saved the republic by exposing Catiline, much to the annoyance of Pompey.

All these political gyrations resolved nothing, for Pompey was still the key figure. But contrary to expectation, on returning to Italy in 62, Pompey disbanded his army and asked only that the Senate reward his veterans and legalize his settlement in the East.

Relieved of the prospect of another military dictator, the Senate proceeded to act in a way that drove Pompey, Crassus, and Caesar into a political alliance. It refused to reward Pompey's veterans or ratify his Eastern settlement. It took action to restrict the powers of provincial tax farmers, a step that threatened one of the main sources of Crassus' immense wealth. It placed every possible obstacle in the way of the election of Caesar to the consulship. Equally frustrated, the three joined in an informal agreement, the First Triumvirate, designed to ensure that each obtained what he wished. Assured of the support of Pompey and Crassus, Caesar won the consulship for the year 59. Once in office, he took steps to satisfy his fellow triumvirs.

Having finished his term as consul, Caesar went to Gaul as proconsul—his reward from the alliance with Pompey and Crassus. There he remained from 58 to 49, during which time he conquered Gaul and added it to the empire. The triumvirate held together uneasily through these years, due in large part to Caesar's efforts. The marriage of his daughter, Julia, to Pompey gave him a personal tie with one member of the triumvirate, and his long-standing friendship with Crassus also helped to sustain the alliance. But Crassus was killed in 53 in a futile bid for glory in the form of a war against the Parthians. A showdown between Caesar and Pompey then became inevitable. The climax came at the end of Caesar's proconsulship in Gaul, when he sought to run again for the consulship for 48. Desirous of getting him out of office so that he could be prosecuted, the Senate blocked this move and called on Pompey to defend the state. Caesar decided to rebel. In 49 B.C. he led his legions across the Rubicon River separating Gaul from Italy and plunged Rome into civil war.

Caesar's seasoned veterans made short work of Pompey's much larger forces, smashing them first in Italy, then in Spain, and finally in the Greek peninsula. Pompey fled to Egypt, where he was murdered and his head sent to Caesar, who then used this crime against a Roman citizen as an excuse to intervene in Egyptian politics, where a struggle for control of the crown was in progress. Caesar decided to support the claims of Cleopatra against her brother-husband, Ptolemy XII, perhaps prompted by the fact that he had become her lover, but he may well have had another motive. Egypt was the last important Hellenistic kingdom still not under Roman control. By putting the young princess on the throne, he perhaps hoped to tap the country's fabulous riches. Thus he dallied in Egypt until Cleopatra was in control as queen. During 47 and 46 Caesar continued his march through the empire—Asia, Africa, Spain—hunting down Pompey's allies. When he returned to Rome in 45 B.C., he was undisputed master of the Roman world.

Caesar's first move upon his return to Rome was to concentrate political power in his own hands. He had himself simultaneously elected dictator, consul, tribune, high priest, and censor. The other magistracies were filled with men of his choice, and the Senate was packed with his appointees. With such power he was virtually a king in the style of Hellenistic monarchs; indeed, some of his contemporaries insisted that it was his intention to establish a monarchy.

Yet Caesar did not gather such vast powers to himself merely for personal gratification. He intended to use them to solve the major problems that had so long plagued the Roman world. He reduced the number of people in Rome dependent on the dole by mounting extensive public works projects and by sending Romans to the provinces as colonists. He provided a police force for the city, thereby ending mob violence. Measures were taken to aid the Italian farmers, and more orderly institutions of local government were established in many towns throughout Italy. New regulations curbed provincial tax collectors and governors, and ended many of their abuses.

Caesar tried always to conduct himself personally so as to appear to be the benefactor of all classes and therefore responsible for the welfare of all. But a hard core of conservative senators, aware that his program threatened the existence of the old republican order, was obsessed with the idea of stopping him. Helpless to achieve their goal legally, these would-be guardians of the "right" order had him killed in 44 B.C.

4. THE STRUGGLE FOR SUCCESSION, 44–31 B.C.

Murder proved no way of stopping the disintegration of the republic. The conspirators who assassinated Caesar had mistakenly supposed that his passing would somehow result in the restoration of the old republic. The real question was how to find a successor for Caesar's mantle. Fourteen years of civil war were necessary to produce a new master.

Two candidates quickly emerged as the main contenders for control of Rome. One was Mark Antony (ca. 83–30 B.C.), who had served Caesar as a military commander and who was an experienced politician. The other was an eighteen-year-old named Octavian, whom Caesar had adopted as his son and legal heir. More concerned with Antony, the Senate at first favored Octavian; Cicero was especially important in supporting his cause. But Octavian, soon aware that he was being used as a pawn, entered into a liaison with Antony and another general, Lepidus, dedicated to restoring order and punishing Caesar's murderers. This Second Triumvirate was given virtually absolute legal powers to last five years. Within a year, most of the senatorial party, including Cicero, had been eliminated by a brutal proscription and by a successful military campaign against the armies raised by Caesar's assassins.

After 42 B.C., Antony and Octavian continued the pose of ruling Rome jointly. Actually each was preparing to eliminate the other, although the final reckoning was delayed for ten years. Antony spent these years in the East, where he fell into the clutches of Cleopatra. In 33, he went

so far as to marry her and give his approval to an ambitious program to establish Egyptian hegemony over the East and to install her children by Caesar and himself as rulers of Roman lands. It was enough that Antony already had a Roman wife—no less a person than Octavian's sister; to surrender Roman lands to an Eastern queen made him a traitor as well. Antony's efforts to bolster his declining prestige had little effect; in fact, the most serious such effort, a campaign against the Parthians in 36, ended in humiliating defeat.

Octavian made infinitely better use of his time. While establishing a solid hold on the Western provinces, he conducted a powerful propaganda campaign picturing Antony as a madman, a traitor, and the victim of a crafty Eastern harlot. Finally, in 32 he refused to continue his joint rule with Antony and declared war on Cleopatra. The decisive engagement was fought at Actium in Greece in 31. Octavian's fleet won an easy victory. Octavian pursued his enemies back to Egypt, where Cleopatra made one final attempt to entice a Roman to support her. When Octavian would have none of her favors, she committed suicide, as Antony had already done. This left Octavian undisputed ruler of Rome, his sword having raised him to a position comparable to Caesar's in 46.

5. CONSEQUENCES OF THE CIVIL WARS

Octavian's victory at Actium ended a century of civil war whose impact on Roman society had been revolutionary in the profoundest sense of the word. The turmoil had caused a social upheaval that especially affected the staunchest supporters of the old order. Proscriptions and confiscation of property virtually destroyed the old aristocracy. The bids of ambitious politicians for popular support undermined the morale of the city masses, who turned from respect for the old institutions to hope for material reward. It was a golden opportunity for ambitious, ruthless, yet able men, even of low birth, to gain wealth and political power. These men, willing to accept new ideas as long as their prestige was recognized, were the greatest beneficiaries of the wars.

Compounding this social upheaval, Romans grew weary of war and murder and political intrigue and became increasingly interested in anything that would give them peace and security. A wave of pessimism and hopelessness spread during this period. People turned to pleasure seeking, to new religions, and to foreign philosophies in search of something to live by in the midst of daily violence. Under such circumstances, fewer men were willing to fight for the old order. New ideas found an increasing audience. Moreover, the wars broadened the vision of many Romans, who found the old, narrow Roman patriotism senseless in view of the world within which Rome now operated and of the millions of provincials upon whom her politicians often depended for power. These broader-minded men could hardly be expected to fight to preserve a way of life confined to the city-state.

The period from 133 to 31 B.C. proved still another thing: The traditional system of government simply could not cope with existing problems. Annually elected officials, a Senate of aristocrats, and popular assemblies attended by small numbers of people living in and around Rome failed on numerous occasions to deal with such problems as defending Rome's extensive frontiers, maintaining peace among millions of subjects, and keeping order in the city. Even the most conservative saw that the old government was outmoded and must be replaced if Rome was to survive as mistress of the Mediterranean. The wars showed just as clearly that only capable individuals possessing extensive powers could cope effectively with Rome's political problems. In spite of their disrespect for the law and their heavyhanded methods, a Marius, a Sulla, a Pompey, and a Caesar achieved something positive in this wild century, whereas all others failed.

These fundamental changes in the midst of frenzied, brutal struggles for power justify our saying that a revolution had occurred by 31 B.C. The republican form of government was replaced by a system under which one man guided political life in a vast empire stretching around the Mediterranean.

Selected Reading

Political Developments

*H. H. Scullard, *From the Gracchi to Nero: A History of Rome from 133 B.C. to A.D. 68*, 3rd ed. (Barnes and Noble). The best detailed history of the fall of the republic.

R. E. Smith, *The Failure of the Roman Republic* (1955).

*Ronald Syme, *The Roman Revolution* (Oxford).

*F. R. Cowell, *Cicero and the Roman Republic* (Penguin).

*L. R. Taylor, *Party Politics in the Age of Caesar* (University of California Paperbacks). These four books all present highly significant but different interpretations of the causes of the failure of the Roman Republic; Syme's work is especially provocative.

Economic and Social Developments

Tenney Frank, *An Economic History of Rome*, 2nd ed. rev. (1927). The early chapters of this work provide a good picture of the economic stresses affecting the Roman Republic.

*W. W. Fowler, *Social Life at Rome in the Age of Cicero* (Papermac). A well-rounded picture of Roman society at the end of the republic, drawing heavily on Cicero's letters.

Biographies

Charles Oman, *Seven Statesmen of the Later Republic* (1902). Excellently done short sketches of the Gracchi, Marius, Sulla, Pompey, Crassus, and Cato the Younger.

G. P. Baker, *Sulla the Fortunate: The Dictator* (1927).

David Stockton, *Cicero: A Political Biography* (1971).

Matthias Gelzer, *Caesar: Politician and Statesman* (1968).

Sources

*The Fall of the Roman Republic, trans. Rex Warner (Penguin). A convenient selection of biographies from Plutarch's *Lives* depicting some of the leading figures of the late republican period.

*Cicero, *Selected Works*, trans. M. Grant (Penguin). This work will introduce the reader to a leading statesman of the period and a keen observer of the conditions of the times.

*Caesar, *Gallic Wars*, trans. S. A. Handford (Penguin).

*Caesar, *Civil War*, trans. J. F. Mitchell (Penguin). This and the preceding work will provide an insight into the mentality of the greatest figure of the age.

11

THE ROMAN EMPIRE, 31 B.C.–A.D. 180

During the first and second centuries A.D. the Romans made their most notable contribution to civilization by fashioning a system of government, known as the Roman Empire, that brought peace and prosperity to the entire Mediterranean basin. Its success was so impressive that many would agree with the eighteenth-century historian Edward Gibbon who wrote that, if he had to choose a time when the human condition was happiest, he would without hesitation select the period between A.D. 96–180.

1. THE FOUNDATIONS OF THE IMPERIAL ORDER, 31 B.C.–A.D. 14

The victor at Actium was the architect of the Roman Empire and one of history's greatest statesmen. When Mark Antony and Cleopatra committed suicide after their defeat, Octavian was supreme by virtue of conquest. It was clear, however, that open military dictatorship or monarchy could not endure; one-man rule in any form was offensive to the Senate and people of Rome, who for five hundred years had determined their own destiny through a set of institutions that constituted the Roman Republic. But the past century had also taught that the only hope for the management of the vast, problem-ridden Roman Empire was the concentration of power in the hands of one man.

Octavian's solution, worked out cautiously during his forty-five-year rule, was masterful. It permitted him to rule the Roman world while retaining the outward forms of the republic. The process began in 27 B.C., when Octavian dramatically surrendered all the powers he then held. Theoretically, the republic was restored; power again rested with the Senate, the elected magistrates, and the assemblies. Impressed by this noble gesture, fearful of a recurrence of civil war, and skillfully guided by Octavian, the Senate and people hastened to vote him the power of tribune for life, the authority of the consuls, command over the armies, proconsular authority over most of the provinces, and the highest priestly office. To these powers the grateful citizenry added several honors: first senator, *augustus* ("most revered one"), the title he would use henceforth; *imperator* ("victorious general"); and "father of his country." Some even hinted that he was divine. This array of powers and honors so elevated his authority that he was the *princeps*, the first citizen of Rome in every respect, who without a hint of illegality could do whatever was necessary to rule her. Historians have come to refer to his regime as the *principate* to reflect its unique blend of republican and monarchical ingredients.

Armed with these great powers, Augustus turned to reconstructing the social order of Rome. His chief concern was the demoralized condition of the citizen body, that relatively small group who now had no choice but to rule the vast empire. Adhering to the ancient Roman

This majestic statue of Augustus, created during his reign, was intended to idealize and exalt the man who had restored peace to the Roman world after the troubled times of the late republic. *Photo: Alinari/Art Reference Bureau*

conviction that a class-structured society was healthiest and most effective, Augustus tried to redefine the old class divisions, assigning specific functions and responsibilities to each. Rigid standards of birth, wealth, and conduct were set up for senatorial ranking, and to this elite was assigned a large share in government affairs. They were to hold the chief elective offices in the state, to advise the *princeps*, to serve as governors of specified provinces, and to fill high military and civil posts in the provinces. The equestrian order *(equites)*, made up chiefly of rich traders and industrialists, was entrusted with new positions in the army, the tax system,

and the judicial system. It was to supply bureaucrats to assist the *princeps*. For the plebeians, Augustus hoped to provide order and security. He concentrated on supplying cheap grain, police supervision, and entertainment for Rome's huge population and economic security for the farmers of Italy. The plebeians were expected to play a political role by exercising their powers as voters and to serve as volunteers in the armed forces. Their response was not always what Augustus expected, especially in elections; in fact, the populace seemed to prefer benevolent mastery to responsible collaboration.

To improve the morale and the patriotism of the citizen body, Augustus encouraged a revival of the ancient Roman religion; patronized writers, who turned out masses of propaganda exalting Rome's past greatness and present blessings; and arranged for numerous laws aimed at checking what he considered softening vices — luxury, sexual irregularities, divorce, childless marriages, gambling, and drinking. He also spent immense sums beautifying Rome and providing public services in the hope that its citizens would feel a resurgence of pride in the capital.

Augustus undertook a complete overhaul of the military establishment. The foundation was laid for a professional army by the formation of twenty-five legions recruited from the Roman citizen body for long terms of service. Each legion was complemented by an auxiliary unit composed of noncitizens recruited in the provinces. The total force numbered approximately 300,000 men. Careful discipline, regular pay, and adequate pensions were provided. An elaborate support apparatus of roads, supply depots, and military posts was established. The bulk of this newly constituted army was stationed along Rome's extensive frontier; only the Praetorian Guard, a picked contingent of about 9,000 men, was garrisoned in Italy to serve as the bodyguard for the *princeps*. The chief function of the army was defensive. With the exception of some spirited campaigning on the northern frontier against the Germans, Augustus gave up the idea of offensive warfare and expansion. He began the process of fixing a clear boundary between the Roman and non-Roman worlds. The army's job was to hold that frontier and to strike down elements within the empire who tried to escape Roman domination.

Having provided for peace and defense in the provinces, Augustus attempted to improve the Roman administration. Using his proconsular powers, he began to develop a regular provincial administration that he himself carefully supervised. He selected legates to represent him in each province, paying them adequate salaries in order to reduce their inclination to build personal fortunes by exploiting the provincial subjects. Augustus sent each province a *procurator*, usually an equestrian, to collect taxes and render account to the *princeps*. Under the careful eye of Augustus this set of administrative and financial officials almost immediately brought order to the provinces. The notorious corruption, oppression, and violence of the late republican period disappeared, to be replaced by the Roman peace.

The complex responsibilities of maintaining the army and administering the provinces generated the need for a central administrative machinery manned by professional civil servants. To an amazing degree, Augustus himself and a circle of confidants directed the far-flung operations of the principate. Slowly, however, there emerged a corps of helpers, composed to a large degree of freedmen who had no political attachments and who owed everything to the *princeps*. This addition to the political order was important: The expertise and loyalty of its members tended to make the political services of the senators and the citizen population less crucial.

Although one cannot argue that Augustus had a precise economic policy, the restoration of peace and order produced considerable prosperity. Encouraged by a political regime that provided a sound coinage, developed roads, suppressed piracy and brigandage, and imposed an equitable tax burden, agriculture, trade, and industry demonstrated new vitality.

The one remaining problem was for Augustus to ensure the empire a prosperous, stable future. Only the Senate and people could transmit his powers. Augustus began early to try to ensure his succession. He attempted to combine two distinct ideas. First, he hoped to establish the hereditary principle so that the second *princeps* would enjoy the prestige of descent from Julius Caesar and Augustus. Second, he wanted his successor to have gained the practical experience needed to guide the vast empire. Augustus had no sons. His only daughter, Julia, was three times married to potential heirs. Augustus outlived two of them and her two elder sons. Finally, he chose as his heir his adopted son, Tiberius, who became Julia's third husband and after A.D. 4 was granted ever-greater powers by Augustus. When the *princeps* died in 14, Tiberius was ready to assume full authority.

This brief summary hardly does justice to Augustus' career, whose constructive achievements seem almost a miracle. In part he succeeded because he was not a doctrinaire idealist seeking to create a utopian state; he was a patient, realistic, cautious, hard-working statesman to whom good fortune gave many years to work on his program. He kept certain key ideas central in his political activities: the need to concentrate power in his own hands, the need to honor the ancient political ideals of the Roman citizenry, the need to set positive goals for all elements of a widely diverse population. By working toward these ends, he fashioned a new political order. As it took shape, it elicited from the vital element in the Roman world—the people of Italy—a resurgence of their ancient virtues: patriotism, devotion to public service, loyalty, sobriety. It was this elusive capability for moving men to do what had to be done much more than what he did that best describes the greatness of Augustus.

2. SOLIDIFYING THE AUGUSTAN PRINCIPATE, A.D. 14—96

Between Augustus' death and the end of the first century A.D., the principate was tested by severe pressures and by strong opposition. Outwardly this era was marked by the very thing that Augustus wished to avoid: a clash between the *princeps* and the Senate. This encounter bred fear, uneasiness, and turmoil, especially in the city of Rome.

One of the factors contributing to the tension was the difficulty of finding rulers possessed of the talents needed to run a vast, complex empire while respecting the authority that the Augustan system had entrusted to the Senate and the people. Nearly all Augustus' successors down to A.D. 96 were men of limited abilities who evoked accusations of tyranny and incessant opposition from the Senate. The first four rulers of this era, called the Julio-Claudians, were all related to Augustus. Tiberius (A.D. 14–37) was a cold, suspicious, disillusioned man who repeatedly made brutal assaults on those he suspected of trying to undermine his position. Caligula (A.D. 37–41) was a man lacking completely in political sense; perhaps he was even mad. Claudius (A.D. 41–54) was a scholarly man whose chief interests lay outside Roman aristocratic society. Worst of all was Nero (A.D. 54–68). Cruel, vain, wasteful, he kept Rome in a turmoil in his attempts to satisfy his own desires. He was eventually ousted from office, avoiding assassination by killing himself, but only after he had killed his mother and two wives, disposed of numerous senators, persecuted Christians, made a fool of himself posing as an artist, and emptied the treasury in order to indulge his personal whims.

With Nero's passing the family of Augustus was discredited, and the office of *princeps* was forcefully seized by Vespasian (A.D. 69–79), who had spent most of his life in the army. He and his sons, Titus (A.D. 79–81) and Domitian (A.D. 81–96), called the Flavians, were men of considerable ability, but they had little respect for the Senate and appeared to many to be worse tyrants than Augustus' relatives.

The unhealthy turmoil of the first century A.D. was also due in large part to the imprecise definition of the powers to be exercised by the *princeps* and by the Senate and people. Often the *princeps* exercised his authority to meet some real need only to find his actions interpreted by the Senate as a usurpation of its authority. This posture of suspicion, distrust, and misunderstanding caused the rulers to curb criticism and resistance with a heavy hand. The circle of misunderstanding and hatred was generated in particular by the problem of the succession. As we have seen, Augustus had established conflicting principles: Theoretically, the Senate and people chose the *princeps* by voting to him the powers and rank of first citizen. Augustus, however,

had arranged affairs so that his position was hereditary, and thus it remained until Nero's death, when the army again entered politics. In A.D. 68–69 actual war was waged by various legions seeking to elevate a favored general to power. When Vespasian emerged as the victor, it was obvious the Senate had little to say about the succession. He returned to the hereditary principle of succession, but the old resistance was raised against the Flavians.

In reality, these quarrels that loom so large in the records of the first century A.D. were of minor significance compared to less spectacular developments occurring in the Mediterranean world. Several of the rulers—especially Tiberius, Claudius, and Vespasian—were able statesmen who worked patiently and effectively to increase the power of the *princeps* and to perfect its exercise for constructive ends. They were worthy successors of Augustus, faithful to his broad policy. But their successes slowly eroded the remaining power of the Senate and people who in large part caused this decline by consistently failing to act effectively and intelligently. Their place was taken by an organized bureaucracy whose expertise and devotion to public welfare permitted the rulers to carry out intelligent policies beneficial to the entire empire. They ably defended the frontiers and on occasion extended them, as, for example, when Claudius conquered Britain. The provinces were well administered, and their inhabitants grew to respect the imperial regime. Several rulers extended citizenship to many provincials. Vast public works were undertaken in Rome, in Italy, and in the provinces, and trade, industry, and agriculture were given every possible encouragement. To the majority of men of the Roman world—and increasingly even to the senators—the conclusion that rule by a powerful *princeps* meant order and justice, prosperity, and security was inescapable. These were precious gifts.

3. THE EMPIRE AT ITS PEAK: THE "GOOD EMPERORS," A.D. 96–180

With the death of Domitian in A.D. 96, opposition to the principate virtually disappeared, and

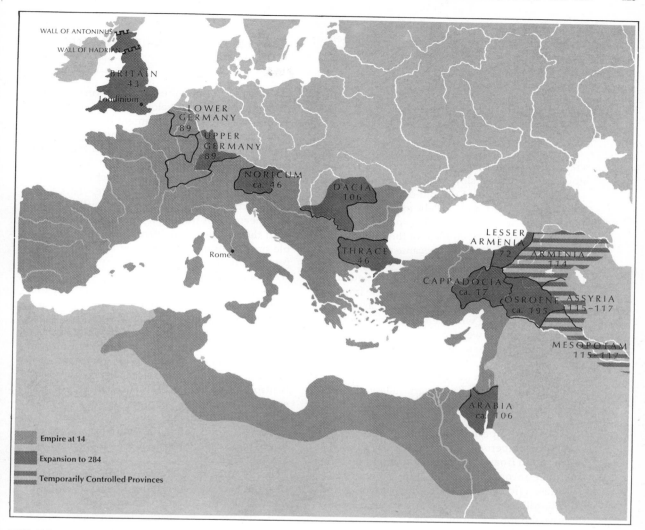

WALL OF ANTONINUS
WALL OF HADRIAN
BRITAIN
43
Londinium
LOWER GERMANY 89
UPPER GERMANY 89
NORICUM ca. 46
DACIA 106
THRACE 46
Rome
LESSER ARMENIA 72
ARMENIA 114
CAPPADOCIA ca. 17
OSROENE ca. 195
ASSYRIA 115–117
MESOPOTAMIA 115–117
ARABIA ca. 106

Empire at 14
Expansion to 284
Temporarily Controlled Provinces

THE ROMAN EMPIRE A. D. 14–284

for roughly the next century, the empire enjoyed a golden age. From the Atlantic to the Euphrates, from Central Europe to deep inside Africa, the *pax romana* became a reality. It was an era characterized by excellent and benevolent rulers, just and efficient administration, internal peace, material prosperity, and stout defense of the frontiers.

Seldom has any era produced rulers more highly praised than the five who ruled from 96 to 180. Nerva (A.D. 96–98) was an elderly man

when chosen to succeed the tyrannical Domitian. Before he died he selected as his heir a native of Spain, Trajan (A.D. 98–117), who won the admiration of the whole Roman world by his respect for the Roman aristocracy, his brilliant military exploits, and his sound, honest administration. Hadrian (A.D. 117–138) was a cultured humanitarian who spent most of his reign traveling throughout the empire promoting the cause of peace and material well-being. Antoninus (A.D. 138–161), by the excellence of his character and intellect, earned the title of "Pius" from the Senate. The crowning glory of the era was Marcus Aurelius (A.D. 161–180), a noted Stoic philosopher who brought a deep sense of duty, willingness to work, and nobility of purpose to the Roman political scene.

The program followed by these "good emperors," as later generations called them, was consistent. Rather early in his reign each took special care to select a successor, adopting a man of ability as a son and slowly increasing his power so that at the death of the old emperor, he was powerfully placed and widely experienced. All these rulers were tactful and respectful toward the senators, who, given most of the high offices and continually consulted, became staunch supporters of the principate, even though their independent power was extremely limited. The "good emperors" steadily developed the imperial bureaucracy. They slowly created a unified body of law for the whole empire. The interests of the provinces were promoted. Citizenship was granted to an ever-larger number of provincials, and humanitarian projects for the aid of the downtrodden in the empire were repeatedly inaugurated. All these rulers allowed local groups extensive freedom as long as that freedom did not threaten the peace. Since the services of the imperial government were costly, the "good emperors" worked tirelessly to establish a sound financial system that would provide adequate income for worthwhile expenditures. All these efforts by the emperors slowly bound the 50 million people of the empire into a commonwealth guided from Rome.

But there was one uncontrollable factor—the frontier. Rome's army, now about 350,000 men, was spread too thinly along it for safety. Trajan tried to safeguard the frontier from the Germans and the Parthians by conquering Dacia and the Tigris-Euphrates Valley. Hadrian reversed this aggressive policy and trusted to strong defense and diplomacy. But by the time of Marcus Aurelius, the problem had still not been solved, and this peace-loving philosopher was forced to spend much of his reign fighting the Germans. When he died, in A.D. 180, a tenuous peace that was cause for grave concern prevailed along the extensive frontier.

4. IMPERIAL GOVERNMENT IN THE SECOND CENTURY

In its mature form in the second century A.D., the principate was a marvelously effective and enlightened system of government that deserves at least a brief description. Throughout this period the Senate and the Roman people in theory still had final authority in the state. In fact, a large part of the ancient republican machinery of the government continued to operate. This kept Roman citizens solidly in touch with a sacred and meaningful tradition. Yet it had little to do with the realities of political life. These venerable organizations had but one function, to approve and legalize the authority of the real wielder of power, the *princeps*.

The *princeps*, or *emperor* (derived from the title *imperator*, the honor voted by soldiers to their victorious general), had assumed a virtual monopoly of executive, legislative, and judicial powers, legally voted each at the beginning of his reign. His key powers were command over all military forces, control of all revenues, and control of legislation. Each also had a huge personal fortune to be spent as he pleased. Each held various honorary titles that exalted him above all others, and most emperors were believed to be especially blessed by the gods, if not actually divine.

The emperors exercised their vast powers through two agencies: the bureaucracy and the army. The bureaucracy was divided into great departments, each headed by an experienced, able official. Below him, the top levels were manned by senators and equestrians, while the lower ranks were filled with educated plebeians or freedmen. Italians and provincials alike were accepted in the civil service, making it a cosmopolitan body.

The army had changed little since Augustus' time. The bulk of the soldiery was recruited for twenty-five-year terms from the citizen population of Italy, although by the second century more provincials were being drawn into the legions. Every effort was made to get good commanders and provide adequate training, pay, and pensions. The soldiers not only played a vital role in defending the empire, but served as transmitters of Roman culture to backward peoples living along the frontiers and to the barbarians beyond.

The support of these two agencies imposed a tremendous financial burden on the state. Salaries for the civil servants and pay, pensions, and provisions for the soldiers made imperative a large, regular income. Added to these expenses were the costs of public services supplied by the government—roads, public buildings, food for the poor of the cities, police forces, and so forth. The emperors of the first and second centuries A.D. succeeded in meeting these financial demands by developing an elaborate but fair tax system. No small part of the tax burden was borne by the provincials as their contribution to the support of their protectors.

The emperors maintained and expanded Augustus' effective provincial administration. By A.D. 180 the empire was divided into roughly forty provinces, some still under the authority of the Senate but most under the *princeps.* A governor was assigned to each with wide powers to keep order, administer justice, and protect Rome's interests, and a *procurator* continued to collect taxes.

The second-century emperors followed Augustus' principle of allowing as much local freedom as possible, and throughout the empire city-states were encouraged to regulate their own affairs. Each city-state and its surrounding territory was ruled by a body of local aristocrats (called *curiales*) who made up a local senate. These senates elected local magistrates, collected local taxes, assumed responsibility for policing and beautifying the city, held courts, and did the many other things necessary for sound government. There can be little doubt that the Romans were inspired to this policy by the model of the Greeks. Where city-states did not already exist—especially in the Western provinces—the Romans founded as many as possible. The second century was truly the culminating age of city-state polity. It must not be thought, however, that the imperial government was totally aloof from local affairs. The emperors themselves and the provincial governors sometimes intervened in local affairs and regulated matters contrary to

local wishes. Once Rome did intervene, the small cities had little hope of resisting.

It is beyond question that by the second century A.D. Rome possessed the essentials of autocratic government. However, government was not despotic; seldom have men with such great power ruled so benevolently or humanely. These emperors were strongly motivated by rather well-defined ideas of what constituted good government and the duty 'of a ruler. They believed that power entailed duty, that power existed so that humanity could be served—a political philosophy based largely on Stoic ideas but also on the theories of men like Plato and on the political practices of men like Alexander the Great. The emperors were also bound by the deep Roman respect for law. The task of an emperor was to operate within the framework of the law, limiting and shaping his powers to fit it. A strong idealism thus drove emperors and their servants: Good government to these men was the first need for civilized life.

5. LIFE IN THE EMPIRE

An elaborate, orderly, powerful government brought peace and stability in which certain patterns of social and economic life flourished. For the majority of the people in the empire, farming was still the fundamental means of livelihood, and the level of agricultural prosperity was high in the second century, for the great cities and the army created a large and steady demand. Especially flourishing were the *latifundia,* nourished by the thriving trade that was the key to imperial prosperity. The reduction of artificial trade barriers, the sound money system, the good roads, and the well-policed seas encouraged the movement of goods to every corner of the empire. The Mediterranean became a busy roadway linking its bordering lands in a common economic system. The traders of the Roman world carried on their activities not only within the confines of the vast empire, but also with India and China. Although a large part of commercial activity involved the exchange of agricultural products, there was a considerable movement of manufactured goods, especially

This relief shows an everyday scene in a Roman household. Food is being prepared and baked in the oven at right. The panel, now in the Musée de Trier, dates from the third century. *Photo: Alinari/Art Reference Bureau*

from the East, where skilled artisans produced a variety of high-quality items much in demand throughout the empire. Industrial production made remarkable progress in the previously backward West, especially in Gaul, Spain, and Africa. These complex international patterns of agriculture, trade, and industry tended to reduce the economic importance and self-sufficiency of Italy, which augured trouble in the future. For the present, probably the level of prosperity of the entire Mediterranean world was greater than it had ever been.

The social system, centered on an urban pattern of life, regained its stability. Rome, of course, was the hub of the entire empire, but many other cities—especially the great Eastern centers like Alexandria, Antioch, Corinth, Ephesus, and Athens—were worthy rivals. In them life was dominated by an aristocracy made up of wealthy landowners, successful traders, and high state officials who used their wealth and prestige to ensure themselves a full share of the comforts of life. And although they sometimes indulged their desires to vulgar excess and were always keenly and arrogantly conscious of their status, these aristocrats, moved by civic pride, poured considerable amounts of talent and wealth into the promotion of the welfare of the cities. Furthermore, the aristocracy was never a closed one; members of the lower classes could enter it by attaining wealth or winning favor with the imperial government.

Below the aristocrats was an array of city dwellers: shopkeepers, skilled artisans, minor officials, hired laborers, servants, slaves, and throngs of idle poor. Some elements of this populace fared fairly well economically and socially, but for many, life was poverty and misery, passed in slums and often dependent upon the state or a rich aristocrat for bare essentials. Still, the city had its compensations: its pageants, its public games, its splendid buildings, its religious ceremonies, its constant excitement.

Those who received the least benefit from the *pax romana* were the peasants who spent their lives tilling the soil. Isolated from the cities, they seldom felt the impact of the forces that gave Roman society its vitality. The major trends in agricultural life encouraged the growth of large estates, a process that increasingly reduced the small independent farmers to dependency on powerful absentee landlords as tenants. These dependent agricultural workers, called *coloni*, were gradually burdened with the greater tax share as well. In effect, the peasantry supported the other classes in Roman society with very little recompense and less hope for a better life.

Slavery played a prominent role in Roman imperial society. In the cities slaves worked in the households of the rich and in the workshops and stalls of artisans and merchants. Nearly every agricultural establishment had slave laborers; some of the large estates depended almost totally on them. So did the mines and the great ceramics factories. Needless to say, the lot of slaves was a hard one and their treatment often brutal, especially where great gangs of them were utilized. There is some evidence, however, that their condition tended to improve. Many were given freedom by masters who in some cases seem to have been moved by moral scruples. Some slaves managed to purchase their freedom and enjoy considerable prosperity practicing trades they had learned as slaves. Numerous funerary inscriptions render praise to slaves for their loyalty and industry, and other literary sources suggest that masters and slaves often associated amicably. Imperial legislation extended several rights to slaves and sought to assure them humane treatment. Despite these signs of a more enlightened view toward slavery, the institution demeaned labor and justified the idleness of many freedmen.

One of the chief social consequences of the Roman imperial order was the degree to which barriers of every kind tumbled to create a cosmopolitan Mediterranean society. The distinction between Roman and non-Roman faded as provincials gained citizenship and wealth. The gulf between national and ethnic groups disappeared as a consequence of the free movement of peoples and the common institutions serving every part of the empire. Religions, philosophies, art forms, and ideas fused in an atmosphere of toleration. Under Roman rule, the Mediterranean basin tended to become one world racially, religiously, culturally, and economically. The Romans provided the synthesizing agency and the chief bond of unity in the form of the imperial government, one of the most humane and beneficent political systems ever devised.

Even a brief description of the Roman world in the second century will elicit admiration for its peace, order, prosperity, and unity. That admiration is warranted, but it must be tempered by certain reservations. The empire had its poverty, its injustices, its oppression, its violence, its greed. The callous disregard shown by the proud, self-satisfied ruling aristocracy for these conditions; the immense power concentrated in the imperial government without any checks; the signs of vulgarization, sterile imitation, and barbarization in the emerging cultural synthesis; the dangerous weaknesses in the economy—all these signs belied the Roman pride and faith that their world was destined to last to eternity.

Suggested Reading

Political History

*M. P. Charlesworth, *The Roman Empire* (Galaxy).

*Harold Mattingly, *Roman Imperial Civilization* (Anchor). Either this or the preceding title will provide a brief survey of Roman imperial history.

*E. T. Salmon, *History of the Roman World from 30 B.C. to A.D. 138* (University Paperbacks). A detailed history of the period, especially good on political developments.

*F. E. Adcock, *Roman Political Ideas and Practices* (Ann Arbor). Helpful in understanding the nature of the Roman imperial system of government and the ideas that inspired it.

Mason Hammond, *The Augustan Principate in Theory and Practice*, rev. ed. (1968).

Mason Hammond, *The Antonine Monarchy* (1959). Although somewhat demanding, these two volumes provide the best characterization of the imperial government.

Economic and Social History

*Jerome Carcopino, *Daily Life in Ancient Rome*, trans. E. O. Lorimer (Yale). A vivid picture of economic and social conditions in the empire.

*Samuel Dill, *Roman Society From Nero to Marcus Aurelius*, 2nd ed. (Meridian). Somewhat old, but still excellent in describing social relationships in the golden age of the empire.

M. I. Rostovtzeff, *Social and Economic History of the Roman World*, 2 vols., 2nd ed. (1957). A classic treatment.

Biography

A. H. M. Jones, *Augustus* (1970).

Stewart Perowne, *Hadrian* (1960).

A. S. L. Farquharson, *Marcus Aurelius* (1951).

Sources

Complete Works of Tacitus, ed. A. J. Church and W. J. Brodribb (Modern Library). Tacitus' *Annals* and *Histories*, both in this edition, provide a lively picture of the first century A.D., written by a conservative not always pleased with the conduct of the emperors.

*Suetonius, *The Twelve Caesars*, trans. Robert Graves (Penguin). A gossipy, personalized sketch of each emperor from Julius Caesar to Domitian.

*Pliny the Younger, *Letters*, trans. Betty Radice (Penguin). Presents an excellent picture of the activities of a Roman provincial governor during Trajan's reign.

12

ROMAN CULTURE

As the Romans were perfecting an imperial government that served the entire Mediterranean world, their intellectual and artistic life reached maturity. Rome played a dual role in the cultural history of the Western world. In certain fields, especially in art, philosophy, and abstract scientific thought, the Romans were not primarily creators; they borrowed from and adapted the Greek tradition, and then disseminated the synthesis among their subjects, especially those in the Western part of the empire. However, the Romans were not entirely imitators. They made major contributions in literature, architecture, engineering, and law—contributions ensuring them an important place in cultural history.

1. THE LONG APPRENTICESHIP

Before 250 B.C. the Romans displayed little interest in cultural pursuits. Their life, strongly influenced by Etruscan models, was simple and conservative. Out of these early centuries emerged a basic orientation that shaped thought and colored cultural achievement for centuries. The Romans became a practical, down-to-earth people, little given to intellectualism or emotionalism. The virtues they admired were sobriety, industry, piety, and responsibility toward family, state, and gods. Originality, creativity, and individuality—all potentially dangerous to stable society but vital to cultural vigor—were little admired or encouraged.

This early Roman outlook on life was shaped by four major forces—family life, agriculture, warfare, and religion. The family structure was dominantly patriarchal. Fathers impressed on other members of the tightly knit families a sense of discipline, obedience, and respect for authority and tradition. Farm life made the early Romans a practical, realistic people, content to live simply and frugally. Constant warfare in defense of Rome deepened the sense of duty and strengthened discipline. But religion had the profoundest effect on thought and action. The Romans' belief that every aspect of life was controlled by numerous gods and spirits instilled in them a deep piety and a sense of dependence on outside forces.

The chief Roman gods at this early date were household and agricultural deities: Janus, the god of the doorway; Vesta, the goddess of the hearth; and the *lares* and *penates*, spirits guarding the productive powers of the family and its lands. The deities who protected civic life were headed by Jupiter and his wife Juno. Conciliating these spirits was life's chief burden. The Romans approached the gods with dignity and reserve. Worship consisted chiefly of sacrificial offerings and long-established prayers. The head of each family led the worship of the family and household gods. The ceremonies in honor of civic gods were conducted by priests who placed great emphasis on the correct performance of traditional ceremonies. Even the least deviation from the proper pattern might anger the gods and bring great misfortune on their worshipers.

Home, farm, battlefield, and altar thus worked together to establish the early Roman outlook and character. The best Roman was a sensible, unemotional, hard-working, disciplined man, willing to accept the world as it was, not especially eager to seek out new things and usually indifferent to speculation.

2. THE HELLENISTIC TIDAL WAVE

Beginning with the conquest of the Greek cities of southern Italy in the first half of the third century and continuing until the end of the second century B.C., these simple Romans experienced a cultural revolution. As a result of their relationships with the Italian Greeks, their wars in the East, and the importation of many Greek slaves into Italy, the Romans slowly became aware of the cultural heritage of the Greek world, particularly in its Hellenistic phase. They were so impressed that during the third and second centuries B.C., they were literally conquered by the culture of their subject peoples.

One of the consequences of this experience was the adoption of a new education system. Previously, the young Roman had been educated at home by his father in family customs, the principles of Roman law, farming, civic duties, and religion. Now that system was replaced by the Hellenistic model. In every respectable Roman household educated Greek slaves were employed to teach young men to read Greek, introduce them to Greek literature and philosophy, and develop in them the skills needed to express their own ideas. Grammar and rhetoric became the touchstones of the new education system and long remained the instruments through which the young were brought into civilized society.

Their fascination with Greek culture soon spurred the Romans to imitation. Epic poems, comedies, tragedies, histories, and even philosophical tracts were produced in Latin. Most early Roman authors copied Greek literary styles slavishly and treated Greek subject matter. But in their work, they perfected Latin expression and laid the groundwork for an independent Latin literature.

In art, the Romans were even more deeply impressed by Greek models. During the wars in the East huge numbers of art pieces were pilfered to decorate Roman villas. Those who could not steal what they wanted hired Eastern artists to turn out copies. Greek styles of architecture and decoration were applied to civic buildings and private dwellings. Rome was transformed into a Hellenistic city.

Even the masses in Rome felt the impact of Greek influences, but they were touched chiefly through religion. The wars of conquest left many people intellectually and emotionally lost. The formal religion of Rome offered little satisfaction. The Eastern religions did. New gods and rituals taken from the Greek civic religions were added to public religion in Rome, but even these additions did not satisfy many. From Eastern slaves they learned about more exciting religions like the worship of Dionysus or Cybele or Isis. All over Italy people joined the Greek and Asian mystery cults in large numbers.

Some Romans, however, fought this cultural revolution. Typical of the conservatives was Cato the Elder, a second-century statesman who spent his life preaching against the Greek way. He argued that Rome was being ruined by the loss of her ancient virtues. But he was fighting a lost cause. Rome was destined by circumstance and choice to be heir to the magnificent Greek cultural patrimony.

During the first century B.C. Roman writers, artists, and thinkers began to put their own stamp on what they had borrowed. Rome's greatest cultural achievements were produced in the years between 100 B.C. and A.D. 180, especially after the accession of Augustus in 31 B.C. After his death there was a brief slackening; the "golden age" had passed. But a second period of considerable activity, often called the "silver age," took place under the "good emperors" (A.D. 96–180). During these three centuries the Romans added enough to what they had borrowed from Greece to permit us to call the product "Greco-Roman culture."

3. LITERATURE

The most impressive and easily appreciated reflection of the Roman cultural genius is found in literature. The chief masterpieces were produced between about 100 B.C. and A.D. 150, but behind the mature works lay a long period of the formation of Latin as a superb instrument of expression. The early Latin writers were deeply indebted to Greek models for both style and content, but as the Roman genius developed, authors demonstrated unique talent. Roman writers poured into their works a depth of personal conviction, a powerful sense of realism, and a passion for instructing and uplifting readers.

Outstanding among all Roman writers is Vergil (70–19 B.C.). Born in rural Italy, he grew to manhood during the last years of the civil wars. Eventually he attracted the attention of Augustus, whose patronage permitted him to devote the last years of his life to writing. Although much of his great talent was poured out in the service of the new Augustan order, it would be erroneous to overemphasize Vergil's role as a propagandist; he wrote out of deep conviction and enthusiasm. His *Georgics* express a strong feeling for nature and for what involvement in pastoral life can mean—especially to those corrupted by the violence and greed surrounding the last days of the republic. Vergil's masterpiece was an epic poem, the *Aeneid*, which glorifies Rome and shows that her rise to mastery of the world was divinely ordered. The plot centers on the adventures of a Trojan hero, Aeneas, who after the fall of Troy was ordered by the gods to establish in Italy a new city destined to rule the world. The noble Aeneas—an ideal Roman—undergoes a series of supreme tests but obeys the divine order. Never was the Roman ideal of the virtuous patriot portrayed with more force and spiritual intensity.

Two other poets, Catullus and Horace, illustrate another side of the Roman character. Catullus (ca. 85–54 B.C.) was a product of high society in the late republican period. His life was lived amid a dissolute, pleasure-seeking crowd of young nobles. Among his many adventures was a love affair with a noble lady who was already married and who eventually jilted him. The experience inspired him to pour forth powerful lyric poetry. Horace (65–8 B.C.), also a lyric poet, enjoyed the patronage of Augustus and was second in influence only to Vergil, whose intimate

friend he was. His best work, the *Odes*, represents his personal reactions to hundreds of situations he met in his lifetime. Although he lacked the fire of Catullus, Horace spoke to a wider circle, his poems reflecting the reactions of an educated, humane Roman to life as a whole—a great spirit looking at the world about him with sanity, intelligence, and wit. He was and remains the ideal of a civilized man.

Lucretius (ca. 95–55 B.C.) demonstrated still another aspect of Roman poetic genius: moral seriousness. A contemporary of Catullus, he was profoundly moved by events of the civil war era. He found his personal salvation in Epicurean philosophy, which he undertook to explain in a long poem called *On the Nature of Things*. With almost missionary zeal Lucretius put poetry to the service of instruction. He made a noble plea to educated Romans to seek in philosophy the bases of moral regeneration. Seldom has a poet shown greater moral earnestness, idealism, and dignity.

Among the lesser poets were Ovid (43 B.C.–A.D. 17), who entertained Augustan high society with his *Art of Love,* a frivolous but amusing poem on the art of seduction, and his *Metamorphoses*, an entertaining, lively rendering of Greek mythological stories into Latin; and Martial (ca. A.D. 38–102) and Juvenal (ca. A.D. 55–140), both of whom revealed the shortcomings of Roman society in their brilliant satires.

Cicero (106–43 B.C.) was the most famous prose writer in Roman history. Although an active lawyer, magistrate, and statesman, he produced a wide variety of writing, of which his speeches form a large part; he made argumentation an art. In addition, Cicero wrote two important essays on political theory, *Republic* and *Laws,* defending Roman republican institutions but pleading for the establishment of a first citizen to guide the state. He also wrote several philosophical tracts that made abstract Greek thought understandable to Roman readers. His numerous *Letters* supply a brilliant picture of Roman politics and society in the first century B.C. This eloquent, learned Roman made Latin prose capable of expressing any idea.

The earliest historical writing in Latin was influenced by Hellenistic models, but the Romans again discovered their own talent. The most influential Roman historian was Livy (59 B.C.–A.D. 17), another of those inspired to creative activity under the Augustan regime. His masterpiece, the immense *History of the Roman Republic,* covers the period 753 B.C. to A.D. 9. Although a large part of the work has been lost, it is clear from what is left that Livy believed Rome had a great historical mission and wished to instruct his readers on the subject. Livy was not a scientific historian, interested only in the truth; his work was a conglomeration of truth and fiction put together to teach a lesson. Nonetheless, it presented with great dramatic impact the men and events that made Rome great over seven centuries.

Less monumental but equally artistic was Tacitus (ca. A.D. 55–117), who wrote about Roman history after Augustus. His *Histories* and *Annals* covered large portions of the period A.D. 14–96. Although Tacitus was a man of senatorial and republican sentiments, prejudiced against the successors of Augustus, he wrote with brilliance and deep moral sense. Another of his works, *Germania,* gives important information about the barbarians, who were soon to play a larger part in Roman life. Suetonius (ca. A.D. 75–150) vividly portrayed the Roman emperors from Caesar to Domitian in his *Lives of the Twelve Caesars.* The works of Greek writers swelled the body of excellent histories. One of the greatest was Polybius, who lived in Rome from 167 to 151 B.C. as a hostage. He became an intimate of the pro-Hellenic Scipionic circle, and, greatly impressed by the Romans, produced a superb work chronicling Rome's rise to world power. Plutarch (ca. A.D. 46–120) provided a brilliant series of biographies of Greek and Roman men in his *Parallel Lives.* Several Romans produced personal memoirs that were of the nature of histories. Probably the best examples were Julius Caesar's *Commentaries on the Gallic Wars* and Marcus Aurelius' *Meditations.*

During the era when Greek ideas and art forms were first sweeping over the Roman world, attempts were made to imitate the magnificent Greek dramatic art. The most outstanding Roman dramatists were Plautus (third century B.C.) and Terence (second). But drama failed to take root among the Romans. Moreover, only occasionally did a fiction writer grace the literary scene. These gaps in the scope of Roman genres suggest that the creation of highly imaginative literature was foreign to the Romans, who had to be tied to reality—to history, to current moral problems, to personal experiences.

This review of Roman literature, touching on only a handful of the best writers, should leave no doubt that Rome stands independent in the history of literature, for her writers handled great subjects in a powerful style, and countless generations in Western Europe in the centuries following Rome's fall were to be introduced to a civilized view of life by reading them.

4. ART

Rome's most impressive and distinctive artistic field was architecture. Greek models predominated, but the Romans added important elements to what they borrowed. They developed concrete as a building material and used it to form the basic structure of most large buildings. They also perfected and put to new uses the arch and the dome, which had been developed earlier in the Near East. These technical advances permitted the Romans to construct larger buildings and to depart from the horizontal lines that characterized Greek architecture.

The Romans achieved their best results in secular public buildings; they were not, like the Greeks, great temple builders. However, they did effect significant modifications of style in temple-building. The Pantheon, built in Rome in the second century A.D., is the greatest round temple ever built. Its domed roof, made of stone, is 142 feet in diameter and is supported by massive concrete walls. A rectangular porch, its roof supported by Greek columns, leads into the rotunda, supplying a pleasing mixture of Greek and Roman architectural ideas.

Much more distinctly Roman were the public baths, amphitheaters, aqueducts, bridges, meeting halls (basilicas), and palaces that appeared in Rome and in many provincial cities during the two centuries following Augustus. The famous Colosseum at Rome, about half of which still

The enormous amphitheater of the Colosseum, built in the center of Rome near the end of the first century, once accommodated 50,000 spectators at the gladiatorial games. Beneath the floor of the arena (visible in this photograph) were chambers where men, animals, and equipment were kept. *Photo: Bruce Davidson/Magnum*

stands, was built to serve the large audiences who loved the games. This concrete structure measures approximately 617 by 512 feet on the outside. The outer wall rises about 160 feet and consists of three tiers of arcades topped by a blank wall. The arcades carry columns executed in the Greek style whose function is purely decorative. Inside is an arena from which rises banks of seats, each giving a good view. Under-

neath the structure is an intricate network of arched passageways and rooms.

The Roman basilica, built in great numbers in cities all over the empire, is especially significant in architectural history because it served as a model for early Christian churches and for most Christian architecture for centuries after the fall of Rome. The basilica was essentially a long hall flanked by side aisles. The walls of the main hall were built higher than the side aisles, allowing windows to be cut in them. The structures show skillful use of the arch; in the Basilica of Maxentius (early fourth century A.D.), a concrete roof was put over a main aisle 80 feet wide. Roman baths, which consisted of a great central court surrounded by numerous smaller rooms, featured arched vaults and passageways. All these buildings are especially impressive because of their size.

Roman sculpture showed less independence from Greek models than did architecture. Although almost every form of sculpture was produced in great quantity everywhere in the empire, the best work done by the Romans was in realistic portraiture and reliefs treating historical incidents. Even statues of emperors were extremely lifelike, accentuating the dignity and manliness of their subjects but avoiding excessive idealization. The historical scenes carved on triumphal arches or the walls of public buildings are almost photographic. What little we know of Roman painting, used chiefly to decorate buildings, reflects this same sense of realism.

5. PHILOSOPHY, SCIENCE, AND RELIGION

Roman philosophers were chiefly engaged in digesting and explaining those portions of the Greek philosophical tradition that seemed applicable to Roman problems, especially to politics and ethics. They carried on the trend already established in the Hellenistic period of concentrating on the application of philosophical principles rather than on speculation. Rome's greatest accomplishment was, therefore, the transmission of part of the Greek philosophical tradition to areas where it was unknown, especially Western Europe.

Four figures represent the main currents in Roman philosophy. Cicero was eclectic, borrowing from many Greek schools of thought and working out a set of ideas he felt were fitted to Roman society in the first century B.C. Lucretius was a disciple of Epicurus who made a powerful plea for intelligent Romans to abandon the superstitions of traditional religion. He argued that a life of learning and withdrawal from the world was the true source of pleasure. Not all Epicureans, however, followed Lucretius' path; many used Epicurean materialism as an excuse for a life of sensual pleasure.

But most intelligent and sensitive Romans found greater attraction in the more sober and serious philosophy of Stoicism, which was the prevailing philosophical force of the first two centuries of the Christian era. Its two most articulate spokesmen were Seneca (ca. 4 B.C.–A.D. 65) and Marcus Aurelius (A.D. 121–180), whose *Meditations* provides a good reflection of Stoic ideas. By arguing for the need for one state and one law, the Stoics also helped to justify the Roman imperial government.

The Romans did not distinguish themselves in pure science. Their interests were practical and nontheoretical, quite in contrast with the bold speculativeness of Greek thought. The Romans "practiced" science by translating Greek concepts into Latin. Perhaps the most significant advance in science in the Roman period resulted from the efforts of scholars, such as Pliny the Elder (ca. A.D. 23–79), Galen (A.D. 131–201), and Ptolemy (ca. A.D. 121–151), to compile great encyclopedias of scientific information derived chiefly from Greek and Hellenistic sources. Through their compilations a considerable part of Greek science was eventually transmitted to Western Europe.

In putting existing scientific knowledge to practical use, however, the Romans were expert. Rome's engineers were unequaled in antiquity; her roads, aqueducts, and bridges have withstood the ages. The technical skills developed by engineers and artisans formed a precious heritage perhaps as important to the West as was the literary, artistic, and philosophical tradition transmitted by Rome.

While the educated upper class of the Roman world absorbed Greek philosophy and science and adjusted its values accordingly, the basic outlook of the great bulk of society was powerfully affected by religion. Roman religious life was greatly enriched during the era 100 B.C.–A.D. 180 by the spread of the emotional Hellenistic mystery religions throughout the empire. The ideas and practices associated with these cults tended to concentrate attention on personal problems and life after death. Their popularity weakened the appeal of the older Roman family and civic religions which once had played a powerful role in shaping Roman thought.

6. LAW

Perhaps Rome's most enduring cultural monument was her law. Although the evolution of

Roman law was not confined to the period between 100 B.C. and A.D. 180, certain developments in this era decided its final character.

The Romans, unable to conceive of a state without a legal basis, had been concerned with law from the beginning of their history. In this respect they were not unique; other ancient peoples, such as the Hebrews, the Mesopotamians, and the Greeks, thought similarly. Roman law was unique in that it continued to grow century after century. Custom was constantly modified by the legislation of the assemblies in the republican period. Even more important, the chief judicial official of the republic, the *praetor*, was allowed to pronounce his interpretation of the law at the beginning of his term. This practice produced a vast but somewhat confused body of judge-made law that needed constant reinterpretation. Moreover, republican Rome began to develop a kind of international law (*lex gentium*) to apply to noncitizen subjects. It was built on ideas derived from the laws of subject peoples, on Roman legal principles and practices, and on the common-sense decisions of judges who had to dispose of cases involving noncitizens.

In the period 100 B.C.–A.D. 180, efforts were made to codify all Roman law into a single, systematic body. This was prompted by many forces. The imperial government, moving toward a unified administration, saw in a unified code a means of exercising authority. The general trend toward removing the distinctions between Romans and non-Romans was also influential. The extensive legislation by the emperors tended to create uniformity. Stoic philosophy, with its emphasis on a universal law of nature, prompted men to think in terms of a consistent body of law for all society. These forces produced a series of notable legal authorities who devoted their lives to the codification of the law, usually with the wholehearted support of the rulers. Their writings became the basis of legal education, so that most lawyers and public administrators adopted a similar view.

The great jurists sought to relate human laws to natural principles, thus providing the legal system a theoretical basis outside human whim. They sought to make the law consistent but flexible. By the end of the second century A.D., the Roman jurists had by no means completed the standardization of Roman law; that would be done only in the sixth century by the emperor Justinian. But they had established its basic principles. Although law could be derived from many sources, it must be related to the universal order of things, that is, to the natural law. It must be supple enough to bend to changing conditions, yet firmly enough based on principle to avoid manipulation by unscrupulous men. It must serve the needs of all men and not a narrow segment of the population. These principles have survived until the present as the highest ideals of all legal systems.

7. THE ROMANS AS SPREADERS OF CULTURE

One final achievement that must be credited to the Romans is perhaps more important than anything else in their cultural history. The Romans developed a special talent for spreading their culture to backward peoples. From the first century B.C. onward, large areas in the Western part of the empire were rapidly transformed into images of Rome. This transformation was of inestimable importance for the future of Western Europe.

Roman soldiers, officials, and merchants, moving freely about the whole empire, were agents of civilization. The government founded towns in far-flung areas of the empire and encouraged Romans to live there and establish schools in them. The study of grammar and rhetoric, literature, and philosophy spread a common store of ideas and set of tastes to the far corners of the empire. Latin and Greek, the administrative languages of the empire, soon became widely known, providing large numbers of people direct access to the Greco-Roman literary tradition. Emperors built roads, aqueducts, temples, and public buildings throughout the provinces, prompting their residents to imitation. The freedom given to scholars, religious missionaries, philosophers, and artists encouraged them to seek out the culturally backward. Rome opened her doors to men with artistic and intellectual talents from all corners of the empire, thus turning all eyes toward a common cultural center and providing a channel for the spread of culture.

Myriad marks of Roman culture remain. The French and Spanish tongues are direct descendants of the Latin learned in the first and second centuries. When the modern traveler comes across an elaborate bath in the city of Bath in western England or a great amphitheater in

France or a Roman bridge at one of a dozen places, he is encountering evidence of the extent of the Romanization of the Western provinces. Luckily for their subjects, the Romans did not adopt the Greek attitude of looking down on foreigners. Instead, the Romans gave their best to all, and in the process spread civilization over a large area of the world previously caught in barbarism.

Suggested Reading

General Surveys
*Edith Hamilton, *The Roman Way* (Norton). A stimulating treatment, slightly distorted by a tendency to compare the Romans unfavorably with the Greeks.

*D. R. Dudley, *Civilization of Rome* (Mentor). A good brief treatment.

Pierre Grimal, *The Civilization of Rome,* trans. W. S. Maguinnes (1963). The best evaluation of the accomplishments of the Romans.

Religion
Franz Altheim, *A History of Roman Religion,* trans. Harold Mattingly. A superlative treatment.

H. J. Rose, *Ancient Roman Religion* (1948). A brief, somewhat oversimplified treatment, providing a clear description of the Roman concepts of deity and of religious practices.

Literature
*H. I. Marrou, *History of Education in Antiquity* (Mentor). An excellent study, relating Roman literary production to the educational process.

*M. Hadas, *History of Latin Literature* (Columbia).

*H. J. Rose, *Handbook of Latin Literature* (Dutton). Either this or the preceding title will provide a concise, well-organized description of the development of Latin literature.

*M. L. W. Laistner, *The Greater Roman Historians* (University of California). A perceptive evaluation of the major Roman historians.

Art
*M. Wheeler, *Roman Art and Architecture* (Praeger). A convenient introduction to a subject about which much has been written.

*F. E. Brown, *Roman Architecture* (Braziller). A superlative treatment.

A. Maiuri, *Roman Painting* (1953). A sound description on a matter about which our knowledge is limited.

L. DeCamp, *The Ancient Engineers* (1970). Although this volume surveys the development of engineering for the entire ancient period, it does full justice to the accomplishments of the Romans.

Law
Fritz Schulz, *History of Roman Legal Science* (1946). Perhaps the best treatment of the development of Roman law.

Sources
Kevin Guinagh and Alfred P. Darjahn, *Latin Literature in Translation,* 2nd ed. (1952). This anthology provides an excellent sampling of Latin literature. It may encourage the reading of some Latin authors in their entirety. Aside from the works of Livy, Polybius, Tacitus, Suetonius, Cicero, and Caesar cited in previous chapters, the following are particularly recommended:

*Vergil, *Aeneid,* trans. C. Day Lewis (Anchor).

*Horace, *Odes and Epodes,* trans. J. P. Clancy (Phoenix).

*Lucretius, *On the Nature of the Universe,* trans. R. E. Latham (Penguin).

*Ovid, *The Metamorphoses,* trans. Rolfe Humphries (Midland Books).

Stoic Philosophy of Seneca: Essays and Letters, trans. M. Hadas (Norton).

*Marcus Aurelius, *Meditations,* trans. J. H. Staniforth (Penguin).

Retrospect
A moment's reflection on the long period covered in this section might help to give it a clearer shape. Few millennia in all history reveal a greater achievement than that extending from the time when the Greeks began to emerge from their Dark Age in about 800 B.C. to the generation that saw the Roman imperial order reach its full maturity about A.D. 160—the epoch from Homer to Marcus Aurelius. We need not list all those magnificent achievements; the intriguing question is *why* this millennium was so fruitful. What was the special quality that gave Greco-Roman civilization its uniqueness and significance in the total stream of history? The answer is at once simple and profound: It was a civilization that made man and his well-being its central concern. Its motto could well be the slogan of Protagoras and the Sophists: "Man is the measure of all things." Socrates formulated its one commandment: "Know thyself." He likewise defined its motor force when he insisted that self-knowledge made men good.

We cannot help being impressed at how much the Greco-Roman world discovered about man and how great were the energies unleashed by that self-knowledge. At grave risk of oversimplification, we might single out a few of these discoveries as being the foundation stones of Greco-Roman civilization, its value-giving, directive forces. First was the rationality of man. Second was the ordered universe that provided the setting for his activities. Third was rational man's capacity for positive good. Fourth was the capability of man to transcend whatever he was at any instant through knowledge and good action. Last was the political nature of man, which gave him no alternative except to join other men to realize his potential to know, to be good, and to outreach his present condition.

Yet this majestic achievement was somehow flawed, even in the minds of its creators. For one thing, the Greeks and the Romans were never completely convinced that their own vision of man was true. They suspected that in him lurked an elusive element of the demonic and that beyond him existed forces he was powerless to control. Their nagging doubts left open profound and disturbing questions: Was it really sufficient to know oneself? Was it possible? Would such knowledge always produce the good?

Moreover, the kind of society that emerged from the centuries-long effort to create a world fit for reasonable, good, enlightened men had some features that were disturbing. The confidence that political action could achieve perfection had given the state—the Greek *polis*, the Hellenistic monarchies, the Roman Republic, the Roman Empire—a dangerous dominance over men at the expense of other dimensions of their existence. The majestic assumptions about man's rationality and capacity for good had given undue power in society to those who managed to acquire the symbols of rationality and good: an education, offices, wealth, and manners. These aristocrats, seldom quite in the Homeric mold, tended to be oblivious to those who had not been enlightened or blessed with power and prestige. The politicized and intellectualized flavor of classical civilization bred in those who wielded power and participated in the mainstream of cultural life a disdain for other kinds of activity—especially labor—and for other kinds of human behavior—especially that emerging from man's emotional nature. The rationalizing of human conduct and of nature bred an intellectual posture that saw things in terms of absolute, fixed forms and found it extremely difficult to accept or to initiate change.

These insights might well have persuaded men living in the second-century Roman Empire of what now seems fairly evident: Classical men had learned much about human nature and that knowledge had liberated man so that a whole new range of talents was unleashed to enliven and beautify the world, but they had not seen man's whole nature. The civilization they constructed thus had inherent limitations arising from their restricted and distorted view of humanity. Perhaps the end product of the classical world is symbolized by a man who revealed his soul to posterity at the very end of the period—the emperor Marcus Aurelius. Marcus Aurelius was the embodiment of classical man: reasonable, good, serious, politically aware, sensitive to others. As ruler over a marvelous political system, he appeared (by classical standards) to have the power to achieve whatever the good of humanity demanded. Yet in his *Meditations* he emerges as the victim of a cruel joke—a man caught up in a mechanical universe running on forever without change, a man who knew and understood but found nothing to do, a man so good that the nature of evil eluded him, a perfect citizen who was destined to the unappetizing business of fending off stupid barbarians. What was there to do but to resign oneself? One suspects that a kind of bloodless, cold, unemotional resignation in the face of what reason and goodness cannot encompass is what classical civilization finally meant. Something of this attitude is apparent in a Greek statue or in the lines spoken by the chorus in some Greek tragedies. For all its accomplishments, the classical world had still not learned enough about man.

But whatever its limitations, classical civilization had changed the course of history. No nation, no people, no civilization of the future could escape its influence—especially not those inhabitants of Europe who first felt the force of civilized life by being drawn into the Greco-Roman world.

III

The Fall of Greco-Roman Civilization A.D. 180-500

During the second century A.D. Greco-Roman civilization had established unchallenged sway over the Mediterranean basin and extended its influence inland from the sea to three continents—Europe, Asia, and Africa. A vast community had been created within which a bewildering variety of peoples was bound together by powerful forces. The political genius of the Romans, embodied in the imperial system of government, furnished the most potent bond of community. Almost as important were the widely shared cultural concepts that created a common system of values. Derived primarily from the Greeks and finding expression in a remarkable literature, art, philosophy, and learning, this cultural force of unity had been adopted by the Hellenistic world and then by the entire Mediterranean world through the Romans. The shared political system and cultural values were powerfully reinforced by a common economy that linked together the many parts of the Mediterranean world in an interdependent material existence. The simultaneous operation of these unifying forces produced one of the most magnificent eras in all human history.

However, no human order, however strong it appears, is perfect, and no community of men, however confident they are of their talents, is safe from change and its tensions. As the second century A.D. drew to an end, serious stresses and strains emerged within the splendid Mediterranean community the Romans had put together. The long process leading to the formation of that community was reversed, and forces of disintegration became dominant. Although Greco-Roman civilization was endowed with great reserves of strength, they were not enough. Within a relatively short time—only about three centuries—a vast transformation occurred in the Mediterranean basin. Greco-Roman civilization was virtually destroyed, eaten away by incurable sicknesses within its body and torn apart by the assaults of barbarians from outside. The disintegration of that civilization has always held a fascination for students of the past, ultimately prompting them to ask why it is that man's greatest achievement—a mature civilization—cannot be made to last. Intriguing as the question might be, however, the fact is that the end of classical civilization left the vast population of the Mediterranean world with no alternative but to set out again to construct new and viable patterns of life.

An era of change and decline of the Roman Empire began with dramatic suddenness during the century following the death of Marcus Aurelius in 180. In vivid contrast to the *pax romana* of the second century, this period was characterized by almost incessant civil war that deeply disturbed the internal order of the empire and increased its vulnerability to outside attack. Amid the political crisis, economic and social maladjustments surfaced to add to the stress. And intellectual and spiritual confusion sapped the capabilities of society to respond to the growing problems. In retrospect it is clear that the foundations of Greco-Roman civilization were being eaten away and that a desperate sickness was engulfing the Mediterranean world.

1. THE POLITICAL CRISIS, A.D. 180–284

The peaceful, humane regime of the "good emperors" suffered an astonishing reversal after Marcus Aurelius, due largely to the incompetence of his son and successor, Commodus (A.D. 180–192). Marcus Aurelius had turned his back on the adoptive system and had had the misfortune of siring an offspring unable to manage the one office that could sustain the *pax romana*. Amid rising dissatisfaction with Commodus, a brutal struggle over the succession ended in the victory of Septimius Severus (A.D. 193–211), a general of African origin whose career had been with the army.

13

THE DECLINE OF THE EMPIRE AND THE RISE OF CHRISTIANITY

The Severi controlled the imperial office until A.D. 235. Their policy was built on Septimius' advice to pamper the troops who had put them in power and forget the rest of the population. These troops were no longer citizen-soldiers drawn chiefly from Italy. Throughout the second century that element had increasingly resisted military service and was replaced by noncitizens recruited in the provinces and by Germanic barbarians. The new soldiers were concerned primarily with material rewards for service. The Severi provided these rewards: larger pay, pensions, citizenship, and career opportunities in the bureaucracy.

The immediate effect of the Severan favoritism toward the army was an era of anarchy lasting from A.D. 235 to 284, as army units, encouraged with promises of new favors from their ambitious generals, repeatedly sought to elevate their favorites to the purple. Civil war, usually ending in the murder of the reigning emperor, became the order of the day. The victorious new emperor made it his prime business to reward the soldiers. New revolts followed. The *pax romana* had turned to ashes.

Behind the warring, a fundamental change was occurring in the political structure of the empire. The "barrack emperors" were a different breed of men from the earlier rulers: By birth products of the frontier provinces and by experience inclined toward total command, they were insensitive to the problems of civil administration and to the needs of the civilian popula-

tion and had little understanding of the fundamental Augustan principle of sharing power with the aristocracies of Rome and the imperial cities. Their major policy concern was with military well-being. Increasingly, administrative posts were filled from the army at the expense of the Italian aristocracy. The emperors moved inexorably toward more thorough regimentation of civilian society and economic productivity to serve military ends. They imposed a heavier and heavier tax burden on the citizenry to support the demands of the army and the enlarged bureaucracy that was required to enact the emperors' expanding role. They intruded ever more decisively into the political affairs of the previously independent city-states, forcing local aristocracies (*curiales*) to siphon money and manpower to the central government away from local interests. They ceased to respect the privileged role of the Italians in imperial affairs, a policy that culminated in A.D. 212 with Caracalla's extending citizenship to all freemen in the empire. Gradually, the autocratic rulers constructed around their office and persons an aura of religious sanctity. The *princeps*, a first citizen on the model of Augustus or Trajan or Hadrian, was becoming a *dominus*, an absolute lord over all Romans, like an Oriental despot.

Despite the sickening brutality and violence of this era—contrasting so sharply with the peace and order of the preceding age—the militarization of society was a realistic response to some crucial problems. The empire was facing a deepening crisis in defense, especially from two of its ancient foes, the Persians and the Germans. In Persia a new dynasty, the Sassanians, much more aggressive than their predecessors, soon engaged the Romans in a protracted and expensive struggle for mastery in Asia. Simultaneously, small German tribes were coalescing into larger groups far more difficult for the Romans to manipulate and restrain. Other peoples pressed the Germans from behind, driving them to the south and west against Rome's fragile defenses. A vigorously led, well-organized society was needed to face these mounting threats. Perhaps we can also applaud the emergence of autocracy because it broadened Roman citizenship, involved more people in the conduct of political life, and reduced the undue influence of the aristocratic Italians in directing the affairs of a cosmopolitan empire.

Yet the path to autocracy was filled with grave dangers to the established constitution. The seizure of the imperial office by military leaders narrowed considerably the political vision of the government. The concentration of power in the hands of the central government ruined local governments, long the real backbone of the empire, and entrusted the conduct of public affairs to a ruthless bureaucracy open to every form of corruption. The militarization of society reduced the freedom of every group. On balance, the transformation of the Roman imperial government into a military autocracy was destructive of the existing order. Greco-Roman civilization had begun to disintegrate at its most crucial point—the political system.

2. ECONOMIC, SOCIAL, AND CULTURAL DISLOCATIONS

The third century was marked by decreased economic production. Most serious was a decline in agricultural output. In part, this was a result of war-bred destruction, which led to the abandonment of lands in many places, especially along the frontiers, where farms were turned over to barbarian settlers who were not expert farmers. But the major causes were deeper. There appears to have been a shortage of agricultural labor, probably due to a population decline in the entire Mediterranean world. Agricultural technology did not advance, so that nothing was done to offset the inevitable soil depletion and erosion that ultimately affects any established agricultural system. The increasing prevalence of *latifundia* was depressive, chiefly because these estates were increasingly supplied with labor by dependent *coloni*.

Trade and industry suffered an even greater depression. Again, the political chaos was a contributing factor. The brigandage, banditry, and piracy that accompanied the civil wars seriously interfered with the movement of goods. The reckless fiscal policy of the emperors of the third century inflicted terrible financial burdens on traders and artisans. A regular policy of debasing the currency as a means of getting money to reward the army caused inflation and removed a basic requirement for vigorous trade—a sound system of exchange. Heavy taxation bore especially hard on the trading class, whose wealth could be easily seized. State regimentation of the economy limited opportunities for new commercial and industrial ventures. And as in agriculture, basic changes in imperial trading and manufacturing patterns now took a toll. Regions such as Gaul and Spain that once needed to import products from the advanced East were gaining self-sufficiency; as a result, the volume of trade declined. The end of Roman geographical expansion offered no new "backward" lands to generate new trade. New capital was scarce because the directive elements in the Roman world preferred to invest wealth in land or in nonproductive city beautification and luxurious living. New talent was likewise wanting; politics and war were always the more respectable careers for citizens. Finally, the aristocratic cast of society precluded any serious thought of generating commercial and industrial growth by elevating the standard of living of the lower-class members of society.

The whole texture of society was changing significantly by the third century. The military autocrats ruthlessly eliminated the aristocrats of Rome and Italy from their ancient places in the central administration and in the army. In cities throughout the empire, local aristocracies were crushed by the burden of taxation and deprived of their control over local affairs by increasing hordes of bureaucrats representing the central authority. Had the lower classes benefited from the decline of the aristocracy, the loss might not have been so serious. But the urban lower classes were increasingly regimented and their social position debased. Artisans and laborers in the cities were forced into compulsory associations (*collegia*) through which their wages and production were tightly controlled in the interests of the state. The peasantry, increasingly driven toward hereditary tenancy, were becoming virtual slaves. These trends in society obviously reduced the benefits of membership in the great Roman community.

Meanwhile, two elements in Roman society drew advantage from the changing order: great landlords and soldiers. The owners of large estates tightened their control on agricultural production and the labor force. The state, interested chiefly in securing revenue and produce from the land, gave the landowners greater freedom to exploit the peasantry and pass on to them the burden of taxation. As their control over the *coloni* increased, the great estateholders moved inexorably toward independence and the satisfaction of their local self-interest, a process that gravely threatened the unity of the Mediterranean community. At the same time, a soldier of ability could work his way to a high position in society, perhaps to the imperial throne. Even the lower ranks of the army enjoyed all kinds of favors not open to other citizens. This elevation of the military element in society had evil effects. On an ever-increasing scale, soldiers were recruited from the most primitive areas of the empire or from among barbarians willing to serve Rome. These people, little acquainted with Roman ideas and institutions, now moved to the leadership of society. The result was a barbarizing of Roman life.

Even more serious was the inability of the Roman world to generate intellectual and spiritual energies to combat the political, economic, and social problems. The third century was one of the least productive periods of the whole classical era. Writers, artists, and thinkers merely imitated the past without any zest or creative power. They seemed to have lost faith in the

Another kind of imperial commemorative monument was the free-standing column, such as the one built in the second century to celebrate the emperor Trajan's victory over the barbarian Dacians. This detail shows Roman soldiers defending their position against a Dacian attack. Such attacks, repeated on all the borders of the empire from the second century on, eventually broke through the frontier. *Photo: Alinari/ Art Reference Bureau*

humanistic, rationalistic values of the Greco-Roman tradition; man and his vaunted powers at last seemed inadequate to the realities of a troubled world.

But the human spirit was seeking refuge and meaning in another realm—religion. The third century was alive with powerful religious currents which together seriously threatened the classical world view. The Oriental mystery faiths, with their personal deities, their promises of eternal salvation, and their emotional rituals, won increasing numbers of adherents at all levels of society. The ancient civic deities of Greece and Rome drew intensified support as well. There was a vast resurgence of interest in astrology and magic. Even philosophy was permeated by a religious, mystical element, as demonstrated by the great vogue of Neoplatonism in the third century, especially after its tenets were systematized by the Egyptian-born Plotinus (A.D. 205–270). Although immensely complex in the form delineated by Plotinus, Neoplatonism basically denied the importance of the material world, characterizing it as unreal and evil-ridden, and asked its adherents to surrender to a contemplative life that would lead them step by step to an ecstatic mystical union with eternal, nonmaterial Reality. In its essence Neoplatonism symbolized the whole spiritual thrust of this age — the search for knowledge and light through a mystical contact with the divine. In this quest human reason played a small part, and many of the old Greco-Roman values seemed to have small relevance.

3. THE BEGINNINGS OF CHRISTIANITY

One particular spiritual movement was destined to reshape history: the religion called Christianity, which made its adherents a "new people" apart from the mainstream of Greco-Roman civilization.

Christianity at its beginning certainly did not seem destined to be a revolutionary force. It began as a splinter movement among the Jews, who had already earned a reputation as adherents of unique religious ideas and as threats to any established order. Christianity arose in a Jewish world that was charged with tension born out of repeated frustrations of the effort to recover lost national independence and out of expectations that eventually God's promise of supremacy for his Chosen People would be fulfilled. Since the destruction of the Hebrew kingdom in 586 B.C. by the Chaldeans, the Jews had dreamed of the day when their political freedom would be restored. The Persians had allowed them to rebuild the Temple in Jerusalem and to sustain a religious community, but that was not sufficient to those who cherished the memory of David and Solomon and who were exhorted by the prophets to stand apart in the world. The Maccabean Revolt in 165 B.C. against the Hellenistic Seleucid kingdom had brought the Jews close to independence, but hope vanished when Rome took over Palestine in 63 B.C. The Romans were generous in conceding religious privileges to the Jews but were suspicious and repressive in the face of any threat of Jewish independence.

The frustration of their national aspiration had by the first century B.C. bred serious division within the Jewish community. Most Jews accepted the idea proclaimed by earlier prophets that a God-sent Messiah would deliver them from their oppressors. And they all sought to abide by the Judaic law as it was interpreted by a special group of learned men called *scribes*. But they disagreed on how to act in the immediate historic setting. The Sadducees, chiefly upperclass Jews, favored compromise with the Romans in the interests of peace and religious freedom so that the Jews could continue to live as a religious community according to Judaic law. The Pharisees, enjoying strong popular backing, were violently opposed to the intrusion of foreign ideas and customs into Jewish life. Smaller groups of radicals opted for more drastic solutions. The Zealots were willing to take up arms against the Romans. The Essenes sought to break through the letter of Hebraic law to spiritual purity and to realize their ideals by withdrawal from the Jewish community into an ascetic life. Added to these groups were innumerable individual prophets, such as John the Baptist, crying out that deliverance was at hand. Of considerable importance were the Jews of the Diaspora — those dispersed by accident or choice to all corners of the Mediterranean world during the centuries prior to Roman rule — who had been strongly influenced by Greco-Roman ideas and tended to incorporate these into their religious views. In many cities they had earned deep respect from the non-Jewish population for their piety and moral earnestness.

Into this complex and highly charged scene came Jesus, born probably in 4 B.C. as the Augustan order was taking shape. When he reached maturity, he went forth among the Jews preaching a message that was grounded in the Judaic tradition but had an appealing freshness. He proclaimed that God's promised kingdom was at hand and that men must immediately prepare for it by repentance and spiritual regeneration based on repudiation of the world and on love for God and men. He did not ask his followers to abandon their Jewish heritage but insisted that they must transcend simple observance of the law and performance of the traditional rituals by opening their hearts to God's grace. To those who repented and accepted his message, he promised eternal salvation. His message attracted an enthusiastic following — but it also earned enemies. His attack on the formalism of Jewish religion and the materialism of religious leaders turned "the scribes and the Pharisees" against him. To them, he was a threat to the whole fabric of historic Judaism. Many of his early followers lost much of their enthusiasm when he made it clear that his mission was not to create or rule an earthly kingdom and that he would not take up the sword to liberate the Jews. This combination of hostility and reduced support ended with his crucifixion by the Romans in the interest of maintaining peace in the Jewish community.

Jesus' death triggered a crucial development. A group of his stoutest disciples was convinced that he had arisen from the dead, proving that he was the Christ ("the annointed"), the Messiah, sacrificed to ensure salvation. This belief set the little band apart from the whole world; in the words of Paul, "We preach Christ crucified, a stumbling block to Jews and folly to the Gentiles . . ." (I Cor. 1:23). A new religion had been born.

4. THE SPREAD OF CHRISTIANITY

The first Christian community in Jerusalem was vigorous, its members observing the Judaic law while also holding to Jesus' precepts. Soon their ideas spread to other cities, where they attracted the attention of Diaspora Jews and Gentile sympathizers with Judaism. Before long, many were asking to join the new community and were being received. This development posed a grave question for the foundling movement: whether or not new converts were to be held to strict observance of Judaic law and practices. There were those in the primitive Christian community who took a conservative position, but others, typified by Peter, leader of the disciples, increasingly insisted on universalizing Christianity so that it would be acceptable to Jew and Gentile alike.

The major figure in the mission to the Gentiles was Paul. A Jew born at Tarsus, where he gained considerable exposure to Greco-Roman thought, he was initially a persecutor of Christians but then was suddenly converted to Christianity. Convinced that he had been marked by the Lord "to carry his name before the Gentiles, and kings, and children of Israel" (Acts 9:15), he began a long career of preaching that took him to Asia Minor, Greece, and eventually Rome. His message emphasized those precepts of Jesus that had universal application — the redemption effected by the Son of God; the need for moral regeneration through faith and love of God and man; salvation as a reward for belief in the Christ; purity of moral life. By the time of his martyrdom in Rome (perhaps about A.D. 67), the thrust toward making Christianity a universal religion had become dominant, and Christianity and Judaism had moved irreparably apart.

Once launched in the Pauline direction, Christianity steadily spread over most parts of the Roman world. During at least the first century after Jesus' death, a series of dedicated missionary preachers working under all kinds of conditions were the chief agents of expansion. They concentrated their efforts in the major cities of the empire, so that Christianity developed chiefly as an urban religion. Often these missionary preachers began their activities in the synagogues of the city. Their efforts usually won a small group of adherents who became self-sustaining "churches" and who labored to win new followers. By the end of the third century, Christian communities existed everywhere in the empire. The heaviest Christian population was in the cities of Egypt, Syria, Palestine, Asia Minor, Greece, and Italy. By A.D. 285, although Christians certainly formed only a small minority of the total population, they had become a potent factor in the Roman world, one far exceeding what might have been expected in view of their early struggles.

The progress of Christianity was not, however, painless and automatic. One obstacle was provided by the Roman government, which viewed the Christians with suspicion and from time to time persecuted them because of their refusal to worship the state gods. This stand made it impossible for them to fulfill many of their civic responsibilities, including army service, and caused the state to view them as lacking in patriotism. Usually the persecutions were local and temporary, although in the third century more serious attempts were made to exterminate Christianity.

The Christians also met opposition of a less official but more menacing nature from various elements of the Roman populace. Among the masses of people there spread a battery of vile rumors about strange beliefs and immoral, bestial practices, rumors fed by the Christian refusal to participate in public religious rites and by their private, semisecret services. Roman intellectuals scorned Christianity, holding up for ridicule its simplistic, illogical concepts. The leaders of the state religion and of the Jewish synagogues constantly charged the Christians with false beliefs and debased practices. These foes of the new religion became especially dangerous during the third-century troubles, when the accusation was often made that false worshipers in society's midst made the gods angry. On occasion, the government itself intervened to protect Christians from violence.

The Christians made difficulties for themselves as well. From the very beginning, there were divisions in their ranks on what constituted right belief and proper usage. The early communities disagreed on the nature of the relationship between Christianity and Judaism. The proper moral posture for a Christian was often a subject for debate, especially because some insisted on a puritanical denial of the world and its pleasures. By the second century and increasingly in the third, Christians disagreed violently on certain fundamental doctrines, thus generating what may be called the first heresies. These conflicts inevitably set Christian against Christian and diverted the faithful from proselytizing.

5. REASONS FOR CHRISTIANITY'S RISE

Yet Christianity grew. Its success was due to many factors, not the least of which were favorable conditions in the Roman Empire. The empire was so knit together that the movement of ideas was easy. Despite isolated cases of persecution, an atmosphere of tolerance generally prevailed. The growing power of centralized government and the decline of city-states weakened civic religions and caused people to seek individual spiritual satisfaction, while the chaos of the third century made the need for personal fulfillment even more urgent. The emergence of a single state uniting many peoples into one society made a religion that would apply to all men regardless of origin or class seem natural.

Another source of Christian strength lay in its appeal as a religion. No matter how far in other directions we push the search for an explanation of its expansion, it is always evident that Christianity won converts primarily because its teachings answered their deepest religious needs. Such ideas as the existence of one almighty, loving, merciful God; his sacrifice of his son to redeem men; eternal salvation based on individual worth; damnation for sinners; and universal brotherhood together supplied a powerful answer to those seeking to know about God's ways toward men. The humanity of Jesus, who had lived on earth not long before, gave an intimacy to Christianity that other religions lacked. Moreover, Christian teachings were dramatically and simply presented in the New Testament, which began to take form immediately after Jesus' death.

Another basic reason for success was the organization that took shape during the first three centuries after Christ. The earliest structure was simple. Christians in a community met to worship in private dwellings for a common meal imitating the last supper of Christ and for prayer and song. Certain individuals were recognized as natural leaders and instructors; later in the first century, they were given titles like *bishop*, *presbyter*, and *elder*. With the passage of time, disputes within the Christian body, persecutions, and increasing wealth led to new problems demanding firmer and larger organization. Authority began to settle in the bishop, who undertook to settle matters of discipline, doctrine, property, and worship, exercising the concept of apostolic succession: By virtue of his ordination, each was the spiritual successor to the original apostles sent forth by Jesus to proclaim the faith. The bishop's authority almost always coincided with the boundaries of a city-state, an indication that the Christians were imitating the political organization of the empire. In some of the larger cities, presbyters, or *priests*, were put in charge of each church, but all priests remained under the authority of the bishop. In effect, the Christian world was evolving toward a structure of self-contained, self-governing units.

Christians never lost sight of their bonds of unity, early forged by Jesus' disciples and the missionary leaders. Later, bishops from large areas met to decide common problems and to apply these decisions in each locality, thus establishing *church councils* with legislative and judicial powers. Before the end of the third century, there was already a movement to establish a final authority. Some of the chief bishops, such as those of Jerusalem, Antioch, Alexandria, and Rome, were exerting considerable influence. The bishop of Rome gained prestige because of Rome's position as capital of the empire but also because of an important doctrine, the *Petrine theory*, that had begun to take shape. According to this doctrine, Jesus had granted Peter a special place as his vicar on earth; Peter had chosen Rome as the seat of that power; and later bishops of Rome exercised the same authority. By A.D 285, Peter's successors, designated as *popes* (derived from the late Latin word for "father"), were turning this claim to spiritual supremacy into active leadership in defining doctrine and prescribing discipline for Christian communities over much of the Roman Empire. And many of these communities were seeking the pope's guidance, especially in doctrinal matters; some accepted his decisions as law. A kind of second Roman Empire was being born, subdivided into well-governed local units and headed by a spiritual "emperor."

Christianity also increased its appeal, especially to the sophisticated upper classes, by developing a systematic, reasoned statement of its fundamental beliefs. This articulation of its doctrine in literary form marked a rather dramatic departure from primitive Christianity. Jesus had preached in Aramaic to an audience that was largely apart from the mainstream of Greco-Roman intellectual and literary life. The early leaders of the new religion were quite open in their rejection of pagan culture, and thus established an anti-intellectual bias in the Christian

This bas-relief shows two major figures of the early Christian Church, the apostles Peter and Paul. *Photo: Alinari/Art Reference Bureau*

community. However, this posture did not survive long. As soon as the Christians began to convert Gentiles, they had to employ Greek and Latin and the modes of thought prevailing in the Roman Empire. By the second century and more pronouncedly in the third, two particular forces spurred the Christians toward intellectualization: the need to answer the accusations of non-Christian intellectuals that the new religion was irrational, and the problem of resolving differences within the Christian ranks on the meaning of basic doctrines. The "apologists" answering the critics and the theologians defining the exact meaning of the faith borrowed heavily from Greco-Roman philosophy, especially the Platonic tradition. The most influential figures in this movement wedding Christian thought and Greco-Roman culture were two scholars from Alexandria, Clement (ca. 150–216) and Origen (ca. 185–254). Their efforts increasingly persuaded Christians that classical learning had been a preparation for the true revelation and was therefore useful in illuminating the meaning of God's word. The absorption of classical learning by Christianity had begun, to the great advantage of Christianity.

For those who were not capable of absorbing the lofty ideas of the theologians, Christianity developed a ritual that could compete on equal terms in a society accustomed to splendid religious pageants, highly emotional practices of worship, and the nonreligious spectacles provided in the circuses. To a large extent this involved adapting existing customs. Churches were built and decorated with art inspired by doctrine. Services were conducted by a clergy in rich attire. The common meal became the center of a ritual that emphasized Christ's sacrifice (the beginning of the Mass). Prayer and music became more elaborate, and ceremonies were instituted for such events as baptism, marriage, and burial. Holidays commemorating the highlights of Jesus' life and the death of early martyrs were celebrated. Although modern men sometimes scoff at this aspect of religious life, splendid public ritual doubtless increased Christianity's appeal, especially to the vast majority of people, for whom religion is a matter more of feeling than of thought.

The Christian movement also developed a strong social consciousness. Jesus in his teachings and his life repeatedly exemplified the need for charity and kindness in dealing with others. This idea received expression in Christian practice almost from the beginning. Christians poured out their resources to help the sick, the poor, criminals, slaves, orphans, widows, and other unfortunates in society. In spite of their belief that happiness came in the hereafter, the early Christians did not close their eyes to earthly affairs.

Yet did the growth of Christianity contribute to the decline of the Roman Empire? In many ways, the Christian was a good Roman. He performed his duties as long as he was not required to deny his god. He paid his taxes and obeyed the emperor. He tried his best to help the unfortunate members of his community. He read books on Christian theology that contained huge portions of Greco-Roman philosophy. He worshiped in a fashion that bore a strong resemblance to non-Christian worship. At least the Christian was not an open rebel, bent on pulling down the established order.

In more important other ways, he was not a good Roman. He served a god who would tolerate no rivals, including Roman emperors who claimed divinity. Believing that his god disapproved of the ways of non-Christian men, he tended to avoid involvement in worldly affairs. His strong sense of sin led him to regard the world, including the Roman Empire, as hardly worth saving. His belief in the omnipotence of God and in human frailty caused him to distrust human reason and man's ability to build a paradise on earth. He thus found little that appealed to him in the basic premise of Greco-Roman civilization: the conviction that enlightened human activity could create a perfect society on earth. The Christian was a devoted, disciplined member of an organization existing independently of the Roman state. Through art, literature, and religious services, the Church kept constantly before him a series of symbols and arguments that made him feel his separateness and his uniqueness. Every Christian convert meant one less Roman citizen in the fullest sense of the word.

What has just been said about Christianity applies to a lesser degree to the other Eastern religions of the third century. The followers of Mithra, Isis, the Unconquerable Sun, and Dionysus all found new ends to serve and gave all their energies in that service. These new religions ate away at the heart of the worldly, politically oriented thinking of Greco-Roman civilization. When men began serving these deities to gain an eternal reward, they lost interest in serving the emperor for worldly prizes.

As the third century drew to a close, Rome and all she stood for seemed destined for quick destruction. Political chaos, external assaults, economic decline, social turmoil, and desertion to foreign religions all coincided to strain the imperial structure to its limit. There was little sign of eventual recovery, for seldom had Roman leadership seemed less inspired and more selfish and brutal.

Suggested Reading

Overview of the Period A.D. 180–500

*Peter Brown, *The World of Late Antiquity, A.D. 150–750* (Harcourt Brace Jovanovich).

A. H. M. Jones, *The Decline of the Ancient World* (1966). This and the preceding work are brilliant brief treatments of the decline of the Roman Empire.

Joseph Vogt, *The Decline of Rome*, trans. J. Sondheimer (1967). The best detailed analysis of the conditions that produced Rome's decline.

*C. G. Starr, *Civilization and the Caesars* (Norton). An excellent discussion of the intellectual revolution accompanying the fall of Rome.

*Donald Kagan, *Decline and Fall of the Roman Empire: Why Did It Collapse?* (Heath).

*Mortimer Chambers, *The Fall of Rome: Can It Be Explained?* (Holt). These two collections offer a variety of explanations by modern scholars of the fall of Rome.

S. Mazzarino, *The End of the Ancient World*, trans. G. Holmes (1966).

*R. M. Haywood, *The Myth of Rome's Fall* (Apollo). This and the preceding work provide excellent summaries of the many approaches to the collapse of the Roman world.

Third-Century Crisis

H. D. M. Parker, *History of the Roman World From A.D. 138 to 337,* 2nd ed. (1958). A detailed political history.

M. I. Rostovtzeff, *Social and Economic History of the Roman Empire,* 2 vols., 2nd ed. (1957). Invaluable in assessing the social and economic problems of the late empire.

*Franz Cumont, *Oriental Religions in Roman Paganism* (Dover). An excellent treatment of the volatile religious situation in the empire.

Rise of Christianity

*Emil Schürer, *History of the Jewish People in the Time of Jesus* (Schocken). A clear, balanced treatment.

*Henry Chadwick, *The Early Church* (Penguin).

*J. G. Davies, *The Early Christian Church* (Anchor). Either this or the preceding title will provide brief surveys of early Christian history.

J. Daniélou and H. I. Marrou, *The First Six Hundred Years* (*The Christian Centuries,* Vol. I), trans. V. Cronin (1964). A longer work by two world-renowned authorities who incorporate the latest scholarship in their survey.

*W. H. Frend, *Martyrdom and Persecution in the Early Church* (Anchor). A splendid treatment of the relationship between the Roman state and the early Christians.

J. Daniélou, *The Development of Christian Doctrine Before the Council of Nicaea* (1964). A well-organized, clearly presented treatment of a complex subject.

E. R. Dodds, *Pagan and Christian in the Age of Anxiety* (1965).

*C. N. Cochrane, *Christianity and Classical Culture* (Galaxy). These two works treat with great insight the relationships and interactions of Christianity and classical culture.

J. A. Jungmann, *The Early Liturgy to the Time of Gregory the Great* (1959). Traces the development of Christian practices of worship from the beginning down to about A.D. 600.

J. G. Davies, *Daily Life in the Early Church* (1952). Provides fascinating glimpses of the simpler aspects of early Christian society.

Sources

New Testament. The best source of information on the primitive Church.

*Eusebius, *History of the Church From Christ to Constantine,* trans. G. A. Williamson (Penguin). An early Christian version of the history of the primitive Church by a fourth-century author.

Early Christian Fathers, trans. C. C. Richardson (1953). A collection presenting selections from the writings of early Christian thinkers.

14

THE DESTRUCTION OF THE ROMAN EMPIRE, 284-500

In A.D. 285 a general named Diocletian seized the imperial throne by force. In itself this was a repetition of what had happened during the preceding century; however, the accession of Diocletian heralded a new period. He and his most important successor, Constantine, undertook a thorough reform of the empire in an attempt to check its steady decline. Their work gave it a reprieve but did not eliminate the basic forces that were eating away the vital centers of Greco-Roman civilization. By the end of the fourth century, the empire was unable to resist the onslaught of the barbarian Germans, who during the next century smashed the empire and brought to an end a whole civilization.

1. THE REFORMS OF DIOCLETIAN AND CONSTANTINE

The way for Diocletian was paved during the years from about 260 to 284, when a series of rulers began the process of curbing the civil wars and pacifying the empire. A Dalmatian by birth and a soldier by experience, Diocletian fit the pattern of so many previous emperors. He did have, however, considerable political talent and a clear insight into the basic problems facing the Roman world. He acted with decisiveness to restore order, stability, and prosperity to the empire.

Disturbed by the chaos the civil wars brought to the succession system and by the ever-increasing responsibility imposed on the single emperor, Diocletian evolved a new arrangement affecting the imperial office aimed at assuring orderly succession and shared responsibility. To himself and another he gave the title *augustus* and established for each a subordinate designated as a *caesar*. When an augustus died, his caesar would succeed to his office and immediately appoint another caesar. In theory the four co-rulers shared the imperium; in practice the burden of administering the empire was divided. It was partitioned into four parts, called *prefectures;* each augustus and caesar assumed full power to govern one of these units with Diocletian providing overall direction.

More significant was Diocletian's effort to solidify the absolute authority of the four co-rulers. He made no pretense of consulting with the Senate and the people. His pronouncements were presented as law. To create a new image, he followed Oriental precedents in making the imperial office appear sacred: He withdrew himself from public view as much as possible and established an elaborate court ritual designed to associate the ruler with divine powers in the exercise of his authority. The traditional *princeps*, first citizen, had disappeared in favor of a charismatic *dominus*, lord, whose will must be obeyed without question.

Diocletian also undertook practical measures to tighten and extend the imperial administrative system. At each of the four courts officials were designated to direct carefully organized administrative departments manned by an ex-

This famous grouping which stands now outside St. Mark's in Venice, shows the augusti Diocletian and Maximian with their caesars, Constantius and Galerius. *Photo: Alinari/Art Reference Bureau*

tensive corps of civil servants. The responsibility of these officials was to see to it that the imperial will was applied promptly and uniformly throughout the empire. The provincial administration within each prefecture was more rigorously organized and made responsive to the central government. The number of provinces was increased, and the provinces were grouped into intermediary administrative units called *dioceses,* of which there were twelve. The building of this bureaucratic hierarchy allowed the central administration to act more directly and more uniformly in local affairs, and it all but ended the active role of local city governments.

Deeply concerned with the military establishment upon which the state was so dependent, Diocletian took steps to increase its effectiveness. He restructured it into two components. One consisted of an infantry army settled along the frontier to absorb the chief blows of outside attackers. The second was a mobile cavalry force held as a reserve to move quickly to meet particular dangers. This reorganization considerably increased the size of the army and raised monumental problems of recruitment and support.

All these imposed an even greater financial burden on the imperial government than it had had to face during the third century. Diocletian met this challenge by reorganizing the financial system. A survey of the empire was undertaken to establish taxable units of land and to identify taxable human beings as a basis for assessments in kind and money. The services of key productive elements in society were also made subject to requisitions by the state. The huge income in produce, money, and services thus collected was then distributed to feed and equip the armies, pay the bureaucrats, and support the court. Diocletian also undertook a massive regimentation of the imperial economy. In 301 he decreed a system of fixed prices and other measures aimed at checking inflationary pressures. To keep producers on their jobs, the gov-

ernment sought to freeze men in their jobs. Peasants, artisans, traders, bureaucrats, and many others were forbidden to change their work, and sons had to step into their fathers' shoes in many occupations. A kind of hereditary caste system was being shaped under imperial direction. Increasingly, citizens of the Roman Empire had but one end for which to live—service to the state.

Diocletian's expanding autocracy sought to focus men's minds on the state through the restoration of religious unity. His reign was marked by a major effort to rally the populace around a worship of the old deities, whose agent the divine emperor was. This policy brought him into conflict with the increasingly numerous and confident Christians who steadfastly refused to make obeisance to these gods or the state that honored them. Their position was intolerable within Diocletian's frame of reference, and a series of punitive decrees in 303 and 304 made death the penalty for defiance. His assault on the Christians was the most serious threat they ever faced from the Roman government. They were to survive and triumph, but Diocletian's persecution symbolized the degree to which religion had come to be viewed as the sustaining force in the Roman imperial regime.

In 305 the aged and ill Diocletian abdicated his power. Although contemporaries, particularly Christians, judged him harshly, his strong measures had proved effective. Internal order was restored, the defenses were holding, the administrative machinery was operating effectively again, and adequate resources were available to the state. Diocletian had established the pattern of government that was to prevail until the empire collapsed. But immediately after his abdication, another series of civil wars erupted, chiefly because his succession scheme did not work. They ended only when Constantine fought his way to control over the entire empire, a goal he did not finally accomplish until 324. Constantine was a worthy successor to Diocletian and carried on most of his policies. He strengthened the armies, tightened bureaucratic controls, further improved the financial machinery, and took more power into his own hands. Through his efforts the absolutist, bureaucratic, militaristic state envisaged by Diocletian—a dominate—was made a reality. The Augustan principate was dead.

Constantine added important elements to the new order. Most significant was his reversal of religious policy in 313, when he and his co-emperor issued the Edict of Milan, granting religious toleration to all in the empire. The edict meant the end of the terrible persecution of Christians that had begun in 303–304 as well as legal recognition of Christianity. Behind the decree was an event of immense importance: the conversion of Constantine himself. During the decisive battle of his career, in 311, he had had a vision that promised him victory if he would display the cross as his insignia. He did this and smashed his enemy. Although in fact he was not baptized until just before his death in 337, after

the edict Constantine gave every indication that he was intent on promoting Christian causes. He poured out money to build churches. He drew clergymen into the councils of state as advisers and extended a variety of special privileges to them. His legislation increasingly reflected Christian teachings in matters such as slavery and marriage. True, he did not openly attack other religions, but he treated them in a way that little encouraged them. Every sign pointed in one direction: that Christianity was the favored religion and that the empire was becoming a Christian state. Contemporary Christians hailed Constantine's conversion as a triumphant fulfillment of God's promise. The evidence suggests, however, that his decision was prompted by powerful political motives. The strength of the Christians had been demonstrated by their resistance to the persecutions of Diocletian. Also, if he could become the servant of the god who gave him victory in battle, would he not be able to unify his subjects and ensure the safety and well-being of his empire? His religious policy therefore was motivated by a desire to put the Christian world view to the service of the state: to make the empire the agency of the Christian god, the emperor his almighty servant, and the citizenry a single community worshiping that god so as to earn his favors. This was not cynical manipulation of religion; it emerged from genuine religious convictions. Constantine was a man of his age, powerfully drawn to religion. His mother, Helen, was a Christian, and his own writings and contemporary testimony indicate that he was deeply moved by Christian ideas. And the evidence used to cast doubts on Constantine's conversion is not very convincing. Deathbed baptisms were usual in his day. His tolerance of paganism reflects the basic fact that he did not have the power to wipe out at will religions that had been practiced for centuries. Constantine was indeed the first Christian emperor both by conviction and in practice. His yoking of the Roman Empire and the Christian community was a momentous event in world history.

Equally momentous was Constantine's decision to build a new capital at the ancient city of Byzantium (which he renamed Constantinople). This action not only created a rival to "old" Rome but also shifted the center of imperial power to the East. The great change was no mere autocratic whim. Rome had been declining in importance in imperial affairs. As early as the second century, men of non-Roman origin had been elevated to the imperial throne, and their local attachments diminished Rome's aura. Also, during the third century the problems of defending the frontiers revealed that Rome was badly located strategically. Diocletian's reorganization of the empire into four prefectures led to the emergence of new centers of political authority. Diocletian established his own headquarters at Nicomedia in Asia Minor, while his co-rulers established their courts in Milan, Sirmium in the Balkans, and Trier in the Rhineland area, choices dictated primarily by military considerations.

In 324, the year that he won the final battle for supremacy, Constantine began construction of his new capital; it was dedicated in 330. He chose the site in part for very practical reasons. It was admirably situated for defense by land and sea. From it the imperial forces had easy access to the most vulnerable and hard-pressed frontiers—the Danube region and the Eastern provinces. The new city was close to the great centers of wealth in the East, whence came the chief resources of the imperial government. And it was situated where Christian strength was greatest, a matter of considerable importance to an emperor identifying himself with a religious minority. Aside from these practical aims, Constantine wished to be free from the restrictive traditions of republicanism and paganism that were entrenched in old Rome as threats to his autocracy and new religious policy.

The full impact of the founding of Constantinople was not immediately obvious. Rome still remained an important city upon which Constantine showered favors, not the least of which was a great Christian church built in honor of St. Peter on Vatican Hill at a site where the bones of the first pope were believed to be buried. Yet the relocation did have a powerful psychological impact on contemporaries. To many who cherished ancient values, it seemed that Constantine had turned the world around, allowing the East

to surpass the West, the Greek to predominate over the Latin. And in the near future, when outsiders threatened to conquer both East and West, the rulers in Constantinople chose to defend "new" Rome and let "old" Rome and the West fall victim to the barbarians.

2. THE LULL BEFORE THE STORM

The vast reorganization of imperial forces carried out by Diocletian and Constantine appeared to have saved the empire: The era from Constantine's death in 337 to the end of the reign of Theodosius (379–395) was one of relative calm and order. There was a fairly regular hereditary succession of emperors, with little civil strife. Agriculture, trade, and industry seemed to hold their own, albeit under rigid state control. Society, carefully manipulated, appeared even content. The Roman political genius seemed again to have saved the civilized world, as in the days of Augustus.

Yet, as is now evident, the old sicknesses persisted. There was no real economic growth. The citizens were more apathetic than ever in supporting the state. Social developments continued to destroy the city aristocracy and depress the peasantry. The menace along the frontiers did not disappear. To these familiar ills were added new ones. The absolutist, militarized state became a monster consuming the wealth of the empire and crushing the spirit of its citizens. The bureaucracy grew more costly, rapacious, corrupt, and inefficient. Regimentation of the economy stifled all enterprise and growth. The imperial policy of favoring Christianity alienated those who still placed trust in the pagan religious tradition. Pagan resentment surfaced during the reign of Julian (360–363), called the "Apostate" by the Christians because he repudiated Christianity and sought to replace it with a restored pagan "church." His effort failed, but it kept alive a fundamental schism in imperial society and thought.

The Julian reaction points up the fact that Christianity did not fulfill the role Constantine expected of it in unifying the state and stirring patriotic fervor. It did continue its triumphant march to dominance, culminating when Theodosius made it the state religion and outlawed all others, but during the fourth century the movement was rent with internal disagreements that promoted disorders. Even during the reign of Constantine, the Christians divided into two warring factions, the Arians and the Orthodox, over the question of the Trinity: The Arians made God the Son subordinate to God the Father, denying the absolute divinity of Christ; the Orthodox insisted that the Son was co-equal with the Father and that the two persons, plus the Holy Spirit, formed a unity. An attempt to settle this quarrel was made at the Council of Nicea in 325. Churchmen from all over the empire met under the auspices of Constantine and agreed on the Nicene Creed, which accepted the Orthodox definition of the nature of Christ. However, the quarrel continued to rage for a century, involving the imperial government as did other "heresies" that divided the Christian community and the empire. Then too, the Constantinian subordination of the Christian Church to the imperial government generated active resistance to imperial domination of Christian life, providing still another source of contention and struggle. In a larger sense, Christianity failed to supply the vitalizing force in the "new" empire; it was a movement with its own ends and strengths, not easily bent to other purposes.

All these signs of deteriorating imperial strength and internal friction were extremely ominous, for a crisis was in the making as the fourth century drew to a close. Its source lay in Central Europe, an area beyond the control of the imperial regime, and involved the Germanic barbarians, whose pressure on Rome's defenses had been constant throughout the fourth century. About 370 a wild horde of Asiatic nomads, the Huns, suddenly swept out of the East across southern Russia. When they approached the Black Sea area, they encountered two settled Germanic nations, the Ostrogoths and the Visigoths. The former were quickly overpowered. The terror-stricken Visigoths begged permission to migrate across the Danube into Roman territory in the Balkans. Their request was granted. The Visigoths were allowed to keep their own king and were promised lands in return for mili-

tary service. When the imperial government failed to provide for their needs, the Visigoths revolted. The emperor Valens marched against them but suffered a smashing defeat at Adrianople in 378. Rome now had a barbarian nation within her boundaries, a nation that she could neither control nor destroy.

3. THE BARBARIAN GERMANS

What and who were these people known as Germans? They have always been designated as "barbarians," a term that is proper if used to characterize the simplicity of their institutions and culture compared with those of the Roman world. The basic Germanic political institution was the *tribe*, composed of a number of *clans* and headed by a *tribal chief*. Heads of clans played a vital role in shaping the chief's decisions, and freemen in the clans had a political voice through an *assembly*. The tribal government concerned itself mainly with war and worship, the clans deciding most other matters. The Germans were primarily hunters and herders, although by the third century A.D., they were beginning to turn to agriculture. In religion, the Germans were polytheistic; they worshiped especially the forces of nature. There was no written Germanic language; what literature they had, mostly stories about the deeds of gods and heroes, was transmitted orally.

But the Germans were not a "backward" people. By the fourth century, small tribal groups were being unified into *nations* ruled over by elected kings enjoying considerable powers, which made it easier for a single ruler to mount heavy attacks on the Roman frontier and more difficult for the Romans to play small group against small group. Within Germanic society there was also developing a unique institution — the war band (*comitatus*) — composed of tested warriors united by pledges made under oath to follow a military chief. These warriors became a kind of aristocracy, practicing war as a way of life and gaining tremendous proficiency in fighting. Also, Germanic society was moving rapidly toward a more advanced agricultural economy, but tillable land was short in the heavy forests of Central Europe. As a consequence, many nations and tribes moved south toward the rich lands of the Roman world. Moreover, agricultural economy was transforming society by creating an aristocracy of landowners and bringing elements of the population into economic dependence on them. These changing conditions made Germanic society dynamic, open to foreign influences, mobile, adaptable.

Between Germans and Romans there was no deep-seated hatred at the moment of their decisive encounter. The Germans were admirers of Greco-Roman civilization, desiring nothing more than to settle within the empire and to become "civilized" so as to enjoy its fruits— especially its material wealth. The Romans on their side respected the Germans for their splendid physical features, their fighting prowess, and their alleged moral excellence and had from at least the time of Augustus permitted them to cross the frontier as long as their movement could be controlled. Large numbers had entered the empire as soldiers and farmers and had quickly become Romanized; many rose to high places in Roman society. Influences from the Roman world also sifted across the frontiers into the Germanic. For example, during the fourth century many Goths were converted to Christianity by Ulfilas, himself a Goth educated in Constantinople. Ulfilas provided a Gothic version of the Bible for his converts, a feat that required the creation of a written language.

It would seem that the barbarian Germans were thus moving peacefully into the mainstream of Greco-Roman civilization and might in the long run have been completely transformed, as some were before A.D. 400. However, the Romans had to be able to prevent too great a flood of Germans from pouring into the empire at once and to dominate those who did enter. Was the Visigothic victory at Adrianople in 378 a sign that Rome had lost that ability? If so, the very existence of the empire would be at stake.

4. THE BARBARIAN INVASIONS AND THE FALL OF THE EMPIRE

The crisis caused by the Visigothic victory was faced by the last great emperor of the united empire, Theodosius. He kept the Visigoths in check by establishing them as *foederati* (allies), assigning them lands in return for their supplying troops for the Roman army. He ensured that they abided by the arrangement and succeeded in confining them to the Balkan area.

Theodosius struggled valiantly with rivals for his throne and eventually eliminated most of them. The machinery of state was kept running, permitting a continued defense of the frontiers. His passing, however, spelled the beginning of the end of the uneasy calm lying over the empire since the time of Diocletian and Constantine. Theodosius was succeeded by two sons, who were assigned the Western and Eastern sections of the empire respectively. Neither had much ability, and both allowed the direction of affairs to fall into the hands of powerful generals, most of whom were Germanic in origin and whose power rested primarily on the loyalty of their Germanic troops. This situation set off a series of power struggles in which the generals sought to manipulate imperial policy for their own advantage.

Its directive force caught up in ceaseless intrigue, the empire lost control over the Germanic hordes pressing in on it. As the fifth century opened, the Visigoths, led by a capable king named Alaric, were playing a dangerous game of selling their services alternately to the emperors in the West and the East. Eventually they turned against the West, having been promised by Constantinople whatever new lands they conquered. Their attacks on Italy necessitated the recall of troops from the British, Rhine, and Danube frontiers, but to no avail. In 410 they captured and sacked Rome—the first time in eight centuries that the city had suffered such a fate. In the meantime, other Germans poured across the undefended frontiers into the heart of the empire.

The invaders were primarily interested in finding lands, not in destroying Roman government and society. The effect of their assault was, however, the dismemberment of the Western part of the empire. Wherever they settled, their kings and warrior nobles became the real rulers, although they often maintained the fiction that they were allies of the Roman government. Angles, Saxons, and Jutes wiped out Roman out-

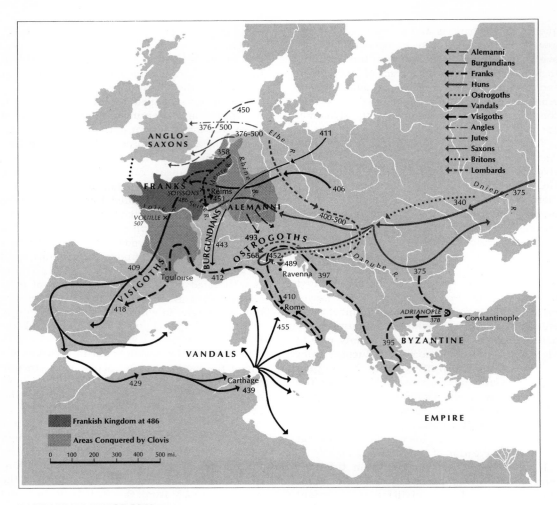

BARBARIAN KINGDOMS 526

posts in Britain and established several petty kingdoms. The Vandals crossed Gaul into Spain; from there, their one great king, Gaiseric, led them into North Africa, where a formidable Vandal kingdom arose. It soon developed enough sea power to allow the Vandals to pillage Rome in 455. After a brief sojourn in Italy, Visigoths settled in southern Gaul. The Burgundians created a kingdom in southeastern Gaul straddling the Rhone Valley. Late in the fifth century the Franks, led by Clovis, a ruthless, able king, seized most of Gaul as their base of power, drove the Visigoths into Spain, and overran the Burgundian kingdom. Italy fell victim to the Germans when the Ostrogoths captured it in 493 and established their king, Theodoric, as ruler. The ferocious Huns under Attila created a huge kingdom north of the Danube from which they harassed the East and then invaded the West in 451–452. Attila's Western invasion was repulsed by a coalition of Roman and German forces. Germanic tribes repeatedly ravaged the territory south of the Danube during the fifth century and hurled themselves at the Eastern provinces.

Unable to bypass Constantinople, they were denied the conquest of the East. Despite this failure, the history of the fifth century really belonged to the Germans; they had won the West.

The magnitude of the Germanic victory is revealed by the slow dissolution of the imperial government in the West. Some of the generals serving the weak emperors fought valiantly to check the invasions and negotiated desperately to turn German against German. Each Germanic nation was usually persuaded to sign a treaty with the Roman government to accept *foederatus* status and nominal Roman overlordship. In fact, however, Rome's allies became independent in the areas assigned to them. The Roman bureaucracy broke down, imperial income dwindled, and the authority of the successors of Augustus disappeared. By 476 the political realities in the West were officially recognized. A German general, Odoacer, deposed the last Western emperor and turned the insignia of imperial office over to the emperor in Constantinople with the advice that there was no longer need for a ruler in the West. In theory, this reunited the empire under the sole authority of the emperor in Constantinople; in practice, the Eastern emperor had virtually no control over the West. The West belonged to the Germans by right of conquest.

5. THE FRUITS OF INVASION

The Germanic invasions of the fifth century affected every aspect of life in the empire, especially the Western part, in a way that spelled the end of Greco-Roman civilization.

The most obvious and important by-product of the invasions was the destruction of imperial government in the West. Gone were the mighty emperors, their courts, their law, their public projects, their armies, their bureaucrats. And the new masters of the West, the Germanic kings and their warriors, were not fitted to take their place. Political chaos settled over the West.

Economically, the invasion was followed by increasing impoverishment. The new overlords were primarily interested in land, and reversion to an agricultural economy was rapid. Cities suffered an especially disastrous decline, some of them shrinking to a fraction of their old population and most of them being stripped of their functions as cultural, administrative, and economic centers. Their decline meant the end of the urban aristocracies that had sustained Greco-Roman civilization in the West. Roman landholders who escaped ousting by German warriors bent their efforts to enlarging their holdings amid the confusion and usually succeeded. Peasants were glad to serve great landowners in return for whatever protection the landowners, be they German or Roman, could offer; as a consequence, the ranks of the dependent peasantry swelled everywhere in the West. Most of the large estates sought self-sufficiency, with the result that the Western empire broke up into thousands of tiny self-contained units that had less and less economic interchange with each other. Trade was drastically reduced, and manufacturing centered more and more in the isolated large estates. All these developments drove standards of living inexorably down toward subsistence level.

The German rulers tried to absorb Roman civilization by learning Latin, patronizing artists and writers, and adopting Roman dress and manners. But the new leaders could do no better than imitate, and all too often their basic barbarism broke through the thin veneer of civilized life. Educated Romans in Italy, Gaul, Spain, and Africa continued to read their classics, study philosophy, send their children to schools, and even write. But their efforts were to no point; no longer was there an opportunity for the cultivated man to serve the government. The cities, long the centers of civilized life, were dead. The agricultural population, increasingly isolated and barbarized, was too provincial to uphold the artistic and intellectual traditions of the old order. The content and spirit of those traditions related to few of the real issues of the new day, and thus were cut off from the vital interaction between the world of learning and art and the world of practical life.

Finally, the Germanic invasions had created a division between East and West. The new political order in the West was markedly different from the imperial regime still surviving in the East. The simple agricultural economy developing in the West set that world apart from the more stable and sophisticated East, undisturbed by the terrors of the invasion period. The Mediterranean community was ruptured; that fact alone was fatal to Greco-Roman civilization.

We must, however, be cautious in assigning the Germanic invasions too great a significance. Destruction of life and property was not excessive, and in most cases the Germans and Romans settled down peacefully side by side. The conquerors were not numerous enough to affect the ethnic composition of the population or the language. The disintegration of the imperial government, economic decline, cultural stagnation, and division of the Mediterranean world had begun before the Germans invaded the empire en masse. What the invasions did was to accelerate these trends and make them irreversible.

6. CHRISTIANITY IN THE LATE EMPIRE

In the face of events bringing virtual ruin to the structure of late imperial society, Christianity showed great resilience and emerged from the ordeal stronger than ever. In some ways this is surprising, given that the fourth century, a glorious period in Christian history, closely identified the Church with imperial society. Great numbers of converts were made from all levels of society, and Christian leaders advanced to prominent positions in it. The wealth of the Christian establishment increased tremendously. The Church in the sense of a visible organization had taken its place as a prominent feature of Greco-Roman society. The fourth-century Roman government gave powerful support to these developments so that the triumphant Church had become to a considerable degree dependent on the rulers. All these successes meant that by 400 the Roman Empire had truly become a Christian Roman Empire, a fact recognized by Theodosius when he legally designated Christianity the state religion.

However, success brought new and serious problems. The avalanche of converts, no longer faced with the terrible possibility that baptism might spell martyrdom, diluted the spiritual fervor of pre-Constantinian Christianity. Discipline within the growing Christian ranks became more difficult. Wealth and power turned the heads of Christian leaders toward dubious ends; a hostile Christian could even describe a late fourth-century bishop of Rome as a "ladies' ear tickler." The influx of pagan ideas and practices with the many inadequately instructed and spiritually lax converts threatened to obliterate Christian practices of worship and doctrines, while generating heresies that divided Christian from Christian. Perhaps the gravest danger facing Christians was control of the Church by emperors faithful to the Constantinian view of the Christian establishment as an instrument to use in the interests of the state. In brief, the advance of Christianity to a central position threatened to deprive the movement of its uniqueness, its zeal, and its sense of mission.

The Christian community of the fourth century proved capable of meeting these challenges, of "reforming" itself to meet the realities of the time. One response was the strengthening of the powers of the clergy, especially the bishops, over individual churches. These powers were used to define Christian behavior and modes of worship more vigorously and to compel Christians to obey the rapidly evolving Christian "law." A major beneficiary of this development was the bishop of Rome, on whom the fourth-century emperors showered wealth and relied to formulate dogma they hoped to impose on the whole empire as a means of combating the divisive heresies of the age. The popes responded by asserting their authority more positively.

During the fourth century Christianity was also able to recapture its spiritual vision. This was the feat of a new breed of men who called themselves "athletes of Christ"—the *monks*. *Monasticism* was born in the late third and early fourth centuries in the deserts of Egypt, to which pious men fled to seek perfection through prayer and mortification of the flesh, inspired by Jesus' command to leave all worldly things behind and sacrifice themselves for him. The spiritual heroics of the desert fathers, exemplified by Anthony, electrified the Christian world. Soon the individual hermits began to gather into communities, or monasteries, and accept rules, or codes of spiritual exercises for achieving perfection. By 400, monasticism had spread over

The sixth-century church of S. Apollinare in Ravenna is a basilica, an adaptation of a Roman architectural style. The central hall (nave) is supported by columns, and its small, high windows are cut above the roof of the side aisles. *Photo: G. E. Kidder Smith*

much of the Roman world and created a new model of the ideal Christian.

In the face of state efforts to control religious life, many fourth-century prelates began to articulate statements that sought to define the limits of imperial authority and religious freedom. Some even argued that Christian society was more important than secular and therefore must be supreme. As the concept of the independence of the Church took shape, it spurred the problem of where ultimate authority in the Church lay. More and more Christians agreed that the bishop of Rome, Peter's successor, was the spiritual leader of the Christian world.

Perhaps the most significant success of the Christian community was its assumption of cultural leadership in the Roman world through an outburst of creative energy. Church building provided one of the chief outlets for the talents

of architects, sculptors, and painters, who developed new modes of conveying the Christian message by appropriating the classical artistic tradition for Christian purposes. Some of the most inspired poetry of the age flowed from the pens of Christians. But the jewel of the period was the theological writing of a remarkable group of intellectuals called the church fathers, especially the Greeks Athanasius, Basil, Gregory of Nyssa, and Gregory Nazianzus. The fruit of their labors was a massive body of literature destined to provide intellectual guidelines for centuries to come. Beginning with a deep faith, they borrowed boldly and creatively from the content and methods of Greco-Roman philosophy to build a consistent, logical, articulate statement of Christian belief. In the process they literally redefined human values and reoriented the end of human existence toward the service of God. They effected an intellectual revolution which overpowered the Greco-Roman world view.

A description of one of their number especially important in Western thought will illustrate the role of the church fathers. He was Augustine

(354–430), bishop of Hippo, in North Africa, two of whose works are especially significant. His *Confessions* recounts the spiritual pilgrimage of an enlightened man through most of the philosophical systems and religions of the ancient world to Christianity. The work not only argues the failure of Greco-Roman philosophy and religion but presents faith as the only adequate response to life. Even more influential was his *City of God*, written to answer pagan charges that the Visigothic sack of Rome in 410 succeeded because the gods were angry at the Romans for becoming Christians. In God's plan for the universe, he said, are two cities. The City of God exists only in the other world; membership will be awarded to men who serve the true faith on earth. In this world is the sinful City of Men, of which the Roman Empire was a part. The coming of Christ established an earthly embodiment of the City of God in the Christian Church. Rome must now pass away to allow men to give the more perfect society their allegiance. Almost immediately, Augustine's interpretation of the cosmos and of history replaced the several world views offered by classical philosophers.

Others worked in more practical ways that supplemented Augustine's intellectual effort. For example, Ambrose (ca. 340–397), bishop of Milan, set forth the basic principles of Christian morality persuasively. Jerome employed his learning to produce a Latin translation of the Bible called the Vulgate, which ensured that Latin would survive as the language of the Church and as a link to classical civilization.

Armed with this vitality, the Church survived the ordeal of the Germanic invasions and the fall of the imperial government amazingly well and emerged the most potent force in society, especially in the West. In many parts of the West, bishops replaced imperial officials as keepers of order, administrators of justice, and caretakers of the unfortunate. Pope Leo I (440–461), for example, served as the virtual governor of Rome and as a forceful diplomat defending the city against the attacks of the Vandals and the Huns. By 500 most of the Germans had been converted to Christianity, and their kings had begun to lend their support to the Church and lean on it for assistance in their efforts to rule. As the focus of life shifted toward rural centers, the Church followed and made considerable progress in incorporating a heretofore neglected peasantry into Christian society. As cultural life collapsed, the monasteries provided havens for study. By 500, the Church loomed as a pillar of order, stability, and strength. At least in the West, it had fallen heir to the leadership of society.

Suggested Reading

Political, Economic, and Social Developments
The general history of the period covered in this chapter is treated in the works of Brown, Jones, and Vogt, cited in Chapter 13. The following works examine more specialized aspects of the period:

J. H. Holland, *Constantine the Great* (1971). A readable, reasonably reliable biography of the crucial figure of the period.

*Jacob Burchkhardt, *The Age of Constantine the Great* (Anchor).

*A. H. M. Jones, *Constantine and the Conversion of Europe* (Collier).

A. Alföldi, *The Conversion of Constantine and Pagan Rome* (1948).

N. H. Baynes, *Constantine the Great and the Christian Church* (1930). This and the preceding three titles treat the crucial matter of the conversion of Constantine from a variety of perspectives.

*John W. Eadie, ed., *The Conversion of Constantine* (Holt, Rinehart and Winston). A collection of materials reflecting ancient and modern interpretations of the significance of Constantine's conversion.

Church History
Again the major developments in church history are traced in the works of Chadwick, Davies, and Daniélou and Marrou, cited in Chapter 13.

A. Momigliano, ed., *Conflict Between Paganism and Christianity in the Fourth Century* (1963). A stimulating treatment, emphasizing the strength of paganism in the fourth century.

H. von Campenhausen, *The Fathers of the Greek Church,* trans. S. Godman (1959), and *The Fathers of the Latin Church,* trans. M. Hoffmann (1964). Clear, accurate summaries of the efforts and of the achievements of Christian thinkers during the patristic age.

D. J. Chitty, *The Desert a City* (1966). A colorful presentation of the origins of monasticism.

Peter Brown, *Augustine of Hippo: A Biography* (1967). A model biography of a key figure.

F. Dvornik, *Early Christian and Byzantine Political Philosophy* (1966). A good introduction to the issues of church-state relationships in the third and fourth centuries.

The Germans

*Francis Owen, *The Germanic People* (Collier).

E. A. Thompson, *The Early Germans* (1965). This and the preceding title give a balanced picture of the nature of Germanic society prior to the invasions.

E. A. Thompson, *A History of Attila and the Huns* (1948). A good study of a fascinating product of the age and his work.

Sources

*Tacitus, *On Britain and Germany,* trans. H. Mattingly (Penguin). A view of the Germans from the perspective of a second-century Roman historian.

*Augustine, *Confessions,* trans. E. B. Pusey (Modern Library).

*Augustine, *City of God,* trans. M. Dodds, 2 vols. (Hafner). These two works will provide an excellent introduction to the seminal ideas of the patristic age.

Sidonius Appollinaris, *Letters,* trans. O. M. Dalton, 2 vols. (1915). Provides a revealing picture of conditions in the West in the era of the Germanic invasions.

Athanasius, *The Life of St. Anthony,* trans. R. T. Meyer (1950). This biography will help to capture the spirit of early monasticism.

Retrospect

At some risk of raising objections on a much disputed question, we can assign the end of Greco-Roman civilization to the years between the deposition of the last Roman emperor in the West (A.D. 476) and the capture of Italy by the Ostrogoths (A.D. 493). The Romans had created a magnificent political order that had brought peace, well-being, and concord to some 50 million people. Why had it not lasted? Within that community an enlightened, sophisticated, esthetically pleasing culture had spread to supply men with a sense of direction, a set of values, and occasion for pleasure. Why was it not sufficient? Any answer to these questions is apt to convince the reader that he has been witness to a great tragedy—almost Greek in character—to be lamented still as it was by some men of the time.

But was the collapse of classical civilization a tragedy? We might conclude that Greco-Roman civilization had become a prison for the human spirit by the third and fourth centuries. Autocratic government, regimented economy, and militarized society may have brought peace and order and security, but the price was heavy. The traditional cultural values seemed to be empty forms from which flowed no inspiration capable of breeding new thought or fresh expression.

The emergence of the Germanic barbarians as a potent force in society may from one perspective have been destructive, but from another, their presence infused society with an element of vitality. Here were fresh doers, learners, experimenters. The rapid rise of Christianity accentuated modes of thought and morality that seemed to lack the sophistication of the concepts governing classical civilization. Again, however, Christianity represented a fresh breeze in the Greco-Roman prison, a new vision of man and his destiny that provided a sense of direction and a reason for acting. The barbarians and the Christians held the key to the future. The promise of man did not die with Greco-Roman civilization.

Moreover, to speak of the fall of that civilization is to utter only a partial truth. When the Roman Empire collapsed, it left behind monuments that would serve as guides to its heirs—a magnificent literature, a great art, model forms of government, a legal system, economic institutions and techniques, moral precepts, philosophical ideals, scientific knowledge, and countless other achievements. In a sense, Greece and Rome did not really die. Little that has happened in the Western world since 476 or 493 can be understood outside its Greco-Roman background. We are all children of the classical world.

IV

The Early Middle Ages
500-1000
Struggle Toward a New Order

The fall of the Roman Empire ended the political, economic, and cultural unity of the Mediterranean world. During the centuries that followed Rome's fall, three new civilizations emerged, each absorbing a part of the Roman world and each extending beyond its boundaries into "new" territory. One of these, the Byzantine, had its center at Constantinople, and continued the Greco-Roman tradition almost unchanged. Byzantine civilization exerted its chief influence in Asia Minor, the Balkans, and European Russia. The second new civilization, the Muslim, or Islamic, began in the Arabian Desert and spread eastward to India and westward across North Africa into Spain. The third new civilization was created by the Germanic invaders of the Roman Empire. Gaul and Italy formed its center, but its influence eventually reached into Germany, Great Britain, Scandinavia, Spain, and the western portions of the Slavic world.

The basic features of these three civilizations were fashioned during the years extending from about 500 to 1000. Because of the chaos and barbarism of the period, it has often been called the "Dark Ages" and was in the past given only cursory attention by historians as an unfortunate hiatus in the story of Western civilization. In many ways it deserves this designation, for the birth pangs of the three new societies were often severe, marked by false starts, and accompanied by a variety of convulsions that spelled human misery. But these outward appearances must not veil the fact that seminal processes were at work in this age: New institutions and ideas that were to mold the modern world were appearing in each society. Equally deserving of notice are the differences that set the life styles of the Byzantine, Muslim, and Western European worlds apart.

The dynamism of this age came from various sources. In all three societies powerful vestiges of Greco-Roman civilization persisted to shape the essential features of the new civilizations. In two of them—the Muslim and the Western European worlds—new peoples supplied a leavening agent. But perhaps it was religion that furnished the chief animating force in this period. Two new universal religions dominated its history and provided the matrix within which old cultural values and new peoples interacted. Christianity finally achieved full power after a somewhat painful period of gestation and became the motor force in the Byzantine Empire and in Germanic Western Europe. Islam, bursting suddenly on the world and becoming established almost immediately as a dominant force by its warlike Arab adherents, affected the destiny of a vast area reaching across southern Asia and North Africa from the Indus Valley to the Atlantic. A meaningful comprehension of the period consequently demands careful attention to the role of religion as a dynamic, creative force in shaping the character of civilizations.

The complex processes that brought the Roman Empire and classical civilization to an end left the East more affluent and better organized than the West, and the two successor civilizations that developed in this area long remained more powerful and more advanced than the Germanic West.

1. BYZANTINE CIVILIZATION: ITS ORIGINS AND POLITICAL HISTORY UNTIL ABOUT 1100

Byzantine civilization originated in the Eastern part of the old Roman Empire, where the established order escaped relatively unscathed from the forces of internal decay and the Germanic invasions. As a consequence, the emperors who ruled in the East after the death of Theodosius in 395 were able to sustain the basic features of the late Roman imperial system even as the Western provinces were being lost. In fact, after the deposition of the last Western emperor in 476, Constantinople acted as if she ruled the old Roman world, even to claiming suzerainty over the newly founded Germanic states.

However, by the sixth century there were signs of a transformation in the East. The emerging civilization is designated as "Byzantine" to distinguish it from its Greco-Roman predecessor. The watershed between the two worlds can perhaps be placed in the reign of Justinian (527–565), often called the last Roman emperor and the first Byzantine.

15

HEIRS TO THE ROMAN EMPIRE:
THE BYZANTINE AND MUSLIM EMPIRES

Justinian's central concern was the restoration of the unity of the old empire. To this end, he set out to reestablish his authority over the Western provinces held by the Germans, an ambition that involved him in war for the greater part of his reign. However, the best that his armies could do was to recapture North Africa from the Vandals, Italy from the Ostrogoths, and a small strip of southeastern Spain from the Visigoths. Gaul, most of Spain, England, and the Danube provinces remained beyond his reach. However, Justinian's Western policy left the Eastern frontiers exposed, and the Sassanid Persians took full advantage of this situation to attack Syria and Palestine and to threaten disaster there. By the end of Justinian's reign, it was clear that imperial forces and resources must be concentrated in the East to hold the areas crucial to the survival of the empire; the Germanic West would have to be abandoned.

Concurrently with this historic decision, a new pattern of life was emerging in the territory ruled from Constantinople. Justinian took important steps to perfect the system of divine-right monarchy originated by Diocletian and Constantine. His chief effort in this direction was to commission a corps of legal experts to codify Roman law into the *Corpus juris civilis*. One of the great monuments of legal science and a work destined to exert considerable influence on the development of law in the future, the code provided legal sanction for a highly centralized, absolutist form of government which stood in sharp contrast to other contemporary systems of government, especially those in the Germanic West.

Religious policies were also changing. Justinian, following the trend in the late empire to completion, claimed that he was the religious as well as the political head of society. This policy was articulated chiefly in an effort to end violent dogmatic quarrels raging in the Eastern Christian world. By issuing edicts defining orthodox doctrine that would be acceptable to all parties, Justinian laid the foundations for a Byzantine Church whose organization, membership, and doctrines were confined to the boundaries of the Byzantine Empire and whose leader was the secular emperor.

Justinian's reign was also the time of the birth of a distinctive Byzantine culture that was oriented primarily toward the ancient Hellenic tradition. In its artistic aspect, it was marked by a merging of Greco-Roman styles with influences from the Near East, especially Persia. The great symbol of this new culture was the magnificent church of Santa Sophia built by Justinian in Constantinople.

Byzantine political history from the reign of Justinian until the First Crusade (1095) is dominated by one theme: the desperate military and diplomatic struggles of the Byzantine state to survive a succession of attacks from beyond its frontiers. These assaults reduced its size and modified the structure of its society so as to accentuate its uniqueness among its neighbors.

A gold medallion struck around 534 to commemorate Justinian's early victories. Cabinet des Médailles, Bibliothéque Nationale. *Photo: Jean Roubier*

Hardly was Justinian dead when the first blow was struck. In 568 the Lombards, a Germanic nation, invaded Italy and seized a considerable portion of the peninsula, leaving only Venice, a corridor of land from Rome to Ravenna, and southern Italy under Byzantine control. Little could be done to stop this assault because the Byzantine Empire was facing a greater menace elsewhere. Late in the sixth century the Sassanids mounted their greatest offensive in the East, seizing Syria, Palestine, and Egypt and advancing through Asia Minor to Constantinople. At the same time the Avars, an Asiatic people who established a state composed largely of Slavs north of the Danube, moved into the Balkans and toward Constantinople. For a moment in the first years of the seventh century it appeared that the empire would perish in the Persian-Avar pincer. But a savior appeared in the person of Heraclius (610–641), who miraculously regrouped Byzantine resources and flung back the enemies in a war of liberation that permanently weakened both.

The dynasty of Heraclius soon had to face an even greater challenge in the form of the rampant Arabs, whose rise to power we shall trace later. During the last half of the seventh century, the Arabs swept into Syria, Palestine, Egypt, and North Africa. By the early 700s they occupied most of Asia Minor, and in 717–718 they placed Constantinople under siege. Again a savior appeared: Leo III the Isaurian (717–741), who rescued the capital and succeeded eventually in liberating Asia Minor. However, the Eastern provinces were permanently lost and the Byzantine Empire was reduced to its basic shape: a state comprising Asia Minor and the Greek peninsula.

Despite Leo III's remarkable victories, the power of the Isaurian dynasty was soon weakened, chiefly as a consequence of its religious policy (see the next section). Meanwhile, the Franks seriously undermined the Byzantine position in Italy, and in 800 the Frankish ruler Charlemagne assumed—with the blessing of the bishop of Rome—the title of emperor, a direct challenge to the universalist claims of the emperors in Constantinople.

In the ninth century the Byzantine Empire was again threatened, this time by the emergence of the Bulgar state in the Balkans. And again the threat of foreign invaders produced a series of strong rulers, the Macedonian dynasty (867–1057), who not only threw back the Bulgars but under the greatest Macedonian, Basil II the Bulgar Slayer (976–1025), destroyed their state and extended Byzantine influence far into the Balkan area and into Russia. Under the Macedonian dynasty Byzantine power was also greatly increased in the East at the expense of the Muslim world.

By the eleventh century the Byzantine state began to suffer decline due in part to internal trouble and in part to still another assault from the outside, this mounted by the Seljuk Turks, who were joined by the emerging Italian city-states and the Normans. To save the empire this time, the emperors appealed to the West, an act that was instrumental in launching the crusades and marked a fateful day in Byzantine history. The empire that had for many centuries withstood repeated attacks by relying on its own internal resources now began to move down a fatal path of dependence on outsiders for defense.

2. BYZANTINE POLITICAL, ECONOMIC, RELIGIOUS, AND CULTURAL LIFE

The ability of the Byzantine Empire to resist these blows stemmed chiefly from the strength of its government, its vast economic resources, and the devotion of its people.

The Byzantine government was an absolute monarchy whose emperor lived amid splendor and ritual that rivaled those of the great rulers of the ancient Near East. He commanded a horde of civil servants, to each of whom was assigned a specialized function, a rank, and a salary. The empire was divided into a number of districts, called *themes,* where officials representing the emperor recruited troops, collected taxes, maintained order, judged cases, and enforced the emperor's edicts. His power was buttressed by a well-organized army and navy, an efficient system of taxation, and a responsive ecclesiastical establishment. Of crucial importance was the army. During the crises brought on by Persian and then Arab attacks from the East, the government abandoned the long tradition of relying on barbarian soldiers and developed an army recruited from the small farmers of Asia Minor, awarding plots of land in return for military service. Commands were entrusted to aristocrats from the same area. For centuries these tough, loyal soldiers stood heroically against repeated attacks on the Byzantine state.

Agriculture formed the backbone of the Byzantine economy. Large estates, farmed by tenants, existed throughout the empire, but the chief strength rested with small landowners. The state took a vital interest in keeping agricultural production high so that taxes could be collected from the farmers, whether large or small, landowner or tenant. Aside from agriculture, the empire enjoyed tremendous commercial activity, and for many centuries Constantinople was the world's chief trading and industrial center. All trade and industry were rigidly controlled by the state. Wages, prices, and profits were carefully fixed. Artisans and merchants were compelled to remain in their trades and hand them

on to their sons. The imperial government itself monopolized many lucrative businesses.

A strong government and a prosperous economy do not, however, fully explain the vitality of the Byzantine Empire. Byzantine life was strongly affected by Christianity, which helped to shape nearly every institution and activity. Perhaps most important, it provided the prime bond linking the populace to the imperial regime and thus supplied the basis for the remarkable loyalty of the imperial subjects. In many important ways, Christians of the Byzantine Empire were like Christians anywhere in basic belief and practice. However, with the passage of time, Byzantine Christianity underwent developments that gave rise to what is now called the Greek Orthodox Church.

The Greek Orthodox were always more completely allied and subjected to the state than Christians in the West. The emperor was accepted as the divinely ordained director of both spiritual and secular life. As a result of this *caesaropapism,* he appointed clergymen, defined dogma, settled theological disputes, imposed discipline on both clergy and laity, and used the wealth of the Church to serve the state. Byzantine religious life was also distinguished by its intense interest in questions of dogma. Quarrels over problems such as the nature of Christ and his relationship to God aroused strong feelings in everyone from the most learned monk to the lowliest artisan and peasant and led to serious political crises on more than one occasion. Greek Orthodoxy placed a tremendous emphasis on rituals, and attempts were sometimes made to curb this tendency. The chief such effort was the iconoclastic struggle that raged from 725 until 843. This quarrel began when Emperor Leo III, backed by part of the clergy, attempted to remove all visual representations (icons) of the deity from the churches and rites, insisting that Christians were worshiping the statues instead of God and thus were guilty of idolatry. But these iconoclasts (icon breakers) ultimately failed, and in 843 the icons were restored. From then on, an elaborate ritualism characterized religious life in the Byzantine Empire. A prominent place was also given to mysticism and emotionalism—religious experiences in which believers were convinced that they could reach and commune directly with God. Monasteries were the chief centers of this type of religious expression, and monks exercised a powerful influence over every aspect of Byzantine life.

These unique characteristics of the emerging Byzantine establishment, added to equally unique developments shaping the Roman Catholic Church, led not surprisingly to a growing division in the Christian world. In part, these differences centered in dogma and ritual, but especially divisive was the ever more bitter quarrel over whether the pope in Rome was superior to or co-equal with the patriarch of Constantinople. By the end of the fourth century, the patriarchs were claiming an equal voice with the bishops of Rome in pronouncing the final word on matters of faith. This claim was stoutly maintained in succeeding centuries, usually with the support of the emperors. The slow drift toward separation on this issue culminated in 1054, when pope and patriarch excommunicated each other and created a schism that to this day has proved irreparable.

The schism between Rome and Constantinople was accentuated by the success of the Greek Orthodox in missionary affairs. From almost the beginning of Byzantine history, Greek missionaries, backed by the imperial government, began to penetrate the vast world of Central and Eastern Europe, eventually converting most of the Slavs in the Balkan peninsula and Russia. Byzantine religious practices, political ideas, and social concepts spread among them. A large portion of the Slavic world was therefore oriented toward Byzantium at a crucial point in the development of Slavic institutions and culture and thus was set apart permanently from Western Europe. The Iron Curtain was not entirely a creation of the twentieth century.

The Byzantine Empire gradually developed its own cultural life, oriented toward the preservation of the classical Greek tradition and its adaptation to the Christian world view. An education system based on the study of classical literature provided the chief avenue of contact with the past. It produced a large number of men, both laymen and ecclesiastics, who were conversant with the literary, scientific, and philosophical masterpieces of ancient Greece and the Hellenistic world. This educated group, often associated with the imperial court, the prime patron of cultural life, also collected copies of the classics, commented on them, and wrote in imitation of them. Their efforts ensured the survival of the Greek classics and their widespread dissemination. As early as the ninth century Muslim scholars began to utilize Byzantine sources to gain access to the classical past, and the cultural renaissance of fourteenth- and fifteenth-century Western Europe depended almost entirely on the Byzantine world to renew its knowledge of ancient Greek culture. The all-pervasive influence of Greek models, however, tended to make Byzantine literature and thought imitative. Probably the most creative figures in Byzantine society were the theologians, whose incessant quarrels over dogma produced a huge volume of writing in which philosophical concepts from the classical tradition were applied to Christian teachings. Byzantine historians, influenced by the models of Herodotus, Thucydides, and Polybius, also produced excellent works. Their skill is illustrated by the work of Michael Psellus (1018–1079), a high official in the imperial regime who chronicled the exploits of the Macedonian emperors, and Anna Comnenus (1083–1148), the daughter of Emperor Alexius I, whose *Alexiad* colorfully describes the career of her illustrious father. Byzantine poets expressed themselves most originally in hymns, some of which can still be heard in Greek Orthodox liturgy.

Byzantine art demonstrated greater distinctiveness; it is perhaps the best mirror of the spirit of the culture. Architecture was the preeminent art. In its basic features, it represents a skillful fusion of Hellenistic and ancient Near Eastern traditions. The style was formed during the fourth and fifth centuries in Egypt, Syria, and Asia Minor and then was elevated to official status by Justinian's building program in sixth-century Constantinople. The great church of Santa Sophia was based on a floor plan derived from the Greco-Roman rectangular basilica upon which was imposed a great central dome after the Persian manner. The glory of this combination lies in the vast internal spaciousness it permits. The dome of Santa Sophia is more than 100 feet across and rises about 180 feet above the floor of the church. Although it rests on four great arches springing from four massive pillars that form the central square of the nave, the dome indeed seems "to hang by a golden chain from heaven," as a contemporary put it. Justinian, upon viewing the completed church, exclaimed: "I have outdone you, O Solomon." The architectural style represented by Santa Sophia was widely imitated, and in the course of time a variation gained considerable popularity: a ground plan based on the Greek cross with its four equal arms, each crowned by a dome, as is the space where the arms cross. The famous church of St. Mark in Venice is an example of this five-domed structure. Byzantine architects also built huge and splendid palaces, most of which have unfortunately disappeared.

Byzantine architecture, for all its technical ingenuity, is incomplete without its decor. The churches and palaces were immense frames for sumptuous decoration. Santa Sophia's interior, for instance, blazed with precious metals, mosaics, paintings, jewels, and fine stone. The techniques and themes of church decoration were especially influenced by Near Eastern traditions. Byzantine mosaics and frescoes, the best examples of which have survived in the churches built in Ravenna in the sixth century, centered primarily on portraying the great chapters of the Christian epic. Byzantine artists made an immense contribution to the development and enrichment of Christian iconography. Their work was never basically concerned with a realistic portrayal of the world; rather they sought to use human, natural, and abstract forms to evoke spiritual understanding. Color, created by glowing combinations of stones, metals, jewels, and paints, played a crucial role in enhancing the impact of every artistic creation.

Byzantine artists did not concentrate all their talents on religious themes; they were noted also as skillful jewelers, goldsmiths, silversmiths, manuscript illuminators, and workers in almost all the other minor arts. In every medium, the same features predominated—the fusion of Greco-Roman and Oriental motifs and styles, the love of elaborate decoration and color, and the preoccupation with symbolism.

3. MUSLIM CIVILIZATION: ORIGIN AND EXPANSION

No less vital was the second civilization that emerged in the East. This was the Muslim civilization, originally the creation of the nomadic inhabitants of the Arabian Desert. Although in the ancient past peoples from this desolate area had powerfully influenced the course of history (the Akkadians, the Assyrians, the Hebrews), no one living about 600 would have guessed that they were soon again to play a major role. Badly divided into numerous competing tribes led by *sheiks*, the desert dwellers, called Bedouins, lived a poverty-stricken nomadic life dependent upon pasturage of animals. Influences from the more advanced civilizations of the Byzantine and Sassanid empires had penetrated the Arab world, especially the cities which served as trading centers along the caravan routes that traversed the desert. The most important was Mecca, a flourishing trading and religious center where many Bedouin tribes came annually to worship at a famous temple called the Kaaba. But these outside influences barely touched the lives of the nonliterate, economically backward, politically divided desert dwellers; they seemed unlikely candidates for international power.

Yet in little more than one generation, this is what they became. The catalyst was a religious prophet, Muhammad, who galvanized the Arab world into unity and jolted it out of its isolation. Muhammad was born in Mecca about 570. Orphaned in his youth, he was brought up by an uncle as a camel-driving trader. Eventually, he entered the service of a rich widow whom he married, thereby ensuring himself a more respectable and leisured career. As a trader, Muhammad appears to have traveled abroad and to have been in constant contact with foreign merchants who came through Mecca. But there is reason to suspect that the decisive aspects of his life were shaped less by these extraneous conditions than by his own introspective, brooding, ascetic spirit, which caused him to spend much of his time in prayer and meditation, often in the solitude of the desert.

When Muhammad was about forty, he suddenly claimed that God—*Allah* in Arabic—had spoken directly to him and named him his prophet. Thereafter he dedicated himself to convincing others that Allah had shown him the way to righteousness and truth.

What did Allah reveal to his prophet? After Muhammad's death some of his associates compiled a book, the *Koran,* containing what was recorded or could be recalled of the prophet's revelations. Many of his teachings were so closely related to Christian and Jewish thought that it is virtually certain he borrowed ideas from these religions. Muhammad said that there is but one god, Allah; his followers must reject their worship of many gods for monotheism. Allah revealed himself bit by bit down through the ages, the Jewish prophets and Jesus all being accepted as his spokesmen. However, Muhammad was the last and greatest prophet, superseding all others, and Muhammadanism was destined to conquer the world. Allah requires

Mohammed replacing the Black Stone of the Kaaba, the sacred building in Mecca to which all Muslims come at least once during their lifetime if they are able. Miniature from an Arabic manuscript. *Photo: Edinburgh University Library*

complete submission to his will; the religion is thus called *Islam,* which means "submission to God." Every true adherent of Islam, called a *Muslim,* must regulate his existence to abide completely by the will of Allah. Those who believe in Allah and obey his orders will gain a happy life after death, while the disobedient and the wicked will be damned forever.

To these simple articles of faith Muhammad added a list of duties required of all believers. All must pray five times daily while facing Mecca, give of their wealth to support the poor, fast during one month of each year, and, if possible, make a pilgrimage to Mecca once in a lifetime. Muhammad also laid down strict rules regulating diet and marriage, prohibiting drinking and gambling, and demanding honesty, fair play, and respect for others. This code of conduct, strongly reminiscent of the Old Testament, injected a strong ethical vein into the new religion. Each man was personally responsible to Allah; there was no church, no clergymen, no sacraments to assist in gaining Allah's favor.

For several years, the preaching of the new prophet netted only a few converts. In fact, Muhammad won many more enemies than followers. By 622 these foes forced him to flee to Yathrib (later renamed Medina, which means "city of the prophet"), north of Mecca. This flight, called the *Hegira*, marked a turning point in the history of the new religion. Feeling spurned and convinced that the will of Allah had been defied by the Meccans, Muhammad began to shape a religious-political community dedicated to punishing sinners and spreading the true religion by force of arms. He molded his converts, mostly Arab nomads from Medina and its vicinity, into an armed political following, held together by the commands of the prophet. By 630 his following was strong enough to recapture Mecca, a feat that persuaded many Arab tribes to join the prophet. During his last years Muhammad also turned his forces against other Arab tribes to compel them to join his community. When he died in 632, he was the leader of a large following of Arabs willing to obey Allah and his prophet.

Muhammad's success in drawing together the Arab world was impressive enough, but even

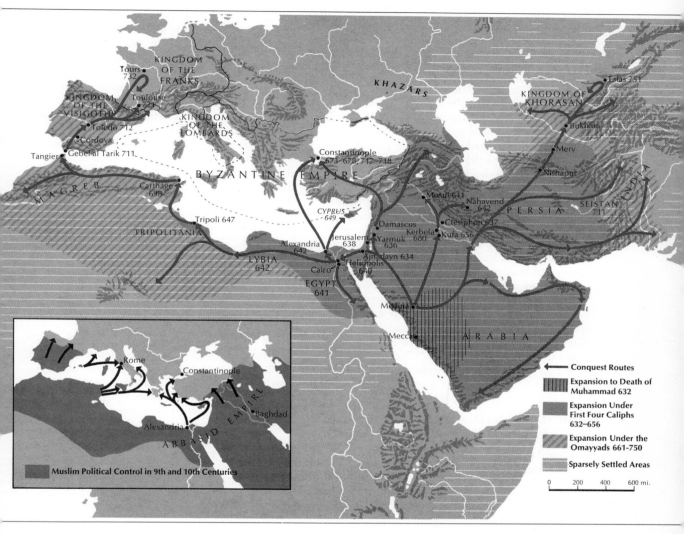

THE EXPANSION OF ISLAM

more astonishing developments were to come. Almost immediately the new "nation" burst out of Arabia and began a series of military conquests that affected most of the civilized world. From 632 to 661, the Arabs destroyed the Persian Empire; wrested the prize provinces of Syria, Palestine, Egypt, and extensive areas of North Africa from the Byzantine Empire; were probing India; and were challenging Byzantine sea power for control of the Mediterranean. After a brief interlude to settle internal problems over

Muslim leadership, the advance resumed. All of North Africa was conquered, and Arab forces pushed into the Indus Valley and the outer reaches of China. An offensive was mounted in Asia Minor that moved closer and closer to Constantinople. Before 700 the Arabs were in virtual control of the Mediterranean. In 711 they crossed from Africa into Europe and quickly overran the Visigothic kingdom in Spain. From there they began to raid Gaul to threaten the Frankish kingdom. But the drive was weakening: In 717 –

718 Arab forces were defeated at Constantinople by Leo III and soon after were driven out of Asia Minor. In 732 — exactly a century after Muhammad's death — the Frankish leader Charles Martel defeated them at Tours in Gaul and halted their further advance in Europe.

The conquest of this vast empire within a century represents one of the great military feats in all history. Several factors played a part in this expansion. For one thing, the Arabs' opponents were weak. The Sassanid Empire was exhausted from its long struggle with the Byzantines. Religious disaffection among the Christians in the eastern Byzantine provinces caused them to welcome the Arabs as liberators from the religious tyranny of the emperors at Constantinople. The conquerors interfered little with local affairs and thus made their overlordship easy to accept. They demonstrated great military prowess; their long training as desert warriors had paid off. Their enthusiasm for their cause was certainly also a factor. Muhammad had said, "Fight and fear not; the gates of Paradise are under the shade of the swords." Their wars were thus holy wars, and the Arabs fought in that spirit.

4. MUSLIM POLITICAL, ECONOMIC, AND CULTURAL PATTERNS

The rapid expansion of the Arabs of course had a profound effect on the Mediterranean world, for nearly a third of the old Roman Empire had been absorbed by the new power. Despite their limited experience, the Arabs managed to establish a new political order to direct the destiny of the vast empire they had won. After Muhammad's death down to 661, his close associates picked one from among them to serve as *caliph*, or successor, to interpret and apply the law as revealed by the prophet. This function gave the caliph vast authority over the political and religious activities of Muslims. In 661, a military leader seized control and made the office of caliph hereditary. The dynasty he founded, known as the Omayyads, ruled until 750. Its center of power was located at Damascus in Syria. The Omayyads had a strong imperialistic bent; they insisted that Islam was the special religion of the Ar-

abs and that the Arab mission was to conquer the world in the name of Allah. But they also realized that the task of ruling what the armies conquered demanded well-developed political institutions. Markedly influenced by Byzantine models, the Omayyads created a centralized court, a bureaucracy, an efficient tax system, and a strong army and navy.

In 750 the Omayyads were overthrown (except in Spain), and the caliphate fell into the hands of the Abbasids, who ruled until 1258. The new dynasty was much more cosmopolitan and held that all Muslims, whether Arab or non-Arab, were equal. The Abbasids' rise to power thus marked the end of Arab domination of the Muslim world. They shifted their capital from Damascus to Bagdad on the Tigris River, close to the heart of the old Persian Empire. In this new atmosphere the militancy that the Arabs represented was greatly diminished, and the energies of the Muslim world were turned inward to develop the potential of the vast empire.

The Abbasids enjoyed a period of great political power, especially in the late eighth and early ninth centuries; the dynasty's most magnificent caliph was Harun al-Rashid (786–809), immortalized in the *Arabian Nights*. But the Muslim Empire lacked permanent stability, perhaps chiefly because of its immense size and diverse population. By the end of the ninth century, Abbasid power began to decline, causing a rapid disintegration of the empire. Rival caliphs were established in Spain, North Africa, Syria, and India and quickly began to compete with each other for a dominant position in the Muslim world. Seeking to protect itself against these rivals, the Abbasid family increasingly placed its trust in Seljuk Turkish mercenary soldiers, barbarians from Central Asia who by 1055 had made the Abbasids their puppets. By that time, Muslim political unity had vanished forever.

The expansion of the Arabs promoted a significant economic revival. The key to this was a network of trade routes stretching from Spain to India and China. Cordoba in Spain, Damascus, Bagdad, and Alexandria, whose merchants and artisans were seldom restricted by Muslim governments, became centers of production. The wealth of the Muslim world at this time exceeded even that of the Byzantine Empire and far outstripped that of Western Europe, which was still dependent upon a backward agricultural economy.

However, religious and cultural developments established the main features of Islamic civilization. The religion of Muhammad demonstrated an amazing power to win converts, usually without force, since Arab conquerors seldom insisted that their subjects accept the new religion. They only imposed a special tax on their non-Muslim subjects for the privilege of retaining their old religion and excluded them from government positions. As the years passed, however, most devotees of other religions— Christians, Jews, Zoroastrians, and Hindus— were converted. Important non-Muslim communities always remained, but they had little influence on the mainstream of life.

Islam itself tended to grow more complex from the ninth century onward as a result of the efforts of theologians and lawyers, who developed a rich body of literature in the form of commentaries on the Koran and on other pronouncements attributed to Muhammad. Their work resulted in an orthodox faith rather far removed from that first proclaimed by the prophet; its adherents were called Sunnite Muslims and constituted the vast majority in the Islamic world. But there were dissenters and heretics, the chief of which were the Shiites, who insisted that the true faith was preserved by Muhammad's blood descendants. Despite these rifts, Islam provided the prime basis for unity in the Muslim world. The religious ties that hold the ''sons of Allah'' together have had a major influence on world affairs to this day.

Muslim expansion also brought about a tremendous cultural revival and joined together in a single society nearly all the world's chief cultural traditions: Greco-Roman, Persian, Mesopotamian, Egyptian, Germanic, Jewish, Indian, and Arabic. The semibarbaric Arab conquerors took these diverse traditions and molded out of them a new culture with its own distinct characteristics. The religious convictions of the Muslims again supplied the unifying force. Since Muhammad had forbidden the translation of the Koran into any other language, all Muslims had

to learn Arabic; and since the Koran contained the final truth, it was necessary to reconcile the knowledge of older cultures with Muslim religious teachings. The response to these challenges was a brilliant outburst of scholarship that rightly allowed the Muslims to claim to be the cultural heirs of the ages.

Many historians would agree that the greatest Muslim achievements were in philosophy and science. Muslim philosophers devoted their efforts chiefly to reconciling Greek philosophy with the teachings of the Koran. At the same time, they wrestled with the contradictions inherent in the Greek tradition, especially those separating Platonic and Aristotelian thought. Their efforts are closely akin to those of the scholastic philosophers of medieval Western Europe (see Chapter 23). In fact, the speculations of the greatest Muslim thinkers, Avicenna (980–1037) and the Spanish Ibn Rushd (1126–1198), known in the West as Averroës, exercised a direct influence on Western scholasticism.

In science, the Muslims' achievements were spectacular. Their efforts as collectors put at their disposal a huge body of scientific information from Greek, Indian, Persian, Mesopotamian, and Egyptian sources—more than scientists had possessed anywhere in the world until modern times. To this they added their own contributions, all of which were made widely available to a large circle of educated people because they were written in Arabic.

In mathematics, the Indian numerical system was adopted and the use of the zero was added to create the Arabic system of numbers which is used almost universally today. A Muslim, al Khwarizmi (ca. 780–850), combined Greek and Indian concepts to create algebra. Astronomy advanced tremendously with the joining of Greek views, such as Ptolemy's, to Persian and Mesopotamian. The works of medical writers like al Razi (865–925) and the philosopher Avicenna represent compilations from numerous sources. Muslim doctors studied diseases, dissected bodies, and experimented with drugs, thereby adding tremendously to the existing body of medical knowledge. Geographers and physicists followed the same course.

Muslim literature also demonstrated great

vigor and variety. Its color, imagination, and emotion are best exemplified by the poetry of Omar Khayyám and the fascinating stories of the *Arabian Nights*, typical of Muslim literature because its stories were collected from nearly all the peoples under Muslim rule.

Like most of Islam's culture, its art reflects a creative synthesis of many traditions. Architectural talents were devoted chiefly to the building of mosques and palaces. The mosques, primarily places for individual prayer rather than community worship, are simple structures whose inner space is often divided by rows of graceful columns creating aisles covered by arches. As a rule, the mosques are covered by domes similar to those of Byzantine churches, above which rise graceful towers (minarets) from which the call to prayer is issued. Before each mosque is an open court containing a purification fountain and surrounded by a covered passageway. The greatest mosques, such as those at Damascus and Cordoba, are beautiful structures marked by delicacy and grace. Surviving palaces, such as the Alcazar at Seville and the Alhambra at Granada, reflect the same architectural style as mosques but are much more elaborate.

Most Muslim buildings are rather bare on the outside but brilliantly decorated inside, especially with paintings and mosaics in splendid colors. Since the use of human and animal forms in religious art was prohibited lest the faithful be tempted to compromise their monotheism, Muslim decorative arts accentuated floral designs and geometric patterns (arabesques). Exquisite artistry also manifested itself in the crafts; Muslim fabrics, tapestries, carpets, leather work, metalwork, weapons, and jewelry were the most prized articles in the medieval world.

Muslim civilization reached its apogee in the ninth and tenth centuries. Thereafter it began to suffer a variety of internal dislocations which sapped its energies and permitted outsiders to take advantage of it. We shall return to these problems in another connection. Despite the afflictions that beset Muslim society, the immense achievements of the preceding centuries ensured its civilization a permanent place in the history of human accomplishment.

5. WESTERN EUROPE AND HER EASTERN NEIGHBORS

The brilliance and vitality of the Byzantine and Muslim civilizations received little competition from the Germanic-Roman portion of the old Roman Empire, which lagged far behind them until the twelfth century. Outwardly, considerable hostility marked the relationship between the West and its more mature Eastern neighbors. During most of the early Middle Ages, both worlds posed threats to the West, although the Muslim danger was far the greater. Religious and linguistic differences promoted discord. Western Christians, who looked on the Muslims as heathens, believed any story of atrocity told about them and distrusted the Byzantines almost as much.

Yet over the gulf passed influences that played a crucial role in shaping the culture emerging in Western Europe. From both Byzantines and Muslims, the West derived an extensive body of technical knowledge, especially for manufacturing and trade, as well as almost all the luxury items that added to its refinement of life during the Middle Ages. Western Europe inherited Roman law from the Byzantine Empire in the form of Justinian's code. The first distinctive architectural style to develop in the West in the Middle Ages, the Romanesque, derived from Byzantine models, as did the sculpture and painting styles used to decorate Romanesque churches. Throughout the Middle Ages and into the Renaissance, Western scholars learned about the splendid culture of ancient Greece from those who played a vital role in preserving it in Constantinople. Muslims passed their large body of philosophical and scientific knowledge to Christians encountered in Spain. This knowledge was the chief leaven in the resurgence of culture in twelfth- and thirteenth-century Western Europe. Finally, European literature received a priceless heritage in the Muslim love poetry.

In short, during these centuries no aspect of Western European civilization escaped the subtle influence of the East. It is a debt often forgotten today, when the West has so far materially outstripped the Near East.

Suggested Reading

Overview

*R. E. Sullivan, *Heirs to the Roman Empire* (Cornell).

*H. St. L. B. Moss, *Birth of the Middle Ages, 395–814* (Galaxy).

*A. R. Lewis, *Emerging Medieval Europe, A.D. 400–1000* (Knopf). This and the two preceding titles will provide useful orientations to the major features of the age covered in this section. Each approaches the era from a unique perspective.

Byzantine Civilization

*J. M. Hussey, *The Byzantine World* (Harper Torchbook).

*Steven Runciman, *Byzantine Civilization* (Meridian). This and the preceding work are splendid introductions to the essential features of Byzantine civilization by renowned scholars.

Georg Ostrogorsky, *History of the Byzantine State,* trans. J. Hussey, rev. ed. (1969). The best full-length history of Byzantium, especially for political history.

*R. Jenkins, *Byzantium, The Imperial Centuries, 610–1071* (Vintage). A detailed survey of the period covered in this chapter.

John W. Barker, *Justinian and the Later Roman Empire* (1966).

Robert Browning, *Justinian and Theodora* (1971). Two stimulating treatments of a crucial age in Byzantine history.

*D. A. Miller, *Imperial Constantinople* (Wiley). A fascinating portrait of the greatest of all medieval cities.

R. M. French, *The Eastern Orthodox Church* (1951). A thorough but dull treatment of an important institution.

*D. T. Rice, *Art in the Byzantine Era* (Praeger). A splendid treatment.

F. Dvornik, *The Slavs: Their Early History and Civilization* (1956).

———, *The Making of Central and Eastern Europe* (1949). These two works amply demonstrate the role that Byzantine civilization played in shaping the Slavic world.

Muslim Civilization

*B. Lewis, *The Arabs in History* (Harper Torchbook). An excellent short introduction.

*P. K. Hitti, *History of the Arabs: From the Earliest Times to the Present,* 8th ed. (Papermac). A standard treatment in detail.

B. Spuler, *The Muslim World,* 3 vols. (1960–69). A masterful synthesis in great detail.

*H. A. R. Gibb, *Mohammedanism: An Historical Survey* (Galaxy). A simple discussion of the basic Islamic religious ideas.

*A. Guillaume, *Islam,* 2nd ed. (Penguin). Especially good on the evolution of the Islamic religion.

*Tor Andrae, *Mohammed, The Man and His Faith* (Harper Torchbook).

M. Rodinson, *Mohammed* (1971). Two judicious biographies that will help to understand one of the world's great figures.

*G. E. von Grunebaum, *Medieval Islam: A Study in Cultural Orientation,* 2nd ed. (Phoenix). A splendid survey of medieval Islamic culture.

East and West in the Early Middle Ages

*Spiros Vryonis, *Byzantium and Europe* (Harcourt).

*K. Bosl, et al., *Eastern and Western Europe in the Middle Ages* (Harcourt).

*A. R. Lewis, ed., *The Islamic World and the West, A.D. 622–1492* (Wiley).

*P. K. Hitti, *Islam and the West: An Historical Cultural Survey* (Anvil). These four works are rich in information clarifying the debt that the West owes the East as a result of interactions in the medieval period.

Sources

*Procopius, *Secret History,* trans. G. A. Williamson (Penguin). A gossipy, scandal-filled picture of the court of Justinian.

*Michael Psellus, *Fourteen Byzantine Rulers,* trans. E. R. Sewter (Penguin). Portraits of the emperors of the Macedonian dynasty.

*The Koran, trans. N. J. Dawood, 2nd rev. ed. (Penguin). The best source for an understanding of the Islamic religion.

16

HEIRS TO THE ROMAN EMPIRE: THE GERMANIC WEST, 500–750

By comparison with the brilliant Byzantine and Muslim civilizations, the third heir to the Roman Empire presented a sorry picture. After 500, the Germanic West was characterized on the surface by strife, confusion, economic backwardness, and cultural decline. In the midst of rampant barbarism, however, creative forces were at work. By 750 new ideas and institutions destined to play a chief role in Europe's history for many centuries had begun to take shape.

1. POLITICAL DEVELOPMENTS

Much of the outward confusion of the period 500 to 750 in the West resulted from the absence of effective political institutions. By 500 the conquering Germans had divided the once unified imperial territory into several independent states: Visigothic, Ostrogothic, Vandal, Burgundian, Frankish, and Anglo-Saxon. Despite their small size relative to the defunct Roman Empire, their lords had never ruled states so large and so diverse in population. The political chaos almost inevitable under such conditions was aggravated by the fact that by 500, political boundaries in the West were highly fluid. Conflicts over territories destroyed some of the weaker Germanic states, and by 750, the political map of the Western world began to take shape in a form highly significant for the future. A new kind of order was being created.

During the first half of the sixth century, two major developments gave this process of recombination impetus. First, large numbers of Slavs moved westward into Central Europe and the Balkan peninsula to replace the Germans who had moved within the Roman Empire. The second and more spectacular development was the rise of the Franks in the West. Prior to 500, they had occupied a small territory in the extreme northern part of Gaul (modern Belgium) along the lower Rhine, where they had been allied with the Roman imperial government as defenders of the frontier. However, their first great king, Clovis (reigned 481–511), transformed the Franks into a crushing military force which he and his immediate successors led to conquer Gaul by 550. In the process, they destroyed the Burgundian kingdom, drove the Visigoths out of Gaul into Spain, and pushed into areas east of the Rhine not previously part of the Roman Empire. Clovis' conversion to orthodox Christianity greatly aided his advance, for the other major Germanic nations were Arian Christians and thus viewed as heretics, while the Franks were accepted as "liberators" by the orthodox Roman population of Gaul. Frankish conquests shaped a large kingdom that embraced peoples with both Roman and German backgrounds, and out of this mixture emerged many of Europe's fundamental political, economic, and social institutions.

Justinian's attempted reconquest of the West in the middle of the sixth century was likewise a decisive step in shaping the new map of Europe. His armies destroyed the Vandal kingdom in

North Africa and the Ostrogothic state in Italy. The Lombards invaded Italy in 568 and established a kingdom embracing a good part of northern Italy, but the Byzantines retained their hold on several areas, notably around Venice, Ravenna, Rome, and in southern Italy. At about the same time, the Avars were imposing their authority over the Slavs in the Danube Basin and in the Balkan area to form another important new state.

There were no further major changes in the political map of Western Europe until the early eighth century, when Muslim forces began to make their presence felt in the West. They destroyed Byzantine power in North Africa, established their control over the Mediterranean seaways, and in 711 wiped out the Visigothic state in Spain, where, except for a few tiny Christian kingdoms in the extreme north, they were to remain supreme for centuries. Thus, by 750, only three Germanic groups survived in the West: the Franks, the Lombards, and the Anglo-Saxon kingdoms in what is today England. The Byzantine Empire still had a foothold in Italy, and in Central Europe the Slavs had established their dominance. This general arrangement of the political map was to remain for a considerable time.

In the Germanic kingdoms surviving in 750, the bases for workable government were being established. In the long run, only two systems were of importance, that of the Anglo-Saxons in England and the Franks on the Continent. We shall return to the Anglo-Saxon political system in Chapter 17; here we shall concentrate our attention on the Franks.

As the Franks established their power in Gaul in the early sixth century, they sought to create an absolute monarchy. Clovis, the first of the Merovingian dynasty, which ruled the Franks until 751, claimed for himself the roles of supreme lawgiver, final judge, sole commander of the armies, and religious director of his subjects, whether Frankish or Roman. He was obviously influenced by Roman concepts, for earlier Germanic kingship had been much more limited. To execute these vast powers, Clovis and his immediate successors borrowed heavily from Roman precedents. They created a central court of offi-

cials, many of whom bore old Roman titles and were assigned comparable duties; and they retained the old Roman territorial divisions of Gaul as the units of local administration. Each district, now called a *county*, was governed by a *count*, appointed by and responsible to the king.

However, the history of the Merovingian dynasty is one of steady decline from the exalted position claimed by Clovis, a decline so drastic that the last Merovingians were dubbed "do-nothing" kings. Many factors explain this failure. The Merovingians could not divest themselves of an ingrained habit of using force to gain their ends, so that they appeared to many as bloodthirsty tyrants. They had a very limited sense of public service and so little managerial ability that their administrative machinery degenerated into virtually a household officialdom caring for the king's personal needs. They persisted in the ancient Germanic custom of treating the state as private property for their male heirs to divide at the end of each reign. By the early eighth century, Clovis' kingdom had split into three distinct subkingdoms as a consequence of repeated division, and the weakening of royal authority allowed other groups to break away. The Merovingians never managed to command sufficient financing to conduct good government. They followed another Germanic practice of allowing each man to be judged by the law under which he was born, be it Frankish, Roman, Burgundian, Visigothic, or whatever, thereby creating more division among a populace already set apart by differences in custom, language, religious practice, and cultural level. All these royal failures were accentuated by the fact that powerful elements in Frankish society persisted in the Germanic tradition of the feud, entire families taking up arms to avenge wrongs done by other families against their members. In the face of this ingrained lawlessness, weak kings were unable to perform even the basic governmental function of maintaining order in the kingdom.

Yet the Merovingian political experience, for all its failures, did establish a limited form of monarchy as an important and necessary political institution. Kings exercised positive powers as leaders of armies, lawgivers, protectors of the

Church, and dispensers of justice. Furthermore, the royal family served as a visible symbol of unity for a diverse group of people thrown together by conquest. Monarchy was taking shape as a visible embodiment of public life at a moment when poor communications, economic fragmentation, and cultural differences created tremendous obstacles to the formation of viable political groupings.

Severely limited in their efforts to create an effective centralized government, the Merovingians were eventually forced to share their power with the great landowners, both lay and ecclesiastical. The emergence of the landed nobility as possessors of political power, one of the major developments of the era, stemmed chiefly from the inability of the kings to sustain an effective taxation system and a professional bureaucracy. When they needed an army or civil servants, they had to depend on subjects who could and would serve at their own expense. Only the great landowners could afford such service, and in return they exacted from the kings grants of land and the right to govern their private estates as they saw fit. Inexorably, a system of private government evolved with the great nobles controlling affairs in their localities and interposing themselves between the central government and the populace. The kings devoted increasing attention to their relationships with the nobility, seeking to purchase their support and limit their independence. The growing power of the nobles was a source of incessant strife in the Merovingian state, for the demarcation between royal authority and noble privilege was imprecise, and the growth of aristocratic control at the expense of royal power was a poor omen for the stability of the monarchy.

This trend was accentuated by the widespread tendency for the weak in society to seek out the protection of the strong. At all levels of society, individuals of their own free will pledged under oath to serve another in return for protection and material support, a process known as *commendation*. These arrangements meant that strong men in society, chiefly the great landowners, built up private followings of *vassals* over whom they exercised considerable governing powers. Here were the roots of the feudal

system. The practice created private jurisdictions that spread political power widely through the noble ranks of society and that fragmented the state into many separate entities.

Thus by 750 the political picture in the Germanic West was a somber one. Only slowly—and accompanied by constant warfare—were the boundaries of the chief powers being defined. Within the several states, royal power had been severely circumscribed, chiefly as a result of the inadequacies of the rulers. Powerful landowners were exerting tremendous political influence at a local level, often irresponsibly. The shape of this new order was a poor substitute for Rome's splendid government, but its full potential for orderly existence had not yet been exploited.

2. ECONOMIC AND SOCIAL LIFE

The economic and social conditions prevailing in the Germanic West between 500 and 750 reflect the same backwardness and depression characteristic of political developments. Although modern scholars have demonstrated that the economic and social order in the West was not so depressed and stagnant as was once thought, still the overall picture was marked by decreasing wealth and shrinking economic activity.

The most notable development of the period was the progressive strangulation of commerce and the industrial life associated with it. Trade and industry were already moribund in the West by the fourth century, as we have seen. In the period of the Germanic invasions (the fifth and sixth centuries), this decline accelerated, especially in the frontier zones of the empire. Moreover, the Germans were not interested in trade, and when they assumed political power they did little to sustain it. Near the Mediterranean, especially in southern Gaul, Spain, Italy, and North Africa, commerce did not suffer so much, and contacts with the richer East were maintained. There was perhaps even a slight quickening of trade after the middle of the sixth century as a result of the political stability brought by Justinian's reconquests and the establishment of the Frankish kingdom. But this modest revival did not persist. Toward the end of the seventh and the beginning of the eighth centuries, trade again contracted, perhaps because of the seizure of control of the Mediterranean by the Muslims or because of more restrictive economic policies introduced by the Byzantine Empire. By 750 there was little circulation of goods in the West, the flow of money was small, city life had deteriorated except where the Church sustained it for administrative reasons, and the skilled artisan class had virtually vanished or had retreated to the large agricultural estates to produce for strictly local consumption.

Economic life had become almost totally agricultural. Possession of land provided not only the key to survival but also the measure of a man's status in society. Agricultural organization tended toward large, self-sufficient estates, called *villas*, a trend that carried over from the later empire's great *latifundia*. Many of the Roman *latifundia* survived the invasions, especially in the areas near the Mediterranean. Where Germanic settlement was heaviest, the Roman estates often disappeared and were replaced by villages inhabited by free landowners. But by the eighth century village establishments were being supplanted by villas which proved to be more economically efficient and politically viable in a disordered age.

The early medieval villa was a farming unit of several hundred acres owned by a noble or by the Church. The owner usually reserved part of this land for his own support. His basic concern was for labor to work the land and to turn its produce into articles he needed. There were still slaves, but a surer labor supply was provided by tenants. Between 500 and 750 increasing numbers of peasants were legally bound to the great estates, given a piece of land from which to derive their own living, and required to work the lord's land and render him dues in return for their tenancy. This pattern of exploitation laid the groundwork for the medieval manor and for serfdom, basic institutions in the future development of Western European civilization.

The villa system is not one that elicits praise; yet in the context of the early Middle Ages, it proved a vital institution. In a time of declining population it allowed an effective concentration of labor. In an age of political chaos it enabled

men to cooperate fruitfully under effective direction. It provided stability for the peasantry by tying them to a piece of land. Even before 700 its potential for economic growth was manifested by the clearance of new lands around some villas, reversing the centuries-long trend toward decreased cultivation.

The social structure in the West also changed to meet new conditions. The direction of change was toward a simpler system than had been characteristic of the Roman world. The distinction between Germans and Romans gradually disappeared. Urban social groups, so vital in the Roman Empire, vanished. The main thrust of social development was toward the creation of a new aristocracy composed of men who proved capable of acquiring land, seizing political power, and grouping dependents around themselves. The new aristocrat was a self-made man, usually crude, aggressive, and lacking in refinement; he was more likely the descendant of the Germanic warrior than the Greco-Roman nobleman. Accompanying the emergence of this new aristocracy was that of a large lower class, chiefly peasants, who were legally tied to the great estates and dependent on a powerful overlord. All but a few freemen, both German and Roman, were swallowed up into this class of the semi-free. Liberty had dubious benefits in an age of political chaos and economic difficulty; protection by a strong man and the security of a piece of land were far more precious.

3. THE CHURCH

Western society needed more than the reshaping of its political, economic, and social structure, for the passing of Greco-Roman civilization posed a threat to moral, spiritual, and cultural standards. To the Church fell the struggle against the barbarism that threatened to engulf Western Europe. It was especially fitted for this task because it had survived the fall of Rome better than had any other institution, carrying over into the new age an appealing, satisfying religious message plus large elements of Greco-Roman culture that found their way into its organization, theology, liturgy, and moral code.

But the Church itself faced great adversity in the West between 500 and 750. It lost the beneficial support of the Roman government. Under the influence of recently Christianized German rulers, it broke into sections that coincided with the boundaries of the Germanic states, which threatened its unity. Moreover, by 750 differences in theology, ritual, and organization had already separated the Greek and Latin churches, and as the Christian world divided its energies, the assaults of Muslims and Slavs rolled back its frontiers.

Even more dangerous was the decay of religious life within the Western Church. The character of Christian leadership had changed drastically. The bishops were especially lax in their religious duties: Most of their energy was devoted to increasing Church lands. As possessors of large holdings, they had the same political duties as did other landowners. And in the unholy competition for the office of bishop, with its land and political power, the strong usually won over the pious. Thereafter, seldom did this worldly figure concern himself with spiritual affairs. As a consequence, discipline in the lower clergy also suffered. The typical priest who dealt directly with the people was unlettered, ignorant of the rudiments of doctrine, unfamiliar with liturgy, and lax in moral life.

Religious life in general reflected its inferior leadership. Recently converted pagans mixed their old religious ideas with Christianity to create bizarre beliefs and practices. Most Christians had but a vague understanding of such ideas as the Incarnation, the Redemption, and the rewards of the good life; their daily life was dominated by efforts to avoid Satan's hordes, who had to be defeated by magic and the intervention of the saints. Church writers of the period complained bitterly about sexual promiscuity, violence, thieving, and general unruliness among Christians. People were in need of instruction and discipline, neither of which was forthcoming from the degraded clergy. Few of these difficulties had been corrected by 750, but a revitalization had begun, chiefly from within the Church itself. In the process of reform, the Church in the West took on a unique character setting it apart from Christian communities elsewhere. And it expanded its role as a dominant directive institution in Western European society.

One of the most significant features of the period was the Church's continued ability to win new converts. We have already noted that most of the Germans accepted Christianity as soon as they came in contact with Roman civilization. Just after the fall of the Western Empire, Clovis and his Franks were converted, thus bringing into the Christian camp the Germanic nation destined to dominate the West. Backed by the Franks, missionaries in the sixth and seventh centuries slowly pushed the Christian frontier eastward from the Rhine. About the same time, the Anglo-Saxons were converted by missionaries converging on England from Rome and from Ireland, which had been converted in the fourth century. In the first half of the eighth century, English and Irish missionaries crossed to the Continent to win new converts on the northern and eastern frontiers of the Frankish kingdom. While the Christian frontier was being pushed outward, the less spectacular task of converting the rural population of the West went forward. As new converts were won, the Church organization was extended to serve their needs. New bishoprics, monasteries, rural churches, and private chapels appeared. By 750 this missionary effort had enfolded most people in the West—Romans and Germans, nobles and peasants, rich and poor—into a common body: the Church.

A second positive achievement of the Church was its growing participation in activities that were not strictly religious. It often shouldered the burden of caring for the weak in society—widows, orphans, cripples, slaves, prisoners. It maintained the only hospitals and schools available. It injected some of its ideas of justice and mercy into the harsh law codes of the era. Each time the Church intervened in these matters, its prestige as a social agency and its influence over society increased. These activities set new standards of social welfare that were to serve as models in reawakening social consciousness in general.

Most notably, the Church proved able to attack the weaknesses within its own body—corruptness and worldliness among the clergy, moral laxness, ignorance, and lack of discipline. Especially important were two corrective institutions that evolved remarkably between 500 and 750: the Roman papacy and the Benedictine monastic order.

The progress of the papacy between 500 and 750 resulted in large part from the strong position established earlier by the successors of St. Peter as defenders of true doctrine and proclaimers of the right Christian law. The barbarian invasions deprived them of imperial support but worked in other ways to enhance their role. They had imposed on them the responsibility of virtually governing the city of Rome and holding the Christian forces in the West together in the face of the triumphant Germans. By the end of the fifth century, the popes were generally recognized as the authoritative spokesmen of the Church in spiritual matters in the West. They responded to their growing prestige by developing a theory of their independence from secular authority. A prime example was Pope Gelasius I's (492–496) famous theory of the two swords. He argued that religious and secular power represented two orders of authority, each established by God to achieve different ends and each independent in its own sphere. This doctrine created the ideological basis for further additions to papal authority and for greater independence from secular authority.

However, conditions in the early sixth century seriously affected the position of the pope. The Ostrogoths, who ruled Italy after 493, were Arians and thus did not recognize his leadership. When Justinian later destroyed the power of the Ostrogoths, the pope came under the authority of the Eastern emperor, whose Greek orientation tended to reduce the importance of Rome in favor of Constantinople. Still later, in 568, the Lombards seized most of Italy from the Byzantines and opened up an era of bloody struggle that made it nearly impossible for the pope to act positively. Finally, his influence was diminished in other Germanic realms as kings and bishops seized control of religious life to make it serve their own ends.

The recovery of the papacy was sparked by the genius of the first great churchman of the Middle Ages, Pope Gregory the Great (590–604).

Descended from a noble Roman family and educated for a political career, Gregory I rejected worldly affairs to become a monk. Eventually, he left his monastic life to serve as a papal diplomat in Constantinople and then to become pope. Coupling deep religious fervor with hardheaded business sense, Gregory pursued the policy of making the pope politically and economically independent while at the same time asserting the authority of the papal office as the fountainhead of spiritual life in the Christian world.

Convinced that wealth was necessary for political and economic independence, Gregory took an active part in the management of papal property in Italy, collecting everything due him, goading his agents into farming better, and acquiring new lands. He used this income to establish full control over the city of Rome and turned it into a little state ruled by the pope. On the basis of his political power, he began to act as an independent agent in the incessant struggles between the Lombards and Byzantines and enhanced his position by playing one side against the other. But Gregory was not simply a wily politician and administrator. His greatest fame came as a spiritual leader. During his busy pontificate, he found time to write important books on theology and church administration. His powerful sermons, circulated in manuscript form, revived the art of preaching in the West. He improved the liturgy. He sought to bestir princes and clergymen to reform their lives. Perhaps his most spectacular achievement was his sponsorship of the conversion of England, which allowed him to organize the new church in England under papal guidance.

Gregory's successors continued his policies. As a consequence, papal political independence and economic strength increased. Obviously, a new force of unity and discipline was emerging, although by 750 it had not yet achieved domination of the Christian West.

Monasticism had been imported from the East as early as the fourth century and had received an enthusiastic reception, so that there were many thriving monastic centers by the fifth century. None was more vital than that in Ireland, where the severe ascetic practices of the East took deep hold. The Irish monasteries became

In this German miniature Benedict supervises the building of a monastery. *Photo: Bayerische Staatsbibliothek, Munich*

and holiness attracted so much attention that he was forced to create a monastery for his followers at Monte Cassino, a village between Rome and Naples. There he put into practice the rule he had devised to govern the community of monks. The rule was so sensible and well fitted to the needs of the period that by 750, the Benedictine monastic system had spread all over the West and had begun to play an important role in revitalizing the whole Christian world.

The Benedictine rule contained several basic principles that explain its success. It established the idea that a community of men could serve God better than a single individual. Such a community must, however, be made up of rigorously selected members. After a long testing period, each new member was required to take vows promising to renounce all personal wealth, to remain chaste, to obey his superiors, and to remain permanently in the community he entered. The rule entrusted absolute authority to an *abbot*, a sensible move in view of the desperate need for discipline in the Church. Probably the most important part of the rule was its provision for an orderly daily routine, consisting of three kinds of activity: eight religious services — not so outrageous a burden when measured alongside some contemporary monastic practices, such as spending one's life atop a pole; four to eight hours of labor, depending on the season and the talents of each monk — cooking, field work, clerical work, the crafts, and teaching; and study. Benedict wrote one final principle into his rule — moderation. He repeatedly cautioned against too strict discipline, advising the abbot to temper his authority with mercy.

Benedict's rule won widespread favor in many parts of Western Europe (and was eventually adopted for women's religious communities), in no small part because of the powerful endorsement given it by Pope Gregory I. By 750 "schools for the service of God," as Benedict called his monasteries, had become the predominant form of monastic life. Their service to society was immense: Monks carved new estates out of Europe's wilderness and made them into the best-managed economic institutions in the West. They taught backward peoples all kinds of technical skills. They taught bewildered Christians

cultural centers and incubators for a powerful missionary movement that during the sixth and early seventh centuries took Irish monks to England and the Continent armed not only with great piety but also with considerable learning. But on the whole, early Western monasticism, perhaps too imitative of the East, failed to sustain its initial vigor. The West needed its own style of monastic life, and another great churchman appeared to answer that need.

Benedict of Nursia (480–543) stands alongside Gregory the Great as a builder. He too was an aristocratic Italian who abandoned his worldly career to become a hermit, but his rigid practices

the basic tenets of the faith and the proper performance of Church rituals. Their devotion, charity, and purity of life inspired others to reform. They bore the brunt of mission work, and they implanted Christianity in many backward areas. They were preservers and transmitters of culture. In a time of uncertainty, they were a small but stable bulwark against barbarism and important shapers of society.

4. THOUGHT AND ART

The depressive characteristics of the age were little conducive to creative thought and expression. Yet these centuries saw developments decisive in determining the cultural future of Western Europe and directing its cultural energies into unique paths.

In the realm of literature and learning, the chief accomplishment was the preservation of classical and patristic Latin literature (the use of Greek had virtually ended in the West). In the sixth century this activity was carried on by both secular society and the Church. Aristocrats in Italy, Gaul, and Spain struggled to maintain the old municipal schools where their sons could learn the traditional Latin rhetoric and grammar and continued to read classical Latin authors. Germanic courts, especially that of the Ostrogoth Theodoric in Italy, actively patronized literature and learning. One of the intellectual luminaries of that court, Boethius, set out to translate the works of Aristotle and Plato into Latin. His famous *Consolation of Philosophy*, written while he was in prison awaiting execution for alleged treason, was a moving defense of learning and rational thought filled with the classical spirit. Another of Theodoric's servants, Cassiodorus, left the court to found a monastery which became famous for its library of classical works, setting an important precedent for the role of monasteries in the preservation of learning.

Before the end of the sixth century, secular society ceased to play this role, and the burden of preservation fell to the Church and primarily to the monasteries. Faithful to Benedict's injunction to serve God by study, the Benedictine monks established schools to teach their neophytes to read and write, copied classical au-

thors and church fathers, compiled textbooks in Latin grammar and rhetoric, and wrote simple commentaries on the old texts to make them understandable. The monastic concerns tended to be narrow, governed by a passion to know God, to understand his word, and to pray well. Thus the monks were selective in their endeavors as preservers. And they felt no compunction about turning the classical heritage to Christian purposes, sometimes distorting classical thought almost beyond recognition. Nonetheless, they did save much of classical Latin literature and patristic writing.

A few creative figures, almost all churchmen, managed to transcend merely preservative activities to produce literary works with unique qualities. One of these was Boethius; another was a Visigothic bishop, Isidore of Seville, who compiled the *Etymologies*, an encyclopedia of information (and misinformation) about nature that encouraged interest in science and organized knowledge. Pope Gregory the Great's important works set forth basic theological concepts in direct, simple terms more suited to the age than the sophisticated presentations of the great fathers from whom he borrowed most of his ideas. A Frankish bishop, Gregory of Tours (ca. 538–594), in his *History of the Franks* demonstrated a real ability to compile and organize historical material. The most outstanding intellectual figure of the age was an English monk named Bede (673–735), whose theological, historical, and biographical writings set high standards of style. His *Ecclesiastical History of the English People* is one of the best pieces of historical writing of the entire Middle Ages.

During this period, the lay world in the main sank into illiteracy. One work that might suggest their patterns of thought has survived this period—the magnificent Anglo-Saxon epic *Beowulf*. The illiteracy of the laity did create one situation of immense cultural significance in Western European history: the language of learning, literature, and religion became different from the *vernacular*, the language that men spoke. This condition was destined for centuries to make learning and letters the property of an elite, chiefly churchmen, and to necessitate the mastery of a foreign tongue in order to join that elite.

And it was destined to keep learning and letters somewhat remote from many of the realities of life.

The art of this period reflects a mixture of old and new. As in every realm of life, Greco-Roman forms persisted in architecture, sculpture, and painting. Many of the churches built in the West followed the basilica plan characteristic of Roman structures. Byzantine architectural forms, given definite shape by Justinian's building program, exerted a strong influence in sixth-century Italy and persisted there to affect building styles in other areas of the West. In sculpture and painting, classical and Byzantine influences tended to merge, so that pictorial art increasingly emphasized symbolic representation of religious motifs. The Germans and Celts added an important ingredient: a distinctive decorative style utilizing animal and geometric forms to create fantastic abstract designs which were employed especially in personal adornments and illuminated manuscripts. A youthful art style was beginning to take shape, and it produced three remarkable illuminated manuscripts that survive from this age: the Irish Book of Durrow (late seventh century), the English Lindisfarne Gospels (eighth century), and the Irish Book of Kells (early ninth century). On the whole, the art of this period reflected considerable freedom from fixed canons and unusual combinations of merging artistic traditions. Artistic expression tended toward abstraction, symbolization, and a search for religious values at the expense of earthly concerns.

By the middle of the eighth century the Western world had by no means emerged from the time of troubles that followed the fall of Rome. Habits of violence, ignorance, poverty, and moral decadence had been ingrained into men's lives and were to affect the conduct of Westerners for many centuries. However, out of the experiences of this period had emerged innovative institutions and patterns of life: monarchy, a new nobility, a stabilized peasantry, an involved Church, the papacy, Benedictine and Celtic monasticism, a treasury of Greco-Roman learning and literature, a new art style. The potential of these forms had not been realized, but their existence ensured the survival of civilized life in the West and compensated to some degree for what had been lost by the fall of Greco-Roman civilization.

Selected Reading

Political, Social, and Economic History

*J. M. Wallace-Haddrill, *The Barbarian West: The Early Middle Ages* (Harper Torchbook). An excellent general survey of the period.

D. T. Rice, ed., *The Dark Age—The Making of European Civilization* (1965). A beautifully illustrated book which points up the contributions of diverse peoples to the new order emerging in the West.

Peter Lasko, *The Kingdom of the Franks: Northwest Europe Before Charlemagne* (1971). A good survey of the emergence of the Merovingian kingdom.

J. M. Wallace-Haddrill, *Early Germanic Kingship in England and on the Continent* (1971). A study that will help greatly in understanding the unique features of monarchy as it developed in the West.

Samuel Dill, *Roman Society in Gaul in the Merovingian Age* (1926). Paints a broad picture of social conditions in the Frankish kingdom in the sixth and seventh centuries.

*Robert Latouche, *The Birth of the Western Economy*, trans. E. M. Wilkinson (Harper Torchbook). Traces in detail the major economic developments of the period.

*Lynn White, Jr., *Medieval Technology and Social Change* (Galaxy). A provocative study that sheds new light on the innovative character of the period.

*Henri Pirenne, *Mohammed and Charlemagne* (Meridian). A seminal study advancing the thesis that Merovingian history was a continuation of Roman civilization and that only the Islamic invasions brought a break with the past.

*A. F. Havighurst, ed., *The Pirenne Thesis: Analysis, Criticism, and Revision* (Heath). A convenient summary of the debate stirred by Pirenne's interpretation of early medieval history.

Church History

*H. Daniel-Rops, *The Church in the Dark Ages*, 2 vols. (Image). A good survey of the major developments affecting the Church in the West during this period.

P. Batiffol, *Saint Gregory the Great* (1929). Provides a full and fair treatment of the role of Gregory I.

Jean Décarreaux, *Monks and Civilization*, trans. C. Haldane (1964). A broad survey of monastic development in the early Middle Ages with special emphasis on the role played by the monks in shaping the new society.

*Justin McCann, *St. Benedict* (Image). An excellent introduction to the origins of the Benedictine monastic movement.

Ludwig Bieler, *Ireland: Harbinger of the Middle Ages* (1963). A brilliant assessment of the nature and role of Irish monasticism.

Cultural History

*M. L. W. Laistner, *Thought and Letters in Western Europe, A.D. 500 to 900* (Cornell). The standard survey of early medieval cultural history, stressing especially classical survivals.

Gustav Schnürer, *Church and Culture in the Middle Ages*, Vol. I, trans. G. Undreiner (1956). An excellent supplement to Laistner, emphasizing the role of the Church in shaping cultural life.

*Jean Leclercq, *Love of Learning and Desire for God: A Study of Monastic Culture* (Mentor). A provocative interpretation of early medieval culture, emphasizing its monastic dimensions.

Sources

*Boethius, *Consolation of Philosophy*, trans. V. E. Watts (Penguin). Illustrates the powerful attraction of classical civilization to a sixth-century scholar.

Gregory the Great, *Pastoral Care*, trans. H. Davis (*Ancient Christian Writers*, No. 11, 1965).

——, *Dialogues*, trans. O. J. Zimmerman (*Fathers of the Church*, Vol. 39, 1959).

——, *Selected Epistles* (*A Select Library of Nicene and Post-Nicene Fathers of the Christian Church*, 2nd Series, Vols. XII–XIII, 1956). A sampling from these works by Gregory I will provide a good introduction to intellectual concerns in the West in the early Middle Ages.

Rule of Monasteries, trans. L. J. Boyle (1949). St. Benedict's rule.

Gregory of Tours, *History of the Franks*, trans. O. M. Dalton, 2 vols. (1927). A dramatic account of Frankish history by a bishop who was involved in it.

*Bede, *The History of the English Church and People*, trans. L. Sherley-Price (Penguin). One of the outstanding literary works of the period by an Anglo-Saxon monk and scholar.

Beowulf, trans. D. Wright (Penguin). A work reflecting the values of the lay nobility of the early Middle Ages.

Lives of the Saints, trans. J. F. Webb (Penguin). A representative collection of one of the most popular literary forms of the early Middle Ages.

17

THE FIRST REVIVAL OF EUROPE, 750–900

By 750, the new institutions and viewpoints forming in the Germanic West had borne only modest fruit. Then, rather suddenly and spectacularly, it enjoyed a revival which was brief in duration—hardly more than a century—but of great historical significance because it established the identity of the West. The revival was the handiwork of a narrow segment of society: on the Continent, a new Frankish royal family, the Carolingians; in England, the kings of Wessex; and in both, other dynamic elements in society, especially clergymen and aristocrats, who clustered around these Germanic ruling houses. Their efforts were promoted and given direction by a vast change in the relationships between the West and its neighbors—Byzantium, Islam, the still pagan Slav and Scandinavian worlds. Although the dreams of this narrow elite were by no means realized, their work had two particularly important results: It made the West visible in the larger world as a coherent unit possessing its own institutions and strengths. And it gave to the West an internal awareness of its civilization. The activities of these men created the first "Europe."

1. THE RISE OF THE CAROLINGIANS

The central figures in Western Europe's first revival were the Carolingians. At first they were only one of the ambitious landowning families that joined other nobles in undermining the authority of the weakening Merovingians. Toward the end of the seventh century, the Carolingians gained hereditary control of one of the key offices in the Merovingian political system, the office of *mayor of the palace* for their home region, the subkingdom of Austrasia. This position gave its holder considerable control over court activities and royal lands, an opportunity that the Carolingians used to increase family wealth and build up a muscular circle of dependents. As their power increased, they shifted their ambitions toward strengthening the central government and expanding their control through it into other subkingdoms. Their decisive moment came in 687, when the mayor of Austrasia, Pepin of Herstal, defeated the rival mayor of Neustria and claimed mayoralty of the entire Frankish kingdom.

Pepin of Herstal's victory was exploited to the fullest by his successors as mayors of the palace, Charles Martel (714–741) and Pepin the Short (741–751), who became the most powerful men in Western Europe, far overshadowing the Merovingian kings whom they served. Both defended the frontiers against hostile invaders, and Charles Martel gained undying fame by defeating the invading Muslim army at Tours in 732. Both tried to improve the royal administration so that justice might be rendered, taxes collected, and the weak protected. Both labored to check the disintegration of the Frankish realm into regional subkingdoms and to recapture for the royal government lands that had been usurped by lay and ecclesiastical nobles or given away foolishly by the weak Merovingians. This policy led to the confiscation of large amounts of Church property, in compensation for which both generously supported missionary work, sought to reform the clergy, and encouraged the improvement of the quality of religious life throughout the kingdom.

Although Charles and Pepin were still only servants of the "do-nothing" Merovingian kings, it became clear as the years passed that the real power lay in the hands of the mayors of the palace. Finally, Pepin took steps to transfer the Frankish crown to his own family. Fearing that a forcible deposition of the Merovingians would arouse hostility among the Franks, who still deeply respected their ancient royal house, Pepin sought the sanction of a higher authority. His choice was a momentous one: He sent an envoy to ask Pope Zachary if it were not right that one who really exercised power should wear the crown. When Zachary approved, Pepin deposed the Merovingian king and had himself elected king of the Franks. The Franks' acceptance of the new dynasty on papal authority was a mark of how great the prestige of the papacy had grown. When Pepin was crowned as King Pepin I in 751, a papal legate was present to anoint him.

Papal sanction of the dynastic change was dictated in considerable part by new and desperate problems facing the bishops of Rome. Since the days of Justinian, Rome had been part of the Byzantine holdings in Italy, and the popes had relied—if sometimes contentiously—on the Byzantine emperors for protection. During the first half of the eighth century, however, the Muslim onslaught made Constantinople increasingly unable to defend its position in Italy. Moreover, the iconoclastic policy adopted by Emperor Leo III was viewed as heretical by the papacy and caused the popes to repudiate the emperors as defenders of the orthodox faith. The decline of Byzantium's power in Italy encouraged her long-time rivals, the Lombards, to take the offensive. But Lombard expansion threatened to engulf Rome and deprive the papacy of its independent control over the city and its extensive property in Italy. The popes needed a new ally and protector. Who could serve better than the rising Carolingians?

In 753–754 Pope Stephen II made a journey to the Frankish court to secure a protector. After long negotiation, an agreement, called the Donation of Pepin, was reached. Pepin promised to ensure papal control over specified territories in Italy, some of which the Lombards already held. Stephen may have persuaded Pepin of the legality of disposing of lands that belonged to others by confronting him with a document known as the Donation of Constantine, a forgery which alleged that Constantine, out of gratitude for having been cured of leprosy, had granted to Pope Sylvester complete control over the Western Empire, especially Rome and Italy. In return for Pepin's grant, Stephen not only reanointed Pepin as king of the Franks but bestowed on him the somewhat vague title of "patricius of Rome," signifying his role as protector of the papacy and of the papal state. Pepin then made two campaigns into Italy and forced the Lombards to surrender some of the territories claimed by the papacy.

The alliance of the Franks and the papacy was truly a landmark. The Frankish kings now ruled by the grace of God bestowed through the papacy. They had assumed the responsibility of safeguarding their realm against all enemies of Christianity and of encouraging their subjects to become more perfect Christians. They had placed themselves under the guidance of the pope, who claimed the power to lead the Christian world. At the same time the papacy had lifted itself to a new position of authority and had established its own political area, the Papal States, within which it could operate in freedom.

2. THE REIGN OF CHARLEMAGNE (768–814)

The preparations made by Charles Martel and Pepin I were brilliantly exploited by Charlemagne (reigned 768–814), who emerges as the first great Western European secular ruler. To his contemporaries he possessed many qualities of greatness: imposing physical stature, courage, generosity, joy for life, intelligence, devotion to family and friends, and deep piety. His actions made him a hero to them.

The energetic, talented Charlemagne was above all a successful war lord. His first notable success came in 774, when he defeated the Lombard king of Italy and annexed all the peninsula except the Byzantine territories in the south and the Papal States, over which he was already protector. Even earlier, Charlemagne had attacked the Saxons who lived on the northeastern frontier of the Frankish kingdom. He finally subdued them after thirty years of struggle, a victory that marked the incorporation of the last major remnant of pagan, barbarian Germans into the Christian, civilized West. His armies also drove down the Danube into the land of the Avars and the Slavs, annexing another large territory. His attack on Muslim Spain resulted initially in his famous defeat at Roncesvalles, but persistent pressure in that direction led to the creation of the militarized border district, the Spanish March, south of the Pyrenees. The stubborn inhabitants of Brittany were beaten into submission. Beyond the new frontiers established by direct conquest, and especially in Central Europe and southern Italy, Charlemagne employed a skillful combination of diplomacy and force to create a large number of tributary peoples who were willing to respect Frankish territory. This aggressive policy permitted Charlemagne to rule over the largest state in the West since the fall of Rome. In all his wars Charlemagne managed to create the impression that he was not merely serving his own greed, but rather overpowering barbarians, pagans, and infidels to save his Christian subjects from grave danger. Popes, poets, and nobles hailed him as "the strong right arm of God."

Charlemagne aimed to set up good government as well as to conquer and made significant innovations in the system his family had taken over from the Merovingians. He supported himself and his large court chiefly by the careful use of royal lands and the booty won in battle. The king's commands, usually arrived at by consultation with the court circle, were executed locally by counts and dukes whom he appointed and rigorously supervised through special officals, called *missi*, sent out from the court to prevent local officials from exploiting their offices for private advantage. He made wide use of commendation to bind not only royal officials but most of the great nobles to him as vassals obligated by oath to serve him loyally. Often he rewarded his vassals with grants of land to be enjoyed as long as they served him faithfully. The growing dependence of the king on feudal usages was especially evident in the military establishment. The eighth century witnessed the emergence of the heavily armored mounted warrior as the chief instrument of warfare. The limited resources of the royal government made it impossible for the king to bear the heavy expenses involved in outfitting and maintaining large armies of mounted warriors. From the time of Charles Martel the rulers relied increasingly on great landowners to perform military service at their own expense; in return, the Carolingians granted them benefices from which the revenues necessary to provide military service could be derived. Charlemagne's military successes were, in no small measure, the fruit of his perfection and of his careful control of this system.

Charlemagne's great distinction as a ruler lay in what he tried to achieve within this old system of government. More than anything else, he sought to institute a regime of order and justice whose sense was derived in large part from Christian ideology. The counts and dukes were instructed to quiet turbulent nobles and to give protection to the weak. Tremendous emphasis was placed on safeguarding each man's rights under the law to which he was born. Charlemagne sought to supplement the existing legal systems by issuing edicts *(capitularies)* affecting nearly every phase of life. For the length of his reign, he once again made monarchy stand for justice, protection, and order.

Moved by a deep personal piety and realizing that the chief thing all his subjects had in common was religion, Charlemagne took the position that his divinely sanctioned royal office imposed on him the prime duty to strengthen and sustain the Church in its task of saving souls. He encouraged missionaries, even using force to compel pagans to accept baptism. He also continued the reform movement begun by Pepin, enacting a large body of laws to strength-

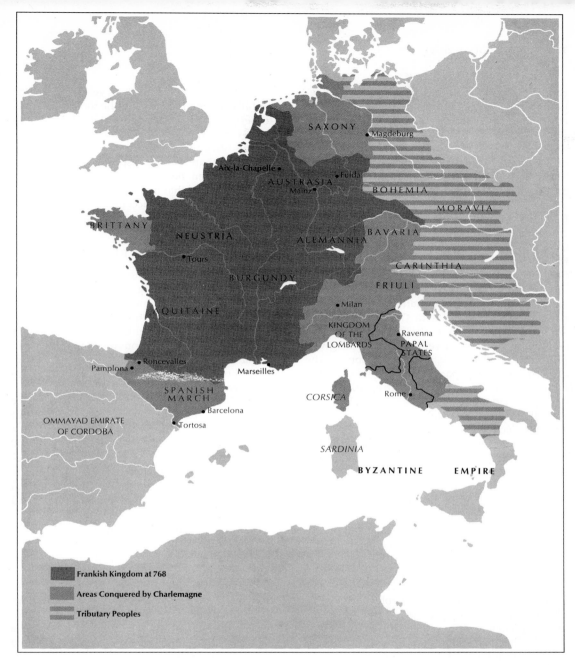

THE EMPIRE OF CHARLEMAGNE

Map labels: Magdeburg, SAXONY, Aix-la-Chapelle, Fulda, AUSTRASIA, Mainz, BOHEMIA, MORAVIA, BRITTANY, NEUSTRIA, ALEMANNIA, BAVARIA, CARINTHIA, FRIULI, Tours, BURGUNDY, Milan, KINGDOM OF THE LOMBARDS, Ravenna, PAPAL STATES, AQUITAINE, Pamplona, Roncevalles, Marseilles, CORSICA, Rome, SPANISH MARCH, OMMAYAD EMIRATE OF CORDOBA, Barcelona, Tortosa, SARDINIA, BYZANTINE EMPIRE

Legend:
Frankish Kingdom at 768
Areas Conquered by Charlemagne
Tributary Peoples

en Church organization, protect its property, impose higher moral and educational standards on the clergy, establish uniform doctrines and rituals, and destroy pagan superstitions. Of course, such an active interest led to constant interven-

tion in every aspect of religious life, from the most mundane problems connected with Church property to the outright appointment of Church officials—and at times to advising the pope on how to conduct himself. In formulating and enacting his religious program, Charlemagne relied heavily on guidance from Rome, so that his effort marked a decisive step in imposing the Roman stamp on the religious life of Western Europe; in this sense he was a major architect of the Roman Catholic Church.

The high point of Charlemagne's career came on Christmas Day, 800. While he was attending a mass in St. Peter's Basilica in Rome, Pope Leo III placed a gold crown on his head and the crowd hailed him as "Augustus, crowned by God, the great and peace-bringing Emperor of the Romans." Charlemagne's biographer, Einhard, claimed that the king was surprised and did not want the new title. But certainly the elevation was a logical culmination of Carolingian policy and in keeping with Charlemagne's position. The new title better fitted his role as conqueror, ruler of diverse peoples, lawgiver, protector of the weak, and champion of the Church and the papacy than did his old title, king of the Franks. It was a fitting tribute for one who had done more than any ruler since the fall of Rome to encourage an ordered world. And it reflected the conviction widely shared in the West that the emperor in the East had failed to protect the Christian world and safeguard the orthodox faith.

In a sense the coronation of 800 was an attempt to revive the Roman Empire in Western Europe; however, the Carolingian Empire was clearly distinct. It came nowhere near embracing the old Roman imperial territory, even in the West. It was based on ideas distinct from those underlying the Roman imperial system. Those who instituted the new empire, especially the churchmen who played a key role in advising Charlemagne, were prompted by Christian idealism. They were convinced it was God's will that all Christians should be joined in a single earthly commonwealth as a new Chosen People under a Christian prince. Charlemagne was the new David ordained by God to ensure the enactment of divine will. This was a vision indebted to Augustine, whose *City of God* was said to have been one of Charlemagne's favorite books. The translation of Augustinian political idealism into a Germanic context was crucial in creating a Western European political consciousness.

Charlemagne ruled fourteen years as emperor, and his actions indicate that he took his new title seriously. He conducted a skillful diplomatic drive that compelled the Eastern emperor to recognize his powers. He also legislated more extensively than before, especially in religious matters. When he died in 814 he left a large, well-ruled state that had moved far in the direction of unity based on acceptance of one emperor and one religion.

3. THE CAROLINGIAN RENAISSANCE

Perhaps the most lasting achievement of the indefatigable Charlemagne was the cultural renaissance that distinguished his age, a revival brought about chiefly through his personal efforts. The motivation behind his cultural policy was pragmatic: He was convinced that the quality of religious and political life could be improved only by the development of better-educated leaders, especially churchmen.

His chief instrument to this end was a palace school which he began in the 780s and 790s but which took on special vigor after he built a splendid church and palace at Aachen about 800 and made that city the center of his political activities. This school attracted the best minds from all over Europe, so that it became a focal point where diverse cultural trends mingled and matured.

In one sense, the palace school served as a locus for study, writing, and discussion of problems. Charlemagne himself was an active participant in these activities. But a more important function was the development of a sound education program. Under the guidance of the Englishman Alcuin, a product of the energetic cultural environment that had produced Bede a century earlier, the school's teachers labored primarily to create the tools and methods of instruction for a proper grounding in the true religion. They sought authentic versions of Scripture, missals, laws, patristic texts, classical authors, church regulations, even Germanic legends—all those precious sources that would guide men to what the Carolingians often spoke of as "the norms of righteousness" which should define and govern Christian life. The court scholars sponsored the compilation of improved textbooks of Latin grammar and spelling and the search for models of good expression in classical authors, copying these model works for their libraries. The Carolingian copyists developed a beautiful script called *Carolingian miniscule*, which provided the base for all modern scripts and typefaces. The workshops where books were produced, called *scriptoria*, likewise developed an impressive style of manuscript illumination that constitutes a major aspect of Carolingian art.

As the tools of education were forged, Charlemagne employed his authority to universalize their use. He insisted that monasteries and bishoprics organize schools and adopt the books and methods developed at the palace school. His efforts led to a significant expansion of education and a greatly increased concern for the quality of teaching in the monastic and episcopal schools. After Charlemagne's death, the palace school declined and cultural leadership passed to these new centers, especially the monastic schools, which sustained through much of the ninth century the Carolingian renaissance.

Although the major energies of the court schoolmen were consumed in gathering and mastering the models of good thought, style, and language, some of them and their contemporaries produced distinguished original works. Einhard's biography of Charlemagne was excellent. Alcuin compiled several important textbooks of grammar and logic and was a lively letter-writer. An Italian, Paul the Deacon, produced a well-organized *History of the Lombards*. Theodulf, a Spaniard, wrote excellent poetry. A succession of theologians prepared impressive commentaries on Scripture and compiled doctrinal tracts pieced together from materials derived from Scriptural and patristic sources. Perhaps the most original mind of the age and the most competent Western theologian since Gregory the Great was an Irishman, John Scotus Erigena, who lived in the Frankish kingdom from 850 to 875. Although the bulk of the work of these and lesser lights was derivative and timid in the face of new ideas, it was infused with an esthetic sense reflecting a genuine appreciation of classical literature. Thus one may speak of a Carolingian humanism mingling with deeply ingrained Christian values.

The Carolingian revival of the plastic arts also grew out of religious concerns. Several fine churches were built, the most splendid of which was Charlemagne's at Aachen. Considerable effort was made to decorate them with mosaics and frescoes. In many ways the best Carolingian art was in miniatures: illuminated manuscripts, ivory carvings for altar adornment, metalwork, jewelry. All Carolingian art mixed diverse traditions: classical, Byzantine, Germanic, Celtic. Again, the men of this age appropriated past styles and formed them into new shapes.

4. THE DISINTEGRATION OF THE CAROLINGIAN EMPIRE

Charlemagne's political empire did not persist long. He did not succeed in developing political institutions capable of surviving him. Especially dangerous was his widespread use of feudal practices in an effort to assure the loyalty and to gain the services of the great nobles. To buy their services he had been forced to grant large blocks of land to them and to concede *immunities* which gave the nobles authority to exercise governing powers over these lands. Charlemagne tried to keep these men faithful to him by having them swear allegiance to him as his vassals, but this arrangement could work for the emperor's benefit only if he were forceful enough to compel his widely scattered vassals to perform the services owed the ruler as their lord. This was a tremendous burden; failure would allow the nobles to escape royal control still in possession of the lands granted to them to secure their loyalty and services. Charlemagne's successors could not manage and paid a disastrous price.

Moreover, Charlemagne's empire was never wholly unified. Germans, Romans, and Slavs were still divided by differences in language and cultural background. The Church, upon which Charlemagne relied so heavily to inspire and guide his subjects to obey and to serve, was actually a doubtful ally. Its leaders in Rome and in the great bishoprics and monasteries scattered over the empire were uneasy about his interference in Church affairs. While aspiring to the same end that he did—an earthly society dedicated to the service of God—many churchmen preferred to lead society themselves rather than bend before a layman. Their independence was a harbinger of bitter conflicts between church and state later in the Middle Ages.

The empire was also threatened by powerful external foes. On the south were the aggressive Muslims, especially strong in sea power, against which the Franks had little defense. On the east the Slavs, under the pressure of new invaders from Asia, the Magyars, pushed relentlessly westward. Finally, the Vikings or Norsemen (Danes, Swedes, and Norwegians) threatened on the north. The Vikings, virtually strangers to Western Europe in the early ninth century, quickly became the greatest danger.

The Vikings were still barbarians and heathens. They had long dwelt along the wild coasts of Scandinavia, surviving chiefly by fishing and piracy. Politically, strong clans played a dominant role, although by 800 loose kingdoms were in the process of formation. In the ninth century, the Vikings began to expand. Traveling by sea in small groups, they spread over an immense area, touching Ireland, England, the whole Atlantic coast of Europe, the southern shores of the North and Baltic seas, Russia, Iceland, Greenland, and probably North America. Wherever they went, they pillaged the land and hauled off vast quantities of loot. In the late ninth and tenth centuries, some of them began to settle permanently in the lands they had been raiding, especially in England, Ireland, France, and Russia, and piracy gave way to trade. The Vikings slowly accepted the religion and culture of Western Europeans, but too late to spare the Carolingian Empire. Charlemagne's successors had to face the full fury of the destructive attacks and found no effective defense against the dreaded raiding parties.

Compounding these external problems, the Carolingian state suffered from inadequate leadership throughout much of the ninth century. Charlemagne's son Louis (814–840) was an indecisive ruler. His strongest impulse was to pursue the universalist ideals embraced by the Carolingian political ideology. This inclination carried him toward a close alliance with powerful churchmen, whose gratitude earned Louis the title "Pious," but who were not averse to bending imperial policy to suit their ends. Equally powerful elements in Frankish society resisted the realization of the imperial idea with its implication of strong central government, and Louis on occasion surrendered to their pressures. The major problem of his reign centered around what provision he would make for his three surviving sons. He was torn between safeguarding the unity of the empire by designating a single successor and observing the ancient Frankish custom of dividing his empire among his heirs. His efforts to compromise these conflicting ideas led his sons to revolt.

Before his death Louis did provide a "kingdom" for each of the three sons and granted to his eldest, Lothair, the title of emperor with a vague authority over the others. Almost immediately the younger sons declared war on Lothair, and in 843 forced him to sign the Treaty of Verdun. This document legalized the division of the empire into three parts: most of modern France, Germany, and Lotharingia (Lorraine), consisting of a narrow band between the west and east kingdoms stretching from the North Sea to Italy. Eventually, there were further divisions that created the kingdoms of Italy and Burgundy.

After 843, Carolingian unity was fatally compromised. Most of the energies of the Carolingian rulers were absorbed in snatching bits of territory from their relatives. The resulting petty wars left little time for problems of religion, justice, internal order, and defense against the mounting attacks of outsiders. The later kings continued the practice of buying support by granting new lands to nobles and conceding political powers to them. This constant diminution of the royal estates and power eventually left the Carolingian rulers powerless to curb the nobility.

High churchmen usually supported the later Carolingian kings and were rewarded by rich royal endowments, but in the long run ecclesiastical support worked against the interests of the Carolingian family. The Church became bolder and bolder in its claims to supremacy over the state. By the middle of the ninth century, the pope was openly claiming superior authority over all Christians—including kings. Pope Nicholas I (858–867) actually tried to exercise these claims by interfering in the private lives of the kings, while at the same time carrying on extensive diplomatic negotiations in an attempt to halt the civil wars raging everywhere, legislating for the whole Church, and taking the lead in spreading Christianity. By 900 the Carolingian dynasty was thoroughly discredited and the empire divided beyond repair. Invaders pillaged Western Europe almost at will. Landed nobles tightened their holds on their small principalities and compelled the lower classes to submit to their petty domination. Even the Church, the last bastion of unity, suffered fragmentation. The dream of Charlemagne and his advisers to make Western Europe a single political unit had foundered in feudalism, a system based on fragmentation.

These obvious failures must not hide the deeper significance of the Carolingian Empire. Germanic rulers—represented by Charlemagne—demonstrated a deepened awareness of a responsibility other than conquering lands for their own private profit. In the centuries following his death, Charlemagne became the ideal prince for medieval Western Europe. His attempt to unify Europe politically was destined to inspire the actions of numerous later medieval rulers. France, Germany, and Italy traced their origin to the Carolingian kingdom and considered themselves its successors. Certain Carolingian techniques of government, especially the practice of creating lord-vassal ties to define the relationship between ruler and ruled, long served as the basis for political life in these successor states. Carolingian law codes persisted for many centuries in some areas of Western Europe. Under its Carolingian champions, the Western Church succeeded in imposing a considerable degree of doctrinal and liturgical uniformity throughout the West and gained important ground in creating an independent state in Italy. The papal role in sanctifying the Carolingians first as kings of the Franks and then as emperors established a significant precedent for the fundamental medieval idea that the state must have the blessing of the Church. The revival of the idea of empire dramatically reaffirmed the tie between Western Europe and classical Rome. The renewed interest in Roman civilization brought about an upsurge of intellectual activity. This Carolingian renaissance was the first of several that brought Western Europeans into more intimate contact with the classical civilizations of Greece and Rome. The true significance of the era must thus be sought in the world of ideas: It was a period when some Western Europeans tried to define what they wanted politically, socially, religiously, and culturally. Although few of their ends were attained at the time, much of later medieval history consists of working out the details of ideas developed in the Carolingian period.

5. EARLY MEDIEVAL ENGLAND

While the Carolingians were shaping much of Western Europe, the small Anglo-Saxon kingdoms of England were undergoing an important transformation. After a long period of fruitless warfare, these kingdoms began to coalesce, chiefly as a result of two outside forces—Christianity and the Viking menace.

England had been Christianized in Roman times, but the Anglo-Saxon invaders wiped out Christianity in the territories they occupied. Late in the sixth century missionaries penetrated England from both Rome and Ireland and within a century reestablished their faith as a common religion in the different kingdoms. For a brief period in the seventh century, Roman and Irish missionaries clashed bitterly for the right to dominate England. Rome won, assuring uniformity of organization, ritual, and doctrine and putting the English in touch with the mainstream of continental religious life.

The threat of the Vikings was a more important unifying force. No area suffered more from their pillaging, especially during the first half of the ninth century, and some Vikings settled permanently in a large northeast territory known as the *Danelaw*. Several of the old Anglo-Saxon kingdoms were swallowed up by the invaders.

The kingdom of Wessex became the center of

resistance and eventually of counterattack against the Vikings. The reign of Alfred the Great (871–899) was the decisive period. He not only stopped Viking expansion, but also laid the groundwork for the reconquest of the Danelaw. His leadership served to revitalize the Church and the dormant English intellectual life, and both accomplishments helped stir up the English against foreigners. During the tenth century Alfred's heirs rewon the Danelaw, pushing the English frontier to about the present boundary between England and Scotland. All the conquered territory and its peoples, including the Danes, were made subjects of a single king, who was no longer king of Wessex but king of England.

The unification of England necessitated a single government system. This system, based on institutions introduced by the Anglo-Saxons in the early fifth century, assumed its final shape by 1000. A king, claiming to be supreme judge, leader of the army, head of the Church, and lawgiver, ruled over the land. Actually, royal power was limited, since the king lacked effective means of exercising his authority. He supported himself and his court chiefly from the income derived from royal estates. Only on rare occasions could he levy a direct tax on his subjects—for instance, several kings collected the Danegeld, levied first in 991 to buy off Viking raiders. For military support, the king depended heavily on knights to whom land had been granted, although he could summon all freemen to serve in the army (called the *fyrd*). He was advised by the *Witan*, an assembly of great nobles and churchmen that in a general way was held to represent all freemen, on matters of great importance such as waging war or enacting new laws. However, a strong king could act without its approval. The whole complex of institutions surrounding him—household officials, fyrd, royal knights, and Witan—made the central govern-

ment important but certainly not strong enough to control political life in all England.

Much more significant was the system of local government that had long been evolving. England was divided into *shires,* of which there were about forty in the tenth century. The king was represented in each by three officials—the *earl,* the *sheriff,* and the *bishop.* The earl had the most rank and prestige, but the sheriff usually conducted most of the royal business. A court was held in each shire twice a year, and all freemen were expected to attend. The king's orders were proclaimed and all civil and criminal cases were handled at this court, where any freeman could bring a complaint. The law administered was customary law, dating from far back in Anglo-Saxon history and known by the local landowners who sat in the court. Each shire was subdivided into *hundreds*, where courts presided over by a royal official met monthly for minor cases. The agricultural villages also had their own courts, usually conducted by great landowners. As a rule, Church business was handled in the shire and hundred courts. This network of local institutions, tied to the central government through royal officials but largely self-sufficient, provided an element of orderly political life in England that was sometimes lacking on the Continent.

However, by 1000 England's political and social institutions were somewhat archaic due to her isolation and thus incapable of adjusting to new conditions stirring everywhere in Western Europe. During the eleventh century England was conquered by the Normans from the Continent who imposed new institutional patterns that "modernized" her society and opened a new era of growth. Perhaps the chief importation was feudalism, which during the ninth and tenth centuries had developed on the Continent as a stabilizing force but which had not emerged in late Anglo-Saxon England.

Suggested Reading

Carolingian History

The general works by Sullivan, Moss, Lewis, and Wallace-Haddrill, cited in Chapters 15 and 16, will be extremely helpful in establishing the broad outlines of Carolingian history.

*Jacques Boussard, *The Civilization of Charlemagne* (1968).

*H. Fichtenau, *The Carolingian Empire: The Age of Charlemagne* (Harper Torchbook).

Donald Bullough, *The Age of Charlemagne* (1965).

Peter Munz, *Life in the Age of Charlemagne* (1969).

R. E. Sullivan, *Aix-la-Chapelle in the Age of Charlemagne* (1963). This and the preceding four works provide interesting overviews of the nature of Carolingian society, emphasizing especially the role played by Charlemagne in shaping its main features. Boussard's book is probably the most comprehensive and up-to-date.

*Richard Winston, *Charlemagne: From the Hammer to the Cross* (Vintage). A good biography of Charlemagne.

F. L. Ganshof, *Frankish Institutions Under Charlemagne*, trans. B. and M. Lyon (1968). Valuable for the insights provided into the nature of Carolingian government.

Georges Duby, *The Early Growth of the European Economy* (1974). The best treatment of Carolingian economy, which can be complemented by Latouche's work, cited in Chapter 16.

*R. E. Sullivan, ed., *The Coronation of Charlemagne: What Did it Signify?* (Heath).

F. L. Ganshof, *The Imperial Coronation of Charlemagne: Theories and Facts* (1949).

Peter Munz, *The Origins of the Carolingian Empire* (1960). This and the two preceding works examine the complicated issues surrounding the imperial coronation from a variety of viewpoints.

E. S. Duckett, *Alcuin, Friend of Charlemagne* (1951).

———, *Carolingian Portraits: A Study in the Ninth Century* (1962). These two works provide valuable insights into the nature of the Carolingian renaissance and the accomplishments of some of its main actors. The fundamental surveys are those of Laistner and Schnürer, cited in Chapter 16.

*Roger Hinks, *Carolingian Art* (Ann Arbor). A thorough treatment.

K. J. Conant, *Carolingian and Romanesque Architecture, 800–1200*, 2nd ed. (1966). A clear description of the main features of Carolingian architecture and its relationship to later developments.

Vikings

*Johannes Bronsted, *The Vikings* (Penguin).

Peter G. Foote and David M. Wilson, *The Viking Achievement: A Survey of the Society and Culture of Early Medieval Scandinavia* (1970). Two excellent descriptions of the major features of Viking civilization; the latter work is perhaps the better.

Anglo-Saxon England

*D. Whiting, *Beginnings of English Society: Anglo-Saxon Period* (Penguin).

*P. Hunter Blair, *Introduction to Anglo-Saxon England* (Cambridge). Two concise, well-organized, clearly written surveys of Anglo-Saxon England.

*E. S. Duckett, *Alfred the Great: The King and His England* (Phoenix). A good account of the accomplishments of a great king.

Sources

The Letters of St. Boniface, trans. E. Emerton (1940). These letters written by an Anglo-Saxon missionary on the Continent throw a great deal of light on conditions in the Frankish world in the first half of the eighth century.

*Einhard, *Life of Charlemagne*, trans. S. E. Turner (Ann Arbor). The essential work by a contemporary on the great emperor.

Son of Charlemagne: A Contemporary Biography of Louis the Pious, trans. A. Cabaniss (1961).

*S. C. Easton and H. Wieruszowski, eds., *The Era of Charlemagne* (Anvil). A selection of documents representative of Carolingian life, accompanied by perceptive commentaries.

D. Whitelock, ed., *English Historical Documents, c. 500–1042* (1952). A collection similar to the preceding one, illustrative of English society in the Anglo-Saxon period.

18

THE FEUDAL AND MANORIAL SYSTEMS

The idealistic dreams that moved a few men to struggle toward a unified Christian Europe in the Carolingian age were blasted by the events of the last half of the ninth century. Amid the wreckage, two institutions emerged to provide a workable base for society: *feudalism* and *manorialism*. Both were products of forces that had been germinating in political, social, and economic life since the fall of the Roman Empire. By the late ninth and tenth centuries, they emerged as the focal organisms of Western European society.

1. ORIGINS AND NATURE OF FEUDALISM

The essential practices that characterized feudalism by the ninth and tenth centuries had their origins deep in the European past. In very simple terms, feudalism grew out of the merging of two traditions: personal dependence and a system of shared rights in land tenure, the first related to the Germanic *comitatus* and the Roman clientage and the second to the Roman tenancy system on the *latifundia*. The confusion and chaos of Western Europe after the Germanic invasions caused these usages to become widespread by the seventh and eighth centuries. In search of a strong protector, many men were happy to engage in a commendation agreement. Likewise, those in search of a livelihood or a way

to enlarge their holdings were willing to accept the use of another's land in return for service. Many small landholders were even willing to surrender ownership of their land to a more powerful man on condition that he would allow them the use of the *benefice*, as such lands were called. The greatest landowners, especially the Church, were eager to free themselves of the obligation of exploiting their extensive holdings by granting benefices to those willing to accept the use of the land in return for some service to the grantor.

As we have noted, the strongest Carolingians vigorously applied these usages as a means of expanding their power, thereby giving them greater universality and more precise legal definition. They required the great men of the realm, especially public officials, to become their vassals and rewarded them with benefices, now called *fiefs*, in return for a variety of services, the chief of which was military. In many cases they also granted their vassals immunities which conceded to them extensive governing powers over their fiefs. Vassalage and benefice came to be interconnected to the point where personal dependence almost always involved an interchange of land, specifically defined obligations, and political rights.

The eclipse of central government after about 850 amid the mounting fury of Saracen (Muslim), Magyar, and Viking raids forced

society to depend more and more on these systems for some political stability. Military security was most essential, and the emerging feudal system was especially suited to this end. A resourceful lord and his warrior vassals were the only effective force capable of defending a locality against the quick-hitting raiders. All who could sought vassalage under a strong lord; every powerful figure tried to find new vassals to swell his military following. To ensure that such arrangements would persist, vassalage and fiefs were made hereditary. Under these circumstances, the holders of fiefs often usurped political functions formerly exercised by the kings and their agents. By the beginning of the tenth century, considerable areas of Europe, especially the northern parts of the old Carolingian Empire, were fragmented into hundreds of small

This view of the medieval fortress at Carcasonne in southern France dramatically illustrates the kind of security that its possessor could offer to those who were his vassals. And it likewise suggests how defiant that same possessor and his followers could be in the face of those who claimed authority over them. *Photo: Bernard G. Silberstein/ Rapho-Guillumette*

private jurisdictions ruled by persons whose relationships were controlled wholly by their private agreements — by feudal contracts. Public authority was too weak and too remote to be effective.

One important point must be added. Long before the beginning of the tenth century, the bulk of the peasant population had already become associated in a condition of dependency with self-sufficient agricultural estates — the villas or, as they came to be called, *manors*. Their dependency was a condition that bound them to serve a possessor of land in the performance of menial services in return for use of a tenancy sufficient to the needs of a family. As a consequence, the peasants were not, properly speaking, participants in the feudal order. Feudalism involved freemen capable of performing the honorable services of fighting and governing and of managing the fiefs that were granted them. It was therefore a sociopolitical system embracing a small class of aristocrats. These same feudal lords and vassals ruled over the peasant population through a set of institutions collectively called *manorialism*.

2. THE FEUDAL CONTRACT

The political bonds involved in the feudal system were defined by the feudal contract. The ritual that evolved to witness such a contract provides a convenient key to the nature of these bonds. One man knelt before another, placed his hands between the other's, and declared himself willing to become his "man." By this voluntary act between two freemen, called *homage*, the first became a vassal and the second a lord. The lord lifted up his new "man" and kissed him, signifying that he accepted him as a vassal. The vassal then swore an oath of *fealty*, binding himself in the sight of God to live up to his obligations; and the lord gave him some object like a banner, a clod of dirt, or a ring. This was called *investiture*. It symbolized the granting of a fief, usually a piece of land, by the lord to the vassal. By the three acts of homage, fealty, and investiture, two individuals bound themselves together in a way that gave to each important rights and imposed on each duties that controlled his political and social activities to a large degree.

The relationship between lord and vassal was intended to last until one party died, unless either broke the contract by some illegal act. By the time the feudal system had reached its full development in the tenth century, the whole arrangement had become hereditary. When a lord died, his eldest son took his place, receiving homage and fealty from his father's vassals and investing them with their fiefs. When a vassal died, his lord accepted his son as a vassal and permitted him to retain the fief of his father. Under these arrangements, lord-vassal relationships continued for generations in the same families, adding considerable stability to the entire system.

The exact obligations of each party differed from place to place in Europe. Generally, however, the lord obligated himself to protect his vassal and give him justice—to use his army to defend a vassal against attack and to maintain a court where the vassal could appear and receive a hearing for any grievances he might have. Put briefly, the feudal contract imposed on the lord the grave responsibility of running a small-scale government for his vassals.

The vassal had equally important obligations. He was expected to conduct himself honorably and loyally toward his lord so as to bring no disgrace upon him—an obligation that generated a special life style in the feudal world. More specifically, he owed his lord four basic obligations: to serve as an armed knight for forty days a year at his own expense; to counsel his lord by serving at his court and performing other political duties; to give *aids* in the form of money payments in certain specific situations (for the ransom of his lord, the knighting of the lord's eldest son, and the marriage dowry of his eldest daughter); and to extend *hospitality* to the lord when he and his entourage visited the fief. In addition, the vassal was obliged to respect certain privileges, called *feudal incidents*, pertaining to the lord by virtue of the fact that he had a vital interest in the fief he had granted to the vassal. The vassal had to maintain the fief in good condition. His heir had to pay an inheritance tax, called a *relief*, when he succeeded to it. The lord had the right of *wardship* over a vassal's minor heir and had to approve the marriage of his daughter, since her husband might someday become heir to the fief. Finally, the vassal was obliged to recognize that if he died without heirs, the fief reverted to the lord.

How were these feudal contracts (which were seldom written down) enforced? When a contract is made in our society, the state stands above the parties as the enforcing agency. In the tenth century there was no effective higher authority; enforcement, too, had to be settled by lords and vassals. The chief instrument was the lord's court, in which the customs that governed feudal contracts in the given area were applied as law. A vassal accused of infidelity to his contract was judged by his "peers"—other vassals—and punished as custom dictated. To this same court every vassal had a right to bring complaints against his lord; again, the vassal's peers judged whether he had redress. Despite this machinery, force was always the final recourse. A lord could call on his other vassals to march against an unfaithful vassal, and a wronged vassal could appeal to his fellow vassals to join him in revolt against an unjust lord. Such wars were numerous in the feudal age.

It would be wrong, however, to picture lords and vassals as seeking any opportunity to start a brawl. In a society that knew no other workable political system, lords were anxious to keep their vassals and gain their services, and vassals were equally anxious to enjoy the protection of a lord. Thus it was to their mutual advantage to live up to the terms of the contract. Then too, in an age when men took religion seriously, there was a good deal of reluctance to break an oath sealed in the presence of God.

3. FEUDALISM AND THE STATE

Feudalism was not contradictory to the good governance of the state, at least in principle. The king was the supreme lord and theoretical owner of all the land in his kingdom. He could at his pleasure accept the vassalage of some of his subjects and grant them fiefs for which they owed him the services previously described. The great vassals of a king could then subdivide their holdings into smaller fiefs and grant them to other men willing to become vassals. This *subinfeudation* could continue until fiefs had been created that were only large enough to permit a single vassal to support himself and fulfill his obligations. In theory, a vast hierarchy was constructed, with the king at the top and with each rank beneath owing allegiance and services to an authority above (see diagram, page 200).

In practice, the feudal system did not work that smoothly. First, if the king or any other lord granted away too much of his land, he had no means at his disposal to compel his vassals to render him the services they owed and thus was powerless to enforce his authority over them. Second, subinfeudation created contradictory loyalties which disturbed the hierarchy. There was nothing to keep a vassal of one lord from becoming the vassal of and accepting a fief from another. To illustrate, let us return to the diagram. Man F, dissatisfied with his status as a simple vassal of E, also does homage to A, B, C, and D in return for fiefs from each one, owing services for each of these fiefs. Suppose A and D go to war. Whom would F serve, since he owes military service to each? Or suppose that by all his deals F acquires control over more land than any of his lords—A, B, C, D, or E. Obviously, he would be in a position to defy them and turn the feudal hierarchy upside down. Subinfeudation, by creating conflicting allegiances, made it impossible for feudalism to operate effectively for the control of a large state. As feudal institutions matured, attempts were made to counteract the fragmentation of authority resulting from subinfeudation by developing *liege homage*, a system whereby a lord required not only his own vassals but also their vassals and subvassals to pledge prime allegiance to him. But this practice developed too late to prevent the atomization of power in early feudal society.

Thus in the areas where feudalism developed first and spread most widely—the kingdom of the West Franks (France) and to a lesser degree in the kingdoms of Burgundy (Arles) and Italy—it seriously weakened royal power in the tenth and eleventh centuries. The kings divided most of their lands into numerous fiefs, and often the royal vassals were conceded immunities or simply usurped rights of government. The kingdoms then were broken into a confusing array of counties, duchies, viscounties, marches, and other principalities over which the weakened kings had little control. Most royal vassals subinfeudated their fiefs to become lords in their own rights. Some managed to maintain control over their vassals. However, others were just as ineffective as the kings in controlling their fiefs and vassals, so that their principalities suffered fragmentation and confusion.

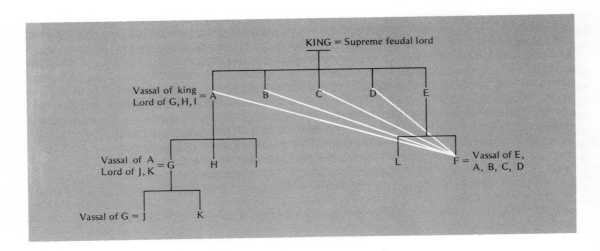

4. FEUDALISM AND THE CHURCH

Feudalism tended to spread outward from France in various ways and with various effects. While it penetrated the kingdom of the East Franks (Germany) very slowly and did not take deep hold until the twelfth century, it tended to destroy royal power and divide the kingdom. Spain became feudalized in the course of the long war to liberate the land from the Muslims; this circumstance provided feudal nobles with an opportunity to become firmly entrenched but also made them dependent on a king for military leadership. Feudalism was brought into England by a conquering king from the Continent, but he used it skillfully to increase royal power. As it penetrated the western Slavic world in the later Middle Ages, feudalism tended to weaken the state to the advantage of the nobles.

Feudalism thus did tend to divide large kingdoms into a series of small jurisdictions, each with its own set of interpersonal relationships, its own laws, and its own instruments of government. If the king were skillful, careful of his resources, and willing to labor at the task, he could exact what was due him and draw strength from the feudal system. If he squandered or lost his resources and could not control his vassals, then his kingdom became weak and divided. In short, feudalism impinged on larger political entities in terms of how it was utilized. Herein lay its danger and its dynamic potential.

Feudalism had a drastic effect on another vital institution in Western society: the Church. Under the guidance of the great Carolingian rulers of the eighth and early ninth centuries, the Church had enjoyed a tremendous upsurge in power and influence, owing to better organization, reform of the clergy, and standardization of ritual and doctrine. The coming of feudalism undid most of this work and pushed the Church into one of its worst periods of decay and inefficiency.

The difficulties of the Church in feudal society stemmed from its position as a great landholder. Much of the land had been acquired in the form of grants from kings and indeed other powerful laymen, who expected the bishops and abbots so favored to render services as did any other vassals. Once having acquired large fiefs, these officials acted as did other feudal landholders: They granted their lands out as fiefs, and thus became lords in their own right. And as lords, they had to concern themselves with protecting their vassals, holding courts, and guarding their interests in general. The consequences were disastrous for the spiritual well-being of Western Europe. Ruling Church officials became preoccupied with secular matters at the expense of their religious duties. Laymen refused to invest any bishop or abbot with a fief unless he had the qualities of a good vassal. In effect, this meant that laymen controlled elections to high offices. The top level of the Church organization thus came to be filled with good fighters and good administrators who had little interest in religious problems. They neglected discipline, education, charity, and moral conduct. The lower clergy sank into ignorance. Religious life in lay society suffered an assortment of evils worse than in any other age in Christian history. Even the pope, who was the head of the Church, did not escape. During the tenth century the papal office was filled with men chosen by powerful feudal lords in central Italy.

One must be somewhat cautious, however, in decrying the abysmal condition of the Church in the feudal age. For its feudalization drew it into intimate contact with the basic institutions and elements of society. This prepared it for an even more decisive role than it had previously enjoyed and gave it a relevance to reality such as it had seldom before had. Perhaps it would not be wrong to say that for the first time since its beginnings Christianity had become fully engaged in the world and was finally in a position where it could move the whole world by bestirring itself.

5. THE FEUDAL NOBILITY

The emergence of the feudal system brought with it the crystallization of Western Europe's nobility as a distinct class. As we have seen, that class was long in the making; its ancestors included the old Roman nobility, the Germanic warriors, the Merovingian landholder politicians, the Carolingian royal vassals. The maturing of feudalism drew these strains together into a class of specialists in warfare and government with a definite role to play in maintaining society. As it took shape, this class developed a style of life impregnated with the usages of feudalism that made it a distinctive, exclusive group almost inaccessible to the rest of Europe's population. Like its fiefs, its place became hereditary, making it self-perpetuating.

In the ninth and tenth centuries that way of life was rough and crude. No better picture of it can be found than in the epic poems written to celebrate it, especially the *Song of Roland* or *The Cid.* The great virtues of the feudal noble were loyalty, bravery, faithfulness, and generosity. Above all, he had prowess: His life centered in a career of fighting for his lord, his lands, his serfs—and his God. From his youth, he learned his craft as an apprentice in the service of one who already knew the art. The culmination of his education was his knighting, an elaborate ceremony surrounded by religious symbolism which ended with his investment with the tools

A knight receives his sword from his lord, here a king, in this early fourteenth-century initial from a Latin Bible manuscript illumination. *Photo: Dean and Chapter of Durham Cathedral, England*

of war. These made him a noble. Of course, he had to sustain himself as a warrior, so that the management of his ancestral lands constituted a part of his education. And he had a political function stemming from his position as the vassal of another and probably as a lord over still others. Therefore, his education had economic and political dimensions.

His style of life was in general crude, which stemmed in part from the economic limitations of society but also from the fact that the feudal world was a man's world. The typical noble residence was a wooden fortress designed for defense rather than comfort. The routine of life featured pursuits typical of soldiering: heavy eating, drinking, gambling, hunting, dancing, wenching, the mock warfare of the tournament, and often real warfare. Usually nobles were illiterate, "reading" by listening to tales of war sung by bards and to the simple preaching of the priests. Marriage was arranged with an eye toward gaining new lands, new vassals, or new political opportunities; seldom was it marred by considerations of sentiment. But the family was another matter, for a household rich in strong sons and nubile daughters possessed a great asset in this world of war, land acquisition, and personal relationships. The nobles were religious in a simple, unintellectual way: They trusted God to take care of them if they were brave and faithful and generous. Their way of expressing their faith was active, impelling them to do something visible to show their piety — build a church, give land to a monastery, go on a pilgrimage, or fight for God.

Under the impact of improving economic conditions, greater order, and new spiritual impulses, the feudal nobility moved toward greater gentility and refinement, and ultimately developed an elaborate code of conduct known as *chivalry* (see Chapter 19). But even in its harsh, crude form, the ethos of the feudal noble constituted a vital factor in Western European history. It nourished a sense of responsibility for the security of society. It engendered independence of action and prowess. All these qualities developed leaders with potential for constructive activity on a scale wider than the fief or petty principality.

6. THE MANORIAL SYSTEM

The feudal nobility was supported by the peasantry, comprising the great bulk of the population and living in a world apart in terms of legal status and social position. By the tenth century, peasant life in most parts of Western Europe was bound up in the manorial system. The manor was an economic unit organized to produce everything needed by its noble possessor and its peasants. It was also a political and social unit providing for the governance of the peasants living there.

The typical manor was an estate of considerable proportions, its exact size being determined by the requirements of self-sufficiency. A workable manor had to have arable land for raising crops, meadowland for hay and pasture, woodland for fuel and building material, and a natural water supply. Some feudal nobles possessed only enough land to constitute one such unit, while others held a fief large enough to incorporate several. One-third to one-half of the manor's tillable soil was reserved as a domain for the lord's support. The rest was divided into small tenancies allotted to the peasants for their own support. The untillable land, like meadows, pastures, and woods, was exploited in common. Under the widely used open-field system, the tillable land was divided into large, unfenced plots that were exploited as units. Each was subdivided into strips of about an acre. The lord reserved a third to a half of these strips in each large field to himself and assigned others to each tenant. In this way everyone got a share of good and bad land.

Farming techniques were crude. Most labor was done by hand, since few peasants could afford to feed oxen, long the chief beast of burden. Teams of oxen for heavy jobs like plowing and hauling farm equipment were communally owned. Most labor was also performed as a common effort. To protect the fertility of the soil, the three-field system was employed over much of Europe. The arable land of each manor was divided into three open fields, lord and tenants having strips in each. Every year and in rotation, one field lay fallow, a second was planted with wheat in the fall, and a third with barley or rye in the spring. In spite of this system, yields were small. Most peasants raised vegetables on the small plots surrounding their huts; these gardens were often very productive because they were fertilized with human and animal waste. Pigs and goats were especially popular because they could live off the woods and wasteland.

Most manufactured goods had to be made on a manor since there was little trade. Although specialized artisans such as blacksmiths, carpenters, and masons sometimes plied their trades there, the peasants were generally required to make and repair needed equipment, buildings, and furnishings. Women, including noble ladies, made clothing, preserved food, concocted medicine, and practiced a dozen other skills.

The center of a manor was a village containing a manor house, peasant huts, a church, granaries, a mill, a bakery, and the like. This village was more than a collection of buildings; it was a community containing a government and a social system. Its governor was the manorial lord, typically a member of the feudal order, who had the power to judge, punish, and exact what he wished from his peasant-subjects. Only rarely did an outside force—the king, a feudal overlord, the Church—succeed in intruding into the manorial jurisdiction. If the lord lived on his manor, he usually exercised his power in person with the aid of a few *bailiffs* drawn from the peasant population. If he lived elsewhere, as many great nobles who possessed numerous manors did, he entrusted management to *stewards* and bailiffs. Each manor had its own governmental institutions—a court, a law, a police force. The law, consisting of a vast body of custom defining every aspect of the relationship between the lord and the peasants, was of crucial importance in regulating manorial life.

The peasant population of a typical manor was divided into complex legal groupings, the exact status of each group being defined in terms of the obligations its members owed to the lord. On some manors, there were slaves who were simply the property of the lord; there were also freemen who rented land and returned payments in money and produce for its use but were otherwise free to do what they wished. The ordinary peasant was a *serf* or *villein* who was bound to the soil and obligated to provide services to the lord at his will, the most important being labor. Serfs almost always held a tenancy from which they could not be dispossessed, making their status a secure one. On some manors, there were peasants who had no tenancy but simply possessed a hut and garden; these *cottars* often owed some kind of service to the lord and sometimes worked for hire, either for the lord or for other peasants. These legal distinctions eventually became meaningless as a result of economic and political conditions on the manors: Because slavery was not economically feasible, most slaves merged into the class of serfs; because the freeman's liberty meant little in a world of limited choices, many of them preferred the security of serfdom.

More important to the peasant than his precise legal status were the obligations he owed to his manorial lord. The chief one was the *corvée*, which required the peasant to spend three days a week tilling the lord's land and occasionally extra time (called *boon work*) at certain seasons such as harvest. The remainder of his time was devoted to his own land. Freemen were not usually subject to the *corvée*. In addition to their regular week's work, the serfs had to keep up the village roads and buildings, transport produce, or do any other maintenance the lord imposed. All peasants were required to render to the lord certain produce; this *taille* amounted to a primitive taxation system. And they had to pay *tithes* to the Church, which often found their way into the hands of the lord. On most manors, the peasants were obliged to pay *banalities* for the use of the mills, ovens, and wine presses over which the lord maintained a monopoly—perhaps because he alone could afford to build these facilities. The lord collected a death tax (*heriot*). A serf whose daughter married outside the manor also paid a tax (*formariage* or *merchet*). There were, of course, fees and fines to be paid by peasants involved in litigation in the manorial court.

It is obvious that the manor provided the lord with considerable opportunities to enrich himself from the peasants. There were, however, limits on his exploitation, as the manor was wholly dependent on them for one prime ingredient of the manorial economy—labor. There was no substitute for human labor and no source for it except manor dwellers. The lord had to act with some justice and benevolence toward his laborers if he hoped to get efficient and constant work from them. The manorial system also supplied considerable security for the peasant. The little surplus that the collectivity could amass was a hedge against the frequent crop failures and plagues that might have meant death to a peasant on his own. The Church was ever-present on the manors, offering its particular kind of solace in the face of life's hardships. In the manorial village, the peasant found an array of pleasures—beer drinking, gaming, singing, dancing—all capable of easing a life of bare subsistence.

Feudalism and manorialism do not usually receive a sympathetic evaluation; the political, social, and economic bases of most other civilized societies seem far superior and considerably more effective. Despite their limitations, however, their operation in the backward society in which they developed was crucial. Each worked to create small associations of men that established stability in an unstable, undisciplined world. Each integrated groups of people from various levels of society and with various talents. These simple collectivities soon demonstrated an immense potential for development. It is not just coincidence that Western European society began a spectacular period of growth *after* feudalism and manorialism had emerged. They constitute the foundation stones the infant Western European society had been struggling to find since the collapse of Greco-Roman civilization.

Suggested Reading

Feudalism

*Carl Stephenson, *Mediaeval Feudalism* (Cornell). A simple, straightforward description.

*F. L. Ganshof, *Feudalism*, trans. P. Grierson (Harper Torchbook). A work stressing the legal aspects of feudalism.

*Marc Bloch, *Feudal Society*, 2 vols. (Phoenix). The classic treatment of the subject, approaching feudal institutions from a sociological perspective.

*John Beeler, *Warfare in Feudal Europe, 730–1200* (Cornell). A thorough survey of military practices related to the feudal world.

Manorialism

N. Neilson, *Medieval Agrarian Economy* (1936). An excellent, brief description of the manorial system.

Georges Duby, *Rural Economy and Country Life in the Medieval West*, trans. C. Poston (1968). This detailed study based on the most recent research is undoubtedly the best work on the nature and evolution of the medieval agricultural system. Duby's major arguments are presented in briefer form in his work cited in Chapter 17.

Marc Bloch, *French Rural History: An Essay on Its Basic Characteristics* (1966). A work that tries to describe the historical roots of the manorial system in France and to trace its evolution.

*H. S. Bennett, *Life on an English Manor* (Cambridge). An engaging picture of manorial life, stressing peasant conditions.

*Eileen Power, *Medieval People*, 10th rev. ed. (University Paperbacks). Delightfully describes typical representatives of medieval social groups; her portrait of a medieval peasant is especially effective.

Sources

*David Herlihy, ed., *The History of Feudalism* (Harper & Row). A highly informative collection of legal, literary, and narrative sources, illustrating the nature of feudal institutions and practices.

The Song of Roland, trans. F. B. Luquiens (Collier).

The Poem of the Cid, trans. L. B. Simpson (University of California). Aside from their literary value, these two medieval epic poems reveal a great deal about the mentality of the feudal nobility.

Retrospect

In a letter written in 593 or 594, Pope Gregory I called his contemporaries' attention to the strife, suffering, destruction, and injustice seen everywhere. "See what has befallen Rome, once mistress of the world," he mourned. "What is there now, I ask, of delight in this world?"

In a way, Gregory supplied the key to the history of the early Middle Ages. Most of what had characterized Greco-Roman civilization had been lost, and society was poorer. One can easily write—as many have—the history of the early Middle Ages in terms of the destruction of classical civilization; from this perspective the era is indeed a dark age.

However, between A.D. 500 and 1000 much happened to replace what had been lost. Three new civilizations—Byzantine, Muslim, and Western European—had been shaped within the confines of the classical world. Each retained precious elements of the old order. Each developed new institutions and ideas to suit its needs and situation. An inventory of what men had fashioned in these difficult centuries gives ample evidence that these "dark" years deserve a decisive place in the continuum of history. By 1000 there were still "things of delight" in the world.

The emergence of three new civilizations was not the only transformation that occurred in the early Middle Ages. In addition to the creative forces at work within each, a new dynamism had developed in the form of interactions among these civilizations. The Greco-Roman world had tended to absorb existing cultures into a unified pattern that stood counterposed to the barbarian world. By 1000 lines of interaction and points of tension existed among civilized societies rather than between the civilized and uncivilized orbits. This was a forceful determinant in the course of future historical development.

The period just reviewed belonged to the East; Byzantium and Islam far surpassed Western Europe in every respect. This little appreciated fact demands attention, for the accomplishments of the Byzantine and Muslim worlds in these centuries gave their peoples a proud sense of contribution to the creation of civilized life that other societies later forgot. None benefited more from the achievements of these leaders than the struggling Western Europeans, whose future glory would have been different had it not been for what they absorbed from the East.

V

The High Middle Ages 1000-1300 The Revival of Europe

An eleventh-century chronicler named Ralph Glaber tells us that many Europeans were convinced that, in accordance with ancient prophecy, the world would come to an end at the end of the first millennium of Christian history, that is, in the year 1000. But, wrote Ralph, when that fateful year passed without the appearance of the Antichrist, "it was as if the very world had shaken itself and cast off its old age." Everywhere, he said, men rivaled each other to build better churches and were filled with new ardor for the faith. This bit of medieval legend, whatever its validity in summing up the actual state of mind of Western Europeans in the late tenth century, provides a fitting introduction to this section. In actual fact, Western Europe did enjoy a sudden revival beginning about 1000 and continuing with unabated vigor until about 1300. This era is often referred to as the High Middle Ages. It is the period in which medieval Western European society reached its full maturity.

As our account of these effervescent, creative centuries unfolds, it should become increasingly clear that the revival of Western European civilization was rooted in certain basic institutions that had been forged during the preceding era: feudalism, manorialism, the Church, the precious treasure of learning stored up by Carolingian scholars. Although primitive in many ways, these institutions and ideas provided basic patterns of organization, social control, thought, and belief which permitted men to apply their energies and intelligences constructively. They were suddenly capable of producing new wealth. They found themselves able to construct larger political entities and to form new class relationships. Their spiritual, intellectual, and esthetic capabilities were expanded so that a wide range of cultural achievements was possible. They found themselves

able to turn outward from their be-
leaguered world to make a major impression on wide areas of the world
heretofore little known to them. In
short, the High Middle Ages was an
era of creative activity that made
Western European civilization a factor
of major significance in the world. The
long centuries of painful experimentation that marked the Early Middle
Ages had clearly ended.

A prime factor in the resurgence of Western
Europe between 1000 and 1300 was a remarkable
economic revival, which was accompanied by
major adjustments of the social order. These
changes had their source at the base of society;
their agents were modest manorial lords, toiling
peasants, peddler merchants, and simple artisans. The more spectacular accomplishments of
the High Middle Ages in politics, religion, and
culture owed a great debt to these simple members of society.

1. POPULATION GROWTH

The forces that generate economic growth in any
society are so complex that they defy clear description, and so it was in Western Europe in the
tenth century. However, one contributing factor
is evident: The population expanded rapidly
until about 1350. This demographic change, reversing the trend since late Roman times, probably began in the ninth century and was felt clear
across Asia to the Far East. The best estimates
suggest that the Western European population
grew from 27 million in 700 to 73 million in 1300
and that the heaviest population concentrations
were centered in the Loire-Seine basins in
France, the Low Countries, northern Italy, and
the Rhine Basin.

The causes of this world-wide growth are obscure. There is some evidence that Eurasia was
relatively free of killer diseases, especially bubonic plague; the destructive aspects of warfare

19
ECONOMIC AND SOCIAL REVIVAL

were curbed; and more food was available. Conditions of relative stability and security may have encouraged population growth. The growing population both put enormous pressures for greater productivity on the agricultural system and provided new hands which could be turned to new economic enterprises.

2. AGRICULTURAL EXPANSION

Perhaps the most important basis of the economic growth from 1000 to 1300 was agricultural production. By the tenth century, the manorial establishment constituted a potent reservoir of managerial ability, trained manpower, and technological skills which permitted a considerable agricultural expansion and stimulated new undertakings in trade and industry. The pressure of a growing population unleashed these latent forces.

The agricultural expansion involved four interrelated developments. First, more land was put under cultivation as a result of an immense amount of land clearance and peasant resettlement. Much of this land clearance simply involved pushing out the boundaries of existing manors, which in the Early Middle Ages stood as cultivated islands in vast stretches of forest, to put newly cleared land to the plow. But many European cultivators, often encouraged by enterprising landlords, moved great distances to settle on the frontiers of Western Europe. The chief areas of colonization were on the German

frontier east of the Elbe River and in Spanish lands being wrested from Muslim control. It appears that the cultivated acreage in Western Europe doubled or trebled between 1000 and 1300; the increase in productivity was equally great.

Second, technological advances greatly increased the efficiency of the labor force, especially by supplying new sources of power. More efficient wheeled plows were perfected. New harnesses, including the shoulder collar, were developed which allowed wider use of the speedier, more efficient horse as a draft animal. Water and wind mills were greatly improved, and complicated power trains (particularly those involving the principle of the crank) were developed to allow the power these mills produced to be applied to such tasks as grinding grain. Human labor freed by these devices was put to more productive uses.

Third, agricultural production was increased by improved methods of tillage and animal husbandry. Irrigation systems were developed in some parts of Western Europe. Agricultural specialization, as in the vineyards of Burgundy and the great sheep-raising granges in England, was made possible by increasing opportunities for exchange that we shall describe later. Greater attention was given to fertilization. The three-field system of tillage spread, which protected the fertility of the soil, promoted efficient use of labor and equipment, and permitted a greater variety of crops to be grown. Better seeds were developed in many parts of Europe to take advantage of local soil and weather conditions. And there were improvements in animal breeds to produce better draft animals and more animal products, such as meat and wool.

Finally, production was expanded as a consequence of what we might call agricultural entrepreneurship. Planning and the adaptation of ancient customs freed labor to clear new lands around existing manors, to apply new tools and techniques, and to dispose profitably of any excess production. Bold foresight resettled groups of peasants on distant lands, and new modes of operation sustained these settlements. Innovative thinking developed new seeds, bred new animals, and launched specialized production. Entrepreneurship, exercised in small and undramatic ways, perhaps provides the key to the greatest agricultural revolution in world history between the neolithic discovery of agriculture and the advent of modern mechanized farming.

3. REVIVAL OF TRADE AND MANUFACTURING

The expansion of agricultural production after 1000 paralleled an economic development of equal magnitude and importance: the revival of trade and manufacturing. Trade had never entirely vanished from the Western European scene, but it had declined steadily from late Roman times. During the late tenth and early eleventh centuries, a revival began that continued until the mid-fourteenth. During this era, commerce became the catalytic force in European economy. Among the factors contributing to the commercial revival were population growth, agricultural expansion, greater political order, outside stimuli, and Western European political, military, and religious expansion. But to these must be added the labors of men whose activities are for the most part unknown to us.

In considerable part, the Europeans' commercial expansion was a story of their ability to break into the flourishing Byzantine and Muslim trading complex and to gain control of a share of it. Western Europe had always remained in contact with the Eastern trade centers, primarily through Byzantine outposts in Venice

and southern Italy. In the tenth century this activity began to quicken. The Venetians took the leading role, steadily enlarging their contacts by sea with Constantinople and bringing an ever-increasing volume of goods to the West. In the eleventh century Pisa's and Genoa's navies loosened Muslim control over the western Mediterranean, and their merchants established trade relations with the Muslims in Spain and North Africa. The successes of the early crusading movement (see Chapter 22) allowed the Italian cities to establish important footholds in eastern Mediterranean Muslim cities in the twelfth century, and the conquest of Constantinople in 1204 during the Fourth Crusade gave the Venetians virtual control over Byzantine trade. By the thirteenth century the efforts of Italian merchants were reinforced by those from coastal cities in France and Spain; collectively they had become the dominant force in Mediterranean trade. The lifeblood of this international trade was luxury items, especially spices and fine cloth. Much of these goods were paid for by European gold, but gradually the Europeans developed products that found a market in the East.

Meanwhile, another window to the East was opened on the northern fringes of the Continent by Viking pirates whose raiding ventures opened a path through the Baltic Sea and along the rivers of Russia to the Black Sea and Constantinople. Traders from many areas of northern Europe eventually followed the Vikings along this route to carry a variety of goods to and from the lands bordering the North and Baltic seas and Constantinople. The focal point of this northern trading complex came to be Flanders and the cities of northern Germany and to a lesser degree English ports. Although the main flow of international trade was between Western Europe and the Byzantine and Muslim East, by the thirteenth century the Europeans developed a long-distance sea trade linking the lands bordering the Baltic and North seas, the Atlantic Ocean, and the Mediterranean.

By no means so spectacular as the expansion of international trade but probably more important was a steady growth of trade within Europe. Its fundamental impetuses were two: the demand of Europe's aristocracy for luxury items

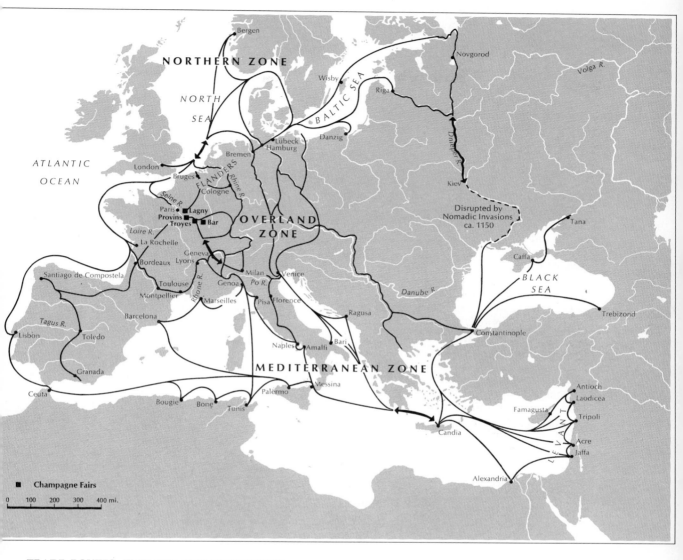

TRADE ROUTES, TWELFTH AND THIRTEENTH CENTURIES

and the needs of manors and towns for the necessities of life.

The aggressive Italian and Flemish merchants took the lead in distributing luxury items from the East across the face of Western Europe. As early as the eleventh century, Italian merchants began moving out of northern Italy into the Rhone and Rhine valleys and onward into France and Germany. Flemish traders penetrated England by the Thames and France and Germany by the Rhine, Scheldt, and Meuse valleys. From these prime arteries an ever-widening network of overland and river routes spread out in all directions. During the twelfth century, the great meeting place of international traders was the fairs of Champagne in France. Here merchants from all Europe came to display their wares to other merchants who in turn carried their purchases to local markets and prize customers. By the thirteenth century the fairs were increasingly giving way to permanent markets established in cities.

Complementing the traffic in luxury items was an ever-growing exchange of goods required by the manorial villages and the towns. Local trade in such items as salt, wine, and metals had always existed, and from the eleventh century onward, it broadened to provide the growing towns with foodstuffs and raw materials and to carry manufactured products of the towns back to the villages. In terms of volume and of the number of people involved, the town-country exchange undoubtedly constituted the larger component of medieval trade.

The expansion of commercial activity in Western Europe promoted the growth of manufacturing. By the twelfth century the towns began to offer opportunities for skilled artisans to make a single product for sale to their fellow townsmen and rural buyers or to merchants who distributed them wherever there was a demand. This kind of manufacturing long remained a vital element of the town economy and put a vast quantity of commonplace goods into trade. Some high-quality items found an international market. By the thirteenth century some areas of Europe, particularly Flanders and northern Italy, had developed more complex manufacturing organizations involving merchant entrepreneurs who "put out" raw materials into the households of hired laborers. This "putting out" system, or "cottage" industry, was especially applied to wool processing, which became international in scope: Raw wool was produced in England and processed into fine cloth in Flanders and northern Italy.

There is no way of ascertaining what the revival of trade and manufacturing meant to the Western European economy in quantitative terms. It is probably safe to venture that by the thirteenth century, Western Europe surpassed the classical world in trade and industry. Agriculture was certainly the most important element in the total economy, but the added wealth created by exchange and expert craftsmanship had decisive importance.

4. ECONOMIC CONSEQUENCES OF INCREASED PRODUCTION

The new level of prosperity generated by the increased agricultural, commercial, and industrial productivity in Western Europe manifested itself in a hundred ways: better homes, bigger churches, more elaborate dress, greater quantities and varieties of food, more art and literature, more leisure. By 1300 the specter of constant poverty and starvation had vanished for most Europeans. But aside from the general increase in wealth, greater productivity had more specific results.

First, economic growth caused the revitalization of city life. Towns had never disappeared from Western Europe. But between the fall of Greco-Roman civilization and about 1000, they became for the most part ecclesiastical, administrative, or defense centers, sparsely populated and economically dependent on agriculture. Between 1000 and 1300, ancient towns grew dramatically in area and population, and new towns appeared in many places. Whereas in 1000 most towns had only a few thousand inhabitants at most, by 1300 there were cities of considerable population: Milan had 200,000 people; Venice, Florence, and Genoa all had at least 100,000; Paris boasted 80,000; and London had some 50,000. By that date perhaps 10 percent of Europe's population lived in urban centers. Significantly, the great bulk of the residents earned their livelihood from trade and manufacturing, thus turning the "new" towns into completely different institutions from the old. The urbanization of Western Europe had begun, never to stop to the present.

In terms of physical growth, most important towns of the era were simply enlargements of older episcopal, monastic, administrative, or military centers. Merchants and then artisans were attracted to these centers for many reasons: security, favor shown them by ruling authorities, access to rivers and roads, availability of buyers. Often they settled haphazardly outside the walls of the old center, their shops, stalls, and households creating a *suburb* (Latin, "under the city"). As commercial activity increased, the walls were extended to enclose the suburbs. Often the suburb marketplace became the focus of urban life. New towns were often established at locations favorable to commerce, and their physical growth resembled that of the old centers.

A second consequence of economic expansion was the growth of a money economy. Money had always circulated in Western Europe, but minimally until the eleventh century. Thereafter its use rapidly expanded to meet the needs of trade. The money economy soon spread to agriculture, where payment in kind had long prevailed as the basis of exchange. Its impact was revolutionary. A whole new form of wealth emerged to challenge the monopoly held by land. Old economic relationships were dissolved and replaced by new. The exploitation of money shaped a new set of economic values.

A third major effect of economic growth was the transformation of manorialism. The market for surplus food provided by the towns gave landlords and peasants money incomes, in return for which they could embellish their lives with products from the town markets. This new potential for profit changed the emphasis on the manors from self-sufficiency to surplus production. And under this pressure, the traditional manorial system began to dissolve.

The dissolution proceeded in two broad directions. In many areas of Western Europe, especially in the twelfth century, landlords began to break their reserved lands into tenancies and rent them to peasants for cash. And they commuted the labor obligations of their serfs and the

One of the signs of the growth of a money economy and of more effective government in the Middle Ages was a change in tax collection; as this enlarged detail from the Canterbury Psalter shows, the officers of the king are collecting taxes in coins rather than in produce or service. *Photo: Master and Fellows, Trinity College, Cambridge*

dues owed them in kind to money payments. Serfs could afford to buy off their obligations because the town market offered them a chance to sell produce and save a little money; they were especially favored because the whole era was inflationary. But many landlords, particularly in the thirteenth century, moved in the opposite direction, expanding their domain and managing its cultivation themselves for profit. A most profitable course was to concentrate on a specialized crop for sale. Lords who did this often displaced peasants from their ancient tenancies, imposed more rigid labor obligations on them, and forced them to work for wages. In either case, the old manorial system vanished over much of Western Europe. In place of the self-contained manors emerged a variety of forms of agricultural exploitation where the concern for profit dominated, an end that could only be achieved by linking the countryside to the towns, their markets, and their money.

The fourth economic change is no surprise: the rise of the profit motive. No longer were men content with self-sufficiency; they worked and planned in order to gain more worldly goods. Western Europeans began to perfect means to achieve this end. High-profit overseas trading ventures were often financed by a non-merchant investor under a contract (called a *commenda*) that provided for sharing the profits after the merchant returned and disposed of the goods. We have already described how landlords manipulated their lands for profit. Lending money for profit (called *usury* by the Church and condemned as a sin) was widespread by the thirteenth century. These are only a few of the multitude of practices that heralded a new economic spirit. A protocapitalist economy was developing.

Finally, Western Europeans had achieved such economic growth by 1300 that they had seized economic leadership in the vast area surrounding the Mediterranean—a leadership that would soon be extended to the world. No longer did Byzantium and Islam stand in the relationship of advanced economic centers to a backward West. As we shall see later, international political factors helped promote the advance of the Europeans, but it is equally obvious that

their enterprise and their methods played a vital role in establishing their economic leadership. It is ironic that their rapid rise was in large part due to their ability to intrude into the richer economies of the East and exploit them for the benefit of the West.

5. SOCIAL CHANGE: THE BOURGEOISIE

The far-reaching economic transformation of the era from 1000 to 1300 had a significant impact on the simple social order that characterized the feudal-manorial world of the tenth century. The most important social development was the emergence of a new class, the *bourgeoisie*. Those engaged in commerce and living in towns found themselves in a society that had no place for them: no legal status, no understanding of their needs, no respect for them. One challenge facing them was to compel the feudal-manorial-ecclesiastical world to recognize and accept them and their activities. Another was to devise rules and techniques for conducting their activities in an orderly, efficient fashion.

As soon as men began to devote full time to commerce and manufacturing, they felt a basic need for personal freedom. Their livelihood depended on freedom to move about in a world that fixed men to fiefs and manors, to dispose of their property at will in a world where property was bound up in an intricate network of obligations, to apply their talent and labor to whatever opportunity arose in a world where long-sanctioned customs dictated how men spent their time and efforts. And so the merchants and the artisans of the towns struggled for personal freedom and were successful in achieving it. Their methods were various: purchase; force; grants won from kings, feudal lords, and bishops; flight. By 1300 simply living in a town meant personal freedom. This freedom constituted a prime legal mark of the new class: Its members were freemen, legally distinct from both aristocrats and serfs.

But personal freedom, although vital, was not sufficient. The merchants and artisans could not operate adequately under the institutions of government and laws of the feudal world. To meet their political and legal needs, the inhabitants of a town often banded together and sought to gain political privileges. Usually the object of their corporate action was a *charter* granted by a king, a feudal lord, or a bishop. Often the charter was not to be had for the asking, but acquiring one grew easier when the power wielders began to appreciate the advantages of having thriving towns in their domains. The typical charter usually recognized the citizen body of the town as a *corporation* that could act and be treated legally as a person. It almost always granted personal freedom to the residents of the town and called for dues in money instead of personal service. Finally, most charters granted the townsmen permission to institute their own local government. In a few cases, especially in Italy, towns gained complete political freedom; such towns, called *communes,* were the exception. More commonly, the townsmen had only the right to regulate local affairs while respecting some higher authority in matters not strictly local.

In shaping political institutions, the townsmen experimented considerably. In most towns there was some degree of popular participation in political life, authority being vested in an elected council. In a typical commune the council usually possessed complete power to legislate, conduct courts, levy taxes, expend money for civic purposes, and negotiate with outside powers. Its only responsibility was to the citizens of the town. Many towns chose a chief administrative official—*mayor, burgomaster, podesta*—who functioned under the supervision of the council. Judicial affairs were entrusted to specially trained judges. Towns with only limited political freedom often had to respect the authority of a royal official or a representative of a feudal lord who exercised many powers in judicial and financial matters. Whatever the form of government, the towns quickly created an elaborate new body of law regulating civic affairs. As a consequence, the bourgeoisie lived in an entirely different legal setting from that of nobles, clergy, and serfs.

A grave problem facing the bourgeoisie was the regulation of economic activity among merchants and artisans, a problem for which the rest of society had no solution. The usual answer was the establishment of *guilds* within each town.

The merchants usually formed a merchant guild while the artisans formed several craft guilds, one for each trade. The merchant guild existed primarily to protect the interests of merchants from outsiders and to restrain the members from taking unfair advantage of one another. Each guild enacted specific rules governing prices to be charged, trading practices to be observed, and the conditions under which trade could be conducted. The craft guilds similarly imposed regulations on their members concerning prices, quality of goods, conditions of labor, and quantity of production. They also controlled the conditions for entering a trade, a power which gave them a vital role in education. Boys began their careers as *apprentices* to a master, working from two to seven years under his guidance and living in his household. The apprentice then became a *journeyman* who worked for hire until he had saved sufficient money and developed adequate skill to open his own shop and become a *master*. Before he acquired that rank, he had to submit his workmanship to a rigid examination by the guild. Along with their regulative functions, merchant and craft guilds had purely social functions. Each usually had its own guildhall, where banquets, pageants, and religious affairs were conducted for the entertainment and edification of the members. Each guild also aided its members when sickness or death struck a family.

New business methods also developed rapidly in the towns. The use of money became typical of the town economy. Sound systems of coinage were developed, especially among the Italian towns, whose coins were used over much of Europe until royal governments finally developed national currency systems. Banks appeared and lent money for interest, supplied bills of exchange to merchants who did not want to carry large sums with them, and provided places of deposit. Although the Church strenuously opposed usury and tried to keep it a function confined to Jewish moneylenders, its struggle was not successful. By the thirteenth century several rich Italian merchant families and the great crusading orders, especially the Templars, conducted large-scale lending ventures. Gradually, the Church modified its position, conceding that great risk justified compensation and that a borrower who did not pay his debt promptly ought to be penalized. Indeed, churchmen were among the best customers of Italian bankers. Insurance was developed to protect merchants against almost any risk. Wholesaling became a regular practice. Bookkeeping systems were devised. In brief, a modern businessman would have been much at home among his medieval predecessors.

For all its success in carving a place for itself in medieval society, the bourgeoisie was still by 1300 not very exalted. The nobility looked down on the new class as uncultured and boorish, an attitude that often caused the bourgeoisie to spend their riches aping the habits of the nobles. The Church officially disapproved of many bourgeois activities as violations of Christian morality. The peasants were suspicious of the sharp practices of the townsmen; the "city slicker" is no recent invention of the rural mind. Still, the bourgeoisie was solidly established in law and was in fact a dynamic factor in the social order. It is worth noting that neither the Byzantine nor the Muslim world produced a comparable class, although trade, manufacturing, and city life in these societies were older and no less vigorous. Perhaps the reason was that the state was too powerful. In the final analysis, the rise of the bourgeoisie in Western Europe was a consequence of successful private initiative carried out by men who operated in a society where there was considerable room for free action.

6. SOCIAL CHANGE: THE FEUDAL ARISTOCRACY AND THE PEASANTRY

This society was also working powerful changes on its older classes. From the late eleventh century on, the nobility increasingly refined its pattern of life as greater wealth afforded it more luxury and leisure. The warrior's code stressing loyalty, bravery, generosity, and military prowess expanded into *chivalry*—a code of behavior brilliantly celebrated in the literature of the troubadors and the writers of romances. Chivalry placed a higher premium on courtly manners than on battlefield prowess. Women became the center of attention as objects of devotion, loyalty,

and sentimental attachment. Even the warrior impulse was transmuted—at least in theory—to a quest for some ideal for which to fight, such as the spread of the true faith or the protection of the weak.

While the noble's life was becoming more complex and refined, economic and political changes were reducing his real power. The evolving money economy created a new kind of wealth that challenged the monopoly of land-based riches. The nobleman's quest for a share of this money wealth led many aristocrats to bargain away their total mastery over the manorial structure in return for cash-paying tenancies. In an era of inflation, the rents lost their value in the long run, so that many nobles were in dire economic straits by the thirteenth century. The development of stronger central governments in many parts of Western Europe reduced the nobleman's role in warfare and government and made the lord-vassal relationship and its attendant mutual obligations less important. The weakening of the lord-vassal nexus tended to narrow the typical aristocrat's interest to people of his own class. By the thirteenth century a nobility of refinement and privilege had evolved out of a class which in the tenth and eleventh centuries was made up of specialists in warfare and governance.

The peasantry was also affected socially by the currents of change. During the twelfth and thirteenth centuries, there was large-scale freeing of serfs, especially in France, England, Flanders, Italy, and western Germany. Some peasants purchased their freedom; some gained it in return for colonizing new lands and others by leaving the manors for the city. A more important cause was the willingness of landlords to surrender their rights to a serf's produce and services for money payments. In much of the West the serf was thus becoming a tenant farmer, enjoying whatever benefits freedom brought, but also losing the paternalistic protection the manorial lord had often extended. In a general way, the tenants prospered, chiefly due to the inflation which raised prices for their produce faster than their rents. However, the economic improvement of the peasant's lot did not elevate his social status; he was still at the bottom of the social scale, perhaps even farther removed from the top than ever because of the increasing complexity and refinement of aristocratic life.

Without question, then, the landlords, peasants, merchants, and artisans had combined their productive efforts to enrich Western Europe between 1000 and 1300. And their diverse economic activities generated not only new wealth but also a battery of economic skills and techniques capable of promoting still more growth. These centuries laid the economic groundwork for the world supremacy of Western Europe. Meanwhile, the social order had shifted into more complex patterns which allowed greater flexibility and adaptability.

Suggested Reading

Overview of the Period 1000–1300

Z. N. Brooke, *A History of Europe from 911 to 1198*, 3rd ed. (1951).

C. W. Previté-Orton, *A History of Europe from 1198 to 1378*, 3rd ed, (1951). These two volumes, successive parts of a series, provide an orderly narrative survey of the period.

*R. W. Southern, *The Making of the Middle Ages* (Yale). A brilliant essay, concentrating on certain "silent" changes affecting society.

*Friedrich Heer, *The Medieval World, 1000–1350* (Mentor). A work that touches most aspects of life in the medieval period in an attempt to prove that Western Europe passed from an "open" to a "closed" society in this era.

R. S. Lopez, *The Birth of Europe* (1967). A masterful interpretation which is more meaningful if the reader has some knowledge of the history of the period.

Economic History

*R. H. Bautier, *The Economic Development of Medieval Europe* (Harcourt, Brace, Jovanovich). The best brief treatment of all phases of economic development in this period.

Georges Duby, *The Early Growth of the European Economy* (1974). Especially strong in outlining agricultural development.

*Henri Pirenne, *Economic and Social History of Medieval Europe* (Harvest). A perceptive survey, although outdated in its interpretations.

Georges Duby, *Rural Economy and Country Life in the Medieval West*, trans. C. Postan (1968). The best comprehensive treatment of agricultural life in the era.

B. H. Slicher van Bath, *Agrarian History of Western Europe, A.D. 500–1850* (1963). An excellent survey, filled with provocative speculations about aspects of agricultural life where the sources tell us little.

*R. S. Lopez, *The Commercial Revolution of the Middle Ages, 950–1350* (Spectrum). A sprightly description of commercial development by a great authority.

Social History

C. Brooke, *The Structure of Medieval Society* (1971).

Charles T. Wood, *The Age of Chivalry: Manners and Morals, 1000–1450* (1970).

*Sidney Painter, *Mediaeval Society* (Cornell).

*P. Boissonnade, *Life and Work in Medieval Europe: The Evolution of the Medieval Economy from the Fifth to the Fifteenth Century* (Harper Torchbook). This and the preceding three titles attempt to paint in broad terms the chief characteristics of the medieval social order. The works of Brooke and Painter provide the most straightforward descriptions of the social order.

*Henri Pirenne, *Medieval Cities* (Anchor).

*Fritz Rorig, *The Medieval Town* (University of California). While awaiting a truly comprehensive synthesis on medieval cities, these two works offer the best picture of the character of medieval urban development.

S. Baldwin, *Business in the Middle Ages* (1937). A brief but excellent summary of the conduct of business in the Middle Ages.

Richard Barber, *The Knight and Chivalry* (1970). An intriguing attempt to reconcile the ideals and realities of the world of chivalry and of the aristocracy of the period.

*U. T. Holmes, *Daily Life in the Twelfth Century* (Wisconsin). An intimate picture of life in Paris as seen by a university student.

Sources

*H. L. Adelson, *Medieval Commerce* (Anvil).

*R. S. Lopez and I. W. Raymond, ed., *Medieval Trade in the Mediterranean World* (Norton). This and the preceding work provide a variety of documents illustrative of the world of commerce in this period.

*J. H. Mundy and Peter Riesenberg, *The Medieval Town* (Anvil). Original sources illustrative of town life in this period.

20

POLITICAL REVIVAL: THE HOLY ROMAN EMPIRE

While Western Europe's lesser men were producing wealth at an astounding rate and rearranging their social relationships into dynamic new patterns, its kings were rebuilding the political order. From 1000 to 1300, royal governments became a positive directive force in society to a degree that had not been reached since the fall of the Roman Empire. The political history of Western Europe in this era centers on the efforts of kings to create and rule extensive political units. These new entities would long persist, some even to the present. The political revival was general in Europe, but its basic patterns were established primarily in Germany, Italy, France, and England.

1. POLITICAL PROBLEMS AND SOLUTIONS

Western Europe's major political problem in the tenth century was the progressive fragmentation of centralized authority. The course of political history in the Early Middle Ages had culminated in the feudal-manorial regime which promoted political localism. Despite the success of that regime in providing local defense and order, its very nature militated against the shaping of collectivities of any size.

Yet in the minds of tenth-century men there existed concepts pointing toward a solution to that problem. There were memories of earlier Germanic "national" groupings—Franks, Lombards, Saxons—and of the universal Christian empire of the Carolingians. In actual existence were the shadowy kingdoms created by the artificial divisions of the Carolingian Empire in the ninth century. Finally, there were examples of large political entities outside Western Europe, the most impressive of which was the Byzantine Empire, which reached its apogee in the tenth century under the Macedonian dynasty.

Given these "models," there remained the problem of discovering an agency capable of redirecting a disintegrating society toward the formation of larger political units. The only possible hope rested with the monarchs of the tenth century. Although woefully weak, they represented an ancient institution everywhere accepted as necessary to right order, and their office was surrounded by an aura of authority derived from religious ideas and traditions of power enshrined in law and custom. Most significant of all, they stood at the apex of the feudal hierarchy with at least theoretical rights to command the loyalty, obedience, and service of their vassals. The political history of the High Middle Ages is basically a story of the struggles of kings to assert their rights as supreme feudal lords and to turn feudal usages into monarchical institutions, which would allow them to control large political entities. While they never eschewed any benefits they could derive from religious and legal precedents supportive of royal power, the kings built their new regimes primarily on a feudal basis; they were first of all feudal monarchs.

2. THE FOUNDING OF THE HOLY ROMAN EMPIRE

The earliest and most spectacular effort at political reconstruction during the period 1000 to 1300 involved the Holy Roman Empire. The chief units that were combined to create it were two kingdoms established by the divisions of the Carolingian Empire. The most important was the kingdom of the East Franks, or Germany, defined by the Treaty of Verdun in 843. A generation later, further divisions of the Carolingian state created the kingdom of Italy. Until the early years of the tenth century, royal power steadily declined in both, and the kingdoms tended to break into smaller principalities. In Germany, the counts and dukes who had once served as representatives of Carolingian royal authority usurped royal power to create virtually independent domains, the chief of which were Saxony, Bavaria, Franconia, Swabia, and Lorraine. In 911 the dukes deposed the Carolingian dynasty and elected one of themselves, Conrad, duke of Franconia, as king. A comparable process but much more violent and confused was occurring in Italy, where the kingdom was torn to bits by local potentates. To complicate the situation, in the late ninth and early tenth centuries Germany was attacked by the Vikings and the Magyars, while Italy felt the lash of the Magyars and the Saracens. Since the only hope of resisting these marauders lay in well-organized local defenses, royal authority and centralized government were further weakened.

In Germany the path toward disintegration and localism was suddenly reversed by a royal dynasty emerging from the duchy of Saxony. When Conrad I died in 918, Henry, duke of Saxony, was elected king. Although Henry I (919–936) concentrated his attention chiefly on the governance of Saxony, his leadership created a solid base of power for his son, Otto the Great (937–973) who made Germany the chief political power in Europe and created the Holy Roman Empire.

Otto I was a man of great vigor and skill whose political concepts were strongly influenced by Carolingian ideas. His most pressing task was to curb the forces that were fragmenting his kingdom. This policy pitted him against the great dukes, and only after years of struggle was royal authority successfully imposed on them. In the course of the struggle he uprooted some of the old ducal families and replaced them with more docile vassals, often his own relatives. Otto's efforts to defend his kingdom were rewarded in 955 at the great Battle of Lechfeld, where the royal armies smashed the Magyar horde so completely that it never again seriously threatened Germany. Not content to trust the safety of his realm to one military victory, he launched a policy of military expansion, colonization, and missionary activity into the Slavic world, a "drive to the East" that continued for centuries—in fact, through the end of World War II.

Otto chose to base his political power on an intimate alliance with the clergy, convinced that clergymen were more loyal to the idea of monarchy than lay nobles. He made large grants of land on what amounted to a feudal basis, creating ecclesiastical fiefs in every corner of Germany, in return for the military and political services he required to sustain his royal authority. To make this policy work, Otto had to be certain of the capabilities and loyalty of the men who filled high ecclesiastical offices. He therefore assumed the power to elect the clergymen who were to receive royal lands and to serve the king. In effect, through lay investiture, the ecclesiastical establishment became an arm of the monarchy much as it had under the strong Carolingian kings.

Successful in uniting and defending his kingdom and served well by his ecclesiastical vassals, Otto made German monarchy the strongest in tenth-century Europe. From this position it was an easy step to dreams of greater power and prestige. These dreams pointed in a predictable direction: the renewal of the Carolingian Empire. Such a course meant involvement in Italy. By the mid-tenth century, many Italians were looking for an outsider to curb internal disorder and external attacks. Among them were the popes, too long captives of the local Roman aristocracy, who yearned for their old independence and realized that only a powerful outsider could restore it. Otto did not remain aloof from this situation, in part because some of his German vassals were fishing in Italy's troubled waters in an effort to increase their power. Following an indecisive venture into Italy in 951, he returned in 961 and assumed the title of "king of Italy." Then he marched on Rome, took the city, and in 962 persuaded Pope John XII to crown him emperor, the title the Carolingians had once held.

Carefully avoiding any claim to Byzantine territory in southern Italy and showing good will by marrying his heir to a Byzantine princess, Otto proceeded to make his power permanent in Rome and northern Italy. Quarrelsome aristocrats were forced to admit his authority and obey his commands. Great churchmen were vested with powers as agents of his administration. Especially significant was his policy toward the papacy. When John XII refused to ac-

Otto I, Holy Roman emperor, is shown in this tenth-century ivory plaque offering a model of Magdeburg Cathedral to Christ in majesty. The Holy Roman emperors, so closely linked with the Church, were its great patrons. *Photo: The Metropolitan Museum of Art, Gift of George Blumenthal, 1941*

cept a subservient position, Otto deposed him and dictated the election of a more pliant successor. The emperor further imposed the rule that no pope would be elected in the future without the consent of the emperor, thus opening an era of German domination of the papacy. As Otto's Italian policy took shape, it became clear that ruling that troubled land would be a major task; and Otto spent most of his later years in Italy trying to ensure his control over the nobles and the papacy.

This renewed Western empire—usually called the Holy Roman Empire—made the emperor at least in theory the head of all Christian princes in the West. Otto of course was actual master only of Germany and Italy, and his huge, multinational empire left his heirs a terrible burden. But for the moment, the ruler of Germany was the greatest political figure in Western Europe.

3. OTTO'S SUCCESSORS AND THE GATHERING OPPOSITION

From Otto I's death in 973 until 1056, a succession of five emperors continued and expanded his policies with considerable success. In Germany the independent spirit of the old duchies was virtually eliminated. The Church was skillfully manipulated to keep it a docile servant of the rulers; in the main it accepted this role willingly. Its contribution to the administration of the realm was supplemented by the development of a corps of secular administrators (called *ministeriales*) recruited from the nonnoble class and completely devoted to royal service. The emperors kept a firm hold on Italy, acting there chiefly through the powerful bishops. Strong pressures continued to be applied in the East, so successfully that by 1056 Poland, Bohemia, and Magyar Hungary all recognized imperial overlordship. On the western frontiers, German domination was established over a significant remnant of the Carolingian Empire, the kingdom of Burgundy.

The Holy Roman Empire remained the most important state in Western Europe, but as it grew, the authority of the emperors inevitably bred opposition. Perhaps most ominous was the growing strength of the German aristocrats who were busy consolidating their hold on the peasantry and building their own alliances with the Church by founding monasteries which they controlled. This strength could potentially be turned against the emperors, whose administrative machinery was not yet effective enough to exert sustained direct control over the aristocrats and who lacked the rights over them permitted by the feudal system, which had not yet made extensive inroads into Germany. The royal office was particularly vulnerable in the face of the nobility because it was elective; despite their efforts the tenth- and eleventh-century rulers had not been able to set aside the ancient Germanic elective principle in favor of hereditary succession, a failure that would soon cost them dearly.

Italy was also a source of growing opposition. The nobles remained resentful of imperial authority. More serious was a new force emerging in Italy: the commercial cities. Waxing richer and stronger from their exploitation of growing opportunities in trade, they sought an independence that could be gained only at the expense of imperial power.

The strength and aggressiveness of the Holy Roman Empire also bred resistance from outsiders. The French in the West and the Slavic kingdoms in the East were hostile and suspicious. Particularly significant was the emergence of a powerful Norman state in southern Italy and Sicily (see Chapter 22), whose ambitious, aggressive leaders by 1050 looked to the north as an area of expansion; and this led them to a confrontation with the Holy Roman emperors.

Finally and most important was a vast reform movement in religious life, which in its ideological aspects challenged the long-prevailing concept that the emperor was the divinely ordained leader of Christian society and in its practical aspects was directed against the feudalization of the Church. Its origins lay in the tenth-century monastic world, especially the Cluniac movement in France (see Chapter 23), one of whose basic principles was that monastic communities should be free from lay control over their property and personnel, for spiritual purity could not be achieved unless monks were separated from all secular influences on their lives. By the mid-

eleventh century, powerful spiritual currents were surging through European society in support of liberty for the Church, spiritual purity in the clergy, and more intense piety among laymen. Ironically, among the most ardent supporters of religious reform was the saintly emperor Henry III (1039–1056), who was seemingly unaware of its implications for his power.

Ultimately, the reform movement found its leadership in Rome. The turning point came when Henry III installed a dedicated reformer, Leo IX (1049–1054), as pope. Under Leo's leadership, the reforming spirit took over the papal court. Its driving force was a monk named Hildebrand, later to be pope as Gregory VII, who gave the movement a more radical, political orientation. He saw the Church as an earthly corporate body which is working out God's will—the salvation of man—and which must become a visible community with its own head, its own law, its own resources, and its own liberty. All Christians, even the greatest princes, must be directed by the pope to the proper execution of their responsibilities in the drama of salvation. Herein lay the radical element of the reform ideology: It denied the role of secular rulers as divinely ordained directors of Christian life.

Beginning with Leo IX, the papacy turned its new ideology into a practical reform program that impinged directly on the existing political and ecclesiastical establishments. Popes began to legislate against the immorality and corruption afflicting the clergy, especially *simony* (buying and selling Church offices) and violation of clerical celibacy. They began to build a centralized administrative machinery to enforce these rules over all Europe. In 1059 a papal decree provided that henceforth popes would be chosen by the College of Cardinals, a body of key officials who assisted the pope in directing the Church administration. The emperor was deprived of any voice in papal elections except to approve what the cardinals decided. Seeking to strengthen its position, the papacy in 1059 formed an alliance with the Normans in southern Italy and Sicily to ensure itself protection from a source other than the emperor.

This aggressive policy naturally generated resistance in many quarters. Immoral clergymen squirmed at talk of reform. Many sincere bishops and abbots, long accustomed to independence, resented Rome's growing interference in local religious affairs. Laymen were uneasy at the prospect of losing the right to appoint Church officials and thus control over its extensive lands. If the popes were successful, the whole feudal order was endangered. Especially vulnerable was the Holy Roman emperor, who relied on a subservient Church as a chief source of power. This formidable opposition might well have blighted the reform movement had it not been for Gregory VII. A strong, willful man of great political ability and courage, he was not afraid to act to achieve what he believed right. Once elected pope in 1073, he moved resolutely to carry through legislation against corrupt clergymen, and he began to remove bishops whom he judged unfit for high office. In 1075 he decreed that lay investiture was illegal, an act that put him on a collision course with all the secular princes of Western Europe. This act opened the investiture struggle, which was destined to have an especially great impact on the Holy Roman Empire.

4. THE INVESTITURE STRUGGLE

During the critical period when the papacy was repudiating the traditional relationship between secular rulers and the Church, the imperial forces were temporarily crippled. Henry III died in 1056, leaving as his successor the child Henry IV, who did not reach his majority until 1065. When he did finally assume full power, Henry showed repeatedly that he fully intended to follow the policies that had made his predecessors strong. Among other things, he proceeded to appoint men of his choice to episcopal office, despite papal attacks on lay investiture.

The break that was sure to come developed in 1075 in connection with a vacant episcopal see in Milan. Henry IV acted decisively to impose his candidate, and late in 1075, Gregory sent Henry a letter ordering him to do penance for violating Church law and threatening him with loss of his office. With the backing of most of the German bishops, Henry replied by declaring that "the false monk" Hildebrand was not even pope, since his election had been improper. Whereupon in 1076 Gregory excommunicated the emperor, suspended him from royal office, and invited the Germans to elect a new king. A considerable number of German nobles and bishops leaped at this opportunity to weaken the king. They commanded Henry to clear himself of excommunication in a personal meeting with the pope to be held in Germany in the near future or suffer deposition.

Henry IV faced a crucial issue. The specific question of lay investiture was no longer so critical as was the broader implication that the pope could claim to judge the emperor unworthy of his office and bring about his deposition. Henry had to offset this claim if he were to save his regime. His next action was tactically brilliant. He set out to intercept Gregory before the pope could reach Germany to preside over the projected meeting. In January 1077, he found Gregory at Canossa in northern Italy. In the garb of a penitent, he begged the pope's forgiveness. Although Gregory realized that to grant this would free a strengthened Henry to continue the imperial policy, he could not abdicate his role as priest. Henry was absolved. The pope had won a moral victory by forcing the most powerful ruler in Europe to admit that he had a superior, but he had apparently lost the war.

Henry moved at once to deal with his most dangerous immediate foes, the German nobility, who persisted in their plans to depose him. The king, however, skillfully and speedily beat down their resistance by force. He then turned to Italy, captured Rome, forced Gregory VII into exile, elevated a supporter to the papal throne, and had himself crowned emperor in 1084. By 1085 it appeared that the empire was saved.

But the victory was a hollow one; the papal challenge had unleashed too many enemies. Henry was unable to hold Rome against the papal allies, led by the Normans, and the papal office was returned to strong and independent hands, especially those of Urban II (1088–1099). In Germany, the nobles kept up their resistance and slowly undermined royal power. Although Henry defended his power valiantly, by the end of his reign he was a virtual fugitive from the rebellious nobles, including his own son.

The
Investiture Struggle:
A Medieval Revolution?

An American medievalist has written that the investiture struggle was one of four "world revolutions" that shaped the Western world. This may seem a little exaggerated in view of the many momentous revolutions occurring later in Western Europe. However, medievalists do in general agree that the investiture struggle was crucial in the course of the history of Western Europe.

One school of investigators sees the struggle as a revolt against a deeply imbedded system governing church property and offices. When the Germans established their mastery over the Western Roman Empire, they brought with them a concept that everything connected with a piece of property belonged to the proprietor. As a consequence, they viewed churches built on lands they occupied as private property and could not conceive of them as belonging to a corporate entity, the Church, as had been the case under Roman law. It was but a simple step from this concept to treating offices associated with churches—priestly, episcopal, abbatial, and even papal—as properties to be disposed of by the possessor as he saw fit. This led to proprietors' controlling appointments to ecclesiastical offices and buying and selling them. Thus emerged the feudal Church, a creation based on Germanic concepts of property. The investiture struggle was in essence an attempt to liberate church property and offices from private ownership and to vest them in corporate hands. The revolutionary implications are obvious: the shifting of vast wealth and thus power from secular to clerical hands and the possibilities of independence open to the corporate Church.

Another and not unrelated view emphasizing the revolutionary nature of the investiture struggle centers on its political implications. Many generations of historians have viewed the clash as an event that condemned Germany and Italy to centuries of internal political chaos and backwardness. They argue that during the period 962–1075 the Holy Roman Empire, representing a limited revival of the Carolingian Empire, had become the strongest, best-organized political unit in Western Europe. Its basic strength derived from a close and mutually beneficial union between church and state. Pope Gregory VII's program worked to detach the German and Italian clergy from the relationship with the emperor with the ultimate consequence of destroying the constitutional basis of the Holy Roman Empire and opening the way for secular nobles to establish independence from the emperor.

Other historians view the investiture struggle more radically—as an effort by an ecclesiastical faction led by Gregory VII to apply a revolutionary sociopolitical ideology. For centuries, Western Europeans had accepted the basic idea that the welfare of Christian society depended upon the actions of divinely ordained rulers whose elevation to office gave them God's blessing to subordinate and direct all society, including the clergy, toward salvation. The royal office combined the functions of both *rex* and *sacerdos*, king and priest, to the end that the divine will be accomplished. The Gregorian party challenged this conception of right order. They insisted it was God's will that the priests should direct society, including its secular rulers, toward its ultimate destiny. The true Christian community—the Church—was a society of the baptized guided by priests whose office gave them the divine grace and wisdom to instruct the faithful according to God's plan. The kings were only agents of the priests, obligated to do the priestly bidding so that right order would be maintained.

Several scholars see the investiture struggle as a revolution less in itself than in its consequences—the fact that it led to a radical change in the governance of the Church. The papacy turned its energies toward defining its powers over the clergy and laity precisely and developing techniques for asserting its claims. The outcome was the papal monarchy and the centralized Church that reached maturity in the thirteenth century and has since remained an important ingredient in Western European society.

Still another group of scholars sees the investiture struggle primarily as a revolutionary shift of the monastic idea that the true path to spiritual improvement involved withdrawal from the world to the holy precincts of a monastery. The investiture struggle directed holy men—exemplified by Gregory VII—to move out of the cloister into the wicked world in order to attack evil and to persuade sinful kings, nobles, bishops, priests, and ordinary men to "convert" to the true Christian life. The investiture problem and its attendant abuses reversed the centuries-long tradition idealizing flight from the world and replaced it with an activist ethos of involvement in worldly affairs.

Whether these issues constitute the "stuff" of real revolution will depend on one's judgment of what is decisive in human affairs. However, when a particular episode in history entails control of property, the constitution of a powerful political entity, the nature of right order in society, the character of ecclesiastical government, and how man acts to change society, then surely revolutionary issues are at stake. One test might be to watch for the extent to which these issues dominated historical development after the investiture struggle.

Henry IV's three successors, who ruled until 1152, could not stem the tide against monarchical power. Imperial political power in Italy nearly disappeared, usurped by independent towns, nobles, and the papacy. The imperial crown tended to become a pawn of warring noble factions, election going to the prince who seemed least likely to exert effective power. Imperial resources were dissipated or usurped, and the administrative machinery broke down. In 1122 Emperor Henry V made peace with the Church over the specific issue of lay investiture by signing the Concordat of Worms, which provided that election to ecclesiastical offices be made by the Church, while the lands and secular powers associated with the office be invested by the ruler. This compromise settlement gave the emperor an effective veto over elections by allowing him to withhold the property of the office. But it also deprived the monarchy of absolute control over its major support.

Although the investiture issue had been set to rest, it had created a crucial problem from the German monarch's point of view: In Germany (and to a lesser extent in Italy) it encouraged the rapid spread of feudalism. Interminable civil wars drove the weak to seek the protection of the strong and the strong to strengthen their hand by marshaling as many followers and as much territory as possible. The desperate emperors often conceded lands and rights in an effort to buy the support of nobles. The emergence of a feudalized Germany left the monarchy out of the picture, for the emperors had traditionally claimed authority on a basis other than feudal rights. By 1152 the Germany monarchy that had been so successful in the tenth and eleventh centuries had lost touch with the new society that had emerged during the investiture struggle. A kingdom that had escaped feudalization in the tenth century had now acquired a feudal structure, and the monarchy had no means of coping with it.

5. THE HOHENSTAUFENS

Despite the destructive impact of the investiture struggle, the Holy Roman Empire survived. At mid-twelfth century a new dynasty, the Hohenstaufens, took up the task of rebuilding the imperial government. The first notable Hohenstaufen was Frederick Barbarossa (1152–1190). Elected king with a remarkable show of unanimity among the warring nobles, Frederick I began from a position of strength, and he set resolutely about establishing a basis for royal power that would fit the new political world in which he lived. In essence, his policy aimed at turning feudalism to royal advantage in order to build a system of government based on secular rather than theocratic principles, principles that Frederick derived in considerable part from the Roman law then enjoying a revival in Western Europe.

His first task was to establish order. He made broad concessions to a few great nobles and allowed them to curb their troublesome vassals, the lesser nobles. The chief beneficiary of this policy was the leader of the traditionally anti-Hohenstaufen faction, Henry of Saxony, who with royal approval became the master of Saxony and Bavaria. But Frederick was careful to define his regalian rights clearly and to insist that his great vassals respect them. To enforce these rights, he gave special attention to increasing his royal domain, much of which was concentrated in Swabia (the Hohenstaufen homeland), and to developing a nonfeudal corps of civil servants. He continued the old imperial policy of turning the German Church to royal support, a policy that entailed royal control of ecclesiastical elections.

Although Frederick's early relations with the papacy were friendly, permitting him to be crowned emperor in 1155, he made it clear that he had no intention of admitting papal supremacy or of allowing the papacy to restrict what he considered to be his rights over the Church. Moreover, he laid down a new set of rules to govern the relationship between the emperor and the rich Italian towns. Henceforth, the towns were to pay regular taxes, accept imperial officials as their rulers, and permit the emperor to coin money and regulate commerce. At one stroke, the freedoms the Italian cities had been fashioning for the previous century were to be denied them.

Once Frederick had made clear his policy with respect to the papacy and the towns, the storm broke. For most of his reign he was forced to fight an imposing array of enemies, led by the papacy. Pope Alexander III (1159–1181), a true heir of Gregory VII, was the main protagonist, and Frederick sought—unsuccessfully—to replace him. With papal encouragement, the Italian towns formed the Lombard League to resist Frederick, and once again the Norman kingdom of Sicily rallied to oppose the emperor. And the German nobles used every chance to limit and defy royal authority. In 1176 at the Battle of Legnano Frederick suffered a crushing military defeat at the hands of the Lombard League, partly because his great German vassals refused to supply troops. In 1177 he gave up his attempt to establish a German pope and recognized Alexander III. In 1183, at the Peace of Constance, the Italian towns came to terms, recognizing Freder-

Emperor Frederick II, a fascinating medieval king, is shown here as a newborn being displayed to the people by his mother, the empress Constance. *Photo: Bürgerbibliothek, Bern*

ick's overlordship in return for certain specific rights, such as choosing their own officials and levying their own taxes. In 1186 he arranged for the marriage of his son Henry to the heiress of the Norman kingdom of Sicily, detoothing one of his most persistent foes. Frederick's sensible compromises had not gained him full control of Italy or subdued the papacy, but his authority was still extensive there and his position as emperor intact. His long-standing policy of trying to live with a few great princes in Germany did not prove wholly successful. Eventually, he had to smash the chief of these, Henry of Saxony. Thereafter, he decided to break up the large principalities and grant the territory to many lesser nobles. This step relieved the immediate danger but in the long run, by further promoting feudalization, proved fatal to royal power.

Frederick Barbarossa's illustrious career ended in 1190 when he drowned while leading the Third Crusade. His son, Henry VI (1190–1197), began as if he would sustain his father's work, fighting a successful war to incorporate into the

empire the kingdom of Sicily, which he claimed by virtue of his marriage to the heiress of that realm. But then instead of concerning himself with establishing effective control over the restless German nobility, he became enmeshed in a series of schemes to extend his power over the Mediterranean to the Holy Land, France, and Spain. As his schemes unfolded, the foes of strong central rule began to join hands. Only a premature death in 1197 relieved him from paying the full price for too great ambition.

For the next two decades the fate of the Holy Roman Empire was determined by the most powerful of all the medieval popes, Innocent III (1198–1216). In 1198 he assumed guardianship over Henry VI's three-year-old heir, Frederick, and in that role took virtual control over the kingdom of Sicily. His concern was to prevent a single Hohenstaufen from ruling Germany and Sicily, a policy that would allow him to restore papal power in central Italy. In Germany the nobles remained loyal to the Hohenstaufens, and elected Philip of Swabia as king. Innocent immediately promoted the claims of another candidate, Otto of Brunswick. This led to a civil war that lasted until 1212 and virtually ruined Germany. Papal diplomacy encouraged the northern Italian towns and the nobles of central Italy to throw off imperial control. The work of Frederick Barbarossa seemed completely ruined; the Holy Roman Empire had become a pawn of the papacy.

In 1212, with the aid of the king of France, Innocent engineered the election of his ward to the kingship of Germany and eventually to the Holy Roman emperorship. Frederick II paid for papal support by making sweeping concessions that returned control of the German Church to the papacy and fortified papal independence in Italy. But he proved no docile servant of the pope. He took up the battle to build a strong Holy Roman Empire with a political skill, ruthless ambition, and personal qualities that made him one of the most intriguing figures in all medieval history. His enemies—and they were many—branded him irreligious, immoral, dishonest, cruel, and Antichrist, while his admirers saw him as a new man driven by a secular spirit quite distinct from that of his era.

Frederick II took a new view toward the Holy Roman Empire. He was little interested in Germany as the base for imperial power; Italy was the focus of his political concern. After becoming ruler of Germany, he remained there only until 1220. He spent these years surrendering royal power. He was as generous to the great feudal princes as to the papacy: He made their fiefs hereditary, gave full rights of government over the fiefs, and even turned over to them the strong position the early Hohenstaufens had established in the towns.

As he progressively disengaged himself from Germany, Frederick turned his energies to building his homeland, Sicily, into a centralized, bureaucratic state where royal power resembled the Byzantine. From this base he sought to extend his control to all of Italy. But this program reopened ancient hostilities. For nearly thirty years a series of able popes backed by the cities battled Frederick II, who fought skillfully and with great flair but lacked the resources to win. Papal prestige was too extensive in Euope for him to form an antipapal alliance. He drew almost no help from the Germans who were too busy enjoying the privileges he had extended them to render help. Frederick II died in 1250 far from realizing his ambitions; in fact, his policy had irreparably damaged any realistic base for imperial authority.

Amid bickering and foreign intervention, the German nobles did not agree on a new king until 1273, when they elected Rudolph of Hapsburg, qualified chiefly by his lack of strength. In the interval 1250 to 1273, known as the Interregnum, the last vestiges of effective imperial power were destroyed. Germany had finally broken to pieces politically. Meanwhile, a French prince, Charles of Anjou, accepting a papal invitation, assumed the crown of the kingdom of Sicily in 1266. In the rest of the peninsula each city, each noble, each churchman went an independent way, respecting no higher authority and feeling no attachment to Italy. The Slavic kingdoms that had so long been under strong German influence were also free. One of the cherished dreams of medieval men—of a Christian empire in which men who held one faith would enjoy one ruler and one law—had failed.

Suggested Reading

The Holy Roman Empire

*Geoffrey Barraclough, *The Origins of Modern Germany* (Capricorn). By far the best treatment of the subject in English.

*James Bryce, *The Holy Roman Empire* (Schocken Books). This classic, originally published in 1864, is still worth reading.

Karl Hampe, *Germany under the Salian and Hohenstaufen Emperors,* trans. R. Bennett (1973). An excellent survey by one of the great German authorities on this period.

*R. W. Herzstein, ed., *The Holy Roman Empire in the Middle Ages: Universal State or German Catastrophe?* (Heath). A selection of modern authorities presenting different interpretations of the nature and fate of the medieval Holy Roman Empire.

L. Salvatorelli, *A Concise History of Italy* (1940). A brief survey of Italian history in this period.

W. Butler, *The Lombard Communes* (1906). An old but useful treatment of the Italian city states that gave the emperors such difficulty.

The Investiture Struggle

G. Tellenbach, *Church, State, and Christian Society at the Time of the Investiture Struggle* (1959). A balanced and comprehensive treatment of the ideological issues involved in the investiture struggle.

*Schafer Williams, ed., *The Gregorian Epoch, Reformation, Revolution, Reaction?* (Heath). A collection of essays by modern authorities treating the nature of the investiture struggle.

Walter Ullmann, *The Growth of Papal Government in the Middle Ages,* 2nd ed. (1962). A controversial but provocative analysis of the papal position in the struggle with the Empire.

Biographies

Peter Munz, *Frederick Barbarossa: A Study in Medieval Politics* (1969).

Thomas C. Van Cleve, *The Emperor Frederick II of Hohenstaufen: Immutator Mundi* (1972).

A. J. Macdonald, *Hildebrand: A Life of Gregory VII* (1932).

Sources

The Correspondence of Gregory VII, trans. E. Emerton (1932). Presents an excellent picture of Gregory's ideas and his efforts to apply them to the reform of Christian society.

Imperial Lives and Letters of the Eleventh Century, trans. T. Mommsen and K. Morrison (1962). A collection of documents that illuminates the imperial position in the struggles of the eleventh century.

Boyd J. Hill, *Medieval Monarchy in Action: The German Empire from Henry I to Henry IV* (1972). The collection of documents appended to this description of the reigns of the first German emperors is invaluable in illustrating the nature of the imperial system of government.

*Otto of Freising, *Deeds of Frederick Barbarossa,* trans. C. C. Mierow and R. Emory (Norton). An account of Frederick I's reign by a contemporary bishop.

21

POLITICAL REVIVAL: ENGLAND AND FRANCE

While the German rulers struggled valiantly but in vain to create a strong state embracing Germany and Italy, political change progressed less dramatically but more effectively in England and France. The rulers of each, chiefly by exploiting feudal rights, slowly built their power to the point where they exercised extensive control over their states, largely because they had created effective institutions of royal government. Strong central government developed in England earlier than in France, but the powers of the French monarchy were ultimately greater — so great, in fact, that France had become the dominant political power in Europe by the end of the thirteenth century.

1. ENGLAND: THE NORMAN CONQUEST

As we have seen, a well-established system of government had evolved in Anglo-Saxon England, reaching its apogee in the tenth century: an effective central government, strong local institutions, a legal system based on customary law, and a military and financial organization that permitted a king like Alfred the Great to defend his people against the Vikings and to impose his authority on most of the country. The kings exercised considerable power directly over their subjects, most of whom were freemen, at a time when royal power was being replaced by the feudal system in many areas on the Continent.

During the eleventh century, Anglo-Saxon monarchy began to show signs of losing its vitality. The rulers' chief local officials, the earls and sheriffs, steadily secured rights of private government. The kings began to grant royal lands to *thegns* who pledged military service in return but often failed to render it. Many freemen were forced to become dependents of the powerful nobles as either vassals or serfs. New Scandinavian inroads undermined royal prestige and encouraged local independence. Canute, a Dane, even took the English crown (1016–1035). He dreamed of drawing England into a vast northern maritime empire, but his plans were foiled by his early death and by ineffective successors.

Edward the Confessor, of the old Anglo-Saxon royal line, then took the throne (1042–1066). His reign was characterized by a rapid deterioration of royal power to the special advantage of the great earls, of whom Godwin of Wessex was the most powerful. When Edward died without heirs, the Witan elected as king Harold, Godwin's son, who was immediately faced with an invasion led by Harald Hardrada, king of Norway, who coveted the English throne. Into this mounting crisis entered William, duke of Normandy. This ambitious chief of a powerful feudal principality and leader of an aggressive nobility laid claim to the English crown on the basis of his distant kinship with Edward. Harald and William chose almost the same moment to assert their claims, forcing a settlement on the battlefield in 1066. King Harold crushed the invading Scandinavians only to meet disaster a short time later, in October, at the Battle of Hastings, where William's Norman knights overpowered the Anglo-Saxon forces and made it possible for their leader to assume the English crown as William I (1066–1087).

William made it clear at his coronation that he would observe Anglo-Saxon customs and exercise all the rights belonging to the Anglo-Saxon kings. This gave his office a far broader theoretical base and a far more extensive claim on his subjects than was the case with continental kings, where feudalism had eroded royal power. To provide the means to exert these rights and powers William took a momentous step: He introduced feudalism into England. William claimed all her land by right of conquest. He set aside about one-sixth of it as the royal domain and granted out most of the rest as fiefs to his Norman followers. In return, they became his vassals, owing him services, chiefly military, in proportion to the size of their fiefs. Most of his direct vassals (called *tenants-in-chief* or *barons*) subinfeudated their lands and acquired their own vassals. William, however, insisted that all subvassals owed first allegiance to the king, thereby establishing a meaningful feudal hierarchy with the king at the head. Through these steps, he not only secured a valuable royal domain but also the military service of about 5,000 knights, enough to ensure his mastery of England, as well as the obedience of her powerful men. In short, the feudal system allowed him to impose a new ruling elite on England in a fashion that gave him as king control over it.

As successor to the Anglo-Saxon kings and chief lord of the feudal hierarchy, William had the authority and resources to lay the groundwork for a strong central government. The Anglo-Saxon Witan was replaced by a feudal body called the *curia regis,* at whose meetings the king's lay and ecclesiastical vassals were expected to judge cases and advise the ruler. William continued to collect the taxes owed the king from Anglo-Saxon times, the chief one being the Danegeld, originally imposed in 991 to provide ransom money to the Danes. In 1086 William's agents compiled the Domesday Book, a survey of England's wealth manor by manor which documented what men had and how much they owed the king. No other monarch in Europe was in a position to reach so directly into the affairs of his subjects; and William developed administrative machinery to exploit that knowledge.

William was careful to retain the local units of administration he had inherited, the Anglo-Saxon shires and hundreds, and to see to it that the local officials, especially the sheriffs, served royal purposes. Through these units he kept in direct touch with large numbers of the English people in the execution of justice, police regulation, and taxation. On the Continent feudal governments had expanded their activities to replace royal government, but in England strong local institutions controlled by the king prevented this development, to the distinct advantage of central authority.

Overlooking no possible source of power and prestige, William acted to attach the Church to his new establishment. William won the support of the reformers and the blessing of the papacy by promising at the time of the conquest to undertake the reform of the badly corrupted Anglo-Saxon Church. Once in control of England, he brought in a Norman, Lanfranc, as archbishop of Canterbury, and Lanfranc considerably improved religious life in England. William was generous in endowing the Church with property and in permitting it liberty to conduct its own courts. However, he never relinquished real control over it, especially in the choice of high ecclesiastical officials. Such a policy risked a quarrel with the Church, but he applied it successfully, which assured him of the immensely valuable support of key church officials.

The Norman conquest was thus a watershed in English history. A disintegrating monarchy was given new political vitality by injecting into its structure certain Continental feudal practices that buttressed the power of the king. The combination of royal and feudal powers provided the king-lord with an opportunity to make himself the real master of England. Moreover, the Normans opened that island to new, invigorating influences. The manorial system with its potential for great agricultural productivity spread rapidly, although it did have the effect of reducing many Anglo-Saxon *ceorls* (freemen with small individual landholdings) to serfdom. New ideas and styles in theology, literature, and art flooded into England to transform Anglo-Saxon culture. Trade relations with the Continent quickened. Contemporaries sometimes lamented that much was lost in the submersion of Anglo-Saxon society, but on the whole England gained from being drawn into the mainstream of Continental life. Her greatest gain was the foundation of a sound political order.

2. GROWTH OF THE MONARCHY

During the next century William's successors were energetic, capable kings who worked hard to develop royal power: the rough, brutal William II (1087–1100); the quiet, prudent, and avaricious Henry I (1100–1135); the ambitious, tempestuous Henry II (1154–1189); and the colorful, romantic ideal knight, Richard I, the Lionhearted (1189–1199). Only one difficult interlude intervened, brought about by a disputed succession in 1135. The twelfth-century kings were men with interests far transcending the governance of England. They managed to expand English influences into Wales, Scotland, and Ireland. William left them with a Continental commitment in Normandy that Henry II expanded into an "empire" embracing half of France. Richard played a leading role in the Third Crusade. These activities made England a major power in twelfth-century Europe. But we must neglect these aspects of English history in order to concentrate on the successful efforts of the kings to perfect effective monarchical government.

One of the major achievements of the twelfth-century English kings, especially Henry I and Henry II, was the formation of an effective central administration, fashioned by combining the old Anglo-Saxon household officials and the feudal *curia regis*. Development moved along two complementary lines. On the one hand, the kings began to draw men from the *curia regis* to serve constantly instead of returning to their private affairs after brief meetings of this body. To this full-time core the kings gradually added

increasing numbers of permanent civil servants, often of nonnoble origin. On the other hand, the kings began to assign specialized functions to this body of permanent servants—the beginnings of departments of administration. During the twelfth century, four specialized groups took shape: the *Exchequer*, for financial administration; the *Treasury*, for guarding and dispensing royal money; the *Chancery*, for issuing royal orders and composing royal correspondence; and the *royal law courts*. So competent did bureaucracy become that Richard I was able to spend most of his reign abroad without any loss of power. It hardly need be added that its growth greatly reduced the dependence of the kings on the political services of their vassals.

So did the kings' management of their military and financial resources. Although they continued to count on the vassals' military service, they maintained the ancient royal right to summon the *fyrd*, the army of all freemen in the realm. And toward the end of the century they began to use mercenary soldiers and to allow vassals to make money payments, called *scutage*, in lieu of service. The financial support of the growing government still depended chiefly on exploitation of the royal domain, and the king's agents were remarkably efficient and even ruthless in administering these estates and in collecting fines and fees. Customs duties were imposed on an ever-wider scale, allowing the kings to capitalize on the growing trade. They also devised ways of imposing direct taxes on income and property.

The kings continued to sustain and strengthen the ancient system of local government. They resisted the ever-present tendency for the sheriffs to usurp royal power for private advantage by using the agencies of the central government to maintain control over the sheriffs and to broaden their activities in support of the king. Henry II was especially effective in providing clearer definitions of the obligations of the sheriffs. Thus the old local institutions of government remained a powerful support of royal authority and a constant barrier against localism.

Beyond all doubt, the most important development of the twelfth century was the formation of a royal judicial system, a development again led and fostered by Henry I and Henry II. Their chief concerns were to increase the number of royal courts, to man them with expert judges, and to encourage them to apply a unified legal code. Henry I began the *circuit court system*, sending itinerant judges at set intervals to shires throughout England to try cases involving the king's interests. By the time of Henry II, this had become a regular practice, and by comparing notes the judges were soon able to erect a common set of principles for deciding cases. A *common law* was in the making. Henry II established the first of England's great central courts, sitting permanently at Westminster to handle

Manuscript illustration showing the murder of Thomas à Becket in the cathedral at Canterbury.
Photo: The Walters Art Gallery, Baltimore

many cases previously heard by the *curia regis*. Soon this body began to divide into specialized courts, like the *court of common pleas* and the *court of the king's bench*. The decisions of these central courts guided the activities of itinerant judges and contributed greatly to uniformity in the royal legal system.

Expanding the jurisdiction of the king's courts meant depriving feudal lords, the Church, manorial courts, and town courts of some of their ancient rights of justice. In this battle the kings and their lawyer-servants showed the greatest ingenuity. The kings usually expanded their authority over criminal cases by legislation that defined new crimes against the peace and ordered royal judges to punish violators. No one complained too loudly, since all society was happy to see violence curbed. Increasing royal control over civil cases, chiefly involving property disputes, was more complicated and met with greater opposition, especially from feudal lords long accustomed to dealing with property disputes in their own courts. Insisting that a man ought not lose his property unjustly (who would disagree?), the king declared that a dissatisfied litigant could purchase a *writ* ordering a royal inquiry into his case. The fertile minds of the royal lawyers soon devised writs that applied to almost every conceivable kind of property dispute. In effect, purchasing a writ amounted to transferring a civil dispute from feudal or manorial courts to royal courts.

To encourage the use of royal courts, Henry II and his lawyers made important innovations that ensured speedier and more efficient judgments. Well-trained experts who excelled feudal barons in their knowledge of the law served as royal judges and lawyers. Court sessions were held regularly when scheduled. Fees were clearly fixed. Corruption and bribery among royal judges were severely punished.

Even more significant was the introduction of the *jury system* in criminal cases. Long before Henry II's reign groups of men had been called together by the king or his officials and required under oath to tell what they knew about some public question. After 1164 Henry applied this idea to criminal cases, having sheriffs call together a *presentment* or *grand* jury for testimony leading to the apprehension of criminals. By the thirteenth century groups of men known as *petit* juries were used to decide guilt or innocence.

The jury system quickly proved superior to traditional practices, which relied on trial by ordeal or by battle to ascertain God's will in proving guilt or innocence. Trial by ordeal required one charged with an offense to submit to a physical test, such as being thrown into water or walking through fire. The outcome revealed the truth: For example, if the accused sank in the water, he was innocent because the water accepted him, but if he floated he was guilty. In trial by battle, the victor won the case. The jury system, emphasizing the evaluation of evidence, proved fairer, more efficient, and more humane. This innovation, together with the other steps taken to improve the judicial process, made royal courts popular. Indeed, nothing increased the prestige of the English monarchy more than the expansion of royal justice.

As one would expect, the feudal lords and the Church chafed under this rapid, aggressive expansion of royal authority. However, during the twelfth century their resistance was sporadic and ineffective. On the whole, the English nobility did more to sustain the growth of strong monarchy than to oppose it and in so doing learned to identify their interests with those of the whole kingdom.

The Church proved a stouter foe than the nobility; throughout the century there were sharp clashes between kings and clergy. William I set the pattern for his successors by richly endowing the Church and supporting its reforming moves, while insisting firmly on royal control of ecclesiastical offices and of a portion of the Church's wealth. During the reign of William II, the Church, led by Anselm, archbishop of Canterbury, challenged the monarchy's right to appoint church officials. This struggle was resolved by the Compromise of Bec in 1106, which allowed the Church to elect its own officials, but reserved to the king the privilege of investing these officials with their lands. A more serious struggle arose when Henry II tried to limit the jurisdiction of Church courts. Thomas à Becket, archbishop of Canterbury, defended the Church's cause so skillfully that an enraged

Henry finally cried out for his murder. Thomas' martyrdom forced the king to concede considerable freedom to the Church in judicial matters. On the whole, however, the English kings exercised a powerful control over the Church, and the Church gave its support to the strengthening of monarchy. England escaped the fatal plague of the Holy Roman Empire—an eternal war with the Church.

3. THE LIMITING OF ROYAL POWER

The remarkable advance of royal power in twelfth-century England ultimately generated a reaction during the thirteenth century. Nobles, churchmen, and the rising bourgeoisie joined hands to compel the kings to recognize a principle inherent in feudal monarchy: that royal power was limited by the "law" of the feudal contract. This challenge marked a major step in establishing constitutional monarchy in England.

The conflict broke into the open during the reign of John (1199–1216). A rash, obstinate tyrant who brought part of his trouble on himself by his inordinate demands on his subjects, John also had the misfortune of having as his enemies two of the most formidable personalities in medieval history, King Philip Augustus of France and Pope Innocent III. Philip captured a considerable part of the French territories under English control in a war that required John to impose a heavy burden of service and taxation on his subjects in a losing cause. Then John became involved in a struggle with Innocent III over the appointment of the archbishop of Canterbury. Again he lost, being forced to acknowledge that he was a vassal of the pope holding England as a fief.

These rebuffs, coupled with a series of tyrannical acts by John, led to a rebellion in 1214 from which he extricated himself only by signing the Magna Carta in 1215. Loudly celebrated by later generations as a charter of liberty, the Magna Carta basically just affirmed the privileges of nobles, churchmen, and townsmen. The king promised to refrain from intruding into certain areas, involving chiefly taxation, the administration of justice, and landholding. The charter was therefore conservative, seeking to limit the expansion of royal power. Its framers had no thought of destroying effective royal government or impeding its capability to maintain order.

John's concession in no way resolved the clash between the king and the privileged. It continued throughout the long reign of his weak, extravagant, foolish son, Henry III (1216–1272), who made problems for himself by relying on Frenchmen for advice, making outlandish concessions to the papacy, and pursuing costly but futile foreign adventures. The exasperated nobles resisted him in a variety of ways: forcing him to reissue Magna Carta, using their influence to compel him to dismiss his foreign advisers, and forming a council of nobles to reform and supervise the operation of royal government. When these efforts failed, they resorted to a major uprising in 1264–1265 led by Simon de Montfort. The rebels won the upper hand temporarily, and de Montfort summoned the nobles, the clergy, and representatives from the towns and shires to a *Parliament* which would establish control over the monarchy. This effort was thwarted by the inability of the rebels to agree and by the actions of Henry's son, Edward, who mustered royal arms and crushed the rebels. However, brute force was hardly an answer to the issues involved in the rebellion.

The astute, capable Edward I (1272–1307) saw that few of the nobles who had opposed John and Henry III wished to end strong monarchy or destroy its institutions. Their protest was against the misuse of royal government and the abuse of ancient rights. More significantly, he recognized that a *community of the realm* had begun to emerge, consisting of great barons, lesser nobles, churchmen, and townsmen, all of whom felt a common interest in the political affairs of England as a nation. This feeling led them to act together in confronting the royal government and to transcend on occasion the narrow confines of feudal contracts, ecclesiastical privileges, and town charters. The community of the realm was the product of English political history since the conquest, of two centuries during which royal power was strong enough to affect all men in a substantial way. Its

emergence provided the basis for the modern English national spirit and for new political institutions through which the community of the realm could find expression.

Edward I's reign represented an attempt to strengthen the central government by taking these views into account. He first took steps to remove complaints that the nobles, clergy, and townsmen had raised about the administrative and judicial systems. Second, a series of fundamental laws was enacted defining more clearly the rights and powers of the crown and how these would be exercised. In general, this legislation, which earned Edward the title of England's Justinian, further limited the power of feudal lords and the Church, while expanding that of the king and his courts, but Edward's political skill usually disarmed protests before they became dangerous.

Edward's chief means of avoiding opposition and one of the major developments in English history was the regular use of Parliament. Advisory bodies, like the Witan and the *curia regis,* had long played a part in English political life, but within a narrow framework of feudal practices. Simon de Montfort's Parliament was a new kind of structure, joining representatives of the shires and towns to the feudal barons and churchmen to create a body claiming to direct the affairs of the realm. Edward I clearly sanctioned this precedent in his Model Parliament of 1295. He commanded that each county and town select two representatives to Parliament to take counsel with the barons and ecclesiastical lords. Such a body was soon accepted as having the power to speak for all Englishmen. Edward called Parliament to serve his own purposes, and especially to get extra money or to have some piece of legislation approved that promised to irk part of the population. For at least another century, the organization of Parliament was vague and its powers were few. Its importance lay in Edward's recognition that he had to listen to the demands of his subjects and in his willingness to create an institution that gave them a voice in government.

Edward's death in 1307 heralded the end of one age and the beginning of another. His career, built upon the work of his predecessors, left England with a sound set of political institutions. The chaos that had threatened to engulf England before 1066 had been replaced by a solidly established monarchy whose authority was widely accepted yet limited by law and ancient custom.

4. FRANCE: ROYAL IMPOTENCE

Monarchical power grew at a slower pace in France than in England and without a decisive turning point comparable to the Norman conquest. In the long run, however, the medieval French kings emerged more powerful than their English counterparts. The kingdom of France was established by the Treaty of Verdun in 843, when the sons of Louis the Pious divided the Carolingian Empire. With the exception of a brief interval, the Carolingians ruled this new kingdom until 987, but their power declined steadily the while, especially because of Viking invasions and the general ineptness of the rulers. Feudalism took root more deeply in France than anywhere else in Western Europe. The kings were still recognized in a vague way as rulers of all France, but real power had settled in the hands of the great vassals who held extensive fiefs from the king, enjoyed the right to govern these lands, and seldom rendered any of the obligations they owed their lord.

In 987 the French nobles and churchmen finally ended the Carolingian dynasty by electing as their king one of the chief feudal lords in France, Hugh Capet, count of Paris. Hugh's descendants, called the Capetians, ruled France without interruption until 1328. They were the architects of French monarchy and a strong French state. Their success, however, was hardly instant. Under the first four Capetians, who ruled to 1108, the kings exercised almost no power outside their own royal domain, a territory around Paris known as Ile de France. The rest of the country remained divided into feudal principalities, some larger and richer than the royal domain.

The real political history of France during the eleventh century must be told in terms of the history of each of these principalities. The dukes, counts, and viscounts who held them made remarkable progress in establishing control over their subvassals, developing institutions that made their power effective, and amassing the military and financial resources needed to perpetuate their supremacy. These powerful royal vassals brought order to their fiefs primarily by utilizing their rights as feudal lords. In brief, they made feudalism an effective instrument for establishing sound government on a small scale. This solidification was most notable in the great fiefs of northern France, especially Normandy, Flanders, Anjou, Maine, Champagne, Burgundy, and Blois. In southern France, feudalism was slower to develop, and fiefs such as Aquitaine, Gascony, and Toulouse remained more chaotic.

The strengthening of the northern principalities created ready-made building blocks which the kings eventually took over along with the power created by the feudal princes.

Until 1108, however, the Capetians had little role in these decisive developments. Aside from their tenuous authority over their domain, the early Capetians succeeded only in keeping monarchy alive, making the throne hereditary, and retaining the support of the Church for the idea of monarchy as an institution common to all who lived in France.

5. THE RESURGENCE OF ROYAL POWER

The period between 1108 and 1223 saw a decisive upturn of Capetian fortunes and a notable advance in the strength of French monarchy. The first accomplishment of the twelfth-century Capetians was the establishment of effective control over Ile de France. Louis VI (1108–1137) was chiefly responsible for this. He set patiently about forcing his vassals there to end their lawlessness and creating an administrative machinery capable of collecting their dues to the king. In the main, he was successful. His control of the royal domain gave him greater ability to play a significant role in the affairs of his vassals outside Ile de France. On occasion he acted as judge in disputes between his vassals, protected weaker ones against stronger, and influenced the succession to fiefs held from the king. Nothing illustrates this new strength better than the decision of the dying duke of Aquitaine to entrust his daughter and heiress, Eleanor, to the protection of his overlord, the king of France. Louis VI promptly married his ward to his son, thereby setting the stage for the annexation of Aquitaine to the royal domain.

Louis VI's successor, Louis VII (1137–1180), lacked the energy and clearheadedness to navigate the murky waters of French feudal politics. Thanks to the able work of his father's administrators, Louis VII did keep a firm hold on the royal domain, but his efforts elsewhere were ineffectual. He proved incapable of controlling Aquitaine, where the feudal nobility acted in complete defiance of the king's will. His participation in the Second Crusade not only won him no glory but cost him a wife and her dowry. The gay, romantic Eleanor accompanied him and was rumored to have dallied with some of the more attractive knights of the crusading army. This scandal was too much for the pious Louis; added to it was the fact that Eleanor had produced no son to assure the survival of the Capetian dynasty. Perhaps Eleanor had had enough too; she is alleged to have said that she discovered she had married a monk instead of a king. In any case, Louis arranged to have the marriage dissolved, with consequences that were dangerous to his power.

The king's major difficulties, however, did not stem from his political and marital ineptness. During his reign the Angevin "empire" emerged as a major threat to the very survival of French monarchy. It was the handiwork of a succession of royal vassals who ruled one of the great fiefs of France, the county of Anjou. The eleventh-century counts of Anjou had been ruthless, ambitious men who had constantly expanded their holdings. By the twelfth century Anjou had become one of the most powerful principalities in France. Count Geoffrey extended the earlier gains, establishing control over Normandy and Brittany by marrying the daughter of Henry I of England, also duke of Normandy. Geoffrey died in 1151; the next year his son and heir, Henry, won the hand of Eleanor, recently repudiated by Louis VII, and acquired her duchy of Aquitaine. For all these territories Henry was a vassal of Louis VII, but obviously his resources far exceeded those of his lord. Then in 1154 this same Henry became king of England as Henry II, further increasing his power and endangering Louis VII.

The French king could do little to check Henry's empire building or his aggression against royal territory and authority. But the next Capetian, Philip II Augustus (1180–1223), met the new challenge successfully. Philip bided his time as long as Henry II lived, only doing what he could to make his burden in ruling his French territories as heavy as possible. This task was made easier by the fact that Eleanor had blessed Henry II with a brood of unruly sons, among them Richard the Lionhearted and John, who delighted in joining their mother in making trouble for their father and husband. With the accession of Richard I, the Lionhearted, Philip began the struggle to break Angevin power. He was finally successful against John, whose conduct alienated many Continental vassals and caused them to turn to John's feudal overlord for justice. When John refused to appear to be judged, Philip declared his fiefs confiscated and proceeded to seize Normandy, Anjou, and parts of northern Aquitaine. His control of these key territories was assured in 1214 by the Battle of Bouvines, where he and his allies, Pope Innocent III and Frederick II of Hohenstaufen, crushed the armies of John and his ally, Otto of Brunswick. As a master of a greatly enlarged royal domain, the king had emerged as the major force in France, a position dramatically different from that of the earlier Capetians.

6. CONSOLIDATION OF ROYAL POWER

Louis VI and Philip II had established the keystones of Capetian policy: careful administration of the royal domain and territorial consolidation. Successful pursuit of these policies characterized the reigns of the later Capetians and account for France's emergence as the strongest state in Europe in the thirteenth century. After Philip II's decisive victory at Bouvines, the French kings added new territories to the royal domain with relative ease, exploiting every possible means to lay hold of them: marriage, purchase, confisca-

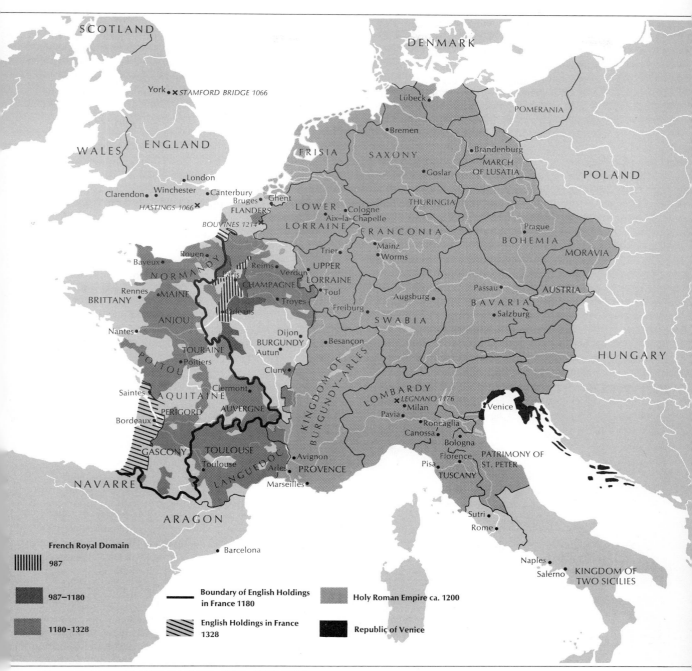

SCOTLAND

DENMARK

York • ✕ *STAMFORD BRIDGE 1066*

Lübeck •

POMERANIA

Bremen •

ENGLAND

FRISIA

SAXONY

Brandenburg •
MARCH
OF LUSATIA

Goslar •

WALES

POLAND

London •

Clarendon • Winchester • • Canterbury
HASTINGS 1066 ✕

Bruges • • Ghent
FLANDERS

BOUVINES 1214 ✕

LOWER
LORRAINE

Cologne •
Aix-la-Chapelle

THURINGIA

FRANCONIA

BOHEMIA

Prague •

MORAVIA

Rouen •

Baveux •

NORMANDY

Paris •

Reims •

Verdun •

UPPER
LORRAINE

Trier •

Mainz •
Worms •

Rennes •
BRITTANY

MAINE

CHAMPAGNE

Troyes •

Toul •

Augsburg •

Passau •

AUSTRIA

BAVARIA

ANJOU

Orleans •

TOURAINE

Freiburg •

SWABIA

Salzburg •

Nantes •

POITOU

Poitiers •

Dijon •
BURGUNDY
Autun •

Besançon •

HUNGARY

Cluny •

Saintes •
AQUITAINE

Clermont •

PERIGORD

AUVERGNE

KINGDOM
OF
BURGUNDY-ARLES

LOMBARDY
✕ *LEGNANO 1176*
 • Milan
Pavia • • Roncaglia
Canossa •

Venice •

Bordeaux •

GASCONY

TOULOUSE

Toulouse •

LANGUEDOC

Avignon •
Arles • PROVENCE

Marseilles •

Bologna •
Florence •
Pisa •

TUSCANY

PATRIMONY OF
ST. PETER

NAVARRE

ARAGON

Sutri •
Rome •

Barcelona •

Naples •
Salerno •   KINGDOM OF
TWO SICILIES

French Royal Domain

||||| 987

▨ 987–1180

▨ 1180–1328

▬▬▬ **Boundary of English Holdings
in France 1180**

▨ **English Holdings in France
1328**

▨ **Holy Roman Empire ca. 1200**

■ **Republic of Venice**

MEDIEVAL ENGLAND, FRANCE, AND GERMANY

tion, escheat. No holding was too small to escape their attention and none too large to defy them. By 1328 most of France had been consolidated under royal control, and she had in fact become a state ruled directly by a king.

The later Capetians, especially Philip II, Louis IX (1226–1270), and Philip IV (1285–1314), constantly increased the power and activity of the royal government. In broad outlines that government resembled the twelfth-century English model, from which the Capetians borrowed heavily. They based their expanding power

The institution of parliament grew up in France as well as in England. Here King Philip IV is shown presiding over a parlement; nobles and churchmen sit to the right and left below the king. *Photo: Bibliothèque Nationale, Paris*

primarily on their rights and obligations as feudal lords, relying also on concepts taken from Roman law and Christian political ideology. The thirteenth- and fourteenth-century kings increased their power chiefly by expanding and modifying primitive institutions bequeathed to them by the earlier Capetians. First, there was the *curia regis,* the meeting of the king's vassals to judge cases for and advise their overlord. Second was the royal household (the *hôtel*), officials who cared for the personal needs of the royal family and its retainers. Finally, there were the *provosts,* who managed the royal estates.

One of the chief accomplishments of Philip II, Louis IX, and Philip IV was the shaping of an effective central administration out of these primitive institutions. Philip II increased the amount of royal business put before the *curia regis,* adding full-time nonfeudal administrators (mostly lawyers) to the staff of feudal vassals. The royal household began to merge with the *curia regis* to serve as a single judicial and administrative body. Paris became the fixed seat of royal government. Louis IX and Philip IV continued to enlarge the activities of the *curia regis* and began to divide it into specialized departments: the *conseil,* a small circle of intimate advisers of the king; the *parlement de Paris,* concerned chiefly with the administration of royal justice; the *chambre des comptes,* which handled financial matters; a *chancery* for producing royal orders and keeping records. By the reign of Philip IV the central administrative system had developed into a complex, sophisticated organism.

As the royal domain grew, the kings were faced with the monumental task of creating a system of local government. The French kings were not so fortunate as the English in this respect; local government had long been monopolized by feudal and manorial lords. Philip II attacked this problem by extensive use of officials known as *baillis* (bailiffs). Usually selected from the nonnoble personnel of his court, these officials were assigned to specific areas in the royal domain to hold courts, collect taxes, and keep order. Succeeding kings expanded the numbers and the activities of the *baillis.* Louis IX established special officers called *enquêteurs* to check on the conduct of the *baillis* and report misdeeds to the central government. The *baillis*, acting in the name of the king, steadily assumed functions once monopolized by feudal nobles and churchmen. All during the thirteenth century (and far beyond) the nobility continued to perform many political functions, sharing the task of governing France with the central authority. But they were no longer at liberty to do what they pleased.

The broadening range of royal activities, especially warfare, placed a heavy financial burden on the kings. A prime source of income remained the royal lands. Feudal dues of all kinds were carefully collected. The thirteenth-century kings were usually willing to allow their vassals to discharge their service obligations by money payments. Special assessments were exacted from the towns, the Church, Jews, foreigners, and anyone else the kings could exploit. Philip IV even resorted to confiscating the wealth of the Templars and to debasing the currency. The Capetians were always short of money, but they managed to raise sufficient income to sustain a strong government.

In the early fourteenth century, the Capetians instituted another practice that strengthened their position. They began to summon representatives of the three classes *(estates)*, nobles, clergymen, and townsmen, from all over their realm to advise them and approve their policies. Philip IV convoked three of these *Estates General*, which always ended in approval of what the king proposed and added tremendous weight to royal power by making it appear that the entire nation approved what the king wished to do. The Estates General was much more the tool of the monarchs than was the English Parliament, largely because the French nobles never stood as a group to resist the king and exact a share of power. Perhaps this was the fruit of the extreme feudalization in the ninth and tenth centuries that had made the French nobles particularistic and independent. Nonetheless, the development of the Estates General was important in uniting the major classes of France under a single government.

While the Capetians were expanding and consolidating their hold on France, they drew valuable assistance from the Church. The kings bestowed considerable wealth on the Church, helped to reform it, took its side in the investiture struggle, and respected its liberties. In return, the Church supported the claims of the Capetians to greater power and lent its wealth and talent to their government. The long, happy relationship did not end until the reign of Philip IV, who became embroiled in a bitter quarrel with Pope Boniface VIII (1294–1303) over the extent of the king's power to tax church property and to judge clergymen. When Boniface commanded Philip to obey papal orders, the king turned French public opinion against Rome, cowed the French clergy into submission, and sent his agents to Rome to capture the pope (see Chapter 26). The mighty head of the Church, so long successful in thwarting the Holy Roman emperors, had suffered a crushing defeat. The explanation is clear: By the early fourteenth century the king of France possessed a power that the pope could not dissolve by simple command.

The victory of Philip IV over Boniface VIII points to a final achievement of the Capetians: an immense prestige. The greatest kings were surrounded by a style that made them stand out in thirteenth-century Europe. Their prestige was best reflected by Louis IX, eventually sainted by the Church. He was lauded as a lover of justice for his subjects, true Christian, gallant knight, crusader, peacemaker, promoter of morality, ideal son, husband, and father—in short, the perfect prince. This aura of superiority added immensely to the authority of the Capetians, proving them as skillful in fashioning an image as in shaping political institutions.

Thus by 1300 England and France had resolved a problem that had persisted since the fall of the Roman Empire—how to create a stable, just political order. The answer was feudal monarchy. In fashioning his power, however, the feudal monarch learned to respect the rights of privileged groups—vassals, churchmen, townsmen—as partners in the tasks of government. The political systems evolved in England and France gave these kingdoms the strength, order, and stability that ensured them a central role in the future of European civilization.

Suggested Reading

England

*C. W. Hollister, *The Making of England, 55 B.C. to 1399* (Heath).

*Christopher Brooke, *From Alfred to Henry III, 871–1272* (Norton). Either of these two brief, well-written surveys will provide an excellent overview of English political development.

*D. M. Stenton, *English Society in the Early Middle Ages (1066–1307)*, 4th ed. (Penguin). A study that succeeds particularly well in relating social, economic, and cultural factors to political history.

*C. W. Hollister, ed., *The Impact of the Norman Conquest* (Wiley). A collection of modern views on the nature and significance of the Norman Conquest.

*G. O. Sayles, *Medieval Foundations of England*, 2nd ed. (Perpetua). A provocative interpretation of constitutional development which has caused a lively debate among historians.

Bryce Lyon, *A Constitutional and Legal History of Medieval England* (1960). A detailed description of the evolution of political institutions and legal structures in medieval England.

*J. C. Holt, *The Making of Magna Carta* (Virginia). A thorough analysis of this great document and its significance.

*G. L. Haskins, *The Growth of English Representative Government* (Perpetua). A clear account of the early history of Parliament.

France

*Robert Fawtier, *The Capetian Kings of France* (St. Martin). The best general account in English.

*Charles Petit-Dutaillis, *The Feudal Monarchy in France and England from the Tenth to the Thirteenth Century*, trans. E. D. Hunt (Harper Torchbook). Especially good in showing parallels in constitutional development between England and France.

A. Luchaire, *Social France in the Time of Philip Augustus* (1912). Paints a broad picture of the social milieu within which the Capetians worked to increase their power.

Biographies

*David Douglas, *William the Conqueror: The Norman Impact Upon England* (University of California).

L. F. Salzmann, *Henry II* (1967).

*Amy Kelly, *Eleanor of Aquitaine and the Four Kings* (Vintage).

David Knowles, *Thomas Becket* (1971).

P. Henderson, *Richard Coeur de Lion* (1958).

W. L. Warren, *King John* (1961).

F. Perry, *St. Louis* (1901).

Sources

D. C. Douglas and G. W. Greenway, eds., *English Historical Documents, 1041–1189* (1953). A splendid collection of materials illustrating the working of English medieval government.

Jean de Joinville, *Life of St. Louis*, trans. René Hague (1955). An assessment by an admiring contemporary of the great French king.

THE MEDIEVAL EXPANSION OF EUROPE

22

The agricultural and commercial growth, the social readjustments, and the political solidification of Western Europe's heartland—Germany, Italy, France, England—created the potential for European expansion. The realization of that potential between 1000 and 1300 is another aspect of the revival of the West. In the three centuries after 1000, Western Europeans brought immense territories under their sway at the expense of the Byzantines, Muslims, Slavs, and Scandinavians. The outward thrust took many forms: missionary activity, commerical penetration, colonization, conquest. The consequence was a major step toward the domination of the world by Western Europeans.

1. MISSIONARY EXPANSION

The missionary urge had been present in the Christian community in the West even during the darkest hours of the Early Middle Ages, bringing considerable numbers of pagans into the fold prior to 1000. After that missionaries moved into new territories from the British Isles, France, Italy, and Germany where Christianity was solidly established by the end of the Carolingian period. The first effort to convert the Scandinavians in the ninth century had been abortive, but it was pursued successfully after the worst of the Viking attacks had subsided. The late tenth and eleventh centuries marked the crucial era in the conversion of Denmark, Nor-

way, and Sweden. In most cases the conversion of the kings was the decisive event. The new Christian kings received invaluable help in their work from pious churchmen, especially from England and Germany, who devoted their careers to proselytizing the Scandinavians. Once Christianity was implanted in Scandinavia, an episcopal organization, often closely linked with Rome, developed.

Meanwhile, Christian forces also moved across the Elbe into the Slavic world, usually with German political backing. Here again, the first expansion came in the Carolingian period, but permanent successes were achieved only when the Holy Roman emperors gave their support to it. During the late tenth and eleventh centuries, the Bohemians, Poles, and Hungarians were gathered into the Roman Catholic fold, while Byzantine missionaries drew the Balkan Slavs, Bulgars, and Russians into the Greek Orthodox orbit. Over a long period Christian influences, again promoted by the Germans and often backed by force, spread along the Baltic to convert the Wends, the Prussians, the Finns, the Livonians, and the Lithuanians.

In the thirteenth century, primarily as a consequence of the crusading movement, Western missionaries ventured all the way to the Mongol Empire and China. Although their labors were ephemeral, their explorations opened vast new prospects. There were also efforts to spread Christianity among the Muslims of North Africa and the Near East, but these proved little susceptible to the Christian message.

Wherever the missionary effort succeeded—Scandinavia, Central Europe, Iceland, the Baltic area—the Church brought learning, literature, and art that often represented the first contact of the new converts with higher civilization. The Church was also often instrumental in shaping political and social institutions in these areas along lines similar to institutional patterns in Western Europe.

2. COLONIZATION AND COMMERCE

While some Western Europeans thrust outward with the cross, others were driven beyond Europe's boundaries primarily by economic interests. As we have discussed, one of the great accomplishments of medieval men during the era from 1000 to 1300 was the opening and colonization of an extensive agricultural frontier on the eastern fringes of Europe—in today's terms, a territory comprising northern Poland, most of East Germany, large areas of Czechoslovakia, and Austria. This Germanic "drive to the East" had the strong backing of the Holy Roman emperors, but in the main it was carried out by landowners and peasants seeking new lands to exploit. Churchmen gave the movement their support because it assured the Christianization of the occupied territories. As the German tide moved eastward, many Slavs brought under German political, religious, and cultural control tended to merge with the Germans and lose their identity.

Likewise, between 1000 and 1300 merchants reached beyond Europe to establish the Western European presence in a much larger world. Italian merchants, powerfully abetted by crusading armies, wrested control of the Mediterranean seaways from the Byzantines and the Muslims, and established trading posts in Constantinople and several Muslim seaports in Syria, Egypt, and North Africa from which they penetrated inland. Northern Europeans, spearheaded by the Vikings, established settlements at Novgorod, Smolensk, and Kiev; from these emerged the Kievan principality that constituted the first effective state in Russia. Scandinavian raiders also settled Iceland and drew it into the European world. After the conquest of Constantinople in 1204 by the armies of the Fourth Crusade, Western European merchants established bridgeheads around the Black Sea which opened access to the cities of Central Asia and China. Italian traders roamed widely across the Asian world, reaping rich profits and reporting the potential of that vast area in travel accounts such as that composed in the late 1200s by the Venetian Marco Polo. A few bold Europeans were finding their way toward the waterways leading to India and the Indies, but their progress was impeded by the Muslim barrier of Egypt, which the crusaders repeatedly but unsuccessfully attacked in the thirteenth century. Simultaneously, Western seafarers were pushing southward along Africa's west coast, drawn chiefly by the fame of the gold mines of Senegal. These many forays by adventuresome, profit-seeking merchants ended Western Europe's isolation and presaged a new age of European expansion.

3. MILITARY EXPANSION IN SPAIN AND SOUTHERN ITALY

The most spectacular form of expansion during the High Middle Ages was military conquest, which added considerable territories to the Western European world and gave temporary control over others. Europeans were impelled by a variety of motives: land hunger, quest for markets, adventure, religious zeal, fear. Military expansionism manifested itself around the whole rim of the European heartland, but the thrust was aimed primarily at Byzantium and Islam, those heirs of the classical world that had so outstripped Western Europe in the Early Middle Ages.

One of the most important focuses of expansion was Spain. When the Moors, (as Muslims are called in Spanish history) conquered the Iberian Peninsula in the eighth century, they failed to subdue a few tiny Christian principalities in the mountainous north. Almost immediately, these petty states—Leon, Castile, Navarre, and Barcelona—began the *Reconquista,* a war of liberation that did not end until 1492 and that drew in Europeans outside the peninsula as early as the Carolingian age. At the beginning of the eleventh century, the powerful Caliphate of Cordova disintegrated, and Muslim Spain broke into numerous warring principalities. This gave the Christians their opportunity, and they turned their energies to a common assault on the Moors. Large numbers of Christian knights from outside Spain, especially from France, joined the fray. The kingdom of Leon-Castile (united in 1037) took the lead and drove to Toledo, capturing it in 1085. After 1085, the Christian frontier was rolled back as a result of Muslim reinforcements called in from Africa, rivalry among the Christian states, and political dissension within them. By the mid-twelfth century, the Christians had renewed their offensive; this time the recently established kingdom of Aragon, which incorporated Barcelona, took the lead. A new kingdom, Portugal, emerged as a result of successful aggression in the west. By 1300 the Christians had occupied all of the peninsula except Granada.

The Reconquista created three major new kingdoms—Castile, Aragon, and Portugal. Each developed its own system of government, although all had certain basic similarities. Monarchy was the basic institution, and the kings steadily gained prestige as a result of their leadership of the Reconquista and Church support of their cause. The resources they gained from the Moors bolstered their power. Newly conquered lands gave them a chance to settle people as farmers or townsmen under conditions that allowed the king to retain his authority. These factors retarded the coming of the feudal system, but eventually, feudal practices not unlike the French did develop. Hereditary fiefs were granted to nobles in return for services, and some vassals gained a large degree of immunity from royal control. The Spanish monarchs sought to develop centralized administrations, well-organized financial systems, and effective courts. Several thirteenth-century kings of Aragon and Castile legislated extensively to define royal powers and appointed local officials, comparable to the French bailiffs, to represent them.

Nobles and townsmen resisted royal attempts to monopolize power, and in the long run, Spanish rulers were compelled to admit limitations

IBERIA 1140

on their authority. The balance between monarchy and specially privileged groups was symbolized by the *Cortes,* a representative body composed of nobles, clergymen, and townsmen. Before the end of the thirteenth century these bodies were being summoned in all the kingdoms to consult with the king. Custom had already sanctioned the right of the Cortes to approve new taxes, address petitions to the king for redressing wrongs, and be consulted in matters of war and peace. Nowhere else in Europe, with the possible exception of England, was there such a well-defined institution for curbing the authority of kings and confronting them with the desires of the vested interests in their realms.

Another area of European military expansion was southern Italy and Sicily. Norman nobles were the aggressors here, intruding into the chaotic Byzantine territory in southern Italy and establishing dominance by the mid-eleventh

The Christian kingdoms of the Iberian peninsula were gradually enlarged by successful military campaigns against the Muslims, shown capturing Christians in this manuscript illustration. *Photo: Fotografía Autorizada por el Patrimonio Nacional, Madrid*

century and snatching Sicily from the Muslims before 1100. In 1130 these feats were given formal recognition when the papacy sanctioned the creation of the Kingdom of Sicily, embracing southern Italy and Sicily. A strong monarchy was soon shaped, incorporating a mixture of feudal, Byzantine, and Muslim practices that made the king virtually absolute, and a brilliant cultural life developed at this meeting place of three worlds. The Kingdom of Sicily passed into Hohenstaufen hands at the end of the twelfth century; then in 1266 the pope invited Charles of Anjou to take over the kingdom. French domination lasted only until 1282, when a rebellion, called the Sicilian Vespers, gave the royal house of Aragon control. These rapid changes of masters, often prompted by outside interests, began to weaken the kingdom and blight its vital cultural and economic life. But it remained in European hands, a prime example of Western military prowess and organizational ability.

4. THE CRUSADES

The expansionist venture that most dramatically illustrates Western European vitality in the High Middle Ages was the crusading movement, a succession of military operations stretching over two centuries that had as its central objective to gain control over Christian holy places. The crusading movement was consequently a war against Islam, although as it evolved, its objectives became more diverse and more complex.

In part, the Western Europeans took up arms because developments in the Near East provided them an opportunity. As the vast Abbasid Empire began to disintegrate into independent caliphates after the ninth century, a major point of weakness in the Muslim armor emerged in Syria and Palestine. The aggressive Fatimid caliphate in Egypt sought to expand in that direction, as did the Byzantine Empire in the late tenth century. In an effort to save their power, the Abbasid caliphs in Bagdad relied increasingly on the Asiatic Seljuk Turks, who by the late eleventh century had also become rivals for this territory. Capitalizing on these conflicting claims, local leaders had established several small principalities in Syria and Palestine, and these rulers were willing to make any arrangement that would thwart the efforts of any stronger contender.

The Byzantine Empire was also undergoing a crisis in the eleventh century. The emperors of the Macedonian dynasty that followed the great Basil II (died 1025) were ineffectual rulers who failed to sustain the defense of the empire, especially by allowing the aristocracy to subordinate the free peasantry, which had long provided the backbone of Byzantine military strength. The Normans wrested southern Italy from imperial control and began to attack Byzantine territories in the Balkans. More seriously, in 1071 Byzantine forces suffered a crushing blow at the Battle of Manzikert from the Seljuk Turks, who in succeeding years conquered most of Asia Minor.

Again Byzantium found a savior in the person of Emperor Alexius Comnenus (1081–1118). His primary task was to recover Asia Minor, a task that appeared more and more possible as Seljuk power began to disintegrate not long after Manzikert. However, Alexius realized that he needed help and began to appeal to the princes and the pope in Western Europe for troops to join in the struggle.

Thus, Byzantine problems and imperial policies stemming from them directed Western European attention toward military ventures in the East. But there would have been no crusading movement without the coincidence of a variety of factors in the West. A long-standing animosity toward Islam was fed by the eleventh-century wars of conquest in Spain and Italy. The Italian cities were eager to advance their commercial interests in the Muslim world. Religious reform engendered the idea that Christians must work collectively and actively to exalt the true faith; and the chivalric nobility—constrained from fighting at home by the advance of effective royal government—found it appealing to turn this religious impulse into the idea of a holy war against the infidel.

The resurgent papacy, enmeshed in the investiture struggle and nourishing dreams of a more effective leadership over Christendom, became the force that merged these many factors into a specific program. Alexius' appeal for help in 1095 opened to Pope Urban II the prospect that in return for channeling military aid to Byzantium against the Muslims, he could gain Byzantine recognition of papal supremacy over the whole Christian world and heal the schism that had separated Rome and Constantinople since 1054. And while helping the Greeks, the pope's soldiers could rewin the holy places, an act pleasing to God and excellent for papal prestige.

After carefully setting the stage, in 1095 Urban delivered a stirring speech at Clermont in France calling for Christian knights to join forces in attacking the Muslims, defending the Christians in the East, and liberating the Holy Land.

The pope's appeal was greeted enthusiastically, especially in France, and a number of feudal potentates (but no kings) gathered separate armies, a development that augured ill for the future. Meanwhile, an undisciplined horde of peasants and artisans stirred to crusading fervor by overenthusiastic preachers proceeded to Constantinople. Before its annihilation, this peasants' crusade aroused hostility along its entire route because of its participants' unruly conduct. By the summer of 1096 the main armies, totaling about 15,000 knights and foot soldiers and a large contingent of hangers-on, began to move eastward, and they converged on Constantinople in the fall and winter. Protracted negotiations, necessitated by lack of coordination and rivalry among the leaders and by misunderstandings between the crusaders and the Byzantine government, finally led to an arrangement that allowed the armies to move forward. Alexius persuaded the crusading leaders to swear an oath of allegiance to him personally and to release to Byzantine control conquered territories that had previously belonged to the empire. In return, he promised to provide supplies and military support.

In the spring of 1097 the crusaders began their march across Asia Minor. One decisive battle at Dorylaeum brushed aside Turkish resistance and allowed the crusaders to pass on toward the Holy Land. Once in Syria, the armies began to split up, chiefly because their leaders were anxious to assure their private fortunes. One group left the main body to establish control over Edessa and its surrounding territory. After the key city of Antioch had been captured in June 1098, a Norman prince, Bohemond, refused to leave it, claiming it as his by right of conquest. Not until July 1099 was Jerusalem captured by the remaining crusaders, who vented their fury on the Muslims by slaughtering hundreds of natives. This great victory made the First Crusade a success.

Jerusalem, Antioch, Edessa, and other key cities were now in the possession of the crusaders. Disregarding their pledge to Alexius to serve as his vassals and a papal plan to create a state subordinate to Rome, the crusaders elected Baldwin of Edessa king of the Latin Kingdom of Jerusalem in 1100. He created a series of fiefs whose holders acquired vassals of their own, creating a typical feudal hierarchy. The king ruled this kingdom with the advice of his vassals, who met regularly at Jerusalem. A Latin patriarch of Jerusalem was installed, subordinating the Christian establishment to Rome. The native population was disturbed very little. Usually their previous local rulers continued to control them under the supervision of the Latin rulers.

The chief problem of the new kingdom was defense. The Latins seized the chief Mediterranean seaports with aid from Italian navies. They built powerful castles at strategic locations in the Holy Land. Before 1130 they established the two great crusading orders, the Knights Templar and the Knights Hospitaler, vowed to defend Christians living in and coming to the Holy Land. Nevertheless, the Christians' position was always weak, and their plight repeatedly persuaded Western Europeans over the next two centuries to go crusading as a way of serving God.

The Second Crusade was prompted by the loss of Edessa in 1144 to the Turks. Papal appeals for action attracted two kings as its leaders: Conrad III, Holy Roman emperor, and Louis VII, king of France. Despite such prestigious leadership, the crusading armies were virtually destroyed by the Turks in Asia Minor. When the two rulers did arrive in the Holy Land with remnants of their forces, their misdirected military efforts aided little in the defense of the Latin kingdom.

During the years following the Second Crusade, a profound change occurred in the Muslim world. A new breed of Muslim leader created a unified state stretching from Syria into Egypt, which replaced the many small, quarreling principalities that had existed when the crusaders first attacked the Holy Land. In 1187 Saladin, the most effective of the new Muslim leaders, captured almost all the Christian holdings except Tyre, a few isolated castles, and the northern counties. The pope called for a new crusade and received the promises of Henry II of England, Philip II of France, and Frederick Barbarossa of Germany to lead armies against Saladin. Frederick left first but was drowned en route. Henry II also died before he could begin his march; however, his successor, Richard the Lionhearted, stepped into his place. He and Philip, almost always at odds, made their way to the East by 1191. Philip, anxious to snatch away Richard's French possessions, stayed on the scene only a minimum time. The colorful English king remained for over a year. After several inconclusive engagements with Saladin, he finally agreed to a truce by which Jerusalem remained in Muslim hands and Christians were allowed to visit it. The Third Crusade did little to improve the Christian position.

The Fourth Crusade, which ultimately made a travesty of the crusading movement, was initially prompted by Pope Innocent III, who was perhaps aware of the weakening of Muslim power that followed Saladin's death in 1193. However, the pope soon lost control over the forces that were raised. To ensure transportation to the East, the crusading leaders became entangled with the Venetians, and the paired interests then agreed to support a claimant to the Byzantine throne in return for trade concessions for Venice and money and troops for the crusaders to attack Egypt. But having ensconced their Byzantine ally in the imperial office, they found him unwilling or unable to deliver on his promises. The crusaders therefore decided to take Constantinople for themselves.

Their attack was successful, and the city fell into Western hands in 1204. The crusaders immediately proclaimed a Latin Empire of Constantinople and elected a Flemish noble as emperor and a Venetian clergyman as patriarch of the Greek Orthodox Church, thus reuniting the Church for the moment. Innocent III approved the whole arrangement. The crusading nobles began immediately to carve out rich fiefs for themselves, especially in the European sector of the Byzantine Empire. The Venetians, who assumed control over the chief port cities of the empire, were the real beneficiaries of the whole undertaking. The Latin Empire of Constantinople survived until 1261. Much of its history was a constant defense of its existence against Greek forces whose leaders kept alive a legitimate Byzantine government in Asia Minor and fought valiantly to oust the usurpers.

After the Fourth Crusade, the movement lost much of its appeal to Europeans. Innocent III organized a fifth crusade, but he died before it got under way in 1217. Its armies attacked Egypt and captured Damietta, a major Mediterranean port. The crusaders could have traded it for Jeru-salem, but greed led them deeper into Egypt, where they were trapped by a Nile flood and destroyed by the Muslims.

Frederick II led the next crusade, chiefly because he wanted to secure possession of the Holy Land, to which he had a legal right by virtue of his marriage to the heiress of the Latin Kingdom of Jerusalem. Frederick's crusade was fraught with difficulties from the very beginning. Because of his refusal to accept papal direction, he was in the bad graces of the papacy when he departed for the Holy Land. Once in the East, he chose to gain his ends by diplomacy rather than by the sword. In 1229 he signed a treaty with the Muslims that restored Jerusalem to the Latins and provided for a cessation of war between Christians and Muslims. This was a great victory, but the way it had been gained outraged many in the Christian West. When Frederick occupied Jerusalem, he was under a sentence of excommunication, and the city was immediately placed under papal interdict.

After this, the turmoil among the Christians in the Latin Kingdom of Jerusalem increased, making it more vulnerable; and in 1244 the Muslims again captured the Holy City. This loss prompted Louis IX of France to organize what amounted to the last major crusade. He spent four years in the Holy Land, but his presence did little to strengthen the Christian position. In fact, his Egyptian campaign increased the danger by providing the opportunity for a strong, aggressive ruling dynasty, the Mamelukes, to establish themselves in Egypt.

The increasing pressure on the Latin Kingdom of Jerusalem was relieved temporarily in the mid-thirteenth century when Christians and Muslims allied against the Mongol threat. Early in the century a great leader, Genghis Khan, had transformed the Mongol nomads of Central Asia into a potent military force that swept over Eurasia and fashioned an empire stretching from China to Central Europe. The Mongol threat began to lessen after 1260, and the old hostilities between Muslim and Christian were renewed. In 1291 the Mamelukes took the last Christian strongholds in the Holy Land. After nearly two centuries, the Latins had finally been ousted from Syria and Palestine; from the whole crusading venture they retained only some Mediterranean islands, specifically Cyprus and Rhodes.

So ended the most overt and dramatic manifestation of medieval Western European expansionism, but its consequences endured. The crusades generated an interaction between East and West which "educated" Europeans to new ideas, products, and styles of life. The ventures extended Western Europe's commercial power. They decisively affected the histories of both the Byzantine Empire and the Muslim world, weakening the former and provoking the latter to a new aggressiveness that was to make an impact on Europe in the Late Middle Ages. Perhaps their most significant consequence was the images of Western Europeans that they created in the Near East: the greedy, faithless, crude warrior; the crafty, grasping merchant; the ambitious, worldly churchman—all of whom would do anything to acquire land, wealth, and power. These images were not to be transformed easily.

5. WESTERN EUROPE AND THE WORLD

By 1300 there were many signs that Western Europe's outward thrust was abating. But certainly the efforts of missionaries, colonizers, merchants, and warriors had immensely changed the relationship between Western Europe and the world. First, the offensive had captured and brought under Western control considerable territory—the Iberian Peninsula, southern Italy and Sicily, the lands between the Elbe and the Oder, much of the Baltic coast, Iceland—as well as the Mediterranean Sea and its crucial trade routes. Second, the expansion had established outposts in the great trading centers of the Near East: Constantinople and the ports of Syria, Palestine, Egypt, and North Africa. Third, Western influences had powerfully affected the development of peoples living on the periphery of the European heartland and drawn them into the Western pattern of civilization. The evolution of Poland, Bohemia, Hungary, and the Scandinavian states was largely determined by European religious patterns, literary and art styles, political practices, agricultural and commercial techniques, educational practices, and value systems. Finally, the Western Europeans exerted an important influence on great powers beyond their direct control. The histories of the Byzantine Empire and the Muslim caliphates between 1000 and 1300 cannot be told without reference to the impact of the Europeans. This was an amazing turnabout considering the impotence of the West vis-à-vis these civilizations prior to 1000.

Suggested Reading

Missionary, Commercial, and Colonial Expansion
Considerable information on commercial and colonial expansion can be found in the economic histories cited in Chapter 19, especially the works of Lopez and Duby.

K. S. Latourette, *A History of the Expansion of Christianity*, Vol. II: *The Thousand Years of Uncertainty, A.D. 500–A.D. 1500* (1938). A detailed survey treating not only the history of missionary work but assessing the impact of the new religion on the converts.

Expansion in Spain, Southern Italy, and Sicily
Rafael Altamira, *A History of Spain from the Beginnings*

to the Present Day, trans. Muna Lee (1949). The early chapters of this history provide the best brief survey of Iberian history.

R. B. Merriman, *The Rise of the Spanish Empire: The Middle Ages* (1918). A detailed account, now somewhat out of date.

H. V. Livermore, *The Origins of Spain and Portugal* (1971). The later chapters of this book treat the *Reconquesta* to mid-twelfth century; the early chapters provide excellent background.

*C. H. Haskins, *The Normans in European History* (Norton). A classic on the role of the Normans in the expansion of Europe.

The Crusades

H. E. Mayer, *The Crusades*, trans J. Gillingham (1972). An excellent brief treatment of this complicated subject.

*Steven Runciman, *A History of the Crusades*, 3 vols. (Harper Torchbook). A study in great detail, enhanced by many provocative interpretations.

*J. A. Brundage, ed., *The Crusades: Motives and Achievements* (Heath). A selection of interpretative essays by authorities on the crusading movement.

D. C. Munro, *The Kingdom of The Crusaders* (1935).

Bon-Ami (pseud.), *Social Change in a Hostile Environment: The Crusaders' Kingdom of Jerusalem* (1969). Either this or the preceding work provides a clear picture of the history of the Latin Kingdom of Jerusalem, although the latter is more provocative.

R. J. H. Jenkins, *The Byzantine Empire on the Eve of the Crusades* (1953). A good assessment of the problems facing the Byzantine Empire as the crusading era began. For a broader view of Byzantine history in this period, reference should be made to the works cited in Chapter 15, especially the study by Ostrogorsky.

S. Lane-Poole, *Saladin and the Fall of the Kingdom of Jerusalem*, 2nd ed. (1926). A stirring account of the deeds of the greatest Muslim leader of the era. Muslim history in general is treated in the works by Hitti and Spuler, cited in Chapter 15.

Sources

The Chronicle of the Slavs by Helmold, Priest of Bosau, trans. F. J. Tschan (1935).

The Chronicle of Henry of Livonia, trans. J. A. Brundage (1961). These two works provide a great deal of insight into the process by which Christianity spread eastward in this era.

J. A. Brundage, ed., *The Crusades: A Documentary Survey* (1962). A fine selection of contemporary accounts of crusading ventures.

William of Tyre, *History of Deeds Done Beyond the Sea*, trans. E. A. Babcock and A. C. Krey, 2 vols. (1943). A massive history of the early crusading movement by a twelfth-century Latin bishop living in the East.

Fulcher of Chartres: Chronicle of the First Crusade, trans. M. E. McGinty (1941).

The Deeds of the Franks and Other Pilgrims to Jerusalem, ed. and trans. R. Hill (1962). Two descriptions of the First Crusade by participants.

Anna Comnenus, *The Alexiad*, trans. E. A. S. Dawes (1928). A long poem by the daughter of the Emperor Alexius I which reflects the impression made on Byzantine society by the crusaders.

Ambroise, *The Crusade of Richard Lion-Heart*, trans. M. J. Hubert and J. L. LaMonte (1941). Treats the most glamorous of all the crusaders.

*Geoffrey de Villehardouin and Jean de Joinville, *Memoirs of the Crusades* (Penguin). Eye-witness accounts of the capture of Constantinople in 1204 and of the exploits of St. Louis during his crusading venture.

Arab Historians of the Crusades, trans. F. Gabrieli (1969). Views of the crusades as seen from the perspective of contemporary Muslims.

23

THE REVIVAL AND TRIUMPH OF THE CHURCH

During the High Middle Ages, potent movements were so changing religious life that with some justice their effect has been characterized as a "reformation." Two aspects of the medieval reformation emerge as the most significant: first, the drive to strengthen the Church as an earthly community by perfecting its organization, defining its teaching, and disciplining its members; and second, the drive to probe more profoundly the spiritual meaning of the Christian message. To some at least, the closest approximation of the City of God on earth had been realized by the thirteenth century when the reformation had run its course.

1. ORIGINS OF THE REFORM MOVEMENT

Perhaps we need not seek further for the origins of the reforming movement of the High Middle Ages than the nature of Christianity itself. Throughout its history it had demonstrated a dynamic quality that dramatized men's imperfections and drove them to perfect their lives. The reforming surge from the tenth century onward was but another manifestation of the search for perfection, aimed specifically against the secularization, immorality, and spiritual insensitivity that had engulfed the feudalized Church. However, more specific factors involved in the reforming movement gave it a unique form.

First was a powerful ferment within the monastic establishment. The monastic spirit emphasized denial of the world, extreme asceticism, contemplation, and mysticism. Drawing on a rich tradition of spiritual concepts related to these practices, the monastic world of the High Middle Ages generated a powerful stream of moral precepts, devotional practices, educational ideals, and emotional perceptions that flowed into and leavened the mainstream of religious life.

A second factor promoting reform was a new intellectualism surging through Western European society that emphasized bringing order out of disorder and establishing norms for human endeavors. This movement promoted religious reform by encouraging men to collect the rich traditions of the faith, to submit them to logical scrutiny in order to eliminate contradictions, and to formulate syntheses that supplied the norms of Christian behavior. The reforms born of this intellectual activity tended to affect church organization, law, doctrine, and discipline.

A third source was popular piety. Reform from this source arose from popular responses to certain simple elements of the faith: the deeds of Jesus, his suffering, the travail of the Virgin, the miracles of the saints, the anticipated pleasures of heaven and the agonies of hell. Popular reform movements often took the form of protest against the power, wealth, and misconduct of the great in society, especially the clergy. They also tended toward excess and often ended in frenzied emotionalism, apocalyptic preaching, revolt, and heresy. Despite these negative aspects, this popular force played a vital role in sustaining and restating Christian idealism in its most exalted form.

Wherever these reforming forces were at work, they all placed a premium on looking back into history for models and ideals. Thus the reformation of the High Middle Ages was deeply rooted in tradition—as perhaps all religious reformations are. Because of the traditionalist spirit surrounding this religious revival, one is sometimes tempted to conclude that there was nothing new in Christian life between 1000 and 1300. In one sense, this is true; every facet of religious change built on the old. But in another sense, everything was new, for the real essence of the reformation of the High Middle Ages consists of the originality with which tradition was interpreted and the vigor with which it was applied to the realities of the world.

Chronologically, the origins of the medieval reformation are traced to the new monastic community established in 910 at Cluny in east-central France. The Cluniac movement, which spread rapidly over Western Europe, represented an attempt to purify Benedictinism by restoring strict observance of the Benedictine rule and freeing monasticism from lay control. Adding to this were powerful religious stirrings in every element of the population in the late tenth and early eleventh centuries: Bishops, kings, nobles, simple priests, and peasants all manifested an urge to purify religious life and to rescue the Church from its perilous position. By the eleventh century the movement found a dramatic focus in the papacy, and thereafter until 1300 the popes charted its major direction. But throughout the eleventh to thirteenth centuries a bewildering array of reform ideas emerged from monasteries, schools, bishoprics, and lay circles.

2. CHURCH ORGANIZATION

A major thrust of the reform movement of the High Middle Ages was toward centralization of the organization of the Church under papal con-

trol. This trend paralleled and outstripped the comparable secular centralization of political control, though its roots date back almost to the beginning of Christian history —Scripture alludes to the ideal of a single community of the faithful. A succession of ecumenical councils and a long series of popes provided precedents for central direction of religious life. But prior to 1000 this was far from a reality; the Church was a confederation of many local churches which recognized a titular head but in fact did what local churchmen—and often laymen—wished.

The situation began to change with the radical papal reformers who came to prominence during the last half of the eleventh century with Hildebrand, later Pope Gregory VII, as their leader. As we noted previously, the Gregorian reformers envisaged the Church as a visible earthly community pursuing a common goal, eternal salvation. This community needed its own head, its own law, its own resources, and its own liberty. On the basis of the ancient Petrine theory, the bishop of Rome was obviously the divinely commissioned head, God's earthly vicar. To him, God entrusted the two kinds of divinely ordained power, spiritual and temporal. The pope held the spiritual sword but vested the temporal in lay princes to be used to promote the quest for salvation. He retained full authority to direct the use of temporal power by any prince and to recall it if spiritual needs so dictated.

Gregory VII acted to convert this ideology into reality. His efforts led him into conflict with secular rulers on the issue of the supremacy of church over state, a struggle which went on long after his death and in which the Church made considerable progress in establishing the principle that the pope was the final arbiter in the world. The Gregorian ideal also pointed toward creating a stronger, more centralized, more universal church organization under papal control. Even before Gregory's papacy, his circle established the College of Cardinals as the body empowered to elect the pope, thereby putting the office beyond lay control. Gregory launched an extensive legislative program, aimed in large part at eliminating abuses that distracted his clergy from pastoral work (simony, marriage, immorality) and practices that limited Church control over personnel and property (lay investiture). Papal legates were sent to all parts of Europe to ferret out and correct clerical abuses and infringements on the Church's liberty. Difficult cases were referred back to Rome for settlement. Special attention was given to papal finances, with the intention of regularizing and increasing income.

Gregory VII did not live to see his program succeed. The immense task he had mapped out met resistance from many quarters, particularly from the bishops and princes, who rightly sensed that their ancient freedoms were threatened. But Gregory's successors pursued his policy with skill and persistence, and step by step through the twelfth and thirteenth centuries an ecclesiastical monarchy was built. This centralizing trend reached a culmination during the pontificates of Innocent III (1198–1216), Honorius III (1216–1227), Gregory IX (1227–1241), and Innocent IV (1243–1254), who headed an immense organization capable of wielding power on a pan-European scale.

These popes were in control of an extensive Church bureaucracy located in Rome and called collectively the papal *curia*. This body was divided into departments dealing with finances, correspondence and records, judicial cases, and the treatment of sinners and was manned by clerical specialists who made careers of papal administration. The College of Cardinals, made up of churchmen especially selected by the pope, sat with the pope in special meetings (called *consistories*) to decide major policies, and often directed the routine administration of the curia. In many areas, clergymen designated as papal *legates* resided for extended periods to control local affairs in the name of Rome; special legates were also sent out often from Rome to perform some specific activity in the interest of the papacy. The legatine system, coupled with the curia's extensive correspondence and the numerous judicial appeals to Rome, kept the popes well informed about local conditions throughout Europe. A huge and constantly increasing income, derived from papal property, gifts, fees, assessments on the laity and the lesser clergy, and other sources, sustained this organization.

Ranked under the pope was the age-old hierarchy of archbishops, bishops, and priests. By 1300 the exact functions of each level were defined in canon law, and papal control over archbishops and bishops was extensive. Each headed a small-scale model of the papal curia, called a *cathedral chapter*, staffed by *canons* who played a significant role in the episcopal election, advised their superior, and directed the administration of his *diocese*. The bishop and canons conducted judicial proceedings, collected and dispensed considerable diocesan income, managed the bishopric's properties, and supervised the parish priests who directed the religious life of laymen.

The centralized church organization imposed a high degree of uniformity on European religious life. Christians participated in the same ceremonies, received the same sacraments, said the same prayers, and were taught the same doctrines. A single code of laws imposed a common discipline. The whole thrust of organizational centralization was toward exalting religious conformity and damning heterodoxy. A manifestation of the growing emphasis on conformity was the development in the thirteenth century of a special papal court, called the *Inquisition*, charged with searching out and punishing heretics. Armed with almost total freedom to devise its own methods of inquiry and impose severe penalties, the Inquisition became a devastating weapon against those who balked at accepting the Church's rules.

The powerful, centralized administration permitted churchmen to extend their influence far beyond religious affairs. Nothing illustrates this better than the role played by Innocent III in European political life, a story replicated by the careers of most of the thirteenth-century popes. We have already observed how he manipulated affairs to make his ward, Frederick II, Holy Roman emperor. After a long quarrel Innocent compelled Philip II of France to take back his second wife, whom he had repudiated the day after their marriage. John of England and several lesser kings were compelled or persuaded to acknowledge themselves as papal vassals. Innocent launched the Fourth Crusade and exercised considerable influence in Byzantine affairs after the capture of Constantinople, and he organized a crushing crusade against the heretical Albigensians in southern France. Innocent made no distinction between religion and politics. He used religious weapons to gain political ends and political pressure to impose his spiritual leadership. When he spoke of his right to exercise "the fullness of power," Innocent meant complete mastery over all aspects of life. And while the pope was acting on the international stage, the extensive hierarchy under his authority was exerting a potent influence on European society at the local level.

3. CANON LAW AND DOCTRINE

Because the success of the whole centralization movement demanded conformity, there was a great surge of activity in the eleventh to thirteenth centuries to standardize law and doctrine. By the eleventh century the Church possessed an immense body of law, much of it dating from earlier periods. Many of its provisions were contradictory, and some no longer applied. Moreover, new difficulties were constantly arising in this era of reform to demand new legal solutions. Guided by Scripture, papal decrees, the acts of church councils, the writings of the early fathers, and the example of the Code of Justinian, church lawyers worked to create a consistent and organized collection of canon law. A decisive figure in this effort was Gratian, who in 1140 published his *Decretum*, a compendium that treated canon law in a strictly logical fashion to remove contradictions and confusions and that immediately became the guide for Church administration and discipline. Among many other things, Gratian's work defined the powers of each rank of the clergy, the jurisdiction of ecclesiastical courts, crimes against the Church and their punishments, the proper use of Church income and property, and the manner of conducting religious ceremonies. Throughout the work ran one predominant idea — the supremacy of the papacy in the governance of the Church. Extensive commentaries on Gratian's work eventually led to new codifications, usually made under papal auspices, and by the end of the thirteenth century, canon law had assumed a form that has persisted with little change to the present.

Church doctrines were even more confused than Church law. Perhaps the decisive figure in the development of a systematic theology was the tempestuous Abelard (1079–1142), constantly in trouble for his criticism of other scholars. He dramatically called attention to the conflicting teachings of Scriptures, the fathers, and tradition on certain key questions and insisted that human reason could resolve these differences. This method of clarifying revealed truth by the use of reason soon came to be known as *scholasticism*, and most theologians quickly adopted it. During the thirteenth century, a series of great scholastic philosophers, the chief of whom was Thomas Aquinas, worked to systematize the Church's teachings and eliminated most of the earlier confusion. In the process, they tried to weave all human knowledge into a unified body related to doctrines, giving the Church a single truth to teach to all.

At the heart of the theological system elaborated during the twelfth and thirteenth centuries stood the doctrine of grace and the sacramental system. According to the theologians, God had created man in order that he might enjoy eternal salvation, human life being but a test of worthiness. His nature corrupted by original sin — the stain imposed on all by the disobedience of Adam and Eve — man was powerless to save himself; only the grace of God could effect this end. That grace was bestowed on man through the sacraments instituted by Christ as an essential part of his mission of redemption.

By the twelfth century the number of sacraments was set at seven, each of which drew its efficacy by virtue of the fact that it was administered by the Church, without whose services no Christian could expect to be saved. *Baptism*, usually administered at infancy, removed the stain of original sin. *Confirmation*, usually received during the difficult years of adolescence, infused into a Christian the Holy Ghost, strengthening his faith and fortifying him against the devil at a particularly critical moment. *Extreme unction*, administered to those in danger of death, strengthened them at the moment they must face the judgment of the Almighty and removed from their souls the stain of minor (or venial) sins. *Marriage* sanctified the wedded state and family life. *Holy orders*, or ordination, conferred on select Christians the

The most solemn moment during the celebration of the Catholic mass is the Consecration, when according to Church doctrine, the wafer of bread, here held aloft by the priest, is changed into the body of Christ. *Photo: The Walters Art Gallery, Baltimore*

priestly powers which permitted them to act as valid successors of Christ and the apostles in teaching the faith and administering the grace-giving sacraments, especially the eucharist and penance. The *eucharist* was the sacrament by which Christ himself was present to the faithful. Its exact nature was not defined until the Fourth Lateran Council in 1215, held under the direction of Innocent III, pronounced the doctrine of *transubstantiation:* When a priest consecrated bread and wine at mass, their substance changed miraculously into the body and blood of Christ, although their external accidents (color, shape, taste, etc.) remained the same. Partaking of this sacrament—receiving communion—infused the grace of Christ's substance into the soul. No punishment was more terrible than excommunication—being cut off from receiving the eucharist. The last sacrament was *penance,* whereby a Christian who confessed his sins to a priest and resolved not to repeat them received God's forgiveness, provided that he made some sacrifice or did some good work assigned by the priest. Since the stain of sin barred one from heaven, Christians constantly needed to resort to the confessional; the Fourth Lateran Council decreed that the faithful must confess at least once a year.

The sacramental system, offering God's saving grace to men and women at the crucial points in their earthly pilgrimage, made the Church the indispensable institution in the drama of salvation. Embroidered on it was a rich array of Church-sanctioned practices and beliefs to facilitate the winning of God's favors. There were prayers and ritual ceremonies that invoked God's help in every conceivable situation. Sacred objects, especially relics, available to almost every Christian possessed powers to draw God and men together. An army of saints filled heaven to plead the cause of humanity with God and to assist in frustrating the hordes of devils that schemed under Satan's command to corrupt men. These adjuncts to the sacramental system were enlarged and enriched during the High Middle Ages, a process that added a powerful emotional dimension to the rather awesome concepts of the sacramental system.

4. MONASTIC REFORM

While the quest for greater order proceeded within the Church, there was an accompanying search for deeper spiritual understanding, centering chiefly in the monastic world which during the High Middle Ages witnessed more intense activity than in any other age in Christian history.

The dominant monastic force during the tenth and eleventh centuries was the Cluniac movement, which sought to restore the primitive purity of the Benedictine rule. In a spiritual sense, the movement placed heavy emphasis on the performance of an elaborate daily round of religious services as the main duty of the monks. The Cluniac liturgy was a splendid model of externalized religion, appealing especially to the feudal aristocracy and having an impact on the religious ethos of that class. Cluniac concepts of piety, clerical conduct, and ecclesiastical governance helped shape the eleventh-century attacks against lay investiture and clerical corruption. However, as the century progressed, the Cluniac Order, increasingly rich and complacent, lost its spiritual leadership to new forces which began to modify and even turn away from the Benedictine ideal of withdrawal into a holy community where men could earn salvation without fear of corruption from contact with the world. These new spiritual movements increasingly sought ways of assuring personal perfection and making monasticism a force that would reshape the world rather than run from it.

The urge for personal perfection generated attempts to return to the practice of the hermit life undertaken by the early desert fathers. The most notable exemplar of this was the Carthusian Order, established in France in the late eleventh century. Selecting the most unattractive sites for monastic houses, the order was never very popular as a result of the severity of its regimen, but it did impress upon an admiring world a model of denial of self and the world.

The new spirit circulating in the monastic world found its most appealing expression in the Cistercian Order, founded in 1098 by a Benedictine who felt that the ancient rule was not being strictly observed. It proved immensely popular, so that by 1300 there were about seven hundred Cistercian monasteries spread over all of Europe. The Cistercians were especially effective in establishing new houses in remote areas, which the labor of the monks quickly turned into rich agricultural establishments. As the order spread, it developed a unique organizational pattern that combined local autonomy and centralized direction. The abbot of each house directed local affairs but was required each year to attend a general meeting at the mother house at Citeaux; these meetings decided policies af-

fecting all houses, and a system of regular visits was developed to see that local houses adhered to general rules. The Cistercian movement exerted powerful influences on all aspects of religious life. Owing largely to the influence of its greatest member, Bernard of Clairvaux, the order became a militant agency seeking to arouse all men to purity and piety. Bernard viewed monastic life as a preparation for action in the cause of God. He insisted that a monk fortified by physical deprivation, long prayer, and contemplation could without fear of corruption go forth into the world to fight sin and spiritual indifference. His life exemplified this idea. During his long career in the order (1113–1153), he was involved in nearly every important event in Europe. His preaching promoted the Second Crusade; he became the papacy's chief support in hunting down corrupt clergymen (he even turned his blasts against a pope or two); he was a relentless foe of any unorthodox or heretical movement; he hounded Europe's kings constantly to improve their lives and their governments; he had no peer as a popular preacher. He and other monks like him—an army of puritanical, industrious soldiers of Christ—penetrated every corner of Europe urging men to be better Christians.

Other movements of the twelfth century contributed to the deepening of religious life and the broadening of the monastic influence on society. An order called the Augustinian Canons was organized to improve the moral quality of the clerics who made up the cathedral chapters. Its rule bound the canons to poverty, prayer, and moral excellence, while allowing them to move about freely as preachers and administrators. This same century saw the founding of the great crusading orders—the Templars, the Hospitalers, and the Teutonic Knights—which played a decisive role in defending Christians in the Holy Land. The military orders also organized numerous charitable agencies to help pious crusaders in the difficult journey to the holy places.

The trend toward involvement in the world became dominant in the early thirteenth century with the establishment of the *mendicant* (begging) orders, the Dominicans and the Franciscans. Both represented a religious response to a new factor in European life, the city, and to the blight that success and wealth visited on earlier monastic movements. The mendicants sought the answer to these challenges in a life in the world and a refusal of any wealth, either individual or corporate. Because they did not confine their members to a fixed residence, the new orders were able to extend the Church's influence in sectors of life where there was tremendous ferment—the cities, the universities, and the courts of the powerful kings.

The Dominican Order was the product of the fertile mind of a Spanish priest named Dominic (1170–1221). During a tour through southern France, where the Albigensian heresy was rampant, he became convinced that orthodoxy would prevail only if preachers learned in theology and free from all suspicion of excessive wealth mingled with the heretics. In 1215 Innocent III authorized him to organize a new order dedicated to the destruction of heresy by preaching. The rule provided for an austere life sustained by begging. Even greater stress was placed on education. Each Dominican was put through a rigorous training program aimed at making him an expert theologian. The Friars Preachers, as the order was called, quickly established themselves as one of the strongest arms of papal power, especially useful in directing the Inquisition against heretics and controlling the teaching of theology in the great universities.

The inspiration for the Franciscan Order was supplied by one of the most appealing figures in all history, Francis of Assisi (1182–1226). The son of a wealthy Italian merchant, Francis established a reputation as a playboy and jovial companion. But while still a young man he underwent a fundamental spiritual conversion that convinced him that he must imitate Christ in a most literal sense and he turned to a life of poverty, preaching, and the performance of charitable works. He was especially effective as a preacher because of his personality, which exuded joy, lightheartedness, and a sympathy for all men. To his contemporaries, he was "God's own troubador," filled with happiness and love. Almost immediately both men and women began to follow him. They surrendered their wealth, worked or begged for a livelihood, and preached a simple message of love for all. In 1210

Francis applied to Innocent III for permission to formalize his work in a religious order. Innocent hesitated, feeling that Francis' demands on his followers were too severe, and perhaps concerned lest the simple message of love and repentance would breed a crop of heretics with little regard for the elaborate machinery that the organized Church supplied for saving souls. Finally, however, he consented to Francis' request. Between then and 1226, when Francis died, the order grew rapidly, spreading to nearly every part of Western Europe and even beyond. Often the Friars Minor met opposition from local clergymen because of their stirring sermons, their exaltation of poverty, and their ability to attract attention. The Franciscans flourished despite this opposition. Their fresh approach to religious life was welcome, especially among the masses.

The mendicant orders were pillars of strength for the thirteenth-century Church. The Dominican Order, emphasizing education and teaching, became the refuge of scholars and preachers, who studied, systematized, and propagated Christian doctrine with a vigor seldom seen in the earlier history of the Church. The simple disciples of Francis, preaching a message of repentance and love, provided an outlet for those dissatisfied with the rigorous, rather formal activities of the organized Church. The friars proved especially useful to the papacy, for they lent themselves to the containment and direction of theological speculation and popular religious ferment.

5. POPULAR RELIGIOUS MOVEMENTS

A confusing array of popular movements and heresies added an important dimension to religious life between 1000 and 1300. Probably they were in part a result of a deeper understanding of the gospel message brought about by more pious and serious priests and monks. The increasing number of articulate and educated laymen in society produced a leadership for such movements. Probably the social and economic pressures resulting from the growth of towns and changes in the manorial order sensitized laymen to injustices and abuses within the Church. Whatever the causes, a powerful urge developed in lay society to live in imitation of the poverty and humility of Jesus.

This new spirit produced numerous individual preachers from all levels of the lay world. Often they succeeded in establishing bands of followers who shared their wealth, engaged in works of charity, cared for the sick, and worshiped after their own style. Some of these leaders spiced their exhortations to live like Christ with passionate attacks on the clergy and the wealth of the Church, thus making anticlericalism a regular part of popular religious movements and leading in extreme cases to overt action. For example, in the mid-twelfth century an Italian monk, Arnold of Brescia, so aroused the populace of Rome against the wealth and secular power of the papacy that he was able to drive the pope out of the city and hold it until the pope persuaded Frederick Barbarossa to depose and execute the radical troublemaker. Often programs that began innocently enough as pious efforts ended by being outlawed and suppressed at the hands of the Church and the political authorities. Intolerance toward heterodoxy and anticlericalism grew as the Church developed the organizational strength to enforce conformity. Two particular movements, the Waldensians and the Cathari (Albigensians), illustrate the nature and fate of many popular reform groups.

The Waldensians were inspired by Peter Waldo, a rich French merchant who in 1173 gave away his wealth and took up a life of poverty in imitation of Christ. His large band of followers took as their only authority the New Testament, refusing to accept the dictates of popes and bishops, who were only men and who because of their wealth were not good Christians. Practicing poverty and a strict moral life that reflected many Cistercian ideas about sobriety, temperance, honesty, and simplicity, the Waldensians went among the people, preaching and praying in vernacular languages, condemning the ordinary clergy, and refusing to admit many of the current teachings of the Church. They developed their own clergy and their own religious services. Eventually they were accused of heresy and attacked by the Church hierarchy. Some

Waldensian groups, especially in France, returned to orthodoxy, but in northern Italy they survived persecution throughout the Middle Ages.

Far more radical were the Cathari, or Albigensians. Their belief originated in the Near East as early as the fourth century, probably from the mixing of Christian and Zoroastrian ideas. It spread slowly westward, finally reaching northern Italy and southern France in the tenth century, and by 1200 it exerted an influence throughout Europe. The Cathari believed that two powers, good and evil, battle constantly for the world and for men. Good was spiritual, while evil was materialistic. True Cathari refused to marry, holding that even reproduction was evil. They ate no meat, milk, or eggs, which are the fruits of sexual union. They owned no property and refused to shed blood. The "perfect," as they called themselves, were certain that they were saved. Allowance was made, however, for weaker men. Second-grade Cathari, called "believers," were permitted to indulge more freely, although every "believer" hoped someday to become a "perfect." Because the Church had wealth and dealt in worldly affairs, it was condemned; and the Cathari developed their own clergy, simple services, and rules of conduct. Needless to say, they were considered heretics from the beginning, and in the thirteenth century the papacy and the French monarchy organized a ferocious crusade that virtually eradicated the movement from its major stronghold in southern France.

6. THE CONSEQUENCES OF THE MEDIEVAL REFORMATION

The religious reformation in the High Middle Ages transformed the Christian establishment in the West. It is perhaps not an exaggeration to say that a "new" Church was created. Traditional patterns were reshaped and reapplied so that they little resembled what they had been. And to them were added new elements that would have been foreign to the apostolic or patristic or Carolingian ages. In sum, the reform created the

Roman Catholic Church that has survived to our day and that has only recently begun to alter its medieval configurations.

One major consequence of the medieval reformation was to furnish the Church with an organization that had the power and resources to impose upon its membership one body of belief, one code of conduct, and one set of religious practices. And not only did this organization have the capability to unify the European population, it also had the intention of imposing conformity; its whole outlook was universal and catholic. The "new" Church therefore worked at achieving conformity, so that by the thirteenth century it was chiefly responsible for providing Western European civilization with its integrating element.

A second major consequence was a revolutionary redefinition of the relation between church and state. Throughout the period 1000 and 1300, Church leaders insisted that it had an independent sphere of activity, an area of liberty into which no other authority could intrude; and indeed it stood superior to all other authorities.

In the society of the High Middle Ages the Church developed immense powers to impose its influence on political, economic, social, and cultural life, and it seldom missed an opportunity to do so. In a larger historical perspective, the Church's quest for independence played a role in defining political freedom. And more significantly, it freed the state to a degree from serving religious ends, thereby opening up to it a new range of activities.

Finally, the medieval reformation articulated an immensely broader range of spiritual possibilities in Christianity. It may be true, as some have insisted, that the totality of Christian spirituality was present from the beginning, but a study of the first millennium of Christian history does not persuade one that believers realized the range of spiritual possibilities available to them. After 1000 the search for meaning in religion produced an amazing array of new spiritual insights. It can be argued that many of the most potent spiritual concepts associated with Christianity date from the High Middle Ages rather than from the apostolic or patristic ages.

Suggested Reading

General Surveys

David Knowles and D. Obolensky, *The Middle Ages* (*The Christian Centuries*, Vol. II) (1968). The most up-to-date survey of all aspects of Church history in this period.

*H. Daniel-Rops, *Cathedral and Crusade*, 2 vols. (Image). A survey full of fascinating details, but some of its interpretations are open to question.

*R. W. Southern, *Western Society and the Church in the Middle Ages* (Penguin). An intriguing overview stressing the relationships between the Church and the secular world.

*J. B. Russell, *A History of Medieval Christianity: Prophecy and Order* (Crowell). A general treatment of Church history focussing on the tensions between the forces of order and of prophetic demands to restructure the world.

Organization, Law, and Doctrine

S. Baldwin, *The Organization of Mediaeval Christianity* (1929). A brief description of the main features of Church organization.

*Geoffrey Barraclough, *The Medieval Papacy* (Harcourt, Brace and World). A compact survey of papal history.

William Barry, *The Papal Monarchy from St. Gregory the Great to Boniface VIII (590–1307)* (1902). A detailed account of the progress toward centralization.

S. R. Packard, *Europe and the Church Under Innocent III* (1968). An excellent picture of the papal government in action at the height of papal power.

W. Ullmann, *Growth of Papal Government in the Middle Ages*, 2nd ed. (1962). A provocative treatment of the ideology that inspired papal activity in the High Middle Ages.

R. C. Mortimer, *Western Canon Law* (1953). Helpful, but far from adequate on a subject that has not yet been adequately treated in English.

E. Vacandard, *The Inquisition* (1908). A good treatment from a Roman Catholic perspective.

Monastic Reform, Popular Religion, and Heresy

*H. B. Workman, *Evolution of the Monastic Ideal from the Earliest Times to the Coming of the Friars* (Beacon). The best general survey of monastic development.

Joan Evans, *Monastic Life at Cluny* (1920).

L. Bouyer, *The Cistercian Heritage* (1958).

W. H. Hinnesbusch, *The History of the Dominican Order*, Vol. I: *Origin and Growth to 1500* (1966).

J. R. H. Moorman, *A History of the Franciscan Order from Its Origin to the Year 1517* (1968). This and the preceding three titles will provide a full picture of the major characteristics of the chief new monastic movements of the High Middle Ages.

*J. B. Russell, *Dissent and Reform in the Early Middle Ages* (Wiley). Traces the major movements of dissent to the twelfth century.

*Norman Cohn, *The Pursuit of the Millennium* (Harper Torchbook). A brilliant study of messianic concepts and their social implications between the eleventh and the thirteenth centuries.

*S. Runciman, *The Medieval Manichee* (Compass). An excellent analysis of Catharism.

J. B. Russell, *Witchcraft in the Middle Ages* (1973). A fascinating aspect of medieval religious life treated with seriousness.

Biographies

L. E. Elliott-Binns, *Innocent III* (1931).

Paul Sabatier, *The Life of St. Francis*, trans. L. S. Houghton (1930).

W. Williams, *Saint Bernard of Clairvaux*, 2nd ed. (1953).

J. Sikes, *Peter Abailard* (1965).

P. F. Mandonnet, *St. Dominic and His World* (1944).

Sources

Selected Letters of Pope Innocent III Concerning England, eds. C. R. Cheyney and W. H. Semple (1953). Provides glimpses of the operation of the papal curia in the thirteenth century.

*Brian Tierney, *The Crisis of Church and State, 1050–1300* (Spectrum). A remarkable collection of materials illustrating contemporary views on church-state relationships.

G. G. Coulton, *Five Centuries of Religion*, 4 vols. (1923–1950). A vast, badly organized collection of source materials illustrating religious life, but full of details which put the reader in touch with the real world of the High Middle Ages.

The Letters of Bernard of Clairvaux, trans. B. S. James (1953). An intimate view of one of the great figures of the age.

Saint Francis of Assisi (1963). A fascinating collection of materials reflecting the reaction of contemporaries to a great saint.

W. Wakerfield and A. P. Evans, eds., *Heresies in the High Middle Ages* (1969). A fascinating introduction to the world of heterodoxy.

24

INTELLECTUAL AND ARTISTIC ACHIEVEMENTS

The crowning achievement of Western Europeans in the High Middle Ages was the original and creative work done in thought, literature, and art. After a long apprenticeship, they came alive culturally and demonstrated a singular genius in all forms of intellectual and esthetic expression. These activities were no less important in establishing Western Europe preeminence than were the remarkable advances in politics, economics, religion, and expansion.

1. A CHRONOLOGICAL OVERVIEW

In 1000 Western European cultural life was at a low ebb. The gains of the Carolingian renaissance had not been lost, but their impact was felt only in the narrow world of the monasteries. The brutal realities of the ninth and tenth centuries were not conducive to vigorous cultural activity. Then, rather suddenly in the eleventh century and extending into the twelfth, there was a spectacular outburst of cultural activity. One famous American medievalist has labeled it "the twelfth-century renaissance," unabashedly claiming for it accomplishments usually attributed to the more famous Renaissance three centuries later.

Whatever we choose to call this renewal, it was a movement marked by great vigor and freshness. The impetus came from many directions: new religious ideas, economic growth, social change, political developments, and wider

contacts with the outside world. The range of cultural activities broadened immensely. New education institutions challenged the monopoly on education held by the monastic schools. Theological speculation quickened, and men began to develop an interest in the study of law and the natural sciences. Literary activity was greatly intensified and took an array of forms: Latin poetry, hymns, history, and drama; vernacular epics, lyric poetry, romances, fables. New artistic concepts found expression in the design and decoration of Romanesque churches and the beginnings of the Gothic style. The twelfth-century renaissance was a remarkably "open" cultural movement, encouraging men to experiment with a wide variety of new ideas, forms, and techniques and drawing into the world of thought, literature, and art not only more churchmen but also important segments of the secular world.

Shortly after 1150 the cultural climate began to change. The buoyant, questing spirit of the revival lost its edge, and men began to concern themselves more with synthesizing their accomplishments. This was especially true in the "sciences": theology, law, studies of the natural world. The prime objective of intellectuals was to reconcile their knowledge with Christian faith in order to produce statements of an ultimate truth. Literary activities became more stylized. In the arts, the thirteenth century was the age of the Gothic, which was a product of an attempt to merge all forms into a style that would reflect the great truths of the faith. This age of synthesis produced the most mature expressions of medieval culture: the theological writings of Aquinas, the poetry of Dante, exquisite Gothic cathedrals, the great romances. But it lacked the spontaneity, the freshness of the twelfth-century renaissance.

2. EDUCATION

There were two cultural spheres in medieval Western European society. The line of demarcation between them was linguistic. In one, Latin was the vehicle of expression. As the official language of the Church, Latin provided the key to the prime sources of the Christian faith: Scripture, the church fathers, the law, the liturgy. When medieval men had something important to say, they said it in Latin. Those who spoke it were the "learned men," and the great majority of them were churchmen. In the other cultural world, the language of the people, the vernacular tongues, prevailed. It developed its own interests, styles, and values. In general, it did not concern itself with the subjects of the Latin world of learning—theology, philosophy, law, science, liturgy, political theory. It tended to reflect lay life, especially that of the aristocracy. The worlds of Latin learning and of vernacular culture were never isolated from one another, but they were enough separated so that ideas and concepts prevailing in one often did not affect the other very seriously.

Since Latin was a language that medieval men had to learn, education was vital to this cultural sphere. In 1000 formal education in Western Europe was confined largely to monastic schools, although there were a few modest cathedral schools and, in Italy, some municipal schools. They touched a narrow segment of the population and cultivated a narrow range of interests. In the eleventh and twelfth centuries they underwent an amazing expansion, due chiefly to the demands of the Church, royal governments, and cities for more literate men capable of handling the growing complexities of administration and commerce. Cathedral and municipal schools, best suited to meet these needs, expanded at a greater rate than did the monastic. Especially in the cathedral schools there was a marked intensification of the study of the seven liberal arts. Three of these arts (called the *trivium*)—grammar, rhetoric, and dialectic—especially captured the interest of the era. Many cathedral schools owed their fame to individual masters who specialized in one of these arts and who worked hard to expand its content and to sharpen the skills associated with it. To a large extent, the subject matter in these disciplines was provided by classical models, so that the schools became centers of a renaissance of classical studies. The other four liberal arts (the *quadrivium*)—arithmetic, geometry, astronomy, music—were not so central to the interests of society, but still their content was constantly expanded, again chiefly as a result of contacts with the classical world.

Toward the end of the twelfth century the monastic, cathedral, and municipal schools no longer met the needs of some elements of society, particularly the masters and students. The accomplishments of these institutions opened up intellectual vistas which abbots and bishops had no utilitarian interest in fostering. Moreover, during the last half of the twelfth century Western Europe was flooded by new knowledge, primarily from the ancient Greek world by way of the Muslims, which challenged existing religious beliefs. The response to these pressures was a new education institution, the university, which in its origin represented a community of scholars seeking to create an independent setting for study. The first universities tended to concentrate on one area of learning: Salerno and Montpellier, for example, on medicine, Bologna on law, Paris on theology.

Universities were founded by the action of either students or faculty, who organized themselves into self-governing corporations, or guilds (the general Latin term for "guild" was *universitas*). At Bologna the students formed a *universitas* because they felt the need for protection against the townsmen. At Paris the teachers of the arts in the Paris episcopal school broke away from the control of the bishop and founded a self-governing body, and later faculties of law, theology, and medicine were added.

The base of the university curriculum was the seven liberal arts, taught by a faculty of several masters rather than only one, as in the cathedral school. The arts program, often lasting six or eight years, usually culminated in a master of arts degree, which entitled its holder to teach. Eventually, a bachelor of arts degree was instituted, requiring four or five years of study but not entitling its holder to teach. The doctor's degree was taken in theology, law, or medicine; at Paris the theology doctorate took at least thirteen years of study. The granting of degrees was another aspect that distinguished the university from earlier institutions.

Teaching consisted chiefly of commenting on texts. Students who could afford to buy a manuscript copy of the authority under discussion made notes of the teacher's comments in the margins of the text. Those without a text tried to copy it as the master read it (thus the origin of the lecture system, since reading from a text was called *lectio*). Examinations at the end of four, six, or thirteen years tested the student's ability to expound on a text or thesis.

At first most university classes were held in rented halls, while students took lodgings in private homes. During the thirteenth century, men of means began to endow establishments for housing and feeding students. Such establishments, called *colleges,* became the centers of most educational activities. The first such institution was the Sorbonne at Paris, endowed in 1258 by Robert de Sorbon, a rich courtier. Usually students and faculty were considered members of the clergy and thus were under the jurisdiction of church courts. This led to endless conflicts between townsmen (who had to tolerate students without being able to control them) and the university community. Medieval students were a tough, rude lot who demanded much and were willing to use almost any means to get what they wanted; some of their exploits make the modern academician thankful for the serenity of the modern university and the seriousness of modern students.

3. THEOLOGY AND PHILOSOPHY

A major portion of the intellectual energies of medieval men of learning was absorbed in a quest for a fuller understanding of the Christian faith. Out of this quest came one of the chief monuments of medieval culture: a body of theology and philosophy that attempted to clarify Christian doctrine and to relate all other branches of knowledge to Christian teaching.

In the eleventh century, ever-increasing attention was devoted to the question of the extent to which human reason could be useful in grasping religious truth. One of the early and influential exponents of this approach was Anselm of Bec (later archbishop of Canterbury), whose aim was to provide a logical proof of the existence of God. Rational inquiry into revealed knowledge reached a decisive point with the career of Peter Abelard (1079–1142). Even as a student, this bold thinker disturbed the intellectual leaders of his generation. His stormy career as a teacher was ruined by a love affair with one of his young pupils, Heloise, and he was forced to spend the rest of his days wandering from monastery to monastery. However, certain of his ideas influenced both his contemporaries and later theologians.

Superbly skilled as a logician, Abelard began to establish a method by which reason could be used to enlarge man's vision of God. In a famous book entitled *Sic et Non (Yes and No)* he set down numerous cases of direct conflicts between authorities on matters of faith. Obviously, only human reason could resolve these. Abelard also developed new insights into how men know. He maintained that the truth consists of concepts formed in the mind from the study of created things, such concepts being the nearest approximation to the perfect knowledge that is God. A philosopher's task is to organize in a logical fashion all that he knows so as to create a mental image of God's universe. The opposition to Abelard's rationalism, led by Bernard of Clairvaux, was strong, and some of his teachings were condemned by the Church before his death. However, his approach to theology soon became predominant, especially after Peter Lombard (1100–1160) used it in his *Sentences*, which undertook to resolve rationally differing doctrinal opinions in order to present a consistent treatment of theology.

The utility of the approach was powerfully enhanced when scholars had to face the vast body of new knowledge that became available in the West during the late twelfth and early thirteenth centuries. Numerous Greek and Muslim philosophical and scientific works were translated into Latin in Spain and Sicily, including most of Aristotle's writings; he quickly became the leading authority on logical methods and scientific learning. This new knowledge posed a serious challenge: Not only did it supply theologians and philosophers with unfamiliar information, but it also confronted them with logically demonstrated systems of truth that directly contradicted basic Christian doctrine. Their recourse lay in a systematic application of reason.

The major concerns of thirteenth-century thought, especially in the universities, centered on this task. Many scholars, collectively called the *scholastics,* labored to master the new knowledge, organize it into a rational system, and reconcile it with Christian doctrine. Differing responses were articulated, often accompanied by bitter quarrels centering on fundamental intellectual issues, especially those posed by Aristotle's philosophical system. These intellectual wars belie the often-stated notion that the Middle Ages was a time of uniformity and conformity in the world of ideas.

The initial reaction to the new knowledge had been fear and suspicion so strong that the teaching of Aristotle was forbidden at Paris, but the knowledge was irresistible, and its study soon became major intellectual fare at the universities. One group, called the Averroists after the famous Muslim thinker, whole-heartedly accepted Aristotelian rationalism, arguing that reason was capable of defining an order of truth that had its own validity irrespective of the tenets of faith. At the opposite pole was a school of thought that rejected the main elements of Aristotelianism and built a philosophical system that strongly reasserted the Platonic tradition and Augustinianism. The most notable figure in this tradition was a Franciscan, Bonaventura (1221–1274), a teacher at Paris and eventually head of the Franciscan Order. Bonaventura argued that reason could not discover the ultimate truth, which must come to man by a mystical illumination. The phenomena of the natural world which the senses and reason comprehend are but symbols of the reality of the divine order.

But the most representative response to the new knowledge was formulated by the succession of scholars who tried to reconcile reason and revelation. By far the most influential advocate of this approach was Thomas Aquinas (1225–1274), an Italian Dominican who spent most of his life studying and teaching at the university in Paris and producing a huge body of theological writing. His chief work, the *Summa Theologiae,* is probably the best product of medieval thought. In this and all his works Thomas begins with the assumption that God created the universe in such a way that all its parts fit together and have a single purpose. Every man has the duty to know God and his works. There are two paths to this knowledge: revelation and reason. The task of the human mind is to seek the truth by applying itself to those things that are the proper subjects for reason while accepting on faith those things that can be learned only by revelation. Thomas accepted on faith the creation, the Trinity, and the Incarnation but applied reason to such problems as the existence of God, immortality, the operation of the natural world, the nature of government, and ethics. If there is a conflict between revelation and reason, it results from faulty reasoning.

Following the rules of logic formulated by Aristotle, and relying heavily on him for knowledge on subjects proper to human reason, Thomas measured the whole realm of human knowledge item after item against the revealed truth. His method consisted of a rigorously applied series of steps: formulation of a truth, statement of all possible contrary positions, demonstration of the fallacies in these, demonstration of the logical validity of the true position. Each single truth in Thomas' system is part of an interlocking structure of thought which relates all things to a perfect truth. The final result of Aquinas' work is a synthesis of all knowledge into one vast structure glorifying God and demonstrating his power.

The Thomistic synthesis perhaps best represents the overall spirit of medieval thought: the quest to integrate existing knowledge into a single structure; new knowledge was seldom a concern. Out of this effort there emerged a bent toward closely reasoned, highly organized learning that was destined to play a major role in the future of thought in Western Europe. During the Middle Ages, however, there was an important limitation on rationalism: Reason was always controlled, disciplined, and channeled by revealed truth and was therefore not free to seek where it would. It had always to test its findings against the teachings of Christianity.

4. SCIENCE, LAW, AND POLITICAL THEORY

The scientific work of medieval scholars seems pale by the standards of our age, and indeed their accomplishments were limited. Even in the thirteenth century, when European thinkers had at their disposal the excellent scientific works of Greek and Muslim authorities, they made little effort to correct errors inherited from Scripture, mythology, and popular lore or to pursue new knowledge about the natural world. This lack of interest was largely due to the intellectual preoccupation of the age with subordinating all knowledge to revealed truth.

Occasionally, however, the medieval world did produce men with a true scientific spirit. An important group, most of them Franciscans, centered at Oxford in the thirteenth century; Robert Grosseteste (1168–1253) and his pupil Roger Bacon (ca. 1214–1294) were its most distinguished members. These men insisted on the necessity of experiments to ascertain the truth about the natural world. Bacon argued that most scholastics put too much trust in ancient authorities and himself engaged in experimentation, especially in optics. Although his work was far from outstanding, he and his fellow scientists prepared the ground for the later revolutionary explosion of scientific knowledge.

Actually, during the Middle Ages there was a steady increase in practical knowledge of medicine, mechanics, and plant and animal life, but it was merely accumulated without thought for scientific method as it is conceived of today. A typical example is alchemy. The efforts to change base metals into gold by a variety of magical practices unearthed a great deal of information on the nature of metals and how to handle them. Yet no one thought to change the direction of his work from seeking the formula for gold to looking at what might be done with some of the discoveries.

The study of law was pursued avidly during the twelfth and thirteenth centuries, especially at the University of Bologna. We have previously noted the work of the canon lawyers and in particular Gratian, who in his *Decretum* created a model compendium of canon law. A long succession of twelfth- and thirteenth-century canon lawyers continued the work of compilation and commentary grounded in a rational approach; their labors produced a highly sophisticated body of law that found widespread application in the governance of the Church. The chief concern in civil law was the Code of Justinian, which began to be studied in the eleventh century after a long period of neglect in the West. Civil lawyers spent most of their time writing commentaries (called *glosses*) on the code to try to elucidate its intention and relate its principles to existing society. Their work had a great impact on the kind of law the rising monarchies administered in their realms.

Political theorists in the High Middle Ages produced a rich harvest. They were spurred by a variety of influences: the Christian concept of the nature of the state and society (especially as articulated by Augustine), the conflict between church and state, the need to justify the powers and actions of the new monarchies, the revival of Roman law, the recovery of classical Greek and Roman works on political theory (notably Aristotle). In the eleventh and twelfth centuries, political thought tended to reassert the Augustinian idea that the state was a divinely ordained organism established to curb man's sinful nature, the ruler being God's agent for correcting men. Under the impact of classical ideas, this concept gradually changed.

Thomas Aquinas argued that the state is a manifestation of natural law, instituted to fulfill man's nature, and is therefore necessary, good, and constructive. To function properly, it must be made up of classes, each with a specific function. Peasants and artisans must work, nobles must rule, and priests must pray and administer the sacraments. The function of the state and the ruler is to see that each does his duty and gets his reward; this is justice. A tyrannical king, a merchant who charges unfair prices, a banker who charges interest, a lazy or rebellious peasant are all guilty of injustice in that they are depriving someone in the community of his due. Aquinas placed upon the ruler the heavy responsibility of discovering the principles of natural law that God has ordained to regulate human society and applying them in a way that would produce a human community in accord with the divine order.

5. LITERATURE

The world of learning produced its own vast body of literature, chiefly in Latin, concerned with theology, law, science, and philosophy. That literature was rivaled by another body, produced to instruct and entertain a broader audience.

Much of this second kind of literature was also written in Latin, chiefly by clergymen who learned the tongue as a part of their professional preparation. Although classical influences were strong, there were fresh and innovative aspects of medieval Latin literature. The vocabulary was constantly being infused with new words and meanings, and inherited literary forms were modified considerably. Probably the best Latin literature of the High Middle Ages was lyric poetry on religious themes, often composed to serve the religious liturgy, especially as hymns. The most moving Latin poetry employed a new verse technique based on rhyme and accent rather than on long and short vowels, the classical technique. The new style also lent itself well to nonreligious themes as in the numerous student songs, called collectively Goliardic poetry, celebrating drinking, sensual love, gambling, and a variety of other worldly subjects. From 1000 to 1300 there was also a great outpouring of historical literature and biography written in Latin, some of it marked by keen observation of contemporary events, good organization, and excellent style.

But it is vernacular literature, written in the tongues that Europeans spoke in their daily lives, that represents the best of the High Middle Ages, for here we can see the literary genius of Western Europeans coming to maturity. Most vernacular works were produced to entertain the feudal nobility. One of the earliest forms of this literature was the epic, or *chanson de geste*, a song recounting the deeds of great warriors and based on oral tradition. The great Anglo-Saxon epic *Beowulf* is largely rooted in pre-Christian Germanic society. So are the Scandinavian sagas, the *Poetic Edda* and the *Prose Edda of Snorri Sturlson*, not written down until the twelfth and thirteenth centuries but reflecting a much earlier society of violence and paganism. The chief Germanic epic, the *Nibelungenlied*, composed about 1200, likewise reflects a tradition dating back to the time of the Germanic invasions. The most representative *chansons de geste* were produced in France, the best known being the *Song of Roland*, written about 1100. Its subject is Charlemagne's expedition to Spain in 778 to attack the Muslims, an expedition that ended in the defeat of the Frankish forces at Roncesvalles. However, the unknown author adorned the event and the hero, Roland, with the ideals and customs of eleventh-century feudal Europe. The writer of the *Song of the Cid*, the Spanish counterpart of the French epic, likewise embroidered on a famous knight's deeds fighting the Muslims.

The epic genre was soon rivaled by a new vernacular literary form, the lyric, which during the twelfth and thirteenth centuries enjoyed a tremendous vogue among the nobility. It developed first in Provence, in southern France, from where it spread over most of Europe. Its creators, called *troubadors*, were for the most part aristocrats who found their inspiration in love for a lady (usually married to someone else) rather than in the action-filled, bloody world of the *chansons de geste*. The troubador reflected a whole new set of values in the feudal world. His poetry, based on his personal emotions—longing for love or a sign of recognition from the beloved, suffering from a lack of it, anticipating the consummation of his love—became an instrument for self-understanding, feeling, and refinement, for the rules of "the gay science," as the art of love was called, demanded a mode of conduct that would be pleasing to the ladies. As the lyric style spread (lyric poets in northern France were called *trouvères* and in Germany *minnesänger*), its forms tended to become highly stylized, the concept of love more ethereal and elevated. The lyric writers (some four hundred have been identified for the twelfth and thirteenth centuries) left an indelible mark on both the feudal world and Western European literary history. They developed a new vehicle for self-identification, charting a new set of values and emotions quite unknown to the classical world and absolutely anathema to the early Christian view.

Before the end of the twelfth century, the epic and lyric traditions had merged to produce a third type of vernacular literature, the *romance*. This was a story, combining love with high adventure, written to entertain nobles. The love aspect was treated in an exaggerated manner. The adventure element centered on three broad themes: the deeds of Charlemagne, the adventures of King Arthur and his knights, and the actions of Greek and Roman heroes. These basic plots were used with complete disregard for historical accuracy. A reader might find Alexander the Great fighting the Seljuk Turks, attending mass, and engaging in a tournament. Many romances were run of the mill, comparable to the bulk of modern novels and movies. A few writers, however, fashioned works with enduring appeal. Among them was Chrétien de Troyes, a twelfth-century French author whose treatment of the Arthurian material established a powerful picture of the ideal knight. Another, the thirteenth-century German Gottfried von Strasbourg, gives a masterful revelation in *Tristan* of the meaning of love in the lives of two who were its prisoners. *Parzival*, by his countryman Wolfram von Eschenbach, is an appealing picture of a man in pursuit of unobtainable desire, symbolized by the Holy Grail.

While the epics, lyrics, and romances were being written, sung, and read by nobles, the middle class was producing dramas and *fabliaux*. Medieval drama had its origin as a part of church liturgy; dramatized parts of services eventually moved outside the church into the marketplace. By the thirteenth century the guilds had taken over the responsibility for producing these dramas on religious festivals. Several types were popular: mystery plays, enacting scenes from the Bible; miracle plays, treating the highlights of saints' lives; morality plays, personifying human virtues and vices. The *fabliaux* were short tales recited in public squares for the entertainment of the crowds. Whatever the subject—it could be almost anything—the *fabliau* was always close to city life, faithfully representing everyday events in the lives of ordinary people. It was often filled with vulgar humor and satire aimed especially at priests and women. The most famous collection of *fabliaux* was the *Romance of Reynard the Fox* made up of stories in which animals symbolize people and human characteristics.

Of the many writers during the High Middle Ages one genius, Dante Alighieri (1265–1321), towers above all others. He was to literature what Thomas Aquinas was to theology. Dante was a product of Florence, actively engaging in political life in that city and eventually suffering exile. It was while in exile that he wrote the masterpiece the *Divine Comedy*. Outwardly it is an account of Dante's journey through hell, purgatory, and heaven. Guided through the first two by Vergil and through heaven by Beatrice, he is permitted to see all things from the depths of hell to God himself. Inwardly, it is a tapestry woven of the many threads that run through medieval literature. Dante is a philosopher, presenting with consummate skill the medieval idea that all things in the universe are ordered by God. He is a mystic, yearning to the depths of his soul to catch a glimpse of God. He is a love poet; Beatrice, his guide in heaven, is a symbol of human love, which purifies and uplifts man. He is a scientist, incorporating many medieval ideas about the structure of the physical universe. He is an admirer of Greek and Roman classicists, although he has to condemn them to hell as non-Christians. He is a keen political observer, full of fierce partisanship. On his long journey from the gates of hell to its very pit, where Lucifer chews up three great traitors, Brutus, Cassius, and Judas, Dante discusses with Vergil nearly every kind of sin, showing a deep understanding of human nature and its weaknesses. Few artists have grasped human life and human aspirations more fully or written of them with greater impact.

6. THE ARTS

The High Middle Ages marked one of the decisive epochs in the history of art. Two major styles, Romanesque and Gothic, were perfected between 1000 and 1300. A great spate of building adorned almost every town and village with impressive new structures. Most of these were churches, for the Church was the prime agency promoting artistic endeavor. Architecture was queen; the other arts were used to adorn structures.

The Romanesque and Gothic styles were the fruits of a long artistic evolution. The starting point of medieval church architecture was the Roman basilica, the rectangular meeting hall. The early Christians placed their altars in the semicircular *apse* at the rear and conducted the mass there. The *nave* provided seating for the faithful. A lateral aisle, called the *transept*, sometimes crossed the nave just in front of the apse, so that the early church took the form of a cross. Over the centuries, the classic mold of church architecture and the art that decorated it was considerably modified by influences from the Byzantine, Germanic, and Celtic worlds and by new creative forces emerging from daily life. During the High Middle Ages artists finally succeeded in blending these many tributaries into distinctive new styles.

Romanesque architecture first appeared in the late tenth century and flourished through most of the twelfth. Its main features are admirably illustrated by several churches still standing: Notre Dame la Grande in Poitiers, the cathedral of Saint-Sernin in Toulouse, the cathedral at Worms, the Abbey Church of Maria Laach in Germany, and the church of Sant'Ambrogio at Milan. The Romanesque style was characterized both by technical innovations and by a new spirit. The monastic world, especially the Cluniac reformers, played a dominant role in developing and spreading this style, for their emphasis on rituals involving large numbers of monks and their concern with the veneration of relics and pilgrimages dictated churches large enough to house a number of chapels and accommodate great crowds. Architects had also long been concerned with replacing the traditional wooden roofs, which so often were destroyed by fire. The solution was a capacious church built entirely of stone. Round arches were utilized to support the stone barrel vaults thrown over the full length of the nave and side aisles to create the roof. Cross vaults were evolved to cover the area where the nave and transept crossed. Since the stone vaulting exerted a tremendous downward and outward thrust, Romanesque churches had heavy walls and a minimum number of windows. Wherever the walls were pierced for passageways, massive piers spanned by equally massive arches had to be constructed. Thus the typical Romanesque church had an atmosphere of gloom and mystery that was not dispelled by the decorative paintings on piers, arches, and walls. Yet this atmosphere was due as well to the religious mentality that viewed the church as God's citadel standing against a world filled with evil forces, a sacred fortress where men could commune with the mighty God who protected them from the howling demons and the frightening forces of nature.

By the mid-twelfth century the European world was changing rapidly, and the new environment produced a new architectural style, the Gothic. It appeared first in Ile de France, the domain of the Capetians; the earliest full-scale Gothic church was the Abbey Church of St. Denis near Paris, rebuilt 1137–1144 by Abbot Suger, the adviser to kings Louis VI and Louis VII. From here the Gothic style spread over much of Europe; only Italy was little affected, for there by the thirteenth century a classical revival was creating a Renaissance architecture.

The Gothic style evolved out of a desire for height and light in churches, a desire derived largely from new intellectual and spiritual concepts that fostered a more rational view of God and saw his chief attributes in terms of reason, light, and proportion. The Gothic church was an attempt to leave behind the mystery-shrouded, awesome world of the Romanesque and move into the light and purity of paradise—the paradise Dante pictured in poetry. Among the Gothic structures that achieve this effect magnificently are Notre Dame at Paris and the cathedrals at Chartres, Rheims, Amiens, Strasbourg, and Bourges in France; at Lincoln, York, and Salisbury in England; and at Cologne in Germany.

Technically, this transformation was made possible by the pointed arch, which carried

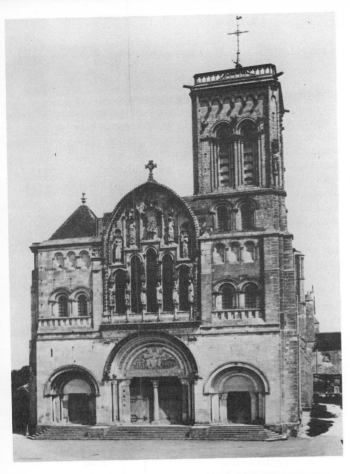

The facade of the Abbey Church at Vezelay in France. Its massive features, highlighted by round arches and heavy walls, provide an excellent example of the Romanesque style of architecture. *Photo: Courtesy, French Government Tourist Office*

thrust downward, and the ribbed vault, used to concentrate the thrust at a few points. Architects were able to combine them to fashion tremendously tall skeletons of stone whose weight flowed to earth through a series of slender pillars. The outward thrust, greatly reduced and concentrated, could be offset by thickened columns at the outside of the building or by flying buttresses, pillars set away from the main structure and joined to it by bracing arches high above the ground. Thin walls, supporting nothing but their own weight, could be filled in between the pillars. More important, light could be let into the structure by great arched windows, often interlaced with delicate decorative stonework, piercing the lofty clerestory and the side aisles and majestic round windows at the ends of the nave and transept. The windows were often filled with many-hued stained-glass figures or scenes that suffused the interior with a breathtaking display of colored light.

Nearly every other visual art was put to work to decorate medieval churches. The exterior of a Romanesque church was generally plain except for the façade, where the great doorways leading to the nave and side aisles provided a setting for sculpture. As illustrated by churches at Arles and Vézelay, these spaces were filled with massive, highly symbolical sculpture portraying human figures, animals, and abstract decorative patterns. A favorite subject was the Last Judgment, in which a stern Christ relegated men to heaven or hell. Within a Romanesque church there was more sculpture, chiefly decoration for the massive piers. The large, flat wall spaces were decorated with frescoes portraying scrip-

The west facade of Chartres, one of the most glorious of the Gothic cathedrals. Structure and decoration are harmonized to give a soaring, upward-striving effect. The great stained glass windows and the delicate stone tracery still further distinguish the Gothic church from the massive, gloomy Romanesque. *Photo: A. F. Kersting*

A detail from the tympanum of the Cathedral of Saint-Lazare at Autun, carved by Giselbertus before 1135. Here are the flat, stylized, clearly defined figures of the Romanesque style. *Photo: Pierre Belzeaux/Rapho-Guillumette*

tural scenes, particularly those that stressed the suffering of Christ and his judgment on men. The style of Romanesque sculpture and painting is a somber one that makes man small, powerless, and dependent; it grips the emotions rather than the mind.

Gothic architecture brought about changes in the other arts. The exteriors of Gothic churches provided innumerable places for decorative sculpture, giving stone carvers an opportunity to experiment with a fantastic array of decorative motifs. Statues were more realistic and human-istic, expressing more the human qualities of Jesus, the Virgin, the apostles, and the saints.

The interior of Gothic churches offered less space for painting and sculpture than did Romanesque churches; decoration was concentrated chiefly on columns and arches. Not images but light fills the Gothic church. The painted walls of the Romanesque church were replaced with stained-glass windows. Their creators drew their themes from scriptural sources, but in their renditions they reflected in amazing detail the daily activities of medieval people. The stained glass at Chartres and in the beautiful Sainte-Chapelle built by Louis IX in Paris enthrall the viewer.

Another art associated with religious activity, music, also developed significantly during the High Middle Ages. Church music consisted primarily of melodies with verses taken from

Scripture (especially the psalms) or composed for liturgical events (such great hymns as *Dies Irae* and *Stabat Mater* came from the Middle Ages). *Gregorian chant* (its alleged inventor was Pope Gregory I) or *plain song* developed as early as the sixth century. At first, the singing was in unison, but over the centuries variations worked on plain song developed into contrapuntal music. The variations required a different scheme of written indications for the music, so that by the eleventh century, the musical notation system still in use today had been developed. By the thirteenth century, complex and moving contrapuntal compositions, rendered by many voices and various instruments, filled the churches with sounds almost as heavenly as the light that poured through the stained glass windows.

The great cathedrals commanded the best artistic talent and the bulk of the wealth that medieval society had to devote to art. However, there were other lines of artistic pursuit. Many feudal castles, massive rather than elegant or comfortable, were built in the Romanesque style. In the towns, especially from the thirteenth century onward, beautiful town halls and guildhalls were constructed, putting Gothic principles to new uses. Some of them were impressive signs that the Church never completely absorbed artistic energies.

These Gothic figures from the south portal of Chartres illustrate the warmth and realism of the style. *Photo: Jean Roubier*

7. THE UNDERLYING SPIRIT OF MEDIEVAL CULTURE

Certainly it is not easy to find a common denominator for Thomas Aquinas, Dante, the architects and sculptors who built the churches at Poitiers, Amiens, and Chartres, the troubadors, the romance writers, and the authors of *fabliaux*. The culture of the High Middle Ages was marked by variety. Medieval cultural life exhibited signs of nearly every attitude or idea present even in modern society, a fact that increasingly has led scholars to insist that modern Western European culture was born in the eleventh to thirteenth centuries.

Most medieval art and thought is permeated by a quest for truth and light beyond the world of men. This reaching out of the mind and the imagination sprang from the almost universal belief that God controlled the universe and that it was man's duty to know and worship him. The artist and the writer stood in awe of God and used their talents humbly to serve him. Medieval culture viewed as a whole, therefore, has an atmosphere of otherworldliness and of surrender to a power beyond human understanding.

Yet, intertwined with this aspiration and submission to the divine there is a warm, sympathetic feeling for humankind. Medieval men believed that man was God's finest creation. Artists and writers were never disdainful of human powers and potentialities. They took joy in presenting man as he was and wrestled constantly with the problem of understanding human nature more fully.

The medieval genius shines most brilliantly in attempts to synthesize these two outlooks. Men seldom felt that otherworldliness and secularism, spirituality and humanism were exclusive terms. Medieval thinkers and artists respected their own powers enough to believe that they could reach out toward God—by building cathedrals higher or by putting together greater *summae* of knowledge or by flights of poetic fancy. Yet they were men of great enough faith to believe that their quest would lead them to a power infinitely greater than themselves.

Suggested Reading

General Surveys

*John W. Baldwin, *The Scholastic Culture of the Middle Ages, 1000–1300* (Heath). A perceptive brief survey.

H. O. Taylor, *The Medieval Mind*, 4th ed., 2 vols. (1949). The best of longer studies written by a nonspecialist with imagination and deep understanding.

*C. H. Haskins, *The Renaissance of the Twelfth Century* (Meridian).

P. Wolff, *The Cultural Awakening*, trans. A. Carter (1969).

*Christopher Brooke, *The Twelfth-Century Renaissance* (Harcourt, Brace, & World). This and the preceding titles cover all aspects of cultural life in the early part of the period. Haskins originally designated these developments as a "renaissance."

Education

*C. H. Haskins, *The Rise of the Universities* (Cornell).

*L. J. Daly, *The Medieval University, 1200–1400* (Sheed and Ward). Two excellent brief surveys of the emergence of the university system.

*H. Wieruszowski, *The Medieval University: Masters, Students, Learning* (Anvil). A brief description accompanied by a fine selection of source materials illustrating the university system.

University Records and Life in the Middle Ages, trans. Lynn Thorndike (1944). Especially good for the picture it presents of student life.

Theology and Philosophy

*D. Knowles, *The Evolution of Medieval Thought* (Vintage). The best brief survey, perhaps stressing too much the continuity between classical and medieval thought.

*Gordon Leff, *Medieval Thought from St. Augustine to Ockham* (Penguin). Another brief survey, perhaps easier to read than Knowles.

Etienne Gilson, *History of Christian Philosophy in the Middle Ages* (1955). A comprehensive survey by the greatest modern authority.

*Richard McKeon, ed., *Selections from Medieval Philosophers*, 2 vols. (Scribners). A representative anthology.

A. C. Pegis, ed., *Introduction to Saint Thomas Aquinas* (Modern Library). Provides a good introduction to the ideas and methodology of the scholastics.

Science, Law, Political Theory

*A. C. Crombie, *Medieval and Early Modern Science*, 2 vols., 2nd ed. (Anchor). A thorough but somewhat technical survey.

R. C. Mortimer, *Western Canon Law* (1953).

P. Vinogradoff, *Roman Law in Medieval Europe*, 2nd ed. (1929). These two works, although not entirely satisfactory, provide insight into legal developments.

*J. B. Morrall, *Political Thought in Medieval Times* (Harper Torchbook).

*Walter Ullmann, *A History of Political Thought: The Middle Ages* (Penguin). Two excellent brief treatments.

Ewart Lewis, *Medieval Political Ideas*, 2 vols. (1954). A fine collection of medieval writings on political theory.

Literature

W. T. Jackson, *The Literature of the Middle Ages* (1960). A convenient introduction to a vast and complex subject. It is perhaps better to read medieval literature itself than about it. The following works are especially recommended:

*Beowulf, trans. David Wright (Penguin).

*Nibelungenlied, trans. A. T. Hatto (Penguin).

*Prose Edda of Snorri Sturlson: Tales from Norse Mythology, trans. J. I. Young (University of California).

*Song of Roland, trans. F. B. Luguiens (Collier).

An Anthology of Medieval Lyrics, ed. A. Flores (1962).

J. A. Symonds, Wine, Women, and Song (1925).

*Medieval Romances, ed. R. S. and L. H. Loomis (Modern Library).

Arthurian Romances by Chrétien de Troyes, trans. W. W. Comfort (1914).

*Aucassin and Nicolette and Other Medieval Romances, ed. E. Mason (Dutton).

*Wolfram von Eschenbach, Parzival, trans. H. M. Mustard and C. E. Passage (Vintage).

*Gottfried von Strassburg, Tristan, trans. A. T. Hatto (Penguin).

*Medieval Mysteries, Moralities and Interludes, ed. V. F. Hopper and G. B. Lakey (Barron).

*Everyman and Medieval Miracle Plays, ed. A. C. Cawley (Dutton).

*Five Comedies of Medieval France, trans. O. Mandel (Dutton).

*The Comedy of Dante Alighieri, trans. D. Sayers and B. Reynolds, 3 vols. (Penguin).

The Arts

H. Focillon, The Art of the West in the Middle Ages, 2 vols. (1963). A great work, made more effective by excellent illustrations.

François Souchal, Art of the Early Middle Ages (1968).

K. J. Conant, Carolingian and Romanesque Architecture, 800–1200 (1959).

A. Grabar and C. Nordenfalk, Romanesque Painting (1958). This and the preceding two titles effectively treat various aspects of Romanesque art.

*A. Martindale, Gothic Art from the Twelfth to the Fifteenth Century (Praeger).

*Robert Branner, Gothic Architecture (Braziller).

*Otto von Simson, The Gothic Cathedral (Harper Torchbook).

*Emile Mâle, The Gothic Image (Harper Torchbook). This and the preceding three titles fully characterize the nature of Gothic art.

Jean Gimpel, The Cathedral Builders, trans. C. F. Barnes, Jr. (1961). Describes the techniques of medieval builders.

*Henry Adams, Mont Saint Michel and Chartres (Anchor). A classic work that contrasts the spirit of Romanesque and Gothic.

*E. Panofsky, Gothic Architecture and Scholasticism (Meridian). A stimulating attempt to interrelate the intellectual and artistic worlds.

*H. Hutter, Medieval Stained Glass (Crown). A good introduction.

Gustav Reese, Music in the Middle Ages (1940). Excellent, although highly technical.

Retrospect

The events upon which attention has been focused in this section were decisive in world history, for the central development of the era from 1000 to 1300 was the rise of Western Europe. The High Middle Ages was distinguished by the remarkable expansion of the primitive society that had been so painfully and tenuously pieced together atop the ruins of classical civilization. At every level of society and in every phase of life, there was sustained, constructive activity that increased wealth, secured order, changed the social structure, expanded mental horizons, deepened understanding of human existence, and enlarged capabilities for expression. The new institutional patterns and ideas that were fashioned during this remarkable age—the youthful national states, the social structure of nobility, peasantry, and bougeoisie, the towns, the Church, the universities, the theology and philosophy, the vernacular literature, the art styles, the commercial and agricultural practices, the laws, the technology—have all survived in their essential forms almost to the present. They are developments basic to an understanding of the later history of Western Europe.

But the era has another, equally important, dimension. While gathering strength internally, Western European society began to impinge on the outside world. The High Middle Ages was the period of the first decisive steps toward the establishment of European preeminence in the world. Those who would understand the situation today would be well served by attempting to identify the ingredients which by 1300 had given Western Europeans the capability to determine the destinies of other peoples. Perhaps never in the entire history of humanity has one civilization demonstrated greater capacity to intrude itself into the lives of other societies for so long a period of time and with such an impact: The political, social, and economic forces that move the peoples of the world today were set in motion in the Western Europe of the High Middle Ages.

In our concentration on the remarkable growth of Western European society and its outward thrust toward other civilizations, we have perhaps not given enough attention to an internal development that may well supply the key to its future history. In considering the High Middle Ages, one is constantly struck by the fact that, as Western European society matured, its institutional and ideological fabric was laced with dichotomies and contradictions. Basic to the political order was tension between strong monarchical government and the privileges and rights of feudal nobles, the Church, and townsmen. Political thought and practice was divided by the clash between the universalism represented by the Holy Roman Empire and the localism inbred in the emergent nations. Engrained in Western European civilization were the contrasting aspirations of church and state. The religious structure was riven by the thrust toward universalism represented by the papacy and the local self-determination claimed by the ancient bishoprics existing all over the West. Everywhere some men struggled to impose uniformity and conformity in religious belief and practice, while others reached out toward personal, individualistic varieties of expression. In the economic realm, commercial towns contended with agricultural villages. On the farms, the traditional forms of collective, manorial exploitation stood juxtaposed with specialized, capitalistic exploitation. In the cities, the guilds sought to impose just prices, common standards of production, and equitable division of business opportunities, while resourceful entrepreneurs tried to follow their private ends. A universal Latin culture competed with localized vernacular cultures. The revealed tenets of the faith were challenged by the dictates of human reason. The world-denying spirit of the monastic world confronted powerful secular, humanistic interests. One is almost forced to conclude that as a consequence of its historical development during the High Middle Ages, Western European civilization in a unique way was compounded of contradictory thrusts. It was like a Gothic cathedral in which height was limited by weight, light met dark, color competed with stark bareness, space was confined by structure.

Can we say perhaps that this juxtaposition of opposites that emerged from 1000 to 1300 constitutes the essence of Western European civilization? Dare we suggest that these medieval contradictions have supplied the Western world with its dynamism? Might we suspect that the history of the West after 1300 may be a story of the resolution of these contradictions: central government versus private interests, rights, and privileges; state versus church, reason versus faith; national states versus universal empire? Perhaps when the West has relieved its inner tensions by resolving these medieval issues, it will have lost its vitality.

VI

The Late Middle Ages
1300-1500

A long sweep of history is sometimes difficult to describe with a single neat phrase. Such is the Late Middle Ages, the era from 1300 to 1500. In the centuries since, historians have labeled it "the dawn of a new era," "the age of the Renaissance," "an age of transition," "the ordeal of transition," "the autumn of the Middle Ages," "the waning of the Middle Ages," "the death of medieval civilization." The descriptions all suggest that change was the keynote of these two centuries — but they also suggest that historians are not at all agreed on the direction of that change. Some emphasize new forces emerging; others stress the dissolution of old ways.

Perhaps we should let those who lived then tell us what was fundamental. Reading the literature and viewing the art of the period, we are struck by the frustration, bitterness, morbidity, and doubt gripping men's minds. Their comments on their world show they sensed that something was amiss; and with few exceptions, they seemed lacking in confidence and incapable of hope. These reactions argue that the dominant theme of the Late Middle Ages must be decline and disintegration rather than renaissance and the onset of modernity. Our description will follow that lead by suggesting that the equilibrium established in the thirteenth century between the numerous dichotomous forces in Western European civilization failed to survive. Perhaps Thomas Aquinas could reconcile revelation and reason, but his successors could not make the blend hold. The architects who built the Gothic cathedral at Amiens might balance height and weight, but their successors who tried to achieve greater height saw their cathedrals crash to earth. The Magna Carta might juxtapose royal authority and baronial right, but that settlement would not keep the peace. And so it was in most aspects of society. The fragile balance of contradictory forces that had been fashioned during the High Middle Ages failed to last. The fourteenth and fifteenth centuries mark a period when men were acutely aware of this failure.

The tensions that began to alter what had been forged in the High Middle Ages were of the essence of civilized life in the West. Tension breeds deterioration—but it also generates new forces in society. They were numerous and powerful, and we must return to them in future discussions. Men living from 1300 to 1500 could not, however, sense their promise as well as we can, gifted as we are with hindsight. To those men, the age was filled with the agonies that mark the passing of the known and familiar.

Politically, the fourteenth and fifteenth centuries were filled with disorder. Such typically medieval institutions as the Holy Roman Empire, the Byzantine Empire, and the feudal monarchies of England, France, and Spain failed to cope with new political problems. Their inadequacies bred civil strife, class struggle, international war, and internal injustice everywhere in Western Europe. Behind much of this trouble lay economic and social problems arising from the growing failure of medieval agricultural and commercial institutions.

1. THE DECLINE OF THE HOLY ROMAN EMPIRE

We have previously traced the efforts made by a succession of rulers between 950 and 1250 to join Germany, Italy, and the western fringes of the Slavic world into a Holy Roman Empire and the powerful opposition, led by the papacy, these efforts generated. The death of the last great emperor, Frederick II, in 1250 marked the beginning of the end: Not only did the empire as an institution disintegrate in the Late Middle Ages; so did the political ideal that had given it a rationale—that a Christian commonwealth could be translated into a secular state.

Frederick II's death opened a quarter century of civil strife, marked by an interregnum caused by the inability of the German nobility to elect an emperor and exacerbated by the incessant

25

POLITICAL, ECONOMIC, AND SOCIAL TENSIONS

intervention of the papacy and of France and England. During this struggle, nobles, clergy, and townsmen successfully extended their independence from central authority. In 1273, long rivalry for the crown ended with the election of Rudolph of Hapsburg (1273–1291), who confined his efforts to increasing his family holdings in the area of modern Austria. His success caused the German princes to repudiate the Hapsburgs in 1308 in favor of Luxembourg's Henry VII (1308–1313), who greatly strengthened his family's position by establishing control over Bohemia. In 1314 Louis IV (1314–1347) of Bavaria was elected out of fear that the house of Luxembourg was getting too powerful. By the attitude they reflected in the election process, the German nobles demonstrated that they would not tolerate a strong ruler; those who desired to gain the imperial office fully realized the situation.

This trend was finally given legal definition by Emperor Charles IV (1347–1378) of Luxembourg. His most important act was to promulgate the famous Golden Bull of 1356, providing that in the future the Holy Roman emperor would be elected by seven German princes designated as the *electors:* the archbishops of Cologne, Trier, and Mainz, and the princes of Saxony, Brandenburg, the Palatinate, and Bohemia. The papacy was excluded from the election process, which was now a strictly German affair.

Each of the electors was granted almost complete independence within his own territory.

After 1356 Germany progressed rapidly toward decentralization. Other princes demanded and gained the same kind of independence enjoyed by the electors, making Germany a confederation of roughly one hundred independent states. The emperor could call together the princes, churchmen, and representatives of the towns in meetings called *diets,* but he lacked any means of enforcing decisions; he had no national army, no tax system, and no court system. Within their small principalities, many princes created stable, well-organized political systems—Germany was not a lawless, ungoverned land by any means. But she did lack unity, and for this she was to pay heavily in early modern times, when she had to meet the competition of the large national states that emerged elsewhere in Europe.

In Italy, the trend toward decentralization after 1250 was even more pronounced. The elected emperor was in theory the ruler of Italy, and from time to time some Italians did seek to have him exert his authority (as Dante's powerful political tract, *On Monarchy,* illustrates). After the early fourteenth century, the emperors seldom even tried to exert any influence, and a welter of independent states of all sizes and descriptions emerged. Among them, five stand forth as important.

In southern Italy the old Norman state, now called the Kingdom of Naples, was now in decline. Throughout most of the Late Middle Ages, its destiny was controlled by outsiders, especially France and Aragon, who contested for it bitterly in order to capitalize on its wealth and strategic position. The Papal States dominated central Italy, their independence firmly established through the efforts of the great thirteenth-century popes, but papal overlordship was bitterly resisted by the local nobility. It was badly compromised by the long residency of the popes at Avignon (1309–1377) and by the Great Schism that followed (see Chapter 26). When the papacy was finally reestablished in Rome early in the fifteenth century, that authority was restored by a succession of popes who used all the tactics of power politics and intrigue to impose a despotic regime. These activities made them powerful, but ruined their reputation as spiritual leaders throughout most of Europe.

The other "major" powers in Italy were the northern city-states of Milan, Venice, and Florence. They accomplished much between 1300 and 1500 that would eventually exert a major influence on all of Western Europe; these were the golden years of their Renaissance. The city-states were preeminently the products of commercial and industrial activity, which made them unique in the West. After the death of Frederick II, they battled one another for land, trading advantages, power, and security. Internally, they tended to move from considerable citizen participation toward one-man or oligarchical rule, a trend encouraged by the pressures of intercity warfare and class strife within each city. Milan was taken over by a despot early in the fourteenth century when the Visconti family established its power. Visconti domination, which made Milan rich and powerful, lasted until 1447, when the Sforzas replaced them. Florence resisted despotism longer, but an aggressive banking family, the Medici, established control in the city shortly after 1430. Venice always remained subject to an oligarchy of rich merchants whose methods did not differ greatly from those of the despots. The turbulent, strife-filled times promoted notable progress in the arts of war and diplomacy. The new style of politics, described brilliantly in Machiavelli's

The Prince, tended to stress the absolute sovereignty of the state, its right to create its own moral sanctions, its superiority over its subjects. Many historians see these developments as prototypes for modern Western diplomacy and power politics.

Despite the vitality of the Italian Renaissance states, their history in the Late Middle Ages has a tragic dimension. The fragmentation of the peninsula doomed Italy to weakness in the face of the more integrated Spain and France and even the larger German principalities. When Charles VIII of France was called into Italy by the Sforza ruler of Milan in order to gain advantage for his city, his invasion in 1494 opened a long era during which the many states of Italy became pawns in European power politics.

2. THE FAILURE OF FEUDAL MONARCHY IN FRANCE, ENGLAND, AND SPAIN

After 1300 England, France, and the Iberian kingdoms encountered troubles nearly as serious as those of the Holy Roman Empire. As the fourteenth century progressed, their feudal monarchies began to show signs of instability and inadequacy. Kings were not content to share power, and nobles, clergy, and townsmen were unwilling to surrender more of their privileges. Kings lacked the power and resources to solve the major problems caused by wars and economic crises, and the vested interests were not blessed with vision great enough to face them. The result was a heightening of tension in each kingdom, a situation that led inevitably to civil wars that pitted the crown against the nobles and noble factions against each other. Under unbearable strain, the essential features of feudal monarchy and the concepts that animated the political order of the High Middle Ages slowly broke down.

The evolution of France and England from 1300 to 1500 must be dealt with together because the histories of the two center around a single event, the Hundred Years' War (1337–1453). This struggle was an extension of a conflict between England and France that had begun in the twelfth century and climaxed in the decisive French victory won by Philip II over John of England in 1214. The Treaty of Paris (1259) recog-

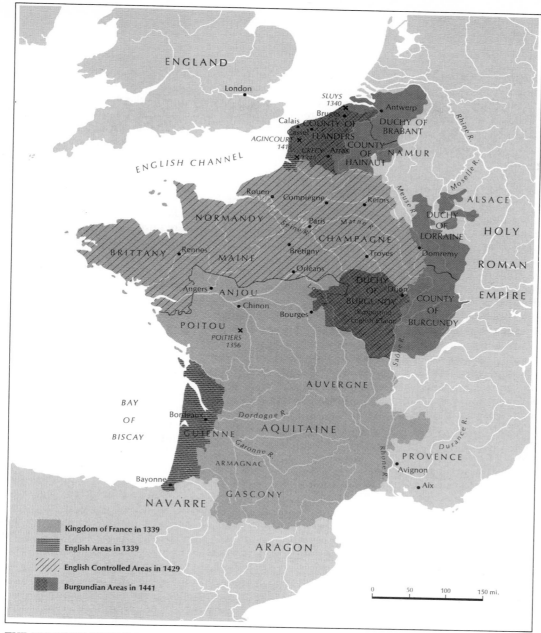

THE HUNDRED YEARS' WAR

Map legend:
- Kingdom of France in 1339
- English Areas in 1339
- English Controlled Areas in 1429
- Burgundian Areas in 1441

nized the control of the French king over the northern part of the old Angevin Empire but left England still in control of much of the old duchy of Aquitaine, including Guienne and Gascony. This settlement only bred continued rivalry. Edward III (1327–1377) finally acted to settle the issue. He was uneasy over the steady progress made by the French kings in extending their control over France. Aquitaine was vulnerable, since the English kings held it as a fief from the kings of France. So also was the county of Flanders, long the object of French ambitions and a focus of England's economic interests: She supplied much of the raw wool used by Flemish manufacturers and the king depended heavily on customs duties collected on the export of wool. Also French support of the Scots' resistance bitterly concerned England, especially after the Scots virtually assured their independence at the decisive battle of Bannockburn in 1314.

Soon after Edward became king, the moment was ripe for a blow against France. In 1328 the last member of the Capetian house died, and Philip of Valois, a man of little ability, succeeded to the throne as Philip VI. Edward struck boldly after careful steps to create a good army and to build up a system of alliances against the king of France. He announced in 1337 that he was claiming the French throne since he was Philip IV's grandson while Philip VI was only a nephew. Philip VI answered by pronouncing Edward a rebellious vassal and confiscating his fief.

The first phase of the Hundred Years' War lasted until 1360 and was nearly fatal to France. English ships won control of the Channel, and English armies, made up largely of nonnoble longbowmen and pikemen, cut to pieces the flower of French feudal nobility in two great battles at Crécy (1346) and Poitiers (1356). The crowning blow came at the battle of Poitiers, when John of France (1350–1364) was captured and carried off to England. Without a king, France was plunged into crisis. Charles, John's son, tried to carry on as regent, but his authority was challenged on every side. The Estates General undertook extensive reforms aimed at curbing royal taxation, correcting abuses in the royal government, and putting controls on royal civil servants. A peasant revolt, called the *Jacquerie* uprising, broke out in 1358 in protest against taxes and war losses. Bands of soldiers ran wild over France. The nobles sought greedily to extend their privileges. Charles finally crushed the rebellious Estates General by force, while the terrified nobles smashed the peasants. John bought his release by signing a humiliating peace with the English in 1360, giving Edward III full title to Guienne.

The next phase of the war, extending from 1364 to 1415, was marked by little decisive fighting but by tremendous internal dissension in each kingdom. France enjoyed a brief recovery under the rule of Charles V (1364–1380), who re-

built France's military strength and increased royal income. Using these resources skillfully, he slowly weakened England's hold on Guienne. However, his work was not continued by his pitiful successor, Charles VI (1380–1422), who took the throne as a minor. His regency was dominated by his greedy uncles, of whom Philip, duke of Burgundy, was the most powerful; on reaching his majority, Charles fell under the spell of his brother Louis, duke of Orléans. Moreover, he began to suffer from spells of insanity and each required the reinstitution of a regency. The Burgundians and the Armagnacs (partisans of the duke of Orléans) competed bitterly for control of the regency and the kingdom. By the early fifteenth century their rivalry divided the nobility into two great camps that plunged France into civil chaos in an incredible display of violence, greed, and selfishness. The final proof of the political bankruptcy of the nobility came when the Burgundians and the Armagnacs each began to dicker with the English to help destroy the other.

England was hardly less troubled during these years. Edward III ruled until 1377 amid increasing trouble. To wage war against France, he needed money, and the easiest way to get it was to call Parliament. Frequent meetings resulted in the rapid development of parliamentary organization. The *House of Lords*, comprising the great feudal barons and high churchmen, separated from the *House of Commons*, made up of townsmen and of the lesser gentry representing the counties. Each house steadily increased its powers. Aside from extensive control over taxation, Parliament began to gain a voice in spending money, controlling royal officials, and initiating legislation.

The stormy reign of Edward's successor, Richard II (1377–1399), was filled with civil strife arising from dissatisfaction with royal government. A great Peasants' Revolt broke out in 1381 and had to be crushed by force. The nobles, acting in Parliament, tried hard to limit royal power, and when Richard resisted their efforts, he was charged with tyranny and deposed by Parliament. Henry IV (1399–1413) of Lancaster was elected in his place—an event that made the monarch more than ever responsible to Parliament. However, Parliament proved neither capable of directing the kingdom nor willing to trust the king to do so. It became a forum for factional agitation aimed at dominating the king in order to secure greater privileges. Often the parliamentary struggles ended in civil strife which became endemic in English society.

Henry V (1413–1422) hastened both England and France along their troubled paths by reopening the Hundred Years' War. Desirous of distracting his nobles from efforts to curb his authority and assured that he would find support among France's warring factions, he invaded her in 1415. He crushed a French army at Agincourt in 1415 and then captured a series of key west-central cities. The Burgundians and Armagnacs tried to use the English to destroy one another, and eventually, the Burgundians allied with Henry V, permitting him to force the humiliating Treaty of Troyes on Charles VI in 1420. By its terms Henry married Charles' daughter; he or his successor was to rule France when Charles died; and until then he would act as regent for the mad Charles. Most of France north of the Loire River was in English hands.

But the English were not to enjoy their dominance for long. After both Henry V and Charles VI died in 1422, leaving the nine-month-old Henry VI as king of both nations, the French made a spectacular recovery. It was inspired by a new hard-to-define feeling of patriotism, of love for France and hatred for foreigners. The chief beneficiary was the son of Charles VI, soon to be known as Charles VII, who after 1420 was a virtual prisoner of the Armagnac faction. In 1428 a simple peasant girl, Joan of Arc, came to him claiming God had revealed to her that Charles must free France from the English and assume the throne. Her pleas bestirred the dispirited Charles and pumped new confidence into the French soldiers loyal to him. Joan herself was present with the army that captured Orléans in 1429, the first French victory for many years, and on the strength of it she persuaded Charles that he should brave the English danger to go to Rheims to be crowned.

From 1429 to 1453 the French won victory after victory, until the English held only the city of Calais in France. But Joan did not live to see these victories. In 1430 she was captured by Burgundian troops, turned over to the English, tried

by the Church for heresy, and burned at the stake in Rouen in 1431. Yet, the maid of Lorraine lived on as a symbol to rally the French.

The reign of Charles VII saw a great revival of royal power. He was not a strong ruler, but he was served by excellent ministers who guided him wisely. A strong, well-trained army was created and paid for by the king, who thus ended his dependence on the sort of useless feudal army that had failed so badly at Crécy, Poitiers, and Agincourt. In 1439 the Estates General voted Charles the power to impose at will a direct tax on persons, the *taille*. Charles VII became the focal point of political life. The bitter taste of defeat, of disorder, of irresponsibility on the part of great nobles compelled everyone to turn to the king for leadership. When he died in 1461, his son, Louis XI (1461–1483), inherited a solid base from which to rule. His accession marked the beginning of a new era.

England was in a less happy state. Strife among rival factions of nobles contending to dominate weak kings finally led to the Wars of the Roses, so called because the opposing forces adopted the white and red rose as their symbols. This struggle had its origins during the reign of Henry VI (1422–1461). Because he became king in infancy, there was a long regency. Moreover, his family, the Lancastrians, had been elevated to the throne by parliamentary action and did not have as strong a hereditary claim to the throne as did their foes, the Yorkists, who insisted that the crown belonged to them as a result of their closer kinship to Edward III. The final blow was an attack of insanity that Henry suffered after reaching his majority. Two major factions of nobles, formed around the rival Lancastrian and Yorkist claimants to the throne, locked in a deadly struggle. The basic issue was simply power and the benefits it could bring. While this civil war raged, the regular processes of orderly government were neglected. Tyranny, intrigue, murder, confiscation of property, and pursuit of private ends were the order of the day, perpetrated by nobles acting through bands of armed retainers. Henry VI and his supporters held the crown until finally defeated by Edward of York, who as Edward IV (1461–1483) tried to restore royal authority. The Lancastrians refused to accept his rule and kept the struggle going.

Edward was succeeded by his twelve-year-old son, Edward V, but within three months the young king's uncle seized the throne as Richard III. He tried vigorously to restore order in England, but he could neither dispel the view that he was a usurper nor blunt the hatred of the Lancastrians. Finally in 1485, Henry Tudor, a Lancastrian, defeated Richard in a pitched battle at Bosworth Field and assumed the throne as Henry VII. Although his claim to the crown was extremely tenuous, the nation, weary of civil disorder, was willing to follow anyone who promised to restore peace and security. The old noble factions had been decimated. Henry was therefore free to do much as he pleased. He used the opportunity to end the feudal state and create a strong central government that united the English people into a nation.

The three major Iberian kingdoms—Aragon, Castile, and Portugal—also had their difficulties during the Late Middle Ages. By 1300 the holy war against the Muslims ceased to be the significant factor in Spanish affairs, for they had been confined to the narrow territory of Granada. The Christian kingdoms then turned on one another, competing bitterly for territory. Added to these wars was the almost constant civil strife within each kingdom that replicated the kinds and the causes of the struggles in England and France. Castile was especially plagued by a long series of disputed successions that undermined royal authority. Aragon's internal order was compromised by the aggressive overseas policy pursued by her kings, especially in Italy, a policy seldom favored by the nobility, and by conflict between the landed and the commercial interests. These senseless quarrels finally began to abate when in 1469 the heiress of Castile, Isabella, married Ferdinand, the heir of Aragon. In 1479, when this couple had succeeded to both thrones, they quickly took steps to end the strife and unify their lands into a single state.

Portuguese kings did not meet such violent resistance as did the other Iberian kings, and they gained considerable internal support because of their heroic struggle to prevent Castile from absorbing Portugal. They also promoted commercial interests throughout the fifteenth century, backing Portuguese merchants who expanded southward along the African coast and found lucrative markets.

3. EASTERN EUROPE AND THE MEDITERRANEAN WORLD

The Byzantine Empire never fully recovered from the attacks of the Seljuk Turks in the late eleventh century and the capture of Constantinople by Western Europeans in 1204 during the Fourth Crusade. After the Europeans were finally ousted in 1261 and Greek emperors again assumed power, a fatal illness seemed to afflict the empire. Civil stife slowly sapped the strength of its government. The Italian city-states, led by Venice, deprived the empire of much of its trade, and bit by bit its territory was pared away, especially by the Ottoman Turks, a rising Muslim power. The emperors of the fourteenth and fifteenth centuries appealed desperately to the West for help but received little, since Western Europeans were too enmeshed in their own rivalries. Finally, in 1453 Constantinople was captured by the Ottomans, ending forever the power that had so long shielded Europe.

The Ottoman victory marked the reappearance of an aggressive Muslim force threatening Western Christendom, a danger long dormant. The disintegration of the vast Muslim Empire and the resulting internal rivalries had removed most of the pressure of Muslim expansion and prepared the way for the European counterattack during the Crusades. Upheavals continued to shake the Muslim world after the crusading movement had subsided; the chief cause was the intrusion of non-Muslim Asiatics. In the thirteenth century the already weak Abbasid dynasty disappeared before the avalanche of the Mongols led by Genghis Khan and his successors. When the Mongol threat began to recede by the end of the century, the Muslim portions of the Mongol Empire broke into rival principalities. One of the most powerful was that of the Ottoman Turks in Asia Minor.

The Ottoman Turks, distantly related to the Seljuks, were Asiatic nomads who had been uprooted by the Mongols and pushed westward. Permitted to settle in Asia Minor in the thirteenth century by the Seljuk Turks, the new-

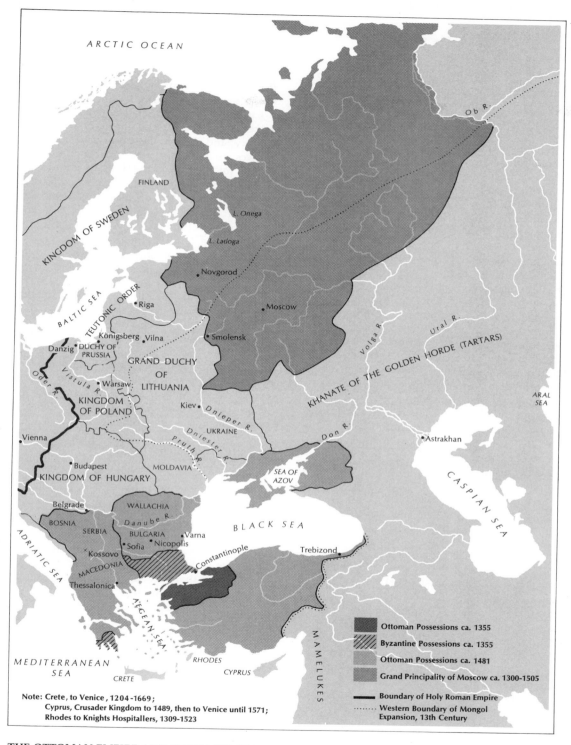

ARCTIC OCEAN

KINGDOM OF SWEDEN

FINLAND

L. Onega

L. Ladoga

BALTIC SEA

TEUTONIC ORDER

Riga

Königsberg

Vilna

Danzig

DUCHY OF PRUSSIA

Novgorod

Moscow

Smolensk

GRAND DUCHY OF LITHUANIA

Oder R.

Vistula R.

Warsaw

KINGDOM OF POLAND

Kiev

Dnieper R.

Volga R.

Ural R.

KHANATE OF THE GOLDEN HORDE (TARTARS)

ARAL SEA

Vienna

Budapest

MOLDAVIA

Dniester R.

Pruth R.

UKRAINE

Don R.

Astrakhan

KINGDOM OF HUNGARY

SEA OF AZOV

CASPIAN SEA

Belgrade

WALLACHIA

Danube R.

BLACK SEA

BOSNIA

SERBIA

BULGARIA

Varna

Sofia

Nicopolis

Kossovo

MACEDONIA

Constantinople

Trebizond

ADRIATIC SEA

Thessalonica

AEGEAN SEA

MAMELUKES

MEDITERRANEAN SEA

RHODES

CYPRUS

CRETE

Note: Crete, to Venice, 1204-1669;
Cyprus, Crusader Kingdom to 1489, then to Venice until 1571;
Rhodes to Knights Hospitallers, 1309-1523

Ottoman Possessions ca. 1355

Byzantine Possessions ca. 1355

Ottoman Possessions ca. 1481

Grand Principality of Moscow ca. 1300-1505

Boundary of Holy Roman Empire

Western Boundary of Mongol Expansion, 13th Century

THE OTTOMAN EMPIRE AND RUSSIA TO 1505

comers had accepted Islam and adopted many of the ways of Muslim society. Within a short time the Ottomans had established their independence. Their first great ruler was Osman, or Othman (1290–1326), whence the term "Ottoman." The new state began to expand almost immediately, and by the end of the fourteenth century the Ottomans had taken over Asia Minor and gained control of most of the Balkans as well.

Early in the fifteenth century Ottoman power was nearly destroyed by Tamerlane, a Mongol warrior who sought to reconstruct the empire of Genghis Khan. But Tamerlane's death in 1405 was followed by a sudden collapse of his empire. The Ottomans soon recovered from these defeats and returned to their attack on Byzantium and the Balkans. With Constantinople captured, early in the sixteenth century they conquered Syria, Palestine, and Egypt, creating a state that stretched from the Danube to the Nile. As the Middle Ages ended, the Ottomans loomed as a major threat to Western Europe.

Central and Eastern Europe began to assume a modern shape in the wake of the decline of the Holy Roman and Byzantine empires. The south coast of the Baltic Sea was dominated by Germans, an expansion spearheaded by the crusading order of the Teutonic Knights who brought traders, missionaries, and agricultural colonists in their wake. Their presence filled the Slavs of Central Europe with an abiding distrust for and fear of the Germans. The Germanic threat resulted in a union of the ruling houses of Poland and Lithuania under the Lithuanian prince Jagiello, who married a Polish princess and governed both states as King Ladislas II (1386–1434). The house of Jagiello exerted considerable military pressure on the Baltic Germans and the Russian states to the east during much of the fifteenth century, but it never succeeded in creating an effective government for its huge kingdom. To the south, Hungary continued to develop, but her energies were increasingly absorbed in defending herself against the Ottoman Turks and holding back ambitious German nobles bent on taking the Hungarian throne. Until the Ottomans seized control of the Balkans at the end of the fourteenth century, a flourishing Serbian kingdom dominated that area; after its destruction, the Hungarians stood as Western Europe's outpost against the Turks.

Farther east, the Mongol *khans* (emperors) had seized much of Russia during the thirteenth century and forced the numerous conquered princes to become subordinates and collect tribute for them from the Russian populace. In the fourteenth century the princes of Moscow gained the privilege of collecting these sums from all the other Russian princes, and they used this function skillfully to begin building a strong state. Early in the fifteenth century they rejected the overlordship of the khans, whose power was rapidly deteriorating, and started a series of wars for the purpose of Muscovite expansion and liberation. Ivan III (reigned 1462–1505) finally broke the Mongol hold on Russia and compelled most Russian princes to accept his authority. After the fall of Constantinople, the Muscovites claimed they were the heirs of the Byzantine tradition and the protectors of the Greek Orthodox religion. Ivan III began calling himself *tsar*, which implied that he was the successor of the caesars. This sense of protecting an ancient heritage gave Russia a new mission that would help solidify her into a powerful nation in the future.

4. ECONOMIC AND SOCIAL TENSIONS

Responsible in part for the political difficulties were basic economic and social problems troubling most areas of Europe. In brief, the entire economic system was suffering from a series of contractions that curbed growth and promoted social disequilibrium.

Especially damaging during the fourteenth and fifteenth centuries was the leveling off of commercial expansion, long the vital factor in Western European economic growth. The incessant warfare upset established trade processes. Europe's population ceased growing, probably because of recurrent famines and the epidemic of bubonic plague, the Black Death, which between 1347 and 1350 wiped out nearly one-third of the population and perhaps more in the cities. The rise of Ottoman power made it more difficult for Western Europeans to penetrate new geographical areas. There was a shortage of capital. The independent cities that had been the sources of medieval commercial growth lacked the manpower, the wealth, and the political strength to offset these numerous difficulties. Persistent cooperation among commercial cities for mutual benefit proved nearly impossible. The most successful effort of this kind was the Hanseatic League, which linked together about seventy cities in northern Germany, Scandinavia, and the Low Countries. But ultimately the league declined, chiefly because its members refused to sacrifice local interests. All these limitations on commerce did not mean that the fourteenth and fifteenth centuries enjoyed none of the benefits of trade; however, trade did not grow so fast as it previously had; in many areas it declined.

Industry experienced a comparable constriction. The guild system, which had once promoted the growth of industry, grew increasingly restrictive. Seeking to protect their monopoly on production in each city, the guilds passed rules excluding the products of outsiders. They barred technical changes that seemed to threaten their members, and they turned away new applicants or admitted them at inferior rank. Often their pricing arrangements were unrealistic. Such practices curtailed production and discouraged expansion into new kinds of industry.

Agricultural production, the foundation of the European economy, likewise suffered a depression. Widespread warfare ravaged many lands, and there is some evidence that a climatic change hurt growing conditions in many regions. The eastern frontier was closed, limiting areas for colonization and new land clearance. Especially crucial was the impact of the Black Death, which not only decimated the rural labor force, but also sharply reduced the city market. Under these pressures the old manorial system continued to break up. Since landowners across much of Western Europe became interested in money income, they manipulated rents and imposed on their peasant tenants whatever remnants of the old manorial dues system they could. Some also resorted to enclosing their land and using hired labor to farm it.

Economic dislocation and contraction led to considerable social tension and disturbance in the Late Middle Ages. In a general way, the social structure lost its earlier mobility. The aristocracy's status as the wealthiest segment in society was challenged by the rising capitalist entrepreneurs in commerce, industry, and finance. Its monopoly on warfare was destroyed by the nonnoble professional soldier. The nobles completely discredited themselves politically by their attempts to seize power for their own interests; then ultimately and perhaps most significantly, they turned to the monarchs to sanction and protect their privileges. With the old bases

A German guild meeting in the fifteenth century. In this period the guild rules limiting the amount of production began to stifle innovation and depress economic activity. *Photo: Kupferstichkabinett, Staatliche Museen der Stiftung, Berlin*

of social preeminence dissolving, the nobility of the Late Middle Ages turned increasingly to ruthless exploitation of its lands and to costly indulgence in a mode of life based on an exaggerated version of chivalry. It closed ranks and sought to control and exploit other groups who might threaten its position, as did the capitalists. Disadvantaged groups chafed under these circumstances and often resorted to violence to better their lot.

Although the virtual disappearance of serfdom improved the social position of most peasants in Western Europe, their status deteriorated in other ways. They were thrown more and more on their own economically. As tenants they could no longer appeal to a lord in times of war and famine. Royal taxes fell heavily on them, and the wars they thus paid for often ravaged their farms, especially in France, Italy, and Germany. Declining prices coincided with reduced opportunities in the troubled cities and closed frontiers. Peasants expressed their discontent by frequent and violent rebellions that often reached frightening proportions, like the *Jacquerie* uprising in France in 1358 and the Peasants' Revolt of 1381 in England. The rebels always cried out for justice and punished their oppressors savagely; but their fervor seldom supported a positive program, and they were usually brutally crushed by kings, nobles, and clergymen acting in concert.

Equally unhappy were certain elements of the bourgeoisie, especially in Flanders and Italy. Many artisans were reduced to the ranks of laborers for hire and lost the political power they had enjoyed in the twelfth and thirteenth centuries. The rich entrepreneurs more and more dominated political life in the cities. The monopolistic guilds often excluded new artisans from the trades, leaving them with little means of livelihood. The laborers and the unemployed frequently resorted to mob violence, but with no more success than the peasants.

The social group making the greatest advance in the fourteenth and fifteenth centuries was an elite segment of the bourgeoisie engaged in capitalistic ventures, again particularly in northern Italy and Flanders although also in France, England, and parts of Germany and Spain. The success of this group is exemplified by the Med-

ici and the Bardi in Italy, the Fuggers in southern Germany, Jacques Coeur of France, and some of the entrepreneurs associated with the Hanseatic League, which monopolized trade in the Baltic and North seas. Members of this group accrued huge fortunes in such fields as banking, money-lending, and the wool industry. They seized political control of most city governments and found increasing favor with kings. Culturally they were able to patronize the advancing cause of the humanists and to set standards of fashion. In a sense, this group now represented the bourgeoisie; others who had formerly been counted in this class—simple artisans and small shopkeepers—were emerging as a group apart, a laboring class. The new bourgeoisie was destined to play a major role in the future of the West.

More and more it became obvious that the solution to the economic and social problems of the era lay with a stronger central government. Nobles, peasants, capitalists, industrial workers—all pressed the government to impose controls on trade, industry, agriculture, and the class structure. In countries such as England and France, kings responded to this pressure and began regulating economic and social conditions on a national scale. This trend was proof of the passing of medieval society, which had been built on social stratification, economic localism, and group protection of vested interests.

By approximately 1450 the worst of the economic and social stresses of the Late Middle Ages were over, and there were signs of recovery everywhere. Aside from the return of political order accompanying the restoration of royal authority, the population had begun to grow again. The agricultural system became increasingly stable, chiefly on the basis of a system of renting that bound landlord and peasant together on a money basis. New technological advances were being made and were being applied more widely—water mills in the textile industry, better mining techniques, printing, improved shipbuilding, the compass, the astrolabe, gunpowder. New frontiers were opening by way of the seas that washed Europe's western shores. All these forces pointed toward new growth in Western Europe. It was obvious, however, that this growth would be achieved in ways different from those that prevailed in medieval Europe.

Suggested Reading

Overview of the Period 1300–1500

*R. E. Lerner, *The Age of Adversity: The Fourteenth Century* (Cornell).

*Margaret Aston, *The Fifteenth Century: The Prospect of Europe* (Harcourt, Brace & World). This and the preceding work succeed remarkably well in capturing the major trends of the age.

W. K. Ferguson, *Europe in Transition, 1300–1520* (1962). The best detailed treatment.

*J. Huizinga, *The Waning of the Middle Ages* (Anchor). Explores the psychological changes affecting society in a troubled time.

The Holy Roman Empire

*Geoffrey Barraclough, *The Origins of Modern Germany* (Capricorn).

*James Bryce, *The Holy Roman Empire* (Schocken Books). These two works, already cited in Chapter 20, continue the story of the decline of the Holy Roman Empire.

*Hans Baron, *Crisis of the Early Italian Renaissance: Civic Humanism and Republican Liberty in an Age of Classicism and Tyranny*, rev. ed. (Princeton).

*Gene A. Brucker, *Renaissance Florence* (Wiley).

David Herlihy, *Pisa in the Early Renaissance* (1958).

D. Muir, *A History of Milan under the Visconti* (1924).

*F. C. Lane, *Venice: A Maritime Republic* (Johns Hopkins). Since there is no satisfactory general history of Italy in the Later Middle Ages, one must turn to the histories of individual cities—which exist in abundance. The above will be especially helpful.

*G. Mattingly, *Renaissance Diplomacy* (Penguin). A brilliant analysis of Italian intercity relationships.

England, France, and Spain

*E. Perroy, *The Hundred Years' War* (Capricorn). A thorough treatment not only of military history but also of internal developments in France and England.

*A. R. Myers, *England in the Late Middle Ages, 1307–1536* (Penguin). An excellent survey.

*George Holmes, *The Later Middle Ages, 1272–1485* (Norton). Especially good on economic and social history.

P. S. Lewis, *Late Medieval France: The Polity* (1968). One of the few works in English on French political development.

*J. H. Elliott, *Imperial Spain* (Mentor). Excellent for the end of this period. More comprehensive are the works of Merriman and Altamira, cited in Chapter 22.

The Eastern Mediterranean and Eastern Europe

S. Runciman, *The Fall of Constantinople, 1453* (1965). A splendid portrayal of the last days of the Byzantine Empire. A broader view of Byzantine history in the era can be found in the work of Ostrogorsky, cited in Chapter 15.

P. Wittek, *The Rise of the Ottoman Empire* (1958). A good treatment, which should be supplemented by the more general treatments of Muslim history presented in the works of Hitti and Spuler, cited in Chapter 15.

*M. Prawdin, *The Mongol Empire*, 2nd ed. (Free Press). A vivid account, putting the Mongols in a good light.

F. Dvornik, *The Making of Central Europe* (1949).

———, *The Slavs: Their Early History and Civilization* (1956). Two extremely useful studies of the evolution of Slavic society.

G. Vernadsky, *The Origins of Russia* (1959). A brilliant treatment.

Economic and Social History

The best treatments of these subjects are contained in the general economic histories cited in Chapter 19. The following specialized studies will complement them.

P. Dollinger, *The German Hansa*, trans. D. S. Ault and S. H. Steinberg (1970).

*W. M. Boswky, ed., *The Black Death: A Turning Point in History?* (Holt, Rinehart, and Winston).

*Raymond de Roover, *The Rise and Decline of the Medici Bank, 1397–1494* (Norton).

*Sylvia Thrupp, *The Merchant Class of Medieval London* (Ann Arbor).

R. L. Kilgour, *The Decline of Chivalry* (1937).

Sources

*Jean Froissart, *Chronicles of England, France, and Spain* (Dutton). A fascinating picture of society caught up in the Hundred Years' War.

*Chaucer, *Canterbury Tales*, trans. Nevill Coghill (Penguin). An entertaining view of English society around 1400.

*William Langland, *Piers the Ploughman*, trans. J. F. Goodridge (Penguin). A poem reflecting the bitter resentment felt by the lower classes of England against the powerful.

R. Pernoud, ed., *Joan of Arc, by Herself and Her Witnesses* (1966). Creates a fascinating picture of a key figure in late medieval France from contemporary sources.

*Johannes Nohl, ed., *The Black Death: A Chronicle of the Plague Compiled from Contemporary Sources* (American Century).

26

THE DECLINE OF THE CHURCH

The tensions that beset Western European political, social, and economic institutions in the fourteenth and fifteenth centuries afflicted the Church even more severely. After 1300 this powerful institution, which had earlier influenced all aspects of human activity, found itself increasingly incapable of guiding men. Its teachings, its system of government, and its leaders were subjected to merciless criticism and to open defiance. And the Church failed to discover new resources with which to meet these criticisms, thereby dooming itself to a reactionary role in society.

1. THE DECLINE OF THE PAPACY

The decline of the Church in the fourteenth and fifteenth centuries was most obvious in the case of the papacy. The apogee of papal power came during the pontificate of Boniface VIII (1294–1303), the proud, ambitious heir to the immense prestige that the great popes of the thirteenth century had built. Perhaps this power inflamed what Dante called Boniface's "prideful fever." For when "the prince of the new Pharisees" was faced with challenges to it, he reacted with vanity and exaggerated claims of authority.

His first serious setback came at the hands of the powerful kings of England and France, Edward I and Philip IV. Each proposed to impose new taxes on the Church in his realm in order to war against the other. Boniface responded with

a papal bull, *Clericis laicos*, maintaining that only with papal consent could any taxes be laid upon the Church. Edward and Philip defied him and took steps to cut off all revenues from their kingdoms to Rome. Boniface had to retreat from his position, something the popes were not accustomed to doing.

Before long he was involved in a new quarrel with Philip IV, this time over the question of the proper courts for trying clergymen. Again the strong-minded pope stated his case in a way that outraged Philip. In the bull *Unam sanctam*, Boniface spoke to the issue by insisting that the French king and all men must subject themselves to the pope to be saved. Philip counterattacked violently. He turned public opinion in France against the pope by blatantly distorting the papal position and finally sent some of his henchmen to Italy to capture Boniface. Philip's agents were successful, and the pope escaped what might have been an even more painful defeat by dying. Peter's successor had suffered a humiliating defeat by a political leader able to reject papal guidance on the running of his kingdom.

Philip IV capitalized on his victory by arranging for the election of a Frenchman as pope. Aware that he would be unwelcome in the turbulent Papal States, the new pope took up residence at Avignon in 1309, and until 1377 this city remained the residence of the papacy. During these years of what the Italian writer Petrarch called the "Babylonian Captivity," the popes were accused, unfairly, of being pawns of the French kings. The English, who were engaged in the Hundred Years' War with the French, took steps to reduce papal control over ecclesiastical affairs. The German emperors and princes were equally defiant. Many Christians were troubled by the fact that the pope's claim to power was based on succession to St. Peter as bishop of Rome, not Avignon. These critics were not impressed by the plea of the papacy that Rome was not safe; neither had it been for Peter nor for many earlier popes. The Babylonian Captivity caused scholars and writers to raise major questions regarding church government and to arrive at answers that challenged papal supremacy.

The Avignon popes were not idle during these years, however. Several of them succeeded in pushing papal control over church organization to its greatest height. They increased the number of offices which they could fill with their own appointees. They collected taxes with great vigor and even discovered new sources of income. They steadily increased the number of cases that had to be appealed to papal courts and derived a huge income from this activity. They enlarged the papal bureaucracy beyond anything previously known. In terms of revenues, subordinates, and business transactions, the Avignon popes were actually the most powerful men in Europe.

However, this emphasis on organizational affairs did the papacy more harm than good in terms of prestige. Abuses of the worst kind began to plague the papal government. The increasing horde of papal bureaucrats engaged in every type of corruption, such as selling offices and accepting bribes. Many buyers of Church offices were interested only in income and never went near the office; absenteeism thus became a major problem. Bishops and abbots in all parts of Europe resented growing papal interference in local Church affairs and tried to escape papal control, often by turning to their kings, who gladly protected them—for a price. Papal taxation aroused bitterness everywhere. Edward III of England reflected the dislike of the money-grabbing popes when he said: "The successor of the Apostles was ordered to lead the Lord's

sheep to the pasture, not to fleece them." Much of this wealth clergymen spent on luxurious living, which aroused the bitter anger of the many in Europe whose lot was poverty. The popes at Avignon were not entirely responsible for this situation. Corruption and moral laxness are problems any huge organization has to face. But the popes did nothing to correct them, and as a result, they were blamed for them.

The Babylonian Captivity finally ended in 1377 with the return of the pope to Rome. But this move led to the election by a part of the College of Cardinals of a second pope, who continued to live at Avignon. Thus began the Great Schism, forty years in which the Church was headed by two (and sometimes three) popes directing two administrations, two tax systems, two sets of Church courts. Everyone was at a loss to know who was the right pope. Corruption increased. Rival popes played politics furiously, each seeking to gain enough allies to oust the other. Many Europeans—and especially princes—thought in terms of obeying the pope who offered the best political deal. Few took seriously the claim of either pope to be spiritual leader of Europe; popes who competed with one another and encouraged the division of Christendom seemed little better than greedy politicians.

Before the schism was many years old, serious men began to search for a way of ending the division. Eventually, it was agreed that a general council should be called to end the schism and reform the clergy. According to the advocates of the conciliar theory, an assembly of bishops possessed an authority superior even to the pope's. This ancient idea seemed revolutionary in the context of the Late Middle Ages and threatened the concept of papal supremacy. Four councils were held between 1409 and 1449, all stormy affairs marked by interminable negotiations. They failed to find a new way of governing the Church, although the second council, held at Constance (1414–1418), did end the schism and reestablish a single pope. Thereafter, the popes generally devoted sharp attention to controlling the councils and ending this dangerous threat to papal authority—not too difficult a task, since they were often split by quarrels

among clergymen representing different nations. Perhaps the most significant efforts of the popes were the concessions they began to make to monarchs in return for support of papal rather than conciliar governance of the Church. For example, the pope accepted the Pragmatic Sanction of Bourges, issued in 1438 by Charles VII, which, when accepted by the papacy, gave the French monarch extensive rights over ecclesiastical income and the clergy. Comparable agreements worked out with other rulers seriously limited papal power and hastened a trend toward the creation of "national" churches.

Probably the greatest failure of the councils was their inability to institute meaningful reform. Despite numerous attempts to enact reforming legislation, the members of the councils were never able to agree on a practical reform program. When the last council disbanded in 1449, most people had lost confidence in this means of revitalizing the Church. The greatest influence of the conciliar movement was indirect: It opened the Church's organization to question and caused many to conclude that the papacy was not necessarily sacred.

The popes of the last half of the fifteenth century concentrated on strengthening their control over the Papal States in Italy and competing in the many power struggles raging in Italy in this period. To all outward appearances each was a secular prince, scheming, bribing, and brawling to get what he desired for himself, his family, and his friends and enjoying a luxurious existence. A few led scandalous lives and several became patrons of Renaissance artists and writers who were openly repudiating Christianity in favor of paganism. The popes ceased to draw the respect and veneration of most Christians. No one would deny that the popes were powerful in terms of wealth and political resources. What they had lost was the moral authority that had been their chief source of influence in the thirteenth century, and without that authority, the papacy became a liability to the Church.

In this detail of a fresco by Ambrogio Lorenzetti, Pope Boniface VIII is shown receiving Louis of Toulouse (later canonized) at the papal court. *Photo: Scala*

2. THE DECLINE OF THE CLERGY

Hardly less significant than the prolonged descent of the papacy was the steady decay of the whole body of the clergy. Especially pronounced was the decline of monasticism. Between 1300 and 1500 not a single new order of any importance was established in Western Europe, and the older monastic institutions became increasingly corrupt. Monasteries were no longer a refuge for the spiritually dedicated or a stage from which the zealous could launch their efforts to cleanse religious life.

Except for a few purists, the most powerful orders, the Franciscans and the Dominicans, forgot their ideals of poverty and service and turned instead to the pursuit of wealth and power. Lesser orders followed suit. Strict rules on moral excellence and piety were relaxed to the point where monks and nuns openly broke their vows. Little attention was paid to the kinds of recruits entering monasteries; many were aristocratic ladies who could not find husbands, younger sons without land, and commoners who wanted to escape work. Absentee abbots thought only of garnering monastic incomes. Of course, not all monks were guilty of this laxness and this lack of religious fervor. However, the culprits, as usual, got most of the publicity. One needs to read only a little of the literature of the fourteenth and fifteenth centuries, such as some of the stories in Boccaccio's *Decameron,* to realize that monasticism was held in low repute. Monastic life had come to signify laziness, greed, immorality, and hypocrisy.

The secular clergy, charged with the Church's everyday business, was equally plagued by corruption and moral laxness. The tone was set by the powerful officials of the papal curia, especially the cardinals, whose vast entourages, immense wealth, and talent for political machinations indeed made them "princes of the Church." Many bishops purchased their offices, paying prices that left them little choice but to wring money out of their subjects, and heavy papal taxes tempted them and lesser clergymen to undertake shady financial practices. Some held several offices at once, making it impossible for them to perform the duties of any. Absenteeism was common, many bishops and priests preferring life at Avignon or at a royal court to life in their episcopal sees or parishes. Absentee clergymen often turned their religious duties over to ignorant clerks who were incapable of guiding religious activities. Services, instruction, confessions, preaching, and counseling were slighted, leaving people with religious problems lost and unhappy.

3. OLD PRACTICES AND NEW IDEAS

The Church of the later Middle Ages was weakened also by its inability to accommodate certain heterodox religious trends in Western European society. Chiefly as a result of the intense effort to impose uniformity on religion during the High Middle Ages, after 1300 Roman Catholic belief and religious practices fell into a rather unbending, formal pattern that became increasingly mechanical; most churchmen were content to equate piety with going through the motions of attending services, receiving the sacraments, and obeying the clergy.

Dissatisfaction with this situation was demonstrated in many ways. One of the most important was an increase in the number of mystics, that is, persons who believed they could experience and know God directly through intuitive powers. Mysticism was present throughout the Middle Ages; St. Bernard and St. Francis of Assisi were mystics. But the fourteenth and fifteenth centuries produced an especially large number. Many of the most influential were simple men and women who never wore clerical garb, like Joan of Arc. None was more prominent than Catherine of Siena (1347–1380). At an early age she spoke of visions of Christ and vowed to remain unmarried in order to serve him. For many years she devoted herself to prayer and physical deprivation, but eventually she turned her energies to helping the poor, the sick, criminals, and the downhearted. She also found time to agitate for religious reform and to try to conciliate political quarrels in Italy. When death ended her career at the age of thirty-three, many believed her a saint possessed with powers to heal and to commune personally with Christ. Although she was never seriously at odds with the Church, Catherine practiced a variety of Christianity unfamiliar to contemporary officials of the cult.

The activities of the mystics led to the development of communal movements that operated almost independently of the Church. A prime example was the Brethren of the Common Life (and its female counterpart, the Sisters of the Common Life), founded by a lay preacher named Gerard Groote (1340–1384), who was one of the many spiritual heirs of the great German mystic, Meister Eckhart (1260–1327). This loosely knit movement was a product of a new kind of piety, called the *devotio moderna,* which stressed prayer, love, and direct communion with God. Devotees of the new piety joined together as brothers and sisters in communities where they shared their worldly goods, joined in common worship, confessed their sins to each other, devoted themselves to works of charity, and even produced their own devotional literature. One of the best examples of their literature, still read today as a spiritual guide, is Thomas à Kempis' *Imitation of Christ.* The many communities of Brethren seldom strayed into heresy, but their piety, their puritanical life, and their mysticism set them apart. Not surprisingly, the Brethren were often attacked for spreading dangerous ideas, and some of the most important later reformers of the Church were educated in their schools.

The fourteenth and fifteenth centuries produced a hardier crowd of radicals—usually condemned as heretics—who voiced ideas that provoked many to violent actions against the Church. Some of them were intellectual figures, such as Marsiglio of Padua, whose devastating book, *The Defender of the Peace,* appeared in 1324. Its thesis was that the Church was obligated to fulfill certain spiritual duties but was not entitled to any secular powers. Marsiglio advocated that it be deprived of its wealth and made a branch of government, subservient to the ruler. He argued that the Church as a community of all Christians should be ruled by a council representing all elements in Christian society, not by a clerical hierarchy headed by the pope. This idea was soon to be put into effect in the conciliar movement, which had a profound impact on the ecclesiastical establishment.

Somewhat later, John Wycliffe (1320–1384) delivered even heavier attacks on the Church. This Oxford scholar and teacher entered the ranks of rebellion late in life, apparently moved by a growing tide of anticlericalism and antipapalism emerging in an England troubled by the Hundred Years' War and internal stresses. In his first attacks on the Church he argued that the Church had abused its right to hold property and that all church property should be confiscated by the state. Later he advocated the destruction of the whole clerical hierarchy on the ground that salvation depended not on clergymen but on the power of God; every man was his own priest. Here, of course, he was striking at a keystone of the medieval Church. Wycliffe also attacked many of the religious practices of the Church—elaborate rituals, prayers to saints, veneration of relics, pilgrimages, and the like. He even questioned the validity of the sacraments. He argued that Scripture alone must be the authority for Christian doctrine and translated the Bible into English so that all could read it.

Although Wycliffe was soon condemned as a heretic and forced to leave Oxford, his teachings attracted many followers, known as the Lollards, and for many years Lollard preachers and writers agitated for their master's ideas in England. In time, however, they came to challenge all authority, and the English kings of the fifteenth century joined the clergy in destroying the movement.

Wycliffe's ideas had their most disturbing effect not in England but in Bohemia. The leading disciple there was John Huss (ca. 1373–1415), a priest who taught at the University of Prague. When his preaching of Wycliffe's precepts raised a protest from the clergy and ruling faction, most of whom were German and were passionately hated by the native population, Huss became a national hero of the Bohemians. He also was excommunicated, and he consented to journey to the Council of Constance under a promise of safe-conduct from the German emperor. But there he was imprisoned, tried, and executed as a heretic in 1415. A rebellion broke out immediately in Bohemia and raged until 1436. Crusade after crusade was preached by the

John Huss, the Bohemian religious reformer and national hero, was burned as a heretic in 1415.
Photo: Rosgartenmuseums, Konstanz

papacy against the Hussites; several German armies, led by an emperor who was anxious to reclaim Bohemia, were soundly thrashed by the fanatical Bohemians. Eventually peace was restored when certain religious concessions were granted to the Hussites. However, a faction of the followers of Huss and Wycliffe, called Taborites, was not satisfied by these concessions and became practically a church apart in the last years of the Middle Ages.

Manifestations of religious ferment and frustration took many other forms during the fourteenth and fifteenth centuries. There were any number of fiery preachers proclaiming the end of the world and the coming of God's wrathful judgment. Wildly emotional cults, such as the Flagellants, who whipped one another to atone for the world's sins, preyed on men's religious sensibilities, especially in times of great crisis like the Black Death. Brutal massacres of the Jews in the name of Christian righteousness marred the histories of many cities. Witchcraft flourished on an unprecedented scale. Increasingly men sought assurances of salvation by purchasing indulgences, which ensured that the punishment due for sins would be removed. Never were relics more appealing and more brazenly manipulated, as illustrated by Chaucer's pardoner with his bag full of "pigs' bones." Literature, art, and sermons were preoccupied with death in particularly horrible forms.

Clearly, Europe was in a troubled religious state. Neither the gentle mystics nor the fiery-tongued rebels, neither the adherents of the occult nor the victims of hysteria were at home in the Roman Catholic Church. People were striking out in all directions, questioning ritual, organization, and dogma. But the institution that claimed to care for men's souls either ignored the quest or ruthlessly crushed the discontent. It was failing its central mission: to meet the basic religious needs of its vast flock.

4. THE FAILURE OF INTELLECTUAL LEADERSHIP

The Church suffered another serious blow as a consequence of fundamental shifts in the intellectual development of the Late Middle Ages. This transformation was not dramatic, but it struck a terrible blow at the Church's long monopoly on a supportive intellectual establishment. Outwardly, the life of learning continued down familiar paths. The universities remained the focal points of scholarship and teaching in theology, law, medicine, science, and the arts and provided the major attraction to most intellectuals. The scholastic method, although increasingly pedantic, reigned supreme. But the emphasis in intellectual endeavor underwent a subtle change. The majestic scholastic synthesis of the thirteenth century, exemplified by the works of Thomas Aquinas, failed to hold. It left so many questions unanswered that many thinkers not only despaired of the dream of reconciling revelation and reason but also began to attack the basic proposition that faith and reason were compatible. Synthesis gave way to analysis. Even while the Thomistic synthesis was being hammered out, there were those who

refused to accept it; most adamant were the Averroists, with their unqualified rationalism, a position that persisted throughout the Late Middle Ages.

Shortly after Aquinas' death in 1274, the attack on his position heightened. The Franciscan scholar John Duns Scotus (ca. 1266–1308) argued with great force that God's freedom and power were so exalted that all attempts to describe his attributes rationally imposed untenable limits on him. In effect, Duns Scotus was saying that theology was not a proper matter for rational speculation. This trend of thought was expanded by William of Ockham (ca. 1300–1349), an English Franciscan who taught at Oxford and served in the court of Emperor Louis IV of Bavaria until the Black Death claimed his life. A powerful logician, Ockham assailed the basic rational supports upon which Thomistic theology was constructed. In his mind knowledge of such things as the existence of God and the immortality of the soul came only by intuition and mystical experience. Theology and philosophy thus became separate "sciences," incapable of reconciliation. In defining the realm of reason, Ockham argued that only by sense perception of individual objects could man know; in this respect he was a philosophical nominalist, repudiating the long tradition that ideas constituted the ultimate reality (philosophical realism). Duns Scotus and William of Ockham gained powerful disciples who followed up the assault cn Thomism. The crescendo of attacks shattered the thirteenth-century confidence in one all-embracing truth and with it a powerful prop of the Church.

The disarray among the scholastics encouraged thinkers to take new intellectual paths. Since reason was distinct from faith, political theorists like Marsiglio of Padua constructed new concepts of the governance of church and state which were especially destructive to theologically based justifications of the Church's power. The attack on rational theology nourished mysticism and opened the way for the radical theological concepts of Wycliffe and Huss. Many intellectuals, disillusioned by the barren exercises of late medieval scholasticism, found intellectual sustenance in classical literature and philosophy. Most pregnant for the future was the growing interest in science. Following Ockham's argument that rational inquiry must confine itself to tangible objects, scholars, especially at the universities of Paris and Oxford, produced a considerable body of scientific knowledge and provided significant corrections to Greco-Arabic scientific generalizations. Their efforts laid the groundwork for the revolutionary discoveries of Copernicus, Galileo, and others in the sixteenth and seventeenth centuries. As intellectual life became more pluralistic, the potential for criticism of the Church increased, and the Church's ability to control intellectual activity for its benefit decreased.

5. THE PRESSURE OF NEW FORCES

While the Church decayed from within, it had to contend with powerful forces—many portending a new era in Western Europe—that challenged its leadership and depleted its following. The new, aggressive national states emerging in Western Europe harassed it, as everywhere princes, although still Catholic, sought to limit and dominate it. In England king and Parliament joined in enacting a series of laws to prevent the papacy from taxing church property and controlling ecclesiastical appointments. In France the royal government worked steadily, often with the clergy's help, to establish a "French" church, independent of the papacy and subservient to the crown. In Spain late in the fifteenth century the monarchs even undertook to reform the Church independently of the papacy. As 1500 approached, national churches were becoming a reality at the expense of the universal Church.

The middle class, accepting a capitalistic philosophy, was likewise challenging the Church's social and economic teachings. Many capitalists would have liked to see church wealth put to a different use. Most of them paid no attention to religious arguments against charging interest or on behalf of fair prices. More ominous was their value system, grounded in secularism, the goods of this world, pleasure, individualism, and practicality. These new values combined with economic interests to reduce the hold of the Church on bourgeois energies and wealth.

Finally, a new breed of thinkers, writers, and artists, sometimes called collectively *humanists,* was emerging to criticize, disregard, or repudiate many teachings and practices of the Church. The new humanism, developing first and most vigorously in Italy and then spreading to other parts of Western Europe, was oriented toward the joys and wonders of the physical world. It found its major intellectual sustenance and its esthetic values in classical models. Its setting was urban, and its patronage came chiefly from the emerging bourgeois elite. Its orientation was toward realism and naturalism. Its spirit was individualistic. It generated a critical temper not averse to challenging authority. Wherever the humanistic spirit manifested itself, it was at odds with some of the most basic positions taken by the Church. The progress of humanism thus challenged and weakened the cultural undergirding that had helped sustain the medieval Church.

The combination of internal difficulties and challenging outside forces that undermined the power of the Church in the late Middle Ages demonstrate emphatically that an epoch was ending. Admittedly, the breakup of the medieval empires, the decline of feudal institutions, the dislocation of the class structure, the failure of manorialism and the guild system—all point toward the passing of medieval civilization. However, for centuries the Church had played the leading role in determining what men thought and how they acted. Its weakening position was the surest sign of the end of an epoch in Western European history.

Suggested Reading

Decline of the Church

A. C. Flick, *The Decline of the Medieval Church*, 2 vols. (1930). A detailed narrative account.

L. Elliott-Binns, *History of the Decline and Fall of the Medieval Papacy* (1934). A balanced, thorough account.

T. S. R. Boase, *Boniface VIII* (1933). This excellent biography highlights many of the problems that eventually brought the papacy low.

*Charles T. Wood, ed., *Philip the Fair and Boniface VIII: State vs. Papacy* (Holt, Rinehart & Winston). Presents an interesting variety of interpretations on the significance of a decisive clash between state and church in medieval society.

Yves Renouard, *The Avignon Papacy, 1305–1403*, trans. D. Berthell (1970).

*G. Mollat, *The Popes at Avignon, 1305–1378* (Harper Torchbook). These two treatments, the former brief and the latter more detailed, make clear the impact of the Babylonian Captivity on the papacy.

W. Ullmann, *The Origins of the Great Schism: A Study in Fourteenth Century Ecclesiastical History* (1948). A learned study that provides a careful analysis of the factors producing the Great Schism.

Brian Tierney, *Foundations of the Conciliar Theory* (1955). A careful study stressing the legal basis of conciliar ideas.

New Religious Movements

R. M. Jones, *The Flowering of Mysticism* (1939).

J. M. Clark, *The Great German Mystics: Eckhart, Tauler, and Susa* (1949).

A. Hyma, *The Christian Renaissance: A History of the Devotio Moderna*, 2nd ed. (1965). This and the preceding two titles provide rich insight into late medieval mysticism and the communal movements it produced.

G. Leff, *Heresy in the Later Middle Ages*, 2 vols (1967). A detailed survey of almost every movement that met the disapproval of the Church.

*Norman Cohn, *The Pursuit of the Millennium* (Harper Torchbook). A brilliant description of aberrant movements which disturbed the religious scene in the Late Middle Ages.

*K. B. McFarlane, *The Origins of Religious Dissent in England* (Collier). An excellent evaluation of the role of John Wycliffe as a reformer.

H. Kaminsky, *A History of the Hussite Revolution* (1967). A thorough study of Hussite ideas and their implications in political and social life.

*J. Huizinga, *The Waning of the Middle Ages* (Anchor). A classic that probably succeeds better than any other single work in conveying the religious spirit of the Late Middle Ages.

Sources

*William of Ockham, *Philosophical Writings*, Trans. P. Boehner (Liberal Arts Press). The master logician of the Middle Ages is difficult to manage, but he provides the best insight into the intellectual changes in progress in the Late Middle Ages.

*Marsilius of Padua, *Defensor Pacis*, trans. A. Gerwith (Harper Torchbook).

R. C. Petry, ed., *Late Medieval Mysticism* (1957). An excellent anthology illustrating a major religious movement in the age.

*Thomas à Kempis, *Imitation of Christ*, trans. L. Sherley-Price (Penguin). A classic illustration of medieval mysticism.

M. Spinka, ed., *Advocates of Reform from Wyclif to Erasmus* (1953). A good sampling of the ideas of the most outspoken advocates of reform in the Late Middle Ages.

V. Scudder, *St. Catherine of Siena as Seen in Her Letters* (1905). A precious view of the life of a unique Christian in the Late Middle Ages.

Retrospect

By 1500 there were many signs that Western European society stood again on the threshold of a remarkable era of expansion; that date marked a moment comparable in many ways to the year 1000, when Western Europe made its first great leap forward. Yet it is understandable that most men living in 1500 were dimly, if at all, aware of the great promise before them. Like men in most ages, they were better instructed by the immediate past than by the unrealized future. That immediate past had been a troubled one. Our review of it in the preceding two chapters emphasized the multiple stresses and tensions which affected the basic patterns of civilization characteristic of the Middle Ages. Given the magnitude of these difficulties, it is not surprising that men's thoughts were colored by pessimism and despair and that their reactions to life were marked by excess and violence.

In retrospect, the causes of the troubles of the Late Middle Ages seem fairly clear. The major institutions, thought patterns, and value systems that had been created prior to 1300 as essential to medieval Western European civilization had unstable features that began to emerge after 1300. The medieval political ideal of a Christian commonwealth, institutionalized in the Holy Roman Empire, was flawed by fundamental disagreements about the leadership of the ideal commonwealth and by deep-seated localism. The feudal monarchies were beset by conflicts between royal authority and private privilege. The universal Church, with its central leadership and uniform doctrine, liturgy, and discipline, was challenged by religious localism, new concepts of leadership, and heterodox spiritual visions. Localistic, monopolistic, self-sufficient economic organizations contended with international, profit-seeking, individualistic enterprises. Faith and reason, Latin and vernacular cultures, religious and secular values confronted each other in men's minds. In all these institutional and intellectual contradictions, each opposite side was an integral part of the medieval order. The strength of medieval civilization rested in the balancing of the two. When the balance became unsettled, then strife and turmoil and uncertainty ensued.

In a superficial way, the general situation prevailing between 1300 and 1500 might resemble that which marked the third and fourth centuries of the Christian era, when classical Greco-Roman civilization suffered its fatal decline. In both eras there was violence and tension arising primarily from flaws in the institutions and values basic to their existence. However, a little reflection will reveal that, unlike the situation in the late classical period, the difficulties facing late medieval society arose not from the total exhaustion of an established pattern of civilization, but from the deepening disparity between vital forces vying to establish the dominant tone in Western European civilization. It was not the onset of decrepitude, but the release of vital energies stored up in institutions and concepts that caused the disturbances in the Late Middle Ages. The release of these energies for new growth only awaited the decision to opt for one way or the other between the alternatives posited by medieval Western European civilization: strong central government or private interest, reason or faith, individualistic religious concepts or a universal Church.

By 1500, these contradictions had begun to be resolved. The path toward the future was emerging. Strong monarchy, reason, religious diversity, a pluralistic culture, a capitalistic economy, among other things, were gaining the upper hand. The future of Western European society lay in the development of these patterns as the essence of civilized life; a future that would be spectacular. But as it unfolded, it was never marked by a catastrophic break such as that which signaled the transition from classical to medieval Western European civilization. The wave of Europe's future had already formed in the medieval world. In fact, "modern" Europe was born in the Middle Ages, and its history is unintelligible without a knowledge of the civilization of that period.

VII

The Beginning of Modern Times
Fifteenth and Sixteenth Centuries

In the previous section, we have observed the various tensions and weakening institutions that marked the decline of the medieval world during the fourteenth and fifteenth centuries; now we shall see how the institutions that we have come to call modern grew out of the decaying medieval system.

In place of the declining feudal monarchies and empires there arose the national or territorial state, which became the dominant political institution of the modern era. The first of these national states to emerge were Spain, Portugal, France, and England. From then until now, the history of the Western world has been centered around them and the other national states that were patterned after them.

Europe's medieval economy, characterized by subsistence agriculture, monopolistic guilds, and localism, gave way to capitalistic practices and institutions. The landed aristocracy who had dominated the medieval economy now found themselves challenged and threatened by a new middle class of aggressive entrepreneurs, whose ambition and vitality pushed Europeans out of their own small world into the larger one. The end result was the discovery and domination of much of the rest of the world.

The decline of the Western Christian Church in the last two centuries of the Middle Ages had important repercussions not only on religious institutions and beliefs, but also on the nonreligious thought, the literature, and the arts of the Western European world as well. Theology could no longer command the attention of most of the best minds. Increasingly, they turned to humanistic philosophy and to science—natural and political. Artists became obsessed with the beauties of the physical world. In short, there was a *renaissance* (rebirth) of secularism.

The Western Church itself split, and much of northern Europe became

Protestant. This, in turn, provoked or at least hastened a Roman Catholic revitalization or reformation. The breakup of the powerful Roman Catholic Church, which had so dominated medieval Western Europe, contributed further to the secularization of society.

Since these four great movements—the rise of national states, the rise of a capitalistic economy, the renaissance of secularism, and the Reformation (Protestant and Roman Catholic) occurred primarily during the fifteenth and sixteenth centuries, it may be useful to conceive of the fifteenth as a century of transition and the sixteenth as the first century of the modern era.

In fifteenth-century Europe, at least four royal monarchs succeeded in creating powerful national states. They did so at the expense of the feudal barons who were unable to adjust to changing conditions, and had lost their former necessary function as the main support of the monarchy. The longbow and gun powder had begun to destroy the fighting effectiveness of the mounted armored knight as early as the fourteenth century. At the same time, reviving commerce, bringing with it a moneyed economy and a prosperous middle class, undermined the economic monopoly of the landowning aristocracy. The kings made use of the new, moneyed class and with its support hired standing armies equipped with the new weapons. To legalize their growing power, the kings utilized the principles of Roman law to evade the common law upon which feudal holdings were based. (Roman law considered kings to be sovereigns in whose hands the welfare of all the people was placed.)

Another factor that facilitated the building of nation-states was the rise of a national consciousness based primarily upon language. In each of the lands that are now Spain, Portugal, France, England, Germany, and Italy, one dialect became predominant. Once established, the national vernacular became the instrument for propagating the common traditions, customs, and legends on which national pride and loyalty were built.

THE RISE OF NATIONAL STATES

Although other factors retarded unification in Italy and Germany until the nineteenth century, Spain, Portugal, France, and England were already well on their way to becoming powerful national states in the late fifteenth century.

1. SPAIN

The most powerful and influential of the new states at the opening of the modern era was Spain. The energy and enthusiasm that Spain displayed at this time may be attributed in part, at least, to her long and finally successful struggle against the Moors. By the middle of the thirteenth century the Moors had been driven out of the entire Iberian peninsula except for the southernmost province of Granada. Furthermore, the numerous medieval feudal holdings in what is now Spain had been consolidated into four large kingdoms—Castile, Aragon, Granada, and Navarre (south of the Pyrenees). The marriage of Ferdinand of Aragon and Isabella of Castile in 1469 united for all practical purposes the two largest kingdoms. During their reign (1474–1516)[1] Granada and Navarre were conquered. Thus, within a forty-seven-year span from 1469 to 1516 the Spanish national state was created.

---

[1]Isabella ruled Castile from 1474 to 1504, and Ferdinand ruled Aragon from 1479 to 1516.

Ferdinand and Isabella strove for political and religious unity. In order to suppress further the jealous nobility, they allied themselves with the middle class, leaning heavily upon it for financial and administrative assistance. In return, the joint sovereigns did everything in their power to advance the fortunes of the merchants. Vigorous enforcement of law and order, stabilization of the currency, building of roads and bridges, tariff protection of home industries—all served to advance the economic prosperity of Spain in general and the middle class in particular. This commercial expansion was greatly enhanced in 1492 with the discovery of the New World in the name of Spain. The ensuing profits and loot further strengthened the hands of the Spanish sovereigns by freeing them from dependence upon the Cortes (the representative bodies dominated by the nobility) for funds.

In religious affairs as well Ferdinand and Isabella attained virtually complete unity for their country. Against the two non-Christian groups in their realm, the Jews and the Muslims, the "Catholic Sovereigns" waged a campaign of conversion or extermination. The Jews had long been the object of hatred and persecution in Christian Europe. In part this hatred derived from religious differences, but there was also an economic factor. Church laws against usury had given the Jews a monopoly on moneylending, which high rates of interest rendered very profitable. The envy and hatred of the Christians led

A coin of Ferdinand and Isabella, sovereigns of Spain, most powerful of the new national states. *Photo: American Numismatic Society*

out to the East to make their names and fortunes that her sparse reserves of talent were depleted at home.

Like Spain, Portugal persecuted and expelled her Jews, Muslims, and Protestants. And like Spain her brilliance rapidly waned after the sixteenth century.

3. FRANCE

The reign of Louis XI (1461–1483) may be said to mark the beginning of France as a modern national state. Louis came to the throne of France eight years after the end of the Hundred Years' War with England. His predecessor had used the war emergency to obtain a permanent tax *(taille)* and a standing army for the crown. During the last phase of the war a great upsurge of French national spirit aided by the exploits of Joan of Arc made possible, at long last, the expulsion of the English invaders. Louis XI put these inherited advantages to clever use. First of all, he set

2. PORTUGAL

Next to Spain the most prosperous and energetic national state in the sixteenth century was Portugal. The origins of this state can be traced back

4. ENGLAND

Modern times, so far as English history is concerned, may be said to have begun with the reign of Henry VII (1485–1509), the first of the Tudor dynasty. The political unity of the English national state had been brought about as early as 1066 by William the Conqueror (aided to a considerable degree by geography). However, the feudal system, with its decentralization of administration and society, the Hundred Years' War with France (1337–1453), and the Wars of the Roses (1455–1484) between the rival houses of Lancaster and York, had by the last quarter of the fifteenth century brought England to a state of turmoil bordering on anarchy. Henry Tudor acquired the English throne by victory on the battlefield over the Yorkish king, Richard III, who was slain. Himself a member of the Lancastrian family, Henry ended the bloody dynastic feud by marrying Elizabeth of York.

The most pressing task confronting the strong-willed new monarch was the suppression of the turbulent nobility. The great feudal barons had taken advantage of the decades of civil war and of the long rule of a weak king prior to the war to defy royal authority. They retained their own private armies and overawed the local courts. At once and with great vigor Henry VII proceeded to enforce the laws against livery and maintenance,[3] thereby destroying the illegal feudal armies. Since the regular local courts were too weak to proceed against the nobility, Henry set up his own Court of Star Chamber, which, backed by the royal army, was able to overawe the most powerful barons and bring them to justice and to submission to the crown.

In these undertakings Henry VII had the wholehearted support of the lesser gentry and the middle and lower classes, all of whom yearned for peace and order. The middle class, particularly, desired stability for the sake of its growing business activities, and it was with this class that the Tudors allied themselves. Henry selected many of his counselors and administra-

tors from the ranks of the bourgeoisie. He made favorable commercial treaties with the Netherlands, Denmark, and even with Venice, the jealous queen of the rich Eastern Mediterranean trade. Navigation acts were passed to protect English shippers. Henry's frugality and careful collection and handling of revenues not only were good business, but freed the king of dependence upon Parliament for funds.

Henry VII, unlike Louis XI of France, attempted to protect the interests of the English peasants, who were being forced off the land by the enclosure movement. The landed nobility, taking advantage of the brisk demand for wool, were turning their farming lands into sheep runs. Thousands of dispossessed peasants roamed the countryside as beggars or drifted to the cities looking for work at any price. Laws passed to protect the peasants from dispossession proved to be largely ineffective, however, as anyone traveling through the lush green and frequently untilled English countryside can observe today.

Henry VII died in 1509, prematurely worn out by his arduous labors. But he passed along to his glamorous son, Henry VIII, a united and orderly national state and a well-filled treasury. And under his granddaughter, Elizabeth, England rose to a position of first-rate importance in European and world affairs.

5. GERMANY AND ITALY

Although Germany and Italy have played a vital role in modern European history, they did not achieve political unity at the opening of the modern period. That failure, although it did not prevent them from making important contributions to the arts and sciences, did create political maladjustments that account for much of Europe's modern turmoil, particularly in the twentieth century.

During the fifteenth century, when the Spanish, Portuguese, French, and English peoples were becoming united under powerful national monarchs, the German-speaking peoples remained split up into more than three hundred virtually independent units. The only political bond between them was the impotent government of the Holy Roman Empire. This ramshac-

---

[3]So called from the practice of the peasantry wearing the lord's badge or livery, signifying membership in his private army, in return for the lord's promise to maintain (support) them in courts of justice.

THE FIVE GREAT POWERS

Republic of Florence

Duchy of Milan

Kingdom of Naples

Papal States

Venetian Republic

1 MARCH OF MONTFERRAT
2 MARCH OF MANTUA
3 DUCHY OF MODENA
4 REPUBLIC OF LUCCA
5 COUNTY OF ASTI
6 DUCHY OF FERRARA

ITALY 1454

kle institution—a survival of the organization set up by Charlemagne in 800 and revived by Otto the Great in 962—purported to be a restoration of the old Roman Empire, but it never was. In the Middle Ages, when the Spanish, Portuguese, French, and English sovereigns were consolidating their territories and their authority, the German emperors were frittering away their time and energy trying to bring Italy under their control. While they were away from Germany on these quixotic ventures, the local feudal barons conspired against them, consolidated their own power, and built up hereditary states of their own within the empire. Meanwhile, territory after territory slipped from under the emperor's control, until by the opening of the modern period, the Holy Roman Empire included for all practical purposes only the German-speaking states (plus Czech-speaking Bohemia).

Eventually seven of the emperor's most prominent subjects gained the right to elect him. This elective feature not only diminished the prestige of the emperor, but forced candidates to bribe the electors and bargain and promise away any chance of strengthening the office. Since the emperor had no sure income, he had no military force with which to enforce his will. Even to defend the empire, he was forced to call upon his subject princes to furnish troops. The lawmaking and taxing powers lay in the hands of the Diet, which was composed of three houses: the house of electors, the house of lesser princes, and the house of representatives of the free imperial cities. The Diet had no regular time or place of meeting, and was seldom able to reach agreement on any important question. In the late fifteenth century an imperial court was set up to settle disputes between member states. However, lacking any means of enforcing its decisions, this instrument too proved ineffective.

The one factor that gave any semblance of vitality to the Holy Roman Empire was the Hapsburg family. A Hapsburg was first elected emperor in 1273. After 1438, with only one brief exception, no one but a Hapsburg was elected until the empire finally died at the hand of Napoleon in 1806. By marriage and diplomacy, the Hapsburgs expanded their original Austrian lands until they possessed at the opening of the modern period one of the largest and richest dynastic estates in Europe. Although, therefore, the Holy Roman emperor as emperor was virtually powerless, as head of the house of Hapsburg he was one of the most influential of monarchs. Nevertheless, all efforts of the Hapsburgs to strengthen the central government of the empire foundered on the rocks of German particularism—the local interests of the jealous princes.

Italy's modern history has paralleled to a considerable degree that of Germany. At the opening of the modern period the Italian peninsula was divided into six major independent states without even the pretense of a Holy Roman Empire to unite them. The six were the Kingdom of the Two Sicilies, the Papal States, Florence (Tuscany), Venice, Milan, and Piedmont. The Kingdom of the Two Sicilies, the poorest and most backward of the Italian states, occupied the southern third of the peninsula and the large island of Sicily. During the fifteenth and sixteenth centuries it was a bone of contention over which France and Spain repeatedly fought. The Papal States occupied the central portion of the peninsula. These states were ruled by the pope not only as supreme pontiff, but also as political head. The popes based their claims to political rule over these states upon the Donation of Pepin, the father of Charlemagne, who drove out the Lombards and gave the territory to the pope in 756. Florence and Venice, republics in name, were dominated by rich banking and commercial families. Milan, another thriving center of commerce, was ruled by an autocratic duke. Piedmont, occupying the northwesternmost portion of the peninsula, was the property of the house of Savoy. This mountainous state, which eventually assumed leadership in the unification of Italy, played a relatively minor role in Italian affairs before the nineteenth century.

An important factor accounting for Italian disunity in the first centuries of the modern era was the presence of the Papal States in the strategic center of the peninsula. Fearing the loss of their territories to a national monarch, the popes vigorously opposed all efforts to set up an Italian national state. A second factor was the long tradition of independence and the great commercial prosperity in the thirteenth, fourteenth, and fifteenth centuries of Florence, Venice, and Milan, where a spirit of local rather than national pride and loyalty prevailed. The political division and weakness of the Italians in an age of powerful national states continued to be a standing invitation to aggression against them.

Maximilian of Hapsburg
Mary of Burgundy
} Philip the Handsome

Ferdinand of Aragon
Isabella of Castile
} Joanna the Mad

} Charles V

6. INTERNATIONAL RIVALRIES IN THE AGE OF CHARLES V, 1516–1556

The rise of national states failed to bring peace to Europe. The national monarchs, supported by the bourgeoisie, had justified their own aggrandizement on the grounds that it was necessary to end the interminable feudal wars, and they had in fact established a large measure of internal law and order. However, the little feudal wars were followed by big national and dynastic wars. Throughout the first modern century — the sixteenth — international strife centered around the house of Hapsburg.   *1500*

During most of the first half of the century the house of Hapsburg was headed by Emperor Charles V. Charles V inherited from his parents and four grandparents an array of territories and claims that have been exceeded in history only by those of his son, Philip II. (Charles' family tree has been diagramed at the top of the page.) From his grandfather Maximilian he inherited the Hapsburg provinces generally spoken of as Austria, to which were added in Charles' lifetime Hungary, Bohemia, Moravia, and Silesia. As a Hapsburg, he also inherited a good claim to the imperial crown of the Holy Roman Empire. From his grandmother Mary he inherited the Burgundian lands: the free county of Burgundy (Franche Comté), the Netherlands, Luxembourg, Flanders, Artois, and claims to the duchy of Burgundy and Picardy, which had been seized by Louis XI. From his grandfather Ferdinand he received Aragon, the Kingdom of the Two Sicilies, and numerous islands in the Mediterranean. From his grandmother Isabella he received Castile and a claim to the entire Western Hemisphere based upon the papal Line of Demarcation (1493) and the Treaty of Tordesillas (1494). And from Ferdinand and Isabella jointly, he inherited Granada and Spanish Navarre.

The very size of Charles V's far-flung holdings spelled perpetual trouble. The language problem alone was appalling. To this were added differences in local customs, tastes, and eventually religion. Moreover, Charles V was sure to become involved in all the major international conflicts of Europe. Born and reared in the Netherlands, Charles got himself accepted in Spain only after serious opposition and open revolt. His efforts to strengthen the government of the Holy Roman Empire and to raise money and troops there were frustrated by the local German princes. Finally, the Lutheran revolt further split the empire and shattered completely the personal power of Charles in Germany.

Charles V found himself almost continually at war with Francis I of France. Each feared the other's power. Francis vigorously contested Charles' election as Holy Roman Emperor. They fought over conflicting territorial claims in Italy, the Burgundian lands, and along the French-Spanish border. Charles won nearly all the battles, but was never able to make his victories permanent.

The relations between Charles of Hapsburg and England were limited to a personal family quarrel. When Henry VIII sought an annulment of his marriage to Catherine of Aragon, the aunt of Charles V, Charles used his influence with the pope to block the proceedings, thus touching off a chain of events that ended with the separation of England from the Roman Catholic Church. It was under Charles' son, Philip II, that conflict between Spain and England was brought to a climax.

Among Charles V's more constructive achievements was his marriage to Isabella of Portugal, which brought about a brief union of Spain and Portugal under Philip II, and his repulse of the Ottoman Turks. Early in the sixteenth century, the Turks under Suleiman the Magnificent swept across Hungary and laid siege to Vienna, the capital city of Hapsburg

Austria. It was feared that all Western Christendom might fall to the Muslims. At this point, Charles V rallied the forces of the empire and the Hapsburg provinces, raised the siege of Vienna, and drove the Turks back into Hungary. He also defeated the Muslim Barbary pirates in the Western Mediterranean.

In 1555 Charles V began to divide his holdings between his son, Philip II, and his brother, Ferdinand. To Philip he gave the Burgundian provinces and Spain, with her appanages in Italy, the Mediterranean, and the New World. To Ferdinand he gave the Austrian provinces and successfully promoted his candidacy to the crown of the Holy Roman Empire. Henceforth there were two branches of the Hapsburg dynasty — Austrian and Spanish — both of which would long continue to play important roles in European and world history.

7. SUMMARY — THE POLITICAL MAP OF EUROPE IN 1500

At the beginning of the modern period, then, four powerful national monarchies, those of Spain, Portugal, France, and England, dominated Europe. Germany and Italy were divided into many small states. The German states and Slavic Czech-speaking Bohemia were in the Holy Roman Empire. The Netherlands, owned by the Hapsburgs, was a part of the empire. Switzerland, nominally in the empire, was in reality an independent confederation of semiautonomous cantons. Elsewhere in Europe, Scotland was still independent, and England's control over Ireland was only tenuous. Denmark owned Norway and was in temporary union with Sweden. Poland, including Lithuania, occupied a large stretch of territory east of Germany, but her anemic government made her impotent at home and abroad. Russia, under Ivan III, had just freed herself from Tartar overlordship and as yet counted for little in European or world affairs. The Balkan peninsula was a part of the Ottoman Empire. Hungary was a battlefield fought over by the Hapsburgs and the Ottoman Turks. The four new national states which represented the political wave that the rest of Europe and most of the world would eventually follow had been firmly established. But their new internal strength brought not a more peaceful international order, but war on a larger scale, as symbolized by the continental scope of the operations of Charles V.

Suggested Reading

General — The Modern Era
R. Palmer and J. Colton, *A History of the Modern World*, 4th ed. (1971). Probably the best.

Beginning of Modern Times
*E. P. Cheyney, *The Dawn of the New Era* (Torch). The first volume of the excellent Rise of Modern Europe series.

The New National Monarchies
R. Altamira, *History of Spain from the Beginning to the Present Day* (1930). Best brief survey.
C. E. Nowell, *History of Portugal* (1953). Best in English.
P. Champion, *Louis XI* (1929). Good biography of the "Spider King."
*C. Read, *The Tudors: Personalities and Practical Politics of the Sixteenth Century* (Norton). By a leading specialist.

Germany and Italy
*K. Brandi, *The Emperor Charles V: The Growth and Destiny of a Man and of a World Empire* (Humanities). Best biography of the central political figure of Germany and Europe at the opening of the modern era.
G. Trevelyan, *A Short History of the Italian People from the Barbarian Invasions to the Attainment of Unity* (1920). Brief; well written.

Sources
Comines, *The History of Comines*, trans. Thomas Danett (1897). An eyewitness account of the struggle between Louis XI and Charles the Bold.

Historical Fiction
*Charles Reade, *The Cloister and the Hearth* (Washington Square). About the unwed parents of Erasmus. Vivid pen pictures of life in the fifteenth century.

28

A NEW ECONOMY AND THE EXPANSION OF EUROPE

The rise of the modern national state was closely associated with the rise of a modern capitalistic economy. The royal monarchs who created the national states made great use of the rising middle class in overcoming the feudal aristocracy. The strength of this middle class lay in its capitalistic wealth. The term *capitalism*, stripped to its barest essentials, may be defined as a system of putting money to work to make more money. It involves, among other things, private property, the profit motive, a substantial amount of free enterprise and individual initiative, the hiring of labor, and the lending of money for interest.

1. ROOTS AND BEGINNINGS OF MODERN CAPITALISM

Although we are likely to think of capitalism as a typically modern system of economy, it reached a fairly high development in ancient Greece and Rome. The reader will recall from earlier chapters that trading, banking, and production of certain wares on a capitalistic basis thrived in and among the Greek city-states, particularly in the Hellenistic age. Capitalism developed to a higher degree in the Roman world. For many centuries all roads and all ship lanes in the Western world led to Rome and were protected by Rome. Interest rates came down, and the standard of living went up.

However, the reader will also recall that, with the breakdown of the Roman Empire, capitalistic practices virtually disappeared. Early medieval economy, like early medieval government, was decentralized. Each manorial estate produced almost all its own needs. Agriculture was collectivist or cooperative. Commerce was a mere trickle of luxuries for the rich, and necessities such as iron, implements, and salt. The Church insisted upon the "fair price" rather than competitive pricing, and since it also forbade the lending of money for interest (usury), only the Jews, who were not bound by these dictates, practiced what small-scale lending of money there was.

During the course of the Middle Ages commercial activities and capitalistic practices began to revive. A slight increase may be observed as early as the eleventh century, and by the thirteenth century a pronounced recovery was under way. The Crusades contributed significantly to this revival. The huge movement of men and supplies from Western Europe to the Holy Land enriched the merchants and shippers of Venice and other Italian cities. Many of these set up permanent trading posts in the Near East and introduced the luxuries of the materially more advanced Muslim and Byzantine worlds to Western Europe. The Fourth Crusade, which the Venetians diverted to the looting of Constantinople, was particularly fruitful for rising Western capitalism. The Venetians seized not only a great hoard of gold and silver in the stricken Eastern imperial capital, but also almost half the territory of the Byzantine Empire itself. This wealth flowed into the stream of Western European commerce.

Foremost among the centers of this newly revived commerce and capitalism were the city-states of northern Italy, such as Venice, Genoa, Florence, and Milan. Venice was the queen of the Mediterranean in the thirteenth, fourteenth, and fifteenth centuries. After her chief rival, Genoa, was eliminated in the fourteenth century, she enjoyed a virtual monopoly over the lucrative trade with the East. At the peak of her prosperity, her merchant marine numbered some thirty thousand sailors. Milan was the starting point of the overland traffic across the Alps to northern Europe. In the late fourteenth century she gained control of the port city of Genoa. Florence manufactured large quantities of fine woolen textiles on a capitalistic basis, and in the fourteenth and fifteenth centuries was the banking capital of the Western world. The Medici family alone possessed at one time some two hundred branch banks scattered throughout Western and Central Europe.

In northern Europe, the Hanseatic League, composed of some eighty German Baltic and North Sea cities, enjoyed a brisk trade in such commodities as fish, furs, grain, and timber. In southern Germany and the Rhine Valley, numerous trading centers such as Augsburg, Nuremberg, and Cologne sprang up along the overland route between Italy and northern Europe. Finally, the Netherlands, Paris, and London shared in this early period of revived commercialism.

By the end of the fifteenth century, however, the further growth of European commerce was threatened by a number of obstacles that little feudal fiefs and independent cities were not able to overcome. One was the expense of the trade routes between Europe and the East, which were partly overland, especially after Muslim middlemen had taken their share of the profits. Another was the inadequacy of the gold and silver supply to serve as a satisfactory medium of exchange. A third was the restrictive practices of the guilds. All these obstacles were soon to be overcome.

2. THE AGE OF DISCOVERY

In the late fifteenth and early sixteenth centuries, European mariners made a series of daring voyages in which they discovered not only the New World, but also new and much better routes to the East. These voyages were promoted by the governments and people of the four nation-states along the Atlantic coast. Their principal motive was a desire to by-pass the Venetians, the Muslims, and the land barriers that separated them from the riches of the East. But there was also a powerful outward impetus in the spirit of inquiry and adventure kindled by the Renaissance interest in the secular world, and in the Christian missionary zeal that had always been a spur to expansion.

The first to begin in the fifteenth century were the Portuguese. Pushing steadily down the coast of West Africa they rounded in 1488 the Cape of Good Hope. In 1498 Vasco da Gama, in what was probably the greatest voyage in the history of navigation, reached India, the object of the quest. Vasco da Gama was out of sight of land 93 days — three times as long as Columbus on his voyage to the New World. That the Portuguese knew what they were up to is proved by the fact that Vasco da Gama's return cargo sold for sixty times the cost of the expedition. These glad tidings sent a host of Portuguese adventurers hurrying to the East Indies, where they carved out a huge commercial and political empire.[1] One of these adventurers, Cabral, swinging too far westward, touched the eastern bulge of South America, thus laying the basis for Portugal's claim to Brazil. With the discovery of an all-water route to the East, the commerce of the Italian city-states began to wither. So did that along the overland route from Italy across Germany.

Meanwhile, Spain was sending her mariners westward, for by the late fifteenth century most educated people in Western Europe assumed

---

[1]For conditions in southern Asia at the time of the European intrusion see pp. 404–407.

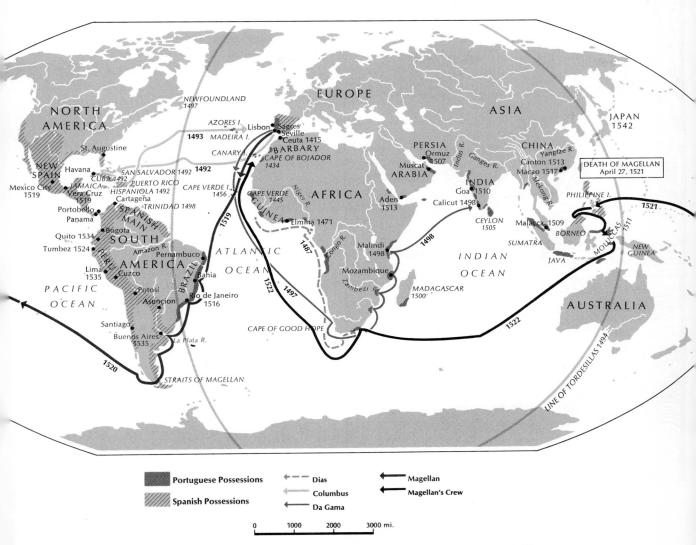

Portuguese Possessions   ←--- **Dias**   ◄━━ **Magellan**

Spanish Possessions   ← **Columbus**   ◄━━━ **Magellan's Crew**

← **Da Gama**

0   1000   2000   3000 mi.

EXPLORATION AND CONQUEST, FIFTEENTH AND SIXTEENTH CENTURIES

that the earth was round, although they greatly underestimated its size. It was therefore believed by many navigators that the East Indies could be reached by sailing west. The first European to attempt it was Christopher Columbus. (Nothing had come of the tenth-century voyages to Greenland and northern America of the roving Norsemen, Eric the Red and Leif Ericson.) Columbus was born in Genoa but moved to Portugal.

When, however, Portugal failed to support his proposed westward voyage, he turned to Queen Isabella of Castile, who gave him the necessary backing. His three ships touched a West Indian island on October 12, 1492. Thinking that the West Indies were islands off the east coast of Asia, Columbus made three further voyages in the hope of by-passing these barriers and sailing on to his real goal, the East Indies. Instead he

Soto, and Coronado explored the southern part of what is now the United States. Balboa crossed the Isthmus of Panama and looked out upon the Pacific Ocean. In 1519 Magellan set out around the world by way of the Strait of Magellan. Although he himself was killed in the Philippines, one of his ships completed the circuit. Also in 1519, Cortez began the conquest of the Aztec Empire in Mexico. In 1531–1532 Pizarro conquered the Inca Indians in Peru.

The other two new national states, England and France, were relatively inactive in discovery and exploration during the fifteenth and early sixteenth centuries. The English crown did, however, sponsor voyages to northern North America by the Italian mariner John Cabot in 1497–1498. These voyages became the basis for England's claims to North America, where she later built a great empire. The French government sponsored Jacques Cartier, who in 1535 sailed up the St. Lawrence to what is now Montreal and claimed Canada for France. Nonetheless, it was not until the seventeenth century that Spain and Portugal were replaced as the world's leading imperial and commercial powers.

3. THE FOUNDING OF THE SPANISH NEW WORLD EMPIRE

Although most of the Western Hemisphere at the beginning of the sixteenth century was sparsely inhabited by primitive and often savage Indian tribes, the Spaniards did find two rich and colorful civilizations: those of the Aztecs in Mexico and the Incas in Peru.

The American aborigines are clearly members of the Mongoloid branch of the human family. They are generally believed to have come from Asia across the Bering Strait, perhaps as long as forty thousand years ago.

The first of these primitive tribes to build a highly civilized society were the Mayas. They are believed to have come into what is now Guatemala and the Yucatán peninsula of southeast Mexico from the northwest about 1000 B.C. Their

was turned back by the South and Central American mainlands and died disappointed, not having realized the magnitude of his discovery.

But others soon realized it, and in the first half of the sixteenth century, Spanish expeditions to the New World multiplied. As previously noted, the pope in 1493 had drawn a line of demarcation dividing the non-Christian world between Spain and Portugal. This line was somewhat altered in favor of Portugal the following year by the Treaty of Tordesillas. Since all of North and South America except the eastern part of Brazil and Greenland fell to Spain, the Spanish sailors continued to move westward. Ponce de Leon, de

civilization reached its height between A.D. 400 and 600. It was a city-state civilization resembling that of ancient Greece approximately a thousand years earlier. Their writing, most of which has been lost, was a combination of pictures and ideographs. Their best art was brightly colored pottery, gems, gold and silver ware, and sculpture. Probably their most remarkable creations were a system of mathematics based on the decimal (actually vigesimal) system and a calendar based upon astronomy, both of which were in advance of those used in contemporary Europe. Their massively walled stone cities were connected by elaborately paved roads. These cities, however, were continually at war with one another, and in the twelfth century the less-civilized but better-organized Toltecs conquered the Mayan city-states much as Philip of Macedon conquered the Greeks.

In the fourteenth century the warlike Aztecs came down from the north and founded a city on an island in Lake Tezcoco—the present Mexico City. From this base they conquered and organized a military empire or confederacy comprising most of what is now southern Mexico. The Aztecs were the Romans of the New World, and like the Romans they acquired most of their culture from the earlier civilization (Mayas). Theirs was the gift of military and political organization. They developed an elaborate, though stern, system of justice. Their religion was important and highly organized. Several thousand priests, both regular and secular, tended the impressive temple and supervised education and morals. The numerous gods, taken mostly from the Mayas, were headed by the terrible war god, whose unquenchable thirst for blood demanded human sacrifice, usually prisoners of war. And yet the rank and file Aztecs were gentle lovers of poetry and art. A flourishing commerce, agriculture, and mining added to the wealth obtained by conquest.

An even more colorful civilization was that of the Incas in the Andean Plateau of South America. In the eleventh century the Inca Indians began to extend their sway over their neighbors until their empire covered an area 1500 miles long and 300 miles wide—including present-day Ecuador, Peru, and parts of Bolivia and Chile.

An elaborate system of roads and communications tied this vast and lofty empire together. Incan society was a combination of benevolent despotism and socialism. The all-powerful Inca (ruler) was treated as a god. However, he had a body of advisers and administrators chosen from the upper classes. All land and all production were owned and directed by the state. The regimented lower classes did all the work under close supervision and shared from the common stores. A high degree of specialization was practiced. Agriculture was well advanced, and huge terracing and irrigation projects had been developed to overcome the difficulties of the Andean terrain. Religious worship, particularly of the sun god, was a beautiful and important feature of national life. Although Incan writing was backward, its art was well advanced. Outstanding were pottery, architecture, textiles, and gold and silver ornamental objects.

Cortez with a band of some six hundred soldiers and eighteen horses overcame the Aztecs by a combination of treachery and superior weapons. He took advantage of the Aztec belief that the Spaniards were ancient gods whose return had long been expected. Once inside the capital city, the Spaniards were too strong to be expelled. They slaughtered and looted the poorly armed Aztecs without mercy. Even more spectacular was the conquest of the Incas. Pizarro enticed the Incan emperor into a conference. At a given signal Pizarro's small but well-armed band of Spanish soldiers fell upon the splendidly dressed but primitively armed Incan troops and slew them by the thousands. Not a Spaniard lost his life. Pizarro promised to free the Incan chieftain in return for a ransom of gold objects sufficient to fill a room seventeen by twenty-two feet to a height of nine feet, plus a larger amount of silver. This ransom was collected and paid, but Pizarro, who never really intended to free the emperor, had him put to death anyway. When this gold and silver, an estimated ten million dollars' worth, reached Spain, the money shortage in Europe was relieved.

Throughout the sixteenth century Spaniards flocked to the New World. By 1607, when the first permanent English colony was founded in North America, a quarter of a million Spaniards

Although there are many Spanish records of their arrival and explorations in the New World, this Aztec manuscript (ca. 1519–1522) is one of the few surviving Indian versions of the coming of the Europeans. This illustration shows Cortez arriving in Mexico. *Photo: La Biblioteca Apostolica Vaticanna, Rome*

had settled in the vast Spanish Empire stretching from what is now Arizona to Cape Horn. A number of distinguished missions and cathedrals had been erected, and several thriving universities had been founded. The native civilizations had been almost wholly destroyed and replaced by the Christian civilization of Spain. Meanwhile, the Portuguese, in addition to reaping a golden harvest from their commerce with the East, were duplicating the Spanish feats on a smaller scale in Brazil.

4. THE COMMERCIAL REVOLUTION

The discovery of the New World and of all-water routes to the Far East resulted in an expansion of European commerce on such a scale that the term *commercial revolution* may accurately be used to describe it. As the main routes shifted from the Mediterranean to the Atlantic, the stranded Italian and German cities decayed, and new commercial centers to the west began to flourish. Contrary to one's expectations, Spain, surfeited with gold and silver from Mexico and Peru, never developed a thriving commercial capitalism. And although Lisbon became the first great terminus of goods pouring in from the East, the Portuguese, like the Spanish, were so preoccupied with their vast overseas empire that they neglected the marketing opportunities in Europe itself.

creased social and political influence. The strongholds of their influence were the towns and cities whose growth paralleled the expansion of commerce. Western European society was becoming more urban — yet another change from the medieval pattern.

As the power of the national monarchs and the middle classes grew, the position of the nobility declined. Their wealth and power were based upon land, and now money was more important. A severe inflation brought on by the great influx of gold and silver into Europe further hurt the nobility in relation to the moneyed bourgeoisie. Not overnight, but slowly and with occasional setbacks over the decades and centuries, the nobility of Western Europe were displaced by the middle classes in political and social influence. Only in England and the Netherlands did they avoid disaster by openly engaging in business operations.

The triumph of the middle class did not bring an immediate improvement in the condition of the lower classes. Indeed, the *nouveaux riches* often proved to be harsher taskmasters than the older aristocracy, who had had time to learn that power brings responsibility. The urban wage earners, no longer protected by the guilds, were especially hard hit by the inflation. In France and England some peasants who had converted their feudal dues to money payments profited, but most of the peasants in Western Europe and all of those in Central and Eastern Europe suffered from the inflation and the general loss of feudal security. The distressed landlords were likely to pass their hardships along to the peasantry. Peasant revolts were common throughout Europe in the sixteenth century. However, the rise of the middle class and the disappearance of feudal class lines produced a more fluid social structure and made possible the future growth of democracy. Money is more easily acquired by the commoner than is blue blood or title.

7. EUROPEAN DOMINATION OF THE GLOBE

Europe's Age of Discovery and the rise of modern capitalistic economy were momentous also for the rest of the world. Much of the Western Hemisphere, southern Asia, and the coastal areas of Africa were quickly brought under European domination. This amazing expansion continued until by the end of the nineteenth century practically the entire world was dominated by Europe and European civilization. Spanish, Portuguese, English, French, and Dutch colonists, followed later by the nationals of all the other European countries, flocked to the New World, taking their Western Christian culture with them. The brilliant Aztec and Incan civilizations of Mexico and Peru were destroyed. The more primitive tribes of American Indians were exterminated, absorbed, or confined to reservations. The Muslim, Hindu, Buddhist, and Confucian civilizations of Asia and Africa were virtually enslaved by the aggressive European imperialists. Modern European history is therefore world history, and the details of European expansion (and eventual contraction) constitute a considerable portion of the history of Western civilization in the modern era.

Thus we see Europe's static, agricultural, collectivist, "fair price" economy transformed into a dynamic, urban, competitive, profit-motivated economy. The rise of capitalism not only changed the nature of European society; it also provided much of the explosive force that enabled tiny Europe to dominate most of the rest of the world.

Suggested Reading

General

H. Heaton, *Economic History of Europe* (1948). Excellent survey.

The Age of Discovery

*C. E. Nowell, *The Great Discoveries and the First Colonial Empires* (Cornell).

S. E. Morison, *Admiral of the Ocean Sea*, 2 vols. (1942). Masterful life of Columbus.

*S. E. Morison, *Christopher Columbus, Mariner* (Mentor). Useful brief account.

Overseas Empires

*W. H. Prescott, *The Conquest of Mexico* (Modern Library). A classic.

*W. H. Prescott, *The Conquest of Peru* (Dolphin). Even better.

*F. Parkman, *Montcalm and Wolfe* (Collier). The best of Parkman's numerous excellent volumes on the French in North America.

The Commercial Revolution

*L. B. Packard, *The Commercial Revolution 1400–1776* (Berkshire). Excellent brief account.

Sources

*R. Hakluyt, *Principal Navigation, Voyages, Traffiques and Discoveries of the English Nation* (Everyman). Colorful contemporary account.

Historical Fiction

*Thomas B. Costain, *The Moneyman* (Permabooks). The story of Jacques Coeur, France's leading merchant and financier of the fifteenth century.

29

THE RENAISSANCE: ITALY

The term *renaissance* means rebirth, and in the development of Western civilization it designates particularly the rebirth of a secular civilization that was inspired in large measure by the civilizations of ancient Greece and Rome. However, *rebirth* implies too sharp a change with the immediate past. Secular interests had never completely died out, even at the peak of the Church's prestige in the Middle Ages; and the revival of secular interests was a gradual process. Furthermore, the Renaissance was not merely a return to pre-Christian culture; new elements that had not existed previously were added. It would be better to regard the Renaissance as an intensification of the secular spirit in Western European thought, literature, and art during the fourteenth, fifteenth, and sixteenth centuries. The key word here is *secular*, meaning that which pertains to this physical world as contrasted with the religious emphasis on the spiritual. The Renaissance began in Italy, where many physical reminders of the glory that was Greece and the grandeur that was Rome had remained.

1. GENERAL NATURE

Probably the most basic of the secular attitudes that characterized the Renaissance was humanism — the focusing of interest on man rather than God. In a period dominated by humanistic concepts, the arts, the sciences, and all forms of intellectual and practical activity tend to be directed toward man. The emphasis on theology, concerned with the nature of God, changes to one on a philosophy centered around the nature and condition of man. During the Renaissance man, not God, was enthroned as lord of the universe. In this respect, Renaissance thought was like that of pagan Greece and Rome and unlike that of the Christian-dominated Middle Ages. The medieval Christian theologians distrusted the flesh as an enemy of the spirit, and human wisdom as a frail thing unable to perceive divine truth by rational processes unless guided by Christian inspiration. But men of the Renaissance, like their Greek and Roman kinsmen, glorified the human form as a thing of beauty and the human intellect as capable of discovering all truth worth knowing.

Humanism extols not only mankind in general but also individual man. Individualism, therefore, was another important facet of the secular spirit of the Renaissance. In this respect, the difference between the medieval and the Renaissance spirit was primarily one of degree. Probably no influence in history has done more than Christianity to elevate the dignity of the individual soul and the individual personality. Christianity taught that even when a sparrow falls God sees and is concerned. How much more then is he concerned for every man, made by him in his own image and for his own glory. But the medieval churchmen feared pride as the deadliest of all the sins. Therefore, they taught that the individual ego must be carefully held in check. Medieval monasticism went so far as to attempt to suppress the individual ego altogether and submerge it in the group. In practice, then, medieval Christianity, like medieval economy, tended to be collectivist. Church artists and writers usually did not sign their names to their work, which was supposed to contribute only to the greater glory of God. Renaissance individualism, like that of Rome, was of the lusty variety. One could hardly imagine a Machiavelli or a Boccaccio hiding his identity. This kind of individualism also gave rise, as in ancient Rome, to excessive men. No more egotistical individual can be found in history than Benvenuto Cellini, liar, thief, murderer, rapist, and one of the most gifted artists of the Renaissance era.

That a Cellini should be not only tolerated but also honored by his contemporaries may be further explained by the fact that he represented another cardinal principle of the Renaissance ideal—versatility. We are reminded of Pericles' all-round man of Athens of the fifth century B.C. and of the broadly educated Roman patrician. The educated man of the Middle Ages was usually a specialist—a theologian or a church artist or administrator. But the most renowned Renaissance schoolmasters taught many subjects in addition to the traditional formal ones—dancing, fencing, poetry, and vernacular languages, to mention a few. Many of the Renaissance universities secularized and broadened the old theology-oriented seven liberal arts and made much greater use of pagan classical literature and philosophy in the curriculum. One of the most popular books in Europe in the sixteenth century was Castiglione's *Book of the Courtier*. The ideal courtier, said Castiglione, is not only a gentleman and a scholar, but also a man of action—a soldier and an athlete. Probably the best illustration of versatility in any age is Leonardo da Vinci. This revered Renaissance figure, one of the most celebrated painters of all time, was also an able sculptor, architect, mathematician, philosopher, inventor, botanist, anatomist, geologist, and engineer.

Finally, the secular Renaissance civilization was urban—again like that of ancient Greece and Rome, but unlike that of the Middle Ages, which was rural. Renaissance writers and artists were more often than not sustained by rich merchants and bankers, first in the revived commercial cities of Italy and later in those of northern Europe.

2. LITERATURE

These secular characteristics of the Renaissance spirit are richly illustrated by the Italian literature of the fourteenth century. The best of that literature was produced by the Tuscan Triumvirate—so called because it consisted of three men who lived in Florence in the old Etruscan province of Tuscany. The first was Dante Alighieri (1265–1321). In an earlier section (see Chapter 24) we discussed Dante as the greatest of the late medieval writers. His masterpiece, the *Divine Comedy*, is so full of medieval Christian lore and theology that it has been called a *Summa Theologiae* in poetry. Nevertheless, there is so much of the secular spirit in the *Divine Comedy* and in Dante's other writings that he belongs also to the Renaissance. In the "Inferno" of the *Divine Comedy*, Dante paints vivid, sensuous word pictures that smack of this world rather than the next. The blazing fires and sulfurous fumes of hell, the cries of lament and curses of the damned come alive in our imagination. Furthermore, the author venerates such pagan classical writers as Vergil and Cicero to a much greater degree than had the medievalists (although a number of medieval writers had tried to make Vergil a Christian).

Dante's other major writings are entirely secular. His love lyrics, written in his native Tuscan vernacular and addressed to Beatrice, are among the most beautiful in any language. In fact, Dante's writings greatly enriched the Florentine dialect and raised it eventually to the status of the national language of Italy.

Dante was also versatile; he was a man of public affairs as well as of letters. An active participant in the turbulent politics of Renaissance Italy, he was exiled from his native Florence when his faction lost out. Dante even went so far as to fill hell in the *Divine Comedy* with his political enemies. His political treatise, *On Monarchy*, argues for a united Italy under the leadership of the Holy Roman Emperor.

Petrarch (1304–1374), the second of the Tuscan Triumvirate, like Dante wrote beautiful love lyrics in the Tuscan vernacular. His exquisite odes and sonnets were poured out for Laura, a noble lady whom he saw at mass and loved from afar. He goes on rapturously about Laura's bosom, arms, face, and feet with most unmedieval abandon. The sonnet is Petrarch's own invention.

Boccaccio (1313–1375) did for Italian prose what Dante and Petrarch did for Italian poetry. In his *Decameron, a collection of one hundred tales or novelettes*, Boccaccio makes no pretense of using Christian restraint. He relates bawdy romances with skill and grace, condoning and even glorifying the seamy side of human nature. Here we have open revolt against the medieval ideal.

3. HUMANISM

Toward the end of the fourteenth century, the original Italian Renaissance literature was stifled by the rise of humanism. Italian humanism was a movement consisting of two rather distinct phases. One was the passionate quest for Greek and Latin literary manuscripts; the other was the development of a many-sided secular philosophy of life.

The search for classical literary manuscripts conflicted with the creation of original Italian literature by siphoning off the interest and energy of the writers. This conflict is illustrated by Petrarch, who rather early in life ceased writing what he called his "worthless" lyrics in order to discover lost classical manuscripts and to copy their style. He did succeed in bringing to light many priceless classical literary gems, but his epic *Africa* (relating the exploits of Scipio Africanus), written in Latin after the style of Vergil's *Aeneid,* lacks spontaneity and is all but forgotten.

Petrarch interested Boccaccio in the recovery of Greek and Latin manuscripts, and the search soon became a fad. Popes, princes, rich merchants, and bankers subsidized the humanists, so called because the pagan Greek and Latin literature dealt with human rather than divine affairs. (Studies concerned with classical literature and language, art, philosophy, and history came to be called the humanities.) In the fifteenth century, Italy was busy with professional humanists hunting, copying, translating, and editing ancient manuscripts.

Meanwhile, the content of the classical masterpieces was influencing the growth of a secular philosophy of life. This phase of humanism had many facets, such as the rise of the concept of the nonmoral state, the revolt in private and social behavior against Christian moral restraints, and the development of a critical or scientific attitude. Machiavelli, in his celebrated *The Prince,* suggested that Christian morals have no place in government. Since men are self-seeking animals, the prince (or ruler or governing officials), to be effective, must be both amoral and ruthless. The prince must assume that his own lieutenants, like all rival princes, are conspiring for his crown. Therefore, his own chief subjects must be set against each other and maneuvered into impotence. Foreign rivals must be deceived and treacherously attacked at the most favorable moment before they can do the same. While Machiavelli was trying to remedy the deplorable reality of a divided Italy overrun and pillaged by more powerful foreign enemies, he also reflected the thinking of a man-centered, secular age. Few books have had more influence on, or been more descriptive of, modern political thought and practice.

The humanistic revolt against Christian restraints on private behavior is illustrated by the fabulous career of Benvenuto Cellini. This gifted Florentine—some say the greatest gold- and silversmith of all time—boasts loudly in his *Autobiography* of his lies, thefts, illicit loves, even of rape and murder. Admittedly Benvenuto Cellini is an extreme case, but the fact that such a character should have been honored in early sixteenth-century society indicates the degree to which Italian Renaissance society had departed from the medieval Christian ideal.

Another facet of the humanistic or secular view of life was the development of an analytic or scientific attitude. When Lorenzo Valla proved by linguistics that the Donation of Constantine was a forgery, the scholarly and secular-minded pope raised no objections, although this was one of the documents upon which the papacy had based its claims to temporal power in the West. In fact, Pope Nicholas V made Valla his secretary. By making this discovery, Valla established himself as the father of modern critical historical scholarship.

4. ART

The renaissance of secularism is vividly illustrated in the Italian visual arts of the fourteenth, fifteenth, and sixteenth centuries. Medieval art in Europe had been closely allied with the Church. Painters deliberately penalized human flesh in order that the spirit might shine forth unimpeded. The figures, nearly always saints, were stiff, haggard, flat, and elongated. The physical world too was blanked out with solid gold backgrounds. The styles were stereotyped.

In the early fourteenth century Giotto, a contemporary of Dante, began to break this medieval mold of artistic custom by humanizing his figures and painting functional landscape backgrounds. Although his magnificent frescoes in the church of St. Francis at Assisi depicting the life of St. Francis were still rather flat, with diffused lighting, this did not make them less decorative—an artistic principle known to ancient Egyptian artists. True, Giotto's subject matter was almost entirely religious, but his treatment of it was such that the secular spirit made definite advances at the expense of the sacred. In the early fifteenth century, Masaccio greatly developed the trend begun by Giotto a century earlier. He increased the illusion of depth by introducing atmospheric perspective and by further developing linear perspective. He also introduced the principle of the known light source, which thereafter replaced diffused light in painting. His nude human forms were further rounded and humanized. His landscape backgrounds were realistic and detailed. With Masaccio, the transition from medieval to Renaissance painting was completed and the stage set for such towering geniuses of the Italian High Renaissance as Leonardo da Vinci, Michelangelo, Raphael, and Titian.

It would be difficult to find a more representative figure of the Italian Renaissance than Leonardo da Vinci (1452–1519). All the colorful facets of the secular spirit are richly illustrated by the career and work of this versatile genius. As a painter, he is probably unsurpassed in any age. Leonardo was an illegitimate child, as were a number of the famous figures of the Renaissance. He was born near Florence and began his career there, but some of his most productive years were spent in the employ of the duke of Milan. He finally followed King Francis I to France, where he died. Like most Renaissance artists, Leonardo dealt primarily with religious subject matter, but, also like the others, his treatment of it was invariably secular and human. In his *Virgin of the Rocks*, for instance, Leonardo creates with exquisite grace and beauty the Virgin Mary and the Christ child. The Virgin, however, is the loveliest of women, and the Christ child is a plump and playful baby boy. The characters are human, not divine. The background is a strange rock formation, naturalistic enough to reveal a keen interest in this material earth, and yet arrestingly abnormal. The plant forms in the background are actually identifiable. Leonardo's *The Last Supper* depicts the reactions of the twelve disciples to Christ's words, "One of you shall betray Me." This celebrated fresco, exhibiting the artist's complete mastery of technique and draftsmanship, is essentially a study in human psychology—a subject in which Leonardo showed a special interest. The famous *Mona Lisa* is not religious in subject matter; it is the portrait of a real woman. The mysterious half-smile—the mouth smiles but the eyes do not—so captivates the viewer that he is likely to overlook other features of the picture, including the hands, which are said to be the most sensitive ever painted. In the *Mona Lisa*, Leonardo, who appears to have been little interested in women in real life, is believed to be probing the universal human nature of womanhood.

Michelangelo (1475–1564) is second only to Leonardo da Vinci as a versatile Italian High Renaissance genius. Since Michelangelo was primarily a sculptor, his painting is sometimes called "painted sculpture." His favorite subject was the virile, muscular male nude. Although a

The breaking of medieval artistic traditions that was to culminate with the glorification of the human form in the great works of the Renaissance began in the fourteenth century with Giotto, whose figures were far more human and who introduced perspective and naturalistic backgrounds. In this fresco, The Flight into Egypt, the subject matter is religious, but the spirit is secular. *Photo: Alinari/Art Reference Bureau*

Florentine, much of his life was spent in Rome, where he labored in the service of the popes. His greatest painting—some say the greatest single painting of all time—was the ceiling fresco in the Vatican Sistine Chapel. The hundreds of individual figures, representing nine scenes from the book of Genesis, marvelously blend together into one harmonious whole. A subdued, blond cast adds to the religious atmosphere of the work. And yet the figures are all vibrant human beings. Later Michelangelo painted the *Last Judgment* as an altarpiece for the same chapel. The Christ in this picture is actually a terrifying, pagan giant, hardly the Jesus of Nazareth of the New Testament and the Christian Church.

Some critics believe Raphael (1483–1520) to be the greatest painter of all time; others say that he merely synthesized the original work of others. The output during his brief life was enormous. His favorite subjects were religious, but his Madonnas were feminine, gracious women and his Christ childs pudgy and mischievous. His best-known paintings, the *Sistine Madonna* and the *Madonna of the Chair*, both in

oil, well illustrate this secular treatment of a sacred theme. Many of his vivid portraits are of lay princes and tycoons. His monumental fresco *The School of Athens* reveals the veneration that Renaissance man felt for the pagan glory of Greece.

The fourth of the great painters of the Italian High Renaissance was Titian (1477–1576). A citizen of Venice, the most prosperous commercial city of the fifteenth century, Titian reflected the secular spirit of the Renaissance to an even greater degree than his three renowned contemporaries. Although a considerable portion of his painting was of religious subjects, his focus was nearly always the pomp and pageantry of the Church rather than its teachings. But a large part of his subject matter was purely secular. The

With Leonardo da Vinci (1452–1519), Renaissance painting reached its peak. In the Virgin of the Rocks, the Virgin is a beautiful woman, and the Christ child is a playful, pudgy boy. The rock formation is authentic, and the plants are identifiable specimens. *Photo: Archives Photographiques, Paris*

The genius of Michelangelo, master sculptor of the Renaissance, is exemplified in this work, the Dying Slave, now in the Louvre, which glorifies both the human form and the human spirit. *Photo: J.B. Harrison*

wealth and brilliance of Venice, overflowing with cargoes of luxurious fabrics, tapestries, and gems from the East, provided a challenging array of sensuous and colorful material for the artist to depict. And in the use of color, particularly vivid yellows, reds, and blues, Titian had no peer. He always painted the hair of his women a reddish-gold hue that has come to be called Titian. His portraits of some of the great lay personages of the sixteenth century, such as Francis I of France, Emperor Charles V, and Philip II of Spain, are masterful character studies. With Titian, the break with medieval painting, begun by Giotto and Masaccio, was completed.

The largest Christian church in the world, St. Peter's Basilica in Rome, was built in the sixteenth and seventeenth centuries at enormous cost. The secular-minded Renaissance architects of St. Peter's were influenced by the styles of pagan Greece and Rome. *Photo: Anderson/Art Reference Bureau*

In sculpture, the artist without peer in any age is Michelangelo. It is true that he had Roman copies of the sculpture of Hellenic Greek masters such as Praxiteles and Scopas to guide and inspire him. But the gifted Florentine was no mere copier. The Greek masterpieces, for all their beauty and grace, were idealized types — half gods, half men. Michelangelo and his lesser-known immediate predecessors and contemporaries added a typically Renaissance characteristic to sculpture: individuality. The statues of the Italian Renaissance are not only human beings, but human individuals. Even Michelangelo's *Pietà*, which represents the mother of Jesus holding the dead body of her son as she looks down piteously, is a study in human emotions. His *Moses* portrays the fierce and rugged strength of man, not God. Moses' beard, as crude as icicles beneath a water tank in the month of January, displays the sculptor's ability deliberately to dis-

tort for effect. The three-dimensional medium of marble enabled Michelangelo to exploit to the full his favorite subject, the masculine nude. Numerous statues of David are used to convey not only the virile muscular power, but also the agile grace of the male animal. His *Dying Slave* is a sublime portrayal of both the human form and the human spirit. Some critics think that the great sculptor's finest genius is displayed in the companion statues of two members of the Medici family—Lorenzo, the contemplative type, and Giuliano, the man of action. In these two pieces the master craftsman and artist exhibits every technique of sculpture. The work of Michelangelo is probably our best example of the Renaissance glorification of man as lord and master of the universe.

The subject of Renaissance sculpture cannot be dismissed without brief mention of the work of Benvenuto Cellini. His work in gold and silver was of an exquisite delicacy that has never been equaled. His most famous larger work is the bronze statue of Perseus holding up the Gorgon's head. In this amazing conglomeration of unrealities, Cellini showed complete disregard of all accepted traditions and standards, yet with happy results. Such bold and original pioneering was typical of the self-confident, secular nature of the Renaissance mind.

Renaissance architecture, like Renaissance sculpture, drew heavily from Greek and Roman sources. From Greece by way of Rome came columns (now merely decorative) and horizontal lines; from Rome came the dome, the arches, and the massiveness that characterized Renaissance buildings. All of these features (except massiveness) represented a revolt against the Gothic architecture of the later Middle Ages, although the Gothic style had never gained much of a foothold in Italy. The two greatest monuments of Italian Renaissance architecture are the cathedral at Florence and St. Peter's basilica in Rome. St. Peter's cannot be called a cathedral, since it has never been the seat of a bishop. The Florentine cathedral, with its gigantic octagonal dome and ornate rectangular façade and bell tower, reflects the influence not only of ancient Rome but of Byzantine and Islamic art as well. But the most grandiose achievement of Renaissance architec-

ture is St. Peter's. This magnificent structure was to the Renaissance era what the Pyramids, the Parthenon, the Colosseum, and the Gothic cathedrals were to their respective epochs. It was built during the sixteenth and early seventeenth centuries at a cost that shook all Western Europe religiously and politically. Its numerous architects drew primarily upon pagan Greek and Roman sources for their inspiration. Even seventeenth-century baroque features eventually entered into its design. Raphael served for a time as chief architect, and Michelangelo designed the dome. One has to step inside St. Peter's to appreciate the breathtaking grandeur of this awesome structure. Its lofty proportions and gigantic pillars, its brilliant paintings and sculptures, its gold, marble, and mosaic decorations all glorify the material things of this world rather than the spiritual aspects of this world and the next. Built by the popes of the Western Church, St. Peter's is really a temple dedicated to the sensuous beauty, earthly pride, and confidence in man that characterized the secular spirit of the Renaissance.

Music was another field of art in which the Italian Renaissance made many original contributions. The chief developments in Renaissance music occurred in the sixteenth century. Instrumental music became popular, and great improvements were made in the instruments. The harpsichord, forerunner of the piano, and the violin family of instruments came into existence. Musical techniques such as major and minor modes, counterpoint (the blending of two contrasting melodies), and polyphony (the interweaving of several melodic lines) rapidly developed. The most illustrious musician of the sixteenth century was Palestrina, chief musician to the pope, and probably the greatest master of polyphonic music of all time. Although most of the music of the Renaissance still centered about the Church, it was now more sensuous and versatile. Moreover, new and entirely secular forms appeared. The madrigal, popular throughout Europe in the late sixteenth century, was a musical rendition of stanzas of secular lyrical poetry. Renaissance musicians laid the foundations for modern classical music in all its major forms—concerto, symphony, sonata, oratorio, opera.

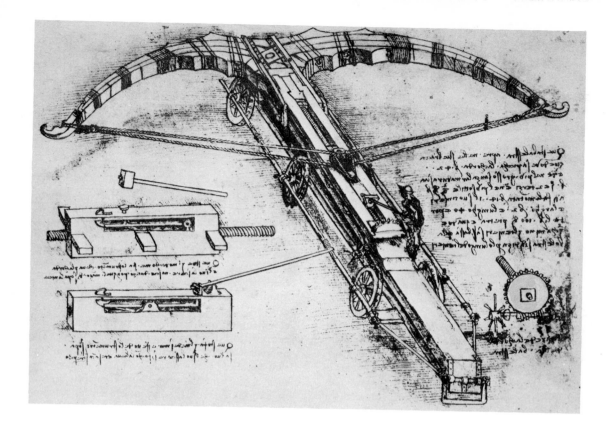

5. SCIENCE

It was almost inevitable that a renewed interest in the physical world, combined with optimism and confidence in the wisdom and self-sufficiency of man, should have resulted in scientific inquiry. Although the flowering of natural science did not occur until the seventeenth and eighteenth centuries, that blossoming sprang from the seedbed of the Renaissance. Leonardo da Vinci, for example, made accurate observations and pondered deeply on such subjects as geology, anatomy, botany, and applied mechanics. His inventions, drawings, and scientific predictions are impressive even today.

In 1543 two of history's most original and provocative scientific works—Copernicus' *Concerning the Revolutions of Celestial Orbs* and Vesalius' *Concerning the Structure of the Human Body*—were published. Both were in large measure products of the free atmosphere of the University of Padua. Copernicus was a Pole, and Vesalius was a Fleming. Both were attracted by the intel-

This drawing from one of Leonardo da Vinci's notebooks shows a giant crossbow that could be operated mechanically. Leonardo wrote backward; you will need to use a mirror to read his notes. Leonardo exemplifies the Renaissance ideal of versatility. Although he is known chiefly as a painter, this illustration depicts his interest in science and technology. *Photo: The Bettmann Archive*

lectual climate of Renaissance Italy, and both attacked long-accepted theories. Copernicus challenged the geocentric theory of Ptolemy (A.D. second century) that the earth is the center of the universe in favor of the heliocentric theory, according to which the sun is the center of the solar system, the earth being only one of many planets revolving around it. Vesalius assaulted the theories of Galen (also second century) concerning the structure of the human body, particularly the heart. Both books raised a storm of opposition, and both were popularly rejected. However, after a century of controversy, Copernicus was to become the father of modern astronomy, Vesalius the father of modern anatomy and physiology. This spirit of scientific inquiry completely supplanted medieval scholasticism. More important, the beginnings made by Leonardo, Copernicus, and Vesalius were to bring forth in the seventeenth century and after an incredible expansion of scientific knowledge.

6. DECLINE

The Italian Renaissance slowly changed and then declined, as the center of Renaissance activity shifted from Italy to northern Europe. This shift closely paralleled that of commerce from the Mediterranean to the Atlantic. When Venice, Florence, and Milan were the most prosperous commercial and banking centers in Europe, they were at the same time the most vigorous seats of Renaissance culture. As their economy stagnated with the shifting of the trade routes to the West, their cultural vigor likewise declined, although Italian art, heavily patronized by the Church, kept its momentum for several generations longer. Literature had declined by the end of the fourteenth century, and humanism by the end of the fifteenth; by the end of the sixteenth century, art too had lost its vigor.

Another factor that undoubtedly contributed to the decline of the Italian Renaissance was the revival of interest in religion, a result of the Protestant and Roman Catholic reformations. Italian humanism, which was more secular and pagan than Northern humanism, was particularly hard hit by the religious revival. It must be remembered also that the Renaissance was in large measure of, by, and for the elite only. The Italian humanists were particularly contemptuous of the masses. Other causes of the decline of the Italian Renaissance are obscure. One frequently reads that the invasion of Italy by the French, Spanish, and German armies and the general military and political instability of the period constituted important factors in the decline. This proposition, however, is difficult to prove. The ancient Greeks and modern Germans—to cite two parallel cases—produced their greatest cultural achievements while they were split up into many political units, and often under adverse conditions such as foreign invasion or civil war. The causes of the decline of brilliant civilizations and epochs remain a challenge to the student of history.

Suggested Reading

General

*M. P. Gilmore, *The World of Humanism, 1453–1517* (Torch). The best single-volume survey.

*W. K. Ferguson, *The Renaissance* (Berkshire). Brief summary by a leading authority.

*J. Burckhardt, *The Civilization of the Renaissance in Italy*, 2 vols. (Torch). A classic that has influenced all subsequent studies of the subject.

Literature, Humanism, Science

J. B. Fletcher, *The Literature of the Italian Renaissance* (1934). Scholarly.

*F. Chabod, *Machiavelli and the Renaissance* (Torch).

*A. Wolf, *A History of Science, Technology, and Philosophy in the Sixteenth and Seventeenth Centuries* (Torch).

The Arts

*H. Wölfflin, *The Art of the Italian Renaissance* (Schocken).

*K. Clark, *Leonardo da Vinci* (Penguin). By a well-known critic.

Sources

*P. Taylor, *The Notebooks of Leonardo da Vinci: A New Selection* (Mentor). Well illustrated.

*B. Castiglione, *The Book of the Courtier* (Anchor). Contemporary textbook for gentlemanly behavior.

*B. Cellini, *Autobiography* (Bantam). The artist's own account of an adventuresome life.

Historical Fiction

*Irving Stone, *The Agony and the Ecstasy* (New American Library). Novel about the life of Michelangelo. Based upon excellent historical research.

30

THE RENAISSANCE: THE NORTH

The Northern Renaissance was in large measure an importation from Italy. Northern European scholars such as Chaucer visited Italy as early as the fourteenth century. By the late fifteenth century, such inspirational journeys to Italy were commonplace. The development of the secular spirit in northern Europe was also furthered by the shifting of trade routes from the Mediterranean to the Atlantic.

1. GENERAL NATURE

Not only was the Northern Renaissance later than the Italian Renaissance, but it was also somewhat different in nature. Painting, sculpture, and architecture played a much less prominent role; humanistic philosophy and literature, on the other hand, were relatively more important. Northern humanism itself, though an importation from Italy, was markedly different in nature. Whereas Italian humanism very frequently represented an open revolt of pagan secularism against Christian ideals, Northern humanism sought, for the most part, to humanize Christianity and thereby to reconcile the sacred and the secular.

2. NORTHERN HUMANISM

The trend to secularism as a basic attitude toward life began in earnest in northern Europe in the late fifteenth century. One of the first evangelists of the new man-centered faith was Johann Reuchlin, a German scholar. After a sojourn in Italy during which he became imbued with the ideas of the Italian humanists, Reuchlin undertook to introduce the new classical learning into Germany. Specifically, he sought to broaden and enrich the university curriculum by establishing the study of the "un-Christian" Hebrew and Greek languages and literature. The Church and university interests vested in the medieval order of things attempted to thwart him, invoking the Inquisition to try him on grounds of heresy. Reuchlin fought back courageously and enlisted a large and enthusiastic following. Eventually the pope condemned him to silence. However, the victory really lay with Reuchlin and his humanist supporters. The tactics and self-centered motives of the churchmen and scholastic pedagogues disgusted most of the genuine scholars and students of the day, and during the first few decades of the sixteenth century the new humanistic curriculum became established in all the major universities of Germany.

Meanwhile, in England a group of Oxford professors was accomplishing with less opposition what Reuchlin had fought for in Germany. John Colet was the most prominent member of this group. He, too, visited Renaissance Italy. In true Northern humanistic fashion he gave a rationalistic slant to his preaching and teaching of the

Scriptures at Oxford. Probably the greatest of Colet's contributions to the new learning was the founding of St. Paul's grammar school in London, with a curriculum devoted largely to the pagan classics. To guarantee its secular orientation, he chose as trustees a guild of London merchants. St. Paul's soon became a model for many other such schools throughout England.

The most famous of the early sixteenth-century English humanists was Sir Thomas More, Lord Chancellor of the Realm. More's *Utopia*, like Plato's *Republic*, blueprinted an earthly, not a heavenly, paradise. In picturing his ideal commonwealth, More indicted the social, religious, and political evils of his own time. Utopia was a socialistic society in which private property and profits were unknown. Much attention was given to public health and education. The economy was planned and cooperative. War was outlawed except in self-defense. Religious free-

The "prince of the humanists," Erasmus, is shown in this fine portrait by the Northern Renaissance painter Hans Holbein. *Photo: Archives Photographiques, Paris*

dom was granted to all but atheists. Although More eventually was to accept death by beheading rather than to recognize Henry VIII as head of the English Church in place of the pope, his ideal society was entirely secular. Man through his own wisdom would create his own perfect world here on earth.

Towering above all the other Northern humanists was Desiderius Erasmus (1466–1536), the intellectual dictator of the sixteenth century. In his efforts to humanize Christianity itself, the "Prince of the Humanists" presented the fundamental issue of Western civilization: Are the basic faith, ideals, and standards of Western civilization human or divine? Erasmus was born in Rotterdam in the Netherlands, the illegitimate son of a priest. Reared as an orphan, he was educated in a school run by the Brethren of the Common Life, a pietistic order of laymen that taught the Greek and Latin classics and emphasized simple inner piety rather than ritual and formal creed. (It is interesting and probably significant that Martin Luther, the great contemporary and adversary of Erasmus, also attended a school of the Brethren of the Common Life.) At the age of twenty-one Erasmus entered an Augustinian monastery (again like Luther) and was eventually ordained. Instead of serving as a priest, however, he spent every possible moment studying his beloved classics—a pursuit he was to continue at the Sorbonne and for the rest of his life.

Erasmus' vast erudition combined with his great personal charm made him a much-sought-after man. His first book was *Adages*, a collection of wise sayings of the Greeks and Romans together with his own comments. It was an immediate success, and other books soon followed. His greatest work was the *Praise of Folly*, in which he ridiculed with subtle humor and delightful satire the ignorance, superstition, credulity, and current practices of his day, particularly those connected with the Church. The folly which he praised was man's very human lightheartedness, his sense of humor. Wherever Erasmus went—France, England, Italy, Switzerland, Germany, the Netherlands—he was received with admiration and awe. No man so advanced the cause of Northern humanism by popularizing the study of the pagan Greek and Latin classics.

In addition to popularizing the new humanistic learning north of the Alps, Erasmus is significant in history for at least two other reasons—his influence on religious and social reform, and his efforts to humanize and intellectualize Christianity. He was at his best when laughing to scorn the abuses and superstitious practices of the Roman Catholic Church. The taking of money from the poor and ignorant masses by wealthy and corrupt churchmen, veneration of relics, and unquestioning belief in the miraculous were in the eyes of Erasmus beneath the contempt of enlightened men. But he was clever enough to sheathe his barbs with humor, thus making them more subtle and effective. Erasmus, however, was no Protestant. When Martin Luther first began his attacks on the Roman Catholic Church, Erasmus thought that he was merely seeking to correct glaring abuses and hailed him as a fellow spirit. But when Erasmus discovered that the German reformer was primarily interested in doctrinal reform and that the Protestants were as dogmatic as the Roman Catholics (actually more so in the early sixteenth century), Erasmus would have nothing more to do with him. The great humanist found it more comfortable to remain in the Roman Catholic Church. The two men ended hurling epithets at each other. Nevertheless, Erasmus' incessant attacks on the abuses in organized Christianity undoubtedly encouraged both the Protestant and the Roman Catholic reformations.

Erasmus' efforts to humanize Christianity, however, are far more significant historically than his campaign to eradicate religious and social abuses. Since the fall of the Roman Empire the great common denominator of Western civilization has been the Christian religion. The vast majority of the members of Western society have subscribed even if they have not lived up to its creeds, ideals, and moral standards. Furthermore, the vitality of these creeds, ideals, and moral standards has derived, in large measure, from the belief that they are of divine origin and sanction. Indeed, it is difficult to conceive of Western civilization as it has developed thus far without this basic faith at its center. This is why Erasmus' questioning of the divine origin and nature of the Christian religion—his efforts to humanize it—is of such deep significance. Although the "Prince of the Humanists" never did specifically say so, the implication running through his writings is that Jesus was a human being—the greatest, best, and most charming man who ever lived, the man we should all try to emulate, but nevertheless man, not God. Erasmus would by-pass formal creed, dogma, ritual, organization, and seek the "historical" Christ. Now, all this is quite appealing to the rationalistic humanist, but it is not quite so simple as it first appears. The historical Christ is a most elusive figure. As a matter of fact, the only documentation we have for Christ is in the New Testament, and if we apply to it the same standards of critical analysis used for other historical documents, its evidence is by no means conclusive. And yet the secondary evidence—the word of mouth and written tradition—is overwhelming. Few historians today would deny the existence of Jesus of Nazareth. However, all we have to go on for the "historical Christ" is the New Testament and the early tradition, and the Christ of both these sources is not the Christ of Erasmus. He is a miracle-working Christ who claimed to be the son and image of God, to have the gift of eternal salvation, who "spake as no other man ever spake." Far simpler to reject Christ as did many of the Italian humanists than to humanize him. Erasmus' attempt was not only the ultimate in the renaissance of secularism, but the beginning of a controversy that has endured until today.

3. THE NATIONAL RENAISSANCE LITERATURES

The national literatures that flourished during this period differed greatly from the literature of the Middle Ages, which in the main (with noteworthy exceptions) centered around religious subjects and was international in viewpoint. Although the literature of the Northern Renaissance owed a great deal to the Italian literature of the fourteenth century, it reached its prime much later—in the sixteenth and early seventeenth centuries. The most important literary developments in this era were in England, France, and Spain.

English Renaissance literature began with Chaucer (1340–1400), who traveled to Italy, became acquainted with Boccaccio, and brought back to England the spirit and much of the technique of the early Italian Renaissance writers. His *Canterbury Tales* are almost an Anglican *Decameron* in charming verse. Salty and very earthy characters from all walks of life parade past us on their way to Canterbury, their human frailties and sins of the flesh forgiven them by the author. Only hypocritical churchmen get the censure of the English Boccaccio, and even they with a light and subtle touch. As in Italy, however, the century following Chaucer was rather barren in a literary sense; it was not until the mid-sixteenth century, the time of Queen Elizabeth I, that his plantings suddenly burst forth in full flower.

The reign of Elizabeth I (1558–1603) was a period of great energy and optimism in England. To the rediscovery of the achievements of ancient Greece and Rome were added the discovery of the New World and of new routes to the riches of the Far East. English seamen such as Drake, Gilbert, and Howard first plundered the Spanish treasure ships, and then crushed the "Invincible Armada" of the world's chief military power, making England mistress of the seas for the next three centuries. English explorers boldly laid the foundations for a future empire in the East and in the West. England's commerce increased, and the standard of living for the middle and upper classes rose sharply. The Queen herself knew how to stimulate national pride centered around her own person. England became "a nest of singing birds" such as the world has never seen or heard. Edmund Spenser's *Faerie Queen* glorified the versatile man of the Italian humanists, particularly the ideal set forth by Castiglione in his *Book of the Courtier.* Christopher Marlowe in his brief life wrote

man-centered plays of such caliber that some critics think he would have achieved the stature of Shakespeare had he lived. His *Tamburlaine the Great* and *Edward II* treat of the worldly drama of royal ambition. The central figure in *The Jew of Malta*, a forerunner of Shylock, is a product of the revived commercial capitalism. *Doctor Faustus* dramatizes the theme, later immortalized by Goethe, of the intellectual who in true Renaissance fashion sold his soul to the devil in return for earthly knowledge and pleasure.

Mightiest of all the artists of the English Renaissance was, of course, William Shakespeare (1564–1616). Shakespeare was born in the same year that Michelangelo died, a fact that ought to remind us that many of the same circumstances that stimulated the Italian artists of the sixteenth century to design St. Peter's and paint the *Sistine Madonna* spurred the English artists to write the *Faerie Queen* and *Hamlet.* So little is known of Shakespeare's life that there is still controversy over whether or not he is actually the author of the poems and plays we attribute to him. Shakespeare wrote some of the world's most beautiful lyrical poetry. His most important work, however, was in the field of drama. Here he was heavily indebted to his contemporary, Christopher Marlowe, as well as to the ancient Greek and Roman dramatists. Marlowe developed the blank verse form, which Shakespeare perfected. In plays such as *Hamlet, Macbeth, Othello, King Lear, Merchant of Venice, As You Like It, Henry IV, Romeo and Juliet,* and *Julius Caesar,* Shakespeare displayed a mastery of every known technique of the dramatic art.

More important for the student of history, he exemplified and dramatized every facet of the secular spirit of the Renaissance. Secular man is Shakespeare's subject matter. Rugged, distinctive human personalities are the heroes and villains of his plays. No human emotion, aspiration, or psychological conflict escapes his eye. On the whole, Shakespeare, unlike the Greek dramatists, makes man the master of his own fate. In addition to making man the center of his universe, Shakespeare illustrates the Renaissance spirit and times in other ways. Admiration for pagan Greece and Rome, a keen interest in new-found lands, the first stirrings of modern natural science, the commercial revolution and social problems arising from the emergence of the capitalistic middle class, the rise of national monarchy and a national patriotic spirit—all enter into the fabric of the plays. In spite of the fact that both the Protestant and the Roman Catholic reformations loomed large in the affairs of England and the rest of Western Europe just before and during Shakespeare's time, he showed little interest in matters of religion. In this respect, too, he was a true child of the Renaissance.

One of Shakespeare's most important contemporaries was Sir Francis Bacon. Though not Shakespeare's peer as an artist, Bacon was nonetheless an intellectual giant. His father, Sir Nicholas Bacon, was one of the chief administrators and advisers of Queen Elizabeth, and Francis spent much of his life seeking political fortune. Finally he succeeded, becoming Lord Chancellor of England, only to be convicted of dishonesty, stripped of his powers, and for a time imprisoned. That his reputation and his own self-esteem could survive such misfortune is indicative of the moral relativism of the Renaissance era. Bacon's intellectual interests were broad, and his knowledge encyclopedic. His *History of the Reign of Henry VII* is still an important source. His *Novum Organum* is one of the first important treatises on modern natural science. Bacon preached the absolute necessity of accurate and unbiased observation in acquiring scientific truth. His major contribution to Renaissance literature is his *Essays,* which he continued to polish and refine as long as he lived. The final result is fifty-eight gems of pithy, salty, practical, and very human wisdom.

The last of the giants of Elizabethan literature was Ben Jonson. This robust personality, a familiar figure in the bohemian taverns of London, could serve as a trooper in the English army and also write "Drink to me only with thine eyes." Jonson was first a connoisseur of classical literature. With exquisite plays reminiscent of the Greek dramatists, he attempted unsuccessfully to reverse the trend toward cheap popularization and sensationalism that had characterized the English stage after the death of Shakespeare. Jonson's death in 1637 marked the end of the most glorious epoch in the history of the world's literature—England's greatest contribution to the Renaissance and the Renaissance spirit.

The two chief figures in French Renaissance literature were François Rabelais and Michel de Montaigne, both of whom lived in the sixteenth century. Rabelais was a renegade priest, a bored physician, and a loving student of the classics. Although he stumbled quite by accident and late in life upon his gift for writing, he turned out to be one of the greatest creative geniuses in the history of literature. His masterpieces are *Pantagruel* and *Gargantua.* They are fantasies about two completely unrestrained giants who wallow and revel unashamedly in all the sensuous and sensual pleasures known to man. These works are an open assault upon Christian moral standards and restraints. The wit is coarse, lewd, and sympathetic toward the frailties of human nature. Rabelais' rich imagery, his marvelous gift of expression, and his graceful artistry combine to make him one of the founding fathers of modern French prose. He shares that honor with his contemporary, John Calvin, whose lucid and incisive Protestant writings Rabelais hated no less than the works of the Roman Catholic theologians and the scholastic philosophers.

Montaigne was a prodigy born of a wealthy family. Like Rabelais, he was an ardent lover of the classics. This, together with the fact that his mother was Jewish and his father Roman Catholic, probably accounts for his skepticism in matters of religion. The result of his life of study and reflection was his *Essays.* Montaigne was a skeptic. To arrive at reliable truth, he believed, one must rid himself of all religious prejudice. He was a moral and spiritual relativist, rejecting all absolutes. Unlike his successors of the eighteenth-century Enlightenment, he distrusted the authority of human reason. Unable to replace the authority of Christian dogma with any other firm conviction, Montaigne was nearly always negative in his conclusions. But he immensely enjoyed this game of intellectual hide-and-seek. In fact, Montaigne believed that the chief purpose of life is pleasure—not the "eat, drink, and be merry" pleasure of Rabelais, but urbane, sophisticated, restrained, intellectual pleasure.

The influence of Montaigne has been enormous—obviously upon essayists from Bacon to Emerson and later, but also upon the development of modern rationalism in general.

Standing out above all others in Spanish Renaissance literature are Miguel de Cervantes and Lope de Vega. Cervantes was a contemporary of Shakespeare, the two dying within a few days of each other in 1616. Cervantes' early life is also obscure. In time he became a soldier of fortune, fought heroically and was wounded in the great naval battle of Lepanto with the Turks, suffered a five-year imprisonment in Algeria, and finally served as a quartermaster for Spain's Invincible Armada. In poverty-stricken later life he settled down to write *Don Quixote*, called by some critics the greatest novel ever written. This masterpiece of Spanish literature relates with urbane grace and humor the adventures of a slightly addled knight who filled his noble head too full of the lore of chivalry, and of his groom, Sancho Panza. Sancho, a squat plebeian on a donkey, and Don Quixote, an emaciated knight on a tall, lean horse, go about Spain from one delightfully charming adventure to another. It is altogether necessary to read a few pages, almost any few pages, of this rollicking fantasy to appreciate the genius of Cervantes. Since all types and classes of people in all parts of Spain are lucidly portrayed, *Don Quixote* is a valuable historical source for descriptions of life in sixteenth-century Spain. But Cervantes does not stop with sixteenth-century Spain; he probes the depths of human nature. All of us are Don Quixotes—at least all of us who are not Sancho Panzas. Cervantes' more immediate purpose was to laugh out of existence what was left of medieval chivalry. He therefore did to feudal society what Erasmus and Rabelais were trying to do to medieval Christianity, and in much the same manner.

Lope de Vega, a contemporary of Ben Jonson, wrote a fabulous number of works in practically every known genre. His plays alone exceed in number those of any other writer, whether we accept the writer's own claim to twenty-two hundred or recognize only the seven-hundred-odd plays that can be accounted for today. Secular man, pictured in every conceivable dramatic situation, is the hero of the great Spanish playwright. Lope de Vega was an ardent Spanish nationalist; he sailed with the Invincible Armada. Like the Elizabethans and other Northern Renaissance writers, he thought that his country and the sixteenth and early seventeenth centuries were an exciting place and time to live.

Thus the writers of the Northern Renaissance had much in common. Their chief interests were contemporary man and the exciting, rapidly expanding material world around them. Their chief inspiration was the pagan classics of Greece and Rome. They were on the whole nationalistic, and wrote in the new national vernaculars. Although the Protestant and Roman Catholic reformations were tearing Western European society apart during the sixteenth and early seventeenth centuries, the men of letters were in the main either apathetic or, as in the case of Rabelais and Montaigne, hostile to theology in general and to Christianity in particular.

4. NORTHERN RENAISSANCE ART

Northern Renaissance art did not equal either the northern literature or the Italian art after which is was largely patterned. It was, however, noteworthy. The best Renaissance painters outside Italy were the Flemings (Belgians) and the Germans. The Van Eyck brothers, Hubert and Jan, lived in Ghent in the Flemish Netherlands in the early fifteenth century. Like Masaccio, their Italian contemporary, they brought to near completion the transition from medieval to Renaissance painting. Their greatest joint work is *Adoration of the Lamb*. Not the least of their contributions to painting was the development of oil as a medium. It was from them that Leonardo da Vinci learned to work in this medium, which he perfected in such masterworks as the *Mona Lisa* and the *Virgin of the Rocks*.

In sixteenth-century Germany, Albert Dürer of Nuremberg and Hans Holbein the Younger of Augsburg were the leading painters. Dürer was primarily a master craftsman of delicate and graceful line. Probably for this reason, his woodcuts and engravings are better than his paintings, and in these media he is without peer in any age. Holbein was a skillful sketcher and woodcutter, but he made his greatest contributions in the field of portrait painting. He painted several portraits of Erasmus and illustrated Erasmus' *Praise of Folly* with pen-and-ink drawings. Many of his most productive years were spent in England in the employ of Henry VIII. Among his greatest portraits are those of Henry VIII, Edward VI, Mary Tudor, and Sir Thomas More. Both Dürer and Holbein were interested primarily in the contemporary things and people of the material world around them.

Renaissance artists did not produce many architectural monuments outside Italy, probably because commercial capitalism had not yet developed sufficiently in northern Europe to finance this more costly type of undertaking. The largest Renaissance structure outside Italy is the vast Escorial near Madrid, which Philip II of Spain built as a royal palace and mausoleum. Its rugged massiveness, rectangular shape, and horizontal lines typify the Renaissance style. Some of the best examples of Northern Renaissance architecture are the Renaissance wing of the Louvre in Paris, which is the world's largest and probably greatest art gallery, and some of the largest chateaux along France's Loire River. This architecture was essentially derivative; the French Renaissance chateaux were really fortresses being played with.

5. PRINTING WITH MOVABLE TYPE

A major Renaissance contribution to the world of intellect and literature was the invention of printing with movable type. In ancient and medieval times manuscripts were written and copied in longhand on parchment or papyrus, a slow and costly process that greatly retarded the dissemination of knowledge. In the fourteenth century printing from carved wooden blocks came to Western Europe from China by way of the Muslim world and Spain. This process too was tedious, costly, and limited. Also from China came paper, made of various fibers, silk, cotton, or flax. Paper was a great improvement over parchment or papyrus for purposes of mass production. (Even the art of printing by movable type itself was a Chinese invention, although

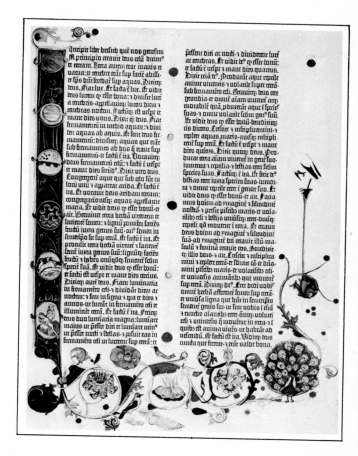

An illuminated page from the Gutenberg Bible, after a facsimile. *Photo: Rare Book Division, New York Public Library, Astor, Lenox, and Tilden Foundations*

this is not believed to have influenced its invention in the Western world.)

Johannes Gutenberg set up the first practical printing press using movable type in Europe at Mainz in western Germany. The Gutenberg forty-two-line Bible printed in 1454 is the earliest known book to be printed by the new process. The invention was an immediate success and spread quickly to all the other countries of Western Europe. It is estimated that by the end of the fifteenth century more than twenty-five thousand separate editions and nearly ten million individual books had been printed. To appreciate the significance of the new invention in

This woodcut of the Four Horsemen from his Apocalypse series (ca. 1497–1498) shows Albert Dürer's skill as a master of delicate, graceful line. Note the artist's signature at center bottom. *Photo: Marburg/Art Reference Bureau*

making knowledge available to the masses, the reader need only reflect for a few moments on the probable cost of this book if it were copied in longhand on parchment or printed from seven hundred hand-carved wooden blocks at present-day wages. As a result of Gutenberg's invention and later improvements few people in the Western world today can excuse their ignorance of good literature on the grounds that it is unavailable.

6. SIGNIFICANCE OF THE RENAISSANCE IN HISTORY

In retrospect, then, it is apparent that the Renaissance was a transition from the God-centered civilization of the Middle Ages to the man-centered, secular civilization of the modern period. In some measure it was a rebirth of the classical civilization of pagan Greece and Rome, but it was not merely that. There was much in the Renaissance that was fresh and original. The rediscovery of the brilliant culture of antiquity and the rising secular spirit with its confidence in man, versatility, egotism, materialism, and individuality combined to produce some of the most beautiful art and literature the world has ever known. In addition, the foundations were laid for the later rise of science. The Renaissance was also a serious challenge to Christianity, directly in Italy and somewhat indirectly in northern Europe. That it did not destroy or palsy Christianity as a dynamic force in Western civilization is due in some measure to the Protestant and Roman Catholic reformations, which revitalized Christianity. To these great movements, which paralleled the Renaissance in its later stages and which were in part provoked by it, we must now turn.

Suggested Reading

General
See items at end of previous chapter.
J. H. Randall, *The Making of the Modern Mind* (1946). Widely used study. Science is the hero, Christianity the villain.

Northern Humanism
E. H. Harbison, *The Christian Scholar in the Age of the Reformation* (1956). By a leading scholar in the field.
*J. Huizinga, *Erasmus and the Age of the Reformation* (Torch). Probably best single volume on Erasmus.

Literature
*H. O. Taylor, *Thought and Expression in the Sixteenth Century* (Collier). Now in five handy volumes, the most appropriate of which for this chapter are *The English Mind* and *The French Mind*.

Art and Printing
O. Benesch, *The Art of the Renaissance in Northern Europe: Its Relation to the Contemporary Spiritual and Intellectual Movements* (1945).
P. Butler, *The Origin of Printing in Europe* (1940).

Sources
*Erasmus, *The Praise of Folly* (Ann Arbor).
*T. More, *Utopia* (Appleton).
*F. Rabelais, *Gargantua and Pantagruel* (Penguin).
*M. de Montaigne, *Autobiography* (Vintage).
*M. de Cervantes, *Don Quixote* (Modern Library).
*G. T. Matthews (ed.), *News and Rumor in Renaissance Europe* (Capricorn). A collection of reports of the agents of the Fugger bankers from all over Western Europe.

31

THE PROTESTANT REFORMATION

The Protestant and Roman Catholic reformations, which split Western Europe into two hostile religious camps, virtually completed the destruction of the medieval synthesis, for this synthesis had centered around the Church. (Russia and the Balkans with their Orthodox Church had never been a part of this synthesis.) The Protestant Reformation had strong political, economic, and intellectual overtones; nevertheless, it was primarily a religious movement. Western Europeans of the sixteenth century were intensely interested in religion. The Church was still at the very center of their lives, and even the unlettered masses knew a good deal about matters of doctrine and ritual. The leaders of both the Protestant and the Roman Catholic reformations were certainly men whose lives were dedicated to religion.

1. BACKGROUND

In the Late Middle Ages there developed within the ranks of the Roman Catholic Church a growing dissatisfaction with some of its fundamental doctrines (see pp. 292–294). Some had come to believe that the Roman Catholic Church had departed so far from the spirit and practices of the apostles and early fathers that it could no longer be considered God's appointed custodian of the Christian religion. They began to define *The Church* to mean the sum total of all those who put their faith in Christ, not any one specif-

ic institution.[1] The Scriptures alone, not the decisions and traditions of an organized church, became for these reformers the sole authoritative source for Christian dogma. Their growing conception of the Christian religion as a direct relationship between man and God tended to lessen the importance of the professional clergy and the sacraments of the Roman Catholic Church. They spoke of the priesthood of all believers. These ideas the reformers believed to be in harmony with those of St. Augustine and the early Church, as well as with those to be found in the Scriptures. They clashed sharply, however, with the beliefs and practices of the Roman Catholic hierarchy of the Late Middle Ages. This doctrinal split within the ranks of organized Western

---

[1]The reformers disputed the Petrine doctrine upon which the popes based much of their claim to headship over the Christian Church. The popes claimed that, as bishops of Rome, they inherited the authority of St. Peter, the first bishop of Rome, whom Christ designated to head his Church. (" . . . thou art Peter and upon this rock I will build my church . . . ," Matthew, 16:18.) The reformers maintained that in the original Greek the word for Peter is *petros*, meaning an individual stone, and that the word for rock is *petra*, meaning a large body of stone. Therefore, they assert, Christ did not mean to say that he would found his Church upon Peter, but upon the faith that Christ was the son of the living God, which Peter had just affirmed.

This cartoon shows John Tetzel, the papal dispenser of indulgences in Germany in 1517. It was in opposition to the doctrine of indulgences that Luther posted the ninety-five theses and advocated open debate of Church policies. The last lines of the jingle at upper left read: "As soon as gold in the basin rings, Right then the soul to heaven springs."
Photo: Lutherhalle, Wittenberg

Christendom was the most fundamental of all the causes of the Reformation.

Other factors, however, contributed to the break within the Roman Catholic Church. Quite apart from matters of doctrine, many abuses had arisen in the Church during the fourteenth and fifteenth centuries when the Church was torn by the Babylonian Captivity, the Great Schism, and the struggles between the popes and the councils (see pp. 288–291). Ignorance and worldliness of the clergy, the sale of Church offices and services (simony), the favoring of relatives for lucrative Church offices (nepotism), the holding by one man of more offices than he could adequately serve (pluralism)—all were subjects of loud and growing complaint. Many of the higher clergy, even the popes, became infected with the secular spirit of the Renaissance. Often they displayed greater interest in humanistic pleasures and pursuits than in feeding their flocks. Eventually the Church hierarchy came to realize the seriousness of these abuses and took drastic steps to remedy them, but not until much of Western Christendom had left the Roman fold.

Politically the rise of national states and of local loyalty to them clashed with the international character of the Church. The national monarchs became increasingly jealous of the pope's claims over their subjects, and in many cases supported native Protestant leaders and movements.

Economic motivation undoubtedly played a significant part. Church taxes drained away to Rome much wealth from the local economy. The rich tax-exempt lands of the Church all over Western Europe excited a great deal of envy. The Church's opposition to usury and its close alliance with the landed aristocracy antagonized the rising capitalistic classes.

Finally, the intellectual activities of the humanists weakened the hold of the Church on many minds. Erasmus and other humanists heaped ridicule on what they considered to be the superstitious beliefs of the Church. Their scholarly translations and critical textual studies exposed errors in the sacred documents upon which the Church based its claims. It must not be assumed, however, that the Protestants were more humanistic than the Roman Catholics. As a matter of fact, the sixteenth-century humanists found the Protestant leaders even more dogmatic and uncongenial than the Roman Catholic hierarchy. However, the humanists unwittingly helped to bring about the Reformation by weakening the position of the Church.

As early as the fourteenth century such reformers as John Wycliffe in England and John Huss in Bohemia had voiced their protests against the Church. By the opening of the sixteenth century the religious, political, economic, and intellectual opposition to the Church had reached explosive proportions. All that was needed for revolt was a dynamic personality to lead it and an incident to set it off.

2. LUTHERANISM

The Protestant Reformation was composed of four major distinct but related movements—Lutheranism, Calvinism, Anglicanism, and Anabaptism. From these four main stems have sprung the hundreds of Protestant denominations that exist today. The Lutheran revolt was first in point of time.

Martin Luther (1483–1546) was the son of an ambitious ex-peasant miner of central Germany. At a boarding school run by the pietistic Brethern of the Common Life he, like his contemporary Erasmus, was introduced to a type of Christianity that emphasized simple piety rather than dogma and ritual. Later at Erfurt University he received a traditional liberal arts education. He was an excellent student. However, upon the completion of his undergraduate course and just as he was ready to begin study of the law, he suddenly renounced the world and entered an Augustinian monastery. This decision was no passing whim. As a child, Luther had been much concerned over the fate of his soul, and throughout his university days, his religious yearning had increased.

But the young friar found no satisfaction in the monastic life of the sixteenth-century Church. He scourged himself, donned beggar's garb, and went out among his former fellow students with sunken cheeks and gleaming, feverish eyes. It was not until, on the advice of a perceptive supervisor of his monastic order, he began to read the writings of St. Augustine and St. Paul that Brother Martin found the answer to

his lifelong quest. On reading in Paul's Letter to the Romans (1:17) "the just shall live by faith," he concluded that here was the true means of salvation—not good works, sacraments, and rituals, but simple faith in Christ. Over a period of years he developed a theology based on this fundamental concept. Gradually he regained his old radiance and energy.

In the meantime Luther had become a member of the faculty of the newly founded University of Wittenberg in Saxony, where he was to remain for the rest of his life. For several years he taught philosophy and theology, quite unaware that his belief in salvation by faith alone was in fundamental conflict with the dogma of his church. Students flocked from afar to listen to him.

One day a friar named John Tetzel came into the vicinity of Wittenberg selling indulgences. According to the doctrine of indulgences, which had grown up in the Late Middle Ages, Christ and the saints, by their good works while on earth, had accumulated in heaven a treasury of excess merit which the pope could apply to the credit of penitent sinners, thereby shortening for them or their loved ones their stay in purgatory. By the opening of the sixteenth century the dispensing of this extra sacramental means of grace had become hardly more than a money-making venture. Huge sums, taken from the credulous all over Europe, were brought to Rome for the construction of St. Peter's or for other costly papal projects.

On October 31, 1517, Martin Luther posted on the church door in Wittenberg ninety-five theses or propositions concerning the doctrine of indulgences, which he proposed to be debated publicly. It did not occur to him that this event would mark the beginning of an upheaval to subside only after nearly half of Western Christendom had broken away from the Roman Catholic Church. He was astonished and at first dismayed to find himself suddenly the national hero of all the various disgruntled elements throughout Germany. When, however, two years later in a public debate at Leipzig Luther finally realized that his position was hopelessly at odds with that of the Church, he lost no time in making the break clean. He published a series of pamphlets in which he violently denounced the pope and his organization, and called upon the German princes to seize the property of the Church and make themselves the heads of the Christian Church in Germany.

A papal bull of excommunication (which Luther publicly burned) soon followed. A few months later Emperor Charles V called the troublesome monk to appear before the Diet of the Holy Roman Empire at Worms (1521). There Luther boldly refused to recant and was outlawed by the highest civil authority in Germany. Although Luther remained under this death sentence with a price on his head for the rest of his life, he was protected by his prince, the elector of Saxony, and by German public opinion.

By this time all Germany was in religious and social turmoil. Nearly everyone with a grievance of any kind was looking to Luther for leadership. Religious zealots, many of them calling themselves Anabaptists, began preaching individualistic and more radical doctrines in his name, and he found it necessary to repudiate them. Taking a somewhat more conservative stand, he decided that only those features of the Roman Catholic Church that were opposed to the Scriptures ought to be rejected. In the early stages of the conflict Erasmus and many other humanists thought they saw in Luther a kindred spirit, but this alliance was short-lived. Erasmus soon found Luther to be as dogmatic and uncompromising in matters of doctrine as the Roman Catholic theologians, if not more so. Erasmus was primarily interested in matters of the intellect, and Luther in those of religious faith. Erasmus found it more convenient and comfortable to remain in the Roman Church, which he had done so much to discredit. He and Luther ended their days hurling recriminations at each other.

Luther also found it necessary to break with a group of rebellious peasants in south Germany. The condition of the peasants was bad and growing worse. The landed aristocracy, themselves losing ground to the rising middle classes, were depriving their peasants of long-established manorial rights such as free use of meadows and woodlands. In 1524 widespread disturbances broke out in southwestern Germany. The next year the peasants published a list of moderate demands; when these were refused, the peasants rebelled in the name of Luther, whom they believed to be against all oppressive authority. Luther, although sympathetic, pleaded with them to refrain from violence. This the peasants refused to do, and when they went on a bloody rampage, killing and burning in Luther's name, he repudiated them and called on the civil authorities to suppress the revolt by force. The alarmed authorities did so with a vengeance.

In the end both sides blamed Luther for the revolt and its painful results. South Germany has remained a Roman Catholic stronghold to this day. Luther was in favor of peaceful social reform, but he believed that successful reform depended upon a change of heart. In short, the first Protestant leader found it necessary quite early in the revolt to make it clear that Protestant Christianity was neither a humanistic philosophy nor a materialistic social reform movement, nor yet a free-for-all for everyone to believe and preach anything he chose.

Luther's new religion, as he eventually formulated it, made the Scriptures the sole authoritative source of Christian dogma. That all might have access to the Bible, he translated it into German.[2] He conceived of the Church as the whole body of believers in Christ, not the Roman Catholic Church or any other specific organization. He abolished the hierarchy of pope, cardinals, and bishops, and reduced the importance of the clergy in general, proclaiming the priesthood of all believers. He made the various secular rulers the heads of the Christian Church in their territories. He abolished monasteries and the celibacy of the clergy. Luther himself married an ex-nun. The ritual of worship was made much simpler. Of the seven sacraments of the Roman Catholic Church, Luther kept only the two he found mentioned as sacraments in the Bible: baptism and the eucharist. He rejected the Roman Catholic

---

[2]Luther's translation was in such excellent German that it had great influence on the standardization of the modern literary German language.

This portrait of Calvin as a young man by an unknown painter reveals his intellectual keenness and his elegant bearing. Calvin was an uncompromising zealot for the Protestant faith. His enemies thought him a kill-joy and a tyrant—a "Protestant pope." His friends and followers considered him the most gentle and inspiring of men. *Photo: Société du Musée Historique de la Réformation, Genéve*

Peace of Augsburg. Each of the more than three hundred German princes was left free to choose between Lutheranism and Roman Catholicism; his subjects were to abide by his choice. Luther himself died in 1546, just before the fighting began. Lutheranism triumphed in the northern half of Germany and soon spread to Denmark, Norway, Sweden, and most of the Baltic provinces (now Latvia, Estonia, and Finland), which were then under Swedish control. In addition, Lutheranism heavily influenced all later Protestant movements.

3. CALVINISM

Calvin shares with Luther the position of first importance in the founding of Protestant Christianity. Born in France in 1509, John Calvin was twenty-six years younger than Luther. He was the son of a lawyer who was secretary to the bishop of Noyon in Picardy. Young Calvin had a radiant personality that made for warm friendships. Long association with aristocratic friends probably accounts for his elegant manners. His father sent him first to the University of Paris for a thorough grounding in the humanities and theology, and then to the best law schools in France, where Calvin ruined his health by overwork. Upon finishing his legal training, he entered upon a humanistic literary career and quickly showed signs of becoming a second Erasmus. Suddenly at the age of twenty-four, he was converted to Protestant Christianity, probably as a result of reading Luther.

The zealous young reformer soon aroused the ire of Roman Catholic authorities in France and of the French government, and was forced to flee

doctrine known as transubstantiation.[3] Luther interpreted the Scriptural passages that refer to the Holy Eucharist, or Lord's Supper, to mean that during the administration of the sacrament Christ's body somehow enters into the bread and the wine, but the bread and wine remain. He denied the Roman Catholic belief that a sacrifice is involved.

The Emperor Charles V was greatly distressed by this religious revolution, which further divided his scattered and chaotic empire. Although determined to suppress the Protestants, he was too busy with his wars against the French and the Turks to make much headway. Nine years of indecisive fighting between the Roman Catholics under Charles V and the Protestants ended in 1555 with the compromise

---

[3]The New Catholic Dictionary defines transubstantiation as "the marvellous and singular changing of the entire substance of the bread into the entire substance of the Body of Christ and of the entire substance of the wine into His Blood."

for his life. Calvin then spent the next two years in hiding writing the first edition of *The Institutes of the Christian Religion.* Published in Basel, Switzerland, when Calvin was only twenty-six years of age, this theological treatise was to become the most influential writing in the history of Protestantism. Its precise and forceful logic reveals not only the fine legal training of the author, but also one of the most powerful intellects in history. Its lucid and facile style had much the same influence on the formulation of modern literary French that Luther's translation of the Bible had on German. It immediately made Calvin an important name in literary and theological circles.

Probably Calvin's most significant contribution to Christian theology is his sublime concept of the majesty of God. To the author of the *Institutes,* the Divine Creator is so majestic and awe-inspiring and man so insignificant by comparison that salvation by election, or *predestination,* as it is more often called, seems to follow logically. According to Calvin, God in the beginning planned the whole universe to the end of time. For unfathomable reasons of his own, God selected those human beings who would be saved and those who would be damned. He planted in the minds of the elect a saving faith in Christ and an insatiable desire to live the Christian life and to bring about the Kingdom of God on earth. In no other way could man acquire this faith and this desire. Calvin based this doctrine upon the Scriptures (particularly the writings of St. Paul), which he considered to be the sole authoritative source for Christian theology. St. Augustine, the most influential of the early Church fathers, and Luther also believed in salvation by election, but neither they nor anyone else had ever spelled out the doctrine so precisely.

Shortly after the publication of the *Institutes,* Calvin went to Geneva. That city, like most of the rest of Switzerland, was in the throes of religious and political revolt brought on partly by the influence of Luther and the native Swiss reformer, Ulrich Zwingli (1484–1531). The Protestant leaders in Geneva immediately recognized in Calvin a natural leader and with difficulty persuaded the gifted but modest young man to remain there and make Geneva a model city of

God on earth. Calvin, by sheer force of personality and intellect, soon rose to a position of virtual dictatorship over the city. He brought the town council, which was remarkably democratic and representative for the sixteenth century, under the dominance of a consistory composed of Protestant pastors and laymen. In other words, Geneva became a theocracy. Under Calvin's leadership, the town council and the consistory set up a strict system of blue laws. Churchgoing was compulsory. Dancing, cardplaying, theatergoing, drinking, gambling, and swearing—all were forbidden. Enforcement was vigorous, and penalties severe, even for the sixteenth century. The most famous penalty was the burning of Michael Servetus, an eccentric amateur scientist and theologian whom the Roman Catholic Church had already condemned to death for heresy.[4] Servetus escaped his Catholic persecutors and came to Geneva for the purpose of destroying Calvin and his works. Calvin had warned him to stay away on pain of death; when Servetus arrived, he was seized, tried, convicted, and burned at the stake.

A strong minority in Geneva had no use for Calvin, his theology, or his blue laws. To them Calvin was a kill-joy, a bigot, and a tyrant, a verdict that has found its way into many textbooks. The majority of the Genevans, on the other hand, practically worshiped their leader; they considered him the most brilliant, inspiring, sympathetic, kindly, and gentle of men. Protestant Christians came from many countries to sit at the feet of Calvin and to study at the University of Geneva, which he founded. John Knox, who came from Scotland to study under Calvin, called the Genevan theocracy "the most perfect school of life that was ever on earth since the days of the apostles."

Calvinist ritual was even simpler than that of the Lutherans. The worship service consisted of preaching, praying, and psalm-singing. Like Luther, Calvin retained only two of the seven

---

[4]The most serious of Servetus' heretical views was his denial of the Trinity, which cast doubt on the divinity of Christ.

sacraments—baptism and the Holy Eucharist, or Lord's Supper. But to Calvin, Christ was present only in spirit in the bread and wine, and only for the elect. Calvin patterned his system of church government after that of the very earliest church as described in the Bible (Acts of the Apostles). The local churches were governed by laymen called *elders* who were elected by the congregations. A measure of unity in faith and practices was maintained by means of a hierarchy of representative assemblies.

Calvinism became dominant in most of Switzerland (Swiss Reformed), the Dutch Netherlands (Dutch Reformed), Scotland (Presbyterian), and the German Palatinate. It also had a strong minority following in England (the Puritans), and a smaller but vigorous following in France (the Huguenots), Bohemia, Hungary, and Poland. The Calvinists played an important part in the founding of the United States, particularly the Puritans in New England, the Dutch Reformed in New York, and the Scotch-Irish Presbyterians along the frontiers of all the original states. Such well-known denominations in present-day America as the Congregationalists, the Presbyterians, and the Baptists are Calvinist in origin. The Calvinists were the most zealous and evangelical of all the major early Protestant groups. In later years they made a strong appeal to the rising middle classes. Wherever they were found, they were a powerful influence for the growth of democracy and for public education.

4. ANGLICANISM

The occasion, though not the cause, of the beginning of the Reformation in England was the desire of Henry VIII (1509–1547) for a male heir. Catherine of Aragon, to whom he had been married for eighteen years, had given him only a daughter, Mary. When it became apparent that Catherine would have no more children, Henry decided to ask the pope to annul the marriage. The pope, however, was in no position to grant the annulment. Catherine was the aunt of the Emperor Charles V, whose troops were at that very moment in control of the city of Rome. When Henry finally realized the pope was not going to accommodate him, he took matters into his own hands. At his bidding a subservient Parliament passed the Act of Supremacy, making the king of England, not the pope, head of the Church in England. Later the monasteries, strongholds of papal influence, were dissolved. Meanwhile, Thomas Cranmer, whom Henry made archbishop of Canterbury, had arranged the annulment, and Henry had married Anne Boleyn. (He was to marry six times in all.) Henry was, of course, excommunicated by the pope.

But Henry VIII was no Protestant. In the days before the annulment controversy the pope had given him the title "Defender of the Faith" for his anti-Lutheran writings. Now he had Parliament pass the Six Articles reaffirming the Catholic position on all controversial doctrinal points except that of papal supremacy. Protestants, on the one hand, and Roman Catholics who refused to acknowledge the headship of Henry VIII in place of the pope, were persecuted with equal severity. Death was the penalty for both.

It was during the reign of Henry VIII's young son, Edward VI (1547–1553), that the Anglican Church first became Protestant. Archbishop Cranmer drew up a *Book of Common Prayer* and Forty-two Articles of faith that were definitely Calvinist in flavor. Edward VI was succeeded by his elder sister, Mary (1553–1558), who was the daughter of Catherine of Aragon and a devout Roman Catholic. Mary's ambition was to restore her kingdom to the Roman Catholic fold. Her first step was to marry her cousin, Philip II of Spain, the most powerful champion of resurgent Roman Catholicism in all Europe. Next she asked and received papal forgiveness for her wayward people. Finally, "Bloody Mary" burned at the stake some three hundred Protestants, including Archbishop Cranmer. But Mary's marriage to a man soon to be king of England's most dangerous rival and her persecutions were extremely unpopular in England; in the long run her policies hurt rather than helped the Roman Catholic cause there.

Elizabeth I (1558–1603), the Protestant daughter of Anne Boleyn, followed Mary on the English throne. This high-spirited, cynical, and politically minded queen found theology tiresome. Her chief interest was to find a satisfacto-

WHAT IS THE MEANING OF THE PROTESTANT REFORMATION

Most historians agree that the breakup of the all-powerful medieval Church was probably the most significant factor in bringing the Middle Ages to an end and that the Reformation was, therefore, of major importance in the rise of modern Western civilization. But there the agreement ends. Was the Protestant Reformation spiritual, as its leaders firmly believed, or was it something else—intellectual, political, economic? As the modern Western world has become more and more secular, so have interpretations of the Reformation.

The historians of the Enlightenment of the eighteenth century tended to think of the Protestant Reformation as the religious aspect of the Renaissance. They liked to believe that the early Protestants were seeking intellectual freedom and individualism in their search for theological truth. Whatever might be said about the trend of Protestantism in later centuries, this interpretation of early Protestantism, with the possible exception of certain minor sects, is certainly based upon faulty information. It did not take Erasmus very long to discover that the early Protestant leaders were more dogmatic and less compatible with his humanistic approach to Christianity than was the Roman Catholic hierarchy.

From the mid-nineteenth century to the present day, many historians have thought of the Protestant Reformation in political terms. They have viewed the various religious movements of the sixteenth century as adjuncts of nationalism. They believe it to be significant that the Protestant Reformation began in Germany, where there was no strong central government to protect the German people from exploitation by the Italian papacy. Luther strongly and openly appealed to German nationalism against Rome, and there can be little doubt that his nationalistic appeal gained many followers. By contrast, the strong rulers of France and Spain were able to extract such concessions from the pope as to create what amounted to a Gallican Church and a Spanish Catholic Church. The various Calvinistic churches were generally set up along national lines, such as the Swiss, Dutch, German, and Scottish Reformed churches. And of course the Anglican Church was a national church. All this was in striking contrast to the medieval Church, which had encompassed all of Western and Central Europe. Another popular twentieth-century interpretation has been that of the Freudian psychologists, who have used the theories of Freud to analyze the personalities of the early Protestant leaders, particularly Luther.

Most popular of the secular interpretations of the Protestant Reformation from the late nineteenth century to the present has been the economic interpretation. Those who emphasize this line of thought point out the hunger for the rich lands held by the Roman Church, the resentment over the tax exemption of these lands and over the draining away of money to Rome, and the opposition of the commercial class to the Church's ban on usury. From this viewpoint, Protestantism seemed to promise an end to all these "abuses." The ultimate in economic approaches to explaining the Reformation is that of the Marxists, who regard all religion as the "opiate of the people"—a trick of the "haves" to keep the "have nots" quiet and obedient.

A widely accepted economic interpretation of the Reformation is that of Max Weber, a German sociologist who was strongly influenced by Karl Marx. The Weber thesis was first published in 1904–1905 in two articles entitled "The Protestant Ethic and the Spirit of Capitalism." Weber believed that Protestantism, particularly Calvinism, contributed to the rise of capitalism. It removed the ban on usury, and made possible unlimited profits. The doctrine of salvation by election encouraged its believers to work hard, each in his appointed calling, for the glory of God and for the assurance that he is one of the elect. This hard work, coupled with the asceticism Calvin preached, resulted in growing surpluses which were reinvested in capitalistic enterprises. Weber also offers as evidence the capitalistic successes of the Calvinistic Dutch and Swiss and the Puritans of England and New England. Weber's thesis has won the support of thousands of readers.

His critics, however, have demonstrated his surprising unfamiliarity with the actual writings of the early Protestants. Calvin devoted only 50 out of some 30,000 pages of his published writings to economic matters; Luther devoted about twice as many pages to this topic out of a similar total. Both Calvin and Luther repeatedly warned against the danger of riches and admonished lenders not to take advantage of the poor and distressed. Nowhere did they consider prosperity as a sign of election. The voluminous writings of the seventeenth-century English Puritans continue in a similar vein. Critics of Weber point out that capitalism is much older than Calvinism, and wonder why Weber did not cite the early modern commercial prosperity of Roman Catholic northern Italy, southern and western Germany, or the Belgian Netherlands, or the lack of capitalistic activity in Calvinistic Scotland. Weber's most influential disciple was R. H. Tawney, a British economic historian active in Labour party politics. His *Religion and the Rise of Capitalism*, published in 1926, reveals a great deal more knowledge of history than does Weber, and more subtlety and sophistication, but adheres essentially to the Weber thesis.

It would appear that writers and readers of history tend to impute their own motives to the makers of history—to read the prevailing spirit of their own times into the spirit of earlier epochs. This is particularly true in the field of religious history, where it is impossible to know the hearts of the proclaimers of the various faiths. Historians very frequently reveal their own times more than the times of the period about which they write.

ELIZ

ry compromise that would unify her people. During the course of her long reign the Anglican Church became definitely, but conservatively, Protestant. Cranmer's *Book of Common Prayer* was readopted with slight alterations. The Forty-two Articles were changed to the Thirty-nine. Some of the more controversial doctrinal points that seemed to prevent the various Protestant sects from uniting were reworded. Although celibacy of the clergy was abandoned, the episcopal system (government of the church by bishops) was retained. A rather elaborate ritual was adopted. Two of the sacraments, baptism and the eucharist, were retained.

Although the great majority of the English people appeared to have accepted Elizabeth's compromise settlement, two groups remained dissatisfied. An extreme Calvinist element sought to "purify" the Anglican Church of all remaining traces of Roman Catholicism. These Puritans were to increase in strength until under Oliver Cromwell's leadership in the next century they gained temporary control of the country. The Roman Catholic minority, on the other hand, lost steadily in numbers. The support that some Roman Catholics gave to Philip II's attempt to conquer England and to the effort of Mary, Queen of Scots (a Roman Catholic) to overthrow Elizabeth (see Chapter 32) tainted all of them with the suspicion of treason and played into Elizabeth's hands. By the end of her reign, England was one of the Protestant countries of Europe.

5. THE ANABAPTISTS

Some reformers believed that Luther, Calvin, and the Anglican leaders had not gone far enough. They would break more sharply with all the existing institutions of the early sixteenth century—political, economic, and social as well as religious. Hence the term *radical* is often applied to them. Since these "radicals" were highly individualistic in their approach to religion, it is difficult to generalize about the many sects with their widely differing views and points of emphasis. One of the most commonly held beliefs was their opposition to infant baptism. The true Christian, they believed, was one

who was "born again" and baptized as an adult according to Scripture. Those who had been baptized as infants must be rebaptized. Anabaptism means *re*baptism. The Anabaptists believed that the true church of Christ on earth is a gathered church composed only of born-again Christians (in contrast with the territorial or state churches of the Roman Catholics, Lutherans, Calvinists, and Anglicans which of necessity contain many who are not genuine Christians). The Anabaptists attempted to live lives of uncompromising holiness as dictated by the Bible or by the Holy Spirit speaking directly to each individual. All human institutions are evil. These sects refused to recognize or participate in civil government, take oaths of allegiance, recognize titles, or serve in armed forces. Some practiced a shared or communistic economy. Most of them were poor. They were feared and cruelly persecuted, of course, by all organized secular society, and by Roman Catholics, Lutherans, Calvinists, and Anglicans alike.

A few of the early Anabaptist leaders were violent activists, such as Thomas Müntzer, who inflamed the peasant rebels of southwest Germany, and John of Leyden, who set up a violent dictatorship in Münster in northwest Germany. This bizarre "heavenly Jerusalem" held out for more than a year against besieging Lutheran and Roman Catholic armies. The leaders were then tortured to death and their bodies hung in iron baskets from a church tower for three hundred and fifty years. But the great majority of the Anabaptist leaders were pious and gentle—in fact, pacifists. Conrad Grebel, the first prominent Anabaptist leader, was a humanist from an upper class family of Zurich, Switzerland. Probably the most successful and influential of all the Anabaptist leaders was the convert Menno Simons, a gentle former Roman Catholic priest from the Dutch Netherlands. His followers, the Mennonites, spread throughout much of Western Europe and later the United States. Also in the Anabaptist tradition was the Society of Friends, commonly known as Quakers. Founded by George Fox in England in the mid-seventeenth century, this pietistic and pacifistic sect has spread to many parts of the world. It has furnished two presidents of the United States.

6. SUMMARY

By the end of the third quarter of the sixteenth century, then, Protestantism had triumphed in the northern half of the Germanies, in Scandinavia, in most of the Baltic provinces, in most of Switzerland, in the Dutch Netherlands, Scotland, and England. In addition, it had gained a strong minority following in France, Poland, Bohemia, and Hungary. And, no matter how much the various Protestant denominations might disagree among themselves on minor details, they presented a solid front against the Roman Catholics. All Protestants rejected papal supremacy, the divine sanction of the Roman Church, the celibacy and indelible character of the priesthood, monasticism, and such other characteristic Roman Catholic doctrines as purgatory, transubstantiation, invocation of saints, and veneration of relics. These doctrinal differences between the Protestants and the Roman Catholics were fundamental, and no middle ground for a compromise was ever found. Nor was the Roman Church, notwithstanding its strong comeback, ever able to reconquer the territories in which the Protestants had gained a definite majority. The Reformation split Western Christendom into two sharply defined and hostile camps. In place of the two major divisions into which Christianity had been separated since the early Middle Ages (Eastern Orthodox and Roman Catholic), there were now three.

Suggested Reading

General

*G. R. Elton, *Reformation Europe, 1517–1559* (Torch). Probably the best single volume on the Reformation. Does not include the English Reformation.

H. J. Grimm, *The Reformation Era*, 2nd ed. (1973). Sound and readable.

Lutheranism

*R. H. Bainton, *Here I Stand: A Life of Martin Luther* (Mentor). Combines excellent scholarship with a journalistic style.

Calvinism

*W. Walker, *John Calvin, the Organizer of Reformed Protestantism* (Schocken). Probably still the best single-volume biography of Calvin.

*J. T. McNeil, *The History and Character of Calvinism* (Oxford). By a leading authority.

Anglicanism

*A. G. Dickens, *The English Reformation* (Schocken). Best survey.

*J. J. Scarisbrick, *Henry VIII* (University of California) Best biography.

*J. E. Neale, *Queen Elizabeth I* (Anchor). By a leading authority.

The Anabaptists

F. H. Littell, *The Anabaptist View of the Church* (1952). An excellent brief account.

Sources

*R. H. Bainton, *The Age of the Reformation* (Anvil). A handy selection of excerpts from the writings of important Reformation figures.

*H. E. Bettenson, *Documents of the Christian Church* (Oxford). Another useful selection.

32

THE ROMAN CATHOLIC REFORMATION

The loss of almost half of Western Christendom by the Roman Catholic Church and the threatened loss of the rest touched off a reform movement within the Church. By the middle of the sixteenth century the Roman Catholic reform movement was well under way. The Church was revitalized, and a counteroffensive was launched against the Protestants — one that not only prevented their further encroachment on the Roman Catholic domain, but pushed them back a bit.

1. THE RISE OF A REFORM MOVEMENT

Long before the revolt of Luther and Calvin, there had been a demand for reform by many loyal Roman Catholics. In Spain, around the turn of the sixteenth century, Cardinal Ximenes had forestalled a possible protest movement by enforcing strict discipline upon the clergy and waging bitter warfare against heresy. However, in the rest of Western Christendom, the secular interests of the Renaissance popes and prelates and the popes' fears that a reform council might again challenge the absolute authority of the Holy See prevented effective action. Now, with area after area becoming Protestant, countermeasures of a rather drastic nature became imperative. There were two schools of thought concerning the proper course of action. One, led by the liberal Cardinal Contarini of Venice, advocated compromise and conciliation. Contarini eventually went so far as to meet with Melanch-

thon, a close friend of Luther and an important figure in the Lutheran revolt, in earnest quest of an acceptable compromise. They were unsuccessful; the two religions appeared to be incompatible. The other school of thought was led by the conservative Cardinal Caraffa of Naples. Caraffa believed that many corrupt practices in the Church needed to be reformed, but that no compromise whatever should be made in the dogma. He believed that the Protestants were heretics and could reunite with the Roman Catholic Church only by recanting and submitting to the pope. This is the school of thought that triumphed, and Caraffa became Pope Paul IV. The upshot of this line of thinking was the calling of a Church council at Trent, an imperial city in northern Italy.

2. THE COUNCIL OF TRENT

The Council of Trent, which was in session off and on for eighteen years from 1545 to 1563, was probably the most important council in the history of the Roman Catholic Church. The popes skillfully controlled its membership and voting procedure. The ultimate decisions of the council were in two categories: dogmatic and reformatory. In matters of faith or dogma, all the traditional doctrines of the Church were reaffirmed and redefined, especially controversial ones such as the sacraments, transubstantiation, auricular confession, celibacy of the clergy, monasticism, purgatory, invocation of the saints, veneration of relics, and indulgences. The dogmatic canons and decrees of the council concluded: "Anathema to [accursed be] all heretics! Anathema! Anathema! Anathema!" The council also took stern measures to stop corrupt practices. Simony, nepotism, pluralism, and immorality and ignorance among the clergy were condemned. Schools for the education of the clergy were called for. Bishops were admonished to exercise closer supervision and discipline over the lower clergy. To implement its canons and decrees, the council endorsed the Inquisition, which had recently been set up in Rome to combat heresy, and inaugurated the Index of Forbidden Books to prevent the reading of heretical literature except by authorized persons. Both instruments were placed under papal control and supervision. The Index, periodically revised, proved to be particularly effective. Thus the Roman Catholic Church at last spoke out, selected its weapons, and girded itself for more effective battle against the Protestants. At its service were the militant new Jesuit order and the greatest military power of the sixteenth century, Philip II's Spain.

3. THE SOCIETY OF JESUS

The founder of the Society of Jesus, Ignatius Loyola (1491–1556), was a member of the Spanish lesser nobility, and until early middle life was an obscure and ignorant soldier. In a battle with the French his leg was crushed by a cannon ball. Without benefit of anesthetic, he had it set and, when it grew crooked, twice broken and reset. He remained a cripple for the rest of his life. During the months of agony and convalescence Loyola read lives of the Christian saints and underwent a deep spiritual conversion. He determined to devote his tremendous energies and latent talents to the service of the Roman Catholic Church—to become a soldier of Christ, the Virgin Mary, and the pope. Since his first efforts only revealed his ignorance and got him into trouble with the clerical authorities, he set off for the University of Paris to begin his education. Loyola was, however, not a scholar or theologian, but a man of action. He soon began to

attract a band of followers, with whom he organized the Society of Jesus.

The Jesuit Order, as the Society of Jesus is commonly known, was founded along military lines. A general, elected for life and residing in Rome, issues orders that are transmitted through a hierarchy of officials to the rank and file. Absolute and unquestioning obedience is the first requirement. Loyola admonished his followers, ". . . if she [the Church] shall have defined anything to be black which to our eyes appears to be white, we ought in like manner to pronounce it to be black." Members are urged to cut all earthly ties, even with family and friends, that might divide their loyalties or impede their wholehearted devotion to the work of the order. Applicants for membership are carefully screened. Only those of superior intelligence, sound health, and attractive appearance are chosen. Then follows a two-year testing time, a sort of officer-training school, during which the novices are severely tried and examined for signs of weakness of will or purpose. Those who survive are next given a long and rigorous education as scholastics in preparation for their specialized work. When found to be ready, they are admitted to full-fledged membership as coadjutors. They may now serve as priests, teachers, medics, diplomats, or in almost any other capacity suitable to their talents and training. Whatever their work, it is "all for the greater glory of God," which to the Jesuit means for all practical purposes the Roman Catholic Church. After years of service a few of the most outstanding are admitted to the highest circle. These select few take, in addition to the three Benedictine vows of poverty, chastity, and obedience, a fourth vow of special obedience to the pope. It is from this inner circle that all the high officers of the order are chosen.

For the spiritual guidance and inspiration of the members of the Society, Loyola wrote the *Spiritual Exercises.* Revealing the author's deep understanding of psychology, the *Exercises* guide the member through a solid month of concentrated meditation, a week each on the horrors of sin, the life of Christ to Palm Sunday, his suffering and crucifixion, and his resurrection and ascension. This remarkable work has proved to be a powerful stimulant in time of flagging zeal.

Loyola's high standards, far from deterring applicants, served as a challenge and an attraction. The Society of Jesus grew rapidly. As priests, the Jesuits were nearly always the best trained, the most popular, and the most influential. As teachers, they were usually more highly educated, devoted, and attractive than their competitors. They have always been keenly aware of the power of education, especially for the very young. "Give me the child, and I care not who has the man." The Jesuits soon got control of all education in most Roman Catholic countries.

These dedicated soldiers of Christ also made the best missionaries. In North and South America the dauntless Jesuits went among the Indians, risked and in many cases lost their lives, learned the languages of the natives, lived with them, and converted most of them to Roman Catholic Christianity. In the Far East, Francis Xavier, second only to Loyola himself in Jesuit history, converted tens of thousands.

Not the least important of Jesuit activities was that of gaining the confidence of kings, princes, and other high political personages, and thereby influencing state policy. This militantly zealous order was a powerful stimulant to the wavering cause of Roman Catholicism. In Italy, Spain, Portugal, and Ireland, where Protestantism had only a weak foothold, the Jesuits stamped it out altogether. In France and Belgium they helped to turn the tide against the Protestants. In southern Germany, Poland, and the Austrian Hapsburg lands, all of which seemed to be on the point of going Protestant, the Jesuits reversed the trend and made those lands the strongholds of Roman Catholicism they are today.

4. THE CRUSADE OF CATHOLIC SPAIN

Also at the service of the Roman Catholic Church in its counteroffensive against the Protestants was the world's greatest military power of the sixteenth century—the Spain of Philip II. Emperor Charles V had bequeathed the greater part of his vast empire to his son Philip II (1556–1598). In addition to Spain, Philip's inheritance included the Netherlands, Franche-Comté, Mi-

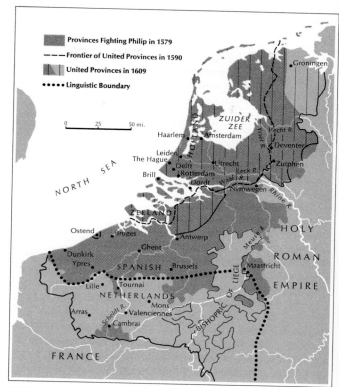

THE NETHERLANDS 1578–1609

lan, the Kingdom of the Two Sicilies, Sardinia, the Balearic Islands, holdings along the west coast of Africa, and the Western Hemisphere. When in 1580 Philip conquered Portugal in the name of his Portuguese mother and became master (at least in name) of Portugal's huge Eastern empire, he exercised legal rule over more of the earth's surface than any other man in history.[1] Philip II, unlike his father, was a native Spaniard. The gold and silver now flowing in a steady stream from the New World and the lucrative commerce of the East Indies and of the busy Netherlands he utilized in the interests of Spain. The Spanish infantry were the best foot

---

[1] Sixty years later Portugal regained her independence.

soldiers of the sixteenth century. Philip II was also a firm believer in the divine rights of monarchy. Ignoring the Cortes and the local rights of Aragon and tending personally to the myriad details of government, the meticulous and stubborn Philip brought Spain under his sway to an extent that Ferdinand and Isabella and Charles V had never been able to do. Little wonder that the king of Spain was the most feared man in Western Christendom.

More important even than Spain in the mind of Philip II, however, was the Roman Catholic Church. He conceived it to be his chief mission in life to use the great wealth and power of Spain to restore the dominion of the Roman Church over all of Western Christendom. In the Netherlands, in England, and in France, Philip II threw the might of Spain on the side of the Roman Catholics in their counteroffensive against the Protestants.

Philip II, unlike his father, Charles V, was considered by the Netherlanders to be an unsympathetic foreigner who taxed their prosperous commerce and industry for the benefit of Spain. The absolutist monarch and his Spanish administrators also overrode the traditional political privileges of the nobles and the cities in the Netherlands. Nonetheless, religion was the foremost cause of dissension. By mid-sixteenth century, nearly half the people in the Netherlands had become Protestant. Most were Calvinists, but a considerable number were Anabaptists. Philip II, who would tolerate no heresy in his empire, took stern measures to stamp out Protestantism. The Inquisition was used to enforce the laws against heresy. In 1566, bands of outraged Protestants began to deface Roman Catholic churches. Philip thereupon dispatched 10,000 Spanish soldiers to reduce the Netherlands to submission. A six-year reign of terror followed, in which thousands were put to death.

Far from being cowed, however, the Netherlanders resisted fiercely. They found a brilliant leader in William of Orange, or William the Silent, as he came to be known. They took to the sea, playing havoc with Spanish commerce and communications. When, in 1580, Philip conquered and annexed Portugal, the hardy Dutch "Sea Beggars" seized the richest parts of the Portuguese Empire in the East Indies. The Spanish infantry quickly overran the ten southern (Belgian) provinces, but against the seven northern (Dutch) provinces, made up largely of islands and peninsulas and skillfully defended by the Dutch fleet, Spain's armies could make little headway. Most of the Protestants soon fled north from the Spanish-occupied southern provinces. Likewise, most of the Roman Catholics fled south from the Protestant-dominated north. In 1579 the ten Roman Catholic southern provinces, fearful of the growing power of the Protestant northern provinces, submitted to the Spanish yoke. The seven northern provinces, however, banded together in the Union of Utrecht and continued the struggle for independence. When in 1584 William the Silent was assassinated by a hireling of Philip II, other able leaders arose to take his place. Finally in 1609, eleven years after Philip's own death, Spain agreed to a twelve-year truce, and in 1648 Spain recognized the complete independence of the Dutch Netherlands, as the seven northern provinces are commonly called. In the seventeenth century the little Dutch republic led the world in commerce and in painting and was second to none in science and philosophy.

Thus Philip II's crusade in the Netherlands was only partly successful. He saved the southern provinces for Spain for another century, and for the Roman Catholic Church, but the Dutch provinces were lost both to Spain and to the Church.

Most grandiose of all Philip II's crusading efforts was his attempt to restore wayward England to the Roman Catholic fold. His first move was to marry England's Roman Catholic queen, Mary Tudor. This was done in 1554, two years before he began his own rule over the Spanish Empire. However, Mary's marriage to the king of a feared and hated rival power and her persecution of English Protestants only increased her own unpopularity and that of the Roman Catholic cause in England. Moreover, the marriage failed to produce an heir. When Mary died in 1558, Philip sought to continue his influence in England by trying to marry her successor, Elizabeth. But Elizabeth, a Protestant and a high-spirited English patriot, refused. Instead, she aided the Dutch Protestant rebels and encouraged English sea dogs to plunder Spain's treasure ships sailing from her New World colonies—indeed, to plunder the colonies themselves.

Eventually Philip II undertook to conquer England by direct military action. In 1588 his "Invincible" Armada sailed forth—130 ships, many of them great galleons. Aboard was a formidable Spanish army. The Armada was to go first to the Netherlands and pick up additional Spanish veterans. In the English Channel it met the somewhat larger English fleet, composed mostly of smaller but swifter and more heavily armed ships. The Spaniards fought well until finally their formation was broken by English fire ships sent into their midst. Once scattered, the Spanish ships were no match for the English fleet. Storms added to the catastrophe. Only about half the ships ever reached Spain by way of northern Scotland, whither they had fled. It was at this point that England began to wrest control of the seas from Spain. Philip II had not only failed to exterminate Protestantism in England, but the Roman Catholic cause there was now tainted with treason, and Protestantism was stronger than ever.

Philip found it more profitable to crusade against the Muslim Turks than against the Protestants. In fact, one of the few clear-cut successes of his career was the great naval victory over the Turks at Lepanto. Under the urging of the pope, Venice, Genoa, and Spain amassed a fleet of more than two hundred vessels under the command of Philip's illegitimate half brother, Don Juan. In 1571 this fleet caught and annihilated the somewhat larger Turkish fleet off Lepanto on the coast of Greece. Never again were the Turks to menace Christendom by sea.

5. THE RELIGIOUS WARS IN FRANCE

In France and Germany the Roman Catholic counteroffensive against Protestantism resulted in bitter religious wars in the late sixteenth and early seventeenth centuries. Crusading Spain

participated in these wars, but here her role was relatively minor and indecisive. In France, Calvinism had made slow but steady progress during the reigns of Francis I (1515–1547) and Henry II (1547–1559) in spite of vigorous persecution by those Roman Catholic monarchs. By 1559 the Huguenots, as the French Calvinists were called, numbered possibly a tenth of the total population. However, since their ranks included many of the prosperous bourgeoisie and some of the greatest noble families of France, their influence was far greater than their numbers would indicate. Enmity between the Huguenots and the Roman Catholics, which had smoldered under the strong rule of Francis I and of Henry II, broke into open and consuming flame under Henry II's three weakling sons, who ruled in succession from 1559 to 1589. All three were dominated by their unscrupulous and ambitious mother, Catherine de Médicis. This situation invited political as well as religious faction and intrigue, and in the civil wars that followed politics and religion were intertwined.

The leadership of the Roman Catholic faction was assumed by the powerful Guise family; that of the Protestants by the influential Bourbon family, who were related to the royal line. The first eight years of fighting were ended in 1570 by an uneasy truce. However, Catherine de Médicis, fearful of the growing influence of the Huguenots, decided to exterminate them all. She was, of course, supported and urged on by the Guises. At a given signal at midnight, August 24, 1572 (St. Bartholomew's Day), the Roman Catholics in Paris fell to slaughtering the Protestants. The massacre soon spread to the provinces and went on for weeks. Thousands of Huguenots were slain. When news of the Massacre of St. Bartholomew reached Madrid, Philip II, who seldom smiled, smiled.

The ablest of the Huguenot leaders, young Henry (Bourbon) of Navarre, escaped and rallied the remaining Protestant forces for the war that was now renewed in earnest. The wealth and energy of the numerous bourgeois and noble members of the Huguenot faction, plus the brilliance of their dashing young leader, offset the superior numbers of the Roman Catholics. Eventually Henry III, the third son of Catherine de Médicis to rule France, organized a moderate Roman Catholic faction to stand between the uncompromising Guise faction and the Protestants. The struggle now became a three-cornered "War of the Three Henrys" (Henry, duke of Guise, Henry of Navarre, and Henry III, king of France). Philip II of Spain threw his support to Henry, duke of Guise. Henry III, now regarding Henry, duke of Guise, as the greater menace to his own royal authority, had him assassinated in 1588. The next year an agent of the Guises assassinated Henry III. This left Protestant Henry of Navarre, by right of succession, King Henry IV of France. However, it was only when he abjured Protestantism four years later and went through the formality of becoming a Roman Catholic that the great majority of his subjects, who were Roman Catholics, allowed him to enter Paris and be legally crowned. "Paris is worth a Mass," he is alleged to have remarked. Five years later (1598) he issued his famous Edict of Nantes (see p. 367), which by granting toleration to the Protestant minority, ended religious strife in France for nearly a century.[2] Once again the crusade of Philip II had stalled.

6. THE THIRTY YEARS' WAR IN GERMANY

The Peace of Augsburg (1555), which had brought to a close the first armed conflict in Germany between the Roman Catholics and the Lutherans, proved to be only an uneasy truce. Since the signing of the treaty, which recognized only Roman Catholics and Lutherans, the Calvinists had made strong headway in several states of the Holy Roman Empire and demanded equal recognition. Furthermore, lands of the Roman Catholic Church were constantly being secularized in Protestant areas in violation of the treaty. On the other hand, the Roman Catholics, becoming more aggressive as a result of the clarification of their position by the Council of Trent

---

[2]The Huguenots rose up in a brief rebellion (1627–29) against Cardinal Richelieu when he removed their military and political privileges (see p. 367).

and the activities of the militant Jesuits, dreamed of exterminating Protestantism in the Holy Roman Empire and recovering all their lost lands and souls. The Protestants in alarm formed a defensive league. The Roman Catholics countered by forming a league of their own.

The increasing tension finally erupted into the Thirty Years' War (1618–1648). In this war the religious issue was complicated and often confused by political and dynastic issues. The individual princes of the empire were struggling to maintain or even increase their independence of the emperor. The Hapsburg dynasty, both Austrian and Spanish, threatened to become so powerful that the apprehensive Bourbons of France entered the war against them. The upshot was that eventually the Roman Catholics, the Holy Roman Emperor, and the Hapsburg dynasty (the emperor was an Austrian Hapsburg) formed one faction against which were arrayed the Protestants, most of the individual princes of the empire, and the Bourbons.

The long-brewing Thirty Years' War began in 1618 when a group of Bohemian noblemen, mostly Calvinists and fearful of losing both their religious and their political rights, declared their Hapsburg ruler deposed and chose the Calvinist elector of the Palatinate as their king. The Hapsburg Holy Roman Emperor, aided by the Roman Catholic League and by Hapsburg and Roman Catholic Spain, took the field and easily crushed both Bohemia and the Palatinate. Hundreds of Calvinist Bohemian noblemen were executed and their property confiscated. Protestantism was outlawed in Bohemia. The Calvinist Palatinate was annexed to Roman Catholic Bavaria. This quick and crushing victory by Roman Catholic and imperial forces frightened not only the Protestant princes of northern Germany, but also the Protestant neighboring states.

In 1625 Lutheran King Christian IV of Denmark, who held numerous bishoprics in Germany that had been illegally secularized, entered the war against the Roman Catholic and imperial forces. Christian IV was aided by English subsidies and numerous German Protestant princes. At this critical juncture a brilliant soldier of fortune, Albrecht von Wallenstein,

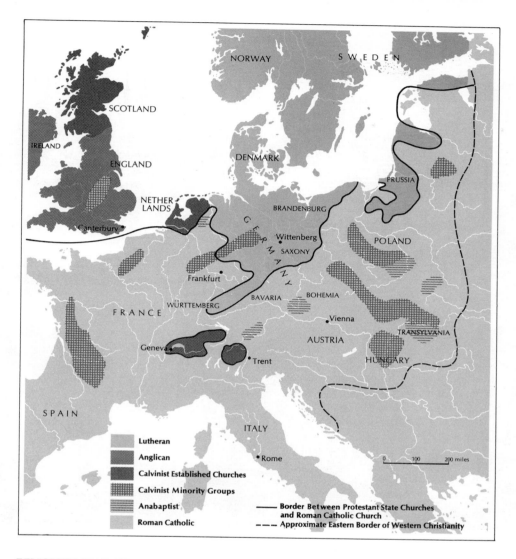

RELIGIOUS MAP OF EUROPE ca. 1560

offered his services to the emperor. This military genius raised a volunteer army of 50,000 adventurers of various nationalities whose only motivation was hope of plunder. Wallenstein's army, together with the regular imperial and Roman Catholic forces, defeated Christian IV and drove him out of Germany. The Danish king was deprived of nearly all his German holdings. Upon the conclusion of this phase of the war in 1629,

the victorious emperor issued the Edict of Restitution, restoring to the Roman Catholic Church all the lands illegally secularized since the Peace of Augsburg—more than a hundred tracts, large and small.

The whole Protestant world was now genuinely alarmed at the resurgent power of the Roman Catholics. The German princes were faced with the loss of their powers to the Holy Roman Em-

peror. The French Bourbons were concerned about the rapidly growing strength of the Hapsburgs. At this juncture another Protestant champion stepped forward—Gustavus Adolphus of Sweden. This Lutheran "Lion of the North" was a military leader of great ability. Furthermore, he was well backed by French gold. Gustavus Adolphus led his army victoriously through the Germanies, gaining allies among the Protestant princes as he went. The Hapsburg emperor hastily recalled the ambitious Wallenstein, whom he had dismissed upon the conclusion of the Danish phase of the war. Two of the ablest military commanders of early modern times now faced each other. In the battle of Lützen (1632) Wallenstein was defeated, but Gustavus Adolphus had been killed and the victory was far from decisive. Fortunately for the Protestants, Wallenstein was dismissed and assassinated two years later. Since the Swedes had failed to turn the tide of the war, France in 1635 threw the full weight of her military might di-

This print shows Magdeburg, where in 1631 one of the battles of the Thirty Years' War was fought. The last and bloodiest of the religious wars that accompanied the Roman Catholic Reformation, the Thirty Years' War, devastated much of Germany and exhausted the participants. *Photo: NYPL Picture Collection*

rectly into the fray. For thirteen more years the war dragged on until all participants were exhausted. The Treaty of Westphalia in 1648 finally brought the struggle to a close.

In general, thanks largely to the intervention of France, the Roman Catholics, the Holy Roman Emperor, and the Hapsburgs suffered a setback. Not only were the Roman Catholics thwarted in their efforts to exterminate Protestantism in Germany, but the Calvinists now gained equal status with the Lutherans and Roman Catholics in the Holy Roman Empire. The Edict of Restitution was nullified. The Holy Roman Empire practically fell apart. According to the terms of the Treaty of Westphalia, each of the more than three hundred individual princes could now make his own treaties. Three of the most important princes, the rulers of Brandenburg, Bavaria, and Saxony, made sizable additions to their territories. Sweden gained strategic territories along the German Baltic and North Sea coasts. France gained the important bishoprics and for-

Legend:

- Austrian Habsburgs
- Spanish Monarchy
- Swedish Dominions
- Brandenburg-Prussia
- Church Lands
- —— Boundary of the Holy Roman Empire

0 100 200 300 miles

SHETLAND I.

NORWAY

Bergen

ORKNEY I.

SCOTLAND

KINGDOM OF
DENMARK AND NORWAY

Edinburgh

DENMARK (TO SWEDEN 1658)

NORTH SEA

Copenhagen

BALTIC S

Belfast

IRELAND

ENGLAND
(COMMONWEALTH
1649-1660
UNITED KINGDOM
1707)

SCHLESWIG

SWEDISH
POMERANIA

Danz

Dublin

Liverpool

HOLSTEIN
Hamburg
Lübeck Stralsund

POMERANIA

Bristol

London

UNITED
PROVINCES

Bremen
Amsterdam
Ryswick
Utrecht

HANOVER

BRANDENBURG
Berlin

VIS

GREAT
POLAND

STOCK

ATLANTIC OCEAN

ENGLISH
CHANNEL

SPANISH
NETH.

Brussels
Cologne

Münster

MINOR
GERMAN STATES

Leipzig

SAXONY

SILESIA

Rouen

Trier

Mainz

Dresden

Breslau

Rennes

Paris

PALATINATE

Metz

BOHEMIA

MORAVIA

Orléans

LORRAINE

ALSACE

Strasbourg

BAVARIA

Augsburg

Prague

FRANCE

FRANCHE
COMTÉ

SWISS CANTONS

Vienna

Bordeaux

Lyons

SAVOY

REP. OF VENICE

HUN

La Coruña

PYRENEES

PIEDMONT

Milan

Parma

Venice

SLAVONIA

León

Montauban

Avignon

Genoa

BOSNIA

Oporto

NAVARRE

Valladolid

Marseilles

CATALONIA

Florence

TUSCANY

Zara

MONTENEGRO

PORTUGAL
(TO SPAIN
1580-1640)

Saragossa

ARAGON

Barcelona

CORSICA
(Genoa)

PAPAL
STATES

Be

Escorial Madrid

CASTILE

Rome

Aquila

ADRIATIC SEA

Lisbon

Toledo

Valencia

BALEARIC I.

Mérida

S P A I N

MINORCA

Bari

Seville

Murcia

MAJORCA

SARDINIA

Naples

NAPLES

Cadiz

Malaga

GIBRALTAR

MEDITERRANEAN

KINGDOM OF THE
TWO SICILIES

IC

Tangier
(Portugal)

Ceuta (Spain)

Palermo

Algiers

SICILY

Oran (Spain)

Tunis

SEA

MALTA (Spain)

FEZ AND MOROCCO

ALGERIA

TUNISIA

B A R B A R Y   S T A T E S

tress cities of Metz, Toul, and Verdun, and the province of Alsace except for the free city of Strasbourg. These former imperial territories gave both Sweden and France a vote in the Diet of the Holy Roman Empire and a say in German affairs. The complete independence of Switzerland and the Dutch Netherlands was officially recognized. The Austrian Hapsburgs retained their hereditary possessions but lost prestige as emperors of a disintegrating Holy Roman Empire. Also, their relative position declined as that of France rose. The Spanish Hapsburgs fared worse. After eleven more years of fighting with France they yielded a strip of the southern Netherlands and another strip along the Spanish border to France. Spain's days of greatness were finished.

The immediate effect of the Thirty Years' War on Germany was disastrous. For three decades hostile German and foreign armies had tramped back and forth across Germany, killing, raping, and looting the defenseless inhabitants. In the wake of Wallenstein's army of 50,000, for instance, swarmed 150,000 camp followers bent on plunder. To the usual horrors of war was added religious fanaticism. Many years would be required for Germany to recover from these wounds.

The Thirty Years' War was the last and the bloodiest of the religious wars that accompanied the Roman Catholic Reformation. Although there would still be much religious strife and controversy, the religious map of Europe henceforth would change very little. In a real sense, then, 1648 marked the end of the era of the Protestant and Roman Catholic reformations. The Roman Catholic Church, by closing ranks, setting its house in order, and availing itself of the militant Jesuit Society, had checked the further spread of Protestantism in Europe, but had been able to win back relatively little that had been lost. Western Christendom was now definitely split into two irreconcilable camps—Roman Catholic and Protestant. After 1648, political rather than religious affairs would occupy center stage in the Western world.

EUROPE 1648

Suggested Reading

General

*G. R. Elton, *Reformation Europe, 1517–1559* (Torch). Has excellent chapters on the Roman Catholic Reformation.

Index and Inquisition

R. Burke, *What Is the Index?* (1952). Gives the Roman Catholic position on censorship.

J. Plaidy, *The Spanish Inquisition, Its Rise, Growth, and End* (Citadel). Good survey.

The Jesuits

H. Boehmer, *The Jesuits,* trans. P. Strodach (1928). Standard survey.

P. Dudon, *St. Ignatius of Loyola* (1949). The best biography by a scholarly, objective Jesuit priest.

The Crusade of Philip II

*R. T. Davies, *The Golden Century of Spain* (Torch). Good survey.

*P. Geyl, *The Revolt of the Netherlands* (Barnes & Noble). Downplays the religious view.

*G. Mattingly, *The Armada* (Sentry). Brilliantly shows the impact of the Armada's failure on all of Europe.

Thirty Years' War

*C. V. Wedgwood, *The Thirty Years' War* (Anchor). The best single volume on the subject. Tries a bit too hard to minimize the war's destructiveness.

Sources

J. Waterworth, *History of the Council of Trent* (1948). Contains the canons and decrees of the council.

*E. M. Burns, *The Counter Reformation* (Anvil). Contains many interesting documents.

Retrospect During the fifteenth and sixteenth centuries, medieval civilization did not abruptly end and modern civilization begin. As a matter of fact, lords and ladies still exist in Western Europe; people still revel in the symbols and pageantry of chivalry; agriculture is still a necessary part of Western economy; and the Christian religion still holds the allegiance of millions. Nevertheless, the world of 1600 was very definitely not the world of 1400.

During these two centuries, the first four national states had come into being, shattering once and for all the theoretical political unity of Western Europe under the Holy Roman Empire and ending the actual independence of thousands of feudal fiefs by bringing them under the authority of the national monarchs.

The revival of commerce and the development of capitalist practices and institutions ended the monopoly of medieval Europe's agricultural economy and of the land-owning class, the nobility. The nobility now faced competition for influence from the new middle class—from merchants, bankers, lawyers. It is true that the bourgeoisie sought most of all to enter the ranks of the nobility, and did so whenever possible, and that the nobility held the upper hand politically and socially for two or three more centuries. But by 1600 class lines had become more fluid. European civilization was becoming more urban. Furthermore, much of the rest of the world had come under European economic and political domination.

Even in the fourteenth century, a secular trend in Western European literature and art could be observed. This turning (or returning) from the sacred, God-centered ideals of the Middle Ages to the secular, man-centered interests of the modern world accelerated during the fifteenth and sixteenth centuries. Western European man had become more self-centered, proud, versatile, and materialistic. These humanistic Renaissance qualities produced, as in ancient Greece and Rome, some of the world's greatest literature and art. They also laid the basis for an era of natural science.

Finally, by 1600 the Christian Church, which in 1400 still monopolized religious life and strongly influenced the intellectual, political, and economic life of Western Europe, was split asunder. This may have been the most important of all the developments that brought the medieval system to an end and ushered in the modern era, for nothing so characterized medieval civilization as the dominance of the Church. By 1600 the Western Christian world had become fragmented. On the other hand, the Protestant and Catholic Reformations revived interest in and allegiance to the Christian religion at a time when Western man appeared to be turning his attention to secularism, nationalism, and capitalistic enterprises. Although Christianty had lost its position of dominance, it continued as a major force in the modern world.

VIII

The Age of Royal Absolutism Seventeenth and Eighteenth Centuries

As we have seen, the kings of Spain, Portugal, France, and England gained the ascendancy over the feudal nobility in the late fifteenth century and welded the first four national states around their own persons. In the sixteenth century, Spain and Portugal were at the peak of their power and affluence. They acquired vast and lucrative colonial empires in the West and in the East. During the reigns of Charles V and Philip II, Spain was the dominant military power in Europe. After Philip's death in 1598, however, Spain's decline was as rapid as had been her rise a century earlier. Although her huge empire in the New World was still intact and although her greatest outpouring of literature and art was yet to come, her military and political power and influence were spent. Portugal's decline was equally precipitous. When in 1580 she was annexed to Spain, the Dutch, then fighting the Spanish for their independence, took advantage of Portugal's misfortune to seize the richest part of her Eastern empire. Although Portugal regained her independence in 1640, she never recovered her sixteenth-century wealth and influence.

The decline of Spain and Portugal left France in a favorable position to dominate Western Europe. Henry IV, the first of the Bourbon line of kings, who ascended the throne in 1589, brought the three decades of religious and political turmoil in France to an end. The Bourbon kings set out to make themselves supreme in France, and France supreme in Europe. In England royal absolutism had reached its peak during the sixteenth century under the vigorous Tudor dynasty. By the opening of the next century, Parliament was ready to challenge the royal authority—and the kings were the politically inept Stuarts. Meanwhile, the French, the English, and the Dutch were preparing to replace the Iberian nations as the leading commercial and colonial empire builders.

In Central and Eastern Europe two vigorous new dynasties—the Hohenzollerns of Prussia and the Romanovs of Russia—began to assert themselves. Their natural enemies were the Austrian Hapsburgs, the Ottoman Turks, the Poles, and the Swedes.

France was the dominant nation in Europe throughout most of the seventeenth and eighteenth centuries. Under Louis XIV royal absolutism not only reached its peak in France but also served as a model that all other monarchs sought to emulate. The well-lighted stage across which the "Sun King" strode was set for him by three able predecessors—Henry IV, Richelieu, and Mazarin.

1. THE RISE OF FRANCE UNDER HENRY IV, RICHELIEU, AND MAZARIN

When Henry IV became king of France in 1589, his country was torn from several decades of bitter religious war. Respect for law and order had broken down. The feudal nobility had in many cases reasserted its own authority. The finances of the central government were in chaos. Roads and bridges were in disrepair. French prestige abroad was at a low ebb; even the city of Paris was garrisoned by the Spanish troops of Philip II.

Henry of Navarre, the first of the Bourbon dynasty to rule France, set out to change all this. The new king, in his prime at the age of thirty-six, was debonair and witty, courageous, generous, optimistic, and democratic in his social life. His slogan, "A chicken in the pot of every peasant for Sunday dinner," was more than an idle phrase; it is little wonder that *Henri Quatre* became the most popular monarch in French history. The romantic Henry had in the Duke of Sully

33

THE DOMINANCE OF FRANCE:
THE AGE OF LOUIS XIV

an able, methodical administrator to serve and steady him. The most urgent task was to restore the authority of the central government. This he set out to do by vigorously suppressing brigandage and enforcing the law. The lesser nobility was brought to heel directly and quickly. The powerful nobility was dealt with more gingerly, but by the end of Henry's reign real headway had been made toward reducing the nobles to obedience to the central government.

Henry and Sully launched a comprehensive program of economic reconstruction. Agriculture and commerce benefited from the increased security of life and property, from the repair of roads, bridges, and harbors, and from the freeing of internal and external commerce of many obstructions and tariff barriers. Marshes were drained for farming. Better breeding methods were introduced. The peasants' livestock and implements were protected against seizure for debt or taxes. New industries producing glass, porcelain, lace, tapestries, and fine leather and textiles were subsidized and protected by the state. Silk culture, which brought vast wealth to France, was introduced. The building of France's overseas empire began in 1608 when Champlain founded Quebec, the first French colony in the New World.

When Henry IV came to the throne, only about one-fourth of the heavy taxes, from which the clergy and the nobility were largely exempted, ever reached the national treasury. The rest went into the pockets of corrupt officials and tax farmers, that is, the collectors who bid a fixed sum for the privilege of collecting the taxes and were permitted to keep anything over and above the contracted amount. Sully was unable to change this vicious system, but by means of careful bookkeeping, efficient administration of expenditures, and elimination of corruption, he was able to show a surplus for the first time in many years.

Another major achievement of Henry's reign was the granting of religious toleration to the Huguenot minority. Although Henry abjured Protestantism in order to gain acceptance as king of an overwhelmingly Roman Catholic nation, the sympathy and probably the faith of this former leader of the Huguenots remained with the Calvinist minority. The Edict of Nantes, which Henry IV issued in 1598, granted not only complete freedom of conscience and limited public worship to the Huguenots, but also civil and political equality. Moreover, they were given military control of some two hundred fortified cities and towns as a guarantee against future oppression. The Edict of Nantes stands as a monument in the bloody and endless struggle for religious freedom—one of the most precious possessions of civilized man. It antedates the work of Roger Williams in Rhode Island by thirty-eight years.

Having laid the foundations for royal supremacy, economic health, and religious toleration, Henry IV in the last years of his reign devoted an increasing amount of attention to foreign affairs.

He talked vaguely from time to time about a sort of league of nations for perpetual peace, but nothing came of it. His specific goal was to make France first secure and then supreme in Europe by weakening the power of the Spanish and Austrian Hapsburgs. In 1610 he readied his armies for a campaign, but just as he was preparing to join them he was assassinated by a fanatical Roman Catholic who doubted his orthodoxy.

After fourteen years of retrogression under Henry IV's Italian wife, Marie de Médicis, and their young and inept son Louis XIII, Cardinal Richelieu gained active control over the government of France. Although technically a mere servant of the fickle Louis XIII, the masterful cardinal made himself so indispensable that for eighteen years (1624–1642) he held firm control over French affairs. Handsome, arrogant, and calculating, Richelieu was a true Machiavellian. His twofold policy, from which he never veered, was to make the royal power supreme in France and France supreme in Europe.

Believing the high nobility and the Huguenots to be the chief threats to royal absolutism, Richelieu crushed them both. He boldly destroyed the castles of the nobles who remained defiant, disbanded their private armies, and hanged a number of the most recalcitrant. The special military and political privileges that the Huguenots enjoyed under the Edict of Nantes were considered by Richelieu to be intolerable, giving them the status of a state within a state. After a bloody two-year struggle, he stripped the Huguenots of these privileges, although he left their religious and civil liberties intact.

In order to by-pass all local political influence, which in some provinces was still strong, the dynamic minister divided France into some thirty administrative districts called *généralités*, each of which was placed under the control of an *intendant*,[1] who was an agent of the crown. So absolute was the power of the *intendants* over local affairs, even of the most minute nature, that they came to be called the "thirty tyrants of France." They were chosen from the ranks of the bourgeoisie and were shifted around frequently

lest they become too sympathetic with the people over whom they ruled. The royal will was thus extended to every part of France.

Although Richelieu was a cardinal in the Roman Catholic Church, he did not hesitate to plunge France into the Thirty Years' War in Germany on the side of the Protestants. His purpose, of course, was to weaken the Hapsburgs, chief rivals of the French Bourbons for European supremacy. As a result of Richelieu's intervention, Protestantism in Germany may have been saved from extermination, but the Hapsburgs were humiliated. When Richelieu died in 1642, he had gone far toward bringing to fruition Henry IV's policies of royal supremacy in France and French supremacy in Europe. Richelieu, however, did not share Henry IV's concern for the common people. Their lot became harder under the imperious and ruthless cardinal, at whose death they rejoiced.

Richelieu was succeeded by his protégé, Cardinal Mazarin. Louis XIII's death in 1643, one year after that of his great minister, left the throne to Louis XIV, a child of five. Mazarin played the same role in the early reign of Louis XIV that Richelieu had played during most of the reign of Louis XIII. From the death of Richelieu in 1642 until his own death in 1661, Mazarin vigorously pursued the policies of his predecessor. The Thirty Years' War was brought to a successful conclusion. All who challenged the crown's absolute authority were crushed.

Although the policies were the same, the methods of carrying them out were quite different. Whereas Richelieu was bold and forthright in dealing with even his most formidable enemies, the Italian-born Mazarin was treacherous, deceitful, and devious. The most noteworthy events during his administration were two uprisings, known as *Frondes*, against his tyranny. The Frondes were revolts of the disgruntled nobility, supported by various other rebellious elements, against the ever-increasing authority of the central government. At times it looked as if the rebels might succeed, but the crafty Mazarin was too much for them. The failure of the Frondes marked the last overt resistance to royal absolutism in France until the French Revolution in 1789. When Cardinal Mazarin died in 1661, he passed along to young Louis XIV a royal

---

[1] The *intendants* existed before Richelieu's time, but he greatly increased their power and functions.

power that was at last absolute and a national state that was easily the first power of Europe.

2. LOUIS XIV AND HIS GOVERNMENT

Louis XIV was twenty-three years of age when, in 1661, he stepped forth as the principal actor on the world's gaudiest stage. Young Louis was well fitted for the part. He had a sound body and a regal bearing. His lack of brilliance and of deep learning were more than offset by a large store of common sense, a sharp memory, a sense of responsibility, and a capacity for hard, tedious work. From his Spanish mother, from Mazarin, and from his tutors he had gained the conviction that he was God's appointed vicegerent for France. In Bishop Bossuet he had the most famous of all theorists and exponents of royal absolutism. Bossuet in numerous writings argued that absolute monarchy is the normal, the most efficient, and the divinely ordained form of government. Furthermore, the royal monarch, the image of God and directly inspired by God, is above human reproach and accountable to God alone. These ideas were the culmination of the thinking of James I of England a half century earlier (see the next chapter). As acted out by Louis, they gained and held the ascendancy throughout the continent of Europe (and far beyond it) during the late seventeenth and most of the eighteenth centuries.

Absolute though he might consider himself (the words *"L' état, c'est moi"* ["I am the state"] are often attributed to him), Louis could not possibly perform all the functions of government personally. Actually, the great bulk of the decisions and details of government were handled by a series of councils and bureaus, and administered locally by the *intendants*. The functions of the chief councils, such as those of state, finances, dispatches, and the privy council, appear on paper to have been overlapping and ill-defined. As supervised by the industrious Louis XIV, however, the administrative machinery worked smoothly and efficiently. In fact, it was the envy of his fellow monarchs and probably constituted his most constructive achievement. There was no semblance of popular participation in government. The role of the people was to serve and obey; in return, they enjoyed reflected glory and received such benefits as the monarch might be willing and able to bestow upon them. The Estates-General was not called once during the seventy-two years of Louis XIV's reign or the fifty-nine-year rule of his successor.

3. THE KING AND HIS COURT: VERSAILLES

In line with Louis XIV's concept of divine right absolutism, he believed that he should have a palace worthy of God's chief vicegerent on earth. Hating tumultuous Paris, congested and crowded with vulgar tradesmen, he selected Versailles, 11 miles southwest of the city, to be the new seat of government. There as many as thirty-five thousand workmen toiled for thirty years, turning the marshes and sandy wastes into the world's most splendid court. The cost was so staggering that Louis destroyed the records. The greatest artists in the land were employed in the creation of the palace and the grounds. The most costly marbles, glass, tapestries, paintings, and inlaid woods were used in profusion in the ornate Baroque style of the period. Hundreds of acres of gardens, parks, walks, canals, and artificial lakes were laid out with mathematical precision. Playing fountains and myriad marble statues formalized the landscape.

Around his court Louis XIV gathered the great nobles of France. Henry IV, Richelieu, and Mazarin had broken their power; Louis XIV turned them into court butterflies. The inevitable jostling for the king's attention, which was the one source of preferment, and the conflicting claims of so much titled rank necessitated the drawing up of an elaborate code of etiquette. The king was dressed and undressed, bathed, and fed by the highest noblemen in the land—all in strict ritual. The household personnel consisted of ten thousand soldiers in brilliant uniforms and four thousand civilians. Nor was the pageant of Versailles mere glitter alone. Louis XIV subsidized or gathered around himself the leading French artists and literary figures. Mansard the architect and Lebrun the painter were the chief designer and decorator, respectively, of the palace. Corneille, Racine, Moliére, La Fontaine, La Rochefoucauld, Saint-Simon, and Madame de

The Palace of Versailles. This chateau built by Louis XIV in the late seventeenth century was designed to be a palace fit for the greatest of all the absolute monarchs. The palace is so huge that no single view can show the whole structure and also the elaborate detail of the baroque style of architecture in which it was built. This frontal view of the center section reveals the detail. *Photo: Bettmann Archive*

Sévigné made Louis XIV's reign the golden age of French literature. (See Chapter 37.)

But there was a reverse side to the coin. Versailles was a showplace, not a comfortable home for the king. It was cold, drafty, and inconvenient. The balls, parades, hunts, and social ritual were not sufficient to absorb the energy of the vivacious and ambitious nobility of France. The court seethed with gossip, scandal, and intrigue. Nor did the hard-toiling, heavily taxed French masses, who were supposed to enjoy the reflected glory of the monarch, always appreciate such extravagant glamor. Indeed, there were increasing expressions of discontent.

4. COLBERT AND THE FRENCH ECONOMY

Louis XIV was fortunate to have at his command during the first half of his reign a prodigious financial manager. Jean Baptiste Colbert was an inordinately ambitious social climber who real-ized that, because of his bourgeois origin, his only means of advancement was through indispensable service to the king. An engine of efficiency, he toiled endlessly, supervising the countless details of the French economy.

Colbert's first and probably his most difficult task was to balance the national budget, which had become badly unbalanced under Richelieu and Mazarin. The careful accounting of receipts and expenditures that Sully had inaugurated three quarters of a century earlier was resumed. Some of the debts that the government had contracted at exorbitant rates of interest were canceled; on others the rates were reduced. Dishonest tax collectors were dismissed and punished.

With Colbert, mercantilism reached its peak. French industries were protected by prohibitive tariffs, while exports and new industries were subsidized. Raw materials, however, were strictly husbanded. Imperial and commercial activities in India and North America were vigorously promoted. It was at this time that Marquette, Joliet, and La Salle explored the Great Lakes and the Mississippi Valley for France. To protect this growing empire and the commerce with it, a large navy was built. But Colbert did not stop with these traditional mercantilist practices. In order to gain a world-wide reputation for the uniformly high quality of French products, all manufacturing was subjected to the most minute regulation and supervision. So many threads of such and such quality and color must go into every inch of this textile and that lace. A veritable army of inspectors enforced the regulations. This extreme phase of mercantilism, the economic adjunct to royal absolutism, has come to be called Colbertism. It achieved its immediate end so far as quality and reputation were concerned, but it stifled initiative and retarded future industrial development. That Colbert was able to balance the budget and achieve general economic prosperity in the face of Louis XIV's lavish expenditures, including the building of Versailles, was a remarkable feat. It is well, however, that Colbert died in 1683, for Louis' wars of aggression eventually wrecked most of the great minister's work. With the exception of the Netherlands, practically all of Europe copied Colbert's policies and techniques during the latter part of the seventeenth and most of the eighteenth centuries.

5. ABSOLUTISM AND RELIGION

It was virtually inevitable that Louis XIV's concepts of divine right monarchy would have religious repercussions. First of all, they ran counter to the claims of the pope. All his life Louis considered himself to be devoutly loyal to the Roman Catholic faith, as were the majority of his subjects. But when it came to matters of church administration Louis was not willing to have his royal authority limited, even by Rome. Numerous conflicts between king and pope led to the calling of a great council of the French clergy in 1682. This council, under the domination of Bishop Bossuet, faithful servant of Louis XIV and famed exponent of the theory of royal absolutism, drew up a statement of Gallican Liberties, special privileges or freedoms of the French church from Roman domination. These were in essence: (1) A church council is superior to the pope. (2) The pope's jurisdiction is supreme only in matters of faith and morals, and his rulings even here are applicable in France only after they have been accepted by the French clergy. (3) The traditional customs and practices of the French church shall be respected. The Gallican Liberties brought the French church to a position close to that of the English church under Henry VIII. They might even have led to eventu-

al separation from Rome had not Louis XIV in later life fallen increasingly under the influence of the Jesuits and his pious mistress, Madame de Maintenon, who were able to rekindle his loyalty to the pope.

Louis' absolutism also ran afoul of the Jansenists, so called because they were followers of a Belgian bishop, Cornelius Jansen. This group represented a Puritan movement within the Roman Catholic Church. The Jansenists had no intention of breaking away from the Church, to which they considered themselves entirely loyal. It was their wish to return to the teachings and practices of the Church in the days of St. Augustine. They emphasized predestination, inner piety, and the ascetic life. A number of intellectuals and people of means were attracted to their ranks, including the dramatist Racine and the mathematician and philosopher Blaise Pascal. At Port Royal near Versailles a group of prominent Jansenists practiced a communal life and established an excellent school that attracted much favorable attention. It was probably fear for the reputation of their own schools that aroused the jealousy of the Jesuits, militant watchdogs over Roman Catholic orthodoxy and papal supremacy. After a long and bitter controversy, the pope was persuaded to declare Jansenism heretical, though no bill of particulars was ever presented. Eventually the Jesuits also aroused against the Jansenists the animosity of Louis XIV, who could tolerate no deviation from his own views even in matters of religion. He outlawed the sect and destroyed its buildings. But he was unable to destroy Jansenism itself, which has continued to exist to the present time.

The chief religious victims of Louis XIV's absolutism were the Huguenots. Ever since Richelieu had removed the military and political privileges they had enjoyed under the Edict of Nantes, the Huguenots had lived quietly as good French citizens, clinging unobtrusively to their Protestant faith. Although the Huguenots numbered not more than one-tenth of the total population of France, many of them were industrious, prosperous, and educated members of the middle class. The Jesuits had little difficulty kindling the ire of Louis XIV against these heretical subjects who had the audacity to consider the king's religion not good enough for themselves. The

Huguenots were subjected to one of the cruelest persecutions in the bloody history of religious intolerance. Barbarous regular army troops were quartered in Huguenot homes and instructed to live licentiously. Students familiar only with twentieth-century civilian armies will need to reflect a little to realize the significance of this move. Whole Huguenot communities would abjure their faith at the approach of the troops. Finally, in 1685 the Edict of Nantes was revoked and the Protestant religion outlawed. Although Huguenots were forbidden to emigrate, many—probably a quarter million—succeeded in doing so, taking much of their wealth and all their economic knowledge and skills with them. Not only were these industrious citizens, the backbone of French commercial and industrial life, lost to France, but they greatly strengthened some of France's rivals and enemies, such as England, the Dutch Netherlands, and Brandenburg, who welcomed them. Forbidden to enter the underpopulated French colonies, many Huguenots helped to people the English colonies in America.

6. LOUIS XIV'S WARS OF AGGRESSION

The Sun King was not content to rule the world's most powerful nation. France was not big enough to satisfy his vanity, ever inflated by the constant flattery of his courtiers. He coveted a wider domain. Louis' immediate and expressed goal was to extend his rule to France's natural frontiers. Since the French boundaries were already delimited by mountains and sea on every side but the northeast, it was in that direction that Louis looked for expansion. He claimed that only the Rhine River would provide France with an adequate natural strategic boundary on that side. This was, of course, pure fiction. River valleys unite rather than separate people; nor have rivers ever proved to be effective military barriers. A glance at the map (p. 000) will quickly reveal that an advance to the Rhine would involve France in war with most of Europe. Between the French frontier and the Rhine lay the Spanish Netherlands, much of the Dutch Netherlands, imperial territory belonging to the Austrian Hapsburgs, and many German states. England, too, would be threatened, and the balance of power upset. But Louis felt himself equal to the task of defeating these powers.

Louis' war minister, Louvois, is often considered the father of modern militarism. Louvois organized France's huge military establishment on a scientific and businesslike basis, replete with supply depots and hospitals. He introduced strict discipline, uniforms, and marching drill. Louis had other distinguished military aides. Vauban was one of the great designers of fortifications and of siege operations. It was a common saying that a city defended by Vauban was safe and that a city besieged by Vauban was doomed. Condé was an able and dashing military leader, and Turenne a masterly planner of campaigns and battles.

During the last four decades of his seventy-two-year reign Louis XIV fought four wars of aggression. In 1667 he unceremoniously sent French armies in to conquer the Spanish (Belgian) Netherlands. Spanish power had declined rapidly since the sixteenth century, and Louis' armies captured one fortress city after another. The Dutch, however, took alarm and formed an alliance with England and Sweden to check the French menace. This array of power in addition to Spain caused Louis to accept a peace that granted him only a slice of the Spanish Netherlands.

The frustrated Grand Monarch determined to punish the upstart prosperous Dutch. He sent huge French armies into the Netherlands. The cause of the Dutch seemed hopeless, and in desperation they opened their dikes. Large portions of their land were flooded, but the French were held at bay. Meanwhile, the power of France frightened Spain, the Holy Roman Emperor, Brandenburg, and several small German states into joining the Dutch in alliance. Louis XIV won many victories over the allies, but when the English Parliament forced Charles II to break his agreement with the French king and join the alliance against him, Louis XIV decided to make peace. Again hapless Spain was the loser, giving up to France the long-coveted Franche-Comté (free county of Burgundy) and another strip of the Spanish Netherlands.

At the end of the Dutch War (1678) Louis XIV stood at the peak of his power. He had defeated all the greatest military powers on the Western European continent and had gained valuable territories. But the tide was about to turn. Turenne was killed near the end of the Dutch War, and the aged Condé retired at the end of war. No comparable generals were found to replace them. Colbert's hard-won surplus and balanced budget were now things of the past, and France's economy was suffering. All Europe had become alarmed by the French aggression. Louis XIV, however, was not statesman enough to perceive the realities of the present. His ever-growing appetite for power was hardly whetted.

No sooner had the Dutch War ended than Louis began trumping up claims to various territories in Alsace and Lorraine and sending in his armed forces to occupy them. The result was another defensive alliance against Louis composed of the Dutch Netherlands, Spain, Sweden, the Holy Roman Emperor, and a number of small German states. The heart of the alliance was William of Orange, stadholder of Holland, and when the redoubtable Dutchman became King William III of England after the Glorious Revolution of 1688, England, too, was brought into alliance against Louis. The alliance was

THE WARS OF LOUIS XIV

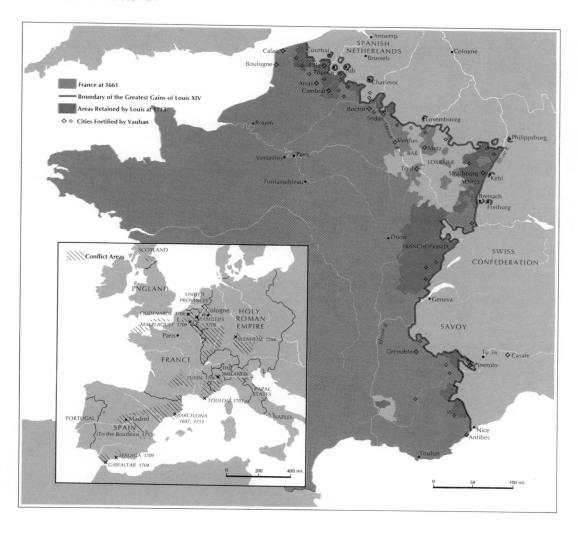

called the League of Augsburg. After nine years of fruitless struggle, Louis accepted a peace giving him only the city of Strasbourg.

But the Sun King, still blinded by pride and greed, was not about to give up. He persuaded the last monarch of the Hapsburg line in Spain just before he died in 1700 to choose one of Louis' grandsons as king. The prospect of Spain and the Spanish Empire joined to the already inordinately powerful French monarchy frightened the other powers of Western Europe into once more forming an alliance against France. This alliance, known as the Grand Alliance, was also engineered by William III; it consisted of England, the Dutch Netherlands, Austria, Brandenburg, several small German states, Savoy, and Portugal. The ensuing War of the Spanish Succession lasted eleven years (1702–1713) and surpassed all previous wars in modern times in destructiveness. The allies, led by the brilliant duke of Marlborough (John Churchill, a direct forebear of Winston Churchill), administered to the French and Spanish armies a series of severe defeats. In 1713 Louis XIV, beaten and exhausted, was forced to accept the Treaty of Utrecht. Although Louis' grandson was permitted to retain the Spanish throne, France yielded Newfoundland, Nova Scotia, and Hudson Bay to Great Britain.[2] Spain gave up Gibraltar and Minorca to Great Britain, and ceded the Belgian Netherlands, Naples, Sardinia, and Milan to Austria. The duke of Savoy received the title of king and the Spanish island of Sicily (which he later exchanged with Austria for Sardinia). The Hohenzollern margrave of Brandenburg was granted the title "king in Prussia," and henceforth his state was called Prussia. Thus the houses of Savoy and Hohenzollern, which later were to create the Italian and the German nations, respectively, added greatly to their prestige. France was somewhat humbled. She was beginning to lose ground overseas to Great Britain, and in Europe she had been halted short of the Rhine. But she was still the most powerful single nation in Europe.

Louis XIV lived only two years after the signing of the Treaty of Utrecht. He had long outlived his popularity. As the body of the grandest of all the absolute monarchs was drawn through the streets of Paris, some of his abused people cursed in the taverns as the coffin passed. A faint scent of revolution was already in the air.

---

[2]The term *Great Britain* replaced the term *England* in 1707 when England and Scotland were united.

Suggested Reading

General
*G. N. Clark, *The Seventeenth Century* (Galaxy). Good brief survey, emphasizing cultural aspects.
*J. B. Wolf, *Emergence of the Great Powers, 1685–1715* (Torch). Scholarly volume in Rise of Modern Europe series.

Rise of France Under Henry IV, Richelieu, and Mazarin
P. F. Willert, *Henry of Navarre* (1902). Still the best biography of Henry IV.
*C. V. Wedgwood, *Richelieu and the French Monarchy* (Collier). Brief but sound.

Louis XIV and His Court
*W. H. Lewis, *The Splendid Century* (Anchor). Very well written.
*J. B. Wolf, *Louis XIV* (Norton). Supersedes all other biographies of Louis XIV.

Religious Affairs
A. J. Grant, *The Huguenots* (1934). Brief and readable.

Sources
*L. R. Saint-Simon, *The Memoirs of the Duc de Saint-Simon* (Macmillan). A disgruntled courtier's detailed eyewitness account of Versailles under Louis XIV.
Marie de Sévigné, *Letters from Madame la Marquise de Sévigné*, ed. and trans. Violet Hammersley (1956). Charmingly written eyewitness account of life at Versailles.

Historical Fiction
*Alexandre Dumas, *The Three Musketeers* (Penguin). Famous novel depicting French life at the time of Richelieu.
Francis Steegmuller, *The Grand Mademoiselle* (1956). Novel about the richest woman in Europe and cousin of Louis XIV. Based upon excellent historical research.

The Dutch Netherlands in the Seventeenth Century

One of the most remarkable phenomena of early modern history was the spectacular achievements of the Dutch Netherlands, sometimes erroneously called Holland. This tiny nation of approximately one million people living for the most part on islands, peninsulas, and land reclaimed from the sea, with a total area a little larger than the state of Maryland, was the commercial, financial, intellectual, and artistic capital of the Western world throughout most of the seventeenth century. It was also the freest and the most democratic country in the world.

The Dutch Republic—or the United Provinces as they were called in the seventeenth century—came into being during the revolt of the Netherlands (low lands) against Spain (1566–1609). Although the ten southern provinces (now Belgium) were conquered by Spain, the seven northern (Dutch) provinces, taking advantage of their geography, their large and skillful navy, and the excellent leadership of William of Orange and his sons, fought stubbornly on to victory against the world's mightiest military power. Far from being exhausted by the long uphill struggle, the Dutch now exhibited an enormous outburst of energy and confidence. The seven provinces were largely self-governing, held together only by a common language and purpose, a rather weak states general, and in time of danger by the leadership of the house of Orange. The province of Holland, where most of the great cities were located, was essentially a merchant oligarchy. The Reformed (Calvinist) Church was established as the state church, but religious minorities such as the Roman Catholics, who constituted about a third of the population, and Jews were treated with tolerance. As a result some of the greatest intellects of Europe found refuge in the United Provinces and contributed to their intellectual vigor. Notable examples are René Descartes from France, John Locke from England, and Baruch Spinoza, whose Jewish family had fled religious persecution in Portugal. A free press enabled the Dutch Netherlands to become the world's chief publisher of books.

But the Dutch during the seventeenth century were producing an impressive array of writers, artists, and scientists of their own. Hugo Grotius' *On the Law of War and Peace* was the first great treatise on international law and has remained a classic on the subject ever since. Joost van den Vondel was the greatest of all Dutch poets. His epic poem *Lucifer* is believed to have served as a model for Milton's *Paradise Lost*. This was the golden age of Dutch painters. While the baroque painters in other countries were glorifying the royalty and the nobility, Jan Vermeer, Franz Hals, and, above all, Rembrandt van Rijn were revealing the true nature of Dutch society by dignifying—sometimes glamorizing—the middle and lower classes. Dutch scientists invented the telescope and the microscope. The first great microscopist, Anton van Leeuwenhoek, discovered blood corpuscles, the cellular structure of living tissue, and bacteria (two hundred years before Pasteur learned how to combat them). The most renowned scientist of the Western world in the seventeenth century was Christian Huygens. Among other things he invented the pendulum clock, man's first means of accurately measuring short intervals of time, and introduced the wave theory of light.

Of all the achievements of the little Dutch Republic during the seventeenth century it was her economic supremacy that most dazzled the rest of the world. The seafaring economy of the Dutch was founded upon the fishing industry. In the fourteenth century the herring had migrated to the waters north of the Netherlands and the Dutch had discovered a secret formula for preserving them. By the time of their revolt from Spain their fishing activities employed some twelve thousand ships and one hundred fifty thousand people. Their experienced sailors played a vital role in the struggle for independence. At the start of the seventeenth century most of the carrying trade of Europe was by the broad-bellied Dutch ships, and Dutch shipyards built more ships than all the other shipyards in Europe combined. During their war for independence the Dutch had taken advantage of Portugal's temporary annexation by Spain to seize Portugal's vast and lucrative Eastern empire. Throughout the seventeenth century the Dutch East India Company, which monopolized this trade, paid annual dividends of up to 200 and 300 percent. Amsterdam replaced Antwerp (in Spanish Netherlands) as the world's busiest port and financial center.

Such wealth, of course, excited the envy of the United Provinces' larger neighbors. But it required several decades of all-out fighting by Louis XIV's France by land and Cromwellian and Stuart England by sea to break the power of the Dutch, near the end of the seventeenth century. Even then, Amsterdam remained Europe's financial capital for another hundred years.

How can we account for such a phenomenon? Was it merely a matter of geography? Does Calvinism promote democracy and education as its founder believed? Does the smallness of a state incite its citizens to greater loyalty and participation? Does the challenge of the sea work its wonders as appears to be the case in ancient Athens, Renaissance Venice, and modern Britain and Japan?

34

THE CLIMAX AND DECLINE OF ABSOLUTISM IN ENGLAND

While Henry IV, Richelieu, Mazarin, and the Sun King perfected royal absolutism in France and set an example for other Continental powers, a world-shaking drama was played out in England. A revolution occurred that established a pattern of limited monarchy that strongly influenced later struggles against absolutism in many parts of the world. That same constitutional struggle also strengthened England's position as one of the great powers of the world.

1. TUDOR ABSOLUTISM

Royal absolutism reached its pinnacle in England during the Tudor period (1485–1603). We have already reviewed the methods of government practiced by Henry VII, Henry VIII, and Elizabeth I to control the political, economic, religious, and cultural destiny of their tight little island (see p. 306).

It is well to recall, however, that Tudor absolutism demanded a tremendous amount of political skill on the part of the rulers. This was particularly so because England had inherited from the Middle Ages a tradition of limitations on royal power. These limitations had taken shape in two highly significant institutions: Parliament and the common law. The great Tudor monarchs had carefully avoided assaulting these institutions openly. Instead they worked with infinite patience and skill to get around the restrictions these institutions might have imposed. For instance, Parliament was consulted

whenever any important and controversial legislation needed to be enacted. By personal persuasion, bribery, skillfully applied compulsion, and patronage the Tudors always managed to get Parliament to do exactly what they wanted. A good part of Tudor success sprang from the fact that their ideas for the good of England happily coincided with the interests of their subjects. Internal peace, religious reform, success in foreign wars were all popular; Englishmen did not think too seriously about how these goals were achieved.

As the Tudor period neared its end, however, there were increasing signs of tension, discontent, and change. Parliament was restive under royal manipulation; many of its leaders were acutely aware that they were being managed. The general consensus which had once approved religious change was giving way to a realization that the initial changes involved in the Tudor reformation had engendered deep-seated differences on religious issues. Especially significant was the growing number of Puritans who believed that the newly established Church of England needed further purification. New economic interests, bent on profit seeking and capitalistic modes of exploitation, were advancing rapidly in the prosperous setting of Tudor England. Most notable was the new country gentry, whose control of land and vigorous economic activity permitted them to replace the old medieval aristocracy as the dominant element in England. This group was impatient with the ancient feudal restraints that still surrounded economic and political life. Equally aggressive and anxious for a larger voice were the burgeoning commercial interests, eager for England to take a more aggressive position in developing overseas trade and in supporting policies that would promote commercial activities at home. Finally, the lessening of the Spanish threat after 1588 removed a unifying bond among Englishmen and reduced their dependence on the crown as the protector of the realm. A major change was in the making in England as the seventeenth century opened.

2. THE FIRST STUARTS (1603–1649)

Despite mounting problems, "Good Queen Bess" ended her reign a beloved ruler. Because there were no immediate heirs, the throne fell to a cousin, James Stuart, king of Scotland. James I (1603–1625) came to England with definite ideas about the royal office; he was a convinced absolutist, believing that God had set him on the English throne with full authority to do as he pleased. Not only did he openly claim absolute power, but he was quick to make an issue of the matter whenever anyone challenged him. But he was woefully ignorant of political realities in England. He gave no evidence that he realized the intricate maneuvering, the hard work, and the many compromises that the Tudors had devoted to the task of making royal power a reality. The combination of rigid absolutist convictions and political ineptitude on the part of the king led to a polarization of political forces in England and to the elevation of practical issues to the realm of principle.

James I began his reign by alienating the Puritans, who had had great hope for sympathetic treatment because the new king had been ruler of Presbyterian Scotland. In fact, James was an avowed Anglican, not inclined to bend any longer before what he considered to be religious radicals. When the Puritans confronted him with their demands, he threatened to harry them out of the country if they did not abide by the regulations of the Church of England. The Puritans were made more desperate by his refusal to become involved in the Thirty Years' War, a policy that appeared to abandon the cause of Protestantism at a moment when its fate was threatened in all of Europe by resurgent Catholic forces. James further aroused religious fears and outraged patriotic sentiments by making peace with Spain, that bastion of Catholic strength which within the memory of men had tried to invade England. As a practitioner of autocratic government, James was a failure. He surrounded himself with incompetent wastrels as councillors and permitted the royal administrative machinery to become ridden with corruption. His constant need for money forced him to turn to Parliament, but he grew angry at parliamentary criticisms of his policies, his conduct, and his advisers. His encounters with Parliament usually ended with its dismissal, and caused many to feel that the king refused to abide by ancient constitutional customs. Without grants of money from Parliament, James turned to means of raising funds that were viewed as illegal. When the courts declared as much, James retaliated by dismissing judges, further confirming the belief that he refused to respect the constitution and the law.

Perhaps the decisive development of James' reign was the tendency for these disagreements and discontents to focus in Parliament, especially in the House of Commons. Theoretically representing all Englishmen, the House of Commons was dominated by well-to-do country gentry, lawyers, and businessmen. On the whole, these men were patriotic, religious, conservative men who seem to have had no idea of triggering a revolution. But they were also men of political experience, intent on sharing with the king the governance of England because they believed that this was the nature of the "constitution." James could not accept the outrageous idea that his power must be shared; each of his acts dramatized his aversion to ancient custom and confirmed the growing opinion that he was defying the established order. As a consequence, his reign was marked by repeated confrontations between crown and Parliament into which religious, administrative, financial, foreign policy, and class issues began to enter.

Under James' successor, Charles I (1625–1649), the conflict developed into civil war.

Charles I was one of a large number of kings in history whose inflexibility and incompetence have precipitated revolution. During the first years of his reign he was forced to summon several Parliaments because of his financial needs, only to dismiss them for demanding that he alter his policy or dismiss his detested advisers. Royal efforts to raise money without parliamentary consent led to new clashes with the courts and the alienation of those upon whom the illegal levies fell. A blundering foreign policy resulted in costly wars but no victories. The sharpening antagonisms led the leaders of Parliament to frame the Petition of Right, which was presented to the king in a session of Parliament he summoned in 1628 in order to raise money. This bold document charged that Charles had acted illegally by imposing martial law in peacetime, taxing arbitrarily, imprisoning citizens without trial, and quartering soldiers with private citizens. It clearly posited the principle upon which Parliament was ready to stand: that even the king must be bound by the law. Desperate for money, Charles accepted the Petition of Right, perhaps without realizing its implications for his autocratic concepts. But when the next Parliament, meeting in 1629, renewed the demand that the Petition be respected, he dissolved it over the bitter protests of its leaders.

For eleven years Charles ruled without Parliament. His opposition was temporarily neutralized, having been deprived of its chief means of exerting pressure on the king. For this respite Charles paid a heavy price and earned a growing circle of enemies, chiefly because of the financial exactions he was forced to impose on his subjects without the approval of Parliament and often in opposition to the courts. Ultimately, however, it was his religious policy that defeated Charles' efforts to rule as an absolute monarch. Under the guidance of his chief adviser, William Laud, archbishop of Canterbury, the royal government mounted a concerted effort to force a rigid Anglicanism on the entire realm. This policy was especially detestable to the Puritans of all persuasions; many of them sought refuge in the New World in hope of finding religious freedom. Even many Anglicans resented Laud's policies, which seemed to

them to smack too much of Roman Catholicism. It was the Scotch Presbyterians who finally faced the challenge directly and precipitated a crisis. In 1639 they revolted against Laud's effort to make them Anglican. Charles had to have money to resist them; the only place to get it was from Parliament. So in 1640 he called a new Parliament.

The first Parliament of 1640, called the Short Parliament, lasted only three weeks. Its leaders angered the king by their threats against his policy, and so the king dissolved it. However, as the Scots continued to press, Charles had to abandon the hope of ruling without Parliament. He summoned the so-called Long Parliament. Once seated, the Long Parliament proceeded to legislate an end to Stuart absolutism. It forced Charles to sacrifice his chief ministers, including Laud. It abolished all the extraordinary courts, including the Star Chamber and the Court of High Commission, which had long been tools with which absolutist kings had dodged the common law. An act was passed requiring the king to call Parliament every three years and curbing his power to dismiss Parliament. Severe limits were imposed on royal taxing power unless Parliament was consulted. To all these assaults on his concept of royal government Charles acceded, chiefly because he realized the inability of his government to face the rebellious Scots without the money which only Parliament could supply.

Up to this point, Parliament had succeeded brilliantly in legislating what amounted to a bloodless revolution. Yet its success did not stay a rapid drift toward more extreme measures. The past record of the Stuarts did not inspire great trust among parliamentary leaders that Charles would respect the new style of government. More significant was a rising spirit of extremism among some elements of Parliament, fed chiefly by religious radicals. These extremists not only became more violent in their assault on monarchy, but they moved rapidly to end Anglicanism "root and branch" in favor of some form of Puritanism. This mounting radicalism cooled the ardor of many influential men who had previously supported the limitation of royal power and drove them toward support of Charles as the symbol of the established order. The division in the parliamentary ranks caused the king to try to restore his control; he went so far in early 1642 as to seek to arrest the leaders of Parliament as a means of ending their meddling in matters that were the royal prerogative. His action was a call to arms, a challenge perhaps not unwelcome to the elements of English society that had for a generation been resisting royal absolutism in all its forms.

Historians have long debated the causes of England's descent into civil war. Some have argued that the issue was a clash between two political philosophies: autocracy versus parliamentary government. Others have seen the issue in terms of the blind, stupid blunders of men in power. Still others are convinced that the struggle was basically religious—an attempt to carry the Reformation beyond the Tudor settlement. Of great vogue in recent years has been the view that the civil war was the political side of an economic revolution which involved the transformation of England from a feudal, agricultural society into a capitalistic, commercial society; the outbreak of armed conflict in 1642 simply marked the final chapter in the effort of the new landed gentry and the commercial class to seize political power to match their economic supremacy. All these issues were involved; yet in the final analysis, the struggle that began in 1642 is best understood as a clash between elements of a ruling class which had lost its community of interest, so long centered in the king.

3. THE CIVIL WAR (1642–1649)

The lines of division that marked the opening of the civil war have not yet been clearly defined. Charles represented himself as the champion of the established order against the political and religious radicals in Parliament. His position won him a considerable following, soon known as Cavaliers, from many elements in society. The backbone of his support came from the great noble families and their extensive clientele and from the country gentry living in the more economically backward areas of northern and western England. The opposition, called the Roundheads, proclaimed their cause as liberty from tyranny, protection of the law, and the safe-guarding of the principles of Protestantism. Roundhead support came from lawyers, the gentry of the south and the east, and the commercial interests; great numbers of these groups were Puritans. To this core was soon joined radical elements from the poor and the oppressed, especially those living in London. Into the intricate matter of choosing sides went a complex array of personal elements—family ties, friendship, personal loyalties, and so forth—much after the fashion of the American Civil War.

The first phase of the war lasted through 1646. In the beginning neither side was prepared militarily, but the royal forces had the upper hand for the moment. Some initial defeats did not, however, deter the Roundheads. The navy sided with them. More significantly, they controlled the richest part of England, including London. And they were in possession of the regular organs of administration, which gave them the great advantage of being able to vote and collect money. In 1643 the Roundhead cause was bolstered by an alliance with the Scots that brought Scottish military forces into the struggle against the king in return for the establishment of Presbyterianism as the religious system for England and Scotland. But Scottish support was not decisive; the outcome of the war ultimately hinged on the ability of the Roundheads to create an effective army. The chief architect of the victorious army was Oliver Cromwell. A farmer with strong Puritan convictions, Cromwell organized a cavalry regiment of disciplined, deeply religious recruits who proved more than a match for the Cavalier forces they faced. His ideas were soon applied to the entire Roundhead force. The result was the New Model Army, made up of selected troops paid and equipped in a businesslike fashion. Upon this force was imposed a strict discipline, strongly colored by Puritan ideas of godliness and sobriety. The New Model Army was deeply imbued with enthusiasm for the Puritan cause. It quickly proved itself superior to the Cavalier army; by 1646 Charles' forces were crushed, and the king himself surrendered to the Scots.

With victory in their grasp, the Roundheads split into factions. The events of the war tended to transfer Roundhead leadership from fairly

This contemporary cartoon satirizes the conflict between Cavaliers and Roundheads, between royal absolutism and parliamentary government, that led to civil war, the execution of the king (Charles I), and eleven years of experimentation in governing England without a king. *Photo: Historical Pictures Service, Chicago*

moderate parliamentarians with a leaning toward Presbyterianism and a willingness to accept limited monarchy to more radical leaders strongly devoted to religious independence and the abolition of the state church. These radicals were centered in the New Model Army, which was the decisive source of power. Religious radicalism nourished political radicalism in the New Model Army, where there was an increasing clamor for more democratic elections, the abolition of monarchy, and the redistribution of property. Fearful that the radicals would assume complete control, the moderate group turned back toward the king, who suddenly discovered considerable enthusiasm for parliamentarianism and Presbyterianism now that the path seemed opened for his return to power. The Independents, with Cromwell in firm control, ended Charles' hope in a single battle in 1648. Convinced of the righteousness of his cause and backed by the victorious New Model Army, Cromwell acted swiftly to ensure the position of the Independents. He forceably purged the Long Parliament of all members not dedicated to his cause, and gave to the so-called Rump Parliament chief authority in the land. The Rump Parliament immediately legislated out of existence the Anglican Church, the House of Lords, and the monarchy. More momentous was the decision to try Charles for treason. Chiefly at Cromwell's urging, the king was judged "a tyrant, traitor, and murderer" and beheaded in 1649, a culmination of the civil war that shocked many Englishmen who had little love for the king but had not contemplated an England without a king.

Olver ſeeking God while the K.
is murthered by his order.

The deep religious fervor of the Puritans and the taint of regicide that lingered throughout the Commonwealth and the Protectorate are satirized here as Oliver Cromwell is shown at prayer while Charles I is being executed. *Photo: NYPL Picture Collection*

4. EXPERIMENTATION IN GOVERNMENT: COMMONWEALTH AND PROTECTORATE (1649–1660)

For eleven years after Charles I's death, Cromwell's forces sought to rule England without a king, experimenting desperately but unsuccessfully to establish a stable order. From the beginning, the Cromwellians represented a minority, and they never gained additional support. Their main strength was concentrated in the army, a fact that was destined to make many Englishmen suspicious.

The first experiment centered around establishing a republican form of government called the Commonwealth. A one-house Parliament was made the supreme authority. It was to be aided by a council of state made up of about forty men who were charged with conducting the daily affairs of government. The men who dominated the Commonwealth were far from radical; in fact, one of their first decisive acts was to silence the ever-more strident voices of the political and religious extremists in the army. Led by Cromwell, the Commonwealth government optimistically began the onerous tasks of reestablishing order and prosperity in England. In different circumstances, Cromwell's policies might have won approval. Somewhat unexpectedly, he showed considerable toleration toward all varieties of Protestantism. He sent his armies into Ireland to crush a long-festering rebellion with such ferocity that the Irish never forgave him. Scotland was likewise brought under firm English control. An aggressive foreign policy, aimed at promoting English commercial and colonial interests, was undertaken. Navigation acts were passed to ensure that trade in England's emerging empire would be monopolized by England. War was waged on the Dutch, and to some extent, England's commercial position vis-à-vis her chief rival was improved. None of these policies, however, helped to popularize the Commonwealth; resistance and criticism grew steadily. The Cromwellian faction never escaped the charge of being regicides, nor were their puritanical religious ideas acceptable to more than a small minority of Englishmen.

Cromwell blamed much of the trouble on what he considered the self-seeking leaders of the Rump Parliament. With characteristic vigor and self-righteousness, he dissolved the Rump by force in 1653. The army and its officers were now completely in power. Cromwell tried appointing a Parliament to lead the Commonwealth. This hand-picked body (called Barebones Parliament in honor of Praise-God Barebones, the first name on the roll) failed to distinguish itself except by a series of extremely radical proposals and was likewise dissolved before the end of 1653. Now even the instrument that had originally stood against tyranny was gone. The tide of revolution had peaked.

Left in complete power, Cromwell and his friends then produced a written constitution entrusting power to a protector. The protector was to be advised by a council and guided by a one-house Parliament elected by property holders from districts of approximately equal population. Cromwell became the first protector late in 1653. When the new Parliament met in 1654 and began to criticize the protector, Cromwell dismissed it. Thereafter he assumed the role of virtual dictator. Although he called later Parliaments, he seldom heeded their advice. He repeatedly found that the Parliaments he called reflected political and religious concepts that ran contrary to the convictions of those who alone could sustain him in power, the "godly" men of the New Model Army. Despite his realization that civilian control of the state alone would assure stability, Cromwell was forced to rely on the army.

To curb disorder, he imposed martial law on England, and placed army officers in full authority in several areas. The rule of these puritanical soldiers was detested by most Englishmen, and so was the man responsible for their actions. Opinion began to run in favor of a restoration of monarchy. In 1657 a majority of the members of Parliament asked Cromwell to become king. Although he refused this honor, he did agree to changes in the constitution that made him protector for life. When he died in 1658, Cromwell had approached as nearly as possible to being king of England without having the formal title. The wheel had come almost full circle since the day Cromwell and his soldiers thought that they had abolished monarchy by executing Charles I.

Perhaps no figure in England's history has caused more debate than Oliver Cromwell. He has been called everything from a religious bigot and bloody tyrant to a champion of democracy. No simple description will ever fit him. Unquestionably, he was a man of great talent, especially capable in warfare and administration. He was driven by strong religious compulsions that made him feel that whatever he did was godly;

he felt obligated to purify Englishmen of those things he considered sinful—gambling, drinking, swearing, ostentatious living, enjoying themselves on Sunday, and staying away from church services. Yet, a tolerant man by the standards of his day, he favored a religious settlement that would allow broad freedom to many groups. Although he frequently resorted to force as a means of solving his problems, he believed in parliamentary government and tried until his dying day to establish it. Certainly England has had few greater patriots. Seldom did Cromwell do anything for his personal gain; his life was lived for England. His failure was largely due to the fact that only a minority of Englishmen were willing to accept Puritanism and republicanism.

At Cromwell's death his son, Richard, became lord protector. This weak figure was soon swept aside by more powerful forces. By 1660 elements of Cromwell's army, backed by considerable segments of the men of property and influence in the realm, brought pressure to bear for restoration of the Stuarts as rulers of England. A new Parliament was elected and negotiations were opened with Charles Stuart, the son of Charles I. By May 1660 all parties were satisfied, and Charles appeared in London in triumph, greeted by a happy people tired of Puritanism and radicalism.

5. THE RESTORATION (1660–1688)

The Restoration of the Stuarts left unresolved the great questions that had been so bitterly fought over since 1603. Neither king nor Parliament had established its supremacy. Religious division had not been wiped out, nor had any principle of toleration been discovered. For twenty-eight years after 1660 these problems continued to disturb England. However, the struggles of the Restoration era proved to be more moderate. Most Englishmen had learned between 1640 and 1660 the bitter price of dogmatism, violence, and tampering with ancient institutions. Moreover, they were weary of struggle, of the flouting of the law, and of the burden of saintliness. They were ready for "a very merry, dancing, drinking, quaffing and unthinkable time." For all his faults, Charles II proved to be a king who won the hearts of his subjects, something the austere, godly Cromwellians had never done.

When Charles became king in 1660, he seemed genuinely interested in working with Parliament. Both he and Parliament were eager for an end to radicalism and experimentalism. In a spirit of compromise and forgiveness, together they repealed the acts of the Commonwealth and the Protectorate. Only a handful of the Cromwellian faction were punished by execution; the spirit of vengeance was in part slaked by digging up and hanging Cromwell's body. Included in the arrangements surrounding Charles' restoration was a generous return of property confiscated during the era of the civil war to the original owners. The whole spirit of this settlement centered in the reestablishment of the wealthy landowners in control of England. The king was assured of a sizable income on a regular basis, but he was deprived of many of the ancient feudal rights that had allowed earlier kings to exact taxes without approval of Parliament. Not only was control of taxation reserved to Parliament, but the Triennial Act was passed to ensure that Parliament would meet at least every three years whether or not the king so wished.

The one matter that defied a satisfactory compromise settlement was religion. Parliament was forced to enact a religious settlement that again bred discord. The settlement was embodied in a series of acts passed in 1661 and 1662 and known as the Clarendon Code, after Charles II's chief adviser, the Earl of Clarendon. These laws reestablished the Anglican Church and threatened to destroy the Independents and Presbyterians. The Act of Uniformity required all clergymen to abide by the Book of Common Prayer or to surrender their livings. The Corporation Act provided that all members of city governments worship in the Church of England. The Conventicle Act made religious meetings other than Anglican illegal, and the Five Mile Act forbade all preachers who were not Anglicans to come within five miles of any city. The Clarendon Code raised immediate dissension within the ranks of the nonconformists, who were once more treated as criminals.

As important as it was in restoring order, the settlement accompanying the restoration of the Stuarts generated its own problems, which continued to keep England agitated. The exact powers of the king and Parliament were still not clearly defined, and religious sentiments were deeply offended by the Clarendon Code. These deep-seated sources of trouble were exacerbated by a series of disasters that befell England shortly after Charles returned to power. Charles became involved in a war with the Dutch, during which the Dutch fleet humiliated the English. In 1665 a plague struck England, and the next year a large part of London was destroyed by fire. Charles II's court became notorious for immorality, and the king earned a reputation as its most profligate member. One member of Parliament, in an obvious reference to Charles' many illegitimate children, proposed that cradles be bought by the government in wholesale lots.

In the minds of some people, England's misfortunes were divine retribution for royal immorality. Public wrath fell on Charles' chief minister, Clarendon, and Parliament forced him out of office. Parliament also grew stingier toward the king, who then turned to Louis XIV of France. In an alliance of 1670, Louis promised him a sizable subsidy provided that Charles join France in a war on the Dutch and work for the restoration of Roman Catholicism in England. But when in 1672 Charles tried to set aside laws against Roman Catholics, Parliament was so outraged that it passed the Test Act (1673), excluding Roman Catholics from all public offices in England. And when Charles joined France in a war against the Dutch in 1672–1674, Parliament again blocked him by refusing financial aid.

By the middle of his reign Charles seemed determined to end the deadlock between crown and Parliament either by dispensing with Parliament altogether or by controlling it. He continued to rely on Louis XIV for money. He succeeded in building a court party devoted to monarchy and Anglicanism. The opposition scornfully dubbed the members of this party *Tories* (a term previously used to designate Irish bandits). An opposing party, committed to parliamentary supremacy and the tolerance of all Protestant groups, was also formed. Members of this party were called *Whigs* (after a term used to designate Scottish horse thieves and murderers). By skillful use of the Tories and with French money, Charles managed to enjoy a great deal of freedom during his later years. Fear that he would use his power to restore Roman Catholicism, however, steadily increased, fanned whenever possible by the Whigs, who used every possible occasion to persuade the English that a "popish plot" was afoot to restore Catholicism. The Whigs centered their efforts in Parliament chiefly on trying to pass an Exclusion Act that would have barred Charles' brother, James, from the throne. Charles kept the bill from passing, but his methods convinced the despairing Whigs that tyranny had returned to England.

Charles' successor, James II, inherited a strong position, based in large part on a parliamentary majority controlled by the king. However, he acted with such reckless abandon that his following soon melted away. His chief mistake was open avowal of Roman Catholicism, the one thing that neither the Tories, the king's supporters, nor the Whigs, his enemies, would tolerate. Early in his reign James was forced to call the army to crush a rebellion. When the danger had passed, he kept the army and began to appoint Roman Catholics as officers, acts that seemed to threaten a forceful imposition of Catholicism. Increasing numbers of Catholics were appointed to high offices in the royal government, and several clergymen favorable to Rome were installed in the chief religious posts. In 1687 James issued the Declaration of Indulgence, which relaxed the restrictions on all religious groups, Dissenters and Roman Catholics alike. Protestants interpreted this act as favorable to Roman Catholics. Finally, in 1688, a son was born to James by his Roman Catholic wife, ensuring that his regime would be perpetuated by a Catholic successor.

This was the last straw. A group of prominent Tories and Whigs, usually bitter political rivals but drawn together by their conservative concerns for property, Anglicanism, and aristocratic domination of politics, invited James' daughter, the Protestant Mary, and her husband, William of Orange, the rulers of the Netherlands, to accept England's throne. William, eager to ensure England's support against the French threat to his country, accepted. When he invaded England late in 1688, the great majority of the people rallied to his side, and James fled to France. For a second time the unhappy Stuarts had been forced off England's throne.

6. THE GLORIOUS REVOLUTION

The flight of James II, unlike the death of Charles I, was not followed by a period of radical political experimentation. Instead, the Glorious Revolution was carried through without bloodshed and recrimination. A series of laws was passed that pacified England and established the basis for her future political development.

The major laws were enacted immediately after the accession of William and Mary. Parliament declared James deposed by virtue of abdicating his office. A new coronation oath was devised requiring William and Mary to swear to abide by decisions of Parliament as well as by the ancient laws of England. The Bill of Rights was passed in 1689. This charter spelled out in detail the laws to which the king must adhere. It laid down Parliament's authority to depose a king and choose a new one. It assured the members of Parliament the right of free speech, immunity from prosecution for statements made in debate, and freedom from royal intervention in elections. It declared illegal a whole series of acts: taxation without consent of Parliament, dispensing with laws, maintaining a standing army in peacetime, requiring excessive bail, depriving citizens of trial in the regular courts, interfering with jurors, and preventing people from petitioning the king. The Toleration Act was also enacted, allowing religious freedom to Puritans and Independents, although still keeping non-Protestants out of public office.

Accepting the crown on the basis of these laws and conditions, William and Mary acted with vigor to dispose of other sources of difficulty. In 1689–1691 William led an army into Ireland, where James was attempting to stir up a rebellion that would put him back on the throne. William crushed the rebels and instituted a policy of depriving Irish Catholics of their land in favor of English landlords. Ireland was thus placed on a colonial status, to be exploited by England.

William also conducted long negotiations to solve the problem of Scotland. These negotiations bore fruit after his death, when Parliament passed the Act of Union (1707), which joined the two kingdoms, gave Scotland a liberal number of seats in Parliament, and guaranteed her Presbyterian religious organization. The Act of Union created a political unit known thereafter as Great Britain.

Probably William's most significant act was to give England a new orientation in foreign affairs. A dedicated enemy of the schemes of Louis XIV to dominate Europe, William threw all of England's resources into the struggle against France. His action was decisive. Not only were Louis XIV's ambitious plans upset, but through these wars England became a great power and was well on the way to acquiring a great empire.

Still another significant issue remained to be settled—the succession problem. Mary died in 1694 and William in 1702, leaving the crown to Anne (1702–1714), another daughter of James II. Even before William's death it was apparent that Anne would have no heirs. To avoid the return of the Roman Catholic Stuarts, Parliament in 1701 passed the Act of Settlement. This law provided that none but Protestants would inherit the English crown. In line with this principle, Parliament designated Sophia of the German state of Hanover, granddaughter of James I, and her heirs as successors to Anne. In spite of strong sentiment in favor of restoring the dynasty of James II, this act was honored in 1714, when George of Hanover became King George I of England.

7. THE EMERGENCE OF THE CABINET SYSTEM

The establishment of parliamentary supremacy in the wake of the Glorious Revolution left unsolved one more major political problem—that of the executive power. How would the daily affairs of government be conducted? Many were afraid to trust this task to the king, fearing that he would regain control over political life. Yet Parliament, composed chiefly of landowners and businessmen, was in no position to take up this burden. During the half century after 1688 a solution was found that permitted Parliament effectively to control the executive branch of the government while still assuring the skillful conduct of state business. The answer lay in the emergence of the cabinet.

English kings had long employed advisers to conduct government affairs and to shape policy. Up to 1688 these ministers had usually been chosen by the king and were responsible to him alone. After the Glorious Revolution it became absolutely necessary for the king to gain parliamentary support for every phase of government policy. From William III's reign onward, therefore, royal ministers were increasingly chosen because of their influence in Parliament. Since Parliament tended to divide into parties that controlled large blocs of votes, it proved wisest for the king to seek out party leaders for posts as ministers and advisers.

After the accession of Anne, this trend developed rapidly. Since Anne and the first Hanoverians, George I (1714–1727) and George II (1727–1760), were unfit for the rigorous job of administering the state, the direction of the government and the formulation of policy fell into the hands of royal ministers who could get the approval of Parliament. This group of ministers slowly learned to accept mutual responsibility for the total operation of the government, which required that they all be members of the same party and stand together in Parliament. While their party held a majority in Parliament, they could enact their program; when they lost control over Parliament, they had to give way to a new cabinet that could control Parliament. One member of the cabinet, the *prime minister*, came to be recognized as the leader and spokesman of the whole group.

Anne relied heavily on the advice of John Churchill, duke of Marlborough, to conduct her government. However, a minister of the first two Georges, Robert Walpole, was the first real prime minister and the first to observe the principles of cabinet government. A Whig member of Parliament for many years, he learned well the potential power of a disciplined party. In 1721 he became George I's chief minister, primarily because of his power in Parliament, and he virtually ran England until 1742. He surrounded himself with men who could control votes in Parliament and followed policies suitable to the interests of his party. A coarse, hard-drinking squire, Walpole was not above bribery and the shameless use of patronage to keep his party strong. His strength in Parliament made him the real ruler of England; even the king could not control or check his dominance. Walpole lost control of Parliament when he tried to keep England out of war with Spain, a policy that was not popular with most Englishmen. Having lost his control of Parliament, Walpole resigned as prime minister in 1742. However, the king had little choice but to appoint another prime minister who could command a majority vote in Parliament. The cabinet, under a prime minister, had taken over the executive branch of the government, exercising that power through a group of parliamentary leaders who devoted themselves to administration but who had to render account for their conduct of state affairs before Parliament.

The Glorious Revolution and the settlement that followed were a turning point in England's history. Two burning issues had been settled to the satisfaction of most Englishmen. Parliament, representing the landed and moneyed interests, replaced the king as supreme authority. Religious toleration was established for all Protestant sects, thus putting an end to religious uniformity. (Roman Catholics, Unitarians, Jews, and atheists were not given the right to worship freely or to exercise fully their rights as Englishmen.) Although much blood had been spilled deciding these issues, England emerged from her revolution with no deep scars. She had managed to hold her own in competition with other powers, especially France, which at the time enjoyed a more stable political system. In fact, England had raised her prestige and power in world affairs during the seventeenth century and entered the eighteenth even stronger than she had been at the death of Elizabeth in 1603. With her political quarrels settled, she was able to increase her status as a world power rapidly during the next two centuries. Her revolution against absolutism and her new constitutional monarchy were destined to serve as models for other nations ready to discard royal absolutism.

Suggested Reading

General Treatments

R. Lockyer, *Tudor and Stuart Britain* (1964). A brilliant survey of the entire period.

*G. M. Trevelyan, *England Under the Stuarts* (21st ed., University Paperbacks). An older work, deeply sympathetic with the parliamentary cause and anti-Stuart, but exciting to read and full of information concerning social history.

*C. Hill, *The Century of Revolution, 1607–1714* (Norton). A treatment of the period from a Marxist perspective providing fresh insight into economic factors involved in the English Revolution.

*J. R. Tanner, *English Constitutional Conflicts in the Seventeenth Century* (Cambridge). Provides an excellent description of the major constitutional issues surrounding the English Revolution.

*W. Haller, *The Rise of Puritanism* (Harper Torchbook). A perceptive treatment of the religious forces at work in seventeenth-century England.

*L. Stone, *The Causes of the English Revolution, 1529–1642* (Harper Torchbook). An excellent review of modern interpretations of the causes of the English Revolution.

The First Stuarts, the Civil War, the Age of Cromwell

*C. V. Wedgwood, *The King's Peace, 1637–1641* (Collier); *The King's War, 1641–1647* (Collier); and *A Coffin for King Charles* (Collier). Masterful treatments of the crucial years of the English civil war, distinguished by brilliant writing.

*C. V. Wedgwood, *Life of Cromwell* (Collier). An excellent account of Cromwell's life.

*R. E. Boyer, ed., *Oliver Cromwell and the Puritan Revolution: Failure or a Faith* (Heath). A collection of essays representing the conflicting views of modern historians concerning Cromwell's accomplishment.

*M. Walzer, *The Revolution of the Saints: A Study of the Origins of Radical Politics* (Atheneum). An excellent account of the radical elements that played a part in the English Revolution.

C. Hill, *The World Turned Upside Down: Radical Ideas During the English Revolution* (1972). A brilliant treatment of the "lunatic" fringe of seventeenth-century England and the special influence this element had on the course of the English Revolution.

The Restoration, the Glorious Revolution, and the Aftermath

*G. M. Trevelyan, *The English Revolution, 1688–1689* (Galaxy). A penetrating analysis of the events of 1688–1689 and their significance.

*G. Straka, ed., *The Revolution of 1688; Whig Triumph or Palace Revolution* (Heath). A good collection of conflicting interpretations of the Glorious Revolution.

*P. Laslett, *The World We Have Lost* (Scribner). A splendid evocation of English society about 1700.

Sources

Carl Stephenson and Frederick George Marcham, eds., *Sources of English Constitutional History* (1937). A rich collection of key political documents, including the Petition of Right and the Bill of Rights, which spell out the issues of the English Revolution.

*John Locke, *Two Treatises of Government* (many editions). The classic statement of the political ideology that inspired the English Revolution and especially the Glorious Revolution.

*Samuel Pepys, *Diary* (Harper Torchbook). A fascinating eyewitness picture of English social life during the Restoration period.

35

THE RISE OF PRUSSIA AND RUSSIA

The most significant political developments in Central and Eastern Europe during the seventeenth and eighteenth centuries were the rise of Prussia and Russia. At the opening of the seventeenth century, the two chief powers in Central and Eastern Europe were the Ottoman and Hapsburg empires. Although the Muslim Ottoman Turks had been restrained by the Hapsburgs in the sixteenth century on both land and sea, they were about to renew their effort to conquer Christian Europe. The Austrian Hapsburgs, in addition to disputing the control of Southeastern Europe with the Turks, dominated the Holy Roman Empire, which included all the German states. In Northeastern Europe, Sweden, Prussia, Poland, and Russia competed for hegemony. Among all these powers, Prussia and Russia had hitherto been the least conspicuous in world affairs.

1. THE EARLY HOHENZOLLERNS

The history of Prussia is in large measure the history of the Hohenzollern family. This aggressive and prolific dynasty was first heard of in the tenth century. At that time the Hohenzollerns were obscure counts ruling over the castle of Zollern and a tiny bit of surrounding territory in southwest Germany just north of the Swiss border. In the twelfth century they became burgraves of Nuremberg, an important commercial city in Bavaria. Early in the fifteenth century the Holy Roman Emperor, looking for an able ruler

for the mark of Brandenburg, a military province near the exposed northeastern border of the empire, chose the head of the house of Hohenzollern. Although its ruler was one of the seven electors of the Holy Roman Emperor, Brandenburg was a bleak and thinly populated little province. Yet around this nucleus the Hohenzollerns built the important state of Prussia, and later the German Empire—the world's most powerful and feared nation.

From the time the Hohenzollerns became margraves of Brandenburg (1415) until they were finally overthrown at the end of World War I in 1918, they followed a threefold policy from which they never veered: militarism and territorial aggrandizement; paternal despotism; and centralized bureaucracy. No state in modern times has been so wedded to militarism as a cardinal feature of national life and policy as that of the Hohenzollerns, and few modern states have been more autocratic in their government and society.

Early in the seventeenth century Brandenburg began to expand. In 1609 the Hohenzollerns inherited three little provinces in and near the Rhine Valley far to the west, and nine years later they inherited East Prussia, a fief of Poland on the Baltic far to the east. In 1640 Frederick William, the Great Elector, one of the ablest of all the Hohenzollerns, became margrave and began filling in the territorial gaps. His first move was to take Brandenburg out of the Thirty Years' War, which had been devastating the Germanies for the past twenty-two years. While the other ad-

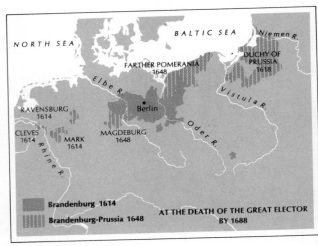

THE GROWTH OF PRUSSIA 1417–1807

versaries, France, Sweden, the Hapsburgs, and many of the small German states, exhausted themselves in eight more years of struggle, Brandenburg recouped her strength and resources. Reentering the war shortly before its end, she was in a position to demand and get valuable territories. According to the terms of the Treaty of Westphalia (1648), Brandenburg received Eastern Pomerania, a sizable strip of territory that gave her valuable frontage on the Baltic, the large bishopric of Magdeburg, which straddled the Elbe, and several smaller bishoprics. Shortly afterward Frederick William gained the independence of East Prussia from Poland.

The Great Elector centralized and administered the governments of his scattered territories with energy and skill. He protected the native industries, improved communications, and aided agriculture. In a most intolerant age he followed a policy of religious toleration. When Louis XIV revoked the Edict of Nantes in 1685, Frederick William welcomed thousands of industrious Huguenots to Brandenburg. At the death of the Great Elector in 1688, Brandenburg was on the road to becoming a great power.

The next Hohenzollern, Frederick I (1688–1713), acquired the title of king for the dynasty. The Hapsburg Holy Roman Emperor in 1701 granted Frederick the title in return for aid against Louis XIV in the War of the Spanish Succession. Frederick I chose Prussia rather than Brandenburg for the name of his kingdom, since Prussia was outside the Holy Roman Empire and a free sovereign state. Hence Brandenburg became Prussia.

From 1713 to 1740 Prussia was ruled by a vigorous militaristic autocrat, Frederick William I (since he was the first Frederick William to be king). Unquestioned absolutism, machinelike centralized bureaucratic administration, and above all militarism were his obsessions. He built the Prussian army into the most efficient and one of the largest fighting forces in Europe. And yet Frederick William was so efficient and miserly that he was also able to pass along to his talented son a well-filled treasury.

The talented son, the future Frederick the Great, was a "problem" child. An ardent lover of music, literature, and philosophy, young Frederick hated militarism and governmental details. He even attempted to flee the country to escape the stern discipline of his disgruntled father. Arrested, he was forced to undergo exceptionally rigorous training from the bottom up in the army and the government services. Eventually Frederick became enamored of both, and Frederick William I died happy, sure that the Hohenzollern state would pass into good hands.

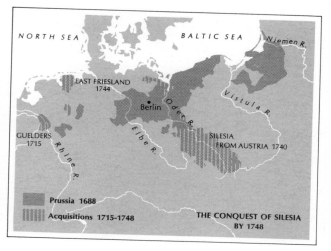

THE CONQUEST OF SILESIA
BY 1748

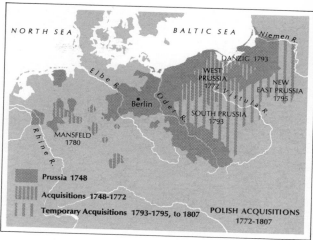

POLISH ACQUISITIONS
1772–1807

2. THE EMERGENCE OF PRUSSIA AS A GREAT POWER UNDER FREDERICK THE GREAT, 1740–1786

In the same year that Frederick II became king of Prussia (1740), the beautiful and gracious young Maria Theresa became archduchess of the Austrian Hapsburg dominions. These dominions included, in addition to the Austrian lands, the Kingdom of Hungary and the triune crown of Bohemia, Moravia, and Silesia. Maria Theresa's father, Emperor Charles VI, had spent much time in his last years attempting to safeguard his daughter's accession to the Hapsburg throne. He succeeded in obtaining the signatures of virtually every European sovereign, including the king of Prussia, to a document called the Pragmatic Sanction, which guaranteed the integrity of Maria Theresa's crown and territories. Two months after Charles VI died, however, Frederick II, without a declaration of war, marched his troops into and seized Silesia, one of the richest of the Hapsburg provinces. This Machiavellian act of the young Prussian king plunged most of the major European states into a series of wars for the mastery of Central Europe. Bavaria, Saxony, France, and Spain rushed in to despoil Maria Theresa of her territories. Only Great Britain and the Dutch Netherlands took the side of Austria. Great Britain was a bitter rival of France in

India and North America, and she was also concerned for the Austrian Netherlands, with which she enjoyed a profitable trade, and for Hanover, whose ruling family now sat on the British throne. The Dutch were fearful of renewed French aggression in their direction.

The War of the Austrian Succession lasted for eight years (1740–1748). Maria Theresa successfully repelled the Bavarians, Saxons, French, and Spaniards, but she was unable to dislodge Frederick II from Silesia. Frederick, on his part, cynically deserted his allies as soon as he had achieved his own purposes. The Treaty of Aix-la-Chapelle in 1748 brought the hostilities to an end. Frederick retained Silesia, and Maria Theresa's husband, Francis of Lorraine, was recognized as Holy Roman Emperor. The only real gainer from the war was Frederick II. Silesia, a fertile province inhabited by more than a million German-speaking people, nearly doubled the population and resources of Prussia.

The Hapsburgs, however, had no intention of being thus despoiled of one of their fairest provinces by the upstart Hohenzollerns. Proud rulers over territories many times the size and population of Prussia and for centuries emperors of the Holy Roman Empire, of which Prussia was but a member state, they viewed the Hohenzollerns with condescension. Maria Theresa's able diplo-

THE GROWTH OF RUSSIA IN THE WEST

mat, Count Kaunitz, was soon at work lining up allies. Saxony, Sweden, Russia, and even France were won over. Spain, now ruled by the Bourbons, later followed France into the alliance. This time, however, Great Britain took the side of Prussia. She did this in order to oppose her archenemy France, with whom she was already at war in India and North America, and to safeguard Hanover. This double shifting of alliances came to be called the Diplomatic Revolution. Since Great Britain was Prussia's only ally and since her aid was limited to subsidies and to tying down French forces overseas, the opposition was certain of victory over Frederick II. They were already dividing up his territories, leaving him only the little original Hohenzollern province of Brandenburg.

But Frederick was not one to wait for his enemies to strike first. As soon as he became aware of their designs, he opened hostilities by overrunning Saxony. Thus began the Seven Years'

War (1756–1763), the bloodiest war in history up to that time. Frederick, with his slender resources, soon found himself at bay; the four greatest military powers on the continent of Europe were closing in on him from all directions. The Austrians advanced from the south, the Russians from the east, the Swedes from the north, and the French from the west. Hurling his disciplined but ever-dwindling army against first one and then another of his enemies, Frederick held them off for seven years. His lightning marches, tricky maneuvers, and indefatigable tenacity in the face of seemingly hopeless odds won for him the title, "the Great." But after six years the end appeared to be near. His treasury was empty, his manpower exhausted, much of his territory laid waste. The Russians even captured and burned his capital, Berlin. Then suddenly fortune changed. In 1762 the Russian Tsarina Elizabeth, one of his bitterest enemies, died and was succeeded by the weakling Peter III,

who was an ardent admirer of Frederick II and who put Russia's forces at the disposal of Prussia. Although Peter III was soon murdered by a group of his own officers and court nobility and Russia withdrew from the war, the remaining allies had no further stomach for the fight. The Peace of Hubertusburg in 1763 left things as they were at the beginning of the war, Prussia retaining the controversial Silesia. In the same year the Treaty of Paris brought to a close the colonial struggle between Great Britain and France in India and North America, leaving Great Britain master of both.

Having so narrowly escaped destruction, Frederick the Great spent the remaining twenty-three years of his life reconstructing his war-ravaged territories. His career as an enlightened despot will be surveyed in Chapter 38. He encouraged agriculture, subsidized and protected industry, and invited immigrants into his well-governed territories. At no time, though, did he

neglect his war machine. In 1772 he joined Austria and Russia in the first partition of Poland. Frederick took West Prussia, thus joining East Prussia with the main body of the Prussian state. When Frederick II died in 1786, Prussia had been raised to the status of a great power, sharing equally with Austria the leadership of Central Europe. During his reign Prussia's size and population had more than doubled, and her military exploits pointed to a spectacular future.

3. RUSSIA BEFORE PETER THE GREAT

While Prussia was becoming a great power in Central Europe, Russia was rising to prominence to the east. The first shaping of some of the Slavic tribes of Eastern Europe into what eventually became the Russian national state was begun by Viking invaders in the ninth century. These intrepid seamen moved out from their Scandinavian homes in all directions—

across the Atlantic, into the Mediterranean, and up the rivers of what are now England, France, Germany, and Russia (the word *Russia* is apparently derived from the Swedish word for rower). Their most important commercial and political center in Eastern Europe was Kiev, which became Russia's first capital. Eventually the Norse adopted the Slavic culture of their subjects.

In the tenth century Christianity was brought to Russia by missionaries from Constantinople. This is probably the most significant development in Russian history, for through the influence of the Greek Orthodox Church, whose headquarters were in Constantinople, Russia became a semi-Oriental Byzantine civilization and was cut off from the Greco-Roman and Roman Catholic culture common to the countries of Central and Western Europe. English, Spanish, Polish, and Swedish churchmen were constantly traveling to Rome, where they associated with churchmen from Italy, Hungary, France, and Germany. Russian churchmen, on the other hand, traveled to Constantinople, where they encountered only Greek, Serbian, Bulgarian, and Rumanian churchmen of the Balkan Peninsula.

Second in importance only to Greek Orthodox Christianity in the infusion of Oriental influence into Russian civilization was the Tartar conquest of the thirteenth century. Around the turn of the thirteenth century the Mongol conqueror Genghis Khan (1162–1227) had established a vast empire in Eastern Asia. Shortly after his death the Golden Horde, as the Mongol warriors were called, swept westward into Christian Europe. The thirteenth-century Europeans were no match for the Tartars. Russia was easily overrun, and in 1241 a combined German and Polish army was defeated at Liegnitz in the heart of Central Europe. All Christian Europe appeared to be at the mercy of the invaders. At that moment, however, the great khan died in Eastern Asia, and the Tartar commander withdrew his forces to Russia and hastened back to seize his share of the spoils. The Golden Horde never resumed its triumphal surge westward, but for two and a half centuries it inundated Russia. Although there was little mixing of blood between the Mongol Tartars and the Caucasian

Russians, there was considerable mixing of cultures. When the Mongol tide finally receded near the end of the fifteenth century, a deposit of such characteristically Oriental traits as backward-looking conservatism, fatalism, female seclusion, and absolutism in government had been added to the Byzantine cultural influence.

During the Tartar occupation the grand dukes of Muscovy managed to ingratiate themselves with their Mongol masters and build up their own influence and power. Moscow replaced Kiev as the political center of Russia. The first of the grand dukes of Muscovy under whom Russia took on the shape of a modern national state was Ivan III (1462–1505). In 1480 Ivan III defeated the rapidly declining Tartars and limited their power in Russia to the southeastern area. Ivan greatly extended his sway both to the north and to the west by military conquest. A momentous event in Ivan III's reign was his marriage to Sophia Palaeologus, heiress to the now-defunct Byzantine (Eastern Roman) Empire. Ivan immediately declared himself successor to the Eastern Roman Caesars—hence the title Tsar. When he died, the foundations of a Russian national state had been laid.

Ivan IV (1533–1584) the Terrible added both to the authority of the Russian tsars and to the territories over which they ruled. He destroyed the remaining power of the Tartars in southeastern Russia and annexed most of their territory. The Ottoman Turks, however, seized the strategic Tartar territory north of the Black Sea. Although Ivan IV established trade relations with England by way of the White Sea and the Arctic Ocean, his efforts to gain a foothold on the Baltic were frustrated by Sweden and Poland. It was during Ivan IV's reign that Russia's conquest of Siberia was begun. Half a century later the Russian flag was planted on the shores of the Pacific.

The twenty-nine years following the death of Ivan IV are known as the Time of Troubles (1584–1613). Weak rulers and disputed successions resulted in such anarchy that the Poles were able to capture Moscow and hold it briefly. To end the political chaos, a group of leading nobles in 1613 chose Michael Romanov as tsar. The Romanov dynasty was to rule Russia until the Communist revolution of 1917. Throughout the seventeenth century, Russia under the early Romanovs slowly but gradually established commercial and cultural contacts with the West. Increasing numbers of traders, craftsmen, and adventurers from Central and Western Europe, particularly Germany, came to Russia to seek their fortunes. Thus the stage was set for Russia to become Westernized and a first-rate European power. This was done during the reign of Peter the Great.

4. RUSSIA UNDER PETER THE GREAT, 1689–1725

Peter I (1689–1725)[1] was a physical giant full of mental vitality and primitive animal instincts and emotions. At the age of seventeen he seized the reins of government from his elder sister. For the next thirty-six years he devoted his boundless energy to the twofold policy of Westernizing Russia and of gaining windows to the West on the Baltic and Black seas.

During Peter's youth he had come in contact with foreign craftsmen in Moscow and had become enamored of Western technology, particularly shipbuilding. In 1697 the twenty-five-year-old tsar made a grand tour of Western Europe, seeking allies against the Turks and firsthand knowledge of Western ways. He failed to gain any allies, but he learned a great deal about Western customs and techniques, which he proceeded to introduce into Russia. In Prussia, Peter studied one of the world's most efficient military organizations; in the Dutch Netherlands, shipbuilding; in England, shipbuilding, commerce, and finance.

On his way to Italy from Vienna he was suddenly called home by the revolt of his bodyguard. Slicing off hundreds of heads by his own hand, he crushed the revolt with a ruthlessness that cowed all potential troublemakers. To make his authority as absolute as that of the most au-tocratic Western European monarchs, he adopted their bureaucratic system in both central and local government. Western technicians were brought to Russia in large numbers, and new industries were subsidized and protected by mercantilist policies. Western, particularly French, social customs were introduced to the upper and middle classes of Russian society. Women were brought out of seclusion, and the long beards and flowing Oriental robes of the men were banned. These reforms hardly touched the peasant masses, who were increasingly tied down in a system of serfdom bordering on slavery—a process that had been going on in Russia throughout the sixteenth and seventeenth centuries. When the patriarch of the Russian Orthodox Church opposed the tsar's authority and some of his Westernizing policies, Peter abolished the patriarchate. He placed at the head of the church a Holy Synod composed of a committee of bishops and presided over by a lay procurator-general, all appointed by the tsar. Henceforth, the Orthodox Church was a powerful instrument of the Russian government. But Peter the Great's chief concern was always his military establishment. He built a navy and patterned his conscript army after that of Prussia. By the end of his reign, Russia had one of the major fighting forces of Europe.

When Peter became tsar, Russia had no warm-water access to the West. Sweden held the coveted shores of the Baltic Sea, and the Ottoman Turks occupied the territory north of the Black Sea. Peter's efforts to dislodge these "natural" enemies were only partly successful. He did manage to seize Azov on the Black Sea from the Turks and hold it for fourteen years, but the Turks were still too strong for the Russians and blocked them off from the Black Sea for another half century. Against Sweden Peter was more successful. In 1697 the fifteen-year-old Charles XII came to the throne of Sweden, which since the reign of Gustavus Adolphus in the early seventeenth century had been the greatest military power in Northern Europe. Hoping to take advantage of Charles XII's youth, Peter formed an alliance with Denmark and Poland for the purpose of despoiling Sweden of valuable territories. Charles, however, proved to be a first-rate

---

[1]In 1682 Peter I, at the age of ten, technically became joint ruler with his elder brother, Ivan V, who was mentally incompetent. Until 1689, however, his rule was only nominal, and that date is usually considered to be the beginning of his reign.

military genius. Not waiting for his enemies to ready their plans, he struck first at Denmark and forced her to sue for peace. Marching rapidly into Russia, he crushed a Russian army much larger than his own at Narva. Instead of pursuing the demoralized forces of Peter, however, he turned to Poland, defeated the Polish army, and placed a puppet king on the Polish throne. After spending seven years rearranging the affairs of Poland, Charles, known as the "Madman of the North," at last turned his attention once more to Russia. But Peter had used the seven years of grace to rebuild his forces. He retreated before the advancing Swedes deep into the vast interior of Russia, scorching the earth behind him. In 1709 the forces of Charles XII, decimated by hunger and disease, were brought to bay and shattered at Poltava, in southern Russia. Charles escaped with a remnant of his army to Turkey, but the military strength of Sweden was spent. Nine years later Charles XII was killed fighting in Norway. By the Treaty of Nystad in 1721, Russia received the Swedish Baltic provinces of Livonia, Estonia, Ingria, and Karelia. On the Neva River near the Baltic Peter built a new modern capital, St. Petersburg, facing the West. At his death in 1725, Russia was a great and growing power ready to play a major role in European affairs.

5. RUSSIA UNDER CATHERINE THE GREAT, 1762–1796

Peter the Great was followed by a succession of weak or mediocre rulers. After an interval of thirty-seven years, Catherine the Great (1762–1796) ascended the Russian throne. Catherine was an obscure princess from one of the little German states. She had been married for political reasons to young Peter III, grandson of Peter the Great, while he was still heir to the Russian crown. After he became tsar, Peter III, a weakling, quickly alienated all classes of his subjects. The astute Catherine, meanwhile, was becoming a good Russian, popularizing herself with her people. She was also reading widely from classical and French eighteenth-century authors. Less than a year after her husband became tsar, Catherine conspired with a group of aristocratic army officers, who murdered Peter and declared Catherine tsarina of Russia.

The Machiavellian tsarina prided herself on being an enlightened despot, as was fashionable in the late eighteenth century. She carried on a lively correspondence with Voltaire, D'Alembert, Frederick the Great, and other leading members of the eighteenth-century intelligentsia. She invited Diderot to St. Petersburg and became his friend and patron. She talked learnedly about freedom, education, and reform, and soon after her seizure of the throne, she called a commission to study the question of reforms. All this made good salon talk, but none of it was translated into deeds. No one knew better than Catherine, as she admitted to a confidant, that an enlightened populace would endanger the position of all despots. The desperation of the peasants led to one of the greatest "slave" insurrections in history. Under the able leadership of a Don Cossack, Pugachev, hundreds of thousands of peasants rose against their masters. The rebellion was put down with difficulty. The cruel repression left the Russian serf really a slave.

The chief significance of Catherine the Great in history lies in her aggressive foreign policy. Peter the Great had reached the Baltic by despoiling the Swedes. Catherine reached the Black Sea, the Balkan Peninsula, and the heart of Europe by defeating the Turks and destroying Poland. In two major wars between 1768 and 1792 Catherine defeated the Turks (something that Peter the Great had never been able to do) and seized all of their territory north of the Black Sea as far west as the Balkan Peninsula. Russia also gained a vague protectorate over the Christians in the Ottoman Empire, which gave her a standing opportunity to meddle in the internal affairs of the Turks. But Catherine fell short of her real goal, Constantinople. So certain was she of winning the old Byzantine capital on the Bosporus, which the Russian tsars had coveted since the days of Ivan III, that she named her second grandson Constantine. However, turning aside to join Prussia and Austria in the partitioning of the remainder of the Polish state, Catherine died before she could resume her drive on Constantinople. Already in 1772 Rus-

L'ENJAMBÉE IMPERIALE.

Constantinople

Russie

Catherine the Great's territorial ambitions are satirized in this cartoon, which shows her leaping toward a coveted goal, Constantinople, as the pope and other European leaders look on in dismay.
Photo: NYPL Picture Collection

sia, Prussia, and Austria had seized strips of Poland. In 1793 Russia and Prussia enlarged their holdings, and in 1795 the three powers divided among themselves the remainder of the once huge Poland. Catherine's share, which was about two-thirds of the total, brought Russia's western boundary deep into Central Europe. The second and third partitions of Poland and concern over the French Revolution, which began in 1789, absorbed Catherine's energies during the last years of her life. When she finally died in 1796, Russia was a nation ominous in size and power, and a major factor in European and world affairs.

6. THE DISAPPEARANCE OF POLAND AND THE DECLINE OF SWEDEN AND THE OTTOMAN EMPIRE

Poland, at the opening of the eighteenth century, was the third largest country in Europe, exceeded in size only by Russia and Sweden. In the sixteenth and seventeenth centuries it had appeared that she would become a major power. Taking advantage of Russia's Time of Troubles (1584–1613), the Poles had captured Moscow. In the latter part of the century they had saved Vienna from the Turks.

Actually, however, the Polish nation was far from strong. Sprawling over a large area be-

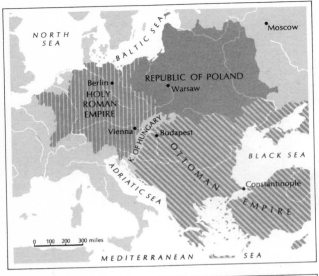

AGING EMPIRES (HOLY ROMAN EMPIRE, POLAND, OTTOMAN EMPIRE) AND NEW POWERS (AUSTRIA, PRUSSIA, RUSSIAN EMPIRE)

tween Russia and the German states, she enjoyed no natural boundaries either in the east or the west. The eastern half of her territory was inhabited by Russian-speaking people. Her northern provinces were peopled largely by Latvians, Lithuanians, and Germans. There were also many Germans in the west. Religious cleavages followed the language lines. The Poles themselves were militantly Roman Catholic under strong Jesuit influence. Some of the Rus-

sians were Orthodox and some were Uniates (orthodox Christians who recognized the headship of the Roman pope). The Latvians and Germans were mostly Lutherans, as were some of the Lithuanians. In the cities lived many Jews.

Moreover, there was no strong middle class to vitalize Poland's economy. In the Late Middle Ages a sizable overland commerce between the Black and the Baltic seas had flowed across Poland. But with the shifting of commercial routes and centers to the west in the early sixteenth century, Poland's commerce had withered like that of Italy and the German states. Furthermore, the Polish nobility, jealous of its own power and fearful of an alliance between the bourgeoisie and the king, deliberately penalized commerce with severe restrictions. The great mass of the people were serfs, tilling the soil of the powerful nobility.

In the face of so many divisive forces, only a strong central government could have made Poland a stable national state. But here lay Poland's greatest weakness. The kingship was elective, and the great nobles who held the elective power saw to it that no strong king ever came to the throne. During the eighteenth century the kings were all foreigners or puppets of foreign powers. The legislative Diet was completely monopolized by the nobility. In order to safeguard each nobleman's rights, unanimity was required for the passage of every measure. This meant that any nobleman could veto any proposed law (liberum veto). In addition, any nobleman could disband ("explode") the Diet and cancel all its acts. This system guaranteed virtual political anarchy. National spirit was weak. The all-powerful nobles were far more concerned for their own private interests than for the well-being of the nation.

It would have been surprising had such a power vacuum as eighteenth-century Poland not invited the aggression of her ambitious neighbors. In 1772 Catherine the Great and Frederick the Great bargained to take slices of Polish territory. The somewhat less greedy Maria Theresa of Austria, fearful of being outdistanced by Russia and Prussia, joined them, although her slice was beyond the Carpathian Mountains. Russia took a strip occupied by White Russians, and Prussia took West Prussia, joining up East Prussia with Brandenburg. This aggression at long last stirred the Poles to action. Sweeping reforms were passed improving the condition of the peasants and the bourgeoisie and giving the king and the Diet power to act effectively. But it was too late. Russia and Prussia were determined to prevent the emergence of a vigorous Polish nation. In 1793 they marched in and seized additional slices of territory. The Poles, under the leadership of Thaddeus Kosciusko, now flew to arms, although the arms were often only agricultural implements. They were no match for the professional armies of Russia, Prussia, and Austria, who in 1795 divided the remainder of Poland among themselves. Russia's share of Poland, about two-thirds of the total, was inhabited largely by Russian-speaking people. Austria's share was inhabited by Roman Catholics, as was Austria itself. Prussia's share, however, except for part of West Prussia, was inhabited for the most part by people who were neither linguistically nor religiously akin to the Prussians and who proved to be a fruitful source for future trouble.

Poland was not the only victim in Eastern Europe of the rise of Prussia and Russia. Sweden and the Ottoman Empire declined, both relatively and actually. Sweden had become the dominant military power in Northern and Eastern Europe under Gustavus Adolphus in the early seventeenth century. At the opening of the eighteenth century she was second only to Russia in size among the nations of Europe, holding large areas east and south of the Baltic in addition to the homeland. However, her population and resources were too small to hold for long such far-flung territories, which were coveted by ambitious and growing Prussia and Russia. Charles XII made a spectacular effort to hold them, but in the end he lost all his trans-Baltic territories except Finland, and dissipated Sweden's strength in so doing. Sweden has never been a major power since.

The Ottoman Turks, after reaching the gates of Vienna early in the sixteenth century and again late in the seventeenth century, weakened rapidly. The Treaty of Karlowitz in 1699 limited their power in Europe to the Balkan Peninsula and a strip of territory north of the Black Sea. Their two serious defeats at the hands of Catherine the Great marked the beginning of the breakup of the Ottoman Empire. By the end of the eighteenth century, the three dominant powers in Central and Eastern Europe were the relatively static Austrian Hapsburg Empire and the two rapidly rising military despotisms — Prussia and Russia.

Suggested Reading

General

*J. B. Wolf, *The Emergence of the Great Powers, 1685–1715* (Torch).

*P. Roberts, *The Quest for Security, 1715–1740* (Torch).

*W. L. Dorn, *Competition for Empire, 1740–1763* (Torch).

*L. Gershoy, *From Despotism to Revolution, 1763–1789* (Torch). All four are scholarly volumes in the Rise of Modern Europe series.

Rise of Prussia

*S. B. Fay, *The Rise of Brandenburg-Prussia to 1786* (Berkshire). Good brief survey.

H. Holborn, *A History of Modern Germany 1648–1840* (1966). Volume II of Holborn's history of modern Germany. Best on the subject.

G. P. Gooch, *Frederick the Great, the Ruler, the Writer, the Man* (1947). Probably the best all-around biography of Frederick the Great.

Rise of Russia

M. T. Florinsky, *Russia: A History and an Interpretation*, 2 vols. (1953). Best survey of Russian history to 1917.

*V. Klyuchevsky, *Peter the Great* (Vintage). Probably the best biography of Peter I.

*G. S. Thomson, *Catherine the Great and the Expansion of Russia* (Collier). Brief but scholarly.

Disappearance of Poland and Decline of Sweden and Ottoman Empire

O. Halecki, *A History of Poland*, rev. ed. (1961). Sound coverage of the partitions.

J. A. Gade, *Charles the Twelfth* (1916). Best biography.

*L. S. Stavrianos, *The Balkans Since 1453* (Holt, Rinehart and Winston). Brief but sound account of the decline of the Ottoman Empire.

36

OVERSEAS COLONIZATION AND COMPETITION FOR EMPIRE

During the age of royal absolutism, the European nations intensified their competition for overseas possessions and commerce. Whereas Spain and Portugal had led the way beyond the Atlantic frontier during the sixteenth century, England, France, and the Netherlands threw themselves vigorously into colonizing and commercial expansion in various quarters of the globe during the seventeenth and eighteenth centuries. The newcomers indeed outstripped their older rivals and established themselves as the leading European imperial powers. As large as the world beyond Western Europe was, the competition for it led to struggles among the leading European powers; the outcome of these struggles decisively affected the power relationships among the competing nations. And while the Europeans colonized, traded, and competed around the globe, European civilization spread with them, impacting with varying results on the native populations encountered by the Europeans. The seventeenth and eighteenth centuries marked a decisive turning point in the establishment of Western European domination over much of the world.

1. THE NEW WORLD: THE ENGLISH, THE FRENCH, AND THE DUTCH

One of the areas attracting the English, French, and Dutch was the New World, where all three nations established thriving colonies during the seventeenth century and eventually became embroiled in bitter rivalry for dominance. The Northern European nations had their appetites whetted by the fabulous profits reaped from the New World by the Spanish and the Portuguese during the sixteenth century. These two powers retained their vast empires in Central and South America during the seventeenth and eighteenth centuries and continued to earn a rich reward from their enterprises. But the days of vast gold and silver hauls were soon over, and the Spanish and Portuguese turned their energies toward creating large plantations worked by oppressed natives and imported slaves to produce products marketable in Western Europe. Their presence in South and Central America forced the attention of the English, French, and Dutch toward North America and the Caribbean area.

The English were the most successful colonizers in North America. The initial ventures were undertaken by joint stock companies specifically chartered by the royal government to plant settlements in the New World. The first English colony was established at Jamestown, Virginia, in 1607. It soon attracted a large population and developed a thriving economy based on tobacco growing. Only a little later, in 1620, a group of Puritans, despairing of finding religious freedom in Stuart England, founded a colony at Plymouth. This struggling colony was quickly overshadowed by the efforts of the Massachusetts Bay Company. Its first colony was located at Salem. However, the Puritan-dominated company soon moved its headquarters from

England to Boston, around which there developed a vigorous community, made up largely of emigrants from England. New colonizing ventures, often inspired by resentment against the strong-handed political and religious dictates of the governors of the company, were undertaken from the Massachusetts base. Independent colonies were founded in Connecticut and Rhode Island, the latter under the leadership of Roger Williams, an especially strong advocate of religious freedom. Migrants from Massachusetts, reenforced by increasing numbers of Englishmen, also settled in New Hampshire and Maine.

Other colonies were established by proprietors, that is, individuals to whom the English king gave large grants of land. Maryland was established in 1632 through the efforts of Lord Baltimore, who tried to make his colony a refuge for Catholics. In 1663 eight English gentlemen were given proprietary rights over Carolina, and two centers of colonization were established shortly thereafter. In 1664 the English captured the Dutch colony of New Netherland, whereupon Charles II made his brother, the duke of York, its proprietor. Thus New York came into existence as an English colony. In 1681 William Penn received a grant from which grew the colony of Pennsylvania, where Penn hoped Quakers would find refuge. New Jersey and Delaware grew out of grants to various other proprietors. When in 1733 a colony was established in Georgia, England controlled the Atlantic seaboard from Maine to the Spanish colony in Florida. Her seaboard colonies, established under a variety of circumstances, very quickly began to enjoy a considerable independence that permitted them to take advantage of local circumstances and to develop a stable, prosperous order which showed remarkable potential for growth.

The English were also active elsewhere in the Western Hemisphere. English explorers and traders, seeking to establish a profitable trade in furs, penetrated into the Hudson Bay area in Canada. Flourishing colonies were established in the West Indies, the chief ones being Barbados, Jamaica, and Bermuda. In this area the English concentrated on developing highly profitable sugar plantations utilizing Negro slaves as a labor supply. At first, these Caribbean colonies appeared more valuable than did the seaboard colonies to the north.

Although no less interested and ambitious, France was not so successful as England in colonizing North America. Her first American colony was established by Samuel de Champlain at Quebec on the St. Lawrence River in 1608, only a year after the founding of Jamestown. Although Champlain explored the whole St. Lawrence Valley to the Great Lakes, settlers were slow to come from France to live in Canada. Most of those who did leave France preferred to settle in the West Indies, where France had also established colonies. Not until the reign of Louis XIV did the French turn to a more vigorous policy. Colbert, Louis' economic minister, put all of New France under royal administration and sent the Comte de Frontenac off to the New World as governor. Frontenac exerted every effort to increase France's possessions. During the last quarter of the seventeenth century, explorers and missionaries such as La Salle, Joliet, and Marquette explored the Mississippi Valley, allowing France to claim a huge territory, called Louisiana, which stretched from the Great Lakes to the Gulf of Mexico and included extensive lands on either side of the Mississippi. Territorially, the French holdings in North America were much larger than those of the English.

Efforts to attract settlers to this rich territory were unsuccessful. France closed her empire to non-Catholics, thus excluding the element that had been so important in populating England's colonies—the religiously dissatisfied. The French government, by making extensive grants to aristocrats, made it difficult for the lower classes to get land overseas. The excellent trading opportunities in the fur business attracted more attention than the less profitable pursuit of agriculture. French settlements were thus few and far between in the territory stretching from New Orleans to the mouth of the St. Lawrence. When England seized France's American empire in 1763, perhaps no more than eighty thousand people lived in New France, and most of these were in the St. Lawrence Valley.

Even this sparse population left its mark. The Roman Catholic Church was established firmly in New France. Missionaries were active converting the Indians. The French language was spoken everywhere. Larger communities, such as Quebec and New Orleans, imitated the ways of French society. Even today the influence of these early French colonists can be seen along the St. Lawrence Valley and in Louisiana.

The Dutch attempted to join the other powers in colonizing the North American wilds. In 1621 the Dutch West India Company was chartered to undertake colonization and commerce in the New World. In 1624 a colony was planted on Manhattan Island. Soon other Dutch communities were established in the Hudson Valley and on the Connecticut and Delaware rivers. The Dutch enjoyed only limited success, since Dutch interest and effort were concentrated chiefly on the more profitable East Indies. And in 1664 the English seized New Netherland during a war with the Dutch, ending Dutch colonization in North America.

2. EUROPEAN PENETRATION OF THE FAR EAST

The nations that colonized North America in the seventeenth and eighteenth centuries—England, France, and the Netherlands—were equally aggressive in the Far East. Portugal had established her supremacy there in the sixteenth century, building a commercial empire based upon control of a few key ports. Spain had sought to enter the Far East, but had not progressed beyond the Philippines.

By 1600 Portugal had begun to lose her dominant position. Ruled by Spain from 1580 to 1640, she was unable to protect her empire. The enterprising Dutch, who were successfully freeing themselves from Spanish control, were the chief beneficiaries. Early in the seventeenth century all the competing Dutch companies interested in Far Eastern trade were joined into a single Dutch East India Company, to which the Dutch government gave almost complete freedom of action. The company soon drove the Portuguese out of the Spice Islands, which became the center of the Dutch Empire. In 1641 Malacca on the Malay Peninsula was seized, giving the Dutch control of the seas around the East Indies. Ceylon and the Celebes were captured. The English tried to seize a share of this rich area, but were driven out by the Dutch as early as 1623. To safeguard the sea route to the Indies, the Dutch established a colony at the Cape of Good Hope in South Africa. To watch its interest in the Indies, the Dutch East India Company established a governor-general in Java, who in turn set up several other governmental centers in the island empire.

For years after, the Dutch continued to profit from their holdings in the Indies. They demonstrated remarkable skill in utilizing the native agricultural economy to produce commodities such as spices that were in great demand in Western Europe. Consequently, their presence disturbed very little the existing patterns of life in the area. The Dutch also made attempts to penetrate China and Japan, but both countries refused to deal with them and were too strong to permit entrance by force.

The English, although shut out of the East Indies by the Dutch, made rapid progress toward replacing the Portuguese in India. The English East India Company was chartered in 1600 and given a monopoly of English trade in the East. This company concentrated chiefly on India, slowly forcing the Portuguese to let English traders into that rich land. The company founded its own "factories" (trading posts) at key locations—Surat, Madras, Bombay, and Calcutta. For a long time the East India Company was content to exploit the trading opportunities available in these cities; the merchants interfered little with Indian affairs and had little influence on Indian society.

Rather belatedly, the French entered the competition in the Far East. Again it took the farsighted Colbert to see what France was missing. He organized a French East India Company (1664), which soon established a French outpost at Pondicherry in India. From this center the French company built up a prosperous trade that returned large profits.

3. THE IMPACT OF EUROPEAN EXPANSION: THE NATIVE AMERICANS

The increasing presence of European colonists and traders around the world during the seventeenth and eighteenth centuries had a significant impact on the native populations of the areas to which Europeans went. In many ways these encounters between Europeans and natives set a pattern that was destined to impose a bitter heritage on the modern world.

Of all the non-Europeans who felt the impact of the white man, the native Americans—the American Indians—were perhaps most immediately and directly affected. Their patterns of life, ranging from the highly sophisticated civilizations of the Incas in Peru and the Aztecs and Mayas in Mexico and Central America to the simple pastoral and hunting cultures of the North American Indians, were irreparably disrupted by the onslaught of the intruders.

We have already seen the destructive impact of the Spanish and Portuguese *conquistadors* on the Aztecs, Mayas, and Incas. During the seventeenth and eighteenth centuries, the dislocation continued. Spanish and Portuguese mercantilist policies cast the Indians into the role of laborers on the expanding plantation system and in the mining enterprises from which the Europeans drew huge profits. Although the native Europeans were few in number, they dominated political, economic, and social life with little respect for the established practices of native life. However, the new masters were not totally insensitive to their new minions. Especially through their missionary activities, they gave the native Americans not only a new religion but also an introduction to advanced technical skills and even access to a rudimentary education. The paternalistic policy of the Spanish and the Portuguese had the long-range effect of imposing a semblance of Iberian and Catholic culture on the native Indians; a living monument of this process is the language structure of modern Latin America.

Despite their indifference to established native American culture, the Europeans in Latin America were never numerous enough to exterminate the native Americans or their cultures. Inexorably, their blood and their culture intermingled with those of the native Americans. As a result, significant elements of native American culture survived, especially in family structure, agricultural techniques, art motifs, and even religion. Although the ancient Indian civilizations of Central and South America were forever disrupted, enough Indian culture survived to give Latin American society a special hybrid character that has survived to this day. This uniqueness will forever constitute a monument to native Americans.

The Indians of North America suffered a less dramatic but perhaps ultimately more ignominious fate at the hands of the Europeans than did the native Americans of Central and South America. Generally speaking, they were fewer in number and less advanced than were the Indians of Latin America. Their meager economic resources, their primitive institutions, and their ancient political rivalries limited their capacity to resist the onslaught of the French and English intruders.

On the whole, the French policy toward the Indians that inhabited their vast North American empire was not particularly disruptive, chiefly because there were not many French settlers in the New World. The chief French encounter with the Indians centered in the fur trade, a process that enticed the Indians into a new kind of economic activity and introduced into their world such European products as guns and liquor but that did not usually result in French control of their lives. The French also expended great efforts to Christianize the Indians. In general, the French and the Indians lived peaceably together to the point where the Indians joined the French as allies in the Anglo-French struggle for dominance in North America, a choice that boded ill for the Indians in the wake of the French defeat in the mid-eighteenth century.

The English settlers pursued a more ruthless policy toward the native Americans. From the beginning the English came to occupy and exploit the land of North America. Their intent demanded that they displace the natives by whatever means possible. Although English-Indian relationships were occasionally marked by friendliness and mutual assistance, a harsher pattern evolved as the number of white settlers increased. The burgeoning seaboard population began to assert inexorable pressure on the Indians aimed at exterminating them or driving them from their lands. As a consequence, the Indian began to disappear from the "new" America; his demise was often accompanied by brutality and every form of conniving on the part of his tormenters, who began to speak of themselves as "Americans." In an effort to protect their lands, the Indians often fought back savagely. Their resistance nourished a feeling among the white men that the native Americans were bloodthirsty, inferior savages whose extermination would best serve everyone's interest. The British government struggled from afar to establish a more enlightened Indian policy aimed at respecting Indian rights to their lands and at dealing with them honorably in resolving conflicts; this effort was especially intense after the French and Indian War, which resulted in English control of the vast Indian stronghold lying between the Appalachians and the Mississippi. But the westward bound, land-hungry Americans, abetted by greedy land speculators, paid little heed to the Indian policy of the British government and proceeded with the grim business of displacing or exterminating the Indians. After the American Revolution there was nothing to restrain the movement of the white men into the huge Indian world west of the Appalachians. As the frontier moved West, the native American was progressively driven ahead of it or exterminated.

4. THE IMPACT OF EUROPEAN EXPANSION: INDIAN CIVILIZATION

In contrast with the New World, the impact of the Europeans was minimal on the peoples of the Far East. Few Europeans went to that part of the world as colonists. Those few who did isolated themselves in a few trading depots located in the seaboard cities of India and the East Indies, where their contacts with the natives were slight. The limited impact of the Europeans on the Far East resulted primarily from the fact that there they encountered ancient cultures, solidly founded and not inferior to those of Western Europe. A brief discussion of Indian civilization will illustrate why the European impact was minimal.

When the Europeans first began their penetration of India, they were confronted by a situation rare in her long history: the presence of a unified political system embracing the entire subcontinent. Political unity had been imposed by the Moguls, a branch of the Mongol horde of Tamerlane that had begun to penetrate India about 1500. By the reign of Akbar (1556–1605), the Moguls had subdued most of the petty principalities into which India had long been divided. Muslim by faith and the bearers of a foreign culture, the Mogul emperors held their power throughout the seventeenth century chiefly because of their tolerant attitude toward native Indian civilization. But their success represented a relatively rare episode in Indian history. Since the beginnings of Indian civilization in the third millennium B.C., foreign invaders had repeatedly tried to unite the peninsula, only to be frustrated by the racial, linguistic, and geographical barriers that fragmented this vast and populous land. For long stretches of time, Indian political life was dominated by numerous petty princes. A tradition of strong political organization was therefore not a decisive element in Indian civilization. Its strength lay elsewhere, in institutions and beliefs that were affected very little by the presence of outsiders, including Europeans.

Indian society in the sixteenth and seventeenth centuries gained its cohesion primarily from three interrelated and very ancient institutions—the village, the family, and the caste system. With the exception of a small minority of the population living in the coastal cities, the great mass of Indians lived in self-sufficient agricultural villages under the authority of the Brahmins (priests), whose role we will examine in a moment. Each village was made up of several families. Every family was a tightly knit unit held together by blood ties, common ownership and exploitation of the land, and religion. Each village had its own government, amazingly democratic in its operation. The villages sometimes had to pay taxes to a faraway central authority, but seldom did that authority significantly influence the course of village life.

Even more fundamental in the life of each Indian was the caste system. Its origins were ancient and are still poorly understood. Long before the beginning of the Christian era, Indian society had been stratified into groups, each with its own customs, responsibilities, and rights. The system steadily became more complicated and more rigid. In ancient times there were four broad castes: the priests, the aristocratic warriors, the small landowners and artisans, and the laborers. The untouchables were those having no caste. As the centuries passed, numerous subgroups were created within each broad caste, and the rules regulating the conduct of each group became constantly more elaborate. By the time Europeans became acquainted with Indian society, there were hundreds of caste groups. Almost every occupational group in India constituted a special caste. Elaborate rules defining every detail of life within the caste and of relationships with other groups had been evolved. A member of a caste had his life clearly cut out for him from birth. Education, marriage, occupation, manners, dress, and nearly everything else were clearly defined. Obviously, this institution gave the individual little freedom, but just as obviously it provided him with a definite place in society and established a remarkably stable and unchanging social order.

The strength of the Indian caste system lay in the religious sanctions that stood behind it; every Indian accepted the system that bound him to his present lot because he believed that that system was the earthly embodiment of the divine order of the universe. More than anything else, religion gave Indian civilization its distinctive qualities and made most Indians immune to Western influences.

That religious system was already ancient when the Europeans first began settling in India. Several religious traditions, some dating back to the beginnings of Indian civilization, had merged to create the main body of Indian religious thought. By 500 B.C. a basic set of assumptions had been clearly formulated by religious and philosophical leaders and set down in a body of philosophical literature called the Upanishads. From the Upanishads later developed the chief religious systems of India (except Mohammedanism, which entered India from the outside). A brief description of the

The flowering of Indian civilization under the Mogul emperors is revealed in splendid architectural monuments such as the Taj Mahal, in glorious poetry, and in exquisite painted miniatures such as this one, which shows the emperor Akbar on a hunt. *Photo: The Victoria and Albert Museum, London*

basic ideas contained in the Upanishads is the best starting place for an understanding of Indian religion.

The ancient Indian thinkers agreed that the universe is permeated by a spiritual force that creates and animates everything. This spiritual force is the only thing that is real. The world that man sees and experiences is merely an illusion, representing the spirit entrapped in material things. The destiny of spirits born to the flesh is to escape back to the perfect world of pure spirit.

At a certain stage on their way to perfection spirits are born into the material world. Once made flesh, spirits become excessively attached to earthly existence, piling up a record of activities not befitting a pure spirit. This record must be atoned for before a spirit achieves its ultimate perfection. When death parts the spirit from its earthly prison, the soul carries its record with it. Therefore, the spirit must be reincarnated in some earthly form to continue its purification. The form that rebirth takes depends on the record of a spirit's previous activities; forces beyond man's control assign him to a status in this world and demand that he keep that status. Rebirth may occur many times, each time putting the spirit in a different shape and presenting it with new tests. Eventually, the spirit will end its dependence on the material world and be freed from reincarnation. Toward that perfect state all things are destined.

Hinduism was by far the most significant religion that grew out of the concepts discussed previously. The great spiritual force, which the philosophers said directed the universe, became gods. Most Hindus worship many gods, although three predominate: Brahma the Creator, Vishnu the Preserver, and Siva the Destroyer. No matter how many different gods are worshiped, the Hindu believes they are all part of a single spiritual order and thus in no sense competitive. To honor these gods, an elaborate set of rituals has developed over the centuries, chiefly under the guidance of the Brahmins, or priests, who play a leading role in Indian society because they are necessary to approach the gods in the proper way.

Hindus take literally the idea that a part of the divine spirit dwells in every creature. This has led to the development of a complicated list of prohibitions against killing and eating animals, doing violence to other men, and mistreating one's own body. Since detachment from the world is a way of freeing the spirit, Hindus are strongly ascetic, often withdrawing from daily life for fasting, prayer, and chastisement of the flesh. All Hindus believe in reincarnation, and consider the caste system to be the earthly form of this truth. Each caste is a kind of religious order representing a stage into which spirits are born on the path to perfection. It becomes every Hindu's religious duty to accept his caste and fulfill all the obligations attached to it. In the ascending structure of the caste system, each grade represents a step nearer to spiritual perfection and liberation from the material world. The untouchable is the least pure of all humans and must suffer burdens equal to his impurity. The Brahmin at the top of the caste system is nearest to perfection and is about to end the cycle of rebirth, a status that gives Brahmins the wisdom to control earthly society. The orthodox Hindu therefore accepts the established social system in India as a vital part of his religion and feels that to change it would be to tamper with the divine order.

Hinduism places a heavy emphasis on acceptance of one's lot and upon close observation of all the rituals and laws connected with one's earthly station. The good Hindu believes, worships, observes the law, and waits until repeated reincarnation delivers him. It is one of the most formalistic religions in the world.

However, the powerful stream of Indian religious life did not confine itself to that one channel. Buddhism, for example, illustrates how the basic set of beliefs that we have just noted could produce a different religion. Buddhism drew its original inspiration from the teachings of Gautama Buddha (ca. 563–483 B.C.). Buddha, the son of a prince, was well educated in the philosophical ideas of the Upanishads. Rejecting his princely heritage to become a religious leader, Buddha preached a doctrine according to which men freed themselves from the suffering of this world by moral activity. He believed that all suffering was caused by the desire for things that did not befit human beings. To help men free themselves from such desires, Buddha laid down an enlightened moral code, called the Eightfold Path, which stressed love of others, good works, and rejection of sensual pleasures. By following this code Buddha felt that a man could help himself along the road to spiritual freedom. Buddha did not reject reincarnation; he taught merely that a morally strong man could speed up his own deliverance.

Buddha's teachings, originally an ethical protest against Hindu religious practices, were soon turned into a religion. His disciples, organizing themselves into monastic groups, turned Buddha into a god, began worshiping his statues, and devised rituals to give expression to his teachings. The new religion took deep roots in India and flourished for many centuries. Eventually, it fell into decline and by 1500 virtually disappeared there. In part this was due to the fact that several foreign invaders of India were converts to Buddhism, causing it to gain a reputation as a foreign religion. However, before it died in India, Buddhism had gained a foothold abroad, especially in China. In its new home it flourished and spread, until today it is one of the major religions of the world, practiced nearly everywhere in the Far East except India. Buddhism left its mark on India despite its disappearance there. Its moral earnestness, its explanation of suffering, and its denial of this world all became part of the Indian religious tradition.

Indian religion accounted for many things about the civilization that the Europeans met in India in the early modern period. Indians were inclined to accept this world passively, feeling that the individual's destiny lay elsewhere. Progress, competition for wealth, and the search for new things were not attractive to them. The good Indian took what life gave him reverently and humbly. He was not impressed by the Europeans, for he was convinced that he had reflected as keenly and deeply as they about human problems and had arrived at answers superior to theirs. He could point to a remarkable art and literature to prove (to his own satisfaction, at least) the superiority of his way of life. Nothing the European could bring him would, in his mind, improve upon his institutions and ideas. He therefore refused to be agitated by the advent of the Europeans. They, in turn, found that a few hundred soldiers and a few cannon could not shake the Indian's confidence in his village and family life, his caste system, and his religion. Only slowly and almost

imperceptibly did the European way of life make any significant impression on the East.

5. THE IMPACT OF EUROPEAN EXPANSION: SUB-SAHARAN AFRICA

Too infrequently noted is the fact that the expansion of Europe in the seventeenth and eighteenth centuries had a significant impact on Africa. On that vast continent the European influence was exercised by a tiny number of white men who changed the course of African history chiefly by enticing the Africans to serve their interests through trade—especially traffic in human beings.

The centuries prior to 1500 had been highly significant in shaping the destiny of sub-Saharan Africa. That period witnessed the formation of a number of prosperous states spread across a wide belt of territory south of the Sahara from the Atlantic to the Indian Ocean and then far southward along that inviting sea. These states—Ghana, Mali, Songhay, the kingdoms of Hausaland, and the Swahili city-states—were strongly influenced by Muslim religion, culture, and technology from North Africa; however, in all of them the imprint of much older native African cultures was strongly felt, producing an amazingly cosmopolitan culture, especially in the brilliant cities that dominated these states. The remarkable affluence of these states depended on a vigorous trans-Saharan and Indian Ocean trade that carried gold, ivory, slaves, and many other products northward to the Muslim Empire and Europe and eastward to India. In fact, many of these states were brought into existence by enterprising native chieftans who organized extensive realms so as to control more effectively the trading ventures that brought such great riches. Because their existence depended so heavily on trade and because the techniques their rulers borrowed to assert their power had little impact on the great bulk of the native population, these African states tended to be unstable. Nonetheless, their creation and their active intercourse with outside cultures marked an important stage in the development of Africa and its involvement with the larger world. Farther to the south, beyond the sphere of Muslim influence, the native population continued its simple agricultural existence according to ancient customs, as yet little touched by developments to the north.

These developments in pre-1500 sub-Saharan Africa created a situation that made Africa particularly susceptible to the onslaught of the Western Europeans, chiefly because the destiny of so many African states was tied directly to trade with the outside world. Coming by sea to the coastal areas of sub-Saharan Africa, the Europeans almost instantly caused a redirection of trade routes from the traditional trans-Saharan routes toward Western Europe and the expanding European empires in the New World and the Far East. The newcomers made little effort to settle in sub-Saharan Africa, partly because the Africans resisted their settlement but more importantly because they could get what they wanted by doing little more than establishing a few trading posts in the coastal cities of Africa. What they wanted were the valuable raw materials of Africa and then before long the Africans themselves — as slaves to perform the arduous labor of creating a rich agricultural establishment in the New World. Throughout the seventeenth and eighteenth centuries massive numbers of black Africans were uprooted from their native soil, often as a result of the efforts of their black compatriots, sold into the hands of English, French, Dutch, Portuguese, Spanish, and American slave traders, and distributed under inhuman conditions far and wide to toil as chattels in the service of white landowners intent on exploiting the vast agricultural potential of the New World.

As the Europeans opened markets along the coasts of sub-Saharan Africa, significant political alignments occurred in Africa. African kingdoms along the Gold Coast flourished as a result of their domination of trade flowing from inland into the hands of European traders. Often the ruling elements of these kingdoms became prime agents in supplying slaves to the Europeans, leading them to intervene among inland tribes to find slaves to sell. Native chiefs living inland likewise became caught up in the slave trade. Armed with deadly weapons from Europe, the native tribes began to wage war on one another

as a means of procuring slaves. The Europeans asserted subtle influences on the coastal states in order to enhance their own trading interests, thus promoting a slow deterioration of the capability of the Africans to control their own destiny. As the demand for slaves increased and the prices commanded by the African slave suppliers rose, European traders moved farther and farther south along the west coast of Africa to turn the attention of more and more native Africans toward serving European trading interests, especially slavery, with the same disruptive consequences. European influences, especially Portuguese, on the east coast of Africa were equally disruptive of the brilliant Swahili civilization flourishing there. Only deep in the central part of Africa did the native population remain relatively free of the impact of European intrusion.

On the whole, the development of sub-Saharan Africa was seriously impeded by the encounter of its peoples with the Western Europeans during the seventeenth and eighteenth centuries. Africa's human resources were depleted, her resources plundered, and her political and social structures disoriented. The Europeans gave little in return, especially when compared to what the Muslims of North Africa had contributed to the enrichment of sub-Saharan Africa prior to 1500. Despite the traumatic consequences of European expansion in this era, the Africans retained many elements of their native tradition, which would later reassert itself as a significant aspect of the revival of Africa. And those who were uprooted from Africa in this period took much with them to add important elements to the civilization that was forming in the New World, where they were laboring as slaves.

6. THE STRUGGLE FOR OVERSEAS EMPIRE

In spite of nearly empty continents to occupy in the New World and rich trading opportunities to exploit in the highly civilized East and in sub-Saharan Africa, the aggressive European nations could not keep out of one another's way in their overseas expansion. In the sixteenth century the competition had begun with Dutch and English assaults on the Spanish and Portuguese empires.

By the end of the seventeenth century the struggle for overseas empires entered a critical phase and progressed rapidly toward a decision in the eighteenth.

This struggle did not arise because the world overseas had become too crowded with Europeans. As mercantilists, the colonial and commercial powers of the eighteenth century believed that their wealth and self-sufficiency depended on absolute control of territories overseas and that they could strike a mortal blow at their European foes by depriving them of their colonies. Every European war was, therefore, extended overseas, and every major settlement of a European war included a redistribution of overseas possessions.

The Dutch were the first to engage in serious competition with other European powers. As we have previously noted, they began to dismember the Portuguese Empire in the Far East in the sixteenth century. England soon followed the Dutch lead. Although her attacks on the Spanish Empire in the New World were not especially profitable, England did succeed in seizing most of Portugal's Indian holdings during the seventeenth century.

By the middle of the seventeenth century, the rivalry between the English and the Dutch began to increase. As early as 1651 England passed her first Navigation Act, providing that all goods coming to and from England and her overseas possessions would be carried in English ships. This struck a blow at Dutch commercial power, which concentrated on providing shipping services for other nations. It also encouraged the growth of the English navy, badly neglected by the first two Stuart kings. On three different occasions between 1651 and 1688 England engaged the Dutch in warfare. In general, these wars were not decisive. England did annex New Netherland in 1664, but gave the Dutch territory elsewhere. Probably the chief result of the wars was to add to the growing strength of the English navy. Eventually, the English and the Dutch began to see that France was the chief threat to both. The result was an alliance in 1689, when William of Orange became king of England. By that time the Netherlands was no longer the major sea power in Europe. The Dutch were content to keep their already established holdings, letting the other nations compete for the rest of the world.

The Dutch and the English had real cause for alarm. Louis XIV threw France wholeheartedly into the competition for overseas possessions in Canada, Louisiana, the West Indies, and India—all areas near to England's centers of operation. From 1689 until 1763 England and France fought each other regularly in Europe, and each engagement had its repercussions abroad.

Several times during the War of the League of Augsburg (1688–1697), the English and the French engaged forces in North America, where the war was called King William's War. Neither in Europe nor in America was the action decisive, and no changes were made in the holdings of either combatant. England had more success during the War of the Spanish Succession (1702–1713). In North America, where the struggle was called Queen Anne's War, England captured Arcadia (Nova Scotia) and received recognition of her claims to Newfoundland and Hudson Bay. From France's ally, Spain, she received Gibralter and Minorca, assuring her entrance into the Mediterranean. Spain also granted to England the right to supply Spain's colonies with slaves (the *asiento*) and the privilege of sending one ship a year to the Spanish colonies in America. These concessions ended Spain's long effort to close her empire to outsiders and gave England the advantage over other nations in exploiting Spanish overseas holdings.

From 1713 to 1740 England and France remained at peace. During this calm neither nation was idle in overseas matters. France, realizing the weakness of her position, was especially active in North America. She tried to protect her holdings from English sea power by building a strong fort at Louisburg at the mouth of the St. Lawrence. She also began constructing a series of forts designed to keep the English colonists pinned to the Atlantic seaboard. England concentrated her efforts on widening the commercial breach she had made in Spain's empire in 1713. A new European war in 1740, the War of the Austrian Succession, led to a sharp conflict between England and France in America (King George's War) and in India. At the end of the

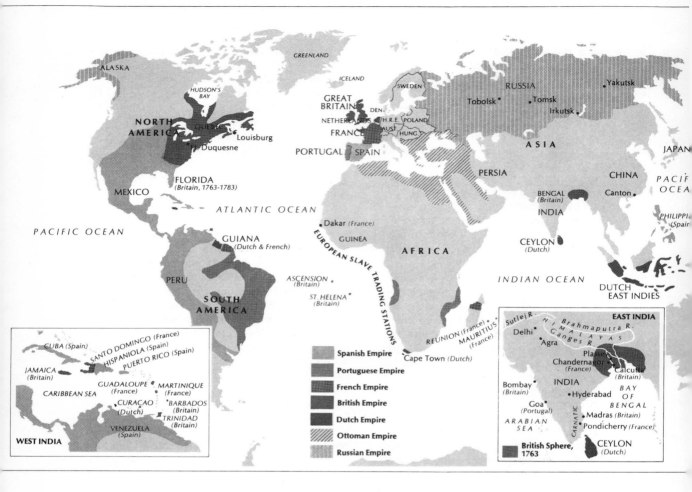

THE WORLD IN 1763

war in 1748 each power restored its spoils to the other, England giving up Louisburg and France restoring Madras.

An eight-year truce ensued in Europe, each side preparing desperately for the struggle that everyone knew would soon reopen. In North America, France went back to her policy of building a barrier against the westward expansion of the English colonies. Already the colonists were pushing across the Appalachians into the Ohio Valley, claiming the territory as part of their original grants from the English crown. The inevitable clash came in 1755, when the British tried to stop the French from occupying Fort

Duquesne at the present site of Pittsburgh. The issue was clearly joined; one power must destroy the other in America.

In India a no less dramatic struggle was shaping. France had entered the scene later than England but had made steady progress up to 1740. Growing English sea power then made France's position precarious. To offset this disadvantage, the French governor of Pondicherry, François Dupleix, decided to take advantage of the internal chaos in India resulting from the decline of Mogul authority. In return for concessions favorable to France, he supplied troops and made promises to whatever political faction in India gave him the best advantage. The policy netted France a claim to most of southern India. Dupleix soon found his match in a lowly clerk of the British East India Company named Robert Clive, who began to fight fire with fire. Spending money liberally and making even greater promises to the Indians, Clive built a counteralliance of Indian princes and wrung generous concessions from them for his company. Soon an undeclared war was on in India. Dupleix was recalled to France in 1754, chiefly because his company did not trust his high-handed methods. The showdown began in 1756, when an Indian prince attacked the British garrison in Calcutta. Having captured the garrison, the prince put 146 Englishmen into a tiny cell; by the next morning 123 were dead in this "Black Hole" of Calcutta. Clive decided to avenge this atrocity.

Thus, at the opening of the Seven Years' War (French and Indian War in America) in 1756 France and England were pitted against each other on three continents. We have previously examined the course of that war in Europe (see Chapter 35). England, led by William Pitt, threw her chief efforts into the naval and colonial war and won a smashing victory. In North America the French held their own until 1757. The superior British forces, supported by the navy, overpowered the French outposts one by one. The decisive blow came, in 1759, when the British captured Quebec, opening all Canada to the British. British naval units captured the chief French holdings in the West Indies. In India, Robert Clive gave the British as great a victory as Quebec. Using his military resources brilliantly and gaining invaluable help from the navy, he smashed France's Indian allies and captured her trading centers. When Pondicherry fell in 1761,

France was ruined in India. Perhaps even more important, Clive had added large territories to England's sphere of influence by conquering several native Indian states.

The Seven Years' War ended in 1763 with the Treaty of Paris. France surrendered Canada and all Louisiana east of the Mississippi (except New Orleans) to England. Spain, who had been an ally of France, ceded Florida to England. By a special treaty France compensated Spain for this loss by giving her the rest of Louisiana (west of the Mississippi). All French possessions in the West Indies except Guadeloupe and Martinique also fell to England. France's empire in India likewise went to Britain. The French were permitted to enjoy trading privileges in India and to keep Pondicherry, but Britain controlled the chief centers of trade, ending any hope of a French recovery of power there.

The Treaty of Paris closed an era in European expansion. Although the Dutch and the Spanish still had extensive holdings abroad, Great Britain had fought her way to supremacy in colonial and commercial affairs. She could now turn to the exploitation of her empire.

Since Columbus' voyage the Europeans had wrought an important change around the world. Energetic colonizers had planted European civilization on the soil of the New World. Enterprising merchants had begun to tap the wealth of a considerable part of the Far East and of sub-Sahara Africa. European patterns of civilization had begun to alter the lives of peoples who had developed their own cultures long before the Europeans came. For good or bad, the Europeanization of the world had begun. And European history never again ceased to have a world-wide scope.

Suggested Reading

European Overseas Colonization

*J. H. Parry, *The Establishment of European Hegemony, 1415–1715: Trade and Exploration in the Age of the Renaissance* (Harper Torchbook). A thorough general treatment.

H. E. Bolton and T. M. Marshall, *The Colonization of North America* (1924). A careful, balanced study of the colonizing efforts of the European powers in North America.

*C. H. Haring, *The Spanish Empire in America* (Harbinger). A splendid picture of the Spanish role in the New World.

*W. H. McNeill, *The Rise of the West* (Mentor). A provocative view of the expansion of Europe from a global perspective.

The Impact of European Expansion

P. Radin, *The Story of the American Indian*, rev. ed., (1944). A good introduction to a neglected subject.

K. S. Latourette, *A Short History of the Far East*, 4th ed., (1964). A sweeping review of a complicated subject by a sympathetic scholar.

*R. Thapar and P. Spear, *A History of India*, 2 vols. (Pelican). An excellent survey in some detail of India's long and complex history.

*H. G. Rawlinson, *India, A Short Cultural History* (Praeger). This well-informed survey will provide a grasp of the major elements of India's rich cultural tradition.

*J. S. Hutton, *Caste in India*, 3rd ed., (Oxford). This work will clarify many aspects of the complex social system so vital to Indian life.

*K. M. Sen, *Hinduism* (Penguin). A clear description of the major elements constituting India's most important religion.

*E. Conze, *Buddhism: Its Essence and Development* (Harper Torchbook). A good introduction.

H. A. Gailey, *History of Africa: From the Earliest Times in 1800* (1970). A balanced, well-organized treatment of a complex subject.

J. Maquet, *Civilization of Black Africa* (1972). Provides a sense of the unique and significant features of the cultures of the native Africans.

Imperial Rivalry

*W. L. Dorn, *Competition for Empire, 1740–1763* (Harper Torchbook). A splendid treatment of the conflict for control of the world in the critical period.

*F. Parkman, *Parkman Reader*, ed. S. Morison (Little Brown Paperback). This work will provide a good introduction to the work of the nineteenth-century American historian whose many works provided a vivid picture of the Anglo-French struggle for dominance in North America.

37

CLASSICISM, BAROQUE, PIETISM

The spirit of royal absolutism, with its exaltation of kings, princes, and attendant nobility, and also its concern for order and form, was reflected in the literature, the arts, and certain religious movements of the seventeenth and eighteenth centuries. The prevailing styles were classicism in literature and music and baroque in painting and architecture. Pietistic religious movements passively accepted royal absolutism as a form of government. Absolutism had its direct apologists in the field of political theory.

1. THE PHILOSOPHY OF ABSOLUTISM

In our twentieth-century concern for popular government we sometimes forget the service performed in early modern times by the royal monarchs. It was they who suppressed feudal turbulence, established law and order, and molded the first national states. Some were incompetent and some were predatory. However, the tragic example of Poland and the Holy Roman Empire, where the monarchs were dominated by the nobility and the local princes, would seem to indicate that in the first three centuries of the modern era, the absolutist kings generally served a useful, and possibly necessary, function. Their role was appreciated and defended by many of their subjects. We have already encountered Bishop Bossuet's eloquent defense of Louis XIV's claims to be God's duly ordained vicegerent on earth, and James I's espousal of divine right monarchy.

The seventeenth-century thinker Thomas Hobbes, dismayed by the civil strife then raging in England (the Puritan Revolution), decided that only absolute government could maintain law and order. In his *Leviathan* (1651), Hobbes theorized that basically selfish men for their own protection contracted with a prince to rule them; but, once having made the compact, they could not revoke it.[1] To be effective, the prince must be all-powerful, controlling even the religion of his subjects. The great Dutch political theorist Hugo Grotius argued not only for absolute governmental authority within the state, but also for absolute sovereignty and equality of all states large and small. His chief work, *The Law of War and Peace* (1625), was one of the earliest and probably the most influential of all treatises on international law. It was the outgrowth of Grotius' experiences during the revolt of the Netherlands against Spain and of his observation of some of the horrors of the Thirty Years' War in Germany. Both Hobbes and Grotius believed royal absolutism to be in accordance with the natural law.

2. THE GOLDEN AGE OF FRENCH LITERATURE

The reign of Louis XIV (1643–1715), which marked the apogee of royal absolutism in France

---

[1]While proffering the social-contract theory of government, Hobbes did not believe that it actually occurred as a historical event.

This photograph of the interior of the church at Ottobeuren, Munich, shows the elaborate, gaudy splendor of the baroque style, the hallmark of the age of royal absolutism and affluence. *Photo: Hirmer Verlag*

and indeed in all Europe, was also the golden age of French literature. The elegance, the sense of order, and the formalism of the court of the Grand Monarch were all reflected in the literature of the period, sometimes called the Augustan or the classical period of French literature. It was in the field of the drama that the French writers attained their greatest success. Corneille wrote elegant tragedies in the style of and often on the same subjects as the ancient Greek tragedies. The struggles of man against himself and against the universe furnish the dramatic conflicts. Corneille's craftsmanship and style are handsomely polished, though often exalted and exaggerated.

Even more exquisitely polished were the perfectly rhymed and metered couplets of Racine's tragedies: *Andromaque* relates the tragic story of Hector's wife after the death of her husband at the hands of Achilles and the ensuing fall of Troy. *Phèdre* is about the wife of the legendary Greek king Theseus who falls in love with her stepson. This story had also been the subject of plays by Euripides, Sophocles, and Seneca. As with the Greek and Roman dramatists, abnormal love was a favorite theme with the French playwrights of the seventeenth century. Racine, an ardent Jansenist, turned later in life to religious subjects.

One of the greatest of all the French dramatists was Molière. In his charming and profound comedies—such as *Tartuffe, Le Misanthrope,* and *Les Femmes Savantes (The Learned Ladies)*—Molière devastatingly portrays and satirizes the false, the stupid, and the pompous among men: egotists, pedants, social climbers, false priests, quack physicians. The tragic conflicts and the personality types of Corneille, Racine, and Molière are universal and eternal.

Other major French writers of the age of Louis XIV were Blaise Pascal, the scientist and mathematician who also wrote the marvelously styled *Provincial Letters* against the Jesuits and the deeply reflective *Pensées (Thoughts)*; Madame de Sévigné, who wrote almost two thousand letters to her daughter, each a work of art; and the Duke de Saint-Simon, who spent the latter part of his life writing forty volumes of *Mémoires*. Madame de Sévigné and the Duke de Saint-Simon, both of whom were eyewitnesses of the court of Louis XIV, constitute two of the most important sources we have for the history and the life of that period.

The common denominator among all these writers is their emphasis upon and mastery of elegant and graceful form. In this they reflect the spirit of royal absolutism at its height. However, the form is valued not merely for its own sake, but as an artistic clothing for subtle and critical thought. French literature in the late seventeenth century overshadowed that of all other countries of Europe, much as did French military and political influence. The lucid and graceful French language became the fashionable language of most of the royal courts and courtiers on the European continent.

French literature in the eighteenth century continued for the most part in the classical vein. Voltaire wrote dramas and poems carefully tailored to the dictates of classical formalism. His prose works exalted logic and the ideals of Greece and Rome. Only Rousseau among the major eighteenth-century French writers departed from the classical spirit to anticipate the romanticism of a later era. Voltaire and Rousseau, however, are much more important for the philosophic content of their works than for their literary artistry, and will be more fully examined in the following chapter, "The Intellectual Revolution."

3. THE ENGLISH CLASSICAL WRITERS

Next to France, England produced the most important literature in the seventeenth and early eighteenth centuries, and like the French the English authors generally wrote in the classical vein. The giant of English letters in the mid-seventeenth century was John Milton. This learned Puritan was steeped in the literature of ancient Greece and Rome. His exquisite lyrics *L'Allegro* and *Il Penseroso* and incomparable elegy, *Lycidas,* are thickly strewn with references to classical mythology. The conscientious Milton contributed much of his great talent and energy to public affairs. During the Puritan Revolution he went blind working as pamphleteer for the Puritan cause and as secretary for Oliver Cromwell. The chief literary product of this period of his life is *Areopagitica,* probably the noblest defense of freedom of the press ever penned. Milton's masterpiece is *Paradise Lost,* written in his blindness and after the restoration of the Stuart kings had ruined his public career. *Paradise Lost* is a poem of epic proportions based on the Genesis account of the rebellion of Satan against God and the temptation and fall of man. This grandiose theme is treated in stately blank verse of formal elegance. Even in this deeply religious work, holy writ is interwoven with classical pagan myth.

The two greatest poets to succeed Milton were John Dryden in the late seventeenth century and Alexander Pope in the early eighteenth century. Both were satirists, both displayed a massive knowledge of Greek and Roman lore, and both wrote chiefly in the formal rhymed couplets typical of the classical period. In the precision of their form, as in the sharpness of their satire, their appeal was to reason rather than to emotion. In these respects they resemble the great French classicist Voltaire, whom they preceded by a few decades.

The eighteenth century in English literature was an age of great prose. Following the upheavals of the seventeenth century, the Puritan and Glorious revolutions, it was a time of political and religious bitterness and bickering. In pungent and incisive prose Jonathan Swift, in his *Gulliver's Travels* and political essays, and Richard Sheridan in his numerous dramas, pilloried the fops, pedants, bigots, and frauds of the day, much as Molière had done a century earlier across the channel. It was in the eighteenth century that the English novel was born. Samuel Richardson, in *Clarissa Harlowe,* and Henry Fielding, in *Tom Jones,* used this medium to analyze human personality, emotions, and psychology, just as Corneille and Racine had used the poetic drama in France for the same purpose.

In the eighteenth century several writers— Robert Burns in Great Britain, Rousseau in France, Schiller and Goethe in Germany—anticipated romanticism (see pp. 530–538). But the prevailing spirit in eighteenth- as in seventeenth-century literature was classical. Precision, formalism, and ofttimes elegance marked the style. Ancient Greece and Rome furnished the models. The appeal was generally to reason. The royal monarchs and their courts had little to fear from this literature, even from the poetic and dramatic works of Voltaire. They could derive comfort from its formal order and laugh with the rest of the world at its satire, which was aimed at mankind in general rather than at ruling regimes.

4. BAROQUE PAINTING AND ARCHITECTURE

If the literature of the seventeenth and eighteenth centuries did not offend the absolutist kings and their aristocratic courtiers, the visual arts of the period usually glorified them. The dominant style of painting and architecture was the baroque, which was an elaboration of the classical style of the Renaissance. The baroque style was originally a product of the Roman Catholic Reformation and reflected the resurgence of a revitalized Roman Catholic Church led by the militant Jesuits. Later its massive and ornamental elegance reflected the wealth and power of the absolutist monarchs and their courts, then at the peak of their affluence.

The most popular of the baroque painters of the early seventeenth century was the Fleming Peter Paul Rubens. After studying the work of the Italian High Renaissance masters, Rubens returned to Antwerp and painted more than two thousand pictures, many of them huge in size. He operated what amounted to a painting factory, employing dozens of artists who painted in the details designed and sketched by the master. Rubens, a devout Roman Catholic, first painted religious subjects. His sculpturesque and sensational *Descent from the Cross* undoubtedly reveals the influence of Michelangelo. His later subjects were pagan mythology, court life, and especially voluptuous nude women—all painted in the most brilliant and sensuous colors. All these subjects appear in his most ambitious work—twenty-three colossal scenes (mostly imaginary) from the life of Marie de Médicis, widow of King Henry IV of France. Seldom, if

Rembrant's The Polish Rider (ca. 1655), a work of the later life of this great baroque artist, has a moving depth and subtlety: The rider, alert to dangers we can only imagine, seems about to move past our view as he follows a curving path across the canvas. *Photo: Copyright The Frick Collection, New York*

ever, has a dull and colorless woman been more glamorized in paint.

Spain boasted two of the greatest seventeenth-century baroque painters: El Greco and Velásquez. El Greco, whose real name was Domenikos Theotokopoulos, was a native of the Greek island of Crete (hence "The Greek"). After studying the Italian Renaissance masters, he settled down in Toledo and developed a style of his own, usually called mannerism or expressionism. By deliberate distortion and exaggeration he achieved sensational effect. *View of Toledo, St. Jerome in His Study,* and *Christ at Gethsemane* illustrate his genius. El Greco's favorite subject

Tiepolo, Venetian by birth and training, a master of light and color, was famous for his skill at illusionistic ceiling decoration, one of the hallmarks of the baroque and rococo styles. This painting of Perseus and Andromeda shows the grace and delicacy of his work. *Photo: Copyright The Frick Collection, New York*

was the reinvigorated Church of the Roman Catholic Reformation. Considered to be a madman by his contemporaries, he is now regarded as the forerunner, if not the founder, of several schools of nineteenth- and twentieth-century painting. Velásquez was a painter of great versatility. Although much of his earlier work was of a religious nature, he also painted genre subjects (depicting the life of the common people) and, later, portraits. He is considered one of the greatest of portrait painters. As official court painter, he exalted and glorified the Spanish royalty and ruling classes at a time when they

had really passed their peak in world affairs. Velásquez was one of the chief pioneers of modern art; it was from him that the nineteenth-century impressionists and realists received much of their inspiration.

France's chief contribution to baroque painting was Nicolas Poussin, who spent most of his life in Italy studying the Renaissance masters. Although his biblical and mythological scenes are much more serene and subtle than the works of Rubens and El Greco, they are more vibrant and pulsating than the Italian Renaissance paintings that inspired them. They must, therefore, be classified as baroque in style. Some critics think that Poussin's magnificent landscapes have never been surpassed.

In eighteenth-century Great Britain Reynolds, Gainsborough, Romney, and Lawrence (who lived and painted well into the nineteenth century) vied with each other for commissions to paint the portraits of royalty and aristocracy. The result was plumes, jewels, buckles, silks, brocades, and laces in dripping profusion. This flattering of royalty and aristocracy, however, did not go unchallenged. Hogarth in Great Britain and Goya in Spain in the eighteenth and early nineteenth centuries pitilessly satirized the excesses and abuses of aristocratic society. Their brushes matched the pens of Swift and Sheridan.

Only in the Dutch Netherlands did the age of the baroque fail to reflect the ascendancy of royalty. Here in the busy ports and marketplaces commerce was king, and the great Dutch painters of the seventeenth century, notably Frans Hals and Rembrandt van Rijn, portrayed the bourgeoisie and the common people. Hals was one of the first great realistic genre painters. Rembrandt is universally recognized as one of the greatest artistic geniuses of all time. One of his favorite subjects was the Dutch bourgeoisie. He was not a popularizer, however, and he suffered many personal hardships rather than compromise the sincerity of his art. The tragic toll of these hardships is strikingly revealed in a series of magnificent self-portraits. As a portrayer of character he has never been surpassed, perhaps not even equaled. His mastery of light and shade (*chiaroscuro*) made it seem as if the very souls of his subjects were illumined. *Syndics of the Cloth Guild, Night Watch,* and *Anatomy Lesson of Dr. Tulp* are among his most powerful portrait studies. These three paintings also vividly depict the commercial prosperity, the festive urban life, and the growing interest in natural science, respectively, in the seventeenth-century Dutch Netherlands. Rembrandt's glowing idealization of people and landscapes anticipates the age of romanticism of the early nineteenth century.

Baroque architecture, like baroque painting, was an elaboration and ornamentation of the classical style of the Renaissance, and a product of the Roman Catholic Reformation. In the late sixteenth, seventeenth, and eighteenth centuries Jesuit churches sprang up all over the Roman Catholic world. The most important and one of the best examples of the baroque style is the Jesuit parent church, Il Gesù, in Rome. Also, like the painting, baroque architecture was later used to represent the gaudy splendor of the seventeenth- and eighteenth-century absolute monarchs and their courts.

Towering over all other monuments of baroque architecture, much as did St. Peter's over all other Renaissance structures, was the Versailles Palace of Louis XIV. The exterior of Versailles is designed in long, horizontal classic lines. The interior is lavishly decorated with richly colored marbles, mosaics, inlaid woods, gilt, silver, silk, velvet, and brocade. The salons and halls are lighted with ceiling-to-floor windows and mirrors and crystal chandeliers holding thousands of candles. The palace faces hundreds of acres of groves, walks, pools, terraces, fountains, statues, flowerbeds, and clipped shrubs—all laid out in formal geometric patterns.

So dazzling was this symbol of royal absolutism that many European monarchs attempted to copy it. The most successful attempt was Maria Theresa's Schönbrunn Palace in Vienna. As late as the mid-nineteenth century, mad King Ludwig of Bavaria was building three palaces in the style of Versailles. One, Herrenchiemsee, is a remarkable duplication.

Two other notable examples of baroque architecture, seen by thousands of tourists in Paris, are the Hôtel des Invalides (Old Soldiers' Home)

with its magnificent dome, and the Luxembourg Palace and Gardens. In England Sir Christopher Wren was the greatest architect of the baroque period. The great fire that destroyed most of the heart of London in 1666 provided Wren with an opportunity to build numerous baroque structures. His masterpiece is St. Paul's Cathedral, with its lofty dome and columns.

In the eighteenth century, architecture tended to become more feminine and less massive, relying heavily upon multiple curves and lacy shell-like ornamentation. This style is usually referred to as rococo. One of the best examples is Frederick the Great's Sans Souci Palace at Potsdam. The rococo style, like the baroque, represented an age of aristocratic affluence.

5. THE GREAT AGE OF CLASSICAL MUSIC

The classical spirit pervaded the music of the seventeenth and eighteenth centuries as it did the literature and the visual arts; and, like the literature and the visual arts, seventeenth- and eighteenth-century music was an outgrowth of Renaissance developments.[2] The piano and the violin family of instruments, whose forebears appeared in the sixteenth century, developed rapidly in the seventeenth. In the late seventeenth and early eighteenth centuries, three Italian families, the Amati, the Guarnieri, and the Stradivari, fashioned the finest violins ever made. The seventeenth century was also marked by the rise of the opera. Alessandro Scarlatti in Italy, Lully in France, and Purcell in England popularized this grandiose combination of music and drama. The eighteenth was the great century of classical music—the age of Bach, Handel, Haydn, Mozart, and Beethoven.

Johann Sebastian Bach (1685–1750) was a member of a German family long distinguished in music. Noted in his own lifetime chiefly as an organist, he composed a vast array of great mu-

---

[2]Some music historians designate the music of the seventeenth and early eighteenth centuries, including that of Bach and Handel, as baroque, which was a forerunner of the classical.

sic for organ, harpsichord and clavichord (forerunner of the piano), orchestra, and chorus, much of which has been lost. Most of Bach's compositions were religiously inspired, and he holds the same position in Protestant music that the sixteenth-century Palestrina does in music of the Roman Catholic Church. Bach was not widely appreciated in his own day. It was not until Felix Mendelssohn in the nineteenth century "discovered" him that he became widely known. Today Bach is considered one of the greatest creative geniuses of all time—comparable to Leonardo da Vinci, Shakespeare, and Cervantes.

George Frederick Handel (1685–1759) was born in central Germany in the same year as Bach and not many miles distant. He studied Italian opera in Germany and Italy, and wrote forty-six operas himself. He became court musician of the elector of Hanover, and when the elector became King George I of England, Handel followed him there. Handel wrote an enormous quantity of music, both instrumental and vocal. All of it is marked by dignity, formal elegance, and melodious harmony—fitting for and appreciated in an age of royal splendor. His best-known work is the majestic oratorio *The Messiah*, heard every Christmas season.

Franz Joseph Haydn (1732–1809), unlike Handel, was primarily interested in instrumental music; he was the chief originator of the symphony. During his long career in Vienna, which he helped to make the music capital of the world, he wrote more than a hundred symphonies in addition to scores of compositions of

This painting of the Mozart family shows the great musical genius as a boy with his parents. Original in Mozart's Wohnhaus, Salzburg. *Photo: Internationale Stiftung Mozarteum, Salzburg*

other forms of music, particularly chamber music. It was in his hands that orchestral music really came into its own. All his work is in the formal, classical style. As a friend of the younger Mozart, Haydn probably learned more than he taught.

Wolfgang Amadeus Mozart (1756–1791) is regarded by many students as the greatest musical genius of all time. Born in Salzburg, he spent most of his adult life in Vienna. Mozart began composing at the age of five (possibly four), and gave public concerts on the harpsichord at the age of six. At twelve he wrote an opera. Before his untimely death at the age of thirty-five, he wrote more than six hundred compositions in all the known musical forms. Symphonies, chamber music, and piano sonatas and concertos were his favorite forms. His best-known operas are *The Marriage of Figaro, Don Giovanni,* and *The Magic Flute.* In the masterful hands of Mozart the classical style reached the peak of its perfection. Never was music so clear, melodic, precise, and logical. However, Mozart's material rewards in this world were few. Although the courts of many kings, princes, and aristocrats were graced by his marvelous music, whose spirit accorded with the formalism and authoritative orderliness of an age of absolutism, his opulent patrons gave him little money or honor. Even their servants looked down on him, and he was buried in a pauper's grave.

Upon the stage set by Bach, Handel, Haydn, and Mozart emerged the greatest figure in the history of music, Ludwig van Beethoven (1770–1827). Beethoven's dynamic genius overflowed the bounds of any school or style. However, his training, his earlier work, and his fundamental style and form were classical. Beethoven, like so many geniuses, lived a tempestuous, trouble-filled life. He was born in Bonn in the German Rhineland of Flemish ancestry (hence the "van"). High-strung, poor, unsocial, and frustratingly ambitious, he suffered in his early prime the greatest calamity that could befall a musical genius — deafness. At the age of twenty-two, he went to Vienna, where he lived the rest of his life. Although Beethoven studied under Haydn, the greatest influence in his life was Mozart, to whose work his earlier compositions

bear a marked resemblance. To the classical style, however, the mature Beethoven added spontaneous and sometimes noisy emotion, thereby becoming the founder of the romantic style of a later generation. Beethoven lived through the upheavals of the French Revolution, Napoleon, and the surge of nationalism that overthrew the Napoleonic dictatorship. His keen interest in these dramatic events is revealed in his music (see p. 537). Beethoven did not write voluminously; however, his nine symphonies, chamber music, and numerous piano sonatas and concertos constitute the best-loved music in history.

6. PIETISM IN RELIGION

Royal political authority was passively accepted by a number of pietistic religious sects that arose during the seventeenth and eighteenth centuries.

We have already observed the Jansenist movement within the Roman Catholic Church in France in the seventeenth century (see p. 369). Although the Jansenists were by no means oblivious to the political and social issues of the day and actually participated in the Fronde uprising against Mazarin's tyranny, they were fundamentally a Puritanical pietistic group, seeking communion with God through prayer, meditation, and mild asceticism. Early in the eighteenth century Louis XIV, under the influence of the Jesuits, outlawed the Jansenists and destroyed their buildings. At the same time the pope declared them to be heretics. However, the spirit of Jansenism continued to exist.

In Germany Philipp Spener (1635–1705) and Count Zinzendorf (1700–1760) became leaders of pietist movements of considerable dimensions. Spener, a Lutheran pastor, recoiled from the formal officiousness that his church had fallen into after the heated religious strife of the sixteenth and early seventeenth centuries. He minimized dogma and external forms in favor of inner piety and holy living. His largely Lutheran following included some of the leading intellects of Germany. Count Zinzendorf, a well-to-do Saxon nobleman, undertook to restore the Bohemian Brethren, the persecuted and scattered followers of the early fifteenth-century reformer John Huss. He called his group the Moravian Brethren. The Moravians, too, shunned intricate dogma and formal ritual. They set up model communities based upon brotherly love, frugal living, hard work, and inner piety. Count Zinzendorf migrated to America and founded Moravian communities at Bethlehem and other Pennsylvania towns. Later many Moravian ("Pennsylvania Dutch") Germans migrated southward along the Appalachian piedmont as far as Georgia, planting settlements, such as Winston-Salem in North Carolina, along the way.

In Lutheran Sweden, Emanuel Swedenborg (1688–1772), a distinguished scientist, inventor, and public servant, founded a movement somewhat like the Moravian Brethren, based upon his visions, which he took to be direct revelations of God. Swedenborg wrote several learned theological works stressing inner and outward piety and individual communion with God. His followers, who called themselves the Church of the New Jerusalem, also came in considerable numbers to America.

England, however, was the seat of the most widespread and influential pietistic movements of the seventeenth and eighteenth centuries. The first was the Society of Friends, or the Quakers, as they were generally called, founded by George Fox (1624–1691). Fox, a man of great energy and stubborn independence, detested formalism in religion as well as in society and government. He believed that true Christianity is an individual matter—a matter of plain, pious living and of private communion with God under the guidance of divine "inner light." Opposed to war, to rank, and to intolerance, the Quakers refused military service, the use of titles, and the taking of oaths. In these respects the Quakers were different from most of the other pietists. They were considered dangerous to the established order and were severely persecuted. Probably the most prominent of the early Quakers was William Penn, a wealthy aristocrat, who in 1682 founded Pennsylvania as a refuge for members of the sect. Pennsylvania and the Quakers both prospered.

A more moderate and popular pietist movement was Methodism. The prime mover in Methodism was John Wesley (1703–1791). While studying for the Anglican ministry at Oxford, John Wesley and a little band of his fellow students became disillusioned at the coldness and spiritual emptiness that had fallen upon the Anglican Church following the exciting religious controversies of the seventeenth century. They also deplored its subservience to the government and to the aristocracy. Wesley's little group began holding prayer meetings and visiting the poor and the sick. Their lives were such examples of piety and moderate regularity that their fellow students branded them "Methodists" in derision. After leaving Oxford, John Wesley and his brother, Charles, spent two years in the newly founded American colony of Georgia, trying unsuccessfully to convert the Indians. In Georgia they came in contact with some German pietists and became converted to a more fervent, evangelical type of Christianity. This they took with them back to England. When the Anglican churches closed their doors to John Wesley, he preached emotional sermons in the streets and fields. A tireless and dynamic soul-stirrer, he rode horseback from one end of England to the other until well into his eighties. Charles Wesley wrote more than 6,500 hymns. George Whitefield, the most eloquent of all the early Methodists, electrified tens of thousands in England and America and converted many to pietistic Christianity. The real founder of Methodism in the American colonies was Francis Asbury (1745–1816), who duplicated in many respects the work of John Wesley in England. The Methodists played a prominent part in the two "Great Awakenings" in America—the first in the 1730s and 40s and the second at the opening of the nineteenth century. In both England and America the Methodists grew rapidly in numbers, mostly among the middle and lower classes.

The various pietist groups were definitely not political revolutionaries. They were intensely interested in social reform—in education, health and sanitation, temperance, penal reform, and abolition of the slave trade. But they hoped to achieve these reforms by private charity rather than political action. They tended to accommodate themselves to absolute monarchy in the belief that spiritual and social conditions could be improved within that framework of government. John Wesley, for instance, though deeply interested in social reform in the American colo-nies, did not sympathize with their struggle for independence. It was not the pietists, but their contemporary rationalistic philosophers of the Enlightenment (see the following chapter), who helped to bring on the revolutionary era that toppled the thrones of many absolute monarchs and chastised or frightened the rest.

Suggested Reading

General
*C. J. Friedrich, *The Age of the Baroque, 1610–1660* (Torch). In Rise of Modern Europe series. Good chapters on the arts in the seventeenth century.
A. Guérard, *The Life and Death of an Ideal: France in the Classical Age* (1928). Well written.

Philosophy of Idealism
J. N. Figgis, *The Divine Right of Kings*, 2nd ed. (1922).
*H. Rosenberg, *Bureaucracy, Aristocracy, and Autocracy, the Prussian Experience, 1660–1815* (Beacon).

Classical Literature
C. H. C. Wright, *French Classicism* (1970).
*R. F. Jones, *The Seventeenth Century* (Stanford University). Good survey of English literature.

Baroque Art
D. N. Robb and J. J. Garrison, *Art in the Western World*, 3rd ed. (1953). Excellent survey. Well illustrated.

Classical Music
E. J. Stringham, *Listening to Music Creatively*, 2nd ed. (1959). Written by a learned musicologist for the layman.

Pietism
W. C. Braithwaite, *The Beginnings of Quakerism* (1912).
*F. J. McConnell, *John Wesley* (Apex). Popularly written by a leading scholar.

Sources
*J. B. Racine, *Three Plays* (Phoenix).
*Molière, *Eight Plays* (Modern Library).
*H. Fielding, *Tom Jones* (Modern Library).

Retrospect

The seventeenth and eighteenth centuries were the apogee of royal absolutism as a form of government in the Western world. With few exceptions, it was the nations ruled by absolutist kings that achieved the greatest successes during those two centuries. The most noteworthy exceptions were England and the Dutch Netherlands.

Under Henry IV, Richelieu, Mazarin, and Louis XIV, the Bourbon monarchy achieved a degree of absolutism in France that was virtually complete and a hegemony in Europe that has seldom, if ever, been equaled. European history during the years 1661–1715 has come to be called the age of Louis XIV. Louis and his court were the envy of all other monarchs, who sought to emulate them. France possessed a military strength so great that the major states of Western and Central Europe working in combination held her in check only with difficulty.

France's only real rival for European and world hegemony in the seventeenth century was England. There royal absolutism had reached its peak during the sixteenth century under the vigorous and politically crafty Tudor rulers. The Stuart kings, who came to the throne in 1603 when Elizabeth I died childless, were full of fine absolutist theories but were politically inept. They soon found themselves in a running fight, mostly over money matters, with Parliament, stronghold of the landed and commercial interests. In a showdown—the Puritan Revolution—the parliamentary forces, under the able leadership of Oliver Cromwell, triumphed. Before the century had ended one Stuart king had been executed, another invited to the throne on terms, and a third driven out of the country. During the course of the seventeenth and eighteenth centuries England's parliamentary and cabinet system gradually took shape. The landed and commercial interests now in control of the English government, however, were no less aggressive in foreign and colonial affairs than had been the royal monarchs. In fact, they were more so.

The most significant political developments in Central and Eastern Europe during the seventeenth and eighteenth centuries were the rise of two military despotisms—Prussia and Russia. The Hohenzollerns of Prussia, consistently pursuing the policies of royal absolutism, militarism, and territorial aggrandizement, more than doubled their territory and population and challenged Austria for the leadership of the German-speaking world. Russia under Peter the Great and Catherine the Great became Westernized, decisively defeated Sweden and the Ottoman Turks, and gained valuable territory facing the West. Poland disappeared from the map, carved up by Russia, Prussia, and Austria.

While Prussia, Russia, and Austria were struggling for the mastery of Central and Eastern Europe, the French, the English, and the Dutch were competing for dominance in North America and Asia. In this contest the English emerged victorious in North America and India, and the Dutch in the East Indies. The English found it relatively easy to drive the primitive Indians out of eastern North America and colonize the continent with Europeans. In Asia the English and the Dutch easily defeated the technologically backward natives, but found it next to impossible to Europeanize peoples steeped in cultures and religions more ancient than those of the West.

The baroque and the classical styles prevailed in literature and the arts in Western Europe throughout most of the seventeenth and eighteenth centuries. These styles generally harmonized with and often exalted the absolutist monarchs and their courts. And the numerous pietist and quietist religious sects that arose during this period passively accepted, for the most part, the political authority of the absolutist governments.

IX

The Era of the French Revolution
1776-1830

The late eighteenth century was an era of revolution in the Western world, both in Europe and in America. Although the royal monarchs had reached the apogee of their power during the seventeenth and eighteenth centuries — everywhere in Europe except England and the Dutch Netherlands — European society remained essentially feudal. The feudal nobility were still powerful in government, and their social supremacy remained virtually complete.

The Christian churches, too, were still powerful in the late eighteenth century. Although the Roman Catholic Church had suffered a loss of influence as a result of the renaissance of secularism and had lost much of its territory as a result of the Protestant Reformation, it still had a strong voice in government and society in predominantly Catholic countries, and had lost none of its spirit of intolerance. The various Protestant churches had adopted quite similar poses wherever they were established. In Eastern Europe, the Orthodox Church had not been touched by either the Renaissance or the Reformation. The clergy there, particularly the upper clergy, like the nobility, enjoyed unchanged the privileged position they had had for hundreds of years.

Meanwhile, new forces were rising to challenge those entrenched elements. The theory of royal absolutism itself came under heavy attack from political theorists. The nobility in Northern and Western Europe felt increasing pressure from the bourgeoisie as the tempo of commerce, capitalistic enterprises, and urban growth steadily increased. The peasantry, too, and even the wage earners were becoming increasingly restive. The clergy found their theological and intellectual influence undermined during these centuries by the rise of natural science and of rationalistic and empiricist philosophies based upon science.

When the privileged classes steadfastly refused to yield or even to bend to these new forces, a series of revolutionary upheavals ensued—the American and the French revolutions, and the exploits of Napoleon. The whole Western world was involved, and the changes brought about by these upheavals reached every area and every level of society.

The so-called intellectual revolution of the eighteenth century marked the triumph of a philosophy of materialistic rationalism and empiricism known as the Enlightenment. This philosophy was based largely upon a scientific attitude brought on by the rise of natural science.

1. THE PIONEER SCIENCE: ASTRONOMY

The first branch of modern natural science to attract systematic attention was astronomy. The founder of modern astronomy was Nicolaus Copernicus (1473–1543), a German-speaking native of Poland whose real name was Kopernik. Like so many other Northern European scholars in the fifteenth century, he crossed the Alps to study in an Italian Renaissance university. It was from his Italian teachers that he received the ideas which led to his revolutionary concept of the structure of the universe. After returning to Poland, he spent the rest of his life in an attempt to prove that the sun, not the earth was the center of the solar system and that the earth and all other planets revolved around the sun while rotating on their own axes. Although this idea had been held by a number of Greek astronomers of the third and second centuries before Christ, it had never gained wide acceptance. For at least thirteen hundred years the Western world had accepted the conclusions of the Hellenistic astronomer Claudius Ptolemy (A.D. second century). The Ptolemaic system, which placed the earth at the center of the universe, satisfied the

38

THE INTELLECTUAL REVOLUTION

senses and seemed to agree with certain statements in the Bible. The medieval Christian theologians, therefore, had come to regard the Ptolemaic system as the Christian view of the physical universe.

Copernicus was quite aware that his startling conclusions would arouse both the ridicule of laymen and the ire of churchmen. It was only near the end of his life that he could be persuaded to publish his views, and the first copy of his book, *Concerning the Revolutions of Celestial Orbs*, reached him on the day of his death. Roman Catholic and Protestant leaders alike denounced the Copernican system as illogical, unbiblical, and unsettling to the Christian faith.

But the new idea could not be suppressed. Nearly a century after Copernicus, a German astronomer, Kepler, with the benefit of additional data, showed convincingly that Copernicus was fundamentally right. However, the exact movements of the heavenly bodies, Kepler discovered, were not quite what Copernicus had believed them to be: the planets revolve around the sun in elliptical rather than circular orbits. Shortly thereafter Galileo (1564–1642), one of the truly great heroes of science and the first to use the telescope in astronomical observation, won over most contemporary scientists to the Copernican theory. Nonetheless, Galileo too was ridiculed and suffered much persecution from the clerical authorities.

The uphill trail blazed by Copernicus, Kepler, and Galileo was continued on to its lofty peak by Sir Isaac Newton (1642–1727). Newton was a

frail boy, the son of a poor English farmer. As a student at Cambridge University he was distinguished enough in mathematics to be chosen to stay on as professor after his graduation. Shortly thereafter, while still in his early twenties, Newton came forth with some of the most tremendous discoveries in the history of science, or indeed of the human intellect. He is probably best known for the law of universal attraction, or gravitation. The concept matured and was refined in Newton's mind over a period of years. As it finally appeared in his *Principia (The Mathematical Principles of Natural Knowledge)*, the law is stated with marvelous simplicity and precision: "Every particle of matter in the universe attracts every other particle with a force varying inversely as the square of the distance between them and directly proportional to the product of their masses." This law, so simply expressed, applied equally to the movement of a planet and a berry falling from a bush. The secret of the physical universe appeared to have been solved—a universe of perfect stability and precision. The modest Newton was so overcome by the grandeur of this law that he was unable to complete the confirming calculations, a task that he turned over to a trusted assistant. Two centuries were to elapse before Albert Einstein would raise grave doubts about the truth of Newton's theory.

Newton, in addition to his teaching and his prodigious scientific achievements, found time to perform public service. He became a member of Parliament and served for many years as active director of the royal mint. He was knighted by Queen Anne. The knighting of Newton as contrasted with the ridicule and persecution suffered by Copernicus and Galileo illustrates the progress that had been made by the scientific attitude between the sixteenth and the eighteenth centuries.

2. OTHER SCIENCES

Astronomy was only the first of many fields of modern natural science that came into being as Western man shifted the center of his interest from spiritual and moral matters to material things. In the seventeenth and eighteenth centuries such a galaxy of great names and discoveries appeared in the various branches of natural sci-

ence that we can mention here only a few of the most significant.

In the sixteenth century Vesalius, a Fleming living in Italy, wrote the first comprehensive textbook on the structure of the human body to be based on careful observation. Because he dissected many human bodies in order to make his observations, he ran into serious opposition from clerical authorities. In disgust he gave up his scientific studies and became the personal physician of Emperor Charles V. In the seventeenth century William Harvey, an Englishman who also studied in Italy, discovered the major principles of the circulatory system, thus making it possible for surgeons to operate on the human body with somewhat less fatal consequences than had previously been the case. Vesalius and Harvey are regarded as the founders of the science of anatomy.

The founding fathers of biological science were Linnaeus, the Swedish botanist, and Buffon, the French zoologist, both of whom lived in the eighteenth century. Since the varieties of plant and animal life are so enormous, one of the major problems in this field of knowledge is that of classification and nomenclature. Linnaeus worked out a system of names for the various species in both the plant and animal kingdoms that is still in use. He also worked out a system of classification of plant life that is partly used by botanists today. Buffon made important contributions to the classification of the animal kingdom and wrote a natural history in forty-four volumes.

An Irish nobleman, Robert Boyle (seventeenth century), laid the foundations for the modern physical sciences by attacking many false assumptions inherited from the ancients and by beginning the systematic search for the basic physical elements. He discovered the law of gases, which still bears his name. Following Boyle's

Galileo is shown here in dialogue with the duke of Tuscany and other learned men in 1632, arguing the merits of the Ptolemaic versus the Copernican theories of the structure of the universe. It was Galileo who, despite considerable persecution by the Church, established the Copernican system as the true one. *Photo: NYPL Picture Collection*

lead, Lavoisier in France (eighteenth century) discovered twenty-three of the basic elements. He also discovered the secrets of combustion and formulated the law of the conservation of matter. Lavoisier is generally considered to be the father of modern chemistry. (He was beheaded by the terrorists during the French Revolution on a false political charge.) Probably the most important developments in the founding of modern physics were the discoveries connected with electricity. A number of men, including Benjamin Franklin, contributed bits of knowledge concerning electricity, but it was the Italian physicist Volta (1745–1827) who first harnessed electricity by inventing the storage battery. The versatile Newton discovered the basic secrets of light, thereby founding the science of optics. He also made important contributions to hydrostatics and hydrodynamics and formulated the three laws of motion (which had been conceived earlier by Galileo). James Hutton, a Scottish farmer in quest of better agricultural techniques, made observations that led him to the conclusion that the earth's surface has been undergoing gradual changes over eons of time. His *Theory of the Earth*, which appeared toward the end of the eighteenth century, is the first systematic treatise on geology.

3. THE TOOLS OF SCIENCE

Meanwhile, the tools necessary for the ever more rapid progress of natural science were being invented. The language in which science is expressed is mathematics. In the early seventeenth century a Scotsman, Sir John Napier, invented logarithms, by which the process of multiplying and dividing huge numbers is greatly simplified. Shortly afterward the system was applied to the slide rule. About the same time, René Descartes, a Frenchman, adopted the symbols now used in algebra, and devised analytic geometry, a method of combining and interchanging algebra and geometry. In the latter part of the seventeenth century, sometimes called the century of genius, Newton and the German Wilhelm Leibnitz, working independently, invented calculus, upon which many of the most intri-

cate processes of advanced science and engineering are dependent.

During the seventeenth and eighteenth centuries some of the basic physical scientific instruments were invented. Both the telescope and the microscope were products of the Dutch Netherlands. However, it was Galileo who first used the telescope in systematic astronomical observations. Leeuwenhoek, a Dutchman, was the chief pioneer in the use of the microscope. He discovered bacteria two hundred years before Pasteur learned how to combat them; he also observed the cellular structure of plant and animal tissue, the structure of the blood, and its circulation through the capillary system. Another Dutchman, Huygens, invented the pendulum clock, making possible for the first time in history the precise measurement of small intervals of time. A German, Fahrenheit, greatly improved the thermometer and adopted the scale that bears his name.

It is interesting that the universities played little or no part in this great drama. Nearly all of them were controlled by the churches, either Roman Catholic or Protestant. They looked askance at science. It was the scientific academies that played a significant role in the advancement of science. The earliest and most important of these were the Royal Society in England, chartered in 1662 by Charles II, and the Académie des Sciences in France, founded by Colbert four years later. These organizations and others patterned after them furnished laboratories, granted subsidies, brought scientists together to exchange ideas, published their findings, and encouraged scientific achievement generally.

4. THE ENLIGHTENMENT

The discovery of so many marvelous new truths concerning the physical universe could hardly have failed to make a strong impact upon the direction of the thinking of Western man. From the fifth century A.D. to the fifteenth, Christian theology and its various ramifications had engaged the best minds in the Western world. Christian spiritual and moral concepts pervaded the philosophy, letters, arts, and customs of Western civilization, and set it off from all other civilizations. In the fifteenth and sixteenth centuries, the Renaissance had rediscovered the secular pagan civilizations of Greece and Rome and popularized them in the West. Western philosophy and literature became humanistic, and its art sensuous. In the seventeenth and eighteenth centuries, Western man's interests, now predominantly secular, began to focus on science. Not only, as we have seen, did one spectacular discovery follow another, but eminent scientists such as Sir Francis Bacon, René Descartes, and Sir Isaac Newton devoted much thought and writing to scientific methodology and theory. The scientific attitude began to replace the Christian religion as the distinguishing characteristic of Western civilization.

But Western thinkers did not limit their attention exclusively to science. They began to speculate on the broader meaning of science—its ethical, political, social, and economic implications. These speculations gave rise to a philosophical movement which in the eighteenth century came to be called the Enlightenment. Many thinkers contributed to the philosophy of the Enlightenment. Three of the most influential were René Descartes, John Locke, and Voltaire.

Descartes (1596–1650), in addition to his major contributions to mathematics, was one of the first to ponder and write on scientific theory and methodology. His *Discourse on Method* was a landmark in the rise of the scientific spirit. It is an eloquent defense of the value of abstract reasoning. He would question all authority no matter how venerable—be it Aristotle or the Bible. From a few simple and self-evident truths he would derive further truths by a process of deductive reasoning. "I think, therefore I am," he believed to be a safe starting point. Descartes thought the whole material universe can be understood in terms of extension and motion. "Give me extension and motion," said Descartes, "and I will create the universe." Only mind and spirit are exempt from the mechanical laws. Though either commonplace or outworn and discarded today, the basic ideas of Cartesian philosophy were revolutionary in the seventeenth century. By challenging all established authority, by accepting as truth only what could be known by reason, and by assuming a purely mechanical, physical universe, Descartes clashed head on with the Christian concepts of divine revelation and divine Providence, which had prevailed for so many centuries in the Western world.

John Locke (1632–1704) went a step further. This rugged English thinker would not exempt even the mind from the mechanical laws of the material universe. In his *Essay Concerning Human Understanding*, Locke pictured the human brain at birth as a blank sheet of paper on which nothing would ever be written except by sense perception and reason. This concept ruled out

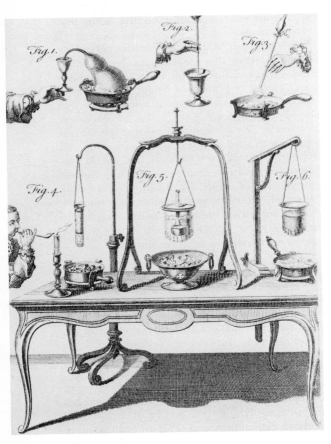

This eighteenth-century English engraving shows some of the new physical tools for scientific study being developed during this period. *Photo: NYPL Picture Collection*

innate ideas as well as revelation. Thus the mechanization of the whole universe was complete. Locke was the first behavioristic psychologist. Although Descartes' rationalism (pursuit of truth through reason) and Locke's empiricism (pursuit of knowledge through observation and experience) were by no means the same, they were one in rejecting divine revelation and authority. Both contributed heavily to the philosophy of the Enlightenment.

Of all the leading figures of the Enlightenment, Voltaire (1694–1778) was the most influential. It was his skillful pen that popularized the deep and original ideas of Locke. Voltaire, the son of a Paris lawyer, became the idol of the French intelligentsia while still in his early twenties. His versatile mind was sparkling; his wit was mordant. An outspoken critic, he soon ran afoul of both church and state authorities. First he was imprisoned in the Bastille; later he was exiled to England. There he encountered the ideas of Locke and Newton and came to admire English parliamentary government and tolerance. Slipping back into France, he was hidden for a time and protected by a wealthy woman who became his mistress. Voltaire's facile mind and pen were never idle. He wrote poetry, drama, history, essays, letters, and scientific treatises — ninety volumes in all. The special target of his cynical wit was Christianity. Few men in history have dominated their age intellectually as Voltaire dominated the eighteenth century. He became the chief spokesman for the *philosophes* or philosophers of the Enlightenment.

Although the *philosophes* differed widely among themselves in matters of detail, the basic elements of their philosophy may be summarized briefly as follows:

EMPIRICAL KNOWLEDGE

All we know and all we can ever know is what we perceive through our senses and interpret with our reason. There are no such things as innate ideas or revealed truth.

MECHANISTIC UNIVERSE

The whole universe and everything in it, including man, are governed by a few simple and unchangeable laws. Anyone who thinks he can change one of these laws — can by praying, for instance, bring down the rain on his parched crops and perchance on his neighbor's unroofed house — is a dupe of his own egotism.

PERFECTIBILITY OF MAN

Man is naturally rational and good, but the proponents of mystic religions have distorted his thinking and given him guilt complexes by preaching false doctrines of original sin and divine moral laws. Rid man's mind of this rubbish, said the philosophers, and he can and will build for himself a perfect society.

GOODNESS OF NATURE

Nature is good and beautiful in its simplicity. Man has corrupted it with his complex political, social, and religious restrictions. A move back to nature would be a move toward wholesome vigor and freedom.

DEISM

This wonderful mechanism called the universe could not have come into being by accident. Some infinite Divine Being must have created it and set it in motion. However, the finite mind of man cannot comprehend the infinite. Therefore, God is unknowable. Furthermore, God, having set his perfect mechanical laws in motion, will never tamper with them nor interfere in the affairs of man. He is impersonal.

In the eighteenth century these ideas came to be generally accepted by the intelligentsia throughout the Western world. A host of French philosophers joined Voltaire in contributing to Diderot's *Encyclopedia*. This gigantic work undertook to explore the whole world of knowledge. It was not objective, however, for the articles were interlarded with the rationalistic and empiricist views of the writers.

Somewhat different from the other philosophers of the Enlightenment, though second only to Voltaire in influence on eighteenth-century thought, was Jean-Jacques Rousseau (1712–1778). One of the most original thinkers and charming writers of all time, Rousseau crusaded for a return to nature—beautiful, pure, simple nature. The message struck home to a society weary of arbitrary and often corrupt governmental bureaucracy and an oppressively artificial and elaborate code of social etiquette. Rousseau was lionized. Great ladies, including the Queen of France, began playing milkmaid. In his novel *La Nouvelle Héloïse*, Rousseau extolled the beauties of free love and uninhibited emotion. In *Emile* he expounded the "natural" way of rearing and educating children. He would let children do what they like and teach them "practical" knowledge. Although Rousseau agreed with his fellow philosophers of the Enlightenment on deism, the mechanistic universe, the perfectibility of man, and the goodness of nature, he differed sharply with them on the matter of reason. Rousseau placed his faith in emotion, feeling, and intuition, rather than in reason. In this he was a forerunner of the romantic spirit and expounded its principles nearly a century before that movement reached its peak.

5. CONFLICT BETWEEN THE PHILOSOPHERS OF THE ENLIGHTENMENT AND THE CHRISTIAN THEOLOGIANS

It is readily apparent that the beliefs of the philosophers of the Enlightenment were diametrically opposed to the doctrines of the Christian churches—Roman Catholic, Protestant, and Orthodox alike. In contrast to the unknowable, impersonal God of the deists, Christian theologians taught that God took on human form and revealed himself to the finite mind of man in the personality of Jesus Christ. Furthermore, they maintained that God is interested in each one of his special creatures—that not a sparrow falls but that he sees and is concerned. To the empirical knowledge of the materialistic rationalists Christian theologians would add divine truth revealed by God, either through Christ, the Bible, and the Church or directly, as in the case of the saints, the prophets, and sometimes even ordinary Christians. They would make the mechanistic universe subject to a miracle-working, prayer-answering Creator. They argued that, if God could create the laws of the material

universe, he certainly could change them or set them aside if he so desired. Or he might envoke any of the myriads of natural laws that were unknown to man. Christian theologians regarded the concept of the natural goodness of man as erroneous. They taught instead that man is a fallen creature, that all inherit Adam's original sin, that man must be "born again" of the spirit in order to attain eternal life. Some theologians argued that the philosophy of the Enlightenment was itself a religion, based on faith. Since it has never been demonstrated that man is naturally good or that if freed from the influence of mystic religion, he can and will build for himself an earthly paradise, these things must be taken on faith—faith that in others the philosophers were so quick to scorn.

Unfortunately the eighteenth-century battle for the minds of men was not limited to honorable debate. Both sides resorted to the tactics of smear and persecution. It is difficult, if not impossible, to determine which side struck the first low blow. The philosophers, often on the flimsiest of scientific evidence and with little knowledge of the Christian religion, would ridicule the miraculous and mystic teachings of the Bible and the churches. Pleading for tolerance, they proved themselves most intolerant of Christian doctrines they did not accept or understand. Voltaire devoted much time and space to pointing out scientific errors in the Bible. "*Ecrasez l'infâme*" ("Crush the infamous thing") was his life motto. The "infamous thing" was, of course, Christianity. Christian theologians, on the other hand, found it much easier to denounce the materialistic rationalists than to answer their arguments. In countries like France and Italy, where the churchmen were strongly entrenched in government, they did not hesitate to persecute the philosophers of the Enlightenment, censor their writings, or even to interrupt the work of scientists. The churchmen were often so ignorant and so corrupt that they laid themselves open to the attacks of their enemies and almost invited the defeat they suffered in the struggle for intellectual leadership.

The materialistic rationalists won this struggle, and the French Revolution was in large measure an attempt to translate their ideas into practical institutions. It was not until the late nineteenth century that Christian theologians began to realize the true strength of their religion, to concentrate on spiritual and moral issues, and to rally their forces for a stronger stand (see Chapter 47).[1]

6. POLITICAL AND ECONOMIC ASPECTS OF THE ENLIGHTENMENT

The philosophers of the Enlightenment devoted a good deal of thought to matters of government. If man is by nature a rational and good creature, then surely, if given the opportunity, he can quickly devise for himself efficient and benevolent political institutions. Corrupt tyrannies were no longer tolerable. Of the numerous "enlightened" thinkers in the field of political science, three stand out above the others in influence. They are Locke, Montesquieu, and Rousseau. Locke's most eloquent plea was for the natural rights of man, which are life, liberty, and property. He theorizes, in his *Two Treatises of Civil Government*, that to safeguard these rights man voluntarily contracted to surrender a certain amount of his sovereignty to government. The powers of the government, however, whether it be monarchical or popular, are strictly limited. No government may violate the individual's right to life, liberty, and property. If it does, the people who set it up can and should overthrow it. These ideas were fundamental in the thinking of the makers of both the French and the American revolutions. Jefferson wrote many of Locke's ideas into the Declaration of Independence, frequently using his exact words. They likewise appear in the American Constitution and in numerous French declarations of liberty.

Baron de Montesquieu (1689–1755) was less a theorizer than a discerning student of history and shrewd analyst of political systems. His masterpiece is *The Spirit of the Laws*. Although a great admirer of the English government after the Glorious Revolution, Montesquieu came to the conclusion that different types of government are best suited to various conditions. For instance, absolute monarchy is best for countries of vast area, limited monarchy for countries of moderate size like France, and republics for small states like Venice or ancient Athens. Not only did he approve of Locke's doctrine of limited sovereignty, but he specified how it can best be secured—by a separation of powers and a system of checks and balances. The powers and functions of government should be equally divided among king, lords, and commons, each one being checked by the other two. This was probably Montesquieu's greatest practical contribution to the science of government. The principle was incorporated into the American Constitution—kings, lords, and commons becoming executive, judicial, and legislative branches of government.

The real father of the theory of modern democracy was not Locke or Montesquieu, both of whom distrusted rule by the masses, but Rousseau. This morbid, erratic genius based the conclusions in his *Social Contract* and in his *Second Discourse* upon pure imagination. Man in his state of noble savagery was free, equal, and happy. It was only when some men began marking off plots of ground saying "this is mine" that inequality began. In order to restore their lost freedom and happiness, men entered into a compact, each with all the others, surrendering their individual liberty to the whole. Since sovereignty is indivisible, the general will is all-powerful. Although Rousseau never made it clear just how the general will would actually operate in practice, he apparently assumed that the individual would be free by virtue of being part of the general will. Rousseau's influence on the leaders of the second and more radical phase of the French Revolution was great. But since it is only a short step from this kind of unrestrained government to state-worshipping dictatorship, the influence of Rousseau is also clearly seen in the Fascist and Communist systems of the twentieth century.

---

[1]The pietists, of course, concentrated on spiritual and moral issues. For the most part, however, they made their impact upon the lower classes rather than the intelligentsia, who were the chief protagonists in the debates over the philosophy of the Enlightenment. And only in England did the pietists gain a mass following even among the lower classes.

It is interesting that neither Rousseau nor any of the other philosophers of the Enlightenment advocated equal rights for women. The honor of being the first in modern times to write on this subject belongs to Mary Wollstonecraft (mother-in-law of the English poet Shelley). In 1792 she published *Vindication of the Rights of Women.* But her plea for equal rights for all human beings fell on deaf ears for half a century.

Some of the eighteenth-century planners of the better life through reason turned their thoughts to economics. Since the late fifteenth century, mercantilism had been the dominant economic theory and practice in Western Europe. This system of regulated nationalistic economy reached its peak in the seventeenth century. Only the Dutch Netherlands held out for free trade. But if, according to the fundamental assumptions of the Enlightenment, the universe is run by a few simple mechanical laws, why should there not be a similar natural order in the field of economics? A group of French Physiocrats, led by Quesnay, personal physician to Louis XV, began to teach that economics has its own set of natural laws, that the most basic of these laws is that of supply and demand, and that these laws operate best when commerce is freed from governmental regulation. This doctrine came to be known as that of *laissez faire* (or free trade and enterprise).

The chief formalizer of the theory of laissez faire was Adam Smith, a Scottish professor of philosophy who associated with the Physiocrats while sojourning in France. His *The Wealth of Nations*, published in 1776, has remained the bible of laissez-faire economics ever since. The ideas of the French Physiocrats and Adam Smith strongly influenced the leaders of the American and French revolutions.

7. THE ENLIGHTENED DESPOTS

The philosophy of the Enlightenment was by no means a monopoly of the intelligentsia. By the middle of the eighteenth century, it had become a fad. Many members of the nobility prided themselves on being followers of Voltaire (probably in most cases without realizing the practical implications of his philosophy). And nearly every country on the European continent was ruled by an "enlightened despot." As a matter of fact, Voltaire, who held the ignorant populace in contempt, believed enlightened despotism to be the most effective form of government.

The most sensational of the enlightened despots was Frederick the Great of Prussia (1740–1786). Frederick had from boyhood loved music, poetry, and philosophy. At the end of the Seven Years' War (1756–1763), the second of his two wars of aggression, he settled down as a model philosopher-king and attempted to apply the laws of reason to statecraft. Frederick was an avid reader of the French philosophers. He even invited Voltaire to visit him at Potsdam, but Prussia was not big enough to hold two such egos at once. The two quarreled and, after several years, parted.

The philosopher-king, who was, of course, a deist, made much of religious toleration. However, he continued to penalize the Jews and never ceased to ridicule Christians of all denominations. He was a strong advocate of public education, although he spent very little on it in comparison with what he spent on his army. The centralized Prussian bureaucracy became the most efficient government in Europe. True to the prevailing thought of the Enlightenment, however, he had no faith in popular self-government. Nor did he make a move to free the serfs or to end the feudal system in Prussia. Probably the most lasting of Frederick's contributions to Prussia were his codification of the law and improvements in the administration of justice. In the field of economy, Frederick was a mercantilist, although he did share the Physiocrats' appreciation of the importance of agriculture. Prussia's economy prospered increasingly during the last two decades of his reign. All in all, Prussia under Frederick the Great seemed to vindicate the contention of the philosophers of the Enlightenment that the rule of reason will quickly and painlessly usher in the good life.

The most sincere of all the enlightened despots was Joseph II of Austria (1780–1790). Unfortunately, he lacked the practical sagacity of Frederick the Great. His well-meaning but ill-conceived efforts to centralize the administration of the far-flung Hapsburg territories, to replace the numerous languages of his subjects with German, to secularize the strongly entrenched Roman Catholic Church, and to free the serfs in a society still based upon feudalism, all backfired.

More successful were the enlightened despots of Sweden, Tuscany, Sardinia, Spain, and Portugal. Even in Russia, Catherine the Great talked and played at enlightened despotism, although she did nothing to put the theories into practice. Significantly, France alone of the great powers on the continent failed to produce an enlightened ruler. Upon attaining the French throne in 1774, the well-meaning Louis XVI appointed the Physiocrat Turgot as minister of finances. Turgot, a friend of Voltaire, initiated a program of sweeping reforms that might have forestalled the French Revolution. However, within two years' time the powerfully entrenched vested interests persuaded the weak-willed king to dismiss him.

Although enlightened despotism achieved enough spectacular successes to gladden the hearts of some of the philosophers of the Enlightenment, the system soon exhibited two fundamental weaknesses. One was the egotism of the ambitious monarchs, which kept Europe in a state of almost constant war. The second was the uncertainty of hereditary succession. In every case, the benevolent despots were succeeded by despots less benevolent, if not outright malevolent or degenerate. And in any case the people had no choice. Europe's feudal society was not to be thus easily and painlessly reformed.

Suggested Reading

General
J. H. Randall, *The Making of the Modern Mind* (1940). Popularly written intellectual history of Western civilization.

The Rise of Natural Science
W. C. Dampier, *A History of Science and Its Relations with Philosophy and Religion* (1949). Probably the best general survey.

*A. N. Whitehead, *Science and the Modern World* (Free Press). By a distinguished twentieth-century philosopher.

The Enlightenment
*P. Gay, *The Enlightenment: An Interpretation*. Vol. I: *The Rise of Modern Paganism* (Vintage). Vol. II: *The Science of Freedom* (1969). Detailed treatment by a leading authority.

*C. Becker, *The Heavenly City of the Eighteenth Century Philosophers* (Yale). Delightful, thought-provoking little volume by a leading historian.

Sources
*R. Descartes, *Discourse on Method* (Liberal Arts). History-making because it was one of the first such studies.

*J. Locke, *Essay Concerning Human Understanding* (Gateway). The first approach to behavioral psychology.

*————, *Two Treatises of Government* (Hafner). Classic plea for limited, contractual government.

*C. Montesquieu, *The Spirit of the Laws* (Hafner).

*Voltaire, *The Portable Voltaire* (Viking). A good selection of his highly readable work.

*J. J. Rousseau, *Social Contract* (Hafner). Rousseau's political masterpiece.

*————, *Emile, Julie and Other Writings* (Barron). *Emile* is the first textbook on "progressive" education.

39

THE AMERICAN REVOLUTION

The political and social ideas of the Enlightenment received their first test and their first application in a somewhat unexpected quarter—the British colonies in America. The American Revolution was a highly significant step in a series of events that altered the political structure of the Western European world by striking down the absolutist concepts of government that had prevailed since about 1500. The bold experiments of the Americans in justifying their rebellion and in shaping new political institutions served as an inspiration and a model for other nations. Placed in its proper setting, the American Revolution was one of the major events in modern world history.

1. AMERICAN COLONIAL SOCIETY

The American Revolution was a complex movement, but behind all its complexity lay one fundamental fact. During the century and a half prior to 1776, American society had become different and separate from British and European societies. America was in the process of becom-

The quarrel of the American colonists with Great Britain was marked by violence and violent propaganda on both sides. This rendering of the shooting of Americans by British troops in Boston in 1770 was engraved, printed, and sold by Paul Revere. *Photo: The Metropolitan Museum of Art, Gift of Mrs. Russell Sage, 1910*

ing independent long before 1776; the revolution was the culmination of this process.

To the American of 1776, probably the most obvious sign of living in a world apart from Europe was the bustling economy that had been created in a wilderness, an accomplishment that had to be attributed to hard work and ingenuity on the part of the colonists.

The backbone of the colonial economy was the diversified agricultural system. The small, independently owned farms of New England and the middle colonies were complemented by the great plantations of certain areas of the South worked by slaves. The system produced a large variety of crops: grain, tobacco, rice, indigo, vegetables, fruit, and many others, which not only fed the rapidly growing population of the colonies, but also supplied a surplus for export. Off to the west lay vast areas of land yet unexploited, an economic opportunity unknown in Europe.

The Americans had by no means neglected commerce and industry. Colonial merchants, especially in New England and the middle colonies, did a thriving business within America. They also reached across the seas to Great Britain, to the West Indies, and to the continent of Europe. The bulk of the overseas trade was in colonial raw materials, such as tobacco and lumber, which were shipped to Britain and Europe in exchange for manufactured goods and slaves. However, by 1776 the colonists were producing manufactured goods in spite of British protest. Numerous fortunes were made in New England by producing rum from West Indian molasses. A thriving shipbuilding industry also existed. Of course the colonists were not self-sufficient, but neither were they absolutely dependent on Great Britain and Europe. American entrepreneurs were intent on protecting and expanding their own interests. And they were ever more determined to do so without constraints.

America's population—about 2.5 million in 1776—was organized in a class structure outwardly similar to that of Great Britain. An aristocracy of rich merchants and planters, which dominated economic life, politics, religion, and manners, was conscious of its position and sought to retain it. A large, enterprising group of independent farmers, shopkeepers, artisans, and professional men was ranked below the aristocrats. There were some day laborers, tenant farmers, and indentured servants, who were condemned to the lower rank of society. And there were the Negro slaves. But this class structure was not nearly so inflexible as that of Europe. Almost none of Europe's aristocracy emigrated to America; the family trees of most of the aristocratic colonial families would not stand close examination. American aristocracy was based on wealth rather than on blood. It was possible for an enterprising and lucky man of the lower classes to attain aristocratic rank by amassing a fortune. The frontier also offered an escape to men of humble origin who resented aristocratic dictation. Colonial conditions thus loosened the bonds of aristocratic society and supplied a large measure of freedom for men of lesser rank and means.

Probably the sharpest differences between the new and old worlds were in political life. Although each American colony had its own government, a common pattern had developed by 1776. Each colony had a governor who represented the authority of the British crown and who was usually chosen by the king. Each colony (except Pennsylvania) had a two-house legislature. The lower house was elected by property owners, while the upper house was usually appointed by the British king or by the governor. The powers of the colonial legislatures were never clearly defined, but in general they were extensive in local affairs and in taxation. The governors had nearly absolute powers of veto over these bodies, but since they were at the mercy of the legislatures for salaries and funds, they were not usually in a position to exercise these powers. The colonists had a system of courts patterned after British courts and enjoyed the rights of Englishmen as incorporated in English common law.

In actual operation, colonial governments grew accustomed to a wide range of freedom, and the colonists increasingly felt that it was their right to decide their own political fate. Prior to 1776 the colonists would have admitted that the British government had authority over them; yet when it came to specific issues, they would have argued that their own governments must have a voice in making decisions. One hundred and fifty years of experience in self-government had created a breach wider than the Atlantic between Great Britain and her colonies.

Colonial religious life was unique. In spite of the fact that the colonies paid taxes to support churches that were often intolerant and dictatorial, there was still greater religious freedom than in most of Europe. Puritanism flourished more vigorously in colonial New England than in Europe. Alongside such established religions as Puritanism and Anglicanism, there was room for Presbyterians, Quakers, Lutherans, Dutch Reformed, Roman Catholics, and Jews. And during the Great Awakening in the eighteenth century, a number of evangelical religions such as Methodism took root.

Prior to 1776 the colonists distinguished themselves least in cultural activities. They did establish colleges and lower schools in an attempt to prepare men for careers in colonial society. Newspapers appeared in many areas. The rudiments of a distinctly American architectural style emerged. But little was produced in literature and art that is worthy of note; in the final analysis colonial cultural life was still tied to that of Europe. Perhaps the most astounding development in colonial America was the ability of the colonists to keep abreast of Europe's chief cultural movements. Neither the sea barrier nor language nor the rigorous life in the colonies prevented Americans from absorbing the ideas of the Enlightenment and the implications of the new science.

Although there were by 1776 wide differences between American and British society, these differences did not spell revolution. Most Americans were still Englishmen and still closely attached to a European tradition. Their economic ideas, their political system, their religion, and their social concepts were fundamentally European, adapted to fit a new environment, but not magically transformed into something new. Their revolt was inspired by the conviction that Britain was violating the very tradition the colonists had inherited from her. The revolution was not a case of the Americans repudiating Europe; it was more nearly a case of the Americans seeking to put into practice some of Europe's most prized and most advanced concepts in order to fulfill the promise of the society they had planted and nourished in the New World.

2. THE QUARREL WITH GREAT BRITAIN

The numerous forces working to create a unique society in colonial America were little understood in Great Britain. Throughout most of the seventeenth century, the British were completely occupied with the painful struggle to decide the seat of authority and the nature of the political system. During the next century, England became a complacent nation, ruled by a narrow aristocracy not especially sensitive to new ideas and the need for change. The ruling forces in Great Britain subscribed fully to mercantilist principles with respect to colonial possessions: A great power should try to export more than it imported. Colonies were valuable in realizing that goal insofar as they could supply raw materials which the mother country would otherwise have to buy elsewhere and could furnish markets for the manufactured goods produced by the more advanced economic system of the mother country. America was thus viewed by England as a source of scarce products and a market for manufactured goods. The major question from the English point of view was how to ensure that America served these ends. The essence of England's policy was spelled out

in the Navigation Acts, passed originally in 1650 and 1651 and then renewed in 1660 and 1663. These laws required that certain "enumerated" items produced in America had to be sold in England, that the colonists must purchase manufactured goods only in England, and that all shipping from the colonies had to be carried in British or colonial ships. In a broad way, these acts implied that the mother country would control the colonial economy and determine the direction of its growth to suit her own interests. There was no intention on the part of the English to pillage the colonies; rather, the assumption was that the colonists would benefit from conformity to British direction.

For a long time, Great Britain's policy caused little friction with the Americans. The early colonial economy, rich in raw materials and lacking much manufacturing, benefited by having a ready outlet for colonial products and a sure source of manufactured goods. The British were extremely lax in administering colonial policy, with the consequence that many enterprising colonials found themselves in an advantageous position. They enjoyed a privileged position in the British economy, while finding ample opportunity to trade directly with other nations in total disregard of British regulations. During most of the first half of the eighteenth century, many colonials, especially New Englanders, ignored the laws requiring the purchase of manufactured goods and the sale of raw materials in England and built up a far-reaching trading enterprise chiefly profitable to themselves. British laxity and American enterprise combined to promote the development of strictly American economic interests that had little relevance to England's interests and needs.

The long succession of eighteenth-century wars that pitted England against France, culminating in the Seven Years' War, brought a change in England's policy after 1763. England's success in these wars greatly enlarged her holdings in America and awakened her to the potential of her vast holdings. A subtle change was affecting imperial thinking everywhere in Europe, one that stressed the importance of possessing territory rather than the older concept of exploiting trade as a source of power and wealth.

The events of the Seven Years' War in America, marked by a refusal of the Americans to raise troops and money, by their blatant trafficking with the enemy, and by their open defiance of royal authority, made England realize how inadequate her system of colonial control was. The long struggle with France also left England with a huge debt, incurred in part to save Americans from the French and the Indians; in the minds of English taxpayers, it was time for the ungrateful colonials to pay up. An overhaul of colonial policy, aimed at more effective control in support of England's interests, was in order. However, the colonials were hardly in a mood to comply after so long enjoying the freedom to do what they wished. Very quickly after 1763 a bitter struggle developed that led the colonials to rebellion, a declaration of independence, and victory.

The strife began when Britain enacted the Grenville (1764–1765) and Townshend (1767) acts, named after the British political leaders who steered them through Parliament. These measures were inspired by a desire on the part of England to raise money and to tighten colonial administration. The laws closed the trans-Allegheny frontier to further settlement, laid duties on numerous imports into the colonies, provided taxes on business documents (the Stamp Tax), prohibited various kinds of manufacturing in the colonies, imposed regulations on colonial money, and established British military and naval forces in the colonies at the expense of the colonial citizenry. Along with these new regulations went an enlargement of the policing forces in the colonies that seriously impeded the ability of the Americans to flout British regulations.

The Americans immediately began to fight back with fiery speeches, boycotts, protest meetings (such as the Stamp Act Congress), and violence. From the American perspective, the British victory in the wars of the first half of the eighteenth century had stemmed largely from the colonial contribution, and therefore it was unjust to force the colonials to pay the cost. The Americans complained bitterly that they were being taxed without representation in Parliament and that their own legislatures, long the chief source of governing regulations, were be-

ing completely disregarded. Britain's new imperial policy was broad enough to affect nearly all the colonists and thus drove them to greater unity than had previously existed. A depression following the Seven Years' War exacerbated American anger and discontent.

The vigor of American resistance forced England to modify some of the more inflammatory provisions of the new colonial policy, but did not basically change the thrust of her effort to tighten her control over the colonies and reap a larger profit from them. By 1768 she was compelled to send troops to America to enforce her will, and she had empowered her officials to seize property in ways that paid little heed to British law. Clearly, England's conduct suggested that she considered her colonists less than full British citizens. The Americans likewise grew more radical in their position; one suspects that John Adams was right when he said that the revolution was effected in the minds and hearts of men before the war commenced. Many Americans became convinced that the British were bent on depriving them of their traditional English liberties while stealing their wealth through taxation enacted without their consent. Increasingly in the American mind such an assault on liberty and property was a violation of the fundamental laws of nature and cause enough for resistance of any kind. Independence and self-government appeared to be the only alternative to the policy of a government that seemed less appreciative of its own sacred principles than did the Americans.

After 1773, the incessant quarreling quickened in tempo to the point of crisis. Angered by the conduct of the Boston "Indians," who destroyed a cargo of tea belonging to the British East India Company, Parliament passed the "Intolerable Acts." This legislation closed the port of Boston, placed Massachusetts under the control of a military commander, quartered troops in Boston homes, and threatened those suspected of a major crime with transportation to Britain for trial in the English courts. As if this were not serious enough, Parliament then passed the Quebec Act, which provided for joining all the territory north of the Ohio River and west of the

Alleghenies to the province of Quebec, establishing a nonrepresentative royal administration for this province, and granting toleration to French Catholics.

This new legislation provided the leaders of the colonial resistance—men such as Samuel Adams, long an advocate of radical measures— with an opportunity to organize an impressive display of protest and to convert discontent into action. At the instigation of some Virginia legislators at odds with the royal governor of Virginia, the First Continental Congress was summoned in 1774 to meet in Philadelphia. Inspired by radical leaders, the delegates adopted a bold statement that proclaimed the Intolerable Acts illegal, stated that Parliament had violated men's natural rights, and recommended resistance to England. The increasing reference to "natural rights" in the arguments of the colonists was momentous. It signified that many colonials believed in a natural law superior to English law and in a right, perhaps even an obligation, to revolt if the English violated that natural law. Here was a principle that could breed revolution. The ties with England were not yet broken, but they were under an extreme strain.

In England, a few statesmen realized the danger of the situation, but they could not muster enough parliamentary support for conciliatory policies aimed at reassuring that considerable segment of the colonial population still unready to break with England. Rather, the English government showed a determination to enforce the Intolerable Acts; in fact, new measures were enacted to increase English control. Both England and the colonists began to prepare for war. Hostilities opened in April 1775 with skirmishes at Lexington and Concord. In May 1775 the Second Continental Congress, led by men ready to declare independence, took steps to organize the war that had already started and appointed George Washington as commander of the American armies.

Colonial opinion had heretofore lagged behind the radical leaders who wanted a break with England, but once the shooting started it rapidly caught up. There was a rising cry for independence. The most potent statement to that effect was delivered by Thomas Paine in his pamphlet *Common Sense*, which appeared early in 1776. His stirring assault on monarchy and its evils and his scathing denunciation of British greed fired the growing appeal of republicanism and fed the expanding national pride of all manner of men who had once thought of themselves just as Englishmen living in America. Only independence could satisfy these sentiments. The English helped by pushing their war plans vigorously and by declaring the colonists rebels. The English pressure inevitably forced the colonial leaders to realize that foreign aid was needed; and that help could only be gained if the Americans broke with England and stood as an independent nation.

Popular sentiment in favor of independence finally made itself felt in 1776, when various colonies instructed their delegations to the Second Continental Congress to break with Britain. On July 4, 1776, Congress issued the Declaration of Independence, the work of Thomas Jefferson, one of the radical leaders. Its magnificent preamble, leaning heavily on the political philosophy of John Locke and the European disciples of the Enlightenment, stated in strong words the doctrines of natural rights and government by contract. The British government had violated these rights and thus had no claim on the allegiance of its subjects, who were entitled to form a new contract to ensure their rights. The Declaration of Independence elevated the struggle above a petty rebellion against legally constituted authority. It made America's struggle that of all "enlightened" men. Not only did it clarify the issues of 1776, but it inspired later generations to strike for liberty in the name of rights so fundamental that they were beyond the authority of any government.

3. THE AMERICAN REVOLUTION

Only a few words can be devoted to the American struggle for independence. Although Britain's power seemed overwhelming, her advantage was offset by poor leadership, distance, and commitments elsewhere. The chief problem of the Americans was overcoming disunity. Many loyalists, or Tories, did not approve of the war against Great Britain. And those in favor of the revolution often disagreed about the course that the new nation should take. These divisions were almost miraculously set aside long enough to press the cause of independence to a successful conclusion. In no small way success rested with the leadership provided by men like George Washington, Thomas Jefferson, Benjamin Franklin, and John Adams, who demonstrated unsuspected talents in leading armies, organizing resources, solidifying popular support, and negotiating with foreign powers.

When the war opened in 1775, the British were unprepared and had to withdraw from Boston to gather their resources, an event the Americans interpreted as a victory. Pushing their initial advantage, the Americans undertook an unsuccessful campaign against Canada in late 1775. By July 1776, Britain was ready to attack, and seized New York as a base of operations. The following months marked the darkest hours of the revolutionary cause. Washington's pitifully small army, poorly fed and armed, was hounded through New Jersey and Delaware; only the caution of the British commander, General Howe, saved it from destruction. Washington did manage to strike blows at Trenton and Princeton in the winter, but these victories were valuable chiefly in keeping up American morale.

The turning point came in 1777, when the British attempted to split the colonies by capturing the Hudson Valley. Their strategy consisted of driving down from Canada and up from New York. General John Burgoyne led the British armies from Canada. Under constant attack from the Americans, his progress was anything but spectacular. No help came from the south. Howe occupied himself in the useless capture of Philadelphia. While he enjoyed that victory, Burgoyne's effort turned into a disaster. Finally, in October 1777, he surrendered at Saratoga.

American spirits rose rapidly as a result of this victory. Its chief effect was to swing the French to the American cause. France, moved by a desire to see Great Britain defeated and by a genuine sympathy for America's cause, had unofficially been offering help to the colonists since 1775. However, she had not committed herself fully, fearing that the Americans would either patch up their quarrel with the British or would

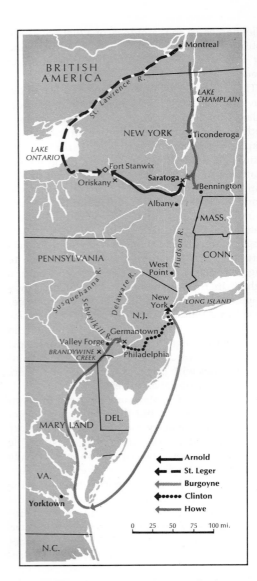

REVOLUTIONARY WAR CAMPAIGNS

be defeated, leaving France in a war from which nothing could be won. The victory at Saratoga convinced France that America had a chance for victory. In 1778 a formal alliance was agreed upon, and France began to supply needed money, ships, and troops. In the wake of Saratoga and the French commitment, other European powers showed increasing friendliness toward

America and hostility toward Britain. Spain and the Dutch eventually declared war on Britain. The British now had a world war on their hands; the pressure on America was considerably relieved.

After 1777 fighting in America was spread over a wide area. The British withdrew from Philadelphia and concentrated large forces in New York. Washington's army was chiefly engaged in containing these forces. The British threw their offensive effort into a campaign in the South, trying in 1780–1781 to capture the Carolinas and Virginia. This campaign ended in a disastrous defeat at Yorktown, Virginia, in October 1781, Americans and French both sharing in the victory. This was the last major battle of the war, although hostilities officially continued until 1783. By 1781 Britain was anxious to end a war that threatened her position all around the world.

Peace negotiations were conducted in Paris. The American delegation, led by Benjamin Franklin, was sent with instructions to follow French leadership and to make no separate treaty with Britain. However, France, eager to deliver Britain a few more blows, was in no hurry to conclude the war. Moreover, she had hopes of reannexing the territories in North America that she had given up in 1763, since the new American nation as yet had no legal claim to these lands. Having detected the French intentions, the American delegates disregarded their instructions and made a separate peace with the British. By the terms of the Treaty of Paris, 1783, Britain recognized America's independence and ceded to her all territories east of the Mississippi from the Great Lakes to Spanish Florida. The Americans agreed to honor all debts owed Britain and to make restoration to the Tories who had suffered during the war. The French, unwilling now to continue the war on their own, also agreed to these terms. The new American nation had won a magnificent victory.

4. REVOLUTION AND THE DEMOCRATIZATION OF AMERICAN SOCIETY

The American Revolution involved more than a successful war against Great Britain. Some Americans had drawn back in 1775–1776 at the prospect of dissolving the existing social and political order and building a new one. However, once the decision for independence was taken, there was no turning back. As the war progressed, moves were made to construct new institutions for America. In the years following 1776 the Americans showed a genius for combining traditional patterns of life with radical new ideas. Their revolution did not uproot the old social order completely in the name of any radical doctrine; yet it did incorporate into the new order some of the most advanced ideas of the Enlightenment.

The first important efforts at reconstruction were made on the state level (as the colonies were called after July 4, 1776). New state governments, based on British principles of government and on colonial political experience, were created in all the colonies. The framers of these governments sought to create a political order that would protect men's liberties without becoming tyrannical. Nearly every state drew up a written constitution carefully defining the structure and functions of government. Elaborate bills of rights, stressing traditional English liberties, were included in the constitutions. Since sovereignty rested with the people, elections were provided for all officials. Two-house legislatures were established, the lower houses being controlled by property-holding voters and the upper houses being selected by the lower chambers. Legislatures were armed with extensive powers to control and check executive officials, who were universally suspected of being the chief instigators of tyranny. Independent judiciaries were almost universally adopted. The whole philosophy of separation of powers was thereby incorporated into the new state governments, signifying a strong conviction that the powers of government must be limited by constitutional safeguards. Taken as a whole, the state constitutions framed between 1776 and 1780 inaugurated a degree of popular control over government unknown in the contemporary world, although none of them was completely democratic.

The revolution affected changes in other areas of life as significant as those altering the political structure. Several states took steps to disestab-lish state-supported churches, to institute reli-gious toleration, and in general to separate polit-ical and religious life. Many states passed new land laws that tended to make it easier to gain ownership of property. Especially significant was the abolition of primogeniture, which re-quired that the eldest son receive all his father's land. Slavery was abolished in some Northern states, in part at least because this institution seemed out of place in a society dedicated to the principles of the Declaration of Independence. All these liberalizing movements pointed to-ward greater freedom in the future.

Quite accidentally, the revolution had an important leveling effect in terms of the distri-bution of wealth. An inflation, caused by the efforts of the Americans to pay for the war with paper money, wiped out fortunes, aided debt-ors, and allowed new fortunes to be built. Many established merchants suffered heavy losses from the disturbance of foreign trade, but new opportunities in trade and industry emerged once America was free from the British commer-cial system. Small farmers flourished during the war, bolstered by easy money and high prices. Under these varied pressures, the prerevolution-ary social order did not survive intact. Again, a greater degree of social equality and personal freedom emerged to characterize life in the new nation.

5. LAUNCHING THE NEW NATION

Even more challenging to the Americans was the problem of creating a central government cap-able of organizing the struggle for indepen-dence. Perhaps there were some who accepted in theory the Enlightenment dream that the best government was a small republic, but the reali-ties of a war for survival, the dangers inherent in a world of large and ambitious nations, and the bonds of unity existing among the people who had carved a new destiny out of the wilderness of the New World compelled the Americans soon after the opening of the war to begin think-ing of fashioning a common government. Move-ment in this direction always had to contend with the existence of the thirteen separate states,

each commanding a considerable loyalty and each the proud possessor of a long tradition of independent action in the face of the English government.

The first attempt at forming a national govern-ment was the work of the Second Continental Congress, dominated by the radical leadership that had framed the Declaration of Indepen-dence. These men had a deep distrust for strong government over which the populace had no control. On the basis of this conviction, they shaped the Articles of Confederation in 1777 and secured its acceptance by all the states by 1781. A national congress in which each state had one vote was created and given considerable author-ity to conduct foreign affairs, declare war, issue money, raise armies, fix weights and measures, and borrow money. The executive branch of the government was entrusted to a committee of thirteen, selected by congress. However, con-gress lacked the essential powers to tax and to regulate commerce, and on most vital issues its decisions had to be submitted to the states for final approval. The Articles of Confederation thus established a loose union of thirteen nearly independent states headed by a central govern-ment that could not compel them to do anything but could only encourage them to cooperate.

The Articles of Confederation survived until 1789. The central government made some deci-sions of lasting importance, such as provisions for the use of the public lands west of the Al-leghenies. On the whole, however, the govern-ment was weak and indecisive, especially after the victory over England removed the cohesive force of war as the reason for its existence. Little was done to curb the aggressive policies of Britain and Spain to the west. The grievous economic problems of the new nation were un-resolved. The states, free to pursue their indi-vidual policies in economic affairs, often worked at cross-purposes. Some of them seriously threat-ened property rights, but the most dangerous action of the states was their issuance of nearly worthless paper money that inflated prices, ben-efited debtors, and nearly wiped out the for-tunes of the wealthy.

In the face of the mounting evidence of the inadequacies of the confederation, there was rising sentiment for a stronger central government. Many grew certain that too little government was as bad as too much. And many began to think "continentally," as Alexander Hamilton put it, seeing issues that far transcended the selfish provincialism so often manifested in the government established by the Articles of Confederation. This new feeling, constantly challenged by the old fears of too-strong central government and the pride of the states, finally led in May 1787 to the summoning of a convention to consider revising the Articles of Confederation. Those present were chiefly men of wealth and position, not a little disturbed by some of the radical moves being taken in the states they represented. This fact has sometimes led to the

George Washington and the Federalists are satirized in this cartoon, which illustrates the controversy that soon developed in the new nation over the issue of the extent of the central government's power. *Photo: Brown Brothers*

conclusion that the American constitution was framed by men bent on creating an instrument to safeguard the interests of the privileged few. Although there may be some truth in this position, the delegates were also patriots interested in safeguarding all Americans and men with firm convictions, drawn chiefly from the philosophy of the Enlightenment, about what government ought to be.

The convention immediately decided to scrap the Articles of Confederation and to write a new constitution. Once this task was undertaken, the delegates found themselves in broad agreement on many vital matters. They agreed that a written constitution enumerating the powers of the central government was necessary, that there must be popular control over the central government, and that every government must have built-in checks, necessitating the separation of powers of the various branches. No one believed that the states should be stripped of all power,

yet all were convinced that the central government must have certain powers to deal independently with matters affecting national interests.

Working from these premises, the delegates quickly arrived at a basic framework for a new government. A two-house legislature, a president, and a national judiciary were to be established. Each branch was provided with specific functions, and an elaborate system of internal checks was provided to prevent any branch from exercising too much power. The powers of the national government in certain specific areas were enumerated, while all other matters were reserved to the states. The federal government was given clearly stated authority to coerce the states in those matters over which it had jurisdiction, and to ensure a degree of flexibility, provisions were made for amending the constitution.

In spite of broad agreement, there were a few crucial points over which the delegates long debated. One centered around finding a way to safeguard the interests of the small states against the large. This issue was settled by providing that seats in the House of Representatives would be apportioned according to population (with slaves counting three-fifths as much as freemen), while the Senate would be made up of two senators from each state, whatever its size. Another problem was the method of choosing the president. Many wanted a strong executive but were fearful of allowing the populace to select him. It was finally agreed that the president would be chosen for four years by a special electoral college, the members of which were to be chosen by the states.

The new document was handed over to the states for ratification with the provision that when nine states approved, the new government would go into effect. The constitution aroused stormy discussion within the states. However, one by one they fell into line. On June 21, 1788, the ninth state, New Hampshire, approved the constitution, and the new government was officially in existence. In the next month the crucial states of Virginia and New York accepted the constitution, and thus ensured that it would be put into actual operation. Rhode Island held out until May 1790. Several

states added a condition to their acceptance of the constitution, asking that a bill of rights guaranteeing fundamental liberties be added. This condition was filled shortly after the government was set up by the addition of the first ten amendments to the constitution (1791).

The new government began operation in 1789 with George Washington as President and with men who were committed to the new Constitution (Federalists) in control of Congress. During the next decade the new government proved its worth. Congress provided legislation which filled in many crucial details of the governmental system that had been touched on in only a general way in the Constitution: a bill of rights, a system of federal courts, and executive departments to assist the President in discharging his responsibilities. Taxes were levied and collected, and public credit was established when the central government assumed state debts and funded its obligations on a sound basis. Although not gifted with great political wisdom, George Washington conducted himself in a way that gave dignity and independent stature to the executive branch of the government, thus ensuring effective direction of national affairs while allaying deep-seated fears of executive tyranny. Two of his cabinet members, Alexander Hamilton, Secretary of the Treasury, and Thomas Jefferson, Secretary of State, proved to be skilled and devoted servants of the new nation. Hamilton's economic policies helped to restore prosperity, and Jefferson's foreign policy permitted the new nation to steer a perilous path of neutrality through the stormy international waters disturbed by the French Revolution.

Despite the successes of the new government under Washington and his successor, John Adams, there was mounting discontent with the Federalists who dominated it. The Federalists made it increasingly clear, especially through the policies promoted by Alexander Hamilton, that they intended to make the central government as strong as possible. Aristocratic in his political philosophy, Hamilton was convinced that what the new nation needed most was order and that only a powerful central government based on the support of men of wealth could provide that order. He fashioned a national economic policy intended to favor the wealthy and to tie their interests to a strong central government. His policy aroused opposition not only from economic self-interest on the part of those not favored by it, but also from philosophical principles rooted in fear of strong government, belief in human equality, and trust in the political wisdom of common men—ideas powerfully reinforced by the issues raised by the French Revolution. Those who opposed the Federalists began to rally around Thomas Jefferson, likewise an aristocrat but almost always at odds with Hamilton, especially on philosophical issues. A new political party, called the Republicans (not to be confused with the present Republican party, founded in 1854), took shape under Jefferson's leadership. The emergence of political parties added an element to the new government that the constitution makers had not foreseen. Although the Republican challenge to the Federalists failed in 1796, when John Quincy Adams was elected president, the new party won in 1800. In a close and bitter contest, Jefferson won the presidency in what he called the "Revolution of 1800." Perhaps it would be more accurate to say that this election completed the revolution begun twenty-five years earlier. It furnished the final proof of the workability of the new government, since it demonstrated that the voters con-

trolled the government and that they did not have to rebel to make their voices heard. If the founding fathers thought they had created a government to serve the interests of the few (which they probably did not) and if the Hamiltonian Federalists felt that only the few could adequately run the new nation (which they probably did not), they were disabused of that idea by Jefferson's victory in 1800.

Between 1775 and 1800 the Americans had put on an impressive display for the world. They had asserted their rights against tyranny by force of arms, and demonstrated that no government was sacred once it began to oppress men. They had then proceeded in a rational fashion to establish thirteen state governments and a national government that were capable of action yet were restricted from abusing the inalienable rights of men. Furthermore, an ingenious federal system was worked out whereby state and national governments coexisted. These governments proved sensitive to popular control and made the exercise of popular sovereignty a fact. Everywhere liberal, enlightened men saw their dreams becoming a reality in America. Here was inspiration and guidance for those who might like to change society elsewhere. The revolutionary era was launched in practice as well as in theory.

Suggested Reading

Colonial Society

The emergence of colonial American society and the articulation of its unique features have been cause for endless debate among historians. A vast literature has developed on the subject. The following four works will provide a good orientation on the subject and an introduction to some of the divergent views:

C. L. Ver Steeg, *The Formative Years, 1607–1763* (1964).

C. Nettels, *The Roots of American Civilization: A History of American Colonial Life*, 2nd ed. (1963).

*D. J. Boorstin, *The Americans: The Colonial Experience* (Vintage).

*M. Kraus, *The Atlantic Civilization* (Cornell).

The Revolution

*E. S. Morgan, *The Birth of the Republic, 1763–1789* (University of Chicago). A well-constructed, balanced review of the major events of the period.

*J. C. Miller, *Origins of the American Revolution* (Stanford). An exploration of the major forces that produced the revolution reflecting the best of modern scholarly judgment on this complex and much debated problem.

*B. Knollenberg, *Origins of the American Revolution, 1759–1766*, rev. ed. (Free Press). An excellent complement to the preceding work.

*L. H. Gipson, *The Coming of the Revolution, 1763–1775* (Harper Torchbook). An interpretation of the coming of the revolution from a British perspective.

B. Bailyn, *The Ideological Origins of the American Revolution* (1967). A brilliant analysis of the political ideas that created the revolutionary spirit in America.

*C. Becker, *The Declaration of Independence: A Study in the History of Political Ideas* (Vintage). A perceptive analysis of the Declaration that helps to clarify the ideas that sparked revolutionary actions and that played such an important role in establishing the new nation.

*R. B. Morris, *The American Revolution Reconsidered* (Harper Torchbook). An excellent evaluation of the conflicting interpretations of the nature and significance of the American Revolution that have been developed by modern scholars.

*H. Peckham, *The War of Independence: A Military History* (University of Chicago). A fine story of the course of the Revolutionary War.

*S. F. Bemis, *The Diplomacy of the American Revolution*, 3rd ed. (Midland Books). A full treatment of a crucial aspect of the American struggle for independence.

The New Nation

*M. Jensen, *The New Nation: A History of the United States During the Confederation, 1781–1789* (Vintage). A thorough review of events in this crucial era that casts the government under the Articles in a better light than is usual.

*M. Farrand, *The Framing of the Constitution of the United States* (Yale).

*C. Van Doren, *The Great Rehearsal* (Compass). This and the preceding title skillfully evoke the drama and clarify the issues involved in the Constitutional Convention.

*C. A. Beard, *An Economic Interpretation of the Constitution of the United States* (Free Press). A seminal interpretation of the constitution arguing that the new government was shaped by a minority of wealthy men seeking to protect their interests. Originally published in 1913, this book has provoked long and heated debate.

*J. C. Miller, *The Federalist Era, 1789–1801* (Harper Torchbook). A thorough study of the crucial first years of the new Republic.

Sources

*Thomas Paine, *Common Sense and Other Political Writings*, ed. N. F. Adkins (Liberal Arts Press). A prime document for understanding the feelings of some men who made the revolution.

*Alexander Hamilton, *et al.*, *Federalist Papers* (many editions). The best source for sampling the ideas and issues that surrounded the formation of the Constitution.

40

THE FRENCH REVOLUTION, 1789-1799

During the long reign of Louis XV (1715–1774), French prestige declined steadily from the lofty heights it had reached under his predecessor. Louis XV was a lazy, selfish, and cynical man who lavished more time and money on his mistresses, Madame de Pompadour and Madame du Barry, than on affairs of state. His participation in the War of the Austrian Succession and the Seven Years' War resulted only in disgraceful defeats and the loss of France's empire in India and North America to Great Britain. His successor inherited an unbalanced budget and a discontented populace. Young Louis XVI (1774–1792), though well-meaning, reasonably intelligent, and of good moral character, was not the man to restore the prestige of the throne. He was awkward, shy, and weak-willed when the situation called for decision. His reign was ended by one of the greatest and most far-reaching upheavals in the history of Western civilization—the French Revolution.

1. THE LAST DAYS OF THE OLD REGIME IN FRANCE

France at the succession of Louis XVI, though somewhat weakened by the defeats and failures of Louis XV, was still the richest and most influential nation in the world. During the course of the eighteenth century, her commerce and prosperity had steadily increased. Half of all the specie in Europe was to be found in France.

With the possible exception of Great Britain, she enjoyed the highest standard of living of any of the great powers. It is not, therefore, to desperation born of poverty that one must look as an explanation for the French Revolution, but rather to frustration caused by existing institutions—social, religious, political, economic—that had failed to adjust to changing conditions.

French society on the eve of the French Revolution was divided into three distinct classes or *estates*. The First Estate was the clergy, numbering approximately 100,000 out of a total population of some 23 million. The Roman Catholic Church in France owned about 10 percent of the land—the best land—and from its lands and tithes and fees enjoyed an income probably half as large as that of the government itself. It controlled all educational institutions and censored the press. It monopolized public worship and continued to harass all other religious groups at a time when the spirit of religious tolerance was rising throughout most of the Western world. The clergy itself was sharply divided. The upper clergy—the bishops and the abbots—were rich and powerful. They were drawn exclusively from the ranks of the aristocracy and were generally looked upon by most of the lower clergy and the common people as parasites. The lower clergy—the priests and the monks—came from the lower classes. The income of the priests was modest. They shared the lives of the people they served and were generally popular, but they had almost no influence on Church policy.

The Second Estate was the nobility, numbering approximately 400,000. Since the death of Louis XIV in 1715, the French nobility had recouped most of its power and influence at the expense of the king and of the bourgeoisie. All the high government posts were now held by the nobility. These offices, many of them just useless sinecures, carried handsome salaries and pensions. The nobility owned approximately 20 percent of the land of France, but was exempt from all direct taxation. The richest of them lived at Versailles as absentee landlords, where they hunted, intrigued, made love, and read the books of the philosophers of the Enlightenment. They were reputed to possess the best manners and the worst morals of any class in Europe. The most haughty of the nobility—the most jealous of their rights—were the newcomers, the noblesse de la robe (nobility of the gown). These were former rich bourgeois who had purchased judgeships in one of the high law courts.

The Third Estate was composed of commoners—the bourgeoisie, the proleteriat, and the peasantry—and comprised about 96 percent of the total population. Of all the social and economic groups in France in 1789, the bourgeoisie were probably the most frustrated. These were business and professional people, the bankers, merchants, shopkeepers, lawyers who had grown into a middle class between the nobility and the peasantry. By the late eighteenth century, the upper French bourgeoisie had gone as far as their wits and energy could take them. They had become richer by far than most of the nobility, only to find the highest levels of government and society closed to them.

The proletariat—the city wage earners—were not a class-conscious group such as we find in modern industrial society. Many of them were servants of the rich and tended to identify with their masters. Nevertheless, there was enough distress among the proletariat to create tensions—tensions that would increase with the maladjustments caused by the revolution. During the course of the eighteenth century, the price of bread had risen three times as fast as wages. Paris was the only city in France with a proletariat large enough to make its influence strongly felt. There, about 300,000 citizens (about half the total population of the city) could be classified as proletarians, and there they would play a significant role in the revolution.

At least 90 percent of the French people in 1789 were peasants, tillers of the soil. Although they were probably better off than the peasants of any other country in Europe (they owned at least 30 percent of the land, and serfdom had virtually disappeared), they were on the whole discontented. Most peasant-owned land was subject to feudal dues. Probably a majority of the peasants owned no land at all but were sharecroppers who gave up 50 percent of their produce to the lord in addition to the feudal dues (the fees paid by the peasant for use of the lord's mill, oven, wine press, and breeding stock, death taxes, inheritance taxes, sale of property taxes). Not only was the peasant forbidden to hunt; he could not even protect his crops from the lord's hunting parties—nor, for that matter, from the game itself. Although the French peasant no longer had to donate his labor to the lord, he still was required to furnish so many days' labor for roads and public works. On him fell nearly all the direct taxes levied by the national government—heavy in the extreme.

The life of the peasant too had not changed much since the Middle Ages, except that he was no longer a serf. He lived in little rural villages, the houses close together and the livestock frequently under the same roof. The house usually consisted of one room, with a dirt floor, thatched roof, and neither chimney nor glass windows. His daily diet was made up almost entirely of dark bread and wine; meat was reserved for special occasions. Entertainment centered around the Church. On Sundays and holy days, of which there were many, his attire and attitude were festive and gay. The ambitious young French peasant, unlike the peasants in most of the rest of Europe, did have opportunities for advancement. He could buy some land, become a priest or the lord's steward, a blacksmith or innkeeper, or try his fortune in the city. Only relatively few, of course, would succeed.

The government of France was arbitrary. The king's decree was law. The Estates General, the

French counterpart of the British Parliament, had not met for nearly two centuries. Justice was capricious and corrupt. There were 237 different codes of law to confuse the litigants. There were no juries as in Great Britain. The king could arrest and imprison at will (although Louis XV and Louis XVI seldom did). The judges of the thirteen superior courts, called *parlements*, purchased or inherited their titles. Torture was still used. The arbitrariness and inherent injustice of this system, which had long been taken for granted, seemed intolerable to the readers of Voltaire and Rousseau.

The breakdown of the old regime in France began in the field of finance. Louis XVI had inherited a large and constantly growing national debt. It was not excessive for a rich nation like France; Great Britain and the Netherlands had higher per capita debts. But, when combined with the exemption of the nobility and the clergy and much of the bourgeoisie from direct taxation and the extravagant cost of maintaining the military establishment and servicing the national debt (most of which had been incurred by past wars), it spelled eventual bankruptcy. Furthermore, France was still burdened with the corrupt system of tax collection (called tax farming) that allowed much revenue to be diverted from the treasury into the pockets of private collectors.

Upon assuming the throne Louis XVI appointed the Physiocrat Turgot, a friend of Voltaire, as minister of finance. Turgot initiated a series of sweeping reforms designed to clean up the mess. However, those with vested interests in the old system brought about his dismissal at the end of two years, and his reform measures were rescinded. A succession of ministers then tried all kinds of palliatives, such as borrowing, pump-priming expenditures, better bookkeeping, but to no avail. By 1786 the debt was 3 billion livres,[1] and the annual deficit had reached 125 million. Bankers refused to lend the govern-

ment more money. In a desperate effort to save his regime, Louis called an Assembly of Notables in 1787 in an attempt to persuade the nobles and the clergy to consent to be taxed. But the privileged orders refused, and demanded, instead, a meeting of the Estates General, thinking that they could control it and thereby save their privileges. Pressured by a virtual revolt of his own nobility, the king gave in.

2. THE TRIUMPH OF THE THIRD ESTATE

During the early months of 1789 elections were held for members of the Estates General. All France was agog with excitement. Voltaire and Rousseau had done their work; it was generally believed that man could quickly construct an earthly paradise if given a chance.

Since the Estates General had not met for a hundred and seventy-five years, no one quite knew the procedure. Hundreds of pamphlets appeared, and there was widespread public debate. By tradition, each of the three estates, the clergy, the nobility, and the commoners, elected their own representatives. All males who had reached the age of twenty-five and paid taxes were permitted to vote. Since the Third Estate, including the bourgeoisie, the peasantry, and the proletariat, comprised more than nine-tenths of the total population, it was given as many seats as the other two combined. This large representation for the Third Estate was not believed to be especially significant at the time, since again by tradition the three estates sat separately, and each group had one vote.

By April 1789, the delegates began to arrive at Versailles. Good will prevailed. Violent revolution was far from anyone's mind. The delegates came armed only with *cahiers*, the lists of grievances that had been called for by the king. Of the six hundred representatives of the Third Estate, not one was a peasant. Except for a handful of liberal clergy and nobles who were elected to the Third Estate, they were all bourgeois. Nearly all the members of the Third Estate, as well as many members of the two privileged estates, were fully acquainted with and enamored of the philosophy of the Enlightenment.

---

[1]The livre was technically worth about 20 cents, but its purchasing power in the eighteenth century was much greater than that of the mid-twentieth-century American dollar.

The first formal session was held on May 5. Immediately a sharp debate began over the method of voting. The two privileged estates demanded that, according to custom, the three estates meet separately and vote by order, that is, each estate cast one vote. This would mean that all attacks on privilege and inequality would be defeated by a vote of two to one. The Third Estate, already becoming disillusioned by the snobbish attitude of the royal court and of some of the members of the first two estates, demanded that the voting be by head. The three estates would meet jointly, each individual member casting one vote. This would mean that all measures for fundamental reform would pass, for not only did the Third Estate have as many members as the other two combined, but a number of liberal clergy and noblemen sympathized with the common people and the cause of reform. Both sides realized that the outcome of this issue would be decisive.

On June 17, after six weeks of fruitless haggling, the Third Estate declared itself to be the National Assembly of France and invited the other two estates to join it in the enactment of legislation. Three days later, on June 20, when the members of the Third Estate arrived at their meeting hall, they found it locked and guarded by royal troops. Adjourning to a nearby building used as an indoor tennis court, they took the "Tennis Court Oath," vowing never to disband until France had a constitution. It was the Third Estate's first act of defiance. On June 23 the king met with the three estates in a royal session at which he offered many liberal reforms but commanded the estates once and for all to meet separately and vote by order. The king, his ministers, and members of the first two estates filed out, but the representatives of the Third Estate defiantly remained seated. When the royal master of ceremonies returned to remind them of the king's orders, Mirabeau, a liberal nobleman elected by the Third Estate, jumped to his feet and shouted, "Go and tell those who sent you that we are here by the will of the people and will not leave this place except at the point of the bayonet!" When the startled courtier repeated these words to his master, Louis XVI, with characteristic weakness, replied, "They mean to stay. Well damn it, let them stay." A few days later he reversed himself and ordered the three estates to meet jointly and vote by head.

The Third Estate had thus won the first round. However, alarming news soon began to arrive that the king was calling the professional troops of the frontier garrison to Versailles. It appeared that he was at last preparing to use force. At this critical juncture, the Parisians countered the threat of force with force. On July 14, a riotous mob marched on and destroyed the Bastille, a gloomy old fortress prison in the workingmen's quarter that symbolized the arbitrary tyranny of the old regime. (July 14 has long been celebrated as the French national holiday.) This show of force stayed the king's hand.

Throughout the remainder of July and August the spirit of violence spread from Paris to the rest of France, where it had been only desultory hitherto. Many nobles fled from France for their lives (the *émigrés*), and feudalism, for all practical purposes, came to an end. Since the peasants feared reprisals from the nobility and believed a widespread rumor that the nobles were raising brigand bands against them, this period is known as the Great Fear. The legal end of feudalism came on August 4, when, during a hysterical night session of the National Assembly, one nobleman after another stood up and renounced his feudal rights and privileges.

Three weeks later, August 26, the National Assembly proclaimed the Declaration of the Rights of Man and the Citizen. This document, which followed the English Bill of Rights by an even hundred years and preceded the American Bill of Rights by two years, was replete with the phrases of the philosophers of the Enlightenment. "Men are born and remain free and equal in rights." The natural rights of man were declared to be "liberty, property, security, and resistance to oppression." Liberty of opinion "even in religion," freedom of the press, and freedom from arbitrary arrest were all proclaimed. Thus, within a span of three weeks' time, August 4 to August 26, 1789, two of the most constructive achievements of the revolution—or of modern history, for that matter—were proclaimed: the end of feudalism and the individual freedom and legal equality of all Frenchmen.

This engraving commemorates the storming of the Bastille, hated symbol of arbitrary government and royal and aristocratic tyranny. The day of its destruction by the Parisian mob, July 14, has long been celebrated as the French national holiday.
Photo: Bibliothèque Nationale/Estampes

The forces of privilege and reaction, however, still had to be brought to terms. The king not only refused to sign the August decrees, but began once more to assemble troops around Versailles and Paris. In answer to this new threat of force, a huge mob of Parisian women on October 5 and 6 marched the 10 miles out to Versailles, surrounded the palace, and with the help of the bourgeois National Guard forced the king to accompany them to the city, where he became a virtual prisoner of the populace. As the carriage bearing the royal family rolled toward Paris, the surrounding mob shouted jubilantly, "We have the baker, the baker's wife, and the little cook boy! Now we shall have bread!" A few days later, the National Assembly moved its sessions to Paris, where it came increasingly under the influence of the radical populace of the great city. The Third Estate had triumphed.

3. MAKING FRANCE AN "ENLIGHTENED" MONARCHY

The National Assembly could now at last settle down to the task of making France over in the image of Voltaire and Montesquieu. During the next two years the Assembly passed a series of sweeping reforms that may be conveniently classified as follows:

JUDICIAL

The *parlements*, and the manorial and ecclesiastical courts with their arbitrary procedures and overlapping jurisdictions were swept away. An orderly system of lower and higher courts was established. The administration of justice was decentralized and democratized. Judges were to be elected for six-year terms. Torture was abolished. In criminal cases juries were to be used for the first time in French history.

ECONOMIC

In accordance with the doctrine of laissez faire, guilds, labor unions, and trading associations were abolished. All occupations were declared open to all classes. Feudal obligations, including labor on the public roads, had already come to an end on the night of August 4. Internal tolls and customs were abolished.

FINANCIAL

The complex and unequal taxes, direct and indirect, were swept away. They were replaced by a tax on land and a tax on the profits of trade and industry. Both were uniform and no one was exempt. Tax farming was, at long last, abolished. Expenditures were henceforth to be authorized only by the national legislature. To meet the pressing financial needs of the government, the National Assembly issued paper money called *assignats* to the value of 400 million livres. To back up this paper money, the property of the Roman Catholic Church, valued at approximately that amount, was confiscated.

RELIGIOUS

The seizure of property was the first step toward the nationalization of the Church. Monasticism was abolished. The secular clergy was to be elected by the people (including non-Roman Catholics) and their salaries paid by the state. The bishops were reduced in number, wealth, and power. They were no longer to be invested by the pope. These measures were incorporated in the Civil Constitution of the Clergy, to which all the members of the clergy were required to take an oath of allegiance in order to perform their functions and draw their salaries. The pope, whose control over the organization and the clergy of the French church would have been broken, declared the Civil Constitution of the Clergy to be founded upon heretical principles and ordered the clergy to refuse to take the oath of allegiance. A majority of the clergy, including nearly all the bishops, followed the pope's command. The defection of the "nonjuring clergy" and of thousands of their devoted parishioners was the first serious split in the ranks of the revolutionists.

POLITICAL

Under the new constitution, which was completed in 1791, the central government was patterned after the ideas of Montesquieu. Judicial, legislative, and executive powers were separated. Lawmaking was given to the single-chamber Legislative Assembly of 745 members elected for two-year terms. Voting, however, was limited to males at least twenty-five years of age who paid taxes equivalent to three days' wages. It is estimated that some 4 million adult males ("active" citizens) could meet these qualifications and that some 2 million remained "passive" citizens. Actually to sit in the Legislative Assembly required the payment of taxes amounting to 54 livres. Only some 70,000 Frenchmen could meet this qualification, and the weight of power fell to the bourgeoisie. The king was granted a suspensive veto over all but financial and constitutional measures, but three successive legislatures could pass a bill over the king's veto. The conduct of foreign relations was left in the hands of the king, but he could not declare war or make treaties without the consent of the Legislative Assembly. The king's expenditures were limited to a sum voted by the legislative body. France was greatly decentralized. For purposes of local government and administration, the country was divided into eighty-three departments, each of which was administered by a small elected assembly. The execution of the national laws was placed almost entirely in the hands of the local authorities.

In October 1791, the National Assembly, having completed its work, gave way to the Legislative Assembly, which had recently been elected under the new constitution. Had Voltaire and Montesquieu been alive, they would have had every right to say, "I told you so." Within a brief span of two years and with very little bloodshed, France had been made over. The monarchy had been limited and "enlightened." The Roman Catholic Church had been subordinated to the state. Feudalism had come to an end. Individual rights and liberties and legal equality had been defined and established. But would Rousseau have been happy? Did the general will now prevail?

4. FOREIGN WAR AND THE FAILURE OF THE MODERATE REGIME

The new government so optimistically launched was expected to last forever. Actually, it lasted less than a year. Although the Legislative Assembly, elected under the restricted suffrage provisions of the new constitution, was made up largely of moderate men, it probably represented the wishes and interests of the great majority of the French people. The chief gainers in the French Revolution thus far had been the bourgeoisie and the peasants. The bourgeoisie had gained political control over the country and greater social mobility. Most of the peasants, who constituted the bulk of the French population, could now vote, and all of them were at last free from feudal obligations. To the many peasant landowners who owned their land before the revolution were now added a few others who had seized the lands of émigré nobles or had purchased confiscated Church lands. Most of the bourgeoisie and the landowning peasants were satisfied and wished to see the revolution stop where it was, lest they lose their sacred property and their political dominance.

However, there were other groups that were quite dissatisfied. The royal family, the aristocracy, most of the clergy, and the army officers yearned for the restoration of their privileges. On the other hand, many of the city proletariat and some of the poorest peasants wished to see the revolution continued in a more radical way. They had gained little except theoretical rights and legal equality. Owning no property, they could not vote. Yet they had supplied much of the physical force that had saved the Third Estate and made the moderate reforms possible.

Leadership for these disgruntled groups was found among the intelligentsia who were disciples of Rousseau. These intellectual radicals would be satisfied with nothing less than the overthrow of the monarchy and extension of the revolution.

The radical groups, although a definite minority of the French people, were well organized and ably led. In the Legislative Assembly itself, the most liberal or radical group was the Girondins, so called because many of their leaders came from the vicinity of Bordeaux in the department of Gironde. Outside the assembly numerous clubs, of which the Jacobin Club became the most influential, were formed to debate and plan political matters. Although the Jacobins were and remained predominantly intellectual bourgeoisie and were moderate at first, they gradually became the most radical group in France. Three Jacobin leaders came to tower over all others. Jean Paul Marat, Swiss by birth, was an inordinately ambitious and frustrated physician and scientist turned popular journalist. His was the gift of rabble-rousing journalism. He incessantly demanded the beheading of all those leaders who opposed the further extension of the revolution. Georges Jacques Danton, a former lawyer in the king's council, was a thundering orator of great energy and ability. Maximilien de Robespierre was also a lawyer. This eloquent and sincere man was a fanatical disciple of Rousseau, bent upon the establishment of a deistic republic.

Events soon played into the hands of the radicals. The kings of Austria and Prussia, fearful of the spread of revolutionary ideas to their own lands and urged on by the French émigrés, began to make threatening moves and to issue meddlesome warnings to the French revolutionaries. In France the reactionaries believed that a successful war would enhance the prestige and power of the throne and that a defeat would result in the restoration of the old regime. Most of the radicals believed that war would expose the inefficiency and disloyalty of the king and bring about his downfall. When, therefore, in April 1792 Louis XVI appeared before the Legislative Assembly to request a declaration of war against Austria and Prussia, only seven negative votes were cast. Thus lightly was begun a war that was to last twenty-three years and embroil most of the Western world.

The French armies, leaderless since nearly all the high-ranking officers were members of the nobility and had either fled or been deposed, were badly defeated. As the Austrian and Prussian armies advanced toward Paris, there was panic in the city. The king, who had already forfeited his popularity when he attempted to flee the country in June 1791, was now rightly suspected of being in treasonable communication with the enemy. On August 10, 1792, a huge Parisian mob advanced on the king's palace. The royal family fled for its life to the Legislative Assembly. The interior of the palace was wrecked, and several hundred of the Swiss guard were slain. The Legislative Assembly suspended and imprisoned Louis XVI and called elections for a national convention to draw up a new constitution to take the place of the one that had just failed.

5. THE TRIUMPH OF THE RADICALS AND THE REIGN OF TERROR

The elections to the constitutional convention took place in an atmosphere of panic and violence. During the interim between the overthrow of the limited monarchy and the meeting of the convention, Danton assumed emergency leadership of the nation. Feverishly he superintended the gathering of recruits and rushed them to the front. As the recruits were preparing to leave Paris, rumors spread that their wives and children would be murdered by the reactionary clergy and nobles. Violent elements began murdering members of the nonjuring clergy and reactionary nobles who were being held in the prisons of Paris. During the first three weeks of September 1792, more than a thousand such victims were massacred. In the elections to the National Convention, held amid this hysteria, the radicals won a sweeping victory. Most of the conservative elements prudently stayed away from the polls.

In the Legislative Assembly the Girondins had been the Leftist group.[2] In the National Convention they found themselves on the extreme Right. The new Left was made up of the Jacobin followers of Marat, Danton, and Robespierre, mostly from the city of Paris. They came to be called the Mountain, since they occupied the highest seats in the convention hall. This radical convention, elected for the purpose of drawing up a new constitution, was to rule France for the next three years (1792–1795) — the most exciting years of the revolution.

The first act of the National Convention was to declare France a republic. The next move was to dispose of the king. After a fair trial he was found unquestionably guilty of treasonable communication with the enemy and sent to the guillotine — an instrument adopted by the revolutionists for the more mechanical and humane beheading of the condemned. The execution of Louis XVI, accompanied by proclamations of world revolution by the evangelical Jacobins, sent a shudder of horror through the royal courts of Europe. Furthermore, the hastily recruited French revolutionary armies, which had checked the Austrians and Prussians at Valmy in September 1792, had taken the offensive and overrun the Austrian Netherlands.

Austria and Prussia were now joined by Great Britain, the Dutch Netherlands, Spain, Portugal, Sardinia, and Naples in a great coalition bent upon the destruction of the French Revolution and the restoration of the old regime. The French armies were unable to stand up to such an array of armed might. But the defeats and invasions were not the worst disasters to confront the revolutionary government. The ignorant peasants of the Vendée region in western France, who had been stirred up by the nonjuring clergy, rebelled against the radical government. The rebellion spread until some sixty of the eighty-three departments were involved. Major provincial cities such as Bordeaux, Lyons, and Marseilles were in revolt. Toulon, the chief French naval base on the Mediterranean, invited in the British fleet. Inside the convention itself, many

---

[2]The present political connotation of the terms "right" and "left" derives from this period. In the revolutionary assemblies the conservatives sat quite by chance on the speaker's right, the liberals and radicals on his left.

The execution of Marie Antoinette in Paris, October 1793. The deaths of the members of the French royal family and of many of the nobility frightened the French opponents of the revolution into supporting the radical regime against the foreign invaders.
Photo: Bibliothèque Nationale/Estampes

of the moderate Girondins were sympathetic to the rebels.

Faced with what seemed to be inevitable disaster to their radical cause and indeed to the revolution itself, the leaders of the Mountain decided on drastic action. Since the Paris Commune, as the city government was called, was already completely controlled by the radicals, the Mountain leaders conspired with it to incite a mob. On June 2, 1793, the National Convention, now dominated by the left wing and surrounded by a threatening Paris mob, voted the expulsion and arrest of twenty-nine Girondin leaders. Having thus silenced all opposition within the convention, the radical leaders and their followers inaugurated a reign of terror against their political enemies. Their goals were to unite France and to save and extend the revolution.

For efficiency, the National Convention delegated unlimited powers to a Committee of Public Safety, composed of twelve men working in secret. The most influential member of this all-powerful committee was Robespierre. At its call was the Committee of General Security, a national police force. A Revolutionary Tribunal was set up to try, condemn, and execute suspects without the usual legal procedure and as quickly as possible. Members of the National Convention were sent out in pairs to carry the Terror to every nook and cranny of France. Although tens of thousands of persons, possibly half a million, were imprisoned during the Reign of Terror, only some 16,000 are believed to have been executed. The drastic policy was remarkable successful. The disaffected elements were quickly silenced, and the rebellions quelled. The defense of the republic was entrusted to Lazare Carnot. A *levée en masse* was ordered. All men, women, and children were called to the colors. The able-bodied young men were rapidly trained and rushed to the front. Everyone else contributed his bit to the war effort on the home front. This common activity for defense of country produced a high state of morale—the first mass na-

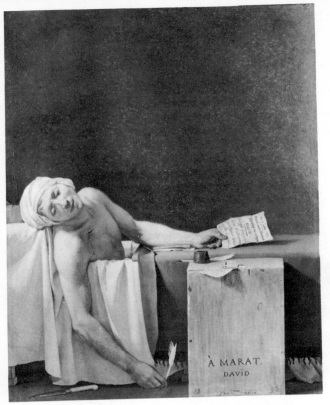

This well-known painting by the French artist David shows the death of Marat, one of the chief leaders of the radical second phase of the revolution. *Photo: Musées Royaux des Beaux-Arts de Belgique, Brussels*

tional patriotism in history. Able new officers were found. The armies of the coalition were defeated on every front and hurled back beyond the frontiers.

6. ROBESPIERRE'S UTOPIA OF ROUSSEAU

While Robespierre and his associates were saving the revolution, they were also busy extending it to more radical ground. A fanatical disciple of Rousseau, Robespierre was determined to make France a deistic utopian republic where virtue and fraternity would reign supreme. During the emergency of 1793 a maximum price was placed upon the necessities of life for the protection of the consumer, particularly the city proletariat. Efforts were made to control inflation by forcing people to accept the badly inflated *assignats* at their face value. The lands of the émigrés were confiscated and sold in two- or three-acre farms to the peasants. Since these farms

could be paid for over a long period of time, almost every French peasant could now become a landowner, and most of them did. France became a nation of peasant proprietors. The metric system was adopted; the Louvre Palace was turned into an art gallery; the national library and national archives were founded; a law (never implemented) provided for a comprehensive national system of public education. Women adopted the flowing robes and hair styles of ancient Greece. Silk knee breeches, the symbol of aristocracy, gave way to trousers. Rich and poor alike took pride in being *sans culottes* (without knee breeches). Titles of all kinds were discarded for Citizen and Citizeness.

One of Robespierre's greatest ambitions was to replace Christianity in France with the deistic religion of the Enlightenment. A group of his followers, mistakenly thinking him an atheist, set up an actress of questionable morals in Notre Dame as goddess of reason. Robespierre, however, was planning the establishment of the worship of the Supreme Being in the fashion of Rousseau. In an elaborate ceremony, Robespierre, wearing a sky-blue coat and carrying a bouquet of red roses, led a procession across Paris to the scene of the closing festivities. Thus was inaugurated the "Republic of Virtue." Thousands of Christian churches were closed. Even the calendar was de-Christianized by eliminating Sundays. The months were made equal and named after the seasons. The year I was dated from September 22, 1792, the date of the declaration of the republic.

Meanwhile, discontent with Robespierre and his policies was increasing. The defeat of the invading armies of the coalition and the suppression of the internal rebellion appeared to most people to remove the justification for the Terror, yet the Terror was intensified. Robespierre felt that the republic of virtue for which he yearned had eluded him. When Danton counseled moderation, Robespierre sent even him and his most prominent followers to the guillotine. No one, not even the members of the National Convention, felt safe any longer. Finally, in July 1794, the convention found the courage and the leadership to overthrow Robespierre and send him to his own guillotine.

7. REACTION AND THE RISE OF NAPOLEON

Since Robespierre was overthrown on July 27, which was 9 Thermidor by the revolutionary calendar, the reaction that followed is known as the Thermidorian Reaction. The propertied bourgeoisie, who quickly gained control of things, had been frightened and angered by the restrictive measures of Robespierre's regime. All such measures still in force were repealed. The Terror was brought to an end, and the chief terrorists executed. Armed bands of bourgeois hirelings went around for some time beating or killing Jacobins. The populace, weary of discipline and restraints, reveled in an orgy of licentious living. In 1795 the National Convention finally got around to the task for which it had been elected three years earlier: the drawing up of a new constitution. The constitution reflected the conservative reaction. Only property owners could vote for members of the legislative bodies. Executive functions were placed in the hands of five directors, who were chosen for five-year terms by the two legislative bodies. In October 1795, the National Convention turned over its powers to the Directory, the name that was given to the new government.

The most significant development of the period of the Directory, 1795–1799, was the rise to power of Napoleon Bonaparte. The directors, though men of reasonable competence, were unable to restore peace and political and social tranquillity. Though peace had already been made with Spain and Prussia, war with Great Britain, Austria, and Sardinia dragged on. Government finances were chaotic, and brigandage was rife. More and more people longed for a strong man who could bring peace abroad and order at home. Napoleon proved to be the man, and the story of his rise to power will be told in the next chapter. When in November 1799 Napoleon overthrew the Directory and made himself dictator, the French Revolution had run full cycle from absolute Bourbon monarchy to absolute Napoleonic dictatorship. France had failed by popular democratic processes to establish the utopia promised by Voltaire, Montesquieu, and Rousseau. She would now try to achieve it by the dictatorship of a genius.

Suggested Reading

General

*R. R. Palmer, *The Age of the Democratic Revolution*, 2 vols. (Princeton). Best single study of the French revolutionary era. A challenge for the ambitious student.

*C. Brinton, *A Decade of Revolution, 1789–1799* (Torch). Excellent survey.

*C. Brinton, *The Anatomy of Revolution* (Vintage). Seeks to discover a common pattern in revolutions by comparing the English, American, French, and Russian revolutions. Fascinating.

Last Days of the Old Regime and First Phase of the Revolution

E. J. Lowell, *The Eve of the French Revolution* (1892). A lucid masterpiece.

*G. Lefèbvre, *The Coming of the French Revolution* (Vintage). By one of France's leading authorities. Covers first phase of the revolution.

Second Phase

*R. R. Palmer, *Twelve Who Ruled: The Committee of Public Safety During the Terror* (Princeton). Best book on the Reign of Terror.

*J. M. Thompson, *Robespierre and the French Revolution* (Collier). Brief biography by leading authority.

Sources

Madame de Campan, *Memoirs* (1883). Vivid eyewitness account of court of Louis XVI by lady-in-waiting to Marie Antoinette.

E. Higgins, *The French Revolution as Told by Contemporaries* (1938). Skillfully weaves together the story from eyewitness accounts.

Historical Fiction

*Charles Dickens, *A Tale of Two Cities* (Collier). Famous novel based on the French Revolution.

*Daphne Du Maurier, *The Glassblowers* (Pocket Book). This fine novel based upon excellent historical research brings the revolution very close to the reader.

41

THE ERA OF NAPOLEON, 1799-1815

No individual in modern times has enjoyed a more meteoric career than Napoleon Bonaparte, the modern counterpart of Alexander the Great and Julius Caesar. He was essentially a product of the Enlightenment and the French Revolution. His mission was to consolidate the revolution in France and to spread its "enlightened" concepts and many of its institutions to most of the rest of Europe.

1. NAPOLEON'S RISE TO POWER

Napoleon was born on the French island of Corsica in 1769. Corsicans speak Italian, and Napoleon never learned to speak French without an accent. At the age of nine he was sent to a military school in France. Here he was made fun of by his schoolmates because of his foreign accent and his small size. Already suffering from megalomania, he withdrew into himself, studied history, geography, and mathematics, and dreamed of future greatness. At sixteen he received his commission as second lieutenant of artillery. During several years of boring garrison duty he

Portrait of Napoleon by David. Napoleon Bonaparte has never been surpassed as a military and political genius. The popular image of Napoleon as a conqueror often neglects the constructive aspects of his career. As a child of the Enlightenment Napoleon created many efficient political and social institutions. *Photo: Girandon/Rapho-Guillumette*

stuffed his photographic mind with history, the classics, and the philosophy of the Enlightenment, particularly that of Rousseau. Had it not been for the French Revolution, his rather humble, foreign birth would probably have made it impossible for him to have risen very far.

Napoleon's first big chance came in 1793 at the siege of Toulon, France's Mediterranean naval base, which had gone over to the side of the British. Since most of the regular army officers were nobles and had fled the country or been deposed, the young Napoleon was given an opportunity to try his plan for the recapture of the base. It worked brilliantly, and he attracted the attention of some important people, including General Paul Barras, who was to become one of the five directors. These contacts paid off two years later on 13 Vendémiaire (October 5, 1795). When the National Convention completed the constitution setting up the government of the Directory, the members of the convention, fearful of losing power after so much bloodshed, decreed that two-thirds of the members of the new legislative bodies must be chosen from among themselves. This decree angered a great many disgruntled people who, for one reason or another, wished to see an entirely new government come in. Royalist leaders seized the opportunity to arouse a huge Paris mob against the convention. In the emergency the convention appointed General Barras to defend it. Barras, in turn, called upon Napoleon, whose prowess with artillery he had observed at Toulon. Although the details of the fracas are uncertain, it would appear that Napoleon masterminded the defense of the convention. (Barras and Napoleon in their memoirs both claim the leading role and belittle the part played by the other.) An artillery expert with no love for the French people, the ambitious Corsican had long before decided that the way to handle a mob was to let it have a "whiff of grapeshot." A few such whiffs from his skillfully placed artillery dispersed the mob, and Napoleon became the hero of the convention.

The day of 13 Vendémiaire made Napoleon a prominent figure. Although he was now only twenty-six, he demanded and got the command of the Army of the Interior. As an astute student of history, he realized that glamour and power could be won only in the field. Therefore, he requested and received command of the Army of Italy—the French army still fighting the Austrians and Sardinians in northern Italy. Napoleon's dynamism and skill quickly galvanized the lethargic French forces, who defeated the Austrians and Sardinians and forced them to sue for peace. Nor was the young general any less skilled in diplomacy and propaganda. He personally negotiated a favorable peace with Austria (a function that really belonged to the newly created French Directory), and sent back glowing reports of his exploits.

Soon the name Napoleon Bonaparte was on everyone's lips. The Directory, grappling with the unheroic problems left by the preceding revolutionary bodies, was concerned for its own existence. Fearing the presence of a popular and ambitious young general in France, it was only too glad to accede to Bonaparte's request to lead an expedition to Egypt as a means of striking at the British Empire. Napoleon's chief purposes in going to Egypt were personal and psychological. He sensed that the time was not yet ripe to overthrow the government, that exploits far away in the mystic East would greatly enhance his reputation, and that during his absence from France crises would arise enabling him to play the role of the returning savior. He was right. His victories in Egypt were of no military importance, but they did add to his personal glamour. The only

achievement of real importance was the discovery by a French officer of the Rosetta Stone, which unlocked the secrets of the ancient Egyptian language and history.

Meanwhile, Great Britain persuaded Austria and Russia to join her in a second coalition against France. This was what Napoleon was looking for. His fleet having been destroyed by the British squadron under Lord Nelson, Napoleon deserted his army in Egypt and slipped back to France with a few chosen followers. The timing was perfect. General Bonaparte conspired with various members of the government, and with the additional support of armed forces under his command, overthrew the Directory, setting himself up as dictator. This coup d'état occurred on 18 Brumaire (November 9, 1799). Napoleon was only thirty years of age.

2. THE CONSULATE—PEACE AND REFORM, 1799–1804

Having seized absolute power by conspiracy and force, Napoleon drew up a constitution to conceal his dictatorship under the cloak of parliamentary forms. He gave himself the title of First Consul with the power to appoint key civilian and military personnel (giving him control over the armed forces), declare war and make treaties, and initiate all legislation through a hand-picked Council of State. Two other consuls without any significant powers served as camouflage. Two legislative bodies were selected from a list of candidates elected by all adult French males. But since they could not propose new laws, their power was very limited. Thus the voters were led to believe that they were participating in the government, whereas in reality their voice was but faintly heard. Local government was again brought under the strict control of the central government by placing each of the eighty-three departments into which France was divided under the control of a powerful agent of the central government called a *prefect*.

The First Consul's initial project was to restore law and order at home and peace abroad. The Directory had never been able to suppress brigandage. Life and property were not safe. Napoleon sent out military detachments that quickly put an end to lawlessness and restored the authority of the government, much to the satisfaction of law-abiding citizens. He lost no time in making a treaty (1800) with the United States, bringing to an end a two-year undeclared naval war that had grown out of French seizures of American vessels and the pro-British and anti-French policies of John Adams' administration. Slipping over the Alps with a French army, the First Consul crushed the Austrian army in northern Italy in the battle of Marengo, knocking Austria out of the Second Coalition. Tsar Paul of Russia was cajoled with flattery and promises into making peace. Even Great Britain was persuaded to sign the Peace of Amiens in 1802, which, however, was to last little more than a year.

The young dictator next proceeded to create by enlightened despotism the permanent institutions that the revolutionary leaders had been unable to establish by the processes of popular government. Of all Napoleon's reforms, the one of which he was the most proud was his Civil Code. The National Convention had set up a commission of lawyers to reduce to order the 237 different legal codes in use in France, but this commission had been unable to complete its work. Shortly after seizing power, Napoleon appointed his own commission of legal experts to draw up a uniform code. When his experts proved to be unequal to the task, Napoleon threw himself into the project. The result was the Code Napoleon, which has been adopted by most of the nations that have since come into existence throughout the world. Later codes set in order criminal and commercial law. These achievements won for Napoleon the title "the Second Justinian."

The First Consul proved himself to be an astute financier. The numerous government notes, bonds, and obligations, all depreciated, were called in and uniformly refunded. Efficient agents of the central government fairly assessed and collected the taxes. Strict economy in expenditures made it possible to balance the French budget for the first time in more than a century. Napoleon capped France's financial structure with the Bank of France, a seminational bank privately owned but regulated by the state. The bank handled government funds and was given certain monopolistic privileges such as the issuing of paper money. It established branches all over France and grew so strong that it later became a powerful influence on the government itself. French businessmen, however, never quite trusted Napoleon; they always felt uneasy about what the dictator's next arbitrary move might be.

Napoleon was keenly aware of the importance of religion. "Always treat the pope," he counseled his diplomats, "as if he had 200,000 men." He himself was a Voltairian deist and a cynical moral relativist, believing that God was "always on the side with the most cannon." One of his first steps was to make peace with the pope and end the ten-year struggle between the French revolutionary governments and the Roman Catholic Church. After arduous negotiations, the First Consul and the pope signed the Concordat of 1801, which was to govern the relations between the French state and the Roman Catholic Church until the beginning of the twentieth century. The Roman Catholic religion was declared to be the religion of the majority of the French people. The state was to appoint the bishops, but only the pope could invest them in their offices. The bishops were to appoint and discipline the lower clergy, thus restoring the traditional episcopal principle of the Roman Church. The salaries of the clergy were to be paid by the state, and the clergy were to take an oath of allegiance to the state. The pope accepted the permanent loss of church property seized by the National Assembly. Once the pope's signature was on the document, Napoleon, in his characteristic manner, violated its spirit by adding "organic articles" that further subordinated the church to the state. According to these articles, the state was to pay the salaries of Protestant as well as Roman Catholic clergy, and all clergy were placed under the "police powers" of the state. Nevertheless, the pope gained firmer control over the Gallican Church than he had enjoyed since the Late Middle Ages. Napoleon, on the other hand, ended the religious cleavage that had harassed France since the early days of the revolution.

Napoleon was also interested in pedagogy. All French schools were brought under the control of a national board of education called the University of France. One of the most important elements in his educational system was the *lycée*, an institution that combined what in the United States would be the last two years of high school with the first two years of college. In addition, professional and technical schools were established. Napoleon had a low opinion of female education and of feminine mentality in general. Actually, he was chiefly interested in educational institutions as agencies of propaganda for the molding of loyal and efficient soldiers and citizens. But the educational institutions he created have served France well.

Napoleon's one outstanding failure during the period of the Consulate was his effort to restore France's lost empire in North America. He successfully pressured the weak Spanish government into returning the vast Louisiana territory to France. But his plans to secure the approaches to Louisiana miscarried when yellow fever and native resistance wrought havoc with a costly French expedition to Santo Domingo. Realizing that war with Great Britain was about to be renewed and that he could not hold Louisiana, he offered to sell it to the United States. President Jefferson eagerly accepted the offer, paying some $16 million for what is now a third of the United States.

With the exception of the overseas imperial venture, the first five years of Napoleon's dictatorship were spectacularly successful. The dictatorship itself was mild. Law and order at home and peace abroad had been attained. Financial stability, equal and efficient justice, religious tranquillity, and the foundations of an effective educational system had all been achieved. Public morale was high. In 1804, as in 1791, the worshippers of Voltaire's materialistic rationalism must have felt vindicated. The benevolent genius on horseback seemed to have ushered in the utopia of human reason that the National Assembly appeared to have achieved a little more than a decade earlier. However, 1804 like 1791 was only a prelude to an era of war, violence, disillusionment, and reaction. Napoleon was not satisfied with his accomplishments. He yearned for more glory. In 1804 he crowned himself Emperor of the French and sought further fields to conquer.

3. THE EMPIRE—WAR AND CONQUEST

Great Britain, France's inveterate foe, had become increasingly alarmed at Napoleon's growing strength. The French dictator had not only continued to build up his military forces, but had taken advantage of the Peace of Amiens to further his commercial and imperial schemes at Great Britain's expense. Before the end of 1803 the British government declared war and the next year joined with Austria and Russia to form a third coalition against France. This was what Napoleon expected and wanted. He soon appeared at the English Channel at the head of a force sufficient to conquer the British Isles, if only the 24-mile water barrier could be crossed. In the Channel, however, lay the world's mightiest fleet, commanded by the greatest of all Britain's admirals, Lord Nelson. Napoleon was unable to figure out any way to get past it. Meanwhile, he was watching the movements of the Austrians and Russians and readying his own army. When the time was ripe he suddenly marched his army eastward, surrounded an exposed Austrian army at Ulm in southwest Germany, and forced it to surrender. But the day after Ulm, Lord Nelson sighted the combined French and Spanish fleets off Cape Trafalgar on the southwest point of Spain and annihilated them (October 21, 1805). Although Nelson was killed early in the battle, his victory saved Great Britain from the menace of a Napoleonic invasion and limited the scope of the French emperor's conquests to the continent of Europe. Trafalgar was one of the decisive battles of all time.

On land, however, Napoleon seemed invincible. Moving his army eastward from Ulm, he met and crushed the oncoming combined forces of Austria and Russia at Austerlitz. Austria immediately sued for peace, and the demoralized Russians retreated toward their home country. At this juncture Prussia declared war on Napoleon. The time was inopportune, and the Prussian army, which under Frederick the Great had held most of Europe at bay, was no match for Napoleon. At Jena and Auerstädt Napoleon overwhelmed and virtually destroyed the Prussian forces (1806). Two weeks later the French were in Berlin. Hearing that the Russian troops were re-forming in Poland, Napoleon moved eastward to meet them. After being held to a draw by the Russians in a blinding snowstorm at Eylau, he defeated them decisively a few months later in the great battle of Friedland (1807). Tsar Alexander I now sued for peace. Although the Treaties of Tilsit (July 1807) were technically between equals, they actually left Napoleon master of the European continent and Alexander I only a junior partner. Russia was given a free hand to deal with Turkey in Eastern Europe, but was not permitted to take Constantinople, the prize the Russians most desired. In return for a dominant hand in Eastern Europe, Alexander promised to join Napoleon against Great Britain, and to force Sweden to do so. Tilsit recognized the changes that Napoleon had already made in Central and Western Europe and left him free to make any others he wished.

Between 1806 and 1808 Napoleon remade the map of Europe. The puppet Duchy of Warsaw was created out of part of Prussia's (and later, part of Austria's) Polish territory. Prussia's territory west of the Elbe was made a part of the kingdom of Westphalia, over which Napoleon's youngest brother, Jerome, was made king. Prussia was thus virtually halved in size. The Holy Roman Empire was at long last abolished, and its hundreds of little principalities greatly consolidated. A strip of German territory along the North Sea was annexed outright to France. The rest of German territory west of the Elbe was brought into the Confederation of the Rhine, with Napoleon as protector. Napoleon's younger brother, Louis, was made king of Holland, but when Louis began to favor the interests of his Dutch subjects over those of the French Empire, Napoleon deposed him and annexed his territory to France. The whole Italian peninsula was brought under French dominance. Northwestern Italy down to and including Rome was annexed outright. Marshal Murat and Napoleon's sister Caroline were made king and queen of Naples. The northeastern third of the peninsula was made into the kingdom of Italy, with Napoleon as king and his stepson, Eugene, as viceroy. The coastal areas along the northeastern Adriatic Sea were detached from Austria and annexed to France. In 1808 Napoleon overthrew the weak Spanish royal house and made his elder brother, Joseph, king of Spain. Shortly before, the Portu-

By 1808, when this Gillray cartoon called "The Valley of the Shadow of Death" was published in England, Napoleon had remade the map of Europe and was the object of mass resentment: From the left, King Joseph sinks in the Ditch of Styx as the Spanish avenger leaps across with the Portuguese wolf; the British lion and the Sicilian terrier attack from the front and the Russian bear from behind; and from the Lethean Ditch in the foreground, the Rhenish Confederation of starved rats crawl out, Dutch frogs spit out their spite, the American rattlesnake shakes his tail, and the Prussian scarecrow attempts to fly. From above, the "Roman Meteor" descends in bolts of lightning, the "Turkish New Moon" rises, the spirit of Charles XII of Sweden descends with raised sword, and the "Imperial Eagle" (Germany) emerges from the clouds. *Photo: Prints Division, New York Public Library, Astor, Lenox, and Tilden Foundations*

guese royal family had fled to Brazil at the approach of a conquering French army. Denmark (including Norway) became Napoleon's most faithful ally.

Thus, by 1808, all Europe except the British Isles was under French control or French influence. No other conqueror has so dominated Europe. In all those territories under direct French control, Napoleon's "enlightened" institutions and administrative efficiency were introduced. The rest of Europe, impressed with the effectiveness of the French revolutionary ideas

Napoleon's Russian Campaign
June to December 1812

EUROPE 1810

and institutions, adopted many of them voluntarily. And yet this mighty Napoleonic empire was to last less than five years.

4. DECLINE AND FALL OF THE EMPIRE

A number of factors contributed to the decline and fall of the Napoleonic empire. One of the most obvious was British sea power. Because of it, Great Britain alone of the European powers was able to withstand the Napoleonic military onslaught. After Trafalgar dashed Napoleon's hopes of invading the British Isles, he sought the destruction of "perfidious Albion" by economic pressure. In order to wreck the economy of the "nation of shopkeepers" he attempted to blockade the entire continent of Europe against British shipping. All British goods were confiscated. French privateers were set upon British merchant ships. These measures, known as "the Continental System," did cause Great Britain grave distress. However, with her control of the sea, she was able to apply a more effective counterblockade against the Napoleon-dominated Continent. While wrestling with Napoleon she was able even to hold her own in the War of 1812 with the United States, which attempted to resist the British maritime restrictions. Since Europe was almost entirely dependent upon Great Britain for manufactured goods and tropical products, the Continental System created ever-increasing resentment against Napoleon's rule.

Another factor that undermined the Napoleonic empire was the rise of a national spirit among the subject peoples. The mass spirit of intense patriotism or nationalism, which had its origin in France during the *levée en masse* of 1793, spread to the rest of Europe in the wake of Napoleon's conquering armies. The first people to rebel openly against the French yoke were the proud Spaniards. Hardly had Napoleon's brother Joseph been placed on the Spanish throne when his unwilling subjects rose up and chased him out of Madrid. The superior French armies, even when led by Napoleon himself, were ineffective against the hit-and-run guerrilla tactics invented by the Spaniards. The British

government, observing Napoleon's predicament in Spain, sent an army under Arthur Wellesley, the future duke of Wellington, to exploit the situation. Spain became a running abscess that drained away much of Napoleon's military strength. Meanwhile, Prussia, after the humiliation of Jena, had begun a rejuvenation under the leadership of Baron vom Stein. Partly in secret and partly in the open, the Prussians modernized their army and their civil institutions and prepared for the day of liberation. In 1809 Austria declared war on Napoleon in a premature effort to free herself from subservience to the French emperor. Although Austria was once more defeated, the heroic valor with which her armies fought served notice of the rising spirit of national pride and resistance. Napoleon could no longer enjoy the advantage of fighting with soldiers fired with the heady wine of nationalism against lethargic professional armies.

A third factor in the decline of the French colossus was Napoleon himself. He began to slow down — to lose his magic touch. Symptoms of the stomach cancer or ulcer from which he is believed to have died began to appear. As his enemies one after another adopted his winning tactics, he failed to come up with better ones.

The beginning of the end was a disastrous campaign against Russia in 1812. When Alexander I wearied of the hardships of the Continental System and opened his ports to the British, Napoleon, against the advice of his closest associates, decided to conquer Russia. Amassing an army of 600,000, the mightiest army ever assembled up to that time, he plunged into the vastness of Russia. Many of his troops, however, were unwilling conscripts from the puppet states. The Russian army retreated into the interior of the huge country, following a scorched-earth policy and drawing Napoleon ever farther from his base of supplies. Finally, after the bloody battle of Borodino about 75 miles from Moscow, Napoleon's hosts entered the city. But Alexander I refused to make peace. A fire destroyed much of Moscow, leaving the invaders without shelter in the face of approaching winter. Napoleon began his retreat too late. The Russian winter caught his forces burdened down with loot. Tens of thousands froze or starved. Russian Cossacks, riding out of the blizzards, cut down or captured other thousands. Of the 600,000 men who marched into Russia, only some 20,000 escaped.

Napoleon dashed back to France to raise fresh conscripts, but the flower of French manhood was gone. One nation after another rose up to join the Russians in a war of liberation. At Leipzig in central Germany, in October 1813, Napoleon was at last decisively defeated. The next year the allies entered Paris and exiled Napoleon to the island of Elba, off the coast of Italy. When the allies began to squabble over the peace settlement, Napoleon escaped back to France and raised another army, but he was finally defeated by the duke of Wellington and the Prussians under Marshal Blücher at Waterloo in Belgium, June 1815. This time he was imprisoned on the island of St. Helena in the South Atlantic, where six years later he died.

5. NAPOLEON'S IMPACT ON LATIN AMERICA – REVOLUTION AND INDEPENDENCE

One vast area outside Europe upon which the impact of Napoleon was strong and immediate was Latin America. During the eighteenth century, discontent with colonial rule had been steadily mounting in the Spanish and Portuguese colonial empires in North and South America. Like the thirteen English colonies in North America, resentment was directed primarily against economic and political restrictions. As the native-born "Creoles" had come to outnumber the Spanish- and Portuguese-born settlers, the ties of loyalty to the mother countries had become more and more tenuous. The liberal writings of the French and British philosophers of the Enlightenment were smuggled into Latin America and made their converts, particularly among young intellectuals. These liberal Latin Americans could not help being impressed by the successful revolt of the English colonies to the north and the setting up of a liberal New World republic. The French Revolution had an even more profound influence on them. When, therefore, Napoleon overthrew Ferdinand VII of Spain and placed his own brother, Joseph Bonaparte, on the Spanish throne, the

sentiments of loyalty on the part of the colonies for the mother country, which were already weak, quickly became quite confused.

By 1810 the colonies were in open revolt. As with the English colonists three decades earlier, the cause of the Latin American revolutionists seemed hopeless. In addition to the regular Spanish troops, they had to struggle against most of the wealthy Spanish settlers and the local Roman Catholic hierarchy. Eventually two brilliant young leaders, Simón Bolívar and José San Martín, emerged to overcome the seemingly impossible obstacles and to lead the South American revolutionists to success. By 1822 the independence of Spanish South America was won. In the same year the issue was decided in Spain's Central American colonies and in Mexico, which then included the southwest quarter of what is now the United States. In all the former Spanish colonies, republics were established, although a long period of troubled apprenticeship preceded the establishment of reasonably stable popular governments. As a matter of fact, real stability has continued to be a problem for Central and South American nations.

In the huge Portuguese colony of Brazil, the independence movement was delayed by the flight of the Portuguese royal family to Brazil in 1807. However, the return of the king to Portugal six years after Napoleon's fall and the efforts of the Portuguese government to reimpose the colonial status on Brazil quickly fanned the embers of revolt into flame. In 1822 the Portuguese king's son, Pedro, whom he had left behind as regent, yielded to native pressure and declared himself king of independent Brazil. In all of independent Latin America the Code Napoleon was adopted as the basis of civil law, and the impact of the Enlightenment on political institutions was clearly visible.

6. SIGNIFICANCE OF THE FRENCH REVOLUTION AND NAPOLEON

The French Revolution and its Napoleonic sequel had a profound effect upon the course of history. Like Pandora when she lifted the lid of that fateful box they let loose forces and ideas

Who Was Napoleon?

No man in modern times—if indeed, in all history—has displayed more military and political genius than Napoleon Bonaparte. He was a dreamer and planner of grandiose projects and yet the master of exact practical detail. His memory was photographic; his energy seemed inexhaustible. He possessed charisma—that combination of personal dynamism and charm that enabled him to dominate and lead virtually all those with whom he came in contact. The French Revolution, by pulling down the pillars of a venerable society, presented him with a building opportunity, the like of which would not have happened again, as he himself admitted, in another thousand years. To what ends did he use this unparalleled talent and opportunity?

This is a difficult question to answer. Napoleon made it more difficult by spending much of the last six years of his life on St. Helena dictating his reminiscences, in which he dressed up his record for the historian. According to him, he was a true child of the Enlightenment and heir to the French Revolution—to the principles of liberty, equality, fraternity. His loyalty was to France, but at the same time he loved all mankind. Above all, he was a man of peace. His wars were all in defense of France and of the principles of the Revolution. There can be little question that there is some truth in these assertions, but unfortunately there is so much untruth that it is by his deeds rather than his words that we must judge him.

Napoleon cannot be rightly accused of destroying a popular constitutional regime that had been set up during the course of the revolution. The Directory, which Napoleon overthrew, had already violated the constitution upon which it was based. It had refused to accept the results of every election that had been held during the course of its existence. Moreover, it had failed to achieve either law and order in France or peace abroad. It had been unable to balance the national budget or to stabilize the currency. In short, it had not been able to consummate the revolution. Public opinion, as revealed by all the elections held during the Directory, showed a strong preference for monarchy. A powerful group of conspirators was already looking for the right man to lead a coup d'état when Napoleon returned from Egypt. If Napoleon had not overthrown the Directory, somebody else would have, and the ensuing dictatorship probably would have been harsher and certainly less efficient. On the other hand, there was no widespread popular clamor for Napoleon, as he would have us believe. His fame among the masses at that time was not that great.

Napoleon's best claims to greatness in history lie in his constructive reforms during the period of the Consulate, 1799–1804. He was the last and by far the greatest of the enlightened despots. His achievement of peace, law and order, administrative efficiency, prosperity, and social tranquillity, his legal codes, the Concordat of 1801, his educational institutions, his sound financial measures constitute a record of political and social reform probably unparalleled in history. They vividly reflect the influence of the Enlightenment. Nor should the fact that many, if not all, of these reforms were already under consideration or under way and that other men played an important part in bringing them to fruition detract from Napoleon's role. It was his energy, imagination, sense of the practical and the possible, and political skill that were primarily responsible for bringing them into being.

The empire is another matter. It was a decade of almost constant war, and all but the last few months of it was on soil other than French. It is difficult to accept Napoleon's claim that his wars and conquests were solely defensive. It is true that many of Napoleon's reforms, such as the Code Napoleon, administrative efficiency, religious toleration, and the weakening of feudalism followed in the wake of his conquering armies. But these benefits were offset by heavy exactions of conscripts and property for the benefit of the French. Likewise, the emperor's boast of creating a European state or confederation was more than nullified by the nationalism that he aroused everywhere in emulation of that of the French. Finally, the Napoleonic empire illustrated a weakness of all dictatorships—dependence upon a mortal man. There was no one to take the great man's place.

So what of Napoleon? Was he a great genius? He was. Did he achieve any lasting humanitarian reforms? He did. Was he a child of the Enlightenment and the heir to the French Revolution? In some measure he was—especially in his youth. But being human, he grew old and fell victim to the great truth that Lord Acton has so well stated, "power corrupts and absolute power corrupts absolutely." The great enemy that Napoleon could never conquer was his own ego.

that have influenced and ofttimes shaken the world ever since, especially the revolutionary ideals of *Liberty, Equality, Fraternity.* Originally conceived in the eighteenth century by the philosophers of the Enlightenment, they were born materially in the American and French revolutions, and developed and spread by Napoleon.

Liberty, of course, has been one of the chief quests of the human race from its beginning to the present and has never at any time been perfectly attained. In the era of the French Revolution, the ideal of liberty meant freedom from arbitrary authority—political, religious, economic, or social. It meant freedom of speech, press, conscience, assembly, person, and profession, and the sacredness of property. During the moderate first phase of the French Revolution, a great deal of progress toward these goals was made; in the tumultuous and bloody second phase, a good deal was lost. Under Napoleon's dictatorship there was no political liberty. However, he claimed that the efficiency, prosperity,

and honor of his regime more than made up for the lack of popular government, for which, he believed, the world was not yet ready.

Equality meant essentially equality under the law and equality of opportunity for gain and advancement. It was only during the brief dominance of Robespierre that the absolute social equality of all citizens became a cult. Its impracticability was soon evident. Napoleon's law codes were a great boon to the more moderate and practical kind of equality.

Fraternity manifested itself in the mass movements (sometimes violent) for reform, in the comradeship in the conscripted armies, and above all in the new popular and dynamic spirit of nationalism. These forces, released by the American and French revolutions, spread first to the rest of Europe, then to Latin America, and eventually to the rest of the world. Much of the history of the world since the era of the French Revolution has centered around these forces at work.

Suggested Reading

General

*G. Bruun, *Europe and the French Imperium, 1799–1814* (Torch). Excellent volume in the Rise of Modern Europe series.

*G. Lefèbvre, *Napoleon,* 2 vols (Columbia University Press). Scholarly treatment by a leading authority.

*H. Butterfield, *Napoleon* (Collier). Good brief biography.

The Consulate

R. B. Holtman, *Napoleonic Propaganda* (1950). Reveals a clever and important aspect of a dictator.

The Empire

*C. Brinton, *The Lives of Talleyrand* (Norton). Excellent, but a little too sympathetic.

P. Guedalla, *Wellington* (1931). Popularly written biography of Napoleon's greatest nemesis.

*W. S. Robertson, *The Rise of the Spanish-American Republics* (Collier). Good brief account.

Sources

*J. C. Herold, *The Mind of Napoleon* (Collier). Good selection of Napoleon's quoted words.

*A. de Caulincourt, *With Napoleon in Russia* (Universal Library). Vivid account of Napoleon's Russian campaign by one of his aides-de-camp.

Historical Fiction

*Leo Tolstoy, *War and Peace* (Penguin). Sometimes called the world's greatest novel; based on excellent historical research.

42

AFTERMATH: RESTORATION AND REACTION, 1815 - 1830

The overthrow of Napoleon in 1815 brought to an end, in Europe at least, the heroic and tumultuous epoch that had begun in 1789 with the meeting of the Estates General. The intervening twenty-six years had been filled with great expectation, experimentation, turmoil, and war. Now there was mass disillusionment and weariness. The European royalty and aristocracy, at long last triumphant over revolutionary France, were determined to put an end not only to the Mirabeaus, Robespierres, and Napoleons, but also to the ideas of Voltaire and Rousseau. In order to achieve this goal, to redraw the mutilated map of Europe, and to set the clock back as far as was practically possible, the leaders of the victorious powers gathered at the Austrian capital of Vienna in the autumn of 1814. To this conference also flocked representatives of every state in Europe, hundreds of dispossessed princes, agents of every conceivable interest, and adventurers.

1. THE CONGRESS OF VIENNA (1814—1815)

The Congress of Vienna, which never actually met in formal session, was dominated by the four major victors over Napoleon. Great Britain was represented by her able foreign minister, Lord Castlereagh. Prussia's mediocre king, Frederick William III, headed his own delegation, as did Russia's tsar, the idealistic young Alexander

I. Austria's emperor, Francis I, played host to the assembled great. However, the real leader of the Austrian delegation, and, indeed, the dominant figure of the whole congress, was the Austrian chancellor, Prince Klemens von Metternich. As a guiding principle upon which to base their decisions, the conferees decided upon "legitimacy." This meant that in redistributing various territories, attention would be paid not to the desires or interests of the people concerned, but to the legal claims of the former and future sovereigns. Many of the decisions formalized at Vienna had already been made by the four major powers shortly before and after Napoleon's overthrow in April 1814.

Thanks in no small measure to the presence of the clever and able Talleyrand, France, the cause of all the turmoil, got off very lightly. Prussia would have severely punished and weakened France, but her three major colleagues were fearful of upsetting the balance of power. Already saddled with the restored Bourbons, France was merely reduced to the boundaries she had possessed before her annexations during the wars of the revolutionary era. The Congress of Vienna had originally imposed no indemnity upon France. But because of Napoleon's return from Elba in the midst of the congress and his hundred-day fling that ended at Waterloo, the four great powers compelled France to cede the Saar Basin to Prussia, to pay an indemnity of $140 million, and to return the art treasures stolen by Napoleon from the various galleries of Europe. To contain France within her frontiers and to discourage future French aggression, Prussia was given a sizable block of territory along the Rhine, the Austrian Netherlands (Belgium) was annexed to the Dutch Netherlands, and Piedmont was enlarged by the annexation of the city-state of Genoa.

To safeguard her empire, Great Britain sought a balance of power on the Continent and the acquisition of certain strategic territories. Because of her complete mastery over the seas, she could have helped herself to any of the colonial possessions of France or the Napoleonic puppet states that she desired. However, she limited herself to Helgoland in the North Sea, Malta, and the Ionian Islands in the Mediterranean, several small French and Spanish territories in the West Indies and the Indian Ocean, and the Dutch colonies of Ceylon off the tip of India, the Cape of Good Hope, and part of Dutch Guiana in South America.

Prussia, in addition to her valuable gains in the Rhineland, annexed Westphalia and Swedish Pomerania. In return for a portion of her Polish territory including the city of Warsaw, which she ceded to Russia, she annexed two-fifths of Saxony. These changes considerably strengthened and consolidated Prussia's territories and made her more homogeneously German and Western. However, her Rhineland territory was not contiguous to the homeland—a situation that invited further aggression.

Russia received Finland from Sweden. Sweden got Norway from Denmark in return. Russia's acquisition of most of Prussia's Polish territory made the great majority of the Polish-speaking people subjects of Russia and brought Russia farther into the heart of Central Europe.

Austria, in exchange for the Belgian Netherlands, took the two rich Italian provinces of Lombardy and Venetia. Austrian princes were placed on the thrones of three other Italian states: Modena, Parma, and Tuscany. This preeminence in Italy, together with the presidency over the German Confederation, made Austria the dominant power in Central Europe. Her mastery over Italy and Germany was made possible by their political division and weakness.

The Italian Peninsula was left divided into eight separate states with no common political ties. In the words of Metternich, Italy was "only a geographical expression."

The Holy Roman Empire, which Napoleon had destroyed, was not restored, but in its place was erected the equally weak and ineffective German Confederation. Napoleon's consolidation of the more than three hundred German states into thirty-nine was allowed to stand, bringing the German people that much more political unity. However, Metternich saw to it that the government of the German Confederation was powerless and under the permanent presidency of Austria.

Thus were the peoples and territories of Europe moved about by the great powers at Vienna like pawns on a chessboard, in complete disregard for the wishes of the people or for the spirit of nationalism that was now an increasingly virile force.

2. THE CONCERT OF EUROPE—FIRST RIFTS IN THE METTERNICH SYSTEM

Metternich and his colleagues, pleased with their work, set up machinery for perpetuating it. Conveniently at hand was the Holy Alliance, conceived by Alexander I to establish and safeguard the principles of the Christian religion. Russia (Orthodox), Austria (Roman Catholic), and Prussia (Protestant), representing the three major branches of Christendom, were to form the nucleus of the alliance. All the Christian states of Europe were invited to join, and only Great Britain and the Papal States did not. Metternich considered the Holy Alliance a "sonorous nothing," but saw in it an opportunity for influencing the tsar. Intended by Alexander I as a bulwark of Christianity, the Holy Alliance became under Metternich's influence a symbol of reaction and repression.

Much more earthly an agency for perpetuating the Vienna settlements was the Quadruple Alliance. This was a military alliance of Austria, Russia, Prussia, and Great Britain created in November 1815, for the purpose of guaranteeing for twenty years the territorial boundaries estab-

Boundary of the German Confederation

0   100   200 miles

FINLAND
(Russia, 1808)

St. Pe

KINGDOM OF NORWAY
AND SWEDEN

Novgorod

Reval

Oslo•

•Stockholm

Riga•

SCOTLAND

•Edinburgh

NORTH SEA

LITHUA

•Copenhagen
DENMARK

BALTIC SEA

EAST
PRUSSIA
Danzig•

UNITED KINGDOM
OF GREAT BRITAIN AND IRELAND

Niemen R.

IRELAND   •Dublin

ENGLAND

SCHLESWIG
HELIGOLAND
(Britain)
HOLSTEIN

•Hamburg

P

S

Vistula R.

Berlin•

•Warsaw

KINGDOM OF
POLAND
(1815-1831)

WALES

KINGDOM OF THE
NETHERLANDS

HANOVER

Elbe

•London

BELGIUM
(Ind. 1831)

•Cologne

SAXON
STATES   SAXONY

Oder

Breslau•

GALICIA

LUX

HESSE

Cracow•

Dni

ENGLISH CHANNEL

Prague•

•Rouen

Seine R.

Metz•

LORRAINE

WÜRT-
TEMBERG

BAVARIA

Vienna•

AUSTRIAN EMPIRE

ATLANTIC OCEAN

•Paris

Strasbourg•

BADEN

•Munich

AUSTRIA

•Budapest

TRANSYLVANIA

Loire R.

ALSACE

•Tours

F R A N C E

Berne
SWITZERLAND

TYROL

HUNGARY

CROATIA

•Bordeaux

Rhone R.

•Lyons

LOM-
BARDY

VENETIA

Belgrade•

WALLACH
(Autonomous

•Toulouse

SAVOY

Milan•

Po R.

BOSNIA

SERBIA
*(Autonomous
1829)*

Danube

PYRENEES

Nice•

PARMA

MODENA

DALMATIA

•Sofia   BU

•Marseilles

Genoa•

LUCCA

•Madrid

•Barcelona

Toulon•

•Burgos

Ebro R.

PORTUGAL

SPAIN

Tagus R.

Lisbon•

•Valencia

•Seville

Cadiz•

•Gibraltar *(Britain)*

ELBA

CORSICA
(France)

TUSCANY

PAPAL
STATES

•Rome

MONTE-
NEGRO

Salonica•

O
T
T
O

•Naples

BALEARIC I.
(Spain)

SARDINIA

KINGDOM OF THE
TWO SICILIES

IONIAN I.
(Britain)

GREECE
(Independent 1829

A

•Algiers

Palermo•

SICILY

MALTA
(Britain)

ADRIATIC SEA

MOROCCO

ALGERIA *(France, 1830)*

TUNIS
(Turkish)

*MALTA
(Britain)*

MEDITERRANEAN SEA

TRIPOLI

TRIPOLI

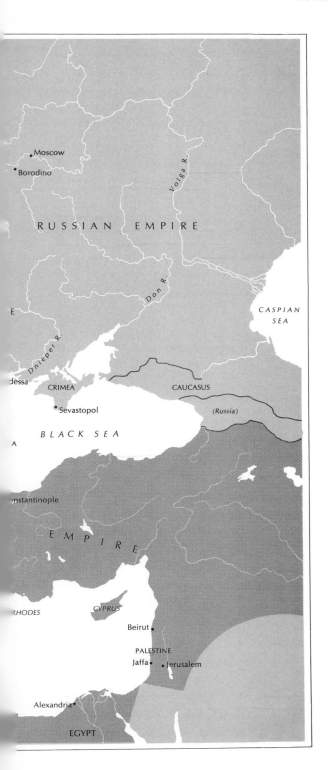

EUROPE 1815

lished by the Vienna settlement. <u>Metternich was determined to make of the alliance an international military police force that would spy out and suppress any liberal or national movements.</u> It was arranged that the four member powers should hold periodic congresses to carry out the purposes of the alliance.

The first congress was held at Aix-la-Chapelle in northwest Germany in 1818. The purpose was to arrange the withdrawal of occupation forces from French soil. Since France had demonstrated good behavior under the restored Bourbon king, Louis XVIII, she was not only freed of occupying forces, but was admitted to the Quadruple Alliance, which thereupon became the Quintuple Alliance. Congresses at Troppau in 1820 and at Laibach in 1821, both on Austrian soil, concerned themselves with an insurrection that had broken out in Naples against the tyrannical Bourbon king, Ferdinand I. An Austrian army was authorized to put down the insurrection and reestablish the hated Ferdinand I upon his throne. The Neapolitan liberal volunteers, no match for the Austrian regulars, were soon defeated, and their leaders executed, imprisoned, or exiled. What turned out to be the last of the congresses met in 1822 at Verona, in Austria's Italian province of Venetia, to deal with a liberal revolt in Spain against the reactionary tyrant Ferdinand VII. With the sanction of the Congress of Verona a French army crossed the Pyrenees and easily put down the rebellion.

The bloody vengeance that Ferdinand took upon the liberal rebels revolted the French soldiers who had restored him. However, the first of the alliance powers to repudiate the Metternich system was not France but Great Britain. At the Troppau congress, she clearly indicated her opposition to interfering in the internal affairs of other states. When the Verona congress decided, over her protest, upon intervention in Spain, Britain's representative withdrew from the congress. It was the first sign of dissension within the concert of Europe.

The Metternich system soon received further blows, some from unexpected quarters. At the Congress of Verona, the like-minded Austrians,

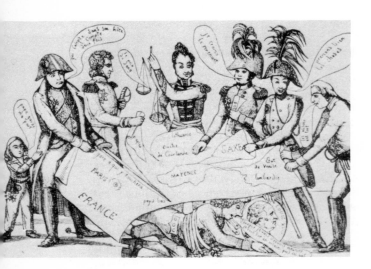

Guided by Metternich, the assembled rulers and diplomats at the Congress of Vienna (1814–1815) traded territories and rearranged the map of Europe in a cynical great-power contest for dominance of the Continent after the defeat of Napoleon. *Photo: Historical Pictures Service, Chicago*

Russians, and Prussians had been alarmed not only by the rebellion in the Spanish homeland, but also by the revolt of Spain's New World colonies. The brilliant success of the thirteen English colonies was bad enough; it must not be repeated in Latin America. When the corrupt government of Ferdinand VII proved incapable of putting down the revolt, Alexander I, with Metternich's blessing, proposed to send a Russian fleet to help coerce the colonies. Great Britain, enjoying a lucrative trade with the rebellious colonies, did not wish to see them restored to Spanish dominion and commercial monopoly. Her foreign minister, Canning, who had succeeded Castlereagh in 1822, proposed to the government of the United States that Great Britain and the United States issue a joint statement against interference by the "Holy Alliance" in the affairs of the Western Hemisphere. To President Monroe and to his confidants, ex-Presidents Madison and Jefferson, this seemed a good idea. However, Secretary of State John

Quincy Adams foresaw that the time might come when the United States would wish to invoke such a policy alone, perhaps even against Great Britain. The British would support the policy of the United States anyway because of their own self-interest.

Adams convinced Monroe that the United States should proclaim the policy alone. When, therefore, the President in his message to Congress, in December 1823, announced what has come to be called the Monroe Doctrine, it was the Adams rather than the Canning version. Monroe stated simply that the United States would regard any interference on the part of European powers in the affairs of the Western Hemisphere as an "unfriendly act." The United States was at the time, of course, a new and relatively weak nation, but Canning's immediate support of the American policy killed any further thought of "Holy Alliance" intervention in the New World, for Great Britain was the unchallenged mistress of the seas. The Monroe Doctrine was more than just a blow to Metternichism in Europe. It guaranteed the independence of Latin America and marked the beginning of active participation by the United States in affairs beyond her own immediate shores.

The next successful blow at repressive tyranny was struck by the Greeks against their Muslim Turkish overlords. The Greek revolt of 1821–1829 is an excellent example of the influence of the past in world affairs. The Greeks had been treated no worse by their Turkish masters than the rest of the Christian European subjects of the Sultan—the Serbs, the Bulgarians, or the Rumanians. However, the Greeks, unlike the others, had the memory of a glorious past to spur them on to heroism. Even so, the valiant efforts of the Greeks were not sufficient to resist the power of the whole Ottoman Empire. By 1827 they were on the point of being hopelessly crushed.

Meanwhile, the sympathies of the great powers were being aroused for the courageous Christian Greeks, who were being cruelly massacred by the Muslim Turks. Russia, Great Britain, and France in particular displayed a growing concern over the events in Greece. Russia's Orthodox Christian religion was the same as that of the Greeks. Furthermore, the Russians had long desired Constantinople, which controlled her natural strategic and commercial outlet to the Mediterranean. Great Britain was concerned over the possibility of Russia's dominance in the Near East. In addition, the ruling classes in Great Britain and France were steeped in the classical culture of ancient Greece. Lord Byron, the most popular literary figure in Europe, lost his life fighting as a volunteer for Greece.

In 1827 these three powers, over Metternich's protest, intervened in the Greek revolt and defeated the Turks on land and sea. The Treaty of Adrianople in 1829 granted independence to most of the Greeks on the home peninsula and local autonomy to the Serbs and Rumanians. The successful revolt of the Greeks was a victory for the resurging revolutionary principles of liberalism and nationalism. The intervention of Russia, Great Britain, and France demolished the already battered concert of Europe. The Treaty of Adrianople also hastened the disintegration of the once powerful Ottoman Empire.

The year 1830 was a bad one for Metternich. Successful revolutions in France and Belgium undid two of the settlements at Vienna. News of the revolution in France (which will be described in the next section) set off the revolt in Brussels. The union forced upon Belgium and the Netherlands at Vienna had never been a happy one, and Belgian discontent with Dutch rule had been mounting for fifteen years. In addition to differences in language, the Belgians were Roman Catholic, whereas the Dutch were predominately Calvinist. The Belgian economy was based on industry, the Dutch on commerce. Belgium, more populous than the Netherlands, was not given her fair share of representation in the government. When the halfhearted efforts of the Dutch failed to suppress the revolt, Austria and Russia threatened to intervene in the interests of legitimacy and tranquillity. They were deterred by British and French support of Belgian independence. By 1830, then, Metternich's international system of reaction and repression was definitely breached. It was events in France that disturbed the watchdogs over the status quo the most.

3. THE BOURBON RESTORATION IN FRANCE

When the victorious armies of the coalition powers entered France and deposed Napoleon in the spring of 1814, they brought "in their baggage" the members of the Bourbon royal family who had fled the revolution. In their wake trooped the émigré nobility. A younger brother of the guillotined Louis XVI was placed on the throne as Louis XVIII. (The son of Louis XVI, who had died in prison in 1795, without having ruled, was considered to be Louis XVII.) The "restored" Bourbon king was now fifty-nine years of age and too fat and gouty to walk unassisted. He had traveled much and unwillingly during the long, lean years of his exile. When Napoleon returned from Elba in 1815, Louis XVIII had to flee once more. After Waterloo he returned to his throne, which he considered "the most comfortable of armchairs," determined to do nothing that might force him to leave it again.

Upon assuming the throne, Louis XVIII issued a charter, or constitution, that retained Napoleon's administrative and legal system, and civil and religious liberty. Lawmaking was placed in the hands of a two-chamber legislature. The upper house was made hereditary, and the lower house was elected by a highly restricted electorate. Only those who paid direct annual taxes of 300 francs ($60) could vote; this limited the suffrage to about 100,000 out of a total population of nearly 30,000,000. The lower house could be prorogued or dissolved by the king. Since the king also appointed and controlled his own ministers and the host of civilian and military officials, carried on foreign relations, controlled the military forces, and enforced the laws, his power was only slightly limited by the charter.

Louis XVIII set out to use his powers with moderation in order that tranquillity might be restored. There were no wholesale punishments of revolutionary leaders. The peasant and bourgeois purchasers of church and noble lands were not dispossessed. However, most of the returned émigrés were of a different spirit. They came back from their unhappy exile angry and vengeful, demanding their old privileges and indemnification for their lands. Their leader was the king's younger brother, the Comte d'Artois —a typical Bourbon who had "never learned anything and never forgotten anything." The reactionaries controlled both houses of the national legislature, since even in the lower elected house, suffrage restrictions heavily favored the aristocracy and the *nouveaux riches*. Louis XVIII found it increasingly difficult to hold these fire-eating reactionaries in check. Shortly before he died in 1824, he warned his incorrigible brother of the danger to the Bourbon dynasty if he did not adopt a more moderate attitude.

Unfortunately, <u>Charles X</u>, as the Comte d'Artois now styled himself, was a stranger to moderation. He quickly aroused animosity against his regime to an explosive pitch. The Napoleonic generals who had brought so much glory to France were immediately retired from duty. An indemnity was voted the émigrés for their confiscated lands, the money to be raised by reducing the interest on government bonds from 5 percent to 3 percent. This angered the upper bourgeoisie, who were the chief bondholders. The peasants were alarmed by a proposed establishment of primogeniture, which seemed to endanger the principle of equality and the security of land titles. The Jesuits were brought back to France, and favors were bestowed upon the Roman Catholic Church. Opposition mounted rapidly. By 1827 Charles X had lost his majority in both houses of the national legislature. Totally blind to the political realities of the day, he twice dissolved the lower chamber and attempted to force the election of a friendly majority by censoring the press and using official pressure on the electorate. The hostile majorities only increased in number.

Finally in July 1830 the king decided to end the parliamentary regime and rule as a dictator. In a set of ordinances he dissolved the newly elected chamber, called for new elections, restricted the suffrage so drastically that only about 25,000 very rich citizens could vote, and abolished completely the freedom of the press. These tyrannical measures set off an uprising in Paris. The Parisian proletariat erected barricades in the streets that the disaffected rank and file of the army were "unable" to break. After three days of desultory fighting, the insurgents had the upper hand, and the last Bourbon king of France was on his way to exile in England. A group of moderate opposition members of the lower chamber now set themselves up as a provisional government and named a new king: Louis Philippe, head of the house of Orléans and a cousin of the departed Bourbon. Louis Philippe, a well-known moderate liberal and friend of the middle class, was accepted by the great majority of the people of France. The French people in July 1830, therefore, showed Metternich and the rest of the world that the spirit of the French Revolution was not dead, but for fifteen years had been only dormant.

4. RESTORATION AND REPRESSION IN THE GERMANIES

In Central and Eastern Europe, particularly in the Germanies, Italy, and Russia, the Metternich system was more secure. The Germanies in 1815 consisted of thirty-seven little states and two large ones—Prussia and Austria. In all of them the influence of Metternich was strong. At the Congress of Vienna the Austrian prime minister had seen to it that the Germanies were reconstructed in such a way that German nationalism and liberalism would be thwarted. The German Confederation was an improvement over the old Holy Roman Empire, which Napoleon had destroyed, only in the sense that Napoleon's consolidation of the more than three hundred states down to thirty-nine was allowed to stand. The boundaries remained the same. The Diet was only a gathering and debating place for the representatives of the rulers of the thirty-nine states. The confederation had no treasury and no army at its command. There was not even a flag to symbolize its German national character. Reactionary Austria enjoyed a permanent presidency over it.

The German nationalism and liberalism that existed in 1815 centered primarily in the little states, some of whose rulers defied Metternich by granting liberal constitutions. The national and liberal activities here were largely the work of university students and professors, who shortly after 1815 began to form *Burschenschaften,* or brotherhoods, for the purpose of promoting German nationalism, liberalism, and the Christian religion. In 1817 in commemoration of the three hundredth anniversary of Luther's publication of his ninety-five theses, the *Burschenschaften* staged a giant festival at Wartburg, where Luther had hidden and had begun his translation of the Bible. Although the festivities were primarily religious in character, enough enthusiasm for German nationalism and liberalism was displayed to fill Metternich with anxiety. The murder two years later of a reactionary propagandist by a fanatical student gave Metternich his opportunity to strike. Calling together the princes of the leading German states at Carlsbad, he joined them in drawing up a set of harsh decrees designed to crush the embryonic national and liberal movements. The *Burschenschaften* were outlawed. Strict censorship was established. Classrooms and libraries were supervised. Liberal students and professors were terrorized by spies and police. The Carlsbad Decrees succeeded in suppressing for a number of years this first outcropping of the revolutionary spirit in Germany since the overthrow of Napoleon. The spirit, however, was not really suppressed; it was merely driven underground.

In Prussia the militaristic, paternalistic, despotic Hohenzollerns reigned. Behind them stood the equally reactionary landed aristocracy, the *Junkers.* In fact these sword-bearing, monocled Junkers, who ruled feudal-fashion over their peasants, officered the Prussian army, and filled the key posts in the civil service and administration, constituted the dominant factor in Prussian history in the nineteenth century. These military lords hated not only liberalism in any form, but also German nationalism. They did not wish to see virile, martial Prussia contaminated by association with the German states that were now infected with the French disease of liberalism. The *Burschenschaften* made slight headway in Prussia. It was only in the economic field that German unity received any encouragement from Prussia. Because her territory was separated into two noncontiguous segments, Prussia in 1819

began making commercial treaties with her smaller German neighbors, providing for the free flow of trade among them. By 1834 nearly all the states of the German Confederation except Austria had joined the Prussian-sponsored *Zollverein* (customs union). Though it was not so intended, the *Zollverein* proved to be a forerunner of German political unity under Prussian leadership.

As was to be expected, Metternichism reached its height in Austria. The spirit of the French Revolution and Napoleon, with the one exception of nationalism, had hardly touched the Hapsburg state and its feudal society. In addition to the natural conservatism of the Hapsburgs and their chief minister, Austria had a language problem that caused her rulers to fear liberalism and its companion nationalism like the plague. Austria proper is German-speaking, but during the sixteenth, seventeenth, and eighteenth centuries the Hapsburgs had annexed territories inhabited by Hungarian (Magyar), Czech, Slovak, Ruthenian, Polish, Rumanian, Serb, Croat, and Slovene language groups. In 1815 two Italian-speaking provinces were added. Before 1789 these various language groups remained quiet under their feudal lords, the Hapsburg dynasty, and the Roman Catholic Church. However, with the mass nationalism, based largely on language, that followed in the wake of the French Revolution, they began to stir with national consciousness.

Metternich saw clearly that if this new force was not suppressed, the Hapsburg state would fall apart. Furthermore, nationalism unchecked would cause Austria to lose her dominance over Germany and Italy. The various German and Italian states would be drawn together into powerful national states from which Austria would be excluded, for most of the people in the Hapsburg state were neither German- nor Italian-speaking. When these facts are considered, it is not surprising that Austria in 1815 was the most reactionary state in Europe save Russia. In the Hapsburg provinces Metternich's police and spies were everywhere. Permission to enter or to leave the country was made very difficult, lest dangerous ideas be brought in from the West. Classrooms, libraries, bookstores, and organizations of all kinds were supervised with suspicion. Censorship covered even music (in the country of Mozart and Beethoven) for fear that musical notes would be used as a cryptic code for conveying revolutionary ideas. On the surface, these policies appeared for some time to succeed. Nevertheless, Metternich was aware that the Hapsburg state stood on shaky ground.

5. RESTORATION AND REPRESSION IN ITALY

Austria's domination over Italy was even more complete than over Germany. Lombardy and Venetia were annexed outright. Modena, Parma, and Tuscany were ruled by Austrian princes. The Papal States and Naples were under Austria's protection and guidance in both domestic and foreign affairs. In all these states the deposed aristocracy and clericals trooped back, full of hatred for French institutions and for the Italian liberals who had cooperated with Napoleon. Nearly all the Italian intelligentsia were soon in prison or in exile. In the Papal States the Inquisition and the Index were restored, and such Napoleonic innovations as street lighting were done away with. Of all the Italian states, only Piedmont in the extreme northwest was free of direct Austrian control, but even here the restored heads of the house of Savoy were so reactionary as to cause Metternich only pleasure.

In considering Italy to be "safe," however, Metternich failed to reckon with the influence of history. Italy had had a glorious past. As the seat of the Roman Empire, it had ruled the Western world for many centuries. During the Middle Ages all roads still led to Rome, which was then the head of Western Christendom. In the fourteenth and fifteenth centuries Italy held the economic and cultural leadership of the West. Venice was queen of the seas and Florence was the center of the banking world. Both were fabulously rich in money and in culture.

The extraordinary brilliance of Venice, Florence, Milan, Rome, Pisa, Siena, Ravenna, and many other Italian city-states in the Renaissance period tended to develop a local rather than a national pride. This local patriotism was in large measure responsible for Italy's division and weakness in early modern times. However, the French Revolution and Napoleon brought to Italy a new kind of nationalism and reawakened memories of past exploits. Very soon after 1815 Italian liberals began to form secret societies, called *Carbonari* (charcoal burners), which met at night around charcoal fires to plot freedom from Austrian and local tyranny and to plan for national unification. In the early thirties a romantic young intellectual, Giuseppe Mazzini, organized the Young Italy society, which was dedicated to the task of achieving a free, united, and liberal Italian nation. Although the first uprisings inspired by the Carbonari and Young Italy were crushed by Austrian arms, the Italian national movement once aroused could not so easily be suppressed.

6. REACTION AND REPRESSION IN RUSSIA

Even primitive, autocratic, semi-Asiatic Russia had not escaped the influence of the French Revolution and Napoleon. She had joined in the second, third, fourth, and fifth coalitions against France, had been invaded and ravaged as far as Moscow in 1812, and had played a major role in the wars of liberation against Napoleon in 1813–1814. Meanwhile, her young tsar, Alexander I, and many of his aristocratic young army officers had picked up romantic and liberal ideas from the West. But Russia was not yet ripe for Western liberalism. She was a vast agricultural nation with a feudal social structure and a very small urban bourgeoisie that could serve as a liberal base. The Orthodox Christian Church, dominated by an upper clergy drawn from the aristocracy, was a handy governmental agency for controlling the masses. The unstable Alexander I soon fell under the influence of Metternich and of his own reactionary boyar magnates, and repented of his liberalism. He sought atonement for his sins by volunteering to stamp out liberal movements in Naples, Spain, and Latin America. He did, however, remain a romantic idealist as long as he lived.

There was no trace of romanticism whatever in Nicholas I, Alexander's younger brother, who succeeded him in 1825. Nicholas was a hand-

This illustration shows Italians being shot for reading Mazzini's writings; it epitomizes the spirit of reaction and repression that characterized the years after the defeat of Napoleon, when the great powers of Europe tried to restore the old order and stifle the new currents of liberalism and nationalism. *Photo: Historical Pictures Service, Chicago*

some, austere autocrat whose military career wedded him to the concepts of discipline and authority. A quixotic revolt by a group of young liberal officers on the occasion of his ascension to the throne and a full-scale revolt against Russian tyranny by his Polish subjects in 1831 further embittered him against liberalism in any form. Both revolts were crushed with an iron hand. For thirty years (1825–1855) Nicholas I was to stand as the perfect symbol of absolute reaction and the armed guardian of the Metternich system. Russia, of all the great powers of Europe, was the least affected by the spirit of the French Revolution. When at the end of the nineteenth century she did begin to yield to liberal and revolutionary forces, it was with disorder and violence.

But in Western and Central Europe it was obvious by 1830 that the liberal and national forces created or released by the Intellectual and the French revolutions and spread by Napoleon were not dead, but only temporarily repressed. Greece, Belgium, and most of Spain's New World colonies had gained their freedom. The restored French Bourbons had been overthrown. In Great Britain the Reform Bill of 1832 opened a new liberal era (see pp. 502–503). The fifteen years of restoration, reaction, and repression that followed the overthrow of Napoleon proved, therefore, to be only a brief interlude. By 1830 the revolutionary forces of liberalism and nationalism were once more on the march.

Suggested Reading

General
*F. Artz, *Reaction and Revolution, 1814–1832* (Torch). Scholarly volume in Rise of Modern Europe series.
*A. J. May, *The Age of Metternich, 1814–1848* (Berkshire). Good brief survey.

The Congress of Vienna
*H. Nicolson, *The Congress of Vienna: A Study in Allied Unity 1812–22* (Compass). Best single volume on subject. Attractively written.
*C. Brinton, *The Lives of Talleyrand* (Norton). Lively and sympathetic biography of one of the leading participants.

The Concert of Europe
*D. Perkins, *Hands Off! A History of the Monroe Doctrine* (Little, Brown). Popularly written account by foremost authority on the subject.

Bourbon Restoration in France
F. Artz, *France Under the Bourbon Restoration, 1814–1830* (1931). Scholarly and detailed.

Reaction in Central and Eastern Europe
K. C. Pinson, *Modern Germany: Its History and Civilization* (1954). A sound survey with good but brief coverage of the period 1815–1830.
J. C. Legge, ed., *Rhyme and Revolution in Germany: A Study in German History, Life, Literature, and Character, 1813–1850* (1918). Scholarly and entertaining.
*A. J. P. Taylor, *The Hapsburg Monarchy, 1809–1918* (Torch). Lively and scholarly.
*R. Albrecht-Carrié, *Italy from Napoleon to Mussolini* (Collier). Excellent brief survey.
*A. G. Mazour, *The First Russian Revolution, 1825* (Stanford). By a leading authority.

Retrospect

The era of the French Revolution was a period of one of the greatest — some historians think *the* greatest — political and social upheavals in history. It was a time of high expectation and excitement. In a matter of weeks, and sometimes days, the kind of fundamental changes that usually require centuries took place. Time-honored institutions, privileges, and customs toppled. Wealth, power, and rights were redistributed. Specifically, the story begins with Copernicus and ends with Metternich.

The French and American revolutions were preceded and in part, at least, induced by an intellectual revolution — the triumph of the philosophy of the Enlightenment. The Enlightenment, in turn, was based upon the concepts of modern natural science. When, therefore, Copernicus in the sixteenth century attacked the long-accepted beliefs concerning the structure of the solar system, he set off a chain reaction. The Christian churchmen who had allowed their theology to become enmeshed in ancient theories of astronomy and physics, which were now questioned, tried to silence Copernicus and his disciples. But they could not. During the course of the seventeenth and eighteenth centuries, the new science prevailed. Indeed, the intellectual world of the West became fascinated with the scientific attitude.

Thinkers like Descartes, Locke, and Voltaire, armed with the new discoveries of science, developed and popularized the philosophy of the Enlightenment. The materialistic, rationalistic, humanistic, deistic concepts of the Enlightenment clashed with the theology of the Christian theologians of the eighteenth century, who were no match for their adversaries. The philosophy of the Enlightenment also advocated limited constitutional government and laissez-faire economics. The widespread acceptance of these ideas played a major role in bringing about the American and the French revolutions.

The American Revolution was primarily a matter of the thirteen English colonies winning their independence from the mother country. A great deal of political and social equality already existed in the colonies—probably more than anywhere else in the world. Nevertheless, there were some further political and social changes. The revolutionary leaders like Franklin, Jefferson, and John Adams were ardent disciples of the Enlightenment. As a result of the revolution, loyalist lands were redistributed, and the royal governors and their aristocratic councils gave way to the more democratic legislatures. The new constitution was filled with the ideas and phrases of Locke, Montesquieu, and Rousseau.

The influence of the Enlightenment on the French Revolution is even more obvious. French society on the eve of the revolution was still essentially feudal, with its privileged clergy and nobility. Government was arbitrary. The Church was intolerant and oppressive. The crisis of the old regime in France, however, occurred in the field of finance. Because the two privileged estates refused to surrender any of their exemptions from direct taxation, the government was forced to declare bankruptcy. And it was the calling of the Estates General for the first time in one hundred and seventy-five years in an attempt to solve the financial problem that triggered the French Revolution.

The French Revolution began modestly enough, but when the two privileged estates refused the demands of the bourgeois-dominated Third Estate for equal representation, the king sided with them and threatened to use force. At this juncture the lower classes rose up with a display of violence of their own and stayed the king's hand. The result was a victory for the Third Estate. A series of sweeping reforms ensued—the end of feudalism, the Declaration of the Rights of Man, and the drawing up of a liberal but moderate constitution.

But the nobility and the clergy were not willing to see their privileges so easily lost. Nor were the radical disciples of Rousseau convinced that the revolution had gone far enough. They wished to see the principles of Liberty, Equality, Fraternity extended not only throughout France, but throughout the world. When Austria and Prussia intervened in behalf of the French royalty and nobility, the radicals deposed and beheaded Louis XVI. All the great powers of Europe except Russia formed a coalition for the purpose of ending this threat to the established order. The revolutionary radicals, now in control, inaugurated a Reign of Terror for the purpose of uniting and mobilizing the nation. It was remarkably successful; the internal enemies of the revolution were terrorized into silence or support, and the foreign enemies were defeated and driven back beyond the frontiers. The radicals, led by Robespierre, were now able to make France over into what they believed was the image of Rousseau.

But no one seemed able to consummate the revolution and restore tranquillity. Robespierre and his faction were overthrown by the bourgeois moderates, and the terror ended, but the moderates, too, proved unable to bring peace at home and abroad. That task remained for Napoleon Bonaparte, one of the greatest political geniuses of all time. His mission was to build practical institutions based upon the ideas of the Enlightenment and the reforms of the revolution and to spread those ideas and institutions abroad. After achieving these goals in large measure during his spectacular fifteen-year dictatorship, he was finally defeated and overthrown by a combination of all the great powers of Europe. These powers, under the leadership of Metternich, undertook to push the historical clock as far back as they could, but their efforts met with only partial and temporary success. The ideas of the Enlightenment and the French Revolution were resurgent within a very few years and have remained powerful forces in the world ever since.

X

The Industrial Revolution First Phase: The Dominance of the Middle Class 1830-1871

While the French Revolution was releasing upon the world the explosive forces of liberalism and nationalism, the Industrial Revolution was introducing to the Western world new techniques of working and living. Indeed, most of the world history in the nineteenth and twentieth centuries has centered around these three forces—liberalism of various hues, nationalism first moderate and then aggressive, and industrialism with its manifold facets and problems. And if we broaden our concept of the Industrial Revolution to include the onrush of science, with which it was closely associated, we may venture to give it first place among all the forces that have influenced Western civilization since the era of the French Revolution. Beginning in Great Britain near the end of the eighteenth century, the Industrial Revolution spread first to Belgium and France, then to the United States, and eventually to most of the rest of the world. Everywhere it drastically changed the pattern of life.

The industrial bourgeoisie, who owned and benefited from the new power machines, rose to a position of great wealth and power, justifying their good fortune with theories of laissez-faire economics. The proletariat, on the other hand, unable to compete with the machines, found themselves insecure and perplexed. Their distress eventually led the masses to organize, take up new theories of economics, and demand and get an increased share in government and in society. From approximately 1830 to 1871, the bourgeoisie were generally in control in the industrialized countries. From 1871 to 1914, the masses were moving toward the top. Meanwhile, science and technology were reshaping life and thought.

Without, therefore, minimizing such dynamic forces as liberalism and nationalism, what better title can be given the history of the nineteenth century than "The Industrial Revolution—First Phase: The Dominance of the Middle Class, 1830–1871; Second Phase: The Emergence of the Masses, 1871–1914"? In this part we shall examine the bourgeois-dominated first phase of the Industrial Revolution. Our examination, of course, will not be limited to matters of technology and economics. It will include the development of those two great forces unleashed by the French Revolution—liberalism and nationalism—together with a look at the prevailing trends in the arts and letters during the period 1830–1871.

The term "Industrial Revolution" has come into general use to indicate the shifting of production from hand tools powered by muscles, wind, and water to machinery powered by steam, combustion, electricity, and atomic fission. This, of course, was not an abrupt change. An increase in the tempo of technological development can be observed in Western Europe as early as the seventeenth century. The tempo is still accelerating, and the technology is still spreading to the rest of the world. This shift in the means of production first occurred in significant measure in Great Britain during the last few decades of the eighteenth century and the first few of the nineteenth. Great Britain possessed an abundance of coal and iron and of liquid capital which her merchants and wool growers had amassed from her lucrative commerce. She also possessed the world's greatest merchant marine and the navy to protect it. During the course of the eighteenth century and the era of the French Revolution, Britain's colonial empire had become the world's largest, supplying the mother country with abundant markets and sources for raw materials. Also during the course of the eighteenth century, an agricultural revolution in Britain (described later in this chapter) drove thousands of small farmers from the land to the cities where they provided the industrial entrepreneurs with a cheap supply of labor. Furthermore, since 1688, Great Britain had enjoyed a stable government

43

THE INDUSTRIAL REVOLUTION

dominated by the capitalistic classes—landowners, merchants, bankers. Finally, the demand for more manufactured goods was strong. For reasons not clear, the population in Europe and Asia began to increase markedly about the middle of the seventeenth century. Thus, by the middle of the eighteenth century, there were new millions of people to be fed, clothed, and housed.

1. THE COMING OF THE MACHINE

The textile industry was the first to become mechanized. In 1733 John Kay invented the flying shuttle, which doubled the speed of weaving cloth. In 1764 James Hargreaves, a humble English carpenter, hit upon the idea of hitching eight spindles to his wife's spinning wheel, instead of one. The result was the spinning jenny (named after his daughter Jenny). The number of spindles was soon multiplied. Five years later Richard Arkwright, a barber, patented the water frame, a system of rollers driven by water power which spun a much finer and firmer thread than the jenny. In 1779 Samuel Crompton, combining the principles of the spinning jenny and the water frame, produced the hybrid spinning mule—a great improvement over both. In 1785 an Anglican clergyman, Edmund Cartwright, invented the power loom.

The mechanization of both spinning and weaving greatly increased the demand for cotton. The meeting of this demand was made possible by a young American, Eli Whitney, who in 1793 invented the cotton gin. Removing the lint from the seeds by hand was a tedious process; one man could separate only five or six pounds a day. Cotton was therefore grown only in small patches. Whitney's gin not only made possible an adequate supply of cotton for Britain's mills, but also brought into existence the huge cotton plantations, worked by Negro slaves, in the American South.

Meanwhile, a new source of power was found to help water drive the new machines. In 1769 James Watt, a University of Glasgow repairman-mechanic, invented the first steam engine that could be used to drive machinery. The power that could be generated by the steam engine was almost unlimited. Constant improvements in the making of iron and the mining of coal led to the production of still better machines and guaranteed a sufficient supply of fuel to drive them.

Man now had the capacity to produce a practically boundless supply of goods. The enormous significance of these and other inventions for the future could not, of course, be seen at the time they were made. And today we have become so accustomed to them it is easy to forget their importance. However, the fact is that the inventors of these basic machines and processes were responsible for the coming of a new era. It is true that most of the principles and some of the processes were known in ancient and medieval times, but it was men like Hargreaves and Watt, aided by the favorable political and social setting (and by earlier experimenters), who developed the practical working machines. Most of these inventors were humble amateurs who endured discouragement, scorn, and sometimes bankruptcy and persecution. One of the few exceptions was Richard Arkwright, who rose from barbering to wealth and knighthood.

2. THE REVOLUTION IN TRANSPORTATION AND COMMUNICATIONS

An integral and necessary part of the Industrial Revolution was the improvement of transportation and communications. Otherwise, sufficient quantities of raw materials to feed the hungry machines and adequate markets to absorb the finished products would not have been available. The last decades of the eighteenth century and the first decades of the nineteenth were a time of road and canal building in Great Britain, France, and the United States. Roads had long been good in France, but in Great Britain and of course in the sprawling, young United States they were notoriously poor. Around the turn of the century Thomas Telford and John McAdam in Great Britain pioneered in the construction of well-drained and surfaced roads. In America Albert Gallatin inspired the construction of the Cumberland Road, or Old National Pike, which, begun in 1811, reached from Maryland to Illinois by 1852. In Great Britain canals were particularly useful in transportation of coal. However, the most important canal constructed in this period was the Erie, completed in 1825. The Erie Canal opened up the Great Lakes region to lucrative world communications and assured the primacy of New York City as America's chief port and metropolis.

Nevertheless, the real revolution in transportation came with the application of Watt's steam engine to locomotion. In 1807 Robert Fulton, capitalizing on the failures and partial successes of others, steamed his *Clermont* the 150 miles up the Hudson from New York to Albany in thirty-two hours. Twelve years later the *Savannah* crossed the Atlantic in twenty-nine days, using part steam and part sail. This was by no means record time, but in 1838, when the *Great Western* crossed the Atlantic in fifteen days entirely by steam, the last doubts as to the practicability of the steamship were dispelled.

Meanwhile, George Stephenson in Great Britain was developing the first successful locomotive. In 1825 he made his first convincing demonstration by hauling a train of thirty-four cars 25 miles at 12 miles an hour. Five years later his *Rocket* was pulling cars at the rate of 29 miles an hour. The horse was on the way out as a carrier.

The middle decades of the nineteenth century were a period of great railroad building in Northwestern Europe and the United States. Construction of the Baltimore and Ohio was begun in 1828, and two years later a few miles were opened for traffic. In 1855 Chicago, soon to become the world's leading railroad center, was reached by the New York Central system. By 1869 the Union Pacific had connected the Atlantic with the Pacific. All the while speed and efficiency were rapidly increasing.

Communications were developing faster yet. Until 1844 communications were no speedier than transportation except for a special courier service by horse or a crude system of signaling by semaphore. In that year, however, Samuel F. B. Morse sent a message by wire forty miles from Baltimore to Washington. The telegraph, transmitting messages instantaneously from one end of any length of wire to the other, caught on rapidly. In 1866 a telegraph cable was laid across the Atlantic, enabling news to travel from New York to London as quickly as from New York to Brooklyn. Ten years later Alexander Graham Bell, an American born in Scotland, invented the telephone, and in 1895 Guglielmo Marconi, an Italian, sent the first message by wireless telegraphy.

It is difficult for us today to realize to what degree or how quickly these inventions in the field of transportation and communications shrank the world. Julius Caesar could move his armies as rapidly as George Washington or Napoleon (actually a little more rapidly, thanks to the Roman roads), and Plato could gather news as quickly as Jefferson. Now, in the nineteenth century, far-off places suddenly became near, and strange peoples remained strange only to the primitive, the dull, or the lazy. More and more people, first the rich and then the poor, began to travel and to move their domiciles. The first important effect of the revolution in transportation and communications was to accelerate the Industrial Revolution by greatly facilitating the large-scale mobilization of capital, raw materials, and markets.

3. THE FACTORY SYSTEM

Another basic aspect of the Industrial Revolution was the rise of the factory system. Before the coming of the power machines, goods were produced either by the noncapitalistic craft guilds or under the domestic, or "putting out," system. It is true that some factories, notably the woolen-manufacturing establishments in Florence, came into existence as early as the fourteenth century when commerce and capitalism were reviving, but they were few and small in comparison with those of the machine age. Under the domestic system entrepreneur capitalists would purchase the raw materials and distribute them to numerous craftsmen who would spin, weave, sew, cut, carve, or mold the products by hand in their own cottages. The entrepreneur would then collect the finished products, pay the craftsmen by the piece for their work, and market the wares. The workers under this system enjoyed the advantages of doing as much or as little work as they wished without supervision. They usually carried on farming operations in addition to their craftwork. On the other hand, since they were scattered throughout the countryside, they were unable to bring any group pressure to bear upon the employers or to achieve any uniformity of wage. The smarter and more aggressive entrepreneur could easily cheat them, and wages were very low. The capitalists, too, were limited by this system. The operations were necessarily on a small scale, much time was lost distributing the raw materials from cottage to cottage and collecting the finished products, and uniformity of quality was virtually impossible to attain.

The coming of the power machines made the domestic system of manufacturing not only anti-

quated, but practically impossible The hand-craftsmen discovered that it was hopeless to try to compete with the machines, and since they were unable to buy them, they had to go wherever the machines were located. Thus factories, housing both the machines and the workers, came into existence. Crowded around the factories soon appeared living quarters for the workers and their families, hastily and cheaply built. This was the origin of the modern mill town and industrial city. The rise of the factory system eventually completed the process, begun six or seven hundred years earlier with the revival of commerce, of changing civilization in the commercial and industrialized areas from rural to uban.

4. THE AGRICULTURAL REVOLUTION

During this same period agriculture also was undergoing revolutionary changes in Western Europe and northern America. In the early eighteenth century Charles (Turnip) Townshend, grandfather of the author of the Townshend Acts that had helped to precipitate the American Revolution, began mixing diplomacy and statecraft with agriculture. He demonstrated that increased yields could be obtained through crop rotation and the use of root crops like turnips and clover. His contemporary and compatriot Jethro Tull invented the seed drill, which made it possible to plant seed in rows and thereby ensure better fertilization and cultivation of the soil. Later in the eighteenth century another Englishman, Robert Bakewell, greatly improved the existing types of sheep and cattle by artificial breeding. These new methods were popularized in the late eighteenth century, largely through the efforts of Arthur Young in Britain and the French Physiocrats.

The mechanization of agriculture first began with the reaper, which the American inventor Cyrus McCormick patented in 1834. These improvements in agriculture accelerated the enclosure movement in Great Britain, which had been going on since the sixteenth century. The increased efficiency achieved by the application of the new methods and the consolidation and enclosure of scattered strips and farms meant that

An immigrant family makes cigars in their tenement apartment in New York. The whole family, including the children, worked long hours in austere conditions just to survive. *Photo: Jacob A. Riis, The Jacob A. Riis Collection, Museum of the City of New York*

larger harvests could now be produced by fewer laborers. The result in the most advanced of the industrialized countries was a surplus of farm laborers, who drifted off to the cities to seek jobs in the new factories. The industrial and the agricultural revolutions thus interacted upon each other while they produced an ever-increasing abundance of material goods.

5. THE TRIUMPH OF THE BOURGEOISIE AND THE DISTRESS OF THE PROLETARIAT

The first to profit from the mechanization of industry were the owners of the new machines, the industrial bourgeoisie. Ever since the revival of commerce and capitalism in the eleventh and twelfth centuries, the capitalistic middle class had been gaining ground at the expense of the landed aristocracy. It had been a long, slow process with occasional setbacks. In the fifteenth and sixteenth centuries the middle class had been used as allies by the national monarchs against the feudal lords. In the seventeenth and eighteenth centuries, first in England and then in America and France, the middle class had turned on the king and sharply curtailed his power.

Nonetheless, at the opening of the nineteenth century, the aristocracy in Great Britain and France were still powerful, and everywhere else, except in the United States and in the Netherlands, they were dominant. But the coming of the power machines gave the industrial middle class such a monopoly over the fabrication and transportation of goods in the industrialized countries that they were able to establish their supremacy over the upper *and* lower classes. Driving the handicraftsmen out of business and hiring them on their own terms, the industrial bourgeoisie eventually amassed fortunes vaster than those of the merchant princes before them. With such wealth at their command they gained control not only over their nations' economies, but over government and society as well.

The triumph of the industrial bourgeoisie did not, of course, occur overnight, nor did it occur simultaneously in all countries. It followed the course of the Industrial Revolution—coming first in Great Britain, next in Belgium and France, a little later in the United States, then in Germany, and near the end of the nineteenth century in Central and Eastern Europe, and Japan. By the middle of the twentieth century it was reaching most of the rest of the world. In Great Britain, Belgium, and France, the years approximately from 1830 to 1871 represent an era of industrial middle-class dominance. In the United States, where the growth of industry was a little slower, the industrial bourgeoisie did not gain control until the Civil War (1861–1865) and was not seriously challenged until the turn of the century.

By the same measure that the bourgeoisie gained in the first phase of the Industrial Revolution, the proletariat lost. Men have never been equal since the beginning of organized society. The strong, the clever, the aggressive, and the fortunate have always enjoyed an advantage over their weaker, meeker, or less fortunate fellow-men. Nevertheless, before the coming of the power machines, when workingmen lived by the strength of their muscles, there was a modicum of equality. One man's muscles are not too much stronger than another's. The willing work-

er, with reasonable luck, could hew out some kind of living in competition with his neighbors. No man, however, could compete with steam-driven machines that could do the work of hundreds of men.

The defeated craftsmen and the surplus agricultural workers had no recourse but to flock to the factories to seek employment tending the machines. The rapid increase in population, which had been going on since the middle of the seventeenth century, also swelled the ranks of the industrial proletariat. The owners, under these circumstances, were able to state their own terms. Wages were bid down to the barest subsistence level—sometimes the equivalent of 50 cents for a week of seven eighteen-hour days. Since women and children could tend many of the machines as efficiently as men and could be hired more cheaply, men were replaced by their wives and children. Contracts were made with orphanages for the employment of the children. Little tots too small to dress themselves were marched off before daybreak to work all day in the factories. If they fell behind the pace, they were beaten. Sometimes they were chained to their machines. Crying could be heard at all times in the factories, particularly toward the end of the day. The factories and mines were dark, dirty, and dangerous. The dwellings of the workers were likely to be hovels clustered around smoky, noisy mills or mine entrances. The workers were frequently compelled to spend the pittance they did receive at company stores, paying monopoly prices arbitrarily set by the owners.

Work lost its dignity. The dull, monotonous, robot-like repetition of a single operation on a machine brought the worker none of the satisfaction and pride of skilled craftsmanship. It is true that in the most highly mechanized industrial systems, there was still a considerable amount of skilled craftsmanship left, but even that became tainted with the connotation of the mill. This loss cannot be repaid with any amount of wage increases. Numerous investigations have shown that factory workers are more interested in personal and social dignity and recognition than in wages, hours, and working conditions. These sentiments, of course, were ex-

This woodcut by Gustave Dore portrays the squalor of a London slum in the early nineteenth century.
Photo: Prints Division, New York Public Library, Astor, Lenox, and Tilden Foundations

pressed in more recent years when wages and hours were less cruel.

During the first phase of the Industrial Revolution there was virtually no opportunity for the workers or their children to get an education. The picture of the mid-nineteenth-century industrial proletariat is one of the most dismal in recorded history. Western man, after struggling toward freedom against various forms of tyranny for some six thousand years, was now threatened with a new kind of slavery—slavery to the machine and the machine owner.

Some historians and social scientists maintain that this picture of the distress of the proletariat during the early days of the Industrial Revolution is false, or at least distorted. They undertake to prove by statistics that the early factory workers received higher real wages and enjoyed a better standard of living than they ever had as agricultural workers. There can be little doubt that numbers of workers did move upward in industry and improve their lives. Nor can it be denied that the conditions of work and life among the agricultural poor had always been hard. But statistics often fail when they try to measure human well-being and happiness. The insecurity, the frequent unemployment of the uprooted slum-dwelling factory worker of the early nineteenth century do not appear in statistics. Is a mill hand working seven fourteen-hour days for 50 cents better off than a man plowing, sowing, and reaping, or doing craft work in his own cottage the same number of hours for 25 cents? The question cannot be answered with certainty, but in history, which deals with human beings, statistics need to be supplemented by imagination.

One of the industrial proletarian's first reactions was violence. Throughout the winter of 1811–1812, when the pressure of the Napoleonic war and the blockade against British commerce was added to the maladjustments of the Industrial Revolution, a wave of personal violence and machine-smashing swept throughout Great

Britain (the Luddite riots). This type of reaction to the machine, of course, had no future. Parliament, composed entirely of members of the property-holding classes, quickly made industrial sabotage a capital offense and suppressed violence with a heavy hand. Several dozens of offenders were hanged. Sporadic outbreaks of violence, however, continued for several years. This story was repeated in other countries as the Industrial Revolution spread. In the United States in the middle decades of the nineteenth century, violence broke out among the Irish immigrants working in the anthracite coal mines of eastern Pennsylvania. The exploited miners formed secret terror societies called Molly Maguires. For a number of years they intimidated, even murdered, unpopular bosses and uncooperative nonmembers. They were eventually ferreted out by civil authorities and ruthlessly suppressed.

More peaceful efforts of the industrial proletariat to bring group pressure upon their employers by organizing unions also at first met with defeat. In 1799 and 1800 the British Parliament passed the Combination Acts, which outlawed all labor combinations organized for the purpose of securing better wages, hours, or working conditions. The French and Belgian governments did likewise. In the United States the owners themselves organized for the purpose of breaking up labor unions. Private detectives and police were set upon labor leaders, who were beaten, fired, and blacklisted. It was not until the latter part of the nineteenth century that labor unions were able to make any significant headway. Therefore, during the first phase of the Industrial Revolution, as power machines belched and crunched and ground out ever more and more goods for those able to buy them, and fortunes for their owners, they blighted the lives of tens of thousands of workers, robbing them of the dignity of their labor, and threatening them with a new kind of slavery.

6. NEW ECONOMIC THEORIES — CLASSICAL, LIBERAL, AND UTOPIAN

CLASSICAL THEORY

It was inevitable that the Industrial Revolution should intensify Western man's thinking about economics. Most of the industrial bourgeoisie of the early nineteenth century were self-made men of limited means who had worked hard and risked their possessions in order to succeed. They were likely to feel rather insecure and self-righteous. Though probably not cruel or inhuman, they would have little sympathy with those who might upset their methods and perhaps lower their profits. Seeking intellectual support and justification for their good fortune, they found perfectly suitable the doctrine of laissez faire, which had been developed during the Enlightenment of the eighteenth century. This doctrine had been best stated by the Scottish philosopher Adam Smith in his classic *Wealth of Nations* (1776). The essence of Smith's theory is that economics, like the physical world, has its own natural laws. The most basic of the economic laws is that of supply and demand. When left to operate alone, these laws will keep the economy in balance and in the long run work to the benefit of all. If the sanctity of property and contracts is respected, competition and free enterprise will provide incentive and keep prices down. Government regulations and collective bargaining only impede the workings of the natural laws of economics and destroy incentive. Government therefore should limit its activities in the economic field to the enforcement of order and of contracts, public education and health, national defense, and in rare instances the encouragement of necessary industries that private enterprise does not find profitable. Here was a theory ready-made for the machine owners at a stage in the game when they held all the trump cards. Later, when competition became more severe and complex, the machine owners were to demand and receive a great deal of government protection. But in Great Britain in the early nineteenth century, all that the industrial bourgeoisie needed was an opportunity to exploit its advantage. Little wonder that the *Wealth of Nations* became its bible.

A strong boost was given to laissez-faire thinking by a young Anglican clergyman, Thomas Malthus, who in 1789 published his *Essay on Population*. Malthus argued that, since population increases by a geometric ratio whereas the food supply increases only by an arithmetic ratio, it is a basic natural law that population will outstrip the food supply. This alleged law has two important implications. One is that nothing can be done to improve the lot of the masses. If their condition is temporarily bettered, they will immediately produce children in such numbers that the food supply will be outstripped and starvation will threaten all. Only poverty and privation hold them in check. The second implication is that the rich are not to blame for the misery of the poor; the poor are themselves responsible because of their incontinence. These ideas were so soothing to so many of the book-buying upper classes that Malthus quickly attained fame and wealth.

David Ricardo supplied further ammunition for the free-enterprise economists. Having made a fortune in stock market speculation, Ricardo purchased a seat in Parliament and spent the rest of his life thinking and writing on economics. In *The Principles of Political Economy and Taxation* (1817), he propounded the law of rent and the iron law of wages. Rent is determined by the difference in productivity of land. Take off all restrictions and subsidies, and the poorest land goes out of cultivation, reducing the rent on the more productive lands proportionately. He argued for this idea so forcefully that it played an important part in the repeal of England's Corn Laws, which had maintained the price of grain at an artificially high level. More important in economic thinking was Ricardo's iron law of wages, according to which the natural wage is the subsistence level and the market wage tends to conform to it. Raise the market wage and the workers will multiply so rapidly that soon the law of supply and demand will bring the market wage down below the subsistence level. Then the workers will die off from malnutrition and disease and slow down their reproduction rate. Eventually they will become so scarce as to be able to bid the market wage up above the natural wage. Always, though, the pull is toward the subsistence level. This again was music in the ears of the industrial capitalists.

These thinkers came to be called the classical economists, since they were the first to grapple philosophically with the economic problems of the Industrial Revolution. Their general attitude and assumptions were well expressed by the British Utilitarian philosopher Jeremy Bentham as early as 1789, in his *Principles of Morals and Legislation*. Bentham was an eighteenth-century materialistic rationalist who lived on until 1832, bridging the eighteenth and nineteenth centuries with his life and thought. The Utilitarians believed that the useful is the good and that the chief purpose of government and society is to achieve "the greatest good to the greatest number." But since every individual is the best judge of his own best interests, the surest way to achieve general happiness is to allow each individual to follow his own enlightened self-interest. Individualism, then, is the best safeguard of the general welfare.

LIBERAL THEORY

The early nineteenth-century classical economists who advocated free enterprise and individualism called themselves liberals. However, a new type of liberal, more like the liberal of the twentieth century, soon appeared. The new type of economic liberal, while adhering to the sanctity of private property and to a large measure of individualism, believed that the Industrial Revolution had brought about the need for certain restrictions on both. In fact, Bentham himself came to see the necessity for the state to protect the common weal against overly aggressive individuals. One of the first of the new type of liberal economists was the Swiss historian and philosopher Simonde de Sismondi. In his *New Principles of Political Economy* (1819), Sismondi challenged Bentham's fundamental assumption that the self-interests of the individuals promote the best interests of the common weal. He believed that power machines were interfering with the operation of Adam Smith's laws by glutting certain markets, oppressing labor, and creating monopolies. The true wealth of a nation, Sismondi believed, lay in the equitable distribution of goods and benefits among its citizenry. Therefore, he favored laws that would restrict the amassing of monopolistic fortunes, and divide great estates. He also advocated practices such as profit sharing and long-term job contracts that would give protection and security to the workers.

Probably the most influential of all the new type of economic liberals was John Stuart Mill (1806–1873). Mill, a child prodigy, was brought up to be a good Benthamite. However, he was too sensitive and humanitarian to remain in the hard materialistic camp of the Utilitarians. Moreover, living a generation after Smith, Malthus, Ricardo, and Bentham, he was able to see some of the evil effects of the Industrial Revolution. Although Mill in no wise rejected private property, capitalism, and free enterprise, he believed that in the machine age, restrictions must be instituted by the state for the protection of the poor. Although production is bound by the iron laws of supply and demand, the distribution of goods is not. Public utilities such as railroads and gas and waterworks are natural monopolies and should be owned by the state. The state should provide free compulsory education for all and regulate child labor. He favored income and inheritance taxes as economic equalizers. Mill's chief work on economics, *Principles of Political Economy*, was published in 1848. In his later years he considered himself a socialist, but would hardly be so regarded today. His are the views of many twentieth-century liberals. Mill was also the first influential philosopher in modern times to advocate equal rights for women. His *Subjection of Women*, which appeared in 1869, came to be considered the classic statement on the subject of women's rights.

UTOPIAN SOCIALISM

During the first phase of the Industrial Revolution, the economies of the industrialized countries belonged to the bourgeoisie in thought as well as in deed. The theories of the classical economists enjoyed complete ascendancy. Even such an advanced liberal thinker as John Stuart Mill believed resolutely in private property and the capitalistic system. The hard-pressed proletariat, though increasingly disconcerted, was hardly capable of formulating new economic theories. However, as early as the opening of the nineteenth century, a number of intellectuals began to question the fundamentals of the existing system, such as private property and private enterprise for profit. Since the ideas of these intellectuals were only speculative dreams and offered no practical course of action for the immediate present, their advocates came to be called Utopian Socialists. One of the first Utopian Socialists was the French nobleman Henri de Saint-Simon (1760–1825). He and his followers believed that society should be reorganized on a "Christian" basis, that all should work, and that the inheritance of private property should be abolished. His ideal society would be run according to the formula "from each according to his capacity, to each according to his deserts." Saint-Simon would reward the superior artists, scientists, engineers, and businessmen according to their merits. But he laid down no plan of action for achieving his ideal society.

Charles Fourier (1772–1837), a Frenchman of middle-class origin, would do away with economic competition, the source of so much evil. Production, both agricultural and industrial, would be carried on by voluntary cooperatives whose members would pool their resources and live in communal apartment houses. Distribution of goods and profits would be based upon the formula: workers, five-twelfths; capitalists, four-twelfths; management, three-twelfths. Fourier's elaborate plans included many quixotic ideas and some others that have found their way into practice.

A step forward in socialistic thinking was taken by Louis Blanc (1811–1882), another middle-class Frenchman. Louis Blanc would abolish the evils of selfish competitive capitalism by setting up a system of social workshops. The government would lend money to voluntary workingmen's cooperatives, which would establish and run the workshops. Distribution of the proceeds would be according to the formula, "from each according to his ability, to each according to his need," the formula later adopted by Karl Marx.

A different kind of Utopian was Robert Owen (1771–1858). Born in Wales, Owen quickly made an industrial fortune in Manchester and bought large cotton mills in New Lanark, Scotland. In partnership with Jeremy Bentham, he set out early in the nineteenth century to make New

Lanark a model socialist utopia. Wages were raised, hours shortened, working conditions improved, child labor abolished, educational and recreational facilities provided, sickness and old-age insurance established. Owen spent the rest of his life and fortune drawing plans for and setting up model socialistic communities. Several were set up in America, notably New Harmony, Indiana. All failed; nor was Owen's benevolent example followed by other industrialists. Obviously, mankind, after thousands of years of competing for private gain, was not yet ready suddenly to start living and working for the common weal.

The Utopian Socialists were all strongly influenced by the materialistic rationalism of the eighteenth-century Enlightenment. All were vigorously opposed to existing organized religion, although Saint-Simon believed that his ideal society should be dominated by a new social Christianity—a brand of Christianity that had never yet been tried. None of the Utopian Socialists had any real influence on his own time. They did, however, start a trend of economic thought that was to become influential later.

It was not until the second phase of the Industrial Revolution (1871–1914), when the masses began to stir and to move, that a virile type of socialism would arise. This later socialism would be a state socialism for the most part and would bear the stamp of Karl Marx. Meanwhile, the industrial bourgeoisie established its control over the economy and the government in the industrialized countries—a control that until 1871 was not seriously challenged.

Suggested Reading

General

H. Heaton, *Economic History of Europe* (1948). Excellent chapters on Industrial Revolution.

*P. Deane, *The First Industrial Revolution* (Cambridge University). Brief up-to-date account.

The Coming of the Machine

*A. Usher, *A History of Mechanical Inventions* (Beacon). Best single volume on the subject. Well illustrated.

Social and Political Consequences

J. L. Hammond and B. Hammond, *The Bleak Age* (1947). Depicts the horrors of the industrial workers during the first phase of the Industrial Revolution.

*T. S. Ashton, *The Industrial Revolution: 1760–1830* (Galaxy). Repudiates the Hammonds. Plays down the hardships of the industrial workers as a result of the Industrial Revolution.

New Economic Theories

*L. Mumford, *The Story of the Utopias* (Compass). Popularly written history of socialistic thought during first phase of Industrial Revolution.

H. W. Laidler, *A History of Socialist Thought* (1927). Good chapters on the early socialists.

Sources

*A. Smith, *The Wealth of Nations* (Modern Library). The classical economists' bible.

*T. R. Malthus, *An Essay on the Principles of Population as It Affects the Improvement of Society*, 2 vols. (Everyman). A classic of great influence.

*J. S. Mill, *On Liberty: Representative Government; Utilitarianism; Autobiography* (Liberal Arts). Basic writings of this influential liberal thinker of first phase of Industrial Revolution.

44

TRIUMPH OF BOURGEOIS LIBERALISM

Liberalism is a very difficult term to define. It is of various hues, and from time to time changes its complexion. In general, the term "liberalism" implies a belief in a wider distribution of this world's goods and privileges. During the first three quarters of the nineteenth century, liberalism was closely associated with the middle classes, particularly the industrial bourgeoisie. It was usually strong in those areas where the Industrial Revolution was advanced, and weak where the Industrial Revolution was retarded. In addition to the industrial and commercial bourgeoisie (both great and small), intellectuals and professional people were likely to be liberal. The voice of the industrial proletariat, which after 1871 would be demanding a more radical kind of liberalism, was as yet scarcely heard. The chief wellsprings of this early liberalism were the philosophy of the Enlightenment and the English, American, and French revolutions.

1. GENERAL NATURE OF NINETEENTH-CENTURY LIBERALISM

The middle-class liberals of the nineteenth century prior to 1871 believed in popular government limited by a restricted suffrage and by constitutional guarantees of the rights of the individual. The role of the government should be that of a passive policeman, enforcing laws and contracts. Government should interfere in economic life as little as possible, leaving that realm to private enterprise. The nineteenth-century liberals were also anticlerical; that is, they opposed the interference in government by organized religion. Sometimes, reflecting the influence of the Enlightenment, they were not only anticlerical, but antireligious. Until 1871 the liberals were usually nationalists, since nationalism at that time was primarily concerned with freeing peoples from alien rule and uniting them under one flag, or, where this had already been accomplished, defending the nation's interests. The chief opponents of the nineteenth-century liberals were the vested interests of an earlier day—the aristocracy, the clergy, the military—seeking to retain their favored positions. The peasantry (a term and status applicable in Europe but not in the United States) was still generally conservative, strongly influenced by the clergy and sometimes by the aristocracy, and not very active in politics. The French peasants, most of whom owned their own land, were extremely conservative.

After 1871 the nature of liberalism was to change. The industrial bourgeoisie, having acquired wealth and power, had by now become a vested interest itself and was hostile to further political and social changes. Its members joined, for the most part, the ranks of the conservatives. Their place in the liberal ranks was taken by the

The citizens of Naples joined most of the other states of Italy in rebellion and even sent troops to aid the northern areas — Venetia and Lombardy — in revolt against their Austrian overlords. This drawing showing a barricade on a Naples street in May 1848 just before an attack appeared that year in the Illustrated London News. *Photo: Historical Pictures Service, Chicago*

bulk of the industrial proletariat, which was at last becoming politically active. The new liberals (now chiefly the lower middle classes, the intelligentsia, and the proletariat) began to advocate a greatly increased amount of government interference in economic affairs in behalf of the masses. They also adopted a somewhat different attitude toward nationalism. After 1871 nationalism in the West, having in large measure attained its goals of achieving free and united national states, tended to become aggressive and militaristic. This type of nationalism posed a threat to liberal democracy. After 1871, therefore, liberalism tended to be internationalist, although in times of international crisis and war, nationalism continued to rally the loyalty of all classes.

The period from 1830 to 1871, then, was a time of triumph for bourgeois liberalism in Great Britain, the United States, and France, the first major countries to become industrialized. In Central Europe, where the Industrial Revolution was more retarded, this period marked middle-class liberalism's rise but not its triumph. In Eastern Europe the Industrial Revolution and bourgeois liberalism did not appear until after 1871.

2. POLITICAL AND SOCIAL REFORM IN GREAT BRITAIN, 1832–1867

In Great Britain, the cradle of the Industrial Revolution, the industrial bourgeoisie began to bid for power soon after the Napoleonic wars came to an end. Although Great Britain had been since the thirteenth century the home of the rule of law and of representative government, her government in 1815 was far from democratic. The suffrage was so severely restricted by property qualifications that only about 5 percent of the adult males could vote. Furthermore, the industrial cities of the north, which had grown

up since the last distribution of seats in Parliament, were not represented at all. Both houses of Parliament were therefore monopolized by the landed aristocracy. It must be remembered, however, that the cleavage between the middle class and the aristocracy was not so sharp in Great Britain as on the Continent. The law of primogeniture in Great Britain granted the eldest son the entire landed estate and permitted him alone to assume the title. The younger sons sought careers in the church, in the military, or in business. This brought about much intermingling between the upper and the middle classes. The long-sustained prosperity of British commerce had produced a merchant class wealthy enough to purchase respectability, lands, and sometimes titles. The aristocracy frequently invested in commercial enterprises and later in industry. Before 1830 the two great political parties, the Whigs and the Tories, were hardly more than two rival groups of noble families. These facts help to explain why the great political and social struggles in nineteenth-century Britain, though sometimes bitter, lacked the violence of those on the Continent.

A period of economic depression and unrest in Great Britain followed the ending of the Napoleonic wars in 1815. For twenty-two years, with only one brief interruption, Britain had been engaged in a desperate struggle with France, a struggle that was economic as well as military. Meanwhile, her industrial expansion had gone on apace. The war's end found British warehouses piled high with unsold goods. Thousands of returning veterans found no jobs. Strikes and riots, which had begun during Napoleon's blockade, increased. The conservative Tory party, which had seen the country through the war, was strongly entrenched in power. Both the Tories and the slightly more liberal Whigs were still badly frightened by the specter of French revolutionary Jacobinism. The government therefore took strong measures against the restless workers. The writs of habeas corpus were suspended. The climax came in 1819, when troops fired upon a proletarian throng that had assembled outside Manchester to listen to reform speeches. A number were killed and hundreds injured in this "Peterloo Massacre."

Within a few years, however, as the postwar crisis of depression and unrest eased, the Tory government yielded slightly to the pressure for reform. We have already seen how Foreign Secretary Canning by 1822 had deserted Metternich's reactionary concert of Europe and aided independence movements in Latin America and Greece. During the 1820s the navigation laws were somewhat relaxed and the tariff slightly lowered. The Combination Laws were partially repealed, permitting laborers to organize unions, though not to strike. The civil disabilities against nonconforming Protestants and Roman Catholics were removed, permitting them to participate in political life on an equal basis with Anglicans. These measures, however, welcome as they were, did not get at the fundamental issue: a broadening of popular participation in the government. The pressure for suffrage reform continued to mount, particularly from the industrial bourgeoisie, which was gaining rapidly in wealth. Finally in 1830 the Whigs, long out of power, made common cause with the bourgeois liberals and drove the Tory government from office.

The new prime minister, Earl Grey, immediately introduced and forced through Parliament the Reform Bill of 1832. This bill redistributed the seats in the House of Commons, taking away many from the "rotten boroughs" (once-important towns that had dwindled in population or even disappeared) and giving them to the industrial cities of the north. The suffrage was extended to all those who owned or rented property with an annual value of £10 ($50). It is estimated that the number of voters was thereby increased from approximately 450,000 to 800,000 out of a total population of some 16,500,000. The great majority of the newly enfranchised were members of the urban middle class. Although on the surface the Reform Bill of 1832 appears rather innocuous, it represents a great turning point in British history. The long era of dominance of landed aristocracy had ended and that of the industrial bourgeoisie had begun. The supremacy of the House of Commons over the House of Lords, which had opposed the Reform Bill, was established. A new period of political and social reform had opened.

Both political parties recognized the new era. The Whig party, dominated by the industrial bourgeoisie but containing a right wing of liberal aristocrats and a left wing of intellectual radicals, changed its name to the Liberal party—liberal of course in the pre-1871 sense. For the next half century the Liberals were dominant, under the leadership of such personalities as Lords Grey, Russell, and Palmerston, and eventually William E. Gladstone. The Tory party was still predominantly the party of the landed aristocracy, but it contained some bourgeois elements, and its more liberal wing, led first by Sir Robert Peel and later by Benjamin Disraeli, was now in the ascendancy. The somewhat discredited name "Tory" was changed to Conservative.

Both parties, conscious of the rising importance of public opinion, supported a series of reforms. In 1833 slavery was abolished in the British Empire with compensation for the owners. This achievement was made much easier by the fact that there were no slaves in Britain itself. The Municipal Corporations Act applied the principles of the Reform Bill of 1832 to local government. The barbarous penal code was reformed, reducing the number of capital offenses to three and generally softening the punishment of criminals. The penny post increased the circulation of mail and literature. Parliament granted small but gradually increasing subsidies to the schools, most of which were run by the Anglican Church. Between 1833 and 1847 Parliament passed a series of laws that prohibited the employment in textile mills of children under nine and limited the hours of older children and of women to ten hours a day. The employment of women and children in underground mines was prohibited. In 1846 the Corn Laws (the import tariff on grain) were repealed, greatly reducing the price of bread.

It must be remembered that these reforms were not the work of the masses but of the bourgeois liberals in conjunction with a liberal minority of the aristocracy and a few intellectual radicals. The only reform movement initiated by the proletariat in this period of bourgeois domination came to naught. This was the Chartist movement. The hard-pressed industrial proletariat, bitterly aware that it had been by-passed by the Reform Bill of 1832 and that it was not sharing in the unprecedented national prosperity, was dissatisfied with the reforms of the bourgeois liberals. In 1838 proletarian leaders drew up a People's Charter, which demanded (1) universal male suffrage, (2) the secret ballot, (3) removal of property qualifications for members of Parliament, (4) pay for members of Parliament, (5) annual elections, and (6) equal electoral districts. The charter was twice presented to Parliament and twice summarily rejected. In 1848, when much of the European continent was ablaze with revolution, the Chartists planned a monster petition and demonstration in London. The frightened government prepared to use force. However, only a few mild disorders followed the third rejection, and the movement came to an end. Nevertheless, the Chartist movement had its influence. Before many decades had passed, all the demands in the charter had been enacted into law except that for annual elections. The most immediate result was to make both political parties aware of the growing influence of the proletariat and of the advisability of winning its favor.

This awareness increased as the numbers and the restlessness of the proletariat increased. During the 1860s William E. Gladstone, a more advanced type of liberal, rose to the leadership of the Liberal party. In 1866 he introduced a reform bill that would have enfranchised large numbers of the proletariat. Although the bill was defeated and the Liberal ministry was forced to resign, the narrowness of the defeat plus the agitation of the workingmen, which now reached ominous proportions, convinced the rising young leader of the Conservatives, Benjamin Disraeli, that the reform was inevitable. The shrewd Disraeli decided to seize credit for the inevitable. The result was the Reform Bill of 1867, which, as amended by the Liberals, gave the franchise to the great majority of the urban proletariat. The Reform Bill of 1867, which doubled the electorate, marked the beginning of a new era in British history. Henceforth, the industrial bourgeoisie would have to share power with the industrial proletariat. Liberalism now took on a new and more radical meaning. It is a tribute to British moderation and to Britain's long tradition of the

rule of law that such a revolutionary change should have taken place with so little violence.

3. JEFFERSONIAN AND JACKSONIAN DEMOCRACY IN THE UNITED STATES

The march of liberal democracy in the United States did not follow the European pattern. In America there was never an entrenched aristocracy that had to be overcome as in Europe. The European immigrants who peopled the United States were almost entirely from the middle and especially the lower ranks of society, and they were determined to prevent the rise in America of a class system such as the one from which they had fled. The rough frontier situation in America aided them in their efforts. In the primitive American forests and prairies, blood and title counted for little; muscle and energy counted for much. These factors, in addition to the British heritage of the rule of law, which most of the early settlers brought with them, and the able leadership they developed within their own ranks, sent democracy in America racing on ahead of that in Europe. Nor was American democracy so closely associated with or dependent upon the Industrial Revolution as in Europe. Although the first factory was set up in America by Samuel Slater in Rhode Island, as early as 1791, the growth of machine industry was at first quite slow. Although the French and British blockades during the Napoleonic wars and the War of 1812 with Britain cut the United States off from British manufactures and caused much American commercial capital to be diverted to manufacturing, it was not until after the Civil War (1861–1865) that industrialism in the United States became so advanced that the industrial bourgeoisie was able to gain dominance in politics and society.

The advance of democracy in the young American republic received a great boost with the election of Thomas Jefferson as president in 1800. The coming to power of this democratic theorist—the author of the Declaration of Independence—ended an era of the ascendancy of the well-to-do under Presidents Washington and Adams. Although the rich and the well-born raised a cry of anguish at the triumph of Jeffer-

Andrew Jackson, frontier fighter and popular hero, on his way to Washington after his election to the presidency in 1828. This engraving was done by Howard Pyle for an issue of Harper's Weekly in 1881. *Photo: Library of Congress*

son, he was really a moderate man. It was not so much his radical acts as president as it was his democratic attitudes and principles that made his administration significant. The third president was a scholarly philosopher of liberty and democracy, not a rabble rouser. The toiling masses never felt comfortable around the elegant Virginian.

The first real man of the people to take the helm of the young republic was Andrew Jackson. A rawboned dueler, Indian fighter, and militia commander, Jackson rose from poverty to leadership on the Tennessee frontier. He emerged as the hero of the War of 1812. Without formal education, "Old Hickory" possessed qualities of leadership and a flair for vote getting. His election to the presidency in 1828 is often referred to as a revolution. However, the revolution of 1828,

like that of 1800, was not so much a matter of deeds as of attitudes and spirit. The people's champion did attack and destroy the greatest concentration of private capital in the country, the national bank. He also tackled and crushed such formidable political giants of a more conservative nature as John C. Calhoun and Henry Clay. But there were no radical measures.

In the Jacksonian era, democracy was advancing as new states without property qualifications for voting were rapidly being admitted to the Union and as the older states were eliminating property qualifications from their voting requirements. However, the property requirement had never been a serious limitation to democracy in America, since land was so plentiful and cheap that almost everybody was a property owner. The revolution of 1828 was a revolution only in the sense that for the first time a man came to the White House whom the common people could consider one of their own number. Henceforth, if undemocratic men or causes should triumph in the United States, it would not be because of the system, but because free men would fail to take the time and trouble to inform themselves of the issues and to go to the polls to vote.

Industrialization never constituted the threat to the laboring man in the United States that it did in Europe. Although one could find mill and mine conditions in America that rivaled those in Europe, there was too much free land in nineteenth-century America to permit the machine owners to exploit the workers too much for too long. It is not strange, therefore, that the United States was in advance of Europe in the women's rights movement. This movement, which began in the 1840s somewhat as an adjunct of the abolition crusade, found a dynamic leader in 1850—Susan B. Anthony. Her demands and actions, considered to be dangerously radical at the time, began to bear fruit before two decades had passed.

The chief blight on democracy in the United States was the existence of Negro slavery in the Southern states. This curse not only cast a shadow over the whole American scene, but threatened the life of the nation itself. But this story belongs to the next chapter.

4. THE BOURGEOIS MONARCHY AND THE REVOLUTION OF 1848 IN FRANCE

The rise of liberalism on the continent of Europe was much more turbulent than in Great Britain and the United States. Here industrialization occurred later than in Great Britain, and the forces of privilege and reaction were more strongly entrenched than in the United States.

The Industrial Revolution came to France during the reign of Louis Philippe (1830–1848). This member of the house of Orléans had been placed on the throne by the Parisian middle classes after the tyrannical Charles X, the last of the Bourbons, had been overthrown in the Revolution of 1830. Louis Philippe, recognizing that a new era of middle-class dominance had come to France, catered to this class. He assumed the role of the "Citizen King," casting aside the trappings of royalty and donning those of the Parisian bourgeoisie. His eighteen-year reign came to be called the bourgeois monarchy. His twofold policy, from which he never veered, was order and prosperity at home and peace abroad. One of his first acts was to lower the taxpaying requirements for voting from 300 francs ($60) to 200 francs ($40) per year. This raised the electorate from approximately 100,000 to 250,000 in a nation of some 32,000,000 people and placed political control firmly in the hands of the middle class. Louis Philippe's chief minister during the last eight years of his reign was François Guizot, one of the most eminent historians and teachers France has ever produced. Guizot's policies were identical with those of Louis Philippe. He was a thoroughgoing liberal of the pre-1871 bourgeois variety. He believed in government by the property-owning classes, particularly the bourgeoisie. He therefore opposed any further extension of the suffrage, even to members of the intelligentsia like himself. Meanwhile, France continued to prosper, as the government pursued its policy of order and peace and encouragement to growing industry.

But beneath the surface, things were not going so smoothly. The national prosperity was not shared by the industrial proletariat, who suffered the usual hardships, insecurity, and maladjustments that always accompanied the advent of industrialization. Slums mushroomed in Paris and the industrial cities of the northeast. The distressed proletariat clamored for the right to vote and the right to organize unions, but got neither. The growing discontent centered around the chief minister. Guizot, a Protestant, was busily establishing a system of secular education in a Roman Catholic country. Even the policy of peace was becoming tiresome to a people used to national glamour and heroics.

The mounting discontent came to a climax in February 1848, when the government prohibited the holding of a reform banquet. Street brawling broke out in Paris. Louis Philippe attempted to quiet the mob by dismissing the hated Guizot, but the appeasement failed. A shot fired during a brawl between a mob and the troops guarding the residence of Guizot unnerved the troops, who fired a murderous volley into the mob and set off a full-scale insurrection. Barricades flew up all over Paris, and when the disaffected national guardsmen began going over to the rebels, Louis Philippe followed Guizot into exile in England.

The Paris proletariat had triumphed, but only for a fleeting moment. A group of bourgeois liberals hastily set up a provisional government in which the only prominent radical member was the Socialist Louis Blanc. The provisional government immediately called for the election by universal male suffrage of an assembly to draw up a new constitution. Under the pressure of the Paris proletariat, the provisional government admitted the workingmen to the national guard, thereby arming them, and set up emergency-relief national workshops. The workshops, however, were a parody on those outlined by Louis Blanc, who cried that they were deliberately planned so as to ensure their failure. Workers of all kinds were paid the equivalent of 40 cents a day to work on hastily arranged projects, and when more workers enrolled than could be used, the surplus workers were paid 30 cents a day to remain idle. Loafers and unemployed of all kinds, of course, rushed in by tens of thousands to receive the 30 cents. The resulting demoralization of labor and the cost to the taxpayers thoroughly frightened all property owners, the peasants as well as the bourgeoisie.

The elections held in April 1848 resulted in an overwhelming victory for the conservative republicans and limited monarchists, thanks to the conservatism of the landowning peasants, who constituted the great majority of the French population. The Socialists were crushed. Even in Paris, their only real stronghold, they won a mere handful of seats.

One of the first acts of the newly elected constitutional assembly was to abolish the national workshops. The workers were told either to join the army or to go look for work in the provinces. The desperate Paris proletariat flew to arms and the barricades. "Better to die from bullets than from starvation!" For four days all-out war raged in the streets of Paris between the proletariat, armed with national guard rifles, and the regular army of the conservative constitutional assembly, using artillery in addition to small arms. When the last barricade had been destroyed, some fifteen hundred, mostly workingmen, had been killed. Several hundred were sent overseas to French colonial prisons. Louis Blanc fled to Great Britain. The bloody "June Days" widened the cleavage between radical urban Paris and conservative rural France — a cleavage that has long complicated France's public life.

The inexperienced constitutional assembly hurriedly drew up a constitution establishing the Second French Republic. (The First French Republic had been declared by the revolutionists in 1792 and had been overthrown by Napoleon in 1804.) Legislative power was given to a single-chamber legislature elected by universal male suffrage. All executive and administrative powers were placed in the hands of a president, also elected by universal male suffrage. The April elections had shown that in nineteenth-century France, with her millions of conservative landowning peasants, private property need not fear universal suffrage. No system of checks and balances between the two branches of government was provided. The first presidential election, in December 1848, resulted in a sweeping victory for Louis Napoleon Bonaparte, nephew of Napoleon Bonaparte, as president. It took this ambitious and clever politician only three years to destroy the weak constitution and to establish himself as dictator — a dictator conscious that he had been brought to power by the property-owning bourgeoisie and peasantry.

The Revolution of 1848 in France was the first violent reaction of the industrial proletariat against bourgeois liberalism. The proletariat was too small as yet to make any headway outside Paris. The revolution shattered against the solid mass of landowning peasantry allied with the propertied bourgeoisie. Its bloody suppression left a heritage of proletarian bitterness that would cloud the future of France.

5. THE REVOLUTION OF 1848 IN CENTRAL EUROPE

The February explosion in Paris set Central Europe aflame with revolt. However, the Revolution of 1848 in Central Europe was quite different from that in France. The Revolution of 1848 in France was a revolt of the Paris industrial proletariat led by intellectual radicals against the bourgeois liberalism that had been dominant since 1830. The Revolution of 1848 in Central Europe was a rising of the intelligentsia and the middle classes with a little support from the proletariat against the aristocracy and royalty. In 1848 the Industrial Revolution was just coming to Central Europe; the industrial bourgeoisie and proletariat were both few and weak. Their role in the liberal movement was secondary to that of the intelligentsia — chiefly university professors, students, and journalists. Furthermore, in 1848 the cause of liberalism in Central Europe was mixed up with that of nationalism. The two forces frequently conflicted with each other, nationalism proving to be the more virile of the two. Both causes failed for the time being, and the story of their failure can be told here only in brief and general terms.

The most crucial center of revolution was Vienna. This beautiful metropolis was the seat of the Hapsburg government, which not only ruled over the various language groups of the Austrian Empire, but dominated both the German Confederation and Italy. When early in March 1848 news of the events in Paris arrived in Vienna, the long-repressed student liberals began rioting in the streets and clamoring for an

In Central Europe in 1848, liberal sentiment emerged in the form of public demonstrations by the intelligentsia—particularly the university students. Here in June of 1848 German students convene at Wartburg. *Photo: Copyright Staatsbibliothek, Berlin*

end to the Metternich system. As the uprising gained in momentum, Metternich was forced to flee for his life. The Hapsburg emperor, Ferdinand I, hastily abolished the repressive laws and promised constitutional representative government. However, he too was soon forced to flee his own capital. Meanwhile the Magyàrs in Hungary, under the leadership of the eloquent Louis Kossuth, set up a liberal autonomous Hungary. The Czechs did the same in Bohemia and called for a Pan-Slavic congress to meet at Prague. In Austria's Italian provinces of Lombardy and Venetia the rebellious populace drove the Austrian garrisons into defensive fortresses and declared their independence. Most of the other Italian states adopted liberal constitutions

and prepared to dispatch troops to the aid of Lombardy and Venetia. By June 1848, it appeared that the Hapsburg Empire would become liberalized, fall apart along national (language group) lines, or both.

In Berlin, the capital of Prussia, the news from Paris and Vienna set the liberals demonstrating in the streets. The well-meaning but vacillating Hohenzollern king, Frederick William IV, promised a liberal constitution and support for German national unity. As in Paris, an unauthorized volley into the mob set off bloody street fighting, which the king ended by making further concessions to the liberals. Hohenzollern Prussia, like Hapsburg Austria, appeared for the moment to be on the road to liberal popular government.

Meanwhile, in the rest of the German states, a group of self-appointed liberals called for a popularly elected assembly to meet at Frankfurt for the purpose of constructing a liberal German nation. This was a task so formidable that no one then or since has been able to accomplish it.[1] The drawing up of a code of individual rights and liberties for a people who had never known any was itself a time-consuming undertaking. The two questions confronting the Frankfurt Assembly were whether the German-speaking portions of the multilingual Hapsburg Empire should be included in the projected German nation, and who should head the new nation. Tied in with the Austrian question was that of religion. With Austria (and Bohemia, which was alleged to be predominantly German), the Roman Catholics would predominate, and without Austria and Bohemia, the Protestants. For eleven precious months these knotty problems were debated. Eventually Austria virtually excluded herself by refusing to consider coming into the new German nation without her non-German provinces. By a narrow margin it was decided to offer the emperorship to the king of Prussia. But now it was too late. The situation in Vienna and Berlin had drastically changed.

In Austria the inexperience and weakness of the liberals and the rivalries and conflicts among the various language groups played into the hands of the Hapsburgs. Skillfully playing off one language group against another, the Austrian rulers beat down the liberal and national revolts one after the other. In Hungary they had the help of the reactionary Nicholas I of Russia, whose army crushed the rebels. In Italy a united effort of the various states failed to materialize. Only the kingdom of Sardinia sent significant aid to Lombardy and Venetia. Austrian arms easily prevailed. Everywhere in Italy except in the kingdom of Sardinia, liberalism and nationalism were crushed.

In Prussia, too, the liberals were weak and inexperienced. The unstable Frederick William IV, after his first uncertainty, gradually fell under the influence of his militaristic and reactionary Junker advisers. Further stiffened by the news from Vienna that the Hapsburgs had re-gained their autocratic position, he spurned the German crown offered him by the Frankfurt Assembly, and replaced the constitution drawn up by Prussian liberals with one that was a travesty of liberalism.

The Hohenzollerns' rejection of the crown of a united liberal Germany blasted the hopes of the Frankfurt Assembly. When a few of the most determined attempted to continue their efforts, they were dispersed by Prussian troops. Many of the discouraged German liberals fled to America and became known as the Forty-eighters. Some of them, like Carl Schurz, played a distinguished role in liberal causes in America. The failure of the liberals to unite Germany in 1848 may be explained in large measure by the weakness of the industrial bourgeoisie and proletariat, who were as yet few in number. When the Industrial Revolution did make its influence seriously felt in Central Europe after midcentury, nationalism rather than liberalism would be its chief beneficiary.[2]

6. EMANCIPATION IN RUSSIA

Russia remained untouched by the Industrial Revolution and bourgeois liberalism in the period 1830–1871, when these two forces were triumphing in Western Europe and emerging in Central Europe. Her few liberal reforms at this time came at the hands of the benevolent tsar, Alexander II (1855–1881). Most noteworthy of his acts was the emancipation of the serfs, who constituted a majority of Russia's population. This was done in 1861—one year before President Lincoln issued his Emancipation Proclamation in the United States. The serfs did not get their lands free, however. The land was given over to collective groups called *mirs*, and the ex-serfs were compelled to pay the government redemption dues for a period of forty-nine years. Since they received only the poorest lands, their economic condition was really worse than before. Alexander decreed some legal and

---

[1]The Weimar Republic, 1919–1933, was liberal, but it was virtually forced upon Germany by the victorious World War I Allies, who refused to make peace with the Hohenzollern Empire, and it lasted little more than a decade. (See Chapters 54 and 56.)

---

[2]The rulers of the Netherlands, Belgium, Denmark (including Norway), and Switzerland granted new and more liberal constitutions in 1848–1849.

administrative reforms, but for the most part these became dead letters in the hands of hostile aristocratic administrators. In the absence of political and social liberalization such as that which could be seen in Western Europe, Russia's intelligentsia tended to become defeatist and violent. The resulting nihilism and terrorism were direct antecedents to Russia's twentieth-century upheavals.

The first phase of the Industrial Revolution, 1830–1871, then, was marked by the continued advance of democracy in the United States, the triumph of bourgeois liberalism in Great Britain and France, and the beginnings of moderate liberalism in Central Europe. Eastern Europe and the rest of the world were not yet directly affected by industrialization or the bourgeois liberalism that followed in its wake.

Suggested Reading

General
*W. L. Langer, *Political and Social Upheaval, 1832–1852* (Torch). Latest volume in the scholarly Rise of Modern Europe series.
*J. S. Schapiro, *Liberalism: Its Meaning and History* (Anvil). Good brief summary.

Reform in Great Britain
*G. M. Trevelyan, *British History in the Nineteenth Century and After, 1792–1919* (Torch). By an excellent historian and writer.
W. P. Hall, *Mr. Gladstone* (1931). Scholarly and well written.
*H. Pearson, *Disraeli: His Life and Personality* (Universal). Popularly written.

Jefferson and Jackson
*C. G. Bowers, *Jefferson and Hamilton, the Struggle for Democracy in America* (Sentry). Written in a popular style. Jefferson is the hero.
*A. M. Schlesinger, Jr., *The Age of Jackson* (Little, Brown). Scholarly and well written.

*A. de Tocqueville, *Democracy in America* (Vintage). Astute observations by a brilliant French visitor.

The Bourgeois Monarchy in France
*J. B. Wolf, *France, 1814–1919: The Rise of a Liberal Democratic Society* (Torch). Excellent survey.
A. Guérard, *French Civilization in the Nineteenth Century* (1914). Thoughtfully and gracefully written brief analysis.

The Revolution of 1848
*Priscilla Robertson, *The Revolutions of 1848: A Social History* (Torch). Scholarly and lucid.
*L. B. Namier, *1848: The Revolution of the Intellectuals* (Anchor). An eminent historian shows how nationalism wrecked the liberal movement.

Emancipation in Russia
*W. T. Mosse, *Alexander II and the Modernization of Russia* (Collier). Good brief account.

45

THE DEVELOPMENT OF NATIONALISM IN FRANCE AND THE UNITED STATES

One of the most dynamic forces in the world of the nineteenth and twentieth centuries is nationalism. The variety of nationalism that we have known in the past two centuries was born in the French Revolution and nurtured by the Industrial Revolution. Until around 1871, it was relatively moderate and usually associated with liberalism; since 1871, it has tended to become malignant and aggressive, ofttimes at war with liberalism. Before 1871 it was limited for the most part to Europe and America; since 1871 it has spread to Asia and Africa without losing its vigor in the West.

1. THE NATURE OF NATIONALISM

Nationalism may be defined as a feeling of loyalty to one's country. What are the essential factors that contribute to this feeling? What makes a German a German or a Pole a Pole even when there is no German or Polish national state?

By far the most important factor is language. Language is so basic to a people's culture that it is often mistaken for race. For instance, one sometimes hears of the various races of the Austrian Empire, and the language groups there themselves often considered themselves racial groups, although it is impossible to establish anything more than a cultural identity based largely on language. Language brings people together in understanding and separates them from those they cannot understand. Probably second in importance is a historical tradition of

unity. The Belgians with their two languages and the Swiss with their three languages and two religions illustrate the importance of this factor. Religion can be a powerful factor, too, though not so important as language. The German Empire with its common language came and held together in spite of a serious religious cleavage, and the Austrian Empire fell apart along language lines in spite of a common religion and a long tradition of unity under the Hapsburgs. (In the long run, of course, religion may prove to be a more enduring force in history than nationalism itself.) Territorial compactness and natural boundaries are frequently contributing factors in nationalism.

The first group loyalty was probably to family, tribe, and clan, and to the territory occupied by them; then to language dialect groups. Loyalty to one's own kin and close associates and to the scenes of one's childhood is a natural thing. Loyalty to a large group or area like France or the United States requires conscious education. In Europe in the thirteenth, fourteenth, and fifteenth centuries, the kings of France, England, Spain, and Portugal, aided by the rising middle class and by the ascendancy of one dialect over the others, created by conquest and consolidation the first four national states. Until the French Revolution, however, national loyalty was chiefly centered upon the ruling monarch or dynasty and was limited for the most part to the educated upper classes who participated in the government of the nation. The French Revolu-

From 1848 to 1870, Napoleaon III was the most influential man in the world. As he grew older and his health failed, he came more and more under the influence of his Spanish wife, the elegant Eugénie. *Photo: The Bettmann Archive*

tion gave birth to a new and more virile kind of nationalism. The establishment of equal rights and popular representative government, together with the abolition of old provincial boundary lines, brought the masses of people into direct partnership with the national government. Universal conscription into the revolutionary armies, which were raised first to save France from the invaders and later to spread abroad the blessings of the French Revolution, gave the people a sense of fraternity in a righteous cause—a crusade. Nationalism became a religion. Such mass dynamism made the revolutionary and Napoleonic armies irresistible. Nationalism soon spread to the other peoples of Europe. Since the French Revolution, nationalism has been an ever-expanding force, increasing in scope as more and more people become aware of and participate in national affairs, and increasing in power as science and technology provide the national patriots with the tools to achieve their nationalistic purposes.

2. THE SECOND EMPIRE OF NAPOLEON III: YEARS OF SUCCESS, 1852–1859

Nationalism was both used and advanced by Napoleon III of France, the most influential figure in world affairs from 1848 to 1870. Louis Napoleon Bonaparte was the nephew of Napoleon. His father was Louis Bonaparte, younger brother of Napoleon and king of Holland, his mother was Hortense, daughter of Napoleon's first wife, Josephine Beauharnais. After the overthrow of his father and his uncle, young Louis Napoleon lived in Switzerland, Germany, and Italy, a political exile from France. Very early he developed ideas of grandeur, particularly after the death of Napoleon's only son in 1832 left him the head of the Bonaparte dynasty. On two occasions, in 1836 and again in 1840, the ambitious young adventurer attempted revolutions against the government of Louis Philippe. Both attempts were ludicrous failures. After the second, he was placed in prison, where he spent

six years writing propaganda tracts. In 1846 he escaped to Britain. The Revolution of 1848 presented the tireless schemer with his great opportunity. Using his illustrious name with consummate skill and appealing to all classes of Frenchmen, he was overwhelmingly elected president of the Second French Republic. The first eleven of his twenty-two years of prominence were years of spectacular success. Everything "the man of destiny" touched seemed to turn to gold.

No sooner had Louis Napoleon taken the oath as president, swearing to uphold and defend the constitution of the republic, than he started working to destroy it and make himself emperor. A gifted politician, he managed to take credit for all popular measures and to push the blame

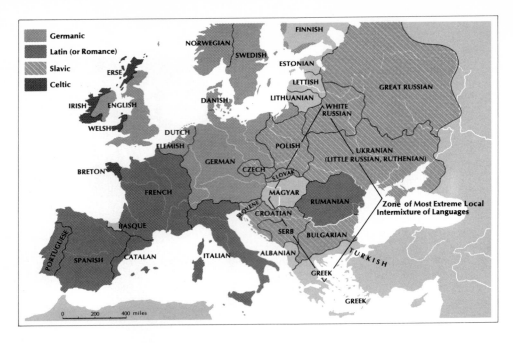

LANGUAGES OF EUROPE

for all unpopular acts of government onto the reactionary and leaderless legislative body. By judicious appointments and dismissals, he soon filled all key military and civilian administrative offices with his own supporters. A master showman, he posed as a friend of the urban and rural masses. The bourgeoisie liked his stand for law and order. He made a particularly firm alliance with the Roman Catholic Church by sending French troops to restore the pope to his throne, from which he had been driven by the Italian revolutionists of 1848, and by helping the Church regain control of French education. After three years of careful preparation, Louis Napoleon seized dictatorial powers for himself in an almost bloodless coup d'état on December 2, 1851. The few courageous liberals such as Adolphe Thiers and Victor Hugo, who attempted to save the republic, were quietly arrested and deported. Exactly one year later, the French president had himself crowned Emperor Napoleon III. (Napoleon Bonaparte's son, who died in 1832 without having ruled, was declared to be Napoleon II.) It would appear that a great majority of the French people approved the deed.

Napoleon III considered himself heir to the spirit of Napoleon Bonaparte, who, he claimed, was a true child of the French Revolution. The new Napoleon believed in government by a powerful tribune (himself) based upon the popular will. This tribune would rise above all parties and rally all factions in a vigorous and benevolent program. Napoleon III was a supreme nationalist, seeking at all times to enhance the prestige of the French nation at home and abroad. The government of the Second Empire was actually a veiled dictatorship. All power, civilian and military, judicial and legislative, as well as executive, resided in the emperor. The veil was a legislative body elected by universal male suffrage. By manipulating the electoral machinery, by official pressure, and by a system of official candidates, Napoleon III was able to control the elections. The legislative body had no control over the ministry. It could not even initiate legislation, this function being performed by the Council of State, appointed by the emperor. On occasion the emperor would seek the "advice" of the people by means of a plebiscite. In many ways, Napoleon III was the first dictator of the kind we have come to know in the twentieth century.

The second Napoleon was an economic liberal in the pre-1871 sense. He encouraged and dramatized the rapid expansion of the Industrial Revolution in France. Two giant investment banking corporations, the Crédit Mobilier and the Crédit Foncier, mobilized huge amounts of capital that were poured into industry, railroads, and real estate. The Bank of France was expanded until each of the country's eighty-six departments (three in Algeria) had at least one branch. The emperor's free-trade policies culminated in the Cobden Treaty with Great Britain, 1860, which lowered the tariff on British manufactures in return for lower British rates on French products, of which wine was the most important. This was the heyday of the French industrial and financial bourgeoisie, which amassed great fortunes, sometimes, as in other countries, by means that would not bear inspection.

The urban proletariat was not overlooked by the benevolent dictator. Hospitals, nurseries, and homes for the aged were built. Although prices were rising steadily with the general prosperity, the price of bread for the wage earners was kept low by government subsidies. A system of voluntary social insurance was instituted for workingmen. Cooperatives were encouraged, and labor unions with limited rights to strike were partially legalized for the first time. The peasants were aided by free trade, more and better roads, railroads, canals, the draining of swamps, and study and practice of scientific breeding. The landowning farmers liked the law and order and sacredness of private property.

All classes, except the liberal republicans, loved the return of court pageantry. Banquets, parades, balls, and spectacles kindled memories of a glorious Gallic past—of Louis XIV and the first Napoleon. Under the guidance of Baron Haussmann, Paris was rebuilt into the world's most beautiful city. In Napoleon III's reign its population increased from approximately 1 million to 2 million. At the center of the court of the Second Empire was the glamorous Empress Eugénie. When Louis Napoleon usurped the French throne, his prospects were held in such low esteem that no royal family in Europe would furnish him a wife. In 1853 he married the Spanish Eugénie de Montijo, of noble but not royal rank. Although she was never popular with the French people, the world of fashion and royalty

was soon deferring to her. Paris has remained the world leader of style and elegance ever since. In 1855 thousands of Europe's great, including Queen Victoria, attended Napoleon's Paris Exposition to view the marvels of the Second Empire.

The peak of France's revived national prestige was reached during the Crimean War, 1854–1856. Like his uncle, the second Napoleon was not satisfied with spectacular domestic achievements. He yearned for farther fields to conquer. His opportunity came when Tsar Nicholas I of Russia attempted to dismember the Ottoman Empire, "the sick man of Europe," and to achieve Russia's historic goal: Constantinople and access to the world through the Turkish Straits. France did not relish the prospect of an ambitious new rival in the Mediterranean. (Great Britain, with her vast holdings and interests in the Near and Far East, was even more sensitive to this threat than was France.) A second source of Franco-Russian conflict arose when the tsar, as the great champion of Orthodox Christianity, attempted to gain a protectorate over all Christians in the Ottoman Empire and over the Christian holy places in the Turkish province of Palestine. France had been since the Crusades the leading champion of Roman Catholic interests in the Near East, including the Christian shrines in the Holy Land. And Napoleon III's strongest ally in France was the Roman Church. The Crimean War is sometimes spoken of as a purely useless and trivial war. In a sense all wars are useless, but in Russia's quest for an outlet through Constantinople, the rivalry of the great powers for control of the strategic Middle East, and the conflict between Orthodox and Roman Catholic Christianity, we have three of the most enduring issues in history—issues that are still with us. A fourth issue was personal and national. Nicholas I alone of the European monarchs had refused to recognize the French usurper as an equal.

In 1853 the Russian army and navy suddenly attacked the Turks. Early the next year Great Britain and France sent their naval and military forces into the Black Sea and laid siege to Russia's naval base, Sebastopol, on the Crimean Peninsula. Sardinia came into the war to gain the friendship of France and Great Britain. Austria

At the height of its splendor and vitality in 1855 the Second Empire drew the major personages of Europe, including Queen Victoria, to the great Paris exhibition of French scientific and industrial progress held by Napoleon III. This engraving published in the Illustrated London News that year shows the interior of the industrial exposition building being prepared by workmen. *Photo: NYPL Picture Collection*

maintained a hostile, and Prussia a friendly, neutrality toward Russia. The war was fought with gross inefficiency on both sides. The only real hero was the British nurse Florence Nightingale, whose efforts helped to inspire the creation of the International Red Cross a few years later (1864). Nicholas I died in 1855, humiliated by the knowledge that his creaking military machine was going to fail. The Peace of Paris in 1856 prohibited Russia's naval forces on the Black Sea and maintained the integrity of the Ottoman Empire. The autonomy of Serbia and the Rumanian provinces of Moldavia and Wallachia under the suzerainty of Turkey was guaranteed by the great powers. The Roman Catholics were left in control of their shrines in the Holy Land. Great Britain at long last agreed to neutral rights on the high seas. The chief immediate beneficiary of the Crimean War was Napoleon III. His troops had fought better than the Russians or the British. He played host to the peace conference, which, of course, he made a colorful spectacle. French national patriotism was now at fever pitch and French prestige abroad at its highest point since the days of the Sun King, Louis XIV. Nationalism itself received a real boost as other peoples observed its success in France.

3. THE SECOND EMPIRE OF NAPOLEON III: YEARS OF FAILURE, 1859–1870

By 1859 the second Napoleon had obtained not only the loyalty of the great majority of his own people, but also a clear hegemony in the affairs of the European continent. France was prosperous and powerful. Then things began to go wrong. Suffering from a painful physical ailment (diagnosed as a stone in the bladder), he aged prematurely. The dynamic force of nationalism, which he understood and used so well in France, he greatly underestimated abroad. In his efforts to control the Italian and German national movements he failed dismally—in the latter case fatally.

The first serious blunder came in 1859, when he made war on Austria in behalf of Italian freedom. (The details of this war belong to the following chapter.) The defeat of Austria set off a frenzy of Italian nationalism that threatened to dispossess all the rulers of the local states of Italy, including the pope. This alarmed and angered the French Roman Catholics, who blamed Napoleon. But when the French emperor deserted the Italian nationalists in the midst of the campaign, with the agreed-upon job only half done, he further alienated the French liberals, who were already unsympathetic to him.

The booming prosperity subsided after 1860. The Cobden Treaty, signed in that year, flooded France with cheap British manufactured goods with which the less advanced French industries could not compete. The French textile industry also suffered heavily as a result of the American Civil War, which cut off its cotton supply. Both the industrial bourgeoisie and proletariat were hard hit. Overexpansion and speculation began to take their toll.

One of Napoleon's most grandiose projects, one that brought much woe to France then and later, was the restoration of an overseas empire. The French have been conspicuously inept at colonial imperialism. For one thing, the French people have always shown a marked disinclination to leave *la belle France* and make their homes elsewhere. The few who have gone to the French colonies have usually gone not as colonists, but as governors, adventurers, and exploiters. And more often than not they have been royally hated by the natives. During the Second Empire the conquest and annexation of Algeria, first begun by Charles X, was completed. French influence was extended in Syria, Senegal, and China. The seizure of Indochina was begun. Numerous islands in the Southwest Pacific were acquired. These aggrandizements, though adding to the national ego and prestige, brought France little immediate profit and much trouble.

By far the most ambitious of Napoleon's imperial schemes and the most momentous failure was the attempted conquest and annexation of Mexico. In 1855 the corrupt Mexican dictator, Santa Anna, backed by the military, the big landowners, and the Roman Catholic Church, was overthrown by the democratic liberals under the leadership of the gifted native Indian, Benito Juárez. The Juárez regime instituted sweeping reforms in behalf of individual civil liberties. It attacked all special privilege, particularly the privileges of the Roman Catholic Church, whose vast lands were confiscated. And as an emergency measure it suspended for two years the payment of interest on foreign debts.

The last act presented Napoleon III with his opportunity. Joining with the other two chief creditors, Great Britain and Spain, he seized several Mexican ports in 1862, ostensibly to collect the debts. As soon as the British and the Spaniards saw that Napoleon had more ambitious plans in mind, they withdrew. The French armies then marched on to Mexico City, drove the Juárez government into the hinterland, and set up a Hapsburg prince, Maximilian, as puppet emperor for France. The government of the United States protested vigorously in the name of the Monroe Doctrine, but, embroiled in its own Civil War, it could do no more. As soon as the Civil War ended early in 1865, the American government dispatched victorious Union troops to the Mexican border. Napoleon III, now hardpressed at home, agreed to withdraw his troops.

No sooner had the last French soldiers left Mexico City in 1867 than the Juárez forces captured and shot the well-meaning puppet, Emperor Maximilian. The Mexican fiasco greatly added to the growing unpopularity of Napoleon III with the French people.

More serious was the fact that the Mexican venture tied Napoleon's hands while events of grave consequence to France were occurring across the Rhine. The story of Bismarck's creation of the mighty German Empire will be told in the following chapter. Here it is necessary to relate only that Napoleon completely misjudged the situation, and was repeatedly outmaneuvered by Bismarck. When he attempted to retard the rapid growth of Prussia and to offset it by annexing Luxembourg, Belgium, and the left bank of the Rhine, he was helpless in the face of Prussian military power, since the best part of his own military force was in Mexico.

The distracted emperor attempted to allay the mounting discontent of the liberals. Beginning in 1859, he made one concession after another to liberal parliamentary government, until by 1870 the Second Empire was, on paper, at least, a limited constitutional monarchy similar to that of Great Britain. But 1870 was too late. The showdown with Bismarck's rapidly forming German nation was at hand. The sick and discouraged Napoleon III blundered into a war with Germany for which his armies were woefully unprepared (see pp. 527–529). He was defeated and captured, and his government was overthrown.

4. THE RAPID EXPANSION OF THE UNITED STATES

Between 1800 and 1870 the United States was the most rapidly growing nation in the world, both in area and in population. The purchase of the Louisiana Territory by Thomas Jefferson from Napoleon in 1803 for some $16 million doubled the original area of the United States. In 1819 Florida was purchased from Spain for $5 million (after two little chunks of west Florida had been seized in 1810 and 1813). Texas, which was even bigger then than now, was annexed in 1845. The next year the Oregon Country, including the present states of Oregon, Washington, and Idaho, was annexed after the settlement of a long-standing dispute with Great Britain. The annexation of Texas resulted in a war with Mexico, 1846–1848. After a quick and easy victory, the United States took a huge block of Mexican territory, comprising the present states of California, Arizona, New Mexico, Nevada, Utah, and parts of Colorado and Wyoming. This territory was enlarged to the south in 1853 by the Gadsden Purchase from Mexico ($10 million). These additions within a period of fifty years more than trebled the original territory of the young American nation.

Meanwhile, the growth in population was keeping pace with the increase in area. Between 1800 and 1870 the population of the United States increased from approximately 5 million to 40 million. Added to the high rate of natural increase was an ever-increasing tide of immigration from Europe. After 1840 the largest immigrant groups were the Irish, most of whom settled in the cities of the Northeast, and the Germans, most of whom pushed on to the fertile lands of the Middle West. The absorption and Americanization of these millions of people of varied background are one of the miracles of nineteenth-century nationalism.

The War of 1812 with Great Britain, sometimes called the Second War for Independence, resulted in an upsurge of American national spirit. A new crop of nationally minded statesmen arose, the ablest of whom were Henry Clay, John C. Calhoun, and Daniel Webster. Even more dramatic was Andrew Jackson, symbol of the rugged American frontier. The Western frontier itself was one of the greatest of the nationalizing influences. To it came people from all the seaboard states and from abroad who looked to the national government rather than to the states for protection, for roads and canals, and for land titles. Chief Justice John Marshall and Justice Joseph Story handed down from the Supreme Court bench opinion after opinion establishing the authority of the national government over the states.

It was in this period also that American culture began to free itself from strictly European influences. The American Indian began to be idealized by Henry Wadsworth Longfellow and James Fenimore Cooper. Washington Irving's pen made the legends of American colonial days enchanting. Gilbert Stuart and Charles Willson Peale made idealized portraits of American heroes. Probably the greatest nationalist influence of all was the little red schoolhouse, where rich and poor, German and Pole mingled and learned the American version of civilization and world affairs.

5. THE STRUGGLE OVER SLAVERY

Over the world's most democratic and rapidly growing nation, however, hung a dark cloud that grew more menacing until it produced a destructive and well-nigh fatal storm. This cloud was the growing national cleavage over the existence in the Southern states of Negro slavery. Slavery was totally incompatible with American ideals and traditions. By the beginning of the nineteenth century, it had been banished from European society, although serfdom remained in the Hapsburg territories until 1848 and in Russia until 1861.

The first boatload of Negroes was brought to Virginia in 1619, one year before the Pilgrims landed at Plymouth Rock. Because of the tremendous amount of labor required to clear the American wilderness, the African slave trade flourished throughout the colonial period. By the time of the American Revolution, Negro slaves constituted approximately one-fifth of the total population of the thirteen colonies. Slavery was recognized and protected by the national constitution. Because of the climate and the diversified economy, however, slavery was proving to be unprofitable in the Northern states, and between 1777 and 1804 all the states north of Maryland passed emancipation laws. South of the Mason and Dixon line (the boundary between Maryland and Pennsylvania), where agriculture reigned supreme, slavery continued to be profitable and prevalent. But by 1789 most Americans, in the South as well as in the North, detested the institution. After the Revolution scores of antislavery societies were founded, the great majority of them in the South. It appeared that slavery in America was on its way to an early and peaceful end.

Some unforeseen developments, however, changed the attitude of the South toward emancipation, and a sharp line was drawn between the North and the South over the slavery issue. The first of these developments was Whitney's invention of the cotton gin in 1793. This machine made the raising of cotton so profitable that soon large cotton plantations worked by Negro slaves grew up throughout the South. The American South became the chief supplier of Britain's textile mills. Whereas in 1793 cotton exports from the United States were a mere trickle, by 1800 they had risen to over 30,000 five-hundred-pound bales valued at some $5 million. By 1859 they had risen to some 4,500,000 bales valued at over $200 million—well over half the total value of American exports. At the same time the Negro population increased from some 700,000 in 1790 to nearly 4,000,000 in 1860, nearly all of it slave and all the slaves in the South. By the mid-nineteenth century, the Negro slaves outnumbered the whites in South Carolina and Mississippi, and in the rest of the deep South slaves were about equal in number to the whites. By 1830 the Southern economy had become so wedded to cotton and to Negro slavery that the Southern antislavery movement faltered, and the defense of slavery gained momentum. Even more important than economic considerations in the development of proslavery sentiment in the South was the social problem. The Southern whites did not believe that they could absorb into their society or even live alongside so many free Negroes. Opposition to emancipation was even stronger among the poor whites than among the slaveowners.

This serious North-South cleavage over slavery was greatly aggravated in 1831 by the appearance in the North of a violent abolition movement under the leadership of William Lloyd Garrison and by an alarming slave insurrection in Virginia under the leadership of a Negro preacher, Nat Turner. By coincidence, both events occurred in the same year. As Garrison's abolition movement gained momentum in the North—although not without widespread opposition—the South became increasingly frightened and angry. Every conceivable argument—from the Bible, history, Plato, Shakespeare, and the Constitution—was advanced to justify slavery. John C. Calhoun, the South's leading statesman and former extreme American nationalist, assumed the leadership of the Southern defense.

The critical issue was the extension of slavery to the Western territories. The population of the Northern states, with their growing industry, was rapidly outstripping that of the South. The immigrants pouring in from Europe avoided the slavery-ridden South almost to a man. The vast and fertile Northwest was filling up much more rapidly than the more limited Southwest; and whether the settlers in the Northwest came from north of the Mason-Dixon line or from Europe, they were determined to have none of slavery. As the Northwestern territories clamored for statehood, the Southerners took alarm. Already they were hopelessly outnumbered in the House of Representatives, whose membership is based upon population. Their only security in the national government lay in the Senate, where each state has two members. The Southerners did everything in their power to slow down the settlement of the West and insisted that the admission of every free state must be accompanied by the admission of a slave state in order that equality in the Senate be maintained. Henry Clay managed to stall off an open break by his Missouri Compromise in 1820 and by his compromise of 1850. But both measures were only makeshift. Time and tide were on the side of the North. Geography, population, the growth of industrialization, and the march of liberalism in the Western world were irresistible.

By 1852 the statesmen of moderation, Clay, Calhoun, and Webster, were dead, and younger and more uncompromising men came to power on both sides. In 1854 the Republican party was founded as a strictly Northern party committed to the restriction and ultimate extinction of slavery. In 1860, with Abraham Lincoln as its candidate, it won a sweeping victory over the Democrats, now split between North and South over the question of slavery. Lincoln's assurance that he would never molest slavery where it already existed but would only oppose its further extension offered the South little comfort. The violent abolitionists were growing stronger in the North every day. The strictly Northern Republican party was now in power. What guarantee would the South have, once it lost its last stronghold, that of equality in the Senate? Who would succeed Lincoln? Rather than accept an inferior status in the nation and face the prospect of eventually having some 4 million black slaves forcibly freed in their midst, eleven Southern states (about half the territory of the Union and a third of its population) seceded and set up an independent government.

When it became clear that the Southern Confederacy meant to make the separation permanent, Lincoln proceeded to restore the Union by military force. The North had an overwhelming preponderance in population, wealth, industry, transportation, and naval power. But the South enjoyed brilliant military leadership and the further advantage of fighting on its own soil for what it believed to be the survival of its white civilization.

The war lasted four bloody years. For three of the four years it looked as if the Union could not be restored. Indeed, but for the genius, the character, and the personality of Lincoln, it is possible that it might not have been restored. But after numerous discordant elements in the North were brought together, Great Britain and France tactfully neutralized, and the winning commanders and strategy found, the Southern armies were finally crushed.

Slavery was abolished and the authority of the national government restored, never to be seriously threatened since. However, the war left a legacy of sectional bitterness that was greatly deepened by the harsh policy of reconstruction followed by the victorious North. The conciliatory Lincoln was assassinated just five days after the war ended. The radical Republican congressional leaders, who now gained control of the government, treated the defeated and devastated South as a conquered province, forcing upon it twelve years of military occupation, political and economic exploitation, and Negro supremacy. In time, however, these wounds too healed over, but not entirely.

The victory of the North in the American Civil War was another great victory for nationalism. It was also a victory for the pre-1871 variety of liberalism, since it brought into power the Northern industrial bourgeoisie, who upon the death of Lincoln gained control of the now dominant Republican party. Thus in the United States, as in France, nationalism and bourgeois liberalism joined hands during the first phase of the Industrial Revolution.

Suggested Reading

General
*R. C. Binkley, *Realism and Nationalism, 1853–1871* (Torch). Excellent volume in the Rise of Modern Europe series.
C. J. H. Hayes, *Historical Evolution of Modern Nationalism* (1931). Classic by leading authority on the subject.

The Second Empire of Napoleon III
*J. M. Thompson, *Louis Napoleon and the Second Empire* (Norton). Scholarly survey.
A. Guérard, *Napoleon III: An Interpretation* (1943). Excellent, brief biography.
*C. B. Woodham-Smith, *The Reason Why* (Compass). Brilliant analysis of the Crimean War.

Expansion of the United States
*R. A. Billington, *The Westward Movement in the United States* (Van Nostrand, Reinhold). By a leading authority.
*B. de Voto, *Across the Wide Missouri* (Sentry). Excellent account written in dramatic and popular vein.

The Struggle over Slavery in the United States
W. E. Dodd, *The Cotton Kingdom* (1919). A little gem — vivid picture of life and thought in the American slave states.
J. G. Randall, *The Civil War and Reconstruction* (1937). Perceptive study by a leading scholar.
B. Thomas, *Abraham Lincoln* (1952). Best biography of Lincoln.

Historical Fiction
*William Styron, *The Confessions of Nat Turner* (Signet). Although fictional in form, this is a scholarly analysis of the slave mind. Excellent.

46

THE TRIUMPH OF NATIONALISM IN ITALY AND GERMANY

The failure of the Revolution of 1848 in Central Europe and the harsh repression that followed appeared to dash the hopes of liberalism and nationalism in both Italy and Germany. The forces of nationalism, however, were only stung to greater energy. Within a surprisingly short time after the disappointments of 1848, both the Italian and the German people were moving rapidly toward national unity.

1. CAVOUR PLANS ITALIAN UNITY

Before 1848 three different plans for uniting Italy into a sovereign state had been proposed; each had its own following. One plan was to make Italy a liberal democratic republic. This was the plan of Giuseppe Mazzini, an inspiring speaker and writer but not a very practical organizer or man of action. His movement was called Young Italy. The second plan was to form an Italian confederacy under the leadership of the pope. The third plan was to make Italy a limited monarchy under the leadership of the house of Savoy, the ruling dynasty in the kingdom of Sardinia. During the Revolution of 1848 the first two plans were discredited. Mazzini's chaotic Roman Republic, which he set up after the rebellious populace had driven out the pope, outraged the Roman Catholic world and was overthrown by a French army of Louis Napoleon. After this experience the pope bitterly opposed the unification of Italy, fearing that it would mean the loss of his political control over the Papal States.

On the other hand, the heroic role played by the kingdom of Sardinia in battling the Austrians against hopeless odds won for the house of Savoy the devotion and confidence of most Italian nationalists. However, the powerful Austrians were still in Lombardy and Venetia, the unsympathetic pope still ruled the Papal States, and the rest of the Italian states were weak and divided. Despite the new prestige of Sardinia, therefore, the task of uniting Italy required the work of a genius. He soon appeared: Camillo Benso, Count di Cavour (1810–1861).

Cavour was a member of a well-to-do noble family of Piedmont in the kingdom of Sardinia. (The kingdom of Sardinia was composed of Piedmont, the large island of Sardinia, and the little French-speaking provinces of Savoy and Nice.) Young Cavour showed such liberal tendencies that he was soon in trouble with both military and civilian authorities. Resigning his commission in the army, he traveled widely in Great Britain and France, where he developed great admiration for liberal constitutional monarchy. Back in Piedmont, Cavour proved himself to be an able businessman. He turned his ancestral estates into models of scientific agriculture and organized successful railroad and steamship companies and chemical and fertilizer factories. Shortly before the Revolution of 1848, he founded a newspaper called *Il Risorgimento (The Res-*

Guiseppe Garibaldi, the most colorful of all the makers of the Italian nation, is shown in this painting, made from a sketch drawn on the spot, during the siege of Rome in the first abortive attempts at Italian unification between 1848 and 1850. *Photo: Prints Division, New York Public Library, Astor, Lenox, and Tilden Foundations*

urrection), which never ceased to preach Italian unity, even through the discouragements of defeat. In 1850 the tireless Italian patriot was made minister of commerce and agriculture, and two years later prime minister of Sardinia.

From the moment Cavour became prime minister in 1852, he devoted all his prodigious energy to the seemingly impossible task of driving Austria out of Italy and creating a liberal Italian national monarchy. For seven years he strove to make Sardinia a model state that the others would be proud to follow. Though often sorely vexed by the self-interest of political factions and tempted to use dictatorial methods, he carefully respected the liberal constitution that had been drawn up in 1848. On the economic front, he applied his own private business efficiency to the economy of the state. Cavour was particu-

larly interested in building railroads that ran through the various Italian states, believing that economic unity would facilitate political unity. The budget was balanced. Although taxes were high, the taxpayers were prosperous and confident that the money was being put to good use. The religious problem was a difficult one for Cavour. The numerous and powerful Roman Catholic clergy in Sardinia strongly opposed his liberal reforms and his plans for uniting Italy. Cavour, a nominal Roman Catholic, believed in "a free church in a free state." Special legal privileges for the clergy were abolished. The Jesuits were banished from Sardinia. Most of the monastic establishments were abolished and their properties confiscated. The remaining Church property was made subject to taxation. Cavour, of course, could not have survived the clerical storm that followed had he not been sustained, as he was in all his measures, by his sovereign, King Victor Emmanuel II. Finally, the great minister built an efficient and, considering the size of the country, a large army.

Cavour saw clearly that Sardinia, a state of fewer than 5 million people, could never defeat Austria alone. It must be done in alliance with a great power. Since Napoleon III's Second Empire was the only great power that might be interested, Cavour sent the efficient Sardinian army into the Crimean War in the hopes of winning French sympathy. The plan worked, and at the Paris Peace Conference in 1856, he was given an opportunity to state impressively to the world Italy's case against Austria. Also of help was Orsini, a fanatical Italian patriot who attempted to assassinate Napoleon III in 1858. At his trial Orsini declared that other such attempts would be made in the future unless Napoleon helped Italy become united. The romantic French emperor, himself of Italian stock, was impressed. A few months later, Napoleon met the Sardinian prime minister at Plombières, a French spa, and there Cavour persuaded him to fight Austria. Sardinia would provoke Austria into a declaration of war; France would come in and help Sardinia drive the Austrians out of Lombardy and Venetia, which would then be annexed to the kingdom of Sardinia. In payment, Sardinia would cede the two little French-speaking provinces of Savoy and Nice to France. Cavour left Plombières satisfied that his life's ambition was about to be accomplished.

2. THE MAKING OF THE ITALIAN NATION

When everything was in readiness in April 1859, Cavour easily provoked unsuspecting Austria into a declaration of war. To Austria's surprise, French armies poured across the Alps to fight alongside the Sardinians. In the two bloody battles of Magenta and Solferino, the Austrians were defeated and driven out of Lombardy. But, to the dismay of Cavour, Napoleon suddenly made a separate peace with Austria (the Agreement of Villafranca) on condition that Sardinia receive Lombardy but not Venetia. Napoleon appears to have been motivated by the surprising bloodiness of the battles, the threatening attitude of Prussia, who mobilized troops in the Rhineland, and the anger of the French Roman Catholics, who feared that the wild outburst of nationalism all over Italy following the victories over Austria threatened the independence of the Papal States.

Cavour, his hopes apparently dashed with victory within grasp, lost his poise for the only time in his life. He wanted to carry on the war alone to certain defeat but was restrained by King Victor Emmanuel. He resigned as prime minister, but was soon recalled to direct the complex and fast-moving events. News of Magenta and Solferino set all Italy agog with nationalistic fervor. Early in 1860, under Cavour's behind-the-scenes direction, Tuscany, Modena, Parma, and Romagna (the northernmost of the Papal States) joined the kingdom of Sardinia, bringing together all of northern Italy except Venetia. However, with Austria in Venetia and French troops protecting the pope in central Italy, it looked as if the unification movement must now come to a halt.

At this juncture, the rawboned Giuseppe Garibaldi, the most colorful of all the makers of the Italian nation, performed a daring exploit. With a thousand civilian warriors dressed in red shirts and slouch hats, he sailed aboard two little Piedmontese ships for southern Italy. His goal was the conquest of the kingdom of the Two Sicilies, the largest and most populous of the Italian states, with a regular army of 124,000 men and a sizable navy. Cavour officially condemned the seemingly foolhardy expedition of the thousand, but secretly aided it. Garibaldi's exploits read like a fairy story. He conquered the large island of Sicily, including Palermo, once the largest city in Europe, crossed the Strait of Messina, and entered triumphantly into Naples. The opposing troops, of course, had little heart for their cause and deserted to Garibaldi by the thousands after his first victories. Moving northward in the direction of Rome, Garibaldi defeated the last Neapolitan forces.

Fearful that the daring but undiplomatic Garibaldi would march on Rome and bring down the armies of all of Roman Catholic Europe on the rapidly forming Italian nation, Cavour made the last and most difficult decision of his life. He sent the Sardinian army southward and seized all the pope's remaining territory except the Patrimony of St. Peter (Rome and the territory immediately surrounding it). When Victor Emmanuel at the head of his army approached the forces of Garibaldi, the gallant warrior and

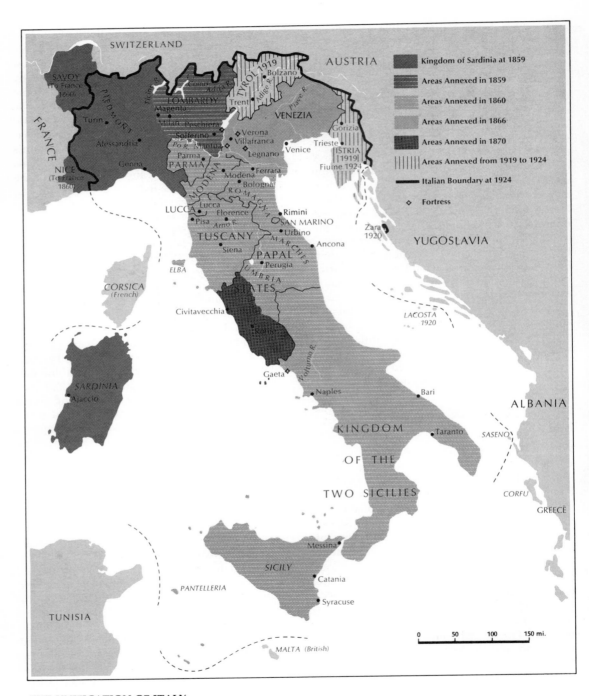

SWITZERLAND

AUSTRIA

	Kingdom of Sardinia at 1859
	Areas Annexed in 1859
	Areas Annexed in 1860
	Areas Annexed in 1866
	Areas Annexed in 1870
	Areas Annexed from 1919 to 1924
	Italian Boundary at 1924
◇	Fortress

SAVOY
(To France
1860)

PIEMONT

TYROL 1919

Bolzano

LOMBARDY

Trent

Magenta

Adige R.

Milan   Peschiera

Comp

Adda R.

Ticino R.

Plave R.

VENEZIA

Turin

Solferino

P. R. Mantua

Alessandria

Villafranca

Verona

Venice

Trieste

Gorizia

ISTRIA
[1919]

Genoa

Parma

Legnano

NICE
(To France
1860)

PARMA

MODENA

Modena

Ferrara

Fiume 1924

Zara
1920

YUGOSLAVIA

FRANCE

Bologna

ROMAGNA

LUCCA

Lucca

Florence

Rimini

SAN MARINO

Pisa

Arno R.

Urbino

Ancona

TUSCANY

MARCHES

CORSICA
(French)

Siena

PAPAL

Perugia

ELBA

UMBRIA

STATES

Civitavecchia

LACOSTA
1920

SARDINIA

Gaeta

Garigliano R.

Ajaccio

Naples

Bari

ALBANIA

KINGDOM

Taranto

SASENO

OF   THE

CORFU

TWO   SICILIES

GREECE

Messina

SICILY

Catania

PANTELLERIA

Syracuse

TUNISIA

0   50   100   150 mi.

MALTA (British)

THE UNIFICATION OF ITALY

patriot submitted to his king and retired to the rocky island of Caprera. The kingdom of Italy was formally declared in March 1861, with Victor Emmanuel II as king and the liberal Sardinian Constitution of 1848 as the national charter. The red, white, and green Sardinian flag now flew over all of Italy from the Alps to Sicily except Venetia and Rome. Those two provinces were not joined to the Italian state until 1866 and 1870, respectively, when, as we shall soon see, first Austria and then France was defeated by Prussia.

Cavour did not live to enjoy the fruits of his labors. Less than three months after the birth of his beloved Italian nation, he was dead, exhausted by his prodigious efforts and achievements. Paunchy, with ill-fitting glasses and a myopic stare, he was anything but impressive in appearance. Neither was he an orator. "I cannot make a speech," he once truthfully said, "but I can make Italy." The new nation was a monument to his genius and to the spirit of liberal nationalism.

3. THE HOHENZOLLERNS ASSUME THE LEADERSHIP OF A GERMAN NATIONAL MOVEMENT

During the decade of the 1850s, both liberalism and nationalism began to make rapid headway in the German states. It was then that industrialization in this area began in earnest. In Prussia the rise of an industrial bourgeoisie and an industrial proletariat, both classes imbued with liberalism (of different hues) and German nationalism, challenged for the first time the dominance of the Junker aristocracy, who abhorred liberalism of any hue and whose national loyalty was limited strictly to Prussia. It was also in the decade of the 1850s that the "Prussian School" of historians, Droysen, Sybel, and Treitschke, began to write ponderous works setting forth the German version of history. They were strongly influenced by the philosophy of Hegel (1770–1831), who had preached eloquently a version of history based on national cultures. Every epoch is characterized by a dominant spirit, said Hegel. The modern era belongs to the German spir-

it of liberty through disciplined order. Hegel, in turn, was undoubtedly influenced in part by the earlier German philosopher Herder (1744–1803). This was the beginning of the German master-race concept.

The flowering of this superior German national culture required the political unity of the German people. However, the experiences of 1848–1849 had demonstrated that, without the support of Prussia and her autocratic rulers, the Hohenzollerns, a German national movement could not succeed. The conversion of the Hohenzollerns and the Prussian Junkers to German nationalism was facilitated by the "Humiliation of Olmütz" in 1850. Shortly after the vacillating Frederick William IV had spurned the German national crown offered him by the Frankfurt Assembly in the spring of 1849, he attempted to reorganize the German Confederation under Prussian leadership. The Hapsburg government of Austria, now completely recovered from its embarrassments of 1848–1849, mobilized its superior army and ordered him to cease. At the town of Olmütz in Austrian territory, he abjectly yielded. After this, the Hohenzollerns and more and more of the proud Junkers sought an opportunity to avenge the national insult to Prussia and replace Austria as leader of the Germanies.

In 1858 the unstable mind of Frederick William IV gave way, and his younger brother, who three years later became King William I, assumed the headship of the Prussian government as regent. Unlike his romantic and idealistic brother, William I was a militarist. His first move was to rejuvenate and greatly strengthen the Prussian military machine. As minister of war he appointed an able organizer, Albrecht von Roon; and, as chief of staff, Helmuth von Moltke, one of the greatest strategists and tacticians of modern times. But their plans to make the Prussian army the most powerful military force in the world required large sums of money. The liberals, now strong in the Prussian Landtag, began to take alarm. Might not this all-powerful military machine be used to suppress liberalism? The liberals hoped that by holding up the military budget, they might bargain for a stronger role for the legislature in the Prussian government. After several years of haggling, the liberals in 1862 finally defeated the military budget. Liberalism and nationalism had collided head-on. William I, unskilled in and unsympathetic with parliamentary government, threatened to resign. As a last resort, on the advice of Roon and Moltke, he called to the chancellorship the one man who could and would force through the military program, Otto Eduard Leopold von Bismarck.

4. BISMARCK WELDS THE NORTH GERMAN CONFEDERATION

The man thus called to the head of the Prussian government at this critical time was to remain there for the next twenty-eight years. He stamped his iron will and his domineering personality not only on Prussia and Germany, but also to a considerable degree on the rest of Europe and the world. Bismarck was a typical Prussian Junker. A blond giant with boundless energy, he was a firm believer in militarism and autocratic government. He had been a dueling, drinking university student, too restless for the academic life. Administrative work in the Prussian government had also failed to challenge him. Back on his ancestral estates he was a hard-riding, hard-drinking country squire, lording it over his peasants and his neighbors. He detested liberalism in any form. He also detested German nationalism, which until 1849 was closely associated with liberalism. His loyalty was to Prussia alone. The other German states he considered weak and effeminate, unfit for union with virile, militaristic, autocratic Prussia. He had deplored Frederick William IV's temporizing with the liberals in 1848 and was pleased at his humiliation at the hands of reactionary Austria. Bismarck's views on liberalism never changed as long as he lived. But his attitude toward German nationalism underwent a sudden and complete reversal when, as Prussia's delegate to the Diet of the German Confederation at Frankfurt, he saw at first hand how Austria dominated Prussia. He became an ardent German nationalist—an enthusiast not for a union of German states, but for a Prussianized Germany from which Austria would be exclud-

ed. As ambassador to Russia and to France, he gained valuable experiences for the key role he was to play in Germany.

Upon assuming the chancellorship of Prussia in 1862, Bismarck, with the backing of the king and the army, defied the liberal opposition in the Landtag, violated the constitution without hesitation, and collected illegally the funds necessary for the military program. "Not by speeches and majority resolutions," said Bismarck, "are the great questions of the time decided—that was the mistake of 1848 and 1849—but by blood and iron." He came to be known as the "Iron Chancellor." Prussian liberalism was crushed. Bismarck declared that a few glorious victories won on foreign soil would turn the Prussian liberals into fervent German nationalists. This prediction soon came true.

The new army created by Bismarck, Roon, and Moltke was the most scientifically efficient military machine that had ever been devised. Behind it was a state and a people long conditioned mentally and physically to military discipline. The Junker officers were used to command; the tow-headed privates and noncoms, mostly from the peasantry, were accustomed to obey. The latest and best equipment was provided. The whole machine worked with clock-like precision under the direction of a general staff. The subordinate officers were well versed in tactics and strategy and could be trusted to use their own judgment in local situations. The privates were well trained to fight in scattered, loose-order formations that made poor targets for the enemy. For the next three quarters of a century, this army was first the envy of, then the model for, the military machines of the other great world powers.

Bismarck lost little time in putting his new military machine to work. An opportunity soon presented itself in the form of a dispute with Denmark over the long-standing and complex Schleswig-Holstein question. Schleswig and Holstein were two little provinces lying between Prussia and Denmark. Their population was partly German-speaking and partly Danish-speaking. Since 1815 they had been ruled by the king of Denmark, though they had not been incorporated into Denmark. In 1863 the Danish

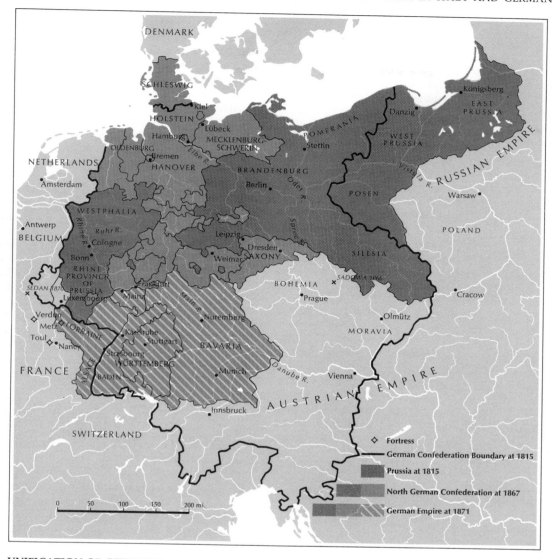

UNIFICATION OF GERMANY

king suddenly annexed Schleswig outright. Bismarck, seeing an opportunity to test the Prussian army, to annex some territory, and also to embroil Austria, declared war on Denmark (1864). Since Holstein was a member of the German Confederation, Austria dared not hold back lest the leadership of the confederation pass to Prussia. The string of Danish fortresses across the narrow peninsula, expected to block any invader for two years, was carried by the Prussian army in two weeks. Denmark sued for peace. Bismarck made the peace settlement as complicated as possible. By the terms of the Convention of Gastein, to which he persuaded Austria to agree, Schleswig and Holstein were to be ruled jointly by Prussia and Austria. Schleswig, however, was to occupied by Prussia; Holstein by Austria. This unworkable arrangement

Bismarck soon used to stir up trouble with Austria.

Confident now that the Prussian army was all that he had hoped and expected, Bismarck devoted the two years following the Danish War to feverish preparations for war with Austria. His first task was to obtain the support or the neutrality of the other three continental powers, Italy, Russia, and France. Prussia had been the first great power to recognize the new kingdom of Italy. Now, promising her Venetia, Bismarck drew her into an alliance against Austria. It was always a cardinal principle of Bismarck to maintain friendly relations with Russia (at Prussia's back door). When Russia's Polish subjects revolted once more in 1863, Prussia alone of the great powers supported Russia. Of course Prussia had several million Polish subjects of her own to worry about. Bismarck neutralized Napoleon III by personal persuasion and deception. Visiting the French emperor at Biarritz, he dangled all sorts of vague possibilities before him, such as the annexation by France of Belgium and Luxembourg. Napoleon completely misjudged the military power of Prussia. He believed either that Austria would win the coming war or that an exhausting stalemate would enable France to arbitrate the peace to her own advantage. Bismarck encouraged him in these misconceptions. By the spring of 1866, with everything in readiness, Bismarck created by threats and maneuvers a state of alarm in Austria. Finally, the Austrian government, realizing that it would require Austria twice as long as Prussia to mobilize her forces and fearing a sudden knockout blow, mobilized her army. Pretending that this was an act of war, Bismarck sent the Prussian army into Holstein, from which the Austrian forces were compelled to flee. Austria thereupon declared war.

In the Austro-Prussian War, most of the little German states supported Austria. Their military forces, however, were quickly crushed beneath the Prussian steamroller. The world was astounded by the rapidity and ease with which Moltke's armies overwhelmed Austria, a nation of twice the size and population of Prussia and long the dominant power in Central Europe. Although the war is sometimes called the Seven Weeks' War, the issue was really decided in less than three weeks. Quickly taking the offensive, the Prussians soon brought the Austrians to bay in northern Bohemia. The Battle of Königgrätz (or Sadowa, as it is sometimes called) was one of the most decisive battles in history. The Austrians fought bravely, but, standing in close formation, they were mowed down by the Prussian infantry, which lay on the ground and fired from behind rocks and trees. The Prussians' breech-loading needle guns fired six times to the Austrian muzzle-loaders' once. As the Prussians marched rapidly toward Vienna, the Hapsburg government sued for peace. William I, Roon, and Moltke wanted to crush Austria, but Bismarck was looking into the future. He saw that Austria was now harmless to Prussia and would make a valuable ally or at least friend in Prussia's future wars. Restraining his king and his generals, he made the terms of the Treaty of Prague extremely lenient. Austria was to pay Prussia a very small indemnity and to accept the rearrangement of Germany by Prussia. She was also forced to cede Venetia to Italy as Italy's reward for fighting on the side of Prussia.

Following the victory over Austria, Bismarck reorganized Germany. Hanover, Nassau, Frankfurt, and Hesse-Cassel were annexed to Prussia outright, bridging the gap between Rhenish Prussia and the main body. The remaining twenty states north of the Main River were bound to Prussia in a North German Confederation. The confederation was completely dominated by Prussia, which alone constituted four-fifths of its area and population. Prussia's king and prime minister were made president and chancellor of the confederation, for which Bismarck drafted the constitution.

Its government was, of course, fundamentally autocratic. The chief administrative officer was the chancellor (Bismarck), who was responsible only to the king of Prussia as president, by whom he was appointed. The legislative body was composed of the Bundesrat, whose members were really ambassadors of the twenty-two state governments, and the Reichstag, whose members were elected by universal male suffrage. All new laws required the approval of both bodies. The Bundesrat was the more influential of the two. The Reichstag had no control over the chancellor and his cabinet, as in Great Britain, and little control over the budget and the army and navy. If the Reichstag failed to vote a new budget, the old one automatically continued in force. This undemocratic document later became the constitution of the German Empire.

Meanwhile, the former liberals in the Prussian Landtag, caught up in the nationalistic fervor following the victory over Austria, repented of their sins of having opposed Bismarck and voted him exoneration for having violated the constitution. The four predominantly Roman Catholic states south of the Main River (Bavaria, Württemberg, Baden, and part of Hesse-Darmstadt) were left out of the North German Confederation at the insistence of Napoleon III and because Bismarck preferred to have them come in later by their own choice. He would not have long to wait.

5. THE FRANCO-GERMAN WAR AND THE CREATION OF THE GERMAN EMPIRE

From the time Bismarck took up the German nationalist cause, he anticipated that France would have to be defeated before the German nation could emerge full-grown. France, he reasoned, long the dominant power on the European continent, would not stand idle while a potentially more powerful rival grew up overnight across the Rhine.

Napoleon III had been badly deceived as to the outcome of the Austro-Prussian War. Too late he realized his error and attempted to safeguard French security. He demanded that the four predominantly Roman Catholic German states south of the Main River be left out of the new German nation and that France receive some German territory west of the Rhine to offset Prussia's sudden expansion. As we have seen, the first proposal suited Bismarck's purposes; he was certain he could get the south German states at a convenient time later. But he stood adamant against the cession of any German territory to France. He pointed out to Napoleon the hard truth that, whereas the victorious Prussian army was nearby and ready for action, the best part of the French army was in Mexico.

Both powers began to prepare for a showdown that appeared to be inevitable and not too far in the future. The Prussian army was refitted and enlarged, and the forces of the other twenty-one states in the North German Confederation integrated with it. Mistakes revealed in the Austrian war were noted and corrected. Napoleon III, for his part, recalled his army from Mexico and made efforts to renovate and enlarge the French military machine. These efforts, however, were crippled and delayed by the liberals in the Chamber of Deputies, who feared that Napoleon would use the strengthened army to crush the reviving French liberalism. Only a watered-down army-improvement bill was passed.

By 1870 Bismarck was eager for a military confrontation with France. The army of the North German Confederation was at its peak. William I was getting old, and his more liberal son, the future Frederick III, had little use for Bismarck. The French army reforms, on the other hand, were just beginning and would not be completed until 1873.

Bismarck's opportunity came when the Spanish crown was offered to a Hohenzollern prince. Bismarck persuaded the reluctant prince to accept the Spanish offer, and the French immediately took alarm at the prospect of being surrounded by Hohenzollerns. Heavy French pressure was exerted on Prussia, to which both the prince and King William I yielded. However, the French ministers were still not satisfied. They had only the spoken word of the aged king of Prussia. Furthermore, Bismarck was continuing to press the Hohenzollern candidacy for the throne of Spain. Foreign Minister Duc de Gramont ordered the French ambassador to demand assurance from the Prussian king that a Hohenzollern would never sit on the throne of Spain. William I politely refused this unreasonable demand. He wired a detailed account of this interview, which took place at Ems, to Bismarck in Berlin. The chancellor saw an opportunity to provoke the French into war. Cleverly editing the Ems dispatch so as to make it appear that the French ambassador and the Prussian king had insulted each other, he published it to the world. The French government, walking into Bismarck's trap, declared war.

This rare photograph shows Otto von Bismarck, the "Iron Chancellor," on his way to the palace at Berlin as an elderly man. The German Empire bore in large measure the stamp of his personality and ideals.
Photo: The Bettmann Archive

The prevailing world military opinion was that this time Prussia had overreached herself and that Bismarck's work would be undone. But, as in the case of the Austro-Prussian War, the military might of Prussia was grossly underestimated. That of France was overestimated. The sordid character that underlay the surface glamour of Napoleon III's long dictatorship was quickly revealed. The usurper had surrounded himself with conspirators and adventurers like himself. Graft and corruption had robbed the army of its vital necessities. There was confusion everywhere. Men could not find their units; horses were without saddles, guns without ammunition. The French were able to mobilize only 300,000 troops to face the 800,000 fully trained and equipped veterans and reservists of Moltke. The four predominantly Roman Catholic South German states, far from joining Roman Catholic France as Napoleon III had hoped, threw in their lot with Protestant, German-speaking Prussia as Bismarck had anticipated.

The issue of the war was decided in a matter of weeks. With scientific precision, Moltke's superior hosts moved into France. The French fought heroically but were overwhelmed. One French army was surrounded at the fortress city of Metz, where it surrendered three months later. Another French army under Marshal MacMahon and Emperor Napoleon III was surrounded at Sedan and surrendered on September 2. Napoleon III himself was one of the captives. When this news reached Paris two days later, the liberals overthrew the government of the Second Empire and declared the Third French Republic. Within a matter of weeks, Paris was surrounded by the Germans. For four months the great city held out; starvation forced it to surrender on January 28, 1871.

Bismarck forced upon stricken and helpless France a treaty designed to cripple her beyond recovery. The Treaty of Frankfurt required France to pay an indemnity of 5 billion francs ($1 billion) in gold. German troops would remain on French soil until this amount was paid in full (which Bismarck mistakenly hoped and expected would take a long time). The province of Alsace and the greater part of Lorraine were ceded to Germany. Although most of the inhabitants of these two border provinces speak a German dialect, their religion is Roman Catholic, and they had long been associated with France, to which they were unquestionably loyal. And since these provinces contained much of France's vital iron reserves, the seizure of Alsace and Lorraine long poisoned Franco-German relations.

On January 18, 1871, while the big German guns were still battering Paris, the heads of the twenty-five German states at war with France met on Bismarck's call at Versailles (behind the German lines) and in the Hall of Mirrors proclaimed William I emperor of the German Empire. The undemocratic constitution that Bismarck had drafted for the North German Confederation became the constitution of the German Empire. Bismarck, of course, became its chancellor, and, unlike Cavour, he lived to rule over his creation for the next nineteen years. The German Empire had now replaced France as the dominant power on the European continent and the chief rival of Great Britain for world hegemony.

The venturesome career of the totalitarian, glory-seeking Second Empire of Napoleon III and to a greater extent the rise of Bismarck's militaristic Prussianized German Empire marked the transition from moderate to malignant nationalism. After 1871 nationalism in the Western world would be less a matter of freeing language groups from alien rule and uniting them under one flag (although some of that still remained) than a matter of military aggrandizement on the part of language groups already free and united. This kind of nationalism was a dangerous foe, rather than a friend, of liberalism.

Suggested Reading

General

*R. C. Binkley, *Realism and Nationalism* (Torch). Scholarly volume in Rise of Modern Europe series.

The Making of the Italian Nation

*R. Albrecht-Carrié, *Italy from Napoleon to Mussolini* (Columbia University). Excellent survey.

G. O. Griffith, *Mazzini: Prophet of Modern Europe* (1932).

W. R. Thayer, *The Life and Times of Cavour*, 2 vols. (1911). A great biography.

G. M. Trevelyan, *Garibaldi's Defense of the Roman Republic, 1848–1849* (1907); *Garibaldi and the Thousand* (1909); *Garibaldi and the Making of Italy, June–No-*

vember, 1860 (1911). These three volumes are scholarly, dramatic, and delightfully written.

The Making of the German Nation

H. Holborn, *A History of Modern Germany* (1959–1969), 3 vols., Vol. III. Detailed, scholarly survey.

*A. J. P. Taylor, *The Course of German History* (Capricorn). Excellent brief survey.

*E. Eych, *Bismarck and the German Empire* (Norton). Best brief biography of the "Iron Chancellor."

The Franco-German War of 1870–1871

R. H. Lord, *The Origins of the War of 1870.* (1924). Makes convincing case that chief responsibility lies with Bismarck.

47

ROMANTICISM IN PHILOSOPHY, LITERATURE, AND THE ARTS

Schools of thought and art do not fall neatly into chronological patterns. Nevertheless, one is frequently able to observe a prevailing vogue that characterizes the culture of a given era. Thus, although romanticism began in the eighteenth century, the prevailing style in that century was still undoubtedly classical. Similarly, although classicism has continued on through the nineteenth century and into the present day, romanticism was unquestionably the dominant spirit in the first three quarters of the nineteenth century.

1. THE NATURE OF ROMANTICISM

The romantic spirit had many facets. But essentially it was a reaction against the rationalism and formalism of the classic spirit. Whereas classicism extolled reason and perfection of form, romanticism appealed to the emotions, to feeling, and to freedom and spontaneity of expression. Whereas the classicist was interested in the natural order and the laws of man and the universe, the romanticist loved to sing of woods and lakes and lovers' lanes and to dream of faraway or imaginary times and places.

Romanticism was associated with and was in large measure a product of the French Revolution and Napoleon. Many classicists had been interested in peacefully reforming society in accordance with the natural law. They did not anticipate the violent upheaval that came, although many of the radical revolutionary leaders and Napoleon believed themselves to be in the tradition of classical Greece and Rome. It was the romanticists, breaking sharply with past forms and traditions and with bold abandon trying the new, who reflected the revolutionary spirit. This does not mean that all romanticists were political radicals, or even liberals. Some, like Shelley and Heine, were. Others, like Edmund Burke and Sir Walter Scott, were conservatives representing a reaction against the excesses of the revolution. Burke (1729–1797) was particularly influential with the more conservative romanticists. Born in Ireland, he spent the last thirty years of his life as a member of the British Parliament. Although he eloquently defended the rights of the American colonists, he warned with equal eloquence against the threat of the philosophers of the Enlightenment and the French revolutionary radicals to destroy much of the precious heritage of Western civilization that had been so long and so painful in the making.

Nationalism was another facet of romanticism. Whether liberal or conservative, the romanticist was likely to be an ardent nationalist of the moderate pre-1871 type. The great poet Lord Byron lost his life fighting for Greek national independence against the Turks. The dreamer and orator Mazzini was called the soul of Italian nationalism. He spent most of his adult life in exile because of his labors for a free and united Italy. Herder, as early as the eighteenth century, had pleaded eloquently for a German national culture. The fraternity and the freedom so common to the national movements before 1871, no less than pride in real or imagined national achievements, gave outlet to the emotions of the romanticist.

Romanticism also represented in the main a reaction against the rationalistic deism of the eighteenth century and a return to mystic religion. With the exception of the Reformation of the sixteenth century, this was the first reversal in the general trend toward secularism, which began as early as the fourteenth, or possibly the thirteenth, century. The Roman Catholic Church had received hard blows in France at the hands

of the Voltairian rationalists and the French Revolutionists, but after 1815 it made a strong comeback both in official status and in popularity. To a generation weary of war and violent change, the Church seemed a rock of stability. In Great Britain the Methodist movement, which had begun in the middle of the eighteenth century, grew rapidly. In the United States much of

The spirit of romanticism that dominated the art and literature of Western Europe during the first half of the nineteenth century was marked by a religious revival and also by an admiration for the simple, rural life which Millet effectively captures in his famous painting, The Angelus. *Photo: Giraudon*

the antislavery movement sprang from moral and religious sources. The revival of religion as part of the romanticism of the early nineteenth century brought about a renewed interest in the Middle Ages. The classicists, almost without exception, had drawn their inspiration from pagan Greece and Rome. Now in the early nineteenth century the Knights of the Round Table and Siegfried and Brünhild came back in style once more. No more perfect example of the romantic spirit can be cited than the novels and verse of Sir Walter Scott, whose subject matter was primarily medieval. Gothic architecture enjoyed a revival. The "Dark Ages" were transformed into the "Age of Faith."

Romanticism was a godsend to the societies of the industrialized countries during the first phase of the Industrial Revolution. Its optimism, its moral and religious idealism, and its nationalism constituted a ready-made justification of life for the prosperous industrial bourgeoisie. For the hard-pressed industrial proletariat, inasmuch as they were able to partake of such cultural luxuries, it provided escapism and spiritual food. If the factory workers dully tending their machines had had nothing but the mechanical universe and the impersonal deistic God of the classicists to sustain them, their lives would have been bleak indeed. Now a few of them at least could dream and hope, and on occasion man barricades.

2. THE PHILOSOPHY OF IDEALISM

Any discussion of romantic thought must, almost of necessity, begin with Rousseau (1712–1778), even though this French genius lived during the heyday of rationalistic classicism and almost a century before romanticism came into full flower. Rousseau, like most of his fellow philosophers of the Enlightenment such as Voltaire, Diderot, Montesquieu, was a deist, believing in the mechanical universe of natural laws. However, he differed sharply with them over the place of reason. Far from believing that man can know only what is perceived through his five senses and interpreted by reason, Rousseau placed his main reliance in feeling, instinct, and emotions. He also anticipated the romantic

movement in his inordinate love of nature. He would stretch himself out on the ground, dig his fingers and toes into the dirt, kiss the earth, and weep for joy. This mad genius was a true romanticist in his revolt against the rules of formal society. Free love, undisciplined childhood and education, the noble savage—all were features of Rousseau's revolt. His influence on later generations has been enormous.

It seems a far cry from the rough genius of Rousseau to the exquisitely ordered mansions of thought of Immanuel Kant (1724–1804), but the German philosopher was admittedly indebted to Rousseau. Kant, who was partly of Scottish ancestry, was a native of Königsberg in East Prussia. A frail and insignificant-looking little man who never traveled more than 50 miles from the place of his birth, he slowly developed into one of the most powerful and influential thinkers of modern times. He was often in difficulty with the Prussian government because of his liberal and unorthodox views. Kant started out as a scientist and always respected the methods of natural science. He was also steeped in the philosophy of the Enlightenment. However, he was not satisfied with the conclusions of the eighteenth-century materialistic rationalists. Eventually he thought on beyond them. Kant came to believe that there are in reality two worlds, not one—the physical realm and the spiritual realm, or the realm of ultimate reality. The first he called the realm of phenomena; the second the realm of noumena. In the physical realm of phenomena the approach to truth of Descartes, Locke, and Voltaire—sense perception and reason—suffices. But in the spiritual realm of noumena, these methods fail. Ultimate spiritual truth may be attained only by faith, conviction, and feeling. Truths in the realm of the noumena, such as the existence of God or the immortality of the soul or the existence of good and evil, cannot be proved by reason. And yet we are justified in believing them because they reinforce our moral sense of right and wrong. His principal work, *Critique of Pure Reason*, was a metaphysical answer of the highest intellectual order to the philosophers of the Enlightenment. These ideas came to be called the philosophy of idealism. Kant and his early nineteenth-century followers represented a sharp reversal in the philosophical trend toward rationalism and materialism, which in a sense began in the thirteenth century with the efforts of Albertus Magnus and Thomas Aquinas to rationalize Christian doctrines.

The most influential of Kant's disciples was Georg Wilhelm Hegel (1770–1831). Hegel's chief interest was the philosophy of history. Like his master, he rejected the mechanistic amoral universe of the Enlightenment. He believed, rather, that a benevolent but impersonal God created and runs the universe, making human society better by a process of purposeful evolution. This is achieved by a dialectical system of thesis, antithesis, and synthesis. Any given system or civilization (thesis) is challenged by its opposite (antithesis). From the struggle emerges a new system containing the best elements of both (synthesis). This synthesis then becomes a new thesis, which when it has served its purpose is challenged by a new antithesis, and so on. Hegel believed that every historical epoch is dominated by a *zeitgeist* (spirit of the time). The zeitgeist of the nineteenth century was German civilization, whose greatest contribution was freedom through disciplined order. Hegel exalted the state. Only in and through the state can the individual find meaning and be free. Hegel's influence on romanticism and on the early nineteenth century in general was probably greater than that of any other thinker. It can readily be seen that he also provided inspiration for some of the "isms" of the twentieth century, such as fascism and communism.

3. ROMANTIC LITERATURE

The spirit of romanticism can be made to come alive in no better way than by a study of the British romantic poets. A number of British writers began to break with classicism during the course of the eighteenth century. The best-known and probably the most representative of these writers was Robert Burns (1759–1796). Born in a humble clay cottage, the Scottish poet lived a carefree life, as undisciplined as if he had been reared in accordance with Rousseau's *Emile.* Burns idealized nature and the rustic rural life

with which he was intimately acquainted. In spontaneous verse written in his native Scottish dialect, he wrote an ode to a field mouse, "Wee, sleekit, cow'rin', tim'rous beastie," which he had turned up with his plow. In *The Cotter's Saturday Night* we are given a charming and sympathetic picture of village life among the poor of Scotland. "Auld Lang Syne" is sung with nostalgia every New Year's Eve by millions throughout the English-speaking world. *John Anderson My Jo* could never have been written by Racine or Alexander Pope.

The romantic spirit, early reflected in the poetry of Robert Burns, reached maturity with William Wordsworth (1770–1850) and Samuel Taylor Coleridge (1772–1834). The two were warm friends. Both were closely associated with the beautiful lake country of northwest England, Wordsworth by birth and Coleridge by adoption. They took a trip to Germany together, where they fell under the influence of Kant. Both, as young men, were ardent social reformers. The two collaborated on *Lyrical Ballads,* which appeared in 1798. *Lyrical Ballads* contains some of the best work of these gifted poets, such as Wordworth's *Tintern Abbey* and Coleridge's *Ancient Mariner.* Both men were masters of versification and poetic expression. They were also lovers and students of nature, and both of them, particularly Wordsworth, were keenly aware of the brooding, mystical presence of the divine. Wordsworth's *Intimations of Immortality* is sublime in its spiritual depth and insight. In their ardent love of nature, their introspective concern for the individual, their preoccupation with the spiritual rather than the material, and their greater attention to substance than to form, Wordsworth and Coleridge broke distinctly with the spirit of classicism.

Once the vogue of romanticism was dignified and popularized in Great Britain by Wordsworth and Coleridge, a host of romantic writers appeared. A younger trio of poetic geniuses of the highest order, Byron, Shelley, and Keats (all of whom lived briefly and died between the years 1788 and 1824), are known and loved wherever the English language is understood. All three gave spontaneous and unrestrained vent to their emotions. Byron and Shelley combined an exquisite esthetic sense with irrepressible revolutionary zeal, defying the forms and customs of society. Keats was a gentler soul, who after a lifelong quest for the beautiful died at the age of twenty-five.

Meanwhile, Sir Walter Scott in novel and verse was devoting his longer life (1771–1832) to glorifying the Middle Ages and his native Scotland. Scott, unlike Bryon and Shelley but like Wordsworth and Coleridge in their mature and mellow later years, was conservative in his attitude toward public affairs.

The last of the British romanticists were Alfred Lord Tennyson (1809–1892) and Robert Browning (1812–1889), who lived on and wrote well into the Victorian era. The young Tennyson's ardent nationalism, exaltation of the Middle Ages in *Idylls of the King,* interest in religion, and essential conservatism were all typically romantic. Browning, deeper and more subtle in thought though less lyrical than Tennyson, paralleled him in many ways.

Across the Atlantic, Longfellow, Cooper, and Irving, as we have seen, were founding an American national literature. In their subject matter, their style, and their attitudes, they reflected the European romantic spirit. In fact, Irving divided his time and his interests between Europe and America. Many other American writers in the early nineteenth century wrote in the romantic vein. We can mention here only a few of the most illustrative. Ralph Waldo Emerson (1803–1882) was considered a religious radical and skeptic in his day. He gave up his Puritan pastorate (by then Unitarian) at Boston's Old North Church because of his heterodoxy. However, in his essays and poems it was the romantic philosophy of Kantian idealism, not the rationalism of the Enlightenment, that he introduced into America. Edgar Allan Poe (1809–1849), short-story writer, literary critic, and romantic poet of a high order, was in a sense an American Shelley, though less ethereal and more morbid. Henry David Thoreau (1817–1862) took Rousseau's back-to-nature idea more seriously than did its author. Rousseau, for all his passion for nature, would never have withdrawn from society for two years to live by Walden Pond in introspective solitude. Emerson, Poe, and Thoreau were all individualists to the point of being mild social revolutionaries. Thoreau preached civil disobedience and allowed himself to be put in jail rather than pay taxes for what he considered to be unworthy causes. The sensitive Poe, enduring oblivion and poverty, turned to drink and an early grave. Emerson weathered a storm of hostility from organized religion and society for his nonconformist views.

Romanticism came to German literature in the latter half of the eighteenth century, partly under the influence of the early British romanticists and partly as a result of the conscious effort of the Germans, led by Herder, to free themselves from bondage to French classical culture. Foremost among all German writers is Johann Wolfgang von Goethe (1749–1832). Like Shakespeare, Leonardo da Vinci, and Beethoven, Goethe is a genius of such proportions that he cannot be confined to any single cultural school or movement. However, insofar as it is possible to classify him, he belongs more nearly to the romantic tradition than to any other, both in time and in spirit. His prodigious energies were devoted essentially to a lifelong (eighty-three years) search for the secrets of happiness and wisdom. His encyclopedic mind delved fruitfully into literature, philosophy, science, and public affairs. His novels, lyrics, essays, scientific and philosophical treatises, and dramas fill a hundred and thirty-two volumes. No writer except Shakespeare has had so many of his lyrics set to music. Goethe's masterpiece is *Faust,* a philosophical drama written in exquisite verse. It is about a medieval scholar who, dissatisfied with the fruits of knowledge, sells his soul to the devil in return for earthly pleasure and wisdom. Goethe explores the depths of human experience and aspiration. *Faust* was sixty years in the making. In his medieval interests, his fresh emotional spontaneity, his love of nature and of individual personality, and his courageous, robust, pioneering spirit, Goethe was a romanticist.

Goethe's friend and protégé, Friedrich Schiller (1759–1805), was more popular in his own day than the master himself. Schiller drew heavily upon the Middle Ages and upon nationalism (when national aspirations were associated with freedom) for his dramas, histories, and lyrics.

William Tell, a drama based upon the Swiss struggle for freedom from Hapsburg tyranny, is probably Schiller's best-known work. Neither Goethe nor Schiller can be considered a German nationalist in the narrow sense; both were universal in their interests and their appeal.

Heinrich Heine (1797–1856) was considered to be Goethe's successor as a writer of German lyrics, though not of Goethe's stature. Most of Heine's voluminous writing was in the field of romantic lyrical poetry. One of his most representative works was an ode to the Silesian weavers who rose up against the hardships caused by the Industrial Revolution, which was just coming to Germany, and were shot down by Prussian troops. Because of the hostility of the various German governments in the age of Metternich to his radical political ideas, Heine exiled himself from Germany. The last twenty-five years of his life were spent in Paris. Many of his later lyrics show a touch of the light gaiety of the French.

One would expect France, the home of Rousseau, the French Revolution, and irrepressible individualists, to be the seat of a flourishing literary romanticism. While this was true in a way,

Another aspect of the arts and literature in the early nineteenth century was a renewed interest in medieval ideals and artistic forms. The Houses of Parliament in London, which were built at this time, were done in a Gothic style. *Photo: A. F. Kersting*

France produced only one romantic writer (Victor Hugo) of the stature of Wordsworth or Shelley. (Goethes, of course, come along only every two or three centuries or so.) Neither did French romanticism attain the glories of French classicism of the seventeenth and eighteenth centuries. François René Chateaubriand (1768–1848), a disillusioned nobleman who began writing during the reign of Napoleon I, was one of the first writers of influence to react against the rationalism of the Enlightenment. His *Genius of Christianity* is a return to mystic religion. He also dreamed and wrote of glorified Indians in faraway tropical America. Honoré de Balzac (1799–1850), the greatest of French novelists, set out to imitate Scott. However, he soon changed his setting from the Middle Ages to contemporary France of the early nineteenth century, becoming one of the first to write about the new industrial bourgeoisie. In nearly one hundred novels and tales, called collectively *The Human Comedy*, he attempted to depict the whole gamut of human nature. Some two thousand characters, many drawn with shrewd insight, parade before us. He foreshadows the realism of a later era. Alexander Dumas the elder (1802–1870) has continued to delight young and old alike with his romantic and melodramatic *The Three Musketeers* and *The Count of Monte Cristo*, painting the haunting afterglow of medieval chivalry. Victor Hugo (1802–1885) in his long and tumultuous life wrote a vast quantity of exquisite lyrics, dramas, essays, and fiction—all in the romantic tradition. His *Hunchback of Notre Dame* is medieval in setting. In *Les Misérables*, sometimes called the greatest of novels, he immortalizes and idealizes the masses of underprivileged mankind, preaching redemption and purification not by planned social reform, but through suffering. We probably should not leave the subject of French romanticism without mentioning Jules Michelet (1798–1874), romantic French historian. In his *History of France* in seventeen volumes he tells the thrilling story of France's long and glorious achievements, usually with skillful historical craftsmanship and always with matchless grace.

The first great figure in Russian literature was the romantic poet Alexander Pushkin (1799–1837). The chief inspiration for his great lyrics, dramas, histories, novels, essays, and tales came from French and British writers, particularly Byron. Because of his revolutionary radicalism (of the French variety), he was for a while exiled by the Russian government to southern Russia. Later he became a Russian nationalist, and took many of his themes from Russian history. His tragic drama *Boris Godunov* (patterned after Shakespeare) is considered to be his masterpiece. Probably Russia's greatest contribution to romantic literature was the work of two of the world's greatest novelists—Ivan Sergyeevich Turgenev (1818–1883) and Feodor Dostoevski (1821–1881). Both were ardent Russian nationalists, but their real love and loyalty were for the Russian common people, particularly the peasants. Because of their radicalism both were arrested. Dostoevski was exiled to Siberia for five years. Turgenev, after eighteen months of house arrest, spent the rest of his life abroad, mostly in Paris. In his masterpiece, *Fathers and Sons*, Turgenev grapples powerfully with the problems of the older conservative Russian generation versus the modern, sophisticated, and radical younger generation. Dostoevski's two greatest novels are *Crime and Punishment* and *The Brothers Karamazov*. In them he delves psychologically and mystically into the problems of evil and purification through suffering. He was deeply religious, but not in any formal or orthodox sense.

4. THE ROMANTIC SPIRIT IN THE ARTS

Words fail miserably to convey the messages and the meanings expressed in the visual and musical arts. This is particularly true of art whose appeal is primarily to the emotions. Brevity, then, will be the soul of our treatment of romantic art.

The leading painters glorified nature, religion, and nationalism. John Constable (1776–1837) in Great Britain, Camille Corot (1796–1875) in France, and George Inness the elder (1825–1894) in the United States painted dreamy, misty landscapes fit to have illustrated the moods of Wordsworth or Thoreau. Their idealizations of rural life would have delighted Rousseau and

Burns. J. M. W. Turner (1775–1851) in England caught the romantic mood in his eerie impressions of seascapes and mythological subjects. Jean François Millet (1814–1875) idealized both the French rural life (*The Sower* and *The Gleaners*) and mystic religion (*The Angelus*). His compatriot, Eugène Delacroix (1798–1863) depicted on canvas Byron's *The Prisoner of Chillon*. On great murals in the Louvre, the library of the Chamber of Deputies, and the Hôtel de Ville he portrayed glorious scenes from the national history of France.

The romantic movement was less pronounced in the field of architecture. Its chief manifestation was a revived interest in the Gothic style. The French, after several centuries of apathy if not scorn for anything associated with medievalism, suddenly showed a renewed interest in their magnificent Gothic monuments. It is significant that the Houses of Parliament constructed in London in the early nineteenth century, when England was rapidly becoming industrialized, were built in the Gothic style.

The romantic spirit was caught and expressed by a host of great musicians. First and foremost was Beethoven (1770–1827), who was not only one of the greatest of classic composers but also the first of the romanticists. His earlier work was in the spirit of his idol, Mozart. In maturity his originality overflowed the bounds of classic forms, becoming freer, more individualistic, and emotional. Beethoven lived through the upheavals of the French Revolution and Napoleon, and his keen interest in these dramatic events is reflected in his music. His Symphony No. 3 ("Eroica") was dedicated to Napoleon, whom Beethoven at first regarded as the embodiment of the democratic ideals of the French Revolution. His Fifth and Seventh symphonies were inspired by the German nationalistic upsurge, which helped to overthrow the French tyrant. Karl Maria von Weber (1786–1826), Franz Schubert (1797–1828), Felix Mendelssohn (1809–1847), and Robert Schumann (1810–1856) carried on in the spirit of the great Beethoven.

These gifted and youthful Germans expressed in their melodic music the same spontaneous and emotional spirit that their contemporaries Byron, Shelley, and Keats were expressing in English verse. A German by adoption was the colorful Hungarian-born Franz Liszt (1811–1886). Liszt is believed to be probably the greatest concert pianist of all time. His glamorous personality and sensational, emotional compositions greatly popularized romantic music. Although Liszt was an international figure, his Hungarian folk music was characteristic of the growing national sentiment of the time. He befriended the youthful Richard Wagner, who later married one of Liszt's illegitimate daughters.

The romantic spirit is nowhere better illustrated than in the work of the Polish-French pianist-composer, Frédéric Chopin (1810–1849). Chopin

This lithograph by Delacroix, a famous French Romantic painter of the first half of the nineteenth century, is an illustration for Goethe's masterpiece, Faust. *Photo: Prints Division, New York Public Library, Astor, Lenox, and Tilden Foundations*

could express his sweet sorrows in lilting nocturnes, his sunny gaiety in bright waltzes and mazurkas, his national patriotism in stirring polonaises, or his deeper, dramatic moods in more formal ballades and concertos—all with equal skill and all in the romantic tradition. Meanwhile, other notable Frenchmen were writing romantic symphonies and operas. Gounod's *Faust* is an operatic version of Goethe's great theme. The haunting melodies of Bizet's (1838–1875) *Carmen* are widely known and sung. The greatest Italian romantic composer was Giuseppe Verdi (1813–1901). His operas *Aida, La Traviata, Il Trovatore,* and *Rigoletto* are still sung every season in opera houses all over the world. Verdi was Italy's national cultural hero during the long, uphill fight for freedom and unity.

Richard Wagner (1813–1883) brought to a dramatic close the romantic era in music. Wagner's tempestuous life, like his music, illustrates and marks the transition from the romantic,

moderately liberal and nationalistic early nineteenth century to the more violent, cynical, and materialistic spirit of the late nineteenth and early twentieth centuries. In his youth Wagner was a radical, and was exiled from Saxony in 1849 for his revolutionary activities. Later he became an extreme German nationalist—even a German "master racist" of the type that has brought so much violence to the twentieth-century world. His operas, though containing some of the world's greatest music, are in the main grandiloquent, strident, and extremely nationalistic. *Tannhäuser, The Meistersingers, Siegfried, Götterdämmerung, Lohengrin,* and *The Ring of the Nibelungs* are an important part of opera repertory today.

Since man is always a complex, emotional, and religious creature and only sometimes rational, the romanticists played a significant role in the eternal quest for an understanding of the mystery and beauty of life.

Suggested Reading

General

R. B. Mowat, *The Romantic Age: Europe in the Early Nineteenth Century, (1937).* Good survey.

J. Barzun, *Classic, Romantic, and Modern* (1962). Spirited defense of romanticism against some of the ridiculous things that have been said about it in recent years.

The Philosophy of Idealism

*C. Brinton, *The Shaping of Modern Thought* (Spectrum). Good chapters on the Romantic period.

Romantic Literature

H. Beers, *A History of English Romanticism in the Nineteenth Century* (1932). Beers has another scholarly volume covering the eighteenth century.

H. Allen, *Israfel: The Life and Times of Edgar Allan Poe* (1949). The best biography of Poe.

N. H. Clement, *Romanticism in France* (1939). A sound survey.

L. Willoughby, *The Romantic Movement in Germany* (1930). Probably the best volume on the subject.

Romanticism in the Arts

M. Raynal, *The Nineteenth Century: Goya to Gauguin* (1951). Beautifully illustrated.

H. Liechtentritt, *Music, History, and Ideas* (1930). Relates music to other aspects of culture.

Sources

*T. V. Smith and M. Grene, eds., *Philosophers Speak for Themselves: Berkeley, Hume, and Kant* (Phoenix). A handy approach to Kant.

*H. Hugo, ed., *The Romantic Reader* (Viking). A good anthology of romantic literature.

Retrospect

Four forces dominated the Western world during the half century that followed the era of the French Revolution. They were the Industrial Revolution, liberalism, nationalism, and romanticism. The last three were in large measure a product of or a reaction to the Enlightenment and the French Revolution.

The Industrial Revolution was a shifting from hand tools to power machinery as a means of production. This sounds rather innocuous, but it is doubtful if any development in history has so changed man's pattern of living. From the earliest civilizations to the mid-eighteenth century, this pattern had changed relatively little. Man had lived and worked by means of his muscles and hand tools. Then man invented spinning and weaving machines and the steam engine to drive them. Once the process began, one invention begat another in rapid order. The Industrial Revolution began in Great Britain, and by 1830 it had proceeded far enough to noticeably affect the social and political order.

The first beneficiaries of the Industrial Revolution were the industrial bourgeoisie—the owners of the machines. Joining the bourgeoisie of an earlier day (the merchants, the bankers, the professional men), they gained control of the government of Great Britain in 1832, as a result of the Reform Bill of that year. In France, the Revolution of 1830 brought in the bourgeois monarchy of Louis Philippe. Since industrialism developed a little more slowly in the United States, the industrial bourgeoisie did not gain control until the Civil War, 1861–1865.

The liberalism of the period 1830–1871 reflected the interests of the bourgeoisie. It also reflected the influence of the Enlightenment and the French Revolution. It advocated constitutional government, civil rights, limited suffrage, and laissez-faire economics. The government was to limit its interference in economic matters to maintenance of law and order, the enforcement of contracts, and protection of property. In Great Britain and France, the first phase of the Industrial Revolution was the heyday of bourgeois liberalism. The United States enjoyed a much more democratic government and society—the most democratic in the world. East of the Rhine, where the Industrial Revolution was slow to spread, liberalism was largely in the hands of the intellectuals until 1871. And they had little to show for their efforts.

Nationalism proved to be a more powerful force than liberalism during the years 1830–1871. The mass nationalism of this period was a product of the French Revolution and Napoleon. The colorful and adventuresome Second Empire of Napoleon III was a manifestation of this type of nationalism. Both French and British nationalism found an outlet in the Crimean War. Nationalism in the United States resulted in the expansion of her boundaries to the Rio Grande River and to the Pacific Ocean. It also beat down the effort of the Southern slave states to secede and split the nation. In Southern Europe and east of the Rhine, where liberalism was still weak, nationalism succeeded in creating the Italian nation and the German nation.

Romanticism, which was the prevailing style in arts and letters during the first phase of the Industrial Revolution, was in large measure a reaction against the classicism of the period of the Enlightenment. It, too, owed a great deal to the French revolutionary upheaval, which smashed old forms and institutions and popularized the quest for the new.

XI

The Industrial Revolution Second Phase: The Emergence of the Masses 1871-1914

The Industrial Revolution, which in the years 1830 to 1871 was still in its youth and limited primarily to Western Europe and the United States, grew to burly manhood between 1871 and 1914 and greatly expanded territorially. In its second phase, sometimes called the Second Industrial Revolution, the industrialized world became obsessed with technology and science, and time-honored moral and spiritual values were called into question.

The industrial proletariat who were so bewildered and oppressed during the first phase of the Industrial Revolution were now numerous enough and experienced enough to make their influence felt. Liberalism, which in the first phase was of the moderate bourgeois variety, began to reflect this proletarian influence, but not enough to satisfy some of the more radical economic thinkers and proletarian leaders.

Nationalism, too, underwent a great change after 1871. Having achieved, in large measure, its constructive purpose of freeing language groups from alien rule and uniting them under one flag during the period 1830 to 1871, it now became more aggressive. The great powers of Europe took advantage of their technical superiority to impose their will on most of the rest of the world that was not already under their domination. This new thrust of imperialism, in turn, precipitated new rivalries among the European powers which played an important part in bringing on World War I.

The arts and letters during the second phase of the Industrial Revolution reflected the preoccupation of the masses with the marvels of science and technology and reflected also the rapidly changing values of the period. Many old forms and styles were discarded. There was much experimentation and great emphasis on the quest for the new — almost anything new.

The year 1871, then, opened a period of ferment that began with great promise and ended in 1914 with the greatest holocaust in history up to that time.

The period 1871–1914 was a time of technological and scientific advancement such as the world had never known. Since the sixteenth century, interest in technology and science had been steadily growing in Western Europe. By the late nineteenth century, discovery and invention begat discovery and invention in geometric ratio. Industry mushroomed, pouring forth an ever-increasing volume of the comforts of life for increasing numbers of people. Transportation and communications were speeded up, making easier the development of huge and far-flung corporate empires. Scientists seemed to be on the verge of solving the last mysteries of the physical universe.

One might assume that theory (science) would precede practice (technology). And today, as technology grows more and more complex, this is largely the case. In the past, however, the opposite has been true more often than not. Man was using the wheel long before he understood the mathematics of the circle. We shall therefore begin this chapter by discussing the growth of technology.

1. THE RAPID GROWTH AND SPREAD OF INDUSTRY

The first phase of the Industrial Revolution has often been called the age of iron; the second phase, the age of steel. Certainly steel has been

48

THE ONRUSH OF TECHNOLOGY AND SCIENCE

the chief sinew of industry and transportation since the latter part of the nineteenth century. Until the mid-nineteenth century, steel was hard to make and very expensive. The discovery of the Bessemer process (1856) and the Thomas-Gilchrist process (1878) of removing impurities from molten iron greatly speeded up and cheapened the production of steel. In 1871 the total annual steel production in the entire world was approximately 1 million tons, of which about half was produced by Great Britain, a fourth by Germany, and an eighth by the United States. By 1914 the world's annual production had increased more than fiftyfold; the United States was producing approximately half the total, Germany a fourth, and Great Britain an eighth. Out of this steel were made tools and machines that constantly increased in numbers and efficiency. By 1914 in the industrialized countries, these increasingly automatic machines fabricated most of the metal, textile, leather, and wood products and produced and processed much of the food.

The power to drive the steel machines was increasing in like proportion. In 1914 probably nine-tenths of the world's industrial power was still provided by the steam engine, which had been vastly improved since the Watt-Boulton model had made its appearance. Other and more efficient power generators, however, were rapidly coming to the fore. Between 1831 and 1882 the dynamo for generating electricity was developed by a number of inventors, the most

important of whom were Michael Faraday (British), the Siemens brothers (Germans), and Thomas A. Edison (American). In 1888 the electric motor was invented by Nikola Tesla, a naturalized American born in Croatia. The first practical internal-combustion engine was invented by Gottlieb Daimler (German) in 1886. One year later he put it to work in the first automobile. In 1892 the diesel engine, efficiently burning cheap crude oil, was invented by Rudolf Diesel (German). The invention of these two engines gave birth to the vast oil industry. Sir Charles Parsons (British) patented the steam turbine in 1884. The turbine proved to be so efficient that it was soon used to drive the largest ships, and eventually to generate most of the world's electric power.

In the last decades of the nineteenth century, pure science was playing an increasingly vital role in industry, and both science and industry were being applied to agriculture. Physics contributed most heavily to the rapidly growing electrical industry. Chemistry made possible such important industries as synthetic dyes, wood pulp, paper, plastics, synthetic fibers, photography, and motion pictures. The electrical and chemical industries were most highly developed in Germany. The mechanization of agriculture made its first big advances in the great grain-growing areas of the United States, Canada, and Australia, although Western Europe was also steadily increasing its agricultural yields through the use of farm machinery and scientific farming techniques.

The Industrial Revolution also spread geographically in this period. In 1871 Great Britain produced more industrial goods than the rest of the world combined. Besides Great Britain, only Belgium and France were well developed industrially. In the United States and Germany, the Industrial Revolution was still in its youth. Between 1871 and 1914, the United States and Germany surpassed Great Britain. By 1914 the Industrial Revolution had penetrated Central and Eastern Europe, Japan, Canada, Australia, and New Zealand; even India had a small textile industry. However, it was still in Western Europe and the United States that most of the world's industry was to be found, and the greater part of Asia, Africa, and Latin America was still not industrialized.

2. THE SPEEDING UP OF TRANSPORT

Between 1871 and 1914 a large part of humanity became mobile. Whereas before 1871 relatively few people had ever seen more of the world than could be seen on a single day's journey by foot or on horseback, by 1914 millions of people were traveling considerable distances, often by rapid conveyance. Even in places like China, Turkey,

This illustration shows the apparatus for making steel by the Bessemer process. Invented in 1856, the Bessemer process (and the Thomas-Gilchrist process, 1878) increased the rate of production and lowered the cost of producing steel, the chief sinew of industry and transportation since the late nineteenth century. *Photo: Historical Pictures Service, Chicago*

and Brazil, trains chugged along, hauling people for distances and at speeds unknown before.

This was the greatest era of railroad building in history. There had been a rather lively building of railroads before 1871 in Western Europe and the United States. However, between 1871 and 1914 the world's mileage more than quintupled. In fact, there has been relatively little railroad building since. The increase in speed and efficiency was proportionate to the increase in mileage.

At the same time, the steamship was making comparable progress, although it had stiff competition from the sailing ship until near the end of the nineteenth century. Steel hulls of great size, turbine engines, and screw propellers, eventually, were too much for the beautiful sails. The opening of the Suez Canal in 1869 and the Panama Canal in 1914, together with the increase in the size and speed of ships, brought the world and its peoples, commodities, and markets much closer together.

During the last three decades of the nineteenth century, the humble bicycle became a common and important means of locomotion, especially in Europe. Millions of people found this cheap and pleasant means of stepping up their speed and radius; many depended upon it to get to and from their work. But the bicycle was not fast enough for the industrial age. When Gottlieb Daimler attached his little combustion engine to a wagon in 1887, the automobile was born. It quickly captured the imagination of daring pioneers. Daimler sold his patent to a French company, and until the end of the century the French led the field in automobile development and production. Leadership passed to America with the founding of the Ford Motor Company in 1903. Henry Ford, who started out as a bicycle mechanic, was the father of two momentous ideas that revolutionized not only the automobile industry, but industry in general. The first was that high wages and cheap products would create markets and profits hitherto undreamed of while permitting the common man to share in the fruits of technology and science. The second was the assembly-line method of mass production (Eli Whitney had introduced the idea of interchangeable parts a century earlier). The rapid growth of the automobile not only made the masses much more mobile, but created vast new industrial empires in oil, rubber, and concrete. Its social and psychological effects are still unfathomed.

Another invention of this period was the airplane. The first successful heavier-then-air flying machine was flown by Wilbur and Orville Wright in 1903 over the sand dunes at Kitty Hawk, North Carolina. Aviation was still in its infancy in 1914, but already its tremendous future was obvious.

3. THE GROWTH OF CORPORATE BUSINESS AND MONOPOLY

At the same time that industry was growing, individual companies were growing larger and combining to form monopolistic mergers or trusts. Such undertakings as railroads, shipping lines, and iron and steel mills were too large for all but a very few individuals to finance. As a rule, therefore, enterprises of this scope were carried on by joint stock companies. Entrepreneur capitalists would raise the necessary capi-

tal outlay by organizing a corporation and selling stock in it to other capitalists. The actual operation of the larger industries would be carried on by hired managers, while the owners of the great industries were far removed from the day-to-day operations. The managers, who hired and fired and supervised the workmen, were working for the absentee owners, and their jobs depended on the amount of profit they could show. They were under constant pressure to pay the workers as little as possible and get from them as much work as possible. The capitalistic owners, often as not banks or insurance companies, rarely came in contact with the workers and their problems. This situation is what later gave rise to the term "soulless corporations."

John D. Rockefeller, shown here with his son, John D., Jr., on Fifth Avenue in New York, built the first huge business monopoly, the Standard Oil Trust, which was to serve as the model for big business all over the world. *Photo: United Press International*

The giant corporations were equally "soulless" in dealing with each other. In this era of unrestrained competition, the big and strong frequently destroyed the small and weak. The premium was on size and strength. The result was combines, mergers, and monopolistic trusts. The organizer of the first monopolistic trust was an American, John D. Rockefeller. Rockefeller began refining oil during the Civil War, and in 1870 organized the Standard Oil Company in Ohio. By shrewd efficiency and ruthless competition, he gained control over so much of the oil-refining business in Ohio and western Pennsylvania that he was able to bargain with the railroads for a lower rate than they charged his competitors. With this advantage he was able either to drive most of his competitors out of business or force them to sell out to him on his own terms. In 1882 he organized his dozens of affiliated companies into the Standard Oil Trust, so-called because the member companies surrendered their stock to nine trustees who made the policies and distributed the profits. This trust dominated the oil business of the entire United States. It could crush smaller competing companies by price cutting. It could fix prices and set wages. It could influence state and national legislation. It could produce more and better oil. It could produce cheaper oil — if it chose. And it could compete with foreign corporations more advantageously than numerous little companies.

The spectacular success of Rockefeller's Standard Oil Trust soon made it the model for many others, particularly in the United States, in Germany, in Japan, and to a lesser extent, in Great Britain. The German monopolistic combinations such as the giant I. G. Farben Industries (chemicals and dyes) were called *cartels*. They received government encouragement and support, particularly in their operations abroad. In Japan three quarters of the nation's industry was controlled by five giant family corporations.

Although the United States began restricting some of the predatory practices of the trusts in 1890, all the industrialized countries encouraged the investment of capital in corporations by passing laws that limited the liability of stockholders to the amount of money invested (hence the "Ltd." usually seen after the name of a British corporation or combine). By 1914 most of the world's industry was controlled by a few great corporations and trusts. Although their stockholders were numbered by the thousands, they were really controlled by a relatively few banks and wealthy individuals. And between the owners of these corporations and the millions of workers, there lay a great gulf.

4. THE ONRUSH OF NATURAL SCIENCE: PHYSICAL AND BIOLOGICAL

Theoretical or "pure" science advanced hand in hand with technology and applied science. The greatest advances in the field of the physical sciences in the nineteenth and early twentieth centuries had to do with discovering the nature of matter, energy, and electricity. John Dalton (1766–1844), a gifted British scientist and teacher of humble origin, started a fruitful line of inquiry by reviving the theory that all matter is composed of atoms. The atomic theory had been introduced by the ancient Greeks, and others had speculated about it from time to time. Dalton got on what turned out be the right track when he came to the conclusion that what distinguishes the various chemical elements is the weight of the atoms of which each element is composed. Building on Dalton's theories, the Russian chemist Dmitri Mendeléev (1834–1907) worked out, around 1870, a periodic chart showing the atomic weight of all the known elements and indicating by gaps in the chart that others remained to be discovered. Both Dalton and Mendeléev thought that the atom was an indivisible solid. But in the 1890s the British physicist Joseph Thomson (1856–1940) and the Dutch physicist Hendrik Lorentz (1853–1928) independently discovered that atoms are composed of still smaller particles, which Lorentz named electrons. Also in the 1890s the German physicist Wilhelm von Roentgen (1845–1923) discovered X-rays, and the French physicist Pierre Curie (1859–1906) and his Polish wife discovered radium and more about radioactivity.

These were marvelous discoveries, but there were still many fundamental secrets concerning the nature of matter yet to be learned. Thomson's theories were further developed early in the twentieth century by another British physicist, Sir Ernest Rutherford (1871–1937). Rutherford conceived of each atom as a miniature solar system, the nucleus being the sun, and the electrons the planets. Furthermore—and this was most startling—Thomson and Rutherford suggested that the neutrons and electrons might not be matter at all but merely positive and negative charges of electricity.

Meanwhile, Albert Einstein (1879–1955), a German physicist who later fled to America, and one of the greatest scientific geniuses of all time, was assailing time-honored concepts not only about the stability of matter, but also about time, space, and motion. The amazing Einstein came up with a formula equating mass and energy: $E = mc^2$ ($E =$ energy in ergs; $m =$ mass in grams; $c =$ the speed of light in centimeters per second). According to this formula, the atomic energy in a lump of coal is some three billion times as great as the energy obtained by burning the coal—a truth that was proved several decades later with the development of the atomic bomb. In 1905 Einstein proposed his theory of relativity, which made time, space, and motion relative to each other and to the observer, not the absolutes they had always been conceived to be. These are only a few of the most basic achievements in the physical sciences in the period 1871–1914. It is little wonder that the intellectual world was fascinated and ordinary men shaken in their beliefs.

The intellectual world was even more interested in and influenced by developments in the biological sciences. Evolution, like the atomic theory, had been suggested by the ancient Greeks and from time to time afterward. With the revival of scientific interests and attitudes in the seventeenth and eighteenth centuries, the thoughts of a number of men turned to the problem of the origin of the present world and its phenomena. By the mid-nineteenth century, the concept of a slow and gradual development of the earth's crust and its inhabitants was not at all uncommon among intellectuals. The time was ripe for a first-rate scientist to supply the evidence. That man was Charles Darwin (1809–1882), the Einstein of the biological sciences.

Darwin was of a distinguished British family. His study of medicine at Edinburgh and theology at Cambridge failed to challenge him. The world of plants and, to a somewhat lesser extent, animals was his first love—or, rather, his consuming passion. In spite of frail health, he turned his prodigious energy and powers of observation and reflection to the amassing of biological knowledge. Gradually he developed his concept of evolution. Of great influence on his thinking was Malthus' *Essay on Population* (1798), which described the struggle of human beings for food and survival, and Sir Charles Lyell's *Principles of Geology* (1830–1833), which was the first really scientific treatise on geology. Lyell demonstrated by the study of fossils the likelihood of a gradual evolution of the earth's crust and of plant and animal forms over eons of time. Darwin published *The Origin of Species* in 1859. In this historic work he described with an impressive array of factual data, convincing reasoning, and lucid prose, the long, slow evolution of present plant and animal species from simpler

A contemporary drawing by the famous American cartoonist Thomas Nast illustrates the controversy stirred up by Charles Darwin. *Photo: NYPL Picture Collection*

Contemporary cartoon by Thomas Nast.
"Gorilla: 'That Man wants to claim my Pedigree. He says he is one of my Descendants.'"

"Mr. Bergh [founder of the A. S. P. C. A.]: 'Now, Mr. Darwin, how could you insult him so?'"

forms through a process of natural selection. In the struggle for survival in nature's jungle, the fittest survived. Those specimens that possessed the more useful characteristics—for instance, the horse with the longer legs—survived to produce more offspring and to transmit their superior qualities, both inherited and acquired, to future generations.[1] Twelve years later (1871) in his *Descent of Man*, he undertook to show how man himself evolved from more primitive species by the same process. Although Darwin's work leaves many fundamental questions unanswered and his belief in the transmission of acquired traits has been pretty well discredited by the German scientist August Weismann and the Austrian monk Gregor Mendel, his main thesis quickly gained general acceptance in the scientific world.

Few books in history have had so much influence as *The Origin of Species* (the religious storm it created in the Western world will be discussed in Chapter 52). The industrial bourgeoisie seized upon Darwin's theory as an explanation and a justification of its own success. Rulers and dominant groups everywhere derived comfort from it. Philosophers, notably Herbert Spencer, undertook to broaden the principle of evolution to make it the key to all truth. Meanwhile, Darwin's brilliant work not only popularized, but significantly contributed to the advancement of the biological sciences.

5. THE DEVELOPMENT OF MEDICAL SCIENCE

Medical science lagged far behind the physical and biological sciences at the opening of the nineteenth century. The seventeenth- and eighteenth-century scientists had made great progress in discovering the secrets of the stars, of

---

[1]The chief apostle of the transmission of acquired characteristics was the French naturalist Jean Baptiste de Lamarck (1744–1829). Darwin was unhappy with this theory, but he did not have sufficient knowledge of the laws of genetics to be able to refute it. The theory was generally accepted in Darwin's time. Darwin did relegate it to a secondary position in his evolutionary hypothesis, however.

the elements, and of plants and animals, but where the ailments of the human body were concerned, they were still holding to theories of the second century A.D. Greek physician Galen. The medical profession was a lowly one. George Washington was bled to death in 1799 by a physician who was following the standard practice of the time.

Much groundwork had been laid, however, for medical progress. In the sixteenth century Vesalius made great advances in the study of human anatomy. In the seventeenth century Harvey discovered the circulatory system, while Leeuwenhoek and Malpighi were using the newly invented microscope to explore the structure of human tissue and to discover the existence of microbes. By the late eighteenth century the British physician Edward Jenner was successfully inoculating against smallpox, though he did not understand the secret of its success. During the 1840s anesthesia was discovered and used successfully. But the whole field of germ diseases and infections was still a mystery.

The secrets of bacteria, their nature and their control, began to be discovered first by the French chemist Louis Pasteur (1822–1895). During the 1860s Pasteur, after indefatigable and imaginative research, discovered that fermentation is caused by bacteria that move through the air and can be destroyed by boiling (or by pasteurization). Later he discovered that many diseases of man and animals are also caused by bacteria and that some of them can be prevented by vaccination. His spectacular services to French agriculture and to mankind made him the most honored man in France. Robert Koch (1843–1910), a humble country doctor in Eastern Germany, hearing of Pasteur's first discoveries, picked up the trail and discovered the germs causing anthrax (a deadly disease of cattle), tuberculosis, sleeping sickness, and many other diseases. He became a professor at the University of Berlin and was awarded the Nobel prize. Also building on Pasteur's foundations was the renowned British surgeon Joseph Lister (1827–1912), who applied the new knowledge of bacteria to the use of antisepsis and eventually asepsis in surgery. His amazing success in controlling infection opened a new era in surgery, and

Lister was raised to the peerage by the British government. The honors bestowed upon Pasteur, Koch, and Lister, in contrast with the persecutions suffered by so many of the sixteenth- and seventeenth-century scientists, are striking evidence of the triumph of science and the scientific spirit in the nineteenth century. In the last decades of that century, the governments of the European and Europeanized countries began to recognize that health is a public matter by passing health and sanitation laws.

6. THE RISE OF SOCIAL SCIENCE

The spectacular successes of the natural sciences in the nineteenth century encouraged scholars to attempt to apply the techniques and principles of natural science to the study of man's mind and of society. The result was the birth of two new sciences, psychology and sociology, both of which soon became popular. The functioning of the mind has, of course, long been a matter of great interest to man. During the vogue of materialistic and mechanistic concepts of the universe in the eighteenth and again in the late nineteenth centuries, the tendency was to make the human brain mechanical in its operations. This mechanistic approach to psychology came to be called behaviorism. John Locke (1632–1704) had laid the foundations for behavioristic psychology by maintaining that man's mind operates mechanically, as does Newton's universe. Locke believed that the human brain at birth is a blank sheet of paper on which nothing would ever be written except by the perceptions of the five senses as interpreted by reason. The first behaviorist to bring psychology into the laboratory was Wilhelm Wundt (1832–1920). In his famous laboratory at Leipzig he and his enthusiastic students tested human reactions and tried all sorts of carefully controlled and measured experiments on cats and dogs, assuming that the findings would also be applicable to human beings.

The Russian scientist Ivan Pavlov (1849–1936), pursuing Wundt's line of attack, excited the intellectual world with the discovery of the conditioned reflex. Pavlov showed meat to a hungry dog and the dog's mouth watered. Then Pavlov rang a bell while showing the meat. Eventually the dog's mouth watered when only the bell was rung. The immediate and fascinating implication was that many of our human responses are purely mechanical reflexes produced by stimuli of which we are often unaware. This was a big step toward the concept of the mechanization of the mind and body of man. The Italian Cesare Lombroso (1836–1909) argued that criminals are born with mental and physical aberrations and are therefore not morally responsible for their acts. The Frenchman Alfred Binet (1857–1911) devised tests for measuring intelligence; variations of his tests are still used today in schools.

The greatest stir of all in the rapidly growing field of psychology was created by the Austrian scientist Sigmund Freud (1856–1939). Freud believed that much neurosis and abnormality are the result of suppressed and frustrated drives of early life, particularly the sex drive—frustrations that then fester in the subconscious. He came to the conclusion that the correct therapy for such neurosis was to bring to the consciousness of the sufferer the facts and circumstances of the original frustration. Freud achieved some remarkable cures, and founded psychoanalysis. His influence on the development of modern psychiatry has been great. The implications of Freud's theories had a profound effect upon pedagogy in the twentieth century, especially in the United States. Many parents and teachers refused to discipline children for fear of frustrating them and giving them Freudian complexes.

It was not psychology, however, but sociology that in the nineteenth century claimed the title, "queen of the social sciences." This new study was founded and named by Auguste Comte (1798–1857), an eccentric Frenchman of great energy and imagination. The history of mankind, said Comte, may be divided into three epochs. The first was religious, when mystical or supernatural explanations were assigned to all phenomena. The second was metaphysical, when general laws and abstract principles were taken as explanatory principles. The third, which man was on the point of entering, was the specific or positive, when the truth would be discovered by the scientific gathering of factual data. Comte had utter scorn for the first and little respect for the second epoch. He believed that man and society are as susceptible to scientific investigation as minerals, plants, and the lower animals. His religion was the worship of humanity, and he had great faith in the future of mankind. These ideas are called *positivism*. Comte's followers, eager and numerous, placed great faith in statistics. They amassed vast arrays of statistical data on every conceivable social problem. They tended to scorn supernatural religion of all kinds, morals and ideals, chronological history, and individual biography.

Second only to Comte in importance in the founding and promotion of sociology was the Englishman Herbert Spencer (1820–1903). Spencer shared Comte's scorn for mystical religion and denied that morals should be based upon religion. He also shared Comte's faith in the progress of man. In his ten-volume *System of Synthetic Philosophy*, Spencer undertook to synthesize all human and social phenomena into one grand evolutionary system.

Man's natural interest in himself and in human society, together with the scientific spirit of the times, guaranteed for the social sciences great popularity. Anthropologists and archeologists dug feverishly into man's physical and cultural past. Political scientists and economists tended to forsake theory for the statistical and "practical." Strenuous efforts were made to make history a social science. Leopold von Ranke (1795–1886) strove to make history coldly scientific and morally neutral. History, he insisted, should be based upon an exhaustive accumulation and analysis of documentary evidence. Ranke's historical attitude and methodology were imported from Germany into the United States. They became the standard in both countries. Efforts were also made to make history topical and statistical, rather than chronological, and to focus upon social trends and forces rather than individuals. During the late nineteenth and early twentieth centuries this approach was very popular, particularly in Germany and the United States.

To a visitor from Mars it must have appeared that the Western world in 1914 was on the brink of Utopia. Better and better machines, driven by greater and greater power, were turning out more and more goods and labor-saving devices every day. Natural scientists appeared to be solving the last mysteries of the material universe. Medical scientists appeared to be banishing pain and disease from the earth. Social scientists were amassing voluminous knowledge about man's mind and his social relationships. The cult of progress enjoyed wide popularity.

Suggested Reading

General

*C. J. H. Hayes, *A Generation of Materialism, 1871–1900* (Torch). One of the best of the scholarly Rise of Modern Europe series.

*L. Mumford, *Technics and Civilization* (Harbinger). Attempt to show the social influence of the rise of technology.

Rapid Growth of Industry

*A. Usher, *A History of Mechanical Inventions* (Beacon). Still the best on the subject.

Growth of Business Monopoly

*Ida M. Tarbell, *History of the Standard Oil Company* (Norton). Written in a popular style, this book helped to inspire Congress to pass more effective antimonopoly legislation.

Onrush of Natural Science

W. P. D. Wightman, *The Growth of Scientific Ideas* (1951). Good for nineteenth century.

*G. Himmelfarb, *Darwin and the Darwinian Revolution* (Norton). A brief useful work.

D. Guthrie, *A History of Medicine* (1948). Good survey.

Sources

*C. Darwin, *On the Origin of Species by Natural Selection and the Descent of Man* (Modern Library). Lucid and fascinating.

*S. Freud, *An Outline of Psychoanalysis* (Norton). A history-making book. Easy to read.

49

THE MOVEMENT OF THE MASSES[1]

The first phase of the Industrial Revolution brought the industrial bourgeoisie to power in the industrialized countries. The industrial proletariat was too small, too impoverished, and too bewildered to make its influence strongly felt. It is true that it had stirred on occasion, as in 1830 and 1848, but it had been suppressed with relative ease. During the second phase of the Industrial Revolution, however, not only the industrial proletariat, its numbers greatly augmented by the rapid growth of industry, but the masses in general began to assert themselves.

1. THE GROWTH OF POPULATION AND THE GREAT MIGRATIONS

Prior to the Industrial Revolution, the population of Europe was largely rural, relatively stable in size, and immobile. During the course of the nineteenth century, it changed drastically in all three respects. The total population of Europe, which had begun to increase moderately but definitely about the middle of the seventeenth century, is believed to have more than doubled during the nineteenth century. At the same time there was a great movement of people from country to city and from Europe to overseas areas, chiefly the United States. These changes were at their peak between 1871 and 1914. For a time it was believed that the world's birth rate had suddenly jumped. It would now appear that this was not true and that, in Europe at least, the

birth rate actually declined after 1871. The revolutionary advances in medicine brought the death rate sharply down; technology and science greatly increased the production and distribution of food; the humble potato fed additional millions as it came into wider use. The movement to the city was brought about by the opportunities in industry and commerce, the growing attractiveness of urban life, and the application of mechanization and science to agriculture, which now required fewer workers to produce greater yields. Urban population exceeded rural in England by 1850, in Germany by 1914, and in the United States by 1920. It is estimated that in the period 1871–1914 more than a hundred million Europeans moved from the country to the city. By 1914 Western civilization was definitely urban.

The overseas migration of Europeans between 1871 and 1914 was phenomenal. Ever since the first settlements in the New World, there had been a sizable trickle of Europeans to the Americas. This trickle had become a flowing stream in the mid-nineteenth century. During the second phase of the Industrial Revolution (1871–1914), it swelled into a rushing torrent. In this brief span of forty-three years, more than 30 million

---

[1]For many of the facts and figures in this chapter the authors are gratefully indebted to Carlton J. H. Hayes, *A Generation of Materialism, 1871–1900* (New York: Harper & Brothers, 1941).

Europeans left their homelands and migrated to the New World or to the British dominion territories. The great bulk of them came to the United States. Never in history had there been such a movement of peoples. The great folk migrations of ancient and medieval times were puny by comparison. These mass migrations were made possible, of course, by the improvements in transportation—railroads and steamships. In addition to the migrations, many more people were now traveling for pleasure. With the coming of the automobile at the turn of the century, so much of mankind took to wheels that tourism eventually became one of the world's biggest businesses. The masses were truly on the move, but not just physically; they were on the move politically, socially, and economically as well.

2. THE MARCH OF DEMOCRACY IN THE UNITED STATES AND GREAT BRITAIN

The period 1830–1871 was marked in most of the Western world by the increasing vogue of liberal, constitutional, and limited government under the domination of the bourgeoisie. The period 1871–1914 was characterized by a surge toward democracy—government of, by, and for the masses. The most democratic nations in the world in 1871 were the United States, Great Britain, France, and Switzerland.

In the United States the great majority of white males had enjoyed the ballot long before the colonies had gained their independence. In 1870 the Fifteenth Amendment granted the recently freed Negroes political equality with the whites, although most of them were illegally denied the ballot in the Southern states. Between 1890 and 1914, eleven Western states gave the ballot to women, and in 1920 the Nineteenth Amendment granted women equal political rights with men. But universal suffrage does not in itself guarantee real democracy. From the death of Lincoln in 1865 until Theodore Roosevelt took office in 1901, the government and the economy of the country were dominated by big business interests that controlled the dominant "Old Guard" wing of the Republican party. Although this was a period of enormous overall economic development, wealth was very unequally distributed. Western and Southern farmers clamored for public regulation of the railroads, upon which they were dependent. Small business, labor, and the consumer demanded protection against the monopolistic practices and prices of the great trusts, which were protected by a prohibitively high tariff. Millions deplored the city slums, the corrupt spoils system in the civil service, and the squandering of natural resources by private interests.

In the years between 1871 and 1914, more than 30 million Europeans migrated from their homelands to settle overseas, most of them in the United States. This photograph of immigrants arriving in New York shows the conditions under which they traveled—jammed together in a small space for a long and sometimes rough sea voyage. *Photo: Museum of the City of New York*

The first great political leader to rally the discontented to a crusade for reform was William Jennings Bryan (1860–1925). Although the silver-tongued Democrat electrified the masses with his eloquence and made three tries for the presidency, he failed to break the grip of the Republican Old Guard. The next great reform crusader to appear on the American political scene was the liberal "progressive" Republican Theodore Roosevelt (1858–1919), who adopted much of Bryan's philosophy (with the appearance of Bryan and Theodore Roosevelt, the term *liberal* took on the post-1871 meaning in America; see pp. 499–501).

No public figure had ever so caught the imagination of the American people as the youthful, swashbuckling, "roughrider," hero of the Spanish-American War, Teddy Roosevelt. After assuming the Presidency in 1901 upon the assassination of McKinley, "T.R.," as he was popularly known, immediately launched a vigorous program of reform. The Interstate Commerce Act of 1887 and the Sherman Anti-Trust Act of 1890, which had lain dormant, were activated. Organized labor was given support in its unequal fight with organized capital. Pure food and drug acts were designed to restrict the corporations and safeguard the public health.

Roosevelt was a strong believer in the conservation of natural resources. More than 200 million acres of forest and mineral lands and water power sites were withheld from private exploitation. He also continued to work for the strengthening of the merit system in the federal civil service. Many of his reform efforts were blocked by Congress and the federal courts, which were still controlled by the Republican Old Guard. Roosevelt firmly believed in the capitalistic system, but he was convinced that the time had come when the superiority of the government over business must be asserted.

When Roosevelt's hand-picked successor, William Howard Taft, exhibited a disappointing lack of zeal in pushing the Progressive reform program and joined hands with the reactionary wing of the Republican party, T.R. ran against him in 1912 with the support of the Progressive Republicans. The split in the Republican ranks

gave the Democrats, under the leadership of Woodrow Wilson (1856–1924), their first clear-cut victory since the Civil War. In fact, many of the Old Guard are believed to have voted for Wilson, whom they did not know, in preference to the "terrible Teddy," whom they did know. Wilson, however, proved to be more liberal than Roosevelt. With the Democrats in control of both houses of Congress, Wilson's administration sharply lowered the tariff, passed the Clayton Anti-Trust Act (more specific than the Sherman Act), gave further encouragement to organized labor, and set up the Federal Reserve Banking System, which removed control of the nation's financial policies from the hands of private interests on Wall Street and placed them in the hands of the federal government.

After woman suffrage was granted in 1920, the biggest flaw remaining in American democracy was the refusal of the Southern states to allow blacks to exercise their constitutional right to vote.

Politically, if not socially, Great Britain, the mother of parliamentary government, kept pace with the United States in the march toward liberal democracy. Britain still had her royalty (though her sovereign was now a figurehead), her lords and ladies, an established Church, and a people very respectful of law and tradition. However, the Reform Bill of 1867 had enfranchised the bulk of the industrial proletariat, and William E. Gladstone's Reform Bill of 1884 enfranchised most of the rural males. After 1884 virtually every male householder or renter in Great Britain could vote. Restricted women suffrage came in 1918 and full suffrage in 1928. The Parliamentary Reform Act of 1911 stripped the House of Lords of most of its former power and made the popularly elected House of Commons supreme. Yet until the end of the nineteenth century, both the Conservative and Liberal parties were controlled by the aristocracy and the wealthy bourgeoisie. Although both parties were fairly benevolent toward the working classes, the large and discontented industrial proletariat wanted its fair share in the government. Between 1881 and 1906 its leaders turned to a program of moderate Socialism, and with the aid of a number of intellectual radicals, notably George Bernard Shaw, H. G. Wells, and Sidney and Beatrice Webb, the Labour party was formed.

In 1906 the rejuvenated Liberal party came to power under the actual, if not official, leadership of the fiery young Welshman David Lloyd George, who also had the backing of the Labour party. Between 1906 and 1911 Lloyd George put through Parliament a revolutionary program of accident, sickness, old-age, and unemployment insurance. To meet this and other increased costs to the government, he forced through the reluctant House of Lords his famous budget of 1909, which shifted the "heaviest burden [of taxation] to the broadest backs." A steeply graduated income tax and high taxes on unearned increment, inheritances, idle parks of the landed aristocracy, and mining royalties struck heavily at the rich. By 1914 Great Britain was well on the road to social and economic as well as political democracy.

Between 1867 and 1909 she granted self-governing dominion status to Canada, Australia, New Zealand, and the Union of South Africa. In 1914 she at long last even granted self-government to Ireland, although the outbreak of World War I in that year delayed its implementation until 1922.

3. DEMOCRATIC ADVANCES ON THE CONTINENT OF EUROPE

During the second phase of the Industrial Revolution, liberal democracy was much less secure in France than in the United States and Great Britain. With the end of the Second Empire of Napoleon III during the Franco-German War of 1870–1871, the Third French Republic was proclaimed. However, the first elections, held in February 1871, after the surrender of Paris, resulted in a sweeping victory for the monarchists. This somewhat surprising result may be explained by the fact that the republican leaders wanted to continue the unpopular and hopeless war with Germany. The city of Paris, made up largely of the liberal bourgeoisie and the radical proletariat, was unwilling to submit to the domination of conservative rural France. It declared its independence from the rest of France and set up its own city government, or commune. Two months (April–May 1871) of fighting, culminating in a week of all-out warfare in the streets of Paris, were required for the rest of the French nation to subdue the Paris Commune. Some 20,000 Parisians were executed and 7,500 were deported. This tragedy further frightened the conservatives.

The royalists, though in the majority, were split into a Bourbon faction and an Orléanist faction, neither of which was willing to yield to the other. Meanwhile, the liberals grew in strength. Finally, in 1875, the frustrated and frightened monarchists consented (by a single vote) to the adoption of a republican constitution. The constitution provided for a Chamber of Deputies elected by universal male suffrage, a Senate elected by a complicated indirect method, and a rather powerless president to be elected by the two legislative bodies. Most of the executive functions of the republic were to be carried on by a cabinet of ministers dependent upon the Chamber of Deputies. It was not until four years later, however, that the liberal republicans under the leadership of the eloquent Léon Gambetta gained actual control of the republic.

But the Third French Republic, so furtively born, was still not safe. Powerful groups were hostile to it. The chief of these were the various factions of monarchists (Bourbons, Orléanists, and Bonapartists), the professional military, the Roman Catholic hierarchy, and large numbers of peasant proprietors. In the late 1880s these factions rallied around a handsome man on horseback, General Boulanger, who became so popular that he might have overthrown the republic had he been bolder and more skillful or had the republican leaders been less courageous. As it turned out, when he was summoned to answer charges of treason against the republic, he fled the country and committed suicide. In the 1890s the antirepublican forces rallied again around a group of army officers who had falsely accused a Jewish army captain, Alfred Dreyfus, and sent him to prison on Devil's Island. This time the enemies of the republic were aided by a rising militant nationalism and anti-Semitism. It required twelve years for the republicans, inspired by the novelist, Emile Zola, to get Dreyfus acquitted and the army officers who had imprisoned him punished. The Dreyfus case strengthened the republic and discredited its enemies.

Democratic government did not work so smoothly in France as in the United States and Great Britain. The Voltairian tradition of extreme individualism, the animosity between clericalist and anticlericalist, the sharp cleavage between radical urban Paris and conservative rural France, lingering provincial loyalty, and a historic suspicion of strong government and high taxes—all contributed to the formation of a multiplicity of political parties. This meant that the cabinet was forced to rely on the support of a precarious combination of parties (a *bloc*) in order to carry on the executive functions of government. In France the Chamber of Deputies could overthrow a cabinet without having to risk an immediate national election, as was the case in Great Britain. As a result, there was a rapid turnover of French ministries. During the forty-three years from 1871 to 1914, no fewer than 51 ministries attempted to govern France. Nevertheless, the French government was not so unstable as it might appear. As cabinets rose and fell, the actual details of administration were carried on with relatively little interruption by a stable civil service, firmly built in the tradition of Richelieu and Napoleon I.

As the twentieth century opened, democratic government in France appeared to be firmly established and increasingly responsive to the will of the masses. Factory laws were giving the workers increased protection. Between 1905 and 1910, a limited program of unemployment, old-age, accident, and sickness insurance was inaugurated. This program of social legislation, however, was only a modest beginning, and the French masses, becoming more politically conscious and active, expressed their discontent in strikes and more votes for the Socialists.

Switzerland is a shining example of what democratic government can do. Surrounded by dangerous potential enemies, split into three language groups (German, French, and Italian)

and two major religions (Calvinist and Roman Catholic), she has nonetheless enjoyed peace and political stability ever since the overthrow of Napoleon in 1815. In 1848 she set up the Swiss Federal Republic, with authority neatly balanced between the central government and the twenty-two cantons, and universal male suffrage—the first permanent universal male suffrage in the world. Under this democratic government the Swiss have been prosperous and progressive.

The peoples of the smaller countries of Northern Europe also witnessed the triumph of democratic government during this period. Belgium adopted universal male suffrage in 1893. Here the weighted vote was established, men of wealth and education getting two or three additional votes. The Dutch Netherlands extended the suffrage in 1887 and again in 1896; in 1917 the suffrage was made universal. Norway adopted universal male suffrage in 1898, Sweden in 1909, and Denmark in 1914. In 1913 Norway became the first European country to grant the vote to women. In these five nations, the traditional respect for government and the relatively high degree of literacy made democracy a vigorous reality.

In Spain and Austria universal male suffrage was granted in 1907, in Italy in 1912, and in all Balkan states except Serbia and Rumania by 1914. In these areas, however, the illiteracy, poverty, and political inexperience of the people combined with a traditional suspicion of all government to make democracy unstable. In Austria, the clashes among the various language groups further hamstrung the functioning of democracy. In Hungary, there was no progress toward liberal democracy at all.

Even in authoritarian and disciplined Germany and autocratic Russia, the increasing clamor of the people for active participation in the government was heard. In order to lessen the appeal of the Socialists to the German workingman, Bismarck in the decade of the 1880s inaugurated a program of social insurance (see pp. 563–565). Nevertheless, in the German elections of 1912, the Social Democratic (workingmen's) party polled approximately one-third of the total vote and became the largest party in the

Reichstag. Universal male suffrage had existed since the setting up of the empire in 1871. But the popularly elected Reichstag lacked the prestige and power of the lower houses in the United States, Great Britain, and France. Nor did it control the cabinet as in Great Britain and France. The cabinet, which administered the executive functions of the government, was responsible only to the Kaiser who remained, in large measure, an autocrat.

In Russia the liberals, taking advantage of Russia's defeat in the Russo-Japanese War of 1904–1905, forced Tsar Nicholas II (1894–1917) to set up a representative Duma, although it too had no real control over the government. In both Germany and Russia between 1871 and 1914, authoritarian government and militaristic nationalism were much stronger forces than was liberal democracy. Therefore, their history will be examined in the following chapter.

Also conspicuously lagging in the march toward democracy in this period was Latin America. Most of this vast area is made up of lofty mountains, arid wastes, or steaming jungle, and the Industrial Revolution had made little headway there. Its masses were poverty-stricken and illiterate. Although its twenty governments were all republics in form (Brazil after 1891 and Cuba after 1900), they were really dictatorships of strong and often violent men.

4. POPULAR EDUCATION AND JOURNALISM

If democratic government was to function effectively, the electorate had to be literate and reasonably well informed, for a democratic government cannot rise and remain very long above the level of the voters who sustain it. Fortunately for democracy, therefore, the second phase of the Industrial Revolution was also a period of great advances in popular education in the industrialized areas. Contributing to this development were urbanization, improvements in transportation, the increase in wealth, and the growing confidence and ambition of the masses.

In 1871 northern Germany and Scandinavia were the only places in the world where practically everyone could read and write. In the United States most of the states had free public elementary schools, but a fifth of the total population was still illiterate (a figure so high because it included the large black population in the South only recently freed from slavery). In Great Britain a third of the people were still illiterate, in France and Belgium a half, in Spain and Italy three-fourths, in Russia and the Balkans nine-tenths, and in Latin America all except a very few. Between 1868 and 1881 national systems of free and compulsory public education were established in nearly all the nations of Western and Central Europe and the United States. For the most part, the systems were as yet limited to elementary schools. Nevertheless, by 1914 illiteracy had practically ceased to exist in Scandinavia, Germany, Great Britain, and the Netherlands. The illiteracy rate was less than 10 percent in the United States, Canada, France, and Belgium. In Italy it had been reduced to 50 percent, in Spain, Russia, and the Balkans to a little more than 50 percent. In Latin America, Argentina and Chile had made noteworthy inroads on the mass illiteracy. Literacy, of course, is only the first step toward education. The enormous and difficult task of really educating the masses remained.

Hardly less potent than public education as an influence on the minds of the restless masses was popular journalism. In 1871 newspapers were relatively few, small, expensive, and written for a limited educated clientele. The London *Times,* probably the world's most influential newspaper, had a daily circulation of some fifty thousand. However, the second phase of the Industrial Revolution — with its improved machinery, transportation, and communications; the growth of liberalism, which stood for freedom of the press; and above all the growing literacy of the masses — brought forth a new kind of newspaper, one that was cheap, sensational, and popular in its appeal. One of the pioneer popular journalists was Joseph Pulitzer (1847–1911), a Hungarian immigrant to the United States. Pulitzer founded the St. Louis *Post Dispatch* and bought and built up the New York *World* until it became the country's biggest newspaper. With screaming headlines, flag-waving patriotism, easy catchy style, sensational news, popular causes and features, and, above all, comics, he made a fortune and became a great influence in politics. His comic strip *The Yellow Kid* was so popular and sought after by other newspapers that it gave the name "yellow journalism" to the new type of publication. In the 1890s William Randolph Hearst built a great newspaper empire patterned after Pulitzer's. In Great Britain Alfred Harmsworth founded the halfpenny popular *Daily Mail*, made a fortune, became Lord Northcliffe, and bought the London *Times* itself. Before the end of the century five newspapers—two in London, two in Paris, and one in Berlin—had a daily circulation of more than a million each. *Le Petit Journal* in Paris had a circulation of more than two and a quarter million. This type of newspaper not only catered to the masses, but also became a powerful molder of public opinion. Hearst boasted, with a modicum of truth, that he manufactured the Spanish-American War. Since the popular newspapers made their money chiefly from advertising rather than from sales, they came increasingly to reflect the viewpoints of their chief advertisers, the great corporations. The big newspapers were themselves, of course, big business. Although they catered to the masses, they did not always represent their interests.

5. LABOR UNIONS AND COOPERATIVES

One of the most important manifestations of the movement of the masses in the second phase of the Industrial Revolution was the formation of labor unions and various types of cooperatives. Democratic legislation, public education, and popular journalism were, for the most part, things done *for* the masses, not *by* them. Labor unions and cooperatives, however, represented direct action by the masses themselves. Wherever industrialization occurred, distressed laborers almost immediately attempted to protect themselves by banding together. However, until around 1871, inexperience, poverty, hostile governments, and unfavorable public opinion caused most of their efforts to fail. Antilabor-union laws were not fully repealed in Great Britain until 1875. In France they were not fully repealed until 1884. In Germany, Bismarck persecuted labor unions until his dismissal in 1890. During the 1870s and early 1880s, the union movement in Europe was limited chiefly to skilled workmen, organized by crafts, who were moderate in their aims and methods.

In the late 1880s unionization spread rapidly to unskilled workmen, cut across craft lines, and adopted socialistic programs (often Marxist) and more violent methods. In Great Britain the labor unions formed the national Trades Union Congress in 1868, and later they became identified with the Labour party, which was founded between 1881 and 1906. In Germany the individual unions formed in 1890 a national organization that was frankly Marxist. In France in 1895 the various unions banded together in the giant CGT (Confédération Générale du Travail—General Confederation of Labor) with an extreme Marxist (syndicalist) program. In the United States the unionization of labor was retarded by the abundance of free land (until the 1890s), and by the influx of cheap labor from Europe. It was not until 1886 that Samuel Gompers, an immigrant from Great Britain, organized the American Federation of Labor, the first successful national labor organization in America. The AFL was a federation of craft unions of skilled workers. It was nonpolitical in its aims and relatively moderate in its methods, and it grew rapidly. By 1914 the proletariat in the industrialized countries was sufficiently large and organized (though only a minority was as yet unionized) to make itself a power to be reckoned with, both in the factories and mines and at the polls.

Meanwhile, a much bigger portion of the masses was participating in the milder cooperatives of various types. In 1910 in Great Britain membership in cooperative retail stores, fraternal insurance (friendly) societies, and credit associations is estimated to have been some 14 million, the great bulk of whom were wage earners. These organizations also provided much-needed social fellowship for the proletariat. In the 1880s Denmark became the home of the agricultural cooperative movement. By 1914 nearly all of Denmark's agricultural commodities were cooperatively produced and marketed, and the movement had spread to most of Northern Europe, to Italy, and to the United States.

6. MARXIAN SOCIALISM

The most radical movement of the masses during the second phase of the Industrial Revolution was Marxian socialism. Strictly speaking, Marxism was not really a movement of the masses, but rather a movement for the masses begun and carried on by small groups, usually intellectuals. Nevertheless, its influence on the masses between 1871 and 1914 was significant, and since 1914 it has been an enormous factor in world history. It was a product and a compound of various nineteenth-century forces—industrialism, materialism, science, Hegelian philosophy, Darwinian concepts, and the momentary confusion and decline of Christianity. Nor should the influence of the eighteenth-century Enlightenment and the French Revolution be overlooked. Its founder, Karl Marx (1818–1883), was a brilliant Prussian Jew who, having attained his Ph.D. in philosophy and history, was denied an academic position. Exiled from Prussia and later from France because of his radical ideas, he spent the last thirty-four years of his life in London. Marx collaborated with his friend Friedrich Engels, son of a wealthy German manufacturer, in writing the *Communist Manifesto* (1848) and *Das Kapital*, the first volume of which appeared in 1867. These two works present the chief fundamentals of the Marxist philosophy, known in the twentieth century as communism. Although Marx's ideas continually evolved and are often contradictory, the salient points of his philosophy are as follows:

ECONOMIC INTERPRETATION OF HISTORY

The good things of life are material. "Religion is the opiate of the people," an ideological veil behind which the "haves" achieve their selfish purposes. The dominant characteristic of a historical epoch is its prevailing system of production, which determines every phase of human culture.

CLASS STRUGGLE

"The history of all hitherto existing society is the history of class struggles"; in ancient times freeman versus slave; in medieval times landlord versus serf; in modern times capital versus labor. The bourgeoisie, having overcome the aristocracy, will in time be displaced by the proletariat.

SURPLUS VALUE

The one fundamental law of capitalist economy is the law of surplus value. The worker, who is paid only a subsistence wage, creates, by his work, value in excess of his wage. This excess value is the source of profit for the capitalist.

INEVITABILITY OF COMMUNISM

The working of the law of surplus value makes it impossible for wages ever to catch up with prices. If wages should be raised, the profit differential working in an accumulative manner will raise even higher the price of the commodity that the worker has to buy back from the capitalist. The capitalists will become richer and fewer; the workers will become poorer and more numerous. Furthermore, the capitalistic system is characterized by alternating periods of prosperity and depression and wars resulting from the rivalries of economic imperialism. Under capitalism, then, the law of surplus value plus boom, bust, and war will finally produce such misery that someday, in a time of depression or war, the workingmen will stage a giant revolution, destroy the capitalistic system, and set up a classless society. Meanwhile, the proletariat must fan the flames of class hatred, sabotage capitalistic governments, and work constantly for their final destruction.

INTERNATIONALISM

Workers in all countries have more in common with each other than they have with the capitalists of their own country. Therefore workers should unite and obliterate national boundary lines in their struggle against the common enemy—the bourgeoisie.

After Marx's death, his followers, though they split into various groups, tended to regard him as a religious prophet. Indeed, Marx appears to have regarded himself somewhat as a prophet, for he spoke in dogmatic absolutes and in grandiose and stirring, though often vague, phraseology. The most important figure to arise among Marx's orthodox followers was the Russian intellectual Nikolai Lenin (1870–1924). Lenin, a much more effective organizer and leader than Marx, advocated a more positive and violent type of revolutionary activity carried on by a small, highly trained, and constantly purged group of dedicated men. Lenin's greatest influence came after 1914 (see Chapter 55). The chief development in Marxism from the death of Marx in 1883 to 1914 was a moderate revisionism, led by the German socialist Eduard Bernstein. The revisionists became tired of working and waiting for the total collapse of capitalism. Things were not going as Marx had predicted. The rich were not becoming fewer nor the poor poorer. In fact, the condition of the workingmen was steadily improving. Bernstein advocated cooperation with the capitalistic classes to obtain all the practical benefits possible for labor here and now and a gradual approach to socialism.

In Germany, where socialism had its greatest success before 1914, the Social Democratic party adopted in practice, if not in theory, this more moderate type of Marxism during the 1890s. By 1914 it was able to poll some 4½ million votes and had become the largest party in Germany. The French Socialists were more radical and violent than the Germans. In 1905 the orthodox and the revisionist wings of the French Socialists joined to form the United Socialist party under the leadership of the scholar-orator, Jean Jaurès. By 1914 they numbered a million and a half voters and had 110 seats in the Chamber of Deputies. Contrary to the expectations of Marx, socialism in Great Britain was weak and mild. Among the earliest British Socialists were George Bernard Shaw, H. G. Wells, and Sidney and Beatrice Webb. These intellectual radicals formed the Fabian Society, which was committed to moderation and gradualism. The Labour party, founded between 1881 and 1906, was also mild and grew slowly before 1914. Neither the Fabian Society nor the Labour party could be called Marx-

ist, although both were influenced by Marx. In the United States, too, the socialist movement was relatively weak and (in retrospect) mild. The first prominent American Socialist, Eugene V. Debs, did manage to poll nearly a million votes in 1912 and again in 1920. In 1920 he conducted his campaign from a jail cell, where he had been placed because of his opposition to America's participation in World War I.

Marxism probably set back the rise of the masses in the Western world by many decades. It frightened the propertied classes, intensified class hatred, and played into the hands of demagogues and dictators at a time when the masses were beginning to gain a greater voice in government, educational advantages, and a larger share of this world's goods and privileges.

7. ANARCHISM

A radical and violent movement that has been falsely associated with Marxist socialism in the minds of many people is anarchism. The two movements are alike in that they are anticapitalist and violent, but they seek opposite goals. Although Marx talked vaguely about the eventual "withering away of the state," Marxists in reality have always striven to make the state omnipotent. Anarchists, by contrast, would do away with the state entirely.

The most influential contributor to anarchist thought and action was Michael Bakunin (1814–1876), a Russian nobleman. Exiled from Russia, he would turn up wherever in Europe antiestablished violence was brewing. He believed that mankind is by nature good. He would destroy all institutions that restrict man—the state, the capitalistic system, the church, the family. And he would do this by direct action—strikes, sabotage, assassination.

The anarchists and their fellow terrorists provided cartoonists with bearded, wild-eyed, bomb-throwing stereotypes. But they were not a laughing matter; among their victims were Tsar Alexander II of Russia in 1881, President Carnot of France in 1894, King Humbert of Italy in 1900, and President McKinley of the United States in 1901.

Suggested Reading

General

*C. J. H. Hayes, *A Generation of Materialism, 1871–1900* (Torch). Has a scholarly, fact-filled chapter, "The Emergence of the Masses."

*C. Cipalla, *The Economic History of World Population* (Penguin). Good brief survey.

Democratic Advances in the United States and Great Britain

*H. Pringle, *Theodore Roosevelt* (Harvest Books). Popularly written.

A. Link, *Woodrow Wilson: The New Freedom* (1956). The second volume of Link's projected eight-volume biography.

R. C. K. Ensor, *England, 1870–1914*, rev. ed. (1949). A standard account.

Democratic Advances on the European Continent

D. W. Brogan, *France Under the Republic* (1940). By a leading authority.

Popular Education and Journalism

P. Monroe, *A Textbook in the History of Education*, rev. ed. (1932). An old standby. Reliable.

C. F. Carr and F. E. Stevens, *Modern Journalism* (1931). Good chapters on the period 1871–1914.

Labor Unions and Cooperatives

W. Galenson, ed., *Comparative Labor Movements* (1952). Best general survey.

Marxism

*I. Berlin, *Karl Marx: His Life and Environment* (Galaxy). Probably the best brief biography.

*A. G. Meyer, *Marxism Since the Communist Manifesto* (Macmillan). Excellent brief survey.

Sources

*K. Marx and F. Engels, *Basic Writings on Politics and Philosophy* (Anchor). A handy selection.

50

MALIGNANT NATIONALISM: MILITARISM

Between 1871 and 1914 much of the enthusiasm and energy of the masses was channeled into the rapidly swelling stream of national patriotic fervor. From its birth during the French Revolution until 1871, mass nationalism had been for the most part relatively mild, constructive, and often defensive. It was usually associated with liberalism and concerned with the achievement of national freedom and unity. After 1871, it became more aggressive and militaristic. Politicians and journalists used it to manipulate public opinion. Generals used it to invigorate their armies. It became in its totality (including the construction and maintenance of huge military establishments, wars, and imperialism) the world's biggest business. Although the new nationalism was a strong and important force in Great Britain, France, and the United States during the second phase of the Industrial Revolution, it was somewhat overshadowed in those countries by the growth of political and economic democracy. In Germany, Russia, and Southeastern Europe, just the reverse was true. There progress toward liberalization and democratization was overshadowed by militaristic nationalism.

1. GENERAL NATURE OF THE NEW NATIONALISM

The chief model and inspiration for the new nationalism was Bismarck's Prussia. At a time when the whole Western world seemed to be moving toward liberalism and democracy, Bismarck had crushed liberal opposition at home. He had also defeated Austria, which had long overshadowed Prussia in the Germanies, and then France, long the foremost military power on the continent of Europe and a nation with a liberal tradition. The autocratic, militaristic German Empire which he welded together was the world's most powerful and seemingly most efficient nation. The Prussian exploits appeared to bear out the evolutionary teachings of Darwin and Spencer with respect to the survival of the fittest. Most of the Prussian liberals who had first opposed Bismarck now repented and sought and received forgiveness. The rest of the world was dazzled and awed by the Prussianized German Empire. Philosophers began to develop new theories to fit the new facts.

Probably the two most influential thinkers in the development of the new nationalistic concepts were Georg Wilhelm Hegel (1770–1831) and Friedrich Nietzsche (1844–1900). We have already seen (see p. 523) how Hegel influenced the Prussian school of historians and the formation of the German Empire through his belief that individual freedom depends upon ordered discipline under a strong state and that the *Zeitgeist* (spirit of the time) of the nineteenth century was the spirit of German civilization. However, Hegel, a disciple of Kant, considered himself a liberal and an idealist and undoubtedly would have disapproved of the excesses to which later German nationalists went in his name. Nietzsche, on the other hand, though neither a nationalist nor a racist, had no use for liberalism and exerted an even more powerful influence upon German nationalists. Nietzsche frankly discarded all liberalism and idealism and considered the Christian religion fit only for slaves. He preached naked force, unbridled self-assertive egotism, the will to power, and the doctrine of the superman. This philosophy was declared to be realism, and its application in statecraft, realpolitik. Most German historians after 1871 shifted from Hegel's moderation to Nietzsche's extremism. Heinrich von Treitschke, the most influential German historian of the time, proclaimed that Germany's victory over France demonstrated the superiority of military autocracy over liberalism. Only strong states ought to exist. Dissident minorities, individualism, and parliamentary inefficiency must not be tolerated.

The new nationalism was by no means limited to Germany. The French historian Hippolyte Taine blamed France's defeat in 1870–1871 on the corrupting influence of liberalism born in the French Revolution and bred during the nineteenth century. He would take France back to the days of the old regime. In Great Britain, Thomas Carlyle in thunderous prose exalted heroes and hero worship, specifically the Prussian variety. Rudyard Kipling put his poetic gifts to use to sing of the glorious British Empire and the "white man's burden" of ruling and civilizing backward peoples. Slavophilism, the cult of the superiority of Slavic culture and Slavic peoples, became popular in Russia. In the United States the new nationalism was symbolized by rough-riding Teddy Roosevelt and his "big stick" diplomacy. Roosevelt was an admirer of the virile German Empire.

The most extreme feature of the new militant nationalism was racism. People of every nation began to think and talk of themselves as a distinct and superior breed. Language was more than ever confused with race. Thus one spoke of the various "races" in the Austro-Hungarian Empire. By far the most popular and serious of all the racial cults was the Aryan myth. The term *Aryan*, which was originally a linguistic term

referring to the ancient Persians (Iranians) and later to all peoples speaking Indo-European languages, was now applied to the Germanic- or Teutonic-speaking peoples or to the Nordic (tall blond) type of Northern European. After Germany's spectacular military triumphs and economic developments under Bismarck, the term *Aryan* came to be applied more specifically to Germans and to the energetic, aggressive, military qualities they were supposed to possess. Oddly, the two chief formulators of the Aryan myth were a Frenchman, Comte de Gobineau, and the renegade Englishman Houston Stewart Chamberlain, who deserted his homeland and became a German citizen. Their ideas, however, were taken much more seriously in Germany than in France or Great Britain. Richard Wagner became a leading racist, repenting of his earlier liberalism to write violent propaganda tracts and to compose grandiose operas stridently extolling the virtues of the early Nordic (German) supermen—Siegfried and the Nibelungs.

The chief immediate victims of the new nationalism were various linguistic minority groups, particularly in Germany, Russia, and Hungary, who were subjected to heavy pressure to give up their native languages and become good Germans, Russians, or Hungarians. The Jews, though not a linguistic group, were also hard hit. In Germany an anti-Semitic party founded in 1887 polled 285,000 votes eleven years later. In Russia during the 1880s the Jews were subjected to such persecutions, including bloody pogroms, that more than a quarter million of them fled, mostly to the United States, in spite of strenuous efforts to prevent their leaving. Another bitter and dangerous fruit of the new nationalism was a series of "pan" movements, particularly pan-Germanism and pan-Slavism. These were moves to bring all German-speaking people under the German flag and all Slavic-speaking people under the Russian flag. If implemented, these programs were certain to lead to wars on a continental if not global scale. In fact, militarism was one of the cardinal features of the new nationalism. After 1871, every nation in Europe except Great Britain undertook to copy the German military system, including universal conscription. Great Britain poured a proportionate amount of faith, effort, and money into her navy. Generals and admirals became ever more popular and influential, and Europe became an armed camp.

2. THE GERMAN EMPIRE UNDER BISMARCK AND KAISER WILHELM II

The center of this new and militant type of nationalism and in many ways its cause was the German Empire. The blood-and-iron method by which it was created by Bismarck and the Prussian military, its autocratic constitution, and its strong-handed leadership, first by the Iron Chancellor and then by Kaiser Wilhelm II, guaranteed that the German Empire would be an enlarged Prussia—a military autocracy. The German Empire possessed the world's most powerful army; a large, energetic, and disciplined population; a rapidly growing industrial machine; and a fervent and restless national spirit. At first it excited the awe and envy, but eventually the fear and hatred, of much of the rest of the world. Bismarck ruled over his creation as chancellor for almost twenty years.

His first concern after the defeat of France and the declaration of the empire in 1870–1871 was to complete the consolidation and nationalization of the German states and people. The law codes, the currencies, and the military forces of the twenty-five lesser states were brought into conformity with those of Prussia. Banking and railroads were brought under the control of the national government. The empire's spawning industry was protected against British competition by a high tariff. The French in Alsace-Lorraine, the Danes in Schleswig, and the more than 3 million Poles in the eastern districts were subjected to severe pressure to give up their language and traditions and to become good Germans. However, Bismarck learned that loyalty was one thing that could not be achieved by force.

Two other groups in Germany excited Bismarck's suspicion and wrath: the Roman Catholics (the Black International) and the Socialists (the Red International). Any German who had a foreign loyalty was intolerable to the imperious Junker. From 1872 to 1878, Bismarck waged an unrelenting campaign against the Roman Catholics which he termed the *Kulturkampf* (battle for civilization). The Jesuits were expelled, civil marriage was made compulsory, and all education, including that of Roman Catholic priests, was brought under state control and largely secularized. When the Roman Catholic clergy and most of the laity, which constituted approximately one-third of the total German population, resisted and rallied to the pope, hundreds of priests and six bishops were arrested. But it was all to no avail. The Roman Catholic Center party in the Reichstag became stronger, and by 1878 Bismarck needed its support for what he considered to be a struggle of greater importance—that against the Socialists. In 1878 upon the accession of a more conciliatory pope, Leo XIII, Bismarck "went to Canossa" and had the most severe of the anti-Catholic legislation repealed.

In the same year he began a twelve-year crusade against the internationally minded Socialists. He outlawed their publications, their organizations, and their meetings, and set the brutal German police force upon them. But he only drove them underground. Throughout the decade of the 1880s, Bismarck sought to undercut the Socialists' appeal to the workingman by setting up a comprehensive system of social insurance. Accident, sickness, and old-age insurance was provided for the industrial proletariat, the funds being raised by compulsory contributions from the workers, the employers, and the state. Although Bismarck's motives were not benevolent or humanitarian and the payments were mere pittances, his measures gave impetus to a trend (first begun by Napoleon III) toward state responsibility for social security. Nevertheless, the Socialists were not appeased, and Bismarck continued to fight them as long as he remained chancellor.

Bismarck's foreign policy after 1871 was one of security and retrenchment. He knew that France would be unforgiving and revengeful, forever seeking an opportunity to regain Alsace and Lorraine. Of France alone he had little fear, but France in league with other powers, particularly Russia and Great Britain, would be formidable. Therefore, his consistent policy was to maintain

Most awesome of the military powers in the years between 1871 and 1914 was the German Empire, whose armies nearly conquered Europe in World War I. Here Kaiser Wilhelm II (center) confers with Generals von Hindenburg and von Ludendorff (left and right). *Photo: The Bettmann Archive*

a close military alliance with Austria-Hungary and cordial relations with Russia and Great Britain. He carefully nurtured British friendship by refraining from naval and imperial rivalry. It is true that Bismarck eventually yielded to the German expansionists and annexed some large chunks of worthless territory in Africa and some islands in the Southwest Pacific, but Britain apparently did not want them. In 1873 Bismarck formed the Three Emperors' League among Germany, Austria-Hungary, and Russia. When the interests of Austria-Hungary and Russia proved to be incompatible, this league was replaced in 1879–1882 by the Triple Alliance among Germany, Austria-Hungary, and Italy. A

separate "reinsurance treaty" of friendship and neutrality was made with Russia. Of course Bismarck did not depend wholly upon diplomacy. Throughout this period, the German military machine was made ever more powerful.

Bismarck's policies provided security for Germany, but only insecurity for France and later other nations. As the industry and wealth of the German Empire came to match and complement the strength of her army, the rest of the world became increasingly uneasy. To make matters worse, the imperious chancellor bullied France and manufactured war scares whenever the military budget was being voted on by the Reichstag. The bitter fruit from these seeds would be harvested later.

In 1888 Wilhelm II (1888–1918) became Kaiser. Wilhelm II was twenty-nine years of age when he ascended the throne of the most powerful nation in the world. He had been brought up in the army, which was his first love. Egotistical and bombastic by nature, he disliked both his father and his mother, the daughter of Queen Victoria. It may be that a withered left arm gave him a sense of inferiority for which he was attempting to compensate. He was a dabbler in theology, history, and the arts, and gave advice and instructions freely to the leading figures in those fields. He was also an eloquent and willing speaker. Soon after ascending the throne he announced, "Everyone who is against me, I shall crush!" In a speech to some young inductees into the army he stated, "In the presence of the socialist agitation it may happen—though God forfend—that I shall order you to shoot down your relations, brothers, yes even parents—but you must obey my commands without murmuring." Nevertheless, Wilhelm II possessed considerable charm and had his generous and humanitarian moments.

The young Kaiser's personality and policies soon clashed with those of Bismarck. In 1890, just two years after he became emperor, Wilhelm II accepted Bismarck's reluctant resignation as chancellor. The immediate cause of the break was a disagreement over the control of the ministry and the repeal of the anti-Socialist laws, which Bismarck wished to be continued. The real reason, however, was that there was simply not room enough in Germany for two such prima donnas.

Bismarck's foreign policy was quickly reversed. The reinsurance treaty with Russia was immediately allowed to lapse, as the Kaiser assumed a keen interest in extending German hegemony over the Balkans and the Ottoman Empire, areas the Russians considered to be vital to their own interests and ambitions. In 1894 Russia formed an alliance with France, the very thing that Bismarck had worked so hard to prevent. Wilhelm II also soon alienated Great Britain. His extension of German influence in the Near East, particularly his Berlin-to-Bagdad railroad project (see pp. 604, 606), threatened an area in which Great Britain had many vital interests and through which ran her "life line" to India and the Far East. In China, too, German interests began to rival those of the British.

It was the Kaiser's naval policy, however, that alarmed the British the most. Wilhelm was an ardent and lifelong navalist. "The waves beat powerfully at our national gates," he cried, "and call us as a great nation to maintain our place in the world. . . ." Germany's "place in the sun" was a favorite phrase of the Hohenzollern emperor. In 1897 Admiral von Tirpitz was made minister of marine. His purpose was to create a German navy equivalent to the army built by Roon and Moltke a generation earlier. He projected, and the Reichstag voted, an enormous naval building program that was steadily increased until in 1908 it called for twenty-eight new battleships of the biggest and latest design. The purpose of this program, which was freely and officially admitted, was to give Germany a battle fleet so great that "a war against the mightiest naval power would endanger the supremacy of that power."

Great Britain, whose food supply as well as her empire depended upon naval supremacy, took utmost alarm. Failing in her efforts to reach an understanding with the Kaiser's government, she launched a huge and costly naval building program of her own. In 1904 she joined France, and in 1907 Russia, in the Triple Entente, which was in reality a defensive military alliance. The interests and policies of Great Britain, France, and Russia had long been so discordant that nothing less than maximum alarm could have brought them together. Thus in seventeen years Wilhelm had undone Bismarck's work and brought about the "encirclement" of the Fatherland by three of the world's greatest powers.

Germany's economic exploits under Bismarck and Wilhelm were no less phenomenal than those in the military realm. In 1871 Great Britain was the world's leading nation in manufacturing and commerce; Germany counted for little in either. By 1914 Germany was a clear second to Great Britain in industry and commerce; in many areas, such as the production of steel and machinery, she had far outstripped her. In the up-and-coming chemical and electrical industries and in scientific agriculture and forestry, Germany was far in advance of all other nations. She was also first in the application of science to industry and in industrial and scientific research. By 1914 her merchant marine had captured the lion's share of the lucrative transatlantic passenger traffic. The Hamburg-American and the North German Lloyd lines (in which the Hohenzollerns were said to be heavy investors) were the biggest steamship companies in the world.

At a time when other industrial nations, particularly the United States, were beginning to restrict the giant monopolistic trusts, the German imperial government was encouraging and subsidizing its cartels in order that they might compete more effectively with foreign companies. More and more of the world's market was captured by German business. "Made in Germany" became a familiar mark from the Andean plateau to the Congo jungles. Germany's population, keeping pace with her economy, increased from 41 million in 1871 to 65 million in 1914. Meanwhile, her heavy emigration (which had reached a peak in the 1880s of some 250,000 a year, most of it to the United States) dwindled to a mere trickle. In 1914 the number of German emigrants was less than the number of workers coming into Germany from neighboring countries. Only the United States was keeping pace with Germany in overall economic advancement.

The industrialization of Germany, although accompanied by the growth of a large and prosperous bourgeoisie and a numerous proletariat, did not produce a tide of liberalism as it did in the other Western industrialized nations. The capitalistic classes, imbued with militaristic nationalism after 1866, allied themselves with the autocratic government. Only the Social Democratic party (workingmen) and the small and weak Progressive party (intellectuals, professionals, and small businessmen) advocated responsible democratic government. But even the Social Democratic party, by 1914 the largest party in the empire, was inundated by the flood of militant nationalism that welled up during the international crises that preceded World War I.

Germany's spectacular achievements between 1871 and 1914 excited the awe and admiration of the rest of the world. However, her continuingly autocratic government in a world where democratic liberalism was on the march, her overweening military power and rapidly growing naval strength, her venture into imperialism, her inordinate nationalism, and her irresponsible, egotistical monarch aroused increasing fear and resentment abroad. Germany's militarism and aggressive nationalism had the effect of intensifying the same forces in the other great powers of Europe.

3. RUSSIA UNDER ALEXANDER III AND NICHOLAS II

Another important state whose malignant nationalism helped to strangle liberalism during the second phase of the Industrial Revolution was the empire of the Russian tsars. A strong wave of dissatisfaction arose during the later years of the long rule of Alexander II (1855–1881). The ex-serfs had been cruelly disappointed by the fruits of emancipation (decreed in 1861). In many ways, their economic condition was worse than before. Another revolt of Russia's Polish subjects in 1863 made Alexander II more reactionary. His failure to follow through with more sweeping reforms after the emancipation of the serfs disappointed the liberals, who were mostly intellectual young aristocrats. In despair over the possibility of reforming the huge, semi-Oriental Russian Empire by orderly methods, these young intellectuals became radical and negativist. They set out to destroy Russia's society, government, and church in order to build a new and modern Russia from the ruins. They called their movement *nihilism* (nothingness). When their efforts were spurned by the illiterate masses whom they were seeking to uplift, a more violent wing of the Nihilists turned to terror and assassination to achieve their ends. Numerous bureaucrats and police officials were slain by terrorists, and Tsar Alexander II himself was killed by a Nihilist bomb just as he was preparing to liberalize the government.

The new tsar, Alexander III (1881–1894), was a harsh, reactionary autocrat. Blaming his father's death on softness, he set out to exterminate all liberalism in Russia. The ruthless Plehve was made head of the secret police, whose agents were soon everywhere. Thousands of liberal suspects were arrested. Some were shot or exiled to Siberia. In his sweeping reactionary program of Russianization, Alexander III relied heavily upon his former tutor Pobedonostsev, whom he made procurator-general of the Holy Synod. As an antidote to Western liberalism, Pobedonos-tsev invoked the most extreme form of Russian nationalism, Slavophilism (love of Slavic culture). According to this cult, the Slavic "races" had a culture of their own, which was different from and superior to that of the West. The salient features of this culture were autocratic government under an omnipotent tsar, a feudalistic agrarian society, and the Orthodox Church. Since Russia was the greatest Slavic power, it was her mission to keep the culture pure and to serve as a model for the lesser Slavic nations and peoples. The censored press, the closely supervised schools, and, above all, the clergy of the Orthodox Church became potent agencies for the propagation of the cult. The great novelist Feodor Dostoevski had been an important proponent of this Russian counterpart to Germany's Aryan myth. Non-Orthodox religions were persecuted. Language minority groups—the Poles, the Baltic peoples, the Finns, and even the Ukrainians—were forced to use the Russian language. We have already observed the treatment of the Jews, for whom the harshest persecution was reserved. Associated with Slavophilism was pan-Slavism, the belief that all the other Slavic-speaking groups (Poles, Czechs, Slovaks, Ruthenians, Serbs, Croats, Slovenes, and Bulgarians) should be brought either under direct Russian control or into federation with Russia. This would result in the dismemberment of the German, Austro-Hungarian, and Ottoman empires, all of which contained Slavic minority groups.

Alexander III was succeeded by Nicholas II (1894–1917), a well-meaning but weak man who was strongly influenced by his neurotic German wife and eventually by the mystic charlatan monk Rasputin. Although Nicholas attempted to continue the policies of his father, he was unable to make them work. During the decade of the 1890s, the Industrial Revolution finally reached Russia, and an industrial bourgeoisie and proletariat emerged. Liberalism and radicalism reappeared among these new classes, and now there was no strong-handed Alexander II to check them. Of the various liberal and radical parties that emerged, the one of greatest significance for the future was the Social Democratic party. This was a Marxist party whose leadership was made up almost entirely of intellectual radicals. Their chief concern was for the industrial proletariat. In 1903 the Social Democrats split into a moderate, gradualist wing called the Mensheviks (minority) and a violent revolutionary wing called the Bolsheviks (majority). The Bolsheviks were led by the brilliant and dynamic Nikolai Lenin, who was living in exile in Switzerland.

Taking advantage of the embarrassment of the tsar's government because of Russia's defeat by Japan in 1904–1905 (see p. 575), the various liberal and radical groups clamored for reform. In July 1904 the hated Plehve was assassinated. In January 1905, some fifteen hundred peaceful demonstrators were shot down in front of the royal palace in St. Petersburg by the tsar's guard. This bloody event, known as Red Sunday, fanned the flames of discontent. In October 1905, a general strike, in which the Menshevik Leon Trotsky played a prominent role, completely paralyzed the country for ten days. Nicholas II, yielding at last, issued a manifesto that promised civil liberties and a popularly elected Duma. However, before the Duma could be elected, the return of the Russian troops from the Far East and a huge loan from Russia's ally, France, strengthened the hand of the tsar. During the next two years he and his advisers succeeded in reducing the Duma to an undemocratically elected body that had no real control over the government. Nevertheless, a break had been made in Russia's autocratic system, and it appeared that the voice of the people was beginning to be heard.

But as in Germany between 1905 and 1914, a series of international crises engulfed the rising liberalism in a torrent of nationalism, militarism, and war. The eventual winners in Russia were not the liberals but the hardy Bolsheviks.

4. NATIONAL MOVEMENTS IN SOUTHEAST EUROPE

While nationalism between 1871 and 1914 was crushing minority language groups in the German and the Russian empires, it was pulling the Austrian and the Ottoman empires apart along language lines. After Austria's defeat by Prussia in 1866, the dominant German minority in Austria felt obliged to take into partnership the aggressive and restless Magyars of Hungary. The

Ausgleich (compromise) of 1867 set up the Dual Monarchy of Austria-Hungary. Each country had its own separate parliament. But the two were united under a common ruler, the head of the house of Hapsburg; common ministries of war, finance, and foreign affairs; and joint delegations from the two parliaments whose duty was to coordinate policies wherever possible. This arrangement was essentially an alliance between the Germans of Austria and the Magyars of Hungary against the Slavic, Rumanian, and Italian language groups, which constituted a majority of the total population of the Dual Monarchy. In effect, the Germans said to the Magyars: "You take care of your minorities [mostly Slavs] and we will take care of ours." (see map p. 605)

Austria followed a relatively moderate policy in dealing with her subject language groups. Cultural autonomy was granted, and the suffrage was gradually extended until in 1907 all adult males were given the vote. However, the subject peoples were more interested in nationalism than in democracy. The various language groups resurrected traditions of a glorious cultural and political past—much of it pure fantasy. The prosperous Czechs of Bohemia were especially adamant. The problem was confounded by the fact that many of the language groups had kinsmen outside the Dual Monarchy whom they wished to join and who deliberately stirred up their disloyalty. Such groups were the Italians, the Poles, the Ruthenians (Ukrainians), the Serbs, and the Rumanians. Parliamentary sessions in Austria frequently degenerated into screaming, inkstand-throwing melees among the various language groups.

Hungary made no pretense of conciliation. The Magyar aristocracy ruled over their Slovak, Rumanian, Serb, and Croat minorities with an iron hand. They also refused to permit their own Magyar masses to participate in the government. The nationalist discontent in Hungary was even greater than it was in Austria; the Croats and Serbs, desirous of joining their independent Serb kinsmen in the formation of a Yugo (southern) Slav state, were particularly troublesome. When explosive nationalism finally blew Austria-Hungary apart in 1914–1918, much of the world was drawn into the conflict.

The Balkan portion of the Ottoman Empire between 1871 and 1914 was a hornets' nest of militant nationalism. The hatred of the Christian Balkan language groups for their Muslim Turkish masters was equaled only by their hatred for each other. The once potent Ottoman Empire crumbled throughout the course of the nineteenth century, and one Balkan language group after another, now aflame with national pride and ambition, emerged as an independent nation. Meanwhile, all the great powers of Europe became involved in the strategic and troubled area of the Near East. Russia, Austria-Hungary, Great Britain, France, Germany, and Italy had important imperial, economic, and military interests in the Balkans. In addition, Russia and Austria-Hungary had serious nationalistic interests there. Russia considered herself as the big brother and protector of the Slavic-speaking Serbs and Bulgarians. Austria-Hungary's large Rumanian and Yugoslav populations desired union with their free kinsmen in Rumania and Serbia. Between 1829 and 1913 first the Greeks, then the Serbs, Rumanians, and Bulgarians, and finally the Albanians gained their independence from the Ottoman Empire. In each case a major crisis occurred among the great powers. These Balkan crises became progressively more severe and finally culminated in World War I (see Chapters 51 and 54).

5. THE NEW NATIONALISM IN GREAT BRITAIN, FRANCE, AND THE UNITED STATES

Malignant nationalism appears to beget malignant nationalism. Great Britain, long the unchallenged mistress of the seas and of the world's commerce, did not relish the appearance of a dangerous rival. In the face of Germany's swift rise to power and prestige, the British took renewed pride in their dominant navy and in their empire, which contained one-fourth of all the earth's territory and people. Many well-to-do Britishers thought themselves to be so superior to the other peoples of Europe that they became the most unpopular of all travelers on the Continent. To some observers, it appeared that Great Britain was as big a bully on the seas and overseas as Germany was on the continent of Europe.

French pride was only intensified by France's defeat at the hands of Germany in 1870–1871. The statue dedicated to the city of Strasbourg in the Place de la Concorde in Paris was draped in perpetual mourning as a constant reminder of the day of revenge. France greatly speeded up her overseas empire building and increased the size of her armed forces until they were larger in proportion to her population than those of the German Empire. She sought and found military allies. When a general strike in 1910 threatened the nation's military security and war preparations, Aristide Briand, himself a radical and former Socialist, did not hesitate to use the armed forces to break it up.

The United States was the slowest of the great powers to catch the new spirit. She had an ocean between herself and the militant nationalism of Europe, and she was still busy exploiting the richest of the continents and absorbing and Americanizing the millions of European immigrants pouring through her gates. Nevertheless, Theodore Roosevelt's "big stick" policy in dealing with the little neighbors to the south, particularly his seizing Panama from a friendly neighbor and afterward boasting of it, smacked of the power politics of Europe. The European powers could see no justification for the claims of the United States to sovereignty over the whole Western Hemisphere. In Latin America, the big Yankee to the north was the most unpopular nation in the world.

When the first shots of World War I sounded in 1914, all groups, including the internationalist socialists (except for a mere handful), rallied to the flags and trumpets of their respective nations. Many promising liberal and democratic movements came to an end, some of them permanently. Aggressive nationalism proved to be a stronger force during the second phase of the Industrial Revolution than liberalism or democracy.

Suggested Reading

General

A. J. P. Taylor, *The Struggle for Mastery in Europe, 1848–1918* (1954). Spirited account of malignant nationalism at work.

*Barbara Tuchman, *The Proud Tower* (Bantam). Brilliant study of the ruling classes in Great Britain, France, Germany, and the United States on the eve of World War I.

General Nature of the New Nationalism

C. J. H. Hayes, *Essays on Nationalism* (1926). By the leading authority on the subject.

*J. Barzun, *Race, a Study in Modern Superstition* (Torch). Thoughtful study of the most extreme form of nationalism.

The German Empire

H. Holborn, *A History of Modern Germany*, Vol. III: 1840–1945 (1969). By a foremost scholar.

*A. J. P. Taylor, *The Course of German History: A Survey of the Development of Germany since 1815* (Capricorn). Brief and lively.

Russia Under Alexander III and Nicholas II

M. Florinski, *Russia: A History and an Interpretation*, 2 vols. (1953). Best general history of Russia in English.

*H. Seton-Watson, *The Decline of Imperial Russia, 1855–1914* (Praeger). Excellent brief account.

Southeast Europe

*A. J. P. Taylor, *The Hapsburg Monarchy, 1809–1918: A History of the Austrian Empire and Austria-Hungary*, rev. ed (Torch). Good brief account.

The New Nationalism in Great Britain, France, and the United States

*C. J. H. Hayes, *A Generation of Materialism, 1871–1900* (Torch). Good chapters covering the Big Three democracies.

*W. Millis, *The Martial Spirit* (Compass). Vivid picture of American nationalism and militarism before World War I.

51

EUROPEAN IMPERIALISM IN ASIA AND AFRICA

Imperialism went hand in hand with the new aggressive type of nationalism. During the second phase of the Industrial Revolution, European power and influence were extended to those portions of the globe which had not previously been affected: the Near, Middle, and Far East, the remaining coastal regions and the whole vast interior of Africa. Europeans even staked out claims over the frozen wastes of Antarctica. This new wave of imperialism was accompanied by increasingly severe friction between the European imperialists and the "native" peoples, and bitter rivalry among the European imperial powers themselves.

1. A NEW BURST OF EUROPEAN EXPANSION

We have already seen that from the fifteenth to the eighteenth centuries, the national monarchies of Europe "discovered" and conquered most of the Western Hemisphere, the west coast of Africa, and Southern Asia. Then from 1763 until 1871 there came a lull in expansion; Europe was busy with revolution and counterrevolution, industrialization, and nation building. The period 1871–1914, however, witnessed a new burst of European expansion that brought practically all the remaining portions of the earth's surface under European influence or domination.

One of the chief impulses behind the new thrust was undoubtedly economic. The rapid expansion of industry in Europe and the United States created a demand for greater markets, new sources for raw materials, and investment outlets for surplus capital. Until Henry Ford demonstrated in the 1920s that low prices and high wages would develop an almost limitless home market, it was generally assumed that the exploitation of home and foreign markets by high prices and low wages was the only way in which industry could succeed. This idea resulted in the acquisition of more and more technologically backward areas by the industrial powers. Furthermore, science and technology gave the industrialized nations such a military advantage that the conquest and control of the nonindustrialized areas was relatively easy.

Probably an even greater impulse to the new imperialism was the new nationalism. Much of the territory seized by the great powers between 1871 and 1914 had no economic value whatever; some, in fact, was an economic liability. However, it flattered the national ego to see its colors spread over the map. It also provided military and naval bases and manpower for the hungry military machines that were an integral part of militant nationalism. In Europe the conservative parties based upon the landed aristocracy were even more imperialistic than the liberal parties based upon industrial and commercial interests. Many of the imperial governors, generals, and admirals came from the conservative aristocracy. National egotism also gave the citizens of the great Western powers a sense of mission; they were bringing the blessings of civilization to backward peoples. Rudyard Kipling expressed the genuine belief of many Westerners when he sang in rhyme of the "white man's burden" to hold in tutelage and to civilize the "lesser breeds" of the earth. The heady wine of nationalism gave the Westerners during the second phase of the Industrial Revolution the same advantage over the Asians and Africans that the French Revolutionists and Napoleon had enjoyed over the rest of continental Europe. It was an advantage that would not last.

Another motivating factor in the new imperialism was the evangelizing zeal of the Christian religion. Christianity has always followed its founder's command, "Go ye into all the world and preach the gospel to every creature," and it has been the most aggressive of all religions. At the very time that it was wavering under attack in its homelands in the West, it was carrying on foreign missionary activity of unprecedented scope and intensity. And it was gaining millions of converts in Asia and Africa. Much of the work of the Christian missionaries was undone by their association in the minds of the natives with economic and nationalistic imperialistic exploiters—how much it is impossible to say.

2. THE EXPLOITATION AND AWAKENING OF CHINA

One of the most important scenes of European imperialism during the second phase of the Industrial Revolution was China. This huge and populous country was the seat of the oldest continuous civilization in the world. For some five thousand years China had been a vast melting pot, absorbing invading peoples and cultures and welding them into a tough but resilient civilization. The military conquerors were always themselves swallowed up or conquered by Chinese culture. By far the greatest influence in molding Chinese civilization was Confucianism. Confucius lived five hundred years before Christ. He was reared in poverty, the son of a youthful mother and an aged father. A prodigy both in scholarship and personality, he attracted a body of devoted disciples who wrote down his sayings. Although he himself never held high

political office, he was revered as a learned man and was the teacher of many who did become officials in government.

The teachings of Confucius really belong to the realm of philosophy rather than religion. The flavor of his life and thought is much more closely akin to that of Socrates, who lived in Greece only a hundred years after Confucius, than to that of the mystic religious leaders such as Christ, Buddha, or Mohammed. Confucius was only vaguely concerned with the Deity, who, he assumed, governs the universe and is on the side of righteousness. On the other hand, he was very much concerned with and very optimistic about man and his ability through reason to build the good life here on earth. Benevolence, righteousness, decorum, wisdom, and faithfulness were the virtues taught by Confucius. These could be developed by the ruling classes and transmitted to the masses by example and persuasion. Confucius was history-minded and held in high esteem the lessons that can be learned from the experiences of the past. He also emphasized family loyalty and filial piety.

Needless to say, the practice of Confucianism, as in all religions, fell far short of the ideal. The use of force was never absent from Chinese government or society. Respect for the past and for family was corrupted into backward-looking ultraconservatism, and an elaborate ritual was built around ancestor worship. Nevertheless, the teachings of Confucius served as a standard that, like Christianity in the West, was at least tacitly accepted by the great majority. The scholar was exalted, not the soldier as in the West. In fact, in no other civilization has the scholar been so revered. For centuries, examinations for the civil service, which was the chief avenue for advancement, were based largely upon the Confucian classics. This guaranteed that the best minds and the ruling classes of China would be steeped in Confucianism. It also guaranteed tight control of government at all levels by the upper classes, since only they had the time and means to prepare for the examinations.

Considering themselves superior to all other peoples, the Chinese gradually isolated themselves. A great wall (never completed) originally

IMPERIALISM IN ASIA 1840–1914

constructed to defend her northern border later symbolized her effort to retain the old and keep out the new. Although they admitted some European traders and Christian missionaries in the sixteenth and seventeenth centuries, they closed their doors rather tightly thereafter. As science, technology, and dynamic capitalism and nationalism developed in the West, China fell far behind in strength and energy. By the nineteenth century her medieval society, under the corrupt and declining Manchu dynasty, constituted a power vacuum that tempted exploitation by the West.

The first Europeans to force themselves upon the Chinese were the British. Going to war in 1839, when Chinese officials interfered with their sale of opium in China, the British, with their modern weapons, easily defeated the Chinese, who were still using medieval arms. By the terms of the Treaty of Nanking (1842), the Chinese ceded Hong Kong to the British, opened many of their ports to foreign trade free of restricting tariffs, and granted the foreigners extraterritorial rights, such as trial by their own courts, on Chinese soil. This was the first of a series of unequal treaties and the signal for all the great Western powers to rush into China and seize what they could. In the ensuing scramble it was the rivalry among the great powers themselves rather than Chinese resistance that saved China from complete loss of independence.

The British got the lion's share. In addition to Hong Kong and concessions in the Canton area of the southeast, they gained a virtual trading monopoly in the Yangtze Valley, which was the richest and most populous part of China. In the north they gained footholds in the capital city of Peking and its port city of Tientsin, in the Shantung Peninsula, and in Manchuria. They gained dominion over Tibet. In the 1880s they seized control of Burma, which owed a tenuous allegiance to China. The French took large areas in Southeast China and Hainan Island as their sphere. In the 1880s they completed the detachment of Indochina from Chinese sovereignty. The Russians took Manchuria as their sphere,

ARCTIC OCEAN

ALASKA
(Purchased by U.S.A.
from Russia, 1867)

BERING SEA

ALEUTIAN I. (U.S.A., 1867)

KAMCHATKA

Lena R.

SEA OF OKHOTSK

SIBERIA

Yakutsk

SAKHALIN

KURILE I.
(Japan, 1875)

Ob R.

Tobolsk

N EMPIRE

KARAFUTO
(Japan, 1905)

AMUR PROVINCE
1858

Khabarovsk

Omsk

Tomsk

L. Baikal

Chita

Amur R.

MARITIME
PROVINCE
(Russia, 1868)

JAPANESE EMPIRE

TRANS-SIBERIAN RAILROAD

Irkutsk

MANCHURIA

Vladivostok
1860

Yenisei R.

Harbin

SEA OF
JAPAN

Urga

Mukden

Tokyo

L. Balkhash

OUTER MONGOLIA
(Autonomous, 1912 Russian Sphere)

INNER MONGOLIA

JEHOL

KOREA
(Japan, 1905, 1910)

1854

Peking

Port Arthur
(Japan, 1905)

Tashkent

1860-65

SINKIANG

Tientsin

Kiao-chow
(Germany, 1898)

RA 1876

Kashgar

PACIFIC OCEAN

1895

Huang Ho

Shanghai
(Britain, 1842)

KASHMIR
1846

TIBET

CHINA

Hankow

Nanking

Ningpo
1842

EAST
CHINA
SEA

PUNJAB

HIMALAYAS

Lhasa

Chungking

Yangtse R.

Foochow

RYUKYU I.

Delhi

NEPAL

BHUTAN

Brahmaputra R.

Amoy

FORMOSA (Japan, 1895)

MARIANA I.
(Germany, 1899)

Ganges R.

YUNNAN

KWANGSI
(French Sphere)

Canton
(Britain, 1842)

PESCADORES (Japan, 1895)

GUAM
(U.S.A., 1898)

INDIA

Calcutta

BURMA
(Britain, 1852, 1885)

Hong Kong (Britain, 1842)

Macao (Portugal, 1557)

Hyderabad

ay

BRITISH INDIA

1852

Hanoi

Kwang-chow
(Lease to France, 1898)

HAINAN

Manila

PHILIPPINE I.
(U.S.A., 1898, 1899)

CAROLINE I.
(Germany, 1899)

Rangoon

ANNAM

FRENCH
INDOCHINA
1884, 1907

YAP

Goa
(Portugal)

Madras

1826

SIAM

Mekong R.

PALAU I.

Pondicherry
(France)

Yanaon
(France)

BAY OF BENGAL

ANDAMAN I.
(Britain)

Bangkok

Saigon

SOUTH
CHINA SEA

Karikal (France)

CEYLON

BRITISH
NORTH BORNEO
1888

NEW GUINEA

KAISER WILHEMSLAND
(Germany, 1884)

MALAY STATES
(Britain, 18   , 1824)

SARAWAK
1888

BORNEO

CELEBES

Singapore
(Britain, 1819)

SUMATRA

DUTCH EAST INDIES

DIAN OCEAN

Batavia

JAVA

TIMOR

(Portugal, 1859)

Darwin

AUSTRALIA

American troops scale a wall in China during the Boxer Rebellion in 1900 in this contemporary photograph. The rebellion was quickly put down with troops from a number of countries interested in keeping China exploitable: Britain, France, Germany, Russia, Italy, Japan, and the United States. *Photo: Brown Brothers*

annexed a large strip of China's northeast coast, including the port of Vladivostok, and became active in Korea. The Germans carved out for themselves much of the strategically located Shantung Peninsula and built a powerful naval base at Kiaochow. In 1894 the rejuvenated and modernized Japanese went to war with China. They easily defeated her and not only took away Formosa and Korea, but forced China to pay a huge indemnity. Even the United States got into the act. The United States had launched upon an imperialist program in the Far East in 1898 by seizing the Philippine Islands and Guam from Spain. Now, fearful for her growing trade with China, she attempted to gain a sphere of influ-ence in Fukien Province and demanded an Open Door policy in China with equal trading oppor-tunities for all. Little if anything came of either of these projects, however.

Meanwhile, Chinese nationalism was being aroused by the Western and Japanese aggres-sions against the "Celestial Empire." The first overt reaction was the Taiping Rebellion of 1851 against the corrupt Manchu dynasty. The re-forming rebels were finally put down thirteen years later by Manchu armies, one of which was organized by an American military adventurer, Frederick Ward, and led by a British general, Charles (Chinese) Gordon. In 1899–1900 a seri-ous uprising against the foreign exploiters, known as the Boxer Rebellion, took place. Thou-sands of Chinese Christians and a number of foreigners were slain. This liberation movement was put down by British, French, German, Rus-sian, Italian, Japanese, and American troops. The nationalist leaders were severely punished, and China was forced to pay the foreign govern-ments a large indemnity.

Meanwhile, a more far-reaching revolutionary movement aimed not only at freeing China from foreign exploitation, but also at modernizing and democratizing her society and government was being organized by Dr. Sun Yat-sen (1866–1925). Sun Yat-sen, the son of a poor Chinese farmer, studied in a British mission school in Hawaii, became a Christian, and later graduated from the British medical school at Hong Kong. Eloquent and dynamic, he organized his followers into the Kuomintang party, which was committed to a three-point program: (1) national independence, (2) democratic government, (3) social justice. In 1911 the reformers launched a revolution against the Manchu dynasty, declared a republic, and elected Sun Yat-sen as provisional president. The revolution swept most of China. The Manchu officials in Peking, their power having evaporated, declared China a republic and abdicated in favor of General Yuan, organizer of the New Army of North China. Early in 1912 the idealistic Sun Yat-sen, in behalf of national unity, and fearful of rising anarchy and war lords within and the possibility of Japanese and Russian intervention from without, yielded to General Yuan. Yuan, however, soon proved to be more interested in power than in liberal reform. When the Kuomintang party won the elections of 1913 he suppressed the party and had its most promising young leader assassinated. Sun Yat-sen, of course, disassociated himself from Yuan's dictatorship and resumed his liberal activities in South China. When World War I opened a new era in 1914, China was torn with revolution and division.

3. THE EMERGENCE OF JAPAN

Japan's reaction to Western intrusion was quite different from that of China. The Japanese people inhabit four large islands and some three thousand small ones stretching along the eastern coast of Asia for a distance of about two thousand miles. Their culture had been greatly influenced by that of the Chinese mainland. However, Buddhism and emperor-worshiping Shintoism, rather than Confucianism, were the two chief religions. Like China, Japan had admitted the sixteenth- and seventeenth-century European traders and Christian missionaries, but had evicted them and closed her doors after observing what was happening everywhere in Asia where Europeans were admitted. At mid-nineteenth century, the Japanese were living in isolation. Their stage of technical knowledge and their feudal society ruled over by military chieftains were quite similar to those of Europe five hundred years earlier.

In 1853, eleven years after the Treaty of Nanking opened up China, an American navy commodore, Matthew C. Perry, steamed into Tokyo Bay and so overawed the Japanese that they opened their ports to shipwrecked American sailors and to American trade. The alert Japanese were much impressed by the technological superiority of the Americans. In 1868, just fifteen years later, a group of forward-looking young Japanese overthrew the existing government and began reorganizing the Japanese government and society along modern Western lines. Taking what they considered to be the best from the various Western nations, they patterned their business methods after those of the United States, their legal system after the French, and their navy after the British. But it was Bismarck's Germany that impressed the Japanese the most. They built a military machine and an authoritarian government and education system on the model of the German Empire.

In an incredibly short time Japan became a modern, industrialized, military, and, on the surface at least, a Westernized power. In 1894, as we have already observed, she attacked China, defeated her with ease, and forced her to pay a large indemnity and to give up Korea (which Japan annexed in 1910) and the island of Formosa. In 1902 Great Britain became the first Western power to treat an Oriental nation as an equal by entering into a military alliance with Japan. Thus strengthened and reassured, Japan attacked Russia in 1904 and, to everyone's surprise, defeated her on land and at sea. As her reward, she took the southern half of Sakhalin Island and Russia's railroad and port concessions in southern Manchuria, thereby becoming the dominant power in that large and valuable section of China. By 1914 Japan was a first-rate Westernized power—industrialized, militaristic, imperialistic. And as in Germany and Russia, liberal democratic trends in Japan were overshadowed and weakened by aggressive nationalism.

4. COMPETITION FOR THE STRATEGIC NEAR AND MIDDLE EAST

The term *Near East* usually refers to the area at the eastern end of the Mediterranean: Egypt, the old Ottoman Empire, and the Balkan Peninsula. In the period 1871–1914, the term *Middle East* usually meant the area of the Persian Gulf, the territory northwest of India, and sometimes Tibet. (By the middle of the twentieth century the term *Middle East* was generally used to designate the whole area from and including Egypt and Turkey to the western borders of India.) Before the development of its oil resources after World War I, this area (with the exception of the Balkan Peninsula) was relatively barren, poor, and sparsely settled. It was inhabited chiefly by Muslims who were hostile to Europeans. The main importance of the area, therefore, was strategic. It is the land bridge between the world's two largest land masses—the continents of Eurasia and Africa. The opening in 1869 of the Suez Canal, which shortened the sailing distance between Western Europe and the Far East by 5,000 miles, doubled the strategic value of the Near and Middle East. Indeed, Suez quickly became probably the most vital single commerical and military focal point in the world.

The Suez Canal was built by a French company between 1859 and 1869. However, in 1875 Great Britain, taking advantage of the Egyptian government's financial distress, purchased the khedive's controlling portion of the canal stock. Seven years later, to quell an anti-European insurrection, the British occupied Egypt with their military forces. The French acquiesced in the establishment of Britain's control over Egypt and the Suez Canal in return for British support of French dominance in Morocco.

Serious competition for the British in the Near East soon came from an unexpected source. Wilhelm II, upon becoming kaiser of the German Empire in 1888, immediately began to show a keen interest in the Ottoman Empire. Sultan Abdul Hamid II (1876–1909) was such a cruel slaughterer of his Christian subjects that he was called in the Western world "Abdul the Damned." Nevertheless, Wilhelm II in 1889 paid Abdul Hamid a visit in Constantinople and declared himself to be the friend and benefactor not only of the Turks, but of all the Muslims. Friendship was followed by economic concessions and German investments in the Ottoman Empire. A second visit by the Kaiser in 1898 led to a concession to Germany to build a railroad from the Bosporus to the Persian Gulf. This, with its European connection, was the famous Berlin-to-Bagdad railroad. The British took alarm. The Bagdad Railroad, with a fortified terminus on the Persian Gulf, would undercut Britain's longer water route to the East and threaten India, Britain's richest colonial prize. A projected branch running down through Syria and Palestine to Hedjaz would menace the Suez Canal itself.

Russia was equally concerned. Since the days of Ivan III in the fifteenth century, one of Russia's major ambitions has been to gain a warm water outlet to the world through the Turkish Straits at Constantinople. As a matter of fact, since the tenth century Russia has looked to Constantinople as the seat and legitimate capital of her Orthodox religion and Byzantine culture. As we have seen, the decay of the Ottoman Empire in the nineteenth century encouraged Russia to try for Constantinople, and only the intervention of Great Britain and France in the Crimean War (1854–1856) prevented her from attaining her goal. Again in 1877–1878 Russia defeated Turkey and threatened to dominate the whole Balkan Peninsula. This time Great Britain and Austria-Hungary forced Russia to submit to a general settlement by the European powers. At the Congress of Berlin, 1878, Russian ambitions in the Near East were once more thwarted. Bismarck's support of Austria-Hungary and Great Britain at the Congress of Berlin marked the beginning of German-Russian estrangement. Russia's defeat by Japan in 1904–1905 caused her to intensify her pressure toward the Middle and Near East. Her southward expansion from Siberia so menaced India that Great Britain in the late nineteenth century and the beginning of the twentieth extended the northwest Indian frontier to the Khyber Pass and crossed over the

A ship passes through the Suez Canal soon after its opening in 1869. By drastically shortening the sailing distance between Western Europe and the Far East, the canal made the Near and Middle East an area of supreme strategic importance. *Photo: Brown Brothers*

Himalayas to checkmate Russian influence in Tibet, Afghanistan, and Persia.

The new German threat in the Near and Middle East, however, caused the British and the Russians to settle their long-standing differences. In 1907 they neutralized Tibet and Afghanistan and divided Persia into three spheres of influence—a Russian sphere in the north, a British sphere in the south, and an "independent" sphere in the center. Great Britain, Russia, and France, now diplomatic allies, prevented the sale of Bagdad Railroad bonds in their respective countries in an effort to embarrass the financing of the costly undertaking. Germany went right ahead, however, with the extension of her influence in the Balkans and the Ottoman Empire. In 1913 Germany dispatched a military mission to Constantinople to reorganize and instruct the Turkish army. The Ottoman Empire's friendship and eventual alliance with Germany was undoubtedly motivated by her greater fear of Russia. By 1914 the area of the Near and Middle East was a giant powder keg with fuses leading to St. Petersburg, Berlin, and London.

5. THE SCRAMBLE FOR AFRICA

At the opening of the nineteenth century, Africa was not the seat of ancient and highly developed civilizations, as was Asia. The brilliant civilizations of Egypt, Carthage, and Rome had long since disappeared. The Muslim religion still existed throughout North Africa, but the once vigorous Muslim civilization was now squalid and tribal except for a few rich potentates. The Portuguese, Spanish, British, and French had trading posts along the gold, ivory, and slave coast on the west. The Dutch and Portuguese had posts and settlements around the southern cape. But most of the huge continent still lay dark and mysterious. By 1871 the African scene had still not changed very much. During the middle decades of the nineteenth century, the interior was explored for the first time, notably by David Livingston, a Scottish missionary, and Henry Morton Stanley, a British journalist. The French had conquered Algeria and made it a part of France, and had pushed up the Senegal River in the west. The British had taken the Cape Colony from the Dutch by the Treaty of Vienna in 1815, and the Dutch settlers had moved northward into the interior. After 1871, however, the tempo of European activity changed drastically. The explorers' tales of strange wild animals and primitive peoples, of jungles, ivory, and gold, excited the imagination of Western European adventurers and evangelical Christians. The new burst of industrialism and nationalism supplied much of the impetus.

After 1871 there took place such a mad scramble for Africa among the powers of Western Europe that by 1914, the only independent areas left were Ethiopia in the east and Liberia in the west. Ethiopia, with French aid, had repulsed an invading Italian army, and Liberia had been sponsored by the United States as a hoped-for receptacle for liberated Negro slaves. The rest of the huge continent had been seized by France, Great Britain, Germany, Portugal, Belgium, Italy, and Spain (listed in the approximate order of size of territory held). (See map, p. 579.) The treatment of the primitive natives was very similar to that accorded the New World Indians in the sixteenth and seventeenth centuries.

The looting of so much territory did not occur, of course, without serious international incidents and crises. One such incident occurred at Fashoda in the Sudan in 1898. A French expedition under Major Marchand, bent on establishing an all-French axis across Africa from west to east, arrived at Fashoda and hoisted the French flag. The British, however, claimed the Sudan as an appendage of Egypt. Furthermore, they were interested in a Cape to Cairo railroad running through all British territory even though they were already blocked by German East Africa. Lord Kitchener therefore hurried down from the north with a superior British force and compelled the French to withdraw.

In South Africa the British fought a major war with the Dutch settlers (1899–1902). When British settlers began to move into Cape Colony af-

ter the Congress of Vienna had ceded it to Great Britain in 1815, the Calvinist Dutch Boers (farmers) who had settled there in the seventeenth century and who wished to live a biblical, patriarchal life trekked northward far into the interior. Eventually the British recognized the independence of the two Boer states, Transvaal and Orange Free State. When, however, the richest gold mines in the world were discovered in the Transvaal in the 1880s, British immigrants (Uitlanders) flooded in. The unwelcome Uitlanders were badly treated by the Dutch Boers. The British empire builder Cecil Rhodes, with the support of powerful interests back home, was determined to brush aside the two little Boer republics. When the able Boer president, Paul Kruger, saw the British intent, he opened hostilities. What the world expected to be an easy victory for the British took three years of all-out military effort involving severe casualties and enormous costs. Britain's treatment of the defeated Boers, however, was lenient. They were taken into partnership in the Union of South Africa; and their war hero, General Botha, was elected the Union's first prime minister. During the course of the struggle, a telegram of congratulation from the German kaiser to President Kruger and the British seizure of a German ship attempting to violate the British blockade caused great tension between Great Britain and Germany. Only the superiority of the British navy, as the Kaiser admitted, prevented him from going to war.

The British navy also proved decisive in two crises over Morocco. In 1905 France, with the approval of Great Britain, Italy, and Spain, began the conquest of Morocco. She claimed that it was necessary because of continual raids by wild Moroccan tribesmen on French Algeria. The German kaiser, seeing an opportunity to assert his own power and possibly to break up the Triple Entente, which France, Great Britain, and Russia were then forming, appeared at the Moroccan port of Tangier on a German warship and indicated his support of Moroccan independence. Great tension followed. At an international conference at Algeciras, France, supported by her own ally, Great Britain, and by Germany's ally, Italy, won a limited control over Morocco. Disorder continued, however, and in

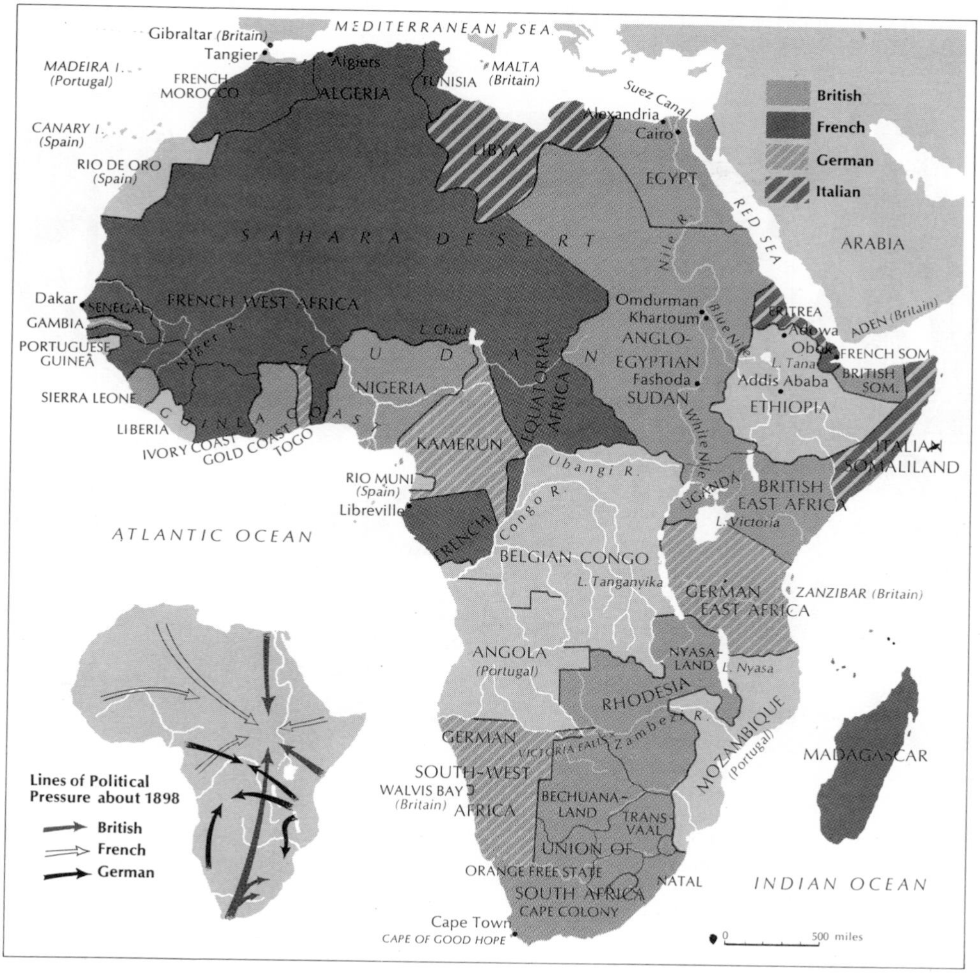
MEDITERRANEAN SEA
Gibraltar (Britain)
Tangier
Algiers
MADEIRA I. (Portugal)
FRENCH MOROCCO
ALGERIA
TUNISIA
MALTA (Britain)
Suez Canal
Alexandria
Cairo
CANARY I. (Spain)
RIO DE ORO (Spain)
LIBYA
EGYPT
British
French
German
Italian
RED SEA
ARABIA
Nile R.
SAHARA DESERT
Dakar
SENEGAL
GAMBIA
PORTUGUESE GUINEA
FRENCH WEST AFRICA
Niger R.
L. Chad
SUDAN
Omdurman
Khartoum
ANGLO-EGYPTIAN SUDAN
Fashoda
Blue Nile
ERITREA
Adowa
Obok
ADEN (Britain)
FRENCH SOM.
BRITISH SOM.
L. Tana
Addis Ababa
ETHIOPIA
SIERRA LEONE
LIBERIA
IVORY COAST
GOLD COAST
TOGO
GULF OF GUINEA
NIGERIA
KAMERUN
EQUATORIAL AFRICA
White Nile
ITALIAN SOMALILAND
RIO MUNI (Spain)
Libreville
Ubangi R.
Congo R.
UGANDA
BRITISH EAST AFRICA
L. Victoria
ATLANTIC OCEAN
FRENCH
BELGIAN CONGO
L. Tanganyika
GERMAN EAST AFRICA
ZANZIBAR (Britain)
ANGOLA (Portugal)
NYASALAND
L. Nyasa
RHODESIA
Zambezi R.
MOZAMBIQUE (Portugal)
MADAGASCAR
Lines of Political Pressure about 1898
British
French
German
GERMAN SOUTH-WEST AFRICA
VICTORIA FALLS
WALVIS BAY (Britain)
BECHUANALAND
TRANSVAAL
UNION OF SOUTH AFRICA
ORANGE FREE STATE
NATAL
CAPE COLONY
INDIAN OCEAN
Cape Town
CAPE OF GOOD HOPE
0
500 miles

AFRICA 1914

1911 France sent a conquering army into Morocco, at which point Germany dispatched a cruiser to the Moroccan port of Agadir. Again tension mounted. In the face of Germany's threat to France, Britain's Chancellor of the Exchequer, Lloyd George, talked loudly of war. Again Germany backed down. Between Germany and Morocco stood the British navy. These two efforts of the Kaiser to drive a wedge between the Entente powers had the effect of driving them closer together. Moreover, his own ally, Italy, had proved uncertain. These two crises growing out of imperialism hastened the coming of World War I.

6. THE BRITISH EMPIRE

Of all the European overseas empires, the British was by far the most successful. Indeed, it was the dazzling size and wealth of the British Empire that helped to excite the other European powers to greater imperialistic activity. By 1914 the British Empire included one-fourth of all the land and people of the earth. In addition to Britain's spheres of influence in China and her African territories, which we have just mentioned, the empire included four great self-governing dominions: Canada, Australia, New Zealand, and the Union of South Africa. It also included

This cartoon, which appeared in Life in 1899, satirizes the attitudes of smug righteousness and superiority with which the Americans, the British, and the European nations extended their dominance over the rest of the world. The United States was dominant in the Western Hemisphere; the European imperialist powers in the Eastern Hemisphere.
Photo: NYPL Picture Collection

British Honduras in Central America; British Guiana in South America; numerous islands in the West Indies; strategic steppingstones along her Mediterranean – Red Sea life line such as Gibraltar, Malta, Cyprus, and Aden; scores of islands in the Atlantic, Pacific, and Indian Oceans; Malaya; Burma; Ceylon; parts of New Guinea and Borneo; and, above all, India. Nor should we forget the English-speaking United States – Britain's prodigal son who made good and who would return more than once in time of need to rescue the mother country.

Great Britain's commerce with her empire was enormous. In 1914 her foreign investments,

most of which were in the empire, totaled $20 billion – one-fourth of the total wealth of the homeland. (By comparison, France had $9 billion invested abroad; Germany, 6. The United States was a debtor nation.) The empire, furthermore, provided lucrative and often glamorous careers for thousands of British governors, army and navy officers, diplomats, and civil servants of every description.

In the latter part of the nineteenth century, Great Britain adopted the policy of granting self-government to the English-speaking portions of her empire. Canada, which had gained self-government in 1849, was granted dominion status in 1867. With dominion status, the only remaining effective bond was allegiance to the British crown. The British governor-general was only a figurehead like the king at home. Australia was made a self-governing dominion in 1901, New Zealand in 1907, and the Union of South Africa in 1910. The policy was successful. All the dominions rallied to the mother country in both world wars.

Great Britain's richest imperial prize was India. India's more than 300 million inhabitants accounted for at least three-fourths of the total population of the whole empire. India was nearly twenty times as large as Great Britain and more than seven times as populous. She was the mother country's best customer and supplied many minerals and raw materials. Until 1858 India was governed by the British East India Company, a private joint stock company. However, the great Sepoy Mutiny of 1857, the first large-scale uprising of the Indians against British rule, caused the British government to take over the government of India from the company. Between 1858 and 1914 Great Britain spent millions of dollars in India on railroads, industries, education, and public health. The enormous growth of India's population, which more than doubled during the period, is testimony to the improvement in the conditions of life under British rule. But, the British took out of India more than they brought in, and they showed no inclination to grant self-government. Indian dis-

satisfaction with British rule mounted steadily. In the late nineteenth century, nationalism, which had provided so much aggressive energy for Europe, was coming to Asia—to India as well as to Japan and China. In 1885 the All Indian Congress party was formed for the purpose of achieving Indian independence. By 1914 it was becoming obvious that India would not remain a placid and profitable colony much longer.

The European world's technology, its dynamic capitalism, and above all its aggressive nationalism had enabled it between 1871 and 1914 to subject most of the rest of the world to its domination. The tail wagged the dog. By 1914 the European world had come to look upon this as a normal and permanent thing. Near the end of the nineteenth century and early in the twentieth century, however, those same forces were coming to Asia and Africa as they had come to Japan a bit earlier. The spirit of nationalism was proving once again to be contagious—ominously this time for the Western imperialists.

Suggested Reading

General

E. M. Winslow, *The Pattern of Imperialism: A Study in Theories of Power* (1948). Demonstrates that imperialism is more political than economic in motivation.

*D. E. Owen, *Imperialism and Nationalism in the Far East* (Berkshire). Good brief survey.

The Exploitation and Awakening of China

*J. K. Fairbank, *The United States and China* (Compass). More than its title indicates. A scholarly, lucid history of China by a leading expert.

*L. Sharman, *Sun Yat-sen: His Life and Its Meaning: A Critical Biography* (Stanford University). One of the few good biographies of China's great liberator.

The Emergence of Japan

*E. A. Reischauer, *Japan: The Story of a Nation* (Knopf). Excellent brief survey.

C. Yanaga, *Japan Since Perry* (1949). Detailed and scholarly.

Competition for the Near and Middle East

S. N. Fisher, *The Middle East: A History*, 2nd ed. (1969). Reliable text.

The Scramble for Africa

G. P. Murdock, *Africa: Its Peoples and Their Culture History* (1959). Good survey.

*H. L. Hoskins, *European Imperialism in Africa* (Berkshire). Good brief survey.

G. Seaver, *David Livingston, His Life and Letters* (1957).

*C. W. de Kiewiet, *A History of South Africa: Social and Economic* (Oxford). A dramatic story.

The British Empire

P. Knaplund, *The British Empire, 1815–1939* (1941). A scholarly survey.

*T. W. Wallbank, *India: A Survey of the Heritage and Growth of Indian Nationalism* (Berkshire). Good brief account.

52
THE CHALLENGE TO CHRISTIANITY

Whatever one's religious faith may be—Christian, Jewish, Buddhist, or rationalistic; orthodox or skeptic; evangelistic or apathetic—he can hardly deny the tremendous influence of religion in history. In the Middle East empires rise and fall, conquerors come and go, but Islam remains, setting the pattern of ideals and thought and, to a considerable degree, the life of the people. The same is true of Hinduism in India and Confucianism in China. In Western civilization the great religious base, the great commonality, is Christianity, with its roots of Judaistic ethics and monotheism. Before the nineteenth century Christianity had withstood many assaults: the Arian heresy in its formative years; conflict between pope and emperor, conflict between the Western and the Eastern churches, and various heresies in the Middle Ages; the Great Schism in the fourteenth and fifteenth centuries; the Protestant Revolt in the sixteenth century; and the rationalistic assault in the eighteenth century. In the latter part of the nineteenth century, however, the Christian religion underwent a challenge more serious and fundamental than any of these.

1. THE VARIOUS FORCES AND INFLUENCES OPPOSED TO MYSTIC RELIGION IN THE PERIOD 1871–1914

Of the various factors and developments during the second phase of the Industrial Revolution that were hostile to mystic or supernatural religion, undoubtedly the most direct and challenging was the rapid growth of science and the scientific spirit. However, there were others. Let us recall a few of the most important that we have observed in the four preceding chapters.

The phenomenal growth of technology and industry was in many ways inimical to religious faith and practices. In the industrialized areas it began to appear that the power machines would soon supply all man's material needs and banish grinding toil from the earth. Preoccupation with creature comforts and pleasure gadgets undreamed of a few years earlier now tended to overshadow interest in the sacred and the spiritual. Dazzling speed did not seem to be conducive to meditation and devotion. The Industrial Revolution also brought about a mass migration of people, from farm to city and from country to country, tearing them loose from old social patterns and institutions, of which the church had long been one of the most important. Members of the flocks became separated from their pastors. And in the growing industrial cities, with their movement and relative excitement, many of the newcomers seemed no longer to need the church for their social life and entertainment.

The liberal and radical political movements of the late nineteenth century were for the most part anticlerical and often antireligious. The established churches in Europe, particularly the Roman Catholic Church, had long been allied with the conservative aristocracy and royalty. Liberals, when they came to power, usually proceeded to attack the powers, the privileges, and the property of the established church. France is a good example. After the revolutionary era had ended with the overthrow of Napoleon, the Roman Catholic Church made a comeback. It allied itself with the Bourbon regime and with Napoleon III's Second Empire and opposed liberal movements, including the setting up of the Third French Republic. The liberal leaders of the Third Republic immediately adopted anticlerical policies. During the 1880s, the Ferry Laws loosened the hold of the Church on education by setting up a rival and favored system of public secular schools, in which the teaching of religion was banned. In 1901 the Associations Law virtually destroyed the Church's schools by outlawing the Roman Catholic teaching orders or associations. In 1905 church and state were conpletely separated. In all the industrialized countries in this period, public secular education made great strides, usually under the sponsorship of liberal parties. Marxist socialism, which began to make headway between 1871 and 1914, was militantly materialistic and atheistic.

A third factor inimical to supernatural religion during the second phase of the Industrial Revolution was the growth of malignant nationalism, which afflicted all the great industrialized powers. Nationalism became itself a religion and drew the allegiance of millions away from their traditional faiths. International Roman Catholicism and international Judaism were prime targets. Between 1872 and 1878, Bismarck waged an unrelenting *Kulturkampf* (battle for civilization) against the Roman Catholic Church in Germany. Bismarck regarded as intolerable the allegiance of millions of German citizens to a non-German pope and the formation of a Roman Catholic political party in Germany. The anti-Semitism that raised its ugly head in many countries at this time may be attributed in part to the resentment against the international character of Judaism and also to racism, which is an extreme form of malignant nationalism. The Dreyfus case in France is an example. Bloody pogroms in Russia drove tens of thousands of Russian and Polish Jews to America. Many Jews themselves, after centuries of dispersion, became nationalistic and started a movement (Zionism) to set up a Jewish national state in Palestine.

2. THE CONFLICT BETWEEN NATURAL SCIENCE AND CHRISTIANITY

With the exception of the evolutionary hypothesis, the challenge to Christianity by natural science was more indirect than direct. The marvelous achievements of the scientists caused many to place great faith in man and in his ability to do for himself whatever needed to be done. The scientific attitude ran counter to the traditional attitude of religious faith. The discovery of more and more of the secrets of the material world made it possible to attribute to natural causes many phenomena that previously had been attributed to divine intervention. Disease germs, for instance, now appeared to be doing things that had long been ascribed to God. In fact, there appeared to many at the end of the nineteenth century to be less and less place and need for God.

The greatest issues between natural science and the Christian religion to be raised in the nineteenth century grew out of Darwin's evolutionary hypothesis. The publication of *The Origin of Species* in 1859 created an immediate religious storm. The proposal of a long, gradual, and seemingly mechanistic evolution of all present species from simpler forms appeared to contradict the account of divine creation given in the first chapter of Genesis. If Darwin should prove to be right and Genesis wrong, what faith could be put in the divine inspiration and the reliability of the rest of the Bible, upon which so much of Christianity depends? The whole process of evolution as suggested by Darwin appeared to leave God out of the affairs of the universe entirely. Any doubt concerning Darwin's place for man in his evolutionary hypothesis was removed twelve years later, when he published *The Descent of Man*. Man, like all other living things, evolved from more primitive species. This appeared to refute not only the biblical account of man's creation, but also God's purpose, according to the Bible, of creating man in his own image as a temple of the Holy Spirit. According to Darwin's hypothesis, in the view of many, man seemed to be just another animal, albeit the highest.

Churchmen throughout Christendom raged against Darwin and his hypothesis. His character and his motives were assailed. His thesis was attacked and ridiculed. Some of the criticism was sound; for example, there is still no empirical evidence for the existence of many of the hypothesized evolutionary stages. A good bit of the theorizing done by Darwin and his contemporaries has since been generally repudiated by most biologists. And although there is abundant evidence of evolution within a given species, neither Darwin nor anyone else has ever demonstrated the evolution of one species out of another—the origin of a species. However, most of the criticism of the churchmen sprang from ignorance, fear, and habits of thought growing out of the uses and abuses of unquestioned authority. Efforts were made, sometimes successful, to suppress the reading of Darwin's books and the teaching of the evolutionary hypothesis in the schools.

Darwin himself, a gentle and modest scholar of the highest order but not a controversialist, refrained for the most part from attacking the churchmen. He merely defended his thesis when he considered it to be incorrectly or unfairly attacked. However, he was not lacking in doughty champions able and willing to assail the forces of religion with the religious forces' own techniques. Thomas Huxley (1825–1895), a biologist, surgeon in the British navy, and president of the Royal Society, popularized Darwin's work in dozens of vigorous and lucid books and pamphlets and heaped withering scorn upon the churchmen. He called himself "Darwin's bulldog." Herbert Spencer was carried away with Darwin's thesis and built a whole system of philosophy around the idea of evolution. Spencer considered evolution the key to all truth and all progress. He was vitriolic in his denunciations of the ideals and practices of the Christian religion, which he regarded as the major enemy of both truth and progress. Ernst Haeckel (1834–1919), a prolific German scientist and popularizer, made great and sometimes ridiculous claims for evolution and for science. He claimed that scientists would very soon be solving all the remaining mysteries of life and even creating life. The conflict between the evolutionists and the Christian churchmen that raged in Western Europe in the last four decades of the nineteenth century did not reach its climax in the United States until the 1920s.

3. THE ASSAULT OF SOCIAL SCIENCE ON CHRISTIANITY

The assault of social science upon Christianity was very much more direct and severe than that of natural science. Social science deals specifically with man and society, as does religion. It was inevitable that two approaches to the same subject from diametrically opposite points of view should come into head-on collision. Also, social science is much less exact than natural science, and social scientists are more given to generalizing and philosophizing on complex subjects with less precise data.

Anthropologists dug into man's distant past to unearth the primtive origins of his culture, of which religion is always an important part. Nearly all of them concluded that religion is based upon primitive superstition. In 1890 Sir James Frazer (1854–1941) published *The Golden Bough*, a vast and fascinating history of early myths, superstitions, and cults from which he believed that present-day religions, including Christianity, are derived. For instance, he shows that it was customary among many primitive tribes to eat their grain god and drink their wine god, hoping thereby to partake of their strength. *The Golden Bough* went through edition after edition, each bigger than the one preceding, until it reached twelve volumes. It is still a good seller in abridged form.

The behavioristic psychologists attempted to mechanize man's mind and his emotions, including religious faith (or "ecstasy," as they sometimes called it). They had man creating God in man's own image in order to have a big brother to lean on in time of need. Some of them saw God as man's creation as a ready answer to the unanswerable.

Historians, many of whom in the period 1871–1914 attempted to make history a social science, assigned natural, usually economic, causes to all religious developments and institutions. The famed German historian of religion Adolf von Harnack (1851–1930) believed Christianity to be an outgrowth of Greek philosophy.

Historians of the warfare between science and religion in this period nearly always made science the hero and religion the villain.

But it was the sociologists who of all the social scientists in the period 1871–1914 were the most persistently and pointedly hostile to religion. Supernatural religion had no place whatever in Comte's positivism, humanity itself being the object of worship. Through volume after volume of Herbert Spencer's sociological writings ran a vein of hostility to mystic religion in general and to Christianity in particular. Mechanical evolution became, for Spencer, the key to all social progress. Even morals evolved. Religious faith retarded social progress and obscured man's vision of the evolutionary social process.

4. THE HIGHER CRITICISM

Finally, the scientific spirit of the second phase of the Industrial Revolution brought forth a number of biblical scholars who subjected the Bible to searching scrutiny and analysis—some for the purpose of establishing its exact meaning, and others for the purpose of detecting error or fraud. This type of scholarship is called "higher criticism."

The first prominent nineteenth-century "higher critic" of the Bible was David Strauss (1808–1874), a Lutheran theologian at the University of Tübingen in Germany. After long years of laborious work, Strauss brought out a *Life of Jesus* in two volumes that stripped Christ of his divinity and undertook to explain in natural terms the miracles and prophecies recorded in the New Testament. Strauss asserted that the New Testament was a very unreliable document, that the authorship of the four Gospels could not be proved, and that the four accounts of the life of Jesus were contradictory.

Much more popular and influential was the charming one-volume *La Vie de Jésus* by Ernest Renan (1823–1892), a French scholar and a Roman Catholic. Renan pictured Christ in solely human and natural terms. Christ was the gentlest, wisest, best, and most charming creature who ever lived. We should all worship him and follow his example. But he was man, not God. Renan attributed Christ's belief in his own divinity to hallucinations. But it was these psychological aberrations that gave him his power and drive and much of his appeal. Renan's *Life of Jesus* was greeted with immediate and continuing enthusiasm by the intellectual world of the late nineteenth and early twentieth centuries. Here at last seemed to be the solution to the most stubborn mystery of all—the answer that the humanistic "scientific" philosophers had long been looking for. It was the rationalization and the humanization of the most influential figure of all time. The work of Strauss and Renan and the numerous other "higher critics" appeared to many to bring religion within the compass of onrushing science.

5. THE CHRISTIAN RESPONSE

The reaction of Christianity to the various nineteenth-century challenges and assaults may be classified under three broad headings: (1) uncompromising rejection, (2) surrender to the challenges and assaults, (3) moderate compromise, or accommodation of the fundamentals of the faith to proved new truth and conditions. On the whole the Roman Catholics were able to meet the challenge more quickly and easily than the Protestants. This is because the Roman Catholics were more centralized and authoritative in their organization than the Protestants and were less dependent upon the Bible (now under attack) for doctrinal authority. The Roman Catholic Church could achieve by papal decree and clerical discipline what the various Protestant denominations, with their less authoritative and sometimes democratic procedures, required years to accomplish. The Eastern Orthodox Christians were not much affected by the nineteenth-century challenges, since they were located mostly in Russia and the Balkan Peninsula, where science and technology arrived only in the last decade of the century, and then very slowly.

The first reaction of Christianity to the new challenges was angry rejection of the new ideas and forces. In 1864 Pope Pius IX (1846–1878) issued a *Syllabus of Errors*, errors that Roman Catholics were to avoid. These errors, eighty in all, included separation of church and state, civil marriage, secular education, freedom of speech and press, religious toleration, liberty of con-

Pope Leo XIII (1878–1903) was the first powerful Christian leader to face up to issues raised by the onrush of science and technology. While clinging steadfastly to the traditional doctrines of the Church, he welcomed new scientific discoveries. He also supported many liberal political and social reform movements. *Photo: UPI*

science, liberalism, and materialism. This list was strengthened and brought up to date by Pius X (1903–1914), who issued another *Syllabus* in 1907 specifically condemning all those Christians who would compromise their doctrines. In 1870 Pius IX called the Vatican council (the first general council since that at Trent in the sixteenth century), which pronounced the doctrine of papal infallibility. According to this doctrine, the pope, when speaking *ex cathedra* (that is, officially *from the chair* of St. Peter) on a matter of faith or morals, is not subject to error. This was the most authoritarian position that the Church and the pope had ever taken, and it came at a time when the intellectual, political, and religious trends seemed to be in the opposite direction. (The pope has used this power only once, as of 1974). In the late nineteenth and early twentieth centuries, the Roman Catholic hierarchy excommunicated numerous members and several priests who had compromised the official doctrines of the Church. By 1914 discipline appeared to have been fairly well restored.

The Protestants had no such disciplinary means and weapons at their disposal. Their difficulties in this respect are illustrated by the failure of the Anglican hierarchy in Great Britain to discipline certain heterodox clergymen. The cases were appealed to the highest secular court; the established Anglican Church, which is subordinate to the British government, was overruled. In Germany, Wilhelm II freely interfered in the affairs of the official Lutheran Church in behalf of compromise (modernist) doctrines. In general, fundamentalism in the Protestant churches was a local or individual matter. However, fundamentalist sects were be no means rare. They interpreted the Bible, including the first chapter of Genesis, literally, and denounced all scientific beliefs that did not accord with it. As science and technology rushed on, the fundamentalist position became harder and harder to maintain.

The second reaction of Christianity to the nineteenth-century challenges and assaults was surrender to them. Many Christians, Roman Catholics and Protestants alike, lost their faith, left their church, and became atheists or agnostics. But many more who lost the traditional faith remained in their church and attempted to change its doctrines. They granted the claims of science and the "higher criticism," and they sympathized with the materialism, liberalism, and extreme nationalism of the day. They continued to go to church, to sing the hymns, to say the prayers, and to recite the creeds, but they did not believe what they sang, said, and recited. They would reject the supernatural and deny the divinity of Christ. They would make the Bible a book of good literature and high ethical ideals; Christ, a great social reformer; and the church, an instrument for the promotion of good will, wholesome fellowship, racial tolerance, temperance, charity, patriotism, and so on. These Christians came to be called *modernists*. The Roman Catholic Church, as we have seen, declared officially against modernism in 1907, and by 1914 it appeared either to have suppressed the modernists in its ranks or driven them under cover. In the various Protestant churches in Europe modernism competed with fundamentalism, both extreme and moderate, and by 1914 modernism tended to gain the upper hand. In the United States modernism in the Protestant churches did not reach its peak until the 1920s and 1930s.

The third reaction of Christianity, the one that appears to prevail today, was moderate compromise: a cheerful acceptance of proved scientific facts and reasonable deductions therefrom together with attempts to harmonize the findings of science with the fundamentals of the Christian faith. This involved the interpretation figuratively of certain passages in the Bible, particularly in the first chapter of Genesis, and the admission of a few errors in various versions of the Bible. On the other hand, it was soon found that many of the anti-Christian claims of the scientists and higher critics had been hasty and ill-founded. Many of the higher critics of this period were anything but scientifically objective, setting out deliberately to debunk the Bible. And the belligerently anti-Christian scientists were, for the most part, not first-rate scholars like Darwin, but second-raters — popularizers and publicists who knew as little about the Christian religion as the militant fundamentalists knew about science. When first-rate men of good will on both sides moved in on the problem, it was discovered that little, if any, conflict existed between the proved facts and principles of science and the fundamental doctrines of the Christian faith. An important feature of this harmonizing Christian reaction was an increased awareness of the responsibility of the Christian churches to participate actively in the social and political problems of the day.

The Roman Catholics were the first to reach this middle position. From 1878 to 1903 the Roman Church was headed by the ablest pope since the thirteenth century, Leo XIII. This elderly, frail, and scholarly man was elected pope at one of the most critical times in the Church's history. It was not thought that he would live long, and he was expected only to hold the rival factions together during his few remaining years, after which a strong pope would be elected. Instead, he lived for twenty-five more years and proved himself to be a brilliant and vigorous theologian, administrator, and statesman.

Leo XIII quickly removed any doubts concerning the willingness of the Roman Catholic Church to compromise its historic doctrines. He proclaimed Thomas Aquinas the official Roman Catholic theologian and philosopher and established numerous centers of higher learning for the study and propagation of Thomistic theology and philosophy. He invited all Protestants and Eastern Orthodox Christians to accept papal supremacy, Roman Catholic doctrines and practices, and to return to the Roman fold. He demanded a privileged status for the Roman Catholic Church in all states, independent of the secular government when in a minority and superior to the secular government when in a majority. On the other hand, Leo XIII welcomed new scientific beliefs on condition that they be proved, opened the Vatican's archives to research scholars, and brought a number of first-rate physicists and the latest scientific equipment to the Vatican observatory. As to the evolution controversy, Leo XIII and his successors gradually took the position that natural science was not the province of the Church and that the Church, therefore, would not make official pronouncements on it; that the evolutionary concept was not in itself repugnant to the doctrines of the Church; that evolution could be taught in the Church's schools as a hypothesis, and, when and if satisfactorily proved, it could be taught as fact; that the first chapter of Genesis should be taken figuratively; and that within these premises belief in evolution was a private and individual matter.

Leo XIII also faced up squarely and boldly to the economic and social challenges of the second phase of the Industrial Revolution. In 1891, in the most famous of all his encyclicals, *Rerum Novarum* (new things), he denounced materialism and Marxian socialism and proclaimed the sanctity of private property. He did, however, declare limits to the use of private property. Labor must not be treated as a commodity; workers must be paid a fair living wage and protected against too long hours, injury, and disease. Leo XIII advocated a wider distribution of property, labor unions for collective bargaining, and farming cooperatives. Roman Catholic labor unions were soon organized to challenge the socialist-dominated unions.

Much — probably most — of Protestantism groped its way slowly, and often painfully, toward a position similar in general to that of Leo

XIII. However, Protestantism never claimed so exalted a place for the church within the state, nor was it ever so firm in its stand on capital and labor.

Early in the twentieth century a number of developments strengthened the hands of the theologians. The discovery by Rutherford and Einstein that the atom is really composed of particles of electricity or energy and Einstein's theory of relativity undermined belief in the stability of matter and confidence in materialism. Natural scientists were no longer so sure of themselves. Many things in the material world, long regarded as certain, suddenly became less certain. The two world wars, the great depression, and the violence of Fascist and Communist dictatorships raised grave doubts concerning some of the optimistic tenets of the social scientists and the modernists.

Shortly after the close of World War I, the brilliant Swiss Protestant theologian and philosopher Karl Barth (1886–1968) began to beckon many disillusioned Western Christians to return to an enlightened fundamentalism. The time had come, said Barth, for the Christian churches to concern themselves less with social and political problems, which he called the worship of and reliance upon man, and to concern themselves more with the worship of God and reliance upon Divine Providence. A neo-Calvinist, Barth believed that God still rules the universe and that the Scriptures are his word to man. Barth's fundamentalism differed from the earlier fundamentalism in that it was propounded in the full light of recent science and philosophy and with an impressive display of intellectualism. Probably Barth's most illustrious follower was Reinhold Niebuhr (1892–1971) in the United States. However, Niebuhr believed that the Christian churches should be actively engaged both in the worship of God and in humanitarian political and social endeavors.

As to evolution, the eminent French scientist Pierre Lecomte du Noüy expressed the views of many intellectual Christians, both Protestant and Roman Catholic, in his *Human Destiny* (1947). Lecomte du Noüy argued impressively that evolution could not have occurred by blind chance, that it must have been divinely guided. The millions of years that God took to create man did not trouble Lecomte du Noüy. Just as a day is long for an insect that has a life span of one day, but short to man, so time that seems long to man would be short to a timeless being like God. Lecomte du Noüy believed that with the appearance of man, evolution ceased to be physical, so far as man was concerned, and became spiritual, Christ being the perfect model. This is a far cry from the fulminations of Huxley and the early fundamentalists. By the time of World War II, the trend in Protestantism appeared to be definitely toward a moderate and somewhat intellectualized fundamentalism.

Protestantism, like Roman Catholicism under Leo XIII, assumed a more direct and organized interest in social problems. The Anglican clergyman, novelist, and historian Charles Kingsley (1819–1875) became so outraged at the lot of the industrial proletariat that he advocated Christian socialism. An English Protestant clergyman, William Booth (1829–1912), founded the Salvation Army, which concentrated on rescue mission work in the industrial slums. The Young Men's Christian Association specialized in wholesome recreation for underprivileged youth; the Quakers, in charities.

Although Eastern Orthodox Christianity was not so seriously challenged in the period 1871–1914 as were Roman Catholic and Protestant Christianity in the more materially advanced West, Orthodox Russia produced one of the foremost Christian social reformers of the time—Count Leo Tolstoy (1828–1910). This wealthy and aristocratic but sensitive literary artist became greatly disturbed by the condition of the wretched poor in Russia's cities. In his book *What Shall We Do Then?* Tolstoy advocates Christian socialism, which he believed to be taught in the four Gospels. The rich should share their goods with the poor and also the physical toil of the poor. Tolstoy practiced his own preaching. Divesting himself of his great wealth, he lived the life of a common laborer and still found time and inspiration to continue writing.

Judaism was affected by the various challenges of the second phase of the Industrial Revolution in much the same way as Christianity. Many Jews drifted away from their religious beliefs and practices entirely. Many others became Reformed Jews (modernists). Those who remained true to the old religion were called Orthodox Jews.

It is an interesting fact that Christianity, so beset on its home grounds by challenges, assaults, and internal divisions during the period 1871–1914, was never more zealous in sending out missionaries to propagate the faith abroad. Roman Catholic, Protestant, and Eastern Orthodox missionaries vied with one another in converting the heathen in Asia and Africa. Probably the most renowned Christian missionary of the early twentieth century was the French Protestant Albert Schweitzer (1875–1965). An eminent philosopher, historian, musician, and surgeon, Schweitzer in 1913 went into the jungles of French Equatorial Africa to spend the rest of his life ministering to the medical needs of the primitive tribesmen and teaching them the Christian message by the example of his life.

By 1914 more than 40 million people outside Western Christendom professed the Christian faith. But since the Christian missionaries to Asia and Africa were often associated in the minds of the native peoples with Western imperialism and exploitation, they frequently aroused resentment. The scope and intensity of this Christian missionary activity, however, is striking evidence of Christianity's continued vitality in the West. Nevertheless, in 1914 Christianity in the West was still on the defensive.

One of the most prominent of the many Christian missionaries active during this period was the French Protestant Dr. Albert Schweitzer, eminent scholar, musician, and physician, who in 1913 at the age of thirty-eight chose to devote the rest of his life to medical missionary work in the jungles of French Equatorial Africa. *Photo: United Press International*

Suggested Reading

General

*C. J. H. Hayes, *A Generation of Materialism, 1871–1900* (Torch). Has an excellent chapter on religious development.

A. Toynbee, *An Historian's Approach to Religion* (1956). A challenging analysis. Lucid style.

The Challenge of Science

*C. C. Gillespie, *Genesis and Geology: The Decades before Darwin* (Torch). Examines pre-Darwin challenges to the Bible.

*W. Irvine, *Apes, Angels, and Victorians* (Meridian). Examines the evolution controversy in a humorous style.

The Higher Criticism

*E. Renan, *Life of Jesus* (Modern Library). Analyzes Jesus in human psychological terms. Very influential.

*A. Schweitzer, *The Quest for the Historical Jesus* (Macmillan). A scholarly work by a famous Christian missionary.

The Christian Response

R. Fülop-Miller, *Leo XIII and Our Times: Might of the Church-Power in the World* (1937). Excellent study.

*P. Lecomte de Noüy, *Human Destiny* (Mentor). Brilliant analysis of the evolutionary hypothesis by a distinguished scientist and Christian layman.

*K. Barth, *The Word of God and the Word of Man* (Torch). Major work by one of Protestantism's leading twentieth century theologians.

*W. Hordern, *Layman's Guide to Protestant Theology* (Macmillan). A handy and reliable guide.

J. W. Parks, *A History of the Jewish People* (1952). A useful survey.

53

DISENCHANTMENT, REALISM, IMPRESSIONISM, MODERNISM

The materialism of science and technology, the cynicism that accompanied the challenged and wavering religious and moral values, and the restlessness of the masses are reflected in the thought and art of the second phase of the Industrial Revolution, 1871–1914. There was no sudden or drastic breaking away from the spirit of idealism and romanticism that prevailed in the thought and art of the bourgeois-dominated first phase of the Industrial Revolution, 1830–1871. Both idealism and romanticism continued on into the second phase, and beyond. Indeed, there were so many divergent trends and schools of thought and art during this period that the term *eclectic* is sometimes used to characterize its culture. Nevertheless, we may detect certain trends that stand out as significant. It is doubly important that we identify these trends, for many of them have continued to the present.

1. THE GENERAL NATURE OF THOUGHT AND ART DURING THE SECOND PHASE OF THE INDUSTRIAL REVOLUTION, 1871–1914

The prevailing idealism and optimism that characterized the thought of the early nineteenth century tended after 1871 to give way to materialism, pragmatism, and pessimism—in spite of material progress never before dreamed of. During the second phase of the Industrial Revolu-

tion, literature was characterized by realism of various types. The arts tended first toward Impressionism and then toward more open revolt against the standards of the past. In music, however, there was a much stronger carry-over of traditional styles and values than in the rest of the arts.

The chief influences behind the new trends were undoubtedly the intellectual and sociological problems created by science and technology. Darwinism, Freudian psychology, and the discontent of the industrial proletariat run through the literature and art of the period like a refrain. Darwinism appeared to many to make man an animal, a brute, struggling for survival in a heartless, competitive world governed by blind chance. This was a sharp break with the romantic idealism that saw man as a child of God, and the world as a thing of beauty governed by a benevolent Divine Being.

The new psychology made man's mind as well as his body mechanical and animal-like. Furthermore, it discovered in the dark subconscious recesses of the mind selfish and brutish desires. These disenchanting concepts represented a radical departure not only from those of the romantic idealists of the early nineteenth century, but also from the ideas of the eighteenth-century philosophers of the Enlightenment, who believed in the essential goodness of nature and the perfectibility of man. The rapid development of technology during the so-called Second Industrial Revolution made the proletariat so numerous and so restless that it could no longer be ignored, either by the bourgeois capitalists or by the writers and artists. The smug all's-right-with-the-world attitude that the writers and painters expressed in the bourgeois-dominated early and mid-nineteenth century tended to give way to sordidly realistic writing and painting about the slums and the uprooted.

Finally, Einstein's relativity theory and the startling ideas of the physicists with respect to the stability of the atom, that is, of matter itself, which came toward the end of this period, heightened the wave of cynicism, disillusionment, and revolt. Nor did the Christian religion, then wavering under heavy assault, give out the guiding light that it had long provided in the Western world. It should be noted, however, that the pessimism that tended to prevail among the thinkers and artists of the second phase of the Industrial Revolution did not always reflect the attitude of the masses, who were at last on the move toward a greater share of this world's material goods and privileges.

2. THE PHILOSOPHY OF DISENCHANTMENT

Although the Darwinian concept of evolution by natural selection made some of the philosophers of the late nineteenth century, such as Thomas Huxley, Herbert Spencer, and Ernst Haeckel, extremely optimistic about man and society evolving ever onward and upward, it had the opposite effect on others. A forerunner of the pessimistic type of materialism that was to have so much influence on the twentieth century was Arthur Schopenhauer (1788–1860). In *The World as Will and Idea,* published in 1819, forty years before *The Origin of Species,* this German thinker set forth the idea that one force governs and motivates the whole world of animate life, and that force is will—the will to survive. The world, therefore, is a cruel and heartless place full of struggling and competing creatures, a place where the strong and fierce devour the weak and gentle. The only possible happiness to be found in it is by ascetic denial and withdrawal. They suffer least who participate least in the hard, competitive world.

This line of thinking (at least a variation of it) was carried to its ultimate by an admirer of Schopenhauer, Friedrich Nietzsche (1844–1900). Nietzsche was a disillusioned German theological student turned philosopher. He was a pain- and nerve-racked genius. Two of his most influential works are *Thus Spake Zarathustra* and *Beyond Good and Evil.* Like Schopenhauer, he believed that the greatest force in the animate world is will. However, this will is not only to survive but, in the strong at least, to achieve power. "The will to power" was Nietzsche's key phrase. If a superior society is to emerge, it will have to come about through the efforts of strong and gifted individuals who will rise to power because of their superior strength, will, and intelligence. Anything that contributes to power is good, be it brute strength, will, boldness, cunning, or intelligence. Whatever leads to weakness is bad, be it gentleness, modesty, generosity, or compassion. The two greatest enemies of the good society are democracy and Christianity. Democracy is the rule of the mediocre masses, cattle. But it was against Christianity that Nietzsche hurled his sharpest invective; he believed Christianity to be the greatest curse of Western civilization: a slave religion that extolls the vices of slavery, such as meekness, compassion, sacrifice, and charity, to compensate for actual weakness. Needless to say, Nietzsche was not very popular with the late nineteenth-century masses, who were obsessed with the marvels and promises of science and technology. However, his influence upon the twentieth century was great. Malignant nationalism, militarism, and fascism drew heavily on his ideas.

Less pessimistic than Schopenhauer's and Nietzsche's cult of the will but equally as materialistic was the philosophy of pragmatism. The chief expounder of this school of thought, which has been so potent and widespread in the twentieth century, was William James (1842–1910), a professor of psychology and philosophy at Harvard University. Pragmatism reflected the uncertainties aroused by atomic physicists around the turn of the century. James rejected all absolutes of logic and religion. Truth is relative depending upon the individual and the circumstances. A thing is true if it works and is useful.

We cannot know ultimate religious or moral truths, for instance, but if a particular religious faith gives an individual confidence and peace of mind, then it is practical and therefore true for him. Thus spiritual, moral, and human values become as relative in the minds of William James and the pragmatists as the physical world in the mind of Albert Einstein.

One of James' most influential disciples was John Dewey (1859–1952), a professor of philosophy at Columbia University. Dewey introduced the principle of pragmatism into the classroom. If, for instance, experimentation proved that children found modeling a bust of Julius Caesar more interesting than learning Latin grammar, as indeed many did, much of the latter was discarded in favor of the former. Or if the statistical studies showed that woodwork or typing was more often used in later life than algebra, then places were found for these useful skills, if necessary, at the expense of algebra. Everyone must be educated both for practical living and for citizenship. Dewey's pragmatism did much to enliven and democratize mass education in an age when the masses were moving to the fore. Unfortunately, in the hands of some of his more extreme disciples who possessed more enthusiasm than wisdom, thousands of twentieth-century classrooms became amusement centers for unrestrained children, large and small. It was in these classrooms that the philosophy of disenchantment—of relativism, cynicism, materialism, pragmatism—was likely to be disseminated by word and example to the masses.

3. REALISTIC LITERATURE

Much of the literature of the second phase of the Industrial Revolution, like the philosophy, reflected the materialism, the cynicism, and the pessimism of the age. However, there was a strong carry-over of romanticism beyond 1871 and into the twentieth century. The romantic poets Victor Hugo, Robert Browning, and Alfred Tennyson lived on until 1885, 1889, and 1892, respectively. Although Browning was a rugged and analytical realist when probing the depths of human psychology and emotions, he tended at times to be an idealist and an optimist, believ-ing that "God's in his heaven, all's right with the world." And although in 1850 the young Tennyson in his *In Memoriam* revealed a religious skepticism bold for the time, in 1889—well into a cynical age—he hoped to see his "Pilot face to face" when he had "crossed the bar." Nevertheless, the prevailing and most significant trend in literature in the period 1871–1914 was realism. It was expressed most generally in the novel and drama rather than poetry. Realism tended to depict the seamy, sordid side of human nature and society. It villainized the smug, *nouveau riche* industrial bourgeoisie and its religious and moral hypocrisy without idealizing the uprooted and distressed proletariat.

France took the lead in realistic literature. Balzac, who died in 1850, though essentially a romantic novelist, had foreshadowed realism. In his scores of novels and tales he subjected the dominant middle class to increasingly exact and severe scrutiny. The first French novelist to catch the full flavor of realism was Gustave Flaubert (1821–1880). His *Madame Bovary* related the illicit sex life of the wife of a small-town French physician in such full and unblushing detail that it scandalized a public not yet accustomed to such unrestrained "realism." *Madame Bovary* became a model to other novelists. Emile Zola (1840–1902), though interested like Flaubert in individual personality, was more concerned with social problems, particularly those created by industrialization. Zola was a bold and radical republican who, it will be remembered, bearded the French military lion and played a prominent role in finally securing justice for Dreyfus. In twenty penetrating but sometimes tedious novels he depicted and analyzed the problems of a changing society. His sympathy was with the industrial proletariat, but he suffered no illusions as to the natural goodness of man, including the distressed lower classes.

The greatest and most influential of the French realistic novelists was Anatole France (1844–1924), whose real name was Jacques Thibault. Anatole France was essentially an Epicurean. With a light touch he satirized the bourgeois society and the Christian religion and morals of the second phase of the Industrial Revolution.

The volume and the influence of his lucid writings were enormous. Three of his best-known novels are *Penguin Island, The Garden of Epicurus,* and *The Revolt of the Angels.* In later life he took an active part as a Socialist in the struggle to improve the status of the lower classes.

Charles Dickens (1812–1870) in Great Britain, like Balzac in France, combined romanticism and realism. In his sentimentality, his moralizing, his optimism, and his spontaneous gush of words he was a romantic. In his zeal for social reform, his pillorying of bourgeois arrogance and corrupt bourgeois institutions, and his graphic and often sordid detailing of the life of the urban proletariat, he was the first of the British realists. In *David Copperfield, Oliver Twist, The Pickwick Papers,* a galaxy of characters of the middle and lower walks of life in industrial Britain parade realistically before us. Thomas Hardy (1840–1928), unlike Dickens, had a completely pessimistic view of the universe. His vivid characters—ordinary English countryside folk— struggle Darwin-like against fate, environment, and their own frail natures without any help from God or Hardy. *The Return of the Native, The Mayor of Casterbridge, and Tess of the D'Urbervilles* are some of the best examples in any language of the realistic novel. H. G. Wells (1866–1946) placed his faith in materialistic science, technology, and social reform. He fascinated a science-obsessed age with novels that made a world of scientific marvels and supermen seem real and at hand. High on Wells' list of outworn institutions that must be discarded before a scientific and socialistic utopia could be created was supernatural religion.

Probably the greatest of all the British realists was George Bernard Shaw (1856–1950). Of Irish birth, Shaw early crossed over to London, where he long remained the gadfly of bourgeois society. In scores of urbane and sophisticated novels, essays, and plays, he charmingly but caustically taunted Christianity, capitalism, and democracy. Shaw was a cynic, a Socialist, and a stark materialist. He was the epitome of late nineteenth-century and early twentieth-century realism.

In the United States, the era of the realistic novel began with the works of Theodore Dreiser (1871–1945). Dreiser was a member of a large German immigrant family who moved about in poverty from place to place in the Middle West, the Roman Catholic father trying unsuccessfully to keep the restless children in line. Dreiser's novels depicted in hard, rough detail the life and the philosophy of the disenchanted and uprooted proletariat, living in a materialistic, industrial world of changing values. His first novel, *Sister Carrie,* which appeared in 1900, was an American industrial version of *Madame Bovary* told with raw unrestraint. To escape poverty, Carrie became the mistress of a succession of men. The progressive degeneration of the characters constitutes the theme of the novel. Editors were so shocked at the frank and open presentation of lurid details that Dreiser had great difficulty getting the book published. The success of *Sister Carrie* was immediate, and other novels in a like vein followed. His masterpiece was *An American Tragedy,* published twenty-five years later. It was not only Dreiser's narrative that startled the generation of the early twentieth century, but his philosophy as well. He pictured an amoral world of materialistic science and technology where human animals struggle for survival, motivated by unedifying Freudian drives. Dreiser's brand of realism, or naturalism, as the more extreme form of realism is sometimes called, became the dominant trend in American fiction as the century progressed.

One of the most influential of the realists was the Norwegian playwright Henrik Ibsen (1828– 1906). A frustrated artist embittered by youthful poverty, Ibsen ridiculed bourgeois society in his popular dramas. In what is probably his best-known play, *A Doll's House,* one of his heroines rebels against the "doll's house" that her stodgy, hypocritical, middle-class husband created for her. In *An Enemy of the People,* Ibsen reveals the fickleness of the masses and their unfitness for democratic government. *Ghosts* deals with the social and personal problems of syphilis.

Ibsen had a wide international following. He was the chief inspiration for the youthful George Bernard Shaw. In Germany, Gerhart Hauptmann (1862–1946) dramatized the dislocation of the proletariat during the early stages of the Industrial Revolution. In Russia, Dostoevski and Turgenev (see p. 536) combined realism with romanticism in much the same manner as did Balzac in France and Dickens in Great Britain. Leo Tolstoy (1828–1910) was more of a realist and dedicated his life and writing almost exclusively to social reform. His masterpiece is *War and Peace*. In this gigantic novel, scores of personalities along with more impersonal social forces so interlace with and influence each other that not even the strongest individual—not even Napoleon—can work his will alone. In his later years Tolstoy sought to combine Christianity with socialism, giving up his great inherited wealth to set a good example. Anton Chekhov (1860–1904) wrote polished but realistic and pessimistic plays about Russian peasant life. Maxim Gorky (1868–1936), up from the proletarian ranks, analyzed the social problems of the Russian masses in his dramas and novels. He was a revolutionary and later a Communist.

Realistic literature, with all its differing varieties, had many things in common. It reflected almost invariably the social dislocation brought about by the Industrial Revolution, particularly in its more advanced second phase. It reflected the materialism of an age of science and technology. It displayed over and over again the influence of Darwin and of Freud. It was increasingly concerned with the disillusionment and cynicism brought about by changing religious and moral values. This last factor is probably the most fundamental and significant of them all.

4. IMPRESSIONISTIC AND MODERN PAINTING AND SCULPTURE

France, the birthplace of realistic literature, was also the chief seat of the impressionistic and modern painting and sculpture that predominated during the second phase of the Industrial Revolution. Impressionism was a mild and sophisticated revolt against the artistic standards that had prevailed since the late fifteenth century. It reflected the intellectual challenge to traditional values and institutions that arose with the startling advances of science in the late nineteenth century. It took its chief inspiration from the seventeenth-century Spanish painters Velásquez and El Greco, from Japanese art, which was rediscovered after 1853, and from new scientific knowledge concerning the nature of color and light. Impressionistic painting was informal, unposed, and random-angled. It sought to convey by studied casualness the impression of a view one gets at a glance. The chief founder of the impressionistic style of painting was the Frenchman Edouard Manet (1832–1883). Among his more illustrious disciples were Claude Monet (1840–1926) and Auguste Renoir (1841–1919) in France, and James McNeill Whistler (1834–1903), an American expatriate in Europe.[1] These artists painted sunlit parks and landscapes, shimmering lakes and rivers, and subtle, sophisticated portraits. They omitted much detail, painting in only suggestive shapes, forms, and colors as first impressions, and leaving the rest to the imagination. Their work was sensuous, decorative, and mildly iconoclastic.

The breach that the impressionists made with the long-established traditions was greatly widened near the end of the nineteenth century and early in the twentieth by more radical modern painters. The new trend was led by Paul Cézanne (1839–1906), a lifelong friend of Emile Zola. Cézanne distorted freely in order to achieve a more powerful effect, and applied thick paint to attain the appearance of solidity and roundness. Going far beyond Cézanne, the gifted but eccentric Frenchman Paul Gauguin (1848–1903) and Dutchman Vincent van Gogh (1853–1890) broke openly with every artistic standard of the past. Gauguin was not interested in painting the literal document of his subject, but only what the subject meant to him. He painted patterns formed in his mind by objects rather than the objects themselves, using the most violent reds, yellows, and greens. He finally went primitive, deserting Western civilization for the South Sea islands. Gauguin's friend, Van Gogh, would squeeze out paint directly from the tube on to the canvas to achieve weird but striking effects. Like Gauguin, Van Gogh was an

---

[1] There were, of course, many other great impressionist painters, such as Hilaire Degas and Henri Toulouse-Lautrec. The interested reader should consult the suggested readings at the end of the chapter for a fuller treatment of this subject.

Paul Cézanne, Still Life with Apples (1895–1898), oil on canvas, 27 x 36½'. *Photo: Lillie P. Bliss Collection, The Museum of Modern Art, New York*

expressionist, freely distorting the images of nature to make them express his own feelings. Cézanne, Gauguin, and Van Gogh were the forerunners of many iconoclastic schools, such as cubism and futurism, that marked twentieth-century painting.

Two of the most influential of the revolutionary modern painters were the Frenchman Henri Matisse (1869–1954) and the Spanish-born (French by adoption) Pablo Picasso (1881–1973), both of whom received their chief inspiration from Cézanne. In some of their work they carried distortion to great extremes. Matisse became enamored with primitive culture. Picasso's figures during one phase of his long career became geometric (hence cubism) and disjointed.

He occasionally gave up color entirely for black and white.

It is characteristic of an age of intellectual revolt and crumbling values (the Hellenistic period was such an age) that the artists turn inward. During the second phase of the Industrial Revolution, painting became highly individualistic. The artists tended to paint such objects as fruit, still life, and mandolins. Furthermore, they turned to figures on the periphery of a disintegrating society, such as prostitutes, solitary drinkers, blind beggars, and circus performers. The figures were separate, not joined. This disjointedness and the symbols of science, machinery, and speed, which were so prominent in this painting, surely represented an age of intellectual revolt against traditional values, of materialistic science and technology, and of mass movement. Unfortunately, much of this painting was so technical and highly specialized that it could be appreciated only by a relatively few, at

Pablo Picasso, Three Musicians (summer 1921), collage Cubism, oil on canvas, 6'7" × 7'3¾". Probably the most influential of all the artistic revolutionaries, Picasso during his long career experimented with many different styles and produced an immense oeuvre that spans both his own personal growth and most of the twentieth century. *Photo: Collection, The Museum of Modern Art, New York, Mrs. Simon Guggenheim Fund*

a time when the many were seeking enlightenment.

The rapid growth of cities and of wealth during the second phase of the Industrial Revolution was responsible for the production of a large quantity of sculpture to decorate the new public buildings, squares, and parks. Most of it was patterned after the styles of the past, either classical or baroque, more often the latter. Probably the two sculptors of the period who most truly reflected the spirit of their own time and of future trends were Constantin Meunier (1831–1905) in Belgium and Auguste Rodin (1840–1917) in France. Meunier was the first great sculptor to recognize the importance of the industrial proletariat. Among his rugged and realistic statues are *The Hammersmith, The Puddler, The Mine Girl,* and *The Old Mine Horse.* Rodin introduced impressionism into sculpture. His most famous statue, *The Thinker,* illustrates not only impressionistic art, but also the influence of the classical, Renaissance, baroque, and romantic styles. Rodin was the forerunner of much of the modern, abstract, and symbolist sculpture of the twentieth century.

5. FUNCTIONAL ARCHITECTURE

The architecture of the period 1871–1914, like the sculpture, combined the old with the new. The prevailing style in the numerous and increasingly large public buildings continued to

Auguste Rodin, Heroic Head (Pierre de Weissart), 1889, bronze. Rodin's powerful figures represent both a new departure in sculpture and a bridge from the nineteenth century to the twentieth, for he brought the impressionistic spirit to sculpture and was the forerunner of much of the abstract and symbolist work of the years between and after the world wars. Norweb Collection, The Cleveland Museum of Art. *Photo: J. Ciliotta*

be classical or baroque. Gothic architecture, which enjoyed a revival in the early part of the nineteenth century, was now limited primarily to university buildings and to churches. Even Byzantine, Moorish, and Oriental models appeared here and there throughout the West as the world was brought closer together by rapid communications.

The first great architect to develop a style appropriate to an age of steel, science, and speed was the American Louis Henry Sullivan (1856–1924). Sullivan pointed out that "Form follows function." That is to say, the style of buildings is determined by their intended use and by the materials used in their construction. This has always been true; Greek, Roman, Gothic buildings served utilitarian purposes, both secular and religious. Furthermore, the columns, posts and lintels, arches, vaults, and heavy walls that characterized these styles were the only known means of supporting massive or lofty structures. But in an age of structural steel this was no longer true. The architectural devices of the past had lost their utility, were purely decorative. And in fast-moving, crowded, and growing New York and Chicago, what sense did horizontal Greek or Moorish lines make? Sullivan designed the steel-supported skyscraper.

But Sullivan and his followers were not satisfied with the principle "Form follows function." They decided that function is the sole purpose of architecture. The application of this principle came to be known as "functional architecture." Structural steel, reinforced concrete, and glass brick made it possible for the functional architects to achieve unbroken horizontal lines impossible to the Greeks, and towering heights combined with gracefulness and light that the medieval Gothic builders could not have contemplated. Furthermore, the spirit of intellectual revolt against the standards and values of the

past gave the architects a freedom to experiment never before enjoyed. Finally, unprecedented wealth and technological advances provided them with the means to execute their ideas. Some of the massive utilitarian structures of this and later periods, such as a number of the railway stations, some of the American skyscrapers like the Philadelphia Savings Fund Society Building and the United Nations Building, and the Firth of Forth, Brooklyn, Golden Gate, and Straits of Mackinac bridges are creditable monuments to an age of materialism.

6. MUSIC OLD AND NEW

Of all the arts, music showed the least responsiveness to the materialistic and scientific spirit of the second phase of the Industrial Revolution. Some of the greatest romantic composers of the first phase lived well on into the second. Wagner lived until 1883, Verdi until 1901. Their ranks were joined in the late nineteenth century by

The American architect Louis Henry Sullivan (1856–1924) was the first to determine that function is the sole purpose of the style of a building. It was he who first designed the steel-supported skyscraper that is the hallmark of twentieth-century cities all over the world. One of his buildings, the Carson-Pirie-Scott Department Store in Chicago, is in use today. *Photo: Hedrich-Blessing*

such great romanticists as Camille Saint-Saëns (1835–1921) in France and Peter Tchaikovsky (1840–1893) in Russia. Nor was there any lessening in the spirit of nationalism in music, which was such an important ingredient of romanticism. We have already seen (Chapters 47 and 50) how Wagner's nationalism became more militant after 1870. Tchaikovsky combined Russian nationalism with his romanticism. More strictly nationalist in their themes and folk tunes were the Russian Nicholas Rimsky-Korsakov (1844–1908); the Czech Anton Dvořák (1841–1904); the Norwegian Edvard Grieg (1843–1907); and the Finn Jean Sibelius (1865–1957). Not only romanticism but also classicism was carried over into the late nineteenth century by the great German composer Johannes Brahms (1833–1897). Spending the last thirty-five years of his life in the Hapsburg capital of Vienna, Brahms became an ardent Hungarian nationalist without giving up loyalty to his native Germany. Probably more than any other musician, Brahms resembles Beethoven in style. Like Beethoven, he combined the classical spirit with the romantic.

The most important innovator in music in the period 1871–1914 was the French composer Claude Debussy (1862–1918). Debussy was the father of impressionistic music. Experimenting with subtle and sophisticated dissonances, he was to music what Manet and Renoir were to painting. Meanwhile, in Germany Richard Strauss (1864–1949) was startling and scandalizing his pre–World War I audiences with his complex and sometimes harshly dissonant "realistic" tone poems. He is often said to have ushered in the "modern" period in music. In Russia Igor Stravinsky (1882–1971) was beginning his long career of composing music that was still more iconoclastic and abstract. He is called the father of the expressionist school. Stravinsky, with his more violent and impetuous dissonances, bears somewhat the same relationship to Debussy as does Picasso to Monet in painting.

The radical, dissonant, and often noisy music of the followers of Debussy surely reflected the spirit of an age of materialistic technology and science, of cynical disenchantment, and of intellectual revolt against traditional values. We must not forget, however, that in any typical concert in the Western world in 1914—or in 1974 for that matter—Mozart, Beethoven, and Schubert would still probably predominate over Debussy and Stravinsky. The new grew up alongside but did not replace the old.

Meanwhile, looming ever larger in the materialistic, cynical, restless mind of the West from 1871 to 1914 was the spirit of nationalism. The character of the nationalism of this period was ominous, now that the aggressive nations were peopled by the "animal masses" of Darwin and Freud—animal masses whose claws and teeth were made ever so much sharper by science and technology.

Suggested Reading

General

*C. Brinton, *The Shaping of the Modern Mind* (Spectrum). This is the latter part of his excellent work, *Ideas and Men*.

The Philosophy of Disenchantment

*W. Kaufmann, *Nietzsche: Philosopher, Psychologist, Antichrist* (Vintage). Excellent biography of Nietzsche.

R. B. Perry, *The Thought and Character of William James*, rev. ed. (1948). By a leading authority on American cultural history.

Realistic Literature

J. W. Cunliffe, *English Literature During the Last Half Century* (1919). The last half century was 1871–1914. Good survey.

*M. Geismar, *Writers in Crisis* (Dutton). Scholarly study of American realistic novelists.

G. E. B. Saintsbury, *A Short History of French Literature*, 7th ed. (1937). Well-known classic.

*M. Slonim, *The Epic of Russian Literature from Its Origins Through Tolstoy* (Oxford). Good coverage of the period 1871–1914.

Impressionism, Functionalism, Modernism in the Arts

M. Raynal, *The Nineteenth Century: Goya to Gauguin* (1951). Beautifully illustrated.

A. Hauser, *The Social History of Art*, 4 Vols. (Random House). Fruitful attempt to relate art to the society that produced it.

*J. M. Richards, *An Introduction to Modern Architecture* (Pelican). Sound brief account.

E. Stringham, *Listening to Music Creatively*, 2nd ed. (1959). Written for the nonspecialist by a leading musicologist.

Retrospect

The growth of technology and science was so rapid in the industrialized countries during the period 1871–1914 that it influenced or overshadowed all other developments. Industrialization also spread during these years from its early base in Western Europe and the United States to Central and Eastern Europe, Japan, and the British dominions. Steel, oil, and electricity joined or superseded the iron and steam of the preceding age. This was the great era of railroad building. The automobile and the airplane appeared. Communications were revolutionized by the telegraph, the telephone, and wireless telegraphy.

Science kept pace with technology. The nature of matter was discovered and it proved to be as shockingly unstable as the old "absolutes" of time, space, and motion. Darwin's evolutionary hypothesis seemed to unlock most of the secrets concerning life on the planet. Medical science had its beginning in this period and the preceding decade. Psychology, sociology, and history made valiant efforts to be scientific. The people in the industrialized countries became fascinated by all this—the masses with the marvels and promises of technology, the intelligentsia with the wonders of science.

The first phase of the Industrial Revolution had belonged to the bourgeoisie. During the second phase, the industrial proletariat, now much more numerous and concentrated in the industrial cities, demanded and got many benefits. Liberalism became much more liberal. By 1914, almost every country in Europe enjoyed universal male suffrage. Liberals abandoned laissez-faire doctrines in favor of government protection for the poor and the weak. Public education and journalism became mass-oriented. But the masses were not waiting for the rather slow processes of government action alone to achieve their demands. By forming cooperatives and labor unions, they were exerting greater pressure on the capitalists by direct action than at the ballot box. The most extreme major effort on behalf of the industrial proletariat during the years 1871 to 1914 was that of the Marxists: Marx and his followers set out to destroy the capitalistic system completely, and create a classless society.

Nationalism also underwent a drastic change during the second phase of the Industrial Revolution. It became much more aggressive and militaristic; it also became the foe of liberalism. Although all the great powers became infected by this new malignant nationalism, it was particularly strong in Germany and Russia, where liberalism had never gained a firm foothold. This new nationalism was the chief impetus behind the new burst of imperialism which by 1914 had brought most of Asia and nearly all of Africa under the domination of Europe. The masses so rapidly gaining their freedoms at home proved to be only too eager to answer the first sound of the trumpet of the new nationalism to go fight the foreign foe.

Meanwhile, the Christian religion, which had for so long been the great commonality—the chief moral and spiritual guide—of Western civilization, underwent its severest test. It was challenged by science, technology, liberalism, and nationalism. And its influence appeared to be on the wane.

The arts and letters during the second phase of the Industrial Revolution also reflected the materialism and the social ferment of the period. The idealism and romanticism of the first phase were, in large measure, replaced by disenchantment, pragmatism, realism, and modernism.

XII

The Era of the Two World Wars 1914-1974

To many observers in 1914 it must have appeared that Western man had finally reached the gates of Utopia. Most of the things for which he had been struggling for thousands of years had finally been achieved. First of all, he appeared to have gained his freedom. Practically everywhere in the Western world males had obtained the suffrage. With the exception of Austria-Hungary and subjected minorities in Germany and Russia, the major language groups had for the most part been consolidated into independent nations, and national pride was at its peak. Furthermore, the Western nations had gained virtually complete domination over the non-Western world.

Technology had reached a stage of development in the Western world (with the exception of Latin America) by 1914 that promised in the not too distant future freedom from material want, hunger, and grinding toil. Most glamorous of all the achievements of Western man by 1914, perhaps, was science. The last secrets of matter, life, man, and society seemed to be on the point of being solved by the natural and social scientists. In fact, man with his mastery of technology and science seemed to be ready to take the place of God — to be able to do all the things that had formerly been expected of God.

We now know, of course, that these were vain or exaggerated hopes and expectations. Western man did not enter the gates of Utopia in 1914, but into the bloodiest and most fear-and-hate-ridden half century in history. This half century was dominated by two world wars and the fear of a third and final atomic world war. Violent fascist and communist dictatorships challenged the disarrayed forces of liberal democracy. Western empires in Asia and Africa crumbled.

How and why did these things happen? Let us keep these questions in mind as we proceed to examine the latest epoch in the history of Western civilization.

The first blow that rocked the twentieth-century world was World War I. To most of mankind, busy with its daily tasks, it seemed to be a sudden and unforeseen disaster. To statesmen and informed students of world affairs, it was the snapping of long-developing tensions.

1. ORIGINS OF THE WAR

World War I began as a showdown between two hostile alliances of European powers: the Triple Alliance, composed of Germany, Austria-Hungary, and Italy; and the Triple Entente, composed of Great Britain, France, and Russia. This system of alliances was begun by Bismarck shortly after the defeat of France and the creation of the German Empire in 1870–1871. In 1873, as a safeguard against a revengeful France, or indeed against any hostile combination against Germany, Bismarck formed the Three Emperors' League, composed of Germany, Austria-Hungary, and Russia. When the interests and ambitions of Austria-Hungary and Russia proved to be incompatible, Bismarck replaced Russia with Italy (1882) to form the Triple Alliance. However, so long as he remained at the head of the German government, he carefully nurtured cordial relations with Russia and also with Great Britain. This policy left France isolated and subject to repeated German bullying.

Bismarck's diplomatic work was quickly undone by Kaiser Wilhelm II, who ascended the

54

WORLD WAR I, 1914-1918

German imperial throne in 1888 and forced Bismarck's resignation two years later. Wilhelm II immediately dropped the friendship pact with Russia and began to antagonize Great Britain by his grandiose schemes in the Near and Far East and by his huge naval building program. France was now able to form an alliance with Russia (1894) and an entente (understanding) with Great Britain (1904). In 1907 the Triple Entente was formed after Great Britain and Russia had settled their long-standing differences in Asia. Only an intense fear of Germany could have reconciled the sharply divergent interests that had long existed among these three powers.

Suspicion, hatred, and fear between the two power combinations mounted steadily. A ruinous armaments race ensued; the powers of the Triple Entente strove desperately to overcome Germany's long lead in land forces, while Germany sought to erase Great Britain's naval advantage. Rivalries and conflicts among the various members of the two alliances cropped up all over the world, threatening to embroil all the other members. In 1905–1906 and again in 1911 two such clashes occurred in Morocco between France and Germany. Two occurred in the Balkan Peninsula between Russia and Austria-Hungary. In 1908 Austria-Hungary suddenly annexed two provinces, Bosnia and Herzegovina, which were inhabited by Serbs and Croats. Serbia had planned to annex these territories, peopled by her own linguistic kinsmen. She

appealed to her big Slavic brother, Russia. Russia threatened Austria-Hungary, whereupon Germany rattled her mighty sword and forced Russia to back down. A second Balkan crisis occurred in 1912–1913. The various Balkan states defeated Turkey and then fought among themselves over the spoils. Victorious Serbia threatened to expand. Austria-Hungary not only thwarted Serbia's expansion to the Adriatic Sea, but threatened to annihilate her. Again Serbia appealed to Russia and again Germany forced Russia to back down. Each of these crises brought the world close to war, increased international tension, and speeded up preparations for a final showdown.

It was in the Balkans that the fatal explosion finally occurred. Here the interests of Russia and Austria-Hungary clashed head-on. The Serbs, Bulgarians, Rumanians, and Greeks were religious (Orthodox) and cultural (Byzantine) kinsmen of the Russians. The Serbs and Bulgarians were also linguistic (Slavic) kinsmen of the Russians. Moreover, the Balkan Peninsula was of great economic and strategic interest to Russia. Since the days of Ivan III in the fifteenth century, Russia had sought control of the Bosporus and Dardanelles (the Turkish Straits) as a water outlet to the West. Austria-Hungary's interests in the Balkans were, perhaps, even more vital than those of Russia. The Dual Monarchy's chief interest in the area grew out of the polyglot nature of its empire. It was composed of numerous lan-

This photograph of the Archduke Franz Ferdinand, heir to the thrones of Austria-Hungary, and his wife was taken as they entered their carriage in Sarajevo on June 28, 1914, just a few minutes before they were assassinated by a Serbian nationalist. *Photo: United Press International*

guage groups, some of which, particularly the Serbs, Croats, Slovenes, and Rumanians, had linguistic kinsmen in the Balkans.

As the Ottoman Empire in the Balkan Peninsula disintegrated in the nineteenth and early twentieth centuries, the various Balkan language groups emerged as independent nations. These free peoples constituted a strong attraction for the members of their language groups in Austria-Hungary, who wished to break loose and join them. This was particularly true of Serbia, which attracted the Hapsburgs' Yugoslav subjects (the Serbs, Croats, and Slovenes). But if the Yugoslavs should join Serbia, Austria-Hungary's other language minorities—Italians, Czechs,

Slovaks, Poles, Rumanians, and Ruthenians—would also demand their freedom from Austrian and Hungarian rule and the Dual Monarchy would fall apart. Austria-Hungary therefore felt that she must control the Balkan Peninsula in self-defense. It was also the only direction in which she could expand, particularly after her exclusion from Germany in 1866. And the militancy that characterized nationalism after 1871 caused all nations to feel that they must expand.

Overlying the clashing interests of Russia and Austria-Hungary in the Balkans were those of Germany and Great Britain. Germany felt she must maintain the integrity of the Dual Monarchy, which was her only effective and reliable ally. Then, too, her own ambitions in the Balkans and the Near and Middle East were great. One of Kaiser Wilhelm II's chief imperial projects was the Berlin-to-Bagdad railway (see p. 565), which would make German power dominant in the Ottoman Empire if not the whole Near and

Middle East. This scheme gravely menaced Great Britain's own imperial life line running through Suez as well as her immediate interests in the Near and Middle East. Germany's project threatened to blight permanently Russia's hopes of gaining an outlet through the Turkish Straits and to cut Russia off strategically from her allies. France and Italy had their own interests in the Balkans and in the Near and Middle East, although their primary concern was their commitments to their respective allies.

When, therefore, a third crisis occurred in the Balkans in the summer of 1914, all the great powers of Europe were automatically involved. The two Moroccan crises, the two Balkan crises,

and the feverish armaments race had brought the tension in Europe to the breaking point. All that was needed was an incident.

2. THE FATAL EXPLOSION

The incident was the shooting at Sarajevo (in Bosnia) of the Austrian Archduke Francis Ferdinand by a Serb on June 28, 1914. The assassination was a deliberate plot involving numerous Serbian army officers. Francis Ferdinand, heir to the Austro-Hungarian throne, was singled out because the Serbs feared that his liberal policy toward the Yugoslavs in Austria-Hungary would allay their discontent, thereby lessening

LANGUAGE GROUPS, AUSTRIA-HUNGARY

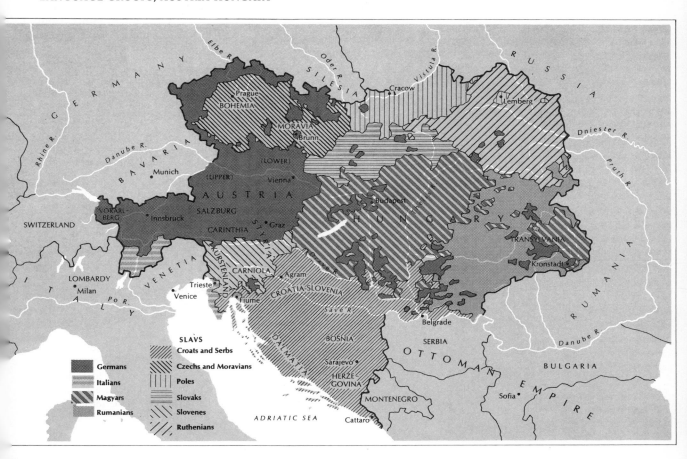

their desire to break away and join Serbia. After the assassination, the government of Austria-Hungary decided to crush Serbia and establish her own dominance in the Balkans once and for all. This would require the backing of Germany, for clearly Russia would not stand aside and allow her Serbian kinsmen and allies to be so treated or her own national interests to be thus violated. At a fateful conference in Berlin eight days after the shooting, Kaiser Wilhelm II gave Austria-Hungary Germany's "blank check." He urged Austria-Hungary to act quickly while world opinion was still outraged by the assassination and promised to support her in any emergency. This promise by the German Kaiser greatly intensified the crisis. Russia would not allow Austria-Hungary to destroy Serbia; Germany would not allow Russia to defeat Austria-Hungary; and France and Great Britain would not allow Germany to defeat Russia, whose support they felt to be indispensable in future dealings with Germany.

Armed with Germany's blank check, Austria-Hungary presented Serbia with an impossible ultimatum. When Serbia failed to yield to all of its terms, Austria-Hungary declared war and invaded Serbia. Russia mobilized her forces against Austria-Hungary and Germany. Germany sent harsh ultimatums to Russia and to France. When Russia failed to reply and France gave an unsatisfactory reply, Germany declared war on Russia on August 1, and on France two days later. The next day, August 4, when German troops violated Belgian neutrality on their way to attack France, Great Britain declared war on Germany. Thus, by August 4, 1914, all the great powers of Europe except Italy were at war. Italy claimed that she was not obligated to aid her allies, Germany and Austria-Hungary, since they were the aggressors. The following year, she entered the war on the side of the Entente powers. To the side of Germany and Austria-Hungary came Turkey and Bulgaria; these were referred to as the Central Powers. To the side of the Entente powers, who came to be called the Allies, eventually came much of the rest of the world—some thirty-two nations in all. This was truly a world war.

In following the tragic events just related, one can hardly fail to be impressed by the great role played by the spirit of malignant nationalism. It was aggressive nationalism that destroyed much of the spiritual unity of Western Christendom, that motivated much of the revived imperial competition, that energized the massive armies, that refused to yield or compromise in times of crisis, that made international law impossible, and produced international anarchy instead.

3. GERMANY'S NEAR TRIUMPH

In a long drawn-out war, the advantage would appear to lie with the Allies in view of their superior manpower and resources and their control of the seas. However, Germany had no intention of fighting a long war, and few world observers saw much possibility of the Allies preventing the superior German army from winning a quick and crushing victory on the mainland of Europe. The German high command had long anticipated the military situation that confronted it in August 1914, and had developed a plan of operation known as the Schlieffen plan. This plan called for a holding action against the slow-moving Russians while the main German forces concentrated on a quick knockout of France, which possessed the only army in the world that gave the Germans any real concern. The main German blow would be a surprise thrust through Belgium, despite a treaty guaranteeing Belgian neutrality, which had been signed by all the great powers, including Germany. Pouring through Belgium, the German army would capture Paris and encircle and destroy the French armies in eastern France. It was calculated that no more than six weeks would be required to crush France. Then the Germans would concentrate on and destroy Russia and with relative ease. Great Britain, her allies gone, would sue for peace.

The Schlieffen plan came near succeeding. Stubborn Belgian resistance held up the Germans long enough for the French to redeploy their forces to the north and for the British to throw their small army across the Channel. Nevertheless, the seemingly irresistible German juggernaut crunched ahead; four weeks after the beginning of hostilities, it was outside Paris

WORLD WAR I

ahead of schedule. At this juncture, the desperate French and British armies turned on the Germans and in the bloody seven-day Battle of the Marne not only defeated them, but drove them back a few miles. Both sides extended their lines from the Swiss border to the North Sea and entrenched. The First Battle of the Marne was one of the decisive battles in history, for it forced

on the Germans a long war of attrition that made possible their ultimate defeat.

An important factor in the German defeat at the Marne was the detachment at the critical moment of 100,000 of their best troops for use against the Russians, who had invaded Germany with unexpected speed. Generals von Hindenburg and Ludendorff, with several divisions, were hastily dispatched to the eastern front. Under their command the reinforced German armies trapped the Russians at Tannenberg and administered a crushing defeat that sent them reeling back into Russia. Meanwhile, the British navy swept the Germans from the surface of the seas and set up a blockade of Germany. However, the Germans quickly discovered Britain's Achilles' heel with a new weapon: the submarine.

In 1915 the Germans staged a holding operation in the west while they delivered a series of hammer blows upon the Russians, driving deep into Russia and inflicting immense casualties. A major Anglo-French effort to come to the aid of the hard-pressed Russians by breaking through the Dardanelles was beaten back with heavy losses. In 1916 Germany returned to the assault in the west. In the nine-month Battle of Verdun, the French held the Germans back, but at an enormous cost in men and supplies. The four-month Battle of the Somme between the British and the Germans was even bloodier. Like Verdun, it ended in a stalemate. In the Battle of Jutland, the biggest naval battle in history up to that time, the British fleet thwarted the effort of the German fleet to break the blockade, but suffered serious losses.

By 1917 Germany and her allies, though beginning to show signs of strain, appeared to be close to victory. French morale dropped at the front and behind the lines; numerous units of the battered army mutinied. The Germans launched an unlimited submarine campaign against Great Britain that soon brought her near starvation. The combined German and Austro-Hungarian forces administered a crushing defeat to Italy. In November 1917, Russia, suffering unbearable hardships at the front and behind the lines, succumbed to the Communist Revolution and soon thereafter withdrew from the war. (The story of the Russian Revolution will be told in the following chapter.) And although the harsh terms forced upon helpless Russia by the Germans in the Treaty of Brest-Litovsk strengthened the resolve of the remaining Allies to fight to the finish, the Germans were now able for the first time in the war to concentrate their full strength on the weary French and British. The prospects for the Allies seemed dim. It was at this critical juncture that the United States entered the war.

4. THE ENTRY OF THE UNITED STATES AND THE VICTORY OF THE ALLIES

When the war had begun in 1914, President Woodrow Wilson had admonished the American people to remain neutral in thought as well as in deed. However, from the beginning, the great majority of public opinion in the United States, as indeed in most of the world, was that Germany and her allies were the aggressors. As Germany came nearer and nearer to victory, most Americans, Republicans and Democrats alike, came increasingly to fear that a German victory would be a world calamity in which the United States would be an eventual victim. To the holders of this view, it would be clearly in the self-interest of the United States to help prevent the fall of France and Great Britain rather than have to face a victorious Germany alone. But the German government eventually gave the United States little choice. Early in the war, the Germans violated American neutrality by using their embassy in Washington as a center for spies and saboteurs to prevent the sale of munitions to Great Britain and France. Early in 1917, the German government, anticipating war with the United States, offered Texas, New Mexico, and Arizona to Mexico as a reward for attacking the United States. Apparently, California was to be offered to Japan. The Zimmermann Note, making this offer, was intercepted by British intelligence and turned over to the United States. For some strange reason, the German government admitted its authenticity.

The sinking of American ships by German submarines, however, provided the immediate impetus for the entry of the United States into the war. When the Germans first began large-scale sinkings of merchant and passenger ships in 1915, President Wilson had protested so vigorously that the Germans finally agreed to desist. Great Britain and France, it is true, had seized some American ships attempting to evade the blockade of Germany, but no lives had been lost and damages had been paid. Early in

1917, the German high command decided to launch an unlimited submarine campaign against enemy and neutral shipping alike. The German leaders fully expected that this course would bring the United States into the war, but they believed that Great Britain and France would be crushed before any appreciable American weight could be brought to bear in Europe. Upon the announcement of this policy, the American government immediately broke off diplomatic relations with Germany. After several American ships had been sunk, Congress, on April 6, at the request of President Wilson, declared war, not on the German people, but on the German imperial government. The vote for war—82 to 6 in the Senate and 373 to 50 in the House of Representatives—probably reflected the opinion of the American people.

Although a full year elapsed before American troops were able to play an important role at the front, the boost in Allied morale was immediate, and the Americans lost no time supplying financial, material, and naval aid. And although the total contribution of the United States to Allied victory was relatively small as compared to that of France and Great Britain, America's role, coming as it did when both sides were approaching exhaustion, was probably decisive. At the beginning of 1918 the race was between Germany and the United States. Germany transferred troops from the Russian front to overwhelm Great Britain and France before large numbers of American troops could arrive, while the United States strove to raise, train, and transport to France sufficient forces to stem the German tide. Again the advantage appeared to lie with Germany.

In March 1918, Field Marshal Ludendorff, now in command of the German armies, launched the first of a series of massive blows on the western front designed to end the war. The British and French were driven back with heavy losses. In desperation, they at long last agreed to a unified command under France's General Ferdinand Foch. The Americans, under General John J. Pershing, also accepted his command. By the middle of June, Ludendorff had launched four great drives, and the Allied lines had been battered so thin that, when the climactic fifth drive

began along the Marne River in mid-July 1918, Ludendorff wired the Kaiser: "If the attack succeeds, the war will be over and we will have won it." When Foch heard the opening German barrage, he wired his government: "If the present German attack succeeds, the war is over and we have lost it." The Germans were stopped by a narrow margin. Foch, now receiving a swelling stream of fresh American troops and armaments, immediately ordered a counterattack. In the Allied counterattack, the tank, developed by the foresight of young Winston Churchill, then First Lord of the British Admiralty, proved to be the breakthrough weapon. German strength and morale waned rapidly; the war was lost.

The first of the Central Powers to go out of the war was Bulgaria, which at the end of September 1918 surrendered to French, British, and Serbian forces operating from the Greek port of Salonika. A month later Turkey surrendered to British imperial forces in the Near East. Austria-Hungary, her various language groups in revolt, surrendered on November 3 to Italian, British, and French forces driving in from Italy. The following day, a full-fledged mutiny that had been brewing for several days broke out in the German navy and quickly spread throughout Germany. On November 11, the German commanders, their armies hopelessly beaten and in full retreat from France and Belgium, accepted Foch's armistice terms, which amounted to outright surrender.

5. THE PEACE SETTLEMENT

The Allied statesmen who gathered in Paris in January 1919 to try to make a lasting peace were confronted with a formidable task. Much of Europe had been shattered by a war of unprecedented scope and destructiveness. Nine million men had been killed in battle. A much larger number had died of diseases traceable to the war. Twenty-one million had been wounded. The financial and material losses were incalculable. No Western power was solvent. (Even the United States, the most fortunate of the Western powers, was saddled with a huge national debt that she has never been able to reduce significantly.) The German, Austro-Hungarian, Ottoman, and Russian empires had collapsed. The British and French empires were seriously weakened. A tenth of the richest part of France had been laid waste. Hate and disillusionment poisoned the atmosphere.

Although all thirty-two of the victorious Allies were represented at the Paris Peace Conference, the great decisions were really made by the leaders of the Big Three: France, Great Britain, and the United States. The French delegation was headed by Premier Georges Clemenceau, the aged "Tiger of France." As host to the conference and head of the nation that had done the most to defeat Germany and that had suffered the most, he expected to dominate the decisions. Leading the British delegation was the eloquent and fiery "Little Welsh Attorney," Prime Minister David Lloyd George. As spokesman for the British Empire, which comprised one-fourth of all the land and people in the world, he also expected to dominate the conference. At the head of the American delegation was President Woodrow Wilson. A fundamental and bitter clash immediately developed between Clemenceau, who wanted a hard peace that would mutilate Germany and make her harmless in the future, and Wilson, who wanted a "just" peace free of vindictiveness of any kind. Specifically, Clemenceau demanded the detachment from Germany of all her territory west of the Rhine and its annexation or control by France. Only by this means, he believed, could the power balance be tipped in favor of France and French security safeguarded against another German assault. Wilson would not tolerate another "Alsace-Lorraine in reverse." In the end he proved to be more eloquent and stubborn than Clemenceau, and to his side eventually came Lloyd George. Great Britain needed the trade of a recovered Germany and did not wish to see France become too dominant on the Continent. The Treaty of Versailles with Germany reflected Wilson's ideas in fundamental principles though not in every detail.

Six months of hard work and bitter wrangling were required to draw up the treaty. Its most important terms were, in brief, as follows: Germany and her allies were forced to accept full responsibility for the war. Germany was compelled to give up all her overseas colonies and concessions. Alsace and Lorraine were returned to France. Three tiny districts were ceded to Belgium, and the Danish-speaking portion of Schleswig was returned to Denmark. The Polish-speaking areas of eastern Germany, most of which had been seized by Prussia in the eighteenth century, were ceded to the resurrected Polish state. With one exception, wherever doubt existed as to the wishes of the people in the affected areas, plebiscites were held to determine their desires. The exception was the Polish Corridor, which was cut along the Vistula River to give Poland an outlet to the sea. Although this territory had been seized from Poland by Frederick the Great and approximately half its population was still Polish-speaking, its cession to Poland severed East Prussia from the main body of Germany and gave Hitler his excuse for beginning World War II.

Germany's army was cut down from the most powerful military machine in history to 100,000 officers and men, who were to be long-term volunteers to prevent a rapid turnover of trained personnel. Her navy was reduced from the world's second greatest to six small battleships, six cruisers, and a larger number of auxiliary vessels. She was permitted no submarines, no military aviation, no poison gas (which she had introduced during the war), and no offensive weapons such as tanks and heavy artillery. Germany's Rhineland was to be permanently demilitarized, and her munitions industries were made subject to Allied inspection. Her general staff was to be dismantled and her top war leaders tried for violations of the rules and customs of war and, if found guilty, punished. (The Kaiser fled to the Netherlands just before Germany collapsed, and the Netherlands refused to give him up.) Germany was prohibited from making economic reprisals against her neighbors and her former enemies. Finally, Germany was held liable for an indemnity that in 1921 was set by an Allied reparations commission at approximately $33 billion. Wilson and Lloyd George believed these terms to be just. Clemenceau considered them to be suicidally lenient.

The treaties with Germany's allies were actually more severe than the Treaty of Versailles because the principle followed in territorial rearrangements was freedom or union of all national language groups, and Germany was more homogeneous linguistically than were her allies. The polyglot Austro-Hungarian Empire was split up along language lines. The Czechs and Slovaks were formed into the new state of Czechoslovakia, which unfortunately also included sizable German and other minorities. The Poles were joined to Poland, the Rumanians to Rumania, the Italians to Italy, and the Serbs, Croats, and Slovenes to Serbia, which now became Yugoslavia. Thus the Dual Monarchy was cut down from a nation of 50 million second in area only to Russia among the nations of Europe to an Austria of 6.5 million German-speaking Austrians and a Hungary of 8 million Magyars. Austria was forbidden to unite with Germany. Bulgaria lost her territory along the Aegean Sea to Greece and became one of the smallest Balkan states. Turkey was shorn of her far-flung non-Turkish territories. The new Turkey included only the Anatolian plateau in Asia and the city of Constantinople and its immediate hinterland in Europe. The new national boundaries, in spite of the painstaking care with which they were drawn up, left many pockets of discontent to breed future conflicts.

6. THE LEAGUE OF NATIONS

Wilson, quite aware of the impossibility of making perfect treaties, placed his chief hopes for peace in an association of nations that would settle peaceably the tensions and conflicts that were certain to arise in the future. Fearful that, if left to future negotiations, the forming of such an association might be shunted aside or put off indefinitely, he insisted that its framework be incorporated in the treaty with Germany. The first twenty-six articles of the Treaty of Versailles therefore constitute the covenant of the League of Nations. Aware also that the United States and some of the other great powers were not yet willing to surrender their absolute sovereignty to a world government, Wilson felt it necessary to settle for a league that lacked the power to compel the major nations to obey its decisions. He hoped and believed that the United States

and the other great powers could be persuaded to join such a league and that it would become a stepping stone to eventual world government.

The central body in the League of Nations, which served as a general clearing house and forum for discussion, was the General Assembly. All members of the league were represented in the General Assembly and each member had one vote. In addition to serving as a discussion forum, the General Assembly supervised the work of numerous specialized agencies and participated in the choosing of members of all the other bodies in the league. The nearest thing the league had to an executive organ was the Council. This was made up of five permanent members and six nonpermanent members chosen for three-year terms on a staggered basis by the General Assembly. The five permanent members were to be the United States, Great Britain, France, Italy, and Japan. The Council was empowered to make decisions and recommendations relative to the prevention of war. Its decisions required unanimity, which meant that all the permanent members possessed a perma-

The "Big Four" as they posed for newsreels at Versailles in 1919. Left to right, David Lloyd George, Vittorio Orlando, Georges Clemenceau, Woodrow Wilson. *Photo: UPI*

ARCTIC OCEAN

NORTH CAPE

Murmansk

Reykjavik

ICELAND
(Denmark)

Narvik

Areas Lost by Germany
Areas Lost by Russia
Areas Lost by Ottoman Empire
Austria-Hungary 1914

0   100   200   300 MILES

NORWAY

SWEDEN

FINLAND

Archan

L. O

L. Ladoga

FAEROE I.
(Denmark)

Helsinki

Leningrad

ORKNEY I.
SCAPA FLOW

Oslo

Reval

Stockholm

ESTONIA

Edinburgh

NORTH SEA

DENMARK

Copenhagen

BALTIC SEA

Riga

LATVIA

LITHUANIA
Memel
Kaunas
Vilna

WHITE
RUSSIAN
S.S.R.

ULSTER

IRISH
FREE STATE

Dublin

GREAT BRITAIN

Liverpool

Hamburg

Bremen

Danzig

EAST
PRUSSIA

POLISH
CORRIDOR

London

ATLANTIC OCEAN

NETHERLANDS
Amsterdam

Rhine

GERMANY

Berlin

POLAND

Brest-
Litovsk

Warsaw

Kiev

Brussels
BELGIUM
Cologne

RUHR

WEIMAR REPUBLIC
Weimar

Weimar

Frankfurt

Prague

GALICIA

Paris

Versailles

LUX

SAAR

Metz

ALSACE-
LORRAINE

Stuttgart

Strasbourg

Munich

CZECHOSLO VAKIA

Dniester R.

BUKO-
VINA

BESSARABIA

FRANCE

SWITZERLAND

Geneva

Locarno

AUSTRIA

Vienna

Budapest

H U N G A R Y

TRANSYLVANIA

U

Bordeaux

Trent

Trieste

Fiume

Y U G O S L A V I A

RUMANIA

Bucharest

DOBR

Marseilles

Florence

CORSICA
(France)

ITALY

Zara
(Italy)

Belgrade

Danube
R.

PORTUGAL

Madrid

SPAIN

Barcelona

Rome

SERBIA

ALBANIA

Sofia

BULGARIA

Lisbon

Naples

SARDINIA

BALEARIC I.
(Spain)

AEGEAN SEA

Seville

Cadiz
Tangier

Gibraltar (Britain)

Algiers

ADRIATIC SEA

Smyrn

Athens

GREECE

SPANISH
MOROCCO

SICILY

MALTA (Britain)

MEDITERRANEAN

DODI

CRETE

MOROCCO
(France)

ALGERIA
(France)

TUNISIA
(France)

SEA

EUROPE 1923

nent veto over its work. Carrying on the day-to-day business of the league was the Secretariat, headed by a secretary-general. Closely associated with the league was the Permanent Court of International Justice, with headquarters at The Hague in the Netherlands. The World Court, as it was generally called, was to settle international legal, but not political, disputes.

The League of Nations had no military forces at its command. Its only teeth, so to speak, were Article X and Article XVI. Article X stated that every member undertook to guarantee the territorial integrity of every other member. This meant that in case one member was attacked, all the other members were morally obligated to come to its aid. However, there was no way to compel them to do so. Article XVI stated that, if a nation went to war in violation of a decision of the league, all the members of the league were to boycott the aggressor. This weapon (economic sanctions) could have been a potent deterrent if faithfully applied. In the last analysis, however, the success of the League of Nations depended primarily upon the support of the Big Three victorious democracies—the United States, Great Britain, and France.

The refusal of the United States to join the League (see pp. 633–634) was a body blow. Great Britain and France immediately lost faith in it and began to pursue their traditional nationalistic aims. Nevertheless, for twelve years the league achieved some noteworthy accomplishments. Sixty-two nations joined it. Germany was admitted in 1926, and the Soviet Union in 1934. The league supervised the carrying out of many of the terms of the treaties, aided tens of thousands of war refugees, gave financial aid to insolvent nations, settled numerous international disputes, promoted international good will, and supported many humanitarian measures. However, in no case did it undertake to discipline a great power, and many observers feared the outcome of such a test. The test came in 1931, when Japan invaded Manchuria. The league's failure to pass it marked the beginning of its end and of the return to war.

Suggested Reading

Origins of World War I

*B. E. Schmitt, *Triple Alliance and Triple Entente* (Berkshire). Brief and lucid by a leading authority.

*S. B. Fay, *Origins of the World War* (Free Press). Favorable to Germany. Fay's scholarly but pro-German works did much to fuel the flames of isolationism in the United States between the two World Wars.

*F. Fischer, *Germany's War Aims in the First World War* (Norton). First published in 1961 by a German historian. Shows Germany's war aims and motives to have been much more aggressive than formerly realized.

The War

*B. Tuchman, *The Guns of August* (Dell). Brilliant account of the immediate background and opening campaigns of World War I. Written in journalistic style.

*C. Falls, *The Great War, 1914–1918* (Capricorn). Probably the best brief account. Factual. Strictly military.

*A. Solzhenitsyn, *August 1914* (Association Press). Inspired, detailed account of the Tannenberg campaign that virtually knocked Russia out of the war, by Russian controversial Nobel prizewinner.

The Peace Settlement

P. Birdsall, *Versailles Twenty Years After* (1939). Scholarly, dispassionate examination of the controversial treaty.

*A. Link, *Wilson, the Diplomatist: A Look at His Major Foreign Policies* (Quadrangle). By the foremost authority on Wilson.

Historical Fiction

*Erich M. Remarque, *All Quiet on the Western Front* (Crest). Has brought home to millions the horrors of trench warfare in World War I.

*Ernest Hemingway, *A Farewell to Arms* (Scribners). Famous novel based upon the author's experiences on the Italian front.

55

THE TRIUMPH OF COMMUNISM IN RUSSIA

One of the most important and ominous of the immediate fruits of World War I was the triumph of communism in Russia. In the postwar years, when the statesmen of the Western democracies were attempting to restore the shattered world of 1914, the Russian Communist leaders were striving to destroy not only Russia's capitalistic, semifeudalistic society, but indeed all Western civilization, based upon Christianity, liberalism, and capitalism, and to create an entirely new civilization based upon the blueprints of Marx and Lenin.

1. THE BOLSHEVIK REVOLUTION OF 1917

The violent Russian upheaval of 1917 was the result of maladjustments and discontent that had been long developing. Russia, except for a handful of intelligentsia, had been virtually bypassed by the great liberalizing movements, such as the Renaissance, the Enlightenment, and the French Revolution, which had influenced Western Europe. The Industrial Revolution, which brought in its wake bourgeois liberalism and proletarian radicalism, reached Russia only in the 1890s. While Western and parts of Central Europe and the United States were becoming industrialized and increasingly liberalized, Russia remained a land of primitive and illiterate peasants, feudal aristocracy, and tsarist autocracy. Many of the frustrated Russian intelligentsia in the latter half of the nineteenth century

turned to terroristic nihilism and then to Marxism (see pp. 557–559). The violent wing of the Russian Marxist party, the Bolsheviks, boycotted the abortive liberal revolution of 1905–1906, seeking instead the total destruction of Russia's existing institutions. The Bolshevik leaders were hunted down by the state police and shot, imprisoned, or exiled. Those who escaped bided their time, many of them abroad, plotting the eventual overthrow of the tsar's government.

The Bolsheviks' opportunity came in 1917. During the first three years of World War I Russia suffered staggering losses at the hands of the superior German armies. Behind the lines the suffering of the civilian population, much of which could be attributed to the corrupt bureaucracy of the tsar, was acute. By 1917 many Russians felt that they had suffered enough. In March of that year a mild revolution in Petrograd[1] overthrew the government of the well-meaning but incompetent Nicholas II and set up a moderate bourgeois regime, in which Alexander Kerensky came to be the leading figure. The Kerensky regime attempted to liberalize the Russian government and to continue the war against Germany in cooperation with the Allies. Both tasks appeared to be beyond the

---

[1]At the beginning of World War I the Russians changed the name of St. Petersburg, which was a German name, to Petrograd, its Russian form. When Lenin died in 1924, it was changed to Leningrad.

capacity of the inexperienced new government. At the front, morale was low, weapons and munitions were nearly spent; at home there was spreading anarchy.

In order to increase the chaos and remove Russia from the war, the German government, in April 1917, transported the top Bolshevik leader, Lenin, from his place of exile in Switzerland to the Russian border. This brilliant and dynamic leader quickly organized the radical forces against the moderate government. A clever phrase-maker, Lenin knew how to appeal to all the disaffected elements. "Peace to the army, land to the peasants, ownership of the factories to the workers!" To Lenin's side in Petrograd flocked the other Bolshevik leaders whom the Kerensky regime, in a conciliatory effort, had released from their various prisons and exiles: Leon Trotsky, Joseph Stalin, and the rest.[2] In November 1917, the Bolsheviks, under Lenin's skillful direction and with perfect timing, overthrew the moderate Kerensky government and set up a Communist dictatorship.

2. EARLY COMMUNIST EXPERIMENTS AND THEIR FAILURE

In order to free the new regime for the enormous task of refashioning Russian society, Lenin immediately opened peace negotiations with the Germans. (The Russian troops were deserting in droves to grab lands and jobs in the new utopia.) The Germans, realizing Russia's helplessness, demanded the harshest of terms. Lenin attempted to stall them off, but when the Germans threatened to march on Petrograd and Moscow, he was forced to sign the Treaty of Brest-Litovsk (March 1918). Russia lost Finland, Estonia, Latvia, Lithuania, the Ukraine, Bessarabia, her Polish provinces, and some of her Trans-Caucasian territory. These lands contained one-third of Russia's European population, three-fourths of her iron, and nine-tenths of her coal. In addition, she was compelled to pay a heavy indemnity.

---

[2]Lenin, Trotsky, and Stalin are assumed names, but these are the names they were and are known by.

But these hard terms were not the end, or the worst, of Lenin's woes. Two years of bitter civil war followed the peace with Germany. The aristocracy, including most of the higher army officers, faced with extermination, flew to arms against the Bolshevik regime. These "white" forces were aided by various other disaffected groups and by French, British, Polish, Japanese, and a few American troops. It was with the greatest of difficulty that the "red" armies, hastily organized by Trotsky, finally liquidated the "whites." In doing so, the Bolsheviks regained the Ukraine. However, a large additional strip of territory was lost to Poland, thanks largely to French armed intervention on the side of the Poles.

In the midst of these disasters, Lenin's Bolshevik regime undertook to create a pilot Marxist state out of the wreckage of the Russian Empire. (For Marxist theory and Lenin's amendments to it, see pp. 558–559.) In place of the tsarist hierarchy, a pyramid of people's councils, or *soviets*, was set up. These councils were elected by universal suffrage but were actually dominated completely by a relatively few Communist Party members. Capitalism was abolished. A barter system of exchange replaced money—the value of the ruble having been destroyed by inflation and devaluation. All industry and commerce were placed under the management of committees of workers responsible to Party commissars. The land, far from being distributed to the peasants, as they had been led to believe, was nationalized and turned over to the management of local peasant committees, who distributed it to individual peasants to be worked by their own labor. All crop surpluses were expropriated by the state.

Russia's war-torn economy was soon in shambles. The workers did not know how to run factories and trains, nor did they know how to distribute goods. When the peasants saw that their surpluses would be seized by the government, they refused to raise more than they needed for themselves. By 1921, some 30 million Russians were threatened with starvation, and in spite of considerable foreign relief, particularly from the United States, many hundreds of thousands did starve. Lenin, a realist, saw the necessity for re-

This rare photograph, taken in 1923 at a Party meeting, shows the feud between Stalin and Trotsky that ended with Trotsky's murder in Mexico in 1940. As the brilliant, eloquent Trotsky speaks, the taciturn Stalin, son of ex-serfs, eyes him coldly from his seat at the right. *Photo: United Press International*

treat. In 1921 he launched the NEP (New Economic Policy), which was a temporary compromise with capitalism. In order to provide incentive, industries employing fewer than twenty workers were permitted to operate under private ownership. These little industrial capitalists were called *nepmen*. Enterprising peasants, called *kulaks*, were permitted to own and rent land and hire laborers. Money and credit were restored. This small-scale capitalistic activity was closely supervised and regulated by the state. However, the NEP provided enough incentive to pull the Russian economy out of chaos. In 1923, just as the new policy was beginning to function, Lenin suffered a paralytic stroke, and died the following year.

3. STALIN AND THE FIVE-YEAR PLANS

Lenin's death precipitated a power struggle among his chief associates. The world assumed that his successor would be Leon Trotsky, who had been the chief organizer of the Red Army

The world's largest dam and hydroelectric power plant, at Dnepropetrovsk on the Dnieper River, at its opening in 1932. It was one of the successfully met goals of the first of the Five-Year plans. *Photo: TASS from Sovfoto*

and had planned its victory over the Whites. A brilliant and eloquent Communist theorist, Trotsky was an apostle of world revolution. Trotsky and the world, however, underestimated Joseph Stalin, executive secretary of the Communist Party. This unobtrusive and taciturn little man was an unscrupulous behind-the-scenes operator. Stalin was the son of poverty-stricken ex-serfs. Expelled from an Orthodox seminary because of his Marxist views and activities, he became a professional revolutionist and terrorist. ("Stalin" is a pseudonym meaning "man of steel.") He was repeatedly arrested and imprisoned and repeatedly escaped. World War I found him in exile in Siberia. Taking advantage of the amnesty granted to all political prisoners by the Kerensky regime in 1917, Stalin hastened to Petrograd, where he became a devoted associate of Lenin. He played a prominent role in the civil war against the Whites and became executive secretary of the Communist Party. In this key position he made himself master of the all-important party machinery. Lenin, in his Testament, declared that Stalin was "too hard, too cruel" to be fit for the headship of the government. Nevertheless, the astute Stalin soon maneuvered himself into absolute dictatorship over Russia. Conspiring with one prominent group of Bolsheviks after another and playing off one faction against another, Stalin crushed Trotsky, had him expelled from the Party and exiled from Russia. In 1940 Trotsky was murdered in Mexico by an agent of Stalin. Eventually Stalin executed most of his top Bolshevik associates and rivals. By 1929 his dictatorship over Russia was complete.

In 1928 Stalin launched the first of a series of five-year plans. These were units of planned economy with certain specific goals or objectives to be achieved every five years. They marked the end of the NEP, which had served its purpose of pulling the Communist economy through its first major crises. The objectives of the first five-year plan were: (1) the elimination of the last remnants of capitalism, (2) the industrialization of the Soviet Union, (3) the collectivization and mechanization of agriculture, and (4) national defense.

Achievement of the first goal meant the liquidation of the nepmen and the kulaks. When tens of thousands of the independent peasant-proprietor kulaks resisted, Stalin ruthlessly exterminated them. The consolidation of their farms into mechanized collectives and the organization of giant state farms went on apace. The state farms were huge outlays up to 300,000 acres in size run by Party managers and hired laborers. Every effort was made to mechanize them. Vast tracts of land in southeast Russia and Siberia were brought under cultivation for the first time. The collective farms were of various types. In the most common type, independent farmers surrendered their lands and horses but retained their houses, gardens, cattle, pigs, and chickens for their own private use. The collective farm was run by elected managers who were instructed and supervised by Party officials. Elimination of the tiny individual tracts, each one of which had been surrounded by ditches or hedgerows, made mechanization possible. A certain amount of the harvest was set aside for taxes, insurance, improvements, and feed. A large part had to be sold to the state at a fixed price. The rest was distributed to the peasant members in proportion to the amount of their original contribution to the collective in land and horses and to the amount and quality of their work. The mechanization of Russia's primitive agriculture required the construction of huge quantities of tractors and farm machinery.

Since the Industrial Revolution was still in its infancy in Russia in 1928, industrialization meant building from the ground up and concentration on producer goods. Western engineers and technicians were lured to Russia with high salaries. Capital was obtained by exporting scarce supplies of wheat, often at ruinously low prices. At the cost of much privation, enormous strides were made. Steel mills, power plants, foundries, mines, refineries, and railroads were built all over the Soviet Union. At Dnepropetrovsk on the Dnieper River, the world's largest dam and hydroelectric power plant were constructed. At the end of 1932, it was announced that all the goals of the first five-year plan had been reached several months ahead of time.

The second five-year plan, which was launched immediately, called for greater production of consumer goods: the gadgets and comforts of life that are usually referred to as the standard of living. These were the things the Russian masses had never had and were now striving for. The second five-year plan got off to a poor start when the Soviet Union suffered a disastrous famine during the first years of its existence (1932–34)—a famine induced by drought, mismanagement, and resistance to collectivation. Stalin admitted to 10 million human victims and the destruction of half of the nation's draft and farm animals. Nevertheless, the dictator pressed vigorously on with his plan.

The economic achievements of Communist Russia have been beyond doubt phenomenal. When the Bolsheviks took over in 1917, Russia was a defeated, war-torn country whose industrialization, though well under way by 1914, was far behind that of the leading industrial nations. Twenty-four years later, when the Germans invaded her in 1941, she was the fourth greatest industrial power in the world; in a number of categories, she had surpassed both Great Britain and Germany and was second only to the United

States. She could never have withstood the German assault had this not been true. Russia's agriculture was no longer primitive but largely mechanized. By the mid-1930s new crop records were established almost every year. Food rationing was abandoned. Most of these achievements had been made since 1928. They were made, of course, at the cost of total loss of individual freedom (although there had never been much freedom in Russia under the tsars), the liquidation of tens of thousands who sought to retain some measure of freedom, and the privation and forced labor of the rest.

4. THE SOVIET POLITICAL SYSTEM

The Bolsheviks, on coming to power, broke the Russian Empire into eleven socialist republics — Russia proper and ten other language or dialect areas. In 1939–1940 five more were added from territories seized by Russia at the outbreak of World War II. The Soviet Union is in theory a union of fifteen (as of 1974) autonomous republics. (U.S.S.R. stands for Union of Soviet Socialist Republics.) Actually, however, Russia itself constitutes at least four-fifths of the total area and population, and the so-called Union is in reality a monolithic autocracy.

The Soviet system of government as originally set up consisted of a pyramid of elected councils — village, district, county, and provincial — culminating in the Union Congress of Soviets, which met once every two years and chose executive and administrative boards. Voting was by show of hands in mass meetings. The urban vote was given more than double the weight of the rural vote, since Bolshevism's chief concern was the industrial proletariat. In 1936 Stalin promulgated a new constitution, which appeared to be more democratic. Voting was to be by secret ballot, the differential between the urban and the rural vote was abolished, and the members of the various soviets in the pyramid were to be elected directly by the local districts. The member republics in the union were allegedly granted complete autonomy.

When one examines the actual functioning of the soviet system, however, he quickly observes that the new constitution, like the old, is entirely farcical as far as democracy is concerned. Only the Communist Party is permitted to engage in organized political activity. It names the official candidates, makes all political policies and platforms, and conducts all election promotion and propaganda. Opposition to the Party's official candidates and program is considered to be disloyal and is ferreted out and crushed by the state police, both secret and regular. The all-powerful Communist Party is organized on an authoritarian basis. The Politburo,[3] sixteen men meeting in secret and responsible only to the Secretariat of the Party, makes all decisions, which are transmitted without question down through the chain of command to the local cells. The real center of power in the Soviet system is the Secretariat of the Communist Party, and the First (or General) Secretary of the Party is the most powerful man in the Soviet Union. Blind and unquestioning obedience to superiors is demanded of all Party members. Party members are carefully selected and trained. As set up by Lenin, the total number has been kept relatively small — in 1973 there were approximately 14½ million out of a total population of nearly 250 million. Those of questionable loyalty or zeal are expelled from the Party. During the late 1930s a series of purges liquidated hundreds of Party members, including a number of the top military and civilian officials in the Soviet Union. Thus constitutions, elections, and elected governmental bodies in Communist Russia are a sham. There is no democracy and no political or civil liberty. The Soviet Union is a dictatorship and a police state.[4]

5. SOVIET EDUCATION, ARTS, AND RELIGION

In 1917 more than 60 percent of the Russian people were illiterate. It was Lenin's belief that a

---

[3]The name of the Politburo was changed to Presidium after World War II.

[4]After the death of Stalin in 1953 Nikita Khrushchev undertook to liberalize the system, but as late as 1974 Nobel prizewinner Alexander Solzhenitsyn was expelled from the Soviet Union for criticizing the government.

Communist state requires an educated populace in order to succeed. Nearly all the top Bolsheviks themselves were educated men—in fact, they would be considered members of the intelligentsia in almost any time or place. Little could be done in the educational field in the first turbulent years of the Communist regime, but education received major attention in Stalin's five-year plans. In 1928 the Communists launched the vastest program of free compulsory secular education in history up to that time. The program covered all levels—elementary, secondary, and higher—for both the young and adults. It included a comprehensive system of technical and on-the-job training. Science and engineering were particularly stressed. By the middle of the twentieth century, Soviet universities and institutes were graduating more than twice as many engineers as were those of the United States, the most materially advanced and technology-conscious capitalistic country. All Soviet engineers were receiving five years of training instead of the four usual in the United States. Of course, Soviet education was interlarded with Communist propaganda, but its standards were high, and it turned out the kinds of trained people who were needed. In 1941 Stalin announced that illiteracy had been banished from Russia. The quality of Soviet education is difficult to assess. It is certain that much of it was crude and makeshift and that the truth was often deliberately distorted. On the other hand, Western assumptions that Soviet science and engineering were too shoddy to produce tanks that would run and planes that would fly, not to speak of nuclear fission, proved to be dangerous miscalculations. Another facet of Soviet education was the emphasis upon physical education. The results of this emphasis became apparent in international athletic competition.

Nor were advanced scholarship and the arts neglected in the Soviet Union. The world's most extensive program of scholarships, prizes, and institutes was inaugurated for the purpose of encouraging and subsidizing superior talent. Soviet musicians, architects, painters, and dancers more than held their own in international competition. American visitors to the Soviet Union were repeatedly surprised at the great interest of the people in the arts and in classical literature. Yet even the arts ran afoul of the Communist police state. All liberal, bourgeois, or capitalistic literature (which was most of it) was heavily censored.[5] Such world-renowned composers as Prokofiev and Shostakovich occasionally fell into official disfavor because of their modern "bourgeois" music. When some powerful commissar decided that the Mendelian law of genetics, which is generally accepted in the world of science, ran counter to the Party line, Soviet geneticists were forced to disclaim it. Such incidents lead one to wonder how long the arts and pure science can flourish in a police state.

One of the most important facets of communism and of its clash with Western civilization is its attitude toward religion. The weakening of Christianity in the late nineteenth century in the face of onrushing science, technology, and malignant nationalism was undoubtedly a major factor in the rise of Marxist materialism. Marx and Lenin both were keenly aware of the importance of religion. They considered it "the opiate of the people"—a concoction of the "haves" to quiet the "have nots" lest they demand and seize their share of this world's goods. But communism is itself, of course, a religion. Stark materialism and class hatred are its basic doctrines. Marx and Lenin are its major prophets, and their writings are its scriptures.

The religious policy of the Bolsheviks, upon gaining power in Russia, was quite similar to that of the French Revolutionists in 1789–1794. All church property was confiscated. The churches themselves were turned into museums or clubs of various kinds, although they were sometimes leased to religious congregations for purposes of worship. No religious instruction whatever was permitted in the schools, which were all public and secular. The churches were forbidden to give organized religious instruction and even to maintain seminaries for the training of their own clergy. On the other hand, the schools were flooded with Communist pro-

---

[5]See p. 662 for persecution of Nobel prizewinners Boris Pasternak and Alexander Solzhenitsyn.

paganda. An oath of atheism is required for membership in the Communist Party. Physical attacks on the clergy and the faithful occurred from time to time, and of course active participation in religious activities was certain to blight a young Russian's career under the Communist regime.

The Communist leaders have always claimed that their harsh treatment of the churches was necessitated by the active opposition of the churches to the Communist government. They claim that when they first came to power they granted religious freedom for the first time in Russian history, but that the churches immediately used this freedom to advocate the overthrow of the very government that granted it. They further claim that churches have always been the tools and agents of capitalistic governments and interests. Whatever truth there may be in these claims, it would appear that religion has remained a great problem and danger to the Soviet regime. Mankind is inherently religious, and churches have nearly always thrived under persecution. Religious groups with international connections, such as the Roman Catholics, Lutherans, and Jews, have attracted sympathy abroad and projected the question of religion into Russia's foreign affairs.

6. SOVIET FOREIGN POLICY

It is Soviet foreign policy that is of greatest concern to the rest of the world. Were the Soviet Union an isolated island, the rest of the world might look upon it as an interesting and perhaps exotic experiment and wish it well. But it is very much in and of the world, to which it has always loomed as an ominous threat. It occupies one-sixth of the land surface of the earth, including the strategic heartland of the world's greatest land mass. It has great physical resources. Its population of some 250 million is rapidly increasing. The Marxist ideology, as modified by Lenin, is activist and violent. What is the foreign policy of the Soviet Union? The rest of the world wants, indeed demands, to know. Is it world conquest, world revolution, or both? These questions are as difficult as they are pressing, partly because of the secretiveness and callous

duplicity of the Soviet police state and partly because of the hysteria that has so often accompanied the quest for the answers.

When the Bolsheviks first took over in 1917, they confidently expected most of the capitalistic governments in the war-weary world to collapse and follow Russia along the path of communism. To encourage them to do so and to avoid fulfillment of the harsh terms of the Treaty of Brest-Litovsk, the Communist leaders began an active campaign of revolutionary infiltration and subversion abroad, particularly in Germany. Although some headway was made in Germany, Bavaria falling under Communist control for a brief time, the only country to go Communist was Hungary, where in 1919 Béla Kun set up a Communist dictatorship that lasted four months. To guide and aid the Communist parties in other countries in the common cause of world revolution, the Bolsheviks set up the Comintern (Communist International) with headquarters in Moscow.

The Western capitalistic powers were as antagonistic to the Soviet Union as was the Soviet Union to them. Thinking that the Bolshevik regime would soon collapse, France, Great Britain, Japan, and the United States landed troops on Russian soil in 1918 and aided the counterrevolutionary White forces. France helped the Poles to seize a large strip of Russian-speaking territory. Great Britain and France organized the anti-Soviet regimes in the countries of Eastern Europe bordering the Soviet Union into a *cordon sanitaire* (health or quarantine belt). For several years, no Western power would recognize the Bolshevik regime. The Soviet Union was refused admission to the League of Nations until 1934, eight years after Germany had been admitted and one year after she had withdrawn under the guidance of Hitler. Even then the Western powers steadfastly refused to cooperate with the Soviet Union in any collective action against the rising Fascist menace.

Nonetheless, the failure of the Communist movements abroad and of the Bolsheviks' early efforts to communize Russia overnight caused the Soviet leaders to adopt a more conciliatory attitude toward the capitalistic powers. The NEP needed foreign commerce and foreign capital in order to function. Great Britain and France yielded to these inducements in 1924. (Germany had recognized the Soviet Union in 1922 in order to frighten her Allied conquerors.) Following the lead of Great Britain and France, one capitalistic state after another recognized the Soviet Union. The United States, which held off until 1933, was the last one to do so.

The five-year plans, which began in 1928, required much Western capital and technical assistance. Therefore, the next ten years represented the high tide of Soviet tractability toward the capitalistic Western democracies. Stalin, unlike Trotsky, was more interested in "socialism in one country" than in world revolution, which he believed would come later. The Comintern was allowed to languish. His foreign minister,

Maxim Litvinov, became a respected and even popular figure in Geneva, Paris, London, and Washington. Of course, the Soviet Union's fear of the growing Nazi German menace after 1933 was a significant factor in her conciliatory attitude toward the capitalistic democracies. This honeymoon ended in 1938 with the Munich crisis (see p. 640). From that time, Stalin was apparently convinced that real cooperation with the Western democracies was impossible. The cooperation forced upon the Soviet Union and most of the capitalistic world by the menace of the Axis during World War II lasted only until victory was assured. Meanwhile, after Hitler came to power in 1933, the greatest threat to both the Soviet Union and the capitalistic democracies was Nazi Germany.

Suggested Reading

The Bolshevik Revolution of 1917
*L. Trotsky, *History of the Russian Revolution* (abridged, Anchor). By one of the two chief leaders of the revolution. Excellent.

*B. Wolfe, *Three Who Made a Revolution* (Delta). Good study of Lenin, Trotsky, and Stalin, for the nonspecialist.

Soviet Political System and History
*L. Fischer, *Life of Lenin* (Colophon). Lucid and objective.

*I. Deutscher, *Stalin: A Political Biography* (Vintage). Not only a scholarly biography of Stalin, but a good history of the whole Communist movement in Russia.

E. H. Carr, *A History of Soviet Russia*, 7 vols. (1950 ff.). The serious student deeply interested in the Soviet Union should know of this work — the most scholarly and definitive study on the subject. The author does not let his sympathy toward the Soviet Union interfere with his objective scholarship.

Soviet Economy, Education, and Religion
*A. Nove, *An Economic History of the U.S.S.R.* (Penguin). The best brief study on the subject.

R. Marshall, *Aspects of Religion in the Soviet Union 1917–1967* (1971). The best book on this difficult subject.

G. S. Counts and N. Lodge, *The Country of the Blind: The Soviet System of Mind Control* (1949). Counts was one of the first Americans to travel extensively in the Soviet Union.

Soviet Foreign Policy
A. Ulam, *Expansion and Coexistence* (1968). Scholarly and objective.

G. Kennan, *Russia and the West Under Lenin and Stalin* (1961). By a former American ambassador to the Soviet Union. Rather harsh toward the Soviet Union.

Life in the Soviet Union
*K. Mehnert, *Soviet Man and His World* (Praeger). Astute observation of the life of the ordinary citizen in the Soviet Union. Finds Soviet man to be more man than Soviet.

*B. Pasternak, *Doctor Zhivago* (Signet). Nobel prizewinning novel depicting life in the Soviet Union by a man who experienced it.

56

THE TRIUMPH OF FASCISM IN ITALY, GERMANY, AND JAPAN

A fruit of World War I more bitter and poisonous for Western democracy even than communism was fascism. We cannot yet know which of these violently antiliberal forces will prove to have the more enduring vigor, but there is no question that fascism constituted the more immediate threat to liberal democracy. It was fascism that broke down the peace settlement and brought on World War II. The first Fascist dictatorship was set up by Mussolini in Italy. But it was Fascist Germany and Japan that became the most virulent threats to world peace.

1. MUSSOLINI CREATES THE FIRST FASCIST STATE

Italy emerged from World War I battered and humiliated. Although she was one of the victorious Allies, her armies had made a poor showing and she had realized few of the grandiose ambitions for which she had entered the war. In the Paris peace settlements she had been awarded the adjacent Italian-speaking areas of Austria-Hungary, but had been denied further acquisitions east of the Adriatic and the Turkish and German provinces in Asia and Africa, some of which she ardently desired. These frustrations were severe blows to Italian national pride.

Italy's weak economy emerged from the war acutely maladjusted. The national debt was huge, and the treasury empty. The inflated currency, together with a shortage of goods, raised prices ruinously. Hundreds of thousands of demobilized veterans could find no jobs. In the summer of 1919, there was widespread disorder. Veterans began seizing and squatting on idle, and sometimes on cultivated, lands. Sit-down strikes developed in the factories. During the winter of 1920–1921, several hundred factories were seized by the workers. Bolshevik agents arrived from Russia to exploit the distress. The Italian government, torn by factions, seemed too weak to prevent the disorder and protect private property. Although the strife diminished and the Communist threat waned before the end of 1921, the landlords and the factory owners were thoroughly frightened. Many of them, and indeed many small business and professional men, longed for vigorous leadership and a strong government. The vigorous leader who stepped forward was Benito Mussolini. The strong government was his Fascist dictatorship.

Mussolini was a dynamic organizer and leader. The son of a humble blacksmith, he became first a teacher and later a radical journalist and agitator. Before World War I he was a pacifistic socialist, but during the war he became a violent nationalist. After the war he began organizing unemployed veterans into a political action group with a socialistic and extremely nationalistic program. During the labor disturbances of 1919–1921, Mussolini stood aside until it be-

Benito Mussolini speaks to a great crowd in Rome after a victory of the Italian forces in Ethiopia, which was conquered as a first step in the Fascist dream of a restoration of the ancient Roman Empire.
Photo: United Press International

came apparent that the radical workingmen's cause would lose; then he threw his support to the capitalists and the landlords. Crying that he was saving Italy from communism and waving the flag of nationalism, Mussolini organized his veterans into terror squads of black-shirted "Fascisti," who beat up the leaderless radical workingmen and their liberal supporters. He thereby gained the support of the frightened capitalists and landed aristocracy. By 1922 Mussolini's Fascist party was strong enough to "march on Rome" and seize control of the faction-paralyzed government. Appointed premier by the weak and distraught King Victor Emmanuel III, Mussolini quickly turned his premiership into a dictatorship. All opposition was

silenced. Only the Fascist party (like the Communist Party in the Soviet Union) could engage in organized political activity. The press and the schools were turned into propaganda agencies. The secret police were everywhere. Eventually, the Chamber of Deputies itself was replaced by Mussolini's hand-picked Fascist political and economic councils.

Italy's economic life was strictly regimented, but in such a way as to favor the capitalistic classes. Private property and profits were carefully protected. All labor unions were abolished except those controlled by the Fascist party. Strikes and lockouts were forbidden. Wages, working conditions, and labor-management disputes were settled by compulsory arbitration under party direction. An elaborate system of planned economy was set up for the purpose of modernizing, coordinating, and increasing Italy's production of both industrial and agricultural goods. The very complicated economic and political machinery that Mussolini created for these purposes was called the corporate state. Under the whip and drive of Mussolini, remarkable increases in production were achieved. Trains began to run on time, the budget was balanced, and the currency was stabilized. But taxes were the highest in the world, and labor's share in the fruits of increased production was small.

Fascism, however, was primarily political in character, not economic. The essence of its ideology was nationalism—malignant nationalism run wild. Mussolini understood the dynamic, energizing quality of this kind of nationalism. His writings and speeches rang with such words as "will," "discipline," "sacrifice," "decision," and "conquest." "The goal," he cried, "is always —Empire! To build a city, to found a colony, to establish an empire, these are the prodigies of the human spirit. . . . We must resolutely abandon the whole liberal phraseology and way of thinking. . . . Discipline. Discipline at home in order that we may present the granite block of a single national will. . . . War alone brings up to the highest tension all human energy and puts the stamp of nobility upon the people who have the courage to meet it." The Fascists adopted the trappings and symbols of ancient Rome. The word "fascism" itself comes from the word "fasces," meaning a bundle of rods surrounding an ax borne by Roman magistrates as a symbol of authority. Here we have the arrogant militaristic nationalism of the late nineteenth century, including the "superman" theory of Carlyle, Wagner, and Nietzsche, come to full flower.

Fascism, of course, clashed head-on with Christianity both in spirit and in deeds. In fact every fundamental principle in Fascist philosophy has its opposite in Christian doctrine: love thy neighbor—hate and conquer thy neighbor; blessed are the meek—blessed are the strong-willed and arrogant; blessed are the peacemakers—blessed are the warmakers. Nevertheless, Mussolini realized the advantage of coming to terms with the powerful Roman Catholic Church and made a treaty with the pope—the Lateran Treaty of 1929. The pope recognized Mussolini's regime. (Since the pope had been despoiled of his territories, 1860–1870, he had refused to rec-

ognize the Italian government.) In return, Mussolini paid him nearly $100 million in cash and government bonds from a hard-pressed national treasury and allowed the teaching of religion by Roman Catholic clergy in the public schools. This seeming accord, however, was uneasy and quarrelsome from the start.

The building of a powerful army and navy and the recovery of Italy's national prestige were always uppermost in Mussolini's thoughts. Fascist Italy's militarism, self-assertiveness, and expansive ambitions played an important part in the breakdown of the peace settlement and the return to war. But before we examine these activities, we must examine the rise and triumph of fascism in Germany and Japan, both of which were more powerful and dangerous to the rest of the world than was Italy.

2. GERMANY REFUSES TO ACCEPT THE PEACE SETTLEMENT

Germany emerged from World War I defeated, humiliated, and angry. As late as July 1918, she had seemed to be invincible; four months later she had been forced to surrender, hopelessly beaten. Then, she was compelled to sign a dictated peace treaty, the terms of which she considered unjust. Furthermore, she was virtually forced to change her form of government by Woodrow Wilson, who refused to negotiate with the Hohenzollern regime. The Weimar Republic (so-called from the city famous for Goethe and Schiller, where its constitution was drawn up), which the Germans set up in 1919, was, on paper, a model of liberal democracy. However, it was lacking in historical precedent and in genuine popular support. The German people, never before having had a democratic government, were inexperienced in its practices. Even worse, the Weimar Republic was set up under the pressure of the victorious Allies, and its leaders were forced to sign the hated Treaty of Versailles. That it was able to function for ten years with reasonable effectiveness was due more to necessity than to inherent strength.

Germany violated many of the disarmament clauses of the Treaty of Versailles from the start. Old military units and organizations continued to function under assumed names. Weapons were hidden away, and many war plants were not dismantled. The 100,000-man army permitted her became the world's best-trained officer corps, which could be quickly expanded into a powerful army. Forbidden weapons such as tanks and artillery were perfected and tested on Russian and Swedish soil. Denied an air force, Germany became the world's leading nation in civil aviation. Her airfields, aircraft factories, and trained pilots and technicians could, of course, easily be converted to military purposes. When the British, in accordance with the treaty, tried to take possession of the German battle fleet interned at Scapa Flow in the British Isles, the German sailors scuttled their ships. Swift, powerful pocket battleships within the 10,000-ton treaty limit were constructed to serve as commerce raiders in the next war. The two most prominent German leaders, Walter Rathenau and Matthias Erzberger, who advocated conciliation with the Western democracies, were assassinated by members of the professional military. The assassins were widely acclaimed as national heroes. When the German people went to the polls for the first time in 1925 to elect a president, their choice was their top military hero, Field Marshal Paul von Hindenburg.

The first overt clash between recalcitrant Germany and the former Allies occurred over reparations. In 1921 the reparations commission that had been established at the Paris peace conference set Germany's reparations bill at approximately $33 billion, to be paid over a long period of time. Although the Germans had been compelled by the Treaty of Versailles to accept in advance liability for whatever figure was set, they received the announcement of this amount with indignation. German governmental and financial leaders boasted both in public and in private that they would never pay it. The Weimar Republic refused to tax heavily the wealth of the great industrialists, and much of their wealth was permitted to leave the country. Germany defaulted on the very first annual payment. To the exasperated French, who were trying desperately to repair the ravages of the war, this was the last straw. In January 1923 French and Belgian troops occupied the Ruhr Valley, Ger-

many's richest industrial area. The Germans fought back sullenly with passive resistance. The French countered by trying to stir up a secession movement from Germany in the Rhineland. Bloodshed between the occupying troops and the civilian population was frequent. Although the occupying forces were unable to collect any reparations, Germany's economy was paralyzed and a wild inflation swept the country. Thus more seeds of bitterness were sown.

After seven months of struggle, the German leaders realized the futility of resistance. In August 1923, Gustav Stresemann became head of the German government and offered conciliation. An international commission headed by Charles G. Dawes of the United States drew up a plan for the withdrawal of the occupying forces, for an international loan to Germany, and for the orderly payment of Germany's reparations installments. Her economy quickly recovered. From 1924 to 1929 Germany was the most prosperous nation in Europe and made her reparations payments as scheduled. In 1929 another international commission headed by Owen D. Young, an American financier, reduced Germany's total liability to the equivalent of a cash payment of $9 billion. However, the world depression struck Germany in that year, and after 1931 no further payments were made.

Meanwhile, under Stresemann's leadership Germany sought a *rapprochement* with her former enemies. In 1925 she signed the Treaty of Locarno with France, Great Britain, Italy, and Belgium, guaranteeing Germany's existing frontiers with France and Belgium. In 1926 Germany was admitted to the League of Nations, and Stresemann was elected president of the Council. But this apparent good will was deceptive. The old German militarism and nationalism, made more malignant by the sting of defeat, were still strong. The spirit of sullen hatred and revenge toward the former Allies filled the hearts of many Germans. Even Stresemann, we now know from his memoirs, was biding his time until Germany was strong enough to reassert herself. He was constantly deceiving the Western democracies and playing one off against the other. However, a far more sinister force was at work in postwar Germany, capitalizing on the economic and social maladjustment and the frustrated militarism and nationalism. This force was National Socialism, organized and led by Adolph Hitler.

3. THE RISE OF HITLER AND NATIONAL SOCIALISM

Adolph Hitler was the neurotic and maladjusted son of a petty middle-aged Austrian customs official and a young, sensitive, unhappily married mother. As a child he already suffered delusions of grandeur. Of an artistic temperament, he went off to Vienna at an early age to seek an artist's career. Denied admission to the art academies for lack of training and too proud to work as a laborer, he lived for years in poverty and sometimes in squalor. He fed his ego with German master-race theories and filled his heart with hatred of the Jews. At the outbreak of World War I Hitler was in Munich, Germany, eking out a living at crude art work such as making posters. The ardent young German nationalist threw himself eagerly into the war, which he considered to be a righteous crusade for the beloved fatherland. Attaining the rank of corporal, he got his first taste for command. When the war ended, he was in a hospital, a victim of poison gas. This may have accounted for the strange, hoarse resonance in his voice that unnerved the listener.

After the war, Hitler frequented beer cellars, haranguing demobilized and unemployed troops and organizing them into violent political action groups. He soon discovered his magnetic powers of oratory and of leadership. The disgruntled and the disenchanted, particularly the frustrated young intellectuals and demobilized lesser army officers, began attaching themselves to Hitler in increasing numbers. He organized them into the National Socialist (Nazi) party. Among his most important early followers were Hermann Goering, who became second in command; Rudolph Hess, who became head of the political section of the party; and Paul Joseph Goebbels, who became the chief Nazi propagandist. As early as 1923 Hitler, in league with the popular war hero Field Marshal Ludendorff, made his first grab for power. It was premature, however, and Hitler was jailed for nearly a year.

While in jail he wrote *Mein Kampf* (My Struggle), which became the Nazi bible.

National Socialism, as outlined in *Mein Kampf*, was the German brand of fascism. In fact, the Nazis were heavily indebted to Mussolini for both ideology and methodology. At the center of its basic philosophy is the German master-race concept. The old Nordic myth of Gobineau and Chamberlain was revived. The terms "German," "Nordic," and "Aryan" were used interchangeably without regard to scientific fact. It was held that the Germans, the only pure representatives of the tall, blond Nordic "race," are superior to and destined to conquer and rule all other peoples. Militarism, indomitable will, pride, aggressiveness, and brute strength were held to be virtues; gentleness, peacefulness, tolerance, pity, and modesty, vices.

As a specific program of action, National Socialism was primarily concerned with foreign affairs. It called for repudiation of the Treaty of Versailles; all-out rearmament; the recovery of all territories, including colonies, lost at the end of World War I; and the annexation of all neighboring German-speaking territories such as Austria, the Netherlands, and most of Switzerland. Then the master race must have *Lebensraum* (living space). This was to be obtained by driving to the east *(Drang nach Osten)*, particularly by conquering and enslaving the Soviet Union. There is little doubt that in the Nazi mind, world domination was the ultimate goal.

The domestic program was vague and contradictory. Trusts and department stores were to be nationalized. Unearned income was to be abolished. Communism was to be destroyed, and labor unions rigidly controlled. Finally, persecution of the Jews was always part and parcel of the Nazi program. Persecution was later changed to extermination. The capitalistic classes never took the socialistic aspects of Hitler's program seriously. As in Italy, they looked to the Fascists to provide strong government, protect property, and control the working classes.

Hitler copied many of Mussolini's techniques. The rank and file of Nazi party members, wearing brown shirts, were organized along military lines as storm troopers. They marched, sang, and intimidated and beat up the opposition. An elite corps of black-shirted "SS" troops supervised and policed the brown shirts. Pagan symbolism was adopted—appropriately, since Nazism represented the antithesis of everything that Christianity stands for. All party members swore unquestioning and undying allegiance to Hitler.

4. THE TRIUMPH OF HITLER

At first National Socialism grew slowly but steadily. From 1925 to 1929, when Germany under Stresemann's leadership was the most prosperous nation in Europe and was being wooed by her former enemies, Nazi party membership grew from 27,000 to 178,000. After the great depression of 1929, which struck Germany along with the rest of the capitalistic world, the Nazis gained rapidly. In the parliamentary elections of 1930 they obtained several million votes and increased their seats in the Reichstag from 12 to 107. They were now strong enough to disrupt the orderly functioning of parliamentary government, and President Hindenburg resorted to ruling by presidential decree. In the presidential election of 1932 Hitler ran as the Nazi candidate. The moderate and liberal parties, which in 1925 had feared and opposed Hindenburg, now persuaded him to run again as the

only man who could stop Hitler (Hindenburg was now eighty-five years old). Hitler got enough votes to force a runoff election against the popular and venerable idol. In the runoff election Hindenburg was elected, but Hitler received more than 13 million votes. In parliamentary elections a few months later, the Nazis obtained 230 out of 608 seats in the Reichstag, the largest number ever held by any party under the Weimar Republic. Hindenburg now offered to make Hitler vice-chancellor, but Hitler, sensing complete dictatorship in the offing, refused.

Meanwhile, the Nazis, under Hitler's instructions, paralyzed Germany's economic and political life with violence. When the chaos threatened to play into the hands of the Communists, in January 1933, Hindenburg offered and Hitler accepted the chancellorship. Franz von Papen, head of the militaristic Nationalist party, was

Hitler reviewing his troops. During the 1930s Hitler's main concern was to remilitarize Germany in preparation for a war of revenge and conquest. The nation and the world were frequently reminded of Germany's growing strength by public displays such as this one. *Photo: UPI*

made vice-chancellor. It was the great industrialists who finally gave the Nazis the necessary support to come to power. Hitler, determined to have nothing less than complete dictatorship, immediately called for parliamentary elections. Now in official control of the state police and the agencies of information in addition to their own highly disciplined party machinery, the Nazis skillfully used every device of propaganda to frighten and confuse the people. Like the Fascists in Italy, they exaggerated and exploited the Communist threat. Five days before the elections, they made use of the burning of the Reichstag building, blaming the Communists. The elections themselves, however, were by secret ballot and were relatively free. The Communists polled 4.8 million votes, the Center (Roman Catholic) party 5.5 million, the Social Democrats (workers and small business and professional men's party) 7.2 million, the Nazis 17 million, and von Papen's Nationalists 3 million. The Nazi and the Nationalist vote combined gave Hitler 52 percent of the seats in the Reichstag. A few days later, Hitler, wearing his Nazi party uniform, appeared before the newly elected Reichstag, from which the Communists were excluded, and demanded dictatorial powers for four years. They were granted with only 94 opposing (Social Democratic) votes. Long before the four years had expired, the moderate parties had been destroyed, and the Nazi dictatorship was complete.

5. NAZI GERMANY

The Reichstag, having voted Hitler dictatorial powers, adjourned, to meet henceforth only on the call of the *Führer* (leader) for the purpose of voting approval of his acts. Hitler disbanded all political parties except the National Socialist party. Freedom of speech, press, and assembly was abolished. An elaborate and all-powerful secret police, the Gestapo, was established under the direction of Heinrich Himmler to spy out and destroy opposition. Hitler's most intense hatred was vented upon the Jews, who were subjected to every conceivable humiliation. As fast as their services could be dispensed with, they were driven out of public and professional life. Eventually, the Nazis embarked upon a program to exterminate all the Jews under their control. It is estimated that by the end of World War II, the Nazis had murdered 6 million Jews out of a world total of 15 million.

The control and molding of thought always held high priority in Nazi activities. Indeed, this appears to be an absolute necessity for any totalitarian dictatorship. Under the direction of Goebbels, minister of propaganda, the German press and radio spewed forth a constant stream of false or distorted information. To read or listen to foreign newspapers or broadcasts was made a crime. An incessant hate campaign was waged against the liberal democratic world. The schools were, of course, Nazified. Only Nazi party members could be school administrators. Unsympathetic teachers were dismissed and punished. Members of Nazi youth organizations were set to spy on their teachers and parents. Textbooks were rewritten to conform to German master-race theories. The burning of liberal books, sometimes even those of Germany's greatest literary figures, such as Goethe and Schiller, became a national fad. The Nazi minister of education admitted that the sole function of education was the creation of Nazis. Hitler wrote in *Mein Kampf* that the German youth's ". . .entire education and development has to be directed at giving him the conviction of being absolutely superior to the others . . . the belief in the invincibility of his entire nationality." The arts were Nazified, only party members or sympathizers being permitted to publish, exhibit, or perform.

Since National Socialism was essentially an anti-Christian religion, the Nazis realized the necessity of controlling the religious establishment. The Lutheran Church, which was the official state church and included more than half the German people in its membership, was easily brought under Nazi domination. Nazi officials turned it into a powerful propaganda agency. The few Lutheran pastors like Martin Niemöller who resisted were thrown into concentration camps. The smaller Protestant denominations met the same fate. Hitler found it much more difficult to deal with the Roman Catholic Church, whose higher authority lay outside Germany. Although he soon signed a concordat with the pope, the terms proved to be unworkable. Roman Catholic clergy, churches, and schools were subjected to constantly increasing pressures, indignities, and physical abuse.

The Nazis rejuvenated and regimented Germany's economic life. The property and the profits of the capitalistic classes were given special consideration. Labor unions were brought under Nazi control, and a system of enforced arbitration of disputes between labor and management was set up along the lines that Mussolini had established in Italy. Strikes and lockouts were forbidden. The entire German economy was forced into the overall pattern and policies of the Nazi government. The vast rearmament program gave employment to millions. Superhighways, airfields, hospitals, and apartment houses were built all over Germany. The most intricate financial trickery was resorted to, but the Nazis expected eventually to finance their huge undertakings out of the spoils of victorious war.

All other activities were subordinated to the prime purpose of making a military comeback. Shortly after assuming power, Hitler took Germany out of the League of Nations and out of the disarmament conference that was in progress in Geneva. Rearmament was pushed as rapidly as possible, and in 1935 Hitler openly repudiated the disarmament clauses of the Treaty of Versailles. In 1936 Hitler remilitarized the Rhineland and sent decisive aid to General Franco's Fascist rebels in Spain (see Chapter 57). The following year he made an alliance with the two other Fascist powers, Italy and Japan. This Berlin-Rome-Tokyo Axis was aimed specifically at the Soviet Union. In reality, it was an aggressive alliance against the non-Fascist world. Before tracing the Fascist aggressions that plunged the world into World War II, however, we must examine briefly the triumph of fascism in the third member of the Axis—Japan.

6. THE TRIUMPH OF FASCISM IN JAPAN

We have already observed (see p. 575) Japan's remarkable modernization and emergence as a great power between 1853 and 1914. She participated in World War I on the side of the Allies and received Germany's island possessions in the Pacific north of the equator as her reward. At the Washington Naval Conference in 1922 she gained a 5:5:3 naval ratio with the United States and Great Britain. That is, for every five capital ships of the United States, Great Britain would have five and Japan three. This represented a significant gain for Japan. Of greater importance, Japan gained a military monopoly in East Asia and the Western Pacific when Great Britain agreed not to fortify anything east of Singapore and the United States agreed not to fortify anything west of Pearl Harbor. Japan in the early 1920s stood at the crossroads. She could use her great energies and skills either to develop her own institutions and raise her standard of living or to become a predatory military state. She could hardly stand still. On her three thousand islands, with a total area no greater than that of the state of California, lived a rapidly increasing population of 60 million. Only 14 percent of Japan's land is arable, and she possesses very few natural resources. Her quickly built industries had overexpanded during the wartime prosperity, and the postwar deflation and sharp competition from her former allies brought severe economic stresses.

Three divergent groups competed for the leadership of postwar Japan. The dominant group was made up of the great industrialists. Seventy-five percent of Japan's industry and capital was concentrated in the hands of five great families, called the *zaibatsu*. This handful of industrial giants had such a stranglehold on the Japanese economy that it was also able to control the highly restricted government. The *zaibatsu*, enjoying this economic and political monopoly, wished to see no fundamental change in Japan's undemocratic society, but advocated instead the peaceful economic penetration of Asia.

The liberals constituted the second group. This faction, with university professors and students providing much of the leadership, set out to broaden the suffrage, which was restricted to the well-to-do, to encourage the more effective unionization of labor, and to diminish the power of the military. Because of the political inexperience and the long tradition of passive submission to authority on the part of the Japanese masses, these were difficult undertakings. They were made more difficult by the activities of a small group of Communists directed from Moscow, who confused liberal reform movements and tainted them with the suspicion of treason. Nevertheless, encouraging progress toward liberal democracy was made. In 1925 the suffrage was broadened. Soon afterward, two liberal political parties appeared. The military budget was reduced. The prestige of the professional military declined to such an extent that many officers ceased wearing their uniforms in public.

The professional military, however, was determined to strengthen and exploit its own traditional power. In the late 1920s a group of restless and ambitious young army officers began to accuse their leaders of softness and plotted to seize control of both the armed forces and the government. When a coup planned for early 1931 was exposed and blocked, the conspirators decided on a bold move to throw the country into such hysteria and confusion that they could seize power. In October 1931 the Japanese army stationed in Manchuria made an unauthorized attack on the Chinese forces and began the conquest of all Manchuria. The next year, 1932, Japanese forces attacked Shanghai, the chief port of China. Once fighting began with huge and potentially dangerous China, war fever and patriotic hysteria swept Japan, just as the army plotters had foreseen. They now assassinated the premier and numerous other government officials and civilian leaders, and cowed the rest into submission. Once in control, the military immediately turned to the destruction of the liberals. Liberal university professors were accused of disloyalty and silenced, dismissed, or imprisoned. As in Italy and Germany, the schools and the press and radio were made organs of propaganda. All democratic processes of government and civil rights were destroyed. The military and state police were given unlimited authority. The *zaibatsu* were corrupted and won over with lush military contracts.

Meanwhile, Japanese armies overran all of Manchuria, which was made into the puppet state of Manchukuo. When the League of Nations declared Japan an aggressor and ordered her to withdraw from Manchuria, she defied the league and instead withdrew from that organization. In 1937 Japan joined the Berlin-Rome Axis. In the same year she began an all-out assault on China proper. By 1937, therefore, the Fascist powers were on the march.

Suggested Reading

Mussolini Creates the First Fascist State

I. Kirkpatrick, *Mussolini: Study of a Demagogue* (1964). Best biography of Mussolini.

H. L. Matthews, *The Fruits of Fascism* (1943). Eyewitness account of fascism in action by New York *Times* reporter.

Postwar Germany

*F. Meinecke, *The German Catastrophe: Reflections and Recollections* (Beacon). Sympathetic account by a leading German historian.

*S. W. Halperin, *Germany Tried Democracy* (Norton). Good brief history of the ill-fated Weimar Republic.

Rise and Triumph of Hitler

*A. Bullock, *Hitler: A Study in Tyranny* (Torch). Best biography of Hitler.

*E. Fromm, *Escape from Freedom* (Avon). Brilliant analysis of the universal urge to accept dictatorship.

Nazi Germany

*W. L. Shirer, *The Rise and Fall of the Third Reich* (Crest). Excellent big book written in a lucid journalistic style.

*———, *Berlin Diary* (Popular). Graphic eyewitness account of Nazi Germany at the beginning of World War II.

*T. Taylor, *Sword and Swastica: Generals and Nazis in the Third Reich* (Quadrangle). Shows the close partnership between the professional military and the Nazis.

Triumph of Fascism in Japan

C. Yanaga, *Japan Since Perry* (1947). Scholarly factual study.

*R. Benedict, *The Chrysanthemum and the Sword* (World). Examines the rôle of the professional military in Japanese fascism and aggression.

57

PARALYSIS OF THE DEMOCRATIC WEST

The fruits of World War I in the democratic West were economic instability, political and social unrest, and intellectual disillusionment. These weaknesses paralyzed the democracies at a time when Western civilization was being seriously challenged by communism and fascism. The efforts of the distraught and disunited democratic powers to appease the Fascist aggressors culminated in World War II.

1. ISOLATIONISM, BOOM, AND BUST IN THE UNITED STATES

The United States emerged from World War I the world's richest and most influential nation. Although her entry into the war at its most critical phase was probably decisive in determining the outcome, she suffered far less war damage than any of the other major participants. President Wilson assumed the leading role in the making of the peace settlements and in the creation of the League of Nations. The rest of the world then looked to the United States to play the major role in supporting the league and maintaining the peace.

When President Wilson returned from Paris in the summer of 1919 and sought to persuade his country to join the League of Nations, he found his political enemies in power. Acceptance by the United States of the league's covenant, which was incorporated into the Treaty of Versailles, required the ratification of the United States Senate by a two-thirds vote. By virtue of a Republican majority of one in the Senate, the chairmanship of the Foreign Relations Committee, through which the treaty must first pass, was held by Wilson's bitterest personal enemy, Henry Cabot Lodge. Lodge was determined to destroy Wilson's handiwork. Indeed, before the exact nature of the league was known and while Wilson was consulting Republican opinion concerning it, Lodge obtained the signatures of thirty-nine senators, more than enough votes to defeat the treaty, to a roundrobin agreeing to vote against whatever proposal Wilson brought back from Paris. Since it appeared that a majority of the American people favored the league in 1919, Lodge decided to defeat the treaty by a flank attack. He therefore attached fourteen amendments that Wilson could not ask the other members of the league to accept. (Some of these deliberately offended Great Britain, and some demanded a privileged position for the United States.) As a matter of fact, had Wilson accepted the obnoxious amendments, Lodge probably would have found other means of defeating the treaty. Wilson set out on a speaking tour to rally American public opinion to the treaty, but suffered a paralytic stroke in the midst of the campaign. As he was unable thereafter to lead the fight for the treaty and was unwilling to give the leadership to others, his opponents easily defeated ratification in the Senate.

Since the American people were never given an opportunity to vote on the league, it is impossible to know what their verdict would have

Jobless and homeless men wait in line for a free meal in New York in 1930. These depression breadlines are part of the reason for the seeming impotence of the democratic nations in the face of the growing Fascist menace. *Photo: United Press International*

been. Such national organizations as the Federal Council of Churches, the American Bar Association, the American Federation of Labor, and the American Bankers Association declared themselves in favor of the league. Some Republican elder statesmen, such as A. L. Lowell, Charles Evans Hughes, and ex-president William Howard Taft, had worked for America's entrance into the league. The league was not an issue in the presidential election of 1920. However, the victor, Warren G. Harding, announced that the league was now a dead issue. And during the cynical and disillusioned decade of the 1920s, American public opinion became overwhelmingly isolationist. When, therefore, during the international crises of the 1930s the league and the harassed British and French governments sought the support of the United States against the fascist aggressors, they sought in vain.

The decade following World War I was a period of unprecedented prosperity in the United States. The all-out war effort brought about a great expansion of American industry and unleashed huge quantities of money and credit. Prices and wages soared. In 1914 the United States had been a debtor nation. She emerged from the war a creditor to most of Europe to the amount of $10 billion, a figure that doubled during the next ten years. Her chief economic competitors came out of the war battered and shaken. Between 1919 and 1929 American production, profits, and purchasing power reached heights never before attained anywhere in the world. However, it was an uneven and unsound prosperity. Agriculture was depressed with surplus commodities and low prices, which meant low purchasing power for great stretches of the South and the Middle West. Nor did wages climb as rapidly as profits and prices in the industrial Northeast. These facts, plus increasing automation, meant growing unemployment and industrial surpluses. Labor unions declined in membership and bargaining power. Foreign markets were killed off by a policy of higher and higher tariffs designed to protect American industry from foreign competition. The government's philosophy of noninterference with free enterprise (except for tariffs) permitted unlimited speculation in the soaring stock market, often with other people's money and with unrestrained use of credit.

The stock market crashed in October 1929. Values tumbled. Thousands of banks and businesses failed. Millions were thrown out of work. The economic depression spread over the entire capitalistic world. For four years the Hoover administration, confident of the essential soundness of laissez-faire economy, refused to permit large-scale government relief measures, expecting and promising that the natural economic laws would soon bring back prosperity. But the depression only deepened.

In the presidential election of 1932 the Democratic candidate, Franklin D. Roosevelt, defeated Hoover by some 7 million votes, ending twelve years of Republican rule. The Roosevelt administration immediately launched a series of sweeping economic and social reforms that came to be called the New Deal. The New Deal was not a radical, new departure, but rather a further advance along the line charted by Theodore Roosevelt's Progressivism and Woodrow Wilson's New Freedom. First of all, emergency measures were taken to relieve the suffering of the 12 million unemployed and their families. The chief of these was the setting up of the huge Public Works Administration, which undertook to avoid the humiliation of the dole by providing useful work of at least some dignity. The

Wagner Act strengthened the position of the labor unions by guaranteeing the right of collective bargaining. Old-age and unemployment insurance was inaugurated. For the desperate farmers, measures were passed that granted debt relief, commodity loans, price supports, and payments for acreage reduction. Deflation was checked by a devaluation of the dollar. Investments and deposits were protected by strict government supervision. Steps were taken to conserve the nation's natural resources against wasteful private exploitation. Gradually, popular confidence was restored and the nation's economy began to prosper again, though far below the boom proportions of the roaring twenties. However, many members of the business community believed that the New Deal discouraged free enterprise and incentive. They thought it was making the United States into a socialistic "welfare state" and argued that the depression eventually would have ended of its own accord through the working of the natural laws of laissez-faire economics. The depression appears to have had no appreciable effect upon the prevailing mood of isolationism in the United States.

2. THE HARASSED BRITISH EMPIRE

Great Britain emerged from World War I a victor. Her greatest prewar military and economic rival was defeated and apparently eliminated as a threat. The British Empire still included one-fourth of all the land and people on the globe. Nevertheless, her economy, her empire, and her world position were shaken beyond recovery. Britain's far-flung possessions in Asia and Africa were beginning to stir restlessly, as the spirit of nationalism, which long had provided the European world with so much of its expansive energy, spread eastward. Great Britain found it advisable to grant freedom to her self-governing dominions, hoping to retain their loyalty. The Statute of Westminster in 1931 gave complete independence and equality with the mother country to Canada, Australia, New Zealand, the Union of South Africa, Newfoundland, and the Irish Free State (free since 1922). These former colonies had been free in reality ever since they had gained dominion status (1867–1922). Now the only remaining legal tie was loyalty to the British crown. The British Empire was thus transformed into the British Empire and Commonwealth. Although the dominions remained loyal (with the exception of Ireland, which severed all relations in 1939), Great Britain could no longer count upon their material support in her world policies, nor could she count upon her restless colonies. Furthermore, Britain was now clearly second to the United States as an industrial and financial power. (It would require many years, however, for British statesmen to readjust their thinking to the reality of their country's reduced position.)

At home, postwar Britain was harassed with acute economic problems. Her national debt had quintupled during the war. She owed the United States a heavy war debt. German submarines had taken a toll of 9 million tons of her ships with their cargoes. Her exports met sharply increased competition in the world markets, particularly from the United States. Rising protective tariffs all over the world hindered her commerce. Her mines and industrial plants were antiquated and in disrepair. Returning servicemen found few jobs. Unemployment hovered around 3 million, a figure that came to be accepted as normal. Government support for the unemployed, sick, aged, and destitute proved to be the most staggering of all Britain's financial problems.

These chronic economic ills were reflected in Great Britain's troubled postwar politics. In 1922 the Conservatives broke up Lloyd George's wartime coalition government of Liberals and Conservatives and won the ensuing parliamentary elections. They sought to restore classical nineteenth-century capitalism by means of rigid retrenchment of government spending, particularly for social services. This policy was so hard on the distressed masses that in 1924 a Labour-Liberal coalition headed by the Labour party leader, Ramsay MacDonald, ousted the Conservatives. The Labour party was now stronger than the Liberal party, and as times grew harder and feelings more bitter, the once great Liberal party was virtually crushed between the more extreme parties—Labour on the left and Conservative on the right.

But the majority of the British people were not yet ready to accept the mildly socialistic program that the Labour party advocated. MacDonald's ministry lasted less than a year. Dependent upon the Liberals for his majority, he was forced to follow a moderate course. When he recognized the Soviet Union and made a commercial treaty with her, the Conservatives were able to capitalize on public suspicion and drive him from power. From 1925 to 1929 the Conservatives wrestled with rising discontent, strikes, and the steady growth of the Labour party. In 1929 a Labour victory, supported by the much dwindled Liberals, again brought Ramsay MacDonald to the head of the government. His moderation in the face of the deepening economic depression, however, caused the majority of his Labour followers to repudiate him two years later. But MacDonald was unwilling to give up the honors of office. In 1931 he therefore formed a National coalition of right-wing Labourites, Liberals, and Conservatives to deal with the mounting domestic and foreign crises. This National coalition was dominated by the Conservatives and MacDonald was now really a captive of the Conservatives until he resigned in 1935. This Conservative-dominated coalition ruled Great Britain until the end of World War II. Before the outbreak of the war, it was on the whole ineffective in dealing with both economic and social maladjustments at home and Fascist aggressions abroad. The Conservative prime ministers Stanley Baldwin and Neville Chamberlain, who followed Ramsay MacDonald as head of the National government appeared still to be living in the nineteenth century.

3. FRUSTRATED FRANCE

Although France enjoyed the advantage of being more self-sufficient economically than Great Britain, she had suffered greater wounds in World War I than had her island neighbor. Most of the fighting had taken place on her soil. A tenth—the most productive tenth—of her land area had been devastated. The retreating Germans had deliberately laid waste much of what had not been destroyed in battle. Orchards were chopped down, and mines were wrecked, many beyond repair. Even more tragic was the loss of life. France, with the lowest birth rate of any major nation in the world, suffered by far the heaviest casualties per capita of any of the combatants. Out of a population of less than 40 million, she suffered almost 1.4 million battle deaths and 1.7 million wounded. These casualties were suffered largely by France's most productive male age groups. The civilian death rate from direct and indirect causes had also been high. France had fewer people in 1918 than in 1914, even after the return of Alsace and Lorraine.

Postwar France was confronted with a staggering job of economic reconstruction and an equally staggering war debt. In addition to her domestic debt, France owed the United States and Great Britain huge amounts. To meet these obligations and to finance the reconstruction, the French government counted on German reparations, but, as we have already seen, practically nothing was forthcoming. Inflation became a chronic headache. A more basic and long-range problem was French industry, which was rapidly falling behind its competitors. The highly individualistic French had not gone in for large-scale corporate industry, as had the Americans, British, and Germans. The little French family industries could not compete with mass production. A like situation prevailed in French agriculture, most of which was carried on on thousands of little family farms too tiny to use machinery profitably. Industrial and agricultural production per worker was lower in France than in any other major Western nation.

Considering the serious plight of France's postwar economy and the habitual disorderliness with which her multiparty democracy traditionally functioned, one is impressed by the remarkable stability of the French government during the decade of the 1920s. From 1919 to 1924, a bloc of conservative parties was in power. It followed an antilabor, probusiness policy. It also favored the Roman Catholic Church and pressed hard for collection of German reparations. Meanwhile, discontent among the laboring classes was mounting. In 1924, the

year of MacDonald's first Labour ministry in Great Britain, the parties of the Left under the leadership of Edouard Herriot were victorious. Like MacDonald, Herriot pursued a prolabor policy, advocating an increase in social services, and soft money. He was also conciliatory toward Russia and Germany. But, also like MacDonald, he lasted less than a year.

From 1926 to 1929, a strong right of center National bloc under the leadership of Raymond Poincaré was in power. Poincaré checked the inflation by rigid retrenchment. Upon his retirement in 1929, however, the increasing pressure of discontent threw the country into political turmoil. No leader or political combination seemed to be capable of dealing with the economic crisis brought on by the world depression, the growing menace of fascism, or the unrest in the French colonies. Ministry followed ministry in rapid succession. Scandals and riots occurred, and Fascist groups appeared. In 1936 the Popular Front, consisting of left-wing parties under the leadership of the mild Socialist Léon Blum, came to power. The Blum ministry obtained a forty-hour week and two weeks' annual vacations with pay for the workers. It also nationalized the Bank of France and the great munitions industries. This was too much for the powerful propertied interests, who drove Blum from office the following year. But the Rightist parties who regained control were unable to agree upon firm policies, domestic or foreign.

Thus France, like Great Britain, in the face of resurgent Nazi Germany, swashbuckling Mussolini, and militaristic Japan, could summon little strength or unity. The propertied classes were unwilling to share their wealth or privileges or to change their nineteenth-century practices. They feared and hated Léon Blum more than they feared Hitler. The working classes felt that they had little to work or fight for. The army was basking in past glory. Seeking to maintain the status quo, the French were defense-minded. They constructed the Maginot Line fortifications along the German border, and formed defensive alliances with Poland, Czechoslovakia, Yugoslavia, and Rumania. These alliances were no stronger than the faith those small countries had in France's ability to defend them, which by the late 1930s was very little.

Therefore when the League of Nations looked to the three formerly potent democratic powers for support in halting Fascist aggression, it found them weak in body and will.

4. THE BREAKDOWN OF THE LEAGUE OF NATIONS

The only international agency that existed for the maintenance of the peace was the League of Nations, which after the defection of the United States was largely dependent upon Great Britain and France for support. For twelve years the league supervised the implementation of the peace treaties, administered relief to tens of thousands of war victims, promoted international good will, and settled numerous international disputes. None of these settlements, however, involved the disciplining of a major power, and thoughtful observers dreaded the time when the league would be called upon to do so.

The first major power to challenge the league was Japan. It will be recalled (see p. 632) that in 1931 the Japanese militarists began the conquest of Manchuria, partly to create a war fever preparatory to setting up a Fascist dictatorship in Japan and partly as the first step in a vast program of conquest. China, the legal owner of Manchuria and a member of the League of Nations, appealed to the league for protection. The league appointed a commission headed by Britain's Earl of Lytton to make an on-the-spot investigation. The Lytton Commission reported that Japan was guilty of aggression, having violated her solemn obligations both as a league member and as a signatory of the Kellogg-Briand Pact of Paris (1928), which outlawed war as an instrument of national policy. Forceful league action, however, would be largely dependent upon Great Britain and France, who were unwilling to act without American support.

The British and French governments realized the seriousness and significance of this first major challenge to the league and to the peace of the world. Soon after the beginning of Japan's aggression, they sought the support of the United States. Secretary of State Henry L. Stimson, fully aware of the significance of the crisis, wholeheartedly approved of joint measures by the three democracies. However, President Hoover, reflecting the isolationist sentiment of American public opinion, would not consent to the use of force, the threat of force, or even economic pressure by the United States. Stimson could offer the British and the French only words of disapproval of Japan's acts. The British and French governments, harassed by their own domestic economic and political problems and the rising menace of fascism in Europe, could not bring themselves to act alone. The league, without their backing, did nothing. It had failed its first major test and was on the way out as a potent force for peace. Japan's successful defiance of the League of Nations convinced Mussolini and Hitler that they could safely launch aggressions of their own.

The deathblow was struck by Mussolini. Late in 1935 the Italian dictator invaded Ethiopia, a large, undeveloped country in East Africa. This was to be the first step in the restoration of the ancient Roman Empire. Ethiopia was a member of the league and appealed to it for protection. Great Britain, concerned for her numerous interests in the Near and Middle East and for her life line to the Far East, now became greatly agitated. Under the leadership of Great Britain and France, the league declared Mussolini to be the aggressor and invoked economic sanctions (Article XVI) against him. A list of commodities that league members were not to sell Mussolini was drawn up. However, the list did not include oil, and it soon became obvious that this was the commodity upon which the success of his aggression depended. But it quickly became apparent that, to be effective, an embargo on oil would require the cooperation of the United States. American exports of oil to Mussolini had trebled since the beginning of his campaign against Ethiopia. When the British and French governments requested the cooperation of the United States in withholding excess oil from Mussolini, Secretary of State Cordell Hull and President Roosevelt were sympathetic. Roosevelt requested the American oil companies to refrain voluntarily from selling Mussolini oil in excess of the normal peacetime amount. But the oil companies refused to comply. Roosevelt then asked Congress to pass legislation restricting the excess sales. A battle ensued between the President and the oil companies for the support of Congress. The oil companies won. The press and public opinion were overwhelmingly isolationist, and Congress, in denying Roosevelt's request, reflected that view. Mussolini got his oil. Britain and France, unwilling to resort to the only other means of stopping him, a shooting war, gave up the league struggle. Mussolini conquered Ethiopia. The League of Nations, for all practical purposes, was dead.

5. APPEASEMENT OF THE FASCIST AGGRESSORS

The most serious consequence of the demise of the League of Nations was the unleashing of Nazi Germany. Since the triumph of the Nazis in 1933, Germany had been feverishly preparing for a military comeback. In March 1936, Hitler ordered his armed forces into the Rhineland, which, according to the Treaty of Versailles, was to be permanently demilitarized. France, recognizing this move as the gravest threat and challenge to herself, called for Great Britain's support. The British offered none. The French fretted and fumed, but in the end did nothing. Hitler had won his gamble. It was France's last opportunity to save herself; a year or two later, Nazi Germany had become too strong.

Fascism's next triumph was in Spain. Modern liberal and industrial civilization had bypassed Spain. Until 1931, she was dominated by the landed aristocracy, a few rich capitalists, aristocratic army officers, and the Roman Catholic Church. The mass of the people were poverty-stricken, illiterate, and landless peasants. Since the turn of the century and particularly since 1918, the pressure of discontent had been rising. In 1931 the dictatorial king yielded, restored the constitution, and granted elections. The liberal and radical groups won such a sweeping victory that the king fled the country. The reformers then proceeded to make over the Spanish nation. They drew up a democratic constitution, granted local autonomy to Catalonia, began a sweeping program of public education, started

to modernize the army by placing promotions on a merit basis, granted religious freedom, seized the lands and schools of the Roman Catholic Church, and planned to break up the great estates into peasant-owned farms.

There was much violence—riots, and attacks on priests, nuns, and private property. After two years, the conservative propertied interests, with the vigorous support of the pope, won the elections by a narrow margin and began to undo the reforms. Early in 1936, however, the liberal and radical parties won again and resumed their drastic reform program. The privileged classes were now desperate. In July 1936, a group of generals led by General Francisco Franco launched an armed rebellion against the government. Although the Rebels enjoyed the advantage of professional military leadership, the regular army, and most of the country's wealth, they were unable to make headway against the Loyalists, who enjoyed the support of the majority of the rank and file of the people.

The Spanish Civil War soon became a battlefield in the world struggle of fascism, liberalism, and communism. Hitler and Mussolini, seeing in it an opportunity to advance the cause of fascism, gain a like-minded ally and a strategic military position, and test their new weapons, sent abundant arms and troops to aid Franco. The Loyalists appealed to the democracies for aid but received none, although a few volunteers from the democracies fought as individuals in the Loyalist cause. The only nation that supported the Loyalists was the Soviet Union, but the amount of aid she could send was quite small and probably did more harm that good, since it tainted the Loyalist cause with the suspicion of communism. After three years of terrific slaughter, Franco and his German and Italian allies beat down the last organized Loyalist resistance. A typical Fascist dictatorship was established over Spain. Liberalism was shattered. The Communist cause in Spain, on the other hand, was strengthened. At the beginning of the civil war, the Communists constituted only a small minority on the Loyalist side. Not a single member of the Loyalist cabinet was a Communist. However, thanks to limited support from the Soviet Union and to the Communists' skill at underground activity, they fared much better in defeat than did the liberals. The world prestige of Fascist Germany and Italy rose while that of the democracies declined further.

The year 1937 was the year of decision—the point of no return on the road to war. As noted previously, in that year the three great Fascist powers formed the Berlin-Rome-Tokyo Axis, which was aimed specifically at the Soviet Union, but was in reality an alliance of these aggressor nations against the rest of the world. In that year the military strength of the Axis powers—their war plants running day and night—forged ahead of that of the rest of the world. They were now out of hand. In that year the Nazis blueprinted their timetable of conquests, and Japan began her all-out assault on China.

Early in 1938 the Nazis' timetable began to function. In March they overran Austria without opposition, annexing the 6½ million Austrians to the German Reich (Empire). Great Britain and France denounced this open aggression and violation of the Treaty of Versailles but did nothing.

Almost immediately Hitler turned his big propaganda guns on his next victim, Czechoslovakia. In constructing this little country out of Austro-Hungarian territory at the end of World War I, the Allied peacemakers had left 3½ million German-speaking people on the Czech side of the border. Although these Sudeten Germans had never been a part of Germany and were separated from Germany by the Sudeten Mountain wall, Hitler now claimed them. His main consideration in attacking Czechoslovakia was military. The Czech republic was allied with France and Russia, and in the coming war that Hitler was planning against those two countries, she could be a threat to the German flank. The "Bohemian bastion" has long been a vital strategic position in Central Europe. Furthermore, the Czech defenses were patterned after those of the French. Possession of them would give the Germans a blueprint of the Maginot Line.

As early as May 1938, Hitler threatened Czechoslovakia. The Czechs, however, surprised him by rushing to their defenses. Hitler spent the next four months arousing his people to readiness for war and softening up the democracies by keeping them in a constant state of tension and alarm. This psychological warfare culminated in a giant Nazi rally at Nuremberg in mid-September. There Hitler screamed to his frenzied followers that if the Sudeten areas were not surrendered to him by October 1, he would march. With France and the Soviet Union standing firm in their alliance with Czechoslovakia, the world anxiously awaited the beginning of a major conflict that was likely to become World War II.

At this juncture, the British Prime Minister Neville Chamberlain took it upon himself to fly to Hitler's retreat at Berchtesgaden and plead for a compromise. The upshot was a conference at Munich on September 29, 1938. The participants were Hitler, Mussolini, Chamberlain, and Premier Edouard Daladier of France. Chamberlain persuaded Daladier to yield to Hitler's demands for the Sudeten areas of Czechoslovakia. Czechoslovakia and the Soviet Union, France's allies, were not consulted. This was one of Hitler's greatest triumphs. By enticing Great Britain and France to abandon France's allies, Czechoslovakia and the Soviet Union, Hitler had driven a wedge between the Soviet Union and the Western democracies. The Soviet leaders never trusted the Western democracies again. Neither did many of the other countries of the world that were watching to see where their greatest safety lay. The Munich "sellout" represented the lowest ebb to which the cause of liberal democracy had ever sunk.

6. THE RETURN TO WAR

Although the four participating powers at Munich had agreed to become joint protectors of what remained of Czechoslovakia, in March 1939, Hitler overran without warning the remainder of the stricken little republic. This crass act of betrayal opened the eyes even of Neville Chamberlain to the fact that fascism could not be appeased. When, therefore, immediately following the rape of Czechoslovakia Hitler threatened Poland, Great Britain and France decided to draw a line. In April 1939, they made a guarantee to Poland that they would come to her aid if she were attacked and resisted the attack. The fat

The chief participants at the Munich Conference pose for the photographer in September 1938. Left to right: Chamberlain, Daladier, Hitler, Mussolini.
Photo: United Press International

was now in the fire. Hitler, however, was not deterred. He was demanding among other things the return to Germany of the Polish Corridor, which separated East Prussia from the rest of Germany, and the city of Danzig, which was governed by the League of Nations. But by now it was apparent to almost everybody that specific Nazi demands were merely excuses for unlimited aggression. Throughout the summer of 1939 the Germans made feverish preparations for war and kept up a drumfire of vilification of

Poland and the democracies. Meanwhile, both sides were bidding for the support of the Soviet Union. But after Munich, Stalin had no confidence in the integrity of the capitalistic democracies. He decided to try to make his own peace with Hitler.

On August 23, 1939, the world was stunned by the signing of a ten-year peace pact by Hitler and Stalin. In return for the Soviet Union's neutrality while Germany conquered Poland, Hitler gave Stalin a free hand to reannex the territories in Eastern Europe, including eastern Poland, that Russia had lost at the end of World War I.

With the Soviet Union safely neutralized, Hitler readied the attack on Poland as quickly as possible. At the last moment the British government instructed its ambassador in Berlin to ask

Hitler what concessions by Poland he would accept to refrain from war. Hitler informed the ambassador that he was not interested in concessions, that his army and his people were ready and eager for war and that he could not disappoint them now. The wires between Warsaw and Berlin were cut, lest the Poles make a last-minute peaceable surrender to Hitler's demands. At dawn on September 1 the Germans launched an all-out attack on Poland by land, sea, and air. Two days later Great Britain and France declared war on Germany, Hitler having ignored their ultimatum to desist. World War II had begun.

Suggested Reading

Isolationism, Boom, Bust in the United States

*F. Allen, *Only Yesterday* (Bantam). Vivid, witty picture of the roaring twenties.

*J. K. Galbraith, *The Great Crash, Nineteen Twenty-nine* (Sentry). By a distinguished economist and lively writer.

*R. Sherwood, *Roosevelt and Hopkins*, 2 vols. (Bantam). Well written. Volume I deals with the Great Depression years and Volume II with the World War II years.

The Harassed British Empire

*D. Thomson, *England in the Twentieth Century, 1914–1963* (Pelican). A good survey.

*R. Graves and A. Hodge, *The Long Weekend: A Social History of Great Britain, 1918–1939* (Norton). A vivid and witty picture of the British ruling classes between the wars.

Frustrated France

*H. Luethy, *France Against Herself* (Meridian). An astute analysis of the paralysis of France in the face of the Nazi menace.

J. Colton, *Léon Blum, Humanist in Politics* (1966). The best biography of Blum.

Appeasement of Fascist Aggression and the Return to War

D. Lee, *Ten Years: The World on Its Way to War, 1930–1940* (1942). A scholarly survey.

*A. Rowse, *Appeasement* (Norton). By a bitter eyewitness of British appeasement efforts.

*H. Thomas, *The Spanish Civil War* (Colophon). Scholarly and objective.

*W. Churchill, *The Gathering Storm* (Bantam). First of Churchill's magnificent six-volume account of World War II. Highly readable.

58

WORLD WAR II, 1939-1945

To much of the disillusioned and paralyzed democratic world, the outbreak of World War II seemed the beginning of the end of liberal Western civilization. What instruments of destruction science and technology had developed since World War I, nobody knew. The Nazis boasted that the German air force was capable of destroying all the cities of the non-Fascist world. For two years these dire fears and threats appeared to be justified. The seemingly invincible German and Japanese military machines swept on to victory after victory.

1. TWO YEARS OF AXIS TRIUMPH

The mechanized might of Nazi Germany overwhelmed Poland in a matter of days. Striking without official warning at dawn, September 1, 1939, the German air force caught the Polish air force on its various airfields and destroyed it on the ground. Thereafter the German *Luftwaffe*, by ravaging Polish cities and communications centers and harassing troop movements, prevented the complete mobilization of the Polish army. Meanwhile, Nazi tanks and infantry poured into Poland from the north, west, and south. Within two weeks' time, Warsaw was surrounded and being pounded to rubble by German artillery. At this juncture, the forces of the Soviet Union, in accordance with the August 23 pact with Hitler, moved into eastern Poland and occupied the Russian-speaking areas seized from her after World War I (see pp. 641–642).

From the beginning of the invasion, the Poles, fighting courageously but hopelessly, cried for help from France and Great Britain. The French and the British mobilized their armies along the German West Wall fortifications, and the British fleet blockaded Germany by sea. But that was all. At that time no fighter planes had the range to fly from French or British bases to Poland and back, and the French and British understandably did not wish to provoke the lightning by bombing German cities. Western military leaders, basing their views on the experiences of World War I, believed it to be suicidal to attack elaborate fortifications. They thought that sooner or later Hitler would be forced to attack the French Maginot Line and would then be destroyed. This thinking was little consolation to the Poles. Warsaw surrendered on September 27, less than a month after the fighting began.

The Soviet Union, in accordance with her agreement with Hitler, proceeded to reannex the remaining territories in Eastern Europe that she had lost at the end of World War I. Shortly after Poland surrendered, the Soviet Union demanded military bases in Estonia, Latvia, and Lithuania. The three little Baltic republics appealed to Hitler, but were told to comply. The following spring they were absorbed politically into the Soviet Union. In October 1939, the Soviet Union demanded three strategic little strips of Finnish territory: the Karelian Isthmus, which put the Finnish border within artillery range of the great city of Leningrad; a strip of territory near the

Russian Arctic port of Murmansk; and the naval base of Hangö, which guarded the sea approaches to Leningrad. The Soviets wanted a thirty-year lease on Hangö; the other territories were to be ceded outright. When the Finnish government refused, the Soviet Union attacked Finland and took these territories by force. In June 1940, while Hitler was busy in Western Europe, the Soviet Union demanded and procured from Rumania the return of Bessarabia. With Bessarabia she also took the little province of northern Bukovina, which she had never previously owned.

Early in April 1940, the Germans suddenly overran Denmark and Norway. The British fleet, attempting to intercept the invasion of Norway, was beaten off with heavy losses by the German air force. Denmark and Norway provided the Nazis with important food, timber, and mineral resources, sea and air bases, and a safe route for vital iron ore coming from Sweden.

On May 10, 1940, the German armies assaulted Luxembourg, the Netherlands, Belgium, and France. Luxembourg offered no resistance. The Netherlands fought heroically, but was overwhelmed in six days. Belgium lasted nineteen days, but when she fell, the French and British armies in Belgium fell with her. Trusting to the Maginot Line to hold along the German border, the British army and a large part of the French army moved into Belgium to support the hardpressed Belgian forces. In a surprise move through the Ardennes forest, powerful German mechanized forces on May 14 smashed through the French defenses at Sedan and drove quickly to the English Channel, cutting off the Belgian, British, and French armies in Belgium. Although some 300,000 British and a few French troops escaped by sea from Dunkirk, all the Belgian troops, the bulk of the French troops together with their weapons and supplies, and the British weapons and supplies were captured.

Only five more days of fighting, June 5–10, were required for the Germans to crush the remaining organized French resistance and turn the French retreat into a disorderly rout. On June 10 Paris was declared an open city. And on that day Mussolini, thinking it safe, declared war on France and Great Britain. On June 16 Marshal

Philippe Pétain became premier of France and the following day dispatched a surrender team to Hitler. On June 25 the "fighting" ceased. The collapse of the French military machine after five days of fighting was the most colossal military debacle in history. It was the one military machine in the world thought to be able to stand up to the Nazis. Hitler forced upon the helpless French a harsh treaty. The northern half of France and all the Atlantic coastal area were placed under German occupation. The unoccupied portion was compelled to disarm and cooperate with Germany. Some 2 million French prisoners were held as hostages to ensure French good behavior. In unoccupied France, Marshal Pétain and Pierre Laval set up a semi-Fascist regime, with headquarters at Vichy, and undertook to cooperate with Hitler.

All Frenchmen did not accept defeat. Many resisted the German army of occupation courageously throughout the war, suffering heavy casualties in so doing. General Charles de Gaulle, having unsuccessfully attempted to warn his superiors of the unreadiness of the French army, escaped to Great Britain and declared himself leader of the Free French. With energy and skill he strove to rally Frenchmen both inside and outside the homeland to resist the Germans and the Vichy collaborators and to restore the dignity and honor of France.

The collapse of France left Great Britain to face the Axis fury alone (except for the Chinese Nationalist forces still holding out against the Japanese in the Chinese interior). Hitler now demanded that she surrender or suffer annihilation. Her situation was desperate. Nearly all her land armaments had been lost at Dunkirk. Against the nearly one hundred and fifty battletried Nazi divisions, she had only one fully equipped division. And although Great Britain did have the English Channel and the world's greatest navy, the fighting around Norway had demonstrated that navies could no longer control narrow waters dominated by a hostile air force. Britain's chief weapon of defense was her relatively small but efficient air force. Not the least of her assets was Winston Churchill, who on May 10, 1940, had at last replaced Neville Chamberlain as prime minister. The dynamic

A view of London in 1941 from the top of St. Paul's Cathedral. During the first three years of World War II, the superior German air force bombed scores of cities in enemy countries, leaving wreckage such as this in its wake. *Photo: United Press International*

and eloquent Churchill defied Hitler. "We shall fight on the beaches; we shall fight on the landing grounds; we shall fight in the fields and in the streets; we shall fight in the hills; we shall never surrender."

Throughout the month of July 1940, Nazi invasion forces gathered along the French coast opposite Britain, 24 miles away. To make the crossing, however, absolute control of the air over the Channel was required. Early in August, there-fore, swarms of German bombers and fighter escorts flew over the Channel, seeking to destroy the British air force and its landing fields. In the ensuing air battles, the British pilots in their swift Spitfires and heavily armed and maneuverable Hurricanes knocked down German planes at the ratio of 2 to 1. Nevertheless, by the end of August the British air forces were facing annihilation by sheer weight of numbers. At this critical juncture, the Nazis suddenly shifted to massive daylight attacks on London, the world's largest city. The destruction and the suffering were immense, but the toll of German planes taken by the British fighters was so great that early in October the Nazis began less effective night attacks. Although the destructive air raids on Great Britain's cities, together with the even more menacing submarine attacks on British shipping, continued until the end of the war, the immediate threat of invasion had now passed (a winter crossing of the Channel would be too risky); the Battle of Britain had been won.

While the Battle of Britain was at its height, Mussolini set in operation his grandiose schemes for conquering an empire. Upon entering the war in June 1940, he had closed the Mediterranean to British shipping. In September his armies moved on Egypt and the Suez Canal from Libya to the west and from Ethiopia to the south. In October his armies attacked Greece from Albania. To meet this threat, Churchill made one of the most daring and farsighted military moves in history. Believing Suez to be the most strategic spot in the world in a global war, he sent half Britain's scarce supply of tanks and artillery around Africa to Egypt while the Nazis stood poised across the Channel for the invasion of Great Britain. Mussolini's forces met disaster everywhere. The Greeks defeated them and drove them back into Albania. A squadron of British torpedo planes delivered a lethal blow to the Italian fleet at its base in southern Italy. During the winter of 1940–1941, the Fascist armies moving on Egypt were completely destroyed by light, mobile British forces. Mussolini's bubble had burst with a feeble plop; henceforth he was hardly more than a prisoner of the German forces that were sent to save him.

When in October 1940 it became evident that Great Britain could not be invaded that year, Hitler ordered his planners to complete blueprints for the earliest possible invasion of the Soviet Union. The conquest of the Soviet Union had always been uppermost in Hitler's thoughts, but he had hoped first to dispose of the French and British threat to his rear. The plans called for an assault date not later than May 15, 1941. But first the Balkan flank was to be secured. Hungary and Rumania joined the Axis Alliance in November 1940, Bulgaria, in March 1941. Immediately, Nazi forces poured into those countries. Yugoslavia and Greece, however, refused to yield, and the Germans attacked them in April 1941. Yugoslavia was overrun in eleven days, Greece in three weeks. British

forces that Churchill had dispatched to Greece were driven out of the peninsula and also off the island of Crete. Suez now appeared to be doomed. It was open to attack from the north; to the west Germany's Afrika Korps, which had been sent to replace the defeated Italians, had driven the British back to the border of Egypt; pro-Nazi movements had broken out in Iraq, Iran, and French Syria. At this point, however, Hitler hurled his main forces against the Soviet Union, giving the British a breathing spell to recoup their strength in the Near and Middle East.

On June 22, 1941, the Germans launched against the Soviet Union the most massive assault in history. They were joined by the Hungarians, the Rumanians, and the Finns. There were one hundred sixty divisions in all (eventually the figure rose to two hundred fifty). And although Stalin was able to throw an equal number of divisions against the invaders, his troops were not so well trained or equipped. Hitler expected to crush Soviet resistance in six weeks; the top British and American military leaders were of the same opinion. The Russians fought with unexpected skill and determination, but the Nazi war machine crunched ever forward until by December 1, it was within sight of Moscow. Leningrad was surrounded, and Rostov, the gateway to the Caucasus oil fields, was captured. The richest and most productive part of the Soviet Union was in German hands. The Russians had suffered such staggering casualties that Hitler announced that the Soviet Union was destroyed and would never rise again. The Japanese, taking him at his word and thinking the golden hour had struck, attacked the United States on December 7, 1941. By that time, however, the Arctic winter and the Soviet counterattacks had forced the Germans to halt and in some places to retreat. The Soviet Union was still alive, and the United States was now in the war.

2. THE ENTRY OF THE UNITED STATES INTO THE WAR

The entry of the United States into the war—the one thing that might conceivably have turned the tide—was not a sudden but a gradual involvement. We have already observed the refusal of the American people to cooperate with the League of Nations in checking Japan in 1931 and Italy in 1935. To make assurance doubly sure, an isolationist Congress in 1935, 1936, and 1937 had passed a series of neutrality laws limiting the powers of the President to carry out his constitutional functions of conducting the nation's foreign relations. At the same time, Congress steadfastly refused to increase the military budget in the face of the rising Fascist menace. During the Munich and Polish crises, President Roosevelt pleaded with Hitler and Mussolini not to plunge the world into war, but the dictators scorned his pleas, realizing that his hands were tied. The outbreak of the war in Europe caused hardly a ripple in the isolationist sentiment of the American public and of Congress. The French army and Maginot Line and the British navy were believed by most of the isolationists to be capable of containing the Nazis.

But suddenly in May–June 1940, the picture drastically changed. The French army and Maginot Line ceased to exist, and the British navy was in grave danger. Much of it would be used up in the defense of Britain in case of invasion. The American people, now seized with consternation, cried for vigorous action. Roosevelt promptly came forward with a three-point program: (1) all-out rearmament, (2) bipartisanship in foreign affairs, (3) all aid to those fighting the Axis (which at the moment meant Great Britain) short of war. There was no opposition to the first proposal, and Congress quickly voted a generous military appropriation. Although there were a few partisan murmurings, Roosevelt activated the second proposal by appointing two prominent internationalist Republicans, Henry L. Stimson and Frank Knox, as secretary of war and secretary of the navy, respectively. Over the aid-to-Britain proposal, however, powerful opposition arose, led largely by stalwart Republican isolationists such as Senator Robert Taft, Colonel R. R. McCormick (publisher of the Chicago *Tribune*), and Charles A. Lindbergh, although a few Democratic isolationists also participated.

The victory of Wendell Willkie, an internationalist Republican, over Robert Taft for the Republican Presidential nomination in July 1940

made it easier for Roosevelt to implement his aid-to-Britain proposal. He immediately dispatched a quantity of World War I arms and ammunition to Britain, and in September 1940, he exchanged fifty World War I destroyers for eight British air and naval bases in the Western Hemisphere. These weapons played an important role in the Battle of Britain. But by the end of the year, Churchill informed Roosevelt that Britain was nearing exhaustion. Thereupon Roosevelt proposed, and in March 1941 Congress passed, the Lend Lease Act, which authorized the President to sell, lend, lease, or give any commodity to any nation whose defense he deemed necessary for the safety of the United States. Congress also voted funds to finance the measure.

The British navy, stretched thin over the world's sea lanes, however, was unable to guard Britain's Lend Lease ships from German submarines. It soon became apparent that if Lend Lease was to achieve its purpose, the ships carrying the goods would have to be convoyed by the American navy. The sinking of an American ship in the South Atlantic by a German submarine led the American government in June and July 1941 to close all Axis consulates and freeze all Axis assets in the United States and begin convoying Lend Lease goods as far as Iceland. Meanwhile, Lend Lease was extended to the Soviet Union when that country was attacked by Germany. In October 1941, two American destroyers on the Iceland convoy run were torpedoed by German submarines with a loss of 126 American lives. Roosevelt stated that "the shooting war has started. And history has recorded who fired the first shot."

In August 1941, Roosevelt and Churchill had met at sea and drawn up the Atlantic Charter, a joint statement of ideals and war purposes. In it appeared such pregnant phrases as: ". . .their countries seek no aggrandizement, territorial or other; . . . they respect the right of all peoples to choose the form of government under which they will live; . . . after the final destruction of the Nazi tyranny, . . . the establishment of a wider and permanent system of general security. . . ." The Soviet Union subscribed to the Atlantic Charter shortly afterward. Thus, by October 1941, the United States was engaged in a shooting—but not yet official—war with Germany and was in a virtual alliance with Great Britain, one of the belligerents. The American people's eyes were on the Atlantic, where at any moment some new German act of aggression might make war official and total.

It was not in the Atlantic, however, but in the Pacific that the history-changing blow was struck; and not by Germany, but by Japan. Early in 1939 the Japanese, having conquered all the populous coastal areas of China and having driven Chiang Kai-shek's forces far into the Chinese interior, turned southward toward the territories of Southeast Asia and the Southwest Pacific. These territories, rich in rubber, tin, rice, copra, and oil, belonged (with the exception of independent Thailand) to France, the Netherlands, Great Britain, and the United States. Since the French, Dutch, and British had their hands full in Europe with the growing Nazi menace, President Roosevelt transferred the American fleet from the Atlantic to Pearl Harbor in Hawaii as a deterrent to further Japanese aggression. He also gave the Japanese the required six months' notice of the termination of the commercial treaty of 1911. These moves appear to have given the Japanese pause.

In 1940, however, after Hitler's conquest of France and the Netherlands and threatened conquest of Great Britain, the Japanese became much bolder. They took advantage of France's helplessness to occupy northern French Indo-China and threatened the Dutch East Indies. The Roosevelt administration, seeking to restrain the Axis with all pressure short of war, now embargoed the shipment of all commodities to Japan except petroleum, and made a loan of $75 million to Chiang Kai-shek. Oil was left out of the embargo for fear the Japanese would immediately strike the oil-rich Dutch East Indies. Again the Japanese halted. But in the following year, 1941, when the Germans overran the Balkans and launched what promised to be a lethal attack on the Soviet Union, the Japanese leaders decided that the day of Axis world triumph was at hand. In July 1941, therefore, they greatly stepped up their war preparations, poured troops into southern Indo-China for an obvious assault on

the Dutch and British East Indies, and launched an all-out propaganda campaign against the United States in the army-controlled press.

The Roosevelt administration, deciding that further conciliation was hopeless, froze all Japanese assets in the United States, which had the effect of embargoing oil. On November 25 the Japanese fleet was ordered to sail for its attack position. The next day the United States, having intercepted and decoded the order, made a final conciliatory offer, which the Japanese government spurned. Roosevelt, realizing that an attack was in motion but not knowing where, sent Emperor Hirohito a last personal plea, which was intercepted and withheld by Japanese army officials. Early Sunday morning on December 7, 1941, a large squadron of Japanese bombers and torpedo planes took off from carriers in a position north of Hawaii and caught by surprise the American fleet anchored in Pearl Harbor. With little loss to themselves, the Japanese planes crippled the American navy in the Pacific, and destroyed the air force in Hawaii on the ground. Later in the day Japan declared the existence of a state of war with the United States. The next day, December 8, the United States Congress declared war on Japan. Three days later, December 11, Germany and Italy, making good their promise to Japan, declared war on the United States. The same day, December 11, the United States replied in kind.

3. CLIMAX AND TURNING POINT OF THE WAR, JUNE–AUGUST 1942

The entry of the United States with her enormous resources and industrial potential, changed the whole complexion of the war. It made possible the turning of the tide. However, many months would be required to mobilize America's resources, and the Axis was determined to win decisively before that mobilization could be achieved. To bring about Allied solidarity, Churchill hastened to Washington, where on January 1, 1942, he and Roosevelt launched the United Nations Alliance. Twenty-six nations, of which the United States, Great Britain, and the Soviet Union were the Big Three, promised to give their all to the common

Early in the hours of Sunday, December 7, 1941, the Japanese attacked Pearl Harbor, Hawaii, and destroyed the Pacific fleet in the harbor and the air force on the ground. This photo shows the U.S.S. California as she went down following the attack. Note the men swarming over the side. *Photo: United Press International*

effort, to make no separate peace, and to abide by the principles of the Atlantic Charter. By the end of the war, the number of member nations had risen to forty-seven.

The now-global war was fought in three major theaters: (1) Russia, (2) the Mediterranean and Western Europe, and (3) the Pacific. The Axis powers made their climactic bid for victory on all three fronts between June and August 1942. The biggest front in terms of numbers of men, weapons, and casualties involved was that in Russia. The Germans, after having been stopped in December 1941 by the Russian winter and the counterattacks, resumed their forward thrust in June 1942, this time in the southern sector. Refreshed and reequipped, they seemed irresistible. By August they had reached the outskirts of Stalingrad on the Volga. Here Stalin ordered a stand: The battle of Stalingrad raged for six months. In February 1943, the Russians, having closed a pincer behind the Germans in Stalingrad, captured all who had not been killed of an army of almost 300,000 men. This was the turning point; the Germans began a slow but general retreat.

The critical battle on the Mediterranean and Western European front was fought in Egypt. General Rommel's tough Afrika Korps in its first drive on Suez in 1941 had been stopped and pushed back into Libya by the British. In June 1942, Rommel, greatly strengthened, struck the British desert forces a shattering blow and chased them in near rout to El Alamein, only 65 miles from Alexandria. Suez seemed doomed, and the British fleet prepared to evacuate the Mediterranean before it could be bottled up. Churchill rushed to the scene and put in a team of winning commanders: Sir Harold Alexander in overall command and Sir Bernard Montgomery as field commander. In August, Rommel assaulted the British positions at El Alamein and was stopped. A race to build up men and supplies ensued; the British, with massive aid from the United States, won. Late in October 1942, Montgomery's superior Eighth Army attacked Rommel's forces, and after a desperate battle drove them back across the desert in defeat. Suez and the Middle East were now saved from the Axis, and for the first time Great Britain and the United States were in a position to assume the offensive.

The war in the Pacific was predominantly naval in character. Three days after Pearl Harbor, Japanese carrier-based torpedo planes struck the British Asiatic fleet a crippling blow in the Gulf of Siam. Now, with unchallenged mastery of the Pacific, the Japanese within the space of a few months were able to conquer with relative ease a vast area in the Southwest Pacific and Southeast Asia. The American islands of Wake, Guam, and the Philippines; British Hong Kong, Malaya, Singapore, and Burma; and the Dutch East Indies were overrun. In May 1942 a strong Japanese fleet was turned back by the American fleet in the Battle of the Coral Sea, northeast of Australia. However, the main Japanese fleet was

EUROPE 1942

Hitler's "Empire"

Allied With Germany

Occupied by the Axis

At War Against the Axis

Relations between the Axis and Vichy France were governed by the Armistice of June 1940, but Germany occupied the whole of France in November 1942.

0   100   200   300 miles

This photograph of the Axis leaders was taken in July 1944. The tide of war had turned against them; within the year, both Hitler and Mussolini would be dead, their countries ruined and defeated. Left to right (foreground): Mussolini, Martin Bormann, Admiral Doenitz, Hitler, Field Marshal Goering.
Photo: United Press International

preparing a major thrust at Hawaii, which could have been taken easily immediately after Pearl Harbor. The United States navy, which was in possession of the Japanese code, massed for an all-out battle. Early in June 1942, just as the Stalingrad and El Alamein campaigns were beginning, the two fleets came within carrier-plane range of each other off Midway Island, a thousand miles west of Hawaii. The climactic Battle of Midway was fought at long range entirely by aircraft and submarines. American planes sank all four of the Japanese carriers, while the Japanese were able to destroy only one of three American carriers. Pounded from the air and without air cover, the Japanese commander ordered a retreat, never to become so bold again. In August 1942, the Americans assumed the offensive by attacking Guadalcanal in the Solomon Islands northeast of Australia. By that time, it was evident that the tide was beginning to turn on all three fronts.

4. VICTORY ON THE RUSSIAN FRONT

Although the greatest crises had passed by the end of 1942, two and a half more years of bloody fighting were required to subdue the Axis. In fact, the defeat of the Axis could not have been achieved at all without a high degree of cooperation among the Big Three allies. President Roosevelt, with his winsome personality, played an important part in maintaining mutual confidence and cooperation among the Allied powers, which were so divergent in their ideologies and specific interests. The chief planners of the coordinated global strategy were Churchill for Great Britain, Stalin for the Soviet Union, and Army Chief of Staff George Catlett Marshall for the United States.

The Battle of Russia was the greatest and most destructive battle in history. Some 9 million men (five hundred divisions) were engaged. For two and a half years after Stalingrad, the Germans were slowly beaten back, doggedly contesting every foot of ground. At last, in April of 1945, the Russians entered Berlin. Along the 1,500 miles between Stalingrad and Berlin lay the wreckage of the greater part of Hitler's war machine, the most powerful engine of destruction the world had ever seen. But the richest and most productive part of the Soviet Union lay devastated. At least 15 million Russians had been killed—possibly many more.

5. VICTORY ON THE MEDITERRANEAN AND WESTERN EUROPEAN FRONT

In November 1942, just as the Germans were beginning to retreat from El Alamein, a combined Anglo-American force under the command of General Dwight D. Eisenhower landed in French North Africa. Early in 1943, the converging forces of Eisenhower and Montgomery cornered the Afrika Korps in Tunisia, where it surrendered in May. In July 1943 the Anglo-Americans conquered the island of Sicily, which they used as a base for the invasion of southern Italy. Mussolini was forced to resign (July 25), and Italy surrendered. However, the peninsula was held by strong German forces. By the end of 1943, the Allies had reached Cassino Pass, about 75 miles south of Rome. At this point, the major objectives in the Mediterranean area had been achieved, and Eisenhower, along with most of his forces, was transferred to Great Britain to command the main Anglo-American thrust across the Channel.

This thrust came on June 6, 1944. Thanks in large measure to complete Allied mastery of the skies, successful landings were made on the Normandy coast. After a rapid buildup, the Anglo-Americans broke out of the beachhead, and before the end of the year cleared practically all of France. Germany, meanwhile, was being pulverized from the air. Early in 1945 the American and British forces, now joined by French units, broke through the German West Wall, crossed the Rhine, and joined hands with the Russians on the Elbe. Germany surrendered on May 8, ending the war in Europe. Near the end, Hitler and several other top Nazis committed suicide, and Mussolini was shot by Italian partisans.

6. VICTORY ON THE PACIFIC FRONT

Early in 1943 American forces under the command of General Douglas MacArthur began with a strong naval escort an island-hopping campaign northwestward from their base in Australia. At the same time, the main American fleet under the command of Admiral Chester Nimitz, now definitely superior to the Japanese fleet, thrust westward from Hawaii toward Japan, capturing the numerous Japanese-held islands in its path. Although the islands, many of them covered by jungles, were bloodily defended, the American forces moved steadily toward Japan itself. In October 1944, the American forces made a bold landing on Leyte Island in the Philippines which brought the Japanese fleet out for a last desperate effort. In history's greatest naval battle, the Battle of Leyte Gulf, the Japanese fleet was annihilated. Cut off, uncovered, and subjected to ceaseless air and sea attacks, Japan was doomed. After Germany surrendered in May 1945, American, British, and Russian troops that had been engaged in the European theater were deployed rapidly to the Far East. In mid-July the atomic bomb, which American and British scientists had been developing for several years, was successfully completed and tested. In order to avoid the heavy and useless casualties that a direct assault on the Japanese home islands would cause, the United States decided to use the bomb to shock Japan into surrender. On August 6, 1945, the first atomic bomb to be used in warfare destroyed the Japanese city of Hiroshima. Two days later, the Soviet Union declared war on Japan and began to overrun Manchuria and northern Korea. The next day,

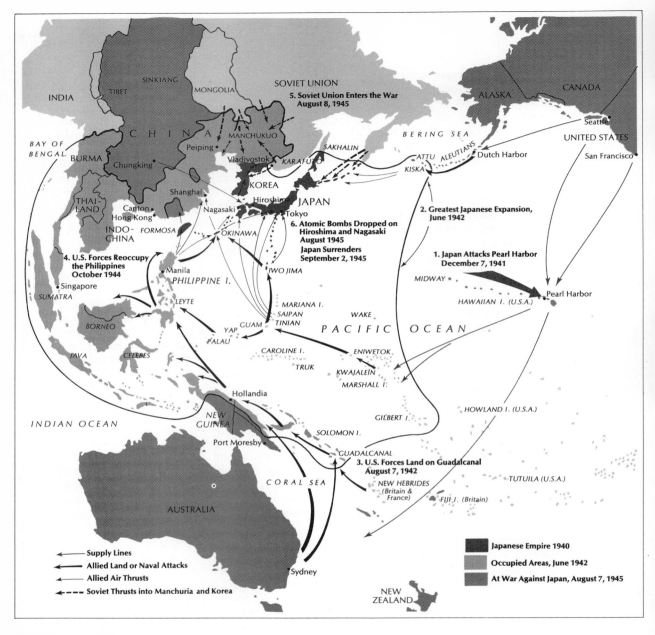

THE PACIFIC WAR

August 9, the second and last atomic bomb then in existence demolished the industrial city of Nagasaki. The Japanese surrendered five days later, August 14, 1945.

World War II had ended. At least 22 million people had been killed, and 34 million had been wounded. Property and moral losses were beyond calculation. Among the casualties was President Roosevelt, who died on April 12, 1945, only a few months before he could have seen the defeat of the Axis, which he had done so much to bring about.

Suggested Reading

General
*B. Liddell Hart, *History of the Second World War*, 2 vols. (Putnam). Best single volume (in original hardback) on the war. Strictly military.

*G. Wright, *The Ordeal of Total War, 1939–1945* (Torch). Thoughtful analysis. Goes far beyond the military aspects.

E. von Manstein, *Lost Victories* (1958). The war from the German point of view, by one of Hitler's ablest generals.

Two Years of Axis Triumph
*M. Bloch, *Strange Defeat: A Statement of Evidence Written in 1940* (Norton). By one of France's most distinguished historians who was executed by the Germans.

*W. Churchill, *Their Finest Hour* (Bantam). The second and the best of Churchill's great six-volume history of the war. Covers the defeat of France and the Battle of Britain.

A. Clark, *Barbarossa* (1964). Good history of the war on the Russian front.

The Entry of the United States
R. Devine, *Reluctant Belligerent: American Entry into World War II* (1969). Good brief survey.

*H. Feis, *The Road to Pearl Harbor: The Coming of the War Between the United States and Japan* (Atheneum). A scholarly work that should dispel much of the nonsense that is written and said about this subject.

Allied Victory
The War Reports of General of the Army George C. Marshall, General of the Army H. H. Arnold, Fleet Admiral Ernest J. King (1947). Official accounts of the chiefs of staff of the U.S. Army, Air Force, and Navy. Marshall's second report is particularly lucid.

*D. D. Eisenhower, *Crusade in Europe* (Dolphin). Popularly written account of the Anglo-American operations in Europe by the commanding general.

*C. Ryan, *The Longest Day* (Crest). Vivid account of the Anglo-American landings in Normandy, June 1944, written in a journalistic style.

59

THE COLD WAR IN EUROPE

In 1945 the leaders of the victorious nations were once again confronted with the task of restoring a shattered world and making a lasting peace. The existence of atomic weapons now made the question of peace a matter of utmost necessity. To act as a watchdog over the peace, the world's leaders, as in 1919, set up an international organization: this time, the United Nations. From the beginning, the work of the UN was seriously hampered by hostility between the United States and the Soviet Union. This hostility, which came to be called the "cold war," pervaded and poisoned every area of postwar international relations.

1. THE UNITED NATIONS

The chief moving force behind the founding of the United Nations was Franklin Roosevelt. Determined to avoid two major mistakes that Wilson had made in creating the League of Nations, Roosevelt (1) saw to it that the UN was born before the war ended and the postwar squabbling among the Allies began, and (2) gave leading roles in the creation of the UN to several important Republicans, so that it would not become a political issue in the United States. The formal launching of the organization took place at a conference in San Francisco in April 1945, a few days after Roosevelt died and less than a month before Germany surrendered.

In structure and procedure, the UN bears a close resemblance to the League of Nations. The General Assembly, in which each member state has one vote, serves as a general clearinghouse and supervisor over the work of all other UN bodies and agencies. Any matter that endangers world peace may be brought to its attention at any time. The UN body that was given special guardianship over the peace is the Security Council. It is composed of five permanent and ten nonpermanent members. The five permanent members are the United States, the Soviet Union, Great Britain, France, and China. The nonpermanent members are elected by the General Assembly for two-year terms.

The fundamental character of the Security Council and, indeed, of the whole UN is really determined by the voting procedure in the Security Council. Any action involving the use of force or the threat of force requires nine votes, including those of all five permanent members. This means that each of the permanent members of the Security Council has a perpetual veto over forceful actions of the UN and cannot be acted against by that body. This crippling veto was incorporated into the charter because the Big Three sponsoring powers—the United States, the Soviet Union, and Great Britain—all were unwilling to submit to the UN's authority. The Soviet Union, finding herself in a constant minority, used the veto to block action to which

The United States representative, Arthur Vandenberg, signs the United Nations Charter in San Francisco in 1945 in the presence of President Truman and other members of the United States government. *Photo: United Press International*

she was opposed more than a hundred times during the first twenty years of the UN's existence.

The Social and Economic Council supervises the work of a number of specialized agencies such as the International Labor Organization (ILO), the United Nations Educational, Scientific, and Cultural Organization (UNESCO), the World Bank, and the International Monetary Fund. The Trusteeship Council is designed to supervise the rule of peoples held under control or trusteeship by other nations, and to promote their independence. The International Court of Justice decides international legal disputes. The day-to-day detailed work of the UN is done by the Secretariat, composed of several thousand full-time professional employees presided over by the Secretary-General, who is appointed by the Security Council and the General Assembly. This important post has been held by Trygve Lie of Norway, by Dag Hammarskjöld of Sweden, by U Thant of Burma and by Curt Waldheim of Austria—all able men. As a permanent headquarters, the UN chose a site in New York City donated by John D. Rockefeller, Jr.

The United Nations has done an enormous amount of work in economic, cultural, and humanitarian fields, most of which has failed to make the headlines. It has assisted in arranging cease-fires in four conflicts between Israel and the Arab states (1949, 1956, 1967, and 1974) and has stopped wars between India and Pakistan, and the Netherlands and Indonesia. It played an important role in checking Communist military aggression in Korea, 1950–1953 (see pp. 678–679). Its biggest failure to date has been its inability to check the free-wheeling policies and actions of the two superpowers—the Soviet Union and the United States, which have threatened to undo the achievements of the UN and engulf the world in atomic war.

2. THE YALTA AGREEMENTS

Soviet-American postwar disagreements first began over the Yalta Agreements. Indeed, the disagreements began even before the fighting in Europe had ended. In February 1945, Roosevelt, Churchill, and Stalin, with their top military and civilian advisers, came together at Yalta in southern Russia for the purpose of coordinating the last Allied blows against the Axis and laying the groundwork for postwar cooperation. The conference marked the culmination of wartime good will and cooperation among the Big Three powers. At the time of the conference, victory was in sight, barring unforeseen disasters; but victory was not so near or so certain that it could be guaranteed without the continued cooperation of the Big Three.

The questions of military strategy were harmoniously worked out by the three military staffs present. The four chief areas of discussion among Roosevelt, Churchill, and Stalin were (1) the UN Charter, (2) Germany, (3) Eastern Europe, and (4) the Far East. Agreements were quickly reached on questions concerning the UN charter, the veto being the chief one. The three conferees also found themselves in close agreement concerning Germany. They agreed on stern measures, including complete de-Nazification with severe punishment for the top Nazis, total demilitarization, the division of the country into four occupation zones, and a long period of occupation by the Allies. Further details were left to a later conference following Germany's surrender.

A sharp cleavage developed over the areas of Eastern Europe that had just been liberated from German control by the Soviet armies. Stalin announced that the territories he had recovered in 1939–1940 (eastern Poland, Lithuania, Latvia, Estonia, strips of Finland, and Bessarabia) were really Russian territories that had been taken from her by force at the end of World War I and that under no condition would they be the subject of discussion. Roosevelt and Churchill did not formally concede these points, but they did not make an issue of them. They were primarily concerned over the fate of western Poland, Hungary, Yugoslavia, Bulgaria, and Rumania—all of which were behind the Soviet lines. (For some reason, the Soviets never overran and occupied Finland, which was a defeated enemy country.)

Roosevelt and Churchill insisted that in accordance with the principles of the Atlantic Charter, to which the Soviet Union had subscribed, these countries must be given complete independence. Stalin argued that these countries had been the doors through which Russia had been invaded in both world wars and that they were vital to the Soviet Union's security. He pointed out that Rumania, Hungary, and Finland had attacked Russia as Hitler's allies, that Bulgaria had cooperated with Hitler as his ally, and that the Soviets' military lines to Germany and Austria ran through Poland, Rumania, and Hungary. Therefore, he asserted, the Soviet Union's security demanded that she maintain a measure of control over these countries. Roosevelt and Churchill were adamant and somehow persuaded Stalin to yield to their position. The official protocol signed at Yalta by Roosevelt, Churchill, and Stalin called for free elections as soon as possible for these liberated peoples of Eastern Europe, with all non-Fascist parties participating. Such elections were almost certain to result in democratic, anti-Communist, and anti-Russian victories.

In regard to the Far East, Roosevelt was guided by the advice of the top American military authorities. It was their purpose to bring the Soviet Union into the Japanese war as soon as possible, thereby saving, it was believed, a million and possibly two million American and British casualties (the atomic bomb was not yet in existence). As payment for the Soviet Union's entry into the Japanese war not later than three months after Germany's surrender, Roosevelt offered Stalin the return of the railroad and port facilities in Manchuria that Japan had taken from Russia in 1905. Also, the Soviet Union was to regain from the Japanese a number of islands north of Japan. Korea was to be given her independence. The United States was to conquer the Japanese in Korea south of the thirty-eighth parallel, and the Soviets were to liberate the portion of Korea lying north of the thirty-eighth parallel. Stalin agreed to these terms, and the Yalta Conference ended with warm cordiality. Within two

At the Yalta Conference, February 1945, Churchill, Roosevelt, and Stalin, representing the Big Three Allied Powers, made a series of agreements concerning the major postwar problems. At the time of the conference, victory over the Axis was in sight. *Photo: United Press International*

weeks after the conference adjourned, however, disputes arose over the agreements, and the United States and the Soviet Union have been in conflict over them ever since.

3. THE SOVIET-AMERICAN CONTROVERSY OVER EASTERN EUROPE

It was over Eastern Europe that Soviet-American accord first broke down. On February 24, 1945, exactly thirteen days after the Yalta Conference

adjourned, the American and British representatives on the Allied Council in Bucharest began to press for the democratization of the Rumanian government, which was a puppet of the Soviet occupying forces. Whereupon the Soviet deputy foreign minister arrived from Moscow and browbeat the Rumanian government into setting up an all-Communist regime. The Soviet government then announced that the Rumanian question was settled. This, of course, was a crass violation of both the spirit and the letter of the Yalta Agreements. A week later the American ambassador to Moscow reported to President Roosevelt that the Soviets were refusing to proceed with the implementation of the Yalta Agreements in regard to Poland.

Whether Stalin had deliberately deceived Roosevelt and Churchill at Yalta or whether he

President Truman is shown here with two wartime leaders, Generals Omar Bradley and George C. Marshall. In 1947 the President appointed Marshall as Secretary of State to implement the Truman Doctrine, which the Secretary supplemented by sponsoring the Marshall Plan for European economic assistance. *Photo: United Press International*

had changed his mind after returning to Moscow is not certain (Stalin's suspicions were aroused by the proposals of certain American and British officials in Europe to violate the Yalta Agreements in regard to Germany). It was now clear, however, that the Soviet Union was determined to keep a tight control over the areas of Eastern Europe that its armies had liberated from the Germans. These Soviet violations of their solemn agreements were a source of great disappointment and worry to Roosevelt, whose physical condition was rapidly worsening. He counseled patience and firmness in dealing with the Soviet Union. There was really nothing else to be done at the time, since the war with Germany and Japan was still in progress and the

areas in Eastern Europe in question were behind the Soviet lines.

President Truman, who succeeded Roosevelt on April 12, 1945, was in favor of a much tougher policy toward the Soviet Union. As soon as the war in Europe had ended, the United States began to press the Soviet Union to sign treaties with the liberated countries of Eastern Europe. After months of haggling, the Soviet Union finally agreed to withdraw her occupying forces from Rumania, Hungary, and Bulgaria within ninety days after the formal signing of the treaties, which took place on February 10, 1947. Long before the expiration of the ninety days, however, Soviet-American relations had drastically worsened.

The immediate occasion for the inauguration of the new policy was the situation in Greece and Turkey, both of which were under severe Soviet pressure. In February 1947, the British government, which had been supporting both Greece and Turkey with troops and money since the end of the war, announced that after March 31 it would be unable to continue to do so. On March 12, 1947, President Truman appeared before Congress and requested authorization to send American military and civilian personnel into Greece and Turkey. "I believe," he said, "that it must be the policy of the United States to support free peoples who are resisting attempted subjugation by armed minorities or by outside pressures." He asked for $400 million to implement the new program, and warned that this was only a starter. Congress greeted this announcement with a standing ovation.

The new policy, which was soon called the Truman Doctrine, meant that the United States would draw a military ring around the Soviet Union and its satellites from Manchuria to Norway. It was the policy of military containment. All real diplomatic negotiations between the United States and the Soviet Union, of course, ceased immediately. The Soviet Union made no further pretense of withdrawing from the areas of Eastern Europe occupied by her troops; instead she tightened the iron curtain that she had drawn around them.

In June 1947, Secretary of State George Catlett Marshall supplemented the Truman Doctrine with the Marshall Plan. This was an offer of comprehensive economic aid to all European countries (except Fascist Spain) who would improve their economies, stabilize their currencies, and cooperate with each other in bringing about general economic recovery. All the countries of Europe except the Soviet Union and her satellites hastened to accept Marshall's terms and American aid. The Soviet Union regarded the Marshall Plan as an American scheme to shore up Europe's and her own tottering capitalism, to lure away the Soviet satellites, and to make the European countries economic dependencies of the United States. She therefore forbade the countries of Eastern Europe under her control or influence to participate. Congress voted $5.3 billion as the first of four installments totaling some $17 billion for Marshall Plan aid. The later installments were trimmed somewhat.

In the fall of 1947 the Soviet Union began a series of vigorous moves to counter the Truman Doctrine and the Marshall Plan. In September 1947, she set up the Communist Information Bureau, or Cominform, the better to coordinate policies of the Soviet Union, Poland, Hungary, Rumania, Bulgaria, Albania, Yugoslavia, and Czechoslovakia. This was in reality a restoration of the old Comintern, which was the Communist International working for world revolution. The following year the Cominform was supplemented by the Council for Economic Mutual Assistance. This was a Soviet Marshall Plan of her own. At the same time the Soviet Union severely tightened her grip on her satellites. The local Communist parties were rigorously purged of moderates and national patriots.

One tragic victim of the stepping-up of the cold war was Czechoslovakia. This little republic, lying geographically between the two armed camps, had tried to remain on friendly terms with both sides. In February 1948, a Soviet-inspired and supported Communist coup overthrew the liberal regime of President Eduard Beneš and drew Czechoslovakia behind the Iron Curtain. Soviet efforts to tighten the reins on Yugoslavia, however, backfired. In March 1948 Communist dictator Marshal Tito severed his ties with Moscow and established relations with the capitalistic West.

After the death of Stalin in 1953, the Soviet government, under the leadership of Nikita Khrushchev, head of the Communist Party, made overtures to the United States to end the cold war. At the same time, it relaxed somewhat its iron grip on the satellites. Some observers optimistically called these overtures and this relaxation the end of the cold war. Unfortunately, this was far from the case. The United States, frustrated and angered by continuing tensions in Germany (see the following section), by the Communist takeover of China, and the costly Korean War (see Chapter 60), quickly spurned the overtures. In the same year that Stalin died, John Foster Dulles became United States Secretary of State in the new Eisenhower administration. It was his belief that communism was a Moscow-directed conspiracy bent upon world conquest. The Truman Doctrine was too tame. The time had come, he proclaimed, to pass over from containment to liberation.

In Eastern Europe itself, long-suppressed discontent in the satellites soon manifested itself. In October 1956, the Polish people elected a native Polish Communist regime to replace the Soviet-endorsed one. At the same time, a massive anti-Communist nationalist revolt broke out in Hungary, only to be bloodily suppressed by the

Soviet army. Khruschev's ambivalent gestures misled some of his own people, who began to speak out and were suppressed. In 1958 Boris Pasternak was officially rebuked for his novel *Doctor Zhivago*, which portrays the Communist revolution in a rather unfavorable light. Under pressure, he declined the Nobel prize for literature.

But now the Soviet government was confronted with another serious problem. Early in 1956 Khrushchev had denounced before startled Communist leaders in Moscow the crimes of Joseph Stalin. This touched off an ideological dispute with the Chinese Communists, who were younger and more evangelical in the Marxist faith than the Russians (see p. 677). They accused the Soviet government of heterodoxy and softness toward the capitalistic, imperialistic West. A rivalry sprang up between the neighboring Communist giants, intensified by the cutting off of desperately needed Soviet economic and technological aid to Peking. The Soviet Union and China share the longest international boundary in the world, much of it subject to dispute. Concern over Red China may have influenced Khrushchev to adopt a still more mellow attitude toward the West. Nevertheless, he blundered into a showdown with the United States in 1962 by attempting to set up Soviet nuclear missiles in Cuba and was forced to make a humiliating retreat.

In October 1964, Khrushchev was suddenly ousted from power by his colleagues in the Party's Central Committee. Leonid Brezhnev replaced him as Party Secretary and therefore as actual head of the government. The new regime rebuked the fallen leader only for his ineffective methods—not his objectives. This was demonstrated in 1968 when the Communist regime in Czechoslovakia, thinking the Soviets had become more relaxed, attempted to pursue a more liberal and independent course; the Soviet army marched in and occupied the country.

Furthermore, Brezhnev pressed vigorously to expand the Soviet Union's presence in the Middle East and the world of the Indian Ocean. At the same time, he succeeded in making lucrative trade deals with the United States and other trade-hungry, inflation-ridden capitalistic nations. In 1973, obviously worried about the growing strength of Communist China and China's improved relations with the United States, he paid a good-will visit to President Nixon and made several pleasant speeches. Unfortunately, the optimism thus aroused among many Americans was short-lived. The massive aid the Russians rendered the Arabs in a fourth Arab-Israeli war in October 1973 precipitated a serious crisis with the United States (see pp. 684–685). Furthermore, the Soviet persecution and banishment of Nobel prizewinner Alexander Solzhenitsyn in 1974 cooled the ardor of many of the Soviets' would-be friends in the West.

4. THE SOVIET-AMERICAN STRUGGLE OVER GERMANY

The biggest prize over which the Soviet Union and the United States struggled in the years immediately after World War II was Germany. The Soviet Union, fearing above everything else a revived and rearmed Germany, was determined to keep her permanently weak and as much as possible under Soviet domination. The United States, on the other hand, having little fear of Germany and seeing in her a valuable potential ally against the Soviet Union, soon set out to restore and rearm her. Fear of a rearmed Germany in alliance with the United States undoubtedly greatly strengthened the Soviet Union's determination to keep Eastern Europe under Soviet control.

The policies and principles to be followed in the government of Germany were agreed upon by the United States, the Soviet Union, and Great Britain at a conference held in Potsdam outside Berlin, in July 1945, shortly after Germany had surrendered. Truman, Stalin, and Clement Attlee, whose Labour party had just defeated Churchill's Conservatives, represented the Big Three. The cordiality that had prevailed at Yalta five months earlier had vanished; suspicion and self-interest reigned instead. On most issues, Truman and Attlee lined up against Stalin.

The Potsdam Agreements tentatively set the eastern boundary of Germany, pending a formal treaty settlement, at the line of the Oder and Neisse rivers (see pp. 664–665). The portion of

Germany lying east of this line, the home of some 6 million Germans, was awarded tentatively to Poland except for the port city of Königsberg in East Prussia and its immediate hinterland, which were awarded to the Soviet Union. The rest of Germany was divided into four occupation zones: American, Russian, British, and French. Berlin, which was in the Russian zone, was divided into four sectors and made the headquarters of a four-power coordinating commission. The four occupying powers were to remove from their zones as reparations war plants and peacetime industrial plants in excess of Germany's peacetime needs. Since the Soviet Union's zone was primarily agricultural, it was agreed at Potsdam that she should have in addition to removals from her own zone, 25 percent of the reparations removed from the three Western zones. The principles agreed upon as the policy to be followed by the four occupying powers in the governing of Germany were the five Ds: demilitarization, deindustrialization, de-Nazification, democratization, and decentralization.

In the implementation of the Potsdam Agreements for governing the four zones, sharp cleavages soon developed among the occupying powers, particularly between the United States and the Soviet Union. The only major question over which there was substantial agreement was that of punishment of the top Nazis. A court consisting of judges and prosecuting attorneys from the four occupying powers was set up at Nuremberg for the purpose. Twelve of the leading Nazis were condemned to death by hanging, seven to long prison terms. But there the four-power unity ceased. The Soviet Union was determined upon a long, hard occupation of Germany. She dropped an iron curtain in front of her zone, proceeded to communize its government and economy, and enforced the five Ds (except for democratization) to the letter. The United States, on the other hand, pursued a lenient policy. The commander of the American zone during the first four years was General Lucius D. Clay. Clay was a great admirer of the German professional military officers and refused to punish them. He was also a believer in free enterprise and big business and soon took steps to restore Germany's private industry. The

problem of de-Nazification he soon turned over to the Germans themselves.

The British Labour government believed that socialization of German industry would be an adequate safeguard against remilitarization and aggression. The French agreed with the harsh policy of the Soviet Union, as indeed did virtually all of Europe. Since, however, the French and the British economies had been wrecked by the war and they were heavily dependent upon the United States, France and Britain were eventually persuaded to support the American policy.

After the inauguration of the Truman Doctrine and the Marshall Plan in the spring of 1947, relations between the United States and the Soviet Union in Germany worsened rapidly. In August 1947 Clay announced a sharp stepping-up of the economy of the American and British zones, which had been merged the previous year. This raised the level far above that prescribed by the Potsdam Agreements and was made possible only by Marshall Plan aid. In December 1947 Secretary of State Marshall, reflecting the new get-tough policy with Russia, walked out of the London Conference of Foreign Ministers, thereby breaking up the four-power arrangement for governing Germany. France, faced with an open East-West break in Germany, reluctantly agreed to merge her zone with those of the United States and Great Britain. The American authorities were now able to set in motion their plans for the creation of an independent West German State.

To the Soviet leaders, this was the last straw. They attempted to dissuade the Western powers from going ahead with the project by blockading the three Western zones of Berlin in the hope of starving them out. For eleven months, June 1948 to May 1949, the Soviets stopped all land traffic across their zone from the West to Berlin. The Western powers defeated the blockade by means of a giant air lift. However, the tension was great.

Meanwhile, the United States proceeded undeterred in the setting up of the German Federal Republic, which began to function in September 1949. It was a liberal democratic government similar to the Weimar Republic. The Christian Democratic party, a slightly right-of-center party with Roman Catholic leanings, won the first

EUROPE 1975

0   100   200   300 miles

ICELAND
ARCTIC OCEAN
LAPLAND
FAEROE I.
(Denmark)
NORWAY
Trondheim
SWEDEN
GULF OF BOTHNIA
FINLAND
Vib
SHETLAND I.
Bergen
Helsinki
Le
Oslo
ORKNEY I.
Göteborg
Tallinn
Stockholm
ESTONIAN S.S.R.
SCOTLAND
Skagerrak
Kattegat
ATLANTIC OCEAN
Edinburgh
NORTH SEA
Riga
LATVIAN S.S.
NORTHERN
IRELAND
UNITED
KINGDOM
DENMARK
Copenhagen
BALTIC SEA
Klaipeda
LITHUANIAN S.S.R.
IRELAND
(EIRE)
Dublin
Kaliningrad (East Prussia)
Liverpool
WALES
Hull
ENGLAND
Hamburg
GERMAN
DEMOCRATIC
REPUBLIC
Szczecin
Gdansk
(Danzig)
BYELO
NETHERLANDS
Vistula R.
Elbe R.
Berlin
Oder R.
POLAND
Warsaw
London
Amsterdam
HANOVER
Rhine R.
Dresden
(Silesia)
Wroclaw
ENGLISH CHANNEL
Brussels
BELGIUM
Cologne
Bonn
GERMANY
BRITTANY
NORMANDY
Rouen
Seine R.
LUX.
Prague
MORAVIA
CZECHOSLOVAKIA
CARPATHIAN
L
Paris
LORRAINE
Strasbourg
GERMAN
FEDERAL
REPUBLIC
BOHEMIA
SLOVAKIA
RUTHENIA
D
Loire R.
ALSACE
BADEN
Munich
BAVARIA
Vienna
Budapest
TRANS
M
Tours
FRANCE
Berne
SWITZERLAND
AUSTRIA
HUNGARY
BAY OF BISCAY
Geneva
Lyons
Rhone R.
Milan
LOMBARDY
Trieste
CROATIA-
SLAVONIA
RUMA
La Coruña
Bordeaux
PIEDMONT
VENEZIA
Venice
BANAT
WALL
GALICIA
GASCONY
Po R.
BOSNIA
YUGOSLAVIA
Belgrade
Da
Oporto
Bilbao
LEÓN
NAVARRE
Genoa
Florence
Sarajevo
SERBIA
BU
PORTUGAL
Ebro R.
OLD CASTILE
ARAGON
PROVENCE
Marseilles
ANDORRA
Toulon
TUSCANY
ADRIATIC SEA
MONTE-
NEGRO
Tirana
Duero R.
Madrid
Tagus R.
SPAIN
CATALONIA
Barcelona
CORSICA
(France)
Rome
CAMPANIA
APULIA
ALBANIA
Sal
Lisbon
NEW CASTILE
Valencia
Palma
ITALY
GREE
Cordoba
LA MANCHA
BALEARIC I.
(Spain)
SARDINIA
(Italy)
Naples
Athe
Seville
ANDALUSIA
Malaga
Gibraltar (Britain)
Palermo
Tangier
Ceuta (Spain)
Melilla
(Spain)
Oran
Algiers
SICILY
Rabat
Tunis
MALTA
Casablanca
Fez
MEDITERRANEAN SEA
MOROCCO
ALGERIA
TUNISIA
Tripoli
Bengazi
TRIPOLITANIA
LIBYA

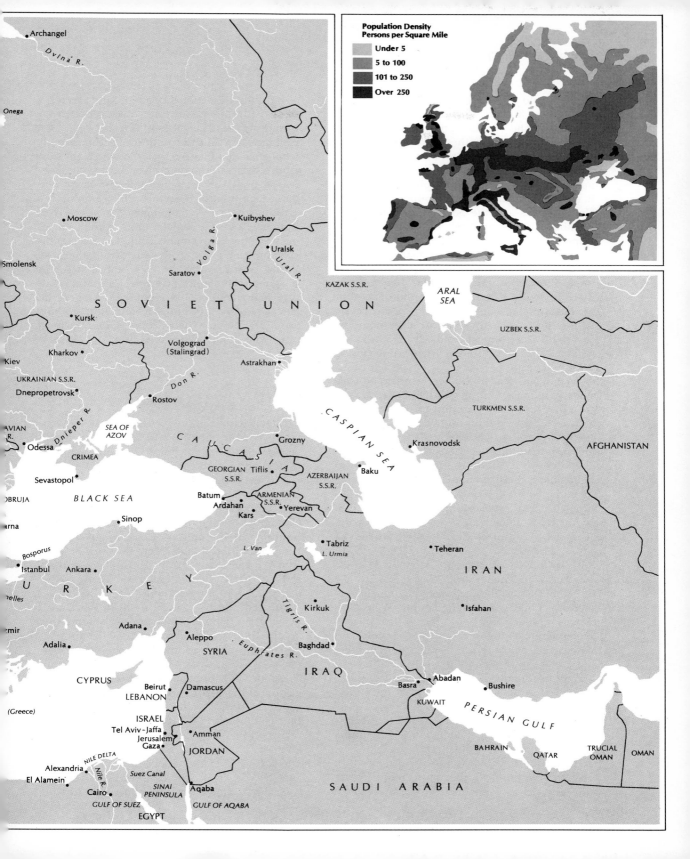

Archangel

Dvina R.

Onega

Moscow • Kuibyshev

Smolensk

Saratov • Uralsk

KAZAK S.S.R.

Volga R.

Ural R.

S O V I E T   U N I O N

Kursk •

Kharkov • Volgograd (Stalingrad) • Astrakhan

ARAL SEA

UZBEK S.S.R.

Kiev •

UKRAINIAN S.S.R.

Don R.

Dnepropetrovsk • • Rostov

Dnieper R.

TURKMEN S.S.R.

AVIAN R. • Odessa

SEA OF AZOV

C A U C A S I A   Grozny

C A S P I A N   S E A   • Krasnovodsk

AFGHANISTAN

CRIMEA

Sevastopol •

GEORGIAN S.S.R. Tiflis • AZERBAIJAN S.S.R. • Baku

OBRUJA

BLACK SEA

Batum • ARMENIAN S.S.R.

rna

Sinop • Ardahan • Kars • Yerevan

L. Van • Tabriz *L. Urmia*

• Teheran

Bosporus

Istanbul • Ankara •

I R A N

elles

U R K E Y

Kirkuk • • Isfahan

Tigris R.

mir

Adana •

Adalia • Aleppo • Baghdad •

Euphrates R.

SYRIA

I R A Q

CYPRUS

Beirut • Damascus • Basra • Abadan • Bushire

LEBANON

KUWAIT

P E R S I A N   G U L F

(Greece)

ISRAEL

Tel Aviv-Jaffa • Amman

Jerusalem • BAHRAIN

Gaza • JORDAN

Alexandria • *NILE DELTA*

El Alamein • *Nile R.* *Suez Canal*

QATAR TRUCIAL OMAN OMAN

SINAI PENINSULA

Cairo • Aqaba

S A U D I   A R A B I A

GULF OF SUEZ *GULF OF AQABA*

EGYPT

election, and its leader, the elderly and pro-Western Dr. Konrad Adenauer, became the first chancellor. The Western powers replaced their military governors with civilian commissioners and relaxed their control over Germany. One month later (October 1949) the Soviet Union set up the German Democratic Republic in its zone. It was a Communist Soviet puppet state. The United States and the Soviet Union feverishly set about to rearm West and East Germany, respectively. However, a fearful France delayed the rearmament of Western Germany until 1955. Severe labor riots against the Communist dictatorship in East Germany in 1953 demonstrated that the Soviet Union could hardly depend on her East German satellite in a showdown. Meanwhile, West Germany's industrial economy recovered by leaps and bounds. By 1957 she had regained her former industrial supremacy in Western Europe.

The Soviets' fear of a powerful rearmed Germany in alliance with the United States was so great that Khrushchev arranged two conferences with President Eisenhower (1955 and 1960) and one with President-elect Kennedy (1961) to try to convince them of the seriousness of the matter in Soviet eyes. When the Americans proved to be adamant, the Communists threatened to resume the Berlin blockade, and in late 1961 constructed a great wall sealing off Communist East Berlin from democratic West Berlin. Scores of would-be escapees died in their attempt to cross the barriers.

In 1963 Konrad Adenauer finally stepped down (at 87) as chancellor of West Germany. His Christian Democratic successors vigorously pursued his policies of strengthening West Germany's military ties with the United States, demanding the reunification of Germany and the recovery of lost territories in Eastern Europe, and a place in the family of nuclear nations. In 1969 Willy Brandt, a Social Democrat, became chancellor and launched Germany on a new course.

His government quickly signed a nuclear nonproliferation treaty that had been long pending, and entered into bilateral talks with East Germany and the Soviet Union. In August 1970 Chancellor Brandt and the Soviet Premier Kosygin signed a treaty renouncing force or the threat of force in international relations, and accepting the existing boundary lines of Eastern Europe including the Oder-Neisse line between East Germany and Poland. An official accompanying letter specified that the treaty left open the possibility of the future reunion of the two Germanies. This possibly momentous treaty was accompanied by trade agreements which promised a greatly stepped-up commerce between West Germany and the Soviet Union. If fully implemented, these agreements could mean a significant turning point in the history of the post-World War II world. In 1974 Brandt suddenly resigned when an East German Communist spy was discovered in his entourage. Brandt was succeeded by his finance minister, Helmut Schmidt. The new chancellor inherited the most prosperous industrial economy of the Western world.

5. THE ATLANTIC COMMUNITY

Challenged by the Soviet Union and by communism at the end of World War II, the European capitalistic nations found their economies, as at the end of World War I, in disarray.

In Great Britain the Labour party swept to victory in elections held in July 1945, just as the war was coming to an end. Clement Attlee succeeded Churchill as prime minister. The problems confronting Britain and the Labour government were indeed formidable. More than half of Great Britain's merchant marine had been sunk; a third of her buildings had been destroyed or damaged; her foreign investments had been liquidated and used up; she owed the United States $18.5 billion; her empire was crumbling. To distribute the burden fairly, the Labour government strictly rationed the short supplies, raised taxes on the rich, and lowered taxes on the poor. It nationalized (1) the Bank of England, (2) the coal mines and the electrical and gas industries, (3) inland transportation, and (4) the steel industry. Altogether, some 20 percent of Britain's economy was socialized. A vast program of social security, public education, public housing, and national health insurance was launched. The dismantling of the British Empire was begun — India, the biggest of all of Britain's colonial prizes, was given her independence in 1947 (see Chapter 60). The six years of Labour rule were years of austerity for the middle and upper classes. However, the general morale of the people was high, and Britain made a more rapid recovery than any other war-ravaged country. By 1948 her production and exports were higher than before the war, and the masses of the people were enjoying more security, services, and material goods than ever before. Millions of British citizens, for instance, were enjoying excellent medical care for the first time in their lives.

Unfortunately, Great Britain's economic condition was fundamentally unsound. The loss of her overseas investments and resources and of the income from most of her prewar shipping, together with the antiquated state of most of her mines and factories, left her far short of the funds needed for war repair, debt repayment, and social services. By 1949 the serious deficit in her balance of trade had become apparent, followed by a weakening of the pound and mounting inflation. Rising discontent enabled Churchill and the Conservatives to return to power in 1951. With the exception of denationalizing the steel and trucking industries, they tampered little with the Labour party's program, most of which the great majority of the British people now clearly favored.

But neither the Conservatives, who governed Britain from 1951 to 1964 and again from 1970 to 1974, nor the Labourites, who governed from 1964 to 1970 and returned to power again in 1974, were able to strengthen Britain's deteriorating economy, which was not yet socialistic but was too restricted to allow free competitive capitalism to function as it had in the nineteenth century. Furthermore, it was difficult for many Britishers to adjust to their greatly diminished place in the world. Many could still remember the glamorous days when Britain ruled the seas and an empire over which the sun never set. But increasing numbers of the young and the poor knew and cared little about past glories. Lawlessness and violence escalated, reaching its peak of intensity in Ulster. There the Roman Catholic minority struggled fiercely to gain equality with the Protestant majority; many of them demanded separation from Britain and union with Ireland. The Protestants fought equally fiercely to maintain their supremacy. Violence begat violence. Hundreds on both sides were killed and hopes for a harmonious society were destroyed for the forseeable future.

France emerged from the war not only ravaged but, unlike Britain, defeated and demoralized. General Charles de Gaulle returned to France in 1944 with the American and British liberators, who gave official recognition to the government he set up in Paris. However, the first postwar elections, held in October 1945, resulted in a sweeping victory for the parties of the Left, with which the authoritarian De Gaulle could not cooperate. Early in 1946 he went into temporary retirement. The Leftist coalition, suspicious of authority, drew up a constitution very similar to that of the Third Republic, with its weak executive. The Fourth Republic, like the Third, was plagued by a multiplicity of parties. In 1947, just as the Leftist coalition was preparing to launch a socialistic reform program similar to that of the British Labour government, France became enmeshed in the sharply intensified Soviet-American cold war. The Communists, constituting about one-fourth of the electorate, deserted the Leftist coalition and supported the Soviet Union. The United States gave strong support to the capitalistic classes and exerted heavy pressure on the Fourth Republic to take the American side in the cold war. The result was a slight swing to the right in French politics and the adherence of a reluctant, frustrated, and divided France to the American cold war camp.

Despite these difficulties the Fourth French Republic proceeded to make some noteworthy changes in French economic and social life. Major banking and insurance facilities, coal mines, gas and electrical utilities were nationalized. Social services, somewhat less comprehensive than those of the British Labour government, were inaugurated. A strong if uneasy economic recovery was achieved. By 1958 the output of goods and services was far in excess of that before World War II. These accomplishments of the Fourth Republic, however, were offset by its unsuccessful effort to hold onto the French Empire. A costly attempt to put down a war for independence in Indochina, which had broken out in 1942, resulted in humiliating defeat for the

French (see p. 681). In 1954 France was forced to grant independence to Indochina. An even costlier war to try to save Algeria, 1954–62, also ended in failure (see p. 685). Meanwhile, France granted independence to Morocco and Tunisia. Her inability to solve the Algerian problem led to the mutiny of the French army in Algeria in May 1958, which brought about the fall of the government and the recall of Charles de Gaulle from his twelve-year retirement. The problems confronting him were formidable—a mutinous army, a disintegrating empire, a seemingly endless war in Algeria, a disgruntled working class, an inflated currency, governmental weakness amounting to anarchy, widespread cynicism.

De Gaulle was probably the only man in France who could have reestablished civilian control over the mutinous army. This he deftly proceeded to do. He drew up a new constitution which greatly strengthened the executive branch of the government, and in December 1958 he was elected first president of this Fifth French Republic by an overwhelming majority. He immediately granted independence to all of France's colonies except Algeria with its large French population. (Algerian independence was granted four years later. All the other colonies

Two of the great postwar European leaders— France's Charles de Gaulle and Germany's Konrad Adenauer—are shown here during a visit of Adenauer to France in 1962. *Photo: United Press International*

except Guinea voted to remain with the French Union.) He undertook to strengthen France's capitalistic economy by means of an austerity program. In spite of widespread strikes and sabotage by the working classes, much of it Communist-inspired, France's economy was soon operating at its highest level in history, and the French masses were enjoying the greatest prosperity they had ever known.

In foreign affairs, De Gaulle set out to restore France's "greatness"—her prestige in world affairs and her hegemony in Western Europe. He also sought to make Western Europe a "third force" independent of both American and Soviet domination. To achieve these ends, he created at great cost an independent nuclear striking force, cultivated cordial relations with Germany, withdrew France's military forces from NATO (see p. 670) because of its domination by the United States, and vetoed Great Britain's entry into the European Common Market (see p. 671) because of her close ties to her Commonwealth associates and to the United States.

For eleven years, these policies worked with remarkable success. France regained much of the stability and prestige she had lost in 1940. De Gaulle's strong role, of course, encountered much opposition, mostly from the extreme Right and the extreme Left. His position and that of France's economy were weakened by massive student and labor union strikes and riots in 1968. When, in early 1969, De Gaulle asked for a vote of confidence from the French people and lost by a narrow margin, he resigned. His successor was Georges Pompidou, who for many years had been De Gaulle's premier. Pompidou continued the policies of De Gaulle until his death in 1974. In the ensuing elections Valery Giscard d'Estaing, a moderate conservative, defeated his Communist-supported Socialist opponent by the narrowest of margins. The Gaullist candidate ran a poor third.

The story of postwar Italy has been somewhat similar to that of France, except that she was much poorer, the corrupting hand of fascism had lain upon her for eighteen years longer, her Communists were more numerous, and no Charles de Gaulle came forth to lead her with a strong hand. By 1948 she appeared to be definitely in the cold war camp of the United States.

Italy's large population and lack of natural resources made her particularly vulnerable to the pressures engendered by the inflation and the energy shortage of the early 1970s.

Of the Western powers, only the United States emerged from World War II virtually unscathed materially. The war had forced billions of dollars into circulation, ended the long depression, and destroyed much of her foreign competition. The end of the war found big business and a high-spending big military machine in close alliance and firmly entrenched. Under Presidents Truman, Eisenhower, Kennedy, Johnson, and Nixon, the United States enjoyed an economic prosperity such as no nation in history had ever experienced. With 6 percent of the world's population she possessed approximately half of the world's wealth and consumed more than a third of the world's energy. A family without an automobile and a television set was looked upon as very poor or eccentric indeed.

That civilization and human well-being depend upon more than material prosperity is clearly illustrated by the fact that during the first three decades after World War II the prosperous American people were harassed by anxiety, unrest, fear, and violence. One of the greatest flaws in American democratic society has always been its failure to integrate its large black population. By 1945 the blacks numbered some 20 million — about a tenth of the total population — and although considerable advancement in material well-being and social equality had been made, the fulfillment was far short of the promise. The curve of expectation was rising faster than the curve of achievement. Returning black World War II veterans were particularly frustrated.

In 1954 the Supreme Court outlawed segregation in the public schools and later specified forced bussing as a means of implementing the decision. In 1964 Congress passed a civil rights act outlawing racial discrimination in private business and services. White resistance to these measures varied in rather close proportion to the number of blacks in the total population — first in the Deep South and second in the large industrial cities of the North. Federal troops and marshals were used to crush white resistance in the South. Millions of whites in the large Northern industrial cities fled to the suburbs, leaving many cities primarily black with black mayors. Massive and bloody riots in these cities, which had taken place every summer since 1964, reached a climax in 1968 following the murder of Dr. Martin Luther King, Jr., the most prominent of the black leaders. The story is far from finished.

But violence in the United States was by no means limited to the blacks. During the decade of the 1960s, youth all over the world was in revolt. However, violence and the crime rate were higher in the United States than in any other country and were increasing constantly. Millions of Americans armed themselves and locked and barricaded their homes at sunset — fearful of going out after dark. President Kennedy was assassinated in 1963 and his brother Robert, a major candidate for the Democratic presidential nomination, in 1968 — both by disgruntled youths. Colleges and universities were scenes of increasing protest, often violent. Some of the contributing factors to this unrest were, undoubtedly, continued racial inequality, widespread poverty alongside great wealth, inflation, pollution and wasteful destruction of natural resources, and growing dissatisfaction with American involvement in the war in Vietnam (see pp. 681–682).

The prosperous American people were seized, from the very beginning of the postwar era, by a morbid fear of the Soviet Union and of communism. Many journals, politicians, and business and professional men exploited this fear. During the early 1950s, Senator Joseph McCarthy of Wisconsin fanned this fear into hysteria. In the eyes of McCarthy and his millions of followers, the American government, defense industries, armed forces, and educational system were honeycombed with Communists and fellow travelers. The word *liberal* became synonymous with *Communist*. Thousands lost their jobs. Neighbor suspected neighbor.

In October 1957, just as McCarthyism was subsiding, the American people were shocked by the news that the Soviet Union had orbited a satellite — Sputnik. The implication was that the lean and eager Russians had forged ahead in nuclear weapons and delivery systems while the soft and contented Americans had slept. The United States had, of course, for some time been working on a satellite of her own, and in 1958 successfully orbited one. In 1960 the Soviet Union and the United States sent men into space and began to race each other to the moon. This race was won by the United States in 1969 at a cost of some $40 billion.

American concern was strongly felt over repeated Communist successes in Asia (see Chapter 60), while closer at home a Communist takeover in Cuba in 1959 caused grave anxiety. Its leader, Fidel Castro, overthrew an American-supported Rightist dictatorship. The American government in 1961 encouraged and aided an unsuccessful attempt by Cuban refugees to overthrow the Castro regime, and the following year, by heavy threats, forced the Soviet Union to dismantle missile bases that she had constructed in Cuba. This was the most frightening of all the confrontations between the two nuclear powers, both of which had the nuclear capacity to destroy all the people on the earth.

Midst all these fears and harassments at home and abroad the prosperous American people in 1973–74 were confronted with their most serious political crisis since the American Civil War. In June 1972, five months before the presidential election, five burglars were caught in the Democratic headquarters in the Watergate apartments in Washington. Evidence quickly tied them to the Republican Committee to Reelect the President and to high officials in the White House. Although the burglars were jailed and indicted and later convicted, legal proof of the higher connections was successfully concealed until after President Nixon's landslide reelection in November. But the pressure of suspicion mounted until in March 1973 the dam broke. President Nixon's White House counsel admitted before a Senate committee his own guilt and accused the President and many of his top White House aides and ranking members of the Republican party of high crimes and misdemeanors, including obstruction of justice, perjury, paying of hush money, violation of civil rights, illegal collection of campaign funds, and dirty tricks during the presidential election campaign that far exceeded the traditional practice of democratic politics—rough and tumble as they are at best. In addition, President Nixon was accused of tax evasion and of using public funds for pri-

vate purposes. Vice President Agnew was convicted of bribery and forced out of office. Numerous high officials in the Nixon administration were forced to resign and were indicted by grand juries. The President himself denied all wrongdoing, but refused to furnish much of the evidence requested by the various investigating committees. Other White House evidence was found to be tampered with. Early in 1974 impeachment proceedings against President Nixon were begun. Finally in August 1974, after the House Judiciary Committee had unanimously voted a bill of impeachment and it had become obvious that the President would be impeached by the full House and convicted by the Senate, Nixon resigned. He was succeeded by Gerald R. Ford, the right-wing conservative Republican leader in the House of Representatives whom Nixon had appointed vice-president in place of Spiro Agnew. Less than a month later the new President forfeited much of his brief honeymoon popularity by suddenly granting Nixon full pardon for all crimes he "may have committed while in office" and for which a special prosecutor was preparing bills of indictment. These events—generally spoken of as Watergate—overshadowed all other activities in the United States and kept the people in an uproar. They were widely believed to have contributed to the spiraling inflation, critical fuel shortage, and economic recession. They also weakened the influence of the United States vis-à-vis her friends and potential enemies.

To buttress her position against the Soviet Union the United States in 1949 took the initiative in creating the North Atlantic Treaty Organization (NATO). This was a defensive military pact signed by the United States, Canada, Great Britain, France, Italy, Portugal, Belgium, the Netherlands, Luxembourg, Denmark, Norway, and Iceland. Greece and Turkey were admitted in 1951, and West Germany in 1955. According to the terms of the pact, all the members were committed to come to the military aid of any member that was attacked. The military effectiveness of this alliance against the Soviet Union was highly dubious apart from the nuclear umbrella provided by the United States.

A more realistic and fruitful step toward union—this time economic—was taken by the

European democracies. In 1958 France's Jean Monnet took the lead in setting up the Common Market. Its original members were France, West Germany, Italy, the Netherlands, Belgium, and Luxembourg. In 1973 Great Britain, Ireland, and Denmark became members. The nine members abolished tariff and immigration barriers among themselves and sought closer coordination of their economies. Considering the venomous hatred and bloody conflicts engendered by selfish nationalism that had for centuries torn Europe, these were historic achievements.

But malignant nationalism was not to be easily harnessed. The slackening of the cold war tensions that followed the death of Stalin in 1953 weakened the appeal of the NATO alliance and probably also of the Common Market. De Gaulle's brand of French nationalism and the dominating position of the United States placed a heavy strain on both alliances. When the Muslim oil sheiks during and after the 1973 Arab-Israeli war quadrupled their prices and curtailed production, the various Western industrial powers and Japan scrambled to make their own deals and policies, each one according to what it believed to be to its own best selfish interest.

Furthermore, by the early 1970s all the capitalistic industrialized nations were suffering seriously from a chronic disease of competitive capitalism — inflation — which threatened to destroy all the remarkable material advances that had been made since the end of World War II. As the frustrated masses saw their hard-earned wages and salaries buying less and less, the governments of the various nations of the Atlantic Community became increasingly insecure.

Suggested Reading

General
*H. Gatzke, *The Present in Perspective: A Look at the World Since 1945*, 3rd ed. (Rand McNally). Good brief survey.

The UN
S. Fenichall and P. Andrews, *United Nations* (1952). Covers the UN's origins, structure, and early functioning.

The Yalta Agreements
*R. Sherwood, *Roosevelt and Hopkins*, Vol. II (Bantam). Sherwood uses the notes of Harry Hopkins, Roosevelt's closest adviser, for an inside, eyewitness account.

Soviet-American Controversy over Eastern Europe
G. Kennan, *Memoirs, 1928–1950* (1967). By the U.S. ambassador to the Soviet Union and chief author of the Truman Doctrine and the Marshall Plan.

*Z. Brzezinski, *The Soviet Bloc: Unity and Conflict* (Praeger). Good brief study of Eastern Europe since World War II.

*M. Djilas, *The New Class* (Praeger). A strong criticism of the ruling bureaucracy in the Soviet Union by a former Yugoslav bureaucrat.

*K. Mehnert, *Soviet Man and His World* (Praeger). Delightful picture of people in the Soviet Union since World War II.

Soviet-American Struggle over Germany
*H. Feis, *Between War and Peace: The Potsdam Conference* (Princeton University). Best study of the Potsdam Conference.

*R. Hiscocks, *The Adenauer Era* (1966). Good history of Germany during the critical and transitional years, 1949–1963.

The Atlantic Community
F. Williams, *Socialist Britain* (1949). A lucid brief study of Britain's first postwar Labour government and its policies and achievements. Sympathetic.

*C. de Gaulle, *The War Memoirs of Charles de Gaulle*, Vol. III, *Salvation, 1944–1946* (Simon and Schuster). Brilliantly written account of the liberation of France and the setting up of the Fourth Republic.

*D. Pickles, *The Fifth French Republic: Institutions and Politics*, 3rd ed. (Praeger). Scholarly study of De Gaulle's France.

*N. Graebner, *Cold War Diplomacy* (Anvil). Excellent brief account of American foreign policy since World War II.

*J. Barzun, *The House of Intellect* (Torch). Sharp examination of the quality of American intellectual life since World War II.

*M. Shanks and J. Lambert, *The Common Market Today — and Tomorrow* (Praeger). A brief, useful study.

*J. K. Galbraith, *The Affluent Society* (Mentor). Keen analysis of the problems of prosperity in the Western World since World War II.

60

THE CHALLENGE OF
THE NON-WESTERN WORLD

Asia was an important area of conflict in the cold war between the United States and the Soviet Union. But it is a serious mistake to think of mid-twentieth-century Asia as a mere pawn in the Soviet-American world struggle. The vast and populous Asian continent was at last astir and out of the control of either the United States or the Soviet Union. Japan, in the latter part of the nineteenth century, had been the first Asian country to adopt Western technology and aggressive nationalism. In the twentieth century the rest of Asia began to move in the same direction. The movement was sharply accelerated by the two world wars. Africa, too, was astir after World War II. She was the last of the continents to throw off the yoke of European imperialism.

1. JAPAN BETWEEN EAST AND WEST

Japan emerged from World War II defeated on sea and land, the shocked victim of history's first two atomic bombs used for military purposes. Since the United States had played by far the major role in the defeat of Japan, she refused to share the occupation and government of the Japanese islands with her former allies. President Truman appointed General Douglas MacArthur Supreme Commander of the Allied Powers in Japan and gave him absolute authority. An allied advisory council was set up to advise MacArthur, but the final decision to accept or to ignore the advice of this body lay with the Supreme Commander, and he paid little or no attention to it.

When the Soviet Union, which had used seventy divisions in crushing the Japanese forces in Manchuria and North Korea and was a next-door neighbor to Japan, realized that she was going to be denied a real part in the control of Japan, she refused for four months to participate in the advisory commissions. MacArthur's only directives came from the United States government, which shortly after the Japanese surrender drew up a four-point policy for postwar Japan: (1) Japan was to be limited to the four "home" islands and some small ones in the immediate vicinity. (2) Japan was to be completely demilitarized. (3) Civil, political, and religious rights and liberties for the Japanese people were to be encouraged. (4) Japan's economy was to be developed for her peacetime needs.

For a year and a half General MacArthur ruled Japan with a firm but liberal and benevolent hand. He was fortunate to have the support of Emperor Hirohito, who urged his people to obey the American commander. A democratic constitution similar to that of Great Britain was drawn up and put into effect. In the first elections under the new constitution, the Social Democrats, who were somewhat similar to the British Labourites, won the largest number of seats in the national legislature. The activities of Japanese labor unions were encouraged, and they became effective for the first time. The five great families who had monopolized Japan's industry and finance disbanded their great business combinations under pressure from the occupation authorities. Demilitarization was carried on apace, including the trial and execution or imprisonment of a number of top war leaders.

Of greatest significance was MacArthur's land-reform program. The great mass of Japanese farmers were poverty-stricken landless sharecroppers, giving up from 50 to 70 percent of their yield to absentee landlords. Laws sponsored by MacArthur forced the landlords to sell to the government all land in excess of 7½ acres (more in less fertile areas). The government, in turn, sold the land in plots of 7½ acres to the tenant farmers, who were given thirty years to pay for them. By the end of 1946 Japan appeared to be on the way to becoming a liberal democracy.

Early in 1947, when the cold war was being stepped up in intensity, General MacArthur suddenly reversed his liberal policy in Japan. He first cracked down on the newly formed labor unions. Industrial decentralization ceased, and land redistribution slowed down. Obviously, the United States was now interested in making Japan, like Germany, a link in the containment chain that she was forging around the Soviet Union. By 1949 the conservative parties were firmly in control of the Japanese government once more.

In 1951 the United States drew up a formal treaty with Japan. The terms granted the United States military bases in Japan and a protectorate over the Ryukyu Islands (including Okinawa) and Japan's former mandated islands in the Pacific. Japan was to pay no indemnity, and was to be free to rearm and to make her own alliances. Although forty-eight nations signed the treaty, India, Burma, the Soviet Union, and the Soviet satellites refused. China was not invited to sign. The Soviet Union complained bitterly that Japan's closest neighbors, the Soviet Union and China, were allowed no part in the making of the treaty and accused the United States of sowing the seeds of future wars by unleashing Japan.

During the 1950s and 1960s Japan made an astounding economic recovery that surpassed even that of West Germany, and like West Germany she received massive American aid. In rebuilding her ruined industries, she adopted the most modern and scientific labor-saving devices. By the mid-1960s Japan was the third greatest industrial power in the world, outranked only by the United States and the Soviet Union, and her people were enjoying a prosperity and a standard of living such as they had never known before. But some observers were apprehensive. Japan has few natural resources. In an area smaller than California, of which only 14 percent is arable, lived more than 100 million people. The large Socialist party was hostile to Japan's close subservience to the United States and to American military bases in Japan and Okinawa. It was also hostile to the renewed concentration of Japanese industry and finance in the hands of the former *zaibatsu* families and to steps leading to the remilitarization of Japan.

2. THE RISE OF COMMUNIST CHINA

Across the Sea of Japan a very different and even more exciting drama was being enacted in China. Here, a massive upheaval involving one-fourth of the world's population took place. Sun Yat-sen, after launching his revolution against both China's foreign exploiters and her own reactionary and conniving government (see pp. 571–575), died in 1925, in the midst of the struggle. His place at the head of the revolutionary Chinese government was taken by his young and vigorous supporter, General Chiang Kai-shek, who soon gained control of all China. Chiang Kai-shek, a professional soldier, was much more interested in making China a powerful and independent nation than in liberalizing her government and society. Under him, the revolutionary Kuomintang party, then dominant in China, swung definitely to the right. When the Chinese Nationalist armies were defeated by the Japanese in 1937–1938 and driven deep into the interior, Chiang Kai-shek and the Kuomintang party were cut off from the chief bases of their liberal support, which were the great coastal cities. Heavily dependent then upon the war lords and landlords of the interior, they swung still further to the right. The long years of rela-

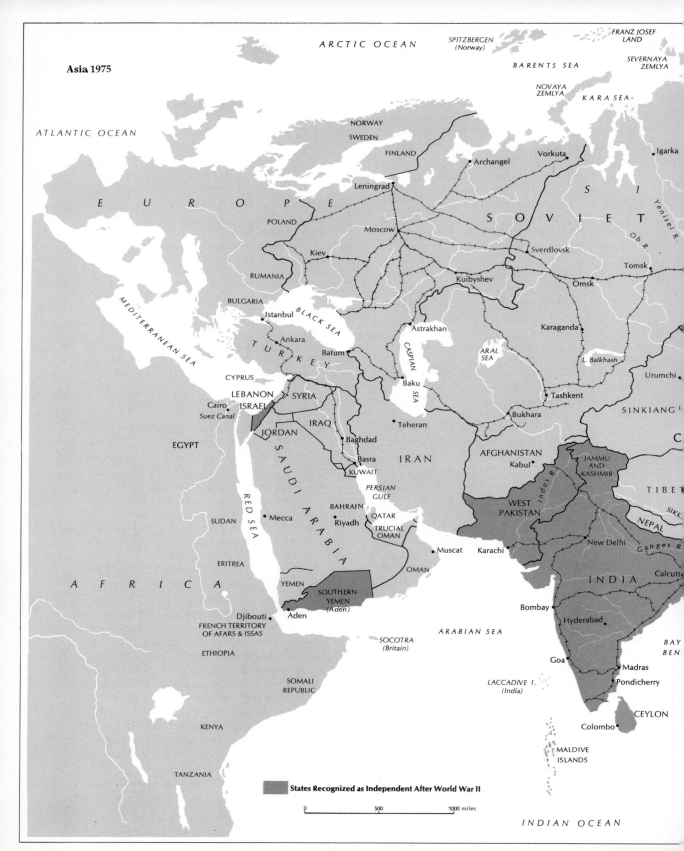

Asia 1975

ARCTIC OCEAN

SPITZBERGEN (Norway)

FRANZ JOSEF LAND

BARENTS SEA

SEVERNAYA ZEMLYA

NOVAYA ZEMLYA

KARA SEA

ATLANTIC OCEAN

NORWAY
SWEDEN
FINLAND

• Archangel
Vorkuta •
Igarka •

• Leningrad

E U R O P E
POLAND
• Kiev
Moscow
• Sverdlovsk
Kuibyshev
Omsk •
Tomsk •
Karaganda

S O V I E T
S I

Yenisei R.
Ob R.

RUMANIA

BULGARIA
Istanbul •
BLACK SEA
Ankara
Batum
TURKEY
Astrakhan •
CASPIAN SEA
Baku •
ARAL SEA
L. Balkhash
Tashkent •
Urumchi •

MEDITERRANEAN SEA

CYPRUS
LEBANON
ISRAEL
Cairo •
Suez Canal

SYRIA
IRAQ
Baghdad •
Basra •
KUWAIT

Teheran •

IRAN

Bukhara •

SINKIANG

C

JORDAN

SAUDI ARABIA

PERSIAN GULF
BAHRAIN
QATAR
Riyadh •
TRUCIAL OMAN

AFGHANISTAN
Kabul •

JAMMU AND KASHMIR

TIBET

EGYPT

SUDAN

RED SEA

Mecca •

Muscat •
Karachi •

WEST PAKISTAN
Indus R.

New Delhi •

NEPAL
SIKK

Ganges R.

ERITREA

OMAN

AFRICA

YEMEN
SOUTHERN YEMEN (Aden)
Aden •
Djibouti •
FRENCH TERRITORY OF AFARS & ISSAS

INDIA
Calcutta

Bombay •

Hyderabad •

ETHIOPIA

SOCOTRA (Britain)

ARABIAN SEA

BAY BEN

Goa •

Madras •
Pondicherry •

SOMALI REPUBLIC

LACCADIVE I. (India)

CEYLON
Colombo •

KENYA

MALDIVE ISLANDS

TANZANIA

States Recognized as Independent After World War II

0   500   1000 miles

INDIAN OCEAN

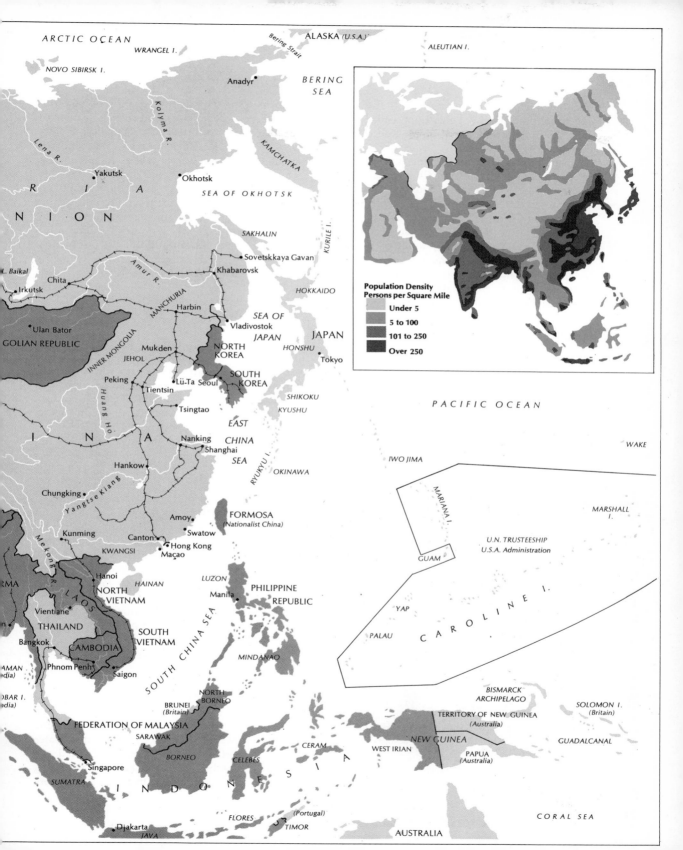

ARCTIC OCEAN

ALASKA (U.S.A.)

WRANGEL I.

ALEUTIAN I.

NOVO SIBIRSK I.

Bering Strait

BERING SEA

Anadyr

Kolyma R.

Lena R.

Yakutsk

KAMCHATKA

Okhotsk

SEA OF OKHOTSK

**Population Density
Persons per Square Mile**

Under 5

5 to 100

101 to 250

Over 250

SAKHALIN

KURILE I.

Amur R.

Sovetskkaya Gavan

Khabarovsk

HOKKAIDO

L. Baikal

Chita

SEA OF

Harbin

Vladivostok

JAPAN

Irkutsk

MANCHURIA

JAPAN

Ulan Bator

HONSHU

Tokyo

GOLIAN REPUBLIC

INNER MONGOLIA

Mukden

NORTH KOREA

JEHOL

Peking

Lü-Ta

SOUTH KOREA

Seoul

SHIKOKU

Tientsin

KYUSHU

Huang Ho

Tsingtao

EAST CHINA SEA

PACIFIC OCEAN

I N A

Nanking

Shanghai

WAKE

Hankow

RYUKYU I.

OKINAWA

IWO JIMA

MARIANA I.

MARSHALL I.

Chungking

Yangtse Kiang

Amoy

FORMOSA
(Nationalist China)

Kunming

Canton

Swatow

U.N. TRUSTEESHIP
U.S.A. Administration

Mekong R.

KWANGSI

Hong Kong

Macao

GUAM

Hanoi

HAINAN

LUZON

PHILIPPINE REPUBLIC

YAP

C A R O L I N E I.

Vientiane

NORTH VIETNAM

Manila

LAOS

PALAU

THAILAND

SOUTH CHINA SEA

SOUTH VIETNAM

Bangkok

CAMBODIA

AMAN
dia)

Phnom Penh

Saigon

MINDANAO

OBAR I.
dia)

BRUNEI
(Britain)

NORTH BORNEO

BISMARCK ARCHIPELAGO

SOLOMON I.
(Britain)

FEDERATION OF MALAYSIA

SARAWAK

TERRITORY OF NEW GUINEA
(Australia)

GUADALCANAL

Singapore

BORNEO

CERAM

WEST IRIAN

NEW GUINEA

SUMATRA

I N D O N E S I A

CELEBES

PAPUA
(Australia)

FLORES

(Portugal)

TIMOR

CORAL SEA

Djakarta

JAVA

AUSTRALIA

tive inactivity at Chungking (1939–1945) had a demoralizing effect not only upon Chiang Kai-shek's military forces, but upon the Kuomintang party leaders themselves.

Meanwhile, a rival movement very different in nature and purpose from Chiang Kai-shek's Kuomintang made rapid headway in China. This movement was communism. During the 1920s, when China's Confucian civilization was crumbling faster than Sun Yat-sen's Western liberalism could replace it, another Western influence moved into the vacuum: Marxist materialism. The hostility that the Western democracies showed to Sun Yat-sen's revolutionary liberal movement greatly encouraged the Chinese Communists. In 1927 the Communists found an able leader in the scholarly and shrewd Mao Tse-tung. This dedicated revolutionary from well-to-do peasant stock had risen to leadership by sheer force of intellect, personality, and energy. Chiang Kai-shek exerted every effort to crush the Chinese Communists—much more, in fact, than to drive out the Japanese invader. During the years 1939–1945, when the Kuomintang forces were inactive in Chungking and getting further and further out of touch with the Chinese masses, Mao Tse-tung's Communists were waging incessant guerrilla warfare against the Japanese and gaining a greater following among the Chinese people.

Following the surrender of Japan in August 1945, a bitter struggle for the control of China ensued between Chiang Kai-shek's Kuomintang forces, now known as the Chinese Nationalists, and the Chinese Communists. In this struggle the United States supported the Nationalists. The American army and navy transported Chiang Kai-shek's forces and seized and held strategic places until Nationalist forces could arrive. Chiang Kai-shek was supplied with American money and weapons. However, the Communists won the support of ever-increasing numbers of the Chinese people. Tens of thousands of people in the populous coastal areas who had endured the Japanese invaders for eight years were outraged when Kuomintang landlords and politicians, having sat the war out in Chungking, returned demanding back rent and back taxes. Morale in the long inactive and graft-ridden Nationalist armies was low, while that in the Communist armies, toughened by the continuous fighting against the Japanese, was high.

Using Japanese weapons that had been left behind by the Russians, and American weapons and munitions that were surrendered by the Nationalists, the Communists began to gain the upper hand in 1947. During 1949 the victorious Communists swept over the entire Chinese mainland. Chiang Kai-shek, with a remnant of his Nationalist forces, mostly officers, fled to the island of Formosa (Taiwan) where after June 1950, they were protected by the United States navy. In 1949 Mao Tse-tung proclaimed the People's Republic of China and the following year formed an alliance with the Soviet Union.

Mao Tse-tung and Ho Chi Minh—two of East Asia's most dynamic leaders since World War II. Under the leadership of men like Mao of China and Ho of North Vietnam the teaming millions in East Asia have been struggling since the end of the Second World War to throw off the last shackles of Western imperialism and to catch up with Western technology. *Photo: Brian Brake/Rapho-Guillumette*

With Soviet aid, he began the enormous task of industrializing and communizing the world's most populous nation.

This formidable undertaking was interrupted shortly after it had begun by China's involvement in the Korean War, 1950–1953 (see the following section). The Chinese Communists were greatly angered by the intervention of the United States, whose navy prevented them from driving Chiang Kai-shek's Nationalist forces from their last stronghold on Taiwan (Formosa) and ending the Chinese civil war. When the United Nations forces, which were mostly American, defeated the North Korean Communists and approached the Manchurian border, the Chinese Communist armies crossed the Yalu River into Korea, drove the Americans back, and stalemated the war. This was a remarkable accomplishment for such an industrially backward country fighting against the world's greatest military power, and it cost the Chinese Communists nearly a million casualties. This feat following the sweeping victories it had just won in China itself filled the young Red regime with pride and confidence.

In 1953 Mao Tse-tung launched his first five-year plan, which was very similar to Stalin's first five-year plan twenty-five years earlier. The Chinese Communists, however, were starting from a much more primitive base than the Russians. Industry and agriculture were both collectivized. The emphasis was on building heavy industry. These were years of bleak austerity, but the Chinese masses had never known anything else. In 1957 the government announced that the first five-year plan had been a great success. Most production quotas had been met or surpassed. The following year it launched its second five-year plan. The vast new goals in industry and agriculture were to be achieved by communizing Chinese society more completely than had ever been attempted in the Soviet Union. The entire population was organized into strictly regimented communes; the ancient and sacred Chinese family structure was drastically altered. China's huge and rapidly growing population was set to building irrigation dams and ditches, steel mills, factories, railroads, schools, and hospitals, and in a frenzied hurry.

Never in history had so vast a revolution been undertaken. It was called "the Great Leap Forward." But the plan was too ambitious. In 1959 a series of droughts and floods produced near famine conditions in many areas. Overzealous local party officials provoked resentment and resistance among the harried populace. The realistic Red leaders slackened the pace and eased the regimentation.

The partial failure of the Great Leap Forward gave rise to ideological differences and set off a power struggle within the Communist Party hierarchy. A moderate group led by Liu Shao-chi, president of the republic and second in command to Party Chairman Mao Tse-tung, wished to slow down the pace of communization, produce more consumer goods, and encourage, at least temporarily, individual initiative, much on the order of the NEP in the early days of the Soviet Union. Mao took a different line. He believed many dangerous remnants of prerevolutionary capitalistic China had still to be destroyed. In 1966 he unleashed tens of thousands of Red Guards—fanatical Communist youths—upon the moderate element in what he called a "cultural revolution," and with the support of the regular army succeeded, after three years of turmoil, in crushing the moderates.

The Chinese Communists' difficulties were intensified by their growing rift with the Soviet Union. An ideological dispute had begun when Khrushchev denounced Stalin in 1956 (see p. 662). Peking accused Moscow of becoming soft toward the capitalistic, imperialistic West. In 1960 the Soviet Union began to withhold promised economic and technological aid from China. By 1964 the two Red giants were vying with each other for allegiance and leadership in the Communist world, hurling epithets at each other and accusing each other of border violations.

In the early years of the regime it was against the United States that Red China directed her greatest hostility. The United States had persistently refused to recognize her and blocked her admission to the United Nations. The American fleet continued to protect Chiang Kai-shek on Taiwan. American arms and armies had prevented Communist regimes from winning complete victories in Korea and Indochina. American military bases in Japan and missile bases in Okinawa menaced China.

In October 1964 Red China exploded her first nuclear device. This event, in addition to China's impressive economic and military growth, appeared to give the Soviets grave concern. They moved many of their best mechanized divisions to the Far East, where in 1968 they clashed with Chinese units along the disputed border. Both Red giants, fearful of each other, sought a détente with the United States. President Nixon in response visited Peking in 1972 and gave up his opposition to the admission of Red China into the United Nations. In the same year he visited Moscow. How much of this apparent détente was shadow and how much was substance, only the future could tell.

3. THE KOREAN WAR

The bitter left-right conflict among the Asiatic peoples and the global cold war struggle between the United States and the Soviet Union merged in Korea to produce a shooting war of major proportions. In August 1945, in accordance with the Yalta Agreements, the forces of the Soviet Union overran Japanese-held Korea north of the thirty-eighth parallel, and the forces of the United States began to occupy Korea south of the thirty-eighth parallel. These moves were supposed to be for the purpose of setting up a free and united Korean nation. However, the Soviet Union immediately proceeded to set up a Communist dictatorship in North Korea. The land was distributed to the peasants, and industry was nationalized. In South Korea the United States authorities sponsored a right-wing government under the leadership of the aged and reactionary Korean patriot Syngman Rhee. Late in 1948 the Soviet forces withdrew from North Korea, leaving behind an energetic Communist regime well armed with the latest Soviet weapons. Six months later the American forces withdrew from South Korea, leaving behind the Syngman Rhee landlord regime armed mostly with the weapons that had been captured from the Japanese. Both the North and South Korean governments talked loudly of conquering each other.

On June 25 (June 24, American time), 1950, North Korea suddenly attacked South Korea. The high-spirited and well-armed North Korean Communists easily defeated the South Koreans. The armies of Syngman Rhee, made up largely of disgruntled landless tenant farmers, melted away. The Truman administration quickly decided that the Communist aggression in Korea was the Soviet Union's first move to conquer the world by military force and that there must not be another Munich. Secretary of State Dean Acheson persuaded the United Nations to take drastic action. Taking advantage of the absence of the Soviet Union's representative, the Security Council called upon all the members of the United Nations to furnish military forces to repel the North Korean aggression and asked President Truman to name the commander of the United Nations forces. Fifty-two of the fifty-nine members of the United Nations voted approval of this action, and a few of them contributed token forces. Truman named General MacArthur to command them. Truman also announced that he had already ordered American forces into the Korean War, that the American navy would protect Chiang Kai-shek's Chinese Nationalists on Taiwan against the Chinese Communists, and that American aid to the French fighting the native Communists in Indochina would be greatly increased.

The forces of the United Nations, mostly Americans, quickly defeated the North Koreans. By late November 1950, MacArthur's forces were approaching the Yalu River, which forms the Korean-Chinese border. At this point Red China entered the war and severely defeated MacArthur's forces, driving them in headlong retreat back down the peninsula. Eventually—January—March 1951—the battle line became stabilized roughly along the thirty-eighth parallel, where the war had started.

MacArthur cried loudly for all available American military forces and for the blockade and bombing of Red China. However, the military authorities in Washington refused the request. They feared involvement in all-out war with the Soviet Union, which hitherto had limited her aid to the North Korean and Chinese Communists to the selling of weapons. The American military authorities were also opposed to stripping the home front and the critical Western European and Middle Eastern areas of defenses. Since the Communist aggression in Korea had been checked, Washington wished to see the Korean War simmer down with a minimum of further casualties. When MacArthur persisted in public criticism of his government's policies and disobeyed the orders of superiors to cease making policy pronouncements, he was relieved in April 1951, both as commander of the United Nations forces in Korea and as supreme commander in Japan.

In June 1951, the Soviet Union, offering her services as an intermediary, proposed the beginning of peace negotiations in Korea. Both sides readily agreed. However, two years of haggling, accompanied by intermittent fighting at the front, ensued before an armistice was finally signed in July 1953. Total casualties—dead, wounded, and missing—are estimated to have been approximately a million and a half on each side, of which some 145,000 were Americans (including 54,000 dead) and 900,000 Chinese Communists. Most of the rest were Koreans. The war ended just about where it had started. However, the first Communist military aggression had been checked with severe punishment. The United Nations had functioned effectively and increased its prestige. Probably of equal significance is the fact that a revolutionary new Asiatic power, Red China, had fought the greatest Western power, the United States, to a standstill. American troops still stand guard along the truce line protecting a reactionary regime in South Korea.

4. THE REVOLT OF SOUTHERN ASIA

The end of World War II found the huge British, Dutch, and French empires in Southern Asia aflame with the spirit of nationalism and revolt. The United States alone of the Western imperial powers escaped direct embroilment in this revolt by granting independence to the Philippines in 1946.

In India, the world's second most populous country, the leader of the independence movement was Mohandas K. Gandhi (1869–1948), one of the most dynamic personalities of the twentieth century. This middle-class Hindu, educated in Great Britain, was a master of the psychology of the Indian masses. His chief tactics were passive resistance and civil disobedience. The British were unable to cope with him. The gentle little Mahatma (Great Spirit), whether sitting at his spinning wheel, subsisting on goat's milk, or fasting in a British prison, was a beloved symbol of national independence not only to India's millions, but also to millions of other Asiatic and African colonials.

Indian nationalism reached its peak during World War II, but Churchill would not hear of Indian independence. "I did not become the king's first minister," said the doughty warrior, "in order to preside over the liquidation of the British Empire." The British Labour party, however, upon coming to power in 1945 immediately announced its determination to grant Indian independence. In 1947 the Hindu portion of India, containing some 350 million (by 1974 more than 500 million) people, became the Dominion of India. In the same year the Muslim portions, with a population of more than 70 million (by 1974 more than 100 million) became the Dominion of Pakistan. Dominion status meant complete independence with voluntary membership in the British Commonwealth of Nations.

Religious and national strife soon broke out between Hindu India and Muslim Pakistan. Gandhi tried to quell the strife, but he was assassinated in 1948 by a fanatical Hindu nationalist. Thus the "Great Spirit" himself became another victim of malignant nationalism. Open war between the two states finally began in 1948 over possession of the disputed state of Kashmir. The United Nations was able to end the shooting, but not the dispute.

One of Gandhi's most devoted followers, Jawaharlal Nehru, a charming, wealthy British-educated Hindu of the highest (Brahmin) caste, became the first prime minister of the independent Union of India. The problems confronting him were staggering. Most of India's

This rubble was once the thriving town of Dong Ha, South Vietnam. Devastation such as this caused by American bombing and shelling of a little country which posed no threat to the United States caused widespread resentment both in the United States and abroad. *Photo: UPI*

millions were poverty-stricken and illiterate. They spoke more than 800 languages and dialects (fewer than 50 percent spoke the official Hindi). Furthermore, their prevailing Hindu religion had long conditioned them to a placid acceptance of the status quo. Nehru inaugurated a liberal and mildly socialistic program somewhat similar to that of the British Labour government. Not the least of his problems was avoiding embroilment in the Soviet-American cold war. However, border clashes with Pakistan and with Red China frightened India into ac-cepting military aid from both the United States and the Soviet Union.

Nehru's great charm and prestige kept India's restive millions fairly quiet. But when he died in 1964, his successors were confronted by rising discontent. In 1966 Nehru's daughter, Mrs. Indira Gandhi, became prime minister. Many Indians felt that the economic and social reform program of the Nehrus was not drastic enough. In spite of sizable loans and much technical assistance from the United States, Great Britain, and the Soviet Union, India's standard of living by 1974 had not kept abreast of her ever-mounting population. Her annual per capita income was still less than $60. In 1974, while millions of her people stood on the brink of starvation, India exploded her first nuclear device, thus boosting her national ego. This unexpected event endangered the nuclear nonproliferation efforts that were being made in the Western world and opened the prospect of many other nations including Germany and Japan developing their own nuclear systems.

Pakistan, divided into two states more than 1,000 miles apart (see map, p. 674), soon became a military dictatorship closely aligned with the United States. In 1971 East Pakistan rebelled against the less populous but dominant West Pakistan and, with the help of India, gained its independence as the Republic of Bangladesh — but not before some three million of its helpless citizens had been slaughtered by the West Pakistani army.

The British Labour government also granted independence to Ceylon, Burma, and Malaya. This left only Hong Kong as a reminder of British imperialism in Asia.

The rich and populous Dutch East Indies declared their independence at the end of World War II. The Dutch resisted fiercely for four years but yielded to pressure from the United Nations. In 1949 the Republic of Indonesia was recognized as an independent nation — a nation of approximately 125 million people living on several thousand tropical islands rich in tin, rubber, oil, and many other valuable products.

Of all the European colonial regimes in Asia, that of the French in Indochina was probably the most predatory and the most hated. Immediately after the surrender of Japan in August 1945, the Indochinese nationalists, under the leadership of Ho Chi Minh, a Russian-trained Communist, proclaimed the independent "democratic" Republic of Vietnam. The returning French imperialists were fiercely resisted by the native Communist nationalists. Heavy fighting ensued, in which the French were aided by American Marshall Plan money. The majority of the Vietnamese people apparently preferred the Communists to the French, and the forces of Ho Chi Minh won victory after victory in spite of American aid to the French.

In 1954 the French government admitted defeat and ceded the northern half of Vietnam to the Communists. Although South Vietnam technically remained a part of the French Union, French influence there quickly vanished. The United States, in accordance with its policy of military containment of communism — both Russian and Chinese — undertook to establish its

power not only in South Vietnam, but in Laos and Cambodia as well, which France had also freed. Vigorous military and financial aid was given to the conservative Ngo Dinh Diem regime in South Vietnam. To many Asians, this policy smacked of the hated Western imperialism. Diem became increasingly unpopular. Almost immediately, he was faced with a rebellion of his own people supported and soon led by the Communists in both South and North Vietnam. No amount of American aid seemed to be able to hold back the tide against the unpopular and faltering Diem regime. In 1963 Diem was overthrown and assassinated by a group of his own officers who set up a harsh military dictatorship of their own. Early in 1965 the Vietnamese Communists with massive material aid from both the Soviet Union and Red China greatly stepped up their war against the American-supported but faltering South Vietnamese forces. The United States retaliated by bombing North Vietnam and increasing its armed forces in South Vietnam to 550,000 men. Vietnam was rapidly being devastated.

Meanwhile, public opinion all over the world, including in the United States itself, was becoming incensed at the wanton destruction. In 1968 representatives of North Vietnam and the United States began long and dreary peace talks in Paris, and the United States ceased bombing North but not South Vietnam. In 1969 Ho Chi Minh died, and the United States began slowly to reduce the size of her forces in Vietnam. This apparent simmering down of the war was marred by the violation by both sides of the territorial integrity of Laos and Cambodia.

Late in 1972 the North Vietnamese made a major frontal assault on the South. The United States with her air and naval power not only broke the back of the attack but literally bombed North Vietnam to its knees, including massive attacks on the capital city of Hanoi. In 1973 the United States withdrew its armed forces from Indochina, but the civil war continued with the United States and the Soviet Union supplying the two sides as at the beginning. The financial cost to the United States of her armed intervention in Indochina has been estimated as high as $575 billion (including future pensions and

Two great charismatic leaders of Asian independence, India's Jawaharlal Nehru and Mahatma Gandhi, are shown during a meeting of the All India Congress in Bombay in 1946. Nehru, who became India's leader after Gandhi was assassinated in 1948, was the first prime minister of the independent Union of India. *Photo: United Press International*

benefits to veterans). Some 50,000 Americans were killed. Millions of Indochinese were killed, maimed, or left homeless — their lands and forests ruined for the foreseeable future.

5. THE EMBATTLED MIDDLE EAST

One of the most explosive areas in the mid-twentieth-century world was the Middle East — that area between and including Egypt and Iran, where East meets West (see map, p. 683). In global terms it is probably the most strategic area in the world. It forms the bridge between the world's two greatest land masses, Eurasia and Africa; and through it pass the chief communication lines between the East and the West. The Middle East is the heart of the Muslim world, which stretches from Morocco to Indonesia and contains nearly 500 million followers of the Prophet. It is also the heart of the tumultuous Arab world. Moreover, the area contains more than half the world's known oil reserves. At mid-twentieth century, the Middle East, the most fought-over area in history, was one of the most sensitive spots in the Soviet-American cold war.

During the early part of the century, while the great European powers competed for control of the Middle East, Arab nationalism was rising. This nationalism was vented first against the British, who were the dominant power in that area. As anti-British hostility mounted in the years between the two world wars, Great Britain began to relax her control. By the end of World War II only Cyprus, Palestine, and the Suez Canal remained in Britain's possession, and the British were bidding strongly for Arab friendship. But continued British possession of the Suez Canal and the admission of tens of thousands of Jews into Palestine under the Balfour Declaration of 1917 proved to be effective barriers to Anglo-Arab accord.

Palestine was the ancient home of the Jews. However, in A.D. 70 they were dispersed by the government of the Roman Empire. In the sev-enth century the Muslim Arabs conquered Palestine and lived there until the twentieth cen-tury—thirteen hundred years. In the late nine-teenth century, the Zionist movement began. This was a movement to restore Palestine as a national home for the Jews. During the anti-Semitic persecutions of the Hitler era, thousands of European Jewish refugees, many of them wealthy, poured into Palestine, buying up the land and dispossessing the Arabs. The whole Arab and Muslim world became incensed.

In 1948 the British Labour government turned Palestine over to the United Nations. The Jews immediately proclaimed the State of Israel and accepted the boundary lines that the United Nations had drawn to divide Palestine between the Jews and the Arabs. The Arab League refused to accept this arrangement, and began hostilities with a view to exterminating the Jewish state. Tiny Israel, however, well armed and well financed, was more than a match for the Arabs. After a year of fighting, the United Nations succeeded in bringing about a truce. Israel had somewhat expanded her original borders, and there were now nearly a million Arab refugees from Israel, Arab nationalism was thoroughly aroused, and border raids recurred as the Arabs

THE ARAB WORLD 1975

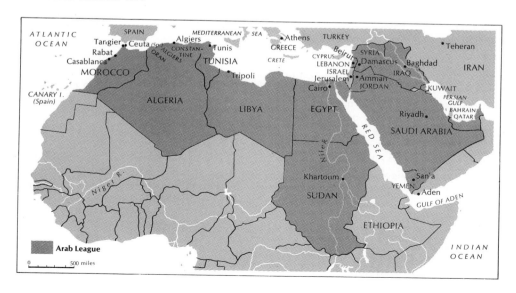

In a lookout post on the Israeli-Lebanon border, Israeli soldiers stand constant duty as sporadic warfare between Israel and her Arab neighbors continues and the tension that has gripped the Middle East since the foundation of the modern state of Israel in 1948 involves the superpowers — the U.S.S.R. and the United States. *Photo: United Press International*

armed for a revival of the struggle. Israel, in the meantime, receiving financial aid from Jews abroad, prospered, built modern cities, introduced irrigation and scientific agriculture, and became a vigorous, democratic, cooperative Western society in the midst of a feudalistic and largely primitive Muslim Arab world.

The Arabs found a vigorous leader when in 1952 a military coup in Egypt brought to power Gamel Abdul Nasser as dictator. Nasser set out to unite the Arab world and inflame it against the West. When he threatened Israel, seized the Suez Canal, and aided France's rebellious subjects in 1956, Israel, Great Britain, and France attacked him. He was saved only by the threatened intervention of the Soviet Union and a counterthreat by the United States, which ended the hostilities. But nothing had been settled. Nasser continued to arouse Arab nationalism against Israel, and the Arab states received a swelling stream of arms from the Soviet Union.

In 1967 Nasser again brought on a showdown. When he blockaded Israel's only port on the Red Sea and Egyptian, Syrian, and Jordanian armies massed along the Israeli borders, the Israelis suddenly attacked them and crushed them in six days' time. The Israelis then occupied Egyptian territory east of the Suez Canal, Syria's Golan Heights, and Jordanian territory west of the Jordan — territories that the Israelis claimed were necessary for their security.

The six-day 1967 war humiliated not only the Arab world but also the Soviet Union, who rushed billions of dollars' worth of arms, including deadly surface-to-air missiles (SAMS), together with thousands of military "advisers," to Egypt and Syria.

As the Israelis were celebrating their Yom Kippur holidays (October 1973), Egypt and Syria, supported by the rest of the Arab states, suddenly attacked them. This time the Arabs, much better armed and trained than before, inflicted serious casualties on the Israelis and pushed them back on all fronts. Several weeks were required for the heavily outnumbered Israelis to recover from their initial shock, receive massive fresh supplies from the United States, and mount offensives of their own. They then crossed the Suez Canal, surrounded an entire Egyptian army, and began advancing on Cairo to the West and Damascus to the East. At this juncture the Soviet Union threatened to enter the war directly. President Nixon alerted the United States armed forces and forced the Israelis to halt their advance. The United Nations helped to arrange a cease-fire.

Ever since the 1967 war most of the world—much of it undoubtedly influenced by its hunger for Arab oil—had supported the Arab states in their demand for the return of all occupied territories. The Israelis, claiming these territories as necessary buffer zones and bargaining pawns, had refused to give them up without adequate guarantees of security, which under the circumstances were hard to envision. Only the United States and the Netherlands supported Israel.

The Arabs now made full use of their oil weapon; they quadrupled the price of their oil, curtailed production, and placed a complete embargo on its shipment to the United States and the Netherlands. These measures added greatly to the strain of inflation that had long gripped the capitalistic world. Japan and the poorer nations of Asia and Africa were particularly distressed. In order to appease the Arabs the United States put such heavy pressure upon the Israelis to yield to Arab demands that Prime Minister Golda Meir resigned and the Israelis felt that the existence of their state was gravely menaced. A cease-fire agreement, 1974, settled nothing, but opened the way to negotiations.

6. THE EMANCIPATION OF AFRICA

Africa was the last of the continents to rise against European imperialism, and the history of Africa since the end of World War II has been largely the story of emancipation from European domination. France and Great Britain, who held the most territory in Africa, were the first to begin to dismantle their vast empires there.

The end of World War II found France's huge North African empire seething with unrest. Its population, largely Muslim, was agitated by the rampaging Arab nationalism in the Middle East. France, in 1956, granted independence to Morocco and Tunisia. The problem of independence or autonomy for Algeria was much more complex because of the presence there of more than a million French settlers who feared reprisals from the 8 million Muslim Algerians.

In 1954 the smoldering Algerian discontent with French rule burst into open revolt—a revolt that the regular French army was unable to quell. In May 1958 the harassed French army in Algeria, fearful that the government of the Fourth Republic was preparing to grant Algerian independence, mutinied and threatened to set up a military dictatorship in France. This emergency brought about the fall of the Fourth French Republic and the recall of Charles de Gaulle. De Gaulle undertook to restore the authority of the government over the army and to placate both the French and the Algerians in Algeria by means of a long-range program of economic and social improvements.

When it soon became evident that the inflamed Algerian Muslims would accept nothing short of complete independence, De Gaulle decided to take this difficult step. Algerian independence was granted in 1962. Meanwhile, he had granted independence to all the other French colonies, most of which were in Africa, and invited them to form a voluntary union with France. All but one, French Guinea, did so.

Great Britain's experiences in Africa following World War II were quite similar to those of the French. In one colony after another, native populations caught the spirit of nationalism and turned in resentment against their white masters. Native terror bands, notably the Mau Mau in Kenya, made British life and property increasingly unsafe. In 1957 Great Britain granted independence to her Gold Coast colony, which became the Republic of Ghana. This proved to be the first step in the eventual freeing of her remaining African colonies. During the next few years one after another of Britain's African territories were freed, until by 1970 only the southern part of Rhodesia remained and that was in a state of rebellion against Great Britain.

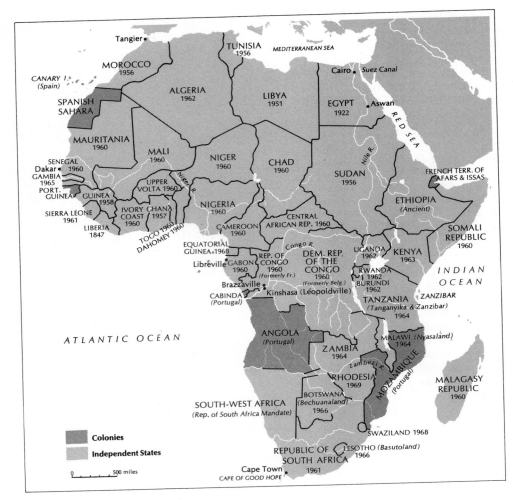

AFRICA 1975

The Dominion of South Africa had, of course, since 1931 (the Statute of Westminster) been completely free. There the prosperous white minority, constituting approximately one-fourth of the total population, clung desperately to its superiority. In 1948 and thereafter the white minority took severe measures to suppress the increasingly restless black majority and to enforce *apartheid* (racial segregation). When in 1961 several of her fellow members of the British Commonwealth censored South Africa because of her racial policies, she withdrew from the Commonwealth, taking her large mandate, South-West Africa, with her.

In 1960 Italy freed Somalia in East Africa and Belgium granted independence to the Congo. Portugal freed her large African colonies in 1974, leaving Fascist Spain the only remaining imperialist nation holding territory in Africa.

The granting of independence, of course, did not bring peace and prosperity to the African people, many of whom were illiterate tribesmen. The boundaries of the African states were drawn in many cases quite arbitrarily by nineteenth-century European imperialists sitting around plush green-topped tables in London or Brussels dividing up the spoils. In the Congo, for instance, tribal warfare flamed up immediately after independence. Russian and Chinese Communist agents moved in to exploit the chaos. UN Secretary-General Dag Hammarskjöld lost his life there in a plane accident while trying to mediate the differences. In Nigeria, the Ibos in the Eastern Region attempted to secede and set up the independent Republic of Biafra. Thousands died in the ensuing struggle, and tens of thousands by starvation. Since the newly freed African people were obviously not ready for democratic government, strong men quickly established themselves as dictators. Only in Kenya was a stable parliamentary system established.

By 1974 Africa's economy was still primarily agricultural despite a sizable development of oil and gas production in Libya, Algeria, and Nigeria, and a beginning of industrialization (mostly foreign) in Ivory Coast. Of course, gold and diamond mining in South Africa was still highly profitable. Africa's rapidly growing population, dependent, for the most part, upon a primitive agriculture, was faced with an increasing threat of hunger and starvation. An unprecedented drought in the huge sub-Sahara region of Northern Africa during the late 1960s and early 1970s brought death by starvation to tens of thousands. Nevertheless, the Africans clearly preferred freedom with its problems to being a part of the "white man's burden."

The expansion of the European world, which began in the fifteenth century, had after five hundred years been very definitely reversed. The non-Western world now challenged the West. And human pride and fecundity threatened both.

7. LATIN AMERICA

Finally, there remains to be examined a large and populous area of the world which is, in a sense, neither East nor West—Latin America. Just as Japan is a highly industrialized Western nation located in the East, Latin America is *in,* but, in many respects, not *of* the West. Her religion and her languages are, of course, Western. But the poverty and the illiteracy of her masses,

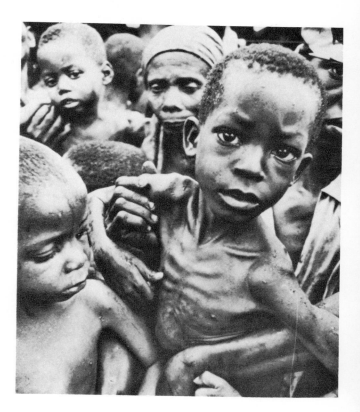

The Nigerian civil war brought unimaginable misery and deprivation to the people of the secessionist province of Biafra. The emergency relief that international organizations managed to get into the country helped but a few of the hundreds of thousands of the starving, most of whom died for lack of food and medical care. *Photo: United Press International*

her underdeveloped economy, and her unstable political institutions more closely resemble Southern Asia and Africa than Western Europe and the United States.

At the end of World War II the governments of the twenty independent Latin American states were all republics in name. In reality, however, most of them were Rightist dictatorships, representing the interests of the well-to-do bourgeoisie, the land-owning classes, and the professional military. The Roman Catholic Church, which during the nineteenth century had been one of the most powerful Rightest forces, had during the twentieth century tended to become much more liberal. In some of the Latin American republics, notably Chile, the Church was now actively engaged in liberal social and economic reform movements. Costa Rica was the most democratic of the republics. In Mexico a stable (though primarily a one-party) democratic regime had since 1934 been pursuing a liberal program of economic, social, and educational reforms.

Throughout most of Latin America the poor, illiterate, and ever more numerous masses became increasingly restive after World War II. Many of them turned to communism, and were encouraged and supported by the Soviet Union. The United States, on the other hand, supported the Rightist governments. In 1954 a military force armed by the United States invaded and overthrew the Leftist government of Guatemala. Ten years later a Rightist military takeover in Brazil was encouraged and applauded by the United States. In 1948 the twenty Latin American "republics" were persuaded to join the United States in an Organization of American States (OAS) for the purpose of resisting outside (Communist) interference. The Latin Americans were primarily interested in economic aid from the United States and were generally disappointed.

In Cuba the policy of the United States backfired. In 1959 the Rightist dictator, Fulgencio Batista, long supported by the United States, was overthrown by the Leftist revolutionary, Fidel Castro. Castro began a sweeping program of social and economic reforms including the seizure of property owned by individuals and corporations of the United States. Fumbling efforts of the United States to overthrow the Castro regime drove it into the arms of the Soviet Union. Cuba became a Communist beachhead in the Western Hemisphere.

In 1970 Chile became the first nation in the world to vote in a Marxist regime. Taking advantage of a split between the conservatives and the moderate liberals, Salvador Allende was elected president (with 36 percent of the vote) and immediately launched a Marxist program. All industrial properties, the biggest of which were owned by United States corporations, were nationalized. The government of the United States determined to destroy the Allende regime. In 1974 the American Central Intelligence Agency admitted that it had spent $11 million bribing Chilean legislators, stirring up labor strife, and supporting rightest elements. In 1973 the Allende regime was overthrown by the professional military which set up a Rightist military dictatorship. Allende and thousands of his followers were executed.

Latin America's writers and artists since World War I have generally reflected these social and political tensions. Many have been Leftists, some have been Marxists. Furthermore, they have tended to break with their European heritage and to glorify their pre-European native cultures—Indianismo. Gabriela Mistral (1889–1957) and Pablo Neruda (1904–1973), Chilean poets, and Miguel Angel Asturias (1889–1974), a Guatemalan novelist, have won the Nobel prize for literature. Neruda was a Marxist. Jorge Luis Borges (1899–) of Argentina has been a Nobel candidate. His subtle and complex poetry and short stories have won world-wide acclaim. He is a liberal and a friend of the United States. Diego Rivera (1886–1957) of Mexico was one of the great muralists of all time. His work glorifies Mexican native Indians and also Marxism. Because of the latter, his murals were removed from Rockefeller Center in New York. Latin America's most significant twentieth-century composer has probably been Heitor Villa-Lobos (1887–1959) of Brazil, whose modern rhythms reflect a renewed interest in the native Indian heritage—an important facet of recent Latin American nationalism.

As the last quarter of the twentieth century opened, Latin America was an area of sharp and dangerous contrasts. Rich natural resources were not being developed and used for the benefit of the rapidly increasing population, which, for the most part, was poor and illiterate. Great modern cities such as Mexico City and Sao Paulo, which rivaled New York and Chicago in size and modernity, stood surrounded by wretched hovels and a depressed countryside. The government of the United States was ready, even eager, to offer financial and technical assistance, but as in Southern Asia and other parts of the world, she continued to support Rightist military regimes that were more interested in retaining their power than in aiding their people.

Suggested Reading

Japan Since 1945

*E. O. Reischauer, *The United States and Japan* (Compass). Lucid picture of Japan since World War II by American ambassador to Japan.

*R. Hall, Jr., *Japan: Industrial Power of Asia* (Searchlight). Excellent study of Japan's remarkable economic recovery.

Rise of Red China

*J. Fairbank, *The United States and China* (Compass). An excellent history of China and her culture and of Chinese-American relations.

*S. Schram, *Mao Tse-tung* (Penguin). Best biography of Mao in English to date.

K. Mehnert, *Peking and Moscow* (1964). Lucid account of the Sino-Soviet rift.

Korean War

*R. Leckie, *Conflict: The History of the Korean War, 1950–1953* (Avon). The best brief account.

Revolt of Southern Asia

*B. Lamb, *India: A World in Transition* (Praeger). A useful brief study.

*M. Gandhi, *Autobiography: The Story of My Experiments with Truth* (Beacon). Reveals the mind of India's chief liberator.

*J. Nehru, *Toward Freedom* (Beacon). Authoritative account of the launching of an independent Indian nation by its chief founder.

*J. McAlister, *Vietnam: The Origins of Revolution* (Doubleday). A scholarly study.

*D. Halberstam, *The Best and the Brightest* (Fawcett). Detailed but fascinating account of the gradual involvement of the United States in the Vietnam morass.

Embattled Middle East

*S. Rondot, *Changing Patterns of the Middle East* (Praeger). A useful study.

*H. Sachar, *The Course of Modern Jewish History* (Dell). Valuable background material for understanding Israel.

Emancipation of Africa

G. P. Murdoch, *Africa: Its Peoples and Their Culture History* (1959). A scholarly study.

*P. Bohannan, *Africa and Africans* (American Museum Science Books). A perceptive and lucid survey.

*H. Kitchen (ed.), *A Handbook of African Affairs* (University Place). The story of the struggle of the various African peoples for independence.

Latin America

*F. Tannenbaum, *Ten Keys to Latin America* (Vintage). Penetrating study of contemporary Latin America by a leading authority, written for the layman.

Conclusion

*A. Toynbee, *A Study of History*, 12 vols. (Galaxy), abridged by D. Somervell, 2. vols. (Laurel) is the most prodigious effort ever made to synthesize and make a meaningful pattern of all human history. The student who reads Somervell's excellent abridgement will be challenged and stimulated.

*W. McNeill, *The Rise of the West: A History of the Human Community* (University of Chicago). A provocative synthesis of world history and civilization. A very different interpretation from that of Toynbee.

*A. N. Whitehead, *Science and the Modern World* (Free Press). A brilliant analysis of the place of science in the twentieth century.

Retrospect

The Europe of 1914 was shattered politically and socially by the two world wars, and much of its science and technology were perverted to destructive purposes. Both wars were essentially the manifestation and the fruits of malignant nationalism. Both were centered around Germany, and it appears that Germany would have won both wars but for the intervention of the United States.

World War I began as a national power showdown between the German Empire on the one hand and France, Russia, and Great Britain on the other. It resulted in the destruction of the German, Russian, and Ottoman empires and the disintegration of the multilingual Austro-Hungarian national state. The British and French empires were both seriously weakened, as indeed were Britain and France themselves. Efforts to make a durable peace and to set up an international organization to keep the peace shattered on the rocks of national self-interests.

During World War I and largely as a result of it, the pioneer Marxist regime was set up in Russia. Quite a different, but equally antiliberal type of dictatorship—fascism—came to power in Germany, Italy, and Japan. These three militant Fascist powers armed themselves and banded together for world conquest. The only powers capable of stopping them—the three great liberal democracies, the United States, Great Britain, and France—were bogged down in depression and disillusionment and were unwilling to cooperate with each other. The League of Nations, without their support, could do nothing. Attempts on the part of the democratic powers to appease the Fascist aggressors resulted in World War II.

During the first two years of World War II, Germany overran all of continental Europe west of Moscow except Sweden, Switzerland, Portugal, and Spain (a Fascist friend). Great Britain narrowly escaped defeat. The most productive part of the Soviet Union was conquered and devastated. By the end of 1941 Japan, thinking the hour of Fascist triumph was at hand, attacked the United States. As in 1917, the entry into the war of the United States, with her enormous industrial resources, turned the tide. The stubborn resistance of the British and the Russian people, of course, made the turning possible. Italy surrendered in 1943, and Germany and Japan two years later. The surrender of Japan was hastened by the dropping of two American atomic bombs, which destroyed two of her major cities. Much of Europe and Japan lay devastated.

As World War II was ending, the victors set up the United Nations. It was obvious to nearly everyone that now that nuclear weapons had arrived, the curbing of irresponsible nationalism was a necessity. The greatest obstacle to the establishment of peace was the intense rivalry of the two remaining world powers, the United States and the Soviet Union, who competed fiercely and dangerously for world hegemony. Meanwhile, the peoples of Asia and Africa freed themselves from all but the last vestiges of Western imperialism. When the oppressed masses in the undeveloped parts of the world attempted to overthrow their own ruling classes and seize a better share of this world's goods and privileges the Soviet Union tried to move in and lead them to communism. The United States, on the other hand, opposing the Soviet Union and communism, invariably supported the Rightest regimes seeking to maintain the status quo.

CONCLUSION
WESTERN CIVILIZATION IN THE TWENTIETH CENTURY

$\mathbf{A}$s we come closer to the present, it becomes more difficult to see and understand and write history. Current events—yesterday's headlines—are not history. Time must elapse before we can gain the perspective necessary to grasp their significance. In mountainous terrain the adjacent hill towers above us and looks big. But as we move away from it, higher hills loom up, and finally lofty mountain ranges emerge, turning our hill into a mole hill. Yet, bearing these pitfalls in mind, let us attempt to identify and explore the highlights of Western civilization in the twentieth century.

1. WAR

Much as we wish it were not so, the history of the twentieth century, perhaps more than any other century, has been dominated by war. World Wars I and II and the lesser wars of the

Guernica by Pablo Picasso. This large mural in black and white by one of the greatest artists of the twentieth century captures some of the worst features of the century—war, terror, brutality, disjointedness, lack of direction, and despair. Guernica was a small Spanish town destroyed by the German air force during the Spanish Civil War. *Photo: Museum of Modern Art*

century not only killed and maimed their tens of millions, but also destroyed nations, empires, and economic systems. Furthermore, they brutalized manners and morals and left in their wake a spirit of disillusionment that strongly influenced philosophy, religion, literature, and the arts. With the advent of nuclear and biological weapons near the end of World War II, war became intolerable. By 1970 the United States and the Soviet Union possessed nuclear bombs that were more than a thousand times as powerful as the two that destroyed Hiroshima and Nagasaki. Each of the two superpowers had stockpiled enough nuclear weapons to kill all the citizens of the other many times over (the explosive power of the two stockpiles was believed to be equivalent to some fifteen tons of TNT for each person on the earth), and yet they continued to pour a major part of their wealth and resources into this race of death. And if nuclear weapons should for any reason prove to be insufficient, wonderful new biological and chemical weapons were reported to be stored and ready for use. War, therefore, was everybody's business.

War in the twentieth century was closely tied to nationalism. During the course of the century empires crumbled, and economic and social systems weakened and changed, but nationalism continued on unabated. Even communism, which was internationalist in theory, became increasingly nationalistic. During the decade of the 1960s the United Nations became less effective in dealing with international problems as nation after nation turned inward for the solution of its own problems, and disarmament talks foundered repeatedly on the rock of national self-interest.

2. TECHNOLOGY

Apart from war, there can be little doubt that Western man's greatest obsession since 1914 has been with technology and science. Industrialization has continued at an ever-increasing pace. Consumer goods have become so plentiful in the Western world and the desire for them has been fanned to such an extent by the advertising industry that by the 1960s, people were rioting over conditions that would be thought luxurious in many parts of the world and that would have been considered normal in the West a few generations earlier. Industrialization was always accompanied by urbanization. At the opening of the century, the great majority of the people in the Western world still lived in rural areas or in small towns. By 1974 only 5 percent of the people in the United States were farmers, and much of their work was mechanized. But people were not just moving from the farms to the cities; the total population was rapidly increasing. At the opening of the modern era (1500) the population of the world is estimated to have been about one-half billion. Three centuries later (1800) it had doubled. One century later (1900) it had doubled again. By 1974 it had more than doubled again and was close to 4 billion. If the present acceleration continues, it will double again by the end of this century. To some observers, the threat of this uncontrolled population increase seemed to be greater than the threat of nuclear destruction.

In July of 1969, man walked on the moon. The United States' Apollo 11 moon mission was launched from Cape Kennedy July 16, 1969; the moon landing was successfully made July 20, and four days later the three astronauts splashed down in the Pacific Ocean. This photograph was taken on the moon. *Photo: NASA*

One of the most serious by-products of the increasing industrialization of the Western world and the increase in population of the whole world was the destruction and pollution of the earth's natural resources. Industrial wastes were poured with abandon into the lakes, the streams, the oceans, and the atmosphere. The decades following World War II were in a real sense the Age of the Bulldozer in the Western world. These monsters chewed up and gouged out hills and mountains, beauty spots and historic sites, forests and farmlands. Millions of productive acres were covered with highways and suburbs. The automobiles, the television sets, and other creature comforts of the Western world, therefore, did not come without a price.

3. SCIENCE

While the consuming masses in the technologically advanced Western world were threatening to consume their own habitat, the intelligentsia of the West were consumed by their fascination with science. During the course of the twentieth century, interest in science has overshadowed all other intellectual interests and has drawn the best brains in the West away from the other disciplines. The main thrust in physics was to continue the probing of the atom, which was begun in the nineteenth century, to discover the last truths concerning the nature of matter. The results tended to be disillusioning. Albert Einstein had undermined the Newtonian world of physical stability with his relativity theory (see p. 547). A more shattering blow was delivered by Max Planck (1858–1947). Although he published his quantum theory in 1900, its full impact was not realized until the decades following World War I. According to this theory, energy is not transmitted in a steady measurable stream, as had long been supposed, but in little unpredictable leaps or packets (quanta), and the behavior of subatomic particles is so irregular and complex that man can never fathom the ultimate secrets of nature by objective observation. This left the materialists and positivists feeling alienated and alone in an uncertain, inscrutable universe. Physicists did, however, find out

enough about the physical universe to produce the atom bomb (1945), orbit the earth (1957), and land on the moon (1969).

The most exciting discoveries in the biological sciences were in the field of genetics. In 1953 the nature of the complicated DNA molecule, which controls the pattern of all living things was discovered. It is assumed that by tampering with this molecule new forms of life may be created, and that given characteristics in man can be controlled. The most beneficial discoveries in the field of biological science during the twentieth century have been those that prevent and cure human ailments. Shortly after World War I viruses were discovered. These organisms are so small that it is not certain whether they are animate or inanimate, but they were proved to be the cause of many diseases, including infantile paralysis, influenza, and the common cold. Vaccines were developed to combat successfully the infantile paralysis virus and a number of others—but the common cold still plagues most of humanity. During the decade of the 1930s the antibiotics, penicillin and the sulfa drugs, were discovered. These "miracle drugs" kill or control the bacteria causing many human infections. Since World War II, drugs have been found useful in treating mental illness, and artificial and transplanted kidneys and hearts have saved or lengthened many lives. The chief drawback in the application of these wonderful discoveries has been their high and continually soaring cost and the shortage of trained personnel to administer them. Some nations, notably Great Britain and Sweden, have recognized the enormous importance of public health by developing comprehensive programs of national health insurance. Communist regimes, of course, have always made the practice of medicine a public rather than a private matter.

In the social sciences, psychology strove to be an experimental laboratory science. Nevertheless, the influence of Freud (see p. 549) continued to be strong. The most important figure in economics between 1914 and 1974 was John Maynard Keynes (1883–1946). In 1936, in the midst of the Great Depression, Keynes published *The General Theory of Employment, Interest and Money* advocating government regulation of the capitalistic system. In times of recession the government should increase the supply of money in circulation by lowering interest rates and by deficit spending on public works. In times of inflationary boom it should restrict the money supply by raising interest rates and by other means. Liberals, not only in Keynes' native Britain but throughout the capitalistic world, accepted his theories, as indeed did many conservatives. But by 1974 it appeared that the Keynesian treatment was too mild to control runaway inflation, which continued to harass and endanger all capitalistic economies. Almost everyone with goods or services to sell—from food and fuel to medicine—had learned how to organize monopolies, create shortages, and set prices.

Of all the social scientists, the sociologists and the anthropologists, as in the late nineteenth century, were the most optimistic and energetic. Like all other social scientists, they attempted to apply the scientific method to the study of human behavior. Max Weber (1864–1920) of Germany set up ideal types or models as a method of analyzing scientifically various sociological problems—a method that has been widely used ever since. Karl Mannheim (1893–1947), a refugee from Nazi Germany to Great Britain, proclaimed the sociology of knowledge—that all ideas are the result of social influence. Anthropologists tended to move from their earlier skull measurements and other physical features to the concept that differing cultures are based essentially on differing ways of interpreting experience and that one culture is not necessarily superior to another. However much the various social scientists might disagree with one another on matters of detail, they were virtually unanimous in agreeing on the importance of religion—not as a manifestation of the divine but as a man-made institution of great social impact. As in the late nineteenth century, they continued their hostility toward the traditional religions such as Judaism and Christianity which were devoted to the worship of God and the quest for divine truth and guidance.

During and after World War II technology and science combined to produce the computer—the mechanical brain. Faith in this device became such a rage, and so many billions were put into

it, that some would call the period since 1945 the Age of the Computer. Since it is a hybrid—a cross between science and technology—perhaps we should call it the thinking mule.

4. PHILOSOPHY

Speculative thought in the Western world during the twentieth century was in large measure a continuation and further development of the philosophy of disenchantment of the late nineteenth century. The factors that had given rise to that philosophy—the depersonalizing effects of natural science in general and Darwinism in particular, the uprooting of the masses by industrialization and urbanization, materialism spawned by technology, and the decline in influence of the Christian religion—continued with increased tempo throughout the first three quarters of the twentieth century. To these factors were added the disillusionment resulting from the two world wars, the Great Depression, and the tensions of the cold war. The influence of all these forces is reflected in the most popular school of philosophy in the twentieth century— existentialism. Existentialism drew heavily from Friedrich Nietzsche (see pp. 562, 591), who was violently anti-Christian and antidemocratic. When Nietzsche said "God is dead," he meant that there are no absolutes. Existential philosophy was also influenced by the mid-nineteenth-century Danish theologian, Sören Kierkegaard, who rejected systematized and institutionalized Christianity in favor of personal inspiration and individual commitment. The most influential spokesman for existentialism has been Jean-Paul Sartre (1905–). Sartre defines his doctrine as an attempt to draw out all the logical implications of a consistent atheism. He rejects all absolute moral laws and values. Man is a finite but free creature responsible only to himself in a universe devoid of purpose. This sophisticated and often vague cult represents a revolt not only against Christianity, but also against such twentieth-century absolutes as Marxism and fascism.

Somewhat more optimistic and humanistic than Sartre and his fellow existentialists were Alfred North Whitehead (1861–1947) and Bertrand Russell (1872–1970) of Great Britain. On the eve of World War I they proclaimed a system of analytic philosophy that spurned any concept that could not be rationally and mathematically expressed. Unlike Sartre, who denied the existence of any meaning, they sought for a rational meaning behind existence. Both were tolerant men. Whitehead became a professor at Harvard University and eventually returned to Christianity, believing that philosophy begins and ends with wonder. Russell, however, became the twentieth century's chief proclaimer of atheism.

5. LITERATURE

The literature of the twentieth century, like the philosophy, was essentially an outgrowth and continuation of the literature of the late nineteenth century. A number of the great realistic writers of the period 1871–1914, such as Shaw and Dreiser, lived and wrote until the middle of the twentieth century. The realism that had shocked many Victorians was succeeded by the more starkly naked naturalism. In the United States Sinclair Lewis (1885–1951), much like Theodore Dreiser, ridiculed both the hypocritical and "Puritanical" bourgeoisie and the stupid, vulgar masses. Babbitt, Elmer Gantry, and Arrowsmith, deflated heroes in Sinclair Lewis' novels by those titles, became stereotypes of typical Americans in the minds of thousands of untypical American readers of books. Eugene O'Neill (1888–1953) wrote plays in which the dramatic tension was maintained by psychological conflict (like those of Anton Chekhov—see p. 594) rather than development of plot and action. Ernest Hemingway (1898–1961) was an existentialist, entertaining his readers with his crisp and sophisticated prose. William Faulkner (1897–1962) with greater depth and artistry tore away the veil woven by civilization to conceal the perverted and animal-like nature of ordinary people. He developed a complex stream-of-consciousness technique.

In Europe, James Joyce (1882–1941), an Irish expatriate in Paris, and T. S. Eliot (1888–1965), an American expatriate in London, developed still further the stream-of-consciousness technique, placing both words and thoughts out of sequence, with dramatic effect. Eliot was one of the few great writers of the twentieth century who revered mystic religion and tradition. He

became a member of the Anglican Church and took seventeenth-century classicism as his literary model. Albert Camus (1913–1960) was in word and deed an apostle of existentialism. A Frenchman born in Algeria, he played a daring role in the French underground in World War II. Like Hemingway's and his own characters, he sought identity as a visceral creative individual in an amoral and purposeless universe.

Earlier in the century, Franz Kafka (1883–1924), a German Jew in Prague, depicted the alienation and frustrations of an intellectual in the World War I era. The haunting, ambiguous quality of his novels symbolizes the uncertainties and fears of his age. Most of his work was published after his death, and it is significant that he enjoyed wide popularity only after World War II, particularly in Germany. Another German novelist, Hermann Hesse (1877–1962), who resembles Kafka in many ways, was equally popular among American college students during the 1950s and 1960s for probably the same reasons. We have already taken note of Boris Pasternak (1890–1960), the Soviet Union's greatest man of letters in the twentieth century. His *Doctor Zhivago*, written in the grand manner of Tolstoy and Dostoevski, portraying the depressive effects of a totalitarian regime on the sensitive individual, was denounced and censored by his government. Of all the great literary figures of the twentieth century, probably the least revolutionary in style and content was Thomas Mann (1875–1955). In his magnificent prose he always revealed his reverence for man. Yet even he was clearly influenced by the philosophers of disenchantment, Schopenhauer and Nietzsche. He was a refugee from Nazi Germany to the United States and eventually to Switzerland. In his last major novel, *Doctor Faustus*, Mann describes the corruption of European humanism in his lifetime. With few exceptions, Western literature in the twentieth century was a literature of protest.

6. THE FINE ARTS

The fine arts in the Western world in the twentieth century, like the philosophy and the literature, have proceeded generally along the guidelines laid down by the artists and writers of the late nineteenth century—disenchantment, rejection of tradition, search for new values. These characteristics have become intensified by the materialism and the uncertainties of the twentieth century.

Without a doubt, the most gifted and influential painter of the twentieth century was Pablo Picasso (1881–1973). A Spaniard, he emigrated to Paris as a young man. There he was influenced by the French post-Impressionists (see pp. 594–595). In order to penetrate the surface and reveal the inner reality of things, Picasso would take his subjects apart—arms, heads, violin parts—and rearrange and distort them for maximum effect. Early in the century, at about the same time that young Whitehead and Russell were proclaiming their analytic philosophy based upon mathematics, Picasso introduced cubism into the world of painting. This was an effort, suggested by Cézanne, to demonstrate the solidity of the material universe by portraying the geometric composition of objects—cubes, cones, and cylinders.

Most twentieth-century painters have attempted to follow or surpass Picasso. Generally they have turned inward, rejecting all tradition, sometimes even disregarding aesthetics, and drawing and painting lines, shapes, and combinations of color to suit their whim or fancy. This type of painting is often called abstract expressionism. Picasso was obviously a genius. Whether his would-be imitators, so busy smashing all tradition and form and values with their depersonalized, disjointed, abstract painting were doing more than reflecting the materialistic times in which they live remains for future critics to determine.

Twentieth-century architecture has been almost entirely in the functional style which was developed near the end of the nineteenth century by Louis Henry Sullivan (see p. 597). Sullivan's most illustrious student was Frank Lloyd Wright (1869–1959). Like his teacher, Wright believed that function is the sole purpose of architecture. He further insisted that form should conform to the materials used and to the setting. He made brilliant use of the cantilever (a projecting member supported at only one end) to achieve striking horizontal lines and an unobstructed spaciousness. These effects were made possible by the tensile strength of steel. Wright combined artistic skill with a Shavian scorn for traditional values and institutions. The most spectacular monuments of functional architecture are, of course, the great bridges and skyscrapers, most of them in the United States.

Twentieth-century music, too, was for the most part a continuation and development of styles formulated during the period 1871–1914. Richard Strauss (1864–1949) and Igor Stravinsky (1882–1971), two of the originators of modern music, lived far into the twentieth century. During the course of the century, music in the Western world became increasingly dissonant, atonal, noisy, and experimental. These qualities probably found their ultimate composer in the Viennese Arnold Schoenberg (1874–1951), who abolished melody and key and replaced the seven-tone scale with one of twelve tones. Probably America's most original contribution to modern music was jazz, a development in which George Gershwin (1898–1937) played an important part. Some other great twentieth-century composers are Béla Bartók (1881–1945) in Hungary, Paul Hindemith (1895–1963) in Germany, and Serge Prokofiev (1891–1953) and Dimitri Shostakovich (1906–) in the Soviet Union.

The prosperous masses, however, with their theater tickets and television sets demanded something more tuneful. After World War II, lyrics from "My Fair Lady" and "The Sound of Music" could be heard on pocket-size transistors throughout the Western world. Meanwhile, the younger masses gyrated to the sound of rock and roll by the Beatles and their successors. Granting membership to the Beatles in the Most Excellent Order of the British Empire in 1965 by Queen Elizabeth II must surely be of historical significance, whatever that significance may be.

7. RELIGION

Theology in the Western world during the twentieth century for the most part reflected the materialism of the age and the influence of existentialist philosophy. Strong efforts were made to update Christian theology by making it a secular philosophy. Paul Tillich (1886–1965), a German Protestant who spent his latter years in the United States, conceived of God as "ultimate truth" and "inner reality." Such traditional terms as "original sin," "salvation," "forgiveness," "immortality," and "atonement" were useful symbols actually referring to personal and social ethics. Harvey Cox (1929–) of Harvard University, in his widely read *The Secular City* (1965), defined Christianity as an endless social revolution. During the decade of the 1960s the phrase "God is dead" enjoyed popularity among quite a number of divinity school teachers and students. The phrase apparently meant a wide variety of things to its various users, including the belief that God is dead. On the other hand, a few powerful voices called for a return to an enlightened orthodoxy, notably Karl Barth (1886–1968) in Switzerland and Reinhold Niebuhr (1892–1971) in the United States, who were neo-Calvinists. God, they said, created the universe and runs it for his holy purpose, but man's selfish pride separates him from God. Only the Christian religion can remove that pride and bring man into God's purpose. Jacques Maritain (1882–1973) in France called for a return to the teachings of St. Thomas Aquinas. These learned men contributed dignity to the continuing claims of traditional Christianity.

But the Christian churches continued to suffer a decline in influence. Many congregations adopted all sorts of devices, including rock sessions, to try to appeal to the young. Strenuous efforts were made to restore the lost unity of Christendom in order that the Christian church might face its enemies with a united front. In 1948 leaders of hundreds of Protestant and Orthodox denominations met in Geneva and set up the World Council of Churches. The most spectacular step in this direction was taken by Pope

John XXIII (1958–1963), head of the largest body of Christians, who called the Second Vatican Council (1962–1965) in the spirit of Christian tolerance and unity. Although John XXIII died during the first year of the council and was succeeded by Paul VI (1963–), who was a less vigorous innovator, the Second Vatican Council introduced an ecumenical spirit into the Roman Catholic Church and a willingness to modernize the ritual and discipline that had been formalized by the Council of Trent in the sixteenth century. Whether such means can check the decline in influence of the Christian religion in the Western world, we cannot know. The dominant concerns of Western man as of 1974 were undoubtedly secular—war, science, technology.

Like Leo XIII, Pope John XXIII (1958–1963) undertook to bring the Roman Church into line with modern conditions. Considered by some observers to be the most important pope in modern times, John XXIII introduced a new spirit of tolerance in the Church which might lead eventually to the restoration of Christian unity. *Photo: United Press International*

8. MANNERS AND MORALS

The obsession of Western man with material values has taken its toll on his traditional manners and morals. The relentless march of technology with its accompanying urbanization, while bringing to the masses many creature comforts, has robbed millions of their manual skills and social contacts, and lost them in the lonely crowd. At the higher levels of industry, corporate man has tended to lose his independence and individual identity. The intricacy and specialization of twentieth-century science has tended to depersonalize the scientist. Furthermore, as the scientist has probed ever more deeply into the nature of the material universe, his findings have led to increased uncertainty rather than to the certainty that was sought and expected. War, of course, has always brutalized those who are engaged in it, but the wars of the twentieth century have vastly exceeded those of the past in size and destructiveness. Most of mankind apparently will discipline their bodies only under duress, and when forced to do so by war or great crisis, will "let themselves go," as it were, afterward. For instance, the Reign of Terror during the French Revolution was followed by the excesses of the Thermidorian Reaction. World War I was followed by the Jazz Age and the so-called lost generation. The expected letdown after World War II was postponed by the Cold War tensions and full-scale wars in China, Korea, and Vietnam. However, in the late 1960s a wave of anarchy swept across the world. The sensitive philosophers, writers, and artists had foreseen and foretold it. Government at all levels staggered. Even national sovereignty was challenged as states and provinces, Flemings, Welsh, Ulsterites, French Canadians, and Biafrans asserted themselves. The crime rate mounted. Political parties and labor unions found themselves unable to control their members. The young, in particular, lacking physical outlets for their excess vitamins, and finding few if any spiritual and moral standards to guide them in this age of anxiety, revolted not only against their parents and teachers and all officials, but also against traditional standards of social and moral behavior. By 1974, Western civilization and its institutions, which had been so long developing—the family, the universities, the courts of law, the church, the state, traditions of social and moral behavior—were being severely tested.

INDEX

Chiang Kai-shek, 648, 673–676
Chiaroscuro, 418–419
Chicago, 490
Child labor, 502
Chile, 688
China: trade with Rome, 125–126; trade with Muslims, 172; medieval Christian missionaries in, 241; trade with West during Middle Ages, 242; in Mongul Empire, 247; repel Dutch in seventeenth century, 402; Buddhism, 407; and nineteenth-century colonialism, 515; isolation of, 571–572; and Western imperialism, 572–575; rise of militant nationalism, 575; attacked by Japan in World War II; 648; Communist Revolution in, 673–677. *See also* People's Republic of China
Chivalry, 202, 216, 245, 286, 336
Chopin, Frédéric, 537–538
Chrétien de Troyes, 266
Christ. *See* Jesus
Christian IV, king of Denmark, 356
Christian Democratic party, in German Federal Republic, 663–666
Christianity: influenced by Zoroastrianism, 53; influenced by Greek mystery cults, 81; and mystery religions, 101; origins and early growth, 144–152; support of Constantine, 152; in fourth century, 153–154; during Germanic invasions, 158–160; and emergence of new civilizations in Early Middle Ages, 164; influence on Byzantine Empire, 167–168; influence on Muhammad, 170; conversion of Franks to, 176; in Early Middle Ages, 179–183; and Carolingian renaissance, 187–193; in Anglo-Saxon England, 193; spread of, in Carolingian age, 193, 200; in feudal society, 196, 199, 200, 202, 204; influence on culture of High Middle Ages, 207–208; eleventh-century reform movement, 221–222; and investiture struggle, 222–225; and medieval missionaries, 241–242; and the crusades, 245–248; during High Middle Ages, 250, 258, 273; role in medieval cultural life,

260–271; problems in Late Middle Ages, 288–295, 297; quest for unity in fifteenth-century Spain, 301; versus Renaissance humanism, 321–322; and Italian Renaissance, 330; challenge of Northern Renaissance to, 331–333, 335, 339; and Calvinism, 344–346; introduced in Russia, 394; and modern science, 431–432, 484; conflict with Enlightenment thinkers, 432, 433, 434–435; and French Revolution, 460; as factor in European imperialism, 571; challenges to, during second phase of Industrial Revolution, 582–589; Nietzsche on, 591; in Soviet Union, 621–622; and Fascism, 626; and existentialism, 694; decline of, in twentieth century, 697. *See also* Orthodox Church; Protestantism; Roman Catholic Church
Christian socialism, 588
Chungking, 676
Church councils, origin, 147
Church fathers, 159–160
Churchill, John, duke of Marlborough, 386
Churchill, Winston: role in World War I, 609; role in World War II, 644–645, 653; role at Yalta Conference, 658–659; return to power in 1951, 667; opposes Indian independence, 679
Church of England, 346, 377, 378
Church of New Jerusalem, 422
Church of S. Apollinare, Ravenna, 159
Church-state relations: in Roman Empire, 145–146, 152, 158; in Byzantine Empire, 165, 167; in Germanic kingdoms, 180; in Carolingian age, 187, 188–190, 191–193; in Anglo-Saxon England, 194; in Holy Roman Empire, 219, 220, 221–225; in medieval England, 230, 232, 233, 234; in medieval France, 235, 239; in medieval Spain, 243; during Reformation of High Middle Ages, 258; and medieval political theory, 264; in Late Middle Ages, 273, 276–277, 288–291, 295; in Russia, under Peter the Great, 395; and Hinduism, 406; in revolutionary America,

446; in revolutionary France, 456, 460; in France, under Napoleon, 465; in France, under Charles X, 480; and nature of nineteenth-century liberalism, 499, 582–583; in Mexico, 515; and unification of Italy, 519, 520; and Third French Republic, 554; in German Empire, 563; in Soviet Union, 621–622; in Fascist Italy, 626; in Nazi Germany, 630–631; in Latin America, 687–688
Cicero, 115–116, 117, 130, 133
Cid, The, 201
Cimon, 73
Circuit court system, 232
Cisalpine Gaul, 111
Cisterian Order, 255, 257
Citeaux, 255
Cities: growth of, in High Middle Ages, 212–213, 214–216; medieval Italian, 210, 221, 225, 227, 278; medieval Spanish, 243
"Citizen King," 505
City-states: Mesopotamian, 8–10, 13, 14; Phoenician, 40; Greek, 60–78, 80, 95–96, 109–110, 111; Roman, 104, 125, 141, 146; and rise of Christianity, 146–147; medieval Italian, 278, 282, 312; Mayan, 315; Swahili, 407; Italian, during Renaissance, 482
Civil Code of Napoleon, 465
Civil Constitution of the Clergy, 456
Civil Rights: struggle for, in United States, 669
Civil War, American, 518
Clans: Minoan, 29; Indo-European, 32; Greek, 60–61, 64, 65; Germanic, 154; Viking, 192
Clarendon Code, 384
Clarendon, earl of, 384
Classical style: and Italian Renaissance literature, 323; and French literature, 415; and English literature, 415–416; in music, 419–431; compared to romanticism, 530, 532
Classical theory of economics, 495
Class struggle, principle of Marxian socialism, 558
Claudius, 122
Clay, Henry, 504, 516, 517
Clay, General Lucius D., 663
Clayton Anti-Trust Act, 553
Cleisthenes, 65–66

relations with Ottoman Empire, 576, 577; conflict with France over Morocco, 578–579. *See also* Germany

German Federal Republic, established, 663–666; and NATO, 670

Germanic invasion, 155–158

Germanic kingdoms: establishment in Roman Empire, 154–158, 160; development in Early Middle Ages, 176–184

Germans: and the Roman Empire, 120, 124, 142, 154, 155; civilization at time of invasions of Roman Empire, 154–155; invasions, 155–158; conversion to Christianity, 160. *See* Germanic kingdoms

Germany: kingdom established by Treaty of Verdun, 192, 219; under Carolingians, 193; feudalism in, 200, 225; colonization of, in High Middle Ages, 209; medieval trade, 210, 211; founding of Holy Roman Empire, 219; under Otto and his successors, 219–222; during investiture struggle, 222–225; under Hohenstauffens, 225–227; political decentralization in Late Middle Ages, 276–277; and Hanseatic League, 285; economic conditions in Late Middle Ages, 284–286; relations with papacy in Late Middle Ages, 289; failure to emerge as national state at beginning of modern period, 306–308, 310; establishment of hereditary states, 308; and Northern Renaissance, 331, 336–337; and Lutheranism, 342–344; and Protestant Reformation, 347, 350, 353; and religious wars of Roman Catholic Reformation, 355; during Thirty Years' War, 356–361; Mongol invasion, 394; and Congress of Vienna, 475; during age of Metternich, 480–482; and Industrial Revolution, 493; during Revolution of 1848, 507–508; triumph of nationalism in, and unification of, 523–529; war with Denmark, 525; during Franco-German War, 527–529; and creation of empire, 529, 561–566, 572, 574, 576, 578–579; nature of malignant nationalism

in, 561–562; role in World War I, 602–611; and Treaty of Versailles, 609–611, 626–627, 631; and League of Nations, 613; and National Socialism, 628–631; role in World War II, 640–653; and Yalta Agreements, 658; post-World War II Soviet-American conflicts over, 662–666. *See also* Holy Roman Empire

Gerousia, 67–68

Gershwin, George, 696

Gestapo, 630

Ghana, 407

Gibbon, Edward, 119

Gibraltar, 374, 409, 580

Gideon, 41

Gilbert, Sir Humphrey, 334

Giotto, 324, 325

Girondins, 457, 458, 459

Giscard d'Estaing, Valery, 668

Gizeh, 19, 27

Gladstone, William E., 502, 503, 553

Glorious Revolution, 385–386

Glosses, medieval, 264

Gobineau, Comte Joseph Arthur de, 562

Godwin, earl of Wessex, 229

Goebbels, Paul Joseph, 628, 630

Goering, Herman, 628

Goethe, Johann Wolfgang von, 334, 416, 534, 535

Golan Heights, 684

Gold Coast, 408, 685

Golden Bull of 1356, 277

Golden Horde, 394

Goliardic poetry, 265

Gompers, Samuel, 557

"Good emperors," 122–124, 140

Gordon, Charles, 574

Gorky, Maxim, 594

Goshen, 40

Gothic style, 260–261, 267–268, 269, 270, 532, 537

Gottfried von Strasbourg, 266

Gounod, Charles François, 538

Goya y Lucientes, Francisco José de, 418

Grace, medieval doctrine of, 253

Gramont, Duc de, 527

Granada, 243, 282, 301, 309

Grand Alliance, 374

Grand jury, in medieval England, 232–233

Granicus, battle of, 92

Gratian, 253, 264

Gravitation, 429

Great Awakening, 422, 440

Great Britain: creation of, under Act of Union, 386; role in Seven Years' War, 391–393; conflicts with American colonies, 441–443; and American Revolution, 443–445; and French Revolution, 458; and Peace of Amiens (1802), 465; war with Napoleon, 466, 469; at Congress of Vienna, 474–477; and Metternich system, 477–478; intervention in Greek revolt against Turks, 479; during first phase of Industrial Revolution, 488–491, 493–495; in Crimean War, 513, 514; growth of democracy during second phase of Industrial Revolution, 553–554; and rise of militant nationalism, 568–569; imperialism in China, 572; imperialism in India, 576–577; imperialism in Africa, 578; Empire, 579–581; role in World War I, 602–611; and League of Nations, 611–613, 638–639; relations with Soviet Union, 622–623; between two world wars, 635–636; role in World War II, 643–653; and Yalta Agreements, 658; since World War II, 666–667, 670–671; involvement in Middle East, 683; involvement in Africa, 685–686. *See also* England

Great Depression, in United States, 635

Great Elector, Frederick William, 389–390

Great Fear, 454

Great Lakes, 371

Great Leap Forward, 677

Great Schism, 278, 289, 341

Great Wall of China, 571–572

Great Western, 490

Grebel, Conrad, 349

Greece, modern: role in World War I, 603–606, 611; role in World War II, 646; Soviet threat to, 660–661; and NATO, 670

Greek League, 71

Greek Orthodox Church, 167, 247, 284, 394

Greeks: influenced by Minoans, 29; trade with Phoenicians, 40; influenced by Lydians, 49; war with Persia, 50, 52; influence on North Africa, 57; influence on

Vienna, 475; attacked by Nazis, 644; since World War II, 670, 671. *See also* Dutch

Neustria, 186

Nevada, 516

Neva River, 396

New Army of North China, 575

New Deal, 635

New Economic Policy (Lenin's), 617, 619, 622–623

Newfoundland, 374, 409, 635–636

New France, 401–402

New Guinea, 580

New Hampshire, 401

New Harmony, Indiana, 498

New Jersey, 401, 444

New Lanark, 497–498

New Mexico, 516

New Model Army, 380, 381, 383

New Netherland, 401, 402, 409

New Orleans, 402

New Stone Age, 4–6. *See* Neolithic

Newton, Sir Isaac, 429–430, 431, 432

New World: discovery of, 301, 313–314; colonization of, 313–316, 400–402; rivalry for, 408–411

New York, 401, 444, 445, 490

New York Central Railroad, 490

New York *World*, 556–557

New Zealand, 579, 580, 635–636

Nibelungenlied, 265

Nibelungs, 562

Nicene Creed, 154

Nice, province of, 519

Nicholas I, pope, 193

Nicholas I, tsar of Russia, 482–483, 508, 513

Nicholas II, tsar of Russia, 556

Nicholas V, pope, 324

Nicomedia, 153

Niebuhr, Reinhold, 588, 697

Niemöller, Martin, 630

Nietzsche, Friedrich, 561, 562, 591, 694

Nigeria, 687

Nightingale, Florence, 514

Nihilism, 566, 615

Nile River Valley, 18–19, 247, 284

Nimitz, Admiral Chester, 653

Ninety-five theses (Luther), 342

Nineveh, 47, 49

Nixon, Richard, 669, 670

Nobility: Minoan, 30; Greek, 60, 63, 65; in Hellenistic age, 96; Merovingian, 178, 184; Caro-lingian, 186, 191, 192, 193; feudal, 200, 201–202, 216–217, 265, 280, 304; and investiture struggle, 222; medieval England, 233, 281–282, 306; medieval France, 235, 239, 280, 304; medieval Spanish, 243, 282; medieval German, 276–277; decline of, during commercial revolution, 319; Bohemian, 356; challenged by rising middle class, 362; and French frondes, 368–369; Polish, 398; and era of French Revolution, 427–428, 452, 457, 460, 479, 480, 485. *See also* Aristocracy

Noblesse de la robe, 452

Nomes, 21

Nominalism, 294

Nonmaterialism, philosophy of, 85–86

Normandy, 231, 235, 236, 653

Normans: challenge to Byzantine Empire, 166; threat to Holy Roman Empire, 221; alliance with papacy in eleventh century, 221; conquest of England, 194, 229–231; and investiture struggle, 222; opposition to Hohenstaufens, 226; establish kingdom in Italy and Sicily, 243–245; struggle with Byzantine Empire over Balkans, 245

Norse, 394

Norsemn, 192, 313. *See also* Vikings

North Africa, 171, 176–177, 178, 210, 242, 248. *See also* Africa

North America. *See* New World; United States; Canada

North Atlantic Treaty Organization (NATO), 670–671

Northcliffe, Lord, 557

North German Confederation, 526, 527

North German Lloyd Steamship Line, 566

Norway: home of Vikings, 192; eleventh-century invasion of England, 229; conversion to Christianity, 241; at beginning of modern period, 310; spread of Lutheranism in, 344; ally of Napoleon, 467; ceded to Sweden at Congress of Vienna, 475; growth of democracy during second phase of Industrial Revolution, 555; overrun by Nazis, 644; and NATO, 670

Notre Dame, cathedral in Paris, 267

Notre Dame la Grande, church at Poitiers, 267

Nova Scotia, 409

Novel, birth of, 416

Novgorod, 242

Nubia, 19, 33, 34, 39

Nuclear weapons, 692

Numidia, 109, 114

Nuremberg, 312, 389

Nuremberg trials, 663

Nystad, Treaty of, 396

Obelisks, 27

Ockham. *See* William Ockham

Octavian. *See* Augustus

Odacer, 157

Oder River, 248

Oder-Neisse line, 662–663, 666

Ohio Valley, 410

Oil, Arab embargo, 685

Oil industry, beginnings of, 542

Okinawa, 673

Old Guard, Republican, 552, 553

"Old Hickory," 504

Old Kingdom, ancient Egypt, 19, 21, 23–24, 25, 26, 27, 33

Old National Pike (Cumberland Road), 490

Old Regime, in France, 451–453

Old Stone Age, 4

Old Testament, 40–41, 42, 43, 98, 170

Olmütz, Humiliation of, 523

Olympic games, 70, 81

Omar Khayyam, 174

Omayyads, 172

O'Neill, Eugene, 695

Open Door policy, 574

Open-field system, 202

Opera, 419, 538

Opium war, 572

Oporto, 304

Optics, 431

Optimates, 113, 114, 115

Oracles, 81

Orange Free State, 578

Ordeal, trial by, 233

Ordination, sacrament of, 253–254

Oregon, 515

Organization of American States (OAS), 688

Oriental despotism, 9, 10

Origen, 147

Origin of Species (Darwin), 547–548, 583–584

Pindar, 79, 82

Piracy, 109, 210, 310

Pisa, 210

Pisistratus, 65

Pitt, William, 411

Pius IX, pope, 585–586

Pius X, pope, 586

Pizarro, Francisco, 314, 315

Plain song, medieval, 270

Planck, Max, 693

Plataea, battle of, 73

Plato, 76, 80, 86–87, 96, 125, 173, 183, 263

Plautus, 131

Plebians, 104, 105, 107, 120

Plebiscites, 107

Pliny the Elder, 133

Plombières, 521

Plotinus, 143–144

Plows, medieval, 209

Plutarch, 113, 131

Plymouth, Massachusetts, 400

Pobedonostsev, 566–567

Podesta, 215

Poe, Edgar Allan, 534

Poetic Edda, 265

Poetry: Greek, 79, 82, 83: Hellenistic, 98; Roman, 129, 130; early Christian, 159; Byzantine, 168; Muslim, 174; feudal, 201; in twelfth-century renaissance, 260; during High Middle Ages, 265–266; Italian Renaissance, 322, 323; in seventeenth-century Dutch Netherlands, 374; English, classical period, 415–416; romantic, 533–536

Pogroms, 562, 583

Poincaré, Raymond, 637

Pointed arch, 267–268

Poitiers, battle of, 280, 281

Poitiers, church of, 270

Poland: in Holy Roman Empire, 220; conversion to Roman Catholic Church, 241; medival colonization, 242; influence of Western Europeans on development, 248; union with Lithuania, 284; at beginning of modern period, 310; and Protestantism in sixteenth century, 346, 350; Jesuits in, 353; independence of East Prussia from, 390; partition of, by Austria, Prussia, and Russia, 396–399, 424; and Treaty of Versailles, 610, 611; role in World War II, 641–642, 643; and Yalta Agreements, 658; So-

viet violation of Yalta Agreements on, 659–660; and Soviet Cominform, 661; elects native Communist regime, 661; and Potsdam Agreements, 663

Polemarch, 64

Polis, Greek: origins, 60–64; Athenian, 64–66; Spartan, 66–68; basic characteristics, 68; in fifth and fourth centuries, 70–78; as cultural center, 79–91; in Hellenistic period, 96, 97; and mystery religions, 101

Polish Corridor, 610, 611

Political parties: origins of, in England, 384–385, 386; emergence of, in United States, 449; in Great Britain during first phase of Industrial Revolution, 501–503

Pollution, 693

Polo, Marco, 242

Poltava, battle of, 396

Polybius, 131, 168

Polyclitus, 85

Polygnotus, 85

Polytheism, 13–14, 23, 52, 80

Pompadour, Madame de, 451

Pompey, 115–116

Pompidou, Georges, 668

Ponce de Leon, 314

Pondicherry, 402, 411

Pontus, 94, 114

Pope, Alexander, 416

Pope. *See* Papacy

Populares, 113, 114–115

Popular Front, in France, 637

Popular piety, and reform movement of High Middle Ages, 250–251

Popular religions, medieval, 250–251, 256–257

Population: growth of, in Middle Ages, 208–209; failure to grow in Late Middle Ages, 284, 285; growth of, in nineteenth-century America, 516; growth of, since seventeenth century, 551; rapid increase in twentieth century, 692–693

Port Royal, 371

Portugal: medieval kingdom, 243, 282; emergence as national state, 299, 300, 304, 310; role in Age of Discovery, 312, 313, 316; and Jesuits, 353; conquered by Philip II, 353; decline as dominant power, 365; and Grand

Alliance, 374; colonization of New World, 400; empire in Far East, 402; slave trade, 408; rivalry for empire in seventeenth and eighteenth centuries, 408, 409; and French Revolution, 458; impact of Napoleon on colonial empire of, 470; and NATO, 670

Positivism, 550, 585

Potsdam Agreements, 662

Potsdam Conference, 662

Pottery, ancient Greek, 79, 83–84, 85

Poussin, Nicolas, 418

Po Valley, 105, 109

Power loom, 489

Praetorian Guard, 120

Praetors, 107, 134

Pragmatic Sanction, 391

Pragmatic Sanction of Bourges, 291

Pragmatism, 591–592

Prague, 507

Prague, Treaty of, 526

Prague, university of, 293

Praxiteles, 85, 87

Predestination, 345

Predynastic Age, in Egypt, 19, 23

Prefect, 464

Prefectures, Roman, 150

Presbyter, 146

Presbyterian Church, 346

Presbyterianism, 381, 440

Presentment jury, medieval English, 232–233

President, United States, 448

Priests: Mesopotamian, 8, 9, 10, 11, 12; Egyptian, 23, 36, 49; Hebrew, 42; Assyrian, 49; Zoroastrianism, 52; Greek, 81; Roman, 107, 128; early Christian, 146, 147; in Early Middle Ages, 180; and reform movement of High Middle Ages, 251, 252; corruption of, in Late Middle Ages, 291–292; Brahmin, 404, 406; in eighteenth-century France, 451

Prime minister, 386

Primogeniture, 446, 501

Prince Henry the Navigator, 317

Princeps, 119, 120, 121, 122, 124, 125, 141, 150

Prince, The (Machiavelli), 278, 323, 501

Princeton, battle of, 444

Principate: established by Augustus, 119–121; in first century A.D., 121–122, in second century A.D., 122–125; change in third century A.D., 141, 152

Printing, 286, 337–339

Procurator, Roman, 121, 125

Progressive party, in Germany, 566

Progressivism, in United States, 553

Prokofiev, Sergei Sergeevich, 621, 696

Proletariat: Republican Rome: 113; in revolutionary France, 452; industrial, 493–495, 501, 502–503, 505–506, 513, 523

Prophets, Hebrew, 42–43, 47, 52, 170

Proprietors, colonial America, 399

Propylaea, 84–85

Prose of Edda Snorri Sturlson, 265

Protagoras, 86, 136

Protectorate, 383

Protestant Reformation, 318, 330, 339, 340–350, 361, 363

Protestants: rise of, 299–300; religious intolerance of, in Spain and Portugal, 303, 304; and Renaissance humanism, 333; role in Thirty Years' War, 356–361; outlawed in France under Louis XIV, 372; and Holy Alliance, 475; and nineteenth-century challenges to Christianity, 585, 586–588; and Nazi Germany, 630; and conflict in Ulster, 667

Provence, 265

Provosts, 238

Prussia: conversion to Christianity, 241; and early Hohenzollerns, 389–390; expansion under Frederick the Great, 391–393; and partition of Poland, 396–399; war with France in 1792, 458; defeated by Napoleon, 406; defeat of Napoleon at Waterloo, 470; role at Congress of Vienna, 474–477; and Metternich system, 477–478, 481; and Revolution of 1848, 507, 508; and Crimean War, 514; role in unification of Germany, 523–527; and Franco-German War, 527–529

"Prussian School" of historians, 523

Psammetichus, 49

Psamtik, 49

Psychoanalysis, foundation of, 549

Psychology, 549, 584, 590, 693

Ptah, 24

Ptolemaic dynasty, 95, 99, 100, 109, 116, 133

Ptolemaic system, 428–429

Ptolemy XII, 116

Ptolemy, Claudius, 100, 133, 428–429

Ptolemy, general of Alexander the Great, 95

Public Works Administration, 635

Pugachev, 396

Pulitzer, Joseph, 556–557

Purcell, Henri, 419

Puritans: and Calvinism, 346, 348, 349; and Jansenism, 371; discontent under Tudors, 377; conflicts with James I, 378; repression under Charles I, 379; in English Civil War, 380; under Cromwell, 382; and Glorious Revolution, 385; colonization of New World, 400–401; in colonial America, 440

Pushkin, Alexander, 536

"Putting out" system, 212, 317, 491

Pyramids, 19, 21, 26, 27

Pythagoras, 85

Quadrivium, 261

Quadruple Alliance, 475–477

Quaestors, 107

Quakers, 349, 401, 422, 440, 588

Quantum theory, 693

Quebec, 367, 401, 402, 411

Quebec Act, 442–443

Queen Anne's War, 409

Quesnay, François, 436

Quintuple Alliance, 477

Ra, 20, 23–24

Rabelais, François, 335

Race riots, in United States, 669

Racine, Jean Baptiste, 369, 371, 415

Racism, 562

Railroads, 490, 544

Ralph Glaber, 207

Ramses II, pharaoh, 36, 39

Ranke, Leopold von, 550

Raphael, 324, 325–326, 328

Rasputin, 567

Rathenau, Walter, 627

Rationalism: Greek, 61, 83, 88, 89–90; Hellenistic, 97; Greco-Roman, 136–137, 143, 144; medieval, 262–264, 273, 294, 297; Cartesian, 432

Ravenna, 159, 169, 177

Realism, in literature, 590, 592–594, 695

Reaper, invention of, 491

Reconquista, 242, 243

Red Army, 616, 617–618

Red China. *See* People's Republic of China

Red Guards, 677

Red International, 563

"Red" Russians, 616

Red Sunday, 567

Reformation, Protestant, 340–350

Reformation, Roman Catholic, 351–361

Reform Bill of 1832, 483, 502, 503

Reform Bill of 1867, 503, 553

Reform Bill of 1884, 553

Reformed Judaism, 588–589

Reichstag, 526–527, 555–556, 630

Reign of Terror, 459, 460, 461

Reincarnation, 406, 407

Reinsurance treaty, 564, 565

Relativity, Theory of, 547, 588, 591, 693

Relief, feudal tax, 198

Religion: Neolithic, 5; Sumerian, 8, 9; Amorite, 11; Mesopotamian, 12–14, 15, 16, 23, 24, 50; Egyptian, 19, 23–25, 26, 27, 28, 33, 36, 37–38, 49; Minoan, 30–31; Hittite, 34–35; ancient Hebrews, 41, 42–43; Assyrian, 49; Zoroastrianism, 51, 52; Greek, 60, 70, 80–81, 90; Hellenistic, 101; Roman, 104, 120, 127, 128–129, 133, 143–144; early Christian, 144–148, 151–152, 153–154; Germanic, 154; Christian, in Byzantine Empire, 165, 167–168; Islam, 170, 172, 173; Christian, in Early Middle Ages, 179–184; Christianity, in High Middle Ages, 250–258; Christianity, in Late Middle Ages, 288–295; Aztec, 315; Inca, 315; Indian, 405–407; in colonial America, 44; as factor in nationalism, 510; revival of, and spirit of romanticism, 531–532; challenges to, during second phase of Industrial Revolution, 582–589; in Soviet Union, 621–622; in Nazi Germany, 630–631; Muslim

Schubert, Franz, 537
Schumann, Robert, 537
Schurz, Carl, 508
Schweitzer, Albert, 589
Science: Mesopotamian, 14, 15–16; Egyptian, 28; Persian, 52; Greek, 79, 88; Hellenistic, 99–101; Roman, 133; Muslim, 173; medieval, 264, 294, 295; in Italian Renaissance, 323–324, 329–330; seventeenth-century Dutch, 374; rise of modern, 428–433; and growth of industry in second phase of Industrial Revolution, 542; growth of, during second phase of Industrial Revolution, 546; as challenge to Christianity, 583–584; in Soviet Union, 621; importance of, in twentieth century, 693–694
Scipio Africanus, 109, 323
Scotch Presbyterians, 379
Scotland: under English control in twelfth century, 231; and Hundred Years' War, 279–280; at beginning of modern period, 310; and Calvinism, 346; Stuart rulers, 378; revolt against Charles I, 379; and English Civil War, 380; under Cromwell, 382; union with England, 386
Scott, Sir Walter, 530, 532, 534
Scribes: Egyptian, 22; Hebrew, 144, 145
Scriptoria, 191
Sculpture: Mesopotamian, 15; Egyptian, 26, 27–28; Minoan, 31; Assyrian, 49; Chaldean, 50; Persian, 52; Greek, 79, 81, 84, 85; Hellenistic, 98, 99; Roman, 133; early Christian, 159; Byzantine, 169, 174; early medieval, 184; romanesque, 268, 269; gothic, 269; Italian Renaissance, 324–325, 326, 327–328; modern, 596
Scutage, 231
"Sea Beggars," 354
Sebastopol, 513
Second Coalition, against France, 465
Second Continental Congress, 443, 446
Second Crusade, 236, 246, 255
Second Empire, of Napoleon III, 512–515
Second Estate, France of Old Regime, 452

Second French Republic, 506
Second Intermediate Period, in ancient Egypt, 22, 33
Second Punic War, 109, 111
Second Triumvirate, 117
Second Vatican Council, 697
Secretariat, of Communist Party, 620
Secretariat, of League of Nations, 613
Secretariat, of United Nations, 657
Secretary-General, of United Nations, 657
Security Council, of United Nations, 656
Sedan, 528
Seed drill, 491
Segregation: outlawed by United States Supreme Court, 669; in South Africa, 686
Seine River, 208
Seleucid kingdom, 95, 109, 110, 111, 144
Seleucus, founder of Seleucid dynasty, 95
Seleucus, second-century geographer, 99
Seljuk Turks, 166, 173, 245, 282
Semites, 8, 10, 13, 14, 39, 45, 47, 55
Senate, Roman, 104, 105, 107, 108, 114, 115–116, 119, 121–122, 124, 125, 150
Senate, Third French Republic, 554
Senate, United States, formation of, 448
Seneca, 33, 415
Senegal, 242, 515
Sennacherib, 47
Senusret III, 21
Sepoy Mutiny of 1857, 581
Septimus Severus, 140–141
Septuagint, 98
Serbia, 284, 479, 514, 568, 603, 604, 605–606. *See also* Yugoslavia
Serfs, 201, 203, 213–214, 216–217, 229, 231, 286, 508, 566
Servetus, Michael, 345
Seth, 25
Seti I, 36, 39
Seventh Crusade, 247
Seven Weeks' War, 526
Seven Years' War, 411, 442
Severi, 141
Sévigné, Madame de, 370, 415
Sforzas, 278
Shakespeare, William, 334
Shamash, 13

Shanghai, 632
Shantung Peninsula, 572, 574
Shaw, George Bernard, 554, 559, 593, 695
Sheiks, Arab, 169
Shelley, Percy Bysshe, 530, 533–534
"Shepherd kings," 33
Sheridan, Richard, 416
Sheriff, 194, 229, 230, 231
Sherman Anti-Trust Act, 553
Shiites, 173
Shiloh, 41
Shintoism, 575
Shires, 194
Short Parliament, 379
Shoshtakovich, Dmitri, 621, 696
Sibelius, Jean, 598
Siberia, 394
Sicilian Vespers, 244
Sicily: in Peloponnesian War, 75; Roman conquest, 108, 109; added to Holy Roman Empire, 227; conquered by Normans, 243–245; competition for in Late Middle Ages, 227, 228; and Treaty of Utrecht, 375; and unification of Italy, 521; in World War II, 653
Sidon, 40
Siegfried, 562
Siemens brothers, 542
Silesia, 309, 391, 393
Simon de Montfort, 234
Simmons, Menno, 349
Simony, 221, 341, 352
Sinai peninsula, 19, 40
Singapore, 650
Sin, Semitic god, 13
Sirmium, 153
Sismondi, Simonde de, 496–497
Sisters of the Common Life, 292
Sistine Chapel, Vatican, 325
Siva the Destroyer, 406
Six Articles, 346
Six Day War (Arab-Israeli), 684
Sixth Crusade, 247
Skeptics, 100
Skyscraper, 597, 696
Slater, Samuel, 503
Slavery: Greek, 61–62, 64–65, 66, 67; Roman, 115, 126–127, 129, 143; and manorialism, 203–204; beginnings of, in New World, 317; eighteenth-century Russia, 396; in English West Indian colonies, 401; African trade in, 407, 408; in colonial America,

xxxi

ABOUT THE AUTHORS

John B. Harrison was born in Lawrenceville, Virginia, and grew up in Rich Square, North Carolina. He received his B.A. and M.A. at the University of North Carolina, and his Ph.D. at the University of Wisconsin. He taught history at Lees Junior College, Jackson, Kentucky, the University of Wisconsin extension, Ohio Northern University, and since 1942 has been teaching at Michigan State University where he is Professor of History. He was Visiting Professor at the University of North Carolina, 1963-1964. Professor Harrison is a member of the American Historical Association and the American Association of University Professors. During four trips to Europe in 1951, 1955, 1960, and 1963, he visited nineteen European countries. He is the author of *This Age of Global Strife* (1952), and of a number of articles and book reviews.

Richard E. Sullivan was born and raised near Doniphan, Nebraska. He received a B.A. degree from the University of Nebraska in 1942, and an M.A. degree and a Ph.D. degree from the University of Illinois in 1947 and 1949 respectively. His doctorate was earned in the field of medieval history. He has taught history at Northeast Missouri State Teachers' College (1949-1954) and at Michigan State University (1954-1970) where he is currently Dean of the College of Arts and Letters. Professor Sullivan held a Fulbright Research Fellowship and a John Simon Guggenheim Fellowship to Belgium in 1961-1962. He is the author of *Coronation of Charlemagne* (1959), *Heirs of the Roman Empire* (1960), and *Aix-la-Chapelle in the Age of Charlemagne* (1963). His articles have appeared in many scholarly journals.

A NOTE ON THE TYPE

The text of this book was set by means of modern photocomposition in a text type called PALATINO. The display types are MICHELANGELO and POST ROMAN BOLD. MICHELANGELO is a companion titling to PALATINO and both are contemporary creations of the German type designer Hermann Zapf. PALATINO is distinguished by broad letters and vigorous, inclined serifs typical of the work of a sixteenth century Italian master of writing. MICHELANGELO expresses the simplicity and clarity of the classic form. Both PALATINO and MICHELANGELO reflect the early Venetian scripts influencing Zapf's creations. POST ROMAN BOLD, a display roman with slight variation of colour, designed by Herbert Post, distinguishes itself by capitals almost without serifs, most of them wide, and a lower case of small, strong, horizontal serifs and short descenders.

This book was composed by American Can Co., Clarinda, Iowa, printed and bound by Kingsport Press, Inc., Kingsport, Tenn.